Tristram and Coote's
Probate Practice

Tristram and Coote's Probate Practice

Twenty-eighth edition

R. F. Yeldham
A District Probate Registrar (Probate Registry of Wales)

J. I. Winegarten
A Master of the Supreme Court (Chancery Division)

T. Synak
of the Capital Taxes Office

Consulting editor

R. B. Rowe
A District Judge of the Principal Registry of the Family Division

Butterworths
London, Dublin and Edinburgh
1995

United Kingdom	Butterworths a Division of Reed Elsevier (UK) Ltd, Halsbury House, 35 Chancery Lane, London WC2A 1EL and 4 Hill Street, EDINBURGH EH2 3JZ
Australia	Butterworths, SYDNEY, MELBOURNE, BRISBANE, ADELAIDE, PERTH, CANBERRA and HOBART
Canada	Butterworths Canada Ltd, TORONTO and VANCOUVER
Ireland	Butterworth (Ireland) Ltd, DUBLIN
Malaysia	Malayan Law Journal Sdn Bhd, KUALA LUMPUR
New Zealand	Butterworths of New Zealand Ltd, WELLINGTON and AUCKLAND
Puerto Rico	Butterworth of Puerto Rico, Inc, SAN JUAN
Singapore	Reed Elsevier (Singapore) Ptd Ltd, SINGAPORE
South Africa	Butterworths Publishers (Pty) Ltd, DURBAN
USA	Butterworth Legal Publishers, CARLSBAD, California and SALEM, New Hampshire

A CIP Catalogue record for this book is available from the British Library.

ISBN 0 406 02895 8

Typeset by Columns Design and Production Services Ltd, Reading, England
Printed in England by Clays Ltd, St Ives plc

Preface

As in every edition of this work since the tenth, this edition aims to provide the profession with a complete account of the practice of non-contentious and contentious probate business. As far as is practicable it is a comprehensive, up-to-date and authoritative source for all practitioners.

Since the last edition there have been numerous changes in the law and practice. The Non-Contentious Probate (Amendment) Rules 1991 reflected the changes made as parts of both the Children Act 1989 (in particular as to who has parental responsibility for a minor) and the Courts and Legal Services Act 1990 (specifically those provisions changing nomenclature of certain judges) came into force. Those Rules also introduced radical changes relating to settled land grants and further extended the powers of district probate registrars. Since then further parts of the Courts and Legal Services Act 1990, in particular the provision as to who may act as commissioners for oaths, have come into effect as has the Law of Property (Miscellaneous Provisions) Act 1994 which, inter alia, vests certain estates in the Public Trustee instead of the President of the Family Division.

The Law Reform (Succession) Act 1995, due to come into force on 1 January 1996, will make changes affecting the intestate succession rights of spouses, hotch pot, the effect of dissolution or annulment of marriage on wills and appointments of guardians and who may apply under the Inheritance (Provision for Family and Dependants) Act 1975.

The important decisions made in the cases of:

- *Re Adams (deceased)* [1990] 2 All ER 97
  relating to revocation of a will by the testator scoring out her signature;
- *Wood v Smith* [1991] 2 All ER 939, [1992] 3 All ER 556
  relating to where a signature may be made by a testator before the will is written out;
- *Re White (deceased), Barker v Gribble* [1990] 3 All ER 1
  relating to alterations to a will and their authentification; and
- *Re Finnemore (deceased)* [1992] 1 All ER 800
  relating to dependant relative revocation of part of a will,

are among the new ones included in this edition.

Additionally, in 1992 there was an important change in the Rules of the Supreme Court 1965 which allowed, for the first time, contentious probate actions to be commenced in Chancery district registries of the High Court throughout the country. Accordingly we have omitted from this edition details of the disposition of offices in the Thomas More Building, the home of the Chancery Registry of the High Court in London.

As regards inheritance tax and Inland Revenue accounts, the Inheritance Tax (Delivery of Accounts) Regulations 1995 increased the threshold for excepted estates to £145,000 in respect of deaths on or after 6 April 1995. Additionally, changes in rates of business and agricultural relief came into effect on 10 March 1992, and revised Inland Revenue accounts were produced in 1993, though their immediate predecessors may still be used.

All the above changes are dealt with as far as is practicable in this edition.

The layout of the text is similar to that of the previous edition but, for the first time, paragraphs have been numbered. Practitioners should find this of assistance particularly in locating cross-references. We have also taken the opportunity of omitting from this edition those passages which relate to every High Court action and which have no specific significance to contentious probate actions. We feel that the practitioner will already know about such matters or, if he does not, he would turn automatically to the White Book. The omission of these passages means that Part II Contentious Probate now concentrates on the practice peculiar to contentious probate proceedings.

In carrying out this work of excision we have also borne in mind the future publication by Lord Woolf of his final report into civil litigation and procedure. It is thought that he will recommend extensive changes to general procedure but will make fewer, if any, changes to those procedures which have (as, for example, in probate proceedings) been formed to meet the requirements of special types of litigation.

The forms in Appendix VI are now available on the disc provided with this book.

The law and practice are generally stated as at 1 August 1995 but various statutes not yet in force, in particular the Law Reform (Succession) Act 1995, are included in the appendices and are dealt with briefly in the text.

September 1995

R. F. YELDHAM
J. I. WINEGARTEN
T. SYNAK
R. B. ROWE

Contents

Note: A summary of contents will be found at the beginning of each Chapter or Appendix

Table of statutes

References in this Table to Halsbury's *Statutes* are to Halsbury's *Statutes of England* (Fourth Edition) showing the volume and page at which the annotated text of the Act will be found.

References in *italic* are to pages of the Appendices; those in **bold** type indicate where a section is set out in part or in full.

Table of statutory instruments

References in *italics* are to pages of the Appendix and those in **bold** type show where a statutory instrument is set out.

Table of cases

Q

R

PARA

T

Table of abbreviations

A & E	Adolphus and Ellis, Queen's Bench Reports
Add	Addams's Ecclesiastical Reports
All ER	All England Law Reports
All ER Rep	All England Law Reports Reprint
B & Ad	Barnewall and Adolphus
Beav	Beavan's Rolls Court
Bos & Pul	Bosanquet and Puller
Bro CC	Brown's Chancery Reports
CA	Court of Appeal
CB	Common Bench Reports
CD, Ch D	Law Reports, Chancery Division
Cox	Cox's Chancery Reports
CPD	Common Pleas Division
Curt	Curteis's Ecclesiastical Reports
Deane Ecc R	Deane's Ecclesiastical Reports
Dea & Sw	Deane and Swabey's Ecclesiastical Reports
De GM & G	De Gex, MacNaughten and Gordon's Chancery Reports
Dick	Dickens's Reports
Dir Ag	Directions to Agents
E & B	Ellis and Blackburn's Reports, Queen's Bench
Eq Cas	Equity Cases
Fam	Family Division, Series of the Law Reports
F & F	Foster and Finlason's NP Reports
Gow NP	Gow's Nisi Prius Cases
Hag Cons	Haggard's Consistory Court Cases
Hag Ecc	Haggard's Ecclesiastical Reports
Hare	Hare's Chancery Reports
HL	House of Lords
Ir Eq Rep	Irish Equity Reports
JP	Justice of the Peace Reports
JP Jo	Justice of the Peace (Weekly Notes of Cases)
Johns & H	Johnson and Hemming's Reports
Jur	Jurist Reports
KB	King's Bench
Knapp	Knapp's Privy Council Cases
LGR	Local Government Reports
LJ	Law Journal Reports

LRIr	Law Reports, Ireland
LRP & D	Law Reports, Probate and Divorce
LT	Law Times Reports
LTJo	Law Times Newspaper
[19] AC	Law Reports, Appeal Cases
[19] Ch	„ „ Chancery Division
[19] KB	„ „ King's Bench Division
[19] P	„ „ Probate, etc, Division
Lee	Lee's Ecclesiastical Cases
Lev	Levinz, KB
M & W	Meeson and Welsby Ex
Moo	Moore's Privy Council Reports
NC	Notes of Cases
NC	Non-Contentious
NCPR	Non-Contentious Probate Rules 1987
NLJ	New Law Journal
PC	Privy Council Cases
PCC	Prerogative Court of Canterbury
PD	Law Reports, Probate Division
P & D ⎱ P & M ⎰	„ „ Probate and Matrimonial
Phill	Phillimore's Ecclesiastical Reports
Phill Ch R	Phillip's Chancery Reports
Plowd	Plowden, KB
Prec C	Precedents in Chancery
P Wms	Peere Williams' Chancery Reports
QBD	Law Reports, Queen's Bench Division
R	The Reports
RR	Revised Reports
Rob	Robertson's Ecclesiastical Reports
RSC	Rules of the Supreme Court
Russ Ch Rep	Russell's Chancery Reports
SCF	Supreme Court Fees
Sim	Simon's Chancery Reports
Sol Jo	Solicitors' Journal
Spinks	Spinks' Ecclesiastical and Admiralty Reports
S & T ⎱ Sw & Tr ⎰	Swabey and Tristram's Reports
Sugd Pow	Sugden on Powers
TLR	Times Law Reports
Vern	Vernon's Chancery Reports
Ves ⎱ Ves Sen ⎰	Vesey's Chancery Reports
WLR	Weekly Law Reports
WN	Weekly Notes
WR	Weekly Reporter
WW & D	Willmore, Woollaston and Davisson, KB or QB
Y & CCC	Young and Collier's Chancery Reports

The Common Form Probate Practice

of the Family Division of the High Court of Justice

Summary

CHAPTER 1

The probate jurisdiction of the Family Division

Summary

Origin, constitution and jurisdiction

Ecclesiastical courts before 1858

1.01 Before the year 1858, jurisdiction to grant or revoke probate of wills or letters of administration of the estates of deceased persons was vested in some 370 ecclesiastical or secular courts or persons in England and Wales in addition to the Prerogative Courts of Canterbury and York[1].

1 For a short account of the origin of this ecclesiastical jurisdiction, see Chapter II of Soward and Willan's *Taxation of Capital* (London, 1919).

1.02 The practice of obtaining representation appears to have been entirely in the hands of a small body called Proctors, who practised before the ecclesiastical courts and who passed on such practice—founded on statutes and the decisions of such courts—to their pupils and successors, verbally or by notes of decisions of cases.

Courts of Probate 1858–1875

1.03 In the year 1857, the Court of Probate Act[1] was passed, under ss. 3 and 4 of which the voluntary and contentious jurisdiction and authority of all ecclesiastical, royal peculiar, peculiar, manorial, and other courts and persons in England, in respect of the granting and revocation of probates and letters of administration ceased, and became vested in the Court of Probate.

1 13 Halsbury's Statutes (3rd edn) 20.

1.04   The Act, which came into operation on 11 January 1858, provided that the Court of Probate should be a court of record and have the same powers throughout all England as the Prerogative Court of the Province of Canterbury had in relation to testamentary matters and effects of deceased persons within its jurisdiction (s. 23).

1.05   The Court of Probate Act established a Principal Probate Registry in London, with jurisdiction throughout England and Wales, and district probate registries with local jurisdiction. The territorial limits on the jurisdiction of the district probate registries were removed in 1926.

Probate Division of High Court 1875

1.06   The Supreme Court of Judicature Act 1873[1] united the principal English courts then existing (including the Court of Probate) into one 'Supreme Court of Judicature', consisting of two permanent divisions, the High Court of Justice and the Court of Appeal. All causes and matters which would have been in the exclusive cognisance of the Court of Probate were assigned to the Probate, Divorce and Admiralty Division of such High Court (s. 34).

1   18 Halsbury's Statutes (2nd edn) 467.

Family Division: transfer of contentious probate jurisdiction to Chancery Division

1.07   By s. 1 of the Administration of Justice Act 1970[1], with effect from 1 October 1971[2], the Probate, Divorce and Admiralty Division was renamed the Family Division, and various alterations were made in the assignment of business to the Divisions of the High Court. Non-contentious, or 'common form', probate business remains assigned to the Family Division, but all other probate business (i.e. contentious business) is now assigned to the Chancery Division. The dividing line between the two jurisdictions is the issue of the writ of summons in a probate action which, together with all subsequent steps in the action, now takes place in the Chancery Division.

1   11 Halsbury's Statutes (4th edn) 616.
2   Administration of Justice Act 1970 (Commencement No. 5) Order 1971, S.I. 1971 No. 1244.

1.08   Section 1 of the Administration of Justice Act 1970 also renamed the Principal Probate Registry as the Principal Registry of the Family Division.

1.09   With effect from 1 January 1982, the relevant provisions of s. 1 of the Administration of Justice Act 1970 have been repealed and re-enacted by s. 61(1)(3) and Sch. 1 to the Supreme Court Act 1981[1].

1   See pp. 797, 851 post.

Statutory limitation of jurisdiction

1.10   Before 1898 the jurisdiction of the Probate Court was confined to the personal estate of a deceased person, but by the Land Transfer Act 1897[1], later replaced by the Administration of Estates Act 1925[2], real estate which was vested in the deceased vested in his personal representative, and the jurisdiction of the probate registries to make grants of representation was extended to real, as well as personal, estate.

1   See p. 730, post.
2   See p. 744, post.

1.11 The jurisdiction of the High Court of Justice in probate matters is now constituted by s. 25 of the Supreme Court Act 1981[1], which provides that the High Court shall have the following probate jurisdiction, i.e. all such jurisdiction in relation to probates and letters of administration as it had immediately before the commencement of the Act[2], and in particular all such contentious and non-contentious jurisdiction as it then had in relation to:

(a) testamentary causes and matters;

(b) the grant, amendment or revocation of probates and letters of administration; and

(c) the real and personal estate of deceased persons.

1 See p. 837, post.
2 Section 25 of the Act came into force on 1 January 1982. Prior to that date probate jurisdiction was regulated by the provisions of s. 20 of the Supreme Court of Judicature (Consolidation) Act 1925: 7 Halsbury's Statutes (3rd edn) 573.

1.12 The section provides further that the court shall, in the exercise of its probate jurisdiction, perform all such duties with respect to the estates of deceased persons as fell to be performed by it immediately before the commencement of the Act[1].

1 Section 25 of the Act came into force on 1 January 1982. Prior to that date probate jurisdiction was regulated by the provisions of s. 20 of the Supreme Court of Judicature (Consolidation) Act 1925: 7 Halsbury's Statutes (3rd edn) 573.

1.13 By s. 5(5) of the Supreme Court Act 1981[1], all jurisdiction vested in the High Court belongs to all divisions alike, without prejudice to the provisions of the Act as to the distribution of business, e.g. s. 61(1) and para. 1(h) of Sch. 1 to the Act which assigns to the Chancery Division, inter alia, the jurisdiction in probate matters other than in respect of non-contentious or common form probate business, and s. 61(1) and para. 3(b)(iv) of Sch. 1 to the Act which assigns to the Family Division non-contentious or common form probate business.

1 See p. 836, post, replacing s. 4(4) of the Supreme Court of Judicature (Consolidation) Act 1925, with effect from 1 January 1982.

1.14 The High Court thus has exclusive jurisdiction in relation to the granting and revocation of probates of wills and letters of administration in England and Wales, save that a county court has the jurisdiction of the High Court in respect of any contentious matter arising in connection with the grant or revocation of probate or administration where the deceased died possessed of estate not exceeding in value, at the date of death, after making allowance for funeral expenses, debts and liabilities, the county court limit[1].

1 County Courts Act 1984, s. 32 as substituted by the Administration of Justice Act 1985, s. 51; see p. 866, post. The county court limit is currently £30,000: County Courts Jurisdiction Order 1981 (S.I. 1981 No. 1123). As to the practice in relation to probate actions in the county court, see Chap. 40.

Function

1.15 By far the largest proportion of the work of the probate registries consists in the issue, in unopposed cases, of grants of representation to the estates of deceased persons, and ancillary matters, such as the preparation of indexes, or 'calendars', of such grants which are available for public search, the issue of copies of grants and of proved wills etc. Such grants are also made in accordance with a judgment or order of the Chancery Division in a probate action. Subject to any decision of the Chancery Division in such an action, it is the function of the probate registry, for the purpose of the issue of a grant of representation, to determine what documents are testamentary, and who is entitled to be constituted the personal representative of the deceased.

Family Division's right of interpretation and construction

1.16   Where it is necessary for the Family Division to consider the terms of testamentary documents for the limited purpose of granting representation, its registries have power to determine a point of construction[1], but are not bound to do so. They may often prefer to make a grant to some suitable person under the court's discretionary powers[2] and leave the question of construction to be decided in the Chancery Division[3].

1 *Re Frogley's Estate* [1905] P 137; *Re Lupton's Estate* [1905] P 321; *Re Fawcett's Estate* [1941] P 85, [1941] 2 All ER 341.
2 I.e. under the Supreme Court Act 1981, s. 116: see p. 845, post.
3 *Re Last's Estate* [1958] P 137, [1958] 1 All ER 316.

1.17   Whereas, prior to 1 January 1983, the court had no general statutory guidance to assist it in the interpretation of wills, the Administration of Justice Act 1982, s. 21 (see p. 854, post) now provides general rules as to the admission of evidence for such purpose. It should, however, be noted that these statutory guidelines apply only in those cases where the testator *dies* on or after 1 January 1983: for a fuller discussion of this provision, see Chap. 3.

Effect of grant in common form

Effect of probate or letters of administration

1.18   A grant of probate obtained in common form in accordance with the practice set out in Part I of this work is accepted in all courts in England and Wales as conclusive evidence of the executor's title, and of the formal validity and the contents of the will: this applies equally to a grant of administration with the will annexed.

1.19   Similarly a grant of letters of administration is accepted in all such courts as conclusive evidence of the title of the administrator as personal representative of the deceased.

Position where grant is revoked

1.20   A grant in common form may, however, be revoked for any one of a number of reasons. It may then be necessary to consider the position of persons who have made payments or dispositions to the personal representative under the grant, and of a grantee who has partially or even wholly administered the estate.

1.21   Under s. 27(2) of the Administration of Estates Act 1925:

> 'Where a representation is revoked, all payments and dispositions made in good faith to a personal representative under the representation before the revocation thereof are a valid discharge to the person making the same; and the personal representative who

acted under the revoked representation may retain and reimburse himself in respect of any payments or dispositions made by him which the person to whom representation is afterwards granted might have properly made.'

1.22   And under s. 27(1) of that Act:

'Every person making or permitting to be made any payment or disposition in good faith under a representation shall be indemnified and protected in so doing, notwithstanding any defect or circumstance whatsoever affecting the validity of the representation.'[1]

1 In *Re Bloch's Estate* [1959] CLY 1251, letters of administration granted to two administrators in 1952 following an order for leave to swear to the death were revoked on evidence that the presumed deceased was alive in 1958. It was held that one of the grantees was entitled to an indemnity under s. 27 of the Administration of Estates Act 1925, but that the other grantee, who had withheld material information in 1952, was not.

1.23   Section 204(1) of the Law of Property Act 1925[1] provides that an order of the court under any statutory or other jurisdiction shall not, as against a purchaser, be invalidated on the ground of want of jurisdiction or of want of any concurrence, consent, notice or service, whether the purchaser has notice of any such want or not.

1   37 Halsbury's Statutes (4th edn) 329.

1.24   A grant of representation is a judicial act, and even if such a grant were held void on the ground of want of jurisdiction the title of a purchaser would be protected by this subsection[1].

1   *Hewson v Shelley* [1914] 2 Ch 13, 10 LT 785.

1.25   Where an administratrix sold and conveyed certain real estate of a deceased and on the discovery of a will of the deceased appointing executors the title of the purchaser was disputed, it was held by the Court of Appeal that the administratrix could sell and convey as she had done and that the purchaser had a good title[1]: see also Administration of Estates Act 1925, s. 37 (validity of conveyance not affected by revocation of grant).

1   *Hewson v Shelley* [1914] 2 Ch 13, 10 LT 785, overruling *Graysbrook v Fox* (1564) 1 Plowd 275, and *Abraham v Conyngham* (1676) Freem KB 445, 2 Lev 182.

1.26   A receipt given by an executor who has obtained probate of a forged will is a good discharge although the probate is later revoked and administration granted to the next of kin of the deceased[1].

1   *Allen v Dundas* (1789) 3 Term Rep 125 (esp at 129, 131). See also *Boxall v Boxall* (1884) 27 Ch D 220.

1.27   The person for the time being clothed by the probate registry with the character of personal representative of the deceased is, and enjoys all the powers of, a personal representative unless and until the grant is revoked or has determined[1].

1   See the judgment of the MR in *Hewson v Shelley*, above.

Probate, or letters of administration with will annexed, in solemn form

1.28   Any person whose interest is adversely affected by a grant of probate, or letters of administration with will annexed, in common form may proceed by a revocation action to put the grantee to proof of the will in solemn form.

1.29   As to the effect of a grant in solemn form, see Chap. 26.

Common form business

1.30   Grants of representation may be applied for either through a practising solicitor [or, when s. 54 and s. 55 of the Courts and Legal Services Act 1990 (see p. 894) come into force, on a day to be appointed, one of the various bodies or persons qualified in accordance with those sections] or in person at the Principal Registry of the Family Division or at any of the district probate registries and sub-registries (see para. **2.58**). Personal applicants may also apply at various probate offices (see p. 1105).

1.31   Certain officers in public departments, conducting business in the interests of the departments, may act as solicitors although not qualified to practise[1].

1   Solicitors Act 1974, ss. 27 and 88.

1.32   The Treasury Solicitor is also empowered by statute to extract a grant on behalf of a member of the public[1].

1   Registrar's Circular, 8 August 1941.

1.33   It is an offence for an unqualified practitioner, unless within an exemption, to take instructions for, or draw or prepare, any papers on which to found or oppose a grant of probate or letters of administration unless he proves that the act was not done for or in expectation of any fee, gain or reward[1].

1   Solicitors Act 1974, s.23.

Definition

1.34   'Non-contentious or common form probate business' is defined by the Supreme Court Act 1981, s. 128[1], as the business of obtaining probate and administration where there is no contention as to the right thereto, including the passing of probates and administrations through the High Court in contentious cases where the contest has been terminated, and all business of a non-contentious nature in matters of testacy and intestacy, not being proceedings in any action, and also the business of lodging caveats against the grant of probate or administration.

1   See p. 847, post.

1.35   The procedure and practice are regulated by statutes, by statutory rules and orders, by the reported cases, and by the practice of the court.

1.36   The statutes which affect the practice of the Division are collected in Appendix I.

Rules

1.37 By s. 127 of the Supreme Court Act 1981[1], the President of the Family Division, with the concurrence of the Lord Chancellor, is given power to make rules of court (known as 'probate rules') for regulating and prescribing the practice and procedure of the High Court with respect to non-contentious or common form probate business. Probate rules (which shall be made by statutory instrument) may make provision for regulating the classes of persons entitled to grants of probate or administration in particular circumstances and the relative priorities of their claims thereto.

1 See p. 847, post.

1.38 Section 84 of the above Act[1] provides that general rules made under that section shall have effect subject to any special rules for the time being in force in relation to proceedings in the Supreme Court of any particular kind. 'Special rules' means rules applying to proceedings of any particular kind in the Supreme Court made by a separate rule-making authority. Consequently, by virtue of these provisions, the Rules of the Supreme Court do not apply to non-contentious probate business[2], except in so far as they are specifically applied to such business by the Non-Contentious Probate Rules (e.g. by rr. 3 and 67). Rule 3 applies the Rules of the Supreme Court, with the necessary modifications, in respect of matters not specifically dealt with in the Non-Contentious Probate Rules.

1 See p. 842, post.
2 Cf. *Re Caspari's Goods* (1896) 75 LT 663.

1.39 The current rules are the Non-Contentious Probate Rules 1987, as amended by the Non-Contentious Probate (Amendment) Rules 1991. These rules govern the practice in the case of death on or after 1 January 1926: where the deceased died before 1 January 1926 the right to a grant is, subject to the provisions of any enactment, to be determined by the principles and rules under which the court would have acted at the date of the death (r. 23).

1.40 The Non-Contentious Probate Rules 1987, as amended, are printed in Appendix II, pp. 923 ff., post.

Table of fees

1.41 By s. 130 of the Supreme Court Act 1981[1], the power of prescribing fees to be taken in non-contentious probate business has been conferred on the Lord Chancellor with the concurrence of the Lord Chief Justice, the Master of the Rolls, the President of the Family Division and the Vice-Chancellor, or of any three of them, together with the concurrence of the Treasury.

1 See p. 848, post.

1.42 The current table of fees to be taken in non-contentious business is contained in the Non-Contentious Probate Fees Order 1981, as amended, which is printed in Appendix III, pp. 961 ff., post.

Grant as evidence of death

1.43   The production of letters of administration is not prima facie evidence of death[1].

1   *Moons v De Bernales* (1826) 1 Russ 301; *Thompson v Donaldson* (1799) 3 Esp 63.

Property for which grant required

Necessity for grant

1.44   The production of a grant of probate or letters of administration or a confirmation from a court in the United Kingdom is necessary to establish the right to recover or receive any part of the estate and effects of any deceased person situate in the United Kingdom[1]. There is an exception in respect of moneys payable under a life assurance policy effected by a person who died domiciled elsewhere than in the United Kingdom: see para. **1.62**, post.

1   Revenue Act 1884, s. 11 (see p. 1097 of the Twenty-Fifth Edition of this work or 17 Halsbury's Statutes (4th edn) 249. This section originally referred to the personal estate, but in relation to deaths on and after 1 January 1898 the requirement applies to real estate as well as personal estate (Land Transfer Act 1897, s. 2 (p. 730, post), now replaced by the Administration of Estates Act 1925, s. 2 (p. 744, post)).

1.45   As to the penalties for administering an estate of a person dying before 13 March 1975, without having obtained a grant of representation, see the Stamp Act 1815, s. 37[1], the Customs and Inland Revenue Act 1881, s. 40[1] and the Finance Act 1894, ss. 6(2), 8(1), (3), (6) and 22(1)(d): in relation to the estates of persons dying after 12 March 1975, for the provisions as to penalties for administering without obtaining a grant or delivering an Inland Revenue account, see the Stamp Act 1815, s. 37 (as amended), the Finance Act 1975, Sch. 4, para. 28 and the Inheritance Tax Act 1984, s. 245[2]: see also *New York Breweries Co Ltd v A-G* [1899] AC 62, HL, and *IRC v Stype Investments (Jersey) Ltd* [1982] Ch 456, [1982] 3 All ER 419, CA, overruling [1981] Ch 367, [1981] 2 All ER 394 (see the text of the following paragraph).

1   See pp. 1095 and 1097 respectively of the Twenty-Fifth Edition of this work or 17 Halsbury's Statutes (4th edn) 234.
2   See p. 908, post.

1.46   As to the liability for capital transfer tax, see the Finance Act 1975, s. 25 and as to the liability for inheritance tax see the Inheritance Tax Act 1984, ss. 199 and 200[1]: under s. 25(6) of the Act of 1975 and under s. 199(4) of the Act of 1984, any person who takes possession of, or intermeddles with or otherwise acts in relation to, property so as to become liable as executor or trustee, and any person to whom the management of property is entrusted on behalf of a person not of full legal capacity, is treated as a person in whom the property is vested, which, under s. 25(5) of the Act of 1975 or s. 200(1) of the Act of 1984, renders him liable for either capital transfer tax or inheritance tax on the value transferred. Where a defendant resident outside the jurisdiction of the English court holding land in England as nominee for the testator during his lifetime had contracted to sell that land on the testator's authority and subsequently removed the proceeds of sale from the jurisdiction following the death of the testator, it was held on appeal that such removal did amount to intermeddling for the purposes of s. 25 of the Finance Act 1975[2] (which section is in the same terms as s. 199(4) of the Inheritance Tax Act 1984).

1 See p. 905, post.
2 *IRC v Stype Investments (Jersey) Ltd* [1982] Ch 456, [1982] 3 All ER 419, CA, overruling [1981] Ch 367, [1981] 2 All ER 394.

Property covered by grant: death before 1898

1.47 Where the deceased died before 1 January 1898, an English grant of representation could be made only where the deceased left personal estate in England, and if there were no such property the court had no jurisdiction to make a grant[1]. Grants were expressed to be of the *personal* estate of the deceased.

1 *Re Tucker's Goods* (1864) 3 Sw &Tr 585.

Death since 1897

1.48 Section 1 of the Administration of Estates Act 1925[1], which applies in the case of death on or after 1 January 1926, provides that real estate to which a deceased was entitled for an interest not ceasing on his death devolves on his death to his personal representative, in like manner as chattels real previously so devolved.

1 See p. 744, post.

1.49 A similar provision was contained in s. 1 of the Land Transfer Act 1897[1], which applied in the case of death on or after 1 January 1898, but prior to 1 January 1926.

1 See p. 730, post.

1.50 Where the death has occurred at any time since 1897 a general grant is accordingly expressed to be of 'all the estate which by law devolves to and vests in the personal representative of the deceased'.

1.51 Section 2(1) of the Administration of Justice Act 1932 gave the court jurisdiction to make a grant of probate or administration notwithstanding that the deceased left no estate (although this Act was repealed, with effect from 1 January 1982 by the Supreme Court Act 1981, it is clear from s. 25 of the Act of 1981[1] that the court still retains power to make such a grant): see paras. **4.209** and **4.210**, post, as to grants where the estate is 'nil'.

1 See p. 837, post.

1.52 By virtue of ss. 2 and 3 of the Administration of Estates Act 1971[1], a grant of representation in the estate of a person who died domiciled in England and Wales which includes a note of such domicile is recognised in Northern Ireland and Scotland as well as in England and Wales, the necessity for resealing such a grant in those countries having been abolished as from 1 January 1972. Grants can also be extended by resealing under the Colonial Probates Acts 1892 and 1927, so as to make title to estate situate in a country to which those Acts have been applied. As to resealing, see Chap. 18.

1 See pp. 800–801, post.

1.53   A grant made in England and Wales in the estate of a person who died domiciled out of England and Wales is proof of title to the estate in England and Wales only.

Limited grants

1.54   When necessary, a grant may be limited to a specified part of the estate: see paras. **4.10** and **4.11**, post, 'Will limited to personalty' and paras. **11.258** ff., post, 'Grants limited as to property'.

Vesting of property prior to issue of grant

1.55   Section 14 of the Law of Property (Miscellaneous Provisions) Act 1994 (see p. 898) came into force on 1 July 1995 (S.I. 1995 No. 1317). It substituted a new s. 9 of the Administration of Estates Act 1925 (see p. 747). The estate of a person dying intestate vests in the Public Trustee until the grant of administration and, similarly, where a testator dies and at the time of his death there is no executor with power to obtain probate of the will, or at any time before probate of the will is granted there ceases to be any executor with power to obtain probate, the estate vests in the Public Trustee until the grant of representation (s. 9(1) and (2), Administration of Estates Act 1925, as substituted).

1.56   The vesting of the estate in the Public Trustee does not confer on him any beneficial interest in, or impose on him any duty, obligation or liability in respect of, the property (s. 9(3), Administration of Estates Act 1925, as substituted).

1.57   Any estate of a person dying before the commencement of s. 14, if it is property to which sub-s. (2) applies, vested in the Public Trustee on the commencement of s. 14 (s. 14(2), Law of Property (Miscellaneous Provisions) Act 1994). Subsection 14(2) applies to property vested in the Probate Judge under s. 9 of the Administration of Estates Act 1925 immediately before the commencement of s. 14 or if it was not so vested but as at commencement of s. 14 there has been no grant of representation in respect of it and there is no executor with power to obtain such a grant (s. 14(3), Law of Property (Miscellaneous Provisions) Act 1994). The remaining provisions of s. 14 relate to how property is treated as vesting in the Public Trustee and how certain things done by or in relation to the Probate Judge and references in relevant enactments or instruments to the Probate Judge shall be treated as done by, or in relation to or references to the Public Trustee (s. 14(4)–(6), Law of Property (Miscellaneous Provisions) Act 1994).

1.58   When an estate has so vested and it is necessary to serve on the Public Trustee a notice to quit the notice should be served direct on the Public Trustee at the Public Trust Office, PO Box 3010, London WC2B 6JS; telephone no: 0171-269 7196[1].

1 *Practice Direction 12 June (1995)*, [1995] 3 All ER 192.

1.59   Before s. 14 of the Law of Property (Miscellaneous Provisions) Act 1994 came into force (on 1 July 1995) and prior to the issue of a grant of representation the real and personal estate of a person who died intestate vested in the Probate Judge, i.e. the President of the Family Division of the High Court[1]. In the case of a person who died testate his property vested from the moment of death in the executor named in his will[2]. But if no executor was appointed and the will does not dispose of the whole estate, the estate vested as in the case of an intestacy until a grant was made[3]. There was no provision by statute for the case where there is no executor but the will disposes of the whole estate.

1 Administration of Estates Act 1925, ss. 9, 55(1)(xv) (see pp. 747, 763, post); *Wirral Borough Council v Smith* (1982) 80 LGR 628, CA.
2 *Woolley v Clark* (1822) 5 B & Ald 744; *Whitehead v Taylor* (1839) 10 Ad & El 210.
3 Administration of Estates Act 1925, s. 9 (see p. 747, post).

Vesting of real estate before grant: death before 1926

1.60 In the case of death after 1897 but before 1 January 1926, real estate in England vested in the heir-at-law in the interval between the death of the deceased and the issue of a grant of representation, equally in cases of testacy and intestacy as the Land Transfer Act 1897[1] made no provision on the subject; but when a grant of representation was made the title of an administrator related back to the time of death both as to real estate (by virtue of s. 1(1) of the Land Transfer Act 1897) and as to personalty[2].

1 See p. 730, post.
2 *Re Pryse's Goods* [1904] P 301.

Property for which grant not required

Estate of British Sovereign

1.61 The court has no jurisdiction to make a grant in respect of the estate of a deceased British Sovereign[1]. A will of the private estates of the Sovereign does not require publication[2].

1 *Re King George III's Goods* (1822) 1 Add 255; *Re King George III's Goods* (1862) 3 Sw & Tr 199.
2 Crown Private Estates Act 1862, s. 5.

Life policies of persons domiciled abroad

1.62 The production of a grant of representation is not necessary to establish the right to receive moneys payable on policies of life assurance effected with any insurance company by a person who dies domiciled elsewhere than in the United Kingdom[1].

1 Revenue Act 1884, s. 11 proviso (see p. 1097 of the Twenty-Fifth edition of this work or 17 Halsbury's Statutes (4th edn) 249).

Jointly owned assets

1.63 Property held by a deceased person on a beneficial joint tenancy where another joint tenant survives him does not devolve upon his personal representative[1], but passes by survivorship to the other joint tenant(s).

1 See, as to real estate, Administration of Estates Act, 1925, ss. 1(1) and 3(4), pp. 744, 745, post.

Nominated assets

1.64 The rules of certain bodies permit depositors to nominate a person or persons to whom the whole or part of the amount standing to their credit shall be payable upon death. Where such a nomination is in force it supersedes the provisions of any will left by the deceased and of the law of distribution upon an intestacy, and payment to the nominee is normally made without production of a grant: see paras. **1.71** and **1.84**, post.

1.65   The requirements of the Wills Act 1837 have no application to such a nomination: see 'Nominations', paras. **3.31** and **3.32**, post.

Liability for inheritance tax or capital transfer tax

1.66   The liability for inheritance tax or capital transfer tax and death duties is unaffected by the fact that the estate may be realised without the extraction of a grant of representation. As regards any such liability the term 'executor' in the Finance Act 1894, and the term 'personal representative' in the Law of Property Act 1925, the Administration of Estates Act 1925, the Finance Act 1975 and the Inheritance Tax Act 1984, includes any person who takes possession of or intermeddles with, the property of the deceased.[1]

1   Finance Act 1894, s. 22(1)(d); Law of Property Act 1925, s. 205(1)(xviii); Administration of Estates Act 1925, s. 55(1)(xi); Inheritance Tax Act 1984, s. 272 and Finance Act 1975, s. 51(1). See also *IRC v Stype Investments (Jersey) Ltd* [1982] Ch 456, [1982] 3 All ER 419, CA, summarised in the text to footnote 2 to para. **1.46**, ante.

Small sums: payment without grant

1.67   Provisions enabling small sums due on a death to be paid or transferred without the production of a grant of representation are included in a large number of public, general and local statutes. The Administration of Estates (Small Payments) Act 1965[1] provides a uniform limit on the amount which may be paid without the production of a grant by virtue of these provisions. The present limit in relation to deaths occurring and nominations effected, on or after 11 May 1984, is £5,000[2]; in the case of a death prior to that date, but on or after 10 August 1975, the limit is £1,500 and in the case of a death prior to that date, but on or after 5 September 1965, the limit remains at £500.

1   See p. 780, post.
2   Administration of Estates (Small Payments) (Increase of Limit) Order 1984 (see p. 922, post).

1.68   It should be noted that in all cases the power to pay without production of a grant is permissive and not obligatory, and does not connote any exemption from inheritance tax or capital transfer tax if the total amount of the estate is such that tax or duty would be payable. In some cases the production of a certificate from the Commissioners of Inland Revenue to the effect that no tax is payable, or that the appropriate tax has been paid, may be required.

1.69   Consular officers of foreign countries with which conventions under the Consular Conventions Act 1949[1] have been concluded may take advantage of these provisions on behalf of nationals of their countries who are not resident in England[2]. As to grants to Consular officers, see paras. **11.104** ff., post.

1   See p. 765, post.
2   Consular Conventions Act 1949, s. 1(2) (see p. 766, post).

1.70 The principal provisions for payment without the production of a grant are set out in the following paragraphs.

Savings banks and savings certificates

1.71 Prior to 1 May 1981 (before 1 May 1979 in respect of Trustee Savings Bank nominations) a depositor in the National Savings Bank or a Trustee Savings Bank, and a holder of National Savings Certificates, being a person who has attained the age of 16, could nominate a person or persons to receive any sum due to the depositor or holder at his death. Since these dates this facility has been withdrawn and the relevant regulations, as amended, now provide respectively that any nomination made after 30 April 1979 (Trustee Savings Bank nominations) or 30 April 1981 (National Savings Bank or Savings Certificate nominations) shall be of no effect[1]. In the case of the National Savings Bank and Savings Certificate nominations made prior to 1 May 1981, there is no limit to the amount which may be nominated, but in the case of Trustee Savings Banks the maximum amount is £1,500 as respects nominations effected on or after 21 November 1975[2] but before 1 May 1979. Nominated sums are paid or transferred to the nominee without the production of a grant of representation, although proof of payment of inheritance tax or capital transfer tax on death, or that none is payable, may be required (see below).

1 National Savings Bank Regulations 1972, regs. 33–38; Trustee Savings Bank Regulations 1972, regs. 11–15; Savings Certificates Regulations 1972, regs. 13–18 as amended.
2 The former limit was £500.

1.72 Where the total amount in the National Savings Bank or a Trustee Savings Bank which forms part of the estate does not exceed £5,000, the production of a grant of representation may be dispensed with and the amount, or any part thereof, may be paid to a person appearing to be entitled to obtain a grant or to be beneficially or otherwise entitled thereto. Similarly, where the total amount payable in respect of Savings Certificates held in the sole name of the deceased does not exceed £5,000, the Director of Savings may grant payment thereof without requiring the production of a grant[1].

1 The original limit in each case was £500. See National Savings Bank Regulations 1972, reg. 40; Trustee Savings Bank Regulations 1972, reg. 18; Savings Certificates Regulations 1972, reg. 20. In respect of sums in the National Savings Bank and Savings Certificates, a limit of £1,500 applies in cases where the death occurred on or after 12 August 1975 (National Savings Bank (Amendment) Regulations 1975; Savings Certificates (Amendment No. 2) Regulations 1975). In the case of Trustee Savings Banks, a limit of £1,500 applies in relation to the estates of persons dying on or after 21 November 1975 (Trustee Savings Bank (Amendment) Regulations 1975). The limit of £1,500 was increased to £5,000, in respect of deaths on or after 11 May 1984: National Savings Bank (Amendment) (No. 2) Regulations 1984 (S.I. 1984 No. 602), Savings Certificates (Amendment) (No. 2) Regulations 1984 (S.I. 1984 No. 603) and see the Administration of Estates (Small Payments) (Increase of Limit) Order 1984, p. 922, post).

1.73 If the value of the 'specified assets' (i.e. the total amount due to the deceased in respect of National Savings Bank accounts, Savings Certificates, Premium Savings Bonds, stock and securities on the National Savings Stock Register (other than those on the portion of the Register kept by Trustee Savings Banks), whether held in the sole name of the deceased or jointly, and the total amount (including bonus or interest) due in respect of savings contracts entered into by the deceased and registered by the Director of Savings) exceeds £25,000, the Director of Savings must, before paying or transferring, without the production of a grant of representation, any amount due in respect of National Savings Bank accounts or Savings Certificates (whether under a nomination or otherwise) require the production of a statement from the Commissioners of Inland Revenue to the effect that no death duties (including inheritance tax or capital transfer tax chargeable on death) are payable in respect of the deceased or that any death duties, inheritance tax or capital transfer tax payable has been paid[1]: this latter requirement no longer applies in the case of Trustee Savings Banks[2].

1 National Savings Bank Regulations 1972, reg. 41; Savings Certificates Regulations 1972, reg. 22; National Savings Stock Register Regulations 1976, reg. 42: all as amended.
2 Trustee Savings Bank Regulations 1972, reg. 19, having been repealed by S.I. 1979 No. 259.

1.74 Although the regulations dealing with National Savings Bank deposits, Savings Certificates and Premium Savings Bonds give the Director of Savings power to dispense with the production of a grant when the amount due in respect of each asset does not exceed £5,000, in practice payment is not made without the production of a grant if the combined total exceeds £5,000, even though the individual items are below this figure.

Premium Savings Bonds

1.75 The production of a grant of representation issued by, or having effect as if granted by, any competent court in the United Kingdom, the Isle of Man or the Channel Islands is sufficient to authorise the Director of Savings to pay over any sum due in respect of Premium Savings Bonds[1].

1 Premium Savings Bonds Regulations 1972, reg. 12.

1.76 Where the amount due does not exceed £5,000 it may, if the Director of Savings thinks fit, be paid over without the production of a grant[1]. Any prize gained by the bonds held by the deceased after his death is taken into account in deciding whether the maximum is exceeded.

1 Premium Savings Bonds Regulations 1972, reg. 13. The original limit of £500 was increased to £1,500 in cases where the death occurred on or after 12 August 1975 by the Premium Savings Bonds (Amendment) Regulations 1975. In respect of deaths on or after 11 May 1984 the limit was further increased to £5,000 by the Premium Savings Bonds (Amendment) Regulations 1984 (S.I. 1984 No. 601).

Savings contracts

1.77 On the death of a contributor under a savings contract with the Director of Savings or a Trustee Savings Bank, the production of a grant of representation granted, or having effect as if granted, by a court in Great Britain, Northern Ireland, the Isle of Man or the Channel Islands is sufficient authority for repayment to, or as directed by, the grantee of the amount due[1].

1 Savings Contracts Regulations 1969, reg. 9.

1.78 If the aggregate amount repayable in respect of such savings contracts does not exceed £5,000, payment may be made, if the authority thinks fit, without the production of a grant of representation[1].

1 Savings Contracts Regulations 1969, reg. 10. The limit of £500 was increased to £1,500, in relation to deaths occurring on or after 12 August 1975, by the Savings Contracts (Amendment) Regulations 1975 and to £5,000 in relation to deaths occurring on or since 11 May 1984 by the Savings Contracts (Amendment) Regulations 1984 (S.I. 1984 No. 599).

Government and savings bank annuities

1.79   Sums not exceeding £5,000 due in respect of 'National Debt' annuities[1] or savings bank annuities[2] may be paid without probate or other proof of title; and sums of any amount in respect of annuities of either class may be paid on production of a grant issued in the Isle of Man or the Channel Islands[3].

1 Government Annuities Act 1929, s. 21, as amended by Administration of Estates (Small Payments) Act 1965, s. 1(1), the Administration of Estates (Small Payments) (Increase of Limit) Order 1975 (see p. 915, post) to £1,500 in relation to deaths on or after 10 August 1975 and the Administration of Estates (Small Payments) (Increase of Limit) Order 1984 (see p. 922, post) to £5,000 in relation to deaths on or after 11 May 1984. In the case of deaths prior to 10 August 1975, the limit is £500.
2 Ibid., s. 57, as amended by ibid.
3 Government Annuities Act 1929, ss. 20, 56.

Government stock

1.80   Government stock in the name of a deceased person not exceeding £5,000 in nominal or actual value (whichever is the less) may be transferred by the Bank of England or Bank of Ireland to the National Savings Stock Register[1]. This enables it to be dealt with under the provisions of the National Savings Stock Register Regulations: see para. **1.81**.

1 National Debt Act 1972, s. 6: the former amount of £1,500 was increased to £5,000 in respect of deaths on or after 11 May 1984 by the Administration of Estates (Small Payments) (Increase of Limit) Order 1984 (see p. 922, post). In relation to deaths before 11 May 1984 but on or after 10 August 1975 the limit was £1,500, in accordance with the Administration of Estates (Small Payments) (Increase of Limit) Order 1975 (see p. 915, post). In the case of deaths prior to 10 August 1975 the limit is £500.

Government stock on National Savings Stock Register

1.81   A holder of stock inscribed on the National Savings Stock Register may nominate (provided the nomination was made before 1 May 1981) the whole or part of his holding in favour of some other person or persons. Since 1 May 1981, the facility to make such nominations has been withdrawn and any nomination made after 30 April 1981 shall be of no effect. On the death of the nominator the Director of Savings will inscribe the nominee(s) as holder of the stock in accordance with the terms of a valid nomination, but if the value of the 'specified assets', as defined by the National Savings Stock Register Regulations 1976, exceeds £25,000 he must first require a certificate from the Commissioners of Inland Revenue as to the payment of inheritance tax, capital transfer tax or death duties[1].

1 National Savings Stock Register Regulations 1976, regs. 32, 36 (as amended) and 40 (as amended).

1.82   If the total combined value of the stock and of any National Savings Bank balances held by the deceased does not exceed £5,000 the stock may be transferred without the production of a grant[1].

1 National Savings Bank Regulations 1972, reg. 40, as amended by the National Savings Bank (Amendment) Regulations 1975, and applied by ibid., reg. 41. See also National Savings Stock Register (Amendment) Regulations 1984 (S.I. 1984 No. 600). The limit of £5,000 applies to dates of death on or after 11 May 1984; a limit of £1,500 applies in relation to deaths before then but on or after 12 August 1975. For earlier deaths, the limit is £500.

Production of unproved wills to Department for National Savings

1.83   In dealing with applications for payment under the provisions set out in the preceding paragraphs without the production of a grant of representation the Department for National Savings will normally accept, in lieu of the original will, a clear photocopy or other facsimile of the will, certified personally by a solicitor to be a true copy of the original. Typewritten copies are not accepted[1].

1   Notice by Department for National Savings: *Law Society's Gazette*, 6 October 1976.

Registered societies

1.84   A member of a trade union, an industrial or provident society or a friendly society, not being under the age of 16, may nominate a person or persons to receive moneys payable at his death up to a maximum of £5,000, and on the death of the member such moneys may be paid or transferred in accordance with the nomination[1].

1   The figure of £5,000 applies to nominations effected on or after 14 September 1984 (see Administration of Estates (Small Payments) (Increase of Limit) Order 1984, p. 922, post). In relation to nominations effected before then but on or after 10 August 1975, the former limit of £500 was increased to £1,500 (Administration of Estates (Small Payments) (Increase of Limit) Order 1975, amending Industrial and Provident Societies Act 1965, s. 23 and Friendly Societies Act 1974, ss. 66–67). See also the Trade Union (Nominations) Regulations 1977 (S.I. 1977 No. 789) and the Trade Unions (Nominations) (Amendment) Regulations 1984 (S.I. 1984 No. 1290).

1.85   On the death of a member of any such body, or of a member of a loan society or building society, whether testate or intestate, payment of amounts not exceeding £5,000 may be made without the production of a grant of representation[1].

1   The figure of £5,000 applies in relation to deaths occurring on or after 11 May 1984 (Administration of Estates (Small Payments) (Increase of Limit) Order 1984, p. 922, post). In relation to deaths occurring on or after 10 August 1975, the former limit of £500 was increased to £1,500 (Industrial and Provident Societies Act 1965, s. 25, Friendly Societies Act 1974, s. 68, Loan Societies Act 1840, s. 11 and Building Societies Act 1962, s. 46 all as amended by Administration of Estates (Small Payments) (Increase of Limit) Order 1975).

Funds in court

1.86   On the death intestate of a person entitled to a fund, or a share of a fund, in court, if the whole estate of the deceased, including the amount in question, does not exceed £5,000 in value and no grant has been extracted, the court may order that the fund or share be paid to the person having the prior right to a grant[1].

1   RSC Ord. 22, r. 11; Court Funds Rules 1987, r. 43; County Court Rules 1981, Ord. 50, r. 12.

Persons incapable of managing their affairs

1.87   On the death of a person who is incapable by reason of mental disorder of managing his property and affairs, where it appears to the Court of Protection that the net value of his estate does not exceed £5,000 that court may, if it thinks fit, provide for the payment of the funeral expenses out of any funds in court standing to the credit of the deceased and order that any such funds, or the balance thereof, or any other property of the deceased remaining under its control be paid or transferred to the personal representative when constituted, or to the person who appears to be entitled to apply for a grant of representation to the estate[1].

1 Court of Protection Rules 1994. The limit is £5,000 as from 1 February 1985. This limit replaced that of £1,500, which figure had replaced that of £500 with effect from 27 August 1975, by the Court of Protection (Amendment) Rules 1975.

National Insurance

1.88 Sums payable by way of benefit under the Social Security Act 1975 to a deceased person who has made a claim therefor or who is alleged to be entitled thereto may be paid or distributed to or amongst persons claiming as personal representatives, legatees, next of kin or creditors, or where the deceased was illegitimate to or amongst other persons, and strict proof of title may in any case be dispensed with.

1.89 The death grant payable by virtue of s. 32 of the Social Security Act 1975 is usually payable to the person who has incurred or intends to incur funeral expenses in connection with the death, and not necessarily to the personal representative. The amount of the grant is not treated as part of the estate of the deceased for any purpose[1].

1 Registrar's Direction (1950) 18 September.

Civil and public service

1.90 Where any sum not exceeding £5,000 in respect of salary, wages or other emoluments or of superannuation benefits is due from a government department on the death of any person, probate or other proof of title may be dispensed with, and the appropriate authority may pay the whole or part of that sum to the personal representatives or to or among the person or persons appearing to be beneficially entitled to the estate of the deceased[1]. The former limit of £1,500 was increased to £5,000 in respect of deaths occurring on or after 11 May 1984, by the Administration of Estates (Small Payments) (Increase of Limit) Order 1984 (p. 922, post). The earlier limit of £500 was increased to £1,500 in relation to deaths occurring on or after 10 August 1975, by the Administration of Estates (Small Payments) (Increase of Limit) Order 1975[2].

1 Superannuation Act 1972, s. 4.
2 See p. 915, post.

1.91 The term 'government department' includes a reference to the bodies listed in Sch. 1 to the Superannuation Act 1972, i.e. certain national museums and galleries, Royal Commissions, etc.

1.92 Similar powers to pay out small amounts without production of a grant apply in respect of: police pensions; firemen's pensions; superannuation allowances or gratuities to teachers or other persons in the educational service, gratuities to their personal representatives or superannuation benefits allotted to their dependants; salary, wages or superannuation benefits due to persons employed in specified public services, local government service and health services; and sums due from the Greater London Council, or other local authority, to a deceased officer or pensioner on account of remuneration, pension, superannuation or other allowance, gratuity or annuity or by way of repayment of superannuation contributions[1].

1 See, e.g., Local Government Act 1972, s. 119, as amended by the Administration of Estates (Small Payments) (Increase of Limit) Order 1975 (p. 915, post) and by the Administration of Estates (Small Payments) (Increase of Limit) Order 1984 (p. 922, post).

Members of Parliament

1.93   Amounts payable in respect of pensions or refund of pensions contributions of deceased members or office holders of the House of Commons may be paid on production of a grant or confirmation issued by any court in the United Kingdom. If the amount payable, excluding any interest, does not exceed £5,000 it may be paid by the trustees of the Parliamentary Contributory Pension Fund without production of a grant, in whole or in part to any person or persons who appear to the trustees to be beneficially entitled to the estate of the deceased, but if written notice of any claim against the estate is received by the trustees before they have made full payment then, except where the sum payable appears to be bona vacantia, they must make no, or no further, payment to anyone other than the personal representative until the claim is satisfied or withdrawn[1].

1   Parliamentary and other Pensions Act 1972, s. 24. The former limit of £500 was increased to £1,500 in relation to deaths occurring on or after 10 August 1975 by the Administration of Estates (Small Payments) (Increase of Limit) Order 1975 (see p. 915, post) and to £5,000 in respect of deaths occurring on or after 11 May 1984 by the Administration of Estates (Small Payments) (Increase of Limit) Order 1984: p. 922, post.

HM Forces

1.94   Amounts not exceeding the present limit of £5,000[1] on account of: army and air force pay or pensions[2], assets in the hands of the military or air force authorities or Secretary of State[3], or standing in the books of the Admiralty to the credit of a deceased naval officer, seaman or marine[4], and on account of a Greenwich Hospital pension[5] may be all paid without production of a grant of representation where the death occurred on or after 11 May 1984. In the case of death prior to 11 May 1984 but after 10 August 1975 a limit of £1,500 applies. In the case of death prior to 10 August 1975, but after 4 September 1965, a limit of £500 applies.

1   See the Administration of Estates (Small Payments) Act 1965, s. 1(1) as amended by the Administration of Estates (Small Payments) (Increase of Limit) Orders 1975 and 1984.
2   Pensions and Yeomanry Pay Act 1884, s. 4, as amended by ibid.
3   Regimental Debts Act 1893, ss. 7, 9, 16, as amended by ibid.
4   Navy and Marines (Property of Deceased) Act 1865, s. 6, as amended by ibid.
5   Greenwich Hospital Act 1942, s. 2, as amended by ibid.

USA Veterans

1.95   Where an agreement is made between the Minister of Social Security and the Administrator of Veterans' Affairs appointed under the law of the United States of America for the administration by the Minister of payments by the Administrator in respect of a resident of the United Kingdom the Minister may, if the aggregate amount or value of the money or investments held on trust for such person at his death does not exceed the sum of £5,000, transfer the same to the persons who would be beneficially entitled if they had formed part of the deceased's estate; but this power cannot be exercised where such money or investments would devolve under any enactment or rule of law as to escheat or bona vacantia[1].

1   USA Veterans' Pensions (Administration) Act 1949, s. 1(3), as amended.

Merchant seamen

1.96 Property of a deceased seaman, dying on or after 11 May 1984, in the hands of the Secretary of State not exceeding £5,000 may be paid or delivered by the Secretary of State without a grant of representation[1].

1 Merchant Shipping Act 1970, s. 66(2), as amended by the Administration of Estates (Small Payments) (Increase of Limit) Orders 1975 and 1984. In the case of death prior to 11 May 1984 but after 10 August 1975 the limit is £1,500 and in the case of death prior to 10 August 1975, but after 4 September 1965, the limit is £500.

Miscellaneous and local Acts

1.97 The following provisions permitting the payment of small sums without production of a grant were amended by s. 1(1) of the Administration of Estates (Small Payments) Act 1965 and further amended by the Administration of Estates (Small Payments) (Increase of Limit) Orders 1975 and 1984[1], by the substitution, in cases where the death occurred on or since 11 May 1984, of a limit of £5,000 for those previously in force[2]:

- Great Western Railway Act 1835, s. 45(8);
- Taff Vale Railway Act 1895, s. 18(10);
- London Midland and Scottish Railway (Road Transport) Act 1924, s. 61(11);
- Southern Railway (Road Transport) Act 1928, s. 99(12);
- London and North Eastern Railway (Road Transport) Act 1924, s. 3(12)(b).

1 See pp. 780 and 915, 922, post.
2 In the case of death before 11 May 1984 but after 10 August 1975 the limit is £1,500 and in the case of death before 10 August 1975, but after 4 September 1965, the limit is £500.

1.98 In those instances where this power originally applied only where the deceased died intestate s. 3 of the Act of 1965 extended it to cases where the deceased left a will.

1.99 A similar increase to £5,000 of the amount which may be disposed of by nomination is effected by s. 2 of the Act (as amended by the Administration of Estates (Small Payments) (Increase of Limit) Orders 1975 and 1984) in the following provisions:

- Great Western Railway Act 1835, s. 45(7);
- Taff Vale Railway Act 1895, s. 18(9);
- London Midland and Scottish Railway Act 1924, s. 61(9);
- Southern Railway Act 1924, s. 99(10).

Power to amend or repeal other provisions for small payments

1.100 Section 5 of the Administration of Estates (Small Payments) Act 1965[1] enables the Treasury by statutory instrument to substitute a limit of £500 for lower limits on the power to pay sums due on death without the production of a grant which appear in any Act (including a local Act) not specifically mentioned in that Act. Similarly any provision in a local Act which was superseded by s. 25(1) of the Local Government Superannuation Act 1953[2] may be repealed. Under these powers the provisions of various local Acts have been amended to provide a limit of £500 (but since increased to £1,500 and £5,000: see following paragraphs), and certain superseded provisions have been repealed, by the Administration of Estates (Small Payments) Order 1967[3].

1 See p. 781, post.
2 19 Halsbury's Statutes (3rd edn) 708: since repealed and replaced by Local Government Act 1972, s. 119.
3 S.I. 1967 No. 1850.

Power to increase the limit

1.101   Section 6 of the Administration of Estates (Small Payments) Act 1965[1] empowers the Treasury, by order made by statutory instrument, to increase the limit of £500 in any of the enactments amended by s. 1 or 2 of that Act and similar statutes containing a limit of £500. Any such order will apply in relation to deaths occurring after the expiration of one month beginning with the date on which the order comes into force or, in the case of nominations, those delivered or made after one month beginning with that date.

1 See p. 782, post.

1.102   As already noted, the power given by s. 6 of the Administration of Estates (Small Payments) Act 1965 to increase the limit of £500 in the enactments amended by ss. 1 and 2 of that Act has been exercised by the Administration of Estates (Small Payments) (Increase of Limit) Orders 1975 and 1984. The present limit is £5,000.

1.103   These Orders similarly increased the limit of £500 to £1,500 and further to £5,000 appearing in a number of other statutes giving similar powers, i.e. the Ministerial Salaries and Members' Pensions Act 1965, s. 14(2), the Forestry Act 1967, Sch. 1, para. 12, the Merchant Shipping Act 1970, s. 66(2), the Superannuation Act 1972, s. 4(1), the Parliamentary and Other Pensions Act 1972, s. 24(1), the National Debt Act 1972, s. 6(1), the Local Government Act 1972, s. 119(1) and the Friendly Societies Act 1974, ss. 66–68.

1.104   The increases apply in relation to deaths occurring on or after 10 August 1975 (£1,500) and 11 May 1984 (£5,000) respectively.

CHAPTER 2
General procedure in registry

Summary

At the Principal Registry

Situation of offices

2.01 Section 105 of the Supreme Court Act 1981[1] provides that application for a grant of probate or administration may be made at the Principal Registry of the Family Division. The Principal Registry is situated at Somerset House, Strand, London, WC2R 1LP. The Probate Department's Public Enquiries telephone number is 0171 936 6983 and the relevant fax number is 0171 936 6946.

1 See p. 843, post.

By whom application made

2.02 Application for a grant may be made through a solicitor[1], duly certificated in accordance with the Solicitors Act 1974[2], acting on behalf of the applicant. Even if the solicitor holds an English practising certificate, he is not entitled to extract a grant unless he gives an address within the jurisdiction of the High Court of Justice[3].

1 NCPR 4(1).
2 41 Halsbury's Statutes (4th edn) 12.
3 NCPR 4(2).

2.03 When s. 54 and s. 55 of the Courts and Legal Services Act 1990 (see pp. 894–896, post) come into force, on a day to be appointed, application may be made through one of the various bodies or persons qualified in accordance with these sections.

2.04 Alternatively, application may be made in person (see paras. **2.81** ff., post).

Settling documents to lead grant

2.05 In any case where it is desired, drafts of the oath or other documents to lead a grant of representation may be submitted to the Probate Department of the

21

Registry for settling. The fee for perusing and settling each document is £5[1]. The settled drafts must be lodged with the papers to lead the grant.

1 NC Probate Fees Order 1981, Fee 12.

2.06   It is not the practice to settle affidavits of facts (e.g. affidavits to lead an order of the district judge, or affidavits as to due execution of wills).

Preliminary order of district judge

2.07   In certain circumstances it is necessary to obtain an order of the district judge prior to the issue of a grant. For a list of such orders, see 'Ex parte applications' (paras. **25.11** and **25.12**, post), where a reference is given to the place at which each type of application is dealt with.

Lodging papers for grant

2.08   The solicitor or his professional or lay agent must leave with the Receiver of Papers in the Probate Department the 'papers to lead the grant', viz., the will and codicils (if any); the oath; the Inland Revenue account unless dispensed with (see Chap. 8 and the Capital Transfer Tax (Delivery of Accounts) Regulations 1981, as amended, p. 920, post), and such affidavits, renunciations, certificates, etc. as may be necessary. Broadly speaking, and subject to specified exceptions, the regulations dispense with the need to deliver an inheritance tax or a capital transfer tax account where the deceased died on or after 1 April 1981, domiciled in the United Kingdom, and the gross value of the estate does not exceed the threshold from time to time prescribed (see Chap. 8). The Receiver gives a receipt for the papers, which must be produced on any subsequent enquiry concerning the case. Before leaving the papers with the Receiver the ad valorem fee, and the fees for any office copies of the grant required by the applicant (see para. **4.243**, post), are paid to the cashier at the Registry, payment being denoted by a machine imprint on a fee sheet. For Table of Fees, see Appendix III, pp. 961 ff., post. Wherever possible probate fees should be paid by cheque. Cheques for fees in respect of applications should be drawn in favour of 'H.M. Paymaster-General'[1].

1 Establishment Officer's Circular, 1 December 1977.

Postal, or document exchange, applications

2.09   Applications through solicitors for all types of grant are accepted by post or document exchange. The registry will deal with all the simpler queries as far as practicable by telephone or through the post or document exchange, although in more complicated cases the solicitor may be requested to call at the registry.

2.10   Applications for the issue or resealing of grants submitted to the Principal Registry by post should be addressed to:

The Receiver of Papers, Probate Department,
Principal Registry of the Family Division,
Somerset House, Strand, London WC2R 1LP.

2.11   The Principal Registry is a member of the British Document Exchange and its box number is DX 396 LONDON/CHANCERY LANE.

2.12 Remittances for fees should be by crossed cheque made payable to 'H.M. Paymaster-General'. Solicitors are requested to state in all communications their reference or the name of the person dealing with the particular matter.

2.13 Where it is necessary for an Inland Revenue account to be assessed in the Capital Taxes Office prior to issue of the grant (e.g. in the case of foreign domicile) the solicitor should deal with this before sending the papers to the registry: the registry will not undertake the transmission of such accounts to the Capital Taxes Office. Similarly, whenever inheritance tax or capital transfer tax is payable on delivery of the account, the amount, as assessed either by the solicitor under the 'self assessment' procedure or by the Capital Taxes Office, must be paid to the Finance Division, Inland Revenue and a receipt endorsed on the account before the probate papers are sent to the Principal Registry.

2.14 Postal remittances for inheritance tax or capital transfer tax payable in England and Wales should be sent to:

Finance Division,
Inland Revenue (A),
Barrington Road,
Worthing, West Sussex,
BN12 4XH. (DX 90950 Worthing 3)

2.15 Solicitors are reminded that the majority of queries on probate applications are in connection with discrepancies between the various documents submitted. Delays will be reduced if the documents are cross-checked for accuracy and consistency of spelling and dates before swearing.

2.16 The submission of original wills and other probate documents and remittances by post (or document exchange) is at the sender's risk. The registry cannot accept any liability in the event of non-delivery[1].

1 *Practice Direction* [1975] 2 All ER 280, [1975] 1 WLR 662.

2.17 It is emphasised by the registry that enquiries as to whether or not an Inland Revenue account must be delivered in any particular case should not be made of the probate registries, but should be made to the Capital Taxes Office, Ferrers House, PO Box 38, Castle Meadow Road, Nottingham NG2 1BB (tel. 0115 9740000, fax 0115 9742432, DX 701201 Nottingham 4)[1].

1 *Practice Direction* [1981] 2 All ER 832, [1981] 1 WLR 1185.

Resealing

2.18 Applications for resealing Colonial grants may be made at the Principal Registry or any district probate registry. The papers may be lodged, or sent by post or document exchange, by any authorised agent (not necessarily a solicitor) on behalf of the grantee (see Chap. 18).

Postal applications from abroad

2.19 The requirement that every solicitor through whom an application for a grant is made must give the address of his place of business within the jurisdiction of the High Court applies equally to applications for grants transmitted through the post or document exchange: such applications can be accepted only from solicitors practising in England or Wales.

2.20 This requirement does not, however, apply to applications for resealing, which may be submitted by post by solicitors and other correspondents from addresses out of England and Wales[1] (see paras. **18.68** ff., post).

1 Secretary's Circular, 29 June 1959.

Procedure in registry

2.21 In the registry, any will or codicil is photographed and notice of the application is at once sent by the Principal Registry to the registry where the central indexes are maintained (currently the Leeds District Probate Registry) and the records are searched to ascertain that no other grant has been made in respect of the same estate, that no other application for a grant is pending and that no caveat has been entered. (As to caveats, see Chap. 23.) The papers are then examined in the Probate Department and, if in order, a form of grant is prepared, to which is attached a photographic copy of the will and codicils (if any). The grant is signed by a probate officer authorised by the President and sealed with the seal of the Family Division. Photographic copies of the grant and will are filed for record purposes, and are available for inspection by the public, and an entry of the grant is recorded in the calendar (i.e. index), which is open for public search (see Chap. 2l).

Issue of grant

2.22 Grants are sent to the extracting solicitor by post or document exchange, except where the application was lodged by a law agent on his behalf. A list of all grants issued during a week is normally available for public inspection in the calendar of grants on the Friday of the following week[1].

1 Registrar's Direction (1973) 17 December: the appearance of the entry in the calendar is delayed in order that the grant may be in the possession of the solicitor by the time the entry appears.

2.23 The grant is sent to the solicitor's address as shown on the fee sheet completed by him. Law agents call at the Sealer's department of the registry to collect their grants.

Form of grant

2.24 From 1 May 1975, grants of letters of administration (with or without will) no longer included a statement of the way in which prior classes, other than executors, were cleared off, nor the capacity, or title, in which administration is granted. No change was made at that time in the form of grants of probate.

2.25 The practice has continued to evolve. It is no longer the practice to show on grants of letters of administration with will how executors have been cleared off, nor on grants of probate how a substituted or conditionally appointed executor has qualified.

2.26 It is emphasised that there should be no change in the form of oath to lead a grant. This must, in accordance with NCPR 8(4), continue to state the way in which prior classes are cleared off, and the relationship and capacity in which the applicants claim to be entitled. Similarly the oath should contain all the relevant facts to show how any substitution has taken effect or how any condition has been satisfied. This applies equally to an oath to lead a second or subsequent grant in an estate, even if it involves repeating details which were included in the oath which led the previous grant.

2.27 It has also become the practice to leave out from grants any unnecessary words or information, such as:

(a) titles such as 'Mr', 'Mrs' or 'Miss';
(b) aliases of the deceased, unless they are required for the purposes of realising assets;
(c) over-full versions of an address; normally only the version required by the post office will be shown;
(d) addresses, other than the last residential address, of the deceased; former addresses will only be shown if specifically requested and a sufficient reason is given;
(e) former names or aliases of a grantee; only the correct current names of a grantee will be shown.

Although the above matters will not be included in the grant, where they are relevant for identification purposes, etc., they should still be dealt with in the oath.

2.28 Any person requiring to ascertain any of the details no longer appearing in a grant may, on payment of a small fee at the registry from which the grant issued, inspect or obtain a copy of the oath sworn by the grantee or grantees[1].

1 *Practice Direction* (1975) 119 Sol Jo 276.

2.29 Following the repeal of s. 30 of the Customs and Inland Revenue Act 1881 by the Finance Act 1975 in relation to deaths occurring after 12 March 1975, grants of representation in the estates of persons dying after that date do not indicate the amount of inheritance tax or capital transfer tax, if any, paid. It is still the probate registry practice, however, for the gross and net values of the estate to be stated in grants of representation, whether the death occurred before, on or after 12 March 1975[1].

1 Registrar's Direction (1975) 14 March.

2.30 The Non-Contentious Probate Fees Order 1981, as amended (see Appendix III, pp. 961 ff., post) provides, inter alia, for the payment of a flat fee of £40 on application for a grant of representation in cases in which the net value of the estate passing under the grant exceeds £10,000 but does not exceed £25,000, a fee of £80 where the net value exceeds £25,000 but does not exceed £40,000, a fee of £150 where the net value exceeds £40,000 but does not exceed £70,000, a fee of £215 where the net value exceeds £70,000 but does not exceed £100,000, and a fee of £300 where the net value exceeds £100,000 but does not exceed £200,000. No fee is payable if the value does not exceed £10,000.

2.31 Consequently in those cases in which an Inland Revenue account is not required to be delivered (see Chap. 8), it will be sufficient to state in the oath to lead the grant the brackets into which the estate falls. Every oath must contain a statement by the applicant as follows:

'To the best of my knowledge, information and belief the gross estate passing under the grant does not exceed/amounts to* £   and that the net estate does not exceed/amounts to* £   [and that this is not a case in which an Inland Revenue Account is required to be delivered]*'

The alternatives marked with an asterisk are to be deleted as appropriate.

2.32   In addition every oath must state the age of the deceased. In those cases in which the exact age is not known, the applicant should give the best estimate he can[1].

1 *Practice Direction* [1981] 2 All ER 832, [1981] 1 WLR 1185.

2.33   In those cases where an Inland Revenue account is delivered and in respect of which specific figures as to the value of the estate are available, those figures should be set out fully in the oath.

2.34   The wording at the foot of the form of grant is now as follows:

'It is hereby certified that it appears from information supplied on the application for this grant that the gross value of the said estate in the United Kingdom   does not exceed/amounts to £ _   and that the net value of such estate does not exceed/ amounts to £   '

2.35   This version is used for *all* grants, deleting the alternatives as appropriate, save that where the death occurred before 13 March 1975, the certificate prescribed by Form 1 in the Non-Contentious Probate Rules 1987 is still used[1].

1 Secretary's Circulars, 23 June 1981 and 23 October 1981.

Solicitor's reference

2.36   If a solicitor includes his office reference immediately following his name at the head of the oath to lead the grant, e.g.:

'Extracted by A B & Co. (ref. WB) (address)'

the reference will be included, following the solicitor's name, at the foot of the grant, without any special request[1].

1 Registrar's Direction (1972) 9 March.

Earliest time for issue of grant

2.37   Except by leave of a district judge, no grant of probate or administration (with will annexed) may issue within seven days of the death of the deceased, and no grant of administration may issue within 14 days thereof[1].

1 NCPR 6(2).

2.38   Such leave is applied for by submitting evidence of the facts (usually on affidavit) to the Probate Department of the Principal Registry.

Expedition of issue of grant

2.39   The registry is prepared to give consideration to requests for special expedition where the issue of a grant is desired as a matter of particular urgency. A verbal request to the Principal of the Probate Department when the papers are lodged, stating the grounds, is sufficient: it is, however, to be noted that special expedition will only be given for cases where some hardship would otherwise result[1].

1 Secretary's Circular, 13 November 1951.

Papers defective

2.40 The notification of any defect in the papers will, wherever possible, indicate the nature of the query. Simple queries may, so far as possible, be dealt with by post or document exchange, but in the case of complicated matters the solicitor may be required to call at the registry[1]. Enquiry should be made at the Probate Department. Law agents are not notified by post or document exchange, but are required to call regularly at the registry to ascertain the progress of the cases in which they are acting as agents for the extracting solicitor.

1 *Practice Direction* [1975] 2 All ER 280, [1975] 1 WLR 662.

2.41 NC Probate Rule 6(1) provides:

'A district judge or registrar shall not allow any grant to issue until all inquiries which he may see fit to make have been answered to his satisfaction.'

Applications to district judge

2.42 A district judge or registrar may require any application to be made by summons to a district judge or registrar in chambers or to a High Court judge in chambers or open court (NCPR 61(1)).

2.43 For the practice as to summonses, see paras. **25.193** ff., post.

2.44 As to appeal from a decision or requirement of a district judge or registrar, see paras. **25.243** ff., post.

Two applications for grant

2.45 Where there are two applications lodged in the same estate a grant cannot be issued until one of the applications is either refused or withdrawn[1]. If the parties are antagonistic, the matter may be brought before the district judge by summons under NCPR 27(6). (For procedure, see paras. **25.193** ff., post.) Unless there is a good reason to the contrary, where the applicants are equally entitled to the grant it is usually made to the first applicant in point of time.

1 Supreme Court Act 1981, s. 107 (see p. 843, post).

Change of solicitor

2.46 Where, after papers have been lodged, the conduct of the case is transferred from the solicitor then acting to another, a notice of change should be filed.

Official errors in grants

2.47 Any grant which is found to be inaccurate or deficient by reason of official error, and is returned to the registry for correction within 14 days of its sealing, will be rewritten, provided it has not been registered. If it is necessary to return a grant for this purpose, all official copies which have been ordered should accompany it.

2.48   In all other cases correction must be made by district judge's order through the Record Keeper's Department[1].

1 Registrar's Direction (1940) 14 November.

Death of grantee before issue of grant

2.49   When the registry is notified of the death of an intended grantee, immediate steps are taken to see whether the grant has been sealed. If the grant has not been sealed, a 'sole grantee' case will be treated as if the application had been withdrawn. Where there are two or more applicants and a grant may properly be made to the survivor(s) alone, the case will be allowed to proceed, a note of the death being made on the documents. A letter from the extracting solicitor, or a death certificate, is acceptable as sufficient evidence of death.

2.50   If the grant has been sealed before notification of death is received, it must stand unless revoked. Revocation is normally appropriate when it is established that the grantee died before the grant was sealed. Evidence of death as in the preceding paragraph should be lodged.

2.51   Where a grant of probate is to be revoked because of the death of one of two or more executors before sealing and a new grant is to be issued to the survivor(s), a combined application for revocation and issue of the new grant may be made (see paras. **17.57–17.59**, post). In this event, no further Inland Revenue account is necessary. Notice of the revocation and issue of the new grant is given by the registry to the Capital Taxes Office.

2.52   It is not possible to apply this procedure to other types of grant because of the varied situations that can arise. However, in suitable cases the swearing of a further oath by the surviving grantee may be dispensed with, its place in the records being taken by a consent by him to the issue of the new grant, endorsed with a cross-reference to the oath filed on the earlier application.

2.53   If the grantee died after the sealing of the grant, then the grant must stand, and the normal procedure for a further grant after the death of the grantee applies.

2.54   There may be cases of doubt when the grantee dies on the day of the date of the grant and it is difficult to establish whether he died before or after the actual sealing. The case of *Re Seaford* [1968] P 53, leaves considerable doubt whether the doctrine of relation back should be extended to transactions such as grants, and suggests rather that the court should do its best on the available evidence to establish the facts. In such cases the district judge will normally require an affidavit on which to make a decision whether to exercise his discretion under NCPR 41 to revoke the grant[1].

1 Registrar's Direction (1975) 19 June.

At district probate registries and sub-registries

Situation of registries

2.55   Section 105 of the Supreme Court Act 1981[1] provides that application for grants of probate or administration and for the revocation of grants may be made to the Principal Registry of the Family Division or to a district probate registry. It is further provided by s. 104 of the Act of 1981[2] that the Lord Chancellor may by order direct that there shall be district probate registries of the High Court at such places and for such districts as are specified in the order.

1 See p. 843, post.
2 See p. 843, post.

2.56   The current list of district probate registries and sub-registries is contained in the District Probate Registries Order 1982 as amended[1] which Order restates, in effect, the scheme for the establishment of district probate registries as set out in Schedule 2 to the Supreme Court of Judicature (Consolidation) Act 1925[2] as confirmed by paragraph 6 of Schedule 6 to the Supreme Court Act 1981.

1 See p. 921, post.
2 7 Halsbury's Statutes (3rd edn) 573.

2.57   The function of sub-registries is to receive applications for grants and transmit them to their parent registries for the issue of the grants.

2.58   District probate registries and sub-registries are now situate at the following places[1]:–

Registries	Sub-registries	Addresses, telephone numbers, fax numbers and document exchange numbers
Birmingham		The Priory Courts, 33 Bull Street, Birmingham B4 6DU tel. 0121 681 3400/3414 fax 0121 681 3404 DX 701990 Birmingham 7
	Stoke on Trent	Combined Court Centre, Bethesda Street, Hanley, Stoke on Trent ST1 3BP tel. 01782 213736 fax 01782 201944 DX 20736 Hanley
Brighton		William Street, Brighton BN2 2LG tel. 01273 684071 fax 01273 688281 DX 98073 Brighton 3
	Maidstone	The Law Courts, Barker Road, Maidstone ME18 8EW tel. 01622 754966 ext. 234/235 DX 51972 Maidstone 2
Bristol		Ground Floor, The Crescent Centre, Temple Back, Bristol BS1 6EP tel. 0117 9273915/9264619 fax 0117 9259377 DX 94400 Bristol 5
	Bodmin	Market Street, Bodmin, Cornwall PL31 2JW tel. 01208 72279 DX 81858 Bodmin
	Exeter	Eastgate House, High Street, Exeter, Devon EX4 3JZ tel. 01392 74515 DX 8380 Exeter
Cardiff – Probate Registry of Wales		PO Box 474, 2 Park Street, Cardiff CF1 1TB tel. 01222 376467/376479 fax 01222 376466 DX 122782 Cardiff 13

Registries	Sub-registries	Addresses, telephone numbers, fax numbers and document exchange numbers
	Bangor	1st Floor, Bron Castell, High Street, Bangor, Gwynedd LL57 1YS tel. 01248 362410 DX 23186 Bangor 2
	Carmarthen	14 King Street, Carmarthen, Dyfed SA31 1BL tel. 01267 236238 DX 51420 Carmarthen
Ipswich		Level 3, Haven House, 17 Lower Brook Street, Ipswich, Suffolk IP4 1DN tel. 01473 253724/259261 fax 01473 280889 DX 3279 Ipswich
	Norwich	Combined Court Building, The Law Courts, Bishopsgate, Norwich NR3 1UR tel. 01603 761776 DX 5202 Norwich
	Peterborough	1st Floor, Crown Buildings, Rivergate PE1 1EJ tel. 01733 62802 DX 12327 Peterborough 1
Leeds		3rd Floor, Coronet House, Queen Street, Leeds LS1 2BA tel. 0113 2431505 fax 0113 2448145 DX 26451 Leeds (Park Square)
	Lincoln	Mill House, Brayford Side North, Lincoln LN1 1YW tel. 01522 523648 DX 11048 Lincoln 1
	Sheffield	The Court House, Castle Street, Sheffield S3 8LW tel. 0114 2729920 DX 26054 Sheffield 2
Liverpool		Queen Elizabeth II Law Courts, Derby Square, Liverpool L2 1XA tel. 0151 236 8264 fax 0151 236 5575 DX 14246 Liverpool
	Chester	5th Floor, Hamilton House, Hamilton Place, Chester CH1 2DA tel. 01244 345082 DX 22162 Chester Northgate
	Lancaster	Mitre House, Church Street, Lancaster LA1 1HE tel. 01524 36625 DX 63509 Lancaster
Manchester		9th Floor, Astley House, 23 Quay Street, Manchester M3 4AT tel. 0161 834 4319 fax 0161 834 5651 DX 14387 Manchester 1
	Nottingham	Upper Ground Floor, Lambert House, Talbot Street, Nottingham NG1 5NR tel. 0115 9414288 fax 0115 9243374 DX 10055 Nottingham
Newcastle upon Tyne		2nd Floor, Plummer House, Croft Street, Newcastle upon Tyne NE1 6NP tel. 0191 261 8383 fax 0191 233 0868 DX 61081 Newcastle upon Tyne
	Carlisle	Courts of Justice, Earl Street, Carlisle CA1 1DJ tel. 01228 21751 DX 63034 Carlisle
	Middlesbrough	Teesside Combined Court Centre, Russell Street, Middlesbrough, Cleveland TS1 2AE tel. 01642 340001/232947 DX 60536 Middlesbrough

Registries	Sub-registries	Addresses, telephone numbers, fax numbers and document exchange numbers
	York	Duncombe Place, York YO1 2EA tel. 01904 624210 fax 01904 624210 DX 61543 York 1
Oxford		10a New Road, Oxford OX1 1LY tel. 01865 241163 fax 01865 204402 DX 4337 Oxford
	Gloucester	2nd Floor, Combined Court Building, Kimbrose Way, Gloucester GL1 2DG tel. 01452 522585 DX 7537 Gloucester 1
	Leicester	Leicester House, 5th Floor, Lee Circle, Leicester LE1 3RE tel. 0116 2538558 DX 13655 Leicester 4
Winchester		4th Floor, Cromwell House, Andover Road, Winchester, Hants SO23 7EW tel. 01962 853046/863771 fax 01962 877371 DX 96900 Winchester 2

District probate registries and sub-registries are open every weekday, except Saturday, from 9.30am until 4pm.

1 The District Probate Registries Order 1982: S.I. 1982 No. 379 as amended (see p. 921, post).

Transfer of records from discontinued registries

2.59 Section 124 of the Supreme Court Act 1981[1] empowers the Lord Chancellor to direct where original wills and other documents which are under the control of the High Court in the Principal Registry or any district probate registry shall be deposited and preserved. Such documents so deposited shall, subject to the control of the High Court and to probate rules (see NCPR 58), be open to inspection.

1 See p. 847, post.

2.60 The records of former district probate registries which have been closed are held at the following registries:

Registry	Date of Closure	Place of Deposit
Blandford	1941	Winchester
Bury St. Edmunds	1928	Ipswich
Chichester	1928	Winchester
Derby	1928	Nottingham
Durham	1969	York
Hereford	1928	Cardiff
Lewes	1969	Brighton
Lichfield	1928	Birmingham
Northampton	1930	Birmingham
Salisbury	1928	Winchester
Shrewsbury	1941	Chester
Taunton*	1933	Exeter
Wells*	1928	Exeter
Wakefield	1969	Leeds
Worcester	1928	Birmingham

*The records of the Taunton and Wells Registries were destroyed with the Exeter records when the Exeter District Probate Registry was demolished by enemy action in 1942.

2.61   The records of those former district probate registries which have been re-classified as probate sub-registries are in general retained at the sub-registries, under the control of the registrar of the parent district registry.

Jurisdiction of district probate registries

2.62   By virtue of s. 105(b) and s. 106(1)[1], it is enacted that applications for grants of probate or administration and for the revocation of grants may be made to a district probate registry, and that any grant made by a district probate registrar shall be made in the name of the High Court under the seal used in the registry.

1 See p. 843, post.

2.63   There are no territorial limitations on the jurisdiction of the respective registries. With the exception noted in the following paragraph, application for a grant may be made at any registry or sub-registry.

Administration pending suit

2.64   A grant of administration pending suit can be made only at the Principal Registry[1]. As to application for an order for such a grant, see paras. **37.01** ff., post.

1 Direction, 1935; NCPR 7(1).

Second or subsequent grants

2.65   There are now no restrictions as to the registries at which application may be made for any type of second or subsequent grant: such a grant may be issued from the registry at which the previous grant was made or from any other probate registry. (Section 153 of the Supreme Court of Judicature (Consolidation) Act 1925, which formerly imposed such restrictions, was repealed by the Administration of Justice Act 1969, s. 28.)

Powers of district probate registrars

2.66   District probate registrars now have, in relation to matters proceeding in the district probate registries, essentially the same powers as the district judges of the Principal Registry (see definition of 'registrar' in NCPR 2(1)).

2.67   No grant may, however, be made by a district probate registrar in any case where there is contention until the contention is disposed of, or in any case where it appears to the district registrar that a grant ought not to be made without the directions of a High Court judge or a district judge of the Principal Registry[1]. In any case where the district probate registrar seeks directions under the aforesaid provision, he is required to send a statement of the matter in question to the Principal Registry for directions[2]. Where directions are sought, a district judge of the Principal Registry may either confirm that the matter be referred to a High Court judge and give directions accordingly or he may direct the district probate registrar to proceed with the matter in accordance with such instructions as are deemed necessary, or direct him to take no further action in relation to the matter[3].

1 Direction, 1935; NCPR 7(1).
2 NCPR 7(2).
3 NCPR 7(3).

2.68 By s. 107 of the Supreme Court Act 1981, it is enacted that:

'Subject to probate rules, no grant in respect of the estate, or part of the estate, of a deceased person shall be made out of the Principal Registry or any district probate registry on any application if, at any time before the making of a grant, it appears to the registrar concerned that some other application has been made in respect of that estate or, as the case may be, that part of it and has not been either refused or withdrawn.'

2.69 Where any direction of a registrar, or any preliminary order, is necessary in connection with the issue of a grant, the application should be made at the registry at which the application for the grant has been, or will be, made.

Application for grant at district registry

2.70 A solicitor makes application for a grant at a district probate registry by lodging at, or sending by post or document exchange to, the registry, or a sub-registry attached to that registry (see para. **2.58**, above) the papers to lead the grant, namely, the will and codicils (if any), the oath, the Inland Revenue account (unless such an account is not required, see Chap. 8) and any affidavits etc., which the particular circumstances of the case may render necessary. A personal applicant may apply for a grant at the registry or sub-registry, or at a probate office (see paras. **2.88** ff., post).

Procedure in district registry

2.71 After the papers have been lodged, the procedure, including the photography of the will and codicils (if any), is similar to that followed in the Principal Registry (see para. **2.21**, above). Notice of the application is at once sent by the registry to the registry where the central indexes of pending grant applications and caveats are kept (currently the Leeds District Probate Registry) and the records are searched in order either to prevent the possibility of two grants issuing in respect of the same estate, or to prevent a grant being issued in an estate where there is another application pending or where a caveat remains effective[1].

1 NCPR 44(4) and 57.

2.72 On receiving confirmation that no impediment has been found and provided that in the meantime the papers have been found to be correct, the grant is issued.

2.73 Sub-registries have no power to issue grants. Where the papers are lodged at a sub-registry, they are forwarded after examination to the appropriate district registry for the issue of the grant. Notice of the application is sent to the searching registry by the sub-registry, but to avoid delay the result of the search is returned direct to the district registry.

2.74 Grants issuing from a district probate registry may be signed either by a district registrar or by a probate officer. All grants are authenticated by the seal of the registry[1].

1 *Practice Direction* (1974) 118 Sol Jo 264.

2.75 As from 3 January 1995 grants issued out of the Probate Registry of Wales are issued in bi-lingual form (corresponding texts in English and Welsh) unless in a particular case it appears to the Registrar to be necessary or expedient to issue the grant in English only[1].

1 *Practice Direction* [1994].

Copy will etc., for Principal Registry

2.76   A copy of every will and codicil proved, and of every grant made, in a district probate registry is filed at the Principal Registry.

Payment of fees and tax

2.77   In the district probate registries and sub-registries fees are taken in cash, preferably by crossed cheque made payable to H.M. Paymaster-General.

2.78   The former practice whereby district probate registries and sub-registries were generally prepared to forward, on behalf of solicitors, Inland Revenue accounts with the remittance to the Inland Revenue has been discontinued. The Inland Revenue account must now be receipted before it is lodged with the oath at the registry or sub-registry. Similarly, if the Inland Revenue account has to be controlled by the Capital Taxes Office before a grant may be issued, the account must be so controlled before it is lodged at the registry or sub-registry[1].

1 *Practice Direction* [1989] 3 All ER 938.

Appeal from district registrar

2.79   Any person aggrieved by a decision or requirement of a district probate registrar may appeal therefrom to a High Court judge[1]. The appeal is by way of summons issued at the Principal Registry: for procedure, see paras. **25.243** ff., below.

1 *Practice Direction* (1974) 118 Sol Jo 264; NCPR 65.

Printed calendar

2.80   A copy of the printed calendar containing a note of every grant passed in England and Wales in each year can be inspected at a district registry.

Personal applications

Personal application for grant

2.81   A personal application for a grant of probate or letters of administration (with or without will) may be made by the person entitled to the grant[1]. There is no financial limit on the value of the estate.

1 NCPR 5(1).

2.82   Except for an application to reseal a Colonial grant a personal applicant may not apply through an agent, whether paid or unpaid, and may not be attended by any person acting or appearing to act as his adviser[1].

1 NCPR 5(2). In this respect, a nominee of a non-trust corporation is regarded as an agent (Secretary's Circular, 2 March 1982). As to grant to the attorney of a person entitled, see paras. **11.31** ff., post.

2.83 A personal application may not be received or proceeded with if it becomes necessary to bring the matter before the court by action or summons, nor if an application has already been made by a solicitor on behalf of the applicant and not withdrawn[1].

1 NCPR 5(3).

2.84 The district judge or registrar has a general discretion to direct that any personal application be not proceeded with[1]. Cases where there is any dispute between interested parties or where the matter presents any unusual complication are unlikely to be suitable for personal application.

1 NCPR 5(3)(c).

Resealing

2.85 An application under NCPR 39 for resealing a Colonial grant may be made at any registry by the grantee himself or by any person authorised in writing to apply on his behalf[1].

1 NCPR 39(1).

2.86 It is not essential in the Principal Registry that the application should be made through the Personal Application Department: if the applicant is able to obtain the requisite documents he may lodge them, properly completed, with, or send them to, the Receiver of Papers in the Probate Department at the Principal Registry (for details of the documents required and the fees, see paras. **18.70–18.72**, post). Alternatively the applicant may avail himself of the services of the Personal Application Department of the Principal Registry. This involves the payment of an additional fee and personal attendance at the department on at least one occasion by the grantee or some person acting on his behalf.

2.87 For the practice in relation to resealing, see Chap. 18.

Where made

2.88 A personal application may be made at the Principal Registry or any district probate registry or sub-registry. There are no territorial limits on the jurisdiction.

2.89 In addition to the probate registries and sub-registries there are nearly one hundred probate offices throughout England and Wales at which personal applications can be accepted and dealt with. These offices are open usually only on one or two days per week, and in general attendance is by appointment only. Applications in which a solicitor is instructed cannot be accepted at a probate office.

2.90 A list giving the location of the probate offices and their respective parent registries (to which all communications should be addressed) is given in Appendix VII, pp. 1105 ff., post.

Procedure

2.91 A booklet giving details of the procedure on a personal application may be obtained from any probate registry or sub-registry. The forms of application may be obtained on request by letter, telephone or personal call, from the nearest registry or sub-registry. These should be completed by the applicant to show full details of the estate left by the deceased, and names and addresses etc., of the deceased and the applicant, and sent to, or handed in at, the registry or sub-registry at which the applicant desires to attend. An applicant wishing to attend at a probate office should send the forms to the registry or sub-registry having control of the particular office. A death certificate and the will (and codicils), if any, left by the deceased should accompany the forms.

2.92   On receipt of the completed forms, notice of an appointment to attend at the chosen registry or office will be sent to the applicant. A second visit is sometimes necessary, and this will be arranged at the time of the first attendance or subsequently.

2.93   The oath, Inland Revenue account (if required) and any other documents necessary in connection with the application are prepared in the registry[1].

1 NCPR 5(6).

2.94   Unless otherwise directed by the district judge or registrar, every oath or affidavit required on a personal application must be sworn by all the deponents before an authorised officer of a probate registry[1].

1 NCPR 5(7).

Fees

2.95   An additional fee (Fee No. 2) is payable in applications for grants or resealing made through the Personal Application Department. For the fees in respect of personal applications, see p. 962, post.

Inheritance tax or capital transfer tax

2.96   In cases where inheritance tax or capital transfer tax is payable the amount of this, as provisionally assessed, must be paid by the applicant before the grant can be issued. As to inheritance tax and capital transfer tax, see Chap. 8.

Administration guarantee

2.97   A guarantee will only be required in one of those very rare cases where a direction has been given under NCPR 68 that the case is to continue to proceed under the Non-Contentious Probate Rules 1954 and where a guarantee is required under those rules., In such a case for the relevant rules and practice reference should be made to pp. 32 and 246 ff. of the 26th edition of this work.

CHAPTER 3
Wills and codicils

Summary

Interpretation of wills

Testator dying before 1 January 1983

3.01 As a book of practice, this work is not primarily concerned with the subject of construction and interpretation of wills (for which see, generally, *Williams on Wills* and other leading textbooks). However, inevitably, for example in relation to the admission of testamentary documents to proof, questions of construction and interpretation do arise. The main difficulty confronting the court in this respect is the extent of evidence admissible by the court as an aid to interpretation. A vast body of case law exists on the subject (reference to some of which is made in this work) from which certain principles have emerged. Broadly, these principles may be summarised as follows. Save in the case of a mentally disabled person (as to which, see paras. **3.430** ff., post), the court has no power to make or rewrite a will for a testator and, so long as there is no legitimate dispute as to its meaning, the court must admit a testator's will as giving effect to his intentions. However, where there is some doubt about the meaning of the will, the court may resort to the 'surrounding circumstances' as an aid in ascertaining its meaning. Generally, however, it is not possible to admit extrinsic evidence merely to show the testator's intention at the time he made the will, unless the will contains a latent ambiguity (e.g. the words used may apply to more than one person or thing), in which case, where evidence of the surrounding circumstances does not resolve the problem, then evidence of the testator's intention may be admitted.

Testator dying on or after 1 January 1983

3.02   In May 1973, the Law Reform Committee produced a report (19th Report of the Law Reform Committee on Interpretation of Wills: Cmnd. 5301) in which the Committee concluded that the existing rules on the question of admission of evidence were too rigid, and recommended that in certain respects those rules should be relaxed and the case law principles replaced by a comprehensive formula. Statutory recognition was given to the (minority) recommendation of the Committee, by the introduction of statutory guidelines, in the form of general rules as to evidence, for the purpose of interpretation of wills. These general rules are contained in s. 21 of the Administration of Justice Act 1982, which provides as follows:

> '21.—(1) This section applies to a will—
> (a) in so far as any part of it is meaningless;
> (b) in so far as the language used in any part of it is ambiguous on the face of it;
> (c) in so far as evidence, other than evidence of the testator's intention, shows that the language used in any part of it is ambiguous in the light of surrounding circumstances.
>   (2) In so far as this section applies to a will extrinsic evidence, including evidence of the testator's intention, may be admitted to assist in its interpretation.'

3.03   Section 21 of the 1982 Act applies only to wills (including codicils) of *testators dying on or after 1 January 1983*. Where death occurs before that date, the principles as outlined above continue to apply.

3.04   The broad effect of the new statutory rules is that all evidence (including evidence of the testator's intention) is admissible to resolve ambiguities or difficulties in a will, whenever executed, of a testator dying on or after 1 January 1983, but that where the wording of the will is clear and plain, then direct evidence of the testator's intention is not admissible. In other words, only in those cases where an ambiguity arises (either directly from the will itself or through other evidence of surrounding circumstances) is direct evidence of the testator's intention to be admitted: the ambiguity must first be established; once established, all extrinsic evidence is admissible to resolve that ambiguity (but not to do more than resolve the ambiguity[1]).

1 *Re Williams, Wiles v Madgin* [1985] 1 All ER 964, [1985] 1 WLR 905.

What documents can be proved

Formal validity of wills; law prior to 1964

Movable estate

3.05   At common law the general rule has been that in order to be admissible to proof in England and Wales a will of movable estate must be shown to have been executed in accordance with the formalities required by the law of the domicile of the testator at the time of his death[1]. Thus, where a testator died domiciled in England and Wales, his will, to be recognised as validly executed, had in general to be executed in accordance with the requirements of s. 9 of the Wills Act 1837.

1 *Re Deshais' Goods* (1865) 4 Sw & Tr 13.

Immovable estate

3.06 A will of immovables had to be executed in accordance with the law of the place where the immovable estate was situated. Thus, whatever the domicile of the testator, in order to be accepted as valid to pass immovable estate in England and Wales, a will had to be executed in accordance with s. 9 of the Wills Act 1837.

Power of appointment

3.07 So much of a will as exercised a power of appointment under an English settlement was admissible to proof in this country if the will was executed in accordance with the Wills Act 1837, even though not executed in accordance with the requirements of the law of the testator's domicile[1] (see also paras. **11.298** ff., post).

1 Wills Act 1837, s. 10 (p. 721, post).

Wills Act 1861

3.08 Exceptions to the above general principles in favour of British subjects were created by the Wills Act 1861 (Lord Kingsdown's Act)[1]. Under this Act a will of *personal estate* made by a person who was a British subject at the time of execution was recognised as formally valid if it was executed in accordance with any of the provisions of s. 1 or 2 thereof (see paras. **3.374** ff., post).

1 See p. 727, post.

3.09 Furthermore, under s. 3 of this Act no will was to be held to be revoked or to have become invalid by reason of a subsequent change of domicile of the testator. This section has been held to be of general application and not to be confined, as were ss. 1 and 2, to the wills of British subjects[1], and accordingly a will, whether of a British subject or of an alien, executed in accordance with the law of the testator's domicile at the time of execution was accepted as validly executed even though not shown to have been executed in accordance with the law of the domicile at the date of death.

1 *Re Groos' Estate* [1904] P 269. This decision has been criticised, but the replacement of the Wills Act 1861 by the Wills Act 1963 renders it of diminishing importance.

3.10 The Wills Act 1861 was repealed as from 1 January 1964[1], but the repeal does not invalidate a will executed before that date in accordance with its provisions[2].

1 Wills Act 1963, s. 7(3).
2 Ibid., s. 7(4).

3.11 As to the Wills Act 1861, see also paras. **3.374** ff., post.

Death on or after 1 January 1964: Wills Act 1963

3.12 The statutory provisions and common law rules summarised above were substantially relaxed, in cases where the testator had any foreign connection or any foreign element arises, by the Wills Act 1963[1].

1 See p. 777, post.

3.13   This Act gave effect to certain recommendations in the Fourth Report of the Private International Law Committee set up in 1957, and enabled H.M. Government to ratify the Convention on the Conflict of Laws relating to the Form of Testamentary Dispositions which was concluded at The Hague in October 1961. The Act deals, in general, only with the formal validity of wills[1] and not with such matters as the capacity to make a will or the substantial validity of dispositions.

1   The term 'will' in the Act includes any testamentary instrument or act: the Act thus applies not only to wills and codicils but also to oral dispositions and any form of deliberate revocation.

3.14   The Act applies only to the wills[1] of testators who die after its commencement (i.e. on or after 1 January 1964), but in relation to persons so dying it applies to wills whether made before or after that time[2]. It applies to all persons, whatever their domicile or nationality. As stated above, the Wills Act 1861 is repealed, with a saving for wills validly executed under it before the repeal.

1   The term 'will' in the Act includes any testamentary instrument or act: the Act thus applies not only to wills and codicils but also to oral dispositions and any form of deliberate revocation.
2   Wills Act 1963, s. 7(4).

3.15   Broadly speaking, the effect of the Act is to enable a testator's will to be accepted as properly executed if it is executed in accordance with the requirements of any system of law which he might reasonably have invoked.

3.16   The internal law of England and Wales, as contained in the Wills Act 1837, as subsequently amended, as to the mode of execution and other formal requirements in connection with wills, is unaffected by the Act of 1963, as are the statutory provisions as to privileged wills.

3.17   Under the general rule contained in s. 1, a will is to be treated as properly executed if its execution conformed to the internal law in force in the territory where it was executed, or in the territory where, at the time of its execution or of the testator's death, he was domiciled or had his habitual residence, or in a state of which, at either of those times, he was a national.

3.18   Section 2 contains additional rules, which are without prejudice to the general rule quoted above, and which apply to:

 (i)   wills executed on board a vessel or aircraft;
 (ii)   wills so far as they dispose of immovable property;
(iii)   wills so far as they revoke earlier wills or provisions therein;
(iv)   wills so far as they exercise powers of appointment.

3.19   For discussion of the Wills Act 1963, see paras. **3.392** ff., post.

International wills

3.20   As to the recognition and admission of wills made in conformity with the Unidroit Convention providing for a Uniform Law on the Form of an International Will (Cmnd. 5956), see paras. **3.446** ff., post.

Privileged wills

3.21   As to the privilege of making informal wills allowed to soldiers, sailors and airmen on actual military service and to seamen at sea, see paras. **3.312** ff., post.

Admissibility of wills to proof: deceased domiciled in England and Wales

3.22   Note.—Except where otherwise stated, the subjects discussed in pp. 41 to 89 are applicable only in cases where the deceased died domiciled in England and Wales, or where, although not so domiciled, for some other reason[1], the internal law of England and Wales as to the execution of testamentary instruments is in question. It should also be noted that, in general, the practice in relation to the proof of wills applies equally in relation to codicils: the term 'will' in the relevant statutes is defined as including codicils. As to wills of testators dying domiciled out of England and Wales, see Chap. 12.

1   E.g., under the Wills Act 1861, or the Wills Act 1963, or where the whole of the estate in England and Wales consists of immovable property.

3.23   Every document purporting to be testamentary, and executed in such a way as to entitle it to be accepted in this country as well executed (see preceding paragraphs) is entitled to proof in the English court if:

(i) it contains a disposition (whether this is operative or not, or is by inference only[1]) of property[2] situate in England and Wales[3]; or

(ii) it appoints an executor or executors[4], even though the executor is dead or renounces probate[5].

1   *Re Messenger's Estate, Chaplin v Ruane* [1937] 1 All ER 355; *Re Skeats, Thain v Gibbs* [1936] Ch 683, [1936] 2 All ER 298; *Re Stevens, Pateman v James* [1952] Ch 323, [1952] 1 All ER 674.
2   There is no property in a dead body, save as is provided by the Human Tissue Act 1961, under which parts of a dead body may be removed for therapeutic purposes or purposes of medical education or research: the executors have a right to possession of the body of a testator and a duty to bury it. A direction, by will, as to its disposition cannot be enforced (*Williams v Williams* (1882) 20 Ch D 659). A coroner has the right to possession of a dead body as soon as he decides to hold an inquest, and this right continues at common law until the inquest is determined (*R v Bristol Coroner, ex p Kerr* [1974] QB 652, [1974] 2 All ER 719).
3   *Re Coode's Goods* (1867) LR 1 P & D 449, 36 LJP & M 129. In this case there was a will disposing of English property only; and a will disposing of foreign property only was held not to be entitled to probate in this country, but it was ordered that a verified copy of the foreign will be filed. In *Stubbings v Clunies-Ross* (1911) 27 TLR 361, where some of the property abroad had been brought to England, probate was allowed of a will disposing only of property abroad. See also *Re Wayland's Estate* [1951] 2 All ER 1041; a Belgian will, disposing only of property in Belgium, admitted to proof together with a later English will dealing only with English property (the latter contained a revocation clause, but it was held that this did not revoke the Belgian will).
4   *Re Jordan's Goods* (1868) LR 1 P & D 555; *Re Leese's Goods* (1862) 2 Sw & Tr 442.
5   *Re Jordan's Goods* (1868) LR 1 P & D 555, 37 LJP & M 22.

3.24   Although a will contains no effective appointment of executors, no revocation, revival or republication clauses, and is entirely inoperative owing to the predecease of all beneficiaries, so that the whole estate devolves as on an intestacy, it must be proved on any application for a grant of representation, because the deceased died testate, notwithstanding that for some purposes he is considered to have died 'intestate'[1].

1   *Re Cuffe, Fooks v Cuffe* [1908] 2 Ch 500, in which case the grant was of administration with the will annexed. See also *Re Sullivan, Dunkley v Sullivan* [1930] 1 Ch 84.

3.25   However unusual or irregular in form such a document may be, if it fulfils the foregoing conditions it may be admitted to proof provided that it is established that it was intended to be testamentary: for reported cases, see para. **33.57**, post: see also 'Nominations', paras. **3.31** and **3.32**, post.

3.26   It should be shown on any application to prove a will that the testator died possessed of some estate in England and Wales; or, if not, that for some sufficient reason it is necessary to prove the will or obtain a grant of representation notwithstanding that the testator left no estate in this country (e.g. for purposes of title to pass a legal estate in land vested in the deceased, or to constitute a personal representative for the purpose of taking or defending legal proceedings: the reason for which the grant is required must in such cases be deposed to in the oath[1]).

1   Registrar's Direction (1932) 30 November.

3.27   As to grants where the deceased left no estate in this country, see paras. **4.209** and **4.210**, post.

Documents not admissible

3.28   A writing executed in the same manner as a will, but merely revoking a former testamentary disposition, is not entitled to probate[1]; but when set up by evidence of execution in accordance with the Wills Act 1837, s. 20, as a revocation, it must be brought in with the papers to lead the grant and filed in the registry: for practice, see para. **6.06**, post.

1   *Re Fraser's Goods* (1869) LR 2 P & D 40; *Toomer v Sobinska* [1907] P 106.

3.29   But if the document does not create a total intestacy, and is confined to the revocation of a codicil, or to one of the several documents which together constituted the will of the deceased, it will be admitted to probate[1].

1   *Re Spracklan's Estate* [1938] 2 All ER 345.

3.30   An instrument merely appointing a guardian has been held not to be entitled to probate[1]. There has, however, been no modern decision on this point, and it is possible that a different view would now be taken.

1   *Re Morton's Goods* (1864) 3 Sw & Tr 422.

Nominations

3.31   A nomination under the rules of a company's pension scheme whereby a member may appoint a nominee to receive moneys which, under the rules, might fall to be paid to his personal representative, although having certain testamentary characteristics, operates by force of the provisions of the rules of the pension scheme and not as a testamentary disposition. Its testamentary characteristics, including the fact that it is ambulatory, do not suffice to make the paper on which it is written a testamentary paper: accordingly, the requirements of the Wills Act 1837 have no application[1].

1   *Re Danish Bacon Co Ltd Staff Pension Fund, Christensen v Arnett* [1971] 1 All ER 486, [1971] 1 WLR 248.

3.32 On the other hand, a nomination under the Industrial and Provident Societies Act 1893, which was invalid as such because the balance to the credit of the depositor exceeded the then limit of £100, being duly executed in accordance with the Wills Act 1837, was held to be admissible as a will[1].

1 *Re Baxter's Goods* [1903] P 12.

Power to direct the making of a will for a mental patient

3.33 See paras. **3.430** ff., post.

Revocation of wills

Revocation of wills: Wills Act 1837

3.34 Under ss. 18 and 20 of the Wills Act 1837[1], a will is revoked:

 (i) by the marriage of the testator after its execution (subject to certain exceptions—see below);
 (ii) by another will or codicil, or a duly executed writing declaring an intention to revoke; or
 (iii) by its being burnt, torn or otherwise destroyed by the testator, or some other person in his presence and by his direction, with the intention of revoking. (See also paras. **33.58–33.76**, post.)

1 See pp. 722, 723, post.

Death on or after 1 January 1964

3.35 Under the Wills Act 1963[1], which applies to testators dying on or after 1 January 1964, a revocation (wholly or partial) of a will or codicil is effective if executed in accordance with the internal law of the place of execution, or of the place where, at the time of execution or of the testator's death, he was domiciled or had his habitual residence, or of a state of which, at either of those times, he was a national; the revocation is also effective if executed in accordance with any law by reference to which the revoked will or provision would be treated as well executed: Wills Act 1963, ss. 1, 2(1)(c). See also 'Wills Act 1963', paras. **3.392** ff., post.

1 See p. 777, post.

Revocation by subsequent marriage

3.36 As from 1 January 1983, on the coming into force of s. 18 of the Administration of Justice Act 1982, certain changes were made in the law relating to:

(a) the *revocation* of a will by the marriage of a testator after its execution; and
(b) the *effect* of dissolution or annulment of a testator's marriage on his will.

These changes result from the implementation of recommendations contained in the 22nd Report of the Law Reform Committee on the Making and Revocation of Wills (Cmnd. 7902: May 1980).

3.37 As regards *revocation*, the relevant date is the date of execution of the will in question.

Will made before 1 January 1983

3.38   'Every will made by a man or woman shall be revoked by his or her marriage (except a will made in exercise of a power of appointment when the real or personal estate thereby appointed would not in default of such appointment pass to his or her heir, customary heir, executor, or administrator, or the person entitled as his or her next-of-kin under the Statute of Distributions).' Wills Act 1837, s. 18, as formerly enacted.

3.39   It has been held that a will is revoked by the subsequent marriage of the testator even though the marriage may be voidable[1].

1 *Re Roberts, Roberts v Roberts* [1978] 3 All ER 225, [1978] 1 WLR 653, CA.

Will made on or after 1 January 1983

3.40   Section 18 of the Administration of Justice Act 1982 provides for the substitution of s. 18 of the Wills Act 1837 by the following:

'(1) Subject to subsections (2) to (4) below, a will shall be revoked by the testator's marriage.

(2) A disposition in a will in exercise of a power of appointment shall take effect notwithstanding the testator's subsequent marriage unless the property so appointed would in default of appointment pass to his personal representatives.

(3) Where it appears from a will that at the time it was made the testator was expecting to be married to a particular person and that he intended that the will should not be revoked by his marriage to that person.

(4) Where it appears from a will that at the time it was made the testator was expecting to be married to a particular person and that he intended that a disposition in the will should not be revoked by his marriage to that person—

(a) that disposition shall take effect notwithstanding the marriage; and

(b) any other disposition in the will shall take effect also, unless it appears from the will that the testator intended the disposition to be revoked by the marriage.'

3.41   As can be seen from the above text, the changes made by the new statutory provision relate to the exceptions (see below) to the revocation of a will by the testator's subsequent marriage, in particular, the earlier references to heirship and the Statute of Distributions in s. 18 of the 1837 Act when dealing with the exception relating to the exercise of a power of appointment are updated; in addition, clarification is given to the point that only the relevant disposition is preserved in such a case and not the whole will (*sub-s. (2)*). But perhaps the most important change is in relation to the exception permitted where a will is made in contemplation of marriage. In respect of *wills (including codicils) made on or after 1 January 1983*, there is now a rebuttable presumption in favour of preservation of the *whole will*, where it appears from the will that it or part of it was intended to survive a particular marriage (*sub-ss. (3) and (4)*).

3.42   These exceptions are dealt with in the text below.

Exceptions

Will made in exercise of power of appointment

3.43   This subject is dealt with in paras. **11.306** ff., post.

Will made in contemplation of marriage

3.44 As referred to above, certain changes affecting this exception were made by s. 18 of the Administration of Justice Act 1982, which section came into force on 1 January 1983. *The changes apply only to wills (including codicils) made on or after 1 January 1983*. The current position is that where a will was executed on or after 1 January 1926 and before 1 January 1983 and is expressed to be made in contemplation of a marriage, then s. 177 of the Law of Property Act 1925 continues to apply, and the will is not revoked by the solemnisation of the marriage. In such a case, the will must show with whom the marriage is contemplated[1]; but it is not essential that the testator should expressly state in the will that it is made in contemplation of marriage: it is sufficient if he gives a practical expression of his contemplation of marriage to a particular person. A gift to 'my fiancee' (whom the testator afterwards married) has been held to be sufficient[2]: although, more recently, it has been held that where a will contains a gift expressed to 'my fiancée', then, in the absence of a specific statement in the will that the gift was made in contemplation of marriage with the fiancée, the provisions of the will must be considered in deciding whether or not the will was revoked by the solemnisation of the marriage[3]. A will leaving the testator's estate to 'E.L.B., my future wife' was held not to have been revoked by the testator's marriage to E.L.B.[4].

1 *Sallis v Jones* [1936] P 43; *Pilot v Gainfort* [1931] P 103; *Re Langston* [1953] P 100, [1953] 1 All ER 928.
2 *Re Langston* [1953] P 100, [1953] 1 All ER 928; see also *Pilot v Gainfort* [1931] P 103 (a will containing a gift to 'D.F.P., my wife' (whom the testator subsequently married) held not to have been revoked by the marriage). See also *Re Gray's Estate* (1963) 107 Sol Jo 156, referred to in para. **33.68**, post.
3 *Re Coleman, Coleman v Coleman* [1976] Ch 1, [1975] 1 All ER 675.
4 *Knight* (1944) (motion).

3.45 For reported cases, see para. **33.68**, post.

3.46 As respects wills made on or after 1 January 1983, s. 177 of the Law of Property Act 1925 is repealed and is replaced by s. 18(3) and (4) of the Wills Act 1837, as substituted by s. 18 of the Administration of Justice Act 1982. The main effect of this change is to introduce a presumption in favour of the preservation of a will if it is shown to be intended to survive a particular marriage. For this purpose, and as an aid to construing the will, extrinsic evidence is admissible (see s. 21 of the Administration of Justice Act 1982, p. 854, post).

3.47 Wills made in contemplation of marriage are sometimes expressed to be conditional upon the intended marriage being solemnised within a stated period. In this event, the oath should state that the contemplated marriage was duly solemnised and give the date of it. If the will contains no such condition it is admissible to proof whether or not the intended marriage takes place, but is revoked in the event of the testator's marriage to any person other than the one with whom the marriage was expressed to be contemplated.

Marriage validated by Marriage (Prohibited Degrees of Relationship) Acts 1907–1931

3.48 A marriage, originally invalid, but validated by one of these Acts, did not revoke any will made before the passing of the particular Act by which it was validated.

Effect of dissolution or annulment of marriage on wills

3.49   The question whether the dissolution or annulment of a testator's marriage should have any effect on a prior-made will of the testator was considered by the Law Reform Committee in 1980 (22nd Report of the Law Reform Committee on the Making and Revocation of Wills: Cmnd. 7902). The majority view of the Committee favoured retention of the basic rule that such a will should survive the divorce or declaration of nullity, but that in respect of gifts to the former spouse the will should be treated as if that spouse had predeceased the testator. A new provision, s. 18A, was introduced into the Wills Act 1837: s. 18A, as amended by s. 53 of the Family Law Act 1986 on 4 April 1988, is as follows:

'(1) Where, after a testator has made a will, a decree of a court of civil jurisdiction in England and Wales dissolves or annuls his marriage or his marriage is dissolved or annulled and the divorce or annulment is entitled to recognition in England and Wales by virtue of Part II of the Family Law Act 1986,—

(a) the will shall take effect as if any appointment of the former spouse as an executor or as the executor and trustee of the will were omitted; and
(b) any devise or bequest to the former spouse shall lapse

except in so far as a contrary intention appears by the will.

(2) Subsection (1)(b) above is without prejudice to any right of the former spouse to apply for financial provision under the Inheritance (Provision for Family and Dependants) Act 1975.

(3) Where—

(a) by the terms of a will an interest in remainder is subject to a life interest; and
(b) the life interest lapses by virtue of subsection (1)(b) above

the interest in remainder shall be treated as if it had not been subject to the life interest and, if it was contingent upon the termination of the life interest, as if it had not been so contingent.' (*But see para.* **3.51**, *post.*)

3.50   It has been held that on the true construction of s. 18A of the Wills Act 1837 if a devise or a bequest to a testator's spouse 'lapsed' because of the parties' divorce, it failed without qualification and irrespective of the consequences. The devise or bequest was not deemed to have failed as if the former wife had predeceased the testator and gifts in the will contingent on the former wife predeceasing the testator did not take effect if she was still alive at the date of his death[1]. (*But see para.* **3.51**, *post.*) Section 18A applies only in respect of wills of testators *dying on or after 1 January 1983*.

1 *Re Sinclair. Lloyds Bank plc v Imperial Cancer Research Fund* [1985] Ch 446, [1985] 1 All ER 1066, CA; overruling *Re Cherrington* [1984] 2 All ER 285, [1984] 1 WLR 772.

3.51   When the Law Reform (Succession) Act 1995 (see p. 900, post) comes into force, with effect from 1 January 1996, s. 18A of the Wills Act 1837 (see paras. **3.49** and **3.50**, ante) is amended by the substitution of new paras. (a) and (b) in sub-s. (1), in the following terms:

'(a) provisions of the will appointing executors or trustees or conferring a power of appointment, if they appoint or confer the power on the former spouse, shall take effect as if the former spouse had died on the date on which the marriage is dissolved or annulled, and
(b) any property which, or an interest in which, is devised or bequeathed to the former spouse shall pass as if the former spouse had died on that date,'

The amended sub-s. (1) will have effect as respects a will made by a person *dying on or after 1 January 1996* (regardless of the date of the will and the date of the dissolution or annulment) (Law Reform (Succession) Act 1995, s. 3(1) and (2)).

Execution of wills—internal law of England and Wales

3.52 As respects *deaths occurring before 1 January 1983*, the manner in which a will must be executed in order to comply with the requirements of the Wills Act 1837, is defined by section 9 of that Act[1], as amended by the Wills Act Amendment Act 1852[2].

1 See p. 720, post.
2 See p. 726, post.

3.53 The strictness of certain of these requirements was relaxed in respect of testators *dying on or after 1 January 1983* as a result of the substitution of a new s. 9 of the Wills Act 1837 and the repeal of the Wills Act Amendment Act 1852 by the Administration of Justice Act 1982, ss. 17, 75 and Sch. 9 Pt. I.

3.54 These changes arose out of recommendations made in the 22nd Report of the Law Reform Committee on the Making and Revocation of Wills (Cmnd. 7902: May 1980), and are as follows:

(a)   the former law governing the position of the testator's signature on the will ('at the foot or end thereof') is relaxed so as to provide that a will may be admitted to proof if it is apparent on its face that the testator intended his signature to validate it, regardless of where on the will the signature was placed; and

(b)   an acknowledgment of his signature by an attesting witness shall have the same effect as his actual signature, so that where, after the signature or acknowledgment by a testator, a witness acknowledges his earlier signature, that acknowledgment will be sufficient.

3.55 In all other respects, the former requirements of s. 9 of the Wills Act 1837 continue to apply and, *subject to the above-mentioned changes*, it is considered, in the absence of any judicial decisions on the interpretation of the new s. 9 of the Wills Act 1837, as substituted by s. 17 of the Administration of Justice Act 1982, that the former case law in general remains relevant.

3.56 See also para. **3.75**, post.

Will to be in writing: no particular form is required

3.57 *As respects deaths of testators on or after 1 January 1983*, s. 9 of the Wills Act 1837, as substituted by the Administration of Justice Act 1982 is as follows:

'No will shall be valid unless—

(a) it is in writing, and signed by the testator, or by some other person in his presence and by his direction; and

(b) it appears that the testator intended by his signature to give effect to the will; and

(c) the signature is made or acknowledged by the testator in the presence of two or more witnesses present at the same time; and

(d) each witness either—

(i) attests and signs the will; or

(ii) acknowledges his signature,

in the presence of the testator (but not necessarily in the presence of any other witness),

but no form of attestation shall be necessary.'

3.58   *As respects deaths of testators before 1 January 1983*, s. 9 of the Wills Act 1837, as formerly enacted, applies and, in addition to the requirement that the will shall be in writing, requires that:

'it shall be signed at the foot or end thereof by the testator or by some other person in his presence and by his direction; and such signature shall be made or acknowledged by the testator in the presence of two or more witnesses present at the same time, and such witnesses shall attest and shall subscribe the will in the presence of the testator, but no form of attestation shall be necessary.'

3.59   The Interpretation Act 1978 provides that in any Act, unless the contrary intention appears, the word *writing* is to be construed as follows:

'*Writing* includes typing, printing, lithography, photography and other modes of representing or reproducing words in a visible form, and expressions referring to writing are construed accordingly.'

3.60   A will in shorthand characters is acceptable[1]. When lodged for probate it should be accompanied by a transcription by some competent person, verified by affidavit.

1   *Orrin v Orrin* (1921) Times, 20 December.

3.61   No particular form is required, but the writing must in some manner express the wishes of the testator as to the disposition of his estate or some part thereof[1], or appoint an executor[2]. The dictated instructions to a solicitor for the preparation of a will, if duly executed, are admissible: see 'Will contained in "instructions" ', para. **3.221**, post.

1   *Re Stevens, Pateman v James* [1952] Ch 323, [1952] 1 All ER 674.
2   *O'Dwyer v Gear* (1859) 1 Sw & Tr 465; *Re Lancaster's Goods* (1859) 1 Sw & Tr 464; *Re Jordan's Goods* (1868) LR 1 P & D 555.

Age of testator

3.62   In the case of a will made on or after 1 January 1970, the testator must be of or over the age of 18 years[1]: in the case of a will made prior to that date the testator must have attained the age of 21 years[2].

1   Wills Act 1837, s. 7, as amended by Family Law Reform Act 1969 (see p. 789, post).
2   Wills Act 1837, s. 7, as originally enacted.

3.63   There is an exception to this rule in the case of a soldier, airman, member of the Royal Navy, or seaman, who, if he is in actual military service, or in the case of a seaman, if he is at sea, may make a valid will if of the age of 14 years and upwards. See paras. **3.315** ff., post, and for reported cases para. **32.07**.

Signature of testator

3.64 '*Signed . . . by the testator*'. A will may be signed by the testator with his name, initials[1], or mark. The words 'Your loving mother' have been held to represent the name of the testatrix and to be a sufficient signature[2].

1 *Re Blewitt's Goods* (1880) 5 PD 116.
2 *Re Cook's Estate, Murison v Cook* [1960] 1 All ER 689, [1960] 1 WLR 353.

Incomplete signature

3.65 A signature left incomplete owing to weakness has been accepted[1]; but where one witness left the presence of the testator before the signature was completed, the testator completing his signature in the presence of the other witness, who subscribed the will in the presence of the testator, the execution was held to be invalid notwithstanding that the testator and the second witness acknowledged their signatures when the first witness returned[2]. It would seem that this decision would no longer be held valid *where the testator's death occurs on or after 1 January 1983* in view of the facility now afforded to a witness to acknowledge his signature (see para. **3.57**, ante).

1 *Re Chalcraft, Chalcraft v Giles* [1948] P 222, [1948] 1 All ER 700.
2 *Re Colling, Lawson v von Winckler* [1972] 3 All ER 729, [1972] 1 WLR 1440. But see now s. 9 of the Wills Act 1837, as substituted by s. 17 of the Administration of Justice Act 1982.

Signature with a dry pen

3.66 Re-execution by the testator going over his signature with a dry pen has been held to be sufficient if in the presence of two witnesses who then attested the re-execution; but if the testator's death occurred before 1 January 1983 the witnesses must re-sign. This action by the testator constitutes an acknowledgment of his signature, a course not open to witnesses where the testator's death occurred before 1 January 1983. (See para. **3.87**, post, and Chap. 33, post.)

In foreign characters

3.67 If the signature is in foreign characters, evidence is required that the deceased signed his name in the (*Greek*) characters, and as to the testator's knowledge of the contents of the will. (See paras. **3.125** ff., post.)

By mark

3.68 The testator's mark, whether accompanied by his name or not[1], is sufficient as a signature. The mark may be made with a pen or with some other instrument. A mark made with a stamp engraved with the testator's name[2] or with a seal engraved with his initials[3] has been held to be a good execution. The mark must be made before the witnesses sign[4] (or sign or acknowledge their signatures where the testator's death occurred on or after 1 January 1983). But a mark made with a seal would require proof that the sealing was intended as a signature and not as a sealing[5]. A thumb-print mark has been accepted[6].

1 *Re Bryce's Goods* (1839) 2 Curt 325.
2 *Jenkins v Gaisford and Thring* (1863) 3 Sw & Tr 93, 32 LJPM & A 122.
3 *Re Emerson's Goods* (1882) 9 LR Ir 443.
4 *White v Jones* (1932) Times, 19 February.
5 *Jenkins v Gaisford and Thring* (1863) 3 Sw & Tr 93, 32 LJPM & A 122.
6 *Re Finn's Estate* (1935) 154 LT 242.

3.69   Where a testator had his hand guided in making his mark, it was held to be a sufficient signature within the Statute of Frauds[1].

1   *Wilson v Beddard* (1841) 12 Sim 28.

3.70   The placing of a wrong name against the mark of the testatrix, where the real name appeared at the commencement of the will, was held not to vitiate the mark[1].

1   *Re Clarke's Goods* (1858) 1 Sw & Tr 22.

3.71   As to the additional wording relating to the testator's knowledge of the contents of the will which should appear in the attestation clause when a will is signed by mark, see para. **3.73**.

By another person

3.72   *'Or by some other person in [the testator's] presence and by his direction'*. When a person signs for a testator by his direction, he may sign either the testator's name or his own name for the purpose of giving effect to such direction[1]. The testator's signature may be made by one of the attesting witnesses[2].

1   *Re Clark's Goods* (1839) 2 Curt 329.
2   *Re Bailey's Goods* (1838) 1 Curt 914; *Smith v Harris* (1845) 1 Rob Eccl 262.

3.73   When a will is signed by direction, the attestation clause should show that the will was signed by another person signing his own or the testator's name, by the direction and in the presence of the testator[1], and (as also in the case of a mark) that it had been read over to the testator and that he appeared thoroughly to understand the same. For reported cases, see para. **33.13**, post.

1   Wills Act 1837, s. 9 (see p. 720, post).

Position of signature

3.74   In respect of the will of a testator who *dies on or after 1 January 1983*, irrespective of the date of execution of the will, s. 9 of the Wills Act 1837, as substituted by s. 17 of the Administration of Justice Act 1982, makes no stipulation as to the position of the testator's signature.

3.75   Where a testator made his signature (intended to give effect to his will) and then wrote out the dispositive part of his will, it all forming one transaction, the Court of Appeal held it to be validly executed (*Wood v Smith* [1993] Ch 9, [1992] 3 All ER 556, CA).

3.76   For *deaths before 1 January 1983*, the testator's signature is required to be *'at the foot or end thereof'*. The Wills Act Amendment Act 1852[1] specifies certain cases in which the position of the testator's signature, though not strictly complying with the term 'at the foot or end thereof', does not on that account invalidate the execution[2]. But a signature in the testimonium clause or in the attestation clause is not necessarily sufficient unless it be shown that the testator intended it for his signature to the will[3]. The court has in each case to look at the document and see whether the signature, wherever it is, is so placed as to show on the face of the will that the testator intended to give effect by that signature to the writing signed as his will[4].

1 See p. 726, post. This Act is now repealed in *respect of deaths of testators on or after 1 January 1983* (Administration of Justice Act 1982, s. 75 and Sch. 9 Pt. I).
2 *Re Usborne's Goods* (1909) 25 TLR 519.
3 *Re Pearn's Goods* (1875) 1 PD 70 (testimonium); *Re Mann's Goods* (1858) 28 LJP & M 19.
4 *Re Hornby* [1946] P 171 at 177, [1946] 2 All ER 150 at 153; see also *Re Long's Estate* [1936] P 166, [1936] 1 All ER 435.

3.77 Signature of the testator at the top of a will with the operative words below has been held not to be a valid execution[1].

1 *Re Stalman* (1931) 145 LT 339; *Re Bercovitz's Estate, Canning v Enever* [1962] 1 All ER 552, [1962] 1 WLR 321. See also Wills Act Amendment Act 1852, s. 1 (p. 726, post): 'no signature . . . shall be operative to give effect to any disposition or direction which is underneath or which follows it'. This Act is now repealed *in respect of deaths of testators on or after 1 January 1983* (Administration of Justice Act 1982, s. 75 and Sch. 9 Pt. I).

3.78 Signature in the margin of the will has in special circumstances been held valid[1]. Signature on the back page or endorsement is acceptable upon strict evidence that it was intended by the testator to be in execution of the will. (See para. **33.14**, post, for reported cases.)

1 *Re Roberts' Estate* [1934] P 102.

Words below signature

3.79 No signature under the Wills Act 1837, or the Wills Act Amendment Act 1852 (i.e. in respect of wills of testators *dying before 1 January 1983*), operates to give effect to any disposition or direction which is underneath or which follows it, nor does it give effect to any disposition or direction inserted after the signature was made (Wills Act Amendment Act 1852, s. 1). Where *death occurs before 1 January 1983*, words below the signature will be excluded from probate even though there is evidence that they were present at the time of execution of the will[1].

1 *Re Evans' Goods* (1923) 128 LT 669.

3.80 Again, where a will of a testator *dying before 1 January 1983* is signed at the foot of the first page only, but for lack of space is continued on the next page, the second page will not be admitted to probate unless there is also a reference, above the signature on the first page, to the subsequent portion which effects incorporation of the latter[1]. See also para. **33.14**, post.

1 Registrar's Direction (1953) 23 April, citing *Re Gee's Goods* (1898) 78 LT 843; *Royle v Harris* [1895] P 163.

Execution by testator on envelope

3.81 A will was written on a paper in the presence of witnesses. The testator then wrote on an envelope 'This is my last Will and Testament' and signed it, the witnesses signed the paper on which the will was written, the testator put both into the envelope and sealed it up. It was held that the will could be properly admitted to probate as duly executed[1]. But in a case where the testator had not signed his will (which had been signed by the witnesses) but had placed it in an envelope bearing the printed words 'The Last Will and Testament of . . . of . . . To . . . Executor. Date . . .' which he had completed by writing in his name and address, the name of the executor and the date, it was held that the name written on the envelope was not put there as a signature, and probate was refused[2].

1 *Re Mann's Goods* [1942] P 146, [1942] 2 All ER 193.
2 *Re Bean's Estate* [1944] P 83, [1944] 2 All ER 348. See also *Re Beadle, Mayes v Beadle* [1974] 1 All ER 493, [1974] 1 WLR 417: signature of testator and one witness at top of single sheet will; will then enclosed in envelope on which testator wrote 'My last will and testament' (followed by his name) 'to Charley and Maisy'; the witnesses signed on the other side of the envelope under a statement that the contents were written in their presence: held, the will was not duly executed.

3.82   A British subject, domiciled in Chile, made his will in Chilean form. The will was signed by the testator but unattested. It was enclosed in a sealed envelope signed by the testator and witnesses, with a statement that the envelope contained the testator's testamentary dispositions. It was held that the testator had executed a will effectual to pass real estate in England in accordance with the Wills Act 1837[1].

1 *Re Nicholls, Hunter v Nicholls* [1921] 2 Ch 11. (As to wills of immovables in the case of deaths on or after 1 January 1964 see also 'Wills of immovables', para. **3.401**, post.)

3.83   The signature of the testator, if not on the paper on which the will is written, must be physically connected with the will[1]. See para. **33.14**, post.

1 *Re Horsford's Goods* (1874) LR 3 P & D 211; *Lewis v Lewis* [1908] P 1 (sheets of paper held together by the hand of the testator); *Re Little, Foster v Cooper* [1960] 1 All ER 387, [1960] 1 WLR 495.

Execution of wrong will

3.84   Where a testator executed a will—intended to be that of another person—as his own by mistake, probate of the will was refused notwithstanding that it contained some testamentary dispositions that were intended by the testator[1].

1 *Re Meyer's Estate* [1908] P 353.

Acknowledgment of signature

3.85   *'Acknowledged by the testator'*. An acknowledgment of the testator's signature may be made expressly by words, by gestures[1], or by implication, e.g. by the testator producing the will, with his signature visibly apparent on the face of it, to the witnesses, who must both be present together[2], and requesting them to subscribe it, or assenting to a like request made by some other person in his presence[3]. Both witnesses must see or have an opportunity of seeing the signature[4]. If the signature was there, and the witnesses had an opportunity of seeing it, it does not matter that they did not actually see it[5]. But in the absence of evidence as to the existence of the signature at the time of execution, proof of the will may be refused[6]. There is no sufficient acknowledgment if the signature of the testator was covered up so that the attesting witnesses could not see it had they looked[7], although it is sufficient if the witnesses could see part of the signature[8]. The acknowledgment must be in the joint presence of the witnesses and before either of them has signed[9] (or signed or acknowledged their signatures *where the testator's death occurred on or since 1 January 1983*).

1 See *Re Hadler's Estate, Goodall v Hadler* (1960) Times, 20 October (testatrix indicated approval by nodding head while witnesses signed).

2 See *Brown v Skirrow* [1902] P 3, and para. **3.96**, post.
3 *Inglesant v Inglesant* (1874) LR 3 P & D 172.
4 *Re Dinmore's Goods* (1853) 2 Rob Eccl 641.
5 *Re MacDonald's Goods* [1942] IR 201.
6 *Fischer v Popham* (1875) LR 3 P & D 246. See, however, *Wright v Sanderson* (1884) 9 PD 149 (codicil pronounced for though witnesses could not say whether signature of testator was there at time of execution).
7 *Re Gunstan's Goods, Blake v Blake* (1882) 7 PD 102; *Re Groffman, Groffman and Block v Groffman* [1969] 2 All ER 108, [1969] 1 WLR 733 (will in testator's coat pocket).
8 *Re Glass' Estate, Hosking v Hutchings* (1961) 105 Sol Jo 612.
9 *Re Davies' Estate, Russell v Delaney* [1951] 1 All ER 920.

3.86 It is of great importance, particularly when the evidence of witnesses is being taken with a view to obtaining a district judge's or registrar's fiat refusing probate, that the affidavits should set out the exact story of what occurred, and should not state merely 'the testator did not sign or acknowledge his signature in our joint presence'. As will be seen from the case law, set out in para. **33.07**, post, it is sufficient—if the signature of the testator appears to have been written first—that the witnesses could have seen it, if they had looked. Unless, therefore, they state affirmatively that they did look, and that the signature was not there; or that the will was folded or covered in such a way that the signature was never visible to them there is a prima facie case for 'acknowledgment'. See also paras. **3.94** and **3.95**, and 'Refusal of Probate', paras. **3.129** ff., post.

Re-execution by acknowledgment

3.87 Subsequent to its execution a testator wrote two interlineations in his will and at the end wrote 'Republished and declared by the testator with the words [*here followed the words interlined*] in the presence of us in his presence and in the presence of each other have subscribed our names as witnesses'. He produced the will to the witness and stated it was necessary for him to republish it. The witnesses signed but the testator did not repeat his signature. It was held that this amounted to an acknowledgment and, the witnesses having signed their names after the acknowledgment, the will as it stood was entitled to be admitted to proof[1].

1 *Re Dewell's Goods* (1853) 1 Ecc & Ad 103, 22 LTOS 124.

3.88 See also *Re White, Barker v Gribble* [1991] Ch 1, [1990] 3 All ER 1. A testator made a will in 1981. In 1984 he decided to alter his will and dictated alterations to another person who copied them by hand onto the will. The testator checked the alterations and then wrote 'Alterations to Will dated 14-12-84' and asked two witnesses to sign it. The testator did not sign the will again although it still bore his signature from the original execution in 1981. It was held that the will could not be admitted to proof in its altered form but only in its original 1981 form.

Competency of witnesses

3.89 Section 14 of the Wills Act 1837[1] provides that if a witness is at the time of execution of the will or at any time thereafter incompetent to be admitted as a witness, the will is not on that account invalid. There is no rule or enactment that a minor may not be a witness.

1 See p. 721, post.

3.90 By s. 15 of that Act[1], any beneficial gift or appointment to a witness, or the husband or wife of a witness, is void, but the witness is competent. If the will is otherwise in order it is therefore valid and operative apart from the gift or appointment in question.

1 See p. 721, post.

3.91 The effect of s. 15 of the Wills Act 1837 is modified by the Wills Act 1968[1]. As to forfeiture of gifts to attesting witnesses or their spouses, see paras. **5.142** ff., post.

1 See p. 787, post.

3.92 A blind person is not a competent witness to a will[1].

1 *Re Gibson* [1949] P 434, [1949] 2 All ER 90.

3.93 A creditor of the testator is a competent witness notwithstanding that the estate is charged with his debt[1], and an executor appointed by the will is also a competent witness[2].

1 Wills Act 1837, s. 16 (p. 721, post).
2 Ibid., s. 17 (p. 721, post).

Presence of witnesses

3.94 '*In the presence of two or more witnesses present at the same time*'. The signature of the testator must be made or acknowledged in the actual visual presence of the witnesses, present at the same time, and before either of them has signed as a witness[1] (or signed or acknowledged their signatures *where the testator's death occurred on or after 1 January 1983*); it is not necessarily sufficient that they were in the same room[2]; nor necessarily conclusive against due execution that they were not[3].

1 *Re Linley. McDonnell v Linley* (1949) 207 LT Jo 372; *Re Davies' Estate, Russell v Delaney* [1951] 1 All ER 920; *Re Colling, Lawson v von Winckler* [1972] 3 All ER 729, [1972] 1 WLR 1440.
2 *Longford v Eyre* (1721) 1 P Wms 740; *Brown v Skirrow* [1902] P 3.
3 *Casson v Dade* (1781) 1 Bro CC 99; *Mulhall v Mulhall* [1936] IR 712: one of the witnesses was in another room, the door between being open, and this was held sufficient.

3.95 The witnesses must have seen, or have had the opportunity of seeing, the testator's signature[1], even though they were unaware of the nature of the document they were asked to sign[2], and they must both subscribe their names (or subscribe or acknowledge their signatures *where the testator's death occurred on or after 1 January 1983*) after this has occurred in their joint presence[3]. The will is not duly executed if the testator acknowledges his signature in the presence of one witness who thereupon signs the will, and subsequently the testator acknowledges his signature in the joint presence of the two witnesses, after which the second witness signs[4] but see para. **3.96**, post.

1 *Re Gunstan's Goods, Blake v Blake* (1882) 7 PD 102; *Re Groffman, Groffman and Block v Groffman* [1969] 2 All ER 108, [1969] 1 WLR 733.
2 *Daintree v Butcher and Fasulo* (1888) 13 PD 67; on appeal 13 PD 102, CA.
3 *Hindmarsh v Charlton* (1861) 8 HL Cas 160.
4 *Wyatt v Berry* [1893] P 5, following *Hindmarsh v Charlton*, above; *Re Colling*, para. **3.94**, above.

Acknowledgment of signature of witness

3.96 Acknowledgment of a previously subscribed signature by a witness is now permitted in respect of the will of a *testator dying on or after 1 January 1983* by virtue of s. 9 of the Wills Act 1837, as substituted by s. 17 of the Administration of Justice Act 1982, but is not a sufficient compliance with the former s. 9 of the Wills Act 1837 (which continues to apply where a testator dies *before* 1 January 1983), because the earlier statutory provision requires the witness to subscribe the will after its production to both the witnesses together[1].

1 *Re Maddock's Goods* (1874) LR 3 P & D 169.

Signature of non-attesting witness

3.97 Where a will bears the signatures of three or more persons, apparently as attesting witnesses, application has sometimes been made for the omission from the probate of one or more of such signatures, on the basis that the signatory did not in fact sign with the intention of attesting the will, the object of the application being to avoid the forfeiture of a gift to such person or his or her spouse under s. 15 of the Wills Act 1837[1].

1 See *Kitcat v King* [1930] P 266 (doubted in *Re Bravda*, below).

3.98 There is a strong presumption that any person whose signature appears at the end of a will signed as an attesting witness, and this presumption must be rebutted before the omission of such a signature will be allowed[1].

1 Senior Registrar's Memorandum, 18 January 1956: see also *Re Bravda's Estate* [1968] 2 All ER 217, [1968] 1 WLR 479, CA.

3.99 In relation to deaths occurring on or after 30 May 1968, however, such applications should normally be unnecessary by virtue of the Wills Act 1968[1], which provides that if a will is duly executed independently of its attestation by a person or persons to whom, or to whose spouse, the will gives any beneficial interest the attestation of such person is to be disregarded for the purpose of s. 15 of the Wills Act 1837. See also paras. **5.142** ff., post.

1 See p. 787, post.

Attestation

3.100 '*Shall attest and shall subscribe the will in the presence of the testator*'. The witnesses must subscribe the will in the presence of the testator after he has signed it, or acknowledged his previously made signature, when all of them were present together; but under English law it is not essential that the witnesses should subscribe in the presence of each other.

3.101 No form of attestation is necessary; but to make a valid subscription and attestation, either the name or initials of each witness, or some mark or name intended to represent his name, must be written or made by him in the presence of the testator[1].

1 *Re Sperling's Goods* (1863) 3 Sw & Tr 272; see also *Hindmarsh v Charlton* (1861) 8 HL Cas 160; *Charlton v Hindmarsh* (1859) 1 Sw & Tr 433.

Attestation by initials

3.102   The initials of the witnesses may be accepted as sufficient attestation, if proved to be intended as signatures in execution of the will[1].

1   *Re Christian's Goods* (1849) 2 Rob Eccl 110: see also *Re Martin's Goods* (1849) 1 Rob Eccl 712.

Presence of testator

3.103   *'In the presence of the testator'*. The testator must have been able to see the witnesses subscribe their names if he had chosen to look[1].

1   *Jenner v Ffinch* (1879) 5 PD 106.

Position of witnesses' signatures

3.104   The attesting witnesses are not required to subscribe their names on any particular part of the will or codicil, provided that the signatures were clearly intended to attest the testator's signature[1]. But if their signatures appear on a separate sheet, it must be shown by affidavit that this sheet was physically connected (e.g. with a pin) with the sheet on which the testator signed[2]. (See Chap. 33, post.)

1   *Davis' Goods* (1843) 3 Curt 748; *Re Chamney's Goods* (1849) 1 Rob Eccl 757; *Re Ellisons' Goods* [1907] 2 IR 480.
2   *Re Whittle*, proved in July 1905; *Re Braddock's Goods* (1876) 1 PD 433; *Lewis v Lewis* [1908] P 1, where the sheets of paper were held together by the testator's hand; *Re Little, Foster v Cooper* [1960] 1 All ER 387, [1960] 1 WLR495.

3.105   A testatrix wrote her will, consisting of the date, dispositive words and her signature, on a small single sheet of paper. There was no attestation clause. On the reverse side, upside down, were written in different handwritings the names of two persons whom it had proved impossible to trace. It was held, applying *Re Peverett's Goods* [1902] P 205, and the maxim *omnia praesumuntur rite esse acta*, that the document was a duly executed will, there being no practical reason why the names should be on the reverse of the document unless for the purpose of attesting the will[1].

1   *Re Denning, Harnett v Elliott* [1958] 2 All ER 1, [1958] 1 WLR 462.

Evidence of execution

Evidence required

3.106   *'But no form of attestation shall be necessary'*. Every will or codicil, however, should contain a statement by the witnesses, called an attestation clause, showing that the will was signed by the testator in the presence of the two witnesses, and that they, afterwards, signed their names thereto in his presence.

Affidavit of execution

3.107   If there is no attestation clause, or where it is not evident by the wording of the clause that the will or codicil has been executed in accordance with the provisions of the statute, or where it appears to the district judge or registrar that there is some doubt about the due execution of the will, an *affidavit of due execution* by at least one of the witnesses is required (see NCPR 12(1)) (Form cf affidavit No. 2) unless the district judge or registrar exercises the discretion given to him under NCPR 12(3) and dispenses with evidence where he is satisfied that the distribution of the estate is not affected by the admission of the will. In considering whether to exercise this discretion the district judge or registrar will require evidence as to who would be entitled to the estate if the will is not admitted.

3.108 Evidence in writing as to the execution of a will or codicil may be given by affidavit or affirmation, sworn or affirmed in accordance with the Oaths Act 1978, or by statutory declaration under the Statutory Declarations Act 1835, s. 16. A documentary statement under the Evidence Act 1938 is not admissible, as it is specifically excluded, for this purpose, by the proviso to s. 3. See also para. **22.01**, post.

3.109 Where the evidence of a witness, or of some other person present at the execution, is required by the district judge or registrar, the deponent must also depose to the manner of execution of the document in question (NCPR 16).

3.110 An affidavit of due execution may be called for in, inter alia, the following circumstances: where the signature of the testator has been placed in the attestation clause or in the testimonium clause (see Form No. 2(a)); in certain cases where the will or codicil has been signed twice; where the testator's signature appears below those of the witnesses (see Form No. 2(e)); where the will is signed by mark or by a person at the direction of the testator (with insufficient attestation clause) (NCPR 12: see Form No. 2(c)); where the purported subscription of a witness is in capital letters or is printed (an affidavit being called for if it appears to the district judge or registrar that there is a doubt as to whether the purported witness did subscribe the will as required or whether his name was written by him or another person before the will was executed, e.g. in anticipation of the will being executed and subscribed by the witness later and in order to show clearly the name of the witness adjacent to the later to be made subscription.

3.111 An affidavit of due execution is not required solely because in a will made on a printed form the words 'his/her' or 'his or her', or the incompleted word 'h. .' appear in the attestation clause, but this does not affect the practice of requiring an affidavit of due execution of any will which is irregular in other respects, or which gives rise to the suspicion that it may not have been duly executed[1].

1 Registrar's Direction (1951) 31 May.

3.112 An affidavit of due execution is not necessary solely because the attestation clause states that the witnesses 'attested' in the presence of the testator: this term is wide enough, when used in this connection, to include subscription[1].

1 *Re Selby-Bigge* [1950] 1 All ER 1009.

Will to be exhibited

3.113 The will and/or codicil/s must be exhibited (not annexed) to the affidavit and endorsed with the exhibit clause, which must be signed by the Commissioner for Oaths. See 'Exhibits', para. **22.11**, post. The district judge or registrar now has a general discretion to allow a facsimile copy of the will (or codicil) to be exhibited in lieu of the original document[1]. Application for authority should be made to the Principal of the Probate Department, or in district probate registry cases to the district registrar. The facsimile copy must be provided at the expense of the applicant.

1 NCPR 10(2).

3.114 Attention is drawn to the different requirements of NCPR 10(1)(a) and 10(1)(b):

(a)   NCPR 10(1)(a) relates to marking the will where it is referred to in the oath in support of the application to prove the will. The will is to be marked by the signatures of the applicant and the person before whom the oath is sworn. It is not to be endorsed with the exhibit clause nor is it to be physically annexed to the oath.

(b)   NCPR 10(1)(b) relates to a will being exhibited to an affidavit, not the oath. Where a will is exhibited to an affidavit RSC Ord. 41, r. 11 also applies. The will in this instance is to be endorsed with the appropriate exhibit clause signed (only) by the person before whom the affidavit is sworn, and is again not to be physically annexed to the oath.

Confirmation of defective will by codicil

3.115 The decided cases go to show that when an earlier document is not executed in accordance with the provisions of the Wills Act 1837 it cannot be rendered a valid testamentary document by reason only of its being contained in the same paper as a later properly attested testamentary document. It can be rendered effective as a testamentary document only by incorporation in the later properly attested testamentary document, there being such reference to it in the later document as to effect such incorporation. (See also 'Republication and revival', paras. **3.166** ff., post.)

3.116 When an earlier document, which purports to have been executed in the presence of two witnesses, has no attestation clause indicating that the requirements of the Wills Act 1837 have been complied with, the lack of such clause is not cured merely by the presence of a later properly attested testamentary document on the same paper, unless the earlier document is referred to, or expressly confirmed by, the later document. In the absence of such reference, it must be proved by affidavit evidence that the earlier document was in fact duly executed.

Affidavit of due execution from a person other than an attesting witness

3.117 Where evidence of due execution is necessary, and both the attesting witnesses are dead, or are not conveniently available, an affidavit as to due execution from any other person who was present at the execution of the will or codicil is acceptable (NCPR 12(1)).

No evidence of due execution available

3.118 NCPR 12(2) is as follows:

> 'If no affidavit can be obtained in accordance with paragraph (1) above, the district judge or registrar may accept evidence on affidavit from any person he may think fit to show that the signature on the will is in the handwriting of the deceased, or of any other matter which may raise a presumption in favour of due execution of the will, and may if he thinks fit require that notice of the application be given to any person who may be prejudiced by the will.'[1]

---

1   *Burgoyne v Showler* (1844) 1 Rob Eccl 5; *Re Thomas's Goods* (1859) 1 Sw & Tr 255; *Re Peverett's Goods* [1902] P 205; *Re Strong's Estate, Strong v Hadden* [1915] P 211. In *Burgoyne v Showler*, Dr Lushington says 'I apprehend that where a will on the face of it appears duly executed, and *there is a clause of attestation of this kind, being not in the strict form*, the presumption must be *omnia rite facta fuisse*. However, if the party is put on proof of the will he is under the necessity of producing the subscribed witnesses and any other evidence, if there be any other, to establish the fact.' The same learned

judge, in *Prudence Wills* (ibid. in note), where the attestation clause of the will was imperfect, said, 'I apprehend that where there is an attestation clause of this description and the names of two witnesses, and the signature of the testratrix, the presumption, in the absence of all evidence, is that the will was duly executed according to the statute'. See also *Vinnicombe v Butler* (1864) 3 Sw & Tr 580. The strength of the presumption varies according to whether the document is regular or irregular in form: see *Re Bercovitz's, Canning v Enever* [1961] 2 All ER 481, [1961] 1 WLR 892.

3.119   If it is sworn that both witnesses are dead, or there is satisfactory evidence that they cannot be traced, and that so far as is known no other person was present at the time of execution of the will, the consents of the persons prejudiced (if they are all sui juris) to the admission of the will to proof will normally be accepted. There should be affidavit evidence as to who such persons are and whether they are all sui juris and their consents, if readily available, should be lodged with the application. If the persons prejudiced are not all sui juris, or do not all consent, or if there is anything in the will which calls for enquiry, the matter should be referred to a district judge or registrar for his directions. Form of affidavit, No. 3; form of consent to proof of will, No. 56.

3.120   If there is no person available to make an affidavit of due execution, evidence of the testator's handwriting should be provided (form of affidavit No. 4). If, in addition, evidence of the handwriting of the witnesses is available, this has often been accepted, in the absence of special features, as sufficient to raise a presumption in favour of due execution.

3.121   If evidence of the testator's handwriting is not procurable, the directions of a district judge or registrar should be obtained.

Recalcitrant witness

3.122   Under s. 122(1) of the Supreme Court Act 1981[1], the High Court may, whether or not any legal proceedings are pending, order any person it reasonably believes has knowledge of any document which is or purports to be testamentary to attend for examination in open court. Failure to attend for examination or to answer any question renders that person guilty of contempt of court[2]. See also para. **27.17**, post.

1   See p. 846, post.
2   Supreme Court Act 1981, s. 122(3).

3.123   Where a will is ex facie duly executed, probate will not necessarily be refused because the witnesses cannot recollect the circumstances[1].

1   *Wright v Sanderson* (1884) 9 PD 149; *Whiting v Turner* (1903) 89 LT 71; *Woodhouse v Balfour* (1887) 13 PD 2; *Re Webb, Smith v Johnston* [1964] 2 All ER 91, [1964] 1 WLR 509.

3.124   The fact that the witnesses were not aware of the nature of the document they attested does not invalidate it[1].

1   *Re Benjamin Estate* (1934) 150 LT 417.

Knowledge and approval

3.125   It is essential to the validity of a will that the testator should know and approve of its contents[1]. Unless suspicion attaches to the document, e.g. where it is signed by mark, or where the signature indicates extreme feebleness, the testator's execution is sufficient evidence of his knowledge and approval[2]. (See also para. **33.16**, post.)

1   *Hastilow v Stobie* (1865) LR 1 P & D 64. See also *Re Simpson, Schaniel v Simpson* (1977) 121 Sol Jo 224; where, through age or infirmity, a testator's capacity is in doubt, the making of the will ought to be witnessed or approved by a medical practitioner.
2   *Guardhouse v Blackburn* (1866) LR 1 P & D 109.

3.126   As to the exclusion of words, etc, inserted by mistake and without the knowledge and approval of the testator, see paras. **3.249** ff. and Chap. 33, post.

Blind or illiterate testator. Affidavit of reading over, etc.
Signature by mark

3.127   If the testator appears to be blind or illiterate, the court requires to be satisfied that he had knowledge of its contents at the time of its execution (NCPR 13). This is also the case where the testator's name is signed by another person, or the will is signed by a cross or other mark only, or where the signature is so imperfectly or badly written or is written in capital letters or is printed in lower case letters as to indicate extreme feebleness or illiteracy on the testator's part, or where for any other reason doubt arises as to whether the testator had knowledge of its contents (ibid.).

3.128   If the attestation clause includes a statement that prior to execution the will was read over to the testator and that he appeared thoroughly to understand the same, this is normally accepted as sufficient to satisfy the requirements of the rule; in the absence of this, an affidavit of due execution showing that the will was read over, or otherwise establishing the testator's knowledge of the contents of the will, is necessary. For forms of affidavit, see Nos. 2(c) and 2(d).

Refusal of probate

Fiat against a will. Probate refused

3.129   NCPR 12(1) provides that where a will (which expression includes any testamentary document) contains no attestation clause, or where the attestation clause is insufficient or it appears to the district judge or registrar that there is some doubt about the due execution of the will, he shall before admitting it to proof require evidence as to execution, subject to his discretion to dispense with such evidence if he is satisfied that the distribution of the estate is not affected by the will.

3.130   Rule 12(1) also provides that if the district judge or registrar, after considering the evidence, is satisfied that the will was not duly executed he shall refuse probate and shall mark the will accordingly. If he is doubtful whether the will was duly executed he may refer the matter to a High Court judge in chambers or open court, a registrar first obtaining the confirmation of a district judge.

3.131   If the evidence shows that the will was not duly executed, affidavits by both the attesting witnesses should normally be obtained.

3.132   The procedure, at the Principal Registry, for obtaining the district judge's marking 'Probate refused' on a testamentary document is as follows:

(a) *Prior to an application for a grant.* An application by a solicitor to a district judge for a document to be marked 'Probate refused' must be made through the Probate Department and, if and when so marked, the refused document must be returned to the Probate Department forthwith together with the affidavits leading to the district judge's fiat, and will not be handed out without the leave of a district judge. Upon the issue of a grant in respect of the estate of the deceased the refused document and its accompanying affidavits will be filed with the oath to lead the grant.

(b) *Simultaneously with the application for a grant.* Where the application for refusal of probate and for a grant are simultaneous, the purported will and the affidavits by the witnesses should be lodged with the remainder of the papers at the Receiver's department[1].

1 Registrar's Direction (1951) 14 June (as revised (1958) 5 July).

3.133 No fees are payable in respect of the district judge's or registrar's fiat, or for filing the affidavits.

3.134 Where the testator died on or after 1 January 1964, although a testamentary document may prove not to have been executed in accordance with the formalities required by the Wills Act 1837, it is treated as properly executed if executed in compliance with any of the alternatives applicable, in the particular circumstances, by virtue of the Wills Act 1963 and the possibility that a will may be admissible to proof under one of the alternatives should be fully considered before applying to have it marked 'Probate refused'. As to the Wills Act 1963, see paras. **3.392** ff., post.

Date of will

3.135 If there is no date to a will, or if there is an imperfect date only, one of the attesting witnesses, or some other person present at the time of execution or able to testify to the date thereof, must supply evidence of the date of execution[1]. If evidence of execution on a definite date cannot be obtained, evidence as to execution between two definite dates should be given, and in such cases evidence from both witnesses is sometimes required. If neither of the attesting witnesses nor any other person can depose to execution between two definite dates, evidence must be given showing that search has been made and no will of presumably later date has been found. (Form of affidavit of search, No. 6.) An affidavit of search may also be required when the witnesses are able to speak only to execution between two dates separated by a substantial period of time.

1 NCPR 14(4).

3.136 If there is no date, or only an imperfect date, on the face of the will but a complete date is given in the endorsement of the will and there is no reason to suppose that this is not the true date of the will, it may be accepted as such and evidence as to the date of execution is not required. A notation of the date appearing in the endorsement will be made by the registry on the face of the will and this will be reproduced on the probate copy[1].

1 Registrar's Circular, 17 May 1968.

3.137 If the date given in the will is not the true date of execution, evidence of the correct date should be given by an attesting witness or some other person present at the execution. If the exact date cannot be spoken to the procedure is as set out above.

3.138   If the date in the endorsement of the will differs from that on the face of the will, affidavit evidence as to the true date of execution is required where the endorsement shows a later date, unless the discrepancy is slight and is not of importance[1].

1 Registrar's Direction (1951) 27 July (amended 1964).

3.139   A notation of the date or period sworn to is made by the registry on the will and probate copy.

3.140   Unless a definite date of execution or execution between definite dates can be deposed to, the affidavits should include a statement as to whether any other person was present at the time of execution.

Two dates on a testamentary document

3.141   Where a testamentary document bears one date at the commencement and a later date at the foot thereof, the later date will generally be accepted as the true date without affidavit evidence.

3.142   Affidavit evidence as to the date is called for in the following circumstances:

(a)   if the later date is in the attestation clause or is not in close connection with the signature, or conflicts with a date on the endorsement if any; or

(b)   if the applicant's title to the grant depends on the later date being the true one[1].

1 Registrar's Direction (1952) 23 May.

Misrecital of date of will

3.143   If a codicil misquotes the date of the will propounded, or of an earlier codicil, an explanatory affidavit must be filed together with an affidavit of search for any other testamentary document.

3.144   If it can be shown that the misquotation is clearly a pure error as to date, there being no other testamentary document to which it might refer, the documents will be admitted to proof, a notation being made on the codicil and the probate copy of the filing of the affidavit as to misrecital of the date.

3.145   Should there be other testamentary documents to which the codicil might refer, other considerations will almost certainly apply; as to which see 'Republication and revival', paras. **3.166** ff. and **34.08**, post, and 'Exclusion of words from probate', paras. **3.249** ff., post.

3.146   If the misrecital is due to a clerical error or a failure to understand the testator's instructions *and the testator died on or after 1 January 1983* an application for an order for rectification under s. 20(1) of the Administration of Justice Act 1982 may be required (see paras. **3.250** ff., post).

Condition of will

3.147   The vestiges or marks of a seal, wafer, pin, paper clip, or fastener, appearing on a will or codicil, raise a suspicion that some further testamentary document may have been at one time attached to it. Although the Rules do not deal with these matters specifically NCPR 6(1) provides that a district judge or registrar shall not allow any grant to issue until all enquiries which he may see fit to make have been answered to his satisfaction and accordingly a district judge or registrar may call for evidence accounting for the same. For this reason a will should not be pinned, or fastened in any other way, to the other papers when these are lodged at the registry.

3.148   If pin or clip marks etc. were caused by documents of a non-testamentary nature being attached to the will or codicil, the production of such documents with a covering certificate to this effect by the solicitor, or other person having knowledge of the facts, may be required: in other cases an affidavit of plight and of search for any other testamentary document may be necessary (see Forms Nos. 5 and 6).

Plight of will

3.149   If the state of the will be such as to suggest that it has been interfered with in any way, or if there is any appearance of attempted revocation by burning, tearing or otherwise destroying, an affidavit of plight is required. (See NCPR 15; Form No. 5.)

Statements admissible

3.150   Statements by a testator, whether made before or after the execution of a will, are admissible to show what papers constituted the will[1].

1   *Gould v Lakes* (1880) 6 PD 1.

Suspicion as to will

3.151   Where a will is propounded which raises the suspicion of the court that it does not express the mind of the testator, the onus is on those who propound it to remove the suspicion. This is not confined only to cases in which the will has been prepared by a person taking a pecuniary benefit under it[1].

1   *Sarat Kumari Debi v Sakhi Chand* (1928) LR 56 Ind App 62, PC. Torn will, pasted together (*Re Hine's Goods* [1893] P 282).

Codicils

Codicils proved with will

3.152   If there be a codicil or codicils, such codicil or codicils must be proved with the will.

3.153   There is an exception to this rule where a codicil, which in no way alters the appointment of executors, is in dispute, and it is necessary for the estate to be administered without delay[1]. In such a case probate of the will only is granted to the executors therein named, the question of the validity of any codicil thereto being reserved. A will and codicil may similarly be admitted to probate limited until the litigation with reference to the other codicil is decided[2].

1 *Lord Sondes* (1836) June; *Boatwright* (1835) December, *Craig* (1812) March and *Hope* (1812) March. In *Cowcher* (1828) June, the court granted probate of a will in common form without any reference to a disputed codicil. See also *Reay v Cowcher* (1829) 2 Hag Ecc 249.
2 *Re Day's Estate* [1940] 2 All ER 544; *Lord Furness* (1943) (Motion).

3.154   Where, exceptionally, a will is admitted to proof notwithstanding a dispute as to the validity of a known existing codicil, it is now the usual practice for an undertaking to be given to the court by the proving executor that he will not dispose of or distribute that part of the estate affected by the codicil until the question as to the validity of the codicil has been determined either inter partes or by order of the court.

3.155   If a will has been proved at a district probate registry the codicil must also be proved there.

Probate of will without a known (valid) codicil

3.156   Probate has been granted of a will and certain codicils only, where there were other codicils in India, it being left open to the executor to prove the latter when they should arrive in England, and he undertaking to do so[1].

1 *Re Robarts' Goods* (1873) LR 3 P & D 110.

Probate of codicil only

3.157   Where a will and first codicil were not forthcoming after the testator's death, the court granted probate of his second codicil, it not having been revoked by any of the modes indicated by s. 20 of the Wills Act 1837[1].

1 *Black v Jobling* (1869) LR 1 P & D 685. Also note the case of *Gardiner v Courthope* (1886) 12 PD 14, where probate was decreed of a document of a codicillary character alone, as of a 'substantive testamentary document', the only other papers found being the drafts of two wills about which no evidence was forthcoming either as to their execution or revocation.

3.158   So also where a will was not forthcoming at the testator's death, the court granted probate of a codicil[1], and where a codicil stated 'Codicil to my last will', but the will could not be found, it was held that the codicil might be proved alone[2].

1 *Re Savage's Goods* (1870) LR 2 P & D 78, 39 LJP & M 25.
2 *Re Clements' Goods* [1892] P 254.

3.159   Where the will has been revoked, viz. by destruction, the court will grant probate of a codicil alone[1].

1 *Re Turner's Goods* (1872) LR 2 P & D 403.

Separate probate of codicil

3.160   If a codicil is discovered after a grant of probate of a will has been made, a separate probate of that codicil will be granted to the executor, provided it does not revoke or alter the appointment of executors made in the will[1]. (For practice, see paras. **16.19** and **16.20**, post.) If the executor who proved the will is dead, the proving executor of the will of the deceased executor should prove the codicil. He is the executor of the will and codicil by transmission of executorship. If different executors are appointed by the codicil, the probate of the will must be brought in and revoked, and a new probate will be granted of the will and codicil together (see 'Revocation', paras. **17.01** ff., post).

1 *Langdon v Rooke* (1841) 1 Notes of Cases 254; *Re Beetson's Goods* (1848) 6 Notes of Cases 13.

3.161 Where letters of administration (with will) have been granted and afterwards a codicil is discovered, the grant must be revoked and a new grant taken, with both the will and codicil annexed.

Will proved abroad, codicil subsequently found

3.162 Where a will had been proved abroad and a codicil was subsequently found, Sir J. Hannen refused to allow the codicil to be proved here until it had been proved in the court where probate of the will had been obtained[1]. But in view of the provisions of the Wills Act 1963[2] (as to which see paras. **3.392** ff., post), it is doubtful whether this decision would now be followed.

1 *Re Miller's Goods* (1883) 8 PD 167; *Re Crawford's Goods* (1890) 15 PD 212.
2 See p. 777, post.

Revocation of codicil

3.163 Where a codicil revoking a will in part is itself revoked, the will remains as altered by the codicil[1]. A codicil which has been revoked by a later codicil must be proved if it alters the terms of the will or of a preceding codicil. If it is known that a codicil has been revoked, but it is not brought in, its production is called for[2]. Should it appear that it was revoked by destruction, it may be admitted to proof as contained in a copy or a reconstruction, by district judge's or registrar's order.

1 *Re Debac's Goods, Sanger v Hart* (1897) 77 LT 374. See also Wills Act 1837, s. 22 (p. 723, post) and *Re Hodgkinson's Goods* [1893] P 339, quoted in para. **33.22**, post.
2 President's Direction (1943) 11 March.

3.164 Before being photographed for the grant the following notations will be made, by the registry, at the foot of each document:

> On the will: 'Partially revoked by codicil dated. . . .' On the codicil: 'The codicil of which this is a copy (or reconstruction) was revoked by destruction.'

The grant will *not* contain the limitation 'until a more authentic copy be proved'[1].

1 Registrar's Direction (1949) 30 July.

Practice in proving codicils

3.165 All the practice set out in the foregoing pages in relation to the proof of wills applies equally in relation to codicils: the term 'will' in the relevant statutes is defined as including codicils[1].

1 E.g., Wills Act 1837, s. 1; Wills Act Amendment Act 1852, s. 3; Wills Act 1963, s. 6(1).

Republication and revival

Republication

3.166   In the absence of a contrary intention, a codicil confirming a will repub-lishes the will, i.e. it has the effect of bringing the will down to the date of the codicil, and effects the same dispositions as if the testator had at that date made a new will containing the dispositions in the original will with the alterations, if any, effected by the codicil[1].

1   *Re Champion, Dudley v Champion* [1893] 1 Ch 101 ; *Re Fraser, Lowther v Fraser* [1904] 1 Ch 726.

3.167   The will and codicil are treated as one document bearing the date of the codicil[1], but where the question is at what date a disposition was 'made' within the meaning of a particular enactment the confirmation of a bequest by a subsequent codicil may not be the dominant consideration, as the question may turn primarily on the construction of the enactment[2].

1   *Re Reeves, Reeves v Pawson* [1928] Ch 351 at 355 (bequest of 'my present lease' applied to new lease acquired after date of the will).
2   See *Berkeley v Berkeley* [1946] AC 555, [1946] 2 All ER 154; *Re Heath's Will Trusts, Hamilton v Lloyds Bank Ltd* [1949] Ch 170, [1949] 1 All ER 199.

3.168   In some instances the doctrine of redating a will by republication is specific-ally excluded by a statutory provision[1].

1   See, for example, ss. 1(7) and 15(8) of the Family Law Reform Act 1969 (pp. 790 and 792, post).

3.169   Provided that the will is sufficiently identified, it is republished by a codicil irrespective of any expression of confirmation, but a will is not republished by a testamentary document not described as a codicil and not containing any reference to the will[1].

1   *Re Smith, Bilke v Roper* (1890) 45 Ch D 632.

3.170   A codicil described as a codicil to a will of a particular date may repub-lish the will even though it be a conditional codicil which is inoperative owing to the non-fulfilment of the condition, and for this purpose such a codicil may be proved[1].

1   *Re Mendes Da Silva's Goods* (1861) 2 Sw & Tr 315.

3.171   The redating of the will by republication will not be applied to the extent that this defeats the testator's intentions[1], e.g. by making void a valid restriction which would be barred by a subsequent statute if the will were brought up to a later date[2].

1   *Re Park, Bott v Chester* [1910] 2 Ch 322.
2   *Re Heath's Will Trusts*, para. **3.167**, above.

3.172   See also Chap. 34, post.

Revival of revoked will or codicil

3.173   A will or codicil, or any part thereof, which has been revoked, can be revived only by re-execution, or by a duly executed codicil showing an intention to revive the earlier document[1].

1 Wills Act 1837, s. 22 (p. 723, post).

3.174   A will or codicil which has been revoked by destruction cannot be revived[1].

1 *Rogers v Goodenough* (1862) 2 Sw & Tr 342; *Re Steele's Goods* (1868) LR 1 P & D 575.

3.175   Where a will or codicil, which has been first partly revoked and subsequently wholly revoked, is revived, the revival does not extend to the portion first revoked unless an intention to that effect appears[1].

1 Wills Act 1837, s. 22 (p. 723, post).

3.176   To revive a revoked will there must be shown an intention to revive[1]; and to determine whether this intention existed, evidence of surrounding circumstances is admissible[2]. A codicil referring to a revoked will only by recital does not revive the will[3].

1 *Re Steele's Goods* (1868) LR 1 P & D 575; *Re Lindsay* (1892) 8 TLR 507; *Goldie v Adam* [1938] P 85, [1938] 1 All ER 586.
2 *Re Davis' Estate* [1952] P 279, [1952] 2 All ER 509.
3 *Re Dennis' Goods* [1891] P 326.

3.177   For reported cases, see para. **34.11**, post.

3.178   Where a will or codicil is revived by a later testamentary document, the two documents are proved in chronological order as a will and codicil, or as the case may be[1].

1 Registrar's Direction (1952) 14 October.

Two wills: effect of codicil confirming earlier will

3.179   Where a testator has made two wills, the earlier of which was revoked by the later, and he subsequently in a codicil refers to or confirms the *earlier* will, delicate points of republication and revival can arise. The question as to which documents are to be proved needs careful consideration, and should preferably be referred to the registry before preparation of the papers to lead a grant. The possibility of rectification of the codicil where appropriate (see paras. **3.250** ff., post) should also be considered.

3.180   It is important to observe that where an earlier will is revived by a codicil, and that will contains a clear revocation clause, any intervening wills are revoked, the revocation clause in the earlier will being incorporated in, and republished by, the codicil[1].

1 *Re Pearson, Rowling v Crowther* [1963] 3 All ER 763, [1963] 1 WLR 1358 applying *Re Baker, Baker v Baker* [1929] 1 Ch 668.

3.181 Where there is any question of doubt as to revocation and as to which documents ought to be proved, the Family Division will admit rather than reject, so that all testamentary documents may be available to the Chancery Division should a question of construction arise.

3.182 See also 'Misrecital of date of will', paras. **3.143** ff., ante; 'Exclusion of words from the probate: rectification and interpretation of wills', paras. **3.249** ff.; and para. **34.11**, post for reported cases.

Two or more wills

Probate of a will contained in two or more papers

3.183 A will need not consist of one document only. There may be two wills not inconsistent with each other[1], or there may be two or more testamentary papers, both or all executed as required by the statute, which, being read together, show a sufficient consensus to constitute one will, not a will and codicils[2].

1 *Re Griffith's Goods* (1872) LR 2 P & D 457; *Re Harris' Goods* (1870) LR 2 P & D 83; *Re Fenwick's Goods* (1867) LR 1 P & D 319; *Simpson v Foxon* [1907] P 54; *Re Todd's Estate* [1926] P 173, 135 LT 381 (English and American wills. Probate granted of both. The original American will was released for probate in America upon an examined and sealed copy being filed in its place).
2 *Re Morgan's Goods* (1867) LR 1 P & D 323; *Re Harris' Goods* (1870) LR 2 P & D 83; *Re Petchell's Goods* (1874) LR 3 P & D 153; *Re Donaldson's Goods* (1873) LR 3 P & D 45; *Deakin v Garvie* (1919) 36 TLR 122, CA.

3.184 As to whether a later will which includes a revocation clause revokes the exercise of a power of appointment in an earlier will, see paras. **11.314** and **33.20** ff., post.

3.185 Where a testator, domiciled in England, made a will in English form containing a statement that the will was intended to deal only with his English estate, it was held that although it included a revocation clause, the will did not revoke an earlier will made in Belgium, dealing only with Belgian property, and valid under s. 1 of the Wills Act 1861[1]. It was also held that both wills could be admitted to proof in England notwithstanding that the Belgian will did not dispose of property in England[2].

1 See p. 727, post.
2 *Re Wayland's Estate* [1951] 2 All ER 1041.

3.186 Where there are two testamentary papers, and the second purports to be a will and not a codicil, the court, in determining whether one or both of them are entitled to probate, is guided by the consideration, not whether the testator intended them both to form his will, but what dispositions of his property, as collected from the language of both documents, he desired to effect. Thus, where a subsequent testamentary paper is only partly inconsistent with one of an earlier date, the earlier instrument is only revoked as to those parts which are inconsistent, and both of the papers are entitled to probate[1].

1 *Lemage v Goodban* (1865) LR 1 P & D 57. But see *Re Carritt's Goods* (1892) 66 LT 379. See also *Re Bagnall, Scale v Willett* [1949] LJR 1; *Re Cocke's Goods* [1960] 2 All ER 289, [1960] 1 WLR 491.

3.187 When the provisions of two testamentary documents, the priority of which is uncertain, and in neither of which express words of revocation occur, are apparently inconsistent, the court will endeavour so to construe the words that, if possible, the two documents may stand together, and both may be admitted to probate as expressing together the whole testamentary intention of the testator[1].

1 *Townsend v Moore* [1905] P 66, CA; *Jones v Treasury Solicitor* (1932) 49 TLR 75 CA, *Re Kernaghan's Goods* [1938] NI 130. See also *Re Phelan* [1972] Fam 33, [1971] 3 All ER 1256, referred to on p. 79, post, and *Re Crannis' Estate, Mansell v Crannis* (1978) 122 Sol Jo 489.

3.188 But where a testator executed on the same day two wills which were inconsistent, both having clauses revoking all previous wills, and there was no evidence as to the order of their execution, it was held that neither will could be admitted, but that the revocatory clauses were effective to revoke an earlier will[1].

1 *Re Howard, Howard v Treasury Solicitor* [1944] P 39.

Two or more wills intended to take effect separately

3.189 Where it appears from the will produced for probate that the testator has made two or more wills, one relating only to his property in England and Wales, and the other (or others) relating only to his property in other countries, and it is the clear intention that they shall take effect separately, then, upon an attested copy of the will (or wills) dealing with property in other countries being filed together with a verifying affidavit, probate will issue of the English will alone[1]. If there is doubt as to whether the intention is clear in such a case it is advisable to refer the matter to the Principal of the Probate Department (London) or the district probate registrar before preparing the papers.

1 *Re Astor's Goods* (1876) 1 PD 150; *Re Callaway's Goods* (1890) 15 PD 147; *Re De 1a Rue's Goods* (1890) 15 PD 185.

3.190 Where a testator made two wills with codicils, the earlier relating to property in the United States, the later to property in England, and appointed executors in the two countries, and the American executors were directed to realise the residue of the American property under the directions of the English executors and hand the proceeds over to them to be dealt with as directed by the English will and codicils, it was decided that the American and English wills were independent documents; that the American will could not confirm a will not then in existence; and that the American will and codicils could not be included in the English probate. Copies of the American documents were ordered to be filed, with an affidavit verifying them, and a note to be appended to the probate that such affidavit had been filed[1].

1 *Re Murray's Goods* [1896] P 65; see also *Re Todd's Goods* [1926] P 173, cited on p. 85, post.

Revocation of will by a later testamentary document

3.191 Although a testamentary document executed as a will may lack a revocatory clause, yet, if it clearly disposes of the whole of the estate, it is held to revoke any testamentary document of an earlier date[1]. A statement in the attestation clause of a codicil, that an earlier codicil 'was thereby revoked', is not effective, the attestation clause being no part of the testamentary portion of the document[2].

1 *Henfrey v Henfrey* (1842) 4 Moo PCC 29: where by a testamentary paper executed as a will, not as a codicil, all the testator's property was given to a certain person, without the appointment of an

executor, such paper operated as a total revocation of a prior will, containing different dispositions, even though an executor may have been appointed by a prior will. For the later paper, being in fact a will disposing of all property, although there is no express revocation of the former will or appointment of an executor, is of necessity a revocation of the former will; *Cadell v Wilcocks* [1898] P 21 (in this case there were three wills: (1) contained an exercise of a power of appointment, (2) no revocatory clause, (3) a disposition of the whole of the estate, no revocatory clause. Held that (3) revoked both (1) and (2) except for the exercise of the power of appointment in (1), and (1) and (3) were proved), and *Thorn v Dickens* [1906] WN 54. A later will was held to indicate the intention of the testatrix to revoke a former will, *Re Fawcett's Estate* [1941] P 85, [1941] 2 All ER 341.
2   *Re Atkinson's Goods* (1883) 8 PD 165.

3.192   It is impossible to lay down any hard and fast rule as to the revocation of an earlier will by a will containing no express revocation clause. The expression 'This is the last will and testament' is not in itself necessarily sufficient, even though there may be a gift of the residue[1]; on the other hand, a will with no revocation clause and no gift of residue has been held to revoke a previous will[2]. The intention of the testator, ascertained from the dispositions in the documents, is the test. The present practice, where the second will contains a clear and complete gift of the whole residue, and is entirely inconsistent with the former, is to regard it as having a revocatory effect; but if there is a lacuna which can be remedied by the admission of a part of the earlier document, and if it appears that this would fulfil the intention of the testator, both are admitted to proof. (For reported cases, see paras. **33.66** ff., post.)

1   *Lemage v Goodban* (1865) LR 1 P & D 57; *Townsend v Moore* [1905] P 66.
2   *Re Bryan's Estate* [1907] P 125.

3.193   Revocation of a will does not of itself necessarily involve revocation of any codicils thereto[1].

1   *Black v Jobling* (1869) LR 1 P & D 685.

3.194   Where there is a paper writing executed in the same manner as a will but merely revoking all testamentary dispositions, it is not entitled to probate, though effective to create an intestacy. The grant will be of letters of administration, with a note thereon that it was so made in consequence of the execution of the document revoking the will[1]. See paras. **3.28** ff., ante, and para. **6.06**, post, as to form of note.

1   *Toomer v Sobinska* [1907] P 106.

Two wills: omission of revocatory clause

3.195   The later of two wills contained a revocatory clause. The earlier will was complete, the later incomplete in that it contained a gift but no named beneficiary, It was held that both documents should be proved, the revocatory clause in the later will to be excluded from probate[1].

1   *Re Brown's (Hope) Goods* [1942] P 136, [1942] 2 All ER 176. See also *Re Cocke's Goods* [1960] 2 All ER 289, [1960] 1 WLR 491. But see *Re Allen* (1962) 106 Sol Jo 115 (later will included a revocation clause, but all dispositive provisions were added after execution of the will. Held, revocation clause was conditional on whole will being effective: the earlier will was therefore not revoked, and probate of the later will was refused).

Two wills: effect of codicil confirming earlier will

3.196   See paras. **3.179–3.182**, ante.

Probate of earlier will

3.197 It is usual for the court to grant probate of the will latest in date; but, if the parties interested under such will have been cited to propound it and do not do so, the court will grant probate in common form of the one preceding it in date[1]. Where a later duly executed will was known to have been made and deposited with a bank but subsequently withdrawn by the testatrix and of which no information was available at her death, probate was ordered of an earlier will and codicil, there being no evidence whether the missing will contained a revocation clause[2].

1 *Palmer and Brown v Dent* (1850) 2 Rob Eccl 284.
2 *Re Wyatt* [1952] 1 All ER 1030.

Conditional will

3.198 If the later will is wholly conditional, e.g. on an event which never occurred, the earlier one will be proved. A revocation clause in a conditional will is effective only if the condition is fulfilled and the whole will operative[1]. See also paras. **3.216** ff., post.

1 *Re Hugo's Goods* (1877) 36 LT 518.

Description in oath

3.199 Where two or more wills are proved as together constituting the true last will, they should be marked 'A', 'B', etc., and described in the oath to lead the grant as 'the true and original last will and testament, as contained in the paper writings marked "A", "B", (etc.)'.

Duplicate wills

Duplicate will

3.200 If a will was executed in duplicate, the executors will prove one part only. If there is a reference in the will produced for probate to execution in duplicate, the executors will be called upon to produce the other part, in order that the two may be collated. The duplicate is returned to the practitioner after examination.

Revocation by the destruction of one part of a duplicate will

3.201 If the other part cannot be produced, its absence will have to be accounted for by affidavit. In respect of the absence of the other part, a question of law may arise: if one part is destroyed by the testator, with the intention of revoking it, the will is thereby revoked, and the other part is not entitled to probate[1]. If the duplicate has been in the testator's possession but cannot be found at his death, there is a prima facie presumption that it has been destroyed animo revocandi[2]. It is provided by NCPR 15 that every circumstance leading to a presumption of revocation by the testator must be accounted for to the satisfaction of the district judge or registrar.

1 *Killican v Lord Parker* (1754) 1 Lee 662; *Boughey v Moreton* (1758) 3 Hag Ecc 191.
2 *Jones v Harding* (1887) 58 LT 60.

Joint and mutual wills

3.202   A joint will is a single instrument executed by two (or more) testators in which each expresses his or her testamentary wishes.

3.203   The term 'mutual will' is commonly used to denote one of two testamentary instruments made respectively by two persons whereby each gives the other corresponding rights in his property although the doctrine of mutual wills can also apply to cases where the two testators leave their property to particular beneficiaries rather than each other (see *Proctor v Dale* [1994] Ch 31, [1993] 4 All ER 129).

3.204   A 'joint and mutual' will is a combination of two mutual wills in a single instrument executed by both testators.

Proof of joint wills

3.205   A joint will disposing only of property jointly owned by the testators is not normally proved until the death of the survivor of them, unless for some reason it is necessary to obtain a grant in the estate of the first to die.

3.206   It was formerly held that a joint will stipulating that its provisions should take effect on the death of both testators could not be proved until both had died[1], but it seems that this decision would not now be followed[2]. A joint will expressed to take effect 'at our death' may be proved on the death of the first to die.

1   *Re Raine's Goods* (1858) 1 Sw & Tr 144.
2   *Re Heys' Estate, Walker v Gaskill* [1914] P 192 at 196. See also *Re Piazzi-Smyth's Goods* [1898] P 7; *Re Hack* (1930) 169 LT Jo 284 (a single will proved with part of a joint will).

3.207   In ordinary cases a joint will is proved in its entirety as the will of the first to die[1]. It remains as the will of the survivor, and, unless superseded by a later will, should be proved again on his death.

1   The practice adopted in *Piazzi-Smyth* (above), of proving only that part of the will which is immediately effective, is not now followed.

3.208   A separate codicil made by one of the testators is proved with the joint will on the death of that testator only.

Practice in proving joint wills

3.209   When a joint will is lodged for proof on the first occasion the practitioner should supply the date of birth of the other testator (or the date of death if he is already dead). An index of joint wills which have been proved in respect of one of the testators is maintained at the registry where the central indexes are maintained (currently the Leeds District Probate Registry) and this information is required to assist in identification of the other testator: a search for any such joint will is included in the search made on every application for a grant of representation.

3.210   The grant in the estate of the second testator must be extracted from the registry at which the will was proved on the first occasion[1]. The applicant should normally 'mark' an office copy of the will, or, if he attends at the registry to swear the oath, he may mark the original will, unless the district judge or registrar has given leave for a facsimile copy of the will to be marked, in lieu of the original, under NCPR 10(2).

1 Secretary's Circular, 10 August 1962.

3.211 If a joint will requires evidence of due execution on being proved on the first occasion, the affidavit should, where practicable, establish that the will was duly executed by both testators[1].

1 Ibid.

Mutual wills—exclusion of direction as to proof

3.212 Two sisters made wills in similar terms, each giving all her estate to her two sisters absolutely, and directed 'that my executors shall not prove this will until after the death of my two sisters'. On the death of the first of the sisters her will was admitted to proof, excluding from the probate the words of this direction[1].

1 *Re O'Connors Estate* [1942] 1 All ER 546: *Re Clayton* (1942) (motion).

Revocation of joint and mutual wills

3.213 Joint wills, mutual wills and joint and mutual wills are all revocable[1], but such wills may also constitute a contract or agreement between the testators, and a revocation by one of them may not be fully effective unless done during the life-time of both of them, with notice to the other, so that he may have the opportunity of altering his own dispositions[2].

1 See *Re Heys' Estate* (para. **3.206**, above), at 197.
2 *Stone v Hoskins* [1905] P 194.

3.214 If after the death of one testator, the survivor revokes his will, the revoca-tion is recognised in the probate registry as operative, but his personal representative may be directed[1] to hold the estate on trust to carry out the terms of the contract, or implied contract (if any), originally made[2]. It does not necessarily follow, because joint or mutual wills are made, that there was a contract: and this is a question to be decided in the Chancery Division[3], the probate registry being con-cerned only with the formal validity of the dispositions.

1 By the Chancery Division.
2 *Dufour v Pereira* (1769) 1 Dick 419; *Stone v Hoskins*, above; *Re Oldham, Hadwen v Myles* [1925] Ch 75 (the probability of a contract is greater if the mutual gifts are for life only); *Re Green, Lindner v Green* [1951] Ch 148, [1950] 2 All ER 913 (the wills themselves may contain a clear indication of a contract); *Re Cleaver, Cleaver v Insley* [1981] 2 All ER 1018, [1981] 1 WLR 939 (the whole evid-ence must be looked at to determine whether there was a definite agreement between the testators: the mere fact that the wills were to the same effect, though a relevant circumstance, was not in itself suffi-cient).
3 *Re Heys' Estate*, above, at 200.

Community of property

3.215 As to probate, where the domicile at the date of the marriage of the deceased was elsewhere than in England and Wales and there was community of property, see para. **4.212**, post.

Conditional wills

3.216 The question whether a testamentary document is conditional or not depends upon the wording of the document itself.

3.217 If a will is clearly expressed to take effect only on the happening, or not happening, of any event, it is conditional. If the testator says, in effect, that he is led to make his will by reason of the uncertainty of life in general, or for some special reason, it is not conditional. But if it is not clear whether the words used import a reason for making a will or impress a conditional character on it, the whole language of the document, and also the surrounding circumstances, must be considered[1]. In 1941 a husband and wife made a joint will to operate 'in the event of our two deaths'. It was contended that the will was conditional upon the husband and wife being killed together in an air-raid. The wife having died from natural causes in 1949, it was held that the will was conditional and, the condition not having been fulfilled, was inoperative[2].

1 *Re Spratt's Goods* [1897] P 28.
2 *Re Govier* [1950] P 237.

3.218 Where a will is made in terms subject to the happening of an event, that event must occur before it can become operative; whereas, if the possibility of an event happening is stated merely as the reason for making the will, the will becomes operative whether the event happens or not. To give an illustration: if a man write, 'should I die tomorrow, my will is' so and so, his death must occur tomorrow to make the document operative; whereas if he write, 'lest I die tomorrow', it will be operative whether he die or not on the morrow[1].

1 *Re Vines's Estate, Vines v Vines* [1910] P 147. Wills pronounced to be conditional in *Parsons v Lanoe* (1748) 1 Ves Sen 189; *Re Winn's Goods* (1861) 2 Sw & Tr 147; *Roberts v Roberts* (1862) 2 Sw & Tr 337; *Re Porter's Goods* (1869) LR 2 P& D 22; see also *Re Smith's Goods* (1869) LR 1 P & D 717: codicil conditional upon assent of wife of deceased. Condition held valid and, wife not assenting, codicil omitted from probate. Wills pronounced to be not conditional in *Re Thorne's Goods* (1865) 4 Sw & Tr 36; *Strauss v Schmidt* (1820) 3 Phillim 209; *Burton v Collingwood* (1832) 4 Hag Ecc 176; *Re Cawthron's Goods* (1863) 3 Sw & Tr 417; *Re Dobson's Goods* (1866) LR 1 P & D 88; *Re Martin's Goods* (1867) LR 1 P & D 380; *Re Mayd's Goods* (1880) 6 PD 17.

3.219 When a question arises whether a conditional will or codicil should be admitted to probate or not, affidavit evidence as to the fulfilment or non-fulfilment of the condition is required before a decision is given, unless it is apparent from the application for the grant that the condition is inoperative. A conditional document which is not admitted to probate and the affidavit evidence, if any, will be filed with the oath to lead the grant. It should be noted that reference in a later conditional testamentary document to an earlier document, which purports to be testamentary, whether such reference is by date or not, and even if the earlier document is not duly executed as a will or codicil, may have the effect of republishing or incorporating the earlier document, and on that ground alone entitle the conditional document to probate, notwithstanding that the condition is not fulfilled[1]. (See also paras. **3.166–3.172**, ante.)

1 Registrar's Direction (1941) 10 March. See *Re Mendes Da Silva's Goods* (1861) 2 Sw & Tr 315.

Lost wills

Probate of lost will

3.220   Probate may be granted of a copy or reconstruction of a lost will. For practice see 'Will lost or not available', paras. **11.11** ff. and **25.46** ff., post.

Will contained in 'instructions'

3.221   Instructions for a will, if duly executed, may be admitted to proof if it is shown that it was the testator's intention so to dispose of his estate up to the time of his death, and upon evidence that there is no other will in existence[1]. Similar evidence is required where the document bears any indication that it was originally intended as a draft.

1 *Hattatt v Hattatt* (1832) 4 Hag Ecc 211; *Whyte v Pollok* (1882) 7 App Cas 400; *Torre v Castle* (1836) 1 Curt 303; *Re Meynell, Meynell v Meynell* [1949] WN 273.

Alterations in wills

3.222   Paragraphs **3.223–3.247** deal with the internal law of England and Wales as to alterations in wills. In the case of persons dying on or after 1 January 1964, consideration should also be given to the provisions of the Wills Act 1963, in connection with unattested alterations, additions, etc., in wills and other testamentary dispositions (whatever their date). The expression 'any testamentary instrument or act' used in the Wills Act 1963 is wide enough to include an alteration, etc. As to this Act, see paras. **3.392** ff., post.

3.223   In all altered wills the prima facie presumption is that the alterations were made after execution of the will.

3.224   The initials of the testator and the witnesses, opposite an alteration, are usually sufficient to rebut this presumption[1]. In the absence of such initials, it must be established that the alteration was made prior to execution, unless it is a minor one or is obviously a mere clerical correction—in which case the initials of the witnesses alone may be sufficient.

1 *Re Wingrove's Goods* (1850) 16 LTOS 347.

3.225   In any case enquiry should always be made if the initials do not appear to be those of the witnesses to the will.

3.226   If it is clear, as a result of such enquiry, or on the face of the will (e.g. by the fact that the alteration bears a date subsequent to that of the will), that the alteration was made after execution, it is not effective unless it is established that the requirements of s. 21 of the Wills Act 1837 were fulfilled. No action is necessary if the alteration is of no practical importance or is in a part of the will which, in the events which have happened, is inoperative.

3.227   If interlineations, interpolations, obliterations, erasures, words or figures written upon erasures, or anything in the nature of an alteration or addition appear in the will, the matter must be considered in two aspects, depending upon whether or not they are verified, as indicated in the following paragraphs.

Verified by testator and witnesses

3.228   Where each alteration has been authenticated in the manner prescribed by s. 21 of the Wills Act 1837. This section provides that no alteration made after execution shall be valid unless executed in the same manner as required for the execution of a will; but the will, with such alteration as part thereof, shall be deemed to be duly executed if—

> 'the signature of the testator and the subscription of the witnesses be made in the margin or in some other part of the will opposite or near to such alteration[1], or at the foot or end of or opposite to a memorandum referring to such alteration' (e.g. a recital of the alteration in the attestation clause) 'and written at the end or some other part of the will.'

1 If an alteration which is unattested forms part of the same sentence in which an attested alteration occurs, it may be admitted to probate (*Wilkinson's Goods* (1881) 6 PD 100).

3.229   The initials of the testator and the attesting witnesses have been held to be sufficient compliance with this provision[1].

1 *Re Martin's Goods* (1849) 1 Rob Eccl 712; *Re Blewitt's Goods* (1880) 5 PD 116; *Re Benn's Goods* [1938] IR 313.

3.230   In any case where the nature or effect of the alteration is not clear on the face of the document the district judge or registrar may require affidavit evidence. As to complete obliterations, see paras. **3.242** ff., post.

Verified by subsequent codicil

3.231   Alterations made in a will, if intended to be final and not merely deliberative[1], can be set up by a codicil made subsequently[2]. The codicil may refer to the alterations in the will by implication only[3].

1 E.g. made in pencil (*Re Adams' Goods* (1872) LR 2 P & D 367).
2 *Tyler v Merchant Taylors' Co* (1890) 15 PD 216.
3 *Re Heath's Goods* [1892] P 253. See *Lushington v Onslow* (1848) 6 Notes of Cases 183 and *Re Bradley's Goods* (1846) 5 Notes of Cases 187.

3.232   The mere circumstance, however, that an alteration has been dated by a testator as before the execution of his will does not alone entitle such alteration to probate[1]. For summary of reported cases, see paras. **32.55** ff., post.

1 *Re Adamson* (1875) LR 3 P & D 253.

Alteration etc., not verified by testator

3.233   Alterations which the testator has neglected to verify by one or other of the foregoing methods are entitled to probate if proof can be adduced that they were made at a period preceding the execution of the will, or if they appear to the district judge or registrar to be of no practical importance.

3.234   When a will contains any obliteration, interlineation or other alteration which is not authenticated in accordance with s. 21 of the Wills Act 1837, or by re-execution of the will or the execution of a codicil, then, unless the alteration is considered by the district judge or registrar to be of no practical importance, evidence to show whether or not it was present at the time of execution is required (NCPR 14(1)).

3.235 Affirmative evidence of this character may be given by an attesting witness who observed the alterations, or whose attention was drawn to them, before or at the time of the execution; by the draftsman of the will, who may be able to depose that the parts apparently interpolated or altered accord with his draft; or by the writer or engrosser of the will, who can prove that he himself made the alterations or additions, either as the correction of his own error in copying, or as a change of intention on the part of the testator previously to the execution of the will. An affidavit from any one of the above persons, or from any other person who is for any other reason qualified to depose affirmatively, is sufficient to entitle the alteration to probate. For forms of affidavit in verification of alterations, see Nos. 7 and 8.

3.236 If the will presents the appearance of having been altered on more than one occasion (e.g. where a passage written in ink of a different colour has itself been deleted or altered) care must be taken in drafting the affidavit. It is not sufficient merely to refer to the deletion of such a passage: the matter must be considered in two stages. The first thing is to deal with the possibility of the words in different ink having been added after the execution of the will. If this is so, or there is no evidence that the words were there at the time of execution they will, subject to any special direction to the contrary, be excluded, and in this situation the question of the subsequent deletion of the words becomes irrelevant. If there is evidence that the words were written prior to the execution of the will the question of their deletion or alteration must then be dealt with.

3.237 This principle also applies where a word or figure appears to have been twice altered: each alteration must be considered separately.

Absence of evidence

3.238 If no affirmative evidence can be obtained, alterations are presumed to have been made after the execution of a will[1], and are excluded from probate unless there are special reasons for a contrary presumption[2]. The presumption of law can be rebutted by evidence of declarations made by the testator before, but not after, the will was executed[3]. If necessary, the matter should be referred to the district judge or registrar for directions as to the form in which the will is to be proved (NCPR 14(1)).

1 But see *Williams v Ashton* (1860) 1 John & H 115, 3 LT 148.
2 *Cooper v Bockett* (1846) 4 Moo PCC 419, 4 Notes of Cases 685. See also Sir H. Jenner's observations in 4 Notes of Cases 695. *Re Cadge's Goods* (1868) LR 1 P & D 543; but see *Re White's Goods* (1860) 30 LJPM & A 55.
3 In *Doe d Shallcross v Palmer* (1851) 16 QB 747, where a holograph will appeared to have been altered by turning a devise of certain cottages to one person in fee into a limitation to him for life, with remainder in fee to another person who was not otherwise provided for in the will, it was held that certain declarations made by the testator before the will was executed that he intended to make a provision by his will for the person to whom the alterations referred, but not specifying the nature of the provision, was evidence to rebut the presumption of law, and proved that the alterations had been made in the will before its execution; *Re Sykes' Goods* (1873) LR 3 P & D 26; *Re Jessop* [1924] P 221. But see *Sugden v Lord St Leonards* (1876) 1 PD 154, CA.

Fiat copy

3.239 When alterations in a will are not admissible to proof, a copy of the will known as a 'fiat copy', reproducing the will in its state at the time of execution, is required (NCPR 11(2) and (3) and for practice, see paras. **4.227** ff., post).

Incomplete obliterations

3.240   If obliterations are so incomplete that the original words or figures can be read or deciphered either with the naked or the assisted eye, the court will restore them and grant probate of them.

3.241   The court will allow the use of artificial means to decipher the original words or figures, but will not generally resort to physical interference with the document[1]. In one case a court expert, appointed to photograph a codicil by the infra-red process in order to ascertain what was underneath slips of paper pasted on the document, reported that he was unable to see what was under the slips by looking at the document, even with the assistance of any modern scientific means known to him, but he had found out what was under the slips by taking an infra-red photograph. It was held that the words and figures under the slips were not 'apparent' within the meaning of s. 21 of the Wills Act 1837, since they could only be read by creating a new document, i.e. the infra-red photograph. The case was, however, held to be one of dependent relative revocation (see below) and, the revocation of the words covered by the slips being ineffective, probate was granted of the codicil in its original form[2].

1   *Ffinch v Combe* [1894] P 191; *Re Gilbert's Goods* [1893] P 183. In the latter case the court ordered the removal of blank paper pasted over words written on the back of a codicil to ascertain whether it amounted to a revocation of the codicil. The pasted paper was not on the actual writing of the codicil.
2   *Re Itter's Goods, Dedman v Godfrey* [1950] P 130, [1950] 1 All ER 68.

Complete obliterations

3.242   If the original words cannot be read either by the naked eye or through extrinsic aid, the court exercises two different principles in its way of dealing with them.

Whole bequest obliterated

3.243   If a testator has obliterated or erased the whole of a bequest or provision in his will, or has completely covered it by paper pasted over it, and has so effectually accomplished his purpose that the passage is not apparent, i.e. cannot be made out on the face of the will, the revocation is complete under s. 21 of the Wills Act 1837, and the court grants probate with a blank where the erasure was[1].

1   *Re Horsford's Goods* (1874) LR 3 P & D 211; *Townley v Watson* (1844) 3 Curt 761.

Part of bequest obliterated. Dependent relative revocation

3.244   But where part of a legacy only, e.g. the amount, has been so covered or obliterated or erased, and has been replaced by other words or figures, the court infers that the testator's intention was only to revoke the original amount in the event of his having effectually substituted another, in which case the doctrine of dependent relative revocation becomes applicable; and by this doctrine, the obliteration or erasure being done with reference to another act, meant to be an effectual disposition, will be a revocation or not according to the effectiveness of the subsequent act. (See also Chap. 33, post.) Where the alteration in the amount, i.e. the relative act, is not executed according to the statute, there is no revocation at all, and the court may restore and grant probate of the original words or figures for which others were sought to be substituted[1].

1   *Brooke v Kent* (1841) 3 Moo PCC 344, 1 Notes of Cases 93; *Re Hall's Goods* (1871) LR 2 P & D 256; *Re Itter, Dedman v Godfrey* [1950] P 130, [1950] 1 All ER 68, cited in para. **3.241**, above.

3.245 In these cases the court will exercise the right of ascertaining aliunde, by parol evidence, what the original words or figures were, in order to restore them[1].

1 *Re Horsford's Goods* (1874) LR 3 P & D 211; *Re Harris' Goods* (1860) 1 Sw & Tr 536; *Re Clark* (1932) 101 LJP 27, 147 LT 240.

3.246 Where, however, the name of a legatee is obliterated and another name substituted after execution, it is not likely that the inference will be drawn in favour of the doctrine of relative revocation in the absence of further evidence as to the testator's intention on substitution of the new name.

3.247 The doctrine of dependent relative revocation applies only where there has been a substitution of other words. The position is different if there is merely an obliteration: in such a case if the obliterated words cannot be made out probate will issue with such parts in blank[1].

1 *Re Ibbetson's Goods* (1839) 2 Curt 337; cf. *Re Horsford's Goods*, above.

Obliteration of testator's signature

3.248 As to when the obliteration of a testator's signature revokes the whole will, see *Re Adams* [1990] Ch 601, [1990] 2 All ER 97 referred to in para. **33.70**, post.

Exclusion of words from the probate: rectification and interpretation of wills

Omission of words

3.249 So that the true will of the deceased may be admitted, the court may exclude from probate words introduced into a testamentary document by mistake or without the instructions or knowledge of the testator[1]. But it has been held that, in respect of deaths prior to 1 January 1983 (see next section, 'Rectification and interpretation of wills') the probate registry has no jurisdiction to insert words[2], nor, by exclusion of words, to correct an omission in the text purely for convenience of construction[3]. In such cases, the court could only rectify, so far as was in its power, by exclusion (e.g. matter inserted in a will owing to a clerical error[4]). In another case, a testator, having executed a home-made will, later executed three further wills. Each contained a revocation clause, appointed as executors the executors and beneficiaries under the first will, and in each the testator disposed of a single holding in a unit trust. These three wills were all attested within a few minutes of each other. It was held that the execution of the later wills was based on a complete misunderstanding by the testator, who intended to supplement the first will. The court has power to admit more than one will if they are not inconsistent, and to omit words if it is satisfied as to the testator's intentions. The revocatory words in the three later wills were ordered to be omitted, and all four documents admitted to probate[5]. (See also Chap. 33, post.)

1 *Re Moore's Goods* [1892] P 378 (omission of revocation clause inserted per incuriam); *Brisco v Baillie and Hamilton* [1902] P 234 (words wrongly describing certain property); *Re Clark* (1932) 147 LT 240 (relationship of legatee wrongly described); *Re Brown's (Hope) Goods* [1942] P 136, [1942] 2 All ER 176 (revocation clause); *Re Swords' Goods* [1952] P 368, [1952] 2 All ER 281; *Re Cocke's Estate* [1960] 2 All ER 289, [1960] 1 WLR 491 (two wills; omission of revocation clause from second, and of clauses in the first where inconsistent with the second); *Re Reade's Goods* [1902] P 75; *Re White's Estate* (1961) 105 Sol Jo 259 (omission from codicil of words mistakenly confirming an earlier will revoked by one later in date).

2 *Harter v Harter* (1873) LR 3 P & D 11, 22; *Re Schott's Goods* [1901] P 190. See also *Re Follett, Barclays Bank Ltd v Dovell* [1955] 2 All ER 22, [1955] 1 WLR 429, CA; *Re Cory, Cory v Morel* [1955] 2 All ER 630, [1955] 1 WLR 725; and *Re Whitrick, Sutcliffe v Sutcliffe* [1957] 2 All ER 467, [1957] 1 WLR 884, as to the power of the Chancery Division to supply missing words for the purpose of construction, and *Re Bacharach's Will Trusts. Minden v Bacharach* [1959] Ch 245, [1958] 3 All ER 618, as to transposition of words in order to make them intelligible.
3 *Re Horrocks, Taylor v Kershaw* [1939] P 198, [1939] 1 All ER 579.
4 *Re Morris, Lloyds Bank Ltd v Peake* [1971] P 62, [1970] 1 All ER 1057.
5 *Re Phelan* [1972] Fam 33, [1971] 3 All ER 1256. See also *Re Crannis' Estate, Mansell v Crannis* (1978) 122 Sol Jo 489 (court directed that a revocation clause contained in a will be omitted from probate as being conditional on an effective disposition of the estate under an earlier testamentary document, which condition had not been fulfilled).

Rectification and interpretation of wills (death on or after 1 January 1983)

3.250   Section 20(1) of the Administration of Justice Act 1982 (see p. 854, post), which came into force on 1 January 1983, provides as follows:

'(1) If a court is satisfied that a will is so expressed that it fails to carry out the testator's intentions, in consequence—
(a) of a clerical error; or
(b) of a failure to understand his instructions,
it may order that the will shall be rectified so as to carry out his intentions.'

3.251   Section 20(2) provides that an application for an order that a will be rectified cannot be made, except with the permission of the court, after the end of the period of six months from the date on which representation with respect to the estate of the deceased is first taken out.

3.252   Section 20(4) provides that in considering when representation was first taken out, a grant limited to settled land or trust property is to be left out of account, and a grant limited to real estate or personal estate is to be left out of account unless a grant limited to the remainder of the estate has previously been made or is made at the same time.

3.253   Section 21 is as follows:

'(1) This section applies to a will—
(a) in so far as any part of it is meaningless;
(b) in so far as the language used in any part of it is ambiguous on the face of it;
(c) in so far as evidence, other than evidence of the testator's intention, shows that the language used in any part of it is ambiguous in the light of surrounding circumstances.

(2) In so far as this section applies to a will extrinsic evidence, including evidence of the testator's intention, may be admitted to assist in its interpretation.'

3.254   Both of these sections apply to a will, whenever made, of a testator who *dies* on or after 1 January 1983, the date upon which the relevant sections came into force. Where it is necessary for the Family Division to consider the terms of a testamentary document for the purpose of admitting that document to probate, the district judge or registrar may need to have recourse to the interpretation provision.

3.255   NCPR 55 provides that an application for an order that a will be rectified by virtue of s. 20(1) of the Administration of Justice Act 1982 may be made to a district judge or registrar, unless a probate action has been commenced.

3.256 The application must be supported by an affidavit, setting out the grounds of the application, together with such evidence as can be adduced as to the testator's intentions and whichever of the following matters are in issue:

(a) in what respects the testator's intentions were not understood; or
(b) the nature of any alleged clerical error.

3.257 Unless otherwise directed, notice of the application must be given to every person having an interest under the will whose interest might be prejudiced by the rectification applied for and any comments in writing by any such person must be exhibited to the affidavit in support of the application.

3.258 If the district judge or registrar is satisfied that, subject to any direction to the contrary, notice has been given to every such person, and that the application is unopposed, he may order that the will be rectified accordingly.

3.259 NCPR 11(2)(b) further provides that where a will has been ordered to be rectified by virtue of s. 20(1) of the Administration of Justice Act 1982, there must be lodged an engrossment of the will in the form in which it is to be proved.

3.260 It has been agreed between the Senior District Judge and the Chief Chancery Master that unopposed applications for rectification of wills may be made to a district judge of the Principal Registry or a registrar of a district probate registry under the authority of NCPR 55 either before or after the issue of the grant.

3.261 Where rectification is ordered under r. 55 after the date of the grant, a memorandum of the order will be annexed to the probate and record copies of the will.

3.262 Where a question of construction also arises, even if unopposed, the application for rectification should be made to the Chancery Division[1].

1 Secretary's Circular, 24 June 1985.

3.263 For a more detailed analysis of the interpretation provision, see paras. **3.02–3.04**, ante. For application in the Chancery Division for rectification of wills, see Chap. 41.

Words of an offensive, libellous or blasphemous nature

3.264 A testator has the right to explain why he has disposed of his property in a certain way, but he is not entitled to use his will as a vehicle for slander[1]. The court will upon application exclude from probate words of an atrocious, offensive or libellous character[2].

1 *Re Hall's Estate* [1943] 2 All ER 159; *Re T's Estate* (1961) 105 Sol Jo 325.
2 *Wartnaby's Goods* (1846) 4 Notes of Cases 476; *Marsh v Marsh* (1860) 1 Sw & Tr 528; *Re White's Estate* [1914] P 153; *Re Bohrmann's Estate* [1938] 1 All ER 271; but see *Re Rawlings' Estate* (1934) 78 Sol Jo 338.

3.265 The court will also exclude words of a blasphemous nature; and the district judge or registrar may refuse to grant probate until the necessary application has been made[1]. The court, however, will not lightly interfere in a man's testamentary affairs, and will not exclude words on these grounds unless they come fully within these categories; nor, it seems, if the words are in any sense dispositive[2].

1 *Re Brown* (1939) (unreported motion).
2 *Curtis v Curtis* (1825) 3 Add 33; see *Re Honywood's Goods* (1871) LR 2 P & D 251; *Re Beech's Estate, Beech v Public Trustee* [1923] P 46, CA (a soldier's will); *Re Caie's Estate* (1927) 43 TLR 697 (words not defamatory of a person); *Re Hall's Estate* [1943] 2 All ER 159.

3.266   For words to be atrocious or offensive they need not necessarily allude to any individual. In *Re Bowker's Goods*[1] the court ordered exclusion of words relating solely to the funeral and disposal of the testator's remains on the ground that such words, which were liable to be published in the press, were 'offensive and objectionable and repugnant to the members of the deceased's family'.

1 [1932] P 93.

3.267   Words ordered to be excluded cannot be expunged from the will itself but will be omitted from the probate copy, and from any copies of the will subsequently ordered[1].

1 *Re Maxwell* (1929) 140 LT 471.

Mode of application for omission of words from probate

3.268   Contested applications for omission of words from probate must be made by summons to a district judge of the Principal Registry[1].

1 *Practice Direction* [1968] 2 All ER 592, [1968] 1 WLR 987. Such an application may, of course, be the subject of a probate action in the Chancery Division: see Chap. 33, post.

3.269   Uncontested applications for the omission of words may be made to the district judge or registrar of the probate registry at which it is proposed to make application for the grant. Any such application may be made ex parte by lodging with the district judge or registrar affidavit evidence (exhibiting the will or codicil in question) together with any consents in writing of persons not under disability who might be prejudiced by the order. If the district judge or registrar is satisfied on the facts and, in the absence of consent, that there is no substantial interest unprotected, he will make the order.

3.270   A district judge or registrar may require an application for the omission of words from probate to be made by summons to a High Court judge in chambers or open court (NCPR 61). A registrar must first refer the matter to a district judge for his confirmation that it be referred to a High Court judge.

3.271   A copy of any order to omit words from probate should be lodged with the application for the grant and will be annexed to the original will and filed with it. A typewritten copy of the will, omitting such part, should be lodged at the Probate Department (Principal Registry), or with the district registrar, for the fiat of a probate officer of the Probate Department or the district registrar to be written in the margin before photography (see also para. **4.182**, post)[1].

1 *Practice Direction* [1968] 2 All ER 592, [1968] 1 WLR 987.

3.272   For practice as to summonses, see paras. **25.223** ff., post.

Incorporation of papers by reference

3.273 Where a testator, in his will or codicil, expressly refers to other existing documents such as deeds, wills, or codicils, of himself or of other persons, or even refers to papers void or invalid per se[1] as carrying out or containing his own dispositions, such documents and papers are considered to be incorporated in and to form part of the will, and are included in the probate. See paras. **32.47** ff., post, for reported cases.

1 *Sheldon v Sheldon* (1844) 3 Notes of Cases 250; *Re Willesford's Goods* (1842) 3 Curt 77; *Re Smartt's Goods* (1845) 4 Notes of Cases 38; *Countess Ferraris v Marquis of Hertford* (1843) 3 Curt 468; *Wood v Goodlake* (1843) 1 Notes of Cases 144, PC; *Re Hakewell's Goods* (1856) Dea & Sw 14; *Re Ash's Goods* (1856) Dea & Sw 181; *Re Bacon's Goods* (1845) 3 Notes of Cases 644.

3.274 But if there is a statement by the testator in the will that the document is not to form part of the will[1], or that its contents are not to create any trust, or are not binding, it is not entitled to probate.

1 *Re Louis, Louis v Treloar* (1916) 32 TLR 313.

Insufficient reference

3.275 The question of incorporation need not be considered if a will or codicil refers to another document in such a manner as to indicate a future intention of the testator to make such a document, for example, 'to such of my friends as I *may* designate in a book or memorandum which will be found with my will', even though a codicil is made after the date the book or memorandum came into existence[1]; or if the reference in the will or codicil be so ambiguous in terms as to prevent the possibility of any document being identified as the one referred to, for example, 'in accordance with any memoranda I may have made'.

1 *Re Smart's Goods* [1902] P 238; *Re Bateman's Will Trusts, Brierley v Perry* [1970] 3 All ER 817, [1970] 1 WLR 1463 (the words 'to such persons and in such proportions as shall be stated by me in a sealed letter' clearly import that the testator may after the date of the will give a sealed letter to the trustees: this is invalid, as an attempt to dispose of the estate by a non-testamentary instrument).

3.276 A testator directed the payment of a sum to trustees under a special declaration of trust, for the benefit of an institution or otherwise as therein contained, executed by him, even in date with the will, or any substitution therefor or modification thereof or addition thereto which he might thereafter make or execute. He executed a deed poll on the same date as the will, in which he declared the trusts upon which the sum was to be held. It was held that the effect of the direction was to give power to change a testamentary disposition by an unexecuted codicil in violation of the Wills Act 1837. A direction to the effect that subsequent declarations should have testamentary validity was not permissible and the gift failed for uncertainty[1]. But a deed, part of which provided for distribution in accordance with possible subsequent memoranda, was incorporated in toto, though the clause as to subsequent memoranda was declared not to be operative[2].

1 *Re Jones' Will Trusts, Jones v Jones* [1942] Ch 328, [1942] 1 All ER 642; *Claire Rich* (1942) (Motion) (a statement in a will that effect was to be given to any wishes the testatrix might express in a memorandum, and to any alterations thereto, provided that they were initialled by her: held, the memorandum was not entitled to incorporation).
2 *Re Edwards' Will Trusts, Dalgleish v Leighton* [1948] Ch 440, [1948] 1 All ER 821.

Sufficient reference. Existence at time of execution of will

3.277   In order that a document referred to in a will or codicil may be entitled to incorporation, it must be evident (1) that it is distinctly identified with the description in the testator's reference, *and* (2) that it was in existence at the time of execution of the will or codicil which refers to it[1].

1   *Singleton v Tomlinson* (1878) 3 App Cas 404; *Re Smart's Goods* [1902] P 238.

3.278   Where a will contained no effective dispositive clause, but the deceased had at the time of writing the will written also several lists of gifts beginning: 'I wish to leave the following amounts', and these lists were found with the will at the time of his death, it was held that there was a sufficient cross reference between the will and the lists, and the will and lists were admitted[1].

1   *Re Saxton, Barclays Bank Ltd v Treasury Solicitor* [1939] 2 All ER 418.

Later than the will but before subsequent codicil

3.279   A document referred to in a will as existing (though not necessarily in these exact words), but which in fact was not existing at the date of the will, is entitled to incorporation if it can be shown to have been in existence at the date of execution of a codicil to the will. But if the terms of the reference in the will indicate a document of a future character, there is no incorporation[1].

1   *Re Mathias' Goods* (1863) 3 Sw & Tr 100; *Re Lady Truro's Goods* (1866) LR 1 P & D 201; *Re Sunderland's Goods* (1866) LR 1 P & D 198; *Re Reid's Goods* (1868) 38 LJP & M 1; *Durham v Northen* [1895] P 66; *Re Smart's Goods* [1902] P 238.

3.280   Similarly, if a document be referred to in a codicil as already existing, though not then in existence, it will be entitled to incorporation if it can be shown to have been made before the execution of a subsequent codicil.

Proof of identity and admissibility of evidence

3.281   Where the reference is not sufficiently precise or particular to identify of itself the document referred to, parol evidence is admissible to show what document answers the description contained in the will or codicil if the description of the document in the will refers definitely to an existing document. If the reference in the will is worded so that it may refer to an existing or future document, parol evidence is not admissible[1], at least, not in respect of a will of a testator dying before 1 January 1983. Where death occurs on or after 1 January 1983, and there is an equivocation in a will, irrespective of the date of its execution, it would seem that extrinsic evidence may be permissible by virtue of s. 21 of the Administration of Justice Act 1982 (see p. 854, post).

1   *Allen v Maddock* (1858) 11 Moo PCC 427; *Re Almosnino's Goods* (1859) 1 Sw & Tr 508; *Re Garnett's Goods* [1894] P 90 (probate refused); *Eyre v Eyre* [1903] P 131. See *University College of North Wales v Taylor* [1908] P 140, CA.

'Wishes'

3.282   The general test to be applied, particularly where the reference is to 'wishes', is:

(a) Are the 'wishes,' etc., expressed, in the terms of the will, to be in the form of a written document[1]?
(b) If so, is such document expressed to be then in existence[2]?
(c) Is it clearly described in the will, without any expression capable of covering a possible substitution[3]?

1 *Re Goodman* (1944) (motion) (Direction, 17 May).
2 *Re Smart's Goods* [1902] P 238 at 241, 242; *Durham v Northen* [1895] P 66 at 67.
3 *University College of North Wales v Taylor* [1908] P 140 at 144; *Allen v Maddock* (1858) 11 Moo PCC 427.

3.283 If 'wishes' are mentioned, but the reference in the will is not to written wishes, no enquiry is made by the registry as to the existence of a document containing them. Evidence as to verbal wishes is not admissible to explain the testator's wishes[1].

1 *Re Hetley, Hetley v Hetley* [1902] 2 Ch 866.

Statement by testator (Inheritance (Provision for Family and Dependants) Act 1975)[1]

3.284 A statement, referred to in a will, containing the reasons why a testator has made particular dispositions or has not made provision for his spouse or dependants, is considered not to be a subject for incorporation, unless it is dispositive. It should be retained by the personal representatives as being a matter between the testator and his spouse or dependants, and for production under s. 21 if an application is made under the Act. For applications under the Inheritance (Provision for Family and Dependants) Act 1975, see Chap. 41.

1 For text, see p. 808, post: this Act applies in relation to the estates of persons dying on or after 1 April 1976; it repealed and replaced the Inheritance (Family Provision) Act 1938, as amended by the Intestates' Estates Act 1952, and the Family Provision Act 1966. The Act is dealt with in detail in Chap. 41, post.

Statutory will forms

3.285 Under s. 179 of the Law of Property Act 1925[1], certain will forms have been prescribed by the Lord Chancellor which may be incorporated in a will by reference only. For forms and manner of reference, see Appendix VII, p. 1095, post.

1 See p. 744, post.

Foreign will confirming English will

3.286 Where an English will ratified and confirmed a foreign will, the latter was held to be incorporated; and where a foreign will confirmed an English one, probate of both was granted[1].

1 *Re Lord Howden's Goods* (1874) 43 LJP 26; *Re Lockhart's Goods* (1893) 69 LT 2l; *Re Harris' Goods* (1870) LR 2 P & D 83; see also *Re Todd's Estate* [1926] P 173 (foreign will (proved with English will) released for proof abroad).

English and foreign wills intended to take effect separately

3.287 For practice in cases where the testator has made two or more independent wills dealing with property in different countries, see paras. **3.189** and **3.190**, ante.

Former will

3.288   Where a testator in his last will referred to a former will of his own enclosed therewith, affirming it as far as any of the provisions therein contained might be applicable to existing circumstances at the time of his death, such former will was admitted to probate, together with the last will of the testator[1].

1 *Re Duff's Goods* (1846) 4 Notes of Cases 474.

Revoked will of another person

3.289   Where a testatrix in her will referred to a revoked will of her late husband, as containing the trusts and purposes to which she wished her own property to be applied, such revoked will was admitted as part of her own[1].

1 *Re Countess of Durham's Goods* (1842) 3 Curt 57, 1 Notes of Cases 365.

Will or codicil not duly executed

3.290   If a testator has made and duly executed a codicil, referring to his will which was not properly executed, the will is entitled to probate by incorporation[1].

1 *Re Claringbull's Goods* (1844) 3 Notes of Cases 1; *Re Hill's Goods* (1846) 4 Notes of Cases 404:
   Allen v Maddock (1858) 11 Moo PCC 427 at 429.

3.291   Similarly, if a testator, in a codicil duly executed, refers to a prior codicil which was not duly attested, the latter is admissible to probate by incorporation[1].

1 *Re Smith's Goods* (1841) 2 Curt 796; *Ingoldby v Ingoldby* (1846) 4 Notes of Cases 493.

Copy of will (original abroad)

3.292   If a testator, in a duly executed codicil, refers to a copy of his will, the original being in another country, probate may be granted of that copy of the will and of the original codicil[1].

1 *Re Mercer's Goods* (1870) LR 2 P & D 91. As to the practice where an original will is not available, see also Chap. 25.

Production of document

3.293   Whenever a will or codicil refers to any list, memorandum, or other document in such a manner as to suggest that such document was in existence at the time the will or codicil referring to it was executed, such document must be produced with a view to ascertaining if it is entitled to probate (NCPR 14(3)) (save that where a will incorporates by reference standard will forms or clauses as contained in a published document, production of that document will not be required in any individual case, unless otherwise directed, if the published document containing the standard forms or clauses (together with as many copies as may be required) has been previously lodged with the Senior District Judge and accepted by him as sufficient lodgment for the purposes – *District Judge's Direction*, 10 April 1995).

3.294   The identity of the document produced as the document referred to in the will or codicil is proved by affidavit, and if it refers, in any way, to the disposition of property[1], the district judge or registrar will decide whether the document is to be incorporated. As to the wording of the oath in such cases, see para. **3.307**, post.

1 See *Re Jones' Goods* (1920) 123 LT 202.

3.295 If a document referred to, as above, in a will or codicil cannot be found, an affidavit of search must be filed. Form of affidavit to be adapted to circumstances, No. 6.

3.296 For summary of cases, see paras. **32.47** ff., post.

Reference to another will

3.297 If a will contains a reference to another will already proved, which under the practice relating to incorporation should be incorporated, the probate of such will should be produced and a note of the name of the deceased and the place and date of such probate will be made by the registry in the margin of the will now being proved and of the probate copy of it.

Deeds

3.298 In the case of deeds as well as of documents not valid per se, the court requires, where possible, that the original be produced. A deed, when proved and registered, can be delivered out.

3.299 Where, for the purposes of applying for a grant of representation, it is necessary for the applicant to produce to the Principal Registry or a district registry an original deed or other instrument, it is the practice of the registry to examine the instrument to ensure that it has been properly executed and duly stamped under the Stamp Act 1891 before proceeding with the application. Where there is any doubt whether the instrument is duly stamped, the applicant will be asked to present the instrument to the Controller of Stamps (Inland Revenue) for adjudication before the issue of the grant[1].

1 *Practice Note* [1978] 1 All ER 1046, [1978] 1 WLR 430 (as extended by Secretary's Circular, 10 September 1987).

3.300 For the purpose of probate the incorporation of a part of, or an extract from, a deed is undesirable; a deed may be incorporated if, in the opinion of a district judge or registrar, it is sufficiently short, but in other cases, the district judge or registrar will direct the filing of an examined copy of the deed, verified by affidavit[1], and this is the more usual procedure. When the deed is in the hands of a person who will not part with it, the court, having no power to enforce its production, will grant probate without it[2].

1 Direction (1936) 21 July; *Re Lansdowne's Goods* (1863) 2 Sw & Tr 194: *Re Dundas's Goods* (1863) 32 LJPM & A 165.
2 *Re Battersbee's Goods* (1852) 2 Rob Eccl 439; *Re Sibthorp's Goods* (1866) LR 1 P & D 106.

Gift to trustees of existing settlement

3.301 Where a will contains a gift to the trustees of an existing settlement which is identified by a date, it is in the discretion of the district judge or registrar to decide whether:

(a)   to take no action;
(b)   to incorporate the settlement; or
(c)   to direct the filing of an examined copy of the settlement in lieu of incorporation.

3.302   The district judges of the Principal Registry are of opinion that the last course will usually be the most convenient[1].

1 Registrar's Direction (1971) 11 March.

Settlement varied by Chancery Division

3.303   Where a testator by his will gave one half of the residuary estate to the trustees of each of two existing settlements on the trusts of the respective settlements, and during the testator's lifetime the settlements were varied in the Chancery Division, it was ordered by the Probate Judge that certified copies of the settlements and of the orders varying them should be included in the probate[1].

1 *Re Seligman* (1936) (unreported motion). See also *Re Dickins' Goods* (1842) 1 Notes of Cases 398; *Re Sibthorp's Goods* (1866) LR 1 P & D 106.

Papers invalid per se

3.304   If the paper in question be invalid and inoperative per se and be made provable by reference only, the court will enforce its production; for, unlike a deed, such a paper must be proved, as a will or codicil is, in order to give it operation and legal existence[1].

1 *Sheldon v Sheldon* (1844) 3 Notes of Cases 250.

Part of document

3.305   Where part only of a document is material, the court does not insist on the whole being proved[1].

1 *Re Dowager Countess of Limerick's Goods* (1850) 2 Rob Eccl 313.

3.306   Although the probate registry may have included in the probate a complete page from a notebook as having been incorporated by the words 'a list of small presents', it is for the court of construction (i.e. the Chancery Division) to decide how much of the contents of the page constitutes the list of small presents[1]: see also Chap. 32, post.

1 *Re Osburn* (1969) 113 Sol Jo 387.

Practice: description in oath

3.307   Any question of incorporation should be decided before the oath to lead the grant is sworn. Where a document is to be incorporated and proved as part of the will, the will should be marked 'A', and the incorporated papers 'B', 'C', etc., and all should be marked with the signatures of the executors and person before whom the oath is sworn. The documents should be described in the executor's oath as 'the will as contained in paper writings marked A and B, etc.'.

3.308 If an incorporated paper or document is to be proved as part of the will or codicil, such document must be included in the probate in its entirety, and be placed immediately after the will or codicil which has incorporated it. Where possible the will and incorporated paper are photographed in the registry in the usual way; where this is impracticable an engrossment of the will and the incorporated paper must be filed, and this copy is then photographed.

Wills admissible otherwise than under Wills Act 1837

3.309 NCPRs 12, 13, 14 and 15[1], which govern the practice as to certain of the matters discussed in the preceding pages of this chapter (i.e. evidence as to due execution of a will; the testator's knowledge and approval of the contents of the will, where this appears doubtful; alterations, etc., in wills; the incorporation of other documents; and the procedure where there is any appearance of attempted revocation), apply where it is sought to establish a will by reference to s. 9 of the Wills Act 1837[2] (as explained by the Wills Act Amendment Act 1852[3] in respect of the will of a testator *dying before 1 January 1983*). It is provided by NCPR 17 that rules 12–15 shall apply only to a will which it is sought to establish by reference to s. 9 of the Wills Act 1837. They do not apply, for example, when proving a will valid under foreign law or admissible by virtue of the Wills Act 1963[4] (except in cases where the internal law of England and Wales is in point); nor to wills made prior to the commencement of the Wills Act 1837 (i.e. 1 January 1838), nor to privileged wills. The terms and validity of all such wills are to be established to the satisfaction of the district judge or registrar (NCPR 17).

1 For text of these rules, see pp. 927 ff., post.
2 See p. 720, post.
3 This Act is dealt with in para. **3.79**, ante.
4 See p. 777, post.

Wills made before Wills Act 1837

Wills made before 1838. Requisites as to execution

3.310 For the making of a valid will disposing of personalty before the Wills Act 1837 came into operation, no solemnities of any kind were necessary. By the Statute of Frauds (29 Car 2, c.3) a will of personalty was required generally to have been reduced into writing in the testator's lifetime; but the document was not required to be in the testator's handwriting, or even to have been signed by him, provided sufficient proof was produced to satisfy the court that it expressed the testator's last wishes regarding the disposition of his personal estate after his death.

3.311 A will made before the Wills Act 1837 came into operation without attesting witnesses, or with one attesting witness only, was admissible to probate. An affidavit of two persons who knew and were well acquainted with the testator's handwriting and mode of subscription in the one case, and of one person similarly acquainted with his handwriting and subscription in the other case, was taken in substitution for full attestation.

Privileged wills

3.312   Before the passing of the Statute of Frauds in 1677, the class of will that could come within the category of privileged wills of soldiers was extremely limited; in fact only a will made by a soldier in actual foreign operations in the field was admitted. A will made by a soldier in a garrison abroad, or besieged in a fortress, while at war was not privileged, according to Swinburne (1677)[1]. Since the Statute of Frauds[2], the privilege has been considerably extended by statute and decisions of the courts[3].

1 *Drummond v Parish* (1843) 3 Curt 522.
2 11 Halsbury's Statutes (4th edn) 205.
3 See paras. **3.338** ff. and **32.27** ff.

3.313   There are several conditions which must be fulfilled before a will can be accepted as a privileged will, e.g.:—the testator must at the time of making the will have been domiciled in England and Wales: he must have been a 'soldier', an 'airman' or a 'seaman' within the meaning of the statute and case law interpretation of these terms; he must have been 'in actual military service' or 'at sea', as the case may be, within the meaning of the Act; and there must be no indication that the document was intended to be no more than a draft, or that the failure to complete it as a testamentary instrument was intentional.

3.314   These matters are dealt with in greater detail in the following pages.

Death on or before 6 February 1918

3.315   The wills of soldiers being 'in actual military service', and of mariners or seamen being 'at sea', were excepted from the operation of the Statute of Frauds by s. 23 thereof[1], and from the Wills Act 1837 by s. 11 thereof[2]. These statutes provided that such persons might dispose of their personal estate as they might have done before these Acts were passed.

1 11 Halsbury's Statutes (4th edn) 205.
2 See p. 721, post.

Death after 6 February 1918

3.316   By s. 3 of the Wills (Soldiers and Sailors) Act 1918[1], the informal wills of soldiers and sailors dying after 6 February 1918, made in circumstances rendering them privileged, were made operative to dispose of real, as well as personal, estate.

1 See p. 733, post.

Navy, Marines and Air Force

3.317   By s. 2 of the Wills (Soldiers and Sailors) Act 1918, s. 11 of the Wills Act 1837 was extended to members of the Royal Naval and Marine Forces not only when at sea but also when so circumstanced that if soldiers they would be in actual military service, and by s. 5(2) of the Act it was provided that the expression 'soldier' therein and in the Wills Act 1837 shall include a member of the Air Force.

Formalities

3.318 The formalities required for making a privileged will are simply a declaration in writing, or orally, of the mode in which the testator wishes his estate to be disposed of after his death.

Nuncupative will

3.319 If the declaration be made orally, the court must have before it evidence sufficient to satisfy it of the substance of the declaration, and of the fact that the testator intended deliberately to give expression to his wishes as to what should be done with his property in the event of his death[1]. The wishes must be intended to convey a request to see that they are acted upon, and not imparted merely as a matter of information or interest[2].

1 *Re Stable, Dalrymple v Campbell* [1919] P 7; *Re Donner's Estate* (1917) 34 TLR 138.
2 *Re Knibbs' Estate, Flay v Trueman* [1962] 2 All ER 829, [1962] 1 WLR 852.

3.320 In one case[1], the court gave effect to an oral declaration of the testator, a soldier in actual military service, upon the evidence contained in the affidavits of two non-commissioned officers in whose presence the declaration was made. In another it admitted to probate a declaration by a merchant seaman who was held to be 'at sea' made in the presence of two witnesses: 'If anything happens to me I want everything to go to mother[2].'

1 *Re Scott's Goods* [1903] P 243.
2 *Re Wilson's Estate, Wilson v Coleclough* [1952] P 92, [1952] 1 All ER 852. See also *Re Jones* [1981] Fam 7, [1981] 1 All ER 1 (declaration made by a soldier on operations in Northern Ireland in presence of witnesses: 'If I don't make it, make sure Anne gets all my stuff', admitted to probate).

3.321 It is immaterial whether the testator knew his declaration would have testamentary effect[1].

1 *Re Spicer, Spicer v Richardson* [1949] P 441, [1949] 2 All ER 659.

3.322 For other reported cases, see para. **32.30**, post.

3.323 For the practice in proving a nuncupative will, see paras. **3.362** ff., post.

Written will

3.324 It is not necessary that a privileged will (if written) should be signed by the testator, or attested by witnesses, to constitute it a valid disposition of a testator's estate.

Legacies to attesting witnesses

3.325 It has been held that a gift in a privileged will to an attesting witness does not fail by virtue of s. 15 of the Wills Act 1837, since witnesses are unnecessary[1]. On the other hand, a gift in the will of a British subject, who died domiciled in England, to the wife of an attesting witness was held to be void notwithstanding that the will, having been made in Scotland, would have been admissible, even though unattested by witnesses, under s. 2 of the Wills Act 1861[2].

1 *Re Limond, Limond v Cunliffe* [1915] 2 Ch 240.
2 *Re Priest, Belfield v Duncan* [1944] Ch 58, [1944] 1 All ER 51.

3.326   As to forfeiture of gifts to attesting witnesses, see paras. **5.142** ff., post.

Revocation

3.327   It would appear that the general rule that a will is revoked by the subsequent marriage of the testator applies also to privileged wills[1]. (As to revocation by subsequent marriage, see paras. **3.36** ff., ante.)

1 *Re Wardrop's Estate* [1917] P 54. (But this case has been doubted as being contrary to *Re Gossage* (below).)

3.328   A soldier can revoke a will with the same freedom from formalities as when making a will[1].

1 *Re Gossage's Estate, Wood v Gossage* [1921] P 194, CA.

Appointment of guardian

3.329   An appointment contained in the privileged will of a soldier, sailor or airman of any person as guardian of the testator's minor children is valid[1].

1 Wills (Soldiers and Sailors) Act 1918, s. 4 (see p. 734, post); *Re Earl of Chichester's Will Trusts, Pelham v Countess of Chichester* [1946] Ch 289, [1946] 1 All ER 722.

Testator under age

3.330   A soldier, sailor or airman in actual military service, or a seaman at sea, may make a will disposing of his personal estate as he might have done before the passing of the Wills Act 1837, i.e. from the age of 14 years[1], and even though not of full age may by will exercise a power of appointment vested in him[2].

1 Wills (Soldiers and Sailors) Act 1918, s. 1 (see p. 733, post); *Re Wernher, Wernher v Beit* [1918] 2 Ch 82. See also paras. **32.28–32.29**, post.
2 *Re Wernher*, above.

3.331   A disposition of real estate by such a person is similarly valid notwithstanding that the testator was at the time of its execution under the age of 18 years[1] (21 years in the case of a will made prior to 1 January 1970[2]).

1 Wills (Soldiers and Sailors) Act 1918, s. 3(1), as amended by Family Law Reform Act 1969, s. 3(1) (see p. 790, post).
2 Ibid., as originally enacted.

3.332   If the testator was under the age of 18 years, or 21 years, as the case may be, when the will was made, this fact should be sworn in the oath, or other affidavit.

3.333   It has been held that a minor aged 19 serving as an officer with the British Army of the Rhine in Germany in May 1954 was a soldier in actual military service, and that a will made by him and executed in accordance with the provisions of s. 9 of the Wills Act 1837 while he was on leave in England was admissible to proof notwithstanding his infancy: although hostilities had ended almost nine years earlier, the forces in Germany were there as a direct result of the surrender and as an occupying force[1].

1 *Re Colman's Estate* [1958] 2 All ER 35, [1958] 1 WLR 457. The Federal Republic of Germany became a sovereign state in 1955, and it seems unlikely that a will made thereafter would be held to be privileged.

3.334 A will which has been made by a person under the age of 18 and which is valid by virtue of s. 11 of the Wills Act 1837 and the Wills (Soldiers and Sailors) Act 1918, may be revoked by the testator notwithstanding that he is still under age, whether or not he would then be entitled to make a privileged will[1]. But once the privilege has been lost, it would seem that a privileged will may be revoked only by those methods available to a non-privileged testator.

1 Family Law Reform Act 1969, s. 3(3) (see p. 790, post).

Domicile outside England and Wales

3.335 Several countries of the British Commonwealth have adopted the Wills Act 1837 to 1918[1] as their law governing testamentary dispositions. Some include s. 11 of the Wills Act 1837, but others have not included that section, so that a will made by a soldier domiciled in a part of the Commonwealth outside England and Wales requires evidence as to its admissibility by the law of domicile as being a privileged will.

1 See pp. 719, 726, 727, 733, post.

3.336 Thus where a will, purporting to be a soldier's privileged will, was proved in Eire (now known as the Republic of Ireland) after an order by the President of the Probate Court in Eire, the registrar directed that an official copy of the order exhibited to the affidavit of an Eireann solicitor be filed with the will on proof in England and that a notation be made on the engrossment 'Affidavit filed that the will is valid by the law of Eire'[1]. Evidence of admissibility by the law of the domicile, if it is outside England and Wales, will always be required and, where the soldier was a minor, it must also deal with this point.

1 *Re Ryan* (1944).

3.337 In the case of testators dying on or after 1 January 1964, reference should also be made to the provisions of the Wills Act 1963 (see paras. **3.392** ff., post).

Privileged wills of the forces of the Crown

3.338 Earlier conceptions of the meaning and extent of the expression 'a soldier in actual military service' were modified by the decision in *Re Wingham*[1], which extended the privilege of making a nuncupative or unexecuted will to a much wider class of members of the armed forces of the Crown than had previously been regarded as falling within the provisions of s. 11 of the Wills Act 1837. The basis of this decision is the finding of the court that the principle enunciated by Sir Herbert Jenner Fust in the case of *Drummond v Parish*[2], that a soldier's privilege under English law is identical with that of the Roman legionary, was fallacious, and that all subsequent decisions are vitiated by the acceptance of this as a fundamental premise.

1 *Re Wingham, Andrews v Wingham* [1949] P 187, [1948] 2 All ER 908.
2 (1843) 3 Curt 522.

3.339 In *Re Wingham* the testator was an officer of the Royal Air Force, who made a will after his arrival in Canada, where he had been sent for the purpose of undergoing his training as a pilot in safety—England being, at the time, under heavy air-attack. The Court of Appeal held that he was entitled to the privilege.

3.340   It seems clear from the tenor of the judgments that any domiciled Englishman actually serving in the armed forces of the Crown whilst there is a state of war between this country and another, or an imminent anticipation of such a state, is within the privileged class.

3.341   But the decision in *Re Wingham* does not confer privilege upon every serving member of the armed forces in peacetime. Where no state of war exists, it is the nature of the duties that the member of the armed forces of the Crown is called upon to perform which determines whether or not he is 'on actual military service' and, provided the service is both active and military, it could be either within the United Kingdom or abroad against a non-conventional military force: all the circumstances must be considered and the matter decided on the facts[1]. So that in *Re Jones*[1], it was held that a British soldier called upon to go out on military patrol in Northern Ireland in 1978, at a time when there was a clandestinely organised insurrection there, was on actual military service and an oral statement made by him to his officers was admitted to probate.

1   *Re Jones* [1981] Fam 7, [1981] 1 All ER 1.

3.342   The position as regards persons who made 'unexecuted' wills during the 1914–18 war is not free from doubt; and owing to the lapse of time it is unlikely that such a case would now arise.

3.343   Generally, the courts seem to adopt the view, when interpreting s. 11 of the Wills Act 1837, that where there is doubt, then such doubt should be resolved in favour of acceptance rather than rejection of the privilege[1].

1   *Re Jones*, above.

3.344   As regards mariners or seamen (when not members of the armed forces of the Crown) whose privilege under the Act arises when 'at sea', an even more liberal interpretation has recently been placed upon this expression, though for different reasons, their rights arising only when they are 'at sea', and irrespective of whether there is a state of war (see para. **3.368**, post).

3.345   The case law is dealt with in para. **32.33**, post.

'In actual military service'

3.346   The words 'actual military service' in s. 11 of the Wills Act 1837 mean 'active military service', and the tests to be applied in ascertaining whether a testator was entitled to the privilege are (a) was he 'on military service', and (b) was such service 'active' in the sense that it was in connection with operations in a war which was or had been in progress or was believed to be imminent[1] or in connection with operations against a clandestinely organised insurrection[2]? These tests are not satisfied by officers on half-pay or men on the reserve or Territorials, when not called up, since they are not actually serving, nor by members of the forces serving in this country or on routine garrison duty overseas, in time of peace, when military operations are not imminent. They are satisfied by all men and women serving or called up for service, in war, whether actively engaged with the enemy or still in training, by non-combatants serving with the forces such as doctors, nurses, chaplains and members of auxiliary services, and by members of the forces who, under stress of war, work at their jobs and also man the defences, such as the Home Guard during the Second World War[3].

1 *Re Wingham*, paras. **3.338–3.339**, above, approving *Re Gossage's Estate, Wood v Gossage* [1921] P 194; *Gattward v Knee* [1902] P 99.
2 Ibid., as extended by *Re Jones*, para. **3.341**, above.
3 *Re Wingham, Andrews v Wingham*, above, per Denning LJ. See also the following earlier cases in which persons were held to be soldiers in actual military service; *Re Donaldson's Goods* (1840) 2 Curt 386 (surgeon); *Re Cory's Goods* (1901) 84 LT 270 (irregular); *Re Stanley's Estate* [1916] P 192 (nurse); *Re Rippon's Estate* [1943] P 61, [1943] 1 All ER 676 (territorial officer recalled for service when war imminent); *Re Rowson's Estate* [1944] 2 All ER 36 (member of WAAF). As to the Home Guard, cf. *Blyth v Lord Advocate* [1945] AC 32, [1944] 2 All ER 375, HL.

3.347 Difficult cases may arise in peace time when a soldier is in, or about to be sent to, a disturbed area where he may be involved in military operations, but it seems that in cases of doubt the serving soldier will be given the benefit of the privilege[1].

1 *Re Wingham. Andrews v Wingham*, above, per Denning LJ, and *Re Jones* [1981] Fam 7, [1981] 1 All ER 1 referred to in the text of para. **3.341** above.

Letters as privileged wills

3.348 As to the admission of a will contained in a letter, the district judge or registrar has a discretion to direct that the whole, or only such part or parts as contain a disposition of the property of the deceased and are necessary for granting probate, shall be admitted to probate. The portions so admitted are to be set out in a 'fiat copy' to be signed by the district judge or registrar[1].

1 *Re Heywood's Estate* [1916] P 47. See also paras. **4.227** ff., post.

3.349 The original letter will be filed, but will not be open to public inspection without leave of a district judge or registrar[1].

1 President's Direction (1939) 20 October.

3.350 An example is a case in which a soldier had already made a formal will; afterwards he wrote a letter to his solicitors stating how he wished his will to be altered and asking them to destroy his will and prepare a new will in the terms of his letter. The letter was admitted to probate as a privileged will[1].

1 *Re Beavis* (1941) (motion).

3.351 In another case a draft will was prepared but not executed, the draft with alterations made by the soldier being sent to his solicitor with a covering letter and a memorandum, both signed by the soldier, and indicating his testamentary wishes. Probate was ordered of the memorandum and the draft will[1].

1 *Re Wood* (1941) October (motion).

3.352 An airman in actual military service wrote on an envelope which was sealed up: 'I wish my brother (A. B.) to have the Savings Certificates contained in this envelope.' On filing affidavits as to handwriting and date, the envelope was proved as a codicil to his will.

3.353   A note on the engrossment was made, as follows: 'Affidavits as to hand-writing and date of codicil, and that the codicil was made while the deceased was an airman in actual military service and that the envelope contained twelve War Savings Certificates'[1].

1 *Re Webster* (1944).

Practice

3.354   In order to prove a soldier's privileged will, an affidavit is required show-ing that, at the date of execution of the will, the testator was 'in actual military service', and it must be stated in the affidavit on what circumstances the applicant relies as constituting the document a privileged will. As a testator can exercise a privilege only if it is at the time allowed him by the law of his domicile, the relev-ant domicile is that at the date of the will[1]. The affidavit must therefore depose to the testator's domicile at the time of making the will[2]. Form of affidavit in support of a privileged will, No. 13.

1 Registrar's Direction (1955) 7 November.
2 President's Direction (1945) 7 May.

Evidence of handwriting of testator

3.355   NCPR 18 is as follows:

> 'Where the deceased died domiciled in England and Wales and it appears to the dis-trict judge or registrar that there is prima facie evidence that a will is one to which section 11 of the Wills Act 1837 applies, the will may be admitted to proof if the dis-trict judge or registrar is satisfied that it was signed by the testator or, if unsigned, that it is in the testator's handwriting.'

3.356   Affidavit evidence identifying the signature, or handwriting, of the will as that of the testator is normally necessary in order to satisfy the requirements of this rule. Form of affidavit of handwriting, No. 4.

3.357   Where a will contains a proper attestation clause and the signatures of the testator and two witnesses, but it is necessary to establish that it is a privileged will (e.g. because the testator was under the age of majority when it was made[1]) affi-davits as to handwriting are not usually called for.

1 See paras. **3.330–3.334**, ante,

Will signed by mark

3.358   When a will made by a soldier while engaged on active service is signed by mark, an affidavit is required showing that the testator had knowledge of the con-tents[1].

1 *Re Hackett's Goods* (1859) 4 Sw & Tr 220.

Alterations

3.359   By NCPR 17, the terms of a privileged will are to be established to the dis-trict judge's or registrar's satisfaction.

3.360 Alterations and interlineations made by the testator, if unattested, are proved by evidence as to his handwriting. If they are in the handwriting of any person other than the testator, it must be proved by affidavit that they were known to and approved of by the testator. The question whether he was still in actual military service will also arise. If there is no evidence obtainable to the contrary, it will be presumed that the alterations were made during the continuance of such service[1].

1 See *Re Tweedale's Goods* (1874) LR 3 P & D 204, as to alterations.

3.361 If the will is attested, evidence as to alterations as required by the Wills Act 1837[1] may be required by the district judge or registrar.

1 See paras. **3.222** ff., ante.

Practice for proving a nuncupative will

3.362 Application for an order admitting to proof a nuncupative will should be made ex parte to the district judge or registrar[1] at the registry at which the application for the grant is being made[2]. The application should normally be supported by the consents of all persons prejudiced who are sui juris, and must be supported by affidavit evidence of the facts (see NCPR 54(3)).

1 NCPR 54(1).
2 NCPR 2(1).

3.363 The oral statement is committed to writing (e.g. 'Oral statement made by A.B. on the   day of   19   in the presence of C. D.' etc.), and is exhibited to the affidavit/s to lead the order, and lodged at the Probate Department at the Principal Registry or with the district probate registrar. The district judge or registrar may, if he thinks fit, direct that the application be made by summons to a district judge or registrar in chambers or to a High Court judge in chambers or open court[1], a reference to a High Court judge by a registrar needing to be confirmed by a district judge.

1 NCPR 61(1).

3.364 When the order is obtained the affidavit/s and the statement in writing are filed with the application for the grant, the statement in writing being subsequently marked as the will by the deponent to the oath and by the person before whom the oath is sworn.

3.365 In the case of a judgment by the court in a probate action the oral statement pronounced for is likewise committed to writing and marked and filed with the application as aforesaid.

Sailors' privileged wills

3.366 The words 'any mariner or seaman being at sea' in s. 11 of the Wills Act 1837 have been defined as shown in the following paragraphs.

'Mariner or seaman'

3.367 The term 'mariner or seaman' includes a purser of a man-of-war[1], a surgeon in the navy[2], a chaplain in the navy, and probably the whole profession, of whatever rank. A merchant seaman is a 'mariner or seaman' within the meaning of the section[3]. A female typist on a liner has been held to be included[4], also a nurse on a hospital ship.

1 *Re Hayes's Goods* (1839) 2 Curt 338.
2 *Re Saunders' Goods* (1865) LR 1 P & D 16.
3 *Morrell v Morrell* (1827) 1 Hag Ecc 51; *Re Milligan's Goods* (1849) 2 Rob Eccl 108; *Re Parker's Goods* (1859) 2 Sw & Tr 375.
4 *Re Hale's Goods* [1915] 2 IR 362.

'At sea'

3.368   The words 'at sea' have been held to mean 'on maritime service', and apply to persons serving on board vessels permanently stationed in a harbour[1], or on service in a river[2]. A will made on shore, but in the course of a voyage, or by the employee of a shipowner between voyages, will be within the section[3]. But it has been held that a pilot on a ship canal is not 'a mariner or seaman at sea' within the meaning of s. 11 unless it is established that the document propounded was made either on board a ship or when proceeding to join, or return from, the ship[4]. A seaman on leave who had not received instructions to join a particular ship, and was not part of the complement of any particular ship, was not 'at sea' within the meaning of s. 11 of the Wills Act 1837[5].

1 *Re M'Murdo's Goods* (1868) LR 1 P & D 540.
2 *Re Patterson's Goods* (1898) 79 LT 123; *Re Austen's Goods* (1853) 2 Rob Eccl 611.
3 *Re Lay's Goods* (1840) 2 Curt 375; *Re Anderson's Estate, Anderson v Downes* [1916] P 49; *Re Newland's Goods* [1952] P 71, [1952] 1 All ER 841; *Re Wilson Estate, Wilson v Coleclough* [1952] P 92, [1952] 1 All ER 852.
4 *Re Barnes' Goods, Hodson v Barnes* (1926) 136 LT 380.
5 *Re Rapley's Estate, Rapley v Rapley* [1983] 3 All ER 248, [1983] 1 WLR 1069.

Practice

3.369   The fact of a privileged will having been made when the testator was 'at sea' must be proved by affidavit, and the same evidence of handwriting and domicile is required as in the case of a soldier in actual military service (see paras. **3.354–3.358**, above).

3.370   The same evidence as to alterations in a sailor's will is required as in the case of a soldier's will (see paras. **3.359–3.361**, above).

Naval and marine forces

3.371   In the case of deaths after 6 February 1918, members of Her Majesty's naval and marine forces are on an equal footing with soldiers with regard to their rights of making privileged wills[1].

1 Wills (Soldiers and Sailors) Act 1918, s. 2 (see p. 733, post).

3.372   The practice as to soldiers' privileged wills is thus equally applicable to the will of a member of such forces not only when he is at sea, but also when he is so circumstanced that if he were a soldier he would be in actual military service within the meaning of s. 11 of the Wills Act 1837.

Naval assets

3.373 A privileged will made by a seaman or marine is effective to pass naval assets if the deceased died after 13 August 1953, and may be directed by the Admiralty to be so effective if he died before that date[1].

1 Navy and Marines (Wills) Act 1953, s. 1 (see p. 773, post).

Wills Act 1861

Wills executed before 1 January 1964 only

3.374 The Wills Act 1861 (Lord Kingsdown's Act) was repealed with effect from 1 January 1964, the date of commencement of the Wills Act 1963[1]. The repeal does not, however, invalidate a will executed before that date[2].

1 Wills Act 1963, s. 7(3) (see p. 779, post).
2 Ibid., s.7(4).

3.375 All the provisions as to the formal validity of wills contained in the Act of 1861 are reproduced in the Act of 1963, with the sole exception of that by which a will of personal estate of a British subject made out of the United Kingdom was held to be well executed if executed in accordance with the law of that part of H.M. dominions where he had his domicile of origin.

3.376 **Note**. The Wills Act 1963 (which applies to persons dying on or after 1 January 1964, whatever the date of the will) is wider in its terms than was the Act of 1861: its provisions are not confined to wills of personal estate, nor to British subjects. The provisions of the Act of 1963 should therefore be relied upon whenever possible, even where a will could also be shown to be valid in accordance with the earlier Act.

3.377 As to the Wills Act 1963, and the practice under it, see paras. **3.392** ff., post.

Wills of British subjects made out of the United Kingdom

3.378 By s. 1 of the Wills Act 1861[1], a will of personal estate *made* (before 1 January 1964) *out of the United Kingdom*[2] by a British subject (including a naturalised British subject[3]), whatever his domicile when the will was made or at the time of his death, is held to be well executed for the purpose of being admitted to probate in England on evidence that it was validly executed (1) by the law of the place where it was made, *or* (2) by the law of the place where the testator was domiciled at the time he made his will, *or* (3) by the law of that part of Her Majesty's dominions where the testator had his domicile of origin[4].

1 See p. 727, post.
2 The expression 'the United Kingdom' excludes the Republic of Ireland: Irish Free State (Consequential Adaptation of Enactments) Order 1923, Art. 2.
3 *Re Gally's Goods* (1876) 1 PD 438. In the case of a naturalised British subject his powers may be restricted by his certificate of naturalisation (*Re Gatti's Goods* (1879) 39 LT 639).
4 This provision is not reproduced in the Wills Act 1963: see para. **3.375**, above.

3.379 The status of British subject must be possessed at the time the will was made[1].

1 *Bloxam v Favre* (1884) 9 PD 130.

3.380   In order to obtain admission of a will of this description, besides the usual formalities, an affidavit as to the British status of the testator must be filed (Form No. 12); and if coming under (1) or (2), an affidavit showing the validity of the will under the law of the foreign place, by a person conversant with that law (Form No. 9); if under (3), an affidavit showing where the testator had his domicile of origin (Form No. 12); and if the law of the place of domicile of origin differs from the law of England and Wales, an affidavit as to the validity of the will by the law of such place.

3.381   Unless the will is in English form the grant will be limited to personalty[1].

1 Registrar's Direction (1953) 5 May.

3.382   A will, invalid by the law of the testator's domicile, but entitled to proof in England and Wales by virtue of s. 1 or 2 of the Wills Act 1861, is regarded by the courts of this country as being a valid and effective disposition of the testator's property to the extent that the law of this country allows the disposition to take effect[1].

1 *Re Manifold, Slater v Chryssaffinis* [1962] Ch 1, [1961] 1 All ER 710.

Wills made in the United Kingdom

3.383   By s. 2 of the Wills Act 1861, a will *made* (before 1 January 1964) *in the United Kingdom*[1] by a British subject, wherever domiciled at the time of making the same or at the time of death, is held to be well executed as to personal estate if valid by the law of that part of the United Kingdom where it was made[2]. In this case, besides the usual formalities, an affidavit as to the British status of the testator, and as to the place where the will was made, must be filed (Form No. 12), together with an affidavit as to the validity of the will (unless it was made in England and Wales or Northern Ireland in proper English form: such a will is normally accepted as valid without further enquiry).

1 See note 2 to para. **3.378**, above.
2 See *Re Cocquerel* [1918] P 4.

3.384   Neither recording nor registration of a Scottish will is in itself an indication that it is valid. Validity can be established only by evidence that confirmation has been issued in respect of the will, or, if no confirmation has issued, by an affidavit of law or other evidence[1].

1 Circular, 7 November 1955.

Change of domicile

3.385   Section 3 of the Wills Act 1861, which provides that subsequent change of domicile does not revoke or render invalid a will, has been held to apply to wills generally and not merely to wills of British subjects[1].

1 *Re Groos' Estate* [1904] P 269.

Isle of Man, Channel Islands and the Republic of Ireland

3.386   Although included in the 'British Isles', the Isle of Man, the Channel Islands and the Republic of Ireland do not form part of the United Kingdom.

Wills Act 1861, generally

3.387   A will made by a British subject, or, indeed by any person, if invalid by the law of his domicile on the ground of incapacity (e.g., on account of minority) is held to be invalid in England, notwithstanding the provisions of the Wills Act 1861[1].

1 Registrar's Direction (1953) 5 May. See also Dicey and Morris, *Conflict of Laws*.

3.388   Where a British subject left a will valid by the law of his domicile, which was revoked by a later will invalid by the law of his domicile, but which could have been proved as valid in accordance with Lord Kingsdown's Act, the court of domicile, when granting probate of the earlier will, retained the later will and refused to give it out. As the distribution of the personal estate in England would be required to be made in accordance with the terms of the will declared valid by the court of the domicile, the registrar held that the grant of probate issued by the court of domicile could be resealed in England[1].

1 *Re Coghlan*, unreported.

3.389   But in a more recent case a testatrix, whose domicile of origin was England but who died domiciled in Cyprus, had made two wills, the earlier valid by the law of Cyprus, the later invalid by that law but executed in accordance with English law. The Cyprus court had granted probate of the earlier will but refused probate of the later. Both wills had been admitted to proof in England. It was held that, as the later will was executed in accordance with the law of the testator's domicile of origin and was thus entitled to proof in England by virtue of s. 1 of the Wills Act 1861, s. 4 of that Act operated, and the earlier will was effectively revoked by the later, which accordingly had dispositive effect in relation to the estate in England[1].

1 *Re Manifold, Slater v Chryssaffinis* [1962] Ch 1, [1961] 1 All ER 710.

British subject

3.390   In considering whether a testator possessed the status of British subject, consideration must be given to the various enactments as to nationality[1].

1 See 4 Halsbury's Laws (4th edn) 399, and the British Nationality Act 1981, 31 Halsbury's Statutes (4th edn) 112. For the purposes of the Wills Act 1963, 'state' is defined by s. 6(1) thereof as a territory or group of territories having its own law of nationality.

3.391   The repeal of the Wills Act 1861, save as regards wills and codicils executed before 1 January 1964, has reduced the number of cases in which this Act is relied upon, but the question of the testator's nationality may also be relevant in deciding whether a will is admissible by virtue of the Wills Act 1963. Under this Act, which applies, whatever the date of the will or codicil, to testators dying on or after 1 January 1964, a testamentary instrument or act is to be treated as properly executed, inter alia, if its execution conformed to the internal law in force in a state[1] of which, either at the time of execution or the time of his death, the testator was a national. For fuller details of this provision, and generally as to the Wills Act 1963, see the following paragraphs.

1 See 4 Halsbury's Laws (4th edn) 399, and the British Nationality Act 1981, 31 Halsbury's Statutes (4th edn) 112. For the purposes of the Wills Act 1963, 'state' is defined by s. 6(1) thereof as a territory or group of territories having its own law of nationality.

Wills Act 1963

3.392   The Wills Act 1963[1] came into operation on 1 January 1964. The Act does not modify the internal law of England and Wales, as contained in the Wills Act 1837 (with subsequent amendments) as to the mode of execution and other formal requirements in connection with testamentary dispositions, but it provides that, in specified circumstances, wills executed in accordance with other systems of law are to be treated as properly executed. The Act does not, in general, deal with the capacity to make a will, or with the substantial validity of testamentary dispositions.

1 For text of Act, see p. 777, post.

To what persons applicable

3.393   The Act applies only to the wills[1] of testators who die after its commencement (i.e. on or after 1 January 1964), but in relation to such persons it applies to wills whether made before or after that time (s. 7(4)). It is not confined to testators of any particular domicile or nationality: its provisions may be used to establish the formal validity of wills of British subjects or aliens, and of testators domiciled either in or out of England and Wales.

1 See 'Definition of "will" ' in the text, below.

Definition of 'will'

3.394   Throughout the Act, the expression 'will' includes any testamentary instrument or act, and 'testator' is to be construed accordingly (s. 6(1)). The Act therefore applies not only to written wills and codicils, but also to oral dispositions as well as to any form of deliberate revocation (see also 'Revocation of wills', paras. **3.404** ff., post). The term 'will' is used in this sense throughout this section of the work.

3.395   A testator, a British subject domiciled in England, purported to execute a holograph will in Switzerland during a brief visit to that country. The purported will was written wholly in the testator's own handwriting on a sheet of hotel notepaper, save for the address which was printed at the top of the sheet. The will was not witnessed. The testator subsequently died in England aged 21 years. By virtue of s. 1 of the Wills Act 1963 (see next paragraph, below) the will could only be treated as properly executed if its execution conformed with the internal law in force in Switzerland. Swiss law provided that a holograph will had to be written by the testator from beginning to end. The will was held to be invalid by reason of its non-compliance with Swiss law[1].

1 *Re Kanani, Engledow v Davidson* (1978) 122 Sol Jo 611.

General rule as to formal validity

3.396   By s. 1 of the Wills Act 1963, a will is to be treated as properly executed if its execution conformed to the internal law[1] in force:

(a)   in the territory where it was executed; or
(b)   in the territory where the testator was domiciled[2], either at the time of its execution or at the time of his death; or

(c)   in the territory where the testator had his habitual residence either at the time of its execution or at the time of his death; or

(d)   in a state[3] of which, either at the time of its execution or at the time of his death, he was a national. (As to the law of nationality, see 'Meaning of "internal law" ', paras. **3.398** ff. post.)

1   See 'Meaning of "internal law" ', below.
2   The Act enabled H.M. Government to ratify the Convention on the Conflict of Laws relating to the Form of Testamentary Dispositions concluded at The Hague in October 1961. The Convention provides (Article I) that the determination whether or not a testator had his domicile in a particular place shall be governed by the law of that place, but in exercise of the power of reservation, the United Kingdom Government, when signing the Convention, reserved the right, in derogation of this provision, to determine in accordance with the lex fori the place where the testator had his domicile. The existing principles of English law as to domicile thus continue to apply in this country.
3   The distinction between 'territory' and 'state' should be noted. A 'state' is defined for the purposes of the Act as a territory or group of territories having its own law of nationality (s. 6(1)). Section 1 refers to 'a' state, and not 'the' state, of which the testator was a national. In the case of a testator having dual nationality the internal law of either state appears to be available to establish formal validity of a will.

Will executed on board vessel or aircraft

3.397   Section 2(1)(a) provides that, without prejudice to s. 1, a will executed on board a vessel or aircraft of any description shall be treated as properly executed if its execution conformed to the internal law in force in the territory with which, having regard to its registration (if any) and other relevant circumstances, the vessel or aircraft may be taken to have been most closely connected. This provision appears to be designed to overcome any doubt as to the actual place of execution of a will made at sea, or in an aircraft in the course of a flight. The reference in s. 2(1)(a) of the Act to a vessel includes a reference to a hovercraft[1].

1   Hovercraft (Application of Enactments) Order 1972.

Meaning of 'internal law'

3.398   In the Act the internal law of a territory or state means the law which would apply in a case where no question of the law in force in any other territory or state arose (s. 6(1)). Any question of reference to the law of any other place, or of renvoi, is thus excluded. The Act does not, however, appear to take away the existing right to prove in this country a will which has been accepted by the court of the country of the deceased's domicile, even if that court accepted the will on some basis other than the internal law of that country (see also 'Domicile out of England and Wales', paras. **3.422** ff., post).

3.399   Where there are two or more systems of internal law as to the formal validity of wills in force in a territory or state, the system to be applied is to be ascertained as follows:

(a)   If there is a rule in force throughout the territory or state indicating which of the systems can properly be applied in the case in question, that rule is to be followed.

(b)   If there is no such rule, the system to be applied is that with which the testator was most closely connected at the relevant time (i.e. the time of his death where the matter is to be determined by reference to circumstances prevailing at his death, and in any other case the time of execution of the will) (s. 6(2)).

3.400 This subsection provides for cases such as that of the United Kingdom and Colonies. Where recourse is to be had to the law of the nationality of a testator who was, at the time of execution of the will, a citizen of the United Kingdom and Colonies, any one of a number of systems of law might otherwise be applicable (e.g. the law of England and Wales, of Scotland, or of a particular colonial territory). Similarly, the subsection applies in the case of a territory or state which applies different systems of law according to the religion, caste, tribe, etc., of testators. If there is no rule in force throughout the territory or state indicating which system can properly be applied to the case in question, it will be necessary to ascertain with which system of law the testator was most closely connected at the relevant time (as defined above), and apply that system. The Act does not define the type of connection, and where this provision is relied upon in connection with the proof of a will, there should be affidavit evidence of the facts by reason of which it is contended that the testator's closest connection, at the time of execution of the will or at the time of death, as the case may require, was with a particular system of law as to the formal validity of wills (see also *Re O'Keefe, Poingdestre v Sherman* [1940] Ch 124, [1940] 1 All ER 216, and 'Practice', paras. **3.425** ff., post).

Wills of immovables

3.401 Under s. 2(1)(b), a will, so far as it disposes of immovable property, is to be treated as properly executed if its execution conformed to the internal law in force in the territory where the property was situated. This provision gave statutory force to the existing law of England and Wales (see note 1, para. **12.36**, post). It should, however, be particularly noted that this is without prejudice to s. 1 of the Act: a will which satisfies any of the tests laid down in that section is to be treated as properly executed, and therefore as effective to pass both movable and immovable property. But even if the will complies with none of these tests, it will still be accepted, so far as it disposes of immovable estate, if executed in accordance with the internal law of the place where the property is situated. In the exceptional case in which this provision entitles a will, which is otherwise invalid, to proof in England and Wales so far as it disposes of immovable estate in this country, it may be necessary for such part of the will only to be admitted to proof in accordance with the practice stated in paras. **11.314** and **12.41**, post.

Exercise of power of appointment

3.402 Section 2(1)(d) contains a provision in relation to the exercise by will of a power of appointment. This, again, is without prejudice to s. 1 of the Act. A will, whether or not admissible to proof by virtue of s. 1, is to be treated as properly executed so far as it exercises a power of appointment, if its execution conformed to the law governing the essential validity of the power (i.e. the 'proper law' of the settlement).

3.403 Under s. 2(2), a will, so far as it exercises a power of appointment, is not to be treated as improperly executed by reason only that its execution was not in accordance with any formal requirements contained in the instrument creating the power. Thus, the exercise by will of the power is valid as to form if the will is validly executed by virtue of either s. 1 or s. 2(1)(d), notwithstanding that additional formal requirements stipulated by the settlement itself may not have been observed. This subsection extended the previously existing provisions of s. 10 of the Wills Act 1837, so as to apply not only to wills admissible under the latter Act, but to all wills admissible under the wider provisions of the Act of 1963.

Revocation of wills

3.404 By the definition in s. 6(1) of the Act the term 'will' includes any testamentary instrument or act. Thus, the effect of the Act is that the revocation of a will, either by a document or by some physical act, is to be accepted as effective if it is executed in conformity with the requirements of any system of law which, by virtue of s. 1 or s. 2(1)(a) thereof, is applicable in the circumstances of the case, or (so far as regards wills of immovables or wills exercising a power of appointment respectively) is applicable by virtue of s. 2(1)(b) or s. 2(1)(d).

3.405 But the Act further provides that the revocation, wholly or in part, of a will which, under the Act, would be treated as properly executed, or the revocation of a provision which, under the Act, would be treated as comprised in a properly executed will, is to be accepted as properly executed if the later will or revocatory act was executed in conformity with *any* law by reference to which the revoked will or provision would itself be so treated (s. 2(1)(c)).

3.406 Thus, even if the revoking instrument or act is not itself executed in a way which would entitle it to recognition under the Act, it is nevertheless effective *as a revocation* if executed in accordance with any system of law which, in the circumstances of the case, could, by virtue of the Act of 1963, be applied in order to establish that the earlier will was validly executed. For example, suppose a testator, while in country A, makes a will in accordance with the forms required by the internal law of that country: a will so executed would be entitled to proof in England whatever the domicile, nationality or residence of the testator (see s. 1 of the Act). If, later, while in country B, he revokes this will by some method which complies with A's internal law, the revocation is effective even though it is not carried out in accordance with the requirements of the law of B or of any other system of law which would be applicable in the circumstances by virtue of s. 1 of the Act. It should be noted, however, that in such an extreme case the revoking instrument or act is effective *only insofar as it revokes the earlier will*: substantive provisions intended to replace those revoked must qualify under s. 1 of the Act in order to be admissible, However, it is possible that in such circumstances the court might hold the revocation to have been conditional, and to depend upon the effectiveness of the substituted provisions: if these are invalid, it might be held that there was no real animus revocandi and that the purported revocation was ineffective (see 'Dependent relative, or conditional, revocation' in paras. **33.65** and **33.76**, post).

3.407 The definition of 'will' in s. 6(1) of this Act includes only *testamentary* instruments or acts. While this clearly includes revocation by a physical act (e.g. destruction animo revocandi), where this is in accordance with the provisions of a relevant law, it would not appear to include revocation by operation of law incidental to some other act, e.g. revocation by subsequent marriage. The internal law of England and Wales as to this is, however, unaffected by the provisions of the Act of 1963.

Alterations in wills

3.408 The definition of 'will' in the Wills Act 1963 (see s. 6(1)) is wide enough to include not only the total or partial revocation of a will or codicil, but also alterations, interlineations, deletions, etc. Accordingly, when considering the form in which a will containing alterations etc. is to be proved, it should be considered (particularly in cases where there is some foreign element, e.g. the testator's domicile, nationality or place of residence) whether the Act enables the alterations to be accepted as properly executed, even if they are neither duly attested nor shown to have been made prior to the execution of the will.

Requirements of foreign law to be treated as formal

3.409   Where, whether in pursuance of the Wills Act 1963 itself or otherwise, a law in force outside the United Kingdom falls to be applied in relation to a will, any requirement of that law whereby special formalities are to be observed by testators answering a particular description, or witnesses to the execution of a will are to possess certain qualifications, is, notwithstanding any rule of that law to the contrary, to be treated as a formal requirement only (s. 3).

Changes of domicile

3.410   Section 4 of the Act provides that the construction of a will shall not be altered by any change in the testator's domicile after its execution. This re-enacts part of s. 3 of the Wills Act 1861: the remainder of that section (which provides that a will is not revoked or rendered invalid by reason of such a change of domicile) is no longer necessary in view of the provisions of s. 1 of the new Act.

Date at which applicable law to be ascertained

3.411   In determining for the purposes of the Act whether or not the execution of a will or other testamentary act conformed to a particular law, regard must be had to the formal requirements of such law *at the time of execution*, any subsequent alteration in the law being normally disregarded. Nevertheless, account may be taken of a subsequent alteration in the law affecting wills executed at that time (i.e. by an enactment having retrospective effect) provided that the effect of such alteration is to enable the will or other testamentary act to be treated as properly executed (s. 6(3)).

Scotland and Northern Ireland

3.412   The Act extends to Scotland and Northern Ireland (s. 7(5)).

3.413   Under s. 32 of the Succession (Scotland) Act 1964 (replacing s. 5 of the Wills Act 1963), as amended by the Administration of Estates Act 1971, s. 7 and Schedule 1, for the purpose of any question arising as to entitlement to any property by virtue of a testamentary disposition to which s. 32 applies, the disposition is, notwithstanding anything in any Act passed before the Succession (Scotland) Act 1964, to be treated as probative.

3.414   Section 32 applies to any testamentary disposition (not being one which would be treated as probative apart from that section) if:

(a)   confirmation of an executor to property disposed of in the disposition has been granted in Scotland; or

(b)   probate, letters of administration or other grant of representation has been issued in England and Wales or Northern Ireland in respect of property disposed of in the disposition and notes the domicile of the deceased in England and Wales or in Northern Ireland, as the case may be, or probate, letters of administration or other grant of representation issued outwith the United

Kingdom in respect of such property has been sealed in Scotland under s. 2 of the Colonial Probates Act 1892.

Repeal of Wills Act 1861

3.415   The Wills Act 1861 is repealed as from 1 January 1964, the date of commencement of the Act of 1963 (s. 7(3)), but any will executed in accordance with its provisions before the repeal is not invalidated (s. 7(4)). All the provisions of the Act of 1861, except that as to wills executed in accordance with the law of a domicile of origin within Her Majesty's dominions, are contained in the Act of 1963, with extended application.

3.416   A will made before 1 January 1964 may still be established as well executed by virtue of the Wills Act 1861, whatever the date of death of the testator, but the restrictions imposed by that Act will operate; i.e. its application to the wills of British subjects only, and the limitation to wills of personal estate. It is accordingly preferable, wherever possible, to establish the formal validity of the will of a testator dying on or after 1 January 1964 under the Wills Act 1963, rather than under the Act of 1861.

Probate practice — effect of Wills Act 1963

3.417   The main effect of the Act is to enable the will of a person dying on or after 1 January 1964 to be accepted as validly executed for the purpose of proof in England and Wales if it is shown to have been executed in accordance with any system of law which, in the circumstances of the particular case, is applicable by virtue of either s. 1 or s. 2 of the Act. The position is summarised in the following paragraphs.

Domicile in England and Wales: Will executed in accordance with Wills Act 1837

3.418   In the case of a testator who dies on or after 1 January 1964, domiciled in England and Wales, leaving a will executed in accordance with s. 9 of the Wills Act 1837, the Act has no effect on the practice, save that it is necessary to consider the circumstances of any possible act of revocation (whether total or partial and whether by document or physical act): for even though not carried out in the manner prescribed by the Wills Act 1837, a revocation is effective if executed in any manner which, under the general rule given in s. 1 of the Act (see 'General rule', para. **3.396**, ante), enables it to be treated as properly executed, or if executed in accordance with any system of law which, under s. 2(1)(c) of the Act, is available in the circumstances of the case (see also 'Revocation of wills', paras. **3.404–3.407**, ante).

3.419   Careful consideration should also be given to apparently unexecuted alterations and additions, in case these may be valid by some other applicable system of law. The onus of proof is on the person propounding the will, and in normal cases where there appears to be no foreign connection the usual principles in cases where wills contain unexecuted alterations etc., are applicable (see paras. **3.222** ff., ante). But if the alterations are material, or if the testator is known to have had some connection with, or even to have visited, other countries, enquiry should be made as to the possibility of establishing that the alterations are valid under some system of law which is available by virtue of the Act. See also 'Alterations', para. **3.408**, above.

Domicile in England and Wales: Will not executed in accordance with Wills Act 1837

3.420   A will not executed in accordance with s. 9 of the Wills Act 1837 should not be regarded as invalid without considering whether it satisfies any of the tests laid down by the Act of 1963. If executed in conformity with any system of law which, in the circumstances, is applicable by virtue of s. 1 or s. 2 of the Act, it is admissible to proof in this country, and affidavit evidence of the facts and, where necessary, of the law of the relevant territory, should be obtained: see also 'Practice', paras. **3.425** ff., post.

3.421   The practice as to the privileged wills of soldiers, sailors, seamen and airmen is not affected by the Act of 1963, except that the latter affords alternative tests, any one of which, if satisfied, will entitle such a will to proof in this country.

Domicile out of England and Wales

3.422   The provisions of the Wills Act 1963 do not derogate from the established practice of accepting without further evidence of formal validity a will which has been proved, or recognised as valid, in the court having jurisdiction at the place where the testator was domiciled at the time of his death (see cases quoted in footnote 1, para. **12.55**, post). A will is also admissible to proof in this country if it is shown to have been executed in accordance with the form required by the internal law of the testator's domicile at the time of death, and the practice stated in paras. **12.54–12.65** is applicable in such cases. In the case of persons dying on or after 1 January 1964, a will, even if not so executed, is admissible if it can be shown that its mode of execution satisfies any other of the tests laid down by s. 1 (or, where applicable, s. 2) of the Act of 1963.

3.423   If the will has been executed in English form (i.e. is properly signed and attested and contains a correctly worded attestation clause showing execution in accordance with s. 9 of the Wills Act 1837) the provisions of the Act of 1963 render affidavit evidence of foreign law unnecessary in cases where it is shown that compliance with the internal law of England and Wales is sufficient to entitle the will to proof. This is the case if:

(a)   the will was executed in England or Wales; or
(b)   the testator's habitual residence either at the date of execution or at the time of his death was in England and Wales; or
(c)   the testator's domicile at the date of execution of the will was in England and Wales; or
(d)   the testator was a British national whose closest connection, either at the time of execution of the will or at the time of his death, was with England and Wales and the English system of internal law as to the formal validity of wills.

3.424   Furthermore, a will in proper English form is normally accepted as valid as to form if:

(a)   the will was made in; or
(b)   the testator's habitual residence either at the date of execution or at the time of his death was in; or

(c)   the testator was at the date of death or at the date of the will a national of; or

(d)   the testator was at the date of death or the date of the will domiciled in:

Northern Ireland, the Republic of Ireland, Australia, Canada or New Zealand[1].

1   Registrar's Direction (1972) 20 November.

Practice

3.425   The practice in proving a will or other testamentary document whose valid-ity it is sought to establish under the Wills Act 1963 is similar to that which applied in relation to wills valid under the Wills Act 1861. There should be affidavit evid-ence as to the relevant facts and, where the law of any territory other than England and Wales, or the countries mentioned in the previous paragraph, is relied upon, then, unless the will has been proved or accepted as valid by the court of such terri-tory, affidavit (or notarial) evidence in accordance with NCPR 19 (see paras. **12.25** ff., post), showing that the execution of the will complied with the internal law of such territory, should be lodged.

3.426   Where a will is shown by a properly authenticated copy issued by a notary practising out of England and Wales to have been executed in his presence, or that of his predecessor, and recorded in his archives at the time of execution, it may be assumed for the purpose of an uncontested application to prove the will in this country, provided that there are no unusual features, that the will is valid as to form by the internal law of the place where it was made[1].

1   *Practice Direction* [1972] 3 All ER 1019, [1972] 1 WLR 1539.

3.427   Where the will has been proved in a territory *other than that of the domicile of the testator at the time of his death*, evidence of law may still be called for not-withstanding the production of an official copy of the probate or other court document establishing this, for it may be that the court in which the will was proved has applied a system of law other than its own internal law as to the formal validity of the will. If reliance is placed on a will having been proved in a court of a territory which is not the territory where the deceased was domiciled at the time of his death, the evidence will need to establish: (a) that the court has applied its own system of internal law as to the formal validity of wills; and (b) the relevant con-nection, with that system of law, under the Wills Act 1963.

3.428   The affidavit (or notarial evidence) of law should deal with the *internal* law of the territory or state[1] concerned, excluding any question of reference to the law of any other country. In order to comply with s. 6(2) of the Act, the affidavit (or notarial evidence) should show whether a single system of law relating to the formal validity of wills obtains throughout the territory or state, or whether there is more than one such system. If the latter is the case, the affidavit (or notarial evid-ence) should also show whether there is in force throughout the territory or state a rule indicating which system is to be applied to the case in question: if so, the expert's opinion as to the validity of the execution of the will etc., should be based on the application of that rule. If there is no such rule, the expert should state upon which system his conclusions are based. In this latter case, it is also necessary to show in the affidavit of facts upon what grounds it is claimed that the deceased was most closely connected at the time of execution of the will or at the time of his death (whichever is the relevant time: see s. 6(2)(b) of the Act) with the system of law referred to in the affidavit (or notarial evidence) of law[2].

1 In cases where the law of the testator's nationality is in point, it should be noted that the Act uses the term 'state', meaning a territory or group of territories having its own law of nationality. See also footnote 3, para. **3.396**, ante.
2 This position appears most likely to arise when applying the law of nationality. For example, in the case of a former citizen of the United Kingdom and Colonies there could be several different systems of internal law as to the formal validity of wills (English, Scottish, the laws of the various Colonies, etc.). It would seem that the territory of origin of the testator need not necessarily be that with which he was most closely connected at the time of execution of the will, or at the time of his death: a person, English by birth, but who had lived in Scotland for most of his life might well have his closest connection with the Scottish system of internal law as to the formal validity of wills. The Wills Act 1963, however, affords several alternative tests, any one of which if satisfied is sufficient to entitle a will to proof in this country, and it will no doubt in many cases be simpler to rely upon the law of the domicile, or of the place of execution of the will or of the habitual residence of the testator, rather than on the more complicated considerations which may arise in dealing with the law of nationality.

3.429 For a form of affidavit of facts under Wills Act 1963, see Appendix VI, No. 10, post.

Will made for mentally disordered person

Power to make will for mentally disordered person

3.430 Section 96(1)(e) of the Mental Health Act 1983[1] (which came into effect on 30 September 1983[2]) empowers a judge having jurisdiction under that Act to order, direct or authorise the execution for a patient (i.e. a person who is incapable, by reason of mental disorder, of managing and administering his property and affairs) of a will or codicil making any provision (whether disposing of property, exercising a power or otherwise) which could be made by a will executed by the patient if he were not mentally disordered.

1 See p. 860, post.
2 Replacing the relevant sections of the Mental Health Act 1959, as amended by the Administration of Justice Act 1969; for which see p. 795, post.

3.431 By s. 96(4) of the Act[1], this power may not be exercised while the patient is a minor, nor unless the judge has reason to believe that he is incapable of making a valid will for himself.

1 See p. 861, post.

3.432 Section 94 of the Act[1] provides that the functions conferred by the Act on a judge are, in general, exercisable by the Lord Chancellor or any nominated judge, but are also exercisable by the Master of the Court of Protection, the Public Trustee or a nominated officer.

1 See p. 859, post.

3.433 The Court of Protection Rules 1994, which came into force on 22 December 1994, replaced the 1984 rules. They include provision as to who may make an application under s. 96(1)(e) of the Act for an order for execution for a patient of a will.

Mode of execution of will

3.434 Section 97(1) of the Act of 1983[1] prescribes the mode of execution of such a will. It must be expressed to be signed by the patient acting by the person authorised by the judge to execute the will for him, and must be signed by such person with the name of the patient and his own name, in the presence of two or more witnesses present at the same time. The witnesses must attest and subscribe the will in the presence of the authorised person, and the will must also be sealed with the official seal of the Court of Protection.

1 See p. 861, post.

3.435 In a Practice Direction issued by the Court of Protection[1] attention was drawn to the following matters:

(a) Section 96(4) of the Act requires that the court must have reason to believe that the patient is incapable of making a valid will for himself. It can be assumed that in most cases the court will require recent evidence of lack of testamentary capacity. If recent evidence is not available, the court may decide to adjourn the application and (if no other evidence can be obtained) call for a report from one of the Lord Chancellor's visitors on this question.

(b) Section 97 of the Act directs how a statutory will is to be executed and attested, and solicitors should consider and submit a suitable form of attestation clause. Statutory wills will not be sealed by the court until they have been correctly executed and attested.

(c) Having regard to s. 97(4) of the principal Act the evidence on the summons should state the patient's domicile, whether any immovable property will be affected by the proposed will, and if so, the situation of that property if already belonging to the patient.

1 Court of Protection *Practice Direction* [1983] 3 All ER 255, sub nom *Practice Note* [1983] 1 WLR 1077.

3.436 The receiver, if not the applicant or one of the applicants, should be given notice of the application. Otherwise, no person should be given notice until the Master has so directed.

3.437 If the receiver is personally interested in the relief sought, or if there is some other reason for having the interests of the patient separately represented, the Master will probably direct that the patient be represented by the Official Solicitor.

3.438 In general, all persons whose interests will be materially affected by proposals should be given notice, but the discretion is wide and will be exercised according to the particular facts of each case.

3.439 The only evidence before the Master will be the evidence filed or referred to in the application. Accordingly, this evidence should give all relevant information necessary for the disposal of the application; full particulars as to the family, property, needs and general circumstances of the patient and the general background of his affairs should be set out, as well as those facts directly giving rise to the application together with the financial circumstances of the application.

3.440   Applications will be heard and determined by the Master unless the Master decides, in accordance with the Court of Protection Rules, to refer the application, or any question arising in the proceedings, to one of the nominated judges.

3.441   The Wills Act 1837 has effect in relation to any such will as if it were a will signed by the patient himself, save that s. 9 (manner of execution and attestation) does not apply, and any later reference in that Act to execution in the manner thereinbefore required is to be construed as a reference to execution in the manner prescribed by s. 97(1) of the Act of 1983.

3.442   In drafting the will, the court assumes that the will is made by the patient during a brief lucid interval and seeks to make a will which that particular patient would have made, acting reasonably on being advised by a competent solicitor. There should be evidence of the patient's capital and income, the expenses of maintaining him, his nature when last of testamentary capacity, and the financial and other circumstances of those who seek to benefit under the will[1].

1 *Re D (J)* [1982] Ch 237, [1982] 2 All ER 37.

3.443   Attention is drawn to the case of *Re C (a patient)* [1991] 3 All ER 866. In this case, in which the patient had been mentally handicapped since birth and had inherited a substantial estate (some £1,600,000) and who would otherwise die intestate, it was held that the court, in exercising its power under s. 95(1)(c) of the Mental Health Act 1983 to make provision for other persons or purposes for whom or to which the patient might be expected to provide if he was not mentally disordered, had jurisdiction to make inter vivos dispositions and direct the execution of a will for the patient on the assumption that he would have been a normal decent person who would have acted in accordance with contemporary standards of morality.

Effect of will

3.444   A will executed as above has, in the case of a patient who is at the time of its execution domiciled in England and Wales, the like effect for all purposes (save in respect of immovable property situate outside England or Wales) as if he were capable of making a valid will and the will had been executed in accordance with the Wills Act 1837.

3.445   In the case of a person domiciled in Scotland or Northern Ireland or outside the United Kingdom at the time of execution of the will, the will is valid only insofar as it relates to any property or matter in respect of which, under the law of his domicile, any question of his testamentary capacity would fall to be determined in accordance with the law of England and Wales[1].

1 Mental Health Act 1983, s. 97(3), (4) (see p. 861, post).

International wills

3.446   Section 27 of, and Schedule 2 to, the Administration of Justice Act 1982[1] introduced into English law a new form of will, the 'international will', so as to enable the United Kingdom to ratify the Unidroit Convention providing a Uniform Law on the Form of an International Will (Cmnd. 5950). The Convention entered into force on 9 February 1978 and instruments of ratification have been deposited by Canada (in relation to the Provinces of Manitoba, Newfoundland, Ontario and Alberta), Ecuador, Libya, Niger, Portugal and Yugoslavia. The Convention has yet to be ratified by the United Kingdom.

1 See pp. 856, 858, post.

Object of Convention

3.447 The prime object of the Convention is the creation of a new form of will which will be valid and recognised by Contracting States as regards form, irrespective of its place of execution or of the nationality, domicile or residence of the testator, provided that it is made in the form prescribed by the provisions of the Convention: these requirements are set out in Schedule 2 to the Administration of Justice Act 1982 (see p. 858, post). The formalities are similar to those laid down by the Wills Act 1837, but with the additional requirement that execution must take place in the presence of an 'authorised person'.

'Authorised persons'

3.448 Section 28(1), (2) of the Administration of Justice Act 1982 is as follows:

'(1) The persons authorised to act in the United Kingdom in connection with international wills are—

(a) solicitors; and
(b) notaries public.

(2) A person who is authorised under section 6(1) of the Commissioners for Oaths Act 1889 to do notarial acts in any foreign country or place is authorised to act there in connection with international wills.'

3.449 The effect of sub-s. (2) above is to designate British Consuls as authorised persons to act in connection with an international will in respect of British nationals abroad.

3.450 It is further provided by s. 28(7) of the 1982 Act, amending s. 10 of the Consular Relations Act 1968, that notarial acts performed for foreign nationals by foreign consuls in the United Kingdom in connection with an international will are also to be recognised.

Form of international will

3.451 Whereas the uniform rules for an international will as set out in the Annex to the Convention (see Schedule 2 to the 1982 Act, p. 858, post) are similar to the requirements of s. 9 of the Wills Act 1837[1] as to form (e.g. the will must be in writing) and as to attestation (the will shall be signed by the testator or by a person on his behalf in the presence of two witnesses), it should be noted that the requirements are not identical. The primary difference is that, in addition to the two witnesses, the testator is required to declare his will in the presence of a person authorised to act in connection with international wills (see above), who is required to attach to the will a certificate, in the form (or substantially in the form) prescribed by the Convention, to the effect that the proper formalities have been performed. Whilst the certificate, in the absence of contrary evidence, is conclusive evidence of the formal validity of the document as a will for the purposes of the

Convention, it is further provided that the omission of (or any irregularity in) the certificate shall not affect the formal validity of the will.

1 See p. 720, post.

3.452   The following additional points are worth noting. The testator, witness and authorised person must sign *at the end of the will*, and the date of the will shall be noted at the end by the authorised person. These requirements are additional to those contained in s. 9 of the Wills Act 1837, as substituted by the Administration of Justice Act 1982[1]. However, the Convention further provides that the invalidity of a will as an international will shall not affect its formal validity as a will of another kind. So it would seem that where the full requirements of the Convention have not been complied with, but the will is validly executed in accordance with s. 9 of the Wills Act 1837, then, although not an international will, it may still be proved under the Wills Act 1837.

1 See p. 720, post.

3.453   The Convention provides that an international will shall be subject to 'the ordinary rules of revocation of wills'. The English rules as to revocation of wills (see paras. **3.34** ff., ante) would seem therefore to apply to an international will.

Deposit of international wills

3.454   Section 28(3) of the Administration of Justice Act 1982[1] provides that an international will may be deposited in a depository designated under s. 23 of the Act for the safe custody of wills of living persons and, once deposited, the provisions relating to the registration of wills as contained in s. 25 and regulations made thereunder shall apply to the will.

1 See p. 856, post.

3.455   As to the deposit and registration of wills of living persons, see Chap. 20.

3.456   **Note**. *Sections 27 and 28 of the Administration of Justice Act 1982[1] (provisions relating to international wills) shall come into force on such date as the Lord Chancellor and the Secretary of State may by Order jointly appoint. No commencement Order has yet been made bringing these sections into operation.*

1 See p. 856, post.

CHAPTER 4

Probates

Summary

Note.—This chapter deals with grants of probate in cases where the deceased died **domiciled in England and Wales**. For the practice in cases where the deceased died domiciled out of England and Wales, see Chap. 12. For interpretation of wills (including codicils), see Chap. 3.

Executors

Executor's title

4.01   An executor derives his title and authority from the will of his testator and not from any grant of probate. The property of the deceased, including any right of action, vests in him on his testator's death, and he can institute an action, as executor, before he proves the will. He cannot obtain a judgment before probate, not because his title depends on probate, but because production of the probate is the only way that he is allowed to prove his title[1]. An executor may be substituted or removed in appropriate circumstances in accordance with s. 50 of the Administration of Justice Act 1985 and the substitute gains his title from the order appointing him (see Chap. 41).

1 *Meyappa Chetty v Supramanian Chetty* [1916] 1 AC 603 at 608; referred to in *Ingall v Moran* [1944] KB 160, [1944] 1 All ER 97. Similarly, the title of an executor to appoint a trustee under s. 36 of the Trustee Act 1925 can be proved only by a grant of representation in the United Kingdom (*Re Crowhurst Park, Sims-Hilditch v Simmons* [1974] 1 All ER 991, [1974] 1 WLR 583, applying *Chetty v Chetty* and *Ingall v Moran*).

Express appointment of executor

4.02   The proceeding which confirms the title of an executor is called proving the will.

4.03   If an executor is appointed he is entitled before all others to prove the will.

4.04   An executor of a will may be expressly nominated, or may be such according to the tenor of the will.

4.05   The appointment may be absolute, when he is constituted immediately without any restriction as to the estate with which he may deal, or limited as to time etc. It may be qualified by limitation as to (1) time, or (2) place, or (3) subject-matter, or the appointment may be conditional or contingent.

4.06   If a testator has, by his will, authorised another person to nominate an executor, probate will be granted to the person nominated[1].

1   *Re Cringan's Goods* (1828) 1 Hag Ecc 548. See also *Re Deichman's Goods* (1842) 3 Curt 123; *Re Ryder's Goods* (1861) 2 Sw & Tr 127. Where the testator appointed as executors two named persons together with such person as they, jointly with the testator's wife, should nominate, but the executors and the wife could not agree, probate was granted to the named executors, power being reserved to the third person when nominated: *Jackson and Gill v Paulet* (1851) 2 Rob Eccl 344.

Limitation as to time

4.07   The appointment may be qualified by limitation as to the time when the person appointed shall begin, or when he shall cease, to be executor. For example, a testator may appoint his son to be executor when he shall attain the age of eighteen years, or he may appoint a person to be executor during the widowhood of his wife, or the minority of his son, or for a period of years after the testator's own death. Where there is no appointment of a person to act before the period limited for the commencement of the office, or after the period limited for its expiration, the court may grant administration (with will) to another person, limited until there is an executor[1], or, if a limited grant of probate has been made, may grant cessate administration (with will) to the person next entitled under NCPR 20 after the period of the appointment has ended.

1   See Supreme Court Act 1981, ss. 118 and 119, p. 845, post. See also paras. **4.30** ff., post, as to minor executors.

Limitation as to place

4.08   An appointment may be limited to a particular place. Thus, where a testator appointed A and B executors in Portugal, and C and D executors in England, it was held that this meant 'limited to estate in Portugal', and that A and B were not entitled to probate in England[1].

1   *Velho v Leite* (1864) 3 Sw & Tr 456.

Limitation as to subject-matter

4.09   The powers of the executor may be limited as to the subject-matter, as where a person is appointed to deal with a particular part of the testator's property only, and at the same time another person is appointed general executor[1]. Where a testator appointed executors except as to property embarked in trade, and then appointed his widow executrix in relation to his business as a licensed victualler, probate was granted to the widow limited to the business[2]. Where, however, a testator appoints A, B and C executors, but as to C as to his literary affairs only, A and

B are granted probate of all the estate, while C is restricted to co-operating with them as to literary affairs. Where A is appointed executor save as to the literary estate and B is appointed executor as to the literary estate only, grants of probate may issue to them, each limited to the relevant part of the estate. See also paras. **11.273** and **11.278**, post.

1 *Lynch v Bellew and Fallon* (1820) 3 Phillim 424.
2 *Re Falkner's Estate* (1915) 113 LT 927.

Will limited to personalty

4.10 Where a will is specifically limited to personal estate and an executor is appointed, his powers must be regarded as limited, and the grant of probate must be limited to personal estate.

4.11 In such a case, no order for a grant limited to part of the estate under NCPR 51 is necessary either in respect of this grant or of any subsequent grant in respect of real estate[1].

7 Registrar's Directions (1947) 15 October and (1958) 24 March.

Conditional appointment

4.12 Where an executor is appointed, provided that he proves the will within three calendar months next after the death of the testator, the day of the death is to be excluded in computing the three-month period[1].

1 *Re Wilmot's Goods* (1834) 1 Curt 1.

4.13 Under s. 61 of the Law of Property Act 1925[1], in all wills etc., made or coming into operation on or after 1 January 1926, unless the context otherwise requires, the expression 'month' means a calendar month[2].

1 See p. 743, post.
2 See also *Re Figgis, Roberts v Maclaren* [1969] 1 Ch 123, [1968] 1 All ER 999 (gift to wife if she should be living 'at the expiration of a period of three months from my death'. It was held that, in accordance with s. 61, Law of Property Act 1925, the period was one of three calendar months, computed in whole days excluding the day of the testator's death. The testator died at 5 a.m. on 9 January: thus the period ended at midnight on 9 April).

4.14 Where a testator has appointed as executor 'A, but if A is not in England at the date of death then such person as A may appoint to act in the settlement of my estate' probate will be granted to A's appointee, upon its being sworn in the oath that A was not in England at the date of death, and production of the appointment by A[1].

1 *Re Andreason* (September 1943, unreported).

4.15 When a person is appointed executor provided a certain condition is satisfied, the oath to lead a grant of probate to such executor should include the facts establishing that the condition was satisfied.

Substituted appointment

4.16 A person may appoint an executor to act alone, or in conjunction with others, or several may be appointed successively. Thus A may be appointed, but if he is unwilling or unable to act (or failing him), B, but if he is unwilling or unable to act (or failing him), C. In such a case A is said to be the instituted executor, and the substituted executor cannot obtain probate until the right of the first named to do so has been superseded, e.g. he has renounced or he is dead. If an instituted executor once accepts the office and afterwards dies, the substitutes are, prima facie, all excluded, because the condition of law (if he is unwilling or unable to act) was extinguished by the acceptance of the instituted executor. See also para. **4.194**, post as to reservation of power to one of two instituted executors.

Two appointments

4.17   If there are two separate appointments of executors in a will, the earlier appointment is held to be revoked by the later appointment of a 'sole executor'. Where in a will executors are named, and a codicil contains the appointment of an executor as 'sole executor', the appointment in the will may be held to be revoked by that in the codicil; but this depends on the exact wording of the documents, and the extent of the dispositions; for example, a woman may be added as 'sole *executrix*'. So where two wills, each of which appointed a sole executor, were together admitted to proof, the second being in the nature of a codicil as regards its dispositions, the judge, with hesitation, granted probate to both executors[1].

1   *Geaves v Price* (1863) 3 Sw & Tr 71.

4.18   In such cases it is advisable to obtain the directions of the district judge or registrar before preparing the papers to lead a grant.

Executor according to the tenor

4.19   An executor according to the tenor of a will is a person, not expressly nominated an executor, who is directed by the will to perform one or more of the duties of an executor[1].

1   *Re Fry's Goods* (1827) 1 Hag Ecc 80; *Re Brown's Goods* (1910) 54 Sol Jo 478.

4.20   The following directions in wills have been held to constitute executorship according to the tenor: a simple direction to pay debts but not out of a particular fund[1]; *trustee* 'to carry out this will'[2]; *trustee* 'to get in the estate and distribute it'[3]; 'to hold and administer all my estate'[4]; 'I appoint A—— and B——' with subsequent reference to executors[5].

1   *Re Cook's Goods* [1902] P 114.
2   *Re Russell's Goods* [1892] P 380; *Re Kirby's Goods* [1902] P 188; *Re Way's Goods* [1901] P 345.
3   *Re Lush's Goods* (1887) 13 PD 20. See also *Kirby*, above; *Re Earl of Leven and Melville's Goods* (1889) 15 PD 22; and *Re Wright's Goods* (1908) 25 TLR 15.
4   *Re Way's Goods*, above.
5   *Re Bradley's Goods* (1883) 8 PD 215.

4.21   In the following cases the recognition of an appointment of an executor according to the tenor was refused: appointment of a *trustee* without any duties as executor[1]; £1 left to the executor and witness, but no executor named[2]; a direction to pay debts out of a particular fund[3].

1   *Re Punchard's Goods* (1872) LR 2 P & D 369, and *Re Lowry's Goods* (1874) 3 P & M 157.
2   *Re Wood's Goods* (1868) 1 P & D 556.
3   *Re Toomy's Goods* (1864) 3 Sw & Tr 562.

4.22   An executor according to the tenor may join in taking probate with an executor nominate[1].

1   *Grant v Leslie* (1819) 3 Phillim 116.

4.23   *In cases of doubt whether the wording of a will is sufficient to constitute a person executor according to the tenor of the will the directions of the district judge or registrar should be taken before preparation of the papers.*

Deceased domiciled abroad

4.24   As to the appointment of executors, or executors according to the tenor, in the wills of persons dying domiciled out of England and Wales, see Chap. 12.

Appointment void for uncertainty

Deaths before 1 January 1983

4.25   Where uncertainty arises from the form of the appointment, such as the appointment of 'any two of my sons'[1], or 'one of my sisters'[2] or 'A or B' with no additional words indicating that the appointment of B is in substitution in certain circumstances, the appointment is void[3], and the question of admission of parol evidence of the intention of the testator does not arise. If the description of the executor is ambiguous[4], incomplete or imperfect[5], the court will sometimes admit parol evidence; but if the correct full names of an existing person are given, evidence is not admissible to show that the testator intended to appoint another person, one of whose names was slightly different[6].

1   *Re Baylis' Goods* (1862) 2 Sw & Tr 613.
2   *Re Blackwell's Goods* (1877) 2 PD 72 (three sisters, but two predeceased the deceased: held, appointment void).
3   *Re Victor-Smith* (1976) April (unreported motion) in which the deceased had by will appointed A or B to be executor and trustee and further provided that if they think fit they can appoint the Westminster Bank Limited or any one of the so-called big five banks to act in conjunction with them as executors: held, on the application of B, the surviving executor, that the appointment was void for uncertainty.
4   *Re Ashton's Goods* [1892] P 83; *Re Hubbuck's Estate* [1905] P 129.
5   As to evidence proving identity in cases of imperfect description, see *Re De Rosaz's Goods* (1877) 2 PD 66; *Re Cooper's Goods* [1899] P 193 (wrong surname, due to draftsman's error, omitted from probate).
6   *Re Peel's Goods* (1870) LR 2 P & D 46.

4.26   A gift to 'M and/or J' has been held to operate as a gift to them as joint tenants: if either did not survive, the other would take the whole gift[1]. Accordingly, an appointment of 'A and/or B' as executors would probably not be held to be void for uncertainty.

1   *Re Lewis, Goronwy v Richards* [1942] Ch 424, [1942] 2 All ER 364.

Deaths on or after 1 January 1983

4.27   The above decisions were made prior to the passing of s. 21 of the Administration of Justice Act 1982, which section provides statutory guidance for the court as to the admission of evidence in the interpretation of wills, whenever made, of testators *dying on or after 1 January 1983*. The section relaxes the former rigid rules of evidence relating to the interpretation of wills, and the section must now be taken into account in respect of wills of testators dying on or after 1 January 1983. For a fuller analysis of s. 21, see paras. **3.02–3.04**, ante.

4.28   *In cases of doubt about the wording of the form of appointment, the directions of the district judge or registrar should be taken before preparation of the papers.*

Who may be executor

4.29   If a person is of full age and capable of making a will he is capable of acting as an executor.

Executor a minor

4.30   If a minor is appointed sole executor, administration for his use and benefit, limited until he shall attain the age of 18 years[1], will be granted:

(1)   Where he has no interest in the residuary estate, to the person entitled to such residuary estate[2].
(2)   Where the minor has a beneficial interest in the residuary estate, to his parents or his guardians with parental responsibility, a second administrator being joined (by nomination) in accordance with the requirements of s. 114(2) of the Supreme Court Act 1981 if there is only one such parent or guardian competent and willing to act, unless it appears to the court to be expedient in all the circumstances to appoint the parent or guardian to act alone.

1   The Family Law Reform Act 1969 (see p. 789, post) reduced the age of majority from 21 to 18 years with effect from 1 January 1970.
2   NCPR 32(1).

4.31   The appointment does not operate to transfer any interest in the property of the deceased to the minor or constitute him a personal representative for any purpose unless and until probate is granted to him[1]. On attaining his majority, he may take or renounce probate, as he wishes. See also 'Sole executor a minor', paras. **11.137** and **11.138**, post.

1   Supreme Court Act 1981, s. 118, p. 845, post.

4.32   Where one of several executors is under age, probate will be granted to the other executors, power being reserved to the minor on attaining full age, when double probate may be granted to him, provided that the number of acting executors is then less than four[1].

1   Supreme Court Act 1981, s. 114(2), p. 844, post.

Executor's title

4.33   An executor's title is not defeasible by bankruptcy, insolvency, or felony[1]; the court has, however, in a proper case a discretion to pass over the prior right of an executor by order under s. 116 of the Supreme Court Act 1981: for practice, see paras. **25.91** ff., post.

1   *Smethurst v Tomlin and Bankes* (1861) 2 Sw & Tr 143; *Re Drawmer's Estate* (1913) 108 LT 732.

Executor incapable

4.34 Mental incapacity is a ground upon which an executor may be excluded from probate[1], but the usual practice where he is sole executor is to make a grant for his use and benefit (see paras. **11.209** ff., post).

1 *Evans v Tyler* (1849) 2 Rob Eccl 128 at 131.

Executor in prison

4.35 For procedure for obtaining a grant where the executor is serving a term of imprisonment, see paras. **11.255** ff. and **25.91** ff., post.

The Public Trustee and trust corporations

4.36 The Public Trustee or a trust corporation, if appointed executor, has power to obtain probate.

4.37 For the practice relating to grants in such cases, see Chap. 9.

Corporation not a trust corporation

4.38 A grant of probate cannot be made to a corporation other than a trust corporation as defined by English law.

4.39 Where a corporation (not being a trust corporation) and an individual are appointed executors the individual's right to probate has priority under NCPR 20, and probate may be granted to the individual only, it being recited in the oath and grant that the corporation is not a trust corporation as defined by NCPR 2(1). Alternatively, application for the grant of probate may be made by the individual alone, with power being reserved to the non-trust corporation: in the latter event, whether or not the status of the corporation is such as to enable it later to extract a grant of double probate will be tested at the time when application is made for the subsequent grant[1].

1 Registrar's Direction (1977) 6 December.

Sole executor a non-trust corporation

4.40 Before a grant can be made under NCPR 36(4)(a) to the nominee or attorney of a corporation (not being a trust corporation) entitled as executor, it must be established that the corporation has power under its constitution to take a grant through its nominee or attorney. This may be established by the production of a copy of the constitution[1].

1 Registrar's Direction (1956) 2 January.

Firm appointed executors

4.41 If a firm of solicitors or a trading firm is appointed executors, the appointment applies only to the members of the firm at the date of the will of the testator, unless a contrary intention is expressed in the will, the appointment being regarded as of the individual members constituting such firm at the date of appointment[1]. In such a case the oath should state that the applicants were partners in the firm in question at the date of the will. All such partners should be accounted for in the same way as if the individual members had been named as executors (e.g. by reciting any renunciation or death, or reserving power to non-proving members of the firm).

1 *Re Fernie's Goods* (1849) 6 Notes of Cases 657. Quaere, where a will appoints a firm of solicitors as executors and that will is subsequently confirmed and republished by a codicil, whether the appointment of the executors should be regarded as of the individual partners of the firm as at the date of the codicil.

4.42   See also paras. **4.193** ff., post, 'Clearing off executors'.

Appointment of firm of solicitors

4.43   A clause in a will appointing the firm of X 'who may act through any partner or partners of that firm or their successors in business at the date of my death not exceeding two in number to be the executors and trustees of this my will' has been held not to be void for uncertainty but, with less than full confidence, construed as an appointment as executors of all the partners in the firm at the date of the testator's death, probate to be granted to two with power reserved to the others. Such clauses cause great difficulty: a wording greatly to be preferred is that suggested by Mr R. T. Oerton[1], viz.: 'I appoint the partners at the date of my death in the firm of X, of . . ., or the firm which at that date has succeeded to and carries on its practice, to be the executors and trustees of this my will (and I express the wish that two and only two of them shall prove my will and act initially in its trusts)', the words in brackets being merely precatory[2].

1 *Law Society's Gazette*, May and June 1967, pp. 244, 343.
2 *Re Horgan* [1971] P 50, [1969] 3 All ER 1570; applying *Re Fernie*, above.

4.44   Variations of the wording suggested in the previous paragraph may result in uncertainty, e.g. 'I appoint two of the partners at the date of my death in the firm of X, of . . .', and it may be possible to save the appointment only by recourse to s. 20 (rectification) or s. 21 (interpretation) of the Administration of Justice Act 1982 — see following paragraph and paras. **3.02–3.04** and **3.250–3.263**, ante.

4.45   The decisions referred to above were made prior to the passing of s. 21 of the Administration of Justice Act 1982, which section provides statutory guidance for the court as to the admission of evidence in the interpretation of wills, whenever made, of *testators dying on or after 1 January 1983*. The section relaxes the former rigid rules of evidence relating to the interpretation of wills, and the section must now be taken into account in respect of wills of *testators dying on or after 1 January 1983*.

4.46   *In cases of doubt about the wording of the form of appointment, the directions of the district judge or registrar should be taken before preparation of the papers.*

An official appointed executor

4.47   Where an executor is designated by his official title, and is not named, the appointment is held to refer to the holder of the office at the date of the death of the testator and not at the date of the will, unless the context indicates otherwise[1]. In this case the oath should include a statement that the applicant was the holder of the office at the date of death.

1 *Re Jones* (1927) 43 TLR 324. See Registrar's Circular, 30 July 1946.

Number of acting executors allowed

4.48 In no case may probate be granted to more than four persons in respect of the same part of the estate of the deceased[1].

1 Supreme Court Act 1981, s. 114(1), see p. 844, post.

4.49 Where four general executors and another executor in respect of the deceased's literary effects were appointed in the will, the court held that four only could take the grant[1].

1 *Re Holland's Estates* [1936] 3 All ER 13.

Reservation of power to non-proving executors

4.50 If several executors are appointed, one or more of them may prove the will without the consent or renunciation of the others, power being reserved to grant probate to the latter whenever they or any of them shall duly apply for the same.

4.51 Notice of the application for probate normally must be given to the executor or executors to whom power is to be reserved (r. 27(1)), unless a district judge or registrar dispenses with the giving of such notice where he is satisfied that it is impracticable or would result in unreasonable delay or expense to give it (r. 27(3)). The oath must state that such notice has been given, unless a district judge or registrar otherwise directs.

4.52 Where leave is sought to dispense with the giving of notice prior to preparing the oath the solicitors through whom the application for the grant is to be made should set out the reasons why the district judge or registrar is being asked to dispense with the giving of notice in a letter. If no preliminary enquiry is made, and the case is one in which notice has not been given to any executor to whom power is to be reserved, the application for the grant must be accompanied by a similar letter[1]. The oath should contain the following paragraph, completed as appropriate to the circumstances:

> 'That notice of this application has been given to the executor(s) to whom power is to be reserved (save . . .)'[2].

1 Registrar's Direction (1987) 21 December.
2 Ibid.

4.53 Where power is to be reserved to executors who are appointed by reference to their being partners in a firm, and not by their names, notice need not be given to them if probate is applied for by another partner in that firm (r. 27(1A)). It should be noted that notice is required to be given to the relevant partners in the firm if the partner executors have been appointed by their names or if the executor applying (or if none of the executors applying) is not also a partner in the firm.

4.54 Where power is to be reserved to partners in a firm, any notice given to them, by an executor applying for probate, of his application, may be given to the partners by sending it to the firm at its principal or last known place of business (r. 27(2)).

4.55 An executor to whom power is reserved may, either during the lifetime or after the death of the proving executor or executors, renounce probate, or prove the testator's will by extracting a grant of double probate (so long as the acting executors are not increased thereby to more than four in number).

4.56   Reservation of power is made only to an executor who is equal in degree. When an executor *for life* takes probate, power is not reserved to the executor substituted upon his decease, but where two executors are appointed, one a full executor, and the other 'for life', a further executor being substituted on the death of the latter, a grant may be made to the two, but as to one for his life only, reserving power to the substituted executor on the death of the executor for life.

Right of proving executors to exercise powers

4.57   Under s. 8 of the Administration of Estates Act 1925:

'(1) Where probate is granted to one or some of two or more persons named as executors, whether or not power is reserved to the others or other to prove, all the powers which are by law conferred on the personal representative may be exercised by the proving executor or executors for the time being and shall be as effectual as if all the persons named as executors had concurred therein.

(2) This section applies whether the testator died before or after the commencement of this Act.'

Sub-s. (2) of s. 2 of the above Act also provides that:

'any conveyance of the real estate may be made by the proving executor or executors for the time being, without an order of the court, and shall be as effectual as if all the persons named as executors had concurred therein.'

Renunciation

4.58   Provided that he has not intermeddled in the estate, an executor may renounce probate. As to renunciation, and retraction of renunciation, see Chap. 15.

Settled land

4.59   In every oath to lead a grant of probate, where the deceased died on or after 1 January 1926, the deponent must swear to the best of his knowledge, information and belief whether there was land vested in the deceased which was settled previously to his death (and not by his will) and which remained settled land notwithstanding his death (NCPR 8(3)).

Probate including settled land

4.60   Before 14 October 1991 a general grant specifically including settled land could have been made in appropriate circumstances. NCPR 29 was amended, with effect from 14 October 1991. As a result all grants issued on or after that date in respect of settled land are grants of administration, are silent as to whether the deceased died testate or intestate and are issued only as separate grants limited to settled land. A person who is entitled to a grant in respect of the free estate and who is also entitled to a grant in respect of settled land must now take separate grants.[1] For practice as to settled land grants, see Chap. 10.

1 Secretary's Circular (2), 26 September 1991.

Probate save and except settled land

4.61 Where there was land vested in the deceased which remained settled land notwithstanding his death, a general executor may take probate save and except settled land. The grant will be in respect of the free estate only, excluding the value of the settled land. (See NCPR 29(3).)

Alteration of general grant to save and except

4.62 As to amendment of a general grant by insertion of the limitation 'save and except settled land', see para. **10.125**, post.

Grant to person other than executor

4.63 If no executor is appointed, or if there is no executor willing or competent to obtain probate, letters of administration, with the will annexed, are granted to some person or persons interested in the estate. (See Chap. 5.)

Transmission of executorship

Chain or transmission of executorship

4.64 A probate does not necessarily cease permanently with the death of the grantee. An executor having taken probate of his own testator's will becomes ipso facto executor, not only of that will, but also of the will of any testator of whom the other was sole, or sole surviving, proving executor, and so on, ad infinitum, upwards[1].

1 Administration of Estates Act 1925, s. 7 (p. 746, post); see *Re Perry's Goods* (1840) 2 Curt 655 (an executor cannot take probate of one will but renounce probate of the other).

4.65 The condition of this rule, however, is that the will of each testator shall have been duly proved in the present High Court or in the Probate Court, or in any of the ecclesiastical or other courts of England which the latter court superseded[1], provided that, in such ecclesiastical or other courts, the grant is not limited in its operation.

1 *Jernegan v Baxter* (1832) 5 Sim 568; contra, *Fowler v Richards* (1828) 5 Russ 39; *Re Gaynor's Goods* (1869) LR 1 P & D 723.

4.66 The office of executor is similarly transmissible downwards ad infinitum, provided that the same condition be observed, viz., that each surviving executor makes a will, which is afterwards duly proved in this country by the executor therein named; and in each case the chain of representation is taken up or handed down, not only in the case of a sole executor, but of more than one, where the survivor of them dies testate[1], and appoints an executor or executors who prove his will.

1 *Re Smith's Goods* (1842) 3 Curt 31.

4.67 Where the original grant of probate was limited to certain property, a chain of representation will continue through a full grant of probate of the will of the sole or last surviving executor[1]; but there would appear to be no chain through a limited grant of probate of the will of a full executor[2]. There is no chain through a grant of probate limited to settled land[3] (issued before 14 October 1991 under the previous practice), nor through a grant to the attorney of an executor[4] (see 'Status of attorney', para. **11.65**, post).

1 *Re Beer's Goods* (1851) 2 Rob Eccl 349; see also Administration of Estates Act 1925, s. 7(4)(a).
2 *Re Bayne's Goods* (1858) 1 Sw & Tr 132; *Re Martin's Goods* (1862) 3 Sw & Tr 1: see also *Re Bridger's Goods* (1878) 4 PD 77. These were all cases of limited grants issued, under the old practice, in the estates of married women. There appears to be no decision on the point since the passing of the Administration of Estates Act 1925, but the same principle still probably applies.
3 Direction, 21 July 1936.
4 Administration of Estates Act 1925, s. 7 (see p. 746, post); *Re Dampier* (1935) May (unreported motion).

4.68   The chain of executorship is not broken by a temporary grant of administration if probate is subsequently granted[1], i.e. the person entitled to take probate as executor must have obtained a grant of probate after the temporary grant has become cessate.

1 Administration of Estates Act 1925, s. 7(3) (see p. 746, post).

4.69   When there are more executors than one, the transmission of the executorship is made through the survivor of the executors who have taken probate of the will[1]. If one executor 'A' proves with power reserved to 'B' who survives 'A' but does not prove, there is a chain of executorship through 'A' that will endure unless and until the executor to whom power was reserved applies for and obtains double probate (see also paras. **4.81** ff., post). Where, pursuant to s. 114(4) of the Supreme Court Act 1981 (see 'Addition of representative after grant has issued', paras. **7.40** ff., post), the court appoints an additional personal representative to act with an executor, the appointment of the additional personal representative does not have the effect of including him in any chain of representation (s. 114(5)). Similarly, where an executor is substituted through an order under s. 50(1)(a) of the Administration of Justice Act 1985, s. 50(2)(a) provides that the appointment does not have the effect of including him in any chain of representation[2].

1 See *Re Lorimer's Goods* (1862) Sw & Tr 471.
2 See p. 865, post.

4.70   In the case of deaths before 1 January 1926, the law as to the chain of representation was contained in the statute 'Executors' (25 Edw 3, Stat 5)[1].

1 6 Halsbury's Statutes (3rd edn) 438.

Chain through resealed colonial grant

4.71   A chain of executorship exists where the Court of Probate in a place to which the Colonial Probates Act 1892 applies has granted probate to an executor (or executors) and such grant has been resealed in England, and where subsequently the same court has granted probate of the will of the executor (or last surviving proving executor) to his executor (or executors), and this grant also has been resealed in England[1].

1 Registrar's Direction (1949) 24 February.

Chain through Northern Irish grant

4.72   Under s. 1(4) of the Administration of Estates Act 1971[1], a grant of probate made in Northern Ireland of the will of a person who died domiciled in Northern Ireland which includes a notation of such domicile is, without resealing, to be treated for the purposes of the law of England and Wales as if it had been originally made by the High Court in England and Wales. Section 7(1) of the Administration of Estates Act 1925 (chain of representation) thus applies to such grants as it applies to grants made in England and Wales.

1   See p. 799, post.

4.73   Section 1 of the Act of 1971 applies in relation to grants made before, as well as after the commencement of that Act[1]. A chain of executorship is thus capable of being created by, or continued through, a Northern Irish grant of probate of the will of a person who dies domiciled in Northern Ireland, provided that the grant contains a statement of such domicile, whether or not the grant has been resealed in England and Wales.

1   Section 1(6); see p. 800, post.

No chain through Scottish confirmation

4.74   The Administration of Estates Act 1971, by s. 12 and Schedule 2, Part I[1], abolished the resealing in Scotland of grants issued in England and Wales and vice versa, as from 1 January 1972. By s. 1(1) and (2) of this Act[2], where a person dies domiciled in Scotland a confirmation granted in respect of all or part of his estate, or a certificate of confirmation relating to one or more items of his estate, which includes in either case a notation of his domicile shall, without resealing, be treated for the purposes of the law of England and Wales (a) if in favour of executors nominate, as a grant of probate, or (b) in any other case, as a grant of letters of administration. It is, however, provided by s. 1(3) that s. 7 of the Administration of Estates Act 1925, which deals with the chain of executorship, shall not, by virtue of s. 1(2)(a), apply on the death of an executor named in a confirmation or certificate of confirmation. Thus, no chain of executorship can be created, nor can one continue, through a Scottish confirmation.

1   See p. 803, post.
2   See p. 799, post.

Transmission of executorship, how evidenced

4.75   The transmission of the executorship is evidenced by the production of each grant of probate forming a link in the chain.

Circumstances in which chain is broken

4.76   The chain of such representation is broken by

(a)   an intestacy; or
(b)   the failure of a testator to appoint an executor; or
(c)   the failure to obtain probate of a will,

but is not broken by a temporary grant of administration if probate is subsequently granted[1].

1   Administration of Estates Act 1925, s. 7(3) (p. 746, post).

4.77   Every person in the chain of representation to a testator has the same rights in respect of the real and personal estate of that testator as the original executor would have had if living; and is, to the extent to which the estate whether real or personal of that testator has come to his hands, answerable as if he were an original executor[1].

1   Administration of Estates Act 1925, s. 7(4) (p. 746, post).

Chain through grant for use and benefit of incapable executor

4.78   The chain of executorship is not broken by letters of administration (with will) of an estate granted for the use and benefit of an executor who has proved the will but has since become incapable. Where such an executor dies without recovering his capacity, the grant, if it has been impounded under the former practice, may be handed out on a district judge's or registrar's order; see paras. **17.67** ff., post.

Executor for life, or for a limited time

4.79   If the executor be appointed for his life, his office is not transmissible to his own executor; and the same observation applies to the case where an executor is appointed to act only until a specified event or contingency shall take place.

4.80   Where there is no limitation in the actual appointment of an executor, but there is a substitution of executors on the happening of certain events, the executorship is transmitted through the executor first appointed should the substituted executors die in his lifetime.

Death of acting executor where power is reserved to another

4.81   Where a grant of probate has been made to one executor, power being reserved to the other executors, on the death of the proving executor intestate or without an executor, if the non-proving executors are not willing to take a grant of double probate, their right may be cleared off by renunciation or citation to enable a grant de bonis non to be made to the person next entitled. Alternatively, application may be made under s. 116 of the Supreme Court Act 1981[1] for a grant de bonis non, limited until the non-proving executors shall obtain a grant. When the other executors obtain probate the limited de bonis non grant becomes cessate[2].

1   See p. 845, post; and para. **25.91** ff., post, as to procedure.
2   *Re Pritchard* (29 July 1937, unreported).

4.82   If the proving executor leaves an executor who proves his will there is a chain of representation which is, however, liable to be broken, as it ceases to apply if the executor to whom power was reserved afterwards exercises his power to take double probate: see Administration of Estates Act 1925, s. 7(1). The non-proving executor may be cited to accept or refuse double probate with a view to the extinction of his rights: see paras. **24.15** ff. and **24.89** ff., post.

Chain in abeyance

4.83 When the only, or surviving, proving executor has died, leaving a will appointing an executor, who for some reason does not prove his testator's will, or renounce probate thereof, a grant may be made, without any order of the district judge or registrar, to a residuary legatee or other person entitled, of the unadministered estate of the original deceased, limited until the executor shall obtain probate of his testator's will. The reasons for his failure to prove his testator's will should be set out in the oath to lead the de bonis non grant.

Executrix during widowhood, or executor for a special purpose

4.84 It would appear that an executrix appointed 'during widowhood', and dying a widow, transmits the executorship to her own executors, but only if there is no substitutional appointment of executors. But it is otherwise if she remarries; since, upon her remarriage, the probate granted to her ceases, and she has then no power of transmitting the executorship. There is no chain of executorship through an executrix appointed 'during *life* or widowhood', even though she dies without remarrying; nor when the executor is appointed to carry on a business or for any special purpose, and the grant is limited for that purpose.

How soon a will can be proved

4.85 By NCPR 6(2) it is provided that:

> 'Except with the leave of a district judge or registrar, no grant of probate or of administration with the will annexed shall issue within seven days of the death of the deceased . . .'

i.e. the probate may not issue at an earlier date than the eighth day after the death of the testator, the day of his death being excluded in the computation. Application for such leave should be made ex parte at the registry from which the grant is to issue. The nature of the evidence required under NCPR 6(2) is a matter for the discretion of the district judge or registrar considering it. An affidavit may not be necessary in all cases, but it is desirable that there should be some supporting document[1].

1 Registrar's Direction (1974) 7 February.

Expedition of grant

4.86 As to expedition of the issue of the grant, see para. **2.39**, ante.

Requirements on proving a will

The executor's oath

4.87 The proving executor swears or affirms (as the case may be) to the identity of the will and the facts of the case in a document called the oath (see NCPR 8, and Forms No. 66 ff.).

4.88 The following paragraphs set out the requirements in an order corresponding to the usual form of oath for executors.

Settling oaths

4.89   If desired, the oath may be submitted in draft for settling by the registry from which the grant is to issue. The settled draft should be lodged with the sworn papers.

4.90   Fee: for perusing and settling, £5[1].

1 NC Probate Fees Order 1981, Fee 12.

Name of deponent

4.91   Care should be taken to ascertain, and include in the oath, the true full name of the deponent, whether or not this is correctly stated in the will.

4.92   If the name of an executor or executrix is misspelt or imperfectly or incompletely stated in the will, the words 'in the will called . . . (*as in will*)' should be added to his or her correct name.

4.93   Where the discrepancy is very slight no further evidence is usually required—e.g. when the two names are identical in sound, as 'Bailey' and 'Bayley'; or, if 'George Smithson' is appointed and his full name is 'George William Smithson'. In such a case it must be sworn in the oath 'George William Smithson, in the will called George Smithson'.

Affidavit of identity

4.94   The district judge or registrar may, in cases where he considers it necessary, require proof, in addition to an assertion in the oath, of the identity of the party applying for the grant (NCPR 6(1)). This proof may take the form of an additional statement in the oath, or a separate 'affidavit of identity', which must refer to the facts as they were at the date of the will, and must dispose of the possibility of there being another person more nearly approaching the description given in the will. (Form of affidavit, No. 14.)

4.95   The following are instances of occasions when such an affidavit is usually necessary.

4.96   *Executor wrongly described in the will*: as 'the elder' or 'the younger'; by a wrong Christian name (e.g. 'William Smithson' is appointed and 'George William Smithson' applies, or 'John Robert Brown' is appointed and 'Robert John Brown' applies, or 'John Robert Brown' is appointed and 'John Richard Brown' applies); or by a wrong surname.

4.97   The use in the will of an incorrect relationship for the executor may require proof of identity, e.g. that there is no person of the relationship stated bearing the name used, or who could have been intended as the executor (see also paras. **4.184** ff., post).

4.98   *Executor imperfectly described in the will*: as 'Colonel Brooks', 'Mr Midwinter', 'Dr Carn'.

4.99   Where the will appoints 'my wife', without giving the name of the wife, the oath should include a statement (if it be the fact) that the deponent was the lawful wife of the deceased at the date of the will; and corresponding wording used if 'my husband' be appointed.

Change of name

4.100 If an executor has changed his name since the date of the will, he should be described in the oath as 'A.B., formerly and in the will called C.D.', and the oath should include evidence in support of the change of name. If the change has been evidenced by a Deed Poll, particulars of this should be given, and the Deed Poll should be produced.

4.101 Where a change of name has been effected by constant use and repute but no Deed Poll has been executed, the oath should state when the change occurred and establish that the deponent has permanently abandoned the old name and uses, and intends to continue to use, only the new name.

4.102 If an executrix has married or remarried since the date of the will, her description should be followed by the words 'formerly ——, spinster', or 'formerly ——, widow', as the case may be.

Address of deponent

4.103 *The true place of residence* (even if only temporary) of every deponent to the oath must be inserted[1]. The full postal address (including the county and post-code) should be used. A *club* or *hotel* will not suffice unless it be the actual residence, in which case this must be sworn to.

1 RSC Order 41, r. 1(4), applied by NCPR 3.

4.104 When an address care of a bank or other accommodation address is given it must be stated in the oath or certified by the solicitor that the deponent has no permanent or better address[1].

1 Direction (1941) 22 July.

4.105 It is not necessary to include the former address of an executor, except where he is imperfectly described in the will and the address is relevant to the question of his identity.

4.106 In the case of a grantee administering the estate in his professional capacity (e.g. a solicitor or a chartered accountant), the professional address of the grantee may be given in the oath and in this event such address will appear in the grant[1].

1 Registrar's Direction (1960) 26 October.

Description of deponent

4.107 The occupation (or, if none, the description) of every deponent must be given in the oath[1]. If the deponent has retired, he should be described by his former occupation prefixed by the word 'retired'. The term 'of independent means' is not accepted: if the deponent has no occupation he should be described as 'of no occupation'[2]. The descriptions 'gentleman', 'esquire' and certain other vague descriptions are not accepted. The description 'Knight' or 'Peer' is sufficient.

1 RSC Order 41, r. 1(4), applied by NCPR 3.
2 Registrar's Direction (1936) 26 May.

4.108   Where a female deponent has an occupation this should be given[1]. If she has no occupation, she should be described as spinster, married woman (or wife of   ), widow, or, if divorced, as a single woman or a feme sole[2].

1 Secretary's Circular, 12 May 1967.
2 The expression feme sole is accepted, except in cases where the title to the grant depends on the status (Registrar's Direction (1963) 20 May).

4.109   The wife or widow of a Knight or Baronet may be described as 'Lady' or 'Dame' unless she has a higher title in her own right[1].

1 Secretary's Circular, 2 March 1955.

Order of executors

4.110   Grants of probate normally name the executors in the order in which they appear in the will. If it is desired to vary this order, the consents of the executors to such variation should preferably be lodged, although if this is not done the grant will nevertheless issue showing the executors in the order in which they appear in the oath.

Description of documents to be proved

4.111   Where two or more wills are together to be proved as the will they are described in the oath as 'the true and original last will and testament as contained in the paper writings marked A, B and C' (as the case may be).

4.112   Where an official copy of a will is to be proved, it is referred to in the oath as 'a sealed and certified copy (*or* an official copy) of the last will and testament'.

4.113   Where the original will is not available and the court has ordered a certain document to be proved in its stead, this document is referred to in the oath as the will 'as contained in a copy (*or* draft) thereof', or 'as contained in the exhibit to the affidavit of   sworn on the —— day of —— 19—', as the case may be, in accordance with the order of the court.

4.114   Where certain documents are to be incorporated with a will or codicil, the will or codicil is described in the oath as 'contained in paper writings marked A, B and C' (as the case may be).

4.115   Where a codicil is proved with the will the words 'with a codicil thereto' must be added after 'last will and testament'.

4.116   Where there is more than one codicil the number must be stated in the oath.

Codicil proved after probate of will

4.117 Where a codicil is to be proved after probate has been granted of the will, the oath refers to it as 'a codicil to the will proved on the —— day of —— at the Registry'.

Marking testamentary documents

4.118 The executor, and the person before whom the oath is sworn, must 'mark' the will and codicils or other testamentary papers by signing their names upon these documents (r. 10). Each document should be marked, but when two documents are written on the same sheet of paper, one marking is sufficient. It is not necessary that the exhibit clause, required on all other occasions when a document (including a will) is exhibited to an affidavit, should be endorsed.

4.119 There is no official requirement that the marking should be made on any particular part of the document, but it should wherever possible be kept away from the text of the will. If there is insufficient space on the face of the document it is often preferable to mark the reverse.

4.120 The marking of a foreign will must be made on the original or copy thereof lodged for probate and not on the translation into English.

4.121 The district judge or registrar may give permission for a facsimile copy to be marked in lieu of the original (r. 10(2)). Application for such permission should be made in advance to the Probate Department or district registrar, as the case may be. The facsimile copy is supplied by the applicant.

4.122 Where permission has been given for a copy to be marked, the oath should recite that the document marked is 'a facsimile copy of the true and original last will and testament'. Both the original will and the copy must be lodged with the papers to lead the grant.

Name of testator. Alias

4.123 A grant should always issue in the true name of the deceased. The inclusion of one or more alternative names (known as alias names) may be necessary because the deceased held assets in a name other than the true full name, or for some other sufficient reason.

'Where it is sought to describe the deceased in a grant by some name in addition to his true name, the applicant shall depose to the true name of the deceased and shall specify some part of the estate which was held in the other name, or give any other reason for the inclusion of the other name in the grant.' (r. 9.)

Change of name

4.124 In the absence of evidence of a change of name, or of any discrepancy in the papers lodged, it is assumed that the name of the deceased given in the sworn documents is the true name. A surname may, however, be abandoned, and another adopted or assumed, in various ways; e.g. by succession or elevation to a title of nobility, by change of name by Royal Licence, or simply by constant use and repute. Subject to any statutory restriction, the law of this country allows any person to assume and use any name, provided that its use is not calculated to deceive and inflict pecuniary loss[1].

1   *Fendall v Goldsmid* (1877) 2 PD 263; *Earl Cowley v Countess Cowley* [1901] AC 450, HL.

4.125   The effect of a Deed Poll is merely to record a change of name in a solemn form which will tend to perpetuate the evidence of the change. A change of name by an adult must involve a conscious decision on his part that he wishes to change his name and be generally known by the new name[1].

1   Dictum of Buckley J, in *Re T (otherwise H) an infant* [1963] Ch 238, [1962] 3 All ER 970, in which case he was dealing with a mother's attempt to change her infant child's surname without the knowledge or consent of the father: see also *Y v Y* [1973] Fam 147, [1973] 2 All ER 574, as to change of child's surname in similar circumstances.

4.126   Where a testator has changed his name since making the will and the change has been recorded by a Deed Poll, he should be described in the oath as 'AB, formerly CD', and it should be recited that he changed his name from CD to AB by Deed Poll, giving its date. The Deed Poll should be produced.

4.127   In the case of a change by use and repute where there has been no Deed Poll, the oath should show when the name was changed and establish that the change was complete and final, and amounted to a total abandonment of the former name and the permanent acquisition of the new name for all purposes. In cases of doubt whether there has been such a complete abandonment of the former name, it is considered in probate practice that the true name remains that in which the birth was registered or, in the case of the surname of a married woman, that of her husband, and the grant should issue in that name, the reputed name being shown as an alias, where necessary.

Will in incorrect name

4.128   If the heading of the will does not give the true full name, in order to deal with the discrepancy it should be sworn in the oath that the true name of the deceased was AB, but that he made (and, if it be so, executed) his will in the name of CD.

4.129   Where the heading of a will gives the true and full name of the testator, but the signature omits names or initials, the grant is issued in the true name alone, unless it is shown in the oath or by affidavit that an alias is required (e.g. for the purpose of administration of assets standing in another name).

4.130   If, apart from any question of such omission, the actual names or initials differ, the true name should be specifically stated in the oath and it should be sworn that the signature is the usual signature of the testator or the discrepancy otherwise accounted for.

4.131   In each of the foregoing cases, the oath must state specifically which is the true name[1].

1   Registrar's Direction (1931) 27 March.

Alias name required in grant

4.132   In cases, whether of testacy or intestacy, where the deceased held property standing in a name other than his true full name, an alias may be included in the grant to facilitate the administration. The oath should depose specifically to the true name and include a statement that the deceased held property in the alternative name or names: at least one item of property in each alternative name must be specified. If the inclusion of an alias is desired for some other reason, this must be deposed to.

Wording of oath

4.133 Whenever an alias is necessary the oath should describe the deceased by his true name, followed by the alternatives (i.e. 'AB otherwise CD'), and the requirements of NCPR 9 (above) must be complied with.

4.134 As an alternative to including the facts in the oath, a separate affidavit of alias may be lodged (Form No. 15).

4.135 In cases of foreign domicile, the name given in the proceedings accompanying the copy will (provided that such name is shown in full and not by initials) may be accepted for the grant unless an alias is shown to be necessary, e.g. because the deceased held securities in England in different names.

4.136 If the testator is described in the will as the 'elder', but has not so subscribed, such description is not to be inserted.

4.137 If the testator is described in the will as the 'younger', but does not so subscribe, he should, notwithstanding, be described as the 'younger', or 'heretofore the younger', as the case may be.

Address of testator

4.138 The residential address of the testator at the time of his death should be given in the oath. The full postal address should be given. If the address given in the oath is a hotel or club it should be confirmed in the oath that it is a residential hotel or club and the deceased resided there.

4.139 Should the address differ from the place of residence stated in the will or codicil, the testator should be identified with the address given in the testamentary document of latest date, by stating that he was 'formerly of' that address, or by accounting for any erroneous description, or former description, of the address, appearing in the will.

4.140 Where the will or codicil contains a temporary address, the testator is described as 'of' his residential address, and 'temporarily of' or 'formerly temporarily of' the address given in the will or codicil.

4.141 If the will or codicil contains no address of the testator, and he is described therein as of, or formerly of, a certain regiment, or of, or formerly of, a certain ship, or by a military or other service number, such description should be included in the oath.

4.142 Where the place of residence of the deceased person cannot be sworn to, the best address available (including an accommodation address) is accepted. But in these circumstances, on an application for a grant, it should be sworn that no better address can be given[1].

---

1 Registrar's Direction (1925) 1 August.

Number of addresses allowed in grant

4.143   Normally only the last residential address of the deceased as shown in the oath will be inserted in the grant. If more addresses are required in the grant, the additional addresses must be deposed to in the oath and a sufficient reason for inclusion of such additional addresses must be given. In no cases will more than four addresses in all be allowed[1].

1   Direction (1939) 23 January.

Description of testator

4.144   Titles of nobility and ecclesiastical titles should be stated in the oath.

4.145   It is not necessary to include in the oath the marital status of the deceased except where this is relevant to the applicant's title to a grant (e.g. for the purpose of clearing off prior classes in administration cases).

Date of death

4.146   The exact date of death, where this is known, must be given in the oath.

4.147   If the *fact* of death is certain, but the exact date unknown, the oath should state that the deceased 'was last seen alive (*or* last known to be alive) on the day of   , and that his dead body was found on the   day of   '[1].

1   *Re Long-Sutton's Estate* [1912] P 97.

4.148   If no direct evidence of death is available but the applicant merely presumes the person to be dead, e.g. from the fact and circumstances of his disappearance, an order giving the applicant leave to swear to the death must be obtained. For the circumstances in which such an order is necessary, and generally as to the practice, see paras. **25.17** ff., post.

4.149   Where an order for leave to swear death has been obtained, the oath should state that the deceased died 'on or since' the date specified in the order, and include particulars of the date and effect of the order and state by whom it was made. For form of oath, see No. 117, which should be adapted as necessary.

4.150   Orders for leave to swear death are retained in the registry. The order may be inspected by the solicitor, who may take notes to enable the particulars to be included in the oath[1].

1   Registrar's Direction (1952) 25 January.

4.151   The date of death in a grant is not prima facie evidence of death[1].

1   *Moons v De Bernales* (1826) 1 Russ 301; *Thompson v Donaldson* (1799) 3 Esp 63.

Evidence of death. Armed forces of the Crown

4.152   *Definite date.* When a certificate from the Ministry of Defence has been received by the next of kin stating death to have occurred on a specific date, on such date being sworn to in the oath no further evidence of death will be required.

4.153 *Indefinite date.* When a certificate, as above, notifies that the deceased was 'missing, believed killed, etc.' or died or was killed 'on or since' a given date or is presumed to have been killed, or in any case where a definite date of death is not, or cannot, be given, the certificate received by the next of kin from the Service Department should be lodged with the papers to lead to a grant[1].

1 Direction (1943) 15 July.

Certificates under Merchant Shipping Acts 1970 and 1979

4.154 The address of the Registry of Shipping and Seamen is P.O. Box 165, Cardiff CF4 5FU (tel. 01222 747333). Evidence of death is provided by the Registrar General of Shipping and Seamen and death certificates are issued in the following instances:

(a) known deaths or losses in United Kingdom ships;
(b) known deaths or losses of citizens of the United Kingdom and Colonies in other ships which call at United Kingdom ports;
(c) known deaths abroad of seamen employed in United Kingdom ships.

4.155 *In respect of deaths occurring before 1 January 1980.* Regulations 3 or 4 and 5 of the Merchant Shipping (Returns of Births and Deaths) Regulations 1972 apply and a certificate in Form RBD6 is issued.

4.156 *In respect of deaths occurring on and after 1 January 1980.* Regulations 3 or 4 and 5 of the Merchant Shipping (Returns of Births and Deaths) Regulations 1979 apply and in those cases a certificate in Form RBD6a is issued.

4.157 Any of these certificates will be accepted as proof of death. All such deaths are recorded in the Marine Register of Deaths at the General Register Office in London, Edinburgh or Belfast and the Isle of Man, as appropriate.

4.158 In cases of presumed death the Registrar General of Shipping and Seamen will issue on request a certified extract from the list of crew on Form RBD7 for merchant ships and Form RBD8 for fishing vessels.

4.159 This is a certificate that the person named was recorded on the copy of the List of Crew required to be maintained ashore by Regulation 16 of the Merchant Shipping (Crew Agreements, Lists of Crew and Discharge of Seamen) Regulations 1972 and by Regulation 15 of the Merchant Shipping (Crew Agreements, Lists of Crew and Discharge of Seamen) (Fishing Vessels) Regulations 1972 and required to be delivered into official custody by Regulations 17 and 16 respectively of these Regulations.

4.160 *In respect of deaths presumed to have occurred before 1 January 1980.* Forms RBD7 and RBD8 will also contain a certificate that the Registrar General of Shipping and Seamen has no information that the person named survived the loss. This certificate will only be given after information has been obtained from the owners, and, if appropriate, from the Consul or other official at or near the place the ship was reported lost. If a body has been landed ashore and a post-mortem examination made by the authorities in that country the certificate will be endorsed as to that fact on the reverse in red ink and imprinted with the office stamp of the General Register Office of Shipping and Seamen. Only certificates so endorsed will be accepted as proof of death. If they are not so endorsed they will be referred by the probate registry to the Registrar General of Shipping and Seamen for confirmation. If confirmed, they will be accepted as proof of death.

4.161 In extremely urgent cases, confirmation will be applied for by telephone. In certain other cases where there may be a supposition of death, although it may not be possible to issue one of the certificates described above, an Inquiry into death can sometimes be held under s. 61 of the Merchant Shipping Act 1970 as amended. Copies of the Report of such an Inquiry may be obtained by the next of kin from the Registry of Shipping and Seamen. Where such a Report is available, it should be referred to the district judge or registrar for his directions whether death has been sufficiently established or whether an application for an order for leave to swear death (see paras. **25.17** ff., post) is necessary.

4.162   *In respect of deaths presumed to have occurred on or after 1 January 1980.* Certified extracts from the Crew Lists will rarely be requested. If there was sufficient evidence available to enable a coroner or statutory enquiry to conclude that death had occurred upon the loss of a ship, then death will be registered and will be included in the class of case mentioned in para. **4.154** at (a) above. A certified extract on Form RBD7 or Form RBD8 in respect of a death on or after 1 January 1980 will, therefore, be no more than evidence that the person named was on board the ship at the time of its loss. It will not itself be evidence that death occurred as a result of the loss of the ship[1].

1 Registrar's Direction (1980) 14 April.

Offshore installations

4.163   Under the Offshore Installations (Logbooks and Registration of Death) Regulations 1972, when a person dies, or is lost in circumstances such that it is reasonable to believe he has died:

(a)   on or from an offshore installation or a lifeboat, life raft, etc. belonging to such an installation; or

(b)   in the neighbourhood of such an installation while engaged in any operation connected therewith,

then, if the death or loss is not required to be registered under the Merchant Shipping Acts, a return of the death or loss is sent to the Registrar General of Shipping and Seamen; a copy thereof is registered by the appropriate Registrar General of Births and Deaths, according to the ordinary residence of the deceased, in the Marine Register; and a certified copy of the entry may be obtained.

4.164   Such returns are the equivalent of the returns made by the master of a ship under the Merchant Shipping Acts, and certificates issued as above may be accepted as proof of death[1].

1 Registrar's Direction (1975) 1 May.

Certificate issued by government departments, etc.

4.165   Certificates of death, and of presumed death, issued from the register kept by the Secretary of State for Trade under s. 55 of the Civil Aviation Act 1949, and deposited with the Registrar General are accepted as evidence of death for the purpose of issuing grants of representation[1].

1 Registrar's Direction (1953) 15 April.

4.166 Certificates of presumed death issued by the Ministry of Defence, and the former India Office, Colonial Office and Commonwealth Relations Office are accepted as sufficient evidence of death[1].

1 President's Direction (1944) 12 May; Registrar's Direction (1949) September.

4.167 It is within the discretion of the Senior District Judge to accept a certificate of death or of presumption of death as sufficient evidence of death notwithstanding that such certificate may not come within the definition of certificates which can be accepted in accordance with existing practice and directions[1].

1 President's Direction (1943) 19 March.

Place of death

4.168 The place of death is no longer included in a grant of representation, and it is unnecessary to state it in the oath.

Age of testator

4.169 The age of the testator must be stated in the oath. If the exact age is not known, then a best estimate should be given[1].

1 *Practice Direction* [1981] 2 All ER 832, [1981] 1 WLR 1185.

Domicile

4.170 Unless otherwise directed by a district judge or registrar, every oath to lead a grant of representation must state where the deceased died domiciled[1].

1 NCPR 8(2). The notional domicile assumed in certain circumstances for the purposes of inheritance tax under s. 267 of the Inheritance Tax Act 1984 (see p. 909, post) is irrelevant for probate purposes: the domicile to be sworn to in the probate documents, and on which the application for the grant should be based, is the deceased's actual domicile at the time of death.

4.171 This requirement is necessitated (among other reasons) by the provisions of ss. 2 and 3 of the Administration of Estates Act 1971[1], which give extended validity to a grant in the estate of a person who dies domiciled in England and Wales provided that the grant includes a statement of such domicile (see paras. **18.23** ff., post).

1 See p. 800, post.

4.172 Where the deceased died domiciled in England and Wales, the expression 'domiciled in England and Wales' should be used, and the statement in the grant will be in this form. If a domicile in England or in Wales is deposed to, the notation in the grant will nevertheless be 'domiciled in England and Wales'.

4.173 For the practice as to a grant where the deceased died domiciled out of England and Wales, see Chap. 12.

Settled land

4.174 Where the testator died on or after 1 January 1926, in every oath the deponent must swear to the best of his knowledge, information and belief whether there was land vested in the deceased which was settled previously to his death (and not by his will) and which remained settled land notwithstanding his death[1].

1 NCPR 8(3).

4.175 For the practice in relation to settled land, see Chap. 10.

Recitation of judgment in a probate action

4.176 When a will has been pronounced for in a probate action, an office copy of the judgment must be lodged with the papers. The following statement should be included in the oath:

> 'That the Honourable Sir . . ., one of the Judges of the Chancery Division, by judgment dated the   day   of   , 19   , in an action entitled "A. against B." pronounced for the force and validity of the said will.'

4.177 Where the court has pronounced for a will or codicil as contained in a copy, draft or reconstruction thereof, the wording of the decree should be followed in the oath: see Form No. 72.

4.178 As to the practice on an application for a full grant following a grant pending suit, see paras. **11.323** and **11.324**, post.

Order on summons

4.179 When an order on summons has been made, the following wording should be used:

> 'That by order of Mr Justice (*or* District Judge *or* Mr District Probate Registrar)   of this Division dated the   day of   19   , it was ordered that   .'

County court judge's order

4.180 When a probate action has been tried in a county court the county court sends a certificate of the judgment to the Principal Registry or a district probate registry. The particulars and effect of the judgment should be recited in the oath.

4.181 The order of the county court judge is not recited in the grant but the grant is noted 'By order of the County Court at   dated the   day of   19 .'

Order for omission of part of will

4.182 If a judgment or order directs the omission from probate of part of the will, a typewritten copy thereof, omitting such part, must be lodged at the registry for the fiat of the district judge or registrar to be written in the margin of the copy—'Let the will (and codicil) be proved in accordance with this copy in pursuance of judge's [or district judge's or registrar's] order dated   19   ', and signed by the probate officer or district probate registrar before photography. A copy of the judgment or order must be lodged with the papers, and is filed with the will[1].

1 *Practice Direction* [1968] 2 All ER 592, [1968] 1 WLR 987.

4.183 As to orders for omission of part of a will, see paras. **3.249–3.272**, ante.

Relationship

4.184 Except in cases where the relationship of the applicant to the deceased is relevant to the question of the former's identity or entitlement to a grant, it need not be stated in the oath.

4.185 Thus, if the full correct name of the executor or beneficiary appears in the appointment in the will it is normally unnecessary to state his relationship to the deceased.

4.186 The following are examples of the circumstances in which the applicant's relationship to the deceased must be stated:

(a) where the appointment of the executor (or beneficiary) is by relationship and not by name (e.g. 'I appoint my son as sole executor'; or 'I leave all my estate to my wife (without naming her)');

(b) where there is some discrepancy or possible ambiguity in the appointment, and inclusion of the relationship assists in establishing the identity of the applicant;

(c) in cases where the applicant's title to a grant depends entirely on his relationship, i.e. where application for administration (with will) is made by a person entitled to the estate undisposed of by the will. Thus, in a case where a will appoints no executor and there is no gift of the residuary estate, the widow of the deceased must depose that she is 'the lawful widow of the deceased and the only person now entitled to the undisposed-of estate', or as the case may be.

4.187 If a testator appoints 'my wife' an executor, and does not name her in any part of the will, an addition should be made to the oath, stating that the applicant was the lawful wife of the testator at the date of the will. If this has been omitted from the oath, a certificate by the solicitor will be accepted if it states that he has seen the marriage certificate, and that it confirms the claim. This applies, mutatis mutandis, in the case of the appointment of 'my husband'.

Executor: capacity in which application made

4.188 The 'capacity' in which proving executors claim the grant is worded, in the oath, in the manner shown in the following list:

When one executor only appointed	'The sole executor.'
When one executrix only appointed	'The sole executrix.'
When executors are all males	'The executors.'
When executors are all females	'The executrixes.'
When some are male and some female	'The executors.'
When one or more of executors appointed has died	'The surviving executor(s)'[1].
When one or more of executors appointed renounces	'One (*or two etc.*) of the executors'[2].
When power is reserved to any executors (*see para.* **4.51** *as to notice to the executor or executors to whom power is reserved and statement in oath*)	'One (*or two etc.*) of the executors.'
When an executor is appointed on attaining the age of [21] years[3]	'The said A. B. having attained the age of [21] years.'

An appointment during life or widowhood, there being also a general executor.	'But as to the said A. B. during life or widowhood.'
When powers of executor are limited to dealing with English property	'The executor for England.'
When an executor is appointed during life, and on his death another is appointed, the latter is described as	'The executor substituted.'
When there is no limitation, for life or otherwise, in the appointment of an executor but other executors are substituted on death, the first-named executor, if he applies is described as	'An executor named in the said will'[4].
When there is no limitation in the actual appointment of executors, and there is also a substitution of executors on certain events	'The executors named in the said will as therein mentioned'[5].
When a codicil cites the death of an executor, or cancels an appointment in the will	'The executors named in the said will.'

1 Where this description applies, it should be so sworn in the oath.
2 The renunciation (see Form No. 183) must be filed.
3 It should be noted that although the age of majority was reduced to 18 with effect from 1 January 1970 (see Family Law Reform Act 1969, s. 1 (p. 789, post)), references in wills, whenever made, to a specific age are unaffected. As to the construction of expressions such as 'full age', 'minor', 'infancy', 'minority', etc. when used in wills, see para. **11.114**, post.
4 Registrar's Direction (1910) 20 June.
5 Registrar's Direction (1912) 25 April.

Individual and company executors

4.189   For procedure and wording of the oath in cases where an individual and a company not being a trust corporation are appointed executors, see para. **4.39**, ante.

Partnership firm, or person holding official position

4.190   For practice, and wording for oath, see paras. **4.41–4.47**.

Trust corporation

4.191   Where a trust corporation is appointed as executor, probate may be granted to the corporation solely, or jointly with an individual: see Chap. 9.

Public Trustee named as co-executor

4.192   Where an executor applies for probate of a will in which the Public Trustee is also appointed an executor, it must be ascertained whether the Public Trustee wishes to act before a grant can be made to the other executor alone[1]. As to grant to the Public Trustee, see paras. **9.54** ff., post.

1 Registrar's Direction (1920) 18 November.

Clearing off executors

4.193   Where a will contains an appointment of an executor, but in certain events (e.g. his predecease, or unwillingness to act etc.) another is substituted, then, on an application for probate by the latter, the oath should describe him as 'the executor named in the will, A. B. mentioned in the said will having died in the lifetime of the deceased' (*or* having renounced probate, etc. as the case may be).

4.194 If power is to be reserved to one or more executors, a statement to that effect should be made in the oath. The oath must state that notice of the application for probate has been given to the executor or executors to whom power is to be reserved, unless the district judge or registrar directs otherwise or dispenses with the giving of such notice or the appointment is by reference to their being partners in a firm and one (or more) of the other partners is applying (see para. **4.51**, ante).

4.195 Where two or more persons are appointed as executors by a will and the identity of at least one of the executors is established but the identity of the other or others is not, on an application being made for a grant of probate by the identified executor it is not normally necessary to determine the identity of the remaining executors or their entitlement to a grant. Application may be made to the district judge or registrar, by letter, under r. 27(3) to dispense with giving notice to the executor or executors to whom power is to be reserved. The executor applying for the grant must, however, include full details relating to the executors in the oath, as this information could be material on an application for a subsequent grant to the estate[1].

1 Registrar's Direction (1977) 6 December.

4.196 Where one executor is a minor the oath should show that power is reserved to him on attaining the age of 18 (see also para. **4.32**, ante). As to grant where the sole executor is a minor, see paras. **4.30–4.31** and **11.137** and **11.138**, post.

4.197 On an application for probate by an executor, the fact that another executor has renounced need not be sworn to in the oath but it is of practical assistance to the registries if it is. The renunciation must be filed.

Amount of estate in oath

4.198 Except in those cases where, pursuant to the Capital Transfer Tax (Delivery of Accounts) Regulations 1981, as amended (see Chap. 8), the need to deliver an account for the purposes of inheritance tax or capital transfer tax has been dispensed with, the oath must state the actual *gross* value of the estate to be covered by the grant, as indicated by the Inland Revenue account.

4.199 In those cases in which an Inland Revenue account is not required to be delivered, it will be sufficient to state in the oath to lead the grant the brackets into which the estate falls. Every oath must contain a statement by the applicant as follows:

'To the best of my knowledge, information and belief the gross estate passing under the grant does not exceed/amounts to* £   and that the net estate does not exceed/amounts to* £   [and that this is not a case in which an Inland Revenue Account is required to be delivered]*'.

The alternatives marked with an asterisk should be deleted as appropriate[1].

1 *Practice Direction* [1981] 2 All ER 832, [1981] 1 WLR 1185. In relation to a death prior to 13 March 1975, a sworn Inland Revenue affidavit is still required.

4.200 The relevant dates and gross limits are:

Death on or after	*Gross limit*
6 April 1995	£145,000
1 April 1991	£125,000
1 April 1990	£115,000
1 April 1989	£100,000
1 April 1987	£70,000
1 April 1983	£40,000
1 April 1981	£25,000

and the relevant net limits and court fees payable are:

Exceeding	*Not exceeding*	*Court fee*
£——	£10,000	(no fee)
£10,000	£25,000	£40
£25,000	£40,000	£80
£40,000	£70,000	£150
£70,000	£100,000	£215
£100,000	£200,000	£300

4.201   The oath may not, in any event, be sworn with the amount of the estate left blank; nor may the amount subsequently be altered without re-swearing.

4.202   A grant in the estate of a person who died domiciled in England and Wales which includes a statement of such domicile is proof of title in Scotland and Northern Ireland as well as in England and Wales[1]. The amount to be sworn in the oath is accordingly the gross value of the estate in the United Kingdom (i.e. in England and Wales, Scotland and Northern Ireland).

1 Administration of Estates Act 1971, ss. 2–3 (see p. 800, post).

4.203   Where the deceased died domiciled in Scotland or Northern Ireland or outside the United Kingdom, it is necessary to include in the Inland Revenue account details of the estate in Great Britain (i.e. in England and Wales and in Scotland), but care must be taken to exclude the value of any Scottish assets in arriving at the figure to be sworn in the oath: this should state that the amount shown is the gross value of the estate 'in England and Wales'. As to the limitation which now appears in a grant made in England and Wales in the estate of a person dying domiciled in Scotland or Northern Ireland, see para. **12.23**, post.

4.204   As to the estate on which probate fees are assessed, see paras. **4.258** ff., post.

4.205   An alteration made by the Capital Taxes Office in the amount of the estate shown in the Inland Revenue account does not normally necessitate amendment of the figure sworn in the oath.

4.206   Amounts in all documents lodged at the probate registries should be expressed in decimal currency whatever the date of death.

Estate not fully ascertained

4.207   It is most important that the value of the estate should, at the outset, be established, but in special circumstances an application is entertained for a grant merely showing property 'so far as can at present be ascertained'. (See para. **8.18**, post.)

4.208 Where it is desired to show the amount 'so far as can at present be ascertained', the figure sworn in the oath should so far as possible be an estimate of the final value of the whole estate, and not merely the total of those assets whose value is known.

Nil estate

4.209 Where it is sought to obtain a grant of representation in respect of a deceased person who left no estate, the oath must include a statement of the purpose for which the grant is required[1].

1 Registrar's Direction (1932) 30 November.

4.210 It is contrary to principle for the court to make a grant of representation in the estate of a person who died domiciled out of England and Wales leaving no assets within the jurisdiction[1].

1 *Aldrich v A-G* [1968] P 281, [1968] 1 All ER 345, in which the grant was sought to enable the applicant to establish his claim to be the father of the deceased.

Estate for purposes of probate or administration

4.211 For the purposes of probate or administration, the local situation of property and the validity of debts and incumbrances for ascertaining the net value of an estate, are determined according to the general principles of English law, any rules or concessions which are peculiar to inheritance tax or capital transfer tax (e.g. under Double Taxation Conventions) being ignored. Thus, all property forming part of the estate must be included, notwithstanding that it may be exempt from inheritance tax or capital transfer tax.

Community of property

4.212 Where, by the law of the place of domicile of the deceased, community of property exists between the deceased and a surviving spouse, the grant will be in respect of the whole estate, but the court fee will be payable in respect of half of it only. The following concluding paragraph to the oath is appropriate and should be used: 'the whole of the estate in England and Wales (or in the United Kingdom, if appropriate) in respect of which a grant is required amounts to the sum of £—— to the best of my knowledge, information and belief; and that £—— (half) ——of that sum has accrued to the surviving spouse by reason of the existence of community of property under the law of the place of domicile of the said deceased at the date of the marriage'[1].

1 Registrar's Direction (1953) 5 May (amended (1968) 11 April). It should be noted, however, that the question whether there is community of property between spouses is not invariably determined by the law of the place of domicile at the date of marriage: see Dicey and Morris, *Conflict of Laws*.

Reversionary interests

4.213 The value of all reversionary interests owned by the deceased must be included in the estate. Unless otherwise expressly provided, the reversionary interest vests absolutely on the death of the testator[1].

1 *Chaffers v Abell* (1839) 3 Jur 577; *Packham v Gregory* (1845) 4 Hare 396; *Re Bennett's Trust* (1857) 3 K & J 280.

4.214   In relation to deaths occurring after 12 March 1975, reversionary interests are, save in certain circumstances, 'excluded property' for the purpose of inheritance tax or capital transfer tax. Nevertheless, the value of any such interest must still be included in the estate for probate purposes. (See also para. **4.261**, post.)

Civil servants' gratuities

4.215   A gratuity granted under the Superannuation Act 1972 on the *death* of a civil servant is, unless a nomination has been effected (see para. **1.64**, ante), included in the amount given in the oath, although such gratuities are not liable to payment of inheritance tax or capital transfer tax or probate fees[1]. However, under the Principal Civil Service Scheme 1972, and Amendment Schemes, the lump sum payable on a civil servant's *ordinary retirement* is receivable as of right. Therefore, in the rare case of a civil servant dying after retirement but before the lump sum has been paid, it will it seems be liable to inheritance tax or capital transfer tax as part of his estate. Gratuities to the personal representatives of deceased school teachers granted under the Teachers Superannuation Acts are part of the estate for the purposes both of inheritance tax or capital transfer tax[2] and of fees. On 1 October 1969 the employees of the Post Office ceased to be civil servants. Lump sums payable in respect of the death of such employees on and after that date are payable as of right under the Post Office Staff Superannuation Scheme, and not under the Superannuation Act 1972. Unless the employee had given a direction to the trustees of the Scheme that the sum should be applied at the absolute discretion of the trustees, the lump sum is part of his estate, and should be included both for the purpose of inheritance tax or capital transfer tax and of probate fees.

1   Direction, 10 November 1910, as revised, 1958. See also NC Probate Fees Order 1981, para. 4.
2   *A-G v Quixley* (1929) 98 LJKB 652.

Property not included

4.216   Since the oath relates only to property passing under the grant, the amount there sworn to should not include property which, although part of the aggregated 'estate' for the purpose of inheritance tax or capital transfer tax, passes otherwise than under the will or intestacy of the deceased, e.g. property passing under a nomination, property passing under a settlement (even if the deceased had, and exercised by his will, a special power of appointment), property held on joint tenancy, and gifts inter vivos. Even where the deceased had a *general* power of appointment, the property should be included only if (1) the power has been exercised by his will, or (2) the property belongs to the estate in default of appointment[1].

1   *O'Grady v Wilmot* [1916] 2 AC 231, HL.

4.217   Payments made under the Social Security Act 1975 in connection with the death of the deceased resulting from an industrial injury, and damages under the Fatal Accidents Act 1976[1], are not included in the amount shown in the oath, but damages awarded under the Law Reform (Miscellaneous Provisions) Act 1934[2] are part of the deceased's estate and liable to inheritance tax or capital transfer tax[3].

1   This Act is a consolidating measure and does not apply to any cause of action arising on a death before 1 September 1976: where a death occurs before that date, the similar provisions of the Fatal Accidents Acts 1846 to 1959, apply.
2   17 Halsbury's Statutes (4th edn) 312; see also p. 765, post.
3   *Feay v Barnwell* [1938] 1 All ER 31.

4.218 The amount sworn to in the oath should not include property which was vested in the deceased as a trustee and not beneficially.

4.219 The amount of the death grant payable by virtue of s. 32 of the Social Security Act 1975 is not regarded as part of the estate for any purpose[1].

1 Registrar's Direction (1950) 18 September.

Notice to Treasury Solicitor

4.220 In any case in which it appears that the Crown is or may be beneficially interested in the estate of a deceased person, notice of the intended application for a grant must be given by the applicant to the Treasury Solicitor. The district judge or registrar may direct that no grant shall issue within 28 days after such notice has been given[1].

1 NCPR 38.

Swearing

4.221 The oath should be sworn or affirmed, if in England and Wales, before a solicitor who holds a current practising certificate, a Commissioner for Oaths or other person authorised to administer oaths (see paras. **22.32** ff., post as to the persons authorised to administer oaths in and at places outside England and Wales).

Copies of wills

4.222 The copy of the will to be annexed to the grant is normally made in the registry by a facsimile reproduction.

4.223 In certain special cases, however, an engrossment or a 'fiat copy' of the will must be lodged by the solicitor.

When copies of wills are necessary

4.224 Where alterations in a will have not been properly set up or the will has been altered after execution; in certain foreign cases, where the will is unsuitable for facsimile reproduction; and in special cases directed by the district judge or registrar, it is necessary to file a copy of the will[1]. Certain wills drawn on paper unsuitable for facsimile reproduction on account of size, and any codicil thereto, must be accompanied by an engrossment copy[2]. The copy is examined in the registry and is then photographed instead of the will (see also 'Fiat copies', below).

1 NCPR 11.
2 The attention of practitioners is drawn to the memorandum issued by the Principal Registry, and published in the *Law Society's Gazette* for February 1956, which is as follows: 'All official copies of wills, whether for insertion in probates or for issue when bespoken afterwards, are now photographed, the system in use in the Principal Registry since 1931 having been extended to all other registries. It would be of assistance to the Probate Registry if solicitors would always bear in mind, when preparing wills, that it is desirable that they should be prepared in a form which lends itself easily to photographic reproduction. The ideal is for the will to be foolscap size, typed in black on white paper. Size of type is not in itself important, as a will in this form can be reproduced without reduction in size or loss of contrast.' A reminder to those preparing wills of the format preferred by the probate registries in order to facilitate facsimile copying appeared in (1974) 124 NLJ 1101.

4.225 Where some of the documents to be proved are not suitable for facsimile reproduction, normally a copy of the whole of the documents must be made and lodged for that purpose. Where, however, one of the documents to be proved is not suitable for such reproduction, the district judge or registrar may direct that a copy of that document only need be made and lodged, the remaining documents being reproduced in facsimile direct for inclusion in the probate copy.

4.226 Typed or written engrossments (including fiat copies) should reproduce as accurately as possible all the features of the original. Great accuracy is essential, and copies containing errors will not be accepted. Strict facsimile reproduction is not necessary, but punctuation, spacing and division into paragraphs of the original must be reproduced and the engrossment must follow continuously from page to page on both sides of the paper[1].

1 NCPR 11(3).

Fiat copies

4.227 Where a will contains alterations or additions which are not admissible, the copy must omit all such alterations by restoring obliterations where they can be read, and omitting additions. Where, however, the obliteration of words is complete, and the words cannot be deciphered, a blank space must be left in the copy. (As to alterations etc., see paras. **3.222** ff., ante.) If necessary the directions of the district judge or registrar should be sought as to the form of the fiat copy.

4.228 A fiat copy will normally be typed bookwise on durable paper following continuously from page to page on both sides of the paper. Single sheets attached together should not be used for the purpose. A space of at least 2 inches should be left at the bottom of the last page for the addition of the 'fiat' signed by the registrar or probate officer.

4.229 To assist in the preparation of fiat copies of testamentary documents, it has been decided that, subject to the district judge's or registrar's discretion, as an alternative to typewritten engrossments, facsimile copies produced by photography or similar process may be used in the following circumstances:

(a) where a complete page or pages are to be excluded;
(b) where words on the same page below the testator's signature can be excluded by masking out;
(c) where the original has been altered but not re-executed or republished and there exists a photocopy of the original executed document[1].

1 *Practice Direction* [1979] 3 All ER 859: see also NCPR 11.

4.230 When a fiat copy of testamentary documents is necessary, a copy of all the documents to be proved is normally required (see above). Where, however, it is necessary for one of several documents to be proved in the form of a fiat copy, the district judge or registrar may direct that a copy of that document only need be prepared, the remaining documents being reproduced in facsimile direct for inclusion in the probate copy. But if, for example, another codicil appears on the same page as the document in respect of which the fiat copy is required it will probably be necessary to provide a fiat copy of all the documents which are to be proved[1].

1 Registrar's Circular, 12 June 1967.

Will re-executed after alteration

4.231 Where a properly executed will has apparently subsequently been altered and re-executed, the practice is to reproduce in facsimile the document itself showing the will in its final form as altered at the time of re-execution. Unless the alterations are initialled by the testator and witnesses to the re-execution, or are referred to in a further attestation clause, evidence in relation to them must be produced. See paras. **3.222** ff., ante.

Foreign cases

4.232 No probate engrossment is normally required of a sealed copy of a will issued by an overseas court, notwithstanding the fact that it may contain extraneous matter; but, when unsuitable for facsimile reproduction, translations of foreign wills may be submitted to the Principal of the Probate Department or a district probate registrar, who will mark the portion required to be copied.

Translations of documents in a foreign language

4.233 These should be certified by an English notary public, or by a British Consul or Vice-Consul. Translations not so verified will be referred to a district judge or registrar as to sufficiency (see para. **12.68**, post).

Wills in the Welsh language

4.234 Where a will is in the Welsh language a translation will normally be made through the Probate Registry of Wales, the will, if necessary, being sent to that registry from the registry at which the papers are lodged. If the applicant so desires, however, to avoid delay or for any other reason, he may lodge a translation verified by the certificate of a notary public or by the affidavit of a private individual, stating his qualifications. The applicant will be reimbursed by the registry from which the grant is to issue for notarial fees not exceeding £2.88 per folio of 72 words[1].

1 Secretary's Circular, 22 July 1985, as amended.

4.235 A copy of the will in Welsh and of the translation into English will be included in the probate without any special request, whether the will is reproduced in facsimile direct or proved in the form of an engrossment or fiat copy.

4.236 Office copies or certified copies of either the document in Welsh or the translation may be issued as requested[1].

1 Registrar's Circular, 20 July 1970.

Incorporated documents

4.237 Where a document is incorporated with the will or codicil, direct facsimile reproduction is used whenever possible. When a copy for such reproduction is required the incorporated document should be copied immediately after the will or codicil which has incorporated it. (See paras. **3.307** and **3.308**, ante.)

Copy to perpetuate pencil writings

4.238 Should a will or any part thereof be written in pencil, a copy of the will or of the pages or sheets containing the pencil writing is made in the registry and the pencil writings are underlined in red ink on the copy, in order to perpetuate them.

Proof of joint wills

4.239   For the practice on proving a joint will, see paras. **3.205–3.211**, ante.

Will of member of the Royal Family

4.240   On the death of a member of the Royal Family it is usual for application to be made to the President of the Family Division for an order that the will be sealed up. Application for such an order is made by summons, which is served on the Treasury Solicitor. The will and Inland Revenue account are examined by an official of the Capital Taxes Office before the papers to lead the grant are lodged.

4.241   No copy of the will is annexed to the grant of probate: the grant bears a notation 'Probate granted without annexing a copy of the will by order of the President dated   '.The usual records of the grant are kept.

4.242   After the will has been sealed up it can be opened only by direction of the President.

Copies of grant for registration

4.243   The executor or administrator may obtain any number of sealed office copies of the grant for the purpose of expediting the registration of the grant, at a fee of 25p for each page, if he applies for them with the application for the grant. The copies will be sent to the solicitor with the original grant.

4.244   He may also obtain copies at any other time, either on personal attendance when the fee is also 25p for each page, or by a postal application when the fee is £2 for the copy grant (including a copy of any will) and 25p for each page of any additional copy or copies.

4.245   Sealed and certified copies of grants and wills may be ordered, if desired.

4.246   The fee for a sealed and certified copy of a grant or will is £1, plus 25p for each page after the first if applied for with the application for the grant or on a personal attendance. If the copies are applied for with the grant application the fee should be recorded on a separate fee sheet. The certified copies will be sent to the extracting solicitor a few days after the grant has issued[1].

1 Establishment Circular, 20 March 1967.

4.247   If a sealed and certified copy is applied for by post (other than on the application for the grant) the fee is £3 for the copy grant (including a copy of any will) and £1 for each additional sealed and certified copy and, for each page after the first of each additional sealed and certified copy, a further fee of 25p.

Copies to be received as proof

4.248   Sealed copies of the grant are accepted as evidence of the grant in all parts of the United Kingdom without further proof[1]. If produced to a limited company in England and Wales they are sufficient proof notwithstanding anything in the articles of the company[2]. The methods of establishing the identity of the deceased with the person registered in the books of the company are unaffected by this system.

1 Supreme Court Act 1981, s. 132 (p. 848, post).
2 Companies Act 1985, s. 187 (8 Halsbury's Statutes (4th edn) 285).

Inland Revenue account

4.249 Unless dispensed with pursuant to the Capital Transfer Tax (Delivery of Accounts) Regulations 1981, as amended, an Inland Revenue account (a sworn Inland Revenue affidavit is required in cases of death prior to 13 March 1975) must be lodged at the registry with the papers to lead the grant. In certain special cases, its prior submission to the Capital Taxes Office is necessary: see paras. **8.147** ff., post. The subject of Inland Revenue accounts is dealt with in detail in Chap. 8.

Fees

Fees on the grant

4.250 For the fees payable on application for a grant of probate or administration, see Appendix III, 'Fees', pp. 959 ff., post.

4.251 Exemption of an asset from inheritance tax or capital transfer tax does not give exemption from court fees unless it is expressly directed by statute or otherwise[1].

1 Direction (1940) 10 April. As to property excluded in assessing the fee for a grant, see paras. **4.216–4.219**, ante.

4.252 At the Principal Registry, all fees in respect of non-contentious business are paid to the cashier in cash or by solicitor's crossed cheque; solicitors are requested to pay fees, wherever possible, by cheque made payable to 'H.M. Paymaster-General'. Payment is denoted by a machine impression on the relevant document or on a fee sheet obtainable at the Registry.

4.253 Refund of overpaid fees at the Principal Registry is made by cheque.

4.254 Similarly, in the district probate registries and sub-registries all fees are paid by cheque, or in cash (preferably by crossed cheque payable to 'H.M. Paymaster-General')[1].

1 Establishment Circular, 1 December 1977.

Remission of probate fees

4.255 Under the NC Probate Fees Order 1981[1], the Lord Chancellor has power to reduce or remit a prescribed fee where it appears that its payment would, owing to the exceptional circumstances of the particular case, involve undue hardship. All requests for reduction or remission of fees payable in the Principal Registry will be referred to the Chief Clerk of the Probate Department; those made in the district probate registries should be referred to the registrar[2]. The power is, however, discretionary and cannot be exercised unless the Lord Chancellor is satisfied that the circumstances of the particular case are exceptional *and* that undue hardship would be involved unless a reduction or remission is made.

1 NC Probate Fees Order 1981, para. 5(1) (see p. 962, post).
2 Registrar's Direction (1976) 22 June, as amended 8 June 1981 and 27 March 1995.

4.256   Where an application for a grant is abandoned and the papers are withdrawn, it is necessary, on any subsequent application, to lodge fresh papers with the Receiver of Papers or district registry and pay full fees. The district judge or registrar has a discretion to reduce or remit the fee paid on the former application[1]. In practice, half the fee is usually returned.

1 NC Probate Fees Order 1981, para. 5(3).

4.257   Where probate of a will is refused (see paras. **3.129** ff., ante), but the same applicant is entitled to a grant in another capacity, it is unnecessary to withdraw the application; the application may proceed under the fee already paid[1]. At the Principal Registry it is important in these circumstances that the further papers are lodged at the stopped applications room in the Probate Department and not with the Receiver of Papers.

1 Senior Registrar's decision, 1 January 1957.

Estate on which fees are assessed

4.258   The fees payable for the issue of a grant of probate or administration (or resealing of a grant, as to which, see Chap. 18) are assessed on the 'assessed value' being the value of the net real and personal estate (excluding settled land if any) passing under the grant as shown either in the Inland Revenue account or affidavit, or, where no account is delivered, in the oath to lead the grant[1]. This provision is not applicable in the case of those applications specified in Fee No. 3 of the Non-Contentious Probate Fees Order 1981, for which a fixed fee of £2 is provided.

1 NC Probate Fees Order 1981, Fee 1, as interpreted by para. 2(1).

4.259   In the case of a person dying domiciled in England and Wales, a grant issued by a probate registry in England and Wales makes title to the whole of the estate situated in the United Kingdom (i.e. in England and Wales, Scotland and Northern Ireland)[1], and all such estate must be disclosed. Probate fees are accordingly assessed on the assessed value of the whole of the estate in the United Kingdom.

1 Administration of Estates Act 1971, ss. 2 and 3 (see p. 800, post).

4.260   A grant in the estate of a person domiciled elsewhere than in England and Wales makes title to the estate in England and Wales only, and probate fees are accordingly charged on the assessed value of such estate. Inheritance tax or capital transfer tax must, however, be paid to the extent to which that tax is chargeable in respect of property (wheresoever situate) (see Chap. 8).

Reversionary interests and fees

4.261   The value of all reversionary interests owned by the deceased must be included in the estate and court fees paid thereon, whether or not inheritance tax or capital transfer tax is payable in respect of those interests. (See also paras. **4.213** and **4.214**, ante.)

Property excluded in assessing fees

4.262 Gratuities granted to the personal representatives of civil servants are exempt from fees[1] but the amount should be included in the amount of the estate sworn in the oath.

1 NC Probate Fees Order 1981, para. 4.

Members of H.M. forces and other persons 'killed in war'

4.263 As regards the estates of members of the armed forces (of whatever rank), and of certain services associated therewith, where the death occurred after 11 March 1952, total exemption from estate duty is allowed by the Finance Act 1952, s. 71, provided that the death resulted from wounds, accident, or disease while on active service, or on other service involving the same risk: in relation to persons dying after 12 March 1975, s. 71 of the Finance Act 1952 is repealed and replaced by para. 1 of Sch. 7 to the Finance Act 1975 as consolidated in the Inheritance Tax Act 1984, s. 154, which provides a similar relief for inheritance tax or capital transfer tax on death. (For practice, see para. **8.117**, post.)

4.264 Fee 3(a) of the NC Probate Fees Order 1981 provides a fixed fee of £2 for a grant in respect of an estate exempt from duty under s. 71 of the Finance Act 1952 or from inheritance tax or capital transfer tax by virtue of the above-mentioned provisions of the Inheritance Tax Act 1984 and the Finance Act 1975. This fee is in practice charged in all cases of death of members of the armed forces or persons dying from war causes if the Ministry of Defence certify that the circumstances of the death were such as to satisfy the conditions of s. 71 of the Act of 1952 or of s. 154 of the Act of 1984 or of Sch. 7, para. 1 of the Act of 1975, as the case may be[1].

1 In *Barty-King v Ministry of Defence* [1979] 2 All ER 80, [1979] STC 218, it was held that, on a true construction of s. 71(1) of the Finance Act 1952, a person 'died from a wound' if in consequence of the wound he died earlier than he would have done had he not sustained the wound, *even though the wound was not the direct or an ascertainable cause of his death*. This decision involves no change in the existing practice.

Filing documents

4.265 No fee is charged for filing the will, codicils, oath, or the Inland Revenue account (if any), or for filing affidavits and other documents to lead an order of the district judge or registrar.

Costs of non-contentious probate proceedings

Solicitors' charges

4.266 The Rules of the Supreme Court (Non-Contentious Probate Costs) 1956, which applied to all non-contentious or common form probate business for which instructions were accepted on or after 1 May 1956 were revoked as from 1 September 1994[1]. A solicitor's charges in such matters are now governed by the Solicitors' (Non-Contentious Business) Remuneration Order 1994[2], which came into force on 1 November 1994 and applies to all non-contentious business for which bills are delivered on or after that date.

1 Rules of the Supreme Court (Amendment) 1994, r. 24 (S.I. 1994 No. 1975).
2 See p. 975, post.

4.267   Under these new rules there are no fixed items or scales of costs for extracting a grant, administering an estate, etc. A solicitor is entitled to charge and be paid[1] such sum as may be fair and reasonable[2] to both solicitor and entitled person[3], having regard in particular to:

(a)   the complexity of the matter or the difficulty or novelty of the questions raised;
(b)   the skill, labour, specialised knowledge and responsibility involved;
(c)   the time spent on the business;
(d)   the number and importance of the documents prepared or perused, without regard to length;
(e)   the place where and the circumstances in which the business or any part thereof is transacted;
(f)   the amount or value of any money or property involved;
(g)   whether any land involved is registered land;
(h)   the importance of the matter to the client; and
(i)   the approval (express or implied) of the entitled person[4] or the express approval of the testator to:
   (i) the solicitor undertaking all or any part of the work giving rise to the costs or
   (ii) the amount of the costs.

1 The funeral, testamentary and administration expenses are a first charge on the estate of a deceased person, whether this is solvent or insolvent: Administration of Estates Act 1925, s. 34(3) and Sch. 1.
2 In determining what is 'fair and reasonable in the circumstances', the sums under article 3 of the Solicitors' (Non-Contentious Business) Remuneration Order 1994 can be cumulative, but there should be no overlapping of allowances. For a large estate, the most important aspect is 'the nature and value of the property involved' and under that heading it is proper to charge as percentages for successive bands of value, the percentage to reduce as the value increases. (*Maltby v D J Freeman & Co* [1978] 2 All ER 913, [1978] 1 WLR 431: in that case where the estate and number of assets were large, the appropriate bands and percentages suggested were as follows: up to £$\frac{1}{4}$ million, 1$\frac{1}{2}$ per cent; from £$\frac{1}{4}$ million to £1 million, $\frac{1}{2}$ per cent; from £1 million to £2$\frac{1}{2}$ million, $\frac{1}{8}$ per cent. It was further suggested that in the case of a smaller estate, the first rate of 1$\frac{1}{2}$ per cent would be too low.)
3 'Entitled person' means a client or an entitled third party, and 'entitled third party' means a residuary beneficiary absolutely and immediately (and not contingently) entitled to an inheritance, where a solicitor has charged the estate for his professional costs for acting in the administration of the estate, and either (a) the only personal representatives are solicitors (whether or not acting in a professional capacity); or (b) the only personal representatives are solicitors acting jointly with partners or employees in a professional capacity.
4 For definition see the Solicitors' (Non-Contentious Business) Remuneration Order 1994, art. 2.

4.268   Notes for the guidance of solicitors in assessing their charges for obtaining grants of representation and administering estates have been issued by the Law Society[1].

1 See *Law Society's Gazette*, 15 October 1980.

4.269   Without prejudice to the client's, or the solicitor's, right to have the solicitor's bill of costs taxed under ss. 70–72 of the Solicitors Act 1974 the entitled person[1] may require the solicitor to obtain a certificate from the Council of the Law

Society in respect of a bill which has been delivered where the costs are not more than £50,000 stating what sum, in the opinion of the Council, would be a fair and reasonable charge for the business covered by the bill (whether it be the sum charged or a lesser sum). In the absence of taxation the sum payable in respect of such costs is the sum stated in the remuneration certificate[2].

1 See fn. 3 to para. **4.267**, ante.
2 The Solicitors' (Non-Contentious Business) Remuneration Order 1994, art. 4.

4.270   Except where the solicitor's costs have been taxed under the Solicitors Act 1974 he must, before bringing proceedings to recover his costs, inform his client in writing of the latter's right under article 8.

Taxation of costs

4.271   Proceedings for the taxation of a solicitor's bill of costs under the Solicitors Act 1974 must be commenced in the Supreme Court Taxing Office[1]: for the practice, see the notes under the Solicitors Act in Volume 2 of the Supreme Court Practice.

1 NCPR 60 excludes taxations in probate matters under the Solicitors Act from the jurisdiction of district judges or registrars or taxing officers of the Family Division.

4.272   On any taxation of costs it is the duty of the solicitor to satisfy the taxing master as to the fairness and reasonableness of his charge.

Legal aid and inter parties costs—non-contentious probate applications

4.273   Legal aid under the Legal Aid Act 1988 may in certain circumstances be given in respect of non-contentious probate matters.

4.274   The solicitor must by regulation file the legal aid certificate and, to obtain payment, lodge his bill of costs for taxation.

4.275   An application for a grant to make title in an action will be regarded as a step in the action, and the solicitor should file his certificate and tax his bill in the Division in which the action is proceeding.

4.276   If the proceedings are confined to the Family Division the certificate should be filed in the Probate Department at the Principal Registry or at the district probate registry where the order for taxation of costs was made.

4.277   With effect from 14 October 1991 the following rule was substituted for NCPR 60:

'60. Every bill of costs, other than a bill delivered by a solicitor to his client which falls to be taxed under the Solicitors Act 1974, shall be referred for taxation—
(a) where the order for taxation was made by a district judge, to a district judge, or to a taxing officer of the Principal Registry authorised to tax costs in accordance with Order 62, rule 19 of the Rules of the Supreme Court 1965;
(b) where the order for taxation was made by a registrar, to that registrar.'

4.278   The bill of costs (and the necessary accompanying papers) must be lodged in the registry where the bill is to be taxed. RSC Ord. 62 is applied with the necessary modifications to taxations under NCPR 60 by NCPR 3. The bill must be lodged within three months after the order for taxation was perfected (RSC Ord. 62, r. 29).

CHAPTER 5

Letters of administration with the will annexed

Summary

Note.—This chapter deals only with grants of administration (with will) in cases where the deceased died **domiciled in England and Wales**. For the practice in cases where the deceased died domiciled elsewhere, see Chap. 12. For interpretation of wills (including codicils), see Chap. 3.

In what circumstances granted

Administration (will)

5.01   Where a will is proved by any person other than an executor, a grant of administration (with the will annexed) is made.

In what circumstances granted

5.02   This form of grant is made in the following instances, inter alia:

(a)   Where no executor has been appointed;

(b)   Where the executor appointed in the will has died in the lifetime of the testator, or after his death without having proved the will;

(c)   Where the executor has renounced probate, or has been cited to accept or refuse a grant and has not appeared to the citation;

(d)   Where the appointment of an executor is void for uncertainty[1];

(e)   Where the court exercises the discretion given to it by s. 116 of the Supreme Court Act 1981[2] to pass over the prior right of the executor and order that a grant be made to some other person[3];

(f)   Where the executor is incompetent by reason of his minority or incapacity; or desires to apply through an attorney. In such cases the grant is normally expressed to be for the use and benefit of the executor, and reserves his right to apply for a grant by means of an appropriate limitation;

(As to grant where the executor is a minor, see paras. **11.137** ff.; where he is incapable, see paras. **11.209** ff., and as to grant to the attorney of an executor, see paras. **11.79** ff.)

(g)   Where a corporation, association or charitable body etc., not being a trust corporation, is appointed as sole executor, when a grant may be made to a nominee or attorney for its use and benefit (see para. **5.201**, post).

1 See paras. **4.25** ff., ante.
2 See p. 845, post.
3 See para. **25.91**, post.

Minority or life interest

5.03   If there is any minority or life interest in the estate, whether arising under the will or under any partial intestacy, administration (with will) may not normally be granted to a single individual, but must be granted to a trust corporation (with or without an individual) or to not less than two individuals[1]. See also Chap. 7, post: the practice there stated applies equally to cases of testacy and intestacy.

1 Supreme Court Act 1981, s. 114(2) (see p. 844, post). As to grants to trust corporations, see Chap. 9.

Order of priority

5.04   Where the deceased died on or after the 1 January 1926 leaving a will, the priority of right to a grant of probate or administration with will annexed is as follows (NCPR 20):

(a)   the executor; (but subject to r. 36(4)(d)) (i.e. where a non-trust corporation is appointed executor jointly with an individual, the individual must first be cleared off before a grant may issue to the nominee or attorney of the non-trust corporation);

(b)   any residuary legatee or devisee holding in trust for any other person;

(c)   any other residuary legatee or devisee (including one for life) or where the residue is not wholly disposed of by the will, any person entitled to share in the undisposed-of residue (including the Treasury Solicitor when claiming bona vacantia on behalf of the Crown) provided that—

   (i)   unless a district judge or registrar otherwise directs, a residuary legatee or devisee whose legacy or devise is vested in interest shall be preferred to one entitled on the happening of a contingency, and

   (ii)   where the residue is not in terms wholly disposed of, the district judge or registrar may, if he is satisfied that the testator has nevertheless disposed of the whole or substantially the whole of the known estate, allow a grant to be made to any legatee or devisee entitled to, or to share in, the estate so disposed of, without regard to the persons entitled to share in any residue not disposed of by the will;

(d)   the personal representative of any residuary legatee or devisee (but not one for life, or one holding in trust for any other person), or of any person entitled to share in any residue not disposed of by the will;

(e)   any other legatee or devisee (including one for life or one holding in trust for any other person) or any creditor of the deceased, provided that, unless a district judge or registrar otherwise directs, a legatee or devisee whose legacy or devise is vested in interest shall be preferred to one entitled on the happening of a contingency;

(f) the personal representative of any other legatee or devisee (but not one for life or one holding in trust for any other person) or of any creditor of the deceased.

5.05 As to the order of priority in cases where the death occurred before 1 January 1926, see paras. **5.225** ff., post.

Number of administrators

5.06 Under s. 114(1) of the Supreme Court Act 1981[1], administration may not be granted to more than four persons in respect of the same part of the estate of a deceased person[2].

1 See p. 844, post.
2 See *Re Holland's Estate* [1936] 3 All ER 13.

Settled land

5.07 For the practice as to grants in respect of settled land, see Chap. 10.

5.08 It has not been possible to issue a general grant specifically including settled land vested in the deceased since 14 October 1991. In all cases since that date separate grants have been necessary[1].

1 Secretary's Circular (2), 26 September 1991.

Executors to be cleared off

5.09 On any application for letters of administration (with will), the oath must show in what way executors are cleared off (e.g. that no executor was named in the will; that the executor died in the lifetime of the testator, or subsequently but without having proved the will; that the executor has renounced probate; etc.). The court will not grant administration (with will) to some other person on the mere consent of the executor: it can do so only on his renunciation or after he has been cited to accept or refuse a grant and has not appeared[1].

1 *Garrard v Garrard* (1871) LR 2 P & D 238.

5.10 The court has, however, in special circumstances, power under s. 116 of the Supreme Court Act 1981 to pass over the prior right of the executor and order that a grant be made to a person having a lower title, or no title, under the rules, to a grant. For practice, see paras. **25.91** ff., post.

Grant for use and benefit of executor

5.11 As to grants for the use and benefit of an executor who: (i) is a minor, see paras. **11.137** ff., post; (ii) is incapable of managing his affairs, see paras. **11.209** ff., post; (iii) has appointed an attorney, see paras. **11.79** ff., post.

5.12 As to grant where the executor is a corporation other than a trust corporation, see paras. **5.201** ff., post.

Persons interested in the residuary estate

5.13   On clearing off executors, letters of administration (with will annexed) are granted to persons interested in the residuary estate in priority to any other person[1].

1 See NCPR 20, classes (b) and (c).

5.14   It is therefore frequently necessary to determine whether a will contains a disposition of the residuary estate: this is sometimes a matter of doubt, particularly in the case of wills drawn without professional assistance, and whenever such doubt arises it is advisable to obtain the decision of a district judge or registrar before preparing the papers to lead the grant[1].

1 A full discussion of the question as to what amounts to a gift of residue will be found in *Williams on Wills*.

5.15   In deciding whether a will contains a gift of the residuary estate a number of factors must be considered. The law is averse to intestacy, particularly where the intention of the testator appears to have been to dispose of his whole estate. On the other hand it has been said[1] that 'it cannot be that, merely with a view to avoiding intestacy, you are to do otherwise than to construe plain words according to their plain meaning. A testator may well intend to die intestate.'

1 *Re Edwards, Jones v Jones* [1906] 1 Ch 570.

5.16   It is necessary therefore to attempt to ascertain the testator's intention; but to constitute a residuary gift this must be expressed in words sufficient to comprise all that is not otherwise disposed of by the will. It is in no way conclusive that the will has disposed, in detail, of everything that the testator then possessed, or possessed at his death: there must be an expression that includes anything, of whatever character, that might have fallen, or may yet fall, into his estate. Some confusion has arisen in the interpretation of the decision in the leading case of *Perrin v Morgan*, referred to below, which decided only that the word 'money' is one of no fixed meaning. It is essential that this word should be judged in its context and with due regard for the ejusdem generis rule; for the more the word is interpolated among legacies of chattels, securities etc., or is followed by other bequests, the less is it capable of being interpreted as 'all I possess'. On the other hand, if it follows the other bequests and is accompanied by some small addition, such as 'all the rest of my money', the presumption is very strong. It is a cardinal rule of construction that words are to be construed in their natural and grammatical sense unless there is something in the context which imposes a different meaning on them[1].

1 *Re Diplock, Wintle v Diplock* [1941] Ch 253, [1941] 1 All ER 193; upheld by the House of Lords sub nom *Chichester Diocesan Fund and Board of Finance Inc v Simpson* [1944] AC 341, [1944] 2 All ER 60.

'Money' or 'moneys'

5.17   Where this expression is used in a will, the sense in which it was used, whether it was the popular or the strict legal sense, and the testator's intention, must be ascertained in each case from the context, the general tenor of the will and the circumstances of the case and of the testator, the standing of the beneficiary in relation to the testator and the provision made for other beneficiaries. If the expression suggests that the word was meant as 'possessions' or the equivalent it may be construed as a residuary bequest, and even a residuary devise. If it is clear that the word was used in relation to a specific gift only, the strict legal interpretation should be applied to that gift[1].

1 *Perrin v Morgan* [1943] AC 399, [1943] 1 All ER 187, HL.

5.18 The following expressions have been held to pass the residuary estate: '*The remainder of my moneys*' (with direction to pay debts etc.)[1]; '*Any saving or money*' in a home-made will[2]; '*All other money, whether invested or in bank*'[3]; '*Estate or property*'[4]; '*All my insurances and private effects*'[5]; '*Rest of my investments*', following other bequests[6].

1 *Re Mellor, Porter v Hindsley* [1929] 1 Ch 446.
2 *Re Rotton, Rotton v Ensor* (1948) 98 L Jo 156.
3 *Re Recknell, White v Carter* [1936] 2 All ER 36.
4 *Hounsell v Dunning* [1902] 1 Ch 512.
5 *Re Smith* (1935) (motion).
6 *Re Craven, Crewsdon v Craven* (1908) 99 LT 390.

5.19 A gift of '*any other personal property*', following a gift of '*any money I may leave*' was held to pass the residuary personal estate and to sweep up a half share of the residuary money fund which had lapsed[1].

1 *Re Barnes's Will Trusts, Prior v Barnes* [1972] 2 All ER 639, [1972] 1 WLR 587, applying *Perrin v Morgan*, above.

5.20 The expression 'effects', even if a residuary gift by reason of the circumstances and context, passes the personal estate only, unless the context strongly suggests otherwise[1]. '*Personal effects*' has been held to pass only physical chattels having some connection with the testator, and not money or securities[2], although in an Irish case[3] in which a testator left his interest in landed property to A, his walking stick to B and all his personal effects to C it was held that the last gift passed the residue of the personal estate.

1 *Hall v Hall* [1892] 1 Ch 361.
2 *Joseph v Phillips* [1934] AC 348.
3 *Re Wolfe's Goods* [1919] 2 IR 491.

5.21 '*The rest and residue of all my belongings*' in a home-made will has been held to mean the whole of the residuary estate both real and personal[1]; when construing an ordinary word like 'belongings' the court should look at the document and express its own view: the practice of referring to authority for ascertaining the construction of a particular document is liable to induce confusion and error[2].

1 *Re Schott's Will Trust, Prause v Malmcrantz* (1968) 112 Sol Jo 335.
2 Ibid., per Stamp J.

Residuary legatee or devisee

5.22 The person named in a will, to whom the 'residue' of the personal estate is left, is called the 'residuary legatee'; while the recipient of the 'residue' of real estate is called the 'residuary devisee', and they are equally entitled to the grant.

Limited gift of residue

5.23   A bequest of residue limited to the residue of the testator's estate 'in England' (or 'the United Kingdom', or 'Great Britain') constitutes a right to a grant to the beneficiary as residuary legatee or devisee. The beneficiary should be described in the oath as the 'residuary legatee in England', or as the case may be.

Virtual disposition of residue

5.24   Where a will contains no residuary disposition in terms, but the testator has nevertheless by enumeration disposed of the whole, or substantially the whole, of his estate as ascertained at the time of the application, a grant may be made to a legatee or devisee entitled to the whole, or part, of the estate so disposed of (NCPR 20(c)(ii)). For practice, see paras. **5.181** ff., post.

Persons entitled

5.25   The following are brief summaries as to the persons who answer certain descriptions used in wills. For fuller details reference should be made to one of the works dealing with wills and their construction.

Relatives

5.26   'To all my relatives' means all persons entitled to share under the Administration of Estates Act 1925 as on an intestacy[1]. Under Part III of the Family Law Reform Act 1987[2], in respect of any disposition by will or codicil made on or after 4 April 1988, references (whether express or implied) to any relationship between two persons are to be construed, unless a contrary intention appears, without regard to whether or not the father and mother of either of them, or the father and mother of any person through whom the relationship is deduced, have or had been married to each other at any time.

1   *Re Bridgen, Chaytor v Edwin* [1938] Ch 205, [1937] 4 All ER 342.
2   See p. 876, post.

Next of kin

5.27   Under s. 50(1) of the Administration of Estates Act 1925, references in a will to statutory next of kin are to be construed, unless the context otherwise requires, as referring to the persons who would take beneficially on an intestacy under that Act. 'For such of my next of kin according to the Statutes of Distribution as shall be living in the United Kingdom at the decease of Z': the testator was survived by a widow and a daughter (Z). It was held that, although the widow was the only next of kin living at the death of Z, on the true construction of the will and having regard to s. 50(1) of the Administration of Estates Act 1925, the gift was to the widow and six relatives (two brothers and four nieces), being the only persons living in the United Kingdom who would have had an interest in the estate if the deceased had died intestate without issue. These seven persons took equally as joint tenants[1].

1   *Re Krawitz's Will Trusts, Krawitz v Crawford* [1959] 3 All ER 793, [1959] 1 WLR 1192.

Heir

5.28   In the absence of any special context a gift of real or personal estate to the 'heir' *of a deceased person* in an instrument coming into operation after 1925 is to be construed as a gift to the person who, at the material date, would have answered the description of 'heir' under the pre-1926 law, whatever the date of death of the deceased person (see Law of Property Act 1925, s. 132). 'To the persons who at the death of my wife are my heirs at law': the testator outlived his wife. It was held that the gift was to the persons who would have been his heirs if he had died at the same time as his wife[1].

1 *Re Hooper, Hooper v Carpenter* [1936] Ch 442, [1936] 1 All ER 277, CA.

5.29 Where there was a gift of both real and personal estate to brothers and sisters 'or their heirs and successors' it was held that no distinction should be drawn between realty and personality, and those entitled under the expression 'heirs and successors' were the persons entitled under the post-1925 law of intestate succession[1].

1 *Re Kilvert, Midland Bank Executor and Trustee Co Ltd v Kilvert* [1957] Ch 388, [1957] 2 All ER 196 (cf. *Re Bourke's Will Trusts, Barclays Bank Trust Co Ltd v Canada Permanent Trust Co* [1980] 1 All ER 219, [1980] 1 WLR 539).

Child; children

5.30 These expressions, when used in a will, and the cases noted here, must be considered in conjunction with the Adoption Acts 1958 and 1968 in respect of deaths prior to 1 January 1976, and the Adoption Act 1976 (the relevant parts of which, as from 1 January 1988, re-enacted and replaced the relevant parts of Sch. 1 to the Children Act 1975) for deaths on or after that date: see subsequent paragraphs of the present chapter. Under Part II of the Family Law Reform Act 1969[1], references to children in deeds, wills etc., made on or after 1 January 1970 are, unless a contrary intention appears, deemed to include a reference to illegitimate children. See also the reference to Part III of the Family Law Reform Act 1987 under 'Relatives' in para. **5.26**, above.

1 See p. 791, post.

5.31 'Children' means issue[1]; 'children' as a class extends to all issue living at the testator's death[2]; 'family' has in one case been held to mean children[3]. 'Issue of our marriage' means children only, and excludes grandchildren[4].

1 *Re Milward's Estate, ex p Midland Rly Co* [1940] Ch 698.
2 *Re Sutcliffe, Alison v Alison* [1934] Ch 219.
3 *Pigg v Clarke* (1876) 3 Ch D 672.
4 *Re Noad, Noad v Noad* [1951] Ch 553, [1951] 1 All ER 467; followed in *Re Bourke's Will Trusts*, above ('surviving issue' held to mean surviving children and not surviving issue of all degrees).

Issue

5.32 As to whether this term can include a child adopted under the law of a foreign country, see *Re Marshall, Barclays Bank Ltd v Marshall*[1]. 'Male issue': unless there is evidence of a contrary intention, the word 'issue' must be given its primary connotation of descendants of all degrees, and 'male issue' (which for this purpose is indistinguishable from 'issue male', a term of art meaning male descendants through the exclusively male line) includes only the sons and remoter male issue in the exclusively male line.

1 [1957] Ch 507, [1957] 3 All ER 172.

Descendants

5.33   The term 'male descendants' is not a term of art, but an expression of ordinary speech, and includes males descended through females as well as through males[1]. The term 'descendants' in a legal document, like other words denoting family relationship which have become terms of art, prima facie denotes only legitimate descendants[2]. Both in legal and ordinary language, the term now means lineal descendants only and excludes collateral relations[3].

1   *Re Du Cros' Settlement, Du Cros Family Trustee Co Ltd v Du Cros* [1961] 3 All ER 193, [1961] 1 WLR 1252; *Re Drake's Will Trusts, Drake v Drake* [1971] Ch 179, [1970] 3 All ER 32.
2   *Sydall v Castings Ltd* [1967] 1 QB 302, [1966] 3 All ER 770.
3   *Re Thurlow, Riddick v Kennard* [1972] Ch 379, [1972] 1 All ER 10.

Nephews and nieces

5.34   A testatrix, after describing certain named nephews and nieces by affinity as 'my nephew' or 'my niece', left her residuary estate to such of her nephews and nieces, great nephews and great nieces as should be living at her death. It was held that as she had described certain nephews by affinity as nephews and as the bulk of her estate came from her husband, whose family she might therefore be expected to benefit, the general rule excluding relatives by affinity was displaced[1].

1   *Re Tylor, Barclays Bank Ltd v Norris* (1968) 112 Sol Jo 486.

Adopted persons

5.35   In relation to events occurring on or after 1 January 1976, the relevant provisions as to the status of adopted children are contained in Part IV of the Adoption Act 1976[1].

1   See pp. 828–831, post. The relevant part of the Act came into force on 1 January 1988 repealing and replacing Sch. 1 to the Children Act 1975.

5.36   The effect of the Act, inter alia, is to restate the provisions of the law relating to adoption orders and succession rights which were contained in Sch. 1 to the Children Act 1975. The following paragraphs briefly summarise the provisions of Part IV of the Act of 1976.

5.37   The adoptions referred to in Part IV of the Act are:

(a)   adoption by an adoption order under s. 12(1) of the Adoption Act 1976;
(b)   adoption by an adoption order under the Children Act 1975, the Adoption Act 1958, the Adoption Act 1950 or any enactment repealed by that Act;
(c)   adoption by an order made in Scotland, Northern Ireland, the Isle of Man or any of the Channel Islands;
(d)   overseas adoptions as defined by s. 72 of the Adoption Act 1976; and
(e)   adoptions recognised by the law of England and Wales and effected under the law of any other country[1].

1   Adoption Act 1976, s. 38.

5.38   A will is treated as made on the date of the testator's death[1].

1   Ibid., s. 46(3).

5.39   Section 39 of the Act deals with the status in law conferred by adoption. As respects things done, or events occurring, after an adoption or after 31 December 1975 (whichever is the later), an adopted child is to be treated in law (subject to certain exceptions set out in Part IV of the Act):

(a)   where the adopters are a married couple, as if he had been born a child of the marriage (whether or not he was actually born after the marriage was solemnised); and

(b)   in any case, as if he had been born to the adopter in wedlock (but not as a child of any actual marriage of the adopter)[1].

1   Ibid., s. 39(1).

5.40   An adopted child is to be treated as if he were not the child of any person other than the adopters or adopter[1].

1   Ibid., s. 39(2).

5.41   The effect of s. 39 is that an adopted child is in no case illegitimate[1].

1   Ibid., s. 39(4).

5.42   In the case of an adoption which was effected before 1 January 1976, the foregoing provisions apply as from 1 January 1976: in the case of later adoptions they apply from the date of the adoption[1].

1   Ibid., s. 39(5).

5.43   Subject to what is stated below, the status in law conferred by s. 39 applies for the construction of enactments or instruments passed or made before the adoption or later, subject to any contrary indication[1].

1   Ibid., s. 39(6).

5.44   A relationship existing by virtue of these provisions may be referred to as an adoptive relationship; a male adopter as the adoptive father; a female adopter as the adoptive mother, and any other relative of any degree under an adoptive relationship as an adoptive relative of that degree[1].

1   Ibid., s. 41.

5.45   Part IV of the Act does not apply to an 'existing' instrument or enactment so far as it contains a disposition of property ('existing' is defined as one made or passed before 1 January 1976); nor does it apply to any public general Act in its application to any disposition of property in an existing instrument or enactment[1]. It must, however, be borne in mind that the death of the testator is the date at which a will or codicil is to be regarded as made[2].

1   Ibid., s. 42(1).
2   Ibid., s. 46(3).

5.46   Sections 16 and 17 of the Adoption Act 1958[1] (which deal, inter alia, with succession rights in relation to adoption orders in respect of deaths occurring before 1 January 1976) were repealed with effect from 1 January 1976, but the repeal does not affect their application to a disposition of property effected by an instrument made before that date[2].

1 For a textual summary of these provisions, see pp. 152–154 of the Twenty-Fourth Edition of this work.
2 Children Act 1975, Sch. 1, para. 5(2); Adoption Act 1976, Sch. 2, para. 6(2), see p. 830, post.

5.47 It is provided that for the purposes of Part IV of the Act of 1976 provisions of the law of intestate succession applicable to the estate of a deceased person are to be treated as if contained in an instrument executed by him, while of full capacity, immediately before his death[1]: as to adoption orders in relation to intestacies, see paras. **6.223** ff., post.

1 Adoption Act 1976, s. 46(4), see p. 830, post.

5.48 Under s. 42 of the Act of 1976, the following rules of construction apply to any instrument made on or after 1 January 1976, so far as it contains a disposition of property. By virtue of s. 39(6)(b) these rules apply to the will or codicil, whenever made, of a testator *dying on or after 1 January 1976*.

5.49 In applying s. 39(1) (adopted child to be treated in law as lawful child of adopter(s)) to a disposition which depends on the date of birth of a child or children of the adoptive parents, the disposition is to be construed as if:

(a) the adopted child had been born on the date of the adoption;
(b) two or more children adopted on the same date had been born on that date in the order of their actual births;

but this does not affect any reference to the age of a child.

5.50 For example, in construing the expression 'the children of A living at my death or born afterwards', a child adopted by A would be treated as if born on the date of adoption, and in the case of a gift to A for life 'until he has a child' and then to his child or children, the gift over would take effect on A's adopting a child.

5.51 The provision under s. 39(2) that an adopted child is to be treated in law as if he were not the child of any person other than the adopter or adopters does not prejudice any interest which was vested in possession in him before the adoption, or any interest expectant on an interest so vested[1]. Where a child is adopted by one of its natural parents as sole adoptive parent, s. 39(2) has no effect as respects entitlement to property depending on relationship to that parent, or as respects anything else depending on that relationship[2]. Thus the child, for property purposes, retains its original relationship to the parent but, by virtue of s. 39(3), ceases to be illegitimate.

1 Adoption Act 1976, s. 42(4), see p. 829, post.
2 Ibid., s. 39(3), see p. 828, post.

5.52 Section 47 of the Act of 1976 provides exceptions from the general rule under s. 39 for various special purposes, e.g. marriage with kindred or affinity, incest, nationality, immigration and citizenship and for certain purposes under the social security legislation. Section 48 provides that entitlement to a pension to or for the benefit of a child which is in payment at the time he is adopted is not affected by s. 39(2).

5.53 Section 44 provides that an adoption does not affect the descent of any peerage or dignity or title of honour, and s. 49 contains a provision transferring to the adopters rights under an insurance policy for funeral expenses effected by the natural parent of a child which is afterwards adopted.

5.54 Part IV of the Act also contains supplemental provisions as to a disposition depending on the date of birth of a child born illegitimate but adopted by one natural parent or legitimated; as to the protection of trustees and personal representatives; as to property devolving with a peerage etc. and in respect of entailed property.

5.55 Part IV of the Act does not apply to Scotland.

5.56 Sections 5, 6, 7, 8(1) and 9 of the Adoption Act 1968[1] and s. 24 of the Children Act 1975 came into force on 23 October 1978. These sections made provision in England and Wales for the making, revocation or annulment of Convention adoption orders and the annulment of certain overseas adoptions regulated by the Convention on Jurisdiction, Applicable Law and Recognition of Decrees Relating to Adoptions concluded at The Hague in 1965. These provisions were replaced by similar provisions contained in s. 17 and Part V of the Adoption Act 1976, which came into force on 1 January 1988.

1 See pp. 788 ff., post.

5.57 Jurisdiction to grant Convention adoption orders in England and Wales is restricted to the High Court. An adoption under the Convention (whether granted in the United Kingdom or in a Convention country), or the revocation or annulment of such an adoption, will be recognised without further formality in all the countries in which the Convention is in force. From 23 October 1978, the Convention applies only to the United Kingdom, Austria and Switzerland, but its scope will be extended as and when its provisions are applied to other countries.

5.58 The effect of the making of an adoption under the Convention is to confer on the child the same status in England and Wales as that conferred on any other adopted person coming within the scope of Part IV of the Act of 1976 (or the former Sch. 1 to the Children Act 1975). Accordingly, from 23 October 1978 adoptions made under the Convention in the United Kingdom, Austria or Switzerland will be recognised in non-contentious probate applications.

5.59 As to the devolution on an intestacy (total or partial) where there has been an adoption, see paras. **6.223** ff., post; as to legitimation following adoption, see paras. **6.242** ff., post; and as to the recognition of overseas adoptions, see paras. **6.257** ff., post.

Inferential gift of residue

5.60 In some cases although there is no actual gift of the residue of the estate the inference of a residuary gift can be drawn from the wording of the will. Where a will named an executor, and proceeded: 'I give and bequeath unto (*the executor*)', it was held that the executor was the residuary legatee and devisee[1]. In another case the words 'I give and bequeath unto (*eleven named persons*)' were followed by a specific gift to one of them. It was held that the eleven were entitled to the whole residuary estate apart from the specific gift[2]. Where a will was on a printed form, and after the printed words 'I give, devise and bequeath' was written 'to my brother W, also sister J, also sister E', it was held that the brother and two sisters took the whole estate[3].

1 *Re Messenger's Estate, Chaplin v Ruane* [1937] 1 All ER 355; *Rycroft v Phelan* (1938) motion.
2 *Re Turner, Carpenter v Staveley* [1949] 2 All ER 935, followed in *Re Davies' Will Trusts, Thomas v Thomas* (1958) 108 L Jo 610.
3 *Re Stevens, Pateman v James* [1952] Ch 323, [1952] 1 All ER 674.

5.61 A testator in his will named his wife as executrix. After the printed words 'I give and bequeath unto' there appeared no names, nor any disposition of property. It was held that the executrix was trustee for the persons entitled on an intestacy (see Administration of Estates Act 1925, ss. 46, 49 and 55(1))[1].

1 *Re Skeats, Thain v Gibbs* [1936] Ch 683, [1936] 2 All ER 298.

Gift to charities

5.62 If a gift to charities is not made to a specified person to hold in trust, the Attorney General has the sole right of representing the alleged charity in proceedings to determine the validity of the gift[1].

1 *Ware v Cumberlege* (1855) 20 Beav 503 at 510; *Practice Note* (1945) 199 LT Jo 72. See also *Strickland v Weldon* (1885) 28 Ch D 426, followed in *Re Belling, Enfield London Borough v Public Trustee* [1967] Ch 425, [1967] 1 All ER 105.

5.63 Under the Charitable Trustees Incorporation Act 1872, the trustees of any charity for religious, educational, literary, scientific or public charitable purposes may apply to the Charity Commissioners for a certificate of registration as a corporate body. If the certificate is granted the trustees become a corporate body able to hold and acquire property, and thereafter all gifts of property to the charity or the trustees or otherwise for the purposes thereof take effect as if made to the incorporated body for the like purposes.

5.64 Where a gift of residue is made to charity generally, or for charitable purposes or objects without specifying particular institutions, the Attorney General has the sole right to represent the beneficial interest of charity. The Treasury Solicitor acts on his behalf in charity matters.

5.65 A bequest of the residue for masses for the repose of souls is a valid gift[1].

1 *Bourne v Keane* [1919] AC 815, 121 LT 426; *Re Caus, Lindeboom v Camille* [1934] Ch 162, and cf. *Gilmour v Coates* [1949] AC 426, [1949] 1 All ER 848.

Gift of residue to hospital

5.66 A gift to a hospital remains valid notwithstanding that the hospital has been taken over under the National Health Service Scheme provided that the original purpose or object of the gift remains, or the work of the hospital continues, and it must be paid to the appropriate management committee[1]. But where a will contained a gift to a home for incurables, to be paid to the general committee, and under the National Health Service Act 1946, the buildings vested in the Minister of Health although the charity retained its endowments, it was held that s. 60 of the

Act did not apply; the gift was payable to the general committee of the charity and not to the Hospital Management Committee[2].

1 *Re Kellner's Will Trusts, Blundell v Royal Cancer Hospital* [1950] Ch 46, [1949] 2 All ER 774; *Re Morgan's Will Trusts, Lewarne v Ministry of Health* [1950] Ch 637, [1950] 1 All ER 1097; *Re Meyer's, London Life Association v St George's Hospital* [1951] Ch 534, [1951] 1 All ER 538; *Re Hunter, Lloyds Bank Ltd v Mistress and Governors of Girton College, Cambridge* [1951] Ch 190, [1951] 1 All ER 58. But see *Re Couchman's Will Trusts, Couchman v Eccles* [1952] Ch 391, [1952] 1 All ER 439; where by his will testator gave a legacy of £100 and a share of the residue of his estate on the death of his wife to the Leominster Orthopaedic Clinic. Testator died on 9 January 1941, and his wife died on 9 June 1949. After the National Health Service Act 1946 came into operation a scheme was approved by the Minister of Health and the said clinic became merged into a special hospital group. On a summons by the trustees of the testator's will to determine the destination of the funds representing the gifts to the clinic, the management committee of the hospital group claimed to be entitled to them. It was held that since the clinic had become merged it had lost its identity and did not come within the definition of 'hospital' in sub-s. (1) of s. 79 of the Act of 1946, and the management committee of the group were not entitled under s. 60(1)(b) of the Act to the funds.
2 *Re Roberts, Re Perkins* (1957) Times, 23 May.

Double gift of residue

5.67 Where a testator in a will written on a printed will form gave the residue of his estate to be divided between St. Peter's Church, Staines, and Oxford University, and then, after the printed words 'I devise and bequeath all my real and personal estate not hereby otherwise disposed of', wrote 'my executors to deal with at their discretion', it was held that the two gifts were not irreconcilable, but that the first gift carried the whole of the testator's estate not disposed of and therefore, provided that the first gift was fully effective, the second was inoperative[1].

1 *Re Gare, Filmer v Carter* [1952] Ch 80, [1951] 2 All ER 863.

5.68 By his will a testator gave all his real and personal estate to his wife 'for her own use and benefit absolutely', and went on to give legacies to nine named persons after her death. The will concluded with a disposition of the real and personal estate not otherwise disposed of upon trust for sale and conversion, the residue, after payment of funeral and testamentary expenses, to go to the issue of certain named persons.

5.69 It was held that the widow took the whole estate absolutely, subject only to the legacies to the nine named persons (following the dictum adopted by Harman J in *Re Gare, Filmer v Carter* (above), that the *general* principle that where a will contains two completely irreconcilable clauses or gifts the later prevails over the earlier, has not been applied to cases of apparently double gifts of *residue*, for the reason that the later gift is meant to sweep up lapsed legacies or shares of residue)[1].

1 *Re Crowther, Houseman v Crowther* (1956) 106 L Jo 658.

Clearing off

Clearing off prior classes

5.70 All persons having a prior right to a grant under NCPR 20 must be cleared off before a grant can be made to a person with a lower title; and the oath must show in what manner the persons with a prior right are cleared off[1].

1 NCPR 8(4).

5.71   In order to clear off a residuary or other beneficiary who attained a vested interest by surviving the deceased, but has subsequently died, the renunciation of his personal representative is necessary. If no such personal representative has been appointed, it is the practice to require the renunciations of all persons entitled to constitute themselves as such (see para. **5.192**, post).

To whom granted

Rule 20, Class (b)

Residuary legatee or devisee in trust

5.72   On clearing off executors (see paras. **5.09** and **5.10**, ante), administration (with will) may be granted to any residuary legatee or devisee holding in trust for any other person[1].

1 *Hutchinson v Lambert and Curling* (1825) 3 Add 27.

5.73   It must be apparent from the will that the residuary estate is given to such person to hold on trusts declared by the will.

Substituted trustees

5.74   If the residuary legatee or devisee in trust has power, under the will, to nominate a trustee in his stead, a grant will be made to the substituted trustee, on the renunciation of the trustee named in the will and production of his disclaimer of the trust. The deed of nomination must also be produced.

5.75   Administration (with will) may be granted to trustees appointed by the court in substitution for the surviving trustees named in the will[1]. The order appointing the new trustees should be lodged with the papers.

1 *Re Woodfall's Goods, Woodfall v Arbuthnot* (1873) LR 3 P & D 108; *Cresswell v Cresswell* (1824) 2 Add 342.

Gift to holder of an office

5.76   A nun in a convent by her will bequeathed her estate to the person who at the time of her death should be, or act as, the abbess of the convent. The will was attested by two other nuns, one of whom subsequently became the abbess.

5.77   It was held that, although it was possible for a legacy to be left beneficially to a person who at the date of death of the testator should occupy a certain position, such a bequest would be extraordinary. In this case the gift was to the official in respect of her office, i.e. in trust for, and as an accretion to the funds of, the convent. Although the witnesses were members of the community they did not obtain any beneficial interest within the terms of s. 15 of the Wills Act 1837[1], and the gift was valid[2].

1 See p. 721, post.
2 *Re Ray's Will Trusts* [1936] Ch 520, [1936] 2 All ER 93.

Secret trust

5.78 Where a testator gave all his property subject to the payment of funeral and testamentary expenses to 'my trustees absolutely, they well knowing my wishes concerning the same', it was held by the Court of Appeal that on its true construction the will gave to the trustees an estate on trust and not a gift conditional on their discharging the wishes communicated to them; oral evidence to the contrary was inadmissible; and therefore the trustees were not beneficially entitled to the residue[1].

1 *Re Rees, Williams v Hopkins* [1950] Ch 204, [1949] 2 All ER 1003.

5.79 A testator left his residuary estate 'unto my trustee absolutely, and I direct him to dispose of the same in accordance with any letters or memoranda which I may leave with this my will, and otherwise in such manner as he may in his absolute discretion think fit'. No letters or memoranda were left with the will. It was held that the words following 'absolutely' imposed some degree of fiduciary obligation or trust. But a gift on trust to be applied in such manner or for such purposes as the trustees might think fit was a trust for unidentified objects and was thus void; accordingly the residuary estate passed to the next of kin of the deceased[1].

1 *Re Pugh's Will Trusts, Marten v Pugh* [1967] 3 All ER 337, [1967] 1 WLR 1262. As to the standard of proof required to establish a secret trust, see *Re Snowden, Smith v Spowage* [1979] Ch 528, [1979] 2 All ER 172.

5.80 But if a testator makes a bequest in unqualified terms, with no reference to trusteeship, but requests distribution in accordance with a memorandum, in terms or circumstances which preclude incorporation of the latter with the will, the gift may be beneficial even though made to a bank[1].

1 *Re Stirling, Union Bank of Scotland v Stirling* [1954] 2 All ER 113, [1954] 1 WLR 763.

Life or minority interests

5.81 If any life or minority interest arises in the estate, administration (with will) must normally be granted to not less than two individuals, or to a trust corporation with or without an individual. In such circumstances if there is only one residuary legatee or devisee in trust, it is usual for application for a grant to be made jointly with a person in the next class of priority (e.g. a residuary legatee or devisee) or, on clearing off the intermediate classes, with a person having a lower title (see also 'Second administrator', paras. **7.12** ff., post).

Rule 20, Class (c)

Any other residuary legatee or devisee, including one for life, or a person entitled to share in undisposed-of estate

5.82 On clearing off executors and residuary legatees and devisees in trust, administration (with will) may be granted to any other residuary legatee or devisee including one for life, or where the residuary estate is not wholly disposed of by the will, to any person entitled to share in the undisposed-of estate.

5.83 Subject to the preference of vested to contingent interests and of persons of full age to guardians of minors (see the following paragraphs) all persons in this class are equally entitled to a grant. Thus:

(a)   a residuary legatee and a residuary devisee have an equal right to the grant, irrespective of the nature of the estate[1];

(b)   if there is a residuary gift of personalty but not of the real estate, persons entitled to share in the estate not disposed of have an equal title to that of the residuary legatee, and similarly in the converse case;

(c)   if the residuary estate was given to two or more persons in specified shares (and not as joint tenants) and the share of one of them has lapsed by his predecease, the surviving residuary legatees have a title equal to that of the persons entitled to share in the undisposed-of estate. (As to lapse of gifts, see paras. **5.133** ff., post).

1 In the event of a dispute, however, if other considerations are equal the practice is to prefer the person having the predominating interest (see paras. **14.24** and **14.25**, post).

5.84   Any of the persons having such equal right may take a grant without the consent of, or notice to, the others. As to the practice in the event of a dispute between persons having an equal right, see paras. **14.08** ff., post.

Preference of vested to contingent interest

5.85   Any residuary beneficiary whose legacy or devise is vested in interest is, unless a district judge or registrar otherwise directs, preferred to one entitled on the happening of a contingency (NCPR 20(c)(i)).

5.86   Thus where a will contains residuary gifts one or some of which are vested in interest and others are contingent, the persons entitled to the vested gifts are entitled to a grant in preference to those whose interest is only contingent. The district judge or registrar has, however, in a proper case power to override this preference and if a direction is sought accordingly the facts should be placed before the Principal of the Probate Department at the Principal Registry, or the district probate registrar, as the case may be. It is advisable to do this before the preparation of the papers to lead the grant.

5.87   Note. *Various decisions are summarised in the following paragraphs on the question whether a gift is vested or contingent.*

Personal representative of child contingent residuary legatee

5.88   Under the residuary devise and bequest contained in a will, one of the children of the testator was entitled to a share contingently on her attaining 25 years. The child married, and died in the lifetime of the testator under 25 years of age, leaving issue surviving. It was held that the gift was a bequest for an interest determinable at her death within the meaning of s. 33, Wills Act 1837, and the section did not apply to her interest[1]. (As to gifts saved by s. 33 of the Wills Act 1837, see also paras. **5.135** ff., post.)

1 *Re Wolson, Wolson v Jackson* [1939] Ch 780, [1939] 3 All ER 852.

Residuary legatee on attaining age of majority. Vesting

5.89   It is frequently necessary to determine whether a gift to a minor, in connection with which there is a reference to the attaining of a specific age, is a contingent or a vested gift. There is a large body of case law on this subject, and reference should be made to *Williams on Wills*, *Theobald on Wills*, or *Jarman on Wills*, and the cases collected there. Care is especially necessary where the gift is to a class.

5.90 Regard must be had to the exact terms of the will, and a distinction should be drawn between: (a) cases in which there is a clear gift to the legatee and also a separate and distinct direction to *pay* when he attains the specified age: in such cases the vesting is not postponed until the age is attained[1], and (b) a gift to an individual at, or upon attaining, or as and when he shall attain, such an age, which, in the absence of other factors (e.g. a gift over, or a gift to the legatee of the intermediate income), is a contingent gift[2].

1 *Re Bartholomew's Trust* (1849) 1 Mac & G 354; *Shrimpton v Shrimpton* (1862) 31 Beav 425.
2 *Hanson v Graham* (1801) 6 Ves 239.

5.91 The following are some of the numerous other factors which may affect vesting: any specific direction in the will as to vesting; a direction to pay after the death of a legatee for life (see also 'Reversions', below), or at the end of a fixed period; a direction to trustees to apply the income at their discretion for maintenance; power to make advances; a reference to the 'share' of a beneficiary; etc.

5.92 A gift to a child on attaining 21 years with a direction that the income is to be paid, after the death of a life tenant and during the child's infancy, to the child's mother for advancement, benefit and education is a contingent and not a vested gift, there being no such complete gift of the entirety of the income to the child as to displace the prima facie contingency arising from the words 'on his attaining the age of 21 years'[1]. But an express direction to pay the whole of the income for the benefit of the child until the attainment of the specified age will vest what would otherwise have been only a contingent gift[2].

1 *Re Rogers, Lloyd's Bank Ltd v Lorvand* [1944] 1 All ER 408.
2 *Re Ussher, Foster v Ussher* [1922] 2 Ch 321.

5.93 As to the construction of expressions in wills denoting full age, minority, etc., under the Family Law Reform Act 1969, see para. **11.114**, post.

Devisee on attaining a certain age

5.94 Under the rule of construction known as the rule in *Phipps v Ackers*, where real estate is devised to A if or when he shall attain a given age, with a gift over in the event of his dying under that age, the attainment of that age is held to be a condition subsequent and not precedent, and A takes an immediate vested estate, subject to being divested on death under that age[1]. But for the rule in *Phipps v Ackers* to apply (i.e. for an interest to subsist as a vested interest liable to be divested rather than as a contingent interest), there must be an express gift over which spells out the conditions on which the gift over will take place and includes among those conditions the counterparts, though not necessarily identical counterparts, of the conditions applicable to the prior gift[2].

1 (1842) 9 Cl & Fin 583.
2 *Re Mallinson Consolidated Trusts, Mallinson v Gooley* [1974] 2 All ER 530, [1974] 1 WLR 1120.

5.95 The rule applies equally to a gift of personal estate and to a gift of mixed real and personal estate[1].

1 *Re Heath, Public Trustee v Heath* [1936] Ch 259.

5.96　If the will purports to defer the vesting until the attainment of an age exceeding 21 years whereby the gift would be rendered void for remoteness, but the gift would not be void if the age specified had been 21, the disposition is for all purposes to be treated as if limited to the age nearest to the specified age which would render the disposition valid[1].

1　Perpetuities and Accumulations Act 1964, s. 4(1) (see p. 779, post).

Reversions

5.97　It has always been assumed that a reversionary interest, following a life interest, vests in the reversioner upon the death of the testator, notwithstanding the fact that the reversioner may die during the lifetime of the life tenant.

5.98　This assumption is generally correct except, e.g., when the reversionary bequest, or second life interest, is qualified by a proviso as to survival, such as 'should he survive', or by the substitution of another beneficiary 'in the event of his death'. In such cases the reversionary interest is held to be contingent during the life of the person enjoying the first life interest, and does not vest until it falls into possession. Should a person whose interest was contingent fail to survive the life tenant his representative cannot obtain a grant; but each case requires to be carefully considered[1].

1　Registrar's Direction (1930) 24 February. See also *Re Douglas's Will Trusts, Lloyds Bank Ltd v Nelson* [1959] 3 All ER 785, [1959] 1 WLR 1212, CA: a bequest to A for life and after his death to B, C and D 'or the survivors or survivor of them' held to refer to those living at the death of A, not of the testator: the gift was thus contingent on survivorship of A.

5.99　The general rule is that a bequest to several persons, or a class, 'or to such of them as shall be living at' a stated time is construed as a vested gift to all, even though this may later involve divesting in favour of those in fact living at the stated time.

5.100　So a gift to A for life, and after his death on trust for B and C or such of them as should be living at the death of the survivor of the testator and A, with a substituted gift in the event of either B or C dying before such survivor leaving issue who attain 21 or, if female, marry, is a vested gift to B and C subject to divesting in certain events[1].

1　*Re Taylor, Lloyds Bank Ltd v Jones* [1957] 3 All ER 56, [1957] 1 WLR 1043.

Preference of persons of full age

5.101　Under NCPR 27(5), unless otherwise directed by a district judge or registrar, administration (with will) is to be granted to a person not under disability in preference to a guardian of a minor entitled in the same degree. When it is desired that a grant should be made to guardians of a minor residuary legatee or devisee (having attained a vested interest notwithstanding the minority) in preference to a person of full age entitled in the same degree, the facts should be placed before the Principal of the Probate Department at the Principal Registry, or the district probate registrar, as the case may be. It is advisable to do this before the preparation of the papers to lead the grant.

Gift of residuary estate on death of a person, no disposition during the lifetime

5.102 The provisions of s. 33 of the Administration of Estates Act 1925[1], as to the sale and conversion of estates in respect of which there is an intestacy, and as to the payment of debts out of the proceeds of such sale, do not apply to a temporary intestacy, such as a deferred reversion (which has not lapsed), when there is no direction as to the intermediate income.

1 See p. 750, post.

5.103 Where under a will the surplus income of the testator's residuary estate was undisposed of during the lifetime of his widow it was (in 1943) held that, under s. 49 of the Administration of Estates Act 1925, she was entitled to the whole of the undisposed-of income until her death[1].

1 *Re Plowman, Westminster Bank Ltd v Plowman* [1943] Ch 269, [1943] 2 All ER 532.

5.104 In the case of death on or after 1 January 1953, however, the fixed net sum taken by a surviving spouse under s. 46(1) of the Administration of Estates Act 1925 (as amended) falls to be reduced by the value of the beneficial interests (other than personal chattels) acquired by the spouse under the terms of the will[1], so that if such beneficial interests were sufficiently large the charge on the intermediate income would disappear.

1 Administration of Estates Act 1925, s. 49(1), as amended (see p. 757, post); but see the effect of the Law Reform (Succession) Act 1995, s. 1(2) (p. 900) on Administration of Estates Act 1925, s. 49 in respect of an intestate dying on or after 1 January 1996.

5.105 As to the converse case where there is a life interest, but no effective gift, see para. **5.173**, post.

Deferred gift of residue

5.106 A gift of residue which is expressly deferred (whether vested, vested subject to being divested, or contingent), as distinct from an immediate gift on a contingency, does not prima facie carry the intermediate income: s. 31(1)(ii) of the Trustee Act 1925 (which provides that if a person interested in a trust fund has not a vested interest on attaining the age of 18 years, the trustees are to pay him the income) applies only where no contrary intention is expressed in the will (see s. 69(2), Trustee Act 1925[1]).

1 *Re Geering, Gulliver v Geering* [1964] Ch 136, [1962] 3 All ER 1043: see also *Re McGeorge, Ratcliffe v McGeorge* [1963] Ch 544, [1963] 1 All ER 519.

Whether gift absolute or for life only

5.107 Despite the general rule that, where there is a clear absolute gift in a will followed by words which purport to confer a power of disposition coupled with a gift over, the absolute gift takes effect and the gift over is void, instances do occur in which an intended absolute gift is, by reason of additional provisions contained in the will, reduced to a life interest.

5.108 The difficulty most frequently occurs in home-made wills, e.g. 'I leave all to my wife and after her death to my children'. To overcome this particular difficulty, since 1 January 1983, the coming into force of s. 22 of the Administration of Justice Act 1982[1], it is provided that in such circumstances there shall be a statutory presumption of an absolute gift in favour of the spouse, except where a contrary intention is shown. *This presumption does not apply where the testator dies before 1 January 1983.* Furthermore, it must be emphasised that the presumption can only arise where the property is left to a spouse with a purported subsequent gift in that property to the testator's issue: it does not arise in, or extend to, other relationships.

1 See p. 854, post.

5.109   Subject to the above limited statutory exception, the following principles have emerged from the case law.

5.110   A gift to a spouse 'for life or until remarriage', with a gift over in the latter event only, is an effective gift over on the death of the life tenant although there has been no remarriage[1], but this is not the case where the gift is absolute, and not limited for life, but only liable to be divested by remarriage[2].

1 *Luxford v Cheeke* (1683) 3 Lev 125.
2 *M'Culloch v M'Culloch* (1862) 3 Giff 606.

5.111   Where a will contains a gift not expressed to be for life, but with a contingent limitation, such as, for example, a gift to the testator's wife 'until her remarriage', and the beneficiary dies without the prescribed contingency having occurred, the question often arises whether the gift is an absolute one or one for life. In such cases the court draws a distinction between cases in which there is a gift over on the happening of the contingency and those in which there is none[1]. A distinction has also been drawn between gifts 'during widowhood' (a state which ceases on death as well as on remarriage) and cases in which such words as 'until remarriage' or 'so long as she remains single and unmarried' are used[2]. The strongest case for an absolute gift is one in which there is no gift over and the limitation is 'until remarriage'. The use of expressions such as 'absolutely', or, conversely, of words implying a gift of income only, is not of itself conclusive, for in interpreting such expressions due weight must be given to the principles enunciated above.

1 See, e.g. *Re Mason, Mason v Mason* [1910] 1 Ch 695; testatrix gave the income of her residuary estate to a daughter 'until she shall marry', followed by a gift over upon marriage. The daughter died unmarried. Held, her interest was *for life* and until marriage, and the gift over took effect.
2 See *Rishton v Cobb* (1839) 5 My & Cr 145; *Re Howard, Taylor v Howard* [1901] 1 Ch 412.

5.112   A gift to a wife 'and her heirs for her and their use and benefit absolutely and for ever' is an absolute gift and not a life interest[1].

1 *Re McElligott, Grant v McElligott* [1944] Ch 216, [1944] 1 All ER 441.

5.113   A gift of residue to A and his executors and administrators or personal representatives is an absolute gift to A and confers no right except on him. If he dies in the lifetime of the testator the legacy or gift lapses, unless it is a gift to a child or other issue of the testator which is saved by s. 33 of the Wills Act 1837. A gift to A *or* his heirs, however, is a substitutional gift, and if A dies in the lifetime of the testator there will be no lapse.

5.114 A gift of 'all the remainder of which I am possessed to my sister . . . and thereafter to her issue' was held to be an absolute gift of the residuary estate to the sister[1].

1 *Re Gouk, Allen v Allen* [1957] 1 All ER 469, [1957] 1 WLR 493 (distinguished in *Re Last* (note 3 to para. **5.117**, below)).

Gift of residue—gift over of 'what remains'

5.115 An absolute gift can be reduced to a gift of a life interest only by clear words cutting down the first gift. The practice is to consider the intentions of the will as a whole[1], although it has been held that 'one cannot annex a course of devolution to a gift once given'[2]. Thus, where a testator gave his residuary estate to his wife 'for her absolute use and benefit so that during her lifetime for the purpose of her maintenance and support she shall have the fullest power to sell and dispose of my estate absolutely', and added a gift over on the wife's death of the portion undisposed of by her, it was held that the wife took an absolute interest, and the part undisposed of passed under her will[3].

1 *Re Thomson's Estate, Herring v Barrow* (1880) 14 Ch D 263; *Re Lupton's Estate* [1905] P 321.
2 *Re Lowman, Devenish v Pester* [1895] 2 Ch 348.
3 *Re Jones, Richards v Jones* [1898] 1 Ch 438 (not followed in *Re Last* [1958]: see footnote 3 to para. **5.117**, below). See also *Re Minchell's Will Trusts* [1964] 2 All ER 47 (the words 'for her lifetime' in a home-made will are not necessarily words of limitation to a life interest only).

5.116 But it was otherwise where the testator by codicil revoked an absolute gift in favour of his wife which he had made by will and substituted another gift to her which on the face of it was absolute, but coupled it with a gift over of what should 'remain undisposed of by her' as it was held that he 'must have intended by the change of phrase to confer a different interest on her'[1].

1 *Re Pounder, Williams v Pounder* (1886) 56 LJ Ch 113.

5.117 In a later case a testatrix wrote in her will 'I give and bequeath unto my brother. . . . All property and everything I have money and otherwise. At his death anything that is left that came from me to go to my late husband's grandchildren (naming them)'. The Treasury Solicitor contended that there was an absolute gift to the brother, which, as he left no kin entitled to share, meant that the estate would go to the Crown as bona vacantia. It was held that, looking at the will as a whole and then seeking to reach the construction which would most effectively express the intentions of the testatrix, the words used were sufficient to cut down the brother's interest from an absolute to a life interest (*Constable v Bull*[1] followed; *Re Sanford, Sanford v Sanford*[2] applied; *Re Gouk* (see above, note 1 to para. **5.114**) distinguished; *Re Jones* (see above, note 3 to para. **5.115**, not followed)[3].

1 (1849) 3 De G & Sm 411.
2 [1901] 1 Ch 939.
3 *Re Last* [1958] P 137, [1958] 1 All ER 316.

Residuary legatee 'during widowhood': form of grant

5.118 If a residuary legatee be appointed 'during widowhood', the grant, though made to her as 'residuary legatee during widowhood' is not limited in terms; consequently it does not cease on her remarriage.

Rule 20, Class (d)

Personal representative of residuary legatee or devisee etc.

5.119   Under NCPR 20(d), the personal representative of a residuary legatee or devisee (*but not one for life, or one holding in trust for any other person*) or of any person entitled to share in residue not disposed of by the will is entitled to a grant on clearing off the prior classes (i.e. executors, residuary legatees and devisees in trust, any other residuary legatee or devisee, including one for life, and any person entitled to share in residue not disposed of by the will).

5.120   A grant may be made to the personal representative of a beneficial residuary legatee or devisee etc. where the interest in the residuary estate vested in the latter by reason of his having survived the testator[1]. The personal representative of a residuary legatee or devisee for life (or of one holding in trust for any other person) has, however, no title to a grant[2]; nor, it seems, has a personal representative of a contingent residuary legatee or devisee who has died without having attained a vested interest.

1 *Jones v Beytagh* (1821) 3 Phillim 635; *Re Ditchfield's Goods* (1870) LR 2 P & D 152; *Re Thirlwall's Goods* (1848) 6 Notes of Cases 44.
2 NCPR 20(d); *Wetdrill v Wright* (1814) 2 Phillim 243.

5.121   Where one of several residuary legatees or devisees or persons entitled to any undisposed-of estate who survived the testator has since died, to enable a grant to be made as of right to his personal representative it is necessary to obtain the renunciations of the surviving residuary legatees and devisees and persons entitled to any undisposed-of estate.

Residuary legatee or devisee

Meaning of residuary legatee extended

5.122   A testator stated in his will, 'I leave M. J. as my residuary legatee'. The real estate was ten times greater than the personalty, and there was no appointment of residuary devisee. It was held that prima facie the words did not apply to real estate, though the application might be extended; and that the context, coupled with the values of the real and personal estate, justified the extension of the words to all the real estate undisposed of[1].

1 *Re Bailey, Barclays Bank Ltd v James* [1945] Ch 191, [1945] 1 All ER 616.

5.123   When a previous gift of residue for life fails (whether such interest becomes vested or not) the residuary legatee is to be described in the oath as the residuary legatee substituted[1].

1 Direction, 31 March 1927.

To substituted residuary legatees or devisees

5.124   If the residuary legatee or devisee for life has died (either in the lifetime or after the death of the testator) the ultimate residuary legatee or devisee should be described in the oath as the residuary legatee or devisee substituted in the will[1]. (For form of oath, see No. 147.)

1 If any life interest subsists, or any minority interest arises, the grant will not normally be made to a sole individual administrator (see para. **5.03**, ante).

To appointee of residuary legatee or devisee for life having power of appointment

5.125 A residuary legatee or devisee for life may have a power of appointing the residue by will or deed. If such power is exercised, the appointees have the same entitlement as if they had been substituted by the testator. Their title is shown by the probate of the will, or the deed, in which the power of appointment is exercised.

5.126 And where a testator by his will bequeathed the whole of his property to his executors, in trust for such persons as a certain married woman named in that will should by deed or will, notwithstanding her coverture, appoint, and she executed a deed of appointment and assignment of all her interest under the will, the court granted administration with the will annexed of the testator's personal estate to the nominees or appointees under the deed, on the renunciation of the executor[1].

1 *Martindale's Goods* (1858) 1 Sw & Tr 8 at 9.

Acceleration of gift otherwise void

5.127 Where there are, in a will, successive limitations of personal or real estate in favour of several persons absolutely, the first of those persons who survives the testator takes absolutely, although he would have taken nothing if any previous legatee had survived and taken. A testatrix by her will gave freeholds absolutely to an individual, subject to the request that whatever of the freeholds should remain after the death of the devisee should be given to a charity. If the individual had survived the testator he would have taken absolutely, as the gift to the charity would have been repugnant and void. But the individual having died in the lifetime of the testator, the doctrine of repugnancy did not apply, and the gift to the charity was accelerated and took effect[1].

1 *Re Dunstan, Dunstan v Dunstan* [1918] 2 Ch 304; *Re Lowman, Devenish v Pester* [1895] 2 Ch 348. See also *Re Riggall, Wildash v Riggall* [1949] WN 491; *Re Bowen, Treasury Solicitor v Bowen* [1949] Ch 67, [1948] 2 All ER 979.

Conditional gift

5.128 Where a testator gave a house (and other assets) to his daughter 'on condition that she will always provide a home for my (other) daughter at the above address', it was held that these words were merely precatory, but that, even if regarded as a condition subsequent, they were void for uncertainty, and the beneficiary took the gift free from any condition[1].

1 *Re Brace, Gurton v Clements* [1954] 2 All ER 354, [1954] 1 WLR 955.

Residuary legatee. Misdescription

5.129 In a case of a devise and bequest for 12 years 'during her widowhood', the legatee was a spinster and had lived with the testator for several years. It was held that the gift was for a period which could never exist, and was ineffective[1]; but where the gift was to the testator's 'wife' during widowhood, though the testator and legatee were not married, it was held that in the circumstances of the case and on the true construction of the will, the gift was valid[2].

1 *Re Gale, Gale v Gale* [1941] Ch 209, [1941] 1 All ER 329. See also *Re Boddington, Boddington v Clairat* (1883) 22 Ch D 597 (gift of an annuity to wife of testator 'so long as she shall continue my widow and unmarried': after the date of the will the marriage was declared null and void by a decree of the Divorce Court. Held, the wife never could be or continue the widow of the testator, and the gift failed).
2 *Re Lynch, Lynch v Lynch* [1943] 1 All ER 168, 168 LT 189.

Residuary legatee as to a moiety

5.130   If the residue of the personalty is given to two persons (not as joint tenants) and the share of one of them has lapsed, a grant may be made either to the remaining residuary legatee or to the person who would have been entitled to the grant in the event of an intestacy.

Residuary legatees as joint tenants

5.131   Where a gift of residue creates a joint tenancy and one of the joint tenants has predeceased the testator, his interest vests in the other joint tenants, and there is no partial intestacy. If the joint tenants survived the testator but all have since died, the personal representative of the survivor of them only would be entitled to a grant.

5.132   It is not the practice of the registries to insist upon a grant being made to two or more individuals in cases where the residuary estate is left to two or more persons as joint tenants, but it may often assist in the administration of the estate for two grantees to be appointed.

Lapse: gifts to child or other issue of testator

5.133   Unless a will shows a contrary intention, a specific bequest or devise normally lapses in the event of the predecease of the beneficiary and falls into the residuary estate.

5.134   A residuary gift, or a share of the residuary estate, given to a person who predeceases the testator normally lapses, subject to any provision to the contrary, and passes as on an intestacy under the provisions of s. 49 of the Administration of Estates Act 1925[1].

1 See p. 757, post.

5.135   But, by virtue of s. 33 of the Wills Act 1837 as originally enacted, where any person, being a child or other issue of the testator, to whom any estate is bequeathed or devised for any estate or interest not determinable at or before his death, dies in the lifetime of the testator leaving any issue living at the death of the testator, the gift does not lapse, but, subject to any contrary intention appearing in the will, takes effect as if the beneficiary had died immediately after the death of the testator. This provision still applies to the will of a testator dying before 1 January 1983 but it has been extended in relation to wills of testators dying on or after that date by the substitution of a new provision which prevents the lapse of testamentary gifts to children or remoter descendants of the testator (including gifts to children or remoter descendants of the testator as a class) who have predeceased their parent by providing that such gifts shall pass to any issue of those children living at the testator's death[1].

1 Administration of Justice Act, 1982, s. 19, replacing Wills Act 1837, s. 33 with effect from 1 January 1983 (see p. 725, post). It must be emphasised that where the testator's death occurred before 1 January 1983, s. 33 does not apply when the gift is to children (or other issue) as a class (*Re Harvey's Estate, Harvey v Gillow* [1893] 1 Ch 567).

5.136   Where the death of the testator occurred before 1 January 1970, references in s. 33 of the Wills Act 1837, to 'child' and 'issue' were confined to legitimate relationships[1], but under s. 16 of the Family Law Reform Act 1969[2], in the case of a testator who dies on or after 1 January 1970 but before 1 January 1983, s. 33 has effect as if:

(a) the reference to a child or other issue of the testator (i.e. the intended beneficiary) included a reference to any illegitimate child of the testator and to anyone who would rank as such issue if he, or some other person through whom he is descended from the testator, had been born legitimate; and

(b) the reference to the issue of the intended beneficiary included a reference to anyone who would rank as such issue if he, or some other person through whom he is descended from the intended beneficiary, had been born legitimate.

---

1 *Dickinson v North Eastern Rly Co* (1863) 9 LT 299. See also *Re Brodie, Barclays Bank Ltd v Dallas* [1967] Ch 818, [1967] 2 All ER 97 (gift to child of testator who was illegitimate at date of will but who became legitimated prior to testator's death by the marriage of his parents: held, notwithstanding death prior to 1 January 1970, gift saved by s. 33).
2 See p. 793, post. In respect of deaths of testators on or after 1 January 1983 this provision is now revoked and replaced by new s. 33(4) of the Wills Act 1837: see p. 726, post.

5.137 In the foregoing provisions, 'illegitimate child' includes an illegitimate child who is a legitimated person within the meaning of the Legitimacy Act 1926 (since repealed and replaced by the Legitimacy Act 1976), or a person recognised by virtue of that Act or at common law as having been legitimated.

5.138 Where the death of the testator occurred on or after 1 January 1983, it is now provided that, for the purposes of the revised s. 33 of the Wills Act 1837, the illegitimacy of any person is to be disregarded[1].

---

1 Administration of Justice Act 1982, s. 19, replacing Wills Act 1837, s. 33 with effect from 1 January 1983 (see p. 725, post). It must be emphasised that where the testator's death occurred before 1 January 1983, s. 33 does not apply when the gift is to children (or other issue) as a class (*Re Harvey's Estate, Harvey v Gillow* [1893] 1 Ch 567).

5.139 Furthermore, it would now seem clear, by virtue of s. 39 of the Adoption Act 1976, that in respect of deaths occurring on or after 1 January 1976, an adopted child is also to be treated as included in the definitions of 'child' and 'issue'.

5.140 It should be noted that *where the testator died before 1 January 1983* a gift which is saved from lapse by this provision falls into the estate of the predeceasing beneficiary and is dealt with under the terms of his will, or under his intestacy, as the case may be: it does not automatically pass to the issue whose survival prevented the lapse of the gift. The persons entitled to take on such an intestacy, and the distribution of the estate, are determined in accordance with the law operating, and the classes existing, at the actual date of death of the predeceasing beneficiary[1]. Conversely, *where the testator dies on or after 1 January 1983*, the gift saved from lapse passes by operation of law directly to the surviving issue[2].

---

1 *Re Hurd, Stott v Stott* [1941] Ch 196, [1941] 1 All ER 238; *Re Basioli, Re Depaoli, McGahey v Depaoli* [1953] Ch 367, [1953] 1 All ER 301; *Re Sutton, Evan v Oliver* [1934] Ch 209.
2 Administration of Justice Act 1982, s. 19, replacing Wills Act 1837, s. 33 with effect from 1 January 1983 (see p. 725, post). It must be emphasised that where the testator's death occurred before 1 January 1983, s. 33 does not apply when the gift is to children (or other issue) as a class (*Re Harvey's Estate, Harvey v Gillow* [1893] 1 Ch 567).

5.141   Subject to any special context in a will, a child *en ventre sa mère* at the date of death of the testator where that death occurred before 1 January 1983 is, it seems, not deemed to be living for the purposes of s. 33 of the Wills Act 1837, and does not preserve its deceased parent's interest. Such a child is entitled by a fictional legal interpretation to be regarded as 'living' or 'born' at some specified point of time only to enable it to take, under the document to which the fictional interpretation is being applied, a benefit to which, if born, it would be entitled[1]. However, it is now provided by new s. 33(4) of the Wills Act 1837[2], as substituted by s. 19 of the Administration of Justice Act 1982, in respect of deaths occurring on or after 1 January 1983, that for the purposes of the revised s. 33 a person conceived before the testator's death and born living thereafter is to be taken to have been living at the testator's death.

1 See *Elliott v Joicey* [1935] AC 209 at 229 ff., HL, disapproving *Re Griffiths' Settlement, Griffiths v Waghorne* [1911] 1 Ch 246. See also *Stern's Will Trusts, Bartlett v Stern* [1962] Ch 732, [1961] 3 All ER 1129.
2 See p. 726, post.

Residuary legatee or any beneficiary a witness. Forfeiture

5.142   It is provided by s. 15 of the Wills Act 1837[1] that a legatee or devisee, whether residuary or specific, who, or whose husband or wife, attests the will, forfeits his or her legacy or devise. In the case of testators dying prior to 30 May 1968, this applies even in the case of an extra or unnecessary witness. There is a strong presumption that any person whose signature appears at the end of a will signed as an attesting witness[2], but if this presumption can be rebutted[3] the court has sometimes ordered that such signature be omitted from the probate[4]. (See also paras. **3.97–3.99**, ante.)

1 See p. 721, post.
2 *Re Bravda's Estate* [1968] 2 All ER 217, [1968] 1 WLR 479, CA.
3 E.g., by there being a substantial break between the attestation by the 'independent' witnesses and the signing by the beneficiaries (see *Re Bravda's Estate*, above).
4 *Re Sharman's Goods* (1869) LR 1 P & D 661; *Re Smith's Goods* (1889) 15 PD 2; *Kitcat v King* [1930] P 266. But see also *Re Limond, Limond v Cunliffe* [1915] 2 Ch 240 (soldier's will); *Aplin v Stone* [1904] 1 Ch 543; *Re Ray* [1936] Ch 520, [1936] 2 All ER 93; *Re Priest, Belfield v Duncan* [1944] Ch 58, [1944] 1 All ER 51.

5.143   Exceptionally, where it is abundantly plain that a testator intended that a beneficiary should take the whole estate, the court may direct that a revocation clause contained in a will be omitted from the probate in order to save the gift from forfeiture under s. 15 of the Wills Act 1837[1].

1 *Re Crannis's Estate, Mansell v Crannis* (1978) 122 Sol Jo 489 (will witnessed by sole beneficiary's spouse).

5.144   In the case of death on or after 30 May 1968, however, s. 15 of the Wills Act 1837 does not operate to cause the forfeiture of a gift to, or to the spouse of, an extra and unnecessary witness. The Wills Act 1968[1] provides that as regards the will, whenever made, of a testator dying on or after that date the attestation of the will by a person to whom, or to whose spouse, there is given or made any such disposition as is described in s. 15 of the Act of 1837 is to be disregarded for the purposes of that section if the will is duly executed without his attestation and without that of any other such person. It should be noted that the forfeiture of a gift to an attesting witness or his or her spouse is not avoided unless the will is attested by at least two 'independent' witnesses.

1 See p. 787, post.

5.145 In as much as s. 15 of the Wills Act 1837 makes void only a *beneficial* legacy or devise given to an attesting witness, or to the husband or wife of such, the rule does not apply to a *trustee* of the residuary estate[1], nor does it apply to a beneficiary under a secret trust[2].

1 *Re Ryder's Goods* (1843) 2 Notes of Cases 462. See also *Re Ray's Will Trusts*, paras. **5.76–5.77**, ante.
2 *Re Young, Young v Young* [1951] Ch 344, [1950] 2 All ER 1245.

5.146 A legatee or devisee who, or whose husband or wife, has witnessed the will does not forfeit the gift if the testator subsequently executes a codicil, attested by other witnesses, which effectively republishes the will[1].

1 *Anderson v Anderson* (1872) LR 13 Eq 381; *Re Trotter, Trotter v Trotter* [1899] 1 Ch 764.

5.147 A charging clause in favour of a professional man amounts to a legacy or gift within the meaning of the section[1].

1 *Re Pooley* (1888) 40 Ch D 1; see also *Re Thorley, Thorley v Massam* [1891] 2 Ch 613.

5.148 The gift is not forfeited where the beneficiary becomes the wife or husband of the attesting witness after the date of the will[1].

1 *Thorpe v Bestwick* (1881) 6 QBD 311.

5.149 Similarly, an attesting witness who is a solicitor, and who is not named in the will as a trustee, but after the death of the testator is appointed by the surviving trustee as a co-trustee, does not forfeit the remuneration given to trustees, or his right to charge for his professional services, under the terms of the will: the true test under s. 15 of the Wills Act 1837 is whether at the time of attestation a benefit is given by the will to an attesting witness[1].

1 *Re Royce's Will Trusts, Tildesley v Tildesley* [1959] Ch 626, [1959] 3 All ER 278.

Effect of forfeiture

5.150 The forfeiture of a share of the residuary estate under s. 15 of the Wills Act 1837 renders the gift of such share null and void, and it is to be treated as undisposed of by the will. It is not a 'failure of the trust' of such share which would bring a substituted gift into operation[1].

1 *Re Doland's Will Trusts, Westminster Bank Ltd v Phillips* [1970] Ch 267, [1969] 3 All ER 713.

Will made in Scotland

5.151 Where a British subject, domiciled in England, executed in Scotland a will which, though holograph, was attested by two witnesses, it was held that a gift to the wife of one of the witnesses was void, notwithstanding that an unattested holograph will would have been valid under s. 2 of the Wills Act 1861[1].

1 *Re Priest, Belfield v Duncan* [1944] Ch 58, [1944] 1 All ER 51.

Privileged wills

5.152 As to gifts to attesting witnesses in privileged wills, see para. **3.325**, ante.

Effect of forfeiture of gift on right to a grant

5.153   NCPR 21 provides that where a gift to any person is void by reason of s. 15 of the Wills Act 1837 such person shall have no right to a grant as a beneficiary named in the will, but this is without prejudice to his right to a grant in any other capacity (e.g. as executor, as a person entitled to share in any undisposed-of estate, or as a creditor).

5.154   Where, because of the forfeiture of a gift under this provision, a grant has to be made to a person entitled in a lower degree, the oath should clear off the disqualified person (e.g. by reciting 'that the residuary bequest and devise in the said will to A. B. is void by reason that he is an attesting witness to the said will' *or* 'that at the date of the said will he was the lawful husband of C. B., an attesting witness to the said will').

5.155   Where application is made by executors for probate of a will, no query is raised by the registry with a view to ascertaining whether a gift fails by reason of s. 15 of the Wills Act 1837 or, in the case of death on or after 30 May 1968, whether it is saved by the Wills Act 1968.

5.156   Where the application is for letters of administration (with will) no query will be raised except where the applicant, or the person through whom the applicant claims, is a witness or presumed witness, or the spouse of such a person. In such circumstances and where there are only two attesting witnesses or presumed witnesses to the will, the grant cannot be made to the applicant in the capacity of a beneficiary under the will unless and until it is established that the gift does not fail. Where there are more than two witnesses or presumed witnesses, and consequently the Act of 1968 may operate to save the gift, then, unless it is apparent from the papers that no other witness is a beneficiary under the will, the solicitor will be asked whether this is so. Where it is apparent, or where the solicitor answers the question in the negative, no evidence as to execution will be called for and the will will be admitted to proof without further enquiry. Where the answer is in the affirmative the application will be stopped, the onus being on the applicant to attempt to establish to the district judge's or registrar's satisfaction, should he wish to do so, that he, or the person through whom he claims, was not a witness to the will. This may involve a dispute with the other beneficiary witness: in this event so far as the application for the grant is concerned the difficulty might be resolved by an application for a grant in the exercise of the court's discretion under s. 116 of the Supreme Court Act 1981 (see p. 845, post). If, but only if, it is formally decided on the evidence that the applicant was not in fact a witness, then his signature should be omitted from the probate copy of the will[1]. (The foregoing does not affect any requirement for proof of execution of the will which arises by reason of circumstances other than the operation of s. 15 of the Wills Act 1837.)

1   Registrar's Direction (1970) 16 November.

Death by murder or manslaughter

5.157   Subject to the limited relief afforded by the Forfeiture Act 1982 (see p. 852, post), a person who feloniously causes the death of another by murder or manslaughter is not permitted, on the grounds of public policy, to benefit from his victim's estate. In any event, the destination of the estate is not a matter to be decided by the probate registry, but application may be made under s. 116 of the

Supreme Court Act 1981 to pass over the guilty person or his personal representative (see paras. **25.91** ff., post) for the purpose of obtaining a grant.

5.158 In what appears to be the first application to come before the court under the Forfeiture Act 1982, the widow, who had been subject to violent physical attacks by the deceased, had killed him during an altercation and was subsequently convicted of manslaughter. It was held that the forfeiture rule applied to preclude her from benefiting under the deceased's will but the purpose of the 1982 Act was to require the court to form a view of the moral culpability attending the killing to see whether the effect of the rule should be modified. The widow had been a loyal wife and having regard to the fact that there were no other persons for whom the deceased had been under any moral duty to provide, it would be unjust for her to be deprived of the benefits conferred on her by his will. The forfeiture rule was accordingly modified to allow her to take under the will[1].

1 *Re K* [1985] Ch 85, [1985] 1 All ER 403.

5.159 On the true construction of s. 2(7) of the 1982 Act, an interest in property 'acquired' before the coming into force of the Act, denoted property which had actually been transferred to the person entitled to it as a result of the operation of the forfeiture rule, or who had acquired an indefeasible right to have it transferred to him, and did not include property which, at the time s. 2(7) came into force, was held by a personal representative who had not completed the administration of the estate[1].

1 *Re K* [1985] Ch 85, [1985] 1 All ER 403.

Murder—effect of forfeiture of beneficial interest

5.160 Where a testatrix, who had bequeathed her whole estate to her daughter, was feloniously killed by the daughter, it was held that, the daughter being disqualified from taking under the will or under the resulting intestacy, the whole estate passed to the surviving son of the deceased, and that no part passed to the Crown as bona vacantia[1].

1 *Re Callaway, Callaway v Treasury Solicitor* [1956] Ch 559, [1956] 2 All ER 451.

Persons entitled to share in undisposed-of estate

Where deceased left a surviving spouse

5.161 In considering who is entitled to a grant under this provision, if the deceased left a surviving spouse, regard must be had to the provisions of the Administration of Estates Act 1925 (as amended by the Intestates' Estates Act 1952 and the Family Provision Act 1966[1]). Where all dispositions in a will fail, the residuary estate is distributed as on a total intestacy (see paras. **6.30** ff., post), but where the will effectively disposes of part of the estate, the provisions of the Administration of Estates Act 1925 apply as modified by s. 49 thereof[2].

1 See p. 786, post.
2 See p. 757, post and fn. 1, para. **5.104**, ante.

5.162 The statutory legacy in favour of the surviving spouse on an intestacy varies according to the date of death of the deceased and whether the deceased left issue surviving.

5.163   Where the death occurred on or after 1 December 1993, the surviving spouse is entitled to the first £125,000 (where the deceased left issue also surviving), or £200,000 (where the deceased left no issue), of the net undisposed-of estate[1], *less* any beneficial interests acquired under the will, other than personal chattels specifically bequeathed; such interests being valued as at the date of death[2]. It is only where the value of the net undisposed-of estate does not exceed the appropriate sum, reduced as above, that it all passes to the surviving spouse.

1   The net value of the undisposed-of residuary estate is found, for the present purpose, by the deduction of the value of the personal chattels, debts, funeral expenses, inheritance tax or capital transfer tax, probate fees and costs of the grant, but not costs of administration.
2   Administration of Estates Act 1925, s. 46(1), as amended by Intestates' Estates Act 1952, s. 1, Family Provision Act 1966, s. 1 and the Family Provision (Intestate Succession) Orders 1977, 1981, 1987 and 1993 (S.I.s 1977 No. 415, 1981 No. 255, 1987 No. 799 and 1993 No. 2906).

5.164   In the case of death occurring on or after 1 June 1987 but before 1 December 1993 the amounts are respectively £75,000 and £125,000; where the death was on or after 1 March 1981 but before 1 June 1987 the amounts are respectively £40,000 and £85,000; where the death was on or after 15 March 1977 but before 1 March 1981 the amounts are respectively £25,000 and £55,000; where the death was on or after 1 July 1972 but before 15 March 1977, the amounts are respectively £15,000 and £40,000; in the case of death on or after 1 January 1967 but before 1 July 1972, they are £8,750 and £30,000; and in the case of death on or after 1 January 1953 but before 1 January 1967, they are £5,000 and £20,000.

5.165   Where the death was before 1 January 1953, and the net value of the undisposed-of estate[1] does not exceed £1,000, the whole passes to the surviving spouse; no deduction is made in respect of the amount (if any) which passes to the spouse under the terms of the will.

1   The net value of the undisposed-of residuary estate is found, for the present purpose, by the deduction of the value of the personal chattels, debts, funeral expenses, inheritance tax or capital transfer tax, probate fees and costs of the grant, but not costs of administration.

5.166   Whatever the date of death is, if the amount of the undisposed-of estate is such that it all passes to the surviving spouse, he or she is the only person entitled to a grant under the provision under discussion. As to the position where the spouse renounces, see para. **5.189**, post.

5.167   If the whole of the undisposed-of estate has vested in a surviving spouse who has since died, the grant may be made to his or her personal representative (NCPR 20(d)).

5.168   Where the net value of the undisposed-of estate, arrived at as aforesaid, exceeds the appropriate statutory figure applicable for a death occurring after 1952, or the sum of £1,000 where the death occurred before 1953, a grant may be made to any person entitled to share in the undisposed-of residue[1]. Where the deceased died after 1952 leaving a spouse and issue, or before 1953 leaving a spouse, a life interest arises in these circumstances, and the grant must accordingly be made to not less than two individuals or to a trust corporation with or without an individual, unless the court thinks it expedient in all the circumstances to appoint a sole administrator[2]. (As to grants to trust corporations, see Chap. 9.)

1 This is the wording of the rule, but in practice the normal order of priority would operate, and, for example, a grant would not be made to children of the deceased without clearing off the surviving spouse.
2 Supreme Court Act 1981, s. 114(2) (see p. 844, post).

5.169 If the surviving spouse has since died, administration (with will) may be granted to any other person taking a beneficial interest in the undisposed-of estate[1].

1 NCPR 20(c).

5.170 If the spouse had acquired an absolute interest in the whole of the undisposed-of estate (i.e. if the testator left no other surviving relative within the degrees mentioned in paras. **6.43–6.73**, post, in case of death before 1 January 1953; or no issue, parent, brother or sister of the whole blood or issue of brother or sister of the whole blood in case of death on or after that date), a grant may be made to the personal representative of the spouse. In such event the classes who would have been entitled to share with the spouse must be specifically cleared off in the oath.

5.171 If the spouse and all other persons entitled to share in the undisposed-of estate have since died, a grant may be made to the personal representative of any of them[1], priority being given in practice to the personal representative of the spouse unless the spouse's interest in the estate has been wholly satisfied.

1 NCPR 20(d).

No surviving spouse

5.172 Where the residuary estate is wholly or partly undisposed of, or has lapsed, and the deceased died leaving no spouse, the order of priority of right to a grant is that applicable in cases of total intestacy (see para. **6.29** table B, post), and is not affected by the amount of the undisposed-of estate. The grant may be made to any person entitled to share in the undisposed-of estate, or, if every such person has since died or is otherwise cleared off, to the personal representative of any such person who has since died. (Form of oath, No. 148.)

Failure of gift over: spouse residuary legatee for life

5.173 Where a testator's will gives his wife a life interest in the residuary estate but there is no gift over or the gift over fails, the provisions of s. 46 of the Administration of Estates Act 1925 have, in accordance with s. 49 of that Act, to be read into the will. The joint effect of the will and the statute is to give the widow a life interest and, subject thereto, the residuary estate stands charged with the immediate payment to her of the statutory legacy under s. 46(1)(i) of the Act, there being no warrant for making it a charge in favour of her personal representative only[1]. Except where the date of death was prior to 1 January 1953 or after 1 January 1996, the statutory sum would presumably be reduced by the value of the beneficial interests acquired by the spouse under the terms of the will (Administration of Estates Act 1925, s. 49(1), as amended).

1 *Re Bowen-Buscarlet's Will Trusts, Nathan v Bowen-Buscarlet* [1972] Ch 463, [1971] 3 All ER 636, following *Re Douglas's Will Trusts, Lloyds Bank Ltd v Nelson* [1959] 2 All ER 620, and not following *Re McKee, Public Trustee v McKee* [1931] 2 Ch 145.

5.174   As to the converse case where there is no disposition during the lifetime of the spouse, see paras. **5.102** ff., ante.

Words of exclusion only

5.175   A testator cannot deprive those who are by law entitled to his estate by words of exclusion only. If he has failed to do this by disposing of his whole property, they are entitled to their share under the law of succession in an intestacy[1].

1   *Re Holmes, Holmes v Holmes* (1890) 62 LT 383; *Sykes v Sykes* (1868) 3 Ch App 301.

Joint tenancy

5.176   When a specific or residuary bequest or devise is made to two or more persons, with no words amounting to severance or partition, the predecease, or incapacity to benefit arising from s. 15 of the Wills Act 1837[1], of one of the beneficiaries does not cause a partial intestacy to arise in respect of the gift. It was given in joint tenancy, and the whole interest vests in the surviving beneficiary or beneficiaries[2] (see also paras. **5.131** and **5.132**, ante).

1   See p. 721, post.
2   Cf. *Young v Davies* (1863) 2 Drew & Sm 167: a gift of 'my shares in . . . to my surviving daughters' held to constitute a joint tenancy.

Disposition of residue not ascertainable

5.177   In cases where the residuary estate is wholly disposed of by the will, but its ultimate disposition is not ascertainable at the time of application for the grant (as, for example, where the residue is left to such only of certain minors as shall attain full age, so as not to vest till then), a beneficial residuary legatee or devisee whose interest is merely contingent is in the same class of priority as one having a vested interest, subject to the preference of the latter where both interests are present.

5.178   Where the residuary estate is not wholly disposed of by the will, a grant may be made to any person entitled to share in the undisposed-of residue, or, if every such person has since died or is otherwise cleared off, to the personal representative of any such person who has died.

5.179   If the terms of the will are such that, though there is a complete disposition of the residue, it is impossible to designate any person as the ultimate residuary beneficiary, the facts should be put before the district judge or registrar for his directions as to whom a grant should be made.

Notice to Treasury Solicitor

5.180   Where the residuary estate is wholly or partly undisposed of and the deceased died without kin entitled to share in the undisposed-of estate, or without known kin entitled to share, notice of the application for the grant must be given to the Treasury Solicitor in accordance with NCPR 38, and an acknowledgment of such notice filed with the papers to lead the grant. Under the same rule the district judge or registrar may direct that no grant shall issue within 28 days after the notice has been given.

Virtual disposition of residue

5.181   Where the residuary estate is not in terms wholly disposed of, but the testator has nevertheless disposed of the whole, or substantially the whole, of the estate as ascertained at the time of the application for a grant, the district judge or registrar may allow a grant to be made (subject to NCPR 38) to any legatee or devisee entitled to, or to share in, the estate so disposed of, without regard to the persons entitled to share in any residue not disposed of by the will (NCPR 20(c)(ii)).

5.182   This provision does not derogate from the right of a person entitled to the undisposed-of estate to obtain a grant if he applies for it, but it frequently facilitates the issue of a grant to a legatee or devisee who has the sole, or a substantial, interest under the terms of the will where the deceased left kin who, although having little or no interest in the estate, would otherwise have to be cleared off.

5.183   In the simplest type of case, where the whole of the estate has been left by enumeration to one or more legatees, and a legatee having a substantial interest applies for the grant, it is sufficient for the oath, in addition to clearing off executors, to include, after the gross amount of the estate, the words 'all of which is disposed of by the said will'. The applicant should be described merely as 'a legatee named in the said will'. Such applications are normally granted as of course without reference to a district judge or registrar. (Form of oath, No. 150.)

5.184   Where not the whole, but substantially the whole, estate is disposed of, the wording should be 'of which £   is disposed of by the said will'. It will be for the district judge or registrar, having regard to the size of the estate and the amount disposed of, to decide whether the facts bring the case within the relevant terms of the rule, and, if so, whether the grant should be made to the applicant. In cases of doubt he may call for more detailed evidence, and may require notice to be given to the persons entitled to the undisposed-of estate.

5.185   If it is clear from the papers that there are kin who would be entitled to share in any undisposed-of estate, the Crown need not be regarded as interested. Unless this is clear, however, the applicant should either provide evidence that there are such kin, or give notice to the Treasury Solicitor in accordance with NCPR 38 (even though the whole of the ascertained estate is disposed of). Where such notice is to be given, the district judge or registrar may direct that no grant shall issue within 28 days after notice has been given in order to give the Treasury Solicitor the opportunity of opposing the making of the grant if he wishes.

5.186   If any person who would be entitled to, or to share in, any undisposed-of estate is a minor it is necessary (unless the court thinks it expedient in all the circumstances to appoint a sole administrator) for the grant to be made to not less than two individuals or to a trust corporation with or without an individual, even though the whole of the known estate has been disposed of.

5.187   In the event of a dispute between a legatee and a person entitled to the undisposed-of estate, the matter is one for decision under NCPR 27(6) (see paras. **14.08** ff., post).

5.188   The term 'legatee' has been used in the foregoing paragraphs to include a devisee.

Rule 20, Class (e)

Specific legatees or devisees and creditors

5.189   On clearing off all prior classes, a grant may be made, without preference, to any specific legatee or devisee (including one for life or one holding in trust for any other person) or any creditor of the deceased. As with residuary beneficiaries, a legatee or devisee whose legacy or devise is vested in interest is preferred to one entitled on the happening of a contingency, unless a district judge or registrar otherwise directs (proviso to NCPR 20(e)). As to whether a gift is vested or contingent see paras. **5.87** ff., ante.

Estate wholly disposed of by the will

5.190   Where the residuary estate is wholly disposed of by the will, the residuary legatee and devisee (or, if he has since died, his personal representative) must be cleared off by renunciation or citation before a grant can be made to a legatee, a devisee or a creditor. For form of oath, see No. 143.

Estate not wholly disposed of by the will

5.191   Where the residuary estate is partly or wholly undisposed of, all persons taking any part of the residue disposed of by the will, and in addition, all persons entitled to share in the undisposed-of estate, or the personal representatives of any that have died, must be similarly cleared off.

Clearing off where no personal representative constituted

5.192   Where a person who had acquired an interest in either the disposed-of residue or in any part of the estate not disposed of has since died, but no personal representative of such person has been constituted, before a grant may be made to a person with an inferior title it is the practice to require the renunciation of all persons who, by reason of their being entitled to constitute themselves the personal representatives of such person, have a potential right to a grant in the estate of the deceased. In case of difficulty in clearing off such persons the directions of the district judge or registrar should be taken.

Undisposed-of estate vested in spouse who has since died

5.193   Where the whole of the undisposed-of estate has vested in the surviving spouse of the deceased, who has since died, a child of the deceased who is also the child of the spouse should constitute himself personal representative of the surviving spouse by taking a leading grant in that estate, and then apply in that capacity for a grant in the estate of the first to die.

Grants to creditors

5.194   The practice in making grants to creditors follows that in making such grants in cases of intestacy (see paras. **6.310** ff., post).

The Crown to be cleared off

5.195   Where the residuary estate is wholly or partly undisposed of and the deceased died without kin entitled to share in the undisposed-of estate, or without known kin entitled to share, the Treasury Solicitor must be given notice in case he wishes to claim bona vacantia on behalf of the Crown (which would enable him to apply for a grant) or the Crown must be specifically cleared off by renunciation or citation before a grant can be made to a person entitled in a lower degree (i.e. to a person entitled under classes (d) or (e) of NCPR 20) (see paras. **6.314** ff., post, as to the practice).

Rule 20, Class (f)

Personal representative of any other legatee or devisee (but not one for life or one holding in trust for any other person) or of any creditor of the deceased

5.196 When all classes entitled in priority, down to and including legatees, devisees and creditors, have been cleared off, a grant may be made, without preference, to the personal representative of any specific legatee or devisee or any creditor of the deceased.

Persons having no interest under the will

5.197 It should be noted that the NCPR 1987, unlike the previous rules, do not include provision for a grant to be made to a member of the nearest class of kin of the deceased having no interest under the will (except where that class is entitled to the estate undisposed of by the will, in respect of which see paras. **5.82** ff., ante).

Miscellaneous grants of administration (with will)

To trust corporation or Public Trustee

5.198 On the renunciation of the executors and the consent of all persons entitled to a grant and of all persons interested in the residuary estate, administration (with will) may be granted to a trust corporation which is neither a beneficiary nor the attorney of a person entitled to a grant. The district judge or registrar has power if he thinks fit to dispense with any such consent.

5.199 Where any of the persons whose consent is required is a minor a special practice operates (see paras. **9.40** ff., post).

5.200 As to grants to trust corporations and the Public Trustee, see Chap. 9.

Nominee or attorney of a corporation (not a trust corporation) appointed executor or trustee or a beneficiary, or being a creditor

5.201 Letters of administration (with will) cannot be granted to a person as nominee of a trust corporation[1]. But where a corporate body (not being a trust corporation) would, if it were an individual, be entitled to a grant, administration for its use and benefit, and limited until further representation be granted, may be granted to its nominee or attorney[2]. In such a case, the following practice is applicable.

1 Supreme Court Act 1981, s. 115(2).
2 NCPR 36(4)(a).

5.202 The nominee or attorney must swear in the oath that the corporation is not a trust corporation as defined by rule 2(1) of the Non-Contentious Probate Rules 1987.

5.203   A sealed, or otherwise authenticated, copy of the resolution of the board of the corporation appointing the nominee, or the instrument appointing the attorney, is required to be filed with the papers when the grant is applied for.

5.204   If the corporation is entitled as executor, it must be established that it has power under its constitution to take a grant through its nominee (e.g. by producing a copy of the constitution[1]).

1 Registrar's Direction (1956) 2 January.

5.205   Where a corporation (not being a trust corporation) or an association or public or charitable or private body of persons is entitled as a beneficiary or creditor, the governing body or committee of management, or other body most completely representing it, may nominate a person or persons to apply for a grant on their behalf, by a resolution under their seal (if any). A copy of the resolution, certified by the secretary or other officer, is brought in with the papers to lead the grant, and the grant is made to the nominee for the use and benefit of the corporation or other body and until further representation be granted.

5.206   Where a body corporate (not being a trust corporation), together with one or more individuals, have been appointed executors of a will, administration (with will) may be granted to their attorney for their use and benefit and 'until further representation be granted'. If the attorney of the body corporate alone applies for a grant, it is necessary to file the renunciation of the individuals (for the reason that probate could be granted to the individuals alone, but not to the body corporate)[1].

1 NCPR 36(4)(d).

5.207   If any minority or life interest arises, a grant cannot normally be made to a single individual, whether as nominee or attorney: two individuals, or a trust corporation with or without an individual, will be appointed, unless it appears to the court to be expedient in all the circumstances to appoint a sole administrator.

Grant to assignee

5.208   NCPR 24 is as follows:

> '(1) Where all the persons entitled to the estate of the deceased (whether under a will or on intestacy) have assigned their whole interest in the estate to one or more persons, the assignee or assignees shall replace, in the order of priority for a grant of administration, the assignor or, if there are two or more assignors, the assignor with the highest priority.
>
> (2) Where there are two or more assignees, administration may be granted with the consent of the others to any one or more (not exceeding four) of them.
>
> (3) In any case where administration is applied for by an assignee the original instrument of assignment shall be produced and a copy of the same lodged in the registry.'

5.209   Any rights prior to that of the assignor or assignors (e.g. of executors and residuary legatees or devisees in trust) must be cleared off before a grant can be made under this rule. Thus, where the deceased left a will, if the executors and residuary legatees or devisees in trust are cleared off, on the execution, by all the persons taking a beneficial interest in the estate, of a deed of assignment of the whole of their interest (whether under the terms of the will or any partial intestacy), administration (with will) may be granted to the assignee or assignees, or to any one or more of them, not exceeding a total of four, with the consent of the others.

5.210 It should be noted that a grant under this provision is not possible if any person beneficially interested in the estate is not sui juris, or for some other reason does not join in the assignment.

5.211 Where any assignee is a minor it is normally necessary for the grant to be made to not less than two individuals or a trust corporation; similarly if the sole assignee is a minor the grant is normally made, on his behalf, to not less than two persons or a trust corporation[1]. As to grants on behalf of minors, see paras. **11.113** ff., post.)

1 Registrar's Circular, 12 June 1967, and see also Supreme Court Act 1981, s. 114(2), p. 844, post.

5.212 Where a grant is sought by one or some only of several assignees a consent to the making of a grant to such person or persons, signed by all the other assignees, must be lodged with the papers (see NCPR 24(2)). Form of consent, No. 57.

5.213 On every application for a grant to an assignee or assignees the original deed of assignment must be produced at the registry for inspection and a copy of the deed lodged for filing: after inspection, the original instrument will be returned to the applicant or his solicitor (NCPR 24(3)).

5.214 It is the practice of the registry to examine the original deed to ensure that it has been properly executed and duly stamped under the Stamp Act 1891 before proceeding with the application. Where there is any doubt whether the instrument is duly stamped, the applicant will be asked to present the instrument to the Controller of Stamps (Inland Revenue) for adjudication before the issue of the grant. To avoid delay in the issue of the grant in such cases, the Commissioners of Inland Revenue have agreed that the applicant may, if so desired, submit the original instrument to the Adjudication Section of the Office of the Controller of Stamps for preliminary noting, endorsement and return, provided that a written undertaking is at the same time given to the Controller by the solicitor applying for the grant of representation that he will, on or immediately after the issue of the grant, re-submit the original instrument to the Controller for formal adjudication and pay the stamp duty (if any) to which the instrument is adjudged liable[1].

1 *Practice Note* [1978] 1 All ER 1046, [1978] 1 WLR 430.

5.215 The Stamp Duty (Exempt Instruments) Regulations 1987 (S.I. 1987 No. 516) came into force on 1 May 1987 and provide that instruments executed on or after that date of a kind specified in the Schedule to the Regulations and which bear a certificate in a form which satisfies the requirements of the Regulations shall be exempt from payment of duty under certain headings in Sch. 1. to the Stamp Act 1891 and ss. 83(2) and 84(8) of the Finance Act 1985. The certificate referred to must be in writing and

(a) either be included in the instrument or be endorsed on or physically attached to it,

(b) contain a sufficient description of;

(i)   the instrument concerned where the certificate is separate but physically attached, and

(ii) the category of the Schedule into which the instrument falls, and

(c) must be signed by the transferor or grantor or by his solicitor or duly authorised agent.

Where it is not signed by the transferor or grantor or his solicitor, it must contain a statement by the signatory of the capacity in which he signs, that he is authorised so to sign and that he gives the certificate from his own knowedge of the facts stated in it. Where a deed of assignment is produced on an application for a grant and is supported by a certificate (as indicated above) it is checked in the registry against the above criteria and the exempt categories set out in the Schedule to the Regulations to establish whether the requirements of the Regulations have been satisfied. The court, however, retains the right to require adjudication if in doubt as to the correctness of the certificate[1].

1 Secretary's Circular, 10 September 1987.

5.216 Form of oath for grant of administration (with will) to assignees, No. 156.

Spes successionis

5.217 The NCPR 1987, unlike the previous rules, make no provision for a grant to issue, where the beneficial interest in the whole estate of the deceased is vested absolutely in a person who has renounced his right to a grant and has consented to administration being granted to the person or persons who would be entitled to his estate if he himself had died intestate. Where the beneficiary does not wish to apply for a grant himself he may now appoint an attorney to apply for a grant for his use and benefit under NCPR 31—see paras. **11.31** ff., post.

To trustee in bankruptcy or under a deed of arrangement

5.218 A right to a grant of administration of the estate of an intestate is not a right which passes to the trustee in bankruptcy of the beneficiary[1].

1 *Re Turner's Goods* (1886) 12 PD 18.

5.219 A trustee in bankruptcy of a beneficiary under a will (or an intestacy) has no title under the probate rules to a grant as such. He cannot be regarded as a trust corporation for the purpose of administering the estate of the deceased (s. 3 of the Law of Property (Amendment) Act 1926 being limited to his duties 'in relation to the property of the bankrupt'). He may, however, in proper cases obtain an order under s. 116 of the Supreme Court Act 1981 (see paras. **14.01** ff., post) for a grant to himself as an individual.

5.220 Such orders and grants will be in the form: 'to A. B. of (*address and occupation*), the trustee of the property of X. Y. a bankrupt, limited to such period as he shall remain trustee of the said property.'

5.221 Where an Official Receiver is acting as trustee, his official title (e.g. the Senior Official Receiver, *or* the Official Receiver, *or* the Assistant Official Receiver of the High Court of Justice, *or* the Official Receiver of the County Court District of   ) should be stated in the oath.

5.222 A trustee under a deed of arrangement may, if the terms of the deed and the circumstances of the case permit, be able to establish title to a grant under NCPR 24 (i.e. as assignee of the only person entitled to the estate). Failing this, he may apply for an order under s. 116 of the Supreme Court Act 1981 (see above). In either event, the grant should describe him as trustee under the deed and be limited to such period as he shall remain trustee[1].

1 Registrar's Direction (1956) 24 July.

5.223 The Chancery Division in its bankruptcy jurisdiction has no power to make an order for administration of a deceased bankrupt's estate until a personal representative has been constituted[1].

1 *Re a Debtor (No 1035 of 1938)* [1939] Ch 594, [1939] 2 All ER 56.

Other grants of administration (with will)

5.224 For the practice in obtaining a grant for the use and benefit of a minor or a person incapable of managing his affairs, or to the attorney of the person entitled to a grant, see Chap. 11; grants in cases where the deceased died domiciled out of England and Wales, see Chap. 12; grants in the exercise of the discretionary power of the Court, see Chap. 14; grants de bonis non and cessate grants, see Chap. 13.

Death before 1 January 1926

5.225 Where the death occurred before 1 January 1926 the right to a grant is still determined, subject to the provisions of any enactment, by the principles and rules in accordance with which the court would have acted at the date of death (NCPR 23).

5.226 The order of priority of right to a grant of administration (with will) is as follows:

Class 1. Residuary legatees and devisees in trust.
Class 2. Residuary legatees and devisees; a residuary legatee or devisee substituted.
Class 3. The personal representatives of residuary legatees or devisees who survived the deceased but have since died.

If the residuary estate is wholly disposed of by the will:

Class 4. The husband or widow (or, if cleared off, the next-of-kin) of the deceased; and legatees, devisees or creditors. No other person is entitled if the residue is fully disposed of.

If the residuary estate is not wholly disposed of, or the residuary gift has lapsed, the order, after Class 3, is as follows:

Class 4. The husband or widow (or, if cleared off, the next-of-kin) of the deceased.
Class 5. The heir-at-law (if there is real estate and the death occurred after 1897). On clearing real estate, the personal representative of the husband.
Class 6. Persons entitled in distribution, not being next-of-kin.
Class 7. The personal representative of the widow, or of the next-of-kin, or of a residuary legatee as to an unlapsed moiety, or of the heir-at-law (where the deceased left real estate and the death was after 1897), or of other persons entitled in distribution.
Class 8. Legatees, devisees or creditors.

Class 9.   The Crown (Treasury Solicitor, Duchy of Lancaster or Duchy of Cornwall).

5.227   Where the residuary estate is not wholly disposed of, or part of a residuary gift has lapsed, the person entitled under the effective disposition and those entitled to the lapsed or undisposed-of residue are equally entitled to a grant.

5.228   Where the deceased left no real estate the right of the heir-at-law, or of his personal representative, should be cleared off in the oath, where necessary, by the statement that the deceased died not possessed of real estate.

Requirements on obtaining administration (with will)

Practice as to will

5.229   The practice as to proof of the will and codicils, alterations, incorporation, etc. is the same as in applications for probate. (See Chaps. 3 and 4.)

Administration (will) oath

Clearing off

5.230   The oath for administration (with the will annexed) should be so worded as to clear off all persons having a prior right to the grant (see NCPR 8(4)), and show the capacity in which the intended administrator is entitled. Thus, it must always be stated that no executors were appointed, or that they are dead or have renounced, as the case may be, in an application for a grant by a person interested in the residue. See also para. **5.192**, ante, as to clearing off where a beneficiary has subsequently died, but no personal representative of such person has been constituted. Forms of oath for administration (with will annexed), Nos. 143–168.

Minority or life interest

5.231   In every oath to lead a grant of administration (with the will annexed), the deponent must state whether there is a life interest or a minority interest, and the district judge or registrar may call for such further evidence as he may require. See NCPR 6(1) and 8(4). See also Chap. 7.

5.232   Where the residuary estate is not wholly disposed of by the will and the deceased left a surviving spouse, regard must be had to the extent of the spouse's statutory entitlement in respect of the undisposed-of estate in deciding whether or not a life interest arises. The spouse's entitlement of £125,000 (where the deceased left issue) or £200,000 (where the deceased left no issue)[1] is diminished by the value of any beneficial interests (other than personal chattels specifically bequeathed) acquired by the spouse under the will[2]. Where the date of death was before 1 January 1953 the spouse is entitled to the first £1,000 of the undisposed-of estate, irrespective of any beneficial interest taken under the will.

1 Or such other sum as is appropriate in case of death prior to 1 December 1993 (see para. **5.164**, ante and Administration of Estates Act 1925, s. 46).
2 Administration of Estates Act 1925, s. 49(1)(aa): see p. 757, post.

5.233 If no minority or life interest arises under the terms of the will, and the gross value of the undisposed-of estate does not exceed the relevant figure, it may be sworn that no minority or life interest arises, and a grant may be made to a sole individual administrator. Where the gross value of the undisposed-of estate is in excess of the appropriate figure but the net value thereof after allowing the permissible deductions (which are set out in para. **6.93**, post) does not exceed this figure, the oath should contain the wording indicated in para. **6.93** in order to justify the statement that no minority or life interest arises.

5.234 The question whether a life interest arises by reason of the amount of the estate in respect of which there is an intestacy must be decided by reference to the total sum wherever situate that will ultimately come into the hands of the administrators. But in case of death after 1952 where the deceased died leaving no issue the interests of the surviving spouse in the undisposed-of estate are absolute. See para. **6.86**, post.

Settled land

5.235 In every oath to lead a grant of administration (with the will annexed) where the deceased died on or after 1 January 1926 the deponent must swear, to the best of his knowledge, information and belief, whether there was land vested in the deceased which was settled previously to his death (and not by his will) and which remained settled land notwithstanding his death (NCPR 8(3)).

Representative grants

5.236 As to the practice on an application for a grant by the personal representatives of a deceased beneficiary, see paras. **6.11** ff., post.

Swearing, descriptions, proof of identity

5.237 The practice as to swearing, and description and age of testators and description of deponents, proof of identity of the deceased, marking the will, amount of estate, etc. is the same as in applications for probate. See Chap. 4.

Form of grant

5.238 This subject is dealt with at paras. **2.24–2.35**, ante.

Guarantee

5.239 The NCPR 1987, unlike the previous rules, make no provision for guarantees. Consequently a guarantee is not required on an application proceeding under the NCPR 1987, which will be every application unless a direction has been given under r. 68 by a High Court judge or district judge or registrar, in any particular case pending on 1 January 1988 (when the NCPR 1987 came into force) that the previous rules shall continue to apply to that particular case.

5.240 The practice as to guarantees on cases proceeding under the previous rules is dealt with in Chapter 6 of the 26th edition of this work.

Facsimile copy or engrossment

5.241 The practice as to facsimile copies or engrossments of the will and codicils (if any) corresponds with that detailed ante, paras. **4.222–4.232**.

Inland Revenue account

5.242   This subject is dealt with in Chap. 8.

Fees

5.243   The fees payable on a grant of letters of administration with the will annexed are the same as in the case of a probate. (See paras. **4.250–4.265**, ante, and Appendix III, p. 959, post.)

Solicitor's charges

5.244   This subject is dealt with in Chapter 4: see paras. **4.266–4.278**, ante.

CHAPTER 6

Letters of administration

Summary

Notes. 1. This chapter deals only with grants of administration in cases where the deceased died **domiciled in England and Wales**. For the practice in cases where the deceased died domiciled elsewhere, see Chap. 12, post.

2. Except where otherwise stated, the practice given in this chapter applies where the date of death of the intestate was on or after 1 January 1926.

In what circumstances granted

6.01   Letters of administration of the estate of a deceased person are granted where the deceased died wholly intestate[1]. The grant is usually required for the purpose of realising and administering the estate of the deceased in the United Kingdom, but a grant may be made where the deceased left no estate[2], but it is for some purpose required to constitute a personal representative of the deceased (e.g. to enable legal proceedings in connection with the estate to be commenced or defended, to make title to estate or property vested in the deceased as trustee, and not beneficially, to enable a new trustee to be appointed, etc.). A grant may also be necessary in respect of settled land vested in the deceased[3].

---

1   Where the deceased left a will appointing no executor and containing no disposition of property in England it has been the practice to regard the will as not entitled to proof in England (see para. **3.23**, ante), but it is considered that where necessary the will may be proved: see *Stubbings v Clunies-Ross* (1911) 27 TLR 361; *Re Wayland's Estate* [1951] 2 All ER 1041, cited at para. **3.23** at fn. 3.
2   As to grant where the deceased left no estate, see paras. **4.209–4.210**, ante.
3   As to grants in respect of settled land, see Chap. 10.

6.02   Letters of administration were also granted in the case of death before 1 January 1926 where the deceased left a will appointing no executor and disposing only of copyhold or other real property which, notwithstanding the Land Transfer Act 1897[1], did not vest in his personal representative, and in case of death before 1 January 1898 where the deceased left a will appointing no executor and containing only a devise of real property, but left personal estate in this country[2].

1 Land Transfer Act 1897, s. 1(4): see p. 730, post. Copyholds were abolished as from 1 January 1926 (Law of Property Act 1922, s. 128).
2 *Re Bootle's Goods* (1874) LR 3 P & D 177.

Letters of administration after citation to propound paper writing

6.03   Letters of administration may be granted to the person entitled to them on an intestacy, notwithstanding that it is suggested that the deceased left a document purporting to be a will, if the executor and all persons interested under the document have been cited to propound it, but have not appeared to the citation[1]. As to citations to propound a will, see paras. **24.33** ff., post.

1 NCPR 48. See *Whiting v Deal and Orchard* (1854) 2 Spinks 57; *Re Jacques' Goods, Perry v Dyke* (1858) 1 Sw & Tr 12; *Re Morton's Goods, Morton v Thorpe* (1863) 3 Sw & Tr 179 at 181, and the cases there referred to. Where the deceased died insane, leaving a will which was, on the face of it, marked with insanity, the court granted administration as on an intestacy, but directed that the will be filed (*Re Bourget's Goods* (1837) 1 Curt 591).

6.04   In such a case it must be sworn in the oath, and the grant will recite, that the deceased died intestate. It is considered in such cases that the order of the court is based on the citor's contention that the deceased died intestate, which contention is confirmed by the order of the court, the default of appearance by the persons cited to propound the document referred to in the citation being tantamount to an admission that the document cannot be set up[1]. Form of oath, No. 130.

1 See also NCPR 48(2).

Letters of administration after judgment pronouncing against a will

6.05   On an application for a grant of letters of administration following a judgment in a probate action pronouncing against the validity of a document purporting to be the last will, the details of the judgment must be recited in the oath, and an office copy of the judgment must be lodged with the papers. The order of the court will be recited in the grant[1]. The practice should follow that set out in para. **4.176**, ante, in cases where a will is pronounced for, mutatis mutandis.

1 Registrar's Direction (1950) 16 January.

Document revoking former wills

6.06   Where the deceased left a duly executed document the sole effect of which is to revoke all previous testamentary dispositions, the grant takes the form of letters of administration, no copy of the document being annexed[1]. The document must be lodged with the papers to lead the grant. The following notation is made on the grant: 'A duly attested instrument made by the deceased on the   day of   19   , revoking all former wills, filed'.

1 *Re Fraser's Goods* (1869) LR 2 P & D 40; *Toomer v Sobinska* [1907] P 106. See also paras. **3.28** and **3.29**, ante.

Preference of living interests

6.07   When the personal representative of a person who, if alive, would have been entitled to a grant in the estate of the deceased, applies for a grant in his representative capacity, regard must be had to the provisions of NCPR 27(5). Unless otherwise directed by a district judge or registrar, administration will be granted to a living person in preference to the personal representative of a deceased person who, if alive, would be entitled in the same degree.

6.08   The oath must, where possible, clear off living interests, i.e. it should be sworn, as the case may be, either that the person whom the applicant represents was the only person entitled to the estate or that all the persons entitled to share in the estate have since died or have renounced. Their respective names, relationships and dates of death should be specified, and it should be stated, where appropriate, that they died without taking a grant in the estate of the deceased.

6.09   Where there are living persons entitled, but it is desired that the grant be made to the personal representative of a deceased beneficiary without clearing off the former by renunciation, the facts should be placed before the Principal at the Principal Registry or the district probate registrar for his directions under r. 27(5).

6.10   As to the position where the deceased left a surviving spouse who has subsequently died, see paras. **6.101–6.106**, post.

Representative grants

6.11   It is the practice to allow one of two or more executors, without reference to the other or others, to take administration of the estate of a deceased whom their testator was entitled to represent. But this rule is not applied to the case of co-administrators, who should take administration in such circumstances jointly[1]. Any one (or normally two if a minority or life interest arises) of two or more co-administrators, however, is allowed to take administration on the other or others renouncing or consenting[2].

1 *Re Nayler's Goods* (1851) 2 Rob Ecc 409, 15 Jur 686.
2 *Hancock v Lightfoot* (1864) 3 Sw & Tr 557. In *Re Crook* (1855) 2 August, Sir John Dodson decreed administration to one of three administrators without notice to the others, of whom one was a lunatic, and the other was resident abroad.

6.12   The oath should state that the applicant is the sole executor (or one of the executors) of the will, or the administrator of the estate, as the case may be, of the person entitled, and should recite the date of the grant and the registry from which it issued. The leading grant, or an official copy of it, should be lodged with the papers: it will be returned with the new grant.

6.13   It is frequently necessary to obtain two grants successively in connection with the administration of the estate of a deceased, one grant being the 'leading' grant which constitutes the applicant as the executor of the will, or administrator of the estate, of a beneficiary who has died.

6.14   In such cases there is no objection to both sets of papers being sworn at the same time, anticipating the title which will be conferred on the applicant by the leading grant. If this course is adopted, the applicant should be described in the oath to lead the grant in the estate of the first to die as 'the sole executor named in the will of the said A. B. deceased' or 'the proposed administrator of the estate of the said A. B. deceased', as the case may be.

6.15 The papers in respect of both applications may be lodged at the registry simultaneously, a note that this has been done being made in the margin of the oaths. If the applications are in order the grants will be made successively, the second a few days after the issue of the leading grant.

Application by attorney administrator for representative grant

6.16 An attorney administrator may obtain a grant in another estate to which he is entitled as personal representative of the deceased without (so far as the probate registries are concerned) any further authority from the donor of the power being necessary[1]. If it is known that a further grant will be required, the power of attorney may, if so desired, be so worded as to authorise the attorney to obtain both grants (see para. **11.74**, post and Form No. 182 for a precedent for such a power of attorney).

1 Registrar's Direction (1974) 11 October.

To whom granted

6.17 The general rule applicable to the grant of letters of administration is that where possible administration is granted to one or more of the persons taking a beneficial interest in the estate of the deceased (see the reference to the probate rules in s. 116(1) of the Supreme Court Act 1981[1] and NCPR 22(1)[2]).

1 See p. 845, post.
2 See p. 929, post.

6.18 In the case of death on or after 1 January 1926 the distribution of the residuary estate of an intestate is regulated by Part IV (i.e. ss. 45–52) of the Administration of Estates Act 1925[1]. This Part of the Act has been amended, as regards deaths occurring on or after 1 January 1953, by the Intestates' Estates Act 1952 and further amended as regards deaths occurring on or after 1 January 1967 by the Family Provision Act 1966. In the case of death on or after 1 January 1970, rights of succession on intestacy were given to illegitimate, as well as legitimate, children of the deceased, and to the natural parents of an illegitimate intestate by Part II of the Family Law Reform Act 1969[2]. As regards deaths on or after 4 April 1988 illegitimacy is not to be taken into account regarding any of the classes of relations entitled to succeed on intestacy, by reason of s. 18 of the Family Law Reform Act 1987[3].

1 See pp. 751 ff., post.
2 See Supreme Court Act 1981, s. 25, p. 837, post.
3 See p. 876, post.

6.19 Where the death occurred prior to 1 January 1926, the former Statutes of Distribution and the Intestates' Estates Acts 1884 and 1890 apply, and the practice thereunder and the special rights of the heir-at-law in relation to real estate, and of the next-of-kin, are still applicable where it is necessary to obtain a grant, (NCPR 23). A summary of the practice applicable in such cases is given post, paras. **6.386** ff.

6.20 The rights of the heir-at-law in respect of real estate would still apply in the now rare case of a person who was of full age but of unsound mind on 1 January 1926 dying intestate and without having recovered his testamentary capacity[1]: see paras. **6.146** and **6.147**, post.

1 Administration of Estates Act 1925, s. 51(2); see p. 761, post.

Number of administrators. Minority or life interest

6.21 By s. 114(1) of the Supreme Court Act 1981[1], the maximum number of persons allowed to take a grant in respect of the same part of the estate[2] is four, and if a minority or a life interest arises under the intestacy, administration must (unless the court in its discretion thinks it expedient in all the circumstances to appoint a sole administrator) be granted to a trust corporation, with or without an individual, or to not less than two individuals[3]. This applies whatever the date of death.

1 See p. 844, post.
2 *Re Holland's Estate* [1936] 3 All ER 13.
3 Section 114(2) of the Supreme Court Act 1981 (p. 844, post).

6.22 As to grants of administration to trust corporations, see Chap. 9 and as to the joinder of a second administrator, see Chap. 7.

Subsequent appointment of additional administrator

6.23 Where a grant has been made to one personal representative other than a trust corporation, or where one of two personal representatives has died, there being a minor beneficiary or a life interest subsisting, an additional administrator may be appointed by a district judge or registrar under s. 114(4) of the Supreme Court Act 1981. The original grant may be noted with the appointment (without any necessity for a new grant), or it may be impounded or revoked as the circumstances of the case require, or as the district judge or registrar may direct. See NCPR 26 and paras. **7.40** ff. and **16.32**, post.

Administrators' power to appoint trustees

6.24 Administrators (with or without will) who have cleared the estate and completed the administration become trustees holding for the beneficiaries, either on an intestacy or under the terms of the will. They have power under the Trustee Act 1925, s. 36, to appoint new trustees to act in their place, but if they do not do so they become trustees in the full sense[1].

1 *Re Cockburn's Will Trusts, Cockburn v Lewis* [1957] Ch 438, [1957] 2 All ER 522, distinguishing *Harvell v Foster* [1954] 2 QB 367, [1954] 2 All ER 736.

Assignment of life interest or reversion

6.25 Persons entitled to life interests, or reversioners entitled after the life tenant, may assign their interests by deed; but before a grant can issue to one administrator it must be proved, by production of the deed, that all the life or reversionary interests have been assigned and have become merged in an absolute interest[1].

1   There is some doubt whether absolute rights under an English intestacy can be disclaimed, and the destination of disclaimed property is uncertain: it is possible that it would vest in the Crown: see *Williams on Wills* and Ing on *Bona Vacantia*: however, the prevailing view would now seem to permit disclaimer and, where all members of a class have disclaimed, to favour the next class of kin in the order of priority in preference to the Crown's bona vacantia claim (*Re Scott, Widdows v Friends of the Clergy Corpn* [1975] 2 All ER 1033, [1975] 1 WLR 1260).

6.26   On application for a grant as sole administrator by a spouse (or other life tenant who is the first person entitled to a grant) to whom the reversioners have assigned all their interests, no renunciation by the reversioners is necessary. On the other hand, the renunciation by a life tenant who has assigned his interest is necessary before a grant can be made to a person of lower title. The facts and the date of the deed must be recited in the oath[1]. Forms of oath, Nos. 90 and 95.

1   Registrar's Directions (1950) 19 December and (1951) 16 July.

6.27   As to the right of a surviving spouse to require the redemption of his or her life interest, see paras. **6.39** ff. and **16.36** ff., post.

6.28   As to the production to the registry of an original deed or other instrument, see paras. **5.213–5.215**, ante.

6.29   TABLES SHOWING THE PERSONS ENTITLED TO THE ESTATE AND TO A GRANT IN THE CASE OF INTESTACY SINCE JANUARY 1926

Note. *When s. 1(1) of the Law Reform (Succession) Act 1995 (see p. 900) comes into force, in respect of an intestate dying on or after 1 January 1996 a spouse will have to survive the intestate for a period of 28 days beginning with the day on which the intestate died, before the spouse acquires a beneficial interest in the estate under s. 46 of the Administration of Estates Act 1925.*

A. Death On or After 1 January 1953 where Deceased left a Surviving Spouse[1]

Intestate leaves	Distribution of estate	Entitled to grant
I. Husband or widow and issue (**net estate not exceeding £125,000**; £75,000 where death on or after 1 June 1987 but before 1 December 1993, £40,000 where death on or after 1 March 1981 but before 1 June 1987; £25,000 where death after 14 March 1977 but before 1 March 1981; £15,000 where death after 30 June 1972 but before 15 March 1977; £8,750 where death after 31 December 1966 but before 1 July 1972; or £5,000 where death before 1 January 1967)[2]	All to husband or widow	Husband or widow

1   As to devolution of the estate of a married woman who has been judicially separated from her husband, see paras. **6.140** ff., post.
2   For method of determining the amount of the 'net estate' for this purpose, see para. **6.92**, post. As to the meaning of 'issue', see note 3 to para. **6.37**, post.

A. Death On or After 1 January 1953 where Deceased left a Surviving Spouse[1]—(*continued*).

Intestate leaves	Distribution of estate	Entitled to grant
II. Husband or widow without issue (**net estate not exceeding £200,000**; £125,000 where death on or after 1 June 1987 but before 1 December 1993; £85,000 where death on or after 1 March 1981 but before 1 June 1987; £55,000 where death after 14 March 1977 but before 1 March 1981; £40,000 where death after 30 June 1972 but before 15 March 1977; £30,000 where death after 31 December 1966 but before 1 July 1972; or £20,000 where death before 1 January 1967)[2]	All to husband or widow	Husband or widow
III. Husband or widow and issue (**net estate exceeding £125,000**, £75,000, £40,000, £25,000, £15,000, £8,750 or £5,000 (whichever is appropriate: see I above))	Husband or widow takes personal chattels, £125,000 (£75,000 where death on or after 1 June 1987 but before 1 December 1993; £40,000 where death on or after 1 March 1981 but before 1 June 1987; £25,000 where death after 14 March 1977 but before 1 March 1981; £15,000 where death after 30 June 1972 but before 15 March 1977; £8,750 where death after 31 December 1966 but before 1 July 1972; or £5,000 where death before 1 January 1967) free of costs and duty, with interest at the appropriate rate[3], and a life interest in half remainder of estate, with reversion to the issue, The other half to the issue absolutely	*Husband or widow and a child

1 As to devolution of the estate of a married woman who has been judicially separated from her husband, see paras. **6.140** ff., post.
2 For method of determining the amount of the 'net estate' for this purpose, see para. **6.92**, post. As to the meaning of 'issue', see note 3 to para. **6.37**, post.
3 The Intestate Succession (Interest and Capitalisation) Order 1977 (Amendment) Order 1983 (S.I. 1983 No. 1374) provides that for the purposes of s. 46(l)(i) of the Administration of Estates Act 1925, as it applies both in respect of persons dying before 1953 and in respect of persons dying after 1952, the rate of interest payable on the statutory legacy until it is paid or appropriated shall be 6 per cent per annum with effect from 1 October 1983. The previous rate of interest was 7 per cent per annum for the period commencing on 15 September 1977 (the Intestate Succession (Interest and Capitalisation) Order 1977, S.I. 1977 No. 1491 which increased the then current rate of 4 per cent per annum or, in the case of persons dying before the coming into operation of the Intestates' Estates Act 1952, 5 per cent per annum). Accordingly, where a statutory legacy remains unpaid for a considerable time, the interest payable on that legacy will need to be calculated at different rates for different periods. For example, where the death occurs after 1952 but before 15 September 1977, the interest to be paid on the statutory legacy will be 4 per cent per annum up to 15 September 1977 and thereafter 7 per cent per annum until 1 October 1983 and thereafter 6 per cent per annum until the legacy is paid or appropriated.

A. Death On or After 1 January 1953 where Deceased left a Surviving Spouse[1]—(*continued*).

Intestate leaves	Distribution of estate	Entitled to grant
IV. Husband or widow without issue (**net estate exceeding £200,000**, £125,000, £85,000, £55,000, £40,000, £30,000 or £20,000 (whichever is appropriate: see II above))[2]	Husband or widow takes personal chattels, £200,000 (£125,000 where death on or after 1 June 1987 but before 1 December 1993; £85,000 where death on or after 1 March 1981 but before 1 June 1987; £55,000 where death after 14 March 1977 but before 1 March 1981; £40,000 where death after 30 June 1972 but before 15 March 1977; £30,000 where death after 31 December 1966 but before 1 July 1972; or £20,000 where death before 1 January 1967) free of costs and duty, with interest at the appropriate rate[3], and one-half of the remainder absolutely. As to the other half, where there are parents[4], to the parents absolutely: where there are no parents, to the brothers and sisters of the whole blood[4] in equal shares, the issue[4] of such as have predeceased the intestate taking per stirpes the share to which their parent would have been entitled.	*Husband or widow
V. Husband or widow without issue, parent, brother or sister of the whole blood or their issue[4] (whatever the amount of the estate)	All to husband or widow	Husband or widow

* See notes at end of tables.

1 As to devolution of the estate of a married woman who has been judicially separated from her husband, see paras. **6.140** ff., post.
2 For method of determining the amount of the 'net estate' for this purpose, see paras. **6.92**, post. As to the meaning of 'issue', see note 3 to para. **6.37**, post.
3 The Intestate Succession (Interest and Capitalisation) Order 1977 (Amendment) Order 1983 (S.I. 1983 No. 1374) provides that for the purposes of s. 46(l)(i) of the Administration of Estates Act 1925, as it applies both in respect of persons dying before 1953 and in respect of persons dying after 1952, the rate of interest payable on the statutory legacy until it is paid or appropriated shall be 6 per cent per annum with effect from 1 October 1983. The previous rate of interest was 7 per cent per annum for the period commencing on 15 September 1977 (the Intestate Succession (Interest and Capitalisation) Order 1977, S.I. 1977 No. 1491 which increased the then current rate of 4 per cent per annum or, in the case of persons dying before the coming into operation of the Intestates' Estates Act 1952, 5 per cent per annum). Accordingly, where a statutory legacy remains unpaid for a considerable time, the interest payable on that legacy will need to be calculated at different rates for different periods. For example, where the death occurs after 1952 but before 15 September 1977, the interest to be paid on the statutory legacy will be 4 per cent per annum up to 15 September 1977 and thereafter 7 per cent per annum until 1 October 1983 and thereafter 6 per cent per annum until the legacy is paid or appropriated.
4 In respect of deaths on or after 4 April 1988 illegitimacy is not to be taken into account: Family Law Reform Act 1987, s. 18.

B. Death On or at any time After 1 January 1926. No Surviving Spouse.

Intestate leaves	Distribution of estate	Entitled to grant
I. Issue only[1]‡	Issue[1] who attain full age or marry under age take equally (children, including illegitimate children when the intestate died on or after 4 April 1988, of predeceasing children taking their parent's share, per stirpes)	*Issue[1]
II. Father or mother[2]‡	Father or mother[2]	Father or mother[2]
III. Father and mother[2]‡	In equal shares	Either or both
IV. Brothers and sisters of the whole blood, and issue of such as died in the lifetime of the intestate‡	Brothers and sisters of the whole blood in equal shares, the issue of such as have predeceased the intestate taking their parent's share, per stirpes	*A person or persons entitled to share in the estate
V. Brothers and sisters of the half blood and issue of such as died in the lifetime of the intestate‡	Brothers and sisters of the half blood in equal shares and issue as in IV	*A person or persons entitled to share in the estate
VI. Grandparents	Grandparents in equal shares	Grandparent (one or more)
VII. Uncles and aunts of the whole blood, and issue of such as died in the lifetime of the intestate‡	Uncles and aunts of the whole blood and issue as in IV	*A person or persons entitled to share in the estate
VIII. Uncles and aunts of the half blood and issue of such as died in the lifetime of the intestate‡	Uncles and aunts of the half blood and issue as in IV	*A person or persons entitled to share in the estate
IX. No blood relation taking an interest as above	(*a*) The Crown, (*b*) Duchy of Lancaster, (*c*) Duchy of Cornwall	(*a*) Treasury Solicitor for the use of Her Majesty (*b*) Solicitor for the Duchy of Lancaster for the use of Her Majesty (*c*) Solicitor for the affairs of the Duchy of Cornwall
X. Creditor		† Creditor

*†‡ See notes at end of tables.

1 Including illegitimate children where the death was on or after 1 January 1970. In the case of deaths prior to this date but after 1926, illegitimate children are entitled only where the deceased left no lawful issue. See also Family Law Reform Act 1987, s. 18, p. 876, post, in respect of deaths on or after 4 April 1988.

2 Including natural parents where the death was on or after 1 January 1970. In the case of deaths prior to this date but after 1926 the natural mother but not the natural father is entitled. See also Family Law Reform Act 1987, s. 18, p. 876, post, in respect of deaths on or after 4 April 1988.

C. Death on or After 1 January 1926, but Before 1 January 1953, where Deceased left a Surviving Spouse[1]

Intestate leaves	Distribution of estate	Entitled to grant
I. Husband or widow (**net estate not exeeding £1,000**)[2]	All to husband or widow	Husband or widow
II. Husband or widow and issue (**net estate exeeding £1,000**)[2]	Husband or widow takes the personal chattels, £1,000 (free of costs and duty) with interest at the appropriate rate[3]. Life interest in half the remainder of estate, with reversion to the issue. As to the other half, to the issue absolutely	*Husband or widow and a child
III. Husband or widow without issue (**net estate exceeding £1,000**)[2]	Husband or widow takes the personal chattels, £1,000 (free of costs and duty) with interest at the appropriate rate[3], life interest in all the remainder of the estate, with reversion to nearest class of blood relations (see Table B, above)	*Husband or widow and a person entitled to share in the estate
IV. Husband or widow but no blood relation within the classes entitled to share (see Table B, above) (whatever the amount of the estate)	All to husband or widow	Husband or widow

* In the event of a minority or life interest arising there must normally be two applicants for the grant; the second person should be a person entitled to share, having a vested interest, but if all of these are cleared off the guardian of a minor entitled to share upon attaining full age may be joined as second applicant. See Chap. 7, post, as to the discretionary power vested in the court to appoint a sole administrator where it is expedient to do so in all the circumstances.

† Upon the renunciation or clearing off of all persons having a prior right to the grant.

‡ As to the interests of legitimated persons, see paras. **6.174** ff. In respect of deaths on or after 4 April 1988 illegitimacy is not to be taken into consideration in respect of the relationships—see Family Law Reform Act 1987, s. 18, p. 876, post.

1 As to devolution of the estate of a married woman who has been judicially separated from her husband see paras. **6.140** ff., post.

2 For method of determining the amount of the 'net estate' for this purpose, see para. **6.92**, post.

3 Intestate Succession (Interest and Capitalisation) Order 1977 (Amendment) Order 1983 (S.I. 1983 No. 1374); see also fn 3, p. 206) ante as to the need to calculate the interest payable at different rates for different periods.

Distribution of an intestate's estate where the death has occurred on or after 1 January 1926

6.30   Where the death of the deceased occurred on or after 1 January 1926, the distribution of the estate on an intestacy is regulated by the Administration of Estates Act 1925, as amended[1].

1 See p. 744, post.

6.31   Under this Act, where the deceased leaves a surviving spouse the latter is entitled to a charge on the residuary estate for a fixed net sum. This sum was originally £1,000[1], but was increased, first by the Intestates' Estates Act 1952[2] in relation to deaths occurring on or after 1 January 1953 to £5,000 (where the deceased also left issue surviving) or £20,000 (where the deceased left no issue), and more recently by the Family Provision Act 1966[3] in relation to deaths on or after 1 January 1967 to £8,750 (where the deceased left issue) or £30,000 (where the deceased left no issue). The last-mentioned Act includes power for the Lord Chancellor to specify larger sums than £8,750 and £30,000 respectively by statutory instrument, to be laid before Parliament in draft (s. 1) and, in exercise of this power, the sums of £15,000 (where the deceased left issue) and £40,000 (where the deceased left no issue) were specified in the case of persons dying on or after 1 July 1972 by the Family Provision (Intestate Succession) Order 1972; increased to the respective sums of £25,000 and £55,000 in the case of persons dying on or after 15 March 1977; and further increased to the respective sums of £40,000 and £85,000 for deaths on or after 1 March 1981; and further increased to £75,000 and £125,000 for deaths on or after 1 June 1987 and further increased to £125,000 and £200,000 for deaths on or after 1 December 1993. **Note**. *See note in heading before table A in para.* **6.29** *about deaths on or after 1 January 1996*[4].

1 Administration of Estates Act 1925, s. 46(1) (as originally enacted: see p. 757, post).
2 See p. 767, post.
3 See p. 786, post.
4 S.I.s 1972 No. 916, 1977 No. 415, 1981 No. 255, 1987 No. 799 and 1993 No. 2906 (see pp. 915, 916, 919, 923, 946, post).

6.32 The relationships entitled to participate in an intestate's estate were in general restricted to lawful blood relationships, but by virtue of the Legitimacy Acts 1926 and 1959, and the Adoption Acts 1958 to 1968, legitimated persons and adopted persons, and persons related to the deceased through a legitimation or an adoption were, in specified circumstances, given rights on an intestacy. And, in relation to deaths after 31 December 1975, the succession rights of adopted and legitimated persons, including the rights of persons related to the deceased through an adoption or a legitimation, are now generally equated to those arising from a lawful blood relationship: see the Adoption Act 1976[1] and the Legitimacy Act 1976[2]. Limited rights of succession on intestacy between illegitimate children and their parents were introduced by the Legitimacy Act 1926, s. 9, and these rights were extended in relation to deaths on or after 1 January 1970 by Part II of the Family Law Reform Act 1969. Details of these provisions are given later in this chapter. Sections 14, 15 and 17 (in Part II) of the Family Law Reform Act 1969 were repealed as from 4 April 1988: see s. 33(4) of the Family Law Reform Act 1987[3]. In respect of intestates dying on or after 4 April 1988, by virtue of s. 18 of the Family Law Reform Act 1987[3] references (however expressed) in Part IV of the Administration of Estates Act 1925 (which deals with the distribution of the estate of an intestate) to any relationship between two persons are to be construed without regard to whether or not the father and mother of either of them, or the father and mother of any person through whom the relationship is deduced, have or had been married to each other at any time. Consequently, *in respect of an intestate dying on or after 4 April 1988 a blood relation in the relevant class is beneficially entitled to (or to share in) the estate and is entitled to apply for letters of administration whether or not the relationship is lawful.* See also para. **6.156**, post.

1 See p. 826, post.
2 See p. 822, post.
3 See p. 876, post.

6.33 By s. 33 of the 1925 Act all the real and personal estate of the intestate is vested in his personal representatives on trust for sale and the payment of funeral, testamentary and administration expenses and debts, and provision for distribution of the residue of the estate is contained in s. 46 of the Act[1].

1 See pp. 750, 752, post.

Court's power to modify provisions for distribution on intestacy

6.34 In respect of the estate of a person dying before 1 April 1976 the court has power, on an application under the Inheritance (Family Provision) Act 1938, as amended[1], to modify the provisions of the laws of distribution on intestacy if it is satisfied that these do not make reasonable provision for the maintenance of a dependant (as defined in the Act). The court is not bound to assume that the intestacy laws always make reasonable provision for dependants. The court also has power to make provision for a surviving former spouse under s. 26 of the Matrimonial Causes Act 1965.

1 13 Halsbury's Statutes (3rd edn) 118.

6.35 In respect of persons dying on or after 1 April 1976 the Inheritance (Family Provision) Act 1938 is replaced by the Inheritance (Provision for Family and Dependants) Act 1975[1], which enables the provisions of a will or the law of intestate succession to be modified in favour of wider classes of relatives and dependants. This Act also replaces s. 26 of the Matrimonial Causes Act 1965.

1 See p. 808, post. Whereas High Court jurisdiction under the Inheritance (Family Provision) Act 1938, as amended, is exercised by the Chancery Division, and jurisdiction under s. 26 of the Matrimonial Causes Act 1965 by the Family Division, either Division may entertain High Court application made under the Inheritance (Provision for Family and Dependants) Act 1975, by virtue of the Rules of the Supreme Court, Order 99; see Chap. 41.

6.36 This subject is dealt with in Chap. 41.

Husband or wife: (a) Death on or after 1 January 1953[1]

[**Note.** *See note in heading before table A in para.* **6.29** *about deaths on or after 1 January 1996.*]

6.37

(1) If the intestate dies leaving a husband or wife, but no issue[2] or parent[3], or brother or sister of the whole blood[4], or issue of brother or sister of the whole blood[4], he or she is entitled to the whole estate, whatever its value.
(2) If the intestate dies leaving a husband or wife and issue[2], the husband or wife is entitled to the personal chattels absolutely[5] and a charge on the residuary estate for a fixed net sum (at present £125,000[6]) free of death duties and costs, with interest thereon at the appropriate rate per annum from the date of death until paid or appropriated[7].
(3) If the intestate dies leaving a husband or wife and one or more of the following: a parent[3], brother or sister of the whole blood[4], or issue of brother or sister of the whole blood[4], but leaves no issue[2], the husband or wife is entitled to the personal chattels and a charge on the residuary estate for a fixed net sum (at present £200,000[8]), free of death duties and costs, with interest thereon at the rate of 6 per cent per annum from the date of death until paid or appropriated[7].

(4) And as to the residue of the estate the husband or wife is entitled to—

    (a) a life interest in one half *where there is issue*[2] *surviving* (on failure of the statutory trusts[9] as to the issue[2] the residue and any statutory accumulations go as though the intestate had left no issue).

    (b) an absolute interest in one half *where there is no issue*[2], but there is a parent[3], or brother or sister of the whole blood[4], or issue of a brother or sister of the whole blood[4], surviving.

1 Section 46, Administration of Estates Act 1925, as amended by the Intestates' Estates Act 1952 and the Family Provision Act 1966: see p. 752, post.
2 In relation to deaths occurring on or after 1 January 1970, the expression 'issue' in relation to the intestate includes illegitimate children and the issue (i.e. lawful descendants) of any such children who predeceased the intestate (Family Law Reform Act 1969, s. 14: see p. 791, post). See also paras. **6.45** ff., post. Section 14 of the Family Law Reform Act 1969 was repealed as from 4 April 1988 by s. 33(4), Sch. 4 of the Family Law Reform Act 1987 (see pp. 880, 881, post) but the repeal does not affect any rights arising under the intestacy of a person dying before the coming into force of the repeal (s. 33(2), Sch. 3, para. 8, Family Law Reform Act 1987; see pp. 879, 881, post). In respect of intestacies on or after 4 April 1988, s. 18 of the Family Law Reform Act 1987 provides that illegitimacy is not to be taken into consideration in determining the rights of succession of an illegitimate person, the rights of succession to the estate of an illegitimate person and the rights of succession through an illegitimate relationship. See also para. **6.156**.
3 In relation to deaths occurring on or after 1 January 1970, the expression 'parents' includes natural parents (Family Law Reform Act 1969, s. 14: see p. 791, post). See also paras. **6.60** ff., post. See also last sentence of fn. 2, above.
4 See last sentence of fn. 2, above.
5 Personal chattels mean carriages, horses, stable furniture and effects (not used for business purposes), motor cars and accessories (not used for business purposes), garden effects, domestic animals, plate, plated articles, linen, china, glass, books, pictures, prints, furniture, jewellery, articles of household or personal use or ornament, musical and scientific instruments and apparatus, wines, liquors and consumable stores, but do not include any chattels used at the death of the intestate for business purposes nor money or securities for money (Administration of Estates Act 1925, s. 55(1)(x), p. 762, post).
6 See para. **6.31** for earlier figures and dates.
7 Intestate Succession (Interest and Capitalisation) Order 1977 (S.I. 1977 No. 1491); but see fn. 3 to para. **6.29**, ante, as to the need to calculate the interest payable at different rates for different periods.
8 See para. **6.31** for earlier figures and dates.
9 See 'Statutory trusts for issue', paras. **6.54** ff., post.

Husband or wife: (b) Death on or after 1 January 1926, but before 1 January 1953[1]

6.38 If the intestate has died leaving a *husband* or a *wife*, he or she is entitled to:

(1) the personal chattels absolutely[2];
(2) a charge on the residuary estate for the net sum of £1,000, free of death duties and costs, with interest on the said sum from the date of death, at the appropriate rate per annum, until paid or appropriated[3];
(3) and, as to the residue of the estate—

    (a) a life interest therein, *when there is no issue*;
    (b) a life interest in one half thereof, *when there is issue surviving*;
    (c) a life interest in the whole of the residue, *if the statutory trusts as to issue fail in the lifetime of the surviving husband or wife*;
    (d) the whole of the residue absolutely, *if the intestate leaves surviving no issue or lawful relative within the degrees mentioned in paras. 6.43–6.73, post*.

1 Administration of Estates Act 1925, s. 46, as originally enacted: see p. 767, post.
2 See fn. 5 to para. **6.37**, ante.
3 See the Intestate Succession (Interest and Capitalisation) Order 1977 (S.I. 1977 No. 1491); see fn. 3 to para. **6.29**, ante, as to the need to calculate the interest payable at different rates for different periods.

Additional rights of surviving spouse

6.39   Section 47A of the Administration of Estates Act 1925, added by the Intestates' Estates Act 1952, gives the surviving spouse of an intestate dying on or after 1 January 1953 a right to require the personal representative of the intestate to redeem the life interest to which he or she may be entitled on the intestacy, by the payment of the capital value thereof, the capital value to be reckoned in accordance with special rules[1].

1   See the Intestate Succession (Interest and Capitalisation) Order 1977 (S.I. 1977 No. 1491); see fn. 3 to para. **6.29**, ante, as to the need to calculate the interest payable at different rates for different periods.

6.40   This right does not affect the entitlement to a grant of administration, as by its nature it cannot be exercised until a personal representative has been constituted.

6.41   Where the surviving spouse is the sole personal representative, the election to redeem his or her life interest is not effective unless written notice thereof is given to the Senior District Judge of the Family Division. For procedure for filing such notice, see paras. **16.36** ff., post.

6.42   Where the estate of an intestate dying on or after 1 January 1953 comprises an interest in a dwelling house in which the surviving spouse was resident at the time of death, the latter may require that the interest in the house be appropriated in or towards the surviving spouse's absolute interest in the estate[1]. The conditions under which this right is exercisable are set out in the Second Schedule to the Intestates' Estates Act 1952 (pp. 768 ff., post).

1   Intestates' Estates Act 1952, s. 5 (p. 767, post); the surviving spouse's right to appropriate the former matrimonial home is exercisable even where the value of the absolute interest of the spouse is less than the value of the home (*Re Phelps, Wells v Phelps* [1980] Ch 275, [1979] 3 All ER 373, CA).

Issue of intestate

6.43   If the intestate dies leaving a *husband or a wife* and *issue*, the issue takes half the residue of the estate (other than personal chattels) remaining after satisfying the spouse's statutory legacy (of £125,000, £75,000, £40,000, £25,000, £15,000, £8,750, £5,000 or £1,000 according to the date of death), and interest thereon; and succeeds to the other half on the death of the surviving husband or wife (both interests being subject to the statutory trusts, see below).

6.44   If the intestate leaves *issue* but no husband or wife the residuary estate is held on the statutory trusts for such issue[1].

1   Administration of Estates Act 1925, s. 46(1)(ii): see p. 753, post.

Rights of illegitimate children

6.45   In the case of death on or after 1 January 1927, where a woman dies leaving no lawful issue but leaving an illegitimate child or children, the latter take the same interest in the estate as if he or they had been born legitimate[1]: see also paras. **6.168** ff., post.

1   Legitimacy Act 1926, s. 9.

6.46 Where the death occurred on or after 1 January 1970 but before 4 April 1988, illegitimate children are, in general, given rights of succession to the estate of either parent on an intestacy equivalent to those of lawful children[1].

1 Family Law Reform Act 1969, Part II (p. 791, post),

6.47 Under s. 14(1) of the Family Law Reform Act 1969[1], where either parent of an illegitimate child dies on or after 1 January 1970 but before 4 April 1988 intestate as respects all or any of his property, the illegitimate child or, if he is dead, his issue, is entitled to take any interest therein to which he or such issue would have been entitled if he had been born legitimate. Accordingly, in such cases Part IV of the Administration of Estates Act 1925 is to have effect as if:

(a) any reference to the issue of the intestate included a reference to any illegitimate child of his and to the issue of any such child; and

(b) any reference to the child or children of the intestate included a reference to any illegitimate child or children of his (s. 14(3)).

1 See p. 791, post.

6.48 The section does not apply to, or affect the right of any person to take, any entailed interest in real or personal property (s. 14(5)). The rights given to illegitimate persons apply only to illegitimate children of the deceased and the issue (i.e. legitimate descendants) of illegitimate children who predeceased the deceased.

6.49 In relation to deaths before 1 January 1976, s. 14(8) of the Family Law Reform Act 1969 provided that the term 'illegitimate child' does not include: (a) an illegitimate child who has been legitimated under the Legitimacy Act 1926, or who by virtue of that Act or at common law is recognised as having been legitimated; or (b) an adopted person under an adoption order made in any part of the United Kingdom, the Isle of Man or the Channel Islands or under an overseas adoption as defined in s. 4(3) of the Adoption Act 1968; the rights of such persons on an intestacy being then provided under the Legitimacy Act 1926 and the Adoption Act 1958, respectively. However, with effect from 1 January 1976, s. 14(8) of the 1969 Act was repealed by the Children Act 1975 and, under Schedule 1 to that Act, it is provided that in relation to deaths after 31 December 1975, a legitimated person and any other person is entitled to the same interest as if the legitimated person had been born legitimate; and an adopted person is treated in law as if he were the lawfully born child of the adopter or adopters, and cannot be illegitimate[1].

1 See p. 822, post.

6.50 The provisions relating to the succession rights of legitimated persons, formerly contained in Sch. 1 to the Children Act 1975, have since been repealed and re-enacted in the Legitimacy Act 1976[1], a consolidating measure; those relating to adopted persons are now contained in the Adoption Act 1976[2]; see paras. **6.174** ff., post.

1 See p. 822, post.
2 See p. 826, post. The provisions formerly contained in Sch. 1 to the Children Act 1975 are re-enacted in the Adoption Act 1976.

6.51 The provisions of s. 14 of the Family Law Reform Act 1969 have no effect on any rights under the intestacy of a person dying before 1 January 1970, the date when the section came into force (s. 14(9)), or on or after 4 April 1988 when that section was repealed by the Family Law Reform Act 1987, s. 33(4), Sch. 4[1].

1 See pp. 880, 881, post.

6.52 *In respect of deaths on or after 4 April 1988*, s. 18 of the Family Law Reform Act 1987 provides that *illegitimacy is not to be taken into consideration in determining the rights of succession of an illegitimate person* or in determining the rights of succession to the estate of an illegitimate person *or the rights of succession through an illegitimate person.*

6.53 For the practice in making grants of administration to persons entitled by virtue of s. 14 of the Family Law Reform Act 1969, see paras. **6.148** ff., post.

Statutory trusts for issue

6.54 Where the death of the intestate occurred on or after 1 January 1970, the statutory trusts for issue are as set out in the following paragraphs.

6.55 If the intestate dies leaving issue (which term includes any illegitimate child or children of his and, where the intestate died before 4 April 1988, the lawful issue of any such child and, where the intestate died on or after 4 April 1988, lawful or illegitimate issue of any such child), then, subject to the rights of the husband or wife of the intestate (if any), the residuary estate is to be held in trust, in equal shares if more than one, for all or any of the legitimate or illegitimate children or child of the intestate, living at the death of the intestate, who attain the age of 18 years or marry under that age, and for all or any of the issue (i.e. lawful issue where the intestate died before 4 April 1988 or lawful or illegitimate issue where he died on or after that date) living at the death of the intestate who attain the age of 18 years or marry under that age, of any legitimate or illegitimate child of the intestate who predeceased the intestate, such issue to take through all degrees, according to their stocks, in equal shares if more than one, the share which their parent would have taken if living at the death of the intestate, and so that no issue shall take whose parent is living at the death of the intestate and so capable of taking[1].

1 Administration of Estates Act 1925, s. 47(1)(i), as amended by Family Law Reform Act 1969, s. 3(2) (p. 754, post) and Family Law Reform Act 1987, s. 18; p. 876, post.

6.56 Where the intestate died before 1 January 1970 the statutory trusts are as set out in s. 47(1) of the Administration of Estates Act 1925, as originally enacted[1].

1 See p. 759, post.

6.57 Before dividing the residue of the estate among the children, the personal representative must bring into account any money or property which, by way of advancement or on the marriage of a child of the intestate, shall have been paid to such child by the intestate, or settled by the intestate for the benefit of such child (including any life or less interest and including property covenanted to be paid or settled). Subject to any contrary intention expressed or appearing from the circumstances of the case, such advances are to be taken as being so paid or settled in or towards satisfaction of the share of such child, or the share which such child would have taken if living at the death of the intestate. They are to be brought into account at a valuation (the value to be reckoned as at the death of the intestate) in accordance with the requirements of the personal representative[1]. But see s. 1, Law Reform (Succession) Act 1995, p. 900, post.

1   Administration of Estates Act 1925, s. 47(1)(iii); p. 759, post.

6.58   If none of the surviving issue of an intestate attain an absolutely vested interest under the foregoing statutory trusts, the residuary estate devolves as if the intestate had died without leaving issue living at the time of his death[1].

1   Ibid., s. 47(2); p. 759, post.

Parents of intestate

6.59   If the intestate dies leaving no spouse or issue[1], but leaving *both parents* surviving, the estate passes to the *father and mother* in equal shares absolutely. If, in such a case, *one parent* only survives, then the estate passes to the surviving *father* or *mother* absolutely.

1   See fn. 2, to para. **6.37**, ante.

Parents of illegitimate child

6.60   Under s. 14(2) of the Family Law Reform Act 1969[1], where an illegitimate child dies intestate on or after 1 January 1970 (but before 4 April 1988, s. 14 of the Family Law Reform Act 1969 being repealed by the Family Law Reform Act 1987 as from that date[2]) each of his parents, if surviving, is entitled to take any interest therein to which he or she would have been entitled if the child had been born legitimate.

1   See p. 791, post,
2   See p. 874, post.

6.61   Accordingly, in relation to such a death, references in Part IV of the Administration of Estates Act 1925, to parents, father or mother, mean, in the case of an intestate who is illegitimate, his natural parents, father or mother, as the case may be.

6.62   It is, however, provided by s. 14(4) of the Family Law Reform Act 1969 that for the purposes of s. 14(2), and of Part IV of the Act of 1925, an illegitimate child is to be presumed not to have been survived by his father unless the contrary is shown.

6.63   In relation to deaths before 1 January 1976, s. 14(8) of the Family Law Reform Act 1969 provided that the expression 'illegitimate child' does not include such a child who is:

(a)   a legitimated person within the meaning of the Legitimacy Act 1926, or a person recognised by virtue of that Act or at common law as having been legitimated; or

(b)   a person adopted under an adoption order made in any part of the United Kingdom, the Isle of Man or the Channel Islands or under an overseas adoption as defined in s. 4(3) of the Adoption Act 1968.

6.64   However, s. 14(8) of the Family Law Reform Act 1969 was repealed with effect from 1 January 1976 by the Children Act 1975, and under Schedule 1 to the latter Act, in relation to deaths after 31 December 1975 a legitimated person, and any other person, is entitled to the same interest as if the legitimated person had been born legitimate. The provisions relating to the succession rights of legitimated persons formerly contained in Sch. 1 to the Children Act 1975 have since been repealed and re-enacted by the Legitimacy Act 1976[1], a consolidating measure. An adopted person is treated in law as if he were the lawfully born child of the adopter or adopters, and cannot be illegitimate[2]. See paras. **6.223** ff., post.

1 See p. 822, post.
2 Adoption Act 1976, s. 39, p. 828, post.

6.65 *In respect of deaths on or after 4 April 1988*, s. 18 of the Family Law Reform Act 1987[1] provides that *illegitimacy is not to be taken into consideration* in determining the rights of succession of an illegitimate person or *in determining the rights of succession to the estate of an illegitimate person* or the rights of succession through an illegitimate person.

1 See p. 876, post.

6.66 As to an application for letters of administration of the estate of an illegitimate person, see paras. **6.267** ff., post.

Protection of personal representatives

6.67 Notwithstanding the amendments of the law effected by Part II of the Family Law Reform Act 1969, trustees or personal representatives could convey or distribute the estate of an intestate to or among the persons entitled thereto without having ascertained that there is no person who is or may be entitled to any interest therein by virtue of s. 14 of that Act, so far as it conferred any interest on illegitimate children or their issue or on the father of an illegitimate child, and were not liable to any such person of whose claim they did not have notice at the time of conveyance or distribution. This did not, however, prejudice the right of any such person to follow the property, or any property representing it, into the hands of any person, other than a purchaser, who may have received it (s. 17). This special protection for trustees and personal representatives ended on 4 April 1988 when s. 17 of the Family Law Reform Act 1969 ceased to have effect pursuant to s. 20 of the Family Law Reform Act 1987[1].

1 See p. 877, post.

Brothers and sisters of the whole blood of the intestate or their issue

6.68 If the intestate dies leaving no spouse or issue or parent, the estate is held on the statutory trusts for *brothers and sisters of the whole blood*; the issue of any such brothers or sisters who predeceased the intestate sharing with them per stirpes. In respect of deaths before 4 April 1988 the relationships must be lawful but in respect of deaths on or after that date this is not necessary (Family Law Reform Act 1987, s. 18[1]).

1 See p. 876, post.

6.69 The statutory trusts for relatives other than issue are in corresponding terms to those for the issue (see above), save that the provision for bringing money or property into account does not apply[1].

1 Administration of Estates Act 1925, s. 47(3); p. 755, post.

Brothers and sisters of the half blood of the intestate or their issue

6.70   If the intestate dies leaving no spouse or issue or parent or brother or sister of the whole blood or their issue, the estate is held on the statutory trusts for *brothers and sisters of the half blood* of the intestate and the issue (taking per stirpes) of any such brothers or sisters who predeceased the intestate. In respect of deaths before 4 April 1988 the relationships must be lawful but in respect of deaths on or after that date this is not necessary (Family Law Reform Act 1987, s. 18[1]).

1 See p. 876, post.

Grandparents of intestate

6.71   Should none of the above-mentioned relations attain absolutely vested interests, then the estate passes to the *grandparents*, and, if more than one survive the intestate, in equal shares absolutely. In respect of deaths before 4 April 1988 the relationships must be lawful but in respect of deaths on or after that date this is not necessary (Family Law Reform Act 1987, s. 18[1]).

1 See p. 876, post.

Uncles and aunts of the intestate and their issue

6.72   Should there be no spouse, issue, parent, brother or sister of the whole or half blood or issue of either, or grandparent, the estate is held on the statutory trusts for the *uncles and aunts of the whole blood* of the intestate (*being brothers or sisters of the whole blood of a parent of the intestate*) and the issue (taking per stirpes) of any such uncles or aunts of the whole blood who predeceased the intestate.

6.73   Should there be no uncles or aunts of the whole blood or their issue, then the estate is held on the statutory trusts for the *uncles and aunts of the half blood* of the intestate (*being brothers or sisters of the half blood of a parent of the intestate*) and the issue (taking per stirpes) of any such uncles and aunts of the half blood who predeceased the intestate.

6.74   In respect of deaths before 4 April 1988 the relationships whether of the whole or half blood, must be lawful but in respect of deaths on or after that date this is not necessary (Family Law Reform Act 1987, s. 18[1]).

1 See p. 876, post.

Surviving spouse. Failure of kin within the classes entitled to share

6.75   Where there is a surviving spouse, but no issue, parent, or brother or sister of the whole blood or their issue, where the death occurred on or after 1 January 1953 (or no kin within the degrees mentioned in table B in para. **6.29**, ante, where the death occurred on or after 1 January 1926, but before 1 January 1953) the estate vests absolutely in the spouse no matter what the amount may be. In respect of deaths on or after 4 April 1988 issue, parent and brother and sister of the whole blood or their issue includes those who are not lawfully related to the intestate (Family Law Reform Act 1987, s. 18[1]).

1 See p. 876, post.

Failure of statutory trusts

6.76   If the statutory trusts in favour of any class of relatives of the intestate fail by reason that none of them attain the age of majority or marry under that age, the estate devolves as though the intestate had left no relative of that class[1].

1 Administration of Estates Act 1925, s. 47(2); see p. 754, post.

No member of primary class surviving

6.77   Where the nearest surviving kin of an intestate are the issue of uncles and aunts of the whole blood, all such uncles and aunts having died in the lifetime of the intestate, the residuary estate is held on the statutory trusts for such issue, notwithstanding that no member of the primary class (i.e. in this case, uncles or aunts of the whole blood) survived the deceased[1].

1 *Re Lockwood, Atherton v Brooke* [1958] Ch 231, [1957] 3 All ER 520.

The Crown, Duchy of Lancaster, or the Duchy of Cornwall

6.78   In default of any person taking an absolute interest under the foregoing provisions, the residuary estate of an intestate passes to the Crown, or to the Duchy of Lancaster, or to the Duke of Cornwall (as the case may be) as bona vacantia, and in lieu of any right to escheat[1].

1 Administration of Estates Act 1925, s. 46(1)(vi); p. 754, post.

Right to the grant

6.79   Subject to s. 116(1) (power of court to pass over prior claims to a grant) and s. 114(2) (number of personal representatives) of the Supreme Court Act 1981, where the deceased died wholly intestate, administration is to be granted to the person entitled thereto in accordance with probate rules[1].

1 Supreme Court Act 1981, s. 116(1); see p. 845, post.

6.80   Rule 22 of the NCPR 1987 provides that the right to the grant shall follow the beneficial interest in the estate, and lays down the order of priority of such right. As to joinder of a second administrator, see Chap. 7.

6.81   As to forfeiture by reason of a felonious act, see paras. **5.157–5.160**, ante; and as to the issue of a grant in special circumstances to a person having no title under r. 22, see paras. **25.91** ff., post.

Grant to surviving spouse

Right of husband or widow

6.82   If the intestate leaves a surviving spouse, he or she is entitled to a grant of letters of administration in priority to any other person[1]. The distribution of the estate under s. 46 of the Administration of Estates Act 1925 (as amended), however, in some cases causes a life interest, and sometimes also minority interests, to arise, which would normally render it necessary for a grant to be made to the spouse jointly with some other person: under s. 114(2) of the Supreme Court Act 1981[2], if there is a minority, or if a life interest arises under the intestacy, then, unless the court considers it expedient in all the circumstances to appoint an individual as sole administrator, the grant must be made to a trust corporation (with or without an individual), or to not less than two individuals. It is suggested that, where the amount of the estate only slightly exceeds the surviving spouse's statutory entitlement or where the minority interest or interests are shortly to terminate on the attainment of majority age, in such circumstances the court may consider it expedient to allow the grant to issue, in the exercise of its discretion, to the surviving spouse alone.

1 NCPR 22(1).
2 See p. 844, post.

6.83 A surviving spouse may take a grant alone where the whole estate of the deceased passes absolutely to the spouse[1], or where, although other persons share with the spouse, no life interest or minority interest arises. As to assignment by the other persons entitled to share in the estate in favour of the surviving spouse, see paras. **6.25** and **6.26**, ante[2].

1 Except where the spouse is himself or herself a minor.
2 Where, in an action concerning the validity of a will, the court pronounced against the will, and terms of compromise, whereby the estate was to be distributed in accordance with the terms of the will, were filed and made a rule of court, letters of administration were granted to the widow alone on its being sworn in the oath that there was no life interest by reason of the provisions of the terms of settlement, notwithstanding that the net estate exceeded the amount of the widow's statutory legacy (*Re Cranfield* (12 June 1950, unreported)). See now the discretionary power vested in the court to appoint a sole administrator where it considers it expedient in all the circumstances to do so, notwithstanding the existence of a life or minority interest; s. 114(2) of the Supreme Court Act 1981 (p. 844, post).

6.84 Although there does not appear to have been any reported case on the question of succession rights of wives of polygamous marriages where succession was governed by English law, it would seem on the basis of the ratio in *Coleman v Shang* [1961] AC 481, [1961] 2 All ER 406, PC (a potentially polygamous marriage celebrated in Ghana between parties domiciled there, *held*: that the widow was entitled to a grant of letters of administration as the deceased husband's widow) and *Re Sehota, Kaur v Kaur* [1978] 3 All ER 385, [1978] 1 WLR 1506 (a wife of a polygamous marriage entitled to claim, as a 'wife', for financial provision from the estate of her deceased husband under the Inheritance (Provision for Family and Dependants) Act 1975) that the terms 'surviving spouse' and 'surviving wife' as contained in s. 46 of the Administration of Estates Act 1925 (as amended) and NCPR 22(1) are sufficiently wide to include the wife of a polygamous marriage.

6.85 The surviving spouse is entitled to the whole estate:

(a) where the net value of the estate, after making the permitted deductions (see para. **6.92**, post) does not exceed:
    (i) *where the deceased died on or after 1 December 1993*: £125,000 where the deceased left issue, or £200,000 where the deceased left no issue[1];
    (ii) *where the deceased died on or after 1 June 1987*: £75,000 where the deceased left issue, or £125,000 where the deceased left no issue[1];
    (iii) *where the deceased died on or after 1 March 1981*: £40,000 where the deceased left issue, or £85,000 where the deceased left no issue[1];

(iv) *where the deceased died on or after 15 March 1977, but before 1 March 1981*: £25,000 where the deceased left issue, or £55,000 where the deceased left no issue[1];

(v) *where the deceased died on or after 1 July 1972 but before 15 March 1977*: £15,000 where the deceased left issue, or £40,000 where the deceased left no issue[1];

(vi) *where the deceased died after 31 December 1966, but before 1 July 1972*: £8,750 where the deceased left issue, or £30,000 where the deceased left no issue[1];

(vii) *where the deceased died after 31 December 1952, but before 1 January 1967*: £5,000 where the deceased left issue, or £20,000 where the deceased left no issue;

(viii) *where the deceased died after 31 December 1925, but before 1 January 1953*: £1,000.

In these cases, the oath should describe the applicant as 'the lawful husband (*or* lawful widow, *as the case may be*) and only person now entitled to the estate'[2]. As to the wording to be included where the gross estate is in excess of the appropriate amount stated above, but the permitted deductions reduce the net estate below this figure, see paras. **6.93** ff., post (Form of oath, No. 87);

(b) where the deceased left no kin within the degrees entitled to share with the spouse, i.e. down to the issue of brothers or sisters of the whole blood, where the death occurred on or after 1 January 1953 (see table A, para. **6.29**, ante); or down to the issue of uncles or aunts of the half blood where the death occurred before 1 January 1953 (see table B, para. **6.29**, ante). The kin should be specifically cleared off in the oath in such cases. The oath should describe the applicant as 'the lawful husband (*or* lawful widow, *as the case may be*) and only person entitled to the estate'.

---

1 In the case of death on or after 1 January 1970 as well as lawful issue, illegitimate children of the intestate and the lawful issue of any who have predeceased the intestate (and, as regards (i) above) in the case of death on or after 4 April 1988 illegitimate as well as lawful issue of any who have predeceased the intestate) are within the definition of 'issue' for this purpose: see fn. 2 to para. **6.37**, ante.
2 Where the net estate exceeds £125,000, but does not exceed £200,000 (or the corresponding lower figures where the date of death was before 1 December 1993), and the deceased died without issue, the oath should state that the deceased died 'without issue or any other person entitled to share in the estate by virtue of any enactment'. Should these words not be included, the oath will be accepted if the applicant's solicitor is prepared to certify to the effect that he is instructed that the deceased died intestate without issue or any other person entitled to share in the estate by virtue of any enactment (Registrar's Circular, 29 July 1977, as amended).

6.86   Where the deceased died on or after 1 January 1953 leaving a surviving spouse, *but no issue*, no life interest arises whatever the amount of the estate, so that, unless the spouse or any person entitled to share with the spouse is a minor, a grant may be made to the surviving spouse alone. In such cases, where the estate is in excess of £200,000 (or the appropriate lower figure where the death was before 1 December 1993), after making the permitted deductions, the applicant should be described as 'the lawful husband (*or* lawful widow) and one of the persons entitled to share in the estate'.

6.87   In every case, whatever the date of death, the oath must state specifically whether any minority, or any life, interest arises under the intestacy (NCPR 8(4)).

6.88   Where the intestate leaves a spouse, the question whether a life interest arises is decided by reference not only to the amount of the estate for which the grant is sought, but to the total sum, wherever situated, that will ultimately come into the possession of the administrators. For example, if it is apparent that there is further estate elsewhere which, with the estate for which the grant is sought, causes a life interest to arise, then the statutory protection of the reversioners must be considered and normally safeguarded by the appointment of two administrators.

Changes in valuation of estate

6.89 Strictly, the question whether the fixed net sum taken by a surviving spouse, with interest, absorbs the whole of the known distributable estate (other than the personal chattels) is determined by reference to the values prevailing not at the date of death of the intestate but at the time of payment or appropriation. For the purpose of deciding the entitlement to a grant, the earlier values are normally accepted by the probate registries, on the footing that any significant change is unlikely. A substantial change in the value of an asset between the date of death and the time of payment or appropriation may, however, change the answer to the question whether the spouse is entitled to the whole of the residuary estate, with appropriate consequences in connection with the application for the grant[1].

1 Secretary's Circular, 9 January 1962.

6.90 This consideration is more likely to arise in relation to an application for a grant de bonis non after the death of the surviving spouse, and is discussed in this connection in paras. **13.38** and **13.39**, post; but in any case where a significant change in the value of an estate, occurring since the death of the intestate, has affected the position as to entitlement to the grant (e.g. where, owing to a fall in value, the spouse is beneficially entitled to the whole of the known estate notwithstanding that the net value at the date of death as shown in the Inland Revenue account suggests the contrary; or where, owing to an increase in value, the converse is the case), a paragraph should be added to the oath stating the circumstances in which it is claimed that the spouse is (or is not) entitled to the whole of the known estate.

Joint grant to spouse and nearest of kin

6.91 A surviving spouse, as the 'only person now entitled to the estate' (the net value not exceeding the amount of the fixed net sum taken by the surviving spouse (see para. **6.31**, ante), may, in appropriate circumstances and if desired, and subject to leave having been obtained under NCPR 25(2) (see paras. **7.17** ff., post), obtain a grant jointly with a person who may be beneficially entitled if further estate falls in. The latter should be described as 'the administrator joined by leave of the district judge or registrar given on . . .'. It should be sworn that no minority or life interest arises, and if the value of the gross estate exceeds the fixed net sum the net estate should be sworn to be below that amount, after making the permitted deductions (see below).

Deductions permitted

6.92 The deductions permitted for the purpose of showing that the net estate does not exceed the fixed net sum provided by the Administration of Estates Act 1925, s. 46 (as amended), are:

(1) the value of the personal chattels (s. 55(1)(x), Administration of Estates Act 1925);

(2)   debts and incumbrances;

(3)   inheritance tax or capital transfer tax or estate duty[1];

(4)   costs incurred or to be incurred (see para. **6.96**);

(5)   the probate fees payable on application for the grant;

(6)   where the death occurred before 1 January 1953, interest on £1,000 from the date of death at the appropriate rate per annum[2].

(Where death occurred on or after 1 January 1953, the interest on the fixed net sum at the appropriate rate per annum is payable primarily out of income and is not a permitted deduction except insofar as the income actually arising from the estate is insufficient for payment of such interest[3].)

1   Limited to tax or duty properly payable out of the estate and not recoverable by the administrator from any other person or out of any other property, e.g. property which the deceased had power to appoint.

2   This is payable out of the corpus of the estate—not the income. See *Re Saunders, Public Trustee v Saunders* [1929] 1 Ch 674. Where the deceased died before 1953, one of the deductions permitted for the purpose of showing that the net estate does not exceed the fixed net sum provided by the Administration of Estates Act 1925, is the interest at the rate of 5 per cent per annum payable from the date of death on the £1,000 statutory legacy in favour of the surviving spouse. The Intestate Succession (Interest and Capitalisation) Order 1977 (Amendment) Order 1993 (S.I. 1983 No. 1374) provides that for the purposes of s. 46(1)(i) of the Administration of Estates Act 1925, the rate of interest payable on the statutory legacy until it is paid or appropriated shall be 6 per cent per annum. The Order came into operation on 15 October 1983. Accordingly, it would seem that in those cases where the deceased died before 1953, the deduction permitted in respect of interest on the statutory legacy will need to be calculated on £1,000 from the date of death up to 15 September 1977 (when the Intestate Succession (Interest and Capitalisation) Order 1977 (S.I. 1977 No. 1491) came into force) at 5 per cent per annum and thereafter until 1 October 1983 at 7 per cent per annum, and thereafter, until the end of the week in which the application for the grant is made (see President's Direction (1945) 18 April), at 6 per cent per annum.

3   Administration of Estates Act 1925, s. 46(4), as amended by the Intestates' Estates Act 1952, p. 767, post, and Registrar's Direction (1960) 17 November.

Deductions to be sworn to in oath

6.93   Where the gross amount of the estate exceeds the fixed net sum of £125,000 (or the appropriate amount in the case of earlier death, as the case may be) but it is reduced below the appropriate amount by these deductions, the oath, after stating the gross value of the estate, should continue 'but that after deduction of the value of the personal chattels, debts, inheritance tax/capital transfer tax/estate duty, costs amounting to £——, probate fees, and (*where the death occurred before 1953*) interest on the sum of £1,000 amounting to £——, the net value of the estate is £——.'

6.94   Only such of these items as are necessary to establish that the net estate is below the relevant figure need be sworn to.

6.95   It is not sufficient merely to swear that the net estate does not exceed the appropriate sum if the gross estate is in excess of that amount.

6.96   The actual amounts of items (4) and (6) in para. **6.92** must be sworn to. The amount permitted to be deducted for solicitors' costs is such sum as is fair and reasonable having regard to the considerations set out in the Solicitors' (Non-Contentious Business) Remuneration Order 1994[1]. In 1980, The Law Society issued notes for guidance on solicitors' costs for obtaining grants of representation and administering estates[2].

1   This order is printed at pp. 975–978.

2   *Law Society's Gazette*, 15 October 1980. See also *Maltby v DJ Freeman & Co* [1978] 2 All ER 913, [1978] 1 WLR 431 (see fn. 2 to para. **4.267**, ante).

6.97   The district judge or registrar must be satisfied that the charge is fair and reasonable before allowing it as a deduction. Costs of administering a trust or of holding the estate during a life interest should be excluded, as should any costs which cannot be forecast with reasonable certainty[1].

1   Registrar's Direction (1960) 28 June.

6.98   The interest, where deductible, may be calculated from the date of death of the deceased to the end of the week in which the application for the grant is made[1].

1   President's Direction (1945) 18 April.

Renunciation etc., of spouse entitled to whole estate

6.99   Where the net value of the estate (after making the deductions referred to in para. **6.92**, ante) does not exceed the fixed net sum taken by the surviving spouse (see para. **6.31**, ante), then if the spouse is cleared off by renunciation or citation[1], the following are equally entitled to a grant; (i) the nearest of kin[2] of the deceased (to be described in the oath as 'the lawful[3] . . . of the said deceased, and a person who may have a beneficial interest in the estate in the event of an accretion thereto') (Form of oath, No. 93); and (ii) creditors (NCPR 22(3)). As to grants to creditors, see para. **6.310**, post.

1   As to citations, see Chap. 24.
2   Where the death occurred after 1925, but before 1953, 'nearest kin' includes all persons in their order under NCPR 22. But where the death occurred after 1952, it is limited to issue, parents, brothers or sisters of the whole blood, and issue of brothers or sisters of the whole blood who predeceased the intestate. See Administration of Estates Act 1925, s. 46, as amended by Intestates' Estates Act 1952, pp. 767 ff., post, and NCPR 22(1)(a)–(d).
3   Or, in the case of death on or after 1 January 1970 but before 4 April 1988, the natural son or daughter or natural father or mother (see paras. **6.45** ff. and **6.60** ff., post). In the case of death on or after 4 April 1988 the relationship of the kin need not be lawful and the word 'lawful' may be omitted.

6.100   If the deceased left a spouse, but no kin within the classes having a potential beneficial interest (see fn. 2 to para. **6.99**, post), on the renunciation of the spouse, a grant may be made to a creditor.

Death of surviving spouse entitled to whole estate

6.101   By virtue of NCPR 22(4), the personal representative of a surviving spouse who was entitled to the whole estate (as ascertained at the time of application for the grant) has the same right to a grant as was possessed by the spouse whilst alive. A grant may therefore be made to the executors or administrators of such spouse. (Form of oath, No. 91.) As to representative grants, see also paras. **6.11–6.15**, ante.

6.102   It follows that, in these circumstances, before a grant can be made to a 'person who may have a beneficial interest' or to a creditor, in accordance with NCPR 22(3), the personal representative of the spouse must be cleared off by renunciation or citation.

6.103   Where no personal representative of the surviving spouse has been constituted, it is not the practice to accept a statement to this effect as sufficient clearance: the renunciation, by the persons first entitled to constitute themselves as such personal representatives, of any right to a grant in the estate of the spouse who died first, is normally required.

6.104   Moreover, where both spouses have died without the survivor of them having taken a grant in the estate of the other, a child who is the child of both spouses cannot obtain a grant in the estate of the first to die without first taking a 'leading grant' in the estate of the survivor. A person renouncing administration in one capacity is precluded from applying in any other capacity[1]; consequently he may not renounce in the capacity of potential personal representative of the survivor and then apply in his other capacity of 'a person who may have a beneficial interest'.

1   NCPR 37(2).

6.105   If, however, such child is not one of the persons entitled to the leading grant (e.g. because of a will made by the surviving spouse) he may, by clearing off such persons, be able to apply as a 'person who may have a beneficial interest'.

6.106   Where the spouse was *not* entitled to the whole residuary estate, any living person sharing in the estate is entitled to a grant in priority to the personal representative of the spouse (see para. **6.110** below).

Joint grant

6.107   Where the net value of the estate, after making the permitted deductions (see para. **6.92**, ante) exceeds the amount of the fixed net sum taken by the surviving spouse (see para. **6.31**, ante) and there is a life or minority interest, a grant will not normally be made to one individual. The surviving spouse should normally apply jointly with one of the persons entitled to share in the estate (Form of oath, No. 88): alternatively a trust corporation may be joined as second administrator, or a grant may be made to a trust corporation alone, on filing the requisite consents (and, where necessary, renunciations). As to joint grants, see also Chap. 7, and as to grants to trust corporations, see Chap. 9.

Renunciation of spouse with life interest

6.108   On the renunciation of a surviving spouse where the amount of the estate is such that he or she has a life interest, a grant may be made to not less than two other of the persons beneficially entitled, or, subject to the necessary consents, to a trust corporation, with or without one of the beneficiaries (see Chap. 9).

6.109   If there is only one other person beneficially entitled to share, an application to join an administrator is required under NCPR 25(2), see paras. **7.17** ff., post.

Death of spouse not entitled to whole estate

6.110   On the death of a surviving spouse who was not beneficially entitled to the whole estate, a grant may be made to one of the other persons beneficially entitled (or, unless the court allows a sole administrator, to not less than two, if there is any minority interest). (Form of oath, No. 94.) A grant may be made to the personal representative of the spouse only on clearing off all other persons entitled to share in the estate[1].

1   NCPR 22(4), proviso.

Death of spouse and all other persons entitled to share

6.111 Where the surviving spouse and all the kin entitled to share with him or her have died, the personal representative of the spouse is normally entitled to a grant in priority to the personal representatives of the other persons who took a beneficial interest, and must be cleared off before the latter can obtain a grant[1]. However, if it is sworn in the oath that the spouse's beneficial interest in the estate has been wholly satisfied, administration may be granted to the personal representative of one of the other persons having a beneficial interest without clearing off the personal representative of the spouse[2].

1 NCPR 22(4); Registrar's Direction (1955) 7 November.
2 Registrar's Direction (1971) 15 November.

Child 'en ventre sa mère'

6.112 A minority interest may arise in the case of a child en ventre sa mère at the time of the death of the deceased, as such child is, for the purposes of s. 46 of the Administration of Estates Act 1925 in the same position as issue living at the date of death[1].

1 Administration of Estates Act 1925, s. 55(2) (p. 763, post).

6.113 The minority interest will arise only in cases where the surviving spouse is not entitled to the whole estate, i.e. in case of death on or after 1 December 1993, where the net value of the estate is over £125,000, and consequently there will also be a life interest: thus the widow of the deceased cannot normally take a grant alone, although the court has a discretion where it is expedient in all the circumstances to appoint a sole administrator[1].

1 See s. 114(2) of the Supreme Court Act 1981, p. 844, post.

6.114 In such a case it should be sworn in the oath that the deceased died leaving an unborn child.

6.115 If a grant is applied for before the child is born and such unborn child is the only 'issue', any second administrator should be joined by district judge's or registrar's order (see also para. **7.27**, post).

Assignment of life interest or reversion

6.116 As to the practice where a spouse entitled to a life interest, or a reversioner, has assigned his or her interest, see paras. **6.25** and **6.26**, ante.

Divorce

6.117 A divorced husband or wife has no title to a grant on the intestacy of his or her former spouse[1], as the relationship of husband and wife no longer existed at the time of death.

1 Except possibly as a creditor or on behalf of a minor.

6.118 A divorced person should be described in the oath as a 'single man' or 'single woman'[1]. The details (including the name and place of the court) and date of the decree absolute must be recited; it must also be sworn that the intestate did not re-marry and, if the decree was not made in England and Wales, an office copy of the decree absolute must be lodged with the papers[2]. (Form of oath, No. 102.)

1 The expression feme sole is not accepted in these circumstances.
2 Registrar's Direction (1972) 18 April and Registrar's Direction (1988) 9 May.

Decree of nullity of marriage

6.119 A voidable (as distinct from a void) marriage subsists until a decree of nullity is made absolute. A decree of nullity granted on or after 1 August 1971 in respect of a voidable marriage operates to annul the marriage only as respects any time after the decree is made absolute. Notwithstanding the decree, the marriage is treated as if it had existed up to that time[1].

1 Matrimonial Causes Act 1973, s. 16, re-enacting Nullity of Marriage Act 1971, s. 5.

6.120 If the marriage of the deceased has been annulled the deceased should be referred to by the status possessed immediately prior to the ceremony, i.e. as a bachelor, spinster, widower, widow, etc., as the case may be. The oath should, however, include particulars of the nullity decree (e.g. 'That the marriage in fact had and solemnised between the deceased and . . . was annulled by final decree of the High Court of Justice in England and Wales [*or* of the . . . County Court *or* as the case may be] dated the . . .') and, if the decree was made outside England and Wales, an official copy of the decree absolute should be lodged with the papers[1].

1 Registrar's Direction (1972) 18 April and Registrar's Direction (1988) 9 May.

Foreign divorce decrees

6.121 Originally the English courts recognised only a divorce granted by the court having jurisdiction at the place where the spouses were domiciled at the date of institution[1] of the divorce proceedings, or a decree made elsewhere which would be accepted as valid by the law of the place where the spouses were then domiciled[2].

1 *Mansell v Mansell* [1967] P 306, [1966] 2 All ER 391; *Leon v Leon* [1967] P 275, [1966] 3 All ER 820.
2 Even this rule was subject to exceptions: see *Middleton v Middleton* [1967] P 62, [1966] 1 All ER 168.

6.122 Since 1 January 1972 the law as to the recognition of divorces and legal separations granted in countries other than England and Wales was contained in the Recognition of Divorces and Legal Separations Act 1971 (as amended by the Domicile and Matrimonial Proceedings Act 1973). The whole of the Recognition of Divorces and Legal Separations Act 1971 and ss. 2, 15 and 16 of the Domicile and Matrimonial Proceedings Act 1973 were repealed and replaced, as from 4 April 1988, by Part II of the Family Law Act 1986[1].

1 See pp. 866 ff., post.

6.123 Section 44 of the 1986 Act provides that for a divorce or annulment obtained in any part of the British Islands to be regarded as effective in any part of the United Kingdom it must have been granted by a court of civil jurisdiction. An exception provided for in s. 44(1), by reference to s. 52(4) and (5)(a), is a divorce which was obtained in the British Islands before 1 January 1974 and was recognised as valid under the rules of law applicable before that date. Section 44(2) provides that, subject to s. 51, the validity of any divorce, annulment or judicial separation granted by a court of civil jurisdiction in any part of the British Islands shall be recognised throughout the United Kingdom.

6.124 Sections 45 to 48 of the Act deal with the recognition of overseas divorces, annulments and legal separations, i.e. those granted in a country outside the British Isles. Such a divorce, annulment or legal separation, if obtained by means of judicial or other proceedings and effective under the law of the country in which it was obtained, is recognised as valid in the United Kingdom if, at the date of the institution of the proceedings in which it was obtained:

(a)   either spouse was habitually resident[1] in that country;
(b)   either spouse was domiciled in that country; or
(c)   either spouse was a national of that country.

1 Habitual residence is to be distinguished from ordinary residence, and is equivalent to the residence to establish domicile, without the element of animus necessary for the purpose of domicile (*Cruse v Chittum* [1974] 2 All ER 940, 4 Fam Law 152). But see *Kapur v Kapur* [1984] FLR 920, [1985] Fam Law 22, where the husband had been resident in England for a period of 12 months preceding the presentation of the petition; it was held that there was no real distinction between 'ordinary' and 'habitual' residence. The fact that the husband had only a restricted right to remain in this country and that the Home Office could refuse his right to remain, did not mean that he was not habitually resident here.

6.125 Section 46(5) provides that, for the purpose of the section, a party to a marriage shall be treated as domiciled in a country if he was domiciled in that country either according to the law of that country in family matters or according to the law of the part of the United Kingdom in which the question of recognition arises.

6.126 Section 46(4) provides that, in the case of an overseas annulment, if the proceedings were commenced after the death of either spouse, the date of death is to be the relevant date for consideration of that party's habitual residence, domicile or nationality.

6.127 Section 47(1) provides that, where there have been cross-proceedings and if the validity of the overseas divorce, annulment or legal separation is otherwise entitled to recognition under Part II of the Act, its validity will also be recognised if either spouse was habitually resident or domiciled in, or was a national of, the country concerned at the commencement of the original proceedings or of the cross-proceedings.

6.128 Section 47(2) provides for the recognition of a divorce which is effective under the law of the country concerned, where that divorce has been obtained by the conversion of a legal separation obtained in the same country and which was entitled to recognition in the United Kingdom.

6.129 Section 48 provides that, for the purpose of deciding whether an overseas divorce etc. obtained by proceedings is entitled to recognition in the United Kingdom, any finding of fact made (whether expressly or impliedly) in the proceedings and on the basis of which jurisdiction was assumed in the proceedings shall—

(a)   if both parties to the marriage took part in the proceedings, be conclusive evidence of the fact found; and
(b)   in any other case be sufficient proof of that fact unless the contrary is shown.

6.130　It is confirmed, in s. 48(2) that the above, in para. **6.129**, includes a finding that either party to the marriage was habitually resident in the country in which the divorce etc. was obtained, or was under the law of that country domiciled there, or was a national of that country.

6.131　It is further confirmed, in s. 48(3) that for the purposes of (a) in para. **6.129** above, a party to the marriage who has appeared in judicial proceedings shall be treated as having taken part in them.

6.132　Section 49 provides that if the overseas country concerned is comprised of territories in which different systems of law are in force in matters of divorce, annulment or legal separation, then as regards habitual residence or domicile or conversion of a legal separation into a divorce, each territory shall be regarded as a separate country. As regards nationality it is necessary for the divorce etc. to be effective throughout the whole country (and not just the territory) in which it was obtained.

Divorce, annulment or legal separation granted otherwise than by a court of law

6.133　Section 46(2) of the Family Law Act 1986 provides that the validity of an overseas divorce, annulment or legal separation obtained otherwise than by proceedings shall be recognised if it is effective under the law of the country in which it was obtained, and, at the date on which it was obtained (or, if it was obtained after the death of one of the spouses, as regards that spouse, the date of his death):

(a)　each party to the marriage was domiciled in that country; or
(b)　either party to the marriage was domiciled in that country and the other party was domiciled in a country under whose law the divorce, annulment or legal separation is recognised as valid;

and provided that neither party to the marriage was habitually resident in the United Kingdom throughout the period of one year immediately preceding the date on which it was obtained (or, if it was obtained after the death of one of the spouses, as regards that spouse, the date of his death).

Divorces etc. granted or obtained before 4 April 1988

6.134　Section 52(1) of the Family Law Act 1986 provides that Part II of the Act applies to—

(a)　a divorce, annulment or judicial separation granted by a court of civil jurisdiction in the British Islands before the date of the commencement, and
(b)　to an overseas divorce, annulment or legal separation obtained before that date,

as well as to one granted or obtained on or after that date, but s. 52(2) provides that the recognition or preclusion of such recognition shall not affect any property to which any person became entitled before that date, or the recognition of the validity of the divorce, annulment or separation if that matter has been decided by any competent court in the British Islands before that date.

6.135　Section 52(5)(a) provides that the following are also recognised in the United Kingdom whether or not entitled to recognition by virtue of any of the preceding provisions of Part II of the Act:

(a) a divorce which was obtained in the British Islands before 1 January 1974 and was recognised as valid under rules of law applicable before that date;

(b) an overseas divorce which was recognised as valid under the Recognition of Divorces and Legal Separations Act 1971 and was not affected by s. 16(2) of the Domicile and Matrimonial Proceedings Act 1973 (proceedings otherwise than in a court of law where both parties resident in United Kingdom);

(c) a divorce of which the decree was registered under s. 1 of the Indian and Colonial Divorce Jurisdiction Act 1926;

(d) a divorce or annulment which was recognised as valid under s. 4 of the Matrimonial Causes (War Marriages) Act 1944; and

(e) an overseas legal separation which was recognised as valid under the Recognition of Divorces and Legal Separations Act 1971.

Practice

6.136 The practice in unopposed probate applications where the validity of a divorce granted in a country other than England and Wales is material is as follows:

(a) A decree of divorce granted by a court in Scotland, Northern Ireland, the Channel Islands or the Isle of Man will be recognised in the same way as a decree granted in England and Wales, irrespective of the domicile of the deceased.

(b) A decree of divorce, whenever granted, by a court in an overseas country will be recognised if the oath shows that at the date of commencement of the proceedings resulting in the decree:

either spouse was habitually resident in that country, or was domiciled in that country, or was a national of that country;
or exceptionally if one of these facts is recorded in the decree itself.

6.137 In all other cases, including a case in which it is alleged that a divorce was obtained by extra-judicial proceedings (unless there is an official document certifying the effect under the law of the relevant country—see s. 51(3)(b) of the 1986 Act), a full statement of the facts should be submitted to a district judge or registrar for decision. The district judge or registrar, after consideration of the facts, will decide whether further evidence of facts or law is necessary.

6.138 In an unopposed application no action by the registry will normally be taken to require evidence that notice of the proceedings, or an opportunity to take part in the proceedings, was given to the respondent. If in any case it appears on the face of the decree that no such notice was given and no such opportunity afforded, or if it appears that recognition of the decree would manifestly be contrary to public policy, the matter should be referred to a district judge or registrar.

6.139 It should also be noted that under the current practice an affidavit of law may not in all cases be necessary. An official copy of the decree of the foreign court, with a notarial, or other properly verified translation (if it is in a foreign language), must be lodged.

Separation order or decree

6.140 On the death intestate, prior to 1 August 1970, of a married woman who had been separated from her husband by a decree of judicial separation or by a separation order, any property acquired by her since the date of the decree or order devolved as if her husband had predeceased her[1]. It was the practice to grant administration limited to that part of her estate to her nearest kin, and if necessary to grant administration of the estate acquired before the date of the decree or order to the husband: see para. **11.296**, post.

1 Matrimonial Causes Act 1965, s. 20(3) (repealed in relation to deaths on or after 1 August 1970 by Matrimonial Proceedings and Property Act 1970, s. 40(3): see now Matrimonial Causes Act 1973, s. 18, p. 806, post). However, the effect of s. 20(3) of the Matrimonial Causes Act 1965 in relation to deaths occurring prior to 1 August 1970 is preserved by Schedule I, Pt. II, para. 13 of the 1973 Act.

6.141   But where the death occurs on or after 1 August 1970:

(a)   If, while a *decree of judicial separation* is in force, either the husband or the wife dies wholly or partly intestate, the estate, or the property as respects which he or she dies intestate (as the case may be), devolves as if the other spouse were then dead[1]. It should be noted that this applies in the case of the death of a judicially separated husband as well as a wife, and that the surviving spouse is excluded from taking on intestacy any estate acquired prior to, as well as after, the date of the decree. The effect of a judicial separation is for this purpose the same as that of a divorce.

(b)   On the other hand, a separation order made in a *magistrates' court* no longer has the effect of depriving the husband of his interest on intestacy in the estate acquired by his wife on or after the date of the separation order[2].

1 Matrimonial Proceedings and Property Act 1970, s. 40(1), since repealed and replaced by Matrimonial Causes Act 1973, s. 18(2) (see p. 806, post).
2 Ibid., s. 40(2): see now Matrimonial Causes Act 1973, s. 18(3).

6.142   Grants limited to a portion of the estate in case of separation by court order or decree are accordingly not appropriate where the death occurred on or after 1 August 1970. For form of oath for administration in the estate of a spouse who has been judicially separated, see Form No. 142.

Separation agreement

6.143   Where a husband and wife have entered into a deed of separation it is uncertain whether a covenant by one party to the marriage not to make any claim on the estate of the other has any effect on the surviving spouse's priority of right to a grant on an intestacy. It would seem that the statutory right to apply continues, but is unlikely to be involved, since it would be of no advantage. However, if the surviving spouse renounces his or her right to administration a grant may be made to the nearest kin, as a person who may have a beneficial interest in the event of an accretion to the estate (see para. **6.99**, ante).

Grant to children or other issue

Statutory rights of next-of-kin and heir-at-law abolished

6.144   In relation to deaths on or after 1 January 1926, the statutory right of the next-of-kin to a grant was abolished by the repealing of 21 Hen. 8, c. 5.

6.145   By s. 33 of the Administration of Estates Act 1925, the real estate of an intestate is to be held by the personal representative upon trust for sale, so that in cases of death on or after 1 January 1926, the heir-at-law has no interest or right in that character, except as stated in the next paragraph; the real estate is treated as personal estate, and the same rules as to distribution apply.

Exception: person of unsound mind on 1 January 1926

6.146 Where, however, the intestate was of full age and unsound mind on 1 January 1926, and thereafter died without recovering his testamentary capacity[1], any beneficial interest in real estate[2], other than chattels real, to which he was entitled at the commencement of the Act and at his death, devolves in accordance with the general law in force before 1926[3]. These circumstances would, of course, be extremely rare today, but the old law applies equally to an undivided share in real estate held immediately before 1 January 1926 by such a person, his interest being for this purpose a 'beneficial interest in real estate' notwithstanding that on that date it became subject to a trust for sale[4]. The personal estate, subject to any settlement by the court, devolves in accordance with the present law. In such circumstances, where there is a preponderance of real estate, the heir-at-law is preferred in an application for a grant. Should such a case still arise, the usual evidence as to heirship (see Forms 20, 21) is required, and it is required to be shown in the oath, and is stated in the grant: 'That the intestate was of full age but of unsound mind on 1 January, 1926, and died, without recovering his testamentary capacity, possessed of real estate'. The grant issues to 'A.B., the heir-at-law'[5].

1 He is not deemed to have recovered his testamentary capacity unless his receiver is discharged (Administration of Estates Act 1925, s. 51(2)).
2 The term includes, for this purpose, not only freehold land but also heritable estates or interests in copyholds (*Re Sirett, Pratt v Burton* [1968] 3 All ER 186, [1969] 1 WLR 60).
3 Administration of Estates Act 1925, s. 51(2), p. 761, post.
4 *Re Bradshaw, Bradshaw v Bradshaw* [1950] Ch 582, [1950] 1 All ER 643, CA distg. *Re Donkin, Public Trustee v Cairns* [1948] Ch 74, [1947] 2 All ER 690.
5 Registrar's Direction (1928) 20 April.

6.147 In the case of preponderance of personal estate the grant issues to the person entitled under the present rules, on showing in the oath: 'That the intestate was of full age but of unsound mind on 1 January 1926 and died, without recovering his testamentary capacity, possessed of real estate, and that C. D. is the heir-at-law'. No consent of or notice to the heir-at-law is necessary.

Grant to children or other issue

6.148 If the intestate has left no widow or husband, as the case may be, the children or other issue of the intestate are entitled to administration—such other issue being children, living at the death of the intestate, of any child, or more remote issue, who predeceased the intestate, and so taking per stirpes their parent's share in the estate: see NCPR 22(1)(b). The oath must clear off the spouse by stating that the intestate died a bachelor or spinster, or a widower or widow, or (if divorced) a single man or single woman. As to divorce, see also paras. **6.117** ff., ante. Form of oath, No. 96.

6.149 The term 'issue' connotes only lawfully born descendants, but there are various statutory provisions which, on an intestacy, give other categories of descendants rights similar to those of the issue, e.g. legitimated children (see 'Legitimated Persons' paras. **6.174** ff., post) and adopted children (see paras. **6.223** ff., post).

6.150 In the case of death on or after 1 January 1970, illegitimate children are placed on an equality with legitimate children so far as regards their right of succession on intestacy to the estate of either parent[1] (see 'Issue of intestate', para. **6.43**, ante).

1 Family Law Reform Act 1969, s. 14 (p. 791, post).

6.151   When the intestate died on or after 1 January 1970 but before 4 April 1988 an illegitimate child should be described in the oath to lead the grant as 'the natural son (*or* daughter) and only person entitled to (*or* one of the persons entitled to share in) the estate', as the case may be. Form of oath, No. 96.

6.152   When the intestate died on or after 1 January 1970 but before 4 April 1988, the *lawful* issue of an illegitimate child of the intestate who died in the lifetime of the latter stands in its parent's place as regards succession to the estate of the intestate, but an illegitimate child of such an illegitimate child has no title except to the estate of its own parent.

6.153   When the intestate died on or after 4 April 1988 it does not matter as regards succession whether the parents of any child or other issue were married to each other at any time[1] and it is sufficient to refer to any such child as the 'son (daughter) of the intestate and only person (one of the persons) entitled to (share in) the estate' and any such other issue as the 'son (daughter) of C. D. the son (daughter) of the said deceased who died before the deceased and only person (one of the persons) entitled to (share in) the estate'[2] or as the case may be.

1 Family Law Reform Act 1987, s. 18 (p. 876, post).
2 Registrar's Direction (1988) 19 April.

6.154   Under s. 21 of the Family Law Reform Act 1987[1], for the purpose of determining the person or persons who would in accordance with probate rules be entitled to a grant of probate or administration in respect of the estate of a deceased person dying on or after 4 April 1988, the deceased is presumed, unless the contrary is shown, not to have been survived by any person related to him whose father and mother were not married to each other at the time of his birth or by any person whose relationship with him is deduced through a person whose father and mother were not married to each other at the time of his birth. The applicant's title, as sworn to in the oath, will be taken as sufficient to rebut any such presumption[2].

1 See p. 878, post.
2 Registrar's Direction (1988) 19 April.

6.155   Under s. 27 of the Family Law Reform Act 1987, where, on or after 4 April 1988, a child is born in England and Wales as the result of the artificial insemination of a woman who was at the time of the insemination a party to a marriage (being a marriage which had not at that time been dissolved or annulled) and was artificially inseminated with the semen of some person other than the other party to the marriage, then, unless it is proved to the satisfaction of any court by which the matter has to be determined that the other party to that marriage did not consent to the insemination, the child is to be treated in law as the child of the parties to that marriage and is not to be treated as the child of any person other than the parties to that marriage[1]. The section does not affect the succession to any dignity or title of honour or render any person capable of succeeding to or transmitting a right to succeed to any such dignity or title[2].

1 See p. 878, post.
2 Family Law Reform Act 1987, s. 27(3), p. 879, post.

6.156 Where a court has made a 'parental order' under s. 30 of the Human Fertilisation and Embryology Act 1990, providing for a child to be treated in law as the child of the parties to a marriage, the Parental Orders (Human Fertilisation and Embryology) Regulations 1994 (S.I. 1994 No. 2767) apply, as from 1 November 1994. Under these Regulations, relevant provisions of the Adoption Act 1976, as modified by the Regulations, are applied. They may be briefly summarised as placing a child in respect of whom a parental order has been made in the same position as if he had been adopted.

6.157 In order to have an absolutely vested interest in an estate, the issue of an intestate must attain the age of majority or marry under that age; otherwise their interest becomes divested and the estate is divisible as if they had not been born (see Administration of Estates Act 1925, s. 47(2)).

6.158 Although a child who marries while under the age of majority is entitled to give a valid receipt for the income of his share in the residuary estate[1], he cannot personally apply for administration until of full age.

1 Law of Property Act 1925, s. 21.

6.159 Those of the issue who share in the estate are all on an equal footing as regards their right to a grant.

6.160 If any person entitled to share in the estate is a minor, a grant must normally be made to not less than two individuals, or to a trust corporation with or without an individual.

6.161 As to joint grants, see Chap. 7. As to grants where all the persons entitled are under age, see Chap. 11, 'Grants for use of minors'.

6.162 As to a grant to a child on the renunciation of a surviving spouse, see para. **6.99**, ante.

Evidence of paternity

6.163 Where the intestate died before 4 April 1988 and the applicant's title to letters of administration depends upon the establishing of an illegitimate relationship (except that with the mother), evidence in support of the claim to the relationship, normally in the form of affidavits, must be lodged at the registry. If a birth certificate is produced which gives the name of the father and shows that the birth was registered on his information or on the authority of a statutory declaration made by him, or if an affiliation order is produced containing a finding of paternity, further evidence as to paternity additional to the statement in the oath is not normally necessary[1]. Where the intestate died on or after 4 April 1988 evidence of paternity will be called for only in exceptional circumstances[2].

1 As from 1 January 1977 a mother may apply for the registration of the father of an illegitimate child on production of an affiliation order naming that person as the putative father (together with the child's consent where he is 16 years or over): Children Act 1975, s. 93, amending Births and Deaths Registration Act 1953, s. 10. See also Civil Evidence Act 1968, s. 12, as amended by Family Law Reform Act 1987, s. 22, from 4 April 1988 which allows an adjudication of paternity made in the course of proceedings brought under the Guardianship of Minors Act 1971 and of proceedings brought by public bodies to constitute prima facie evidence of paternity.
2 Registrar's Direction (1988) 19 April.

Declaration of paternity

6.164   Where necessary it is open to any person who is either domiciled in England and Wales on the date of the application or has been habitually resident[1] in England and Wales throughout the period of one year ending with that date, to apply to the court, under s. 56 of the Family Law Act 1986[2] as substituted by s. 22 of the Family Law Reform Act 1987[3], for a declaration that a person named in the application is or was his parent.

1   See fn. 1 to para. **6.124**, ante.
2   See p. 871, post.
3   See p. 878, post.

Personal representative of child

6.165   Unless otherwise directed by a district judge or registrar, any living person beneficially interested in the estate has a right to the grant superior to that of the personal representative of a child who survived but has subsequently died (NCPR 27(5)).

6.166   If the only child of an intestate dying without a spouse has survived the intestate and died, administration will be granted to his personal representative only if he attained an absolutely vested interest in the estate, i.e., if he died after attaining the age of majority, or married under that age: otherwise the grant is made as though the deceased had died without issue.

6.167   See paras. **6.11–6.15**, ante, as to the practice in applications by personal representatives.

Right of illegitimate child to succeed to mother's estate (death before 1 January 1970)

6.168   By s. 9(1) of the Legitimacy Act 1926, which came into force on 1 January 1927, it was enacted that:

> 'where, after the commencement of this Act, the mother of an illegitimate child, such child not being a legitimated person, dies intestate as respects all or any of her real or personal property, and does not leave any legitimate issue her surviving, the illegitimate child, or, if he is dead, his issue, shall be entitled to take any interest therein to which he or such issue would have been entitled if he had been born legitimate.'

6.169   The children of the deceased and the issue of any deceased child who died before the deceased are next entitled in order of priority to a grant after clearing off the spouse—NCPR 22(1).

6.170   The right to letters of administration arises only where under the relevant statutes the applicant has a beneficial interest. Thus, if the deceased died on or after 1 January 1927, but before 1 January 1970, a spinster (or a widow or divorced woman without any lawful issue) leaving an illegitimate child, a grant may be made to such child. The oath should describe the applicant as the natural son (or daughter) and only person entitled to the estate (or one of the persons entitled to share therein, if the deceased left more than one such child). In the case of a widow or divorced woman it must be sworn that she died without lawful issue.

6.171   The lawful issue of an illegitimate child dying in the lifetime of its mother stands in its parent's place as regards inheritance from the parent's mother, but where the mother of a lawful daughter (who has predeceased her) dies intestate the illegitimate child of such daughter has no claim except to her own (natural) mother's estate.

6.172 Where a married woman dies intestate leaving an illegitimate child or children but no lawful issue, the illegitimate children take the same rights under the intestacy (subject to the interest of the husband of the deceased) as if they had been born legitimate[1].

1 Legitimacy Act 1926, s. 9(1).

Right of illegitimate child to succeed to parent's estate (death after 31 December 1969)

6.173 In the case of deaths on or after 1 January 1970 and before 4 April 1988, s. 9 of the Legitimacy Act 1926 is repealed and replaced by s. 14 of the Family Law Reform Act 1969[1]. As regards deaths on or after 4 April 1988, s. 14 of the Family Law Reform Act 1969 is repealed by s. 33(4) of the Family Law Reform Act 1987[2] but the repeal does not affect any rights arising under the intestacy of a person dying before 4 April 1988: Family Law Reform Act 1987, Sch. 3, para. 8. In respect of deaths on or after 4 April 1988 s. 18 of the Family Law Reform Act 1987 provides that with regard to rights of succession to property on intestacy, illegitimacy is not to be taken into consideration. In relation to deaths on or after 1 January 1970 illegitimate children have, in general, rights of succession on intestacy to the estate of either parent equal to those of lawful children; and this applies whether or not the intestate also left lawful issue (see paras. **6.150–6.154**, ante).

1 See p. 791, post.
2 See p. 880, post.

Legitimated persons

6.174 The Legitimacy Act 1976[1], which came into force on 22 August 1976, consolidates the enactments relating to legitimacy and legitimation. The earlier enactments, now repealed (subject to certain important savings made by Schedule 1 to the 1976 Act), are contained in Schedule 2 to the 1976 Act, and include the Legitimacy Acts 1926 and 1959 and those provisions relating to legitimation formerly contained in Schedule 1 to the Children Act 1975.

1 See p. 822, post.

Legitimation on marriage of parents

6.175 The Legitimacy Act 1926, s. 1[1] enacted that if the parents of an illegitimate child marry or have married one another, whether before or after the commencement of that Act (1 January 1927), the marriage shall (subject to certain conditions), if the father of such child was, or is, at the date of the marriage domiciled in England or Wales, render such child, if living, legitimate from the commencement of the Act, or from the date of the marriage, whichever last happens. Prior to 1 January 1976, however, such legitimation did not enable a person, his spouse, or children, or remoter issue, to take any interest in property, real or personal, except as was expressly provided for in that Act[2], but, in relation to deaths and other events occurring after 31 December 1975, the effect of the coming into force of Schedule 1 to the Children Act 1975 on 1 January 1976 is to place legitimated persons generally in the same position in relation to the devolution of property as if they had been born legitimate: see 'Devolution of property in cases of legitimacy' below.

1 See now Legitimacy Act 1976, s. 2 (p. 822, post).
2 Legitimacy Act 1926, ss. 1(3), 3 to 5.

6.176   The parents of a legitimated person are under a duty to furnish to the Registrar-General within a specified time information with a view to obtaining the re-registration of birth[1].

1 Legitimacy Act 1926, s. 1(4) and Schedule which provisions are since repealed and re-enacted by the Legitimacy Act 1976, s. 9; see also fn. 1 to para. **6.211**, post.

6.177   Section 1(2) of the Legitimacy Act 1926 (which excluded the operation of that Act in the case of an illegitimate person whose father or mother was married to a third person at the time of the birth) was repealed by the Legitimacy Act 1959, which came into force on 29 October 1959. In relation to persons legitimated by virtue of this repeal, the Legitimacy Act 1926 has effect as if for references to the commencement of that Act there were substituted references to the commencement of the Legitimacy Act 1959 (see s. 1(2) of the 1959 Act as preserved by paragraph 2(3) of Schedule 1 to the Legitimacy Act 1976[1]). Accordingly, an illegitimate person, either of whose parents was, at the date of his birth, married to a third person, is rendered legitimate by the marriage of his parents, but the legitimation takes effect only from 29 October 1959 or from the date of the marriage, whichever is the later.

1 See p. 826, post.

Requisites for claiming legitimation

6.178   Where it is necessary to establish that the legitimation took place prior to 29 October 1959 (i.e. by virtue of the Legitimacy Act 1926, as originally enacted), it must be shown that at the date of birth of the person who, it is claimed, was legitimated, neither of his parents was married to a third person.

6.179   It has been held that a child born on the day on which a divorce decree was made absolute was born at a time when the divorced parent was not 'married to a third person' within the meaning of s. 1 of the Act of 1926[1].

1 *Kruhlak v Kruhlak (No 2)* [1958] 2 All ER 294, [1958] 1 WLR 606 (this decision is still relevant in cases where it is necessary to establish that the legitimation took place before 29 October 1959 but it was doubted by the Court of Appeal in *Re Seaford, Seaford v Seifert* [1968] P 53, [1968] 1 All ER 482).

6.180   Until 4 April 1988 s. 45 of the Matrimonial Causes Act 1973[1] provided for the method of application to the court for a declaration of legitimation. That section was repealed from 4 April 1988 by s. 68(2) of the Family Law Act 1986[2] and was replaced with effect from that date by s. 56 of the Family Law Act 1986 as substituted by s. 22 of the Family Law Reform Act 1987[3]. Proceedings begun under s. 45 of the Matrimonial Causes Act 1973 before 4 April 1988 are not affected by the repeal of s. 45—see s. 68(3) of the Family Law Act 1986. Such a declaration or a certificate of re-registration of birth under s. 9 of the Legitimacy Act 1976[4] is accepted as evidence of legitimation in any particular case (see paras. **6.211** ff., post).

1 See p. 806, post.
2 See p. 872, post.
3 See p. 878, post.
4 See p. 824, post.

Devolution of property in cases of legitimation

6.181 *Deaths before 1 January 1976.* Under s. 3(1) of the Act of 1926, subject to the provisions of that Act, a legitimated person and his spouse, children or more remote issue, are entitled to take any interest:

(a)   in the estate of a person dying intestate after the date of the legitimation;

(b)   under any disposition coming into operation after the date of the legitimation[1]; or

(c)   by descent under an entailed interest created after the date of the legitimation;

in like manner as if the legitimated person had been born legitimate. As to the effective date of legitimation, see paras. **6.175** and **6.177**, ante.

1 As to the date on which a disposition 'comes into operation', see para. **6.214**, post.

6.182   Where, however, the right to any property depends on the relative seniority of the children of any person, legitimated children are to rank as if they had been born on the day on which they became legitimated by virtue of the Act; if more than one child became legitimated at the same time, then, as between themselves, they rank in order of seniority (s. 3(2)).

6.183   Section 3(3) deals with property devolving with a dignity or title of honour, which devolves as though the Act had not been passed. Section 3(4) restricts the operation of s. 3 to cases where no contrary intention is expressed in a disposition.

6.184   Under s. 4 of the Act of 1926, where a legitimated person, or a child or remoter issue of a legitimated person, dies intestate as to all or any of his property, the same persons take the same interests therein as they would have been entitled to take if he had been born legitimate.

6.185   Section 5 provides that if an illegitimate person dies after the commencement of the Act of 1926 and before the marriage of his parents, leaving a spouse, children, or remoter issue living at the date of such marriage, then, if that person, if living at the date of marriage of his parents, would have become a legitimated person, the provisions of the Act shall apply as if he had been a legitimated person and the date of the marriage had been the date of legitimation.

6.186   In cases in which legitimation would be effected only by virtue of s. 1 of the Legitimacy Act 1959, i.e. where either of the parents of the illegitimate person was married to a third person at the date of his birth, the foregoing provision applies only where the death occurs after the commencement of the Act of 1959, i.e. on or after 29 October 1959 (Legitimacy Act 1959, s. 1(2)).

6.187   Nothing in the Legitimacy Act 1926 affects the operation or construction of any disposition coming into operation before the commencement of that Act (i.e. 1

January 1927), or any rights under the intestacy of a person dying before that date (s. 10(2)).

6.188   *Deaths after 31 December 1975.* In relation to deaths occurring on or after 1 January 1976 the provisions of the Legitimacy Act 1926 as to the interest taken by legitimated persons, and those claiming through them, on intestacy or under wills and settlements, were replaced by those of the Children Act 1975, Schedule 1 to which contained a complete code replacing earlier provisions as to the treatment of both adopted children and legitimated persons in relation to matters of succession. As regards succession rights arising from legitimation, the relevant provisions of Schedule 1 have since been repealed and replaced by the Legitimacy Act 1976[1].

1 See pp. 822–826, post: the Legitimacy Act 1976, a consolidating measure, came into force on 22 August 1976.

6.189   For the purposes of the 1976 Act a legitimated person means a person legitimated or recognised as legitimated:

(a)   under s. 2 (legitimation by subsequent marriage of parents) or s. 3 (legitimation by extraneous law) of the above Act;
(b)   under s. 1 or 8 of the Legitimacy Act 1926; or
(c)   by a legitimation (whether or not by virtue of the subsequent marriage of his parents) recognised by the law of England and Wales and effected under the law of any other country,

and includes, where the context admits, a person legitimated or recognised as legitimated before the passing of the Children Act 1975 (s. 10(1), (2) of the 1976 Act).

6.190   Section 1(3) of the Act of 1926, which restricted the interests in property taken by a legitimated person to those specified by that Act (see para. **6.181**, ante), was repealed, save in relation to existing instruments, as from 1 January 1976. Sections 3 to 5 of the Legitimacy Act 1926 were similarly repealed by the Children Act 1975.

6.191   Schedule 1 to the Children Act 1975 (now repealed and re-enacted in relation to legitimated persons' rights of succession by the Legitimacy Act 1976) provided rules of construction which are to apply to any instrument other than an 'existing instrument' (defined as one made before 1 January 1976) so far as the instrument contains a disposition of property (s. 5(1) of the 1976 Act). Provisions of the law of intestate succession applicable to the estate of a deceased person are, for this purpose, to be treated as if contained in an instrument executed by the deceased, while of full capacity, immediately before his death (s. 5(2)). The new provisions thus apply to deaths intestate on or after 1 January 1976.

6.192   The general rule is that a legitimated person is to be treated as if he had been born legitimate: s. 5(3) provides that a legitimated person, and any other person, is entitled to take any interest in property as if the legitimated person had been born legitimate.

6.193   Where a disposition depends on the date of birth of a child or children of a parent or parents, it is to be construed as if:

(a)   a legitimated child had been born on the date of its legitimation; and
(b)   two or more children legitimated on the same date had been born on that date in the order of their actual births;

but this does not affect any reference to the child's age (s. 5(4)). Examples of phrases in wills on which this provision could operate are given in s. 5(5).

6.194   Section 5(6) contains a provision similar to s. 5 of the Legitimacy Act 1926: it deals with the case where a child would have been legitimated by the marriage of its parents but for the fact that the child died before the marriage took place. So far as regards the taking of interests by, or in succession to, the spouse, children or remoter issue of the deceased child, a disposition is to be construed as if he was legitimated at the date of his parents' marriage. This provision applies also where a child is adopted by one of its natural parents and his parents intermarry after the child's death.

6.195   Section 4 provides that a child may be legitimated under the Act even though it has previously been adopted by one of its natural parents as sole adopter, but preserves the rights of the child under Part II of Schedule 1 to the Children Act 1975 (which deals with adoptions) under any instrument made prior to the legitimation.

6.196   Section 6 contains provisions dealing with the case where a disposition depends on the date of birth of a child who was born illegitimate but was subsequently legitimated or treated as legitimated; and s. 7 deals with the protection of trustees and personal representatives who distribute property without notice of a legitimation.

6.197   Paragraph 4(3) of Schedule 1 to the 1976 Act provides that, apart from s. 1 (legitimacy of children of certain void marriages (as to which, see below)), nothing in the Act shall affect the devolution of any property which is limited to devolve along with any dignity or title of honour. And, by s. 10(4) of the Act, it is expressly declared that references in the 1976 Act to dispositions of property include references to a disposition by the creation of an entailed interest.

Dispositions made on or after 1 January 1970: illegitimate and legitimated children

6.198   In relation to dispositions of property made on or after 1 January 1970 references, express or implied, for the purpose of indicating beneficiaries, to the child or children of any person are, unless the contrary intention appears, to be construed as, or as including, references to any illegitimate child of such person, and similarly references to persons related in some other manner to any person are to be construed as, or as including, references to a person who would be so related if he, or another person through whom the relationship is traced, had been born legitimate (Family Law Reform Act 1969, s. 15(1)[1]). The provisions in s. 15 of the Family Law Reform Act 1969 do not alter the construction of the words 'heir' or 'heirs' or any expression used to create an entailed interest. Section 15 of the Family Law Reform Act 1969 was repealed on 4 April 1988 by s. 33(4) of the Family Law Reform Act 1987[2] but the repeal does not affect any disposition by will or codicil executed before that date—Sch. 3, para. 9 of the Family Law Reform Act 1987.

1 See p. 792, post.
2 See p. 880, post.

6.199 In respect of dispositions by will or codicil made on or after 4 April 1988 references (whether express or implied) to any relationship between two persons are to be construed, unless the contrary intention appears, without regard to whether or not the father and mother of either of them, or the father and mother of any person through whom the relationship is deduced, have or had been married to each other at any time and s. 19(2) of the 1987 Act declares that the words 'heir' or 'heirs' or any expression which is used to create an entailed interest do not, by themselves, show such a contrary intention.

6.200 Section 15(4) of the 1969 Act provides that references in the foregoing to an illegitimate child include an illegitimate child who is or who becomes a legitimated person within the meaning of the Legitimacy Act 1926 or a person recognised by virtue of that Act or at common law as having been legitimated. However, s. 15(4) is repealed with effect from 1 January 1976, save as respects any instrument passed or made before that date, by the Children Act 1975, Schedule 4, Part II. (As to the interests taken by legitimated persons, see now the Legitimacy Act 1976, ss. 5 and 6[1].)

1 See pp. 823, 824, post.

Declaration of legitimation

6.201 Any person who is either domiciled in England and Wales on the date of the application or has been habitually resident[1] in England and Wales throughout the period of one year ending with that date may make an application to the court for a declaration that he is the legitimate child of his parents or that he has or has not become a legitimated person[2].

1 See fn. 1 to para. **6.124**, ante.
2 Family Law Act 1986, s. 56, as substituted by Family Law Reform Act 1987, s. 22—see p. 871, post.

Children of void marriages

6.202 Under s. 1(1) of the Legitimacy Act 1976[1], a child of a void marriage, whenever born, is to be treated as the legitimate child of its parents if at the time of the act of intercourse resulting in its birth (or at the time of celebration of the marriage, if later) both or either of the parents reasonably believed that the marriage was valid[2]. As from 4 April 1988 for the words 'the act of intercourse resulting in the birth' there were substituted the words 'the insemination resulting in the birth or, where there was no such insemination, the child's conception' and two further subsections were added to s. 1 of the Legitimacy Act 1976, as follows:

'(3) It is hereby declared for the avoidance of doubt that subsection (1) above applies notwithstanding that the belief that the marriage was valid was due to a mistake as to law.

(4) In relation to a child born after the coming into force of section 28 of the Family Law Reform Act 1987, it shall be presumed for the purposes of subsection (1) above, unless the contrary is shown, that one of the parties to the void marriage reasonably believed at the time of the insemination resulting in the birth or, where there was no

such insemination, the child's conception (or at the time of the celebration of the marriage if later) that the marriage was valid.'

(Section 28 of the Family Law Reform Act 1987[3].)

1 See p. 822, post; the 1976 Act repeals and replaces, inter alia, s. 2 of the Legitimacy Act 1959.
2 See *Sheward v A-G* [1964] 2 All ER 324, [1964] 1 WLR 724 (bigamous marriage: court satisfied from evidence of conversations with the mother (who had since died) that she believed she was being validly married by the void ceremony. Declaration of legitimacy made).
3 See p. 879, post

6.203 Under s. 27 of the Family Law Reform Act 1987, where, on or after 4 April 1988, a child is born in England and Wales as the result of the artificial insemination of a woman who was at the time of the insemination a party to a marriage (being a marriage which had not at that time been dissolved or annulled) and was artificially inseminated with the semen of some person other than the other party to the marriage, then, unless it is proved to the satisfaction of any court by which the matter has to be determined that the other party to that marriage did not consent to the insemination, the child is to be treated in law as the child of the parties to that marriage and is not to be treated as the child of any person other than the parties to that marriage[1]. This applies also to void marriages if at the time of the insemination resulting in the birth of the child both or either of the parties reasonably believed that the marriage was valid, there being a presumption unless the contrary is shown, that one of the parties so believed at that time that the marriage was valid[2]. Section 27 of the Family Law Reform Act 1987 does not affect the succession to any dignity or title of honour or render any person capable of succeeding to or transmitting a right to succeed to any such dignity or title[3].

1 Family Law Reform Act 1987, s. 27(1)—see p. 878, post.
2 Ibid, s. 27(2).
3 Ibid, s. 27(3).

6.204 By sub-s. (2), s. 1 of the Legitimacy Act 1976 applies only where the father of the child was domiciled in England and Wales at the time of its birth, or, if he died before its birth, immediately before his death.

6.205 So far as it affects succession to a dignity or title of honour or the devolution of property settled therewith, s. 1 of the Legitimacy Act 1976 applies only to children born on or after 29 October 1959. The section does not affect any rights under the intestacy of a person dying before 29 October 1959 and, except so far as may be necessary to avoid the severance from a dignity or title of honour of property settled therewith, it does not affect the operation or construction of a disposition coming into operation before that date (Schedule 1, paras. 3 and 4).

6.206 However, in the case of persons dying intestate on or after 29 October 1959 and in considering the construction of wills, etc. coming into operation on or after that date, regard should be had to the terms of s. 1 of the 1976 Act in deciding whether or not the deceased left any legitimate issue.

6.207 A child who, by virtue of s. 1 of the Legitimacy Act 1976 (formerly s. 2 of the Legitimacy Act 1959), is entitled to be treated as the legitimate child of his parents may be described as a lawful child in the oath[1].

1 Registrar's Circular, 24 April 1967.

Children of voidable marriages

6.208   Section 16 of the Matrimonial Causes Act 1973 provides that a decree of nullity granted after 31 July 1971 in respect of a voidable marriage shall operate to annul the marriage only as respects any time after the decree has been made absolute, and the marriage shall, notwithstanding the decree, be treated as if it had existed up to that time. Accordingly, any child born during the marriage is the legitimate child of his parents.

6.209   Under s. 11 of the Matrimonial Causes Act 1965[1], any child of a voidable marriage (which is annulled before 1 August 1971) who would have been the legitimate child of the parties to the marriage if it had been dissolved instead of being annulled, is deemed to be their legitimate child notwithstanding the annulment.

1 Section 11 of the Matrimonial Causes Act 1965 is repealed by the Matrimonial Causes Act 1973, s. 54(1)(b) and Schedule 3 thereto, but, in relation to decrees of nullity granted before 1 August 1971, its effect is preserved by the 1973 Act, Schedule I, Pt. II, para. 12.

6.210   It is proper to describe such a child in the oath as a lawful child.

Practice where title depends on legitimation

6.211   In cases where the right of the applicant to a grant depends upon his legitimation, or that of any other person, the following practice should be observed:

1.   If a declaration of legitimation has been obtained from a court of competent jurisdiction, or if the birth has been re-registered under the Legitimacy Act 1926 (since repealed and re-enacted by the Legitimacy Act 1976), the applicant should produce a copy of the declaration or of the amended birth certificate.
2.   If a declaration has not been made or a re-registration effected and it appears that it is open to the applicant to obtain such a declaration or re-registration, he should be required to do so (subject to paragraph 3 below)[1].
3.   If (a) re-registration is impossible, and
       (b) either it is not open to the applicant to obtain a declaration, or to insist on his obtaining a declaration would impose undue hardship,
     the evidence in support of the contention of legitimation should be submitted to a district judge of the Principal Registry, or if the application is to be made in a district probate registry, to the district registrar, for his decision as to its sufficiency. Any case of doubt will be referred by a district registrar to a district judge of the Principal Registry in accordance with NCPR 7(1)(b). If a district judge or registrar is not satisfied he may direct that an application be made by summons to a High Court judge in chambers or open court, with notice to the Attorney General, any such reference by a registrar needing to be confirmed by a district judge.
4.   In any case in which the Crown is or could be beneficially concerned, notice to the Treasury Solicitor must be given under NCPR 38.
5.   Where the applicant produces a declaration or certificate of re-registration, the oath must state that the person who it is claimed has been legitimated is the person referred to in the declaration or re-registration[2].

1 The provisions as to re-registration of the births of legitimated persons are contained in s. 14 of the Births and Deaths Registration Act 1953, as amended (see p. 772, post). Re-registration may be effected only where information with a view thereto is furnished by both parents, unless: (a) the name of a person acknowledging himself to be the father has been entered in the register of births; or (b) the paternity of the legitimated person has been established by an affiliation order or a decree of a

competent court; or (c) a legitimacy declaration has been made. Section 1(1) of the Legitimation (Re-registration of Birth) Act 1957 (since repealed and replaced by para. 6 of Schedule 1 to the Legitimacy Act 1976) extends the provisions of s. 14 of the Births and Deaths Registration Act 1953 and the Schedule to the Legitimacy Act 1926 (since repealed and re-enacted by the Legitimacy Act 1976, s. 9) relating to the re-registration of births of persons legitimated by the subsequent marriage of their parents, to all persons recognised by the law of England and Wales as having been so legitimated, whether or not their legitimation or the recognition thereof was effected under any enactment.

2 *Practice Direction* [1965] 2 All ER 560, [1965] 1 WLR 955.

6.212 The matters to be dealt with in the evidence referred to in sub-para. 3, above, should include the following: whether, at the date of birth of the person who, it is claimed, became legitimated, either of his or her parents was married to a third person; whether the father's name was entered in the certificate of birth; whether there was any affiliation order; whether, at the time of the marriage of the parents, the father was domiciled in England and Wales; particulars of the marriage; whether, and in what manner, the father acknowledged the child to be his own child; whether it was maintained by him; whether it lived with the parents and was brought up as a member of the family; and any other facts relied upon.

6.213 Where an intestate, of unsound mind on and at all times after 1 January 1926 left real estate, the Legitimacy Act 1926 does not have the effect of admitting a person so legitimated to the class of persons who under the pre-1926 law were entitled to take[1].

1 *Re Berrey, Lewis v Berrey* [1936] Ch 274, 105 LJ Ch 38.

6.214 Prior to 1 January 1976 (the coming into force of Schedule 1 to the Children Act 1975) a legitimated person could not take under the will of a testator dying before the date of legitimation, if, apart from such legitimation, he would not have been entitled. The date of coming into operation of the disposition within the meaning of s. 3(1)(b)[1] and s. 10(2)[2] of the Legitimacy Act 1926 is the date of death of the testator and not when some benefit under the will becomes vested or payable[3]. In the case of dispositions made on or after 1 January 1970, however, reference should be made to s. 15 of the Family Law Reform Act 1969 (see p. 792, post); and, as respects events occurring after 31 December 1975, see s. 5 of the Legitimacy Act 1976 (see p. 823, post).

1 Section 3 of the Legitimacy Act 1926 was repealed as from 1 January 1976 by the Children Act 1975, Schedule 4, Pt. II, but as respects instruments disposing of property made prior to that date its effect is preserved by para. 2(1) of Schedule 1 to the Legitimacy Act 1976 (see p. 825, post).
2 Section 10(2) of the Legitimacy Act 1926 was repealed by the Legitimacy Act 1976, but is preserved and re-enacted by para. 2(2) of Schedule 1 to the latter Act (see p. 826, post).
3 *Re Hepworth* [1936] Ch 750, [1936] 2 All ER 1159.

Description of legitimated persons and persons claiming through them

Deaths intestate before, or wills or codicils made before, 4 April 1988
6.215 It is incorrect to describe a legitimated person, or a person related to such a person, in the same way as an ordinary applicant. Where the title to a grant depends on a legitimation which has been properly proved, either in the oath or a separate affidavit, the applicant should be described in the oath as 'the lawful legitimated son (*or* daughter)' or, in the case of other relationships 'the lawful . . . by legitimation'.

6.216 The foregoing applies only in cases where the applicant's title depends on a *legitimation*. A person claiming to have been legitimate at birth who has obtained a declaration of *legitimacy* under s. 45(1) of the Matrimonial Causes Act 1973 or earlier Acts, may be regarded as legitimate or lawful in the fullest sense, and may be so described in the oath[1].

1 Registrar's Circular, 24 April 1967.

Deaths intestate on or after, or wills or codicils made on or after, 4 April 1988
6.217   Where the deceased dies intestate on or after 4 April 1988 or where a will or codicil is made on or after that date, the rights of intestate succession dependent upon the relationship between two persons and references to any relationship between two persons in dispositions by will or codicil are construed, unless the contrary intention appears, without regard to whether or not the father and mother of either of them, or the father and mother of any person through whom the relationship is deduced, have or had been married to each other at any time. Consequently it is not necessary to refer in the oath to the applicant as 'the lawful legitimated . . .' or 'the lawful . . . by legitimation'; reference to the relationship is sufficient.

Effect of foreign legitimation

6.218   By s. 3 of the Legitimacy Act 1976[1] (replacing s. 8(1) of the Legitimacy Act 1926), where the parents of an illegitimate person marry one another and the father of the illegitimate person is not at the time of the marriage domiciled in England and Wales but is domiciled in a country by the law of which the illegitimate person became legitimated by virtue of such subsequent marriage, that person, if living, shall in England and Wales be recognised as having been so legitimated from the date of the marriage notwithstanding that, at the time of his birth, his father was domiciled in a country the law of which did not permit legitimation by subsequent marriage.

1 See p. 822, post.

6.219   The section has no application where the father was at the time of the marriage and of the birth domiciled in a country in which legitimation by subsequent marriage was permitted by law; in such a case different principles apply[1].

1 *Re Hurll, Angelini v Dick* [1952] Ch 722, [1952] 2 All ER 322, where a child born out of wedlock in 1943 but legitimated by the subsequent marriage of his parents, under the law of Italy where the father was domiciled at the date of the child's birth and at the date of the marriage, was held to be a legitimate child of the marriage and could benefit under a will which came into operation in 1939. If legitimation had been under s. 3 of the Legitimacy Act 1976 (replacing s. 8(1) of the Legitimacy Act 1926), it would have been effective only from the date of the marriage: but cf. *Collins v A-G* (1931) 145 LT 551, cited in fn. 1 to para. **6.221**, below, where a declaration of legitimacy was made even though the child had been legitimated by the law of the father's domicile at the date of his birth and the subsequent marriage.

6.220   A child, born before wedlock, of parents domiciled in Holland at her birth, and legitimated by the law of Holland by subsequent marriage of the parents, is entitled to a share in the estate of an intestate dying domiciled in England[1].

1 *Re Goodman's Trust* (1881) 17 Ch D 266.

6.221   A petitioner (a minor) and his father were both domiciled in Germany. When the petitioner was born his father was married to a woman not his mother.

The father was divorced in Germany, and married the mother of the petitioner. By German law the petitioner was legitimate as from the date of such marriage, and it was held that the petitioner should be recognised as legitimated as from that date[1].

1 *Collins v A-G* (1931) 145 LT 551.

6.222 It should be noted that, with effect from 1 January 1976, the rights to property given to legitimated persons, and persons claiming through such persons, under s. 5 of the Legitimacy Act 1976 apply equally to cases of legitimation under s. 2 or 3 of that Act, to legitimation under s. 1 or 8 of the Legitimacy Act 1926 and to legitimation (whether or not by virtue of the subsequent marriage of the parents) recognised by the law of England and Wales and effected under the law of any other country (Legitimacy Act 1976, s. 10(1)).

Adopted persons

6.223 Adoptions were not given effect in English law until the coming into force of the Adoption of Children Act 1926 and it was not until the enactment of the Adoption Act 1950 that rights of succession on intestacy were accorded as between adopters and adopted children.

6.224 In respect of deaths occurring prior to 1 January 1976 the relevant provisions relating to these rights are contained in ss. 16 and 17 of the Adoption Act 1958[1]. For deaths occurring on or after 1 January 1976 the status and rights of succession of adopted persons are to be found in Part IV of the Adoption Act 1976 a consolidating measure which replaced Schedule 1 to the Children Act 1975 from 1 January 1988.

1 See pp. 775, 776, post.

6.225 Being a consolidating measure, the Adoption Act 1976 makes no changes to the substantive law and, therefore, rights of succession of adopted persons continue to be determined by the relevant date of death.

6.226 It should also be noted that, irrespective of the date of death, succession rights are not conferred in those cases where the adoption order made by the authorised court is merely provisional.

Adoption Act 1976: deaths after 31 December 1975

6.227 Section 12(1) of the Adoption Act 1976[1] as amended with effect from 14 October 1991 now defines an adoption order as an order 'giving parental responsibility for a child to the adopters' (Children Act 1989, Sch. 10, para. 3(1)). Section 3 of the Children Act 1989[2], which section also came into force on 14 October 1991, defines 'parental responsibility' for the purpose of that Act. Parental responsibility which any other person has for the child immediately before the making of the order is extinguished (s. 12(3), as amended).

1 See p. 826, post.
2 See p. 882, post.

6.228 Provisions as to the status and property rights conferred by an adoption are contained in Part IV of the Act of 1976[1]. Earlier provisions (in particular ss. 13, 16 and 17 of the Adoption Act 1958[2]) save in relation to things done or events occurring prior to 1 January 1976 were replaced by Schedule 1 to the Children Act 1975 (now replaced by Part IV of the Adoption Act 1976). For the purposes of Part IV of the Adoption Act 1976, adoption means adoption:

(a)   by an adoption order (as defined in s. 72 of the Adoption Act 1976);

(b)   by an order made under the Children Act 1975, the Adoption Act 1958, the Adoption Act 1950 or any enactment repealed by the latter Act;

(c)   by an order made in Scotland, Northern Ireland, the Isle of Man or in any of the Channel Islands;

(d)   which is an overseas adoption (as defined by s. 72 of the Adoption Act 1976)[3]; or

(e)   which is an adoption recognised by the law of England and Wales and effected under the law of any other country.

1 See pp. 828–831, post.
2 See pp. 775–776, post, and textual summary at paras. **6.232** and **6.233**, post.
3 See p. 835, post.

6.229   It should be noted that as from 1 January 1976 or from the date of the adoption (if later) an adopted child is to be treated in law:

(a)   where the adopters are a married couple, as if he had been born as a child of the marriage (whether or not he was in fact born after the marriage was solemnised);

(b)   in any other case, as if he had been born to the adopter in wedlock (but not as a child of any actual marriage of the adopter) (s. 39(1)),

and as if he were not the child of any person other than the adopters or adopter (s. 39(2)).

6.230   Section 42 of the Act of 1976 contains provisions applying to the construction of instruments other than an 'existing' instrument (i.e. one passed or made before 1 January 1976: s. 72). But it is to be borne in mind that, by s. 46(3), a will or codicil is to be taken to have been made on the day of the testator's death. Section 46(4) provides that, for the purposes of Part IV of the Act, provisions of the law of intestate succession applicable to the estate of a deceased person are to be treated as if contained in an instrument executed by him (while of full capacity) immediately before his death.

6.231   The effect of the Act is that on an intestacy (save as to deaths prior to 1 January 1976 when the provisions of s. 16 of the Adoption Act 1958[1] are still applicable) an adopted child is treated as if he were the lawfully born child of his adoptive parents or parent.

1 See p. 775, post.

Adoption Act 1958: deaths prior to 1 January 1976

6.232   By s. 16(1) of the Adoption Act 1958, it is provided that where at any time after the making of an adoption order[1] the adopter or the adopted child or any other person dies intestate as to any property (other than property subject to an entailed interest to which s. 16(2) of the Act does not apply[2]) such property shall devolve in all respects as though the adopted person were the child of the adopter born in lawful wedlock, and not the child of any other person. This section applies equally where the adoption order was made under the Adoption of Children Act 1926 or the Adoption Act 1950, but does not affect the devolution of property on an intestacy where the death occurred before 1 January 1950 (see Adoption Act 1958, Fifth Schedule, para. 4(1) and (2)).

1 The adoption orders to which s. 16 applies include those made (either in England or Scotland) under the Adoption Act 1958 itself, and orders made under the Adoption of Children Act (Northern Ireland) 1950, or any current Northern Irish statute; but the section has no effect in the case of death before 1 January 1950, or after 31 December 1975. Sections 16 and 17 of the Act do not apply in relation to persons dying domiciled in Scotland (see para. **6.263**, post), but similar provisions apply in relation to such persons under ss. 23 and 24 of the Succession (Scotland) Act 1964. Sections 16 and 17, in general, apply in the case of adoption orders made under the authority of the Adoption Act 1968, and of overseas adoptions recognised by virtue of that Act.
2 Section 16(2) of the Act does not apply to dispositions made before the adoption order unless the disposition is made or confirmed on or after 1 April 1959. It does not in any case apply where the adoption takes place after the death of the testator (s. 16(2), s. 17(2) and Fifth Schedule, para. 4(3)). (Compare the position under the Adoption Act 1976, where death occurs after 31 December 1975.)

6.233 Section 17(1) of the Act[1] provides that, for the purposes of the application of the Administration of Estates Act 1925 to the devolution of property in accordance with the provisions of s. 16, an adopted person is deemed to be related to any other person, being a child or adopted child of the adopter (or, in joint adoptions, of either of the adopters):

(a) where he or she was adopted by two spouses jointly and the other person is the child or adopted child of both spouses, as a brother or sister of the whole blood; or

(b) in any other case, as a brother or sister of the half blood.

1 See p. 776, post.

Protection of personal representatives

6.234 Until it was repealed, on 1 January 1988, by the Adoption Act 1976, para. 15 of Sch. 1 to the Children Act 1975 (replacing and extending s. 17(3) of the Adoption Act 1958) afforded protection to personal representatives who conveyed or distributed property in ignorance of the fact that an adoption had been effected or revoked. The personal representatives were protected in respect of claims of which they have had no notice before the conveyance or distribution, but this is without prejudice to the right of a claimant to follow the property into the hands of any person (except a purchaser) who may have received it. Section 45 of the Adoption Act 1976 provides the same protection subject to the same conditions.

Adoptions in Scotland, Northern Ireland, Isle of Man and Channel Islands

6.235 As regards anything done, or any event occurring, on or after 16 July 1964, ss. 16 and 17 of the Adoption Act 1958 apply in the case of adoptions in pursuance of orders made, whether before or on or after that date, in the Isle of Man or any of the Channel Islands by virtue of the Adoption Act 1964, s. 1.

6.236 In relation to things done or events occurring after 31 December 1975 the relevant provisions of s. 1 of the Adoption Act 1964 are repealed by the Children Act 1975. Adoptions by orders made in Scotland, Northern Ireland, the Isle of Man and any of the Channel Islands are now within the definition of 'adoption' for the purposes of Part IV of the Adoption Act 1976 (which replaced Schedule 1 to the Children Act 1975 on 1 January 1988) (see para. **6.228**, ante).

Convention adoption orders

6.237 The Adoption Act 1968[1] together with s. 24 of the Children Act 1975 made provision in England and Wales for the making, revocation or annulment of Convention adoption orders and the annulment of certain overseas adoptions regulated by the Convention on Jurisdiction, Applicable Law and Recognition of Decrees Relating to Adoptions concluded at The Hague in 1965. The Adoption Act 1968 and s. 24 of the Children Act 1975 were repealed on 1 January 1988 by the Adoption Act 1976 and the provisions relating to making and annulling Convention adoption orders are contained in s. 17 and Part V of that Act.

1 See p. 788, post.

6.238 Jurisdiction to grant Convention adoption orders in England and Wales is restricted to the High Court. An adoption under the Convention (whether granted in the United Kingdom or in a Convention country), or the revocation or annulment of such an adoption, will be recognised without further formality in all the countries in which the Convention is in force. As from 23 October 1978, the Convention applies only to the United Kingdom, Austria and Switzerland, but its scope will be extended as and when its provisions are applied to other countries.

6.239 The effect of the making of an adoption under the Convention is to confer on the child the same status in England and Wales as that conferred on any other adopted person coming within the scope of Part IV of the Adoption Act 1976. Accordingly, from 23 October 1978, adoptions made under the Convention in the United Kingdom, Austria or Switzerland are recognised in non-contentious probate applications.

6.240 Certain sections of the 1968 Act, including s. 4, came into force on 1 February 1973[1], and adoptions effected in a number of Commonwealth and other countries have been designated as 'overseas adoptions'[2] to which recognition is to be given in this country: see paras. **6.257** ff., post.

1 Adoption Act 1968 (Commencement No. 1) Order 1973.
2 Adoption (Designation of Overseas Adoptions) Order 1973.

Two adoption orders

6.241 Where an adoption order is made in respect of a person who had been previously adopted, the previous adoption is disregarded for the purposes of succession rights[1].

1 Adoption Act 1958, s. 17(4), repealed as from 1 January 1976 by the Children Act 1976, although its effect was first preserved by para. 3 of the Schedule to the latter Act and is now preserved by para. 6(2) of Sch. 2 to the Adoption Act 1976.

Legitimation following adoption

6.242 Where a person adopted by his father or mother alone has subsequently become a legitimated person on the marriage of his father and mother, the court by which the adoption order was made may, on the application of any of the parties concerned, revoke the order (Adoption Act 1976, s. 52(1)).

6.243   Where a person who became legitimated by virtue of s. 1 of the Legitimacy Act 1959 (as to which, see paras. **6.174–6.177**, ante) had been adopted by his *father and mother* before the commencement of that Act (29 October 1959), the court by which the adoption order was made may, on the application of any of the parties concerned, revoke the order[1].

1   Adoption Act 1976, s. 52(2): see p. 832, post.

6.244   Revocation of an adoption order under either of these provisions does not, however, affect the operation of ss. 16 and 17 of the Adoption Act 1958 in relation to an intestacy which occurred, or a disposition which was made, before the revocation[1].

1   Adoption Act 1960, s. 1(2): see p. 777, post. Adoption Act 1964, s. 1(4); although both these provisions are now repealed by Schedule 4, Pt. I to the Children Act 1975 with effect from 1 January 1976, the court's power to revoke an adoption order when a child has become a legitimated person is unaffected by the 1975 Act: see para. 13 of Schedule 1 to the 1975 Act as re-enacted by s. 4 of the Legitimacy Act 1976, p. 823, post.

6.245   Where a person adopted by his father or mother alone by virtue of a *regulated adoption*[1] has subsequently become a legitimated person on the marriage of his father and mother, the High Court may, upon an application under s. 52(3) of the Adoption Act 1976 by the parties concerned, by order revoke the adoption.

1   'Regulated adoption' is an overseas adoption of a specific description designated in an order of the Secretary of State—see Adoption Act 1976, s. 72(1) and (2).

Right to grant where there has been an adoption

6.246   Under s. 39 of the Adoption Act 1976[1], which applies in relation to deaths occurring on or after 1 January 1976, an adopted child is to be treated in law as the lawful child of the adopter or adopters. This ensures that any person entitled to an interest in an estate on an intestacy by virtue of an adoption is within the appropriate class of entitlement to a grant under NCPR 22.

1   See p. 828, post.

6.247   Under s. 38 of the Act of 1976, the adoptions recognised for this purpose include adoption by an order under the Adoption Act 1950, or any earlier enactment repealed by that Act, the Adoption Act 1958, the Children Act 1975, the Adoption Act 1976, including a Convention adoption under that Act, adoption by orders made in Scotland, Northern Ireland, the Isle of Man or any of the Channel Islands, overseas adoptions as defined by s. 72 of the Adoption Act 1976 and any other adoption recognised by the law of England and Wales and effected under the law of another country.

6.248   Where, in relation to an estate of a person dying intestate prior to 1 January 1976, application is made for a grant of letters of administration, then the relevant provisions of the Adoption Act 1958 continue to apply in determining entitlement to the grant as they apply to the devolution of property on intestacy. Accordingly, when the question arises as to the priority of right to a grant of administration of the estate of an adopted person, of an adopter or of any other person who dies intestate on or after 1 January 1950 the adopted person is in the same position as if he were a child born in lawful wedlock of the adopter or adopters.

6.249   In relation to a death occurring prior to 1 January 1950 no statutory rights of succession are conferred by virtue of an adoption, and therefore neither the adopter nor the adopted person has a right to a grant of letters of administration to the other's estate.

Requirements on obtaining grant

6.250   Where application is made for a grant by a person entitled by virtue of an adoption order it must be shown in the oath to lead the grant that an adoption order has been made under the Acts, the effect of the order, and that it is still subsisting[1].

1   Registrar's Directions (1950) 8 March; (1951) 18 July; (1959) 18 March.

6.251   It is not necessary for a person who applies for a grant in a lower capacity to swear specifically that no adoption order has been made. Persons who, if they existed, would be entitled in priority to the applicant are cleared off by the standard form of clearing given in para. **6.355**, post.

6.252   Where a grant is to be given to a person who is entitled under the Acts, the following descriptions should be used:

(a)   the adopted person   'the lawful adopted son (or daughter)'
(b)   the adopter   'the lawful adopter' or 'one of the lawful adopters'
(c)   any other person   'the lawful brother (or sister) of the whole (or half) blood by adoption'.

6.253   Other degrees of relationship should be described in similar terms. All persons may be described (if so entitled) as being 'entitled to (share in) the estate'. Forms of oath, Nos. 100 and 101.

6.254   Where it is necessary to clear off a person who, because of his adoption, has no interest in an estate in which he would otherwise have participated, the Forms of oath Nos. 98 or 99 may be used. It is not necessary to exhibit or produce the adoption order, and the adopted person should be referred to throughout the documents by the name under which he was known prior to the adoption[1].

1   Registrar's Circular, 2 March 1966.

Adoption orders made outside the United Kingdom

6.255   The provisions of s. 16 of the Adoption Act 1958 originally applied only in the case of adoption orders made by the courts of England and Wales, Scotland and Northern Ireland[1]. Adoption orders made in the Isle of Man and the Channel Islands and 'overseas adoption' orders, as defined in s. 72 of the Adoption Act 1976, are also recognised, and in relation to deaths occurring on or after 1 January 1976, any adoption recognised under the law of England and Wales results in the adopted child being treated for the purposes of succession on intestacy as if he were the lawful child of the adopters or adopter (see paras. **6.223** ff., ante).

1   Adoption Act 1958, ss. 1(1) and 57.

6.256   Earlier decisions to the effect that rights of succession on intestacy were not acquired by virtue of adoptions taking place outside the United Kingdom, for example, if the adopters were not at the time of the adoption domiciled in the country where the adoption took place[1], must now be regarded as modified by the above provisions. It now seems that a child adopted in accordance with the law of the place of domicile of the adopters at the time of the adoption acquires the same rights as would, at the relevant date, be given by law to a child adopted by an order made in England and Wales[2].

1 See *Re Wilson, Grace v Lucas* [1954] Ch 733, [1954] 1 All ER 997.
2 In *Re Varadi* (February 1969, unreported) Payne J made an order on motion for a grant of administration to the attorney of the adopted daughter of the deceased, who died domiciled in England. The daughter had been adopted by the deceased and his wife while they were domiciled in, ordinarily resident in, and nationals of Czechoslovakia, where the daughter was also resident, and there was evidence that the adoption was valid by the law of that country. See also *Re Marshall, Barclays Bank Ltd v Marshall* [1957] Ch 263, [1957] 1 All ER 549; *Re Valentine's Settlement, Valentine v Valentine* [1965] Ch 831, [1965] 2 All ER 226. The decision to the contrary in *Re Wilby* [1956] P 174, [1956] 1 All ER 27, has been criticised. As to whether a child, adopted in accordance with the law of a foreign country in which it and its adoptive parents were then domiciled, can rank as 'issue' of the adopter to enable it to take a share in a gift under an English will, see *Re Marshall, Barclays Bank Ltd v Marshall* [1957] 1 Ch 507, [1957] 3 All ER 172. It was held by a majority of the Court of Appeal that a child adopted in a foreign country will not be recognised as having the status of a child of the adopter for the purposes of an English settlement unless the adopting parents were domiciled in the country concerned at the time of the making of the order (*Re Valentine's Settlement, Valentine v Valentine*, above).

'Overseas adoptions'

6.257   Under Part IV of the Adoption Act 1976[1], 'overseas adoptions' within the meaning of that Part are, for almost all purposes, fully recognised in this country.

1 See p. 828, post: in relation to deaths and other events occurring on or after 1 January 1976.

6.258   By the Adoption (Designation of Overseas Adoptions) Order 1973, which came into operation on 1 February 1973 (the same date as s. 4 of the Adoption Act 1968, since repealed, came into force), adoptions effected in the countries listed overleaf were designated as 'overseas adoptions' for the purposes of that section.

6.259   Consequently, the rights of inheritance on intestacy in relation to adopted persons as provided by Part IV of the Adoption Act 1976, apply where there has been an 'overseas adoption' in a designated country as they would in the case of an adoption order made in the British Isles. Where the applicant for a grant is entitled by virtue of an overseas adoption, the practice set out in paras. **6.250–6.253**, ante, should be followed.

6.260   Adoptions effected in, and in accordance with the law[1] of, the following places have been specified as 'overseas adoptions'. As respects any adoption effected before 1 February 1973 this applies in relation to any place which, at that date, formed part of a country or territory listed overleaf. As respects any adoption effected on or after that date, it applies to any place which, at the time the adoption is effected, forms part of a country or territory which at that time is a country or territory so listed[2].

1 The expression 'law' in this context does not include customary or common law (Adoption (Designation of Overseas Adoptions) Order 1973, art. 3(3)).
2 Ibid., art. 3(2).

Commonwealth countries and United Kingdom dependent territories:

Australia
Bahamas
Barbados
Bermuda
Botswana
British Honduras (now
  Belize)
British Virgin Islands
  (now Tortola)
Canada
Cayman Islands
Republic of Cyprus
Dominica
Fiji

Ghana
Gibraltar
Guyana
Hong Kong
Jamaica
Kenya
Lesotho
Malawi
Malaysia
Malta
Mauritius
Montserrat
New Zealand
Nigeria
Pitcairn

St Christopher (or
  Kitts), Nevis &
  Anguilla
St Vincent
Seychelles
Singapore
Southern Rhodesia
  (now Zimbabwe)
Sri Lanka
Swaziland
Tanzania
Tonga
Trinidad & Tobago
Uganda
Zambia

Other countries and territories:

Austria
Belgium
Denmark (including Greenland and the Faroes)
Finland
France (including Réunion, Martinique, Guadeloupe and French Guyana)
The Federal Republic of Germany and *Land* Berlin (West Berlin)
Greece
Iceland
The Republic of Ireland
Israel
Italy
Luxembourg
The Netherlands (including Surinam and the Antilles)
Norway
Portugal (including the Azores and Madeira)
South Africa and South West Africa
Spain (including the Balearics and the Canary Islands)
Sweden
Switzerland
Turkey
The United States of America
Yugoslavia

Evidence of overseas adoption

6.261   Evidence that an overseas adoption has been effected may be given by the production of a document purporting to be:

(a)   a certified copy of an entry made, in accordance with the law of the country or territory concerned, in a public register relating to the recording of adoptions and showing that the adoption has been effected; or

(b)   a certificate that the adoption has been effected, signed or purporting to be signed by a person authorised by the law of the country or territory concerned to sign such a certificate, or a certified copy of such certificate.

6.262 These provisions are without prejudice to the right to prove in accordance with the Evidence (Foreign, Dominion and Colonial Documents) Act 1933, or the Oaths and Evidence (Overseas Authorities and Countries) Act 1963, or otherwise, that an overseas adoption has been effected[1].

1 Adoption (Designation of Overseas Adoptions) Order 1973, art. 4.

Deceased domiciled in Scotland

6.263 Schedule 2 to the Children Act 1975 which preserved, with certain modifications, the provisions of ss. 23 and 24 of the Succession (Scotland) Act 1964, being provisions which correspond broadly with ss. 16 and 17 of the Adoption Act 1958[1], was repealed from 1 January 1988 by Sch. 4 to the Adoption Act 1976. (See also paras. **6.232** and **6.233**, ante and the Adoption (Scotland) Act 1978.)

1 See pp. 775–776, post.

Grants for the use and benefit of adopted children

6.264 As to the practice in making grants for the use and benefit of adopted children who are under the age of eighteen years, see paras. **11.113** ff., post.

Deceased dying testate

6.265 As to the effect of an adoption order in cases of testacy, see paras. **5.35** ff., ante.

Grant to parents

Father and mother

6.266 If the intestate has left no husband or widow, and no issue[1], then administration will be granted to one or both of the parents: if only one parent survives, then to that one. For form of oath, see No. 103. As to description of the applicant, see para. **6.357**, post.

1 The position is the same if the intestate left issue surviving, but all such issue died without attaining an absolutely vested interest: see paras. **6.55** and **6.58**, ante. As to the meaning of 'issue' in relation to deaths occurring on or after 1 January 1970, see fn. 2 to para. **6.37**, ante.

Parents of illegitimate persons: death after 31 December 1969

6.267 Where the death occurred prior to 1 January 1970, save as provided by s. 9(2) of the Legitimacy Act 1926 (as to which see below), the term 'parent' in the Administration of Estates Act 1925 connotes only a lawful parent: the father of an illegitimate child took no interest in the child's estate on an intestacy, and consequently had no entitlement to a grant of administration.

6.268 Under s. 9(2) of the Legitimacy Act 1926 where an illegitimate child (not being a legitimated person) dies on or after 1 January 1927 wholly or partially intestate, *his mother*, if she survives him, is entitled to take any interest in his estate to which she would have been entitled if the child had been born legitimate and she were the only surviving parent. Section 9(2) was repealed in relation to deaths on or after 1 January 1970, and replaced by s. 14(2) of the Family Law Reform Act 1969, which is as follows:

'(2) Where an illegitimate child dies intestate in respect of all or any of his real or personal estate, *each of his parents*, if surviving, shall be entitled to take any interest therein to which that parent would have been entitled if the child had been born legitimate.'

6.269 Accordingly, in relation to an intestate dying after 31 December 1969 and before 4 April 1988 who is an illegitimate person, any reference in Part IV of the Administration of Estates Act 1925 to his parent, parents, father or mother, is to have effect as if it were a reference to his natural parent, parents, father or mother (s. 14(3)(c)).

6.270 Section 14 of the Family Law Reform Act 1969 was repealed on 4 April 1988 by s. 33(4) of the Family Law Reform Act 1987[1] but the repeal does not affect any rights arising under the intestacy of a person dying before 4 April 1988[2]. In respect of an intestate dying on or after 4 April 1988 s. 18(1) of the Family Law Reform Act 1987 provides that as regards succession to his property illegitimacy is not to be taken into consideration.

1 See p. 880, post.
2 Family Law Reform Act 1987, Sch. 3, para. 8, p. 881, post.

Presumption in relation to natural father and other relatives

6.271 It is provided by s. 14(4) of the Family Law Reform Act 1969 that for the purposes of s. 14(2) of that Act and of Part IV of the Administration of Estates Act 1925 an illegitimate child shall be presumed not to have been survived by his father unless the contrary is shown. Section 14 of the Family Law Reform Act 1969 was repealed from 4 April 1988 but any rights arising under the intestacy of a person dying before that date are not affected. Section 18(2) of the Family Law Reform Act 1987 provides that, in respect of an intestate dying on or after 4 April 1988, there is a rebuttable presumption that a person whose father and mother were not married to each other at the time of his birth was not survived by his father or by any person related to him only through his father. Section 21 of the Family Law Reform Act 1987 creates a rebuttable presumption that, for the purpose of entitlement to a grant of representation of the estate of an intestate dying on or after 4 April 1988, the intestate was not survived by any person related to him whose father and mother were not married to each other at the time of his birth or by any person whose relationship with him is deduced through a person whose father and mother were not married to each other at the time of his birth.

6.272 The applicant's title to a grant of representation, as sworn to in the oath, is sufficient to rebut any of the presumptions referred to in the preceding paragraph[1].

1 Registrar's Direction (1988) 19 April.

6.273 On an application for letters of administration by the natural mother where the death occurred on or after 1 January 1970, it is necessary for her to state in the oath in the normal way whether she is the only person entitled to the estate of the child or one of the persons entitled to share in the estate. Unless she is aware that the child's father is alive it would appear that the presumptions above would entitle her to claim to be the only person entitled to the estate.

Evidence of paternity

6.274   On an application for letters of administration by a person claiming to be the father of an illegitimate child who died on or after 4 April 1988, evidence of paternity will be called for only in exceptional circumstances[1].

1 Registrar's Direction (1988) 19 April.

6.275   If the deceased died before 4 April 1988, evidence in support of the paternity claim (normally in the form of an affidavit) must be lodged at the probate registry. However, if a birth certificate is produced which gives the name of the father and shows that the birth was registered on his information or on the authority of a statutory declaration by him under s. 27 of the Family Law Reform Act 1969, or if an affiliation order is produced containing a finding of paternity, further evidence of paternity additional to the statement in the oath is not normally necessary.

Interest of mother in estate of illegitimate person: death before 1 January 1970

6.276   Where an illegitimate person dies intestate before 1 January 1970, leaving no spouse or issue (and in the case of a female, no natural child) the mother of the intestate is entitled to a grant of administration. It is sufficient for the applicant to depose in the oath that the deceased died intestate a bachelor or spinster, or to clear the spouse and issue, and for the applicant to swear she is 'the natural mother and only person entitled to the estate'. It is unnecessary to describe the deceased as illegitimate[1].

1 Registrar's Direction (1952) 11 March.

Adoptive parents

6.277   In the case of death on or after 1 January 1950, and after the making of an adoption order, s. 16(1) of the Adoption Act 1958, or s. 39 of the Adoption Act 1976 (as the case may be, depending upon the date of death) has the effect of placing an adoptive parent or, in the case of a joint adoption, both the adoptive parents, in the position of lawful parents for the purpose of succession on intestacy to the real and personal estate of the adopted person; accordingly, the adoptive parent has the same priority of right under NCPR 22 to a grant of administration of the estate of an adopted child who dies intestate on or after 1 January 1950 as if he had been a child of the adoptive parent born in lawful wedlock. See paras. **6.250–6.253**, ante, as to the practice in obtaining a grant where the entitlement arises by virtue of an adoption. Form of oath, No. 101.

Personal representative of parents

6.278   On the death of an only surviving parent, there being no surviving husband or wife, or issue, of the intestate, a grant will be made to the personal representative of such parent. In a like case, where both parents have survived and died, a grant may be made to the personal representative of either of them. For form of oath, see No. 104. As to preference of living interests, and grants to personal representatives, see paras. **6.07–6.15**, ante.

Grant to brothers and sisters or their issue

Brothers and sisters of the whole blood or their issue

6.279   If the intestate *dies before 4 April 1988* and leaves no husband or widow, issue or parent, a grant will be made to the brothers and sisters *of the whole blood*, or to the issue of deceased brothers and sisters of the whole blood, taking per stirpes. For form of oath, see Nos. 105 and 106.

6.280   If the deceased *dies on or after 4 April 1988* the relationships need not be lawful, illegitimate relatives having the same rights of succession to property on intestacy as lawful relatives[1], but there is a rebuttable presumption that an illegitimate person was not survived by his father or by any person related to him only through his father[2] and there is a rebuttable presumption that, as regards entitlement to a grant, the deceased left no surviving illegitimate relatives or relatives whose relationship is traced through an illegitimate person[3] (see para. **6.271**, ante). The applicant's title to a grant of representation, as sworn to in the oath, is sufficient to rebut any of these presumptions[4].

1 Family Law Reform Act 1987, s. 18(1).
2 Ibid., s. 18(2).
3 Ibid., s. 21.
4 Registrar's Direction (1988) 19 April.

6.281   If the deceased *died before 4 April 1988* only lawful brothers or sisters of the whole blood (or their issue per stirpes) may succeed and apply, and their lawful status must be sworn to in the oath.

6.282   As regards their rights to a grant, the issue of predeceasing brothers and sisters, taking per stirpes, have an equal claim with surviving brothers and sisters, but it is necessary to show in the oath how their beneficial interest arises (see form of oath, No. 105).

6.283   The practice in making these grants follows in all respects the practice given with regard to children and their issue. As to description of the applicant in the oath, see para. **6.357**, post.

Brothers and sisters of the half blood or their issue

6.284   If the intestate leaves no brother or sister of the whole blood or issue of any deceased brother or sister of the whole blood, administration is granted to the brothers and sisters *of the half blood*, or to the issue of deceased brothers and sisters of the half blood, taking per stirpes. If the deceased died before 4 April 1988 the relationships must be lawful but if the deceased died on or after that date they need not be, in the same way as brothers and sisters of the whole blood (see paras. **6.279** to **6.282**, ante). The practice in making these grants is the same as when granting to the whole blood. For forms of oath, see Nos. 107 and 108.

6.285   In any application for a grant by the half blood it must be sworn in the oath that the deceased died without brother or sister of the whole blood or their issue.

Minority or life interest

6.286 If a minority or a life interest arises under the intestacy, the grant must normally be made to two or more beneficiaries of full age or to a trust corporation (with or without a beneficiary who is of age)[1] (the applicants not exceeding four in number).

1 Supreme Court Act 1981, s. 114(2); see p. 844, post; as to grants to trust corporations, see Chap. 9.

6.287 As to joinder of second administrator, see Chap. 7.

Grant to grandparents

Grandparents

6.288 If the intestate leaves no husband or widow, issue, parent, brother or sister of the whole or half blood or their issue, administration will be granted to one or more of the grandparents. If the deceased died before 4 April 1988 the relationships must be lawful but if the deceased died on or after that date they need not be, in the same way as brothers and sisters of the whole blood (see paras. **6.280** and **6.281**, ante).

6.289 In such a case, the estate is divisible equally among the surviving grand-parents. Subject to the preference of living interests (see paras. **6.07–6.09**), a grant may be made to the personal representative of a grandparent who survived the intestate but has since died.

6.290 As to description of the applicant in the oath, see para. **6.357**, post.

Grant to uncles and aunts or their issue

Uncles and aunts of the whole blood or their issue

6.291 If the intestate has died leaving no husband or widow, issue, parent, brother or sister of the whole or half blood or their issue, or grandparent, administration will be granted to his uncles or aunts *of the whole blood*, being brothers or sisters of the whole blood of a parent of the intestate, or to the issue of any deceased uncle or aunt of the whole blood who predeceased the intestate, the issue taking per stirpes their parent's share in the estate. Such issue have an equal right to the grant with surviving uncles and aunts. If the deceased died before 4 April 1988 the relation-ships must be lawful but if the deceased died on or after that date they need not be, in the same way as brothers and sisters of the whole blood (see paras. **6.280** and **6.281**, ante). For forms of oath, see Nos. 109 and 110.

6.292 The practice in making these grants follows in all respects the practice given with reference to children and their issue.

6.293 As to description of the applicant in the oath, see para. **6.357**, post.

Uncles and aunts of the half blood or their issue

6.294 If the intestate leaves no uncle or aunt of the whole blood or their issue, administration is granted to uncles and aunts *of the half blood*, being brothers or sisters of the half blood of a parent of the intestate, or to the issue of any predeceased uncle or aunt of the half blood, the issue taking per stirpes, and the same practice applies in making these grants as applies when granting to the whole blood. If the deceased died before 4 April 1988 the relationships must be lawful but if the deceased died on or after that date they need not be, in the same way as brothers and sisters of the whole blood (see paras. **6.280** and **6.281**, ante).

6.295   In an application for a grant by uncles or aunts of the half blood or their issue, it is necessary to show in the oath that the intestate died leaving no uncle or aunt of the whole blood nor issue of such uncle or aunt. Second cousins have no interest in an estate or claim to a grant.

Grant to Crown, Duchy of Lancaster, or Duchy of Cornwall

The Crown

6.296   Under NCPR 22(2), in default of any person having a beneficial interest in the estate, the Treasury Solicitor shall be entitled to a grant if he claims bona vacantia on behalf of the Crown. The expression 'the Treasury Solicitor' means the solicitor for the affairs of Her Majesty's Treasury and includes the solicitor for the affairs of the Duchy of Lancaster and the solicitor of the Duchy of Cornwall (NCPR 2).

6.297   If the intestate dies leaving no husband or widow, issue (including, in the case of death on or after 1 January 1970 illegitimate children or their issue), parent, brother or sister of the whole or half blood or their issue, grandparent, or uncle or aunt of the whole or half blood or their issue (including, in the case of death on or after 4 April 1988, any parent, brother, sister, grandparent, uncle, aunt or the issue of any such relative, who is not a lawful relative of the deceased), administration of his estate will be granted to the Treasury Solicitor or the Solicitor for the Duchy of Lancaster or Cornwall.

6.298   Where, as is usually the case, it is not known positively that the deceased left no kin within the classes beneficially entitled to the estate, the Treasury or Duchy Solicitor, after making full enquiries and advertising for kin of the deceased, proceeds by making application for letters of administration under s. 116(1) of the Supreme Court Act 1981, the former procedure of citing the kin having been discontinued[1].

1 For details of the procedure followed by the Treasury Solicitor both prior to, and subsequent to, application for a grant see Ing on *Bona Vacantia*.

6.299   On application for a grant, the Treasury Solicitor, or Solicitor for the Duchy of Lancaster, is not required to deliver any affidavit, statutory declaration, account, certificate, or other statement verified on oath[1]. As to the documents filed in lieu, see para. **9.51**, post. This does not apply to the Solicitor for the Duchy of Cornwall.

1 Administration of Estates Act 1925, s. 30(3) (see p. 750, post).

6.300   Grants made to the Treasury Solicitor and the Solicitor for the Duchy of Lancaster devolve on their successors in office by virtue of the Treasury Solicitor Act 1876[1] and the Duchy of Lancaster Act 1920[2], respectively, and no further grant is necessary when a change occurs in the holder of either of these offices.

1 10 Halsbury's Statutes (4th edn) 271.
2 Ibid., 308.

6.301 Grants made to the Solicitor for the Duchy of Cornwall do not devolve upon his successors in office. They are made to the holder of the office for the time being personally by name and limited until further representation be granted, to enable a new grant to be made to his successor on his death or retirement, should the need arise. Such grants are expressed to be 'for the use of His Royal Highness Charles, Prince of Wales, Duke of Cornwall, in right of his said Duchy'.

Deceased an illegitimate person

6.302 Where an illegitimate person dies on or after 4 April 1988 his illegitimacy is not to be taken into consideration[1] and all the relevant classes of kin (including illegitimate relatives) down to and including uncles and aunts of the half blood and the issue of any such who died before the deceased, in their order of priority are entitled to a grant before the Treasury or Duchy Solicitor.

1 Family Law Reform Act 1987, s. 18(1).

6.303 Where an illegitimate person dies on or after 1 January 1970 but before 4 April 1988 intestate, without leaving a spouse, issue (including illegitimate children or their issue) or parent, letters of administration may be granted to the Treasury Solicitor or the Solicitor for the Duchy of Lancaster or Cornwall, as the case may be, or, upon the renunciation of the Treasury or Duchy Solicitor, to a creditor (NCPR 22(2), (3)).

6.304 To enable the Treasury or Duchy Solicitor, or a creditor, to obtain letters of administration it must be stated (or sworn, in the case of a creditor) that the deceased died intestate 'a bachelor [spinster] [widower] [widow] [single man] [single woman] (as the case may be) without issue, parent, or any other person entitled in priority to share in his/her estate by virtue of any enactment'[1].

1 As to additional wording required where there has been a divorce, see para. **6.118**, ante.

6.305 Where the death of the illegitimate person occurred prior to 1 January 1970 but after 31 December 1926 the more limited rights provided by s. 9 of the Legitimacy Act 1926 apply in place of those given by s. 14 of the Family Law Reform Act 1969: the illegitimate children of a male deceased, and the father of an illegitimate deceased, take no beneficial interest on an intestacy.

Grants to Treasury Solicitor in Foundling Hospital cases

6.306 In a case in which the deceased is known to have been brought up in the Foundling Hospital (the Hospital for the Maintenance and Education of Exposed and Deserted Young Children) and the only evidence as to his true name and that of his natural mother is in the possession of the Governors, an order for a grant to the Treasury Solicitor, if entitled to the estate, may be made under s. 116(1) of the Supreme Court Act 1981.

6.307 The evidence required is as follows:

(a) An affidavit by the Secretary to the Governors swearing that he has disclosed the true name of the deceased and of his natural mother, and all material information in his possession that might lead to the tracing of the mother, to the Solicitor to the Governors.

(b) An affidavit by the Solicitor to the Governors as to the nature of the steps taken by advertisement or otherwise to get in touch with the natural mother, and the result thereof.

6.308   The name of the natural mother need not be disclosed in the evidence and the proceedings will be carried on, and the grant will issue, in the name by which the deceased was known.

6.309   These cases are distinct from the ordinary case of a foundling strictly so called. In such a case nothing is known or can be ascertained as to the foundling's origin, his name will in all probability be that given him by the person or body into whose care he was given when found rather than that of his parents, or mother, and no enquiries or advertisements of any sort would be of the slightest use in tracing kin. In such cases the practice is to apply for a grant under s. 116 on a full statement of the facts[1].

1 Registrar's Direction (1948) 23 December.

Grant to a creditor

Creditor

6.310   On clearing off by renunciation or citation all persons entitled to share in the estate, a grant may be made to a creditor of the deceased (NCPR 22(3)). Form of oath, No. 112.

6.311   As to preference of creditors inter se when several have applied, see paras. **6.374** and **6.375**, post.

Where a spouse survives

6.312   Where the deceased left a surviving spouse who is entitled to the whole of the estate as ascertained at the time of the application for a grant, the renunciation of such spouse (or, if the spouse has since died, of his or her personal representative) is sufficient to enable a grant to be made to a creditor: it is not necessary to clear off persons who may have a beneficial interest in the event of an accretion (see also paras. **6.99–6.103**, ante).

6.313   But where the amount of the estate is such that other persons share beneficially with the surviving spouse, the renunciation of the spouse and all such other persons is necessary.

Deceased having no kin

6.314   Where the Crown has an interest owing to the failure of all kin in the classes entitled to share, the renunciation of the Treasury or Duchy Solicitor is necessary unless there is sufficient evidence that he does not wish to claim bona vacantia on behalf of the Crown. All kin in such classes must be cleared off specifically in the oath by a positive statement that the deceased died 'intestate a bachelor (*or* spinster, widow, widower, single man or single woman, *as the case may be*) without issue, parent, brother or sister of the whole or half blood or issue thereof, grandparent, uncle or aunt of the whole or half blood or issue thereof or any other person entitled to share in the estate by virtue of any enactment'[1].

1 The words from 'or any other person' to the end are necessary only where the date of death was on or after 1 January 1970.

6.315   If, as is the usual case, the applicant is able to swear only that the deceased died without any *known* kin, a citation may be issued against the kin in general and all persons having or claiming any interest in the estate (for practice, see para. **24.25**, post). Notice must also be given to the Treasury Solicitor (see para. **6.359**, post).

6.316   However, if the estate is insolvent, or small in value, application may be made to the district judge or registrar for a grant to the creditor in the exercise of the court's discretionary powers under s. 116(1) of the Supreme Court Act 1981 (see p. 845, post).

6.317   As to grants to creditors where the deceased was an illegitimate person, see paras. **6.302–6.305**, ante.

Specialty or simple contract

6.318   It is a matter of indifference whether the creditor be a creditor by specialty or on simple contract; the amount of the debt is also immaterial, as is the question whether it is statute-barred[1]. These questions become relevant only where there is a contest between two or more creditors for the grant. No special affidavit by the creditor is necessary; he merely swears in the oath that he is 'a creditor of the deceased'.

1 *Coombs v Coombs* (1866) LR 1 P & D 288; *Re Coombs' Goods* (1866) LR 1 P& D 193.

Creditor in equity

6.319   The court will grant administration to a creditor in equity of the estate of the deceased[1], but not to a person who has bought up a debt after the death of the intestate[2].

1 *Re Percy's Goods, Fairlamb* (called *Fairland*) *v Percy* (1875) LR 3 P & D 217; but he was required to take a leading grant.
2 *Baynes v Harrison* (1856) Dea & Sw 15; *Re Coles' Goods, Macnin v Coles* (1863) 3 Sw & Tr 181.

6.320   It should be noted that NCPR 24, which enables a grant to be made to the assignee(s) of the persons having a beneficial interest in the estate, does not enable a grant to be made to the assignee of a creditor of the deceased.

Trustee in bankruptcy or under deed of arrangement

6.321   As to grants to the trustee in bankruptcy of a beneficiary, or to the trustee under a deed of arrangement, see paras. **5.218–5.223**, ante.

Nominees of creditor

6.322   Administration will be granted to the nominee of a county council or other similar body which is a creditor of the deceased, on clearing off all prior rights. The council should by resolution appoint a nominee to apply for the grant on its behalf, and a sealed or certified copy of the resolution must be lodged. Form of appointment of nominee, No. 43.

6.323   The grant is limited for the use and benefit of the council and until further representation be granted. (See also paras. **5.201–5.207**, ante.)

Liquidator of a company

6.324   The official receiver, or other liquidator, of a limited company which is being wound up by court order is empowered by s. 539(2)(f) of the Companies Act 1985 to take out, in his official name, letters of administration of the estate of any deceased contributory (i.e. any person who was liable to contribute to the assets of the company, either in respect of shares not fully paid up or otherwise); and it is provided that any money due from the contributory or his estate shall, for the purpose of the application for such a grant, be deemed to be due to the liquidator, who is thus constituted a creditor of the deceased. The provisions of s. 539(2)(f) apply also in the case of a voluntary liquidation.

Undertaker, for funeral expenses

6.325   The court may enquire as to the circumstances in which the expenses were incurred, and by whose authority the undertaker carried them out, and has given a grant to an undertaker, where he had been commissioned by a person entitled to the estate[1].

1   *Newcombe v Beloe* (1867) LR 1 P & D 314.

6.326   The modern practice is for application to be made for an order for a grant under s. 116 of the Supreme Court Act 1981, as it appears clear that an undertaker is not prima facie a creditor of the deceased. (See also paras. **25.91** ff., post.)

6.327   The funeral expenses of the deceased are, under the Administration of Estates Act 1925, ss. 33(2) and 34(3), a first charge on the estate, and, in the absence of an express contract with some other person, an executor with assets is personally liable under an implied contract to the person furnishing the funeral[1].

1   *Tugwell v Heyman* (1812) 3 Camp 298; *Rogers v Price* (1829) 3 Y & J 28; *Ambrose v Kerrison* (1851) 10 CB 776.

6.328   A husband was formerly liable at common law for the funeral expenses of his deceased wife, and in cases where a stranger commissioned the funeral it was held that he could recover the expenses from the husband[1]. With the enactment of the Married Women's Property Act 1882 and the Law Reform (Married Women and Tortfeasors) Act 1935, however, the foundation for the husband's common law liability has disappeared (except perhaps where the wife's estate is insufficient), and the wife's estate is liable for her funeral expenses in the same way as is the estate of a feme sole[2].

1   See *Ambrose v Kerrison*, above; *Bradshaw v Beard* (1862) 12 CBNS 344.
2   *Rees v Hughes* [1946] KB 517, [1946] 2 All ER 47.

Firm as creditor

6.329   A partnership firm, as distinct from a company, has no separate entity at English law. Each partner acts as agent for the other, or others. In the case of a creditor firm it must be shown in the oath that the individuals named therein are members of the firm. Where application is made by one or more of several partners, it is usually sufficient to include in the oath a statement to the effect that all the remaining partners have been consulted and that they each consent to the application being made.

Minority or life interest

6.330 Where a minority or life interest arises under the intestacy, it will normally be necessary for at least two creditors to apply for the grant, unless the court considers that it would be expedient in all the circumstances to appoint a single creditor. If there is only one creditor, but the court considers two administrators are required, that creditor may apply for a district judge's or registrar's order under NCPR 25(2) for a joint grant with an independent person approved by a district judge or registrar; or (subject to the necessary consent) a trust corporation may be joined as second grantee without the necessity for a district judge's or registrar's order (NCPR 25(3)(b)). (See also Chap. 7.)

Other grants of administration

Grant to person having 'spes successionis'

6.331 It should be noted that, unlike the earlier rules, the NCPR 1987 contain no provision for a grant to a person having spes successionis, i.e. where the beneficial interest in the whole estate of an intestate is vested absolutely in one person, a grant to the person or persons who would be entitled to his estate if he were dead intestate.

6.332 Where the person beneficially interested in the estate does not wish to take a grant, he may now appoint an attorney or attorneys to take a grant for his use and benefit, whether he lives in or outside England and Wales[1].

1 NCPR 31.

Grant to assignee

6.333 NCPR 24 is as follows:

'(1) Where all the persons entitled to the estate of the deceased (whether under a will or on intestacy) have assigned their whole interest in the estate to one or more persons, the assignee or assignees shall replace, in the order of priority for a grant of administration, the assignor or, if there are two or more assignors, the assignor with the highest priority.

(2) Where there are two or more assignees, administration may be granted with the consent of the others to any one or more (not exceeding four) of them.

(3) In any case where administration is applied for by an assignee the original instrument of assignment shall be produced and a copy of the same lodged in the registry.'

6.334 A grant to an assignee or assignees may be made notwithstanding that, prior to the execution of the deed of assignment, more than one person had a beneficial interest in the estate of the deceased, provided that all persons sharing in the estate join in the deed. Where the deceased left a surviving spouse and other kin who share in the estate, all must join in the assignment to enable a grant to be made to an assignee or assignees. This applies also if the amount of the estate is such that the other kin have only a potential beneficial interest in the event of an accretion to the estate[1]: it is only where the deceased left no kin within the classes entitled to share with a surviving spouse on an intestacy that an assignment by the spouse alone will suffice.

1 Senior Registrar's decision (1961) 4 October.

6.335   It should be noted that the rule does not enable a grant to be made to an assignee where any person actually or potentially beneficially interested in the estate is not sui juris, or for some other reason does not join in the assignment.

6.336   Where any assignee is a minor it is normally necessary for the grant to be made to not less than two individuals or a trust corporation: similarly, if the sole assignee is a minor the grant must normally be made, on his behalf, to not less than two persons or a trust corporation[1]. As to grants on behalf of minors, see paras. **11.113** ff., post.

1 Registrar's Circular, 12 June 1967.

6.337   Where a grant is sought by one or some only of several assignees a consent to the making of a grant to such person or persons, signed by all the other assignees, must be lodged with the papers (NCPR 24(2)).

6.338   On every application for a grant to an assignee or assignees the original instrument of assignment must be produced at the registry for inspection and a copy of the instrument for filing at the registry is also required (r. 24(3)). Form of oath, No. 113. As to the practice of the registry on the production of an original instrument, see paras. **5.214** and **5.215**, ante.

Letters of administration where deceased domiciled out of England and Wales

6.339   The practice in making grants of administration where the deceased died domiciled out of England and Wales is set out in Chap. 12.

Grants to trust corporations

6.340   As to grants to trust corporations, see Chap. 9.

Grants to attorneys or guardians

6.341   For the practice in making grants to the attorneys of persons, to the parents or guardians of minors, and on behalf of persons under disability, see Chap. 11.

Administration pending suit or ad colligenda bona

6.342   As to grants of administration pending suit and ad colligenda bona, see paras. **11.318** ff. and **11.335** ff., post.

When issued

Efflux of 14 days from date of death

6.343   Except with the leave of a district judge or registrar, a period of 14 days, excluding the day of the intestate's death, must have elapsed before the letters of administration are allowed to issue (NCPR 6(2)).

6.344   The nature of the evidence required to support an application under r. 6(2) is a matter for the discretion of the district judge or registrar considering it. An affidavit may not be necessary in all cases, but it is desirable that there should be some supporting document.

6.345   As to expedition of grant, see para. **2.39**, ante.

Requirements on obtaining administration

Administrator's oath

6.346   Every application for a grant of letters of administration must be supported by an oath in the form applicable to the circumstances of the case sworn by the applicant, and by such other papers as the district judge or registrar may require (NCPR 8(1)). The oath must state whether, and if so in what manner, all persons having a prior right to a grant have been cleared off (see 'Clearing off', para. **6.355**, post). For forms of oath, see Nos. 87 ff., post.

6.347   The practice as to the name, address, and description or status of the deponent, the name, age and address of the deceased, and the date of death is the same as in the case of an executor's oath. (See paras. **4.91** ff., ante.)

6.348   When an unnecessary renunciation has been lodged with the papers, it is returned to the practitioner. The oath may have to be amended and resworn if such a renunciation has been referred to in it.

6.349   Where a person, who would have had a prior right to a grant, has died without having taken upon himself administration of the estate, this fact must be sworn to in the oath. See also 'Representative grants', paras. **6.11** ff., ante.

Domicile

6.350   Unless the district judge or registrar directs otherwise, the oath must state where the deceased died domiciled (NCPR 8(2)). See 'Domicile', paras. **4.170–4.173**, ante.

Minority or life interest

6.351   In every oath to lead a grant of administration, the deponent must state whether any minority or life interest arises under the intestacy (NCPR 8(4)).

Settled land

6.352   In every oath to lead a grant of administration, where the deceased died on or after 1 January 1926, the deponent must swear to the best of his knowledge, information and belief whether there was land vested in the deceased which was settled previously to his death and which remained settled land notwithstanding his death (NCPR 8(3)). As to grants in respect of settled land, see Chap. 10.

Alias

6.353   Where it is sought to obtain a grant in which the deceased is described by a further name in addition to his true name, the oath, or a supplemental affidavit, must depose to the facts, setting out the true name and that some specified part of the estate was held in the other or giving any other reason for the inclusion of the other name in the grant (NCPR 9). For the practice, see paras. **4.123–4.127** and **4.132–4.135**, ante. Form of affidavit, No. 16.

Judgment or order of High Court judge or district judge or registrar

6.354   Where any judgment or order of a High Court judge, district judge or registrar has been obtained in connection with a grant of administration, e.g. a judgment in a probate action pronouncing against a will; an order under s. 116 of the Supreme Court Act 1981; or an order for leave to swear to the death, particulars of the date of the judgment or order, its effect and by whom it was made, must be included in the oath. The judgment (or an office copy of it) or order and, in ex parte applications, the supporting evidence, must be lodged with the papers.

Clearing off

6.355   Where the death of the intestate occurred on or after 1 January 1970, the alterations in the law of succession under Part II of the Family Law Reform Act 1969 and s. 18 of the Family Law Reform Act 1987 necessitate a more extensive form of clearing off of prior classes than was previously required in many applications for letters of administration. The following table sets out the appropriate wording to be used in the oath:

Clearing off	*Wording* Swear that deceased died:	
Spouse	{ a bachelor a spinster a widower a widow a single man[1] a single woman[1]	
Children or other issue	without issue	
Parents	[or] parent	

Brothers or
    sisters and their
    issue
	[or] brother or
	    sister of the whole
	    [or half] blood or
	    issue thereof
		or any other person
		entitled in priority
		to share in his [her]

Grandparents	[or] grandparent	estate by virtue of any enactment

Uncles and aunts
    and their issue
	or uncle or aunt of
	    the whole [or half]
	    blood or issue thereof	

1 As to the additional wording required in the oath in case of a decree of divorce or nullity, see paras. **6.118** and **6.120**, ante.

6.356   In particular it should be noted: (i) that the words 'or any other person entitled in priority to share in his [her] estate by virtue of any enactment' include not only illegitimate children but also legitimated and adopted children; and (ii) that on the intestacy of a bachelor or spinster, where the application is made other than by a child of the intestate, it will be necessary to clear children[1].

1 *Practice Direction* [1969] 3 All ER 1343, [1969] 1 WLR 1863.

Description of applicant

6.357   Persons applying for administration, where the death occurred after 1925 but before 4 April 1988, are to be described as follows:[1]

A husband as	'the lawful husband'
A wife	'the lawful widow and relict (*or* (if she has remarried) the lawful relict)'.

(Where the net estate, after allowing the permissible deductions, does not exceed £125,000 (or £200,000 if the deceased left no issue)[2] the husband or relict should be further described as 'the only person *now* entitled to the estate'. It is only where it can be sworn that there are no kin within the degrees mentioned in the tables in para. **6.29**, that the spouse can be described as 'the only person entitled to the estate'.

Issue of marriage 'the lawful son (or daughter), and only person entitled to the estate'; or

'the lawful son (or daughter), and one of the persons entitled to share in the estate';

(A child other than a lawful child should be described as 'the natural son *or* daughter', 'the lawful adopted son *or* daughter' or 'the lawful legitimated son *or* daughter', as the case may be[3].)

'the lawful grandson (or granddaughter), and only person entitled to the estate'; or

'the lawful grandson (or granddaughter), and one of the persons entitled to share in the estate'[4]. (In the case of grandchildren or more remote issue, the oath should establish that the applicant has a beneficial interest, i.e. it should show either that the deceased died without child, or that the applicant is 'the lawful [*or* lawful adopted *or* lawful legitimated] son (or daughter) of A. B., the lawful [*or* natural *or* lawful adopted *or* lawful legitimated] son (or daughter) of the said intestate, who died in the lifetime of the said intestate.')

A father
  or
A mother

'the lawful [*or* natural][5] father (or mother), and only person entitled to the estate'; or
'the lawful [*or* natural][5] father (or mother), and one of the persons entitled to share in the estate.'

A brother
  or
A sister

'the lawful brother (or sister) of the whole blood, and only person entitled to the estate'; or
'the lawful brother (or sister) of the whole blood, and one of the persons entitled to share in the estate'.

If there be no brother or sister of the whole blood, nor any issue of such brother or sister, then the half blood is described as 'the lawful brother (or sister) of the half blood, and' etc.

Issue of a brother or
  sister

'the lawful nephew, or great-nephew (or niece), of the whole blood, and only person entitled to the estate'; or
'the lawful nephew, or great-nephew (or niece), of the whole blood, and one of the persons entitled to share in the estate'.

(The oath must also establish that the applicant has a beneficial interest, in a similar manner to that given under 'Issue of marriage', above.)

If there be no brother or sister of the whole blood, or any issue of such brother or sister, then the half blood, if entitled to take a beneficial interest in the estate, is described as 'the lawful nephew, or great-nephew (or niece), of the half blood, and' etc.

A grandparent
{
'the lawful grandfather (or grandmother), and only person entitled to the estate'; or
'the lawful grandfather (or grandmother), and one of the persons entitled to share in the estate'.

An uncle
or
An aunt
{
'the lawful uncle (or aunt) of the whole blood, and only person entitled to the estate'; or
'the lawful uncle (or aunt) of the whole blood, and one of the persons entitled to share in the estate'.

If there be no uncle or aunt (being brother or sister of the whole blood of a parent), or any issue of such uncle or aunt, such person shall be described as 'the lawful uncle (or aunt) of the half blood, and', etc.

Issue of an uncle
or aunt
{
'the lawful cousin german of the whole blood, and only person entitled to the estate'; or
'the lawful cousin german of the whole blood, and one of the persons entitled to share in the estate'.

(The oath must also establish that the applicant has a beneficial interest: see above.)

If there be no uncle or aunt (being brother or sister of the whole blood of a parent), or any issue of such uncle or aunt, such person shall be described as 'the lawful cousin german of the half blood, and' etc.

1 President's Direction (1925) (Non-Contentious Probate).
2 When the intestate died on or after 1 December 1993. For the relevant amounts for earlier dates of death, see para. **6.31**.
3 As to a grant in the case of illegitimacy, adoption or legitimation, see paras. **6.168** ff., **6.223** ff. and **6.174** ff., ante, respectively.
4 As to the practice under which, on the renunciation of the surviving spouse, the issue or other kin may apply as persons 'who may have a beneficial interest in the estate in the event of an accretion thereto', see para. **6.99**, ante.
5 As to grant to a natural parent, see paras. **6.266** ff., ante.

6.358 Where the death occurred on or after 4 April 1988 the description of the applicant as given above may be modified in respect of a wife by describing her as the 'lawful widow', without any reference to 'relict', and in respect of any relative by omitting reference to 'lawful' or 'natural', save that an adopted child should be described as the 'lawful adopted son/daughter' etc.

Notice to the Crown

6.359 In any case in which it appears that the Crown is, or may be, beneficially interested in the estate of the deceased, notice of the intended application for the grant must be given by the applicant to the Treasury Solicitor[1]. The district judge or registrar may direct that no grant shall issue within 28 days after such notice has been given.

1 NCPR 38.

6.360 Any communication received from the Treasury Solicitor in reply to such notice should be lodged with the papers when application is made for the grant.

Amount of estate and swearing

6.361 For the practice as to 'amount of estate' and 'swearing', see 'Executor's oath', paras. **4.198** ff. and **4.221**, ante.

Form of grant

6.362 For practice, see paras. **2.24** ff., ante.

Guarantee

6.363 Section 120 of the Supreme Court Act 1981 (see p. 846, post) allows the High Court to require a guarantee to be given, in accordance with probate rules, as a condition of granting certain administrations.

Circumstances in which guarantee required

6.364 The NCPR 1987 contain no provision relating to a guarantee. Consequently a guarantee may only be required, as a condition of granting administration, in a case which was pending on 1 January 1988 and in which case a High Court judge, district judge or registrar has directed, under r. 68, that the rules in force before 1 January 1988 should continue to apply to that particular case. It is considered that such cases will be extremely rare. If such a direction is given reference should be made to pp. 246 ff. of the 26th edition of this work for the circumstances in which a guarantee is necessary and for the relevant requirements.

Enforcement of guarantee

6.365 The guarantee enures for the benefit of every person interested in the administration of the estate as if contained in a contract under seal made by the sureties with every such person and, where there are two or more sureties, as if they had bound themselves jointly and severally (Supreme Court Act 1981, s. 120(2)).

6.366 However, no action to enforce a guarantee may be brought without leave of the High Court (ibid., s. 120(3)). Application for leave to sue a surety or sureties on the guarantee must, unless otherwise directed by the district judge or registrar under NCPR 61, be made by summons to a district judge of the Principal Registry or the registrar of the district probate registry from which the grant issued. Notice of the application must, in any event, be served on the administrator, the surety and any co-surety (NCPR 40). No assignment of the guarantee is necessary.

6.367 As to the practice in relation to summonses, see paras. **25.223** ff., post. For the procedure to obtain an inventory and account of the estate from a personal representative, see Chap. 19.

Bonds given prior to 1972

6.368   Section 120 of the Supreme Court Act 1981 does not apply in relation to grants of administration made before 1 January 1972, and any administration bond given before that date either under s. 167 of the Supreme Court of Judicature (Consolidation) Act 1925 (as originally enacted) or under the Colonial Probates Act 1892, may be enforced and assigned as it could have been before that date (Supreme Court Act 1981, Sch. 6, para. 10 and Administration of Estates Act 1971, s. 12(5)). For the practice as to assignment of bonds, see paras. **25.202** ff., post.

Resealing of 'Colonial' grants of administration

6.369   Section 11 of the Administration of Estates Act 1971 (see p. 802, post) allows the High Court to require a guarantee to be given, in accordance with probate rules, as a condition of sealing letters of administration, granted in any other country or territory, under the Colonial Probates Acts 1892 and 1927.

6.370   The NCPR 1987 contain no provision relating to a guarantee. For the circumstances in which a guarantee may still be required under the rules in force prior to 1 January 1988 see para. **6.364**, ante.

6.371   The procedure for enforcement of a guarantee given under the former rules on the resealing of a Colonial grant of administration is identical to that set out above in paras. **6.365–6.367** in connection with a guarantee given on an application for an English grant of administration (NCPR 40).

Duties of executor or administrator

6.372   The duties of a personal representative in relation to the administration of the estate of the deceased are set out in s. 25 of the Administration of Estates Act 1925 (see p. 749, post): see also Chap. 19.

Duties of administrator—resealed grant

6.373   A person to whom administration has been granted in a country or territory to which the Colonial Probates Act 1892 applies has, on the grant being resealed in England and Wales, the like duties with respect to the estate of the deceased which is situated in England and Wales and the debts of the deceased which fall to be paid there as are imposed by s. 25 of the Administration of Estates Act 1925 on a personal representative acting under a grant issued in England and Wales, other than the requirement to deliver up the grant to the High Court when required to do so (Administration of Estates Act 1971, s. 11(2)).

Right of retainer and preference of creditors

6.374   Section 10 of the Administration of Estates Act 1971 (which applies in relation to persons dying on or after 1 January 1972 only) abolished the personal representative's right of retainer and his right to prefer creditors.

6.375   However, (1) a personal representative (other than one who has obtained a grant of administration solely by reason of his being a creditor) who, in good faith and at a time when he has no reason to believe that the estate of the deceased is insolvent, pays the debt of any person, including himself, who is a creditor of the estate; and (2) a personal representative who obtains administration solely as a creditor and who, in good faith and at such a time, pays the debt of another creditor of the estate, is not, if it subsequently appears that the estate is insolvent, liable to account to other creditors of the same degree as the paid creditor for the sum so paid (Administration of Estates Act 1971, s. 10(2)). In relation to deaths prior to 1 January 1972 the old law as to retainer and preference continues to apply.

Liability to sureties

6.376 Where letters of administration are obtained by fraud and afterwards revoked the sureties to the administration bond are liable for the acts and defaults of the administrators while the grant is unrevoked[1].

1 *Debendra Nath Dutt v Administrator-General of Bengal* (1908) 99 LT 68, PC.

6.377 Under the law in force prior to 1972 the administrator was required to enter into a bond jointly with the sureties. In such a case it has been held that a personal representative who has cleared the estate and become a trustee of the net residue for the persons beneficially interested does not necessarily and automatically become discharged from his obligations under the bond, nor do the sureties. The duties of an administrator extend where, for example, immediate distribution is impossible owing to the minority of the beneficiary, to retaining the net estate in trust for the minor[1].

1 *Harvell v Foster* [1954] 2 QB 367, [1954] 2 All ER 736.

6.378 An administrator who has cleared the estate and completed the administration is, however, entitled under s. 36 of the Trustee Act 1925 to appoint trustees in his stead (see para. **6.24**, ante).

6.379 The court will not discharge the original sureties and allow others to be substituted[1]: see also 'Substitution of surety', below.

1 *Re Stark's Goods* (1866) LR 1 P & D 76; *Re Cowardin's Goods* (1901) 86 LT 261.

Protection of sureties

6.380 If a surety to a bond has reasonable grounds for anticipating maladministration by an administrator, he is entitled to apply to the court for relief by way of indemnity against his liabilities under his bond[1]. He can also seek relief, in the Chancery Division, under RSC Order 85, r. 2, and Order 29, r. 1. (Semble, this applies also to a surety to an administration guarantee.)

1 *Re Anderson-Berry, Harris v Griffith* [1928] Ch 290, CA.

Substitution of surety

6.381 When, prior to 1972, one surety executed a bond with the assurance that another person named as surety would execute it, the substitution of another person for the second surety, without the consent of the first, was held to invalidate the bond[1]. Consequently, when a fresh surety is substituted in a guarantee, the other surety is required to redeliver the guarantee in order to show his willingness to be joined with the new surety. But this does not apply unless an assurance was given, or there has been substitution of another person for the second surety after the guarantee has been delivered by the other.

1 *Re Cowardin's Goods* (1901) 86 LT 261.

·6.382   The attestation clause or clauses of the guarantee must contain the names or name of the parties or party executing the guarantee.

Inland Revenue accounts

6.383   The subject of Inland Revenue accounts is dealt with post, Chap. 8

Fees

6.384   The fees payable upon grants of administration are the same as for probate: see paras. **4.250–4.265**, ante, and Appendix III, p. 959, post.

Solicitor's charges

6.385   This subject is dealt with in paras. **4.266–4.270**, ante.

Death before 1 January 1926

6.386   The interest of a child or next-of-kin or heir-at-law of the intestate became vested whether he had attained 21 years or not.

Order of priority before 1926

(1)   Husband or widow.
(2)   Husband's representative (subject to the next item).
(3)   Next-of-kin, or heir-at-law* (the latter in preference to the representative of the husband if there is real estate).
(4)   Persons entitled in distribution, though not next-of-kin.
(5)   Representatives of next-of-kin, widow, heir-at-law*, or persons entitled to share in distribution.
(6)   Creditor, if there are kin beneficially entitled who renounce.
(7)   The Crown, Duchy of Lancaster, or of Cornwall (in the case of a bastard or person having no known relations).
(8)   Creditor (if there are no kin).

* Where death occurred before 1 January 1898 the heir-at-law has no right to a grant.

6.387   Administration is granted, subject to the rights of the heir-at-law who is equally entitled (where the deceased died after 1897 and where there is real estate) with the intestate's next-of-kin, in the order following, viz.[1]:

(1)   To *husband or wife* of the intestate.
(2)   To *child or children* (as next-of-kin) of an intestate widower or widow.
(3)   To *grandchild or grandchildren* (as next-of-kin) of widower or widow dying without child.
(4)   To *great-grandchildren* or other descendants (as next-of-kin) of widower or widow dying without child or grandchild.
(5)   To *father* (as next-of-kin) of bachelor or spinster.
      To *father* (as next-of-kin) of widower or widow dying without issue.

Deaths before 1926 only

(6) To *mother* (as next-of-kin) of bachelor or spinster dying without father.
To *mother* (as next-of-kin) of widower or widow dying without issue or father.

(7) To *brothers or sisters* (as next-of-kin) of bachelor or spinster dying without parent.
To *brothers or sisters* (as next-of-kin) of widower or widow dying without issue or parent.

(8) To *grandfathers or grandmothers* (as next-of-kin) of bachelor or spinster dying without parent, brother, or sister.
To *grandfathers or grandmothers* (as next-of-kin) of widower or widow dying without issue or parent, brother, or sister.

(9) To *uncles, aunts, nephews, nieces, great-grandfathers, great-grandmothers* (as next-of-kin) of bachelor or spinster dying without parent or grandparent, brother or sister.
To *uncles, aunts, nephews, nieces, great-grandfathers, great-grandmothers* (as next-of-kin) of widower or widow dying without issue, parent or grandparent, brother or sister.

(10) To *cousins german* (as next-of-kin) of bachelor or spinster dying without parent or grandparent, brother or sister, uncle or aunt, nephew or niece.
To *cousins german* (as next-of-kin) of widower or widow dying without issue, parent or grandparent, brother or sister, uncle or aunt, nephew or niece.

(11) To kin in the next degree of relationship—and so on, progressively.

1 This list includes only those persons who are entitled by relationship or marriage. It should be observed that the term 'next-of-kin' does not include the husband or wife of a deceased.

6.388   The Statute of Distribution[1] provides, as regards classes 2, 3, 4 and 7 above, that in each class the children of members of that class who predeceased the intestate shall be entitled to their parent's share. Such children are entitled to a grant next *after* the members who survived. They take as 'persons entitled in distribution'. This does not apply to classes more remote.

1 17 Halsbury's Statutes (4th edn) 232.

6.389   *Note.*—In the case of death before 1926 relations of the whole and half blood are equally entitled to share.

Distribution of an intestate's personal estate

6.390   The distribution of an intestate's personal estate is, in pre-1926 cases, regulated by the Statute of Distribution, the Statute of Frauds[1]—as amended by 1 Jac. 2, c. 17[2]—and the Intestates' Estates Act 1890[3].

1 11 Halsbury's Statutes (4th edn) 205.
2 9 Halsbury's Statutes (2nd edn) 662.
3 17 Halsbury's Statutes (4th edn) 252.

6.391   The effect of these Acts may be concisely stated as follows:

(a)   If the intestate die leaving a *husband*, he is entitled to all the personal estate.

Deaths before 1926 only

(b)   If the intestate leaves a *wife*, and issue, she is entitled to one-third, and the issue to the remainder; the issue of deceased children sharing with them by representing their stocks.

(c)   If there be no children or their representatives by stocks, and the intestate died before 2 September 1890, the wife is entitled to one-half, and the next-of-kin take the other half. For example, if the intestate leaves a wife and father, a half goes to each. If he leaves a wife, mother, brother and sister, the wife is entitled to half, and the mother, brother and sister take the other half equally among them. If the intestate leaves a wife, mother, brothers and sisters, nephews and nieces, the wife is entitled to half, and the mother, brothers and sisters, and nephews and nieces, being children of a brother or sister who predeceased the intestate, to the other half in equal shares, the nephews or nieces, as representing a deceased brother or sister, sharing per stirpes[1]. By the Intestates' Estates Act 1890[2], if the husband died after 1 September 1890 without issue and the net value of his real and personal estate did not exceed £500, the wife was entitled to the whole, but where it exceeded £500, she had a charge upon the whole estate for £500, with interest at 4 per cent until payment, in addition to her share in the residue of the personal estate. The Act applied, however, only where the husband died wholly intestate[3]; and the rights of the next-of-kin or heir-at-law to a grant were not affected.

1 See *Keilway v Keilway* (1726) 2 Stra 170; *Stanley v Stanley* (1739) 1 Atk 455.
2 17 Halsbury's Statutes (4th edn) 252.
3 *Re Twigg's Estate, Twigg v Black* [1892] 1 Ch 579.

6.392   These Acts were entirely repealed by the Administration of Estates Act 1925[1], as regards deaths after 1925; but by s. 50(2) of that Act it was provided that trusts declared in an inter vivos instrument or will coming into operation before 1 January 1926, by reference to Statutes of Distribution—unless a contrary intention appears therein—shall be construed as referring to the enactments (other than the Intestates' Estates Act 1890), relating to the distribution of the estate of intestates in force immediately before 1 January 1926[2].

1 See p. 744, post.
2 See *Re Hurd, Stott v Stott* [1941] Ch 196, [1941] 1 All ER 238; *Re Sutton, Evans v Oliver* [1934] Ch 209; *Re Sutcliffe, Sutcliffe v Robertshaw* [1929] 1 Ch 123.

6.393   If there be no descendants, father, mother, brother or sister, then, subject to the provisions in her favour stated in the preceding paragraph, the wife is entitled to one-half, and the next-of-kin, i.e. all those in the same degree of kindred, are entitled to the other half equally among them.

6.394   If there be no next-of-kin, or the intestate be a bastard without issue, one-half goes to the wife, and the other half to the Crown.

6.395   *Children* take between or among them equally, grandchildren and more remote descendants taking with them per stirpes.

6.396   *Grandchildren* take per stirpes and not per capita[1], great-grandchildren and more remote descendants taking with them per stirpes.

1 *Re Natt, Walker v Gammage* (1888) 37 Ch D 517.

Deaths before 1926 only

6.397   The same observation applies to further descendants.

6.398   If there be no widow or issue the *father* as next-of-kin takes all the estate.

6.399   So the *mother* (if no father) as *only* next-of-kin takes all, if there be no brothers or sisters, or nephews and nieces taking per stirpes. No other kindred than these is entitled to share with the mother.

6.400   *Brothers and sisters* share among themselves equally, nephews and nieces, being children of brothers or sisters who died in the lifetime of the deceased, taking with them per stirpes; but if no brother or sister survives, nephews and nieces take as next-of-kin, and not by representation. Their right is thus inferior to that of grandparents, and they share per capita with others in the same degree of kinship, e.g. uncles.

6.401   *Grandfathers and grandmothers* share among themselves equally. If there be only one, that one takes all.

6.402   Grandparents do not share with brothers or sisters of deceased.

6.403   *Nephews and nieces* unless entitled to share per stirpes with brothers or sisters, as stated above, share together with uncles, aunts, great-grandfathers and great-grandmothers equally, they being all in the third degree; and so on with other kindred according to their degree, all those in the same degree taking an equal share[1].

1   The special customs of London, the province of York, and certain other places, as to the distribution of the personal estate of intestates were abolished by 19 & 20 Vict. c. 94.

6.404   The Statutes of Distribution do not apply the right to take a deceased parent's share per stirpes to persons beyond nephews and nieces[1], so that as between an uncle and a deceased uncle's child, the former alone would be entitled.

1   The special customs of London, the province of York, and certain other places, as to the distribution of the personal estate of intestates were abolished by 19 & 20 Vict. c. 94.

6.405   For the rules of descent of real estate, see p. 1105, post.

6.406   The following table shows the devolution of personal estate, the entitlement to the grant where there is personal estate, and the priority of the right to the grant of the heir-at-law, when there is real estate.

Deaths before 1926 only

Intestacies—pre-1926 but post-1897

6.407

(sidebar, vertical text) **Deaths before 1926 only**

Devolution of personal estate	Entitlement to grant (subject to rights of the heir-at-law)	Heir-at-law entitlement to grant if real estate
1. *Husband* (all)	(a) Surviving spouse.	Inferior to husband unless there is no personalty and no courtesy title.
2. *Wife* (one-third). Issue (two-thirds) or (after 1890 and if no issue) Wife £500 and half. Next-of-kin (half). If no kin their share falls to the Crown	(b) Personal representative of surviving *husband*, but not of a wife. Next-of-kin in the following classes: (c) Children or, if cleared off, persons entitled in distribution	Inferior to widow. In certain cases, superior to representative of husband.
3. *Children* (grandchildren per stirpes)	Next-of-kin in the following classes:	Superior to kin if *husband* renounces.
4. *Father* (all)	(d) Grandchildren	Equal with next-of-kin (subject to preponderance and (3), above).
5. *Mother* (but sharing equally with brothers and sisters if any, or their *children*, but not grandchildren)	(e) More remote issue (f) Father (g) Mother	Prior to representative of next-of-kin and to persons entitled in distribution, and to
6. *Brothers and sisters* equally (*children* sharing with them per stirpes)*	(h) Brothers or sisters or, if cleared off, persons entitled in distribution though not next-of-kin	husband's representative. His representative prior to kin if real estate only.
7. *Grandparents*, equally	(j) Grandparents	Co-heiresses: both must take in default of
8. *Uncles, aunts, nephews, nieces* (if not sharing with 5 or 6) *and great-grandparents* share equally (no stirpes)	(k) Class (8) opposite (l) Class (9) opposite (m) Next-of-kin of a more remote degree	consent. (The relationship of heir-at-law or co-heiresses is not stated in grants.)
9. All kin of the next degree to (8)	(n) A legal personal representative of one of the class entitled; but the personal representative of a next-of-kin is not entitled before a person entitled in distribution	
10. More remote kin in the same degree		
11. The Crown *Real* estate vests in the heir-at-law subject to the widow's right to the first £500, in total intestacy under the Intestates' Act 1890 if no issue	(o) The Crown (if no kin of any degree) (p) Creditors	

* There is no distinction between the whole and half blood.

Description of grantee. Death occurring before 1926

6.408 Persons applying for administration, where the death occurred before 1926, are to be described in the oath as follows:

A husband as	'the lawful husband'.
A wife	'the lawful widow and relict' or (if remarried) 'the lawful relict'.
A child	'the lawful child, and only next-of-kin', or 'the lawful child, and one of the next-of-kin'.
A father	'the lawful father and next-of-kin'.
A mother	'the lawful mother and only next-of-kin'.
A brother	'the lawful brother'.
A sister	'the lawful sister'.
	If there be no parents living, the brother or sister is further to be described as 'one of the next-of-kin', or the 'only next-of-kin'.
An uncle	'the lawful uncle' { and 'one of the' or
An aunt	'the lawful aunt' { 'only next-of-kin'.
A nephew[1]	'the lawful nephew' { and 'one of the' or
A niece[1]	'the lawful niece' { 'only next-of-kin'.

A grandparent, grandchild[1], cousin, etc., is to be described as 'lawful' and 'one of the next-of-kin', or 'only next-of- kin'.

An heir-at-law	'the heir-at-law'.
An heiress-at-law as	'the heiress-at-law', or 'one of the co-heiresses-at-law'.
An heir according to the custom of gavelkind	'one of the heirs according to the custom of gavelkind.'

1 A nephew, niece or grandchild who is entitled to take, in a higher class than his own, his deceased parent's share, is further described as 'and one of the persons entitled in distribution', and not as 'next-of-kin'.

6.409 If an intestate leaves a brother or sister who is cleared off, and a nephew or niece applies for a grant, he or she should be described not as 'next-of-kin', but as 'the lawful child of A. B., the lawful brother (or sister) of the intestate who died in his lifetime, and as such one of the persons entitled in distribution to his personal estate'.

Practice on application for grant: death prior to 1 January 1926

6.410 For details of the practice applicable in cases where the date of death was prior to 1 January 1926, reference should be made to the 23rd or earlier editions of this work.

CHAPTER 7

Minority or life interests and second administrators

7.01 Sub-sections (2) and (3) of s. 114 of the Supreme Court Act 1981 provide as follows:

'(2) Where under a will or intestacy any beneficiary is a minor or a life interest arises, any grant of administration by the High Court shall be made either to a trust corporation (with or without an individual) or to not less than two individuals, unless it appears to the court to be expedient in all the circumstances to appoint an individual as sole administrator.

(3) For the purpose of determining whether a minority or life interest arises in any particular case, the court may act on such evidence as may be prescribed.'

7.02 It is accordingly provided by NCPR 8(4), that on an application for a grant of administration, with or without the will annexed, the oath shall state whether any minority or life interest arises under the will or intestacy. The district judge or registrar may call for such further evidence as he may require[1].

1 NCPR 6(1).

7.03 The age of majority having been reduced from 21 to 18 years with effect from 1 January 1970[1], the statement in the oath as to the existence or otherwise of a minority must be made with reference to the age of 18.

1 Family Law Reform Act 1969, s. 1 (p. 789, post).

7.04 The general rule therefore is that, unless the court in the exercise of its discretion considers it expedient in all the circumstances to allow the grant to be made to an individual as sole administrator, in every form of grant of administration, including grants ad colligenda bona[1], the grant must be made to at least two administrators, or to a trust corporation, with or without an individual, whenever a minority or life interest arises. The only exceptions to this general rule are a grant of administration pending suit, in which case a sole individual administrator may be appointed notwithstanding the existence of a minority or a life interest[2], a grant to a consular officer under the Consular Conventions Act 1949 (see pp. 765 ff., post) and, it is suggested, in the case of a grant limited to settled land (see Chap. 10).

1 *Re Cizek* (1943) (motion).
2 *Re Haslip* [1958] 2 All ER 275n, [1958] 1 WLR 583.

7.05 The oath must state definitely that *there is or is not a minority interest*, and that *there is or is not a life interest*, or that *there is a minority and a life interest* (when such is the case). A general statement that there is a minority *or* life interest is not accepted. Where, however, two or more persons apply jointly for a grant and it is sworn either that there is a life interest but it is not stated whether or no there is a minority interest, or that there is a minority interest, but it is not stated whether or no there is a life interest, the oath may be accepted without requiring an amendment, provided that a certificate is endorsed thereon stating that there is, or is not, a minority interest, or a life interest, as the case may be[1].

1 Registrar's Direction (1951) 9 July.

7.06 Where a person dies intestate, or partially intestate, leaving a spouse surviving, the question whether a life interest arises by reason of the amount of the estate in respect of which there is an intestacy, is to be decided by reference not only to the amount of the estate for which the grant is sought, but to the total sum, wherever situate, that will ultimately come into the possession of the administrators.

7.07 If it is apparent from the Inland Revenue account, or otherwise, that there is further estate elsewhere, to an amount which, with the estate for which the grant is sought, causes a life interest to arise, the statutory protection of the reversioners must normally be provided by requiring two grantees. As to life or minority interest where the deceased died intestate leaving a surviving spouse, see paras. **6.82** ff., ante.

Foreign domicile

7.08 Where the deceased died domiciled elsewhere than in England and Wales, the statement in the oath as to minority or life interests should be based on the law applicable to the circumstances of the particular case, which law may not necessarily or exclusively be that of the place where the deceased was domiciled (e.g. where the estate consists of, or includes, immovable property situated in a country other than that of the domicile).

Dispensing with second administrator

7.09 The power contained in s. 114(2) of the Supreme Court Act 1981 which enables the court, where a life or minority interest arises, to appoint an individual as sole administrator came into force on 1 January 1982; previously two individuals (or a trust corporation, with or without an individual) was the statutory minimum requirement.

7.10 The district judge or registrar has a complete discretion to dispense with a second administrator, save that he must be satisfied that to appoint a sole individual administrator in any such case appears to be expedient in all the circumstances. No firm or exhaustive guidelines can be given of instances in which the discretionary power will be exercised, but it has been exercised, in the following types of case:

(a) where the proposed administrator is a solicitor or an accountant; or
(b) where the proposed administrator is a surviving spouse and the amount of the estate only slightly exceeds the spouse's statutory entitlement on intestacy; or
(c) where the minority interest relates to a minor who will shortly attain his majority; or
(d) where the proposed administrator is a representative of a local authority.

7.11 The probate rules do not prescribe any formal mode of application for the purpose of obtaining the district judge's or registrar's dispensation. Where the district judge or registrar is to be asked to exercise his discretion under s. 114(2) of the Act of 1981, the facts should be placed before the Principal of the Probate Department at the Principal Registry or the district registrar, as the case may be, and his directions obtained. It is advisable to do this before preparing the papers to lead the grant, although the reasons for the dispensation should be stated in the oath to lead the grant or in a separate affidavit[1].

1 Registrar's Direction (1982) 16 March.

Second administrator

7.12 The second administrator should, where possible, be a person equally entitled to the grant.

7.13 For example, on an intestacy where the deceased left no spouse, a grant may be made to two of the children, or other persons taking a beneficial interest[1]; and where the deceased left a will, on clearing off executors, administration (with will) may be granted to two of the residuary legatees and devisees in trust, or, if none, to two of the other residuary legatees and devisees; or, on clearing off prior classes, to two members of a lower class under NCPR 20 (see para. **5.04**, ante).

1 As to the position when only one child has attained full age, see para. **7.28**, post.

7.14 If there is no person having an equal title to that of the first applicant, a person in the next following class of priority with a beneficial interest in the estate may be joined; e.g. on an intestacy, a spouse may take a grant jointly with a child entitled to share in the estate[1]; and where the deceased died testate, on clearing off the prior classes, a sole beneficial residuary legatee and devisee may join with any other legatee or devisee, or a creditor.

1 See also para. **7.25**, post.

7.15 The oath must include the necessary clearings showing that the second applicant is the person next entitled.

7.16 NCPR 25 provides:

'(1) A person entitled in priority to a grant of administration may, without leave, apply for a grant with a person entitled in a lower degree, provided that there is no other person entitled in a higher degree to the person to be joined, unless every other such person has renounced.

(2) Subject to paragraph (3) below, an application for leave to join with a person entitled in priority to a grant of administration a person having no right or no immediate right thereto shall be made to a district judge or registrar, and shall be supported by an affidavit by the person entitled in priority, the consent of the person proposed to be joined as administrator and such other evidence as the district judge or registrar may direct.

(3) Unless a district judge or registrar otherwise directs, there may without any such application be joined with a person entitled in priority to administration—

(a) any person who is nominated under paragraph (3) of rule 32 or paragraph (3) of rule 35;

(b) a trust corporation.'

Application for order joining co-administrator

7.17 An application for an order of the district judge or registrar for joinder of a co-administrator under NCPR 25 should be made ex parte at the registry at which the application for the grant is to be made by lodging an affidavit by the proposed first administrator setting out the facts, and the consent of the person it is desired to join as co-administrator. At the Principal Registry these documents should be lodged at the Probate Department.

7.18 The district judge or registrar may call for further evidence if he thinks fit[1], and may require any such application to be made by summons to a district judge or registrar in chambers or to a High Court judge, in chambers or open court[2]. If a registrar wishes to refer the matter to a High Court judge he must obtain the confirmation of a district judge of the Principal Registry.

1 NCPR 25(2).
2 NCPR 61(1).

7.19 No fee is payable on the application.

When district judge's or registrar's order not required

7.20 Where the person next entitled to the first applicant has renounced and the second person applying is next in order under NCPR 20, no application for a district judge's or registrar's order is necessary. Any person who appears in r. 22, and who is kin of the deceased, may be joined as second applicant if he has a beneficial interest under the intestacy.

7.21 Where the person first entitled is the only person with parental responsibility (in accordance with r. 32(1)) competent and willing to take a grant under r. 32(1) or (2) for the use and benefit of a minor who has a beneficial interest in the estate, he may nominate a person to act as co-grantee (see paras. **11.200** ff.). A trust corporation may in any case be joined as second grantee without a district judge's or registrar's order, but the consents of all persons entitled to a grant and of all persons interested in the residuary estate are necessary, unless such consents are dispensed with by the district judge or registrar (see NCPR 36(3) and paras. **9.35** ff., post).

7.22 Where the person entitled to the grant is by reason of mental incapacity incapable of managing his affairs and there is only one person competent and willing to take a grant for his use and benefit either under r. 35(2)(a)—the person authorised by the Court of Protection—or, if there is no person so authorised, under r. 35(2)(b) —the lawful attorney of the incapable person acting under a registered enduring power of attorney—or, under r. 35(2)(c)—where there is no such attorney entitled to act or if the attorney has renounced administration for the use and benefit of the incapable person, the person entitled to the residuary estate of the deceased; and a life or minority interest arises, then, unless the district judge or registrar otherwise directs, the person entitled to the grant under either r. 35(2)(a) or r. 35(2)(b) or r. 35(2)(c) may nominate his co-administrator in accordance with r. 35(4). For form of oath see Nos. 160–162 and for form of nomination see No. 63.

7.23 If it is desired to join a person who does not qualify in one of these ways, application should be made to the district judge or registrar as set out in the preceding section.

7.24   Where a grant is to be made to two persons it is immaterial that the applicants represent the interest of a single individual, whether as guardians, attorneys, or otherwise[1]. (But see 'Several branches', paras. **7.36** and **7.37**, post.)

1 President's Direction (1925) November.

Surviving spouse and minor children

7.25   In the case of an intestacy, where the deceased has left a surviving spouse and there are children (all of whom are under age) entitled to share in the estate, if it is shown in the oath that the surviving spouse is the lawful husband (or widow) of the deceased and the parent of the children with parental responsibility for them under s. 2(1) of the Children Act 1989 (or as the case may be), and that there is no guardian of the minor children with parental responsibility for any of them, the surviving spouse may nominate a fit person as co-administrator[1]. For form of oath, see No. 89 and, for nomination, see No. 62. The right to nominate is confined to cases where for the purpose of a grant a second administrator is required. It does not extend to cases in which the purpose is other than to facilitate compliance with s. 114(2) of the Supreme Court Act 1981.

1 NCPR 25(3)(a), and 32(3).

7.26   As to joinder of the Public Trustee or other trust corporation, see paras. **9.09** ff., post.

Child en ventre sa mère

7.27   It would appear that a parent does not acquire parental responsibility under the Children Act 1989 until the child is born and, therefore, until the child is born neither parent may nominate a co-administrator (see also paras. **6.112–6.115**, ante).

Only one child etc. of full age

7.28   Where the deceased has left no spouse, but several children, of whom only one is of full age, an ex parte application, supported by affidavit, should be made to the district judge or registrar for the appointment of the proposed second administrator for the purpose of joining with the child of full age in taking the grant. A person entitled to a grant in his own right will not be appointed on behalf of the minor to enable him to nominate a co-administrator[1].

1 Registrar's Direction (1955) 7 November.

7.29   The practice given in this section is applicable also in cases where kin other than children of the deceased are beneficially entitled, but it should be particularly noted: (i) that where both parents of a minor child with parental responsibility for him are alive they are entitled to apply jointly for a grant on behalf of the child[1]; and (ii) where there is only one parent with parental responsibility competent and willing to take a grant, that parent may apply with a co-administrator and (iii) that if any of the minors has a guardian with parental responsibility for him, such guardian has a right to a grant on behalf of the minor[1]; in other cases the appointment of persons to apply by the district judge or registrar is necessary.

1 NCPR 32(1).

All children under age

7.30   As to the practice in making a grant where all persons entitled to share in the estate are under age, see paras. **11.113** ff., post.

Attorney joined as second administrator

7.31   A limited grant of administration (with or without will) may be made as of course to a person entitled and the attorney of another person equally or next entitled, provided that the person entitled applying consents to a limited grant being made. The grant will be limited until further representation be granted. The consent should be given in writing, and may take the form of specific wording included in the oath. Form of oath, No. 97.

7.32   If the person entitled applying does not consent to such a limitation, the attorney of the person equally or next entitled must be joined by district judge's or registrar's order under NCPR 25(2)[1], and the donor of the power will have no right subsequently to displace his attorney and obtain a grant himself.

1 Registrar's Direction (1949) 22 February.

7.33   On application for such an order, the district judge or registrar will usually require the consent of the donor of the power to an unlimited grant which may permanently exclude him, unless the attorney is expressly appointed for the purpose of being joined with the other person entitled who is applying and no limitation as to the duration of the attorney's powers is mentioned in the appointment.

7.34   This practice does not apply where the person entitled who is applying is an executor: an executor may not take a grant jointly with the attorney of another executor or of a person with a lower title, because the executor is entitled to a grant of probate whereas the grant to the attorney must be of administration (with will).

Attorney of spouse, and a person joined

7.35   Where the attorney of a husband or widow of an intestate applies for a grant jointly with a person having a vested interest in the estate of the intestate, the grant is limited for the use and benefit of the donor of the power and until further representation be granted[1], thus the spouse's priority under NCPR 22 is preserved.

1 Following the principle in *Re Rose* (1940) October.

Several branches

7.36   Where several branches of a family are all under age and equally entitled to a grant, it is desirable, when practicable, that the applicants for a grant should represent the several branches of the family.

7.37   If a member of one branch is of age and entitled in his own right to a grant, it is desirable that the other grantee should represent one of the other branches[1].

1 Registrar's Circular, 14 May 1926.

Joinder of other persons

7.38   Where the whole estate and sole right to a grant vest in one person, as in the case of a universal legatee, but it is desired to join another as co-grantee, a district judge's or registrar's order is required under r. 25(2), unless the co-grantee is a trust corporation. The application for an order is made ex parte, supported by affidavit and the consent of the proposed co-administrator, to the district judge or registrar (NCPR 25). For procedure, see paras. **7.17–7.19**, ante.

Company other than a trust corporation

7.39   On an application for a grant on behalf of a corporate body other than a trust corporation, where a minority or life interest arises, two nominees or attorneys are normally required. (See paras. **5.201–5.207** as to grant.)

Addition of representative after grant has issued

7.40   Section 114(4) of the Supreme Court Act 1981[1] provides that, if there be only one personal representative (not being a trust corporation) then, during the minority of a beneficiary or the subsistence of a life interest, and until the estate is fully administered, the court may (in accordance with probate rules), on the application of any person interested or of the guardian, or receiver of any such person, appoint one or more additional personal representatives to act.

1 See p. 845, post.

7.41   This procedure is not confined to grants of administration: where there is a minority or life interest, an additional personal representative may, if desired, be appointed to act with a sole, or sole surviving, executor[1]. But an appointment of an additional personal representative under s. 114(4) to act with an executor does not have the effect of including him in any chain of representation (s. 114(5)). As to chain of executorship, see paras. **4.64–4.84**, ante.

1 Registrar's Direction (1971) 31 December. As to the meaning of the expression 'personal representative', see *Re Brooks, Public Trustee v White* [1928] Ch 214.

7.42   Although under s. 114(2) of the Supreme Court Act 1981 the general rule is that where there is any minority or life interest administration may not be granted to less than two individuals, s. 114(4) is merely permissive; there is no requirement that on the death of one administrator during the subsistence of a minority or a life interest another must be appointed. Nevertheless, in such circumstances it may often be advantageous to apply for the appointment of an additional personal representative.

Practice

7.43   Under NCPR 26:

'(1) An application under section 114(4) of the Act to add a personal representative shall be made to a district judge or registrar and shall be supported by an affidavit by the applicant, the consent of the person proposed to be added as personal representative and such other evidence as the district judge or registrar may require.

(2) On any such application the district judge or registrar may direct that a note shall be made on the original grant of the addition of a further personal representative, or he may impound or revoke the grant or make such other order as the circumstances of the case may require.'

7.44   The application should be made ex parte at the registry from which the grant issued by lodging an affidavit as to the facts, the consent of the proposed substituted or additional administrator and the grant. At the Principal Registry these documents should be lodged with the Record Keeper.

7.45   The affidavit in support of the application, in addition to giving the details of the grant, should show that there is still a minority or life interest, or, where the grant was originally made to a sole administrator, that such an interest has now arisen.

7.46   Upon the making of the order, the grant and records are noted with the appointment of the substituted or additional administrator.

7.47   No fee is payable in respect of the application.

Substitution or removal of a personal representative

7.48   The power of the High Court to substitute or remove a personal representative, under s. 50 of the Administration of Justice Act 1985, is exercised in the Chancery Division. For the practice see Chap. 41.

CHAPTER 8

Inland Revenue accounts

Summary

Necessity for account

8.01 The Supreme Court Act 1981, s. 109 provides that subject to arrangements made between the President of the Family Division and the Commissioners of Inland Revenue, the High Court shall not make any grant or reseal any grant except on production of an account receipted or certified by the Commissioners of Inland Revenue to show inheritance tax or capital transfer tax payable on delivery of that account has been paid, or that no tax is payable. The Inland Revenue account is ultimately sent by the registry to the Commissioners of Inland Revenue, subsequently to the issue of the grant. The requirement to deliver such an account to the Commissioners is provided by the Inheritance Tax Act (formerly the Capital Transfer Tax Act) 1984, s. 216, which itself consolidated the Finance Act 1975, Sch. 4, para 2[1].

---

1 See p. 907, post. The management and collection of inheritance tax, capital transfer tax and of the former British death duties are by statute vested in the Commissioners of Inland Revenue. The business relative to the tax and to these duties is transacted in a special office of the Inland Revenue Department called the Capital Taxes Office, and enquiries concerning the tax and any of the duties in question should be addressed to the Controller of that Office at Ferrers House, PO Box 38, Castle Meadow Road, Nottingham, NG2 1BB tel. 0115 9740000, Document Exchange: DX 701201 Nottingham 4, Fax: 0115 9742432.

    For some account of the pre-1694 duties payable to the ecclesiastical courts, see Chap. II of Soward and Willan's *Taxation of Capital* (London, 1919).

    A brief history of, and the practice relating to, the probate duty payable before 2 August 1894 will be found in earlier editions of this work. The appropriate forms of affidavit were form B where the gross estate did not exceed £300 and form A for all other cases.

    The law and practice relating to estate duty will be found in the twenty-fourth edition of this work, while the transitional period between the introduction of capital transfer tax on 27 March 1974 and the abolition of estate duty on and after 13 March 1975 is covered by the second (cumulative) supplement to the twenty-fourth edition. Note: the rate at which interest accrues in respect of unpaid estate duty has been altered from time to time in uniformity with the rates of interest accruing on unpaid inheritance and capital transfer tax chargeable on death: see 'Assessment', below.

8.02 The Inheritance Tax (formerly Capital Transfer Tax) Act 1984, s. 256(1), which consolidated the Finance Act 1980, s. 94(1), empowers the Commissioners of Inland Revenue to make regulations inter alia to dispense with this requirement. In pursuance of that power the Capital Transfer Tax (Delivery of Accounts) Regulations 1981[1] as amended[2] provide the concept of the 'excepted estate'. So, if:

— the total gross value of the estate[3] does not exceed £145,000[4]; and
— the estate comprises only property which passes by will or intestacy, by nomination, or by survivorship in joint tenancy; and
— not more than £15,000[5] consists of property situated outside the United Kingdom; and
— the deceased died domiciled in the United Kingdom having made no lifetime gifts chargeable to either inheritance tax[6] or capital transfer tax;

then the estate is an excepted estate and applicants for a grant of representation are not required to deliver an account or to swear to the exact value of the estate to obtain a grant. Instead they are required to swear in the oath as to the limits within which the estate falls. For the purposes of these limits, it is the value of the deceased's beneficial interest, and not the entirety value, of survivorship property which falls to be taken into account. It should be noted that an estate would not be an excepted estate if the deceased had an interest in settled property or had made lifetime transfers which became chargeable with tax by reason or his or her death within seven years thereafter, or (on or after 18 March 1986) had gifted property subject to a reservation which subsisted up to, or within seven years before, the date of death.

1 S.I. 1981 No. 880, which came into operation on 1 August 1981.
2 Capital Transfer Tax (Delivery of Accounts) (No. 3) Regulations 1983, S.I. 1983 No. 1039 with effect from 1 April 1983; and Inheritance Tax (Delivery of Accounts) Regulations 1987, S.I. 1987 No. 1127 with effect from 1 April 1987, S.I. 1989 No. 1078 with effect from 1 April 1989, S.I. 1990 No. 1110 with effect from 1 April 1990, S.I. 1991 No. 1248 with effect from 1 April 1991, and S.I. 1995 No. 1461 with effect from 6 April 1995.
3 Estate for this purpose has the extended meaning as for inheritance tax and capital transfer tax.
4 £125,000 in the case of a death before 6 April 1995; £115,000 in the case of a death before 1 April 1991; £100,000 in the case of a death before 1 April 1990; £70,000 in the case of a death before 1 April 1989; £40,000 in the case of a death before 1 April 1987; £25,000 in the case of a death before 1 April 1983.
5 £10,000 in the case of a death before 1 April 1989; £2,000 in the case of a death before 1 April 1987; £1,000 in the case of a death before 1 April 1983.
6 This is considered in para. **8.12**, post.

8.03 The foregoing procedure may be used in any case where the criterion of an excepted estate is wholly met—not only in the case of first grants which are not limited in nature but also in cases, for example, of applications for grants de bonis non or where a fresh grant is to be made following revocation of an original grant. The Commissioners of Inland Revenue retain the right to call for an account by giving notice in writing within 35 days of the date of issue of the first grant other than a limited grant. If a person, having obtained a grant without delivery of an account, later discovers that the estate is not in fact an excepted estate he or she must deliver an account of all the property comprised in the estate within six months of making that discovery.

Inheritance tax and capital transfer tax

Introduction

8.04   The Finance Act 1986, s. 100 provided that after its Royal Assent the tax charged under the Capital Transfer Tax Act 1984 should be known as inheritance tax, that that Act be cited accordingly, and that all references to capital transfer tax in contemporaneous or earlier enactments have effect as references to inheritance tax. A liability arising before 25 July 1986, then, remains a liability for capital transfer tax.

8.05   The Capital Transfer Tax Act had received its Royal Assent on 31 July 1984 and had been enacted to consolidate the legislation contained in successive Finance Acts from 1975. Statutory references in this chapter will henceforth be to 'the 1984 Act' (and in footnotes to 'IHTA 1984') followed in square brackets by the appropriate reference to earlier provisions prior to consolidation. Inheritance tax and capital transfer tax will be referred to simply as 'tax' unless the context requires otherwise. The following text is of necessity no more than a summary of the more commonly encountered provisions which can apply in connection with the death of an individual. Practitioners are referred in cases where more detailed explanation is required to a standard work such as *Dymond's Capital Taxes*.

Scope of the tax

8.06   The efficacy of the tax depends upon a tree of concepts at the root of which is the—undefined—'disposition'. A liability for tax becomes a possibility if a disposition is a 'transfer of value': that is to say it is made by a person and, as a result, the estate of that person is less than it otherwise would have been[1]. The amount by which the value of the estate is so decreased is known as the 'value transferred'[2]. Most dispositions are transfers of value but some are specifically provided not to be[3]. Moreover no account is taken of 'excluded property'[4]. If a transfer of value is made by an individual (as distinct from a person) and is not an 'exempt transfer'[5] or a potentially exempt transfer[6] then it is a 'chargeable transfer' and tax is chargeable[7] upon the value transferred[8]. The 'exempt transfer' needs no elaboration here; but a 'potentially exempt transfer' would become a chargeable transfer upon the death of the transferor within seven years thereafter.

1   See note 3 to para. **8.02** as to the meaning of 'estate'.
2   IHTA 1984, s. 3(1) [FA 1975, s. 20(2)].
3   IHTA 1984, ss. 10–17 [e.g. FA 1975, ss. 20(4) and 46; FA 1976, ss. 89–92].
4   IHTA 1984, s. 3(2) [FA 1975, s. 20(3)] (see e.g. IHTA 1984, s. 6 [FA 1975, s. 24(2) and Sch. 7, paras. 3(1), 5(1) and 6]).
5   IHTA 1984, ss. 18 ff. [e.g. FA 1975, Sch. 6].
6   IHTA 1984, s. 3A in relation to events on and after 18 March 1986.
7   IHTA 1984, s. 2 [FA 1975, s. 20].
8   IHTA 1984, s. 1 [FA 1975, s. 19] (p. 903, post).

8.07   The foregoing concepts are not apt to apply in connection with an individual's death. But the legislation retrieves the position by providing that on a death tax is to be charged as though, immediately before the death, the deceased had made a transfer of value and the value transferred thereby was equal to the value of the estate immediately before the death[1]. As this notional event to which death gives rise is a transfer of value, and not merely a disposition, it follows that those dispositions ordinarily removed from the charge to tax (by virtue of being dispositions which are not transfers of value) are not so removed in connection with a death.

1 IHTA 1984, s. 4(1) [FA 1975, s. 22(1)] (p. 903, post).

8.08 The rules in relation to transfers of property by individuals and on death are augmented by special rules in relation to transfers of property by the trustees of settlements and by close companies[1].

1 IHTA 1984, Pts. III and IV [FA 1975, ss. 21 and 39 and Sch. 5].

8.09 For the purposes of the tax a person's estate is the aggregate of all the property to which he or she is beneficially entitled, except that the estate immediately before death does not include excluded property[1]. It is to be noted that the word 'property' is not limited in any way and is apt to cover both real and personal property, movable and immovable property wherever situate. Similarly, the phrase 'On the death of any person'[2] is wide enough to extend to persons wherever domiciled. However, property outside the United Kingdom is excluded property if the person beneficially entitled to it is domiciled outside the United Kingdom[3]. Excluded property also includes a reversionary interest, unless it was acquired by the deceased (or by a person previously entitled to it) for a consideration in money or money's worth. There are other exceptions[4] but generally speaking inherited reversions are excluded property unless purchased by a predecessor in title.

1 IHTA 1984, s. 5(1) [FA 1975, s. 23(1)] (p. 903, post).
2 IHTA 1984, s. 4(1) [FA 1975, s. 22(1)].
3 IHTA 1984, s. 6(1) [FA 1975, s. 24(2)] (p. 903, post). The general law of domicile is considered in Chap. 12—but there are provisions for 'deeming' a person to be domiciled in the United Kingdom for the purposes of the tax.
4 IHTA 1984, s. 48 [FA 1975, s. 24(3), FA 1976, s. 120 and FA 1981, s. 104(3)] (p. 904, post).

8.10 Besides excluded property certain other categories of property are removed from the ambit of the tax. So, for example, growing timber (in certain prescribed circumstances) is to be 'left out of account'[1], as is the value attributable to farmworkers' cottages by virtue of their suitability for more general residents[2]; whilst the charge to tax on death under s. 4 of the 1984 Act [FA 1975, s. 22] is specifically not to apply in relation to the death of a person who was, broadly speaking, killed in a war[3] and the Act is not to apply at all as respects Apsley House and the Chevening Estate[4]. And there is other such miscellany.

1 IHTA 1984, s. 125 [FA 1975, Sch. 9] and see under the sub-heading of 'Reliefs'.
2 IHTA 1984, s. 169 [FA 1975, Sch. 10, para. 12(1)].
3 IHTA 1984, s. 154 [FA 1975, Sch. 7. para. 1].
4 IHTA 1984, s. 156 [FA 1981, s. 135 and FA 1982, s. 100].

8.11 On the other hand, a person is to be treated as beneficially entitled to settled property in which he or she has a beneficial interest in possession[1], and to property over which he or she has a general power of disposition and money which he or she may charge on property, in each case other than settled property. (But there is one exception to this exclusion in relation to 'approved' superannuation schemes[2] so that, for example, a death benefit subject to an unexercised or revocably exercised power of nomination forms a part of the deceased's estate.) Additionally, a person is treated as beneficially entitled to any property being the subject of a 'gift with reservation' if the reservation concerned is still subsisting immediately before his or her death[3]. (A gift with reservation is, broadly speaking, a disposal by way of gift on or after 18 March 1986 which is to any extent subject to a reservation in favour of the donor.)

1 IHTA 1984, s. 49(1) [FA 1975, Sch. 5, para 3(1)]. This means broadly a present right of present enjoyment of the property or the income, if any, produced by it. (In *Pearson v IRC* [1981] AC 753, [1980] 2 All ER 479, HL it was held that where the trustees of a settlement have a valid power to accumulate income the beneficiaries entitled in default of exercise of that power are nevertheless prevented from having an interest in possession in the settled property for the purposes of the tax.)
2 IHTA 1984, s. 151(4) [FA 1975, Sch. 5, para. 16(4)].
3 FA 1986, s. 102(3) (p. 911, post).

Lifetime transfers: exemptions

8.12 Tax is chargeable in respect of a person's lifetime chargeable transfers as and when they occur and on a limited cumulative basis. Tax is also chargeable by reason of the death of the transferor within seven years after making such a chargeable transfer and within seven years after making a potentially exempt transfer. Accordingly, a brief outline of exemptions is given for reference[1]:

(a) All transfers between spouses, other than where the donor is domiciled in the United Kingdom but his or her spouse is not. In this case there is a limit to the exemption of £15,000 which was raised to £25,000 as from 27 October 1977, to £50,000 as from 26 March 1980 and to £55,000 as from 9 March 1982.

(b) Annual transfers by a donor up to £3,000 (£1,000 before 6 April 1976; £2,000 after 5 April 1976 and before 6 April 1981), with the amount unused in one year available for carrying forward to the next year only. If a potentially exempt transfer becomes a chargeable transfer (because the transferor fails to survive it by seven years) it is treated as having been made later in the year than any (immediately) chargeable transfer made during the same year[2].

(c) Small outright gifts to any one person, if the total of all gifts made to that person by the transferor during the year does not exceed £250. Prior to 6 April 1981 the £250 small gifts exemption (£100 before 6 April 1980) applied to each donee regardless of the total amount given.

(d) Normal expenditure out of net income (i.e., after deduction of income tax) which leaves the donor sufficient income to maintain his usual standard of living.

(e) Marriage gifts. Maximum £1,000 per donor, but extended to £5,000 where the rnarriage took place before 13 March 1975, or the donor is a parent of either party to the marriage. The maximum limit of £1,000 is extended to £2,500 for a gift made by a more remote ancestor, or by one of the parties to a marriage to the other.

(f) All transfers to United Kingdom charities. It should be noted however that, in relation to deaths before 15 March 1983, the exemption was limited, where the transfer occurred on or within one year before the death of the transferor, to £250,000 (£200,000 for deaths before 9 March 1982 and £100,000 for deaths before 26 March 1980).

(g) All transfers to political parties with two members elected to the House of Commons, or one such member and not less than 150,000 votes, at the general election before the transfer concerned. It should be noted, however, that in relation to deaths before 15 March 1988 the exemption was limited, where the transfer occurred on or within one year before the death of the transferor, to £100,000.

(h) Transfers to heritage bodies, local authorities, government departments and universities and transfers for the public benefit are exempt without limit.

1 IHTA 1984, ss. 18–29 [FA 1975, Sch. 6 as amended].
2 IHTA 1984, s. 19(3A) as inserted by the FA 1986, s. 101(1) and Sch. 19, para. 5.

Rates of tax

8.13 Tax is chargeable if the total for rate exceeds the contemporary threshold, presently £154,000. The total for rate is found by aggregating the value transferred by the instant transfer with the cumulative total of the values transferred by any chargeable transfers made by the transferor within the previous seven years[1]. This does not involve a series of fixed seven year periods but a moving seven year cumulation period from which successive transfers fall away as time passes. The rate of tax chargeable can be summarised as follows:

(a) For deaths on and after 6 April 1995 the rate of tax on values in excess of £154,000 is 40 per cent but there is a taper relief in the form of a percentage reduction in the tax payable in respect of any chargeable transfer which occurred more than three years but less than seven years before the date of death[2]. If the transfer was a chargeable transfer immediately (as distinct from being a potentially exempt transfer) then any tax paid at that time is allowed as a credit against the tax payable in connection with the death. (A chargeable transfer made before 18 March 1986, however, is chargeble at the death rate only if made within three years before the transferor's death.)

(b) For deaths before 15 March 1988 but on or after 18 March 1986 the position is at (a) save that in place of the flat rate of 40 per cent there was a progressively banded table of rates[3].

(c) For deaths before 18 March 1986 but on or after 10 March 1981 the cumulation period was ten years. There were two rate tables and tax in respect of the deceased's estate and any chargeable transfers made within three years before the death were charged according to the first table[4]. All other lifetime chargeable transfers were chargeable according to the second table. Any tax paid under the second table was allowed as a credit pro tanto against tax payable by reason of the transferor's death within three years after the transfer.

(d) For deaths before 10 March 1981 but on or after 13 March 1975 the position was as at (c) save that instead of a moving cumulation period of ten years there was a fixed period which commenced on 27 March 1974.

1 IHTA 1984, s. 7 as amended by the FA 1986, s. 101(1) and Sch. 19, para. 2 [FA 1975, s. 37 as amended by the FA 1981, s. 93(1)].
2 IHTA 1984, s. 7 as amended by the FA 1986, Sch. 19, para. 2.
3 See Appendix IV, pp. 967 ff., post.
4 See Appendix IV, pp. 967 ff., post.

Incidence of tax

8.14 In general, the tax is a charge on the property[1]. But personal or movable property situate in the United Kingdom which was beneficially owned by the deceased immediately before death and vests in the personal representatives is not subject to the Inland Revenue charge; and for this purpose 'personal property' includes leaseholds and undivided shares in land held on trust for sale, whether statutory or not[2].

1 IHTA 1984, s. 237(1) [FA 1975, Sch. 4, para. 20(1)].
2 IHTA 1984, s. 237(3) [FA 1975, Sch. 4, para. 20(3)].

8.15   Thus the tax on the deceased's freely disposable personal estate is a testamentary expense and subject to any express provision in the will is payable with other testamentary expenses out of residue[1] after providing for pecuniary legacies and specific legacies. Much the same applies as respects free realty in the case of deaths on and after 26 July 1983[2]. Tax in respect of real estate and property outside the United Kingdom is a charge on that property.

In the cases of:

— heritage property granted conditional exemption from tax until disposal by sale or otherwise or until a breach of the statutory undertakings under ss. 30 ff. of the 1984 Act [FA 1975, ss. 31 ff. or FA 1976, ss. 76 ff.];

— woodlands left out of account until disposal by sale or otherwise under ss. 125 ff. of the 1984 Act [FA 1975, s. 36 and Sch. 9]

the person liable to pay the tax on any chargeable event with respect to the property is normally the person entitled to receive the proceeds of any sale. If the chargeable event were a sale the tax would be payable from the sale proceeds.

1   *Re Clemow, Yeo v Clemow* [1900] 2 Ch 182 at 195, 'the Court could not have refused to treat Probate Duty as a testamentary expense ... the Estate Duty which takes its place is also a testamentary expense'. Similarly, inheritance tax and capital transfer tax which replace estate duty are testamentary expenses insofar as, like the earlier duties, they are not charged on specific property.
2   IHTA 1984, s. 211 [F(No. 2)A 1983, s. 13] (p. 906, post).

8.16   While the question of the fund for the payment of tax is mainly one of administration, this has now become of importance in the assessment of tax where the estate is partially exempt as to gifts such as to a surviving spouse or charities.

Disclosure of information and payment of tax before issue of grant

8.17   The necessity for an account of the deceased's estate pursuant to the 1984 Act [FA 1975, Part III] and the exceptions from this general rule have already been mentioned at the beginning of this chapter. Part VIII of the 1984 Act [FA 1975, Sch. 4] deals with the administration and collection of the tax. Section 216 [para. 2] requires the personal representatives (other than those applying for a settled land grant and save where the exception already referred to applies) to deliver an account of all the property which formed part of the deceased's estate immediately before the death, 'estate' having the wide meaning in s. 5 [s. 23] of the Act. The personal representatives are liable for the tax on unsettled property and on settled land devolving on or vesting in them. In the case of settled property the trustees of the settlement, inter alia, are liable. Where, however, the personal representatives have paid tax which is a charge on the property, tax shall where occasion requires be repaid to them by the person in whom the property is vested[1]. Tax is due six months after the end of the month in which the death occurs, unless it may be paid by instalments[2]. Personal representatives must deliver the account of the estate within twelve months of the death, or within three months from first acting, if later[3]. Subject to exceptions shown below, they must on delivery of their account pay all the tax for which they are liable[4] and may on such delivery also pay any tax for which they are not liable, if requested by the persons liable therefor. The liability of a personal representative for tax extends to the assets which he has received, or might have received but for his own neglect or default[5]. This condition is most strictly enforced, as is shown by a series of cases relating to estate duty (in relation to which there were similar provisions) in which the probate registrars have declined to allow a grant of representation to issue in default of their fulfilment.

Thus in *Re Beech's Goods* (1904) Times, 9 August, the testator, who died in 1904, had by his will directed his executors—

> 'not to publish or make known after my decease and on proof of my will in any manner whatever the value of my real or personal estate nor any of the provisions contained in this my will, and also to do all in their power to prevent the Government authorities or any other person or persons publishing or divulging the value of my real or personal estate.'

On the strength of this testamentary request, the executors attempted to obtain probate on an Inland Revenue affidavit disclosing a nominal estate only. But the Probate Registry declined to admit the will to probate in the absence of an Inland Revenue affidavit fully disclosing the property passing on the death of the deceased, and this decision was upheld on the matter being referred to the court. The same line was followed in *Re Grimthorpe's Goods, Beal v Grimthorpe* (1905) Times, 8 August, in which the court having ordered the issue of a grant pendente lite, limited to one year's income of the estate, it was, at the outset, sought to proceed on an Inland Revenue affidavit not accounting for the estate duty in respect of the entire personal estate of which the deceased was competent to dispose. Similarly in *Re Horrex* (1910) Times, 9 March, in which case proceedings were being taken against an executor under the Crown Suits, &c., Act 1865[6], an Act applied to the estate duty by the Finance Act 1894, s. 8(1)[7], the court declined to allow the matter to proceed in the absence of an Inland Revenue affidavit complying with the requirements of s. 6(2)[8] of the 1894 Act.

1 IHTA 1984, s. 211 [FA 1975, s. 28; F(No. 2)A 1983, s. 13] (p. 906, post).
2 See paras. **8.21–8.23**, post.
3 IHTA 1984, s. 216(6) [FA 1975, Sch. 4, para. 2(5)] (p. 908, post).
4 IHTA 1984, s. 226(2) [FA 1975, Sch. 4, para. 12(2)] (p. 908, post). See the following cases relating to estate duty: per Kekewich J, in *Re Clemow, Yeo v Clemow* [1900] 2 Ch 18, at 195, 'a will could not be proved without paying the Probate Duty, and it was just the same with administration. . . . In either case the Probate Duty has to be paid. . . . I cannot myself see the difference between the Estate Duty, the payment of which is a necessary incident to the obtaining of the grant.'
   Per Swinfen Eady J, in *Re King, Travers v Kelly* [1904] 1 Ch 363 at 367, 'the Probate Duty was, and now the Estate Duty on personalty is, a payment which must be made before probate can be obtained, and it must be paid on delivering the Inland Revenue affidavit'.
   Per Lord Shaw of Dunfermline, in *Winans v A-G* [1910] AC 27 at 49, 'payment of Estate Duty is made a peremptory condition of probate'.
5 IHTA 1984, ss. 200(1)(a) and 204(1) [FA 1975, ss. 25(5)(a) and 27(1)] (pp. 905, 906, post).
6 8 Halsbury's Statutes (3rd edn) 838.
7 12 Halsbury's Statutes (3rd edn) 472.
8 12 Halsbury's Statutes (3rd edn) 465.

Grants for provisional amounts only

8.18   It is only in the most exceptional cases that any relaxation of the above rule is conceded and that a grant is allowed to issue showing property only 'so far as can at present be ascertained'. But where any particular case is so circumstanced as, in the opinion of the parties, to render it imperative that the grant should issue before full particulars of the deceased's estate can be ascertained, the facts should, in the first instance, be laid before the Controller of the Capital Taxes Office, as an Inland Revenue account disclosing the estate at a provisional figure only will not be accepted by the probate registrars in the absence of the concurrence of the Commissioners of Inland Revenue, which concurrence, however, as above mentioned, is only given in cases of the most exceptional or urgent type. In such cases the applicant for the grant is required to include his best possible estimate, after making full enquiries, of all taxable property wherever situate and not a *nominal* amount. It is not necessary in any such case to give an undertaking to pay any additional fees which may become due to the Registry.

Exceptions

(1) Particular assets not ascertained

8.19   Where the personal representatives, after making the fullest enquiries that are reasonably practicable in the circumstances, are unable to ascertain the exact value of any particular property, their account shall in the first instance be sufficient as regards that property if it contains a statement to that effect, a provisional estimate of the value of the property and an undertaking to deliver a further account of it as soon as its value is ascertained[1].

1   IHTA 1984, s. 216(3)(a) [FA 1975, Sch. 4, para. 2(2)(a)] (p. 907, post).

(2) Exemptions, reliefs and excluded property

8.20   Exemptions and reliefs are considered below. Reference to foreign movable and immovable property and reversionary interests falling within the category of excluded property is made above in connection with the scope of the tax.

(3) Property on which tax may be paid by instalments ('Instalment-option property')

8.21   Where the person paying tax in respect of property in the prescribed categories, by notice in writing to the Commissioners of Inland Revenue elects[1], while the property remains unsold, payment may be made by ten annual instalments (or, in the case of a death before 15 March 1983, by eight yearly or sixteen half-yearly instalments) the first payable six months after the end of the month in which the death occurred. If an account to lead to a grant of representation is not delivered until after the date on which tax has become payable in respect of instalment-option property, the tax on such property so far as already payable and for which the personal representatives are liable must be paid on delivery of the account. On the sale of whole or part, the unpaid tax (or in the case of a sale of part, the proportionate part of the unpaid tax) will become payable together with the accrued interest, although not on a date earlier than the date on which the tax was otherwise due.

1   IHTA 1984, ss. 227 to 229 [FA 1975, Sch. 4, paras. 13 to 15].

8.22   The prescribed categories are:

— land;
— shares or securities which gave the deceased control of the company immediately before the death;
— unquoted shares or securities[1] if:
    (i)   the tax on them, together with the tax on any other property entitled to the instalment option for which the same person is liable, is not less than 20 per cent of that person's total liability, or
    (ii)   the tax cannot be paid in one sum without undue hardship;
— unquoted shares[1] exceeding £20,000 (£5,000 in the case of a death before 15 March 1983) in value provided the holding is not less than 10 per cent of the shares or ordinary shares of the company;

— a business or an interest in a business. The business must be carried on for gain and includes a business carried on in the exercise of a profession or vocation; and

— woodlands.

1 In relation to deaths before 17 March 1987 and on or after 10 March 1992, the term 'unquoted shares and securities' includes shares dealt in on the Unlisted Securities Market.

8.23 Inland Revenue accounts provide for the written election to pay tax in instalments to be exercised. It is understood that the Board of Inland Revenue will accept payment of tax in full notwithstanding an election to pay in instalments. But it is understood too that if the election is not so exercised and tax is paid in full the option will be spent—so that it will not be possible to obtain a refund of tax paid and switch to payment in instalments. Such a failure to exercise the option to pay in instalments can have unwelcome consequences: certain categories of instalment option property carry interest on tax only from the date the instalment concerned becomes due[1]; and so were such property to be sold during the instalment period, and the option to pay in instalments had not been exercised, interest would be payable on the whole amount of the tax from its due date rather than upon so many of the instalments as might by then have become due.

1 IHTA 1984, s. 234 [FA 1975, Sch. 4, para. 16].

Grants on credit

Practice as to grants on credit

8.24 The Commissioners of Inland Revenue may allow the applicant to postpone the payment of tax on such terms as they think fit, where excessive sacrifice would be caused by raising the full tax at once rather than later. In view of the facilities normally available for raising tax, the Commissioners of Inland Revenue use these powers sparingly and only after, and to the extent that, they are fully satisfied that every effort short of excessive sacrifice has been made to raise the tax due. The relief is not given merely because some sacrifice can be shown; the sacrifice envisaged is excessive and must in fact be greater than is customary or normal in prevailing conditions. In such cases application should be made to the Controller of the Capital Taxes Office. The applicant should give full details of the estate, preferably by way of the Inland Revenue account, relate the steps taken and the difficulties encountered in attempting to raise the tax due, and state the maximum amount raisable irrespective of any sacrifice entailed, preferably in the form of a letter from the bank or other source approached. Should the Commissioners of Inland Revenue be willing to postpone the payment of all or part of the tax they will normally require an undertaking as to payment of, and the provision of security for, any postponed tax. Specific proposals for payment within a reasonable time, showing how it is intended to raise the tax, should be made in the application. The availability of the grant obtained after the Commissioners of Inland Revenue have exercised their powers of postponement is not usually restricted, at any rate while any undertaking as to payment is duly observed and any security taken remains adequate.

Current forms

8.25   The current forms of Inland Revenue account (that is to say in relation to deaths on and after 18 March 1986) are shown in the table below. (Forms for capital transfer tax and estate duty are considered below.)

Forms of Inland Revenue account

Forms of account	*Grants for which applicable*
IHT 200 (1993)	Original grant where the deceased died domiciled in some part of the United Kingdom
IHT 201 (1993)	Original grant where the deceased died domiciled outside the United Kingdom
IHT 200	Predecessor of IHT 200 (1993). Still acceptable for use
IHT 201	Predecessor of IHT 201 (1993). Still acceptable for use
IHT 202 (1993)	Original grant where the deceased died domiciled in the United Kingdom and the whole of the estate was situate in the United Kingdom, the deceased had not made any chargeable transfers within 7 years of death and had no interest in settled property, the net estate after exemptions and reliefs does not exceed the inheritance tax threshold at death and the gross estate before exemptions and reliefs does not exceed twice the threshold. [Note: An instructional booklet IHT 210 is available in respect of the above accounts.]
IHT 204	For completion at the request of the Inland Revenue following the issue of an 'excepted estate' grant
Cap A5C	De bonis non, double probate and cessate grants

Forms IHT 200, 201 and 202 (1993)

8.26   These forms are designed to disclose (1) the full name and description of the deceased, together with the dates of birth and death and where it is claimed he or she was domiciled[1]; (2) the full name, address and description of the applicant for the grant; and (3) particulars of the property to be covered by the grant. They then make provision for the deponent to certify the correctness of the accompanying schedules of the property in respect of which tax is payable (or would be payable if tax were payable on estates however small their principal value) and of its value; and of the schedules of the debts and incumbrances which are deductible in arriving at the amounts, if any, chargeable with tax.

1 See Chap. 12. Where a domicile in the United Kingdom is deemed by s. 267 of the 1984 Act [FA 1975, s. 45], p. 909, post, property outside the United Kingdom should be included in Section 4 of the Inland Revenue account IHT 201 so far as Section 3 is not appropriate.

8.27   Any limitation to the grant (or reseal) for which application is made must be indicated in the declaration on page 12 of the IHT 200 (1993) or IHT 201 (1993). Examples of relevant limitations are:

(a)   pending suit or ad colligenda bona;

(b)   limited to prosecuting or defending a specified action;

(c)   limited to, or excluding, a particular part of, or type of estate; such as, realty; personalty; immovable; movable; literary estate; estate in Wales; settled land; or exclusive of settled land.

8.28 In the case of an application for a grant of administration *with will* this should be expressly stated in the declaration on page 12. No reference to codicils to be proved with a will is necessary.

8.29 With the abolition of resealing as between the constituent countries of the United Kingdom by the Administration of Estates Act 1971[1], applications for grants in respect of the estates of persons dying domiciled in any part of the United Kingdom should be made in the country of domicile. The application should be made for a grant covering the assets in all parts of the United Kingdom. Thus in the case of a person dying domiciled in England and Wales, a grant of representation from the High Court in that part of the United Kingdom by reference to an Inland Revenue account IHT 200 will be recognised throughout the United Kingdom of England and Wales, Scotland and Northern Ireland without the necessity for resealing.

1 See p. 799, post.

8.30 The Administration of Estates Act 1971, by s. 12(3) as amended, expressly provides that it does not affect the liability of any person for, or alter the incidence of, tax[1]. For this purpose, Great Britain includes England, Wales and Scotland. It does not include the Channel Islands or the Isle of Man. Since 31 March 1923 the United Kingdom is Great Britain as defined above, and Northern Ireland. Before 22 November 1921 the United Kingdom included the whole of Ireland. For the purpose of death duties, Northern Ireland separated on 22 November 1921, but remained part of the United Kingdom while—what is now—Eire separated on 1 April 1923.

1 See p. 803, post. (FA 1975, Sch. 12, para. 1 and FA 1986, s. 100 secure the extension of the reference to estate duty to capital transfer tax and inheritance tax.)

8.31 Where the deceased has died domiciled in Northern Ireland and no grant of representation has been obtained there, a separate grant may still be extracted in Great Britain limited to that part of Great Britain where application is made[1]. In such a case a separate Inland Revenue account must be delivered to the Capital Taxes Office, Belfast.

1 See Chap. 12—Grant where deceased died domiciled out of England and Wales—post.

8.32 IHT 202 (1993) is a shortened form of Inland Revenue account, provided for use in simple cases as shown in the table of forms. Instructions for completion are provided in IHT 210. However, it should be in view that the applicant for the grant is not allowed to amend the declaration on page 4 of the IHT 202 (1993) relating to settled property and gifts.

8.33 Detailed treatment of the separate sections of IHT 200 (1993) and IHT 201 (1993) will be found under 'Practice—Completion of account'[1]. In subsequent references to the appropriate form to be used for an original grant it should be kept in mind that IHT 200 (1993) is appropriate to a domicile in a part of the United Kingdom (apart from small cases for which IHT 202 (1993) is appropriate) while IHT 201 (1993) should be used in all cases where the deceased died domiciled outside the United Kingdom, even though a domicile in the United Kingdom may be deemed for the purposes of the tax.

1 See paras. **8.47** ff., post.

Settled land[1]

8.34   If the grant is only required for land which was settled before the death and continues to be settled thereafter, the declaration on page 12 should state 'limited to the settled land of which true particulars and value are given in Section 3B'.

1 See Chap. 10, post.

No estate (other than trust property)

8.35   Either IHT 200 (1993) or IHT 201 (1993) is also appropriate in the case of a person who left no estate in the jurisdiction (other than property of which he was a trustee only). Pages 1 and 12 only of the form need to be completed. This applies both to cases where a grant is required in order to deal with trust property, and also to other cases where the grant is sought notwithstanding that the deceased left no estate within the jurisdiction[1]. Where a grant limited to trust property is applied for under the Supreme Court Act 1981, s. 113(1)[2], in a case where the deceased had property of his own in the jurisdiction, the form appropriate to the deceased's own estate should be used, and the applicant should give particulars and value thereof to the best of his knowledge and belief, even if he is not accountable for the relative tax.

1 See Chap. 4—'Requirements on proving a will'—paras. **4.87** ff., ante.
2 See p. 844, post.

Double probate, de bonis non and cessate grants: Cap A5C[1]

8.36   This form is for use in cases whenever the deceased died—at any rate since 1 August 1894—and application is being made for a grant de bonis non, or for a grant of double probate, or for a cessate grant, where the estate to be covered by the new grant was within the operation of the previous grant. If the estate was not within the operation of the previous grant, the form of Inland Revenue account as for an original grant should be used. Among the cases to which Cap A5C is *not* applicable are a full grant following a grant pending suit or ad colligenda bona, a grant caeterorum, and a fresh grant following the revocation of the previous grant.

1 Cap A5C is obtainable on application to the Controller, Capital Taxes Office, Ferrers House, PO Box 38, Castle Meadow Road, Nottingham NG2 1BB, tel. 0115 9740000.

8.37   In cases of second or subsequent grants where it is found that, although the unadministered estate was within the previous grant, yet, for some reason, tax has not been paid on the whole or part of such unadministered estate, the outstanding tax must first be paid and is accepted on a corrective account, for no provision is made for the payment of any tax on the Cap A5C, the summary of this form consisting merely of a certificate showing that the Commissioners of Inland Revenue offer no objection to the issue of the proposed grant.

8.38   The form, when completed, should be sent directly to the appropriate Probate Registry, without prior reference to the Capital Taxes Office. Where the deceased died domiciled in England and Wales or Scotland, the unadministered property situate in the United Kingdom (i.e., in Great Britain and Northern Ireland) should be shown in Account 'A', valued at the date of the account. In all other cases, only the unadministered property situate in Great Britain should be shown.

8.39 In cases where the death concerned occurred before 13 March 1975 estate duty rather than tax would be in point and the foregoing paragraphs should be read accordingly, mutatis mutandis. In cases where the estate was originally accounted for in Ireland, the duty (if any) being United Kingdom estate duty, it is necessary first to obtain from the Revenue Commissioners at Dublin a certificate specifying the unadministered assets and stating that duty was paid (or not payable) thereon.

Second or subsequent grants where Cap A5C not applicable

8.40 In cases of second or subsequent grants where Cap A5C is not applicable, but the full tax was duly paid on the application for the first grant, it is necessary, if a second payment of tax is to be avoided, to obtain a transfer of the receipt and stamp from the original to the new account. Application should be made to the Controller, Capital Taxes Office by a letter accompanying the new account and setting out the circumstances fully. Where the applicant for the new grant did not himself pay the tax, either it must be stated, if such be the fact, that the tax was paid out of moneys forming part of the estate, or a consent to the desired transfer, signed by the person who paid the tax (or, if that person is dead, by his or her legal personal representative), must be annexed[1]. Again, references to 'tax' should be read as references to estate duty where the death occurred before 13 March 1975.

1 This transfer procedure is also appropriate for a first grant when, after an Inland Revenue account has been receipted, the application is rejected by the Registry and a fresh application is being made.

Capital transfer tax and estate duty forms

8.41 In the case of a death on or after 13 March 1975 and before 18 March 1986, capital transfer tax was the relevant tax on death. The forms of account are as follows:

Forms of account	*Grants for which applicable*
Cap 200	Original grant where the deceased died on or after 27 March 1981 domiciled in some part of the United Kingdom.
Cap 201	Original grant where the deceased died on or after 27 March 1981 domiciled outside the United Kingdom.
Cap 200	As for Cap 200 above where the death occurred on or after 13 March 1975 and before 27 March 1981.
Cap 201	As for Cap 201 above where the death occurred on or after 13 March 1975 and before 27 March 1981.
	[*Note*: instructional leaflets Cap 213 (in relation to Cap 200 and 201) and Cap form 213 (in relation to Cap forms 200 and 201) are available.]
Cap 202	Original—full—grant where the deceased died on or after 27 March 1981 domiciled in some part of the United Kingdom, and the estate comprises—only—property passing under the will or intestacy or by nomination or beneficially by survivorship, and all such property was situate in the United Kingdom, and the total net value of the estate after any exemptions and reliefs available does not exceed the contemporary threshold at which tax becomes payable.
Cap Form 202	Available for similar deaths before 27 March 1981.

Cap 204   For completion at the request of the Inland Revenue follow-
                           ing the issue of a grant in an 'excepted estate' (see under
                           'Necessity for account', paras. **8.01** ff., above).
Cap A5C   De bonis non, double probate and cessate grants.

8.42   In the case of a death before 13 March 1975, when estate duty rather than
capital transfer tax was in point, the following forms may be used: forms A–9 when
the deceased died before 16 April 1969 and forms A–10 for deaths between 16
April 1969 and 30 March 1971. For deaths between 31 March 1971 and 12 March
1975 forms A–12, where the deceased was domiciled in some part of the United
Kingdom, and A–13 where he or she was not; and forms A–14, where the deceased
died before 21 March 1972 and A–14A where he or she died on or after that date
and before 13 March 1975, domiciled in Great Britain, leaving gross estate in the
United Kingdom including the whole of any jointly held property and nominated
property not exceeding £12,000 (or £9,000 for deaths before 21 March 1972).

8.43   The Cap A5C has replaced all earlier forms for applications for grants of
double probate, grants de bonis non and cessate grants.

8.44   All other forms of account are obsolete and should not be used.

Practice

Personal application

8.45   Facilities for personal applicants are provided exclusively at registries and
probate offices without limits as to the value of the estate, as explained in Chap. 2.

Where forms may be obtained

8.46   All current forms of account and the booklet of instruction, IHT 210, are
available from the Capital Taxes Office, Ferrers House, PO Box 38, Castle
Meadow Road, Nottingham, NG2 1BB, tel. 0115 9740000.

Completion of account

8.47   IHT 200 (1993) should be used where the deceased died domiciled in the
United Kingdom according to the general law, and the following notes relate to that
form of account.

8.48   The declaration on page 12 should be considered and completed.

8.49   Where the account of the estate includes property with the instalment option
the questions on pages 6, 7 and 8 should be answered to indicate whether or not the
legal personal representatives wish to pay by instalments.

8.50   Enquiries are raised on pages 2, 3 and 8 of the form regarding gifts and other
lifetime dispositions, settled property in which by virtue of or before his or her
death the deceased ceased to have a beneficial interest in possession, nominations
and property in beneficial joint ownership. The applicant must disclose everything
he or she could reasonably be expected to have ascertained by enquiring of the
deceased's relatives, accountants, solicitors, etc. and by investigating the
deceased's records. Certain transfers of value (all of which would be exempt

transfers—see 'Lifetime transfers: exemptions', para. **8.12**, ante) need not be reported. Details of these exceptions are given in Note 1 in the booklet IHT 210 which covers the completion of the account. Where the answers disclose property on which tax is payable (or would be so payable if tax were payable on estates however small their principal value) such property should be included in the appropriate sections of the form.

8.51 These sections numbered as below are arranged to show separately property not subject to the instalment option and property subject to the instalment option, on which tax is payable or would be payable if tax were payable on estates however small their principal value.

8.52 *Section 1* is for details of all lifetime gifts or transfers of value made by the deceased within seven years of death.

8.53 *Section 2* is for all nominated property and survivorship joint property for which the personal representatives are liable to pay the tax (or would be so liable if tax were payable). Section 2A is for property which does not attract the instalment option and Section 2B is for property that does. Each subsection provides for liabilities to be recorded.

8.54 *Section 3* is a schedule of all the property of the deceased within the United Kingdom to which he or she was beneficially entitled and in respect of which the grant is made excluding property over which the deceased had, and had exercised by will, a general power of appointment. Section 3A is for property in respect of which the option to pay tax in instalments is not available and Section 3B is for property in respect of which that option is available: principally land and agricultural and business property. Each subsection provides for incorporation of a schedule of liabilities to be deducted.

8.55 *Section 4* is for all property situate outside the United Kingdom in respect of which the deceased's personal representatives are liable to pay the tax.

8.56 *Section 5* is for all property in which the deceased had a beneficial interest in possession immediately prior to death, including property subject to a general power of appointment exercised by will, together with any gifts with reservation made by the deceased in which the reservation still subsists at death. Provision is made for tax to be paid on delivery of the account by the applicant, together with a provision for a schedule of liabilities, and an option to pay tax by instalments with regard to appropriate property.

8.57 IHT 201 (1993) should be used where the deceased died domiciled outside the United Kingdom according to the general law (notwithstanding that, by virtue of s. 267 of the 1984 Act [FA 1975, s. 45 as modified by the F(No. 2)A 1983, s. 12] he or she might be treated for the purposes of the tax as having been domiciled in the United Kingdom—in which case property situate outside the United Kingdom should be included in Section 4). A statement of the facts establishing a domicile outside the United Kingdom should be annexed to the account[1]. It should indicate the deceased's domicile of origin and provide a brief résumé of his or her life. An additional statement from one or two individuals who were related to or well acquainted with the deceased and who might speak with authority as respects any domicile of choice outside the United Kingdom could usefully be furnished where the domicile of origin was in the United Kingdom or the deceased had lived there at the time of or before his or her death. The case of a married woman has no distinguishing features save where she had already acquired—and had retained—a domicile of dependence by reference to her husband's domicile before 1 January 1974[2]. In such a case it would be necessary to indicate the husband's domicile of origin and give brief particulars of his life in addition to those of the deceased married woman since January 1974.

1 Domicile is explained in Chap. 12: ordinary residence outside the United Kingdom is relevant for the 'exclusion' of Government securities: see fn. 4, para. **8.83**, post.
2 Domicile and Matrimonial Proceedings Act 1973, s. 1: see p. 807, post.

8.58   Particulars should similarly be furnished if it is claimed that the deceased was resident or ordinarily resident outside the United Kingdom.

8.59   Apart from this, pages 1 and 2 are similar to those in IHT 200 (1993). The sections are also similar save that the property required to be included in Section 4 is restricted to that deemed to be situate in the United Kingdom by any double taxation agreement or convention[1] unless a 'deemed domicile' under the provisions of s. 267 of the Act is appropriate, in which case all foreign assets should be detailed. If there is any doubt as to the locality of an asset, the material facts should be disclosed for consideration.

1 See in connection with reliefs, paras. **8.119–8.124**, post.

8.60   Except as indicated, IHT 200 (1993) and 201 (1993) are similar and unless otherwise stated, the following text applies to both types of case.

Valuation

8.61   The value of property is the price it might reasonably be expected to fetch if sold in the open market: s. 160 of the 1984 Act [FA 1975, s. 38]. Detailed rules are also given in Part VI of the 1984 Act [FA 1975, Sch. 10] which provide special rules of valuation. Of particular importance is valuation by reference to 'related property', provided by s. 161 of the 1984 Act [FA 1975, Sch. 10, para. 7]. Related property is property comprised in the estate of a spouse or, by virtue of an exempt transfer made by the transferor or his or her spouse on or after 15 April 1976, is or has been within the preceding five years the property of a charity or one of the political, national or public bodies to which exempt transfers may be made. (In relation to transfers prior to 10 March 1981 related property also includes property comprised in a settlement made before 27 March 1974 by the deceased or his or her spouse in which there was no current interest in possession[1].) In essence the scheme provides that if the value of the deceased's share of property is less than the appropriate proportion of the value of the whole then that proportionate value reckons as the value for tax. So, if the deceased and his or her spouse owned Blackacre in equal shares, and the value of a one-half share of Blackacre was £40,000 and the value of the whole was £100,000, then the value of the deceased's interest for the purposes of the tax is £50,000 (and not £40,000).

1 FA 1975, Sch. 10, para. 7, as modified by FA 1976, s. 103(1) and FA 1981, s. 105.

8.62   Section 163 of the 1984 Act [FA 1975, Sch. 10, para. 5] provides for cases where the property transferred is subject to a fetter—typically, though not exclusively, an option to purchase. In such a case the property is valued without regard to the fetter unless and to the extent that consideration was given for its creation. If the creation of the fetter itself constituted a chargeable transfer then allowance is made for the value thereby transferred.

8.63 Section 171 of the 1984 Act [FA 1975, Sch. 10, para. 9(1)] provides for changes which occur by reason of a person's death. This is important because the deemed transfer of value under s. 4(1) [s. 21(1)] occurs immediately before the death. In consequence of this provision, for example, the proceeds of a policy on the deceased's life payable to personal representatives form part of his or her estate at face value. Equally, the value of a contractual annuity immediately before the death is reduced to nil.

8.64 The question of sales of related property, quoted securities and land— ss. 176, 178 ff. and 190 ff. of the 1984 Act [FA 1975, Sch. 10, Pts II and III]—will be considered later in the context of reliefs (paras. **8.104–8.106**, post).

Section 1: Lifetime gifts on transfers of value:

8.65 Questions regarding gifts made by the deceased within seven years of death and gifts with reservation made after 18 March 1986 must be answered and the relevant details included in this Section or Section 5 as appropriate. The value of each gift is calculated as the loss to the estate caused by the transfer.

Section 2: Nominated and joint property:

8.66 The criteria for valuation provided in Section 3 below are appropriate in this Section also.

Section 3A: Assets

8.67 Quoted shares and securities are normally valued at one-quarter up from the lower to the higher of the quotations for the date of death. Where no prices are available for the date of death, the list for the nearest business day, either before or after the death, may be used at the option of the accounting party. If prices are taken from newspapers, it should be borne in mind that morning newspapers usually give the prices for the previous day. If bargains, other than bargains at special prices, are recorded, however, the valuation may be based on the price at which business was done, if there is only one price, or a price midway between the lowest and the highest of the different prices. Where quotations are ex-dividend, the dividend should be included separately. Where there is no quotation or record of dealings, the value of the stocks or shares should be estimated on the best evidence available. Units of a unit trust should be valued at the manager's bid price. Stocks, shares and other securities which are quoted (listed in the order of appearance in the official list) and dealt in on the Unlisted Securities Market should be shown separately from other securities which are not quoted. All such securities should be listed on form IHT 40 which accompanies the IHT 200 and 201.

8.68 In the case of National Savings Certificates, a letter stating the value should be obtained from the Director of Savings, Savings Certificates Division, Durham. In the absence of such a letter, full details of the certificates should be given.

8.69   A valuation of furniture, etc., should normally be attached, the details including individual values of items valued at £500 and over. It is essential to attach a schedule of any articles for which conditional exemption is claimed as of national, scientific, historic or artistic interest, as to which see para. **8.83**, post, in connection with exemptions from tax.

8.70   In the absence of a professional valuation of an interest in expectancy, a reasoned statement should be attached showing the title to and value of the trust fund, due allowance being made for all factors such as the age of the life tenant.

8.71   Benefits payable under superannuation schemes which have been 'approved' for income tax purposes are not normally liable for tax unless the deceased's personal representatives are entitled as of right or the benefit was subject to the deceased's power of nomination and that power had not been exercised irrevocably.

8.72   An absolute interest in unadministered residue, being a chose in action and thus not carrying the instalment option, should be shown here too (always provided that it is situate in the United Kingdom). The full name and date of death of the first testator or intestate should be provided together with details and values as at the date of the deceased's death, so far as practicable, of the entitlement. The difference between the value of the property constituting the entitlement and the value of the chose in action would normally be negligible. Should a discount be felt appropriate a statement of its pertinent facts, and quantifying the discount, should be furnished.

Section 3A: Liabilities

8.73   The general rule is that in determining the value of the estate, the deceased's liabilities at the date of death shall be taken into account.

8.74   Reasonable funeral expenses including the cost of a tombstone may be deducted, and by concession these include a reasonable amount for mourning for the family and servants. Debts and incumbrances may be deducted but, if they were incurred or created by the deceased, only to the extent that they were incurred for a consideration in money or money's worth. A liability in respect of which there is a right to reimbursement shall be taken into account only to the extent (if any) that reimbursement cannot reasonably be expected to be obtained.

8.75   A liability imposed by law is deductible. This includes the liability of the deceased (whether ascertained or estimated) for income tax and capital gains tax. But otherwise the liability is taken into account only to the extent that it was incurred for consideration in money or money's worth. Moreover, where a debt has been incurred on or after 18 March 1986 and the consideration for that debt consisted of property derived from the deceased directly or indirectly the debt is to be disallowed pro tanto: FA 1986, s. 103.

8.76   Future liabilities are to be valued as at the date of the deceased's death.

Section 3B

8.77   The option to pay tax in instalments has already been considered. Section 3B makes provision for exercising the option and the appropriate box should be marked with a tick. If the instalment facility is to be invoked in respect of some but not all of the property to be included in Section 3B this should be made quite clear—if necessary on a separate schedule. Details of all real and leasehold property, including any such property which is an asset of a business or partnership, should be given by completing form IHT 37. The form provides for inclusion of particulars, such as lettings, which might affect the value of the property concerned.

8.78 If the estate includes a business or an interest in a partnership trading accounts should be provided, showing the position at the date of death, and supplemented by an inventory and valuation of stock and implements. If the goodwill (if any) of such a business is not to be taken over at a price reached in a bargain struck at arm's length, it should be valued according to the custom of the trade or on the basis of the average profits. If there was no goodwill, or goodwill was valueless, a brief explanatory statement should be appended.

Section 4: Foreign property

8.79 So far as respects foreign property particulars should be given as in Section 3. As the value of such property would normally be found in foreign currency and then converted to sterling, the rate of exchange and the source of that rate should be stated. As with Section 3B, it is important to tick the appropriate box relating to the instalment option.

8.80 Debts due to persons resident abroad which are neither due to be discharged in the United Kingdom nor charged on property in the United Kingdom are, so far as possible, deducted from property outside the United Kingdom[1].

1 IHTA 1984, s. 162(5) [FA 1975, Sch. 10, para. 3].

8.81 Where additional expense is incurred in administering or realising property because it is situate out of the United Kingdom an allowance from the value of the property may be made on account of such expense not exceeding 5 per cent of the value[1].

1 IHTA 1984, s. 173 [FA 1975, Sch. 10, para. 9(1)(d)].

Section 5

8.82 Details of assets and liabilities with values (as in Sections 2, 3 and 4) should be shown here according to the titles under which they passed on the death of the deceased. The full name of the settlor or testator and the date of the settlement or other instrument and the date of the testator's death in the case of a will trust should be provided, as should brief particulars of any earlier occasion when the instrument concerned was produced to or discussed with the Capital Taxes Office. Details of any gifts with reservation should also be provided. If tax is to be paid on delivery of the account the funds concerned should be clearly indicated in the appropriate boxes—and here again it is important to tick the appropriate box relating to the instalment option. Otherwise the property should be shown in the alternative boxes and the names, addresses and references shown of the persons liable for the tax chargeable in respect of those funds (or such persons' solicitors or other professional advisers if known).

Exemptions from tax

8.83 Where property, which forms part of the estate passing under the grant of probate or administration, is exempt from tax, its value should be included in the

Inland Revenue account, in order that the true value for the purpose of the grant may be shown, and deducted in the space provided in the account on page 9 as property on which tax is either not payable at all or is not at present payable. In addition to the exemptions in respect of transfers between spouses, to charities and political parties, and gifts for national purposes, considered in para. **8.12**, ante, in connection with lifetime transfers, this applies, inter alia, to the following types of property, which are variously 'exempt', 'conditionally exempt', or 'excluded' from being included for the purpose of ascertaining the tax payable on the rest of the estate—in certain cases with the reservations stated:

(a) Heritage property. Objects of national, scientific, historic or artistic interest, land of scenic, historic or scientific interest; and historic buildings with their adjoining land and associated contents. A claim for conditional exemption must be made and accepted by the Commissioners of Inland Revenue[1]. In addition, transfers to approved maintenance fund settlements for certain heritage property are exempt transfers[2].

(b) Gifts of property of any kind to national heritage bodies such as national or local art galleries or museums, local authorities, government departments and universities.

Gifts for public benefit to bodies not run for profit where the Treasury approves exemption. Such gifts are limited to objects and land as at item (a). In addition, a reasonable maintenance fund may be included[3].

(c) Property situate in the United Kingdom by United Kingdom law but treated as situate elsewhere by virtue of a double taxation convention or agreement where the deceased was domiciled outside the United Kingdom.

(d) Certain British Government securities which are excluded property where the deceased was domiciled and ordinarily resident abroad[4].

(e) Property of which the deceased was life tenant is exempt from tax if it would have been exempt from estate duty under the Finance Act 1894, s. 5(2), duty having been paid thereon in connection with the death of the deceased's spouse, such death having occurred before 13 November 1974. Any apportionment of income received after his or her death to which the estate may be entitled is treated as covered by the exemption[5].

(f) Reversionary interests which have not been acquired by the deceased or by a person previously entitled to it for a consideration in money or money's worth are excluded property.

1 Undertakings are required, inter alia, as to maintenance and retention of the objects in the United Kingdom. Reasonable access for the public must also be provided in all cases: IHTA 1984, ss. 30 ff. [FA 1976, ss. 76 ff. replacing, in relation to deaths on and after 7 April 1976, FA 1975, ss. 31 ff.]. Tax will be chargeable when sold (unless the sale is by private treaty to a national heritage body or similar public body) or on failure to observe the terms of the undertaking imposed as a condition of relief. Claims for exemption or enquiries relating thereto are dealt with by the Capital Taxes Office. Any claim for exemption is investigated after the issue of the grant, and inspection of the objects by Officers of the National Collections is usually necessary. The objects should therefore not be dispersed before inspection has taken place, without adequate notice to the Capital Taxes Office. If any objects were exempted on the ground of national, etc., interest in connection with a previous death, further inspection of those objects may be waived, but the name and date of death of the former owner and, if known, the Capital Taxes Office references to his estate, should be mentioned.

2 IHTA 1984, s. 27 (see also Sch. 4) [FA 1982, s. 95 replacing, in relation to deaths on and after 9 March 1982, the FA 1976, s. 84 which applied to deaths on and after 3 May 1976 as amended with effect from 1 August 1980 by the FA 1980, s. 88. (See also the FA 1982, ss. 93 and 94 and Sch. 16 replacing, in relation to deaths on and after 9 March 1982, the FA 1976, s. 84, amended as aforesaid)].

3 IHTA 1984, ss. 25 and 26 [FA 1975, Sch. 6, paras. 12 and 13]. There is no limit in value, but, as regards gifts for public benefit, undertakings are required, inter alia, as to maintenance, use or disposal and as to reasonable access for the public.

4 Viz. 3½% War Loan; 13% Treasury Stock 1990; 8% Treasury Convertible Stock 1990; 8¾% Treasury Loan 1987–90; 11% Exchequer Loan 1990; 10% Treasury Convertible Stock 1991; 5¾% Funding Loan 1987–91; 2% Index Linked Treasury Stock 1992; 8% Treasury Loan 1992; 10½% Treasury Convertible Loan Stock 1992; 12¾% Treasury Loan 1992; 10% Treasury Loan 1993; 6% Funding Loan 1993; 12½% Treasury Loan 1993; 13¾% Treasury Loan 1993; 9% Treasury Loan 1994; 10% Treasury Loan 1994; 14½% Treasury Loan 1994; 12¾% Treasury Loan 1995; 9% Treasury Loan 1992–96; 13¼% Exchequer Loan 1996; 15¼% Treasury Loan 1996; 8¾% Treasury Loan 1997; 13¼% Treasury Loan 1997; 6¾% Treasury Loan 1995–98; 7¼% Treasury Stock 1998; 15½% Treasury Loan 1998; 9½% Treasury Loan 1999; 8½% Treasury Loan 2000; 9% Conversion Stock 2000; 9½% Conversion Loan 2001; 8% Treasury Stock 2003; 9¾% Conversion Loan 2003; 8% Treasury Loan 2002–06; 8½% Treasury Loan 2007; 9% Treasury Loan 2008; 9% Conversion Loan 2011; 5½% Treasury Stock 2008–12; 9% Treasury Stock 2012; 8% Treasury Stock 2013; 7¾% Treasury Loan 2012–15; 8¾% Treasury Stock 2017; 2½% Index-Linked Treasury Stock 2024.
5 IHTA 1984, Sch. 6, para. 2 [FA 1975, s. 22(4)].

Reliefs

8.84   The several relieving provisions operate for the most part in one of two ways. Most reliefs are given against capital: they reduce the value of the property concerned to produce a net figure to reckon towards the total value of the estate for the purpose of charging tax. But two, the reliefs for double taxation and for successive charges, take the form of reducing the amount of tax chargeable. As with exemptions, reliefs against capital should be recorded on page 9 of the account. The principal reliefs against capital are as follows.

Relevant business property

8.85   Paragraph 1, Sch. 14, Finance (No. 2) Act 1992 (previously s. 104 of the 1984 Act and Sch. 10, para. 2 of the Finance Act 1976) stipulates the rates of relief for the various categories of relevant business property defined in s. 105 [para. 3] of the 1984 Act. From these provisions it can be said that:

— relief is available at 100 per cent with effect from 10 March 1992—previously 50 per cent—for an interest in a business (which includes a partnership interest), for a control holding in a company[1] and, in the case of a death on or after 17 March 1987[2], for a minority holding in an unquoted company which yields not less than 25 per cent of the voting capacity; and
— relief is available at 50 per cent—30 per cent prior to 10 March 1992— for other minority holdings in unquoted companies, for land, buildings, machinery and plant used only or mainly in a company of which the deceased had control or of a partnership in which he or she was a partner, and, in the case of a death on or after 10 March 1981, for those similar assets which, being settled property in which the deceased had a beneficial interest in possession, were used wholly or mainly in a business carried on by the deceased.

1 IHTA 1984, s. 269 as to 'control'.
2 FA 1987, s. 58 and Sch 8, para. 5.

8.86   Where the death occurred on or after 27 October 1977 (the commencement date) but before 15 March 1983, the rate of relief for minority holdings of unquoted shares was 20 per cent. For the relief, securities dealt in on the Unlisted Securities Market were regarded as unquoted shares in relation to deaths before 17 March 1987 and again for deaths on or after 10 March 1992.

8.87   Where the death occurred before 27 October 1977 but on or after 7 April 1976 (the commencement date) the rate of relief for businesses and control holdings was 30 per cent.

8.88   For the purpose of the relief the net value of a business is the value of the assets (including goodwill) reduced by the aggregate liabilities incurred for the purposes of the business. Assets not strictly required for current or future business use are excluded from relief. Assets used wholly or mainly for the personal benefit of the deceased or of a person connected with him are expressly excluded from the terms of the relief.

8.89   For relief to be available, a business must be carried on for gain: it includes a business carried on in the exercise of a profession or vocation. Excluded from relief are a business dealing in stocks and shares, or making or holding investments; a business as a market maker (as defined—formerly, before the Stock Exchange's reforms—'jobber') and the case where a business is subject to a binding contract for sale[1] (including where a partnership share passes to the surviving partners pursuant to a 'buy and sell' agreement).

1 IHTA 1984, s. 113 [FA 1976, Sch. 10, para. 3(4)].

8.90   For the relief to be available it is necessary that the property concerned was owned by the deceased for at least two years prior to the death; or that it replaced other property (or other replaced property) and the transferor owned the various properties for at least two out of the five years preceding the death and each such property would, but for the period of its ownership, qualify for relief; or that it, or the property it replaced, was eligible for relief on an earlier chargeable occasion whereby it became the property of the deceased or his or her spouse.

8.91   If the deceased had inherited the property upon the death of someone else he or she is treated as owning it from the date of that person's death or, if the earlier death was of the deceased's spouse, for any period during which the spouse owned it.

8.92   Business relief applies to farming businesses so far as agricultural relief does not apply. As regards transfers after 9 March 1981, it is not open to claim business relief by forgoing agricultural relief[1]. In general, it applies to transfers of value, i.e. the relief is applied before considering whether and to what extent the interest in the business property is otherwise exempt.

1 IHTA 1984, s. 114 [FA 1981, s. 96(3)(d)].

8.93   Special provisions apply in the following circumstances:

—   where a transfer of value has occurred and the death occurs within seven years thereafter[1];
—   where part of the estate is exempt[2];
—   where the value for tax is reduced pursuant to s. 176 of the 1984 Act [FA 1975, Sch. 10, para. 9A] (sales of related etc. property—see para. **8.106**, post).

1 IHTA 1984, s. 113A and B as inserted by FA 1986, s. 101 and Sch. 19, para. 21 with effect from 18 March 1986.
2 IHTA 1984, s. 39A as inserted by the FA 1986, s. 105 with effect from 18 March 1986.

Agricultural property

8.94 Earlier provisions[1] affording relief for agricultural property were replaced by ss. 115 ff. of the 1984 Act [FA 1981, s. 96 and Sch. 14]. Where a transfer of value, including a transfer on death, made after 9 March 1981 is attributable to agricultural property in the United Kingdom, the Channel Islands or the Isle of Man, the value transferred is reduced for tax purposes provided the prescribed conditions are satisfied.

1 FA 1975, s. 35 and Sch 8, as amended by the FA 1976, s. 74. In relation to deaths prior to 10 March 1981 relief is available only in respect of chargeable transfers. The requirements for relief are: (i) the land must comply with the statutory definition of agricultural property, (ii) the deceased must have been a qualifying working farmer (farming alone or in partnership; employed in farming; director of a company whose main activity is farming in the United Kingdom; undergoing full-time education; or, in receipt of not less than 75 per cent of income from engagement in farming in the United Kingdom) during not less than five of the seven years ending with 5 April immediately preceding the death (special rules apply to retired farmers and to property inherited from a spouse), (iii) the deceased must have occupied the land in question for agricultural purposes for two years immediately preceding the transfer (special provision is made in the case of successive transfers within a two-year period), and (iv) the relief must be applied for within two years of the death (Form 220 obtainable from the Capital Taxes Office should be used). The relief is limited to a maximum of 1,000 acres (rough grazing land counting as one-sixth of its actual area as from 7 April 1976) or £250,000 and is calculated by reducing the agricultural value by half. (Prior to 7 April 1976 the agricultural property was valued at 20 times the rent it would fetch if let so far as it was situated in Great Britain.)

8.95 The property must comply with the statutory definition. For the purpose of relief agricultural property means agricultural land or pasture and includes woodland and any building used in connection with the intensive rearing of livestock or fish if the woodland or building is occupied with agricultural land or pasture and the occupation is ancillary to that of the agricultural land or pasture; and also includes such cottages, farm buildings and farm-houses, together with the land occupied by them, as are of a character appropriate to the property[1]. The cultivation of short rotation coppice is regarded as agriculture for events on or after 6 April 1995[2].

1 IHTA 1984, s. 115(2) [FA 1981, Sch. 14, para. 1(2)].
2 FA 1995, s. 154(2).

8.96 The agricultural property must have been occupied by the transferor for agricultural purposes for the two years immediately preceding the transfer or owned by him or her throughout the seven years immediately preceding the transfer and occupied, by him or herself or another, for agricultural purposes throughout that period[1]. For this purpose:

(a) If the transferor inherited the property on an earlier death, the period of ownership, or occupation if he or she subsequently occupies it, is deemed to have commenced on the date of that death. Where the earlier death is that of the transferor's spouse, the transferor may add to his or her own period of ownership or occupation that of the spouse[2].

(b) Occupation by a company controlled by the transferor is treated as occupation by him; occupation by a Scottish partnership is treated as occupation by the partners[3].

(c) Where the property has been occupied for less than two years, or owned for less than seven years, prior to the transfer but had replaced other agricultural property previously occupied or owned, occupation of the properties for a combined period of two out of the five years, or ownership for a combined period of seven out of the ten years, preceding the transfer will be treated as satisfying the respective conditions. Relief is scaled down if the value of the earlier property on cesser of occupation or ownership is less than the value of the later property when it was first occupied or owned by the transferor[4].

(d) Where property is transferred within two or seven years of an earlier transfer on which it qualified for agricultural relief, or would have done so had the statutory provisions then been in force, the respective occupation or ownership test is regarded as satisfied as regards the second transfer if:

    (i) either transfer took place on death; and

    (ii) the first transfer was made to the second transferor or his or her spouse; and

    (iii) the property was, at the time of the second transfer, occupied for agricultural purposes by either the second transferor or the personal representatives of the first transferor[5].

1 IHTA 1984, s. 117 [FA 1981, Sch. 14, para. 3].
2 IHTA 1984, s. 120 [FA 1981, Sch. 14, paras. 6 and 7].
3 IHTA 1984, s. 119 [FA 1981, Sch. 14, para. 5].
4 IHTA 1984, s. 118 [FA 1981, Sch. 14, para. 4].
5 IHTA 1984, s. 121 [FA 1981, Sch. 14, para. 8].

8.97 Agricultural relief also applies in the case of transfers of controlling holdings of shares and securities, the value of which is not reduced for inheritance tax purposes by reason of a sale within three years of a death, provided that part of the value of the shares or securities can be attributed to agricultural property comprised in the assets of the company and that the conditions as to occupation or ownership referred to above are satisfied by the company in relation to that agricultural property[1]. Provision is similarly made for replacement property and replacement holdings of shares[2].

1 IHTA 1984, ss. 122 and 123 [FA 1981, Sch. 14, paras. 9 to 13].
2 IHTA 1984, s. 123(2) to (4) [FA 1981, Sch. 14, para. 12].

8.98 Relief is given by reducing the value transferred so far as attributable to the agricultural property by 100 per cent—50 per cent prior to 10 March 1992[1]—if immediately prior to the transfer the transferor (or the company in the case of control holdings of shares or securities) had, or could within 12 months have obtained, the right to vacant possession of the property, or the property was let on a tenancy commencing on or after 1 September 1995 and by 50 per cent—30 per cent prior to 10 March 1992[1]—in other cases (20 per cent in respect of transfers before 15 March 1983)[2]. Although let land is normally entitled to relief at 30 (or 20 as aforesaid) per cent, transitional relief at 50 per cent is allowed where it was let prior to 10 March 1981, if and so far as it would have qualified for the 50 per cent agricultural relief under the provisions of the FA 1975, Sch. 8, as amended[3] had it been transferred immediately before 10 March 1981, provided the owner neither had nor could have had the right of vacant possession between 10 March 1981 and the date of transfer[4]. Generally land or shares which are the subject of a contract for sale do not qualify for relief[5].

1 Finance (No. 2) Act 1992, para. 4, Sch. 14.
2 IHTA 1984, s. 116 [FA 1981, Sch. 14, para. 2].
3 See fn. 1, para. **8.94**, ante.
4 IHTA 1984, s. 116(2) to (4) [FA 1981, Sch. 14, para. 2(2) to (4)].
5 IHTA 1984, s. 124 [FA 1981, Sch. 14, para. 2].

8.99 The relief is given without formal claim, and where available there will be no entitlement to business relief.

8.100   In the schedule of real and leasehold property (form Cap 37) the open market value of any agricultural property (which is relevant for all probate and tax purposes) should be shown.

8.101   Special provisions apply in the following circumstances:

— where a transfer of value has occurred and the death occurs within seven years thereafter[1];
— where part of the estate is exempt[2];
— where the value for tax is reduced pursuant to s. 176 of the 1984 Act [FA 1975 Sch. 10, para. 9A] (sales of related etc. property—see para. **8.106**, post).

1 IHTA 1984, s. 124A and B as inserted by FA 1986, s. 101 and Sch. 19, para. 22 with effect from 18 March 1986.
2 IHTA 1984, s. 39A as inserted by FA 1986, s. 105 with effect from 18 March 1986.

Woodlands

8.102   Subject to prescribed conditions, the value of trees or underwood on land in the United Kingdom, which is not eligible for agricultural property relief, is left out of account altogether until its disposal with or apart from the land[1]. An election to claim relief must be made within two years after the death or such longer time as the Board of Inland Revenue might allow[2]. There is no designated form for this purpose. For relief to be available the deceased must have been entitled to the land throughout the five years preceding the death unless he or she became entitled to it other than for consideration in money or money's worth[3].

1 IHTA 1984, s. 125 [FA 1975, Sch. 9, para. 1(1)].
2 IHTA 1984, s. 125(3) [FA 1975, Sch. 9, para. 1(2)].
3 IHTA 1984, s. 125(1)(b) [FA 1975, Sch. 9, para. 5(1)].

8.103   Tax becomes chargeable on the disposal otherwise than on a death of the land or the timber thereon or both[1]. If the disposal is a sale for full consideration tax is charged on the net sale proceeds; otherwise it is charged on the value of the land or timber on the date of its disposal[2]. In either case tax is charged by reference to the last death in connection with which relief was given[3]. If the disposal constitutes a chargeable transfer the value thereby transferred is reduced by the tax paid in connection with the death[4]. If the trees or underwood disposed of would have been eligible for business relief had the death occurred on or after 27 October 1977 the amount on which tax is charged in consequence of a disposal is reduced by 50 per cent[5].

1 IHTA 1984, s. 126 [FA 1975, Sch. 9, para. 2(1)].
2 IHTA 1984, s. 127(1) [FA 1975, Sch. 9, para. 3(1)].
3 IHTA 1984, s. 128 [FA 1975, Sch. 9, para. 3(1)].
4 IHTA 1984, s. 129 [FA 1975, Sch. 9, para. 4].
5 IHTA 1984, s. 127(2) [FA 1975, Sch. 9, para. 3(2) as amended].

Sales of quoted securities within one year after death.

8.104   Sections 178 ff. of the 1984 Act [FA 1975, Sch. 10, Pt. II] provide a scheme whereby if the deceased's portfolio of 'qualifying investments'[1] (broadly speaking quoted securities) valued as at the date of death exceeds the combined values at the death of individual investments retained and the proceeds of sale of others sold during the year after the death then that lower figure is to be substituted in computing the value transferred on the death. There are provisions, inter alia, to counter sales at less than full consideration[2] and to bring capital payments received before the sale into account[3] in calculating the sale proceeds. Moreover, the purchase prices of any securities purchased by the claimant for relief in the same capacity within two months after the last sale are brought into account to mitigate the 'loss' pro tanto[4]. The relief must be claimed by the 'appropriate person'[5] (normally the personal representatives or trustees of the settlement concerned) using form Sect 5.

1 IHTA 1984, s. 178(1) [FA 1975, Sch. 10, para 14(1)].
2 IHTA 1984, s. 179(1)(b) [FA 1975, Sch. 10, para. 15].
3 IHTA 1984, s. 181 [FA 1975, Sch. 10, para. 25].
4 IHTA 1984, s. 180 [FA 1975, Sch. 10, para. 17].
5 IHTA 1984, s. 178(1) [FA 1975, Sch. 10, para. 14(1)].

Sales of interests in land within four years after death

8.105   Sections 190 ff. of the 1984 Act [FA 1975, Sch. 10, Pt. III] as amended by s. 199, Finance Act 1993, provides in relation to deaths on and after 16 March 1990 (within three years for deaths between 7 April 1976 and 15 March 1990) a scheme whereby the proceeds of sale of an interest in land[1] are substituted for the value of the same interest as at the date of death. Though there are superficial similarities with the scheme of relief for quoted securities above, there are important differences. At its simplest, relief is given by substituting the 'sale value'[1,2] for the 'value on death'[1]. But each interest in land sold during the four-year period must be brought into account at its sale value[2]; the 'sale value' means the value on death before adjustment for this relief and any relief for the sale of related etc. property (see below)[3], de minimis differences in value are excluded[4]; provisions are made to ensure a valid comparison between the interest held immediately before the death and the interest sold[5] and to counter sales at less than full consideration[6]; certain non-qualifying sales are excluded from the scheme[6]; and the four-year period may be extended in cases of compulsory acquisition[7]. Relief must be claimed by the 'appropriate person'[8] (normally the personal representatives or trustees of the settlement concerned) but there is no designated form for the purpose.

1 IHTA 1984, s. 190(1) [FA 1975, Sch. 10, para. 31(1)].
2 IHTA 1984, s. 191(1) [FA 1975, Sch. 10, para. 32(1)].
3 IHTA 1984, s. 190(1) [FA 1975, Sch. 10, para. 31(1)].
4 IHTA 1984, s. 191(2) [FA 1975, Sch. 10, para. 32(2)].
5 IHTA 1984, ss. 193 to 195 [FA 1975, Sch. 10, paras. 33 to 35].
6 IHTA 1984, s. 191(3) [FA 1975, Sch. 10, para. 32(3)].
7 IHTA 1984, s. 197 [FA 1975, Sch. 10, para. 38].
8 IHTA 1984, s. 190(1) [FA 1975, Sch. 10, para. 31(1)].

Sales of related etc. property within three years after death

8.106   It was mentioned in para. **8.61**, ante, that property not forming part of the deceased's estate may nevertheless be 'related' property and the value of the deceased's property taken as a proportion of the value of the whole. There can be similar treatment of property comprised in the estate where one part passes under one title and another under another, Blackacre, for example, being comprised partly in the deceased's free estate and partly in a settlement in which he or she had a beneficial interest in possession. Section 176 of the 1984 Act [FA 1975, Sch. 10, para. 9A] provides in relation to deaths on and after 7 April 1976 for these special rules of valuation to be set aside where there is a 'qualifying' sale[1]. Suppose

Blackacre to have been owned as to a one-half share by the deceased and as to the other one-half share by his or her spouse, that other one-half share being 'related property'; or the said Blackacre to have been split as to one-half comprised in the deceased's free estate and the other one-half comprised in a settled title. In each case the value of a one-half share was £50,000 and the value of the whole £120,000. Invoking the special valuation rules the value of the deceased's half share would be £60,000 in each case. Where the relief operates, those values are reduced to £50,000. The sale must be a 'qualifying sale'[1] and there are safeguards against such artifices as sales for less than full consideration and sales between 'connected' persons. And the price obtained on sale must be less than the value for tax as would otherwise have been determined—and after any application of the relief under ss. 190 ff. of the 1984 Act [FA 1975, Sch. 10, Pt. III][2] considered at para. **8.105**, ante. A claim for relief must be made[3] but there is no designated form for the purpose.

1 IHTA 1984, s. 176(1) and (3) [FA 1975, Sch. 10, para. 9A(1) and (3)].
2 IHTA 1984, s. 176(4) [FA 1975, Sch. 10, para. 9A(4)].
3 IHTA 1984, s. 176(2) [FA 1975, Sch. 10, para. 9A(2)].

Falls in value of property transferred within seven years before death

8.107   Provided by ss. 131 ff. of the 1984 Act [FA 1976, s. 99 and Sch. 12] in relation to deaths on and after 7 April 1976, this relief is for the benefit of a transferee who, on the death of the transferor within seven years after the transfer (three years in the case of a death before 18 March 1986) becomes liable for tax at the higher death rate. It should be noted, however, that the relief confers no benefit on any other liable person for it does not substitute a lower figure for the value transferred by the chargeable transfer concerned and so does not alter the lifetime cumulative total of a deceased transferor.

Variations: changes in the distribution of the estate on death

8.108   Sections 142 to 147 of the 1984 Act group together some six items derived from FA 1975, s. 47(1) (as replaced in relation to events on and after 11 April 1978 by FA 1978, s. 68); s. 47(1A) and (1AA); s. 47(1B); s. 47(3) and FA 1976, ss. 121 to 123. Of these six topics it is pertinent to consider, in turn, four.

8.109   *Instruments of variation and disclaimer—s. 142.* Provision is made here for a beneficiary to vary or disclaim benefits from the deceased's estate without, in so doing, incurring a charge to tax. This is secured by treating a variation as though it had been effected by the deceased under the original disposition and by treating a disclaimed benefit as though it had never been conferred[1]. Neither the variation nor the disclaimer is a transfer of value[2]. To be eligible for relief a variation may be made within but not more than two years after the date of death[1]. It must be in writing and executed by all the persons who were to benefit under the terms of the original disposition in relation to the property being re-directed[1]. It should be in a form which identifies the original disposition (commonly the deceased's will) and clearly indicates which property is being re-directed and to whom. A variation must be supported by a written election to that effect given to the Board of Inland Revenue within six months after the date of the instrument. The election must be made by all the persons who made the instrument and, if in consequence more tax is payable in connection with the death, the deceased's legal personal representatives[3]. No form of election is prescribed—indeed it may usefully be incorporated in the instrument itself—but it should be worded so as to make clear that s. 142(1) of the 1984 Act is intended to apply. The provision applies to property, including 'excluded property' passing under a will or intestacy. It applies too to property passing by nomination and survivorship, but not to settled property unless the deceased immediately prior to his or her death had a beneficial interest in possession and a general power of appointment which power had been exercised by will[4].

1 IHTA 1984, s. 142(1).
2 Ibid., s. 17(a).
3 Ibid., s. 142(2).
4 Ibid., s. 142(5).

8.110 The position regarding disclaimers is similar, save that no election is required[1]. The relief is not available in any case where the variation or disclaimer is made for a consideration in money or money's worth save where the consideration is another variation or disclaimer which is itself eligible for relief[2].

1 Ibid., s. 142(2)—which applies in terms only to a 'variation'.
2 Ibid., s. 142(3).

8.111 If a variation fulfilling the conditions considered above confers an interest which comes to an end within two years after the death of the deceased then tax in connection with the death is charged as though the destination of the property which has effect at the end of those two years had had effect from the date of death[1].

1 Ibid., s. 142(4).

8.112 *Non-binding requests—s. 143.* Where a legatee or devisee of property under the deceased's will complies with the testator's wishes that the property concerned be re-directed to a third party, compliance with that wish is not to be a transfer of value[1], provided that such compliance occurs within two years after the death. The funds concerned are treated as bequeathed under the will to the transferee.

1 Ibid., s. 17(b).

8.113 *Settlements with no beneficial interest in possession[1]—s. 144.* The legislation provides not only for taxation in connection with transfers between individuals and transfers on death but also in connection with transfers by trustees of settlements[2]. Provisions are made for a chargeable event to occur in relation to a settlement with no beneficial interest in possession when, inter alia, funds are dealt with by the trustees so that an individual becomes entitled to those funds absolutely or takes a qualifying interest in possession[3] in them. The scheme of relief in this case postulates that the funds have been settled under the deceased's will on trusts under which no beneficial interest in possession subsists; and it secures relief from the charge to tax under those provisions[4] provided that the event concerned occurs within two years after the death of the testator. And, it provides that tax is to be charged in connection with the death as though the testator's will had provided for the property so dealt with to be held as it was after the event concerned[4].

1 I.e., broadly, discretionary trusts.
2 Cf. IHTA 1984, Pt. III.
3 Cf. IHTA 1984, s. 102(1).
4 IHTA 1984, s. 144(2).

8.114 *Orders under the Inheritance (Provision for Family and Dependants) Act 1975*[1]—*s. 146*. It is provided by the 1975 Act, s. 19 that where an order under s. 2 is made the enactments relating inter alia to inheritance tax and capital transfer tax are to have effect subject to that order. This is complemented by s. 146(1) of the 1984 Act [and FA 1976, s. 122(1) in relation to deaths on and after 1 April 1976], which provides that where such an order is made tax is to be charged as though the property affected by that order had devolved on the death in accordance with its terms[2].

1 See p. 808, post. For discussion see Chap. 41, post.
2 IHTA 1984, s. 146(1).

8.115 Further provision is made by reference to orders under s. 10 of the 1975 Act in cases where the property affected by such an order had been the subject of a chargeable transfer before the transferor's death. If the deceased's legal personal representatives claim relief then the tax paid in respect of the value transferred by that chargeable transfer is to be repaid to them and tax is then charged in connection with the death as though that value transferred were left out of account in determining the lifetime cumulative total for the purposes of ascertaining the rate of tax. But the amount concerned, and the tax repayment if claimed, reckon towards the value of the deceased's estate immediately before his or her death[1].

1 Ibid., s. 146(2) and (5).

8.116 Where an order is made staying or dismissing proceedings and the terms contained in the schedule to the order are such that they could have been included in an order under the said s. 2 or s. 10 of the 1975 Act then they are treated for the purposes of the tax as though they had been included in such an order[1].

1 Ibid., s. 146(8).

Death on active service etc.

8.117 Total relief from tax is granted by s. 154(1) of the 1984 Act [FA 1975, Sch. 7, para. 1] in connection with the death of a member of the armed forces of the Crown or any other person subject to the law governing any of those forces by reason of association with or of accompanying any body of those forces including, in relation to any time before 28 July 1981 when the Armed Forces Act 1981[1] was enacted, a member of the women's services. The death must be one which is certified by the appropriate authority[2] as resulting from a wound inflicted, accident occurring or disease contracted at a time when the deceased was on active service against an enemy or on other service of a warlike nature, or which in the opinion of the Treasury involved the same risks as service of a warlike nature, or from a disease contracted at some previous time and due to or hastened by the aggravation of the disease during such period. The usual Inland Revenue account should be completed, the certificate being attached in support of the claim for exemption.

1 C. 55 (which provided, inter alia, for the assimilation of the womens' services).
2 Ministry of Defence, Personnel and Logistics, PL(LS) Legal 1, Room 2/17 Metropole Buildings, Northumberland Avenue, London WC2N 5BL. It is advisable to enclose the deceased's service number, a copy of the death certificate and any supporting medical evidence such as a post mortem report which might be of relevance. See Chap. 4, ante, for probate fees.

8.118 The two remaining reliefs against tax are as follows.

Relief from double taxation

8.119   Agreements or conventions for the avoidance of double taxation made with the United States of America[1], South Africa[2], the Netherlands[3], Switzerland[4], Pakistan[5], Sweden[6], France[7], Italy[8] and the Republic of Ireland[9] provide special rules for determining the situation of property for inheritance tax and capital transfer tax only. Apart from the conventions with the Netherlands and Switzerland, they also provide for credits in respect of overseas tax paid by reference to gifts or on death[10]. They do not affect the situation of property for the purposes of the grant of representation, and the Inland Revenue account should be completed in accordance with the general law regarding the situation of property. Any variation due to the application of an agreement or convention should be made by adjusting the value for tax. Where property of a person domiciled outside the United Kingdom is situate in the United Kingdom under the general law but outside the United Kingdom under an agreement or convention, its value should be deducted as property on which tax is not payable; but if the property is situate outside the United Kingdom under the general law and is taxable only because of the agreement or convention, it should be included in Section 4 of the Inland Revenue account, IHT 201 (1993), with an explanatory note. No adjustment is necessary if an asset is taxable or exempt irrespective of its situation.

1 SR & O 1946 No. 1351; superseded by S.I. 1979 No. 1454 in the case of deaths or transfers after 11 November 1979 but with transitional savings.
2 SR & O 1947 No. 314, as amended by S.I. 1955 No. 424; superseded by S.I. 1979 No. 576 in the case of deaths or transfers after 31 December 1977 but with transitional savings.
3 S.I. 1950 No. 1197; superseded by S.I. 1980 No. 706 in the case of deaths or transfers after 16 June 1980 but with transitional savings.
4 S.I. 1957 No. 426: superseded by S.I. 1994 No. 3214 in the case of deaths or transfers after 6 March 1995.
5 S.I. 1957 No. 1522.
6 S.I. 1961 No. 578, as amended by S.I. 1965 No. 599; superseded by S.I. 1981 No. 840 in the case of deaths or transfers after 19 June 1981.
7 S.I. 1963 No. 1319.
8 S.I. 1968 No. 304.
9 S.I. 1978 No. 1107.
10 Finance Act 1975, Sch. 7, para. 7(6).

8.120   The general law relating to domicile applies (as necessary) in the application of these agreements or conventions. The special rules for tax do not apply for this purpose[1].

1 IHTA 1984, s. 267(2) [FA 1975, s. 45 and Sch. 7, para. 7(6)].

8.121   Where tax similar to inheritance tax or capital transfer tax is chargeable in an overseas territory by reference to death or lifetime transfers of property situated by the law of the United Kingdom in that overseas territory, a credit for that tax is allowed, not exceeding the United Kingdom tax payable on the same property. The overseas tax must be paid[1]. Before 7 April 1976 this relief could only be claimed where an agreement or convention did not apply. On and after that date it and the following further reliefs are alternative to any relief due under an agreement or convention.

1 IHTA 1984, s. 159 [FA 1975, Sch. 7, para. 8].

8.122   In a case where overseas tax is paid on the lines as above, but either the property is situated neither in the United Kingdom nor in the overseas territories charging the overseas tax, or the property is situated in each overseas territory and the United Kingdom, a reduced allowance based on a formula is given[1].

1 IHTA 1984, s. 159(3) [FA 1975, Sch. 7, para. 8(3)].

8.123 Where an allowance is appropriate, a provisional deduction may be taken in the Inland Revenue account if accompanied by a reasoned estimate of the amount of duty or tax payable in the country concerned. The deduction is not to exceed the amount of inheritance tax or capital transfer tax on the property in question.

8.124 Accountable persons may be required to give a written undertaking to produce acceptable evidence of the payment of the tax in the overseas territory and to pay any further inheritance tax or capital transfer tax subsequently found to be payable.

Relief from successive charges ('quick succession relief')

8.125 Where the estate of a person dying after 9 March 1981 has been increased by a chargeable transfer made not more than five years before his death the tax chargeable on the death is reduced by a percentage of the tax charged on the earlier transfer, as follows:

(a)   by 100 per cent if the intervening period was one year or less;
(b)   by 80 per cent if that period was more than one year but not more than two years;
(c)   by 60 per cent if that period was more than two years but not more than three years;
(d)   by 40 per cent if that period was more than three years but not more than four years;
(e)   by 20 per cent if it exceeds four years[1].

1 IHTA 1984, s. 141 [FA 1975, s. 101].

8.126 In the case of deaths prior to 10 March 1981, relief is available only in the case of successive transfers within a period of four years, the percentage reductions being 80, 60, 40 and 20 for deaths within the first, second, third and fourth years respectively. The relief for property chargeable on the later death as settled property is, however, effected by applying the percentage reductions to the value of the settled property as at the later death.

8.127 Where on the earlier occasion tax was reduced or exhausted by an allowance (for example by a prior quick succession relief or by double taxation relief) relief is nevertheless available as though on that earlier occasion tax had been paid in full.

8.128 Where appropriate the relief may be claimed on the Inland Revenue account in the calculation section at the foot of page 10, which should contain a statement showing the property to which the relief applies, the full name and date of death of the prior deceased, where relevant, and the circumstances in which the relief is claimed.

Assessment, payment and delivery

8.129   As already explained, the Inland Revenue account is arranged to show in Sections 3A and 3B the property in respect of which the grant is to be made. Except for liabilities specifically charged on property included in Section 3B or incurred in respect of a business shown in that account, funeral expenses and debts for which the estate is liable are deducted in Section 3A. If there is a deficit in Section 3A this is deducted against the total in Section 3B and vice versa.

8.130   By following the directions on pages 5, 6 and 9, the value of the property on which the assessment is to be based may then be carried through to page 10, while the value of the estate in respect of which the grant is to be made may be carried through to page 11. These two amounts are not necessarily the same. The summary on page 9 provides for exemptions and reliefs to be shown and quantified for subsequent transmission to the summary on page 10[1].

1 See paras. **8.136–8.140**, post, on assessment as to the calculations which may be necessary where part only of an estate is entitled to relief in respect of gifts to a surviving spouse etc.

8.131   In completing Sections 2, 4 and 5, reference may be made to the earlier outline on the scope of the tax. Section 2 is used for joint property accruing by survivorship, donationes mortis causa and property over which the deceased had a general power of appointment such as nominated property (including nominated benefits under a general power conferred by a superannuation scheme). Section 4 is used for property situate outside the United Kingdom, and Section 5 is used for property of all other categories, such as settled property or gifts with reservation. Property passing under different titles should be shown as separate items.

8.132   In certain specific cases the completed account must be forwarded to the Capital Taxes Office for examination and assessment of any tax payable[1]. Otherwise, solicitors should assess the tax and interest payable on delivery of the account by completing pages 10 and 11 of the form.

1 See paras. **8.147** ff., post, as to examination before the grant.

Assessment

8.133   As tax must be paid on delivery of the Inland Revenue account on all property not entitled to the instalment option and any instalments due on instalment option property (in each case for which the personal representatives are liable) care must be taken to include, as a minimum in the assessment, the net value of property in Sections 3 and 4.

8.134   To arrive at the total tax chargeable on the death, the first table—'Summary for determining the chargeable estate'—on page 10 shows, at Total C, the aggregate chargeable transfers including (from Total A) chargeable lifetime transfers. The 'Calculation of Tax' section is used to show, at Total Tax D, the total tax attributable to the death estate having made due allowance for any tax on the chargeable lifetime transfers, based on the scale of tax chargeable on death.[1]

1 The table of rates is in Appendix IV, pp. 967 ff., post.

8.135 In the 'Apportionment of Tax payable on this Account' section on page 11 the value on which tax will be paid on obtaining the grant should be shown. By transferring the figures from Parts B and D and carrying out the numerical operations as indicated by the specimen fractions, the tax to be paid may be calculated.

8.136 Where exemption being claimed on page 9 under one or more of ss. 18 and 23 to 26 of the 1984 Act [FA 1975, Sch. 6, paras. 1 and 10 to 13] (gifts to surviving spouse, etc.) extends to part only of the estate, the calculation of that exemption must have regard to the incidence of the tax. Where the death occurred on or after 7 April 1976[1], 'specific gifts' not bearing their own tax are added together and grossed-up to the tax appropriate to their total value, ignoring all other gifts and residue. If no other part of the estate is chargeable that grossed-up value determines the tax payable.

1 Originally, 'specific gifts' (FA 1975, Sch. 6, para. 23(1)) not bearing their own tax had to be grossed-up at an 'assumed rate' which was the average rate of tax calculated on the basis that no exemption was due. For the same net benefit to a beneficiary this produced a different tax liability as between a legacy which was grossed-up and one which, because it bore its own tax, was not. To ameliorate this, FA 1976, s. 96 introduced a different approach.

8.137 In other cases several steps in the calculation of the taxable part of the estate are necessary as follows:

(1) The specific gifts not bearing their own tax are grossed-up as one unit as above.
(2) The value at 1 is added to specific gifts bearing their own tax and the taxable part of residue (based on the value at 1) to arrive at an initial value for tax.
(3) Specific gifts not bearing their own tax are grossed-up at the rate appropriate to the value found at 2[1].
(4) Using this new grossed-up value for specific gifts not bearing their own tax (as at 3) the chargeable portion of the estate is found by adding the new grossed-up value to the value of specific gifts bearing their own tax and the value of the taxable part of residue (based on the new grossed-up value at 3).

1 The average rate of tax $r = \dfrac{\text{tax on value at 2}}{\text{value at 2}}$. For operation 3, the new grossed-up value of specific gifts not bearing their own tax is given by value of specific gifts $\times \dfrac{1}{1-r}$

8.138 This is the final value of the taxable part of the estate and, in cases to which it applies, the figures thus obtained should be used on page 9 and for the 'Summary' on page 10 of the Inland Revenue account.

8.139 The foregoing procedure undergoes an additional operation in the case of deaths on and after 18 March 1986 where relief for business or agricultural property (or both) is available and the transfer on death is partly exempt. This operation[1] entails reducing specific gifts of business or agricultural property to their values after relief and reducing other specific gifts to the 'appropriate fraction' of their values. This 'appropriate fraction' is X/Y where X is the value of the estate after the relief concerned less the value after relief of any specific gift of business or agricultural property, and Y is the value of the estate before relief less any specific gift also before relief of any business or agricultural property. The grossing procedure is then followed as in the previous paragraph, but using the reduced figures obtained from the process described in this paragraph.

1 IHTA 1984, s. 39A as inserted by FA 1986, s. 105 with respect to transfers of value on and after 18 March 1986.

8.140   Supplementary provisions relate to abatement and the burden of the tax charged[1].

1 IHTA 1984, s. 36 et seq. [FA 1975, Sch. 6, Pt. III]. The amendment of para. 22 (burden of tax) by FA 1976, s. 96(5) is not intended to change the burden of tax as originally enacted].

8.141   Interest on tax on property not entitled to the 'instalment option' is payable from the end of the sixth month after the date of death to the date of payment. The rate of interest is 6 per cent[1] up to and including 31 December 1979, and 9 per cent from 1 January 1980 to 30 November 1982[2], 6 per cent from 1 December 1982 to 30 April 1985[3], 9 per cent from 1 May 1985 to 15 December 1986[4], 8 per cent from 16 December 1986 to 5 June 1987[5], 6 per cent from 6 June 1987 to 5 August 1988[6], 8 per cent from 6 August 1988 to 5 October 1988[7], 9 per cent from 6 October 1988 to 5 July 1989[8], 11 per cent from 6 July 1989 to 5 March 1991[9], 10 per cent from 6 March 1991 to 5 May 1991[10], 9 per cent from 6 May 1991 to 5 July 1991[11], 8 per cent from 6 July 1991 to 5 November 1992[12], 6 per cent from 6 November 1992 to 5 December 1992[13], 5 per cent from 6 December 1992 to 5 January 1994[14], 4 per cent from 6 January 1994 to 5 October 1994[15] and 5 per cent thereafter[16].

1 FA 1975, Sch. 4, para. 19.
2 S.I. 1979 No. 1688.
3 S.I. 1982 No. 1585 and IHTA 1984, s. 233.
4 S.I. 1985 No. 560.
5 S.I. 1986 No. 1944.
6 S.I. 1987 No. 887.
7 S.I. 1988 No. 1280.
8 S.I. 1988 No. 1623.
9 Board's Order June 1989.
10 Board's Order 18 February 1991.
11 Board's Order April 1991.
12 Board's Order 21 June 1991.
13 Board's Order 22 October 1992.
14 Board's Order 20 November 1992.
15 Board's Order 15 December 1993.
16 Board's Order 20 September 1994.

8.142   Interest on the tax on real property and other property entitled to the 'instalment option' is charged in the same way, except that in the case of business assets and unquoted shares in companies (excluding certain investment and dealing companies) and, in the case of deaths after 9 March 1981, property afforded agricultural relief, interest is only charged on each instalment as from the date it falls due (as regards chargeable transfers made before 10 March 1981 a limit of £250,000 is imposed on the value by reference to which tax may be paid by interest free instalments)[1]. Land and buildings held as business assets are entitled to this interest relief.

1   IHTA 1984, s. 234 [FA 1975, Sch. 4, para. 16 as amended by FA 1981, ss. 95 and 96].

8.143   Where the value of the property transferred on the death is such that no tax is payable, 'Nil' should be inserted at the appropriate places before delivery to the Principal or district registry: it is important that this is done, as otherwise the account may not be accepted.

Payment of tax

8.144   Where tax is payable, the assessed Inland Revenue account, the Summary and the tax and interest should first be sent to the Financial Services Office (IHT

Cashiers), Inland Revenue, Barrington Road, Worthing, West Sussex BN12 4XH, DX 90950 Worthing 3 for the Inland Revenue account to be receipted and impressed with the 'Paid' stamp of that Office, or it may be lodged by personal callers only at Somerset House, Strand, London WC2, for payment at the counter. Cheques or money orders should be crossed and made payable to 'Inland Revenue'.

8.145 In small cases, where there is difficulty in raising the money for the tax before the grant by other means, it may be possible to arrange to have the tax paid out of deposits in the National Savings Bank or by encashment of Savings Certificates or Premium Savings Bonds.

8.146 If payment by any of these methods is desired, application should be made by letter to the Controller, Capital Taxes Office, accompanied by the Inland Revenue account and, where appropriate, by the National Savings Bank book, or, in the case of Savings Certificates, by a statement from the Money Order Department of the extent and value of the holding. The Capital Taxes Office makes the necessary arrangements or gives instructions. Some delay in the receipting of the account and consequently in the issue of the grant is inevitable[1].

1 The Commissioners of Inland Revenue may, if they think fit, accept in or towards satisfaction of tax, landed property and objects kept in any building where it appears to be desirable for the objects to remain associated with the building; any picture, print, book, manuscript, work of art, scientific object, etc. which is considered pre-eminent for its national, scientific, historic or artistic interest. Collections of pictures etc. may be treated similarly. (Section 230 of the 1984 Act [FA 1975, Sch, 4, para. 17 as amended] is in point.) Tax should be paid in the usual way. The offer or enquiry should be made to the Controller, Capital Taxes Office.

Examination of account before the grant and delivery

8.147 Although, to avoid delay in obtaining the grant, generally the examination of the Inland Revenue account is deferred until after the grant has been obtained, nevertheless in the following instances the account must be delivered to the Capital Taxes Office before the application for the grant so that the account may be examined and assessed:

(a) where it is claimed that the deceased died domiciled outside the United Kingdom;

(b) where conditional exemption is claimed in respect of objects of national, scientific, historic or artistic interest or in respect of land or buildings of outstanding interest;

(c) where payment of tax is to be made out of a National Savings Bank deposit, or out of the proceeds of National Savings Certificates or Premium Savings Bonds;

(d) where the grant is required only in respect of settled land.

8.148 It is particularly important where an English solicitor is acting for individuals overseas in cases where the deceased is claimed to be domiciled outside the United Kingdom that the papers concerned are delivered to the Capital Taxes Office at the earliest opportunity—not least to avoid the possibility of 'intermeddling' with the estate. Cases of difficulty may still be sent to that office for advice.

8.149 In correspondence with the Capital Taxes Office use of the file number (when known) is always helpful and time-saving, but its absence need cause no special delay to correspondence provided the full name and date of death of the deceased is given.

8.150   The receipted Inland Revenue account is lodged in the registry when application is made for the grant, and is passed by the registry to the Capital Taxes Office for permanent retention.

8.151   A duplicate Inland Revenue account, if delivered to the Inland Revenue, Financial Services Office in Worthing at the time of payment with a letter of request, will be endorsed with a certificate of payment as on the original.

8.152   Evidence of payment for fiscal purposes abroad can be obtained after the issue of the grant, usually on a certified copy of the Inland Revenue account, for which a copying fee may be payable.

Corrective accounts

Practice as to corrective accounts

8.153   Where any correction of the tax paid upon an Inland Revenue account becomes necessary after the grant of representation has issued, the form Cap D–3 is applicable. This should be forwarded for assessment to the Controller of the Capital Taxes Office.

CHAPTER 9

Trust corporations

Definition of trust corporation

9.01 In this work the term 'trust corporation' is used to denote a trust corporation as recognised by the law of England and Wales.

9.02 A trust corporation is defined for the purposes of the Supreme Court Act 1981 as:

'the Public Trustee or a corporation either appointed by the court in any particular case to be a trustee or authorised by rules made under section 4(3) of the Public Trustee Act 1906 to act as custodian trustee'[1].

1 Supreme Court Act 1981, s. 128, replacing the corresponding provision contained in the repealed Supreme Court of Judicature (Consolidation) Act 1925, with effect from 1 January 1982.

9.03 This definition is enlarged by s. 3(1) of the Law of Property (Amendment) Act 1926[1] so as to include the Treasury Solicitor (which includes the Solicitor for the Duchy of Lancaster), the Official Solicitor, and any person holding any other official position prescribed by the Lord Chancellor, and, in relation to the property of a bankrupt and property subject to a deed of arrangement, includes the trustee in bankruptcy and the trustee under the deed respectively, and, in relation to charitable, ecclesiastical and public trusts, also includes any local or public authority so prescribed, and any other corporation, constituted under the laws of the United Kingdom or any part thereof, which satisfies the Lord Chancellor that it undertakes the administration of any such trusts without remuneration, or that by its constitution it is required to apply the whole of its net income, after payment of outgoings, for charitable, ecclesiastical or public purposes, and is prohibited from distributing directly or indirectly any part thereof by way of profits amongst any of its members, and is authorised by him to act in relation to such trusts as a trust corporation.

1 See p. 764, post: although earlier to the Supreme Court Act 1981 in date, this provision is still effective to extend the definition contained in the later Act.

9.04 By virtue of the Church of England Pensions Board (Powers) Measure 1952, s. 6, the Church of England Pensions Board is a trust corporation for these purposes.

323

Definition of custodian trustee

9.05   Rule 30(1) of the Public Trustee Rules 1912, as substituted by the Public Trustee (Custodian Trustee) Rules 1971 and amended by the Public Trustee (Custodian Trustee) Rules 1975, 1976, 1981, 1984 and 1987[1], is as follows:

'The following corporations shall be entitled to act as custodian trustees:

(a) the Treasury Solicitor;

(b) any corporation which:

    (i)   is constituted under the law of the United Kingdom or of any part thereof, or under the law of any other Member State of the European Economic Community or of any part thereof;

    (ii) is empowered by its constitution to undertake trust business (which for the purpose of this rule means the business of acting as trustee under wills and settlements and as executor and administrator) in England and Wales;

    (iii) has one or more places of business in the United Kingdom; and

    (iv) is—

        a company incorporated by special Act of Parliament or Royal Charter, or

        a company registered (with or without limited liability) in the United Kingdom under the Companies Act 1948 or under the Companies Act (Northern Ireland) 1960 or in another Member State of the European Economic Community and having a capital (in stock or shares) for the time being issued of not less than £250,000 (or its equivalent in the currency of the State where the company is registered), of which not less than £100,000 (or its equivalent) has been paid up in cash, or

        a company which is registered without limited liability in the United Kingdom under the Companies Act 1948 or the Companies Act (Northern Ireland) 1960 or in another Member State of the European Economic Community and of which one of the members is a company within any of the classes defined in this sub-paragraph;

(c) any corporation which is incorporated by special Act or Royal Charter or under the Charitable Trustees Incorporation Act 1872 which is empowered by its constitution to act as a trustee for any charitable purposes, but only in relation to trusts in which its constitution empowers it to act;

(d) any corporation which is constituted under the law of the United Kingdom or of any part thereof and having its place of business there, and which is either:

    (i)   established for the purpose of undertaking trust business for the benefit of Her Majesty's Navy, Army, Air Force or Civil Service or of any unit, department, member or association of members thereof, and having among its directors or members any persons appointed or nominated by the Defence Council or any Department of State or any one or more of those Departments, or

    (ii) authorised by the Lord Chancellor to act in relation to any charitable, ecclesiastical or public trusts as a trust corporation, but only in connection with any such trust as is so authorised;

(e) (i) any Regional Health Authority, District Health Authority or special health authority, but only in relation to any trust which the authority is authorised to accept or hold by virtue of section 90 of the National Health Service Act 1977;

    (ii) any preserved Board as defined by section 15(6) of the National Health Service Reorganisation Act 1973, but only in relation to any trust which the board is authorised to accept or hold by virtue of an order made under that section;

(f) the British Gas Corporation or any subsidiary of the British Gas Corporation, but only in relation to a pension scheme or pension fund established or maintained by the Corporation by virtue of section 36 of the Gas Act 1972;

(g) the London Transport Executive, but only in relation to a pension scheme or pension fund—

    (i) which is established or administered by the Executive by virtue of section 6 of the Transport (London) Act 1969, or

    (ii) in relation to which rights, liabilities and functions have been transferred to the Executive by an order under section 74 of the Transport Act 1962 as applied by section 18 of the Transport (London) Act 1969;

(h) any of the following, namely:

    (i) the Greater London Council,

    (ii) the corporation of any London borough (acting by the council),

    (iii) a county council, district council, parish council or community council,

    (iv) the Council of the Isles of Scilly,

    (v) the Common Council of the City of London,

    but only in relation to charitable or public trusts (and not trusts for an ecclesiastical charity or for a charity for the relief of poverty) for the benefit of the inhabitants of the area of the local authority concerned and its neighbourhood, or any part of that area;

(i) any of the following, namely:

    (i) a metropolitan district council or a non-metropolitan county council,

    (ii) the corporation of any London borough (acting by the council),

    (iii) the Common Council of the City of London,

    (iv) the Council of the Isles of Scilly,

    but only in relation to any trust under which property devolves for the sole benefit of a person who occupies residential accommodation provided under section 21(1)(a) of the National Assistance Act 1948 by the local authority concerned or is in the care of that authority; and a corporation acting as a custodian trustee by virtue of this paragraph in relation to any trust shall be entitled to continue so to act in relation to that trust until a new custodian trustee is appointed, notwithstanding that the person concerned ceases to occupy such accommodation or to be in the care of that authority, as the case may be;

(j) the National Coal Board or any subsidiary of the National Coal Board, but only in relation to a scheme or arrangements established under regulations made under section 37 of the Coal Industry Nationalisation Act 1946;

(k) any corporation acting as trustee of the trusts of any pension scheme or pension fund established or maintained by the British Broadcasting Corporation, but only in relation to these trusts.'

1 S.I.s 1971 No. 1894; 1975 No. 1189; 1976 No. 836, 1981 No. 358, 1984 No. 109 and 1987 No. 1891.

9.06 It should be noted that, in addition to certain minor changes, the 1975 amendment to rule 30 of the Public Trustee Rules 1912 enables a corporation constituted under the law of any Member State of the European Economic Community which is empowered by its constitution to undertake trust business, has a place of business in the United Kingdom and complies with the conditions of paragraph (b)(iv) of the rule, to act as custodian trustee and accordingly to obtain a grant of representation in England and Wales in its corporate name.

9.07 The introduction of paragraph (i) into rule 30 by the Public Trustee (Custodian Trustee) Rules 1976 prescribes classes of local authorities entitled to act as custodian trustees (and thereby as trust corporations) in relation to certain trusts, namely in respect of any trust under which property devolves for the sole benefit of a person who occupies residential accommodation provided under section 21(1)(a) of the National Assistance Act 1948 (i.e. persons who by reason of age, infirmity or other circumstances are in need of care and attention) by the local authority concerned or a trust under which property devolves for the sole benefit of a person in the care of the local authority (e.g. a child in care of a local authority): as to the practice to be followed on application being made in these circumstances, see paras. **11.177** ff. and **25.98** ff., post. Where, pursuant to this paragraph, a local authority acts as a custodian trustee, it is entitled to continue so to act until a new custodian trustee is appointed, even though the person concerned has ceased to occupy the accommodation in question or is no longer in the care of that authority. It must be emphasised, however, that this additional right is conferred only in relation to these particular trusts and that it is not available under the general provision (i.e. paragraph (h) of rule 30) whereby a local authority has power to act as a trust corporation in respect of property held upon charitable or public trusts (not being a trust for an ecclesiastical charity or for a charity for the relief of poverty) for the benefit of local inhabitants.

9.08   Where the local authority is not qualified to act as a custodian trustee and is thereby unable to apply for a grant of representation in its corporate name (e.g. where the authority applies for a grant as a creditor of the estate), then application must be made by the local authority through its nominee or attorney (see paras. **5.201–5.207**, ante).

Power to act as executor or administrator

9.09   Section 115(1) of the Supreme Court Act 1981[1] empowers the court to grant probate of a will to a trust corporation named therein as executor, either alone or jointly with any other person named in the will as executor, and to grant administration to a trust corporation either solely or jointly with another person, and empowers the corporation to act accordingly as executor or administrator as the case may be.

1 See p. 845, post.

9.10   The grant is made to the corporation in its corporate name, and is a full grant (unless a limitation is imposed owing to the circumstances of the case).

9.11   No grant may be made to a person as nominee of a trust corporation[1].

1 Supreme Court Act 1981, s. 115(2).

Power to charge remuneration

9.12   The court can empower a trust corporation to charge for its services[1].

1 Trustee Act 1925, s. 42 (38 Halsbury's Statutes (3rd edn) 164); *Re Young's Estate* (1934) 103 LJP 75; *Re Masters, Coutts & Co v Masters* [1953] 1 All ER 19, [1953] 1 WLR 81; *Re Batty* (1950) 17 May (motion). (Westminster Bank Ltd being nominated as co-grantee by the mother, as statutory guardian of an infant, would not act without authority for making its charges. On motion, the court ordered a grant to issue to the mother and the bank with power to the bank to make its charges.)

Resolution appointing person to make the application for grant

9.13 'Any officer authorised for the purpose by a trust corporation or its directors or governing body may, on behalf of the corporation, swear affidavits, give security and do any other act which the court may require with a view to the grant to the corporation of probate or administration; and the acts of an officer so authorised shall be binding on the corporation' (Supreme Court Act 1981, s. 115(3)).

9.14 Where the trust corporation is the holder of an official position, any officer whose name is included on a list filed with the Senior District Judge of persons authorised to make affidavits and sign documents on behalf of the office holder may act as the officer through whom the holder of the official position applies for the grant[1]. Any such list for filing with the Senior District Judge should be lodged with the Secretary of the Principal Registry of the Family Division, Somerset House, Strand, London WC2R 1LP.

1 NCPR 36(2)(a).

9.15 In all other cases a certified copy of the resolution of the trust corporation authorising the officer to make the application must be lodged. If a certified copy of a resolution authorising an officer or officers, identified by the position held, is filed with the Senior District Judge (not in a particular case but as a general authority) it is not necessary to lodge a copy with the application for the grant, otherwise a certified copy of the resolution appointing the officer for the purpose of taking the necessary steps to obtain the grant must be lodged with the papers: the resolution may appoint the officer for one specific case or may take the form of a general appointment either of named officers or of persons holding specified positions in the corporation.

Particulars required in oath

9.16 The officer must depose in the oath that the corporation is a trust corporation as defined by r. 2(1) of the Non-Contentious Probate Rules 1987, and has power to accept a grant: NCPR 36(1).

9.17 The oath must also show how the corporation is entitled to apply, i.e.:

(a) on an application for probate, it must state that the corporation is the sole executor, or one of the executors etc. (as the case may be), as on an application for probate by an individual;

(b) on an application for administration (with will) or administration, it must contain the necessary clearings, and refer to any renunciations and the consents of the persons entitled to a grant and to the residuary estate, as shown in paras. **9.35** ff., post;

(c) on application for a grant as attorney, it must contain a similar wording to that required on application for a grant by an individual appointed as attorney (see paras. **11.79** ff., post);

(d) if reliance is made on a certified copy of a resolution authorising an officer or officers to make the application, which has already been filed with the Senior District Judge, the oath must state that such a certified copy of the resolution of the trust corporation authorising the officer to make the application has been filed with the Senior District Judge, that the officer is therein identified by the position he holds, and that such resolution is still in force[1].

1 NCPR 36(2)(b).

9.18   All renunciations and consents, or the power of attorney, referred to in the oath must be lodged with the papers. Forms of oath, Nos. 67 and 111.

9.19   Where on an application for a grant by a trust corporation, that corporation has been appointed as executor of the will on terms and conditions specifically referred to as being in existence at the date of the will or of its republication, as the case may be, then, provided that the oath contains a statement to the effect that nothing in those terms and conditions limits the corporation's power to take a full grant, it will not normally be necessary to produce them to the registry on the application[1].

1 *Practice Direction* [1981] 2 All ER 1104.

9.20   As a result of the Companies Act 1980, many trust corporations were required to re-register as 'public companies'. The Act of 1980 provided that the name of a public company must end with the words 'public limited company' or its abbreviation 'p.l.c.'. In the case of a company the registered office of which is situated in Wales, the Welsh equivalent 'cwmni cyfyngedig cyhoeddus' or its abbreviation 'c.c.c.' may be used. These requirements are now contained in the Companies Act 1985, s. 25.

9.21   Where a trust corporation applies for a grant using in its name any of these alternatives, it will not be necessary for the oath or the grant to account for any change in the suffix which may have been used in the corporation's appointment, nor will it normally be necessary for the probate registries to require evidence to be produced that the corporation has registered or re-registered under the Act[1].

1 *Practice Direction* [1982] 1 All ER 384, [1982] 1 WLR 214.

Joint grants

9.22   A grant of representation may be made to a trust corporation alone or jointly with an individual. See also Chap. 7.

Trust corporation as executor

9.23   A trust corporation appointed as executor either solely or jointly with one or more individuals may obtain probate or renounce, or power may be reserved to such an executor, as in the case of an individual.

9.24   Form of oath for probate to a trust corporation, No. 67.

Branch office appointed

9.25   When a branch of a bank is appointed executor, the grant is normally made to the bank itself[1]. If the branch office appointed executor is abroad and the head office is in England, a grant of probate should be applied for by the head office. But if the office abroad is not a branch of the trust corporation in England, but has a separate entity, the grant (of administration with will) must be made to its nominee or attorney, which may in some cases be the English bank of which it is an offshoot.

1 *Re White* (1924) July (motion).

Corporations in the Republic of Ireland

9.26 It has been held[1] that a corporation having its head office in the Republic of Ireland, and having obtained power there since the establishment of the Irish Free State to act as an executor, has no power to take a grant of probate in England, as it is not a corporation constituted under the law of the United Kingdom or any part thereof; although a corporation in the Republic of Ireland which obtained its power to act as an executor before the establishment of the Irish Free State is able to take a grant in England.

1 *Re Barlow* [1933] P 184.

9.27 However, it would now appear that a corporation constituted in the Republic of Ireland which qualifies in accordance with the conditions of rule 30 of the Public Trustee Rules 1912 (as substituted by the Public Trustee (Custodian Trustee) Rules 1975 (see paras. **9.05** and **9.06**, ante)) may obtain a grant in its corporate name, the Republic of Ireland being a member state of the European Economic Community[1].

1 *Re Bigger* [1977] Fam 203, [1977] 2 All ER 644.

Renunciation by trust corporation

9.28 As to renunciation of probate or administration by a trust corporation, see paras. **15.09** and **15.10**, post.

Trust corporation as attorney

9.29 A trust corporation appointed by power of attorney for the purpose may apply for administration, or administration (with will), for the use and benefit of an executor or a person entitled to administration (with or without will). No second grantee is required notwithstanding the existence of minority or life interests.

9.30 As to grants to attorneys generally, see paras. **11.31** ff., post.

Trust corporation for use and benefit of minor or incapable person

9.31 Application may be made for the appointment of a trust corporation as a 'person' for the purpose of taking a grant for the use and benefit of a minor (e.g. where a local authority is entitled to act as a custodian trustee under rule 30 of the Public Trustee Rules 1912 in relation to a trust under which property devolves for the sole benefit of a child who is in the care of that authority: see para. **9.05**, ante, for rule 30, and paras. **11.177** ff., post, for the practice to be followed in such cases); but the more usual course is to proceed in accordance with the Registrar's Direction (1952) 25 February—see paras. **9.40** ff., post.

9.32 Where it is desired that a trust corporation shall take a grant for the use and benefit of a person who is incapable of managing his affairs, application should be made to the district judge or registrar for an order under NCPR 35(4) (see para. **11.245**, post). Under that rule the district judge or registrar has power to direct that administration be granted to *two or more* (other) persons.

Trust corporation as administrator (with or without will)

9.33   Where a trust corporation applies for a grant of administration (which includes administration (with will)) *otherwise than as a beneficiary or the attorney of some person*, there must be lodged with the application the consents of all persons entitled to a grant and of all persons interested in the residuary estate of the deceased, unless the district judge or registrar directs that such consents be dispensed with on such terms, if any, as he may think fit[1].

1   NCPR 36(3).

9.34   As to the position when any, or all, of the persons who should consent are minors, see paras. **9.40–9.50**, post.

Administration (with will): consents required

9.35   Where the deceased left a will, to enable a grant to be made to a trust corporation (other than one appointed as executor) all executors named in the will must be cleared off, e.g. by death, renunciation or citation; and, subject to the power of the district judge or registrar to dispense with any consent, the consents of the following to the making of a grant to the corporation must be obtained, where the trust corporation is not applying as a beneficiary or the attorney of some person, and recited in the oath:

(a)   any residuary legatees or devisees holding in trust;
(b)   any residuary legatees or devisees for life;
(c)   the ultimate residuary legatees and devisees (including those entitled on the happening of any contingency), and if the whole or part of the residuary estate is not disposed of by the will, all persons entitled to share in the undisposed-of estate.

Form of consent, No. 58.

9.36   An executor who is also entitled in any of the capacities shown above must consent to the grant in addition to renouncing probate; but except where any beneficiary is a minor (as to which see below) renunciations of administration (with will) are not required.

Administration: consents required

9.37   Similarly, where the trust corporation is not applying as the attorney of some person, where the deceased died intestate, the consents of all persons sharing beneficially in the estate should be obtained and recited in the oath, which must also include the necessary clearings of prior classes as on application by a beneficiary himself. Form of consent, No. 58. Form of oath, No. 111.

9.38   As to the procedure where any person whose consent is required is under age, see the two following paragraphs.

9.39   It is not necessary to obtain the consents of persons having no immediate beneficial interest but who may have an interest in the event of an accretion to the estate: thus, where the deceased left a surviving spouse and the net value of the estate, after allowing the permitted deductions (see para. **6.92**, ante), does not exceed the amount of the 'fixed net sum' due to the spouse[1], the consent of the spouse, to be described as 'the only person now entitled to the estate', is sufficient to enable a trust corporation to obtain administration.

1 See para. **6.31**, ante.

Some person entitled a minor

9.40 Where any person beneficially entitled, whether under a will or an intestacy, is a minor, a consent to the grant by any other person on his behalf is not accepted, as his right to take a grant on attaining full age would be extinguished by the making of a full grant to the trust corporation[1]. All persons of full age whose consents are required under NCPR 36(3) (as set out in paras. **9.35–9.37**, ante) should, in addition to consenting, renounce their right to a grant. The grant to the trust corporation will be limited until the minor (or one or more of them, if more than one) obtains a grant or until further representation be granted[2].

1 *Re Tower* (November 1927, unreported); Registrar's Direction (1952) 14 October.
2 President's Direction (1947) 19 June.

9.41 It should be noted that the grant does not necessarily cease, as in the case of a grant for the use and benefit of a minor, as soon as one minor attains the age of 18.

9.42 It is considered by the district judges and registrars that they have a discretion, in proper cases, to dispense with the renunciations of persons of full age, of a similar nature to their power under r. 36(3) to dispense with consents.

9.43 An order will not be made by a district judge or registrar appointing persons under r. 32(2) on behalf of a minor simply for the purpose of consenting to a trust corporation's application for a grant[1].

1 Direction (1941) 11 December.

All persons entitled under age

9.44 Where all persons entitled to administration are under age, a limited grant may issue as of right to a trust corporation on the consent of all parents with parental responsibility and all guardians with parental responsibility for the minors[1].

1 They being the persons entitled to apply for a grant for the use and benefit of the minors under r. 32(1).

9.45 If there are no persons so qualified, the issue of a grant to a trust corporation is discretionary. The written refusal of the next-of-kin to act may be accepted as sufficient, but if the next nearest of kin are willing to act, consideration should be given to the alternative of having them appointed under r. 32(2) for the purpose of taking a grant.

9.46 Where the deceased died domiciled out of England and Wales, or where all the above persons are abroad, the matter should be referred to a district judge or registrar. For cases of domicile out of England and Wales, see also paras. **11.185** ff., post.)

9.47 A grant to a trust corporation under the above procedure will be limited until one of the minors shall obtain a grant or until further representation be granted.

9.48   Where the only persons entitled to probate as executors are minors, a grant may be made to a trust corporation on the consent of the persons entitled to the residuary estate. If the executors are also persons entitled to the residue, consents on their behalf may be accepted as shown above. If other persons entitled to the residue are not sui juris, the matter should be referred to a district judge or registrar. A grant under this paragraph will be limited until one of the executors shall attain the age of eighteen years.

9.49   A grant to a trust corporation when all the persons entitled are under age will be to the corporation in its own right and not for the use and benefit of the minors[1].

1 Registrar's Direction (1952) 25 February. This Direction must be distinguished from that of (1947) (see para. **9.40**, above), which deals with cases where some only of the persons entitled are under age.

9.50   References in this section to a trust corporation include the Public Trustee.

Treasury Solicitor and Solicitor for the Duchy of Lancaster

9.51   The Treasury Solicitor or Solicitor for the Duchy of Lancaster when taking a grant in his official capacity for the use or benefit of Her Majesty is not required to make an affidavit to lead to the grant: instead, he files a signed Statement containing particulars of the deceased and of the basis on which the grant is sought. He also delivers a signed form of Inland Revenue account[1]. A carbon copy of the Treasury Solicitor's Form of Statement, or of the similar form used by the Solicitor for the Duchy of Lancaster, containing a declaration of the estate and the domicile of deceased, is placed inside the form, and this will go forward to the Capital Taxes Office after the grant has issued[2].

1 Administration of Estates Act 1925, s. 30(3), see p. 750, post.
2 Secretary's Circular, 15 November 1972.

Company in liquidation

9.52   A grant to a company remains operative until the company is finally wound up, the powers of the company being exercised by the liquidator. Unless and until the grant has become inoperative there is no ground for the revocation of such a grant. When a company has been finally wound up, the liquidator is functus officio and has no power either to apply for revocation of the grant, or to consent to its revocation if revocation of it is applied for by an applicant for a subsequent grant.

9.53   The proper course would seem to be not to revoke the grant, which becomes ineffective and inoperative on the winding up of the company. An applicant for a subsequent grant should swear in his oath to lead that grant that the grant to the company has become inoperative by reason of the winding up of the company on the   day of   , and that the file of the company has been marked by the Registrar of Companies 'Company dissolved'; and this statement should be recited in the grant, which will be a grant de bonis non.

The Public Trustee

9.54   The office of Public Trustee was established by the Public Trustee Act 1906[1], which does not extend to Northern Ireland or Scotland.

1 See p. 732, post.

9.55 See paras. **1.55–1.58**, ante as to vesting of estates in the Public Trustee where deceased died intestate or there is no executor with power to obtain probate.

9.56 The Public Trustee is authorised to accept, in his official name, probate or letters of administration of any kind, and either as principal or as agent for any person (Public Trustee Rules 1912, r. 6(c)).

9.57 By virtue of s. 6(1) of the Act, the court may grant probate or letters of adminstration (with or without will) to the Public Trustee by that name, and for this purpose the Public Trustee is to be considered as in law entitled equally with any other person or class of persons to obtain administration (with or without will), save that the consent or citation of the Public Trustee is not required for a grant of administration to any other person, and that, as between the Public Trustee and the husband, widow or next-of-kin of the deceased, the husband, widow or next-of-kin is to be preferred unless for good cause shown to the contrary[1]. The Public Trustee may renounce executorship; but if he takes a grant of probate, he will continue a chain of executorship, if there is such chain[2].

1 Public Trustee Act 1906, s. 6(1): see *Re Woolley's Estate* (1911) 55 Sol Jo 220.
2 President's Instructions, 27 March 1908.

Grants under s. 6 of the Public Trustee Act 1906

9.58 *As administrator with will.* When the Public Trustee applies for letters of administration (with will) he must clear off executors in the usual way; and notice should be given by him to the residuary legatees and devisees, or their representatives, as the case may be, or (if there are no residuary legatees or devisees) to the person or persons entitled to the undisposed-of residue or their representatives, or such of them as can, without delay, be communicated with, intimating that the application for a grant is being made by the Public Trustee, and that unless application for a grant be made, or a caveat be entered, within eight days from the date of the posting of the notices he will proceed with his application without further notice; but, if a person to whom notice is sent is not in the United Kingdom, the period of eight days should be increased by the addition of time sufficient for a reply, by return of post in ordinary course of post, from the place to which the notice is sent[1]. For form of oath, see No. 151. The consents of all such persons should, if possible, be obtained and filed.

1 President's Instructions, 27 March 1908.

9.59 *As administrator.* When the Public Trustee applies for letters of administration notice should be given by him, as above mentioned, to the widower or widow, and all persons sharing in the estate, or their representatives, as the case may be, or such of them as can, without delay, be communicated with[1]. Application to dispense with giving such notice should be referred to a district judge or registrar.

1 President's Instructions, 27 March 1908.

9.60 Should the notice result in another application for a grant being lodged, the question of preference may be dealt with by one of the district judges or registrars.

9.61 If a caveat is entered, the usual practice is followed (see paras. **23.17** ff., post).

9.62   If it is suggested that there is a will, the Public Trustee must first cite the executors and the persons interested thereunder to propound it.

9.63   As to grants where any or all of the persons entitled are minors, see paras. **9.40–9.50**, ante.

Administration under the Public Trustee Act 1906

9.64   Under s. 3(1) of the Public Trustee Act 1906[1], any person who in the opinion of the Public Trustee would be entitled to apply to the court for an order for the administration by the court of an estate of which the Public Trustee is satisfied that the gross capital is less than £1,000, may apply to the Public Trustee to administer the estate. Where such application is made and it appears to the Public Trustee that the beneficiaries are of small means, he shall administer the estate unless he sees good reason for refusing to do so.

1   See p. 732, post.

9.65   Upon receipt of an undertaking by the Public Trustee to administer an estate under this provision, such undertaking is filed, without fee, in the Record Keeper's Department. The record of any existing grant is then noted, also without fee, that 'the Public Trustee has undertaken to administer the estate under s. 3 of the Public Trustee Act 1906'.

9.66   Where such notation appears on the copy of the record no duplicate grant may be issued without special direction of one of the district judges or registrars[1].

1   Registrar's Direction, 3 March 1920.

9.67   Under s. 6(2) of the Public Trustee Act 1906[1], any executor or administrator who has obtained a grant, alone or jointly with others, and notwithstanding that he may have acted in the administration of the estate, may, with the sanction of the court and after such notice to the beneficiaries as the court may direct, transfer the estate to the Public Trustee for administration, either solely or jointly with other continuing executors or administrators (if any).

1   See p. 733, post.

9.68   Application for an order sanctioning such a transfer should be made to the Chancery Division: see Supreme Court Practice under 'Public Trustee Act'.

Oath on behalf of Public Trustee

9.69   Under s. 11(3) of the Public Trustee Act 1906 such person as may be prescribed may, on behalf of the Public Trustee, take any oath or verify any account. The oath is accordingly sworn and the Inland Revenue account (if any) signed by an officer nominated by the Public Trustee for that purpose.

Linlited grant to Public Trustee

9.70   Where the Public Trustee is regarded as entitled to a general grant, but desires to take a limited grant, application should first be made to a district judge or registrar for his directions.

Deceased person domiciled abroad

9.71 The Public Trustee has power to take grants in the cases of persons dying domiciled abroad[1] but is not obliged to do so[2].

1 See *Re Grundt's Estate*; *Re Oetl's Estate* [1915] P 126.
2 In the case of *Re Baltazzi* (1942) October, the Public Trustee, on the advice of the Law Officers of the Crown, refused to take a grant under s. 6 of the Public Trustee Act 1906 as the deceased was domiciled out of England.

Grants on behalf of minor

9.72 The Public Trustee may take a grant for the use of a minor, on being appointed to do so by order of the district judge or registrar: see, however, the alternative procedure set out in paras. **9.33–9.50**, ante.

As attorney

9.73 When a grant is made to the Public Trustee in England as attorney of a person (or persons) other than the Public Trustee of a Commonwealth country, the grant contains the limitation 'until he (or they) shall obtain a grant', or the limitation 'until further representation be granted', according to the requirements of the case[1].

1 Direction (1936) 24 March.

Public Trustee appointed executor

9.74 When an application for probate is made by an executor, the Public Trustee having been appointed as co-executor, it must be ascertained whether the Public Trustee is desirous of acting before a grant can be made to the other executor[1] (and see paras. **4.50–4.56**, ante as to giving notice to an executor to whom power is to be reserved).

1 Direction (1920) 18 November.

CHAPTER 10
Settled land grants

Summary

The necessity for the grant

Settlements before and since the 'Property Acts' of 1925

10.01   Settled land grants were instituted by the 'Property Acts' of 1925 as part of the machinery of the conveyancing system thereby created. As the Acts in question came into force on 1 January 1926, the present chapter is concerned only with deaths on or after that date. It is concerned also only with land in England and Wales.

10.02   Before 1926 a settlement of land might consist of a series of direct limitations to the beneficiaries successively, each in turn taking a legal estate for his life or otherwise; and in such cases the original disposition operated to vest all the legal estates in their due order, as well as the beneficial interests, without further formality on the occasion of any death. Alternatively, the land might be vested in trustees upon trust for the beneficiaries successively, the legal estate remaining in the trustees throughout.

10.03   The first type of settlement was made impossible by s. 1 of the Law of Property Act 1925[1], which provided that the only estates in land capable of existing *at law* are (1) an estate in fee simple absolute in possession, and (2) a term of years absolute. These estates cannot now be split up into successive interests. In the case of settled land, therefore, where there is no absolute beneficial owner, the legal fee simple or leasehold term, the subject of the settlement, must necessarily be vested in someone in a fiduciary capacity. The present system is to entrust the whole legal estate not to ordinary trustees, as under the second type of pre-1926 settlement, but to the tenant for life in possession, provided that he is of full age. If there is no tenant for life of full age, the legal estate is vested for the time being in the trustees of the settlement as a collective 'statutory owner'. For definition of statutory owner, see para. **10.17**, post.)

1   37 Halsbury's Statutes (4th edn) 76.

10.04   Section 9 of the Settled Land Act 1925[1] sets out the settlements or trust instruments deemed for the purpose of the Act to be 'a trust instrument'.

1   48 Halsbury's Statutes (4th edn) 385.

10.05   None of these changes materially affects the beneficial interests, which vest and devolve in substantially the same manner as before.

What is settled land

10.06   In considering the position more closely, it is necessary first to ascertain what land is settled land. This question is dealt with in the opening sections of the Settled Land Act 1925. First, a settlement is defined by s. 1[1], as amended by the Law of Property (Amendment) Act 1926[2]; then, by s. 2[3], land which is or is deemed to be the subject of a settlement is termed settled land. The definition, in conjunction with various subsequent provisions in the Act, dealing with special cases, embraces not only settlements in the narrower sense, whereby the land is 'limited in trust for any persons by way of succession', but also practically every other case where the interest of the beneficial owner for the time being is qualified or restricted. Among the cases so dealt with are entailed interests, minority of the only person absolutely entitled, and absolute interests subject to outstanding charges for jointures or portions.

1   See p. 734, post.
2   37 Halsbury's Statutes (4th edn) 384.
3   See p. 735, post.

10.07   Capital money arising from the sale of settled land, although treated for certain purposes as land or real estate, is not settled land[1]. As to capital money, see paras. **10.57** ff., post.

1   *Re Cartwright, Cartwright v Smith* [1939] Ch 90, [1938] 4 All ER 209, CA.

Land settled on charitable, etc., trusts

10.08   Land vested, or to be vested, in trustees for charitable, ecclesiastical or public trusts or purposes is deemed, by s. 29 of the Settled Land Act 1925[1], to be settled land, and the trustees have, in reference to such land, all the powers, under the Act, of a tenant for life or trustees of a settlement. It follows that a settled land grant may be required on the death of a sole or last surviving trustee in whom the land was vested.

1   48 Halsbury's Statutes (4th edn) 416.

Judicial trustees

10.09   Where there is no tenant for life of a settlement created by will, and no person on whom a tenant for life's powers are conferred by the will, with the result that any Settled Land Act trustees would have under s. 23 of the Settled Land Act 1925[1], all the powers of a tenant for life, but in fact there are no such trustees and no appointment can be obtained out of court, the court will in a proper case appoint a person to be a judicial trustee under s. 1(1) of the Judicial Trustees Act 1896[2]. This may be done by appointing him to be trustee, for the purposes of the Settled Land Act 1925, of the settled land, and directing that in that capacity he shall be a judicial trustee, and by appointing him also judicial trustee of the will[3].

1 48 Halsbury's Statutes (4th edn) 388.
2 48 Halsbury's Statutes (4th edn) 198.
3 *Re Marshall's Will Trusts* [1945] Ch 217, [1945] 1 All ER 550.

Charge on land on joint tenancy

10.10   Land vested in joint tenants and subject to a charge created in consideration of marriage is settled land by virtue of s. 205(1)(xxvi), Law of Property Act 1925[1], and is not subject to the statutory trust under s. 36[2].

1 37 Halsbury's Statutes (4th edn) 332.
2 Ibid., 393; *Re Gaul and Houlston's Contract* [1928] Ch 689, CA.

Land held upon trust for sale

10.11   By s. 1(7) of the Settled Land Act 1925[1], the definition of settled land is not to include land held upon trust for sale. For this purpose, a trust for sale, as defined by s. 117(1)(xxx) (by reference to s. 205(1)(xxix) of the Law of Property Act 1925), means

> 'an immediate binding trust for sale, whether or not exercisable at the request or with the consent of any person, and with or without a power at discretion to postpone the sale.'

The expression 'immediate binding trust for sale' has been the subject of several judicial decisions and much debate in the legal press, with reference to the effect of the existence of some minor interest in the land, such as a jointure under an old settlement, which has priority over the trust for sale[2].

1 See p. 735, post.
2 See, for instance, *Re Leigh's Settled Estates* [1926] Ch 852; *Re Leigh's Settled Estates (No 2)* [1927] 2 Ch 13 (not followed); *Re Ryder and Steadman's Contract* [1927] 2 Ch 62; *Re Parker's Settled Estates, Parker v Parker* [1928] Ch 247; *Re Norton, Pinney v Beauchamp* [1929] 1 Ch 84; *Re Sharpe's Deed of Release, Sharpe and Fox v Gullick* [1939] Ch 51, [1938] 3 All ER 449; *Re Gough, Phillips v Simpson* [1957] Ch 323, [1957] 2 All ER 193.

10.12   By virtue of s. 36 of the Settled Land Act 1925[1], there must always be a trust for sale where the beneficiaries for the time being are tenants in common. The result is that there is a conversion, and the settled land devolves as personalty[2]. The trust must be for sale of the whole property.

1 48 Halsbury's Statutes (4th edn) 427.
2 *Re Kempthorne, Charles v Kempthorne* [1930] 1 Ch 268.

Post-1925 settlements: how effected

10.13   Section 4 of the Settled Land Act 1925[1] provides that every settlement of a legal estate in land inter vivos shall (except as otherwise provided) be effected by two deeds (a vesting deed and a trust instrument), and, if effected in any other way, shall not operate to transfer or create a legal estate. The vesting deed, the contents of which are further regulated by s. 5[2], is to convey the legal estate to the tenant for life or statutory owner (if more than one, as joint tenants) or to declare, if such be already the case, that it is vested in him; the trust instrument declares the trust, appoints the trustees etc. Where the settlement is created by will, the will is for the purposes of the Act the trust instrument (s. 6[3]); s. 9[4] makes similar provision for other special cases, including that of a settlement which does not comply with the requirements of the Act.

1 48 Halsbury's Statutes (4th edn) 377.
2 Ibid., 355.
3 See p. 735, post.
4 48 Halsbury's Statutes (4th edn) 385.

Who is tenant for life

10.14 The tenant for life is defined by ss. 19–21[1] and 117(1)(xxviii)[2]. Two or more joint tenants may in appropriate cases together constitute the tenant for life.

1 48 Halsbury's Statutes (4th edn) 378; see also pp. 736 ff., post.
2 Ibid., 530.

10.15 Where land was conveyed to trustees under a settlement for 99 years, on trust to pay income to A during the term if he should so long live, it was held that A was a person having powers of tenant for life within s. 20(1) of the Settled Land Act, 1925[1].

1 *Re Waleran Settled Estate* [1927] 1 Ch 522.

10.16 A testator under his will gave his wife the option of becoming yearly tenant of real estate at a nominal rent, the tenancy not to be determined during her life, except by her. It was held that if she exercised such option she did not become the tenant for life under s. 20, Settled Land Act 1925[1].

1 *Re Catling, Public Trustee v Catling* [1931] 2 Ch 359.

Statutory owner

10.17 The statutory owner, by s. 117(1)(xxvi)[1], means the trustees of the settlement or other persons who, during a minority, or at any other time when there is no tenant for life, have the powers of a tenant for life under the Act, but excluding cases where the trustees have power, under an order of the court, or otherwise, to convey the land in the name of the tenant for life. This makes it clear that the land *must* be vested in the tenant for life where circumstances permit; there is no option to vest it either in the tenant for life or in the trustees as statutory owner, at choice. The trustees are defined by ss. 30–35[2]. See also paras. **10.74** ff., post.

1 48 Halsbury's Statutes (4th edn) 530.
2 Ibid., 418; see also pp. 738 ff., post.

10.18 When there is a charge on real estate in respect of an annuity payable out of the real estate and the annuitant is still living at the death of the person entitled beneficially to the fee simple in the land, and there is no immediate trust for sale, a grant in respect of settled land may be made on the death of the beneficial owner, the beneficial owner being the tenant for life within the meaning of the Act[1], and the land being still settled land.

1 *Re Buckingham* (1942) September.

Duration of settlements

10.19   By s. 3[1], land not held upon trust for sale which has been subject to a settlement remains settled land so long as any limitation, charge or power of charging under the settlement subsists or is capable of being exercised, or the person who would otherwise be entitled as beneficial owner to call for the legal estate to be vested in him is a minor.

1 See p. 735, post.

One remainderman of full age

10.20   But if a minor remainderman becomes absolutely entitled jointly with a person of full age, it seems that the latter will take the legal estate on the statutory trusts, and, as these include a trust for sale, the land will cease to be settled land (s. 26(4) of the Settled Land Act 1925[1], and s. 19(2) of the Law of Property Act 1925[2]), so that if even one only of several remaindermen is of age the land ceases to be settled land. The last-mentioned section deals in terms only with 'a conveyance of a legal estate' to a minor jointly with a person of full age, but it appears to be intended to govern the procedure in all cases where a minor is beneficially *entitled* in that manner.

1 See p. 738, post.
2 37 Halsbury's Statutes (4th edn) 95.

10.21   A company is held to be a person of full age[1].

1 *Re Carnarvon's Settled Estates* [1927] 1 Ch 138.

Continuing interest, or power of appointment

10.22   Where the tenant for life had some beneficial interest not ceasing at his death, or had a power of appointment which he exercised in such a way as to create further limitations or charges within the meaning of s. 1 of the Settled Land Act 1925[1], the land may continue to be settled land by reason of such interest or appointment.

1 See p. 734, post.

Undivided shares

10.23   If the beneficial interest devolves on a death to persons entitled in undivided shares (even if they are entitled for life only, or are infants), the land ceases to be settled land; for, even where the settlement continues, the land becomes subject to a trust for sale under s. 36 of the Settled Land Act 1925[1].

1 48 Halsbury's Statutes (4th edn) 427.

Compound settlements

10.24   If, on the limitation under a settlement ceasing, the land immediately becomes settled land under another settlement, it does not vest in the general personal representatives of the life tenant; e.g. if A by his will settled land on B for life with remainder to C absolutely, but C died in B's lifetime having devised his real estate to D for life, on B's death the land remains settled land (see *Re Taylor's Estate*[1], and *Re Sharpe's Deed of Release, Sharpe and Fox v Gullick*[2]).

1 [1929] P 260.
2 [1939] Ch 51, [1938] 3 All ER449.

10.25 As to trustees of compound settlements, see paras. **10.82** and **10.83**, post.

Marriage settlement

10.26 An instrument whereby a tenant for life, in consideration of marriage or by way of family arrangement, not being a security for payment of money advanced, makes an assignment of or creates a charge on his interest under the settlement, is deemed to be one of the instruments creating the settlement, and not an assignment for value (Settled Land Act 1925, s. 104(11)[1]).

1 48 Halsbury's Statutes (4th edn) 520.

Pre-1926 settlements

10.27 Settlements of land which were existing on 1 January 1926 were brought into line with the new system by the transitional provisions in the Second Schedule to the Settled Land Act 1925, incorporated by s. 37[1]. The settlement was treated as a trust instrument, and a vesting deed or vesting assent was to be executed as soon as practicable, vesting the legal fee simple or leasehold term, the subject of the settlement—or, if such were already the case, declaring it to be vested—in the tenant for life or statutory owner designated by the Act.

1 48 Halsbury's Statutes (4th edn) 544, 412.

10.28 In normal cases, however, the legal estate vested automatically in the tenant for life or statutory owner at the first moment of 1926, by virtue of the transitional provisions of the Law of Property Act 1925—First Schedule, Part II, paras. 3 and 5[1]. Failure to execute the vesting deed or assent in such cases merely 'paralyses' the statutory powers of dealing with the land (see s. 13 of the Settled Land Act 1925[2]); it does not prevent the legal estate in the land from devolving in the normal way on the personal representative of a deceased person in whom it was in fact vested.

1 37 Halsbury's Statutes (4th edn) 343.
2 48 Halsbury's Statutes (4th edn) 391.

10.29 In a case where land was settled by Private Act with conveyances, the tenant in tail at the date of the Settled Land Act 1925 died intestate in 1930. No trustees were ever appointed for settled land purposes and there was no vesting deed. Letters of administration had been granted save and except settled land to the plaintiff, the eldest son of the tenant in tail. It was held that the Private Act and conveyances constituted one settlement; the court appointed trustees for the purpose of the Settled Land Act, and gave them liberty to apply for a grant limited to settled land[1].

1 *Re Lord Hereford's Settled Estates, Hereford v Devereux* [1932] WN 34.

Dual capacity of tenant for life

10.30   In the ordinary case a tenant for life of full age is concerned with the settled land in a dual capacity. In the first place, he has his beneficial interest in the property, which interest will (normally) cease on his death; in the second place, he is the 'estate owner' of the whole fee simple or term of years, the subject of the settlement, which estate will not cease on his death. For the present purposes, only the latter capacity need be considered, and the tenant for life may be regarded as merely a specialist type of trustee.

Necessity for grant

10.31   Under s. 7(1) of the Settled Land Act 1925, if on the death of a tenant for life or statutory owner, or of the survivor of two or more tenants for life or statutory owners, in whom the land was vested, the land remains settled land, his personal representatives shall hold the land on trust, if and when required so to do, to convey it to the person who becomes the tenant for life or statutory owner[1].

1 Where the land ceases to be settled land on the death of the tenant for life, the legal estate in it passes, on a grant in respect of the free estate, to the general personal representatives of the tenant for life: see 'Land ceasing to be settled land', paras. **10.34** ff., post.

10.32   The expression 'personal representative' means the executor (original or by representation) or administrator for the time being, and where there are special personal representatives for the purpose of settled land, means those personal representatives[1]. This would appear to suggest that in cases where there are no special personal representatives as to settled land, the general personal representatives can convey the land to the person entitled to it; but under the Administration of Estates Act 1925, s. 22[2], and NCPR 29[3], priority of right to a grant in respect of settled land is given to the 'special executors in regard to settled land' and to the trustees of the settlement: it is only on clearing off all trustees that the general personal representative of the tenant for life may take a grant in respect of settled land.

1 Settled Land Act 1925, s. 117(1)(xviii).
2 See p. 748, post.
3 See p. 931, post.

10.33   Under s. 24 of the Administration of Estates Act 1925 the special personal representatives may dispose of the settled land without the concurrence of the general personal representatives, who may likewise dispose of the other property and assets of the deceased without the concurrence of the special personal representatives.

Land ceasing to be settled land

10.34   Where there was settled land vested in the tenant for life which ceased to be settled land on his death (there being no further life interest or outstanding charges and no special circumstances such as minority) the legal estate in the land vests in the general personal representatives of the tenant for life[1]. On its being sworn in the oath 'that there was no land vested in the said deceased which was settled previously to his death (and not by his will) and which remained settled land notwithstanding his death', a normal grant without any reference to the settled land may be taken by the person or persons entitled thereto under his will or intestacy. The value of such land is not included in the amount of the estate shown in the oath.

1 *Re Bridgett and Hayes' Contract* [1928] Ch 163.

10.35 If the deceased tenant for life left no free estate, to enable the legal estate in the land to be passed to the remainderman a general grant may be made[1]: see 'Nil estate', paras. **4.209** and **4.210**, ante.

1 As to the exclusion of such land from a grant to the Treasury Solicitor where the deceased died without known kin, see para. **25.181**, post.

10.36 If all persons with a prior right to a grant are cleared off by renunciation or otherwise, or if their unwillingness to take a grant is established, application may be made by the remainderman[1], or if he is dead, his personal representative[2], for an order for a grant under s. 116 of the Supreme Court Act 1981 (see p. 845, post).

1 *Re Birch's Estate* [1929] P 164; *Re Bordass' Estate* [1929] P 107.
2 *Re Goulden* (1938) December (motion).

Joint tenants

10.37 The interest of a deceased joint tenant, where another tenant survives, is extinguished and does not devolve on the representative of the deceased (see Administration of Estates Act 1925, s. 3(4)). See also 'Land not vested solely in deceased', paras. **10.96** and **10.97**, post. There are also special provisions as to appointments under powers and as to entails.

Representation

10.38 The special rules as to grants of settled land apply only where the land was settled land before the death and remained settled land notwithstanding the death of the tenant for life.

10.39 In such cases a settled land grant is normally necessary on the death of every (sole) life tenant of full age, but not on the death of any other person concerned with the settlement. It should be observed, however, on the one hand, that a settled land grant is neither necessary nor capable of being made in the estate of a life tenant in whom the legal estate was not actually vested (e.g. under a post-1925 settlement where no vesting deed or vesting assent has been executed); and, on the other hand, that such a grant may be required on the death of a person other than a life tenant (e.g. a sole surviving trustee of land held on charitable trusts). A grant, other than a settled land grant, may also be required in some circumstances to enable the land to be dealt with, e.g. in the case of land, settled by will, which had vested in the settlor's executor—though not as settled land—but was not vested by him in a life tenant.

10.40 It is no longer possible to obtain a grant including settled land. Under NCPR 29 as amended, as from 14 October 1991 separate grants must be obtained in respect of the settled land and in respect of the free estate (*Secretary's Circular* (2) 26 September 1991).

10.41 All settled land grants, issued on or after 14 October 1991, are grants of administration only, even if the deceased left a will. Any will left by the deceased is not proved on the settled land grant application (*Secretary's Circular* (2) 26 September 1991).

The practice in settled land grants

10.42   There are various tests to be applied to the trust instrument which may have created settled land, and vested it in a deceased person prior to his death; and these should be considered before an application for a grant relating to settled land is made.

10.43   Is there a trust for sale? If so, is it for immediate sale of the whole of the property, and is it binding on the trustees? In that case there can be no settled land.

10.44   Section 2 of the Settled Land Act 1925[1] states that land which is, or is deemed to be, the subject of a settlement is for the purposes of the Act 'settled land', and s. 3[2] states that land—not held upon trust for sale—which has been subject to a settlement shall be deemed for the purposes of the Act to remain and be settled land, and the settlement shall be subsisting, so long as any limitation, charge, or power of charging subsists, or is capable of being exercised.

1 See p. 735, post.
2 Ibid.

10.45   Section 3(1) of the Administration of Estates Act 1925[1] defines 'real estate', and includes therein real estate held on trust (including settled land) or by way of mortgage or security, but not money to arise under a trust for sale of land, nor money secured or charged on land.

1 See p. 745, post.

10.46   Was the legal estate in the settled land effectively vested in the deceased tenant for life, either under the transitional provisions of the Law of Property Act 1925[1] or by vesting deed or assent? If not, a grant in respect of settled land cannot be made in respect of his estate. The legal estate is vested elsewhere, e.g. (a) (if settled by will) in the personal representative of the settlor (see below); or (b) in a previous tenant for life; or (c) in the trustees of the settlement. In such event the personal representative of the settlor, the personal representative of the previous tenant for life, or the trustees, as the case may be, should convey the legal estate to the present tenant for life or other person entitled thereto.

1 37 Halsbury's Statutes (4th edn) 72.

10.47   If there was settled land vested in the tenant for life at the date of his death, did all life interests or annuities come to an end on or before his death, so that the interest vested absolutely in the remainderman?

10.48   Was there a continuing trust, another life interest, or other charge on the property, after the death of the tenant for life? If not, the land ceased to be settled land and a grant in respect of settled land cannot be made, unless the tenant for life had an absolute or limited power of appointment which he had exercised in such a way as to impose further limitations or charges on the land.

10.49   If at the date of death of the tenant for life there was a continuing trust which has since ceased to exist, a grant is necessary; the date of death of the tenant for life being the material date.

10.50   If there is an absolute gift over, and no outstanding charges, on the death of the tenant for life the land ceases to be settled land on his death, unless there was no remainderman who had attained a vested interest, in which case a grant in respect of settled land can be made.

10.51   If there is more than one remainderman, some being minors, the land vests in such of them as are of age. It ceases to be settled land and a settled land grant cannot be made.

10.52   A *notional* settlement was created on an intestacy where the intestate died (before 1926) leaving real estate and was survived by a widow or husband, and the heir-at-law was under 21 years on 1 January 1926[1].

---

1 *Re Taylor, Pullan v Taylor* [1931] 2 Ch 242.

Vesting of legal estate in first life tenant

10.53   In the case of a settlement by deed, the legal estate should be vested directly in the tenant for life upon trusts which must be declared by a separate deed, trustees for the purposes of the Settled Land Act being appointed. But the position is different in the case of a settlement of land by will. On the issue of a grant in the estate of the settlor, the land settled by the testator vests in his personal representative in the same way as land that is not the subject of any charge or limitation for life. It is liable for the debts of the deceased (see Settled Land Act 1925, s. 8(3)(a)); and these may absorb part, or even the whole, of the land, so that there may remain nothing of the trust estate. When the residue has been ascertained, the legal estate in the land remains vested in the personal representative, and it remains so vested until a vesting assent is executed, even though the testator has by his will appointed his executor to be trustee of the settlement.

10.54   It follows that on the death of a personal representative who has not executed a vesting assent, a de bonis non grant of the testator's estate, including the land (but not as settled land), is necessary in order to provide a personal representative of the settlor, unless there is already one by chain of executorship.

10.55   The only exception is where the tenant for life was in enjoyment of the beneficial interest on 1 January 1926, so that the legal estate vested in him automatically under the transitional provisions of the Law of Property Act 1925 (see paras. **10.27–10.29**, ante)[1].

---

1 Senior Registrar's Memorandum, 13 February 1957: see also *Re Pennant's Will Trusts, Pennant v Ryland* [1970] Ch 75, [1969] 2 All ER 862.

Description of land in grant

10.56   It is not the practice to refer to a vesting deed in the grant. The deed of settlement, or will, alone, is specified in order to show the title of the grantees, e.g. as trustees of the settlement at the date of death of the tenant for life and as such the special executors in respect of the settled land vested in him.

Capital money

10.57   A tenant for life of settled land has under the Settled Land Act 1925, wide powers of management of the land, including power to sell all or part thereof (see s. 38).

10.58   If all or part of the settled land is sold, the proceeds of sale are capital money (see ss. 73–85[1]). Capital money arising under the Act must, in order to be invested or applied in the manner prescribed, be paid, at the option of the tenant for life, either to the trustees of the settlement or into court. Until invested and after investment, for all purposes of disposition, transmission and devolution, it is treated as land and is held for and goes to the same persons and on the same trusts, interests and estates as the land sold, if not disposed of, would have gone under the settlement; and the income will follow the same trusts also[2].

1   48 Halsbury's Statutes (4th edn) 477 ff.
2   *Re Armstrong's Will Trusts, Graham v Armstrong* [1943] Ch 400, [1943] 2 All ER 537.

10.59   With regard to capital money subsisting after 1 January 1926, it seems quite clear that there can be no vesting deed. The Act contemplates a vesting deed only with regard to settled land, and capital money, though deemed to be land for other purposes, is not settled land for the purposes of the Settled Land Act. Under s. 117(1)(xxxi) 'vesting deed' or 'vesting order' means the instrument whereby the settled land is conveyed to or vested in or declared to be vested in the tenant for life or statutory owner, and 'vesting assent' is the instrument whereby a personal representative, after the death of a tenant for life or statutory owner, vests settled land in the person then entitled as tenant for life or statutory owner.

10.60   It follows that where part of the settled land has been sold, only the remaining settled land can be the subject of a settled land grant, and its value alone should appear in such a grant[1]. But if after a sale of settled land by the tenant for life the capital money paid to the trustees is re-invested in land, such land becomes settled land under the settlement and (s. 10[2]) the tenant for life can call upon the trustees to execute a vesting deed vesting the land in him subject to the trusts of the settlement.

1   Registrar's Circular, 1 December 1945.
2   48 Halsbury's Statutes (4th edn) 387.

Grant save and except settled land

When made

10.61   Where there was settled land vested in a deceased person which remained settled land notwithstanding his death, the person entitled to a grant under his will or intestacy in respect of his free estate may take a grant expressly excluding the settled land (NCPR 29(3)). Forms of oath, Nos. 66 and 85.

10.62   The oath should include the statement 'that there was land vested in the said deceased which was settled previously to his death (and not by his will) and which remained settled land notwithstanding his death', but it is unnecessary to include details of the settlement.

No previous grant

10.63 If there has been no previous grant limited to settled land, the practice is in all respects the same as in cases where there was no settled land (see Chap. 4, 5 or 6 as to probate, letters of administration with will, and letters of administration respectively).

Previous grant limited to settled land

10.64 If a grant limited to settled land has previously been extracted, the oath must include details of the former grant (see Form No. 85).

10.65 The further grant may be applied for at the Principal Registry or at any district probate registry. If the subsequent application is made at the Principal Registry, or at a district probate registry other than that from which the previous grant issued, the previous grant, or an office copy of it, must be lodged with the papers.

10.66 Where the deceased left a will, it will have been proved on the application for the grant limited to settled land only if that grant issued before 14 October 1991. On or after that date the grant limited to settled land will have been silent as to whether the deceased left a will or died intestate and if the deceased did leave a will it will not have been proved on that application. Consequently any such will must be proved on the application for the grant excluding the settled land.

10.67 When the settled land grant issued before 14 October 1991 the applicant for the grant save and except settled land may therefore either 'mark' an office copy of the will, or, if the will was proved at the registry at which the subsequent application is made, he may, if desired, attend at the registry to swear the oath and mark the original will or, with leave of the district judge or registrar under r. 10(2), he may mark a facsimile copy of the will.

To whom settled land grant made

10.68 As from 14 October 1991, no provision is made in NCPR 29 for grants of *probate* to issue in respect of settled land. The 'special executors' in regard to settled land constituted by s. 22 of the Administration of Estates Act 1925 still have a prior right to a grant limited to settled land but it is a prior right to a grant of administration.

NCPR 29(2) now reads:

'(2) The person or persons entitled to a grant of administration limited to settled land shall be determined in accordance with the following order of priority:
(i) the special executors in regard to settled land constituted by section 22 of the Administration of Estates Act 1925;
(ii) the trustees of the settlement at the time of the application for the grant; and
(iii) the personal representatives of the deceased.'

10.69 It should be noted that 'the deceased' in (iii) above is the tenant for life.

Special executors

10.70 Section 22 of the Administration of Estates Act 1925 is as follows:

'(1) A testator may appoint, and in default of such express appointment shall be deemed to have appointed, as his special executors in regard to settled land, the persons, if any, who are at his death the trustees of the settlement thereof, and probate may be granted to such trustees specially limited to the settled land.

In this subsection "settled land" means land vested in the testator which was settled previously to his death and not by his will.

(2) A testator may appoint other persons either with or without such trustees as aforesaid or any of them to be his general executors in regard to his other property and assets.'

10.71   It will be seen that 'special executors' can be constituted only where the tenant for life died testate. Such special executors have priority of right to a grant of administration of the estate of the tenant for life, limited to settled land (see NCPR 29(2), above).

10.72   As from 14 October 1991 special executors can only obtain a grant of administration. Where the special executors are applying and they are also the trustees of the settlement at the time of the application for the grant (whether or not there are also other trustees at the time of that application) there appears to be no need for them to produce the will of the tenant for life on the application. They will need to state in the oath that they were the trustees of the settlement at the date of death of the tenant for life and still are trustees of the settlement. They will thereby show that they have both the prior and the next right to a grant.

10.73   However, if the special executors are not also trustees of the settlement at the time of the application for the grant, before they can take a grant in respect of the settled land they must establish their prior right. To do so it will be necessary for them to satisfy the district judge or registrar that not only were they the trustees at the death of the life tenant but also that he died testate. If the will has not been proved previously on an application for a grant of the free estate of the tenant for life it should be produced on the application for the settled land grant. In this circumstance the will is referred to in the oath but it should not be marked by the signatures of the applicants or the person before whom the oath is sworn. The will is not proved on the application for the settled land grant and a copy of it is not annexed to the grant, which is one of administration only. If the district judge or registrar is satisfied that the tenant for life did die testate, the will will be returned to the solicitors so that it may be proved on the application for the grant in respect of the free estate in due course.

Trustees of the settlement

10.74   Only the persons (if any) who were at the death of the tenant for life the *trustees of the settlement* qualify as special executors.

10.75   Section 30 of the Settled Land Act 1925 declares who are trustees of a settlement for the purposes of that Act as follows:

'(1) Subject to the provisions of this Act, the following persons are trustees of a settlement for the purposes of this Act, and are in this Act referred to as the "trustees of the settlement" or "trustees of a settlement", namely—

(i) the persons, if any, who are for the time being under the settlement trustees with power of sale of the settled land (subject or not to the consent of any person), or with power of consent to or approval of the exercise of such a power of sale, or if there are no such persons; then

(ii) the persons, if any, for the time being, who are by the settlement declared to be trustees thereof for the purposes of the Settled Land Acts, 1882 to 1890, or any of them, or this Act, or if there are no such persons; then

(iii) the persons, if any, who are for the time being under the settlement trustees with power of or upon trust for sale of any other land comprised in the settlement and subject to the same limitations as the land to be sold or otherwise dealt with, or with power of consent to or approval of the exercise of such a power of sale, or, if there are no such persons; then

(iv) the persons, if any, who are for the time being under the settlement trustees with future power of sale, or under a future trust for sale of the settled land, or with power of consent to or approval of the exercise of such a future power of sale, and whether the power or trust takes effect in all events or not, or, if there are no such persons; then

(v) the persons, if any, appointed by deed to be trustees of the settlement by all the persons who at the date of the deed were together able, by virtue of their beneficial interests or by the exercise of an equitable power, to dispose of the settled land in equity for the whole estate the subject of the settlement.

(2) Paragraphs (i), (iii) and (iv) of the last preceding subsection take effect in like manner as if the powers therein referred to had not by this Act been made exercisable by the tenant for life or statutory owner.

(3) Where a settlement is created by will, or a settlement has arisen by the effect of an intestacy, and apart from this subsection there would be no trustees for the purposes of this Act of such settlement, then the personal representatives of the deceased[1] shall, until other trustees are appointed, be by virtue of this Act the trustees of the settlement, but where there is a sole personal representative, not being a trust corporation, it shall be obligatory on him to appoint an additional trustee to act with him for the purposes of this Act, and the provisions of the Trustee Act 1925, relating to the appointment of new trustees and the vesting of trust property shall apply accordingly.'

1 I.e., the settlor.

10.76 It will be noted that a requisite of most of the classes under s. 30(1) is power of sale of the settled land, or of other land subject to the same limitations. Persons appointed trustees of the *will* of the settlor are not necessarily trustees of the settlement for the purposes of the Settled Land Act.

Substituted trustees: provisions of Trustee Act 1925

10.77 Section 64(1) of the Trustee Act 1925 enacts that the provisions of that Act with reference to the appointment of new trustees and the discharge and retirement of trustees shall apply to trustees for the purposes of the Settled Land Act 1925 whether the trustees are appointed by the court or by the settlement or under provisions contained in any instrument.

10.78 Under s. 36(1) of the Trustee Act 1925 the person nominated for the purpose by the trust instrument, or if there is none able and willing to act, then the surviving or continuing trustees or trustee for the time being, or the personal representatives of the last surviving or continuing trustee may, by writing, appoint one or more persons (whether or not being the persons exercising the power) to be a trustee or trustees in place of a trustee who is dead, out of the United Kingdom, desires to be discharged, refuses or is unfit to act, is incapable of acting, or is an infant. This power may also be exercised by the sole or last surviving executor (or all the executors) of the last surviving trustee where he or they intend to renounce probate, before so renouncing, and does not constitute intermeddling (Trustee Act 1925, s. 36(5)).

10.79   New trustees appointed under s. 36 have the same powers, authorities and discretions, and may in all respects act, as if originally appointed trustees (ibid., s. 36(7)).

10.80   The personal representative of the sole or last surviving or continuing trustee, although having under s. 18(2) of the Trustee Act 1925 the powers of the sole or last surviving or continuing trustee until new trustees are appointed, has no right to a grant in respect of settled land merely in the capacity of such personal representative.

10.81   Whenever a new trustee for the purposes of the Settled Land Act is appointed, or a Settled Land Act trustee is discharged from the trust without a new trustee being appointed, a deed supplemental to the last or only principal vesting instrument should be executed containing a declaration that the persons therein named, being after the appointment or discharge the trustees of the trust instrument for the purposes of the Act, are the trustees of the settlement (Settled Land Act 1925, s. 35: see also Trustee Act 1925, s. 35(2), as to endorsement of the names and addresses of the trustees of the settlement on the vesting instrument).

Trustees of compound settlements

10.82   Persons who are for the time being trustees for the purposes of the Settled Land Act 1925 of an instrument which is a settlement or is deemed to be a subsisting settlement for the purposes of that Act, are the trustees for the purposes of the Act of any settlement constituted by that instrument and any instruments subsequent in date or operation. Where there are trustees of the instrument under which there is a tenant for life or statutory owner but no trustees of the prior instrument, the trustees of the later instrument are, until the appointment of new trustees of the prior instrument or of the compound settlement, trustees of the compound settlement.

10.83   These provisions apply to instruments coming into operation either before or after the commencement of the Settled Land Act 1925, but are without prejudice to appointments of trustees by the court (see Settled Land Act 1925, s. 31).

Special executors and new trustees applying

10.84   As the special executors are now entitled, under NCPR 29 as amended, to extract only a grant of administration, it follows that new trustees of the settlement appointed after the death of the tenant for life may, where appropriate, join in an application for a grant of administration with the special executors. If new trustees of the settlement appointed after the death of the tenant for life wish to apply for administration without the special executors, the prior right of the special executors to a grant of administration must still be cleared off.

10.85   Practitioners are reminded that any grant in respect of settled land which issues on or after 14 October 1991 will be one of administration. Where the tenant for life died testate the grant will be silent as to his will and a copy of it will not be annexed to the grant.

Personal representative of settlor: when trustee of settlement

10.86   It will be seen from s. 30(3) of the Settled Land Act 1925, quoted at para. **10.75**, that, in the case of a settlement created by will or arising by the effect of an intestacy, where there would otherwise be no trustees of the settlement, the personal representatives of the *settlor* are, until other trustees are appointed, by virtue of the Act the trustees of the settlement.

10.87 Thus, where all the following conditions are fulfilled, viz.:

(a) the settlement was created by will, or arose under an intestacy;
(b) the tenant for life died testate;
(c) there are no other trustees of the settlement; and
(d) the personal representatives of the settlor held office prior to the death of the tenant for life;

the personal representatives of the settlor qualify as the special executors of the tenant for life, and may as such obtain, in accordance with NCPR 29(2), administration in respect of the settled land[1]. It follows that the prior right of such personal representatives to a grant limited to settled land must be cleared off before a grant of administration, so limited, can be made to new trustees of the settlement appointed after the death of the tenant for life.

1 See *Re Gibbings' Estates* [1928] P 28.

10.88 If the personal representatives of the settlor were not appointed until after the death of the tenant for life they do not qualify as special executors, but in default of other trustees may obtain a grant of administration limited to settled land (see para. **10.109**, post).

10.89 The right of the personal representatives of the settlor to be treated as trustees of the settlement does not arise in cases where the settlement was created by deed inter vivos (see Settled Land Act 1925, s. 30(3)).

10.90 On an application for a grant by the personal representatives of the settlor, the oath must show that there are no other trustees of the settlement, and include particulars of the grant (or chain of grants) constituting them, The grant, or an office copy of it, should be produced.

Renunciation or reserving of power

10.91 As special executors can no longer obtain a grant of probate under NCPR 29 as amended from 14 October 1991, it follows that power can no longer be reserved to non-proving executors to obtain a grant of double probate in respect of the settled land. Accordingly, there is no requirement for those special executors who are applying for a grant of administration in respect of the settled land to give any notice of their application to any other special executor who is not joining in the application.

10.92 It would appear to be a consequence of the amendment to NCPR 29 that a special executor to whom power has been reserved, under a grant of probate in respect of settled land issued before 14 October 1991, cannot now extract a grant of double probate in respect of the settled land. Under the amended rule a grant of administration is the only grant that may now issue in respect of settled land. The registries do not issue a grant of administration while there is a grant of probate or a grant of administration (with or without will) in respect of the same estate, in force. Where a special executor to whom power has been reserved under the previous practice wishes to join in the administration of the settled land with the special executor (or special executors) already acting under a grant of probate, it would appear that the existing grant will need to be revoked and a new grant (of administration) taken. Special executors may renounce their right to a grant (now of administration) as before.

10.93   The prior right to a grant given to a trustee of the settlement who was in office at the date of death of the deceased is not cleared off by his subsequent retirement from the trust: his renunciation is necessary before a grant may be made to a person with a lower title.

Rights of general executor

10.94   An executor, who was also a trustee of a settlement of settled land at the time of the death of the testator, may take or join in taking a grant of probate save and except the settled land, without renouncing or losing his right in respect of the settled land. Similarly he may take or join in taking a grant in respect of settled land without renouncing his rights in respect of the general estate[1].

1 See also Administration of Estates Act 1925, s. 23(1), as to the powers of a general executor not wishing to act in relation to settled land.

Several settlements with different trustees

10.95   Should there be several settlements of land with different or varying trustees, a separate grant is made in each case, limited to the settled land under the settlement in question.

Land not vested solely in deceased

10.96   If there are two or more persons entitled to settled land for life as joint tenants, they together constitute the tenant for life for the purpose of the Settled Land Act 1925[1].

1 Settled Land Act 1925, s. 19(2) (48 Halsbury's Statutes (4th edn) 399).

10.97   On the death of any except the last survivor the oath should state that there was no settled land vested 'solely' in him.

Letters of administration limited to settled land

Special executors

10.98   Where the tenant for life in whom settled land was vested dies testate, and the land remained settled land notwithstanding his death, the special executors deemed to have been appointed by him under s. 22 of the Administration of Estates Act 1925, i.e. the persons, if any, who at the date of his death were the trustees of the settlement[1], have a prior right to a grant of administration[2] limited to settled land.

1 For definition of 'trustees of the settlement', see paras. **10.74** ff., ante.
2 NCPR 29(2)(i).

10.99   They may apply for such a grant either before or after probate or administration (with will) save and except settled land has issued to the *general* executors appointed by the tenant for life or other persons entitled to the grant in respect of the free estate.

Surviving trustee and trustee subsequently appointed

10.100 Where a surviving trustee of the settlement at the date of death of the tenant for life has since the death exercised his power of appointing another trustee, administration limited to settled land may be granted to them—see para. **10.84**, ante.

No chain of executorship

10.101 There can be no chain of executorship through a special executor of settled land[1].

1 Registrar's Direction (1936) 21 July.

Grant pending suit limited to settled land

10.102 In a case in which there was a dispute in connection with the will of the tenant for life an order was made under s. 163 of the Supreme Court of Judicature (Consolidation) Act 1925 (since repealed and replaced by s. 117 of the Supreme Court Act 1981), for a grant of administration pending suit to the trustees of the settlement, limited to the settled land, with the right to exercise all the powers of special executors as regards the settled land[1].

1 *Re Earl of St Germans* (1943) (motion).

Proof of will

10.103 As from 14 October 1991, where the deceased left a will it is not proved on any application for a settled land grant. The will is not referred to in the grant and a copy of it is not annexed to the grant. The only circumstance in which the will (not proved previously) need be lodged with the application for the settled land grant appears to be when the special executors applying for the grant are not also trustees of the settlement at the time of the application for the grant—see para. **10.73**, ante.

Second grants

10.104 The second grant and any other subsequent grants may be extracted from the Principal Registry or any district probate registry: not necessarily at the registry from which the first grant was issued.

Renunciation and reservation of power

10.105 As to renunciation by special executors and power being reserved to such executors, see paras. **10.91–10.93**, ante.

Trustees appointed since the death of tenant for life

10.106 The persons next entitled in priority, after special executors, are the trustees of the settlement at the time of the application for the grant.

10.107 In making a grant, trustees appointed by order of the court are on the same footing as trustees appointed by the settlement or by deed.

10.108   As to the power of the surviving or continuing trustees, or the personal representative of the last of such trustees, to appoint new trustees, see paras. **10.77** ff.

Personal representative of settlor

10.109   Where the settlement was created by a will or has arisen under an intestacy, and where there would otherwise be no trustees of the settlement, the personal representatives of the settlor are, until other trustees are appointed, by virtue of the Settled Land Act 1925, the trustees of the settlement[1], a sole personal representative, not being a trust corporation, being however bound to appoint an additional trustee to act with him.

1 Settled Land Act 1925, s. 30(3).

10.110   As to the power of such personal representatives to obtain administration as special executors of the tenant for life when holding such office at the date of his death, see paras. **10.86–10.90**, ante. If they were not in office at that date (for example, when they have subsequently obtained a grant de bonis non in the estate of the settlor, or when they have subsequently become executors of the settlor by chain of representation) and there are no other trustees of the settlement, they may obtain administration limited to settled land as the trustees at the time of application for the grant (NCPR 29(2)(ii)).

Personal representative of tenant for life

10.111   Where there are trustees (or there is a single trustee) of the settlement, the personal representatives of the settlor cannot qualify for a grant by obtaining their renunciation.

10.112   On clearing off all trustees (including the personal representatives of the settlor where there are no other trustees and the settlement arose under a will or intestacy) administration limited to settled land may be granted to the personal representatives of the tenant for life, they having first constituted themselves as such by obtaining a grant save and except settled land[1].

1 NCPR 29(2)(iii).

10.113   Where the settlement is not created by will and does not arise under an intestacy, the personal representatives of the settlor need not be considered: on clearing off the trustees of the settlement, a grant in respect of settled land may be taken by the personal representative of the tenant for life.

10.114   On any application for a grant by the personal representative of the tenant for life, the oath must show how the trustees of the settlement are cleared off (e.g. by stating that none were appointed, or by reciting their death or renunciation). Where the settlement was created by will or arose under an intestacy, in default of other trustees the personal representative of the settlor is the trustee of the settlement[1] and must also be cleared off.

1 Settled Land Act 1925, s. 30(3).

Tenant for life also sole executor of settlor

10.115 Where the tenant for life under the settlement was also the sole executor of the settlor and sole trustee of the settlement, there being on his death no trustee of the settlement and no personal representative of the settlor, a grant limited to settled land may be made to the personal representatives of the tenant for life[1].

1 *Re Saltmarshe* (1941) (motion).

Minority or life interest

10.116 A grant limited to settled land may be made to a single applicant, notwithstanding the existence of a minority or life interest arising under the settlement.

Oath

10.117 Particulars of all previous grants in the estate of the deceased must be given in the oath. (Forms of oath, Nos. 81 to 84.)

Copy of previous grants

10.118 If there has been any previous grant in the estate of the deceased this, or an office copy of it, must be lodged on any application for a subsequent grant, except where application for the latter is made at the district probate registry from which the previous grant issued.

Production of deeds

10.119 The production of the vesting deed, the trust instrument, and any other deeds relating to the settlement (including appointment of new trustees) will be required.

Amount of estate for grant

10.120 The value of the settled land is the amount sworn to in any grant limited to settled land. The details and value of the settled land should be included in the Inland Revenue account even if it is exempt from inheritance or capital transfer tax.

Inland Revenue account

10.121 As to Inland Revenue accounts, see Chap. 8.

Fees

10.122 The fee for a grant limited to settled land is £2[1].

1 NC Probate Fees Order 1981, Fee 3(b).

10.123 The fee for a grant excluding settled land, whether it is extracted first or follows a grant limited to settled land, is the normal fee (Fee 1) calculated on the net amount of the estate covered by the grant[1].

1 NC Probate Fees Order 1981, Fee 3(e).

Amendment of settled land grants

10.124   Grants 'save and except settled land', or limited to settled land, cannot be extended by notation so as to cover the property excluded from the grant: a second grant should be taken[1].

1 Registrar's Circular, 24 November 1926.

10.125   A general grant may be amended by adding the limitation 'save and except settled land' in cases where the value of the settled land was not included in the amount for which the grant was made; this amendment may be made even though the grantee has died, though where the application for amendment is made by a person other than the personal representative of the grantee, the consent of such personal representative is normally necessary.

10.126   The affidavit to lead such an amendment must state whether the settled land is in addition to the property already included in the grant.

10.127   If the value of the settled land was included, in the belief that it was not settled land, the district judge or registrar has a discretion to allow the amendment notwithstanding that the grant was incorrect in amount as well as extent; a suitable notation of the value of the settled land may be made on the grant.

10.128   As grants are no longer issued 'including settled land', separate grants being required in respect of the free estate and settled land, it would appear to be no longer appropriate to amend a general grant by adding the words 'including settled land'. This would appear to be so even where the original grant issued before 14 October 1991 and the value of the settled land had been included in the original grant in the mistaken belief that it was not settled land.

10.129   Application is made through the Record Keeper of the Principal Registry, or at the district probate registry from which the grant issued. For practice, see paras. **16.24** ff., post.

Appointment of special or additional personal representative

10.130   Under s. 23(2) of the Administration of Estates Act 1925[1], the trustees of a settlement or any person beneficially interested thereunder may apply, either before or after a grant of the free estate has issued, for the appointment of a special or additional personal representative in respect of settled land. Such a personal representative, when appointed, is in the same position as if he had originally obtained a grant limited to settled land either in place of, or jointly with, the original personal representative (if any).

1 See p. 748, post.

10.131   Applications under this subsection are extremely rare. The procedure is for prior notice of intention to make the application to be given to the Record Keeper at the Principal Registry (see s. 23(4)), following which application is made in chambers in the Chancery Division for a direction that the application be made in the Family Division. The subsequent application in the latter division is made by summons to a district judge or registrar, supported by affidavit. The direction obtained in the Chancery Division and the existing grant of representation must be lodged on issuing the summons. The question of security (see s. 23(3)) is in the discretion of the district judge or registrar[1].

1 See *Re Clifton's Estate* [1931] P 222. In this case a grant limited to settled land had been made to F and D, trustees of the settlement, as special executors. F subsequently became of unsound mind, and W was appointed as trustee in his place. Under an order on motion the grant was revoked, and a further grant of probate was made to D, with power reserved to F; it was ordered that W be appointed special personal representative with D, and that the grant, when sealed, be noted accordingly.

CHAPTER 11

Limited grants

Summary

Introductory notes

11.01   When necessary, a grant will be limited in duration, in respect of property, or to any special purpose.

11.02   Where by reason of the existence of any limitation in a will, or of any circumstances limiting the operative effect of a will, the inclusion of the whole estate in one grant would be inappropriate, a grant limited so as to include or exclude any part of the estate may be made.

11.03   It is not the practice to allow a person entitled to a general grant to take a limited grant except by special permission[1], and for very strong reasons[2].

---

1   *Re Von Brentano's Estate* [1911] P 172.
2   *Re Lady Somerset's Goods* (1867) LR 1 P & D 350.

11.04   In certain cases an order of a district judge, registrar or High Court judge must first be obtained; in others, such as grants for the use of minors or persons mentally incapable, normally no order is required.

11.05   This chapter sets out under sub-divisions the necessary requirements to obtain the various forms of limited grants.

11.06   For interpretation of wills, see Chap. 3.

Settling oaths

11.07   If desired the oath may be submitted in draft, for settling in the Probate Department of the Principal Registry, if the grant application is to be made there, or in the district probate registry at which the application for the grant is to be made.

11.08   The fee for perusing and settling each document is £5 (NC Probate Fees Order 1981 Fee 12).

11.09   The settled drafts must be lodged with the sworn papers when the grant is applied for.

11.10   In those cases where a draft affidavit (or other document) has not been formally settled, but has been perused and commented upon, the perused draft must also be returned to the registry with the sworn engrossment. See also para. **2.06**.

Will lost or not available

Proof of will as contained in copy or draft

11.11   Where an original will or codicil has been lost, mislaid, destroyed or is not available, application may be made for an order admitting it to proof as contained in a copy, a completed draft, a reconstruction or other evidence of its contents. Such an application is unnecessary where the original will is not available because it is retained in the custody of a foreign court or official (NCPR 54(2)): see 'Will in custody of foreign court or official', para. **11.18**, post.

11.12   All such applications should in the first instance be made ex parte to the district judge or registrar of the registry at which the application for a grant is to be made[1]; but if there is serious opposition it may be necessary for the contents of the will or codicil to be propounded in an action.

1 NCPR 2(1); 54. See *Re Nuttall's Estate* [1955] 2 All ER 921n, [1955] 1 WLR 847.

11.13   The practice in applications of this nature is given in paras. **25.46** ff., post.

11.14   The order of the court normally includes a direction that the grant be limited until the original will or a more authentic copy thereof be proved. The wording of the limitation is adapted according to the circumstances of the case; e.g. where it is known that the original will has been destroyed the wording is 'until a more authentic copy of the will be proved'.

11.15   As to the procedure if the original will is discovered after the issue of the grant, see paras. **13.85** ff., post.

Oath

11.16   The oath should include the details of the order and the limitation appearing in it. (Forms of oath, Nos. 72 and 73.)

11.17   The order and supporting affidavits and other documents should be lodged with the papers to lead the grant.

Will in custody of foreign court or official

11.18   Where the original will is not available because it is retained in the custody of a foreign court or official (e.g. a notary), a duly authenticated copy of the will (i.e. a copy authenticated by the court or official having custody of the original will) may be admitted to proof without any order[1], and no limitation 'until the original will be proved' is included in the grant. See also para. **12.73**, post.

1 NCPR 54(2).

Will damaged

11.19   The following practice applies where a will or codicil is so damaged (e.g. by fire or flood) that it is doubtful whether it can or should be admitted to probate.

11.20   The will or codicil in question should be submitted to the district judge or registrar by leaving it, together with an examined copy (a similar copy being retained by the solicitor), in the Probate Department of the Principal Registry or with the district probate registrar. Where necessary, reference will be made by the Probate Department or the district probate registrar to a district judge of the Principal Registry for a decision whether the damaged will or codicil should be admitted to probate[1].

1 Direction (1941) 22 January, as amended by Secretary's Circular, 27 June 1975.

11.21   If it is quite evident that the document cannot be admitted, owing to its condition, application should be made for an order that a copy or draft be admitted.

11.22   In cases where it is thought the will may be rendered decipherable by some special process the matter should be referred to the district judge or registrar before the document is subjected to any process.

11.23   In every case where there are remains of a document they should be lodged at the registry when application is made, and filed there. No copy, draft, or reconstruction of a testamentary document, or the contents thereof, can be admitted unless by a district judge's or registrar's order, or by other order of the court.

11.24   The evidence necessary to lead such order will depend upon the circumstances, but in every case affidavit evidence as to the facts and the correctness of the copy or draft, or of the contents of the will, is required.

11.25   Whenever a will shows any appearance of attempted revocation by burning, tearing or otherwise, this must be accounted for to the satisfaction of the district judge or registrar[1]. It should therefore be established that the condition of the document was not caused by the action of the testator.

1 NCPR 15.

11.26 The following cases are of interest. A will, blackened and charred, was retrieved folded and intact, but too brittle to be opened, and was subjected to infrared treatment. The photographic reproduction showed the sections placed in their proper order and legible, forming a complete will. The will as contained in the photographic reproduction was admitted to probate[1].

1 *Re Wallace* (1942) Times, 12 March (motion).

11.27 The whole writing of a will had disappeared owing to charring. It was subjected to a process whereby the words written (with a few exceptions) were made decipherable. The court granted probate of the will as contained in a copy made while the will was under the process[1]. See also paras. **3.240–3.247**, ante.

1 *Re Kersley* (1942) (motion).

Practice

11.28 When a will—which is whole—has been damaged but is sufficiently intact to be 'marked' by the applicant and Commissioner for Oaths, the original will should be admitted to probate, and an examined copy of it (not a photograph) filed to perpetuate it. The copy should be supplied by the applicant, and may be written or typewritten. This copy will be filed in place of the original, which will be protected and filed in a special repository, and will bear the same number as the copy. The damaged will, if capable of repair or backing, will be so dealt with at the registry.

11.29 If the damaged will is in such condition that it should not, or cannot, be admitted to probate, by reason of missing words or otherwise, the usual procedure for its admission as contained in a copy or draft, upon a district judge's or registrar's order, should be followed, The limitation in the grant will be 'until a more authentic copy of the will be proved'.

11.30 The district judge or registrar may call for evidence as to due execution of the will and may direct that notice be given to persons prejudiced by the admission of the will.

Grants to attorneys and consular officers

Grants to attorney for the use and benefit of the person entitled

11.31 Rule 31 of the NCPR is as follows:

'(1) Subject to paragraphs (2) and (3) below, the lawfully constituted attorney of a person entitled to a grant may apply for administration for the use and benefit of the donor, and such grant shall be limited until further representation be granted, or in such other way as the district judge or registrar may direct.
    (2) Where the donor referred to in paragraph (1) above is an executor, notice of the application shall be given to any other executor unless such notice is dispensed with by the district judge or registrar.

(3) Where the donor referred to in paragraph (1) above is mentally incapable and the attorney is acting under an enduring power of attorney, the application shall be made in accordance with rule 35.'

11.32   It should be noted that the Non-Contentious Probate Rules 1987, unlike the previous Rules, do not require any leave to be obtained before a grant may issue to the attorney of a person resident in England and Wales.

11.33   It is not obligatory for a person residing out of England and Wales to appoint an attorney: he may, if he desires, obtain a direct grant to himself.

11.34   As to grant to a consular officer in lieu of an attorney, see paras. **11.104** ff., post.

Power of attorney

11.35   A power of attorney for the purpose of obtaining representation to a deceased person remains operative indefinitely unless it is otherwise stated in the document, but if the power is not of recent date, evidence that the circumstances and conditions under which the power was given have not changed may be called for.

11.36   It should be shown in the power of attorney that the purpose of the power is to obtain representation to the estate of the deceased, and the name of the deceased should be specifically stated.

11.37   But there are circumstances in which a general power of attorney containing very extensive authority for the donee may be accepted although the power of attorney was given before the death of the deceased[1]. The direction of a district judge or registrar should be taken as to its acceptance if there is any doubt as to its scope. See also 'General power of attorney', para. **11.59**, post.

1 *Re Barker's Goods* [1891] P 251.

11.38   Where two executors reside in different countries, separate powers of attorney executed by each in similar terms and appointing the same attorney or attorneys are acceptable.

Residence of attorney

11.39   It is not necessary that the attorney reside in England and Wales. He may, though resident abroad, obtain a grant under his power[1].

1 *Re Leeson's Goods* (1859) 1 Sw & Tr 463; but see *Re Reed's Goods* (1864) 2 Sw & Tr 439; and *Re Ballingall's Goods* (1863) 3 Sw & Tr 441n.

Form of power of attorney

11.40   Forms of power of attorney are given in Appendix VI, Nos. 179 to 182.

11.41   It is, however, in the discretion of the district judge or registrar to accept a less formal document[1].

1 *Re Elderton's Goods* (1832) 4 Hag Ecc 210; *Re Ormond's Goods* (1828) 1 Hag Ecc 145; see also the observations of Lord Penzance, in *Re Boyle's Goods* (1864) 3 Sw & Tr 426.

Execution of power

11.42 Section 1 of the Powers of Attorney Act 1971[1] provides that, without pre-judice to any requirement in, or having effect under, any other Act as to the witnessing of instruments creating powers of attorney, an instrument creating a power of attorney shall be signed by, or by direction and in the presence of, the donor of the power. If signed by another person on behalf of the donor two other persons must be present as witnesses and must attest the instrument. It should be noted that, with effect from 30 July 1990, the need for a deed to be sealed by the person executing it has been abolished—see Law of Property (Miscellaneous Provisions) Act 1989, s. 1.

1 See p. 804, post.

11.43 A power of attorney for the purpose of obtaining a grant of representation should be witnessed by a disinterested person. It is exempt from stamp duty if intended to be 'filed in the Probate Division [*now the Family Division*] of the High Court'[1]. If it is a general power authorising the attorney to do other acts in addition to taking the grant, and is required to be returned to the practitioner, it is liable to stamp duty if executed before 19 March 1985[2].

1 Stamp Act 1891, Sch. I.
2 The 50p fixed duty payable on general powers of attorney was repealed in respect of instruments executed on or after 19 March 1985, the 1985 Budget Resolution having statutory effect under the provisions of s. 50 of the Finance Act 1973.

11.44 In Latin countries a married woman as often signs in her maiden name as in that of her husband, the names appearing to be interchangeable. Provided that she is described as the 'Wife of ——', the signature in the maiden name is generally accepted.

Power of attorney given in non-English speaking countries

11.45 The following practice should be followed:

(a) If the power is in the language of such country a translation certified by a competent authority will be required.
(b) If the power is in English it will be accepted if witnessed by a notary or a British consul.
(c) A power in English not witnessed as in (b) will be rejected unless there is evidence (which may take the form of a certificate by the extracting solicitor), or other sufficient indication, that the donor understood English.

11.46 The Republic of South Africa and the Republic of Ireland are regarded as English speaking countries. In cases where the donor appears to be a native of India, Pakistan, Sri Lanka or Malaysia, the requirements stated in (c), above, must be complied with.

11.47 There may be cases of doubt where the power was given in a Commonwealth country or a British possession. Such cases should be referred to a district judge or registrar[1].

1 Registrar's Direction (1949) 17 November.

Notarial copy of power

11.48   When a power of attorney has been deposited with a notary or in a court of law, in accordance with the law of the domicile of the deceased, a notarial copy will be accepted if it is shown by an affidavit of law that such copy, having been prepared by and issued under the hand of the notary, is as valid as the original for the purpose for which it has been made, and would be accepted in place of the original by the court of the domicile[1].

1 *Re Shorts* (1941).

Power deposited at Central Office of Supreme Court

11.49   Prior to 1 October 1971, a power of attorney could be deposited for record purposes at the Central Office of the Supreme Court pursuant to s. 219(1) of the Supreme Court of Judicature (Consolidation) Act 1925 (since repealed). A document purporting to be an office copy of a power of attorney so deposited, or deposited in the Supreme Court of Northern Ireland, or of a power registered in the Books of Council and Session in Scotland, is acceptable without further proof as sufficient evidence of the contents of the original, and of the fact that it has been so deposited or registered.

11.50   The procedure for deposit at the Central Office was abolished by the Powers of Attorney Act 1971[1], but without prejudice to the right to obtain office copies of powers deposited before 1 October 1971; or to the admissibility of such copies as evidence of the contents of the original documents.

1 See p. 804, post.

Admissibility of copy of power of attorney

11.51   The contents of an instrument creating a power of attorney may be proved by a copy which is a reproduction of the original made with a photographic or other device for reproducing documents in facsimile, provided that the copy contains the following certificate or certificates signed by the donor of the power or by a solicitor or a stockbroker (i.e. a member of any stock exchange within the meaning of the Stock Transfer Act 1963, or the Stock Transfer Act (Northern Ireland) 1963):

(a)   a certificate at the end to the effect that the copy is a true and complete copy of the original; and

(b)   if the original instrument consists of two or more pages, a certificate at the end of each page of the copy to the effect that it is a true and complete copy of the corresponding page of the original (Powers of Attorney Act 1971, s. 3(1)[1]).

1 See p. 804, post.

11.52   A copy of a copy of a power of attorney which has been certified as above is acceptable if the further copy is itself certified in the way set out in s. 3(1) (ibid., s. 3(2)).

Protection of donee and other persons on revocation of power

11.53   An attorney acting in pursuance of a power of attorney at a time when it has been revoked incurs no liability, by reason of the revocation, either to the donor or to any other person if at that time he did not know of the revocation (Powers of Attorney Act 1971, s. 5(1)[1]).

1 1 Halsbury's Statutes (4th edn) 65.

11.54 Similarly, where a person, without knowledge of the revocation, deals with the attorney, the transaction between them is, in favour of that person, as valid as if the power had then been in existence (ibid., s. 5(2)).

11.55 Where the interest of a purchaser depends on whether a transaction between the attorney and another person was valid by virtue of s. 5(2), it is to be conclusively presumed in favour of the purchaser that that person did not at the material time know of the revocation if:

(a) the transaction was completed within 12 months of the date on which the power came into operation; or
(b) before or within three months after the completion of the purchase that person makes a statutory declaration that he did not at the material time know of the revocation of the power (ibid., s. 5(4)).

11.56 For the purpose of the foregoing provisions, knowledge of the revocation of a power of attorney includes knowledge of the occurrence of any event, such as the death of the donor, which has the effect of revoking the power (ibid., s. 5(5)).

11.57 These provisions apply to powers of attorney whenever created, but only to acts and transactions on or after 1 October 1971 (ibid., s. 5(7)).

11.58 Section 6 of the Powers of Attorney Act 1971 affords additional protection for transferees of registered securities by an attorney. It is to be conclusively presumed in favour of such a transferee that the power of attorney had not been revoked at the date of the instrument of transfer if a statutory declaration to that effect is made by the attorney on or within three months after that date.

General power of attorney

11.59 A simple form of general power of attorney as follows is set out in Schedule 1 to the Powers of Attorney Act 1971:

> THIS GENERAL POWER OF ATTORNEY is made this   day of
>   19   by AB of
> I appoint CD of
> (*or* CD of   and EF of
> jointly *or* jointly and severally) to be my attorney(s) in accordance with section 10 of the Powers of Attorney Act 1971.
> IN WITNESS etc.'

11.60 Such a power confers on the donee (or donees, acting jointly or jointly and severally, as specified in the power) authority to do, on behalf of the donor, anything which he can lawfully do by an attorney (ibid., s. 10(1)).

Extent of Act

11.61   The provisions of s. 3 of the Act as to the admissibility of copies of powers of attorney extend to Scotland and Northern Ireland. The other provisions of the Act extend to England and Wales only.

Direct appointment necessary

11.62   A direct appointment of an individual (or individuals) or a trust corporation[1] as attorney is necessary, except where a firm is appointed, in which case it must be sworn that the person applying as attorney was a member of that firm at the date of the power.

1   As to grants to a trust corporation where appointed as attorney, see para. **9.29**, ante.

11.63   Where persons are appointed as attorneys successively, e.g. A in the first place, failing him B, and then C—before B or C can apply the person or persons previously mentioned must be cleared off.

Substituted attorney

11.64   If the power of attorney contains a power of substitution, and the attorney has exercised it, the substitute may take the grant[1], and on the substitutional power being executed the first attorney drops out until the substitutional power is revoked, the appointment of the substituted attorney being filed with the original power.

1   *Palliser v Ord* (1724) Bunb 166. An attorney appointed by an attorney was accepted, where it was allowed by the law of the deceased's domicile; *Re Abdul Hamid Bey's Goods* (1898) 78 LT 202.

Status of attorney

11.65   A person acting under a power of attorney has the same status as the donor of the power would have if applying personally[1], except that a chain of executorship is not constituted through the attorney[2], though it is not finally broken. As to chain of executorship generally, see paras. **4.64–4.84**, ante.

1   *Re Rendell, Wood v Rendell* [1901] 1 Ch 230.
2   Administration of Estates Act 1925, s. 7(3) (p. 746, post).

Minority or life interest

11.66   In cases where there is a minority interest or where a life interest arises under the will or intestacy, power should normally be given to a trust corporation, with or without an individual, or to not less than two individuals.

11.67   Where a beneficial minority or life interest arises in an estate, s. 114 of the Supreme Court Act 1981 applies and letters of administration, with will annexed, for the use and benefit of an executor may not be granted to a single individual as attorney[1] or otherwise, unless it appears to the court expedient in all the circumstances to appoint a sole administrator (s. 114(2)).

1   Registrar's Direction (1952) 23 May.

11.68   Where a grant is made to two attorneys, it is immaterial that they represent the interest of a single individual.

Joint grant to person entitled and the attorney of a person equally or next entitled

11.69   For practice in making such grants, see paras. **7.31–7.34**, ante.

Renouncing executor as attorney

11.70   By NCPR 37(1) and (2):

'(1) Renunciation of probate by an executor shall not operate as renunciation of any right which he may have to a grant of administration in some other capacity unless he expressly renounces such right.

(2) Unless a district judge or registrar otherwise directs, no person who has renounced administration in one capacity may obtain a grant thereof in some other capacity.'

11.71   An executor may accordingly renounce probate as executor, and then take a grant of administration as attorney of another executor, or in a personal capacity, provided that he did not previously renounce his right to administration in such lower character.

Limited power

11.72   A power of attorney limited to the administration of a specific portion of the estate is not normally accepted unless good reason is shown to the district judge or registrar and application is made for a grant so limited. It is generally considered that if the donor of the power be entitled to a general grant, his attorney should be empowered to take a grant of the whole estate.

Subsequent application by attorney for representative grant

11.73   An attorney administrator may obtain a grant in another estate to which he is entitled as personal representative of the deceased without the necessity of producing to the probate registry any further authority from his principal[1].

1 Registrar's Direction (1974) 11 October.

11.74   However, if it is known that such a grant will subsequently be necessary, the power of attorney may, if desired, be so worded as to authorise the attorney to obtain both grants. Form of power of attorney for use in such circumstances, No. 182.

Power filed in the registry

11.75   The power of attorney is normally filed permanently in the registry.

11.76   A solicitor lodging a *general* power of attorney, which is required for other purposes, may lodge with it a copy, and request that the original be returned with the grant. The original power must be duly stamped if it was executed before 19 March 1985 (see para. **11.43**, ante). The examined copy is filed with the oath, and the original returned with the grant. A power of attorney limited only for the purpose of obtaining a grant is not returnable[1].

1 Registrar's Direction (1952) 14 March.

11.77   No court fee is payable for examining the copy against the original.

Renunciation

11.78 For practice as to renunciation by an attorney of the right to a grant, see para. **15.33**, post.

Oath of attorney

11.79 The oath should contain all the particulars which would be necessary in the case of a direct grant to the donor of the power. The appropriate limitation must be included. A grant to an attorney is expressd to be for the use and benefit of the donor and the usual limitation required by r. 31(1) is 'until further representation be granted' but, under that rule, the district judge or registrar may direct some other form of limitation. The usual form of limitation in a grant allows a further grant to issue not only to the donor of the original power of attorney, or another attorney appointed by him, but to any other person with an equal title to a grant. The district judge or registrar would not normally allow a further grant to issue to anyone other than the original donor, or an attorney appointed by him in substitution for the original attorney, without good reason being given and without the original attorney or donor being given an opportunity to be heard on the matter. Some other possible forms of limitation are dealt with in the following paragraphs. Forms of oath, Nos. 114–116, 157 and 164.

Grant to the attorney of the sole or surviving executor

11.80 The grant, which takes the form of letters of administration with will annexed, is made to the attorney for the use and benefit of the executor, and limited until further representation be granted (or, if the district judge or registrar so directs, until he shall obtain probate)[1]. For Form of oath, see No. 157.

1 *Re Cassidy's Goods* (1832) 4 Hag Ecc 360. These words signify only that the administrator is the agent of the party constituting him. The grant is virtually for the use and benefit of all persons beneficially interested in the estate: *Chambers v Bicknell* (1843) 2 Hare 536. As to the powers of such an administrator, see *Webb v Kirby* (1856) 7 De GM & G 376, 26 LJ Ch 145. The grant usually follows the terms of the power: *Re Goldsborough's Goods* (1859) 1 Sw & Tr 295 at 297.

Grant to the attorney of all the executors

11.81 If more than one executor is appointed, and the executors jointly appoint the attorney, the grant is limited until further representation be granted (or, if the district judge or registrar so directs, until they (i.e. all of them) shall obtain probate). If the latter limitation has been used and subsequently some, but not all, of them desire to displace the attorney and take probate, and it is established that the other executors have not intermeddled through their attorney, application may be made for revocation of the attorney grant, following which probate may be granted to the executor applying, with power reserved to the others.

11.82 Where the power is given by more than four executors, the limitation in the instrument creating the power if not '. . . until further representation be granted' should be '. . . until any of us, not exceeding four in number, shall obtain. . . .' A power of attorney given by more than four persons bearing the limitation 'until we shall obtain', will not be accepted[1].

1 Registrar's Direction (1952) 14 October.

Death of one of several donors of power

11.83 The position on the death of one of two or more donors of a power of attorney is not free from doubt: it may be that a grant to the attorney of 'A and B, for their use and benefit' would cease to be effective on the death of either of the donors. If the surviving donor revokes the power of attorney the court will revoke the grant to enable a fresh grant to issue to attorneys appointed by him under a further power of attorney[1]. If the grant was limited 'until further representation be granted' a further grant may issue without the need for the first grant to be revoked.

1 *Re Dinshaw's Goods* [1930] P 180.

Grant to attorney of one or some of executors: notice to other executors

11.84 Where two or more executors are named, and an attorney is appointed by one or some, but not all, of them, notice of the application for the grant must be given to the other executors, unless such notice is dispensed with by the district judge or registrar (NCPR 31(2)).

11.85 The notice should be given by leaving it at, or sending it by ordinary prepaid or registered post or recorded delivery to, the last known address of the executors or by document exchange or fax where allowable[1]—see para. **25.232**, post.

1 RSC Order 65, r. 5, applied by NCPR 67.

11.86 The oath, or other evidence, should establish that the notice was so served. It is advisable to lodge a copy of the notice, and any reply received.

11.87 The grant will be limited for the use and benefit of the executor who appointed the attorney and until further representation be granted (or in such other way as the district judge or registrar may direct, e.g. until he, or any of the other executors, shall obtain probate).

Joint grant to attorneys separately appointed

11.88 A joint grant may be made to two attorneys of two executors (each executor appointing his own attorney) for the use and benefit of the executors during their joint lives, so as to cease on the death of either of the executors or the attorneys, or upon either executor obtaining probate. Thus a grant to A the lawful attorney of B and to C the lawful attorney of D, for the use and benefit of the said B and D, during the joint lives of A, B, C and D or until the said B or D shall obtain a grant, would cover every contingency.

Deceased domiciled abroad

11.89 As to grants where the deceased died domiciled out of England and Wales, see Chap. 12.

To the attorney or nominee of executors (corporations)

11.90 As to grants to the attorneys or nominees of non-trust corporations appointed as executors or otherwise entitled, see paras. **4.38–4.40** and **5.201** ff., ante. In all cases where the grant is made for the use and benefit of a non-trust corporation or a foreign corporation, the limitation in the oath and grant is 'until further representation be granted'.

Attorney of a corporation sole

11.91   When a grant is made to the attorney of a corporation sole, e.g. the Public Trustee of a Commonwealth country, such corporation sole need not be named otherwise than by his official title.

No subsequent attorney grant during life of a proving executor

11.92   Administration (with will) is not granted, whilst a proving executor is alive, to the attorney of an executor to whom power has been reserved[1].

1 *Re Wheldon* (1875).

Grant to the attorney of one of several residuary legatees or other persons entitled to administration

11.93   The attorney of one of several residuary legatees may take administration (with will), without notice to the other residuary legatees, and the attorney of one of several persons equally entitled to letters of administration may take administration without notice to the others.

11.94   The limitation in such cases is until further representation be granted, unless the district judge or registrar directs some other form of limitation.

11.95   A grant may be made to two attorneys appointed separately by two persons entitled to administration: see 'Joint grant to attorneys separately appointed', para. **11.88**, ante.

11.96   The attorney of several persons entitled to administration normally takes the grant until further representation be granted. For another possible form of limitation where there are more than four, see 'Grant to attorney of all the executors', paras. **11.81** and **11.82**.

Attorneys of parent or guardian of minors

11.97   A grant to the attorneys of the parents or guardians with parental responsibility for minors, is made for the use and benefit of the minors and until one of them attains the age of 18 years, or until further representation be granted.

Death of the donor or attorney

11.98   An attorney acting in pursuance of a power after the death of the donor incurs no liability if he does not know of the death[1], and transactions by persons who, without knowledge of the death, deal with the attorney are valid[2]. Knowledge of the death of the donor debars the attorney from acting further under his grant. If part of the estate remains unadministered, a de bonis non grant will be required to complete the administration.

1 Powers of Attorney Act 1971, s. 5(1).
2 Ibid., s. 5(2).

11.99   On the death of the attorney before he has completed the administration under his power, a cessate grant is required, another attorney being appointed by the donor of the first power unless he applies for a direct grant.

11.100 As to the position if one of two or more donors dies, see para. **11.83**, ante.

11.101 As to grants de bonis non and cessate grants, see Chap. 13.

'Cessate' grant to attorney

11.102 Where a grant made to one of two attorneys appointed severally has ceased by his death, the other attorney may take a grant under the original power of attorney on swearing that the donor has not revoked the power (see paras. **13.101–13.103**, post).

'De bonis non' grant, after death of attorney

11.103 If there is another person, other than the donor, entitled to share in the estate, and in the same class as the donor and the donor consents, a grant can be made to the other person, but in such a case the grant will be de bonis non, and not cessate.

Grants to consular officers

11.104 Where a national of a state to which s. 1 of the Consular Conventions Act 1949[1] has been applied by Order in Council is entitled to a grant of probate or administration (with or without will), *and is resident out of England*, as an alternative to making a grant to him or his attorney, administration (with or without will) may be granted to a consular officer of the state concerned (Consular Conventions Act 1949, s. 1) provided that the consular officer is not also authorised by a power of attorney by the national to apply for a grant on his behalf and that no other attorney appointed by the national is applying for a grant on his behalf.

1 See p. 765, post.

11.105 The Act has so far been applied to the following countries and states with which conventions have been concluded:

Austria	(operative from		26 December 1963)
Belgium	(	"	1 October 1964)
Bulgaria	(	"	21 December 1968)
Czechoslovakia	(	"	14 October 1976)
Denmark	(	"	23 March 1963)
Federal Republic of Germany	(	"	28 December 1957)
France	(	"	14 January 1954)
Greece	(	"	14 February 1954)
Hungary	(	"	28 November 1971)
Italy	(	"	29 December 1957)
Japan	(	"	10 October 1965)
Mexico	(	"	1 April 1955)
Mongolia	(	"	27 August 1976)
Norway	(	"	30 August 1951)
Poland	(	"	13 August 1971)
Spain	(	"	12 April 1963)
Sweden	(	"	24 September 1952)
USSR	(	"	22 September 1968)
Yugoslavia	(	"	5 May 1966)

11.106   The court has power if it thinks fit to postpone the making of a grant to the consular officer during such period as it considers appropriate in the circumstances (s. 1(1)).

Form of grant

11.107   The grant is made to the consular officer (by his official title) and his successors in office (s. 1(3)), and is limited for the use and benefit of the national and until further representation be granted[1].

1   Registrar's Direction (1952) 31 January.

11.108   A grant may be made to the consular officer alone notwithstanding that a life or minority interest arises (s. 1(4)).

Practice

11.109   Applications by a consular officer of a state to which s. 1 of the Consular Conventions Act 1949 has been applied are dealt with in common form. No order of the court is required unless one is necessary to establish the right of the national whom the officer desires to represent (e.g. an order under NCPR 30 where the deceased died domiciled out of England and Wales[1]).

1   See Chap. 12.

11.110   The oath should show that the applicant is a consular officer of a state with which there is a convention and to which the section has been applied by Order in Council; that the person on whose behalf the officer applies is a national of that state and resides out of England and Wales, and giving his title to a grant as in the case of an application by an attorney; and that no application has been made or is being made by a duly constituted attorney on the national's behalf[1].

1   A charity which is a duly constituted corporation, with power to take representation, is deemed to be a 'person' within the meaning of s. 1 of the Consular Conventions Act 1949 (Registrar's Direction (1954) 13 October).

11.111   In other respects the oath should be worded in a similar way to that to lead a grant to an attorney: see Form No. 164. It will be observed that no consent or authority from the national for whose use and benefit the grant is made is necessary.

Domicile Act 1861

11.112   A similar procedure for the issue of grants to consular officers formerly applied by virtue of s. 4 of the Domicile Act 1861; this section was repealed by s. 8 of the Consular Conventions Act 1949, although Orders in Council made under the earlier Act remain in force until revoked[1]. Application under the earlier Act was to the court by motion.

1   The Administration of Estates by Consular Officers (Estonia) Order in Council 1939 was revoked on 21 June 1978 by the Administration of Estates by Consular Officers (Estonia) (Revocation) Order 1978 (S.I. 1978 No. 779).

Grants for use of minors

Reduction in age of majority

11.113   Under s. 1(1) of the Family Law Reform Act 1969[1], the age of majority was reduced from 21 to 18 years with effect from 1 January 1970[2]. Persons who were already 18, but under 21, years of age on 1 January 1970, attained full age on that date.

1 See p. 789, post.
2 Family Law Reform Act 1969 (Commencement No. 1) Order 1969.

11.114   Section 1(1) of the Family Law Reform Act 1969 applies for the purposes of any rule of law and, unless there is a definition or any indication of a contrary intention (semble, including a reference to a specific age), in any statutory provision, whenever passed or made (except those concerning the Crown, voting matters or taxation, which are dealt with separately) expressions such as 'full age', 'infant', 'infancy', 'minor', 'minority', etc., are to be construed by reference to the age of 18 and not 21. This applies also to any deed, will or other instrument (except a statutory provision) made on or after 1 January 1970. But, notwithstanding any rule of law, a will or codicil executed before 1 January 1970 is not to be treated for this purpose as having been made on or after that date merely because it is confirmed by a codicil executed on or after that date (s. 1(7)). As to the republication of wills see also paras. **3.166** ff., ante, and **34.08** ff., post.

11.115   Persons who have not attained full age may be, and in probate practice are, referred to as minors instead of infants (s. 12).

Intestacies

11.116   Where a person dies intestate on or after 1 January 1970 the statutory trusts for issue and other relatives under s. 47(1)(i) of the Administration of Estates Act 1925[1] are amended by the substitution of the age of 18 for that of 21 as the age at which a minor's interest becomes absolutely vested.

1 See pp. 754, 759, post.

11.117   The Family Law Reform Act 1969 does not affect the statutory trusts in the cases of intestates who died before 1 January 1970 (see s. 3(2)). In such cases the interest of a minor, as before, becomes absolutely vested on his attaining the age of 21 years or marrying while under that age. Pending such vesting, however, trustees have power to apply the income due to a person who has attained the age of 18 to that person himself[1].

1 Family Law Reform Act 1969, Sch. 3, para. 5(2).

Wills and codicils

11.118   The age at which a child's interest under a will becomes vested depends upon: (i) the wording of the will; and (ii) the date of execution of the document in question.

11.119   If there is a specific reference to, or other indication of, the age of 21 this remains the effective age whatever the date of the will or of the death. If there is no definition or indication of a contrary intention, references to 'full age', etc., in the case of wills made on or after 1 January 1970 are to be treated as references to the age of 18. In relation to wills made before 1 January 1970 references to full age, infancy, minority, etc., are to be construed by reference to the age of 21.

11.120   It should be noted that, notwithstanding any rule of law (e.g., the doctrine under which a codicil confirming a will is regarded as bringing the will down to the date of the codicil) a will or codicil is not to be treated for the purposes of s. 1 of the Family Law Reform Act 1969 as made on or after 1 January 1970 merely because, although executed before that date, it has been confirmed by a codicil executed on or after that date (s. 1(7)). The test for this purpose is the actual date of execution of the original document.

Grant where person entitled is a minor

11.121   The practice in making grants for the use and benefit of minors is governed by NCPR 32[1] and the *Practice Direction* of 26 September 1991 ([1991] 4 All ER 562, [1991] 1 WLR 1069).

1   See p. 932, post.

11.122   Briefly, priority of right to a grant for the use and benefit of a minor is given by the rule to a parent with parental responsibility for him or to a guardian with parental responsibility for him. In the absence of such a parent or any such guardian, persons to obtain administration for the use and benefit of the minor must be appointed by district judge's or registrar's order[1].

1   NCPR 32(2).

11.123   Special provisions, which are set out in paras. **11.137–11.145**, post, apply in the case of minors appointed as executors.

Wards of court

11.124   A consequence of a child becoming a ward of court is that during the subsistence of the wardship material decisions relating to his person or his property should not be taken without the concurrence of the High Court or district judge dealing with the wardship. Accordingly, the directions of such judge should be taken when application is made for the appointment of a person to take a grant for a ward of court or for the making of a grant to any person for the use and benefit of a ward. This may involve a formal application to the court dealing with the wardship proceedings by or on behalf of the applicants, but if the wardship proceedings are inactive it may be appropriate for the probate registry in the first instance informally to ascertain the views of the district judge to whom the wardship is assigned[1].

1   Registrar's Direction (1975) 13 October.

Persons of full age equally entitled with minors

11.125   By NCPR 27(5), unless a district judge or registrar otherwise directs, a person of full age entitled to a grant is to be preferred to a guardian of a minor entitled in the same degree. Thus, normally, where one of the persons entitled to a grant is of full age, he or she should apply for the grant in preference to the parents or guardians of a minor. As to the practice in such cases, see Chap. 7.

11.126 Where the only person, or all persons, entitled to the grant are minors, this should be deposed to in the oath to lead the grant. The age of the minors must be given in the oath[1].

1 Registrar's Direction (1863) 18 August.

11.127 If it is desired to obtain the direction of the district judge or registrar under r. 27(5) that a grant may be made to the parents or guardians of a minor in preference to a person of full age, the facts should be put before the Principal of the Probate Department at the Principal Registry, or the district probate registrar, depending upon where the application for the grant is to be made.

Number of applicants required

11.128 It is provided by s. 114(2) of the Supreme Court Act 1981 that whenever a minority or a life interest arises under a will or intestacy, administration shall be granted either to a trust corporation[1] with or without an individual, or to not less than two individuals, unless it appears to the court to be expedient in all the circumstances to appoint an individual as sole administrator.

1 As to grants to trust corporations, see Chap. 9.

11.129 Where a grant is made to two guardians, it is immaterial that they represent the interest of a single individual[1]. However, where several branches of a family, all being under age, are equally entitled to a grant, it is desirable that the applicants should, when practicable, represent the several branches of the family[2].

1 President's Direction (1925) November.
2 Registrar's Direction (1926) 14 May.

11.130 As to nomination of a second administrator where there is only one parent or guardian competent and willing to take a grant, see paras. **11.200** ff., post.

Up to four guardians allowed

11.131 A grant may be made to any number of guardians not exceeding four (see Supreme Court Act 1981, s. 114(1)[1]).

1 See p. 844, post.

Grant to trust corporation

11.132 Where all persons entitled to administration are minors, a limited grant may issue as of right to a trust corporation upon the consents of the parents and guardians with parental responsibility for the minors as shown in NCPR 32(1). If there are no persons so qualified, the making of a grant to a trust corporation is in the discretion of the district judge or registrar.

11.133 Where there is a will and all the executors are minors, a limited grant may be made to a trust corporation on the consent of the persons entitled to the residue. If the executors are also persons entitled to the residue, the practice is similar to that in the case of administration.

11.134   For the practice in making grants to trust corporations in cases of minority, see paras. **9.40–9.50**, ante.

Limitation in grant

11.135   The limitation included in a grant on behalf of one minor is 'for the use and benefit of A.B. limited until he shall attain the age of eighteen years'. Where there is more than one minor, the wording used is 'for the use and benefit of A.B. and C.D. limited until one of them shall attain the age of eighteen years'. In the latter case the grant ceases as soon as one of the minors attains full age; but the death of one of the minors while under the age of 18 years does not render the grant ineffective.

11.136   The appropriate form of limitation should be included in the oath.

Sole executor a minor

11.137   Under NCPR 32(1), a distinction is drawn between cases in which a minor appointed as sole executor has an interest in the residuary estate of the deceased, and those in which he has none. In the latter case, unless otherwise directed by a district judge or registrar, the grant is to be made to the person entitled to the residuary estate for the use and benefit of the minor and limited until he shall attain the age of 18 years. Where, however, a beneficial minority, or a life, interest arises in the estate, s. 114(2) of the Supreme Court Act 1981 applies, which provision will normally require the appointment of not less than two grantees or a trust corporation.

11.138   If a minor is sole executor and also has an interest in the residuary estate, a grant is usually made to both his parents or guardians with parental responsibility for him, or, if there is only one such guardian or parent competent and willing to act, to him and a person nominated by him as co-administrator (see paras. **11.200** ff., post).

Minor executor attaining full age

11.139   Section 118 of the Supreme Court Act 1981[1] is as follows:

> 'Where a testator by his will appoints a minor to be an executor, the appointment shall not operate to vest in the minor the estate, or any part of the estate, of the testator, or to constitute him a personal representative for any purpose, unless and until probate is granted to him in accordance with probate rules.'

1 See p. 845, post.

11.140   A minor executor, on attaining the age of majority, may then as he wishes renounce his right to a grant or take a grant.

One of the executors a minor

11.141   Under NCPR 33(1), where one of two or more executors is a minor, probate may be granted to the other executor or executors, with power reserved of making the like grant to the minor on attaining the age of 18 years.

11.142   Administration (with will) for the use and benefit of the minor executor limited until he attains the age of 18 years may be granted to his parents or guardians having parental responsibility for him in accordance with NCPR 32 if, and only if, the other executors renounce probate or, on being cited to accept or refuse a grant, fail to make an effective application for a grant (NCPR 33(2)); as to citing an executor to accept or refuse a grant, see Chap. 24.

Renunciation of minor's right to a grant

11.143 Where a minor is named as executor, his right to probate on attaining the age of 18 years may not be renounced by any person on his behalf (NCPR 34(1)).

11.144 There are sometimes, however, circumstances in which it is desirable that the superior right of a minor to administration (or administration with will) be renounced so as to enable a grant to be made to a suitable person in a lower category. No person with parental responsibility for a minor, whether a parent or guardian, may renounce on behalf of a minor as of right: a minor's right to a grant of administration (with or without will) may be renounced only by a person appointed in accordance with NCPR 32(2), and authorised to renounce by a district judge or registrar[1].

1 NCPR 34(2).

11.145 Application for appointment of a person for this purpose should be made in the same way as an application for appointment of a person for the purpose of taking a grant (see para. **11.193**, post). It should be shown in the supporting affidavit that the renunciation on behalf of the minor is necessary to facilitate the granting of representation to the estate.

Parents and guardians entitled in priority

11.146 Under NCPR 32(1), where the person to whom a grant of administration (with or without will) would otherwise be made is a minor, the persons primarily entitled to a grant on his behalf are a parent or guardian with parental responsibility for him as shown in NCPR 32(1). This includes the mother of an illegitimate child, the father of an illegitimate child who has acquired parental responsibility under a court order or recorded parental responsibility agreement, an adoptive parent and a guardian appointed by deed, will or court order[1].

1 I.e., the High Court, a county court or a magistrates' court (see the Children Act 1989, s. 5 and Sch. 14, paras. 12, 13 and 14, pp. 883, 892, post).

Grant to parents (including adoptive parents)

11.147 Where a minor (other than one who is a sole executor with no beneficial interest in the estate) is entitled to a grant, administration (with or without will) may be granted, whatever the age of the minor, to both his parents, provided that they each have parental responsibility for him, without any order being necessary.

11.148 The term 'parents' in this context includes adoptive parents.

11.149 NCPR 32(1), as amended with effect from 14 October 1991, no longer requires both parents, if living, to apply jointly for the grant. This change is a consequence of s. 2(7) of the Children Act 1989, which provides:

'(7) Where more than one person has parental responsibility for a child, each of them may act alone and without the other (or others) in meeting that responsibility; but nothing in this Part shall be taken to affect the operation of any enactment which requires the consent of more than one person in a matter affecting the child.'

However, where a minority interest arises under a will or an intestacy, a grant may not normally issue to less than two individuals (Supreme Court Act 1981, s. 114(2)). Accordingly, where both parents have parental responsibility for the minor, they will normally apply jointly for the grant. If one of them is not competent or not willing to take a grant (e.g. because he or she is mentally incapable or has renounced his or her right to take a grant for the use and benefit of the minor) the competent and willing one normally may nominate any fit and proper person to act jointly with him or her in taking the grant (NCPR 32(3) as amended).

11.150   Under s. 2 of the Children Act 1989 a mother of a child has parental responsibility for the child whether or not she and the child's father were married to each other at the time of the child's birth. Accordingly, it is sufficient for her to state in the oath that she is 'the mother of the minor'[1].

1 *Practice Direction* 26 September 1991 ([1991] 4 All ER 562, [1991] 1 WLR 1069).

11.151   A father of a child has parental responsibility for the child under s. 2(1) of the Children Act 1989 provided he and the mother of the child were married to each other at the time of the child's birth. It is provided in s. 2(3) of the Act that references in the Act to a child whose father and mother were, or (as the case may be) were not, married to each other at the time of his birth must be read with s. 1 of the Family Law Reform Act 1987 (which extends their meaning). See p. 874 for s. 1 of the Family Law Reform Act 1987.

11.152   A father of a minor relying on s. 2(1) of the Children Act 1989 must state in the oath that he is 'the father of the minor and has parental responsibility under s. 2(1) of the Children Act 1989'[1].

1 *Practice Direction* 26 September 1991 ([1991] 4 All ER 562, [1991] 1 WLR 1069).

11.153   A father of a child who does not have parental responsibility under s. 2(1) of the Children Act 1989 may acquire parental responsibility in accordance with s. 4 of the Act. Such responsibility may be acquired either by order of the court or by virtue of an agreement between the mother and father of the child made under the Parental Responsibility Agreement Regulations 1991, as amended—see p. 944, post. The oath must state that he is the father of the minor and has parental responsibility 'under an order' or 'under a duly recorded parental responsibility agreement'. A copy of the order or a sealed copy of the agreement recorded in the Principal Registry under the Regulations must be produced[1].

1 *Practice Direction* 26 September 1991 ([1991] 4 All ER 562, [1991] 1 WLR 1069).

11.154   Where the father of a minor was not married to the mother at the time of the child's birth, but has parental responsibility in accordance with paras. 4 or 6 of Sch. 14 to the Children Act 1989 either (a) by virtue of an order under s. 4(1) of the Family Law Reform Act 1987 or (b) by virtue of an order giving him custody or care and control of the child, in force immediately before the commencement of Parts I and II of the Children Act 1989, the oath must state that he is the father of the minor and a parent having parental responsibility by virtue of such an order which was in force immediately before the commencement of the Children Act 1989. A copy of the order must be produced in each instance[1].

1 *Practice Direction* 26 September 1991 ([1991] 4 All ER 562, [1991] 1 WLR 1069).

11.155 An adopter of a child has parental responsibility for the child in accordance with s. 12(1) of the Adoption Act 1976, as amended by s. 88 of the Children Act 1989, and has a right to a grant for the use and benefit of the child under NCPR 32(1)(a)(iii). The oath must state that the applicant is the adopter or one of the adopters of the minor by an order made within the meaning of s. 12 of the Adoption Act 1976. A copy of the order must be produced[1].

1 *Practice Direction* 26 September 1991 ([1991] 4 All ER 562, [1991] 1 WLR 1069).

11.156 Form of oath on application for administration (with will) by both parents, No. 159.

Guardians

11.157 The whole of the Guardianship of Minors Act 1971 was repealed, as from 14 October 1991, by the Children Act 1989, s. 108(7), Sch. 15.

11.158 Under NCPR 32, as amended, with effect from 14 October 1991 a guardian of a minor who is appointed, or deemed to have been appointed, in accordance with s. 5 of the Children Act 1989 or in accordance with paras. 12, 13 or 14 of Sch. 14 to that Act has a right to administration for the use and benefit of the minor limited until he attains the age of 18 years, equal to the right of a parent with parental responsibility for the minor.

11.159 Where the guardian has been appointed in accordance with s. 5 of the Children Act 1989 (see p. 883, post) the oath must state that he or she is a guardian of the minor having parental responsibility by virtue of:

(a) an order made under s. 5 of the Children Act 1989, or
(b) an appointment made by 'AB a parent having parental responsibility for the minor by will' (or 'by deed' as appropriate), or
(c) an appointment made by 'CD a duly appointed guardian having parental responsibility for the minor by will' (or 'by deed' as appropriate).

11.160 Under s. 5(1) of the Children Act 1989, where an application with respect to a child is made to the court by any individual, the court may by order appoint that individual to be the child's guardian if:

(a) the child has no parent with parental responsibility for him; or
(b) a residence order has been made with respect to the child in favour of a parent or guardian of his who has died while the order was in force.

Under s. 5(2) an order may also be made under s. 5(1) in any family proceedings if the court considers that the order should be made even though no application has been made for it.

11.161 Under s. 5(3) of the Children Act 1989 a parent who has parental responsibility for his child may appoint another individual to be the child's guardian in the event of his death and, under s. 5(4), a guardian of a child may appoint another individual to take his place as the child's guardian in the event of his death.

11.162 Under s. 5(5) an appointment made under s. 5(3) or (4) does not have effect unless it is made in writing, is dated and is signed by the person making the appointment or—

(a)   in the case of an appointment made by will which is not signed by the testator, is signed at the direction of the testator in accordance with the requirements of s. 9 of the Wills Act 1837; or

(b)   in any other case, is signed at the direction of the person making the appointment, in his presence and in the presence of two witnesses who each attest the signature.

11.163   Under s. 5(6) a person appointed as a child's guardian under s. 5 shall have parental responsibility for the child concerned and, under s. 5(7), where—

(a)   on the death of any person making an appointment under sub-s. (3) or (4), the child concerned has no parent with parental responsibility for him; or

(b)   immediately before the death of any person making such an appointment, a residence order in his favour was in force with respect to the child,

the appointment takes effect on the death of that person; and, under s. 5(8), where on the death of any person making an appointment under sub-s. (3) or (4)—

(a)   the child concerned has a parent with parental responsibility for him; and
(b)   sub-s. (7)(b) does not apply,

the appointment takes effect when the child no longer has a parent who has parental responsibility for him.

11.164   Under s. 5(9) of the Children Act 1989, sub-ss. (1) and (7) do not apply if the residence order referred to in para. (b) of those subsections was also made in favour of a surviving parent of the child.

11.165   Section 5(10) confirms that nothing in s. 5 is to be taken to prevent an appointment under sub-s. (3) or (4) being made by two or more persons acting jointly.

11.166   Section 5(11) provides that subject to any provision made by rules of court, no court shall exercise the High Court's inherent jurisdiction to appoint a guardian of the estate of any child, and s. 5(12) confirms that where rules of court are made under sub-s. (11) they may prescribe the circumstances in which, and conditions subject to which, an appointment of such a guardian may be made.

11.167   Section 5(13) confirms that a guardian of a child may only be appointed in accordance with the provisions of s. 5 of the Children Act 1989.

11.168   An appointment of a guardian made by a parent or guardian with parental responsibility under s. 5(3) or (4) of the Children Act 1989 revokes an earlier such appointment (including one made in an unrevoked will or codicil) made by the same person in respect of the same child, unless it is clear (whether as the result of an express provision in the later appointment or by any necessary implication) that the purpose of the later appointment is to appoint an additional guardian (Children Act 1989, s. 6(1)). Additionally, an appointment made under s. 5(3) or (4) (including one made in an unrevoked will or codicil) is revoked if the person who made the appointment revokes it by a written and dated instrument which is signed:

(a)   by him; or
(b)   at his direction, in his presence and in the presence of two witnesses who each attest his signature.

(Children Act 1989, s. 6(2)).

In addition, when s. 4 of the Law Reform (Succession) Act 1995 (see p. 902, post) comes into force, an appointment under s. 5(3) or (4) of the Children Act 1989 (including one made in an unrevoked will or codicil) is revoked if the person appointed is the spouse of the person who made the appointment and either:

(a) a decree of a court of civil jurisdiction in England and Wales dissolves or annuls the marriage, or

(b) the marriage is dissolved or annulled and the divorce or annulment is entitled to recognition in England and Wales by virtue of Part II of the Family Law Act 1986,

unless a contrary intention appears by the appointment. This will have effect as respects an appointment made by a person dying on or after 1 January 1996 (regardless of the date of the appointment and the date of the dissolution or annulment).

11.169 A further way to revoke an appointment made under s. 5(3) or (4) (other than one made in a will or codicil) is for the person who made it to destroy the instrument by which it was made or to have some other person destroy that instrument in his presence, in either case with the intention of revoking the appointment (Children Act 1989, s. 6(3)).

11.170 Section 6(4) provides that, for the avoidance of doubt, an appointment under s. 5(3) or (4) made in a will or codicil is revoked if the will or codicil is revoked.

11.171 Section 6(5) provides that a person who is appointed as a guardian under s. 5(3) or (4) may disclaim his appointment by an instrument in writing signed by him and made within a reasonable time of his first knowing that the appointment has taken effect.

11.172 Any appointment of a guardian under s. 5 may be brought to an end at any time by order of the court:

(a) on the application of any person who has parental responsibility for the child;

(b) on the application of the child concerned, with leave of the court; or

(c) in any family proceedings, if the court considers that it should be brought to an end even though no application has been made.

(Children Act 1989, s. 6(7)).

Oath and supporting evidence

11.173 In addition to the appropriate statement in the oath (see para. **11.159**, ante) the order, will or deed (or in the case of a proved will, an official copy of it) must be produced on the application for the grant, together with such further evidence as the district judge or registrar may require in the circumstances of the case. The date of death of the person making the appointment must be included in the oath, as must the date of death of any other person upon whose death the appointment takes place.

11.174 Where the guardian has parental responsibility by virtue of an order made under the now revoked Guardianship of Minors Act 1971, or under the Sexual

Offences Act 1956 or under the High Court's inherent jurisdiction with respect to children which is deemed to be an appointment made and having effect under s. 5 of the Children Act 1989 (by paras. 12 and 13 of Sch. 14 to that Act) the oath must include such information and a copy of the order must also be produced.

11.175   If there is no parent or other guardian with parental responsibility for the minor who is competent and willing to act, the guardian who is may nominate a fit and proper person to act jointly with him in taking the grant, unless the district judge or registrar otherwise directs.

11.176   For forms of oath, see Forms Nos. 120–122 and 159.

Practice on application by local authority in 'care' cases

11.177   Under s. 31(1)(a) of the Children Act 1989, which came into force on 14 October 1991, on the application of any local authority or authorised person, the court may make an order placing the child with respect to whom the application is made in the care of a designated authority.

11.178   Section 33 of the Children Act 1989 also came into force on 14 October 1991. Under s. 33(1), where a care order is made with respect to a child it shall be the duty of the local authority designated by the order to receive the child into their care and keep him in their care while the order remains in force. Section 33(3) provides that while a care order is in force with respect to a child, the local authority designated by the order shall:

(a)   have parental responsibility for the child; and

(b)   have the power (subject to the following provisions of this section) to determine the extent to which a parent or guardian may meet his parental responsibility for him.

11.179   It should be noted that various orders and resolutions made under previous Acts (including the Child Care Act 1980 which was repealed as from 14 October 1991—see Children Act 1989, s. 108(7), Sch. 15) are deemed to be care orders under the Children Act 1989—see Children Act 1989, s. 108(6), Sch. 14, para. 15.

11.180   Where a local authority wishes to apply for a grant of administration for the use and benefit of a minor in its care it should apply under NCPR 32(2) for an order appointing itself to obtain such administration. For applications under NCPR 32(2) see paras. **11.191** and **11.192**, post. A local authority may be considered to be a person within the terms of NCPR 32(2). Where it is not applying as a trust corporation it should normally appoint two nominees or attorneys to make the application for the grant because of the normal requirement of s. 114(2) of the Supreme Court Act 1981 that there be more than one individual grantee.

11.181   A copy of the care order and a copy of the resolution (authenticated by the appropriate officer of the local authority) or the power of attorney appointing the officers of the local authority to apply on the authority's behalf must be lodged with the application.

11.182   Where the local authority qualifies as a custodian trustee under rule 30 of the Public Trustee Rules 1912 and applies as a trust corporation (see paras. **9.01** ff., ante), the oath to lead the grant should, in addition to the usual recitals, state that the local authority is entitled to act as a custodian trustee under the Public Trustee Act 1906 and thereby as a trust corporation as defined by rule 2(1) of the Non-Contentious Probate Rules 1987, and that it has power to accept the grant.

11.183 It should be noted that where the local authority qualifies as a custodian trustee in relation to a trust under which property devolves for the sole benefit of a child in care, the authority is entitled to continue so to act until a new custodian trustee is appointed, notwithstanding that the child has ceased to be in the care of that authority[1].

1 Public Trustee Rules 1912, r. 30(1)(i) (see para. **9.05**, ante).

11.184 The grant is made for the use and benefit of the minor and is normally limited until he attains the age of 18 years or until further representation is granted.

Deceased domiciled out of England and Wales

11.185 Where it is sought to obtain a grant in the estate of a person of foreign domicile for the use and benefit of a minor, regard must be had to the practice as to grants in cases where the deceased was domiciled out of England and Wales; as to which, see Chap. 12. It must be shown whether any person has been entrusted with administration by the court of the place of domicile, or if no one has been entrusted, who is beneficially entitled to the estate by the law of the place of domicile, with the limitations, if any, imposed by that law. A district judge's or registrar's order under NCPR 30 will usually be necessary.

11.186 The provisions of s. 114(2) of the Supreme Court Act 1981[1] apply, and the grant cannot normally be made to a single individual except where the minor is an executor having no beneficial interest in the estate and there is no other minority or life interest, unless the court considers it expedient in all the circumstances to appoint a sole administrator.

1 See p. 844, post.

11.187 If the minor is domiciled in England and Wales, the guardianship is governed by English law whatever the domicile of the deceased. The entitlement to representation, however, will be decided in accordance with NCPR 30 (see Chap. 12).

Deceased domiciled in England and Wales: minors domiciled abroad

11.188 Where the deceased died domiciled in England and Wales, but all the persons entitled to the grant are under age and domiciled out of England and Wales, the grant is made to their guardians lawfully constituted in accordance with the law of the place of their domicile, or to the attorneys of the guardians so constituted.

11.189 Guardianship must be proved by production of a copy of the document by which the guardians have been constituted, duly authenticated by the seal of the court having jurisdiction in the place of the domicile of the minors, or by an affidavit of the law of that place by a person who is conversant with its law. It must be clearly shown in the order that the guardianship is not limited to care of the children, but provides for or implies the custody of their property. Failing this an order appointing persons to obtain administration must be obtained. The domicile of the minors must be sworn to in the oath.

11.190   The requirements of s. 114(2) of the Supreme Court Act 1981 apply, and the application is normally made by two guardians, or, where only one guardian has been constituted, by two attorneys of that guardian, except where the minors are executors with no beneficial interest, and there is no other minority or life interest, or the court considers it expedient in all the circumstances to appoint a sole administrator to act.

Persons appointed to obtain administration

11.191   Application may be made to a district judge or registrar for an order appointing a person or persons to obtain administration for the use and benefit of a minor[1]. Such an application is necessary where the parents do not apply and there is no guardian with parental responsibility. An order may also be applied for, upon good cause shown, where there is a parent or guardian whom it is desired to pass over. A person may be appointed to act jointly with a parent or a guardian. Where there is no such parent or guardian and two grantees are required to be constituted, the proper course is to apply for the appointment of two persons, rather than for the appointment of one with a view to his nominating a co-administrator.

1   NCPR 32(2).

11.192   Appointment of a local authority is also required where application is made by the authority for a grant of administration for the use and benefit of a child in its care (see paras. **11.177–11.184**, ante).

Person appointed for the purpose of renouncing

11.193   It is also necessary to apply for the appointment of a person when it is desired that a minor's right to administration be renounced (NCPR 34(2): see also para. **11.144**, ante). In such case the appointed person must be specifically authorised by the district judge or registrar to renounce. He cannot be authorised to renounce a minor executor's right to probate (see NCPR 34(1)).

Trust corporation

11.194   A trust corporation may be appointed to apply (and must be so appointed where application is made by a local authority for a grant of administration for the use and benefit of a child in its care); but the alternative procedure set out in paras. **9.40–9.48**, ante, is often preferable, as, except where the minor is an executor, the grant is not limited only until he attains the age of 18 years, but until he shall obtain a grant himself. This allows the trust corporation to continue to act as administrator after the minor has attained full age, subject to the latter's right to displace the corporation at any time by taking a grant.

Application for order

11.195   The order appointing persons normally should be obtained before the papers to lead the grant are completed.

11.196   The application is made by lodging an affidavit of the facts sworn by the proposed appointee or appointees, and any supporting documents, in the Probate

Department at the Principal Registry, or, if the application for the grant is to be made at a district probate registry, at that registry[1].

1 NCPR 32(2) and 2(1).

11.197 The affidavit of facts should state whether both parents of the minor are alive, and if so, why they do not apply for the grant; and whether there is any guardian or other person with parental responsibility. If it is desired to pass over any such guardian the reason should be given. The affidavit should also set out the amount of the estate, the ages of the minors[1], whether or not any of them is a ward of court, by whom they are being cared for, the relationship, if any, of the proposed appointees, and any other facts relevant to their suitability. Form of affidavit, No. 19. Where the affidavit is sworn by one of the proposed appointees only, the consent of the other to join in the grant should be lodged.

1 Registrar's Direction (1863) 18 August.

11.198 Any renunciation by guardians or next-of-kin should be lodged with the papers.

11.199 The district judge's or registrar's order and supporting documents if subsequently handed out should be included with the papers to lead the grant when these are lodged at the registry. The oath must include particulars of the order of the registrar. Form of oath, No. 123. No fee is now payable for the order.

Nomination of co-administrator

11.200 Where there is only one parent or guardian with parental responsibility who is competent and willing to take a grant, and, because of the existence of a minority or life interest, the court requires the grant to be made to not less than two persons, the competent and willing one may, unless otherwise directed by the district judge or registrar, nominate a suitable person as co-administrator (NCPR 32(3)).

11.201 It must be sworn in the oath that there is no other parent or guardian with parental responsibility other than the applicant. If there is another such, the first applicant may nominate a co-grantee only where it is established that such other parent or guardian is either incompetent or unwilling to join in the grant. In the latter case, his renunciation or other evidence of unwillingness should be lodged. Forms of oath, Nos. 120 to 122.

11.202 If both parents of the minor are alive they may apply jointly for a grant[1]. If they do not both apply it must be shown to the satisfaction of the district judge or registrar that they do not desire to apply jointly. In the event of contention between the parents it may be necessary for the district judge or registrar to direct that the matter be determined on summons[2].

1 NCPR 32(1).
2 NCPR 61(1).

11.203 The nomination includes a statement as to the fitness of the proposed co-administrator. It is signed by the parent or guardian in the presence of a witness, and filed with the papers to lead the grant. Form of nomination, No. 62.

11.204   Although under the terms of NCPR 32(3) a sole person appointed by the district judge or registrar may nominate a second person as co-administrator, the proper course in most cases where appointment is necessary is for application to be made for the appointment of two persons.

11.205   It should be noted that a person entitled to a grant *in his own right* will not be appointed on behalf of a minor to enable him to nominate a co-administrator (see para. **7.28**, ante).

When parent or guardian of one of several minors may nominate

11.206   NCPR 32(3) restricts the right to nominate a co-administrator to cases where 'there is only one person competent and willing to take a grant under the foregoing provisions of this rule'. Accordingly, when the parent or guardian of one of several minors applies for a grant with a nominated co-administrator, the position as to parents and guardians of the others must be shown in the oath. If any other minor has a parent or a competent guardian with parental responsibility it must be established that such parent or guardian is unwilling to be joined as co-grantee. Cases of doubt should be referred to a district judge or registrar for directions.

Death of one administrator

11.207   As to the power of the district judge or registrar under NCPR 26 to add a further administrator on the death of one of two administrators during the subsistence of a minority interest, see paras. **7.40–7.47**, ante.

Concurrent grant to guardian administrator

11.208   Where guardian administrators, in their representative character, take a grant of administration of the estate of another deceased person, such grant is similarly limited for the use and benefit of the minor on whose behalf they took the original grant, and will cease when the minor comes of age.

Grants for use of persons under disability

Mental incapacity

11.209   Where the person entitled to a grant is incapable of managing his affairs by reason of mental incapacity, administration may be granted for his use and benefit in accordance with NCPR 35.

11.210   This rule is as follows:

'(1) Unless a district judge or registrar otherwise directs, no grant shall be made under this rule unless all persons entitled in the same degree as the incapable person referred to in paragraph (2) below have been cleared off.

(2) Where a district judge or registrar is satisfied that a person entitled to a grant is by reason of mental incapacity incapable of managing his affairs, administration for his use and benefit, limited until further representation be granted or in such other way as the district judge or registrar may direct, may be granted in the following order of priority—

(a) to the person authorised by the Court of Protection to apply for a grant;
(b) where there is no person so authorised, to the lawful attorney of the incapable person acting under a registered enduring power of attorney;

(c) where there is no such attorney entitled to act, or if the attorney shall renounce administration for the use and benefit of the incapable person, to the person entitled to the residuary estate of the deceased.

(3) Where a grant is required to be made to not less than two administrators, and there is only one person competent and willing to take a grant under the foregoing provisions of this rule, administration may, unless a district judge or registrar otherwise directs, be granted to such person jointly with any other person nominated by him.

(4) Notwithstanding the foregoing provisions of this rule, administration for the use and benefit of the incapable person may be granted to such two or more other persons as the district judge or registrar may by order direct.

(5) Notice of an intended application under this rule shall be given to the Court of Protection.'

Other persons having equal right

11.211   Unless otherwise directed by the district judge or registrar, a grant will not be made for the use of a person incapable of managing his affairs without clearing off all other persons equally entitled with him. (See NCPR 35(1).)

11.212   Where one of several persons entitled in the same degree is incapable, application for a grant should wherever possible be made by one or more of the capable persons. If such persons do not wish to act and it is desired that a grant should be made for the use and benefit of the incapable person, the normal procedure is to obtain the renunciations of the capable persons. If there is some difficulty in clearing off such persons, or if for some reason it is sought to prefer the person representing the incapable person, the facts should be put before the district judge or registrar for his directions.

11.213   Where one of several executors named in a will is incapable, probate is granted to the other executors, power being reserved to the incapable executor[1]. The district judge's or registrar's power under r. 35(1) does not enable a grant to be made on behalf of an incapable executor without clearing off other executors who are sui juris[2].

1 *Evans v Tyler* (1849) 2 Rob Eccl 128 at 131.
2 Registrar's Circular, 12 June 1967.

11.214   Where one of two executors is incapable and administration (with will) is granted to the other's attorney, it is limited until further representation be granted, leaving it open for the capable executor to obtain probate and for the incapable one to obtain probate on his recovering his capacity. Form of oath, No. 157, suitably adapted.

Foreign domicile

11.215   Where it is sought to obtain a grant in the estate of a person of foreign domicile for the use and benefit of a person who is incapable of managing his affairs, due regard must be had to the general practice with regard to grants of administration where the deceased died domiciled out of England and Wales[1]. If the applicant for the grant is not the person entrusted with the administration of the estate by the court having jurisdiction at the place where the deceased died domiciled, it must be shown how the incapable person is beneficially entitled to the estate by the law of the place where the deceased died domiciled and how the applicant is entitled to represent the incapable person by that law with the limitation, if any, imposed by that law; alternatively, if the circumstances justify it, the district judge or registrar may order that the grant be made to such person as he thinks fit. In any event, a district judge's or registrar's order must be obtained.

1 See Chap. 12.

Wording of oath

11.216   The oath must state that the person entitled to the grant is a person incapable of managing his affairs. For forms of oath, see Nos. 125 to 127. The date of any relevant order or authorisation is quoted in the oath, and the order or authorisation must be produced; the usual statements as to minority and life interests and settled land must be included (see paras. **6.351** and **6.352**, ante). If any minority or life interest arises, the grant will normally be made to not less than two individuals, or to a trust corporation with or without an individual[1]. If a life or minority interest arises and two administrators are required and if there is only one person competent and willing to take a grant, who is either the person authorised by the Court of Protection or the lawful attorney of the incapable person acting under a registered enduring power of attorney or the person entitled to the residuary estate of the deceased, under r. 35(2), he may nominate his co-administrator under r. 35(3).

1 Supreme Court Act 1981, s. 114(2) (p. 844, post).

11.217   The limitation 'for the use and benefit of' the incapable person 'and until further representation be granted' must be included in the oath.

Person authorised by Court of Protection

11.218   Where the person entitled to the grant is incapable by reason of mental disorder of managing his affairs, priority of right to a grant is given to the person authorised by the Court of Protection under the provisions of the Mental Health Act 1983[1] to apply for the grant[2].

1 28 Halsbury's Statutes (4th edn) 632. Under s. 99 of this Act (which replaces the Mental Health Act 1959 which had replaced the Lunacy Acts 1890 to 1908) the Court of Protection may appoint a receiver for any person who is shown to be incapable by reason of mental disorder of managing and administering his property and affairs, with such powers and duties in relation to the property and affairs of the patient as he may be given by the court pursuant to ss. 95 and 96 of the Act.
   A person who at the commencement of the Mental Health Act 1959 was the committee of the estate of a person of unsound mind so found by inquisition is thereafter deemed to be his receiver appointed under s. 105 of that Act, with such functions in relation to his property and affairs as were exercised by him in relation thereto as such committee (Sixth Schedule, Part IV, para. 26).
2 NCPR 35(2)(a).

11.219   The authority of the Court of Protection confers on the person authorised such powers only as are specified in that authority. An order appointing a receiver is not accepted unless it embodies authority to apply for a grant. A supplemental order must be obtained where this authority is lacking. The order, under the seal of the Court of Protection, must be produced with the application for the grant.

11.220   The authority of the Court of Protection usually contains provision for the appointment of another person (unspecified) as co-administrator with the person named in the event of there being a minority or life interest and the person named in the order can now nominate a second administrator to act with him, unless a district judge or registrar otherwise directs[1].

1 NCPR 35(3).

Notice to Court of Protection

11.221 In cases of mental incapacity, where no person has been authorised by the Court of Protection to apply for a grant, notice of the intended application must be given by the extracting solicitor to that Court[1].

1 NCPR 35(5).

11.222 The notice should be addressed to 'The Court of Protection, Stewart House, Kingsway, London WC2B 6JX'.

11.223 The formal acknowledgment received from the Court of Protection must be lodged with the papers.

11.224 The prior right given by NCPR 35 to a person authorised by the Court of Protection to apply for a grant is sufficiently cleared off by the acknowledgment by that Court of the notice of application, unless it indicates that a person has been, or will be, appointed to apply for the grant[1].

1 Registrar's Direction (1956) 16 July.

Proof of mental incapacity

11.225 In cases of mental incapacity, where the applicant for the grant is not a person authorised by the Court of Protection to apply or an attorney acting under a registered enduring power of attorney, evidence of incapacity must be lodged.

11.226 When the incapable person is a patient who is resident in an institution, the district judges and registrars will normally accept a certificate from the Responsible Medical Officer of the institution in the following terms:

(Name of Institution)

(Name of patient)

I certify that:

1. The above-named patient, who is now residing in this Institution, is in my opinion by reason of mental disorder incapable of managing his property and affairs.
2. In my opinion the above-named patient is unlikely to be fit to manage and administer his property and affairs within a period of three months.

                         (Signed)

Date: *Responsible Medical Officer.*

11.227 In the case of an incapable person who is not resident in an institution the district judges and registrars will normally accept a certificate by the patient's doctor certifying the period in which he has attended the patient in respect of the disability and that, in his opinion, the patient is incapable of managing and administering his property and affairs, and is unlikely to become capable within a period of three months.

11.228   If the Responsible Medical Officer, or the patient's doctor, as the case may be, is unable to give such a certificate, the matter should be referred to the district judge or registrar for directions[1].

1 *Practice Note* [1962] 2 All ER 613, [1962] 1 WLR 738; *Practice Direction* [1969] 1 All ER 494, [1969] 1 WLR 301.

Lawful attorney acting under a registered enduring power of attorney

11.229   Where there is no person authorised by the Court of Protection to apply for a grant, the person next entitled to apply for a grant for the use and benefit of the incapable person is his lawful attorney acting under a registered enduring power of attorney. Notice of the application must be given to the Court of Protection as required by NCPR 35(5).

11.230   A registered enduring power of attorney is one which is in the prescribed form (see the Enduring Powers of Attorney (Prescribed Form) Regulations 1990, which contain saving provisions in respect of powers executed by donors in the forms prescribed by the earlier regulations) and made under the Enduring Powers of Attorney Act 1985 and the Court of Protection (Enduring Powers of Attorney) Rules 1994.

11.231   An enduring power of attorney does not cease when the donor becomes mentally incapable but the powers of the attorney are limited until the power of attorney is registered at the Court of Protection.

11.232   The oath should confirm that no one has been authorised by the Court of Protection to apply for a grant. Form of oath No. 161.

11.233   The original power of attorney, sealed by the Court of Protection, should be lodged with the application for the grant. The production of the original power of attorney sealed with the seal of the Court of Protection, coupled with a statement in the oath that the donor is mentally incapable of managing his affairs, is accepted as sufficient evidence of the incapacity. The power of attorney will be returned by the registry.

11.234   Unless there is a relevant restriction in the power of attorney, the grant will be limited for the use and benefit of the incapable person and until further representation be granted.

Passing over incapable person

11.235   An application to pass over an incapable person, as distinct from making a grant for his use and benefit, must be made under s. 116 of the Supreme Court Act 1981 (see p. 845, post).

Sole executor or residuary legatee or devisee in trust incapable. Grant to residuary legatee

11.236   Where the sole executor or residuary legatee or devisee in trust, as the case may be, is entitled to a grant but is incapable and if no person has been appointed by the Court of Protection and there is no lawful attorney acting under a registered enduring power of attorney (or any such attorney has renounced administration for the use and benefit of the incapable person) a grant will be made to the residuary legatee or devisee named in the will, for the use and benefit of the incapable person and limited until further representation be granted (or otherwise limited as the district judge or registrar may direct). If there be no residuary legatee or devisee, a similar grant will be made to the person entitled to the undisposed-of residuary estate of the deceased[1].

1 NCPR 35(2)(c).

11.237   If a life or minority interest arises and there is only one residuary legatee or devisee or person entitled to the undisposed-of residuary estate who is competent and willing to take a grant, he may nominate his co-administrator, unless the district judge or registrar otherwise directs, under r. 35(3).

11.238   As to the position where there are two or more executors, one of whom is incapable, see 'Other persons having equal right', paras. **11.211–11.214**, ante.

Residuary legatee incapable

11.239   If the sole residuary legatee and devisee is incapable (there being no executor or residuary legatee or devisee in trust), administration (with the will annexed) will be granted for his use and benefit during his incapacity (i) to the person authorised by the Court of Protection, or, if none, (ii) to the lawful attorney of the incapable person acting under a registered enduring power of attorney; or, if none, or if such renounces administration for the use and benefit of the incapable person (iii) to such two or more other persons as the district judge or registrar may by order direct[1] (see paras. **11.245** ff., post).

1 NCPR 35(4).

11.240   As to the position where the will appoints more than one residuary legatee and devisee, see 'Other persons having equal right', paras. **11.211–11.214**, ante.

Only person entitled on intestacy incapable

11.241   In the case of an intestacy, where the only person entitled to the grant is incapable, administration will be granted for his use and benefit and during his incapacity (i) to the person authorised by the Court of Protection or, if none, (ii) to his lawful attorney acting under a registered enduring power of attorney; or, if none, or if such renounces administration for the use and benefit of the incapable person (iii) to such two or more other persons as the district judge or registrar may by order direct (see paras. **11.245** ff., post). For forms of oath, see Nos. 125 to 127.

11.242   As to the position where there is more than one person entitled on an intestacy, see 'Other persons having equal right', paras. **11.211–11.214**, ante.

When spouse of intestate is entitled but incapable

11.243   Where a surviving spouse is incapable, and there is no person authorised by the Court of Protection and no attorney acting under a registered enduring power of attorney, a district judge's or registrar's order is required for a grant to issue to such two or more persons as the district judge or registrar may by order direct, for the use and benefit of the incapable spouse and usually limited until further representation be granted. In view of the spouse's prior right to a grant under NCPR 22(1), this applies whether or not the whole estate vests in the surviving spouse.

11.244   In such a case, notwithstanding that the grantees may themselves have a beneficial interest in the estate, the grant is limited 'for the use and benefit of . . . (*the spouse*) and until further representation be granted' (or in such other way as the district judge or registrar may direct), in order to preserve his or her prior right, under NCPR 22, to a grant in the event of recovery[1].

1 Registrar's Direction (1956) 16 July.

Grant to persons appointed by district judge or registrar

11.245   In cases of mental incapacity where no person has been authorised by the Court of Protection, there is no attorney acting under a registered enduring power of attorney and there is no person entitled to the residuary estate capable of taking a grant, the district judge or registrar may by order direct that a grant for the use and benefit of the incapable person be made to such two or more other persons as he thinks fit[1]. The district judge or registrar may also direct that a grant issue to two or more other persons where there is a person authorised by the Court of Protection, or an attorney acting under a registered enduring power of attorney, or a person entitled to the residuary estate, instead of to such of these persons who would otherwise be entitled to a grant, if he considers it appropriate[1]. Form of oath, No. 127.

1 NCPR 35(4).

11.246   Application for the order of the district judge or registrar is made by lodging an affidavit of the facts at the Probate Department of the Principal Registry, or if the application for the grant is to be made at a district probate registry, at that registry. The acknowledgment of the notice given to the Court of Protection (see para. **11.221**, ante) must also be lodged.

11.247   Instances of circumstances in which such an order is necessary are set out in the following paragraphs.

Only person entitled incapable

11.248   Where the sole person entitled to the estate of the intestate is incapable, a grant may be made, on a district judge's or registrar's order, to two of the next of kin of the incompetent person for his use and benefit limited until further representation be granted (or in such other way as the district judge or registrar may direct).

Surviving spouse incapable; his kin under age; guardian

11.249   Where an intestate's spouse is incapable, and his sole next of kin is a minor, application may be made for an order for a grant to the parents or guardians of the child, for the use and benefit of the spouse and limited until further representation be granted (or in such other way as the district judge or registrar may direct).

To a creditor for the use of person entitled

11.250   If no person has been appointed by the Court of Protection and there is no attorney acting under a registered enduring power of attorney, and all other persons interested in the estate renounce, the court may make a grant for the use and benefit of the incapable person to a creditor[1], or to a stranger[2] by a district judge's or registrar's order but note that now at least two persons are required as grantees under r. 35(4).

1 Cf. *Re Penny's Goods* (1846) 1 Rob Eccl 426.
2 *Re Hastings' Goods* (1877) 4 PD 73; *Re Burrell's Goods* (1858) 1 Sw & Tr 64; *Re Eccles' Goods* (1889) 15 PD 1.

To Scottish curator or foreign committee

11.251 Administration will be granted to a Scottish curator, or to a person appointed by a foreign court to administer the estate[1] but note at least two persons are required as grantees under r. 35(4).

1 *Re Cahill* (1946) 7 June (administration); *Re Towell* (1941).

Supervening incapacity after grant insued

11.252 For the procedure in cases where incapacity has supervened after probate or administration has been granted, see 'Grounds for revocation', and 'Impounding grants', paras. **17.07** ff. and **17.67** ff., post.

Recovery of incapable person

11.253 For practice in obtaining a cessate grant to a formerly incapable person on his recovering his capacity, see paras. **13.111** ff., post.

Physical incapacity

11.254 It should be noted that the NCPR 1987, unlike the previous rules, contain no specific provision for a grant to be issued for the use and benefit of a person physically incapable of managing his affairs. Where a person is suffering from some physical incapacity consideration should be given to him appointing an attorney or attorneys to take a grant for his use and benefit limited until further representation be granted. A person entitled to a grant may now appoint an attorney to take a grant in accordance with r. 31 without leave being required even when the donor is resident in England or Wales (see paras. **11.31** ff., ante).

Grant for use of person serving prison sentence

11.255 The fact that a person is a convicted prisoner does not of itself deprive him of his right to a grant of representation. He may take a grant himself or appoint an attorney to take a grant for his use and benefit (see paras. **11.31** ff., ante) or, if necessary, a grant may be made, under s. 116 of the Supreme Court Act 1981, for his use and benefit[1] — see paras. **25.91** ff., post.

1 Registrar's Direction (1953) 3 March.

11.256 Where the person in prison has appointed an attorney to manage his affairs, the latter would seem to be the most suitable grantee.

11.257   The court may, however, under its statutory powers (now s. 116 of the Supreme Court Act 1981), pass over an executor who is in prison, and make a grant to such person as it may think fit[1]. See para. **25.133**, post.

1 *Re Drawmer's Estate* (1913) 108 LT 732. See also *Re S's Estate* [1968] P 302, [1967] 2 All ER 150, referred to in para. **25.137**, post.

Grants limited as to property

Grant to part of estate only

Limited to part of estate under s. 113 of the Supreme Court Act 1981

11.258   Section 113 of the Supreme Court Act 1981 provides as follows:

'(1) Subject to subsection (2), the High Court may grant probate or administration in respect of any part of the estate of a deceased person, limited in any way the court thinks fit.

(2) Where the estate of a deceased person is known to be insolvent, the grant of representation to it shall not be severed under subsection (1) except as regards a trust estate in which he had no beneficial interest.'

11.259   By NCPR 51 it is ordered:

'An application for an order for a grant under section 113 of the Act to part of an estate may be made to a district judge or registrar, and shall be supported by an affidavit setting out the grounds of the application, and—

(a)   stating whether the estate of the deceased is known to be insolvent; and
(b)   showing how any person entitled to a grant in respect of the whole estate in priority to the applicant has been cleared off.'

11.260   Application for a grant to part of an estate under s. 113 should in all cases be made ex parte to the district judge or registrar of the registry at which the application for the grant is to be made[1]. The application is made by lodging in the Probate Department at the Principal Registry, or at the district probate registry, the affidavit referred to in the rule, together with any renunciations or other supporting documents.

1 See NCPR 2(1).

11.261   A district probate registrar may refer any matter of doubt or difficulty to the Principal Registry for directions[1], and under NCPR 61 a district judge or registrar has power, if he thinks fit, to require the application to be made by summons to a district judge or registrar in chambers or to a High Court judge in chambers or open court, the confirmation by a district judge of a registrar's referral to a High Court judge being necessary. As to applications on summons, see paras. **25.193** ff., post.

1 NCPR 7.

11.262   For examples of cases in which orders have been made, see para. **25.172**.

11.263   A grantee who is entitled to a general grant, but wishes to take one to a chosen part of the estate only, requires an order under r. 51; but a person entitled only to a grant in respect of part of the estate can take that grant as of right. If therefore a grant has been issued in respect of part of the estate by order under r. 51, a grant in respect of the remainder may issue without further order[1].

1 Registrar's Direction (1958) 24 March.

Severance of representation: action against estate of deceased

11.264   Particularly since the passing of the Law Reform (Husband and Wife) Act 1962 cases occur in which it is necessary for a surviving husband or wife to bring an action against the estate of the deceased spouse, and it is therefore inappropriate for the surviving spouse to become the personal representative under an unrestricted grant. The powers of severing the representation given by s. 113 of the Supreme Court Act 1981 do not enable a grant to be made to the spouse limited so as to exclude the defence of an action against the estate[1]. The court prefers the whole administration to be undertaken by the same person, but if in special circumstances it is necessary to apply for a grant limited to the defence of an action the application should be made under s. 116 of the Act of 1981[2]. See also paras. **25.154–25.164**, post.

1 *Re Newsham's Estate* [1967] P 230, [1966] 3 All ER 681.
2 Registrar's Circular, 2 February 1967.

Grant to part of the estate where order under s. 116 of the Supreme Court Act 1981 also required

11.265   The provisions of s. 113 of the Act of 1981 do not enable a grant to part of the estate to be made to a person who is not entitled to a grant under the normal rules of priority (i.e. NCPR 20 and 22). Such a grant may, however, be made by the additional exercise of the court's discretionary power under s. 116 of the Act.

11.266   For practice in applications for an order for a grant under s. 116, see paras. **25.91** ff., post.

Grant to deal with trust property where there is no other estate

11.267   Where a grant is required to deal with trust property vested in the deceased, and there is no other estate for which a grant is required, application may be made for a 'Nil' grant. This grant is made without limitation, and no order is needed unless there are persons with a prior entitlement who will not renounce. For practice, see paras. **4.209** and **4.210**, ante.

Grant to trust property only: principles applied as to choice of grantee

11.268   In making an order for a grant to trust property only, the usual practice has been as follows:

(a)   *Trust created by deed.*—Where the trust was not created by a will, the trustees (either original or substituted) are usually preferred. In the absence of any trustees, application may be made by the personal representative of the last surviving or continuing trustee, or failing such personal representative, by the person beneficially entitled to the property.

(b)   *Trust created by will.*—Where the trust was created by a will the practice has been for the limited grant to be made to the personal representative of the original testator[1]. See also the cases noted in para. **25.172**, post.

1 Application by the cestui que trust has been refused: see *Waterman*, February (1881): the deceased was the surviving executor and trustee of the will of the settlor. It was held that the grant of trust estate must be made to the personal representative of the original deceased, on the grounds that the property was in fact unappropriated residue of the latter's estate.

Fee for grant to trust property only

11.269   The fee for a grant to trust property is £2 (NC Probate Fees Order 1981, Fee 3(c)).

The will to be proved

11.270   In all cases of grants under s. 113, where the deceased has died testate, the will must be proved.

Grant limited in terms of will

General and limited probate

11.271   Where a testator has appointed an executor of his will generally, and another executor for particular purposes, and the general and limited executors apply for probate together, the grant is made in the same instrument, but the powers of each are distinguished; i.e. probate in respect of all the estate is granted to the general executor but the powers of the other executor are limited in the manner specified in the will. See also 'Limitation as to subject-matter', para. **4.09**, ante.

11.272   If the general executor applies for probate before the limited executor, a general grant is made to him, power being reserved of making a limited grant to the other executor[1].

1 But see *Re Wallich's Goods* (1864) 3 Sw & Tr 423, in which case power was not reserved.

Limited grant

11.273   Where, by reason of the existence of any limitation in a will, or of any circumstances limiting the operative effect of a will, the inclusion of the whole estate in one grant would be inappropriate, a grant limited so as to include or exclude any part of the estate will be made. See also 'Grants "save and except" ', paras. **11.279** ff., post.

Order for limited grant

11.274   A grantee who is entitled to a general grant, but wishes to obtain a grant only in respect of (or excluding) a particular part of the estate, must obtain an order for such a grant under s. 113 of the Supreme Court Act 1981 (see p. 844, ante).

11.275   But where a person is entitled only to a grant limited to part of the estate (e.g. a grant limited to personalty), because of the nature of the will, both that grant and any grant in respect of the remainder of the estate may issue without an order under s. 113.

11.276 Similarly, where a grant has been made in respect of part of the estate by order under s. 113, a grant in respect of the remainder of the estate may issue without a further order[1].

1 Registrar's Direction (1958) 24 March.

Oath

11.277 Where an order has been made for a grant to issue for part of the estate only, details of the order must be recited in the oath, and the order and supporting documents must be lodged with the papers to lead the grant[1].

1 Registrar's Circular, 15 December 1930.

11.278 If a limitation is necessary because of the terms of the will, the oath should recite the appointment of executors as given in the will, and the executors should swear to administer the estate to the extent of the powers respectively granted to them.

Grants 'save and except'

Probate or administration (with will) 'save and except'

11.279 If a testator has appointed one executor for a special purpose, or in respect of a specific fund or asset only, and another executor for all other purposes, the latter may take probate save and except the specific purpose or fund. See also para. **4.09**, ante.

11.280 In such circumstances no order is required for severance of the representation. Form of oath, No. 76.

11.281 On the renunciation or failure of the executor appointed for all other purposes, or if there is no such executor, the residuary legatee or devisee may take administration (with will) of the estate of the deceased, save and except as to the special fund or purpose.

Administration save and except

11.282 Similarly, where necessary, a grant of administration may be made by order of the court save and except a particular purpose.

11.283 For practice in relation to obtaining such an order, see 'Grant to part of estate only', paras. **11.258** ff., ante.

Will limited to part of estate: grant to persons entitled on intestacy

11.284 When a testator has made his will limited to particular purposes only, e.g. the administration of a fund or estate vested in himself as trustee, or executor, or limited to his property in a particular country, and has died intestate as to all other property, the persons entitled to his undisposed-of estate may take administration save and except the property disposed of by the will, without waiting for the executor to take a limited grant of probate. It must, however, be clear that the executorship is limited to the property disposed of by the will.

'Caeterorum' grant

11.285   Probate or administration following a grant limited to part of the estate or to a particular purpose is a grant caeterorum, i.e. of all the rest of the estate: it is complementary to the limited grant.

11.286   Where the first grant extracted was a grant 'save and except' a particular part of the estate or purpose, the succeeding grant is a grant limited to the estate or purpose excepted.

Probate 'caeterorum'

11.287   If a testator has appointed one executor for a special purpose or in respect of a specific fund and another executor for all other purposes and effects, and the first-mentioned executor has taken limited probate, the other may take probate of the rest of the testator's estate[1]. Form of oath, No. 77.

---

1   *Re Lord Stanley* (1939) March.

Administration (with will) caeterorum

11.288   If such a limited probate has been granted, and the executor in respect of the rest of the estate is cleared off by renunciation or death, the residuary legatee and devisee, or other person entitled under the normal rules, may obtain administration (with will) of the rest of the estate.

Administration 'caeterorum'

11.289   If a limited grant of probate has been made to an executor in a case where the will was limited to a special purpose, or to estate in a certain country, and the testator died intestate in all other respects, the person entitled to the estate not disposed of may take administration of the rest of the estate.

11.290   Similarly, if administration of only a particular part of the estate has been granted by order under s. 113 of the Supreme Court Act 1981, the person entitled to a general grant may, without further order, take administration of the rest of the estate. Form of oath, No. 177.

Practice

11.291   A grant caeterorum may be applied for at the registry from which the previous limited grant issued, or at any other probate registry.

11.292   The oath must include details of the previous grant, and, in applications proceeding at the Principal Registry or at a district probate registry other than that from which the previous grant issued, the former grant or an office copy of this must be lodged with the papers. The practice as to marking the will is the same as in other cases of second grants where the will has already been proved (see paras. **13.67–13.70**, post).

Married woman's estate after separation

Protection of estate of separated wife

11.293   On the death intestate of a married woman *prior to 1 August 1970*, where the spouses have been separated by a decree of judicial separation or a separation order under the Matrimonial Proceedings (Magistrates' Courts) Act 1960, or the Summary Jurisdiction (Separation and Maintenance) Acts 1895 to 1949, any property which was acquired by, or devolved upon, the wife on or after the date of the decree or order while the separation continued devolved as if her husband had predeceased her[1]. The estate of a married man, however, was not similarly protected.

---

1   Matrimonial Causes Act 1965, s. 20(3) (repealed in relation to deaths on or after 1 August 1970: see Matrimonial Proceedings and Property Act 1970, s. 40(3), since repealed, but its effect is preserved by Schedule I, Part II, para. 13, of the Matrimonial Causes Act 1973, p. 807, post). A *separation* order under the Summary Jurisdiction (Separation and Maintenance) Acts, or under the Matrimonial Proceedings (Magistrates' Courts) Act 1960 while in force, has the effect of a decree of judicial separation, but in relation to deaths on or after 1 August 1970, such an order does not debar one spouse from an interest in the estate of the other on an intestacy (Matrimonial Causes Act 1973, s. 18(3), replacing Matrimonial Proceedings and Property Act 1970, s. 40(2)).

11.294   The provision applied whether the decree or order was obtained at the instance of the wife or of the husband. Where it was obtained by the wife, it applied also to property to which she was entitled in remainder or reversion at the date of the decree or order[1].

---

1   Matrimonial Causes Act 1965, s. 20(3)(b) (repealed: see previous note).

11.295   In the case of death *on or after 1 August 1970* these provisions do not apply. In place thereof, s. 18(2) of the Matrimonial Causes Act 1973[1], replacing s. 40(1) of the Matrimonial Proceedings and Property Act 1970, provides that if, while a decree of judicial separation is in force and the separation is continuing, either of the spouses dies intestate as respects all or part of his estate, the estate, or the property as respects which he or she died intestate, as the case may be, devolves as if the other spouse were then dead. On the other hand, a separation order made in a magistrates' court no longer deprives a husband of his interest in the estate acquired by his wife after the date of the separation order[2].

---

1   See p. 806, post.
2   Matrimonial Causes Act 1973, s. 18(3): p. 806, post.

Practice in granting administration: death prior to 1 August 1970

11.296   Administration, limited to the property acquired by, or devolving on, the wife since the date of the decree or order, may, in such a case, be granted, without any order for a limited grant, to the person or persons who would have been entitled to administration if she had died a widow. Form of oath, No. 141.

11.297   Where administration, limited in this way, has been granted, a caeterorum grant may be taken by her husband, if it is necessary in order to deal with property acquired by the wife before the date of the separation order or decree.

Will in exercise of power of appointment

Power of appointment

11.298   Section 10 of the Wills Act 1837 is as follows:

> 'No appointment made by will, in exercise of any power, shall be valid, unless the same be executed in manner hereinbefore required; and every will executed in manner hereinbefore required shall, so far as respects the execution and attestation thereof, be a valid execution of a power of appointment by will, notwithstanding it shall have been expressly required that a will made in exercise of such power should be executed with some additional or other form of execution or solemnity.'

11.299   There have been numerous legal decisions as to the formal validity of a testamentary exercise of a power of appointment. In relation to a person who dies domiciled out of England and Wales, a will which is formally valid by the law of his domicile is valid to exercise a power of appointment under an English settlement. The latter part of s. 10 of the Wills Act 1837, however, does not in such a case operate to render compliance with any additional formalities required by the provisions of the settlement unnecessary. A will of such a person which is invalid by the law of the domicile and cannot be set up under the Wills Act 1861 (Lord Kingsdown's Act) is admissible to proof, so far only as regards the portion thereof which exercises a power of appointment, if the will is executed in proper English form, i.e. in accordance with s. 9 of the Wills Act 1837[1].

1 See p. 720, post.

Death on or after 1 January 1964: Wills Act 1963

11.300   In the case of persons dying on or after 1 January 1964, s. 1 of the Wills Act 1963[1] provides a number of possible alternative systems of law which can be invoked, in specified circumstances, to establish the formal validity of wills and other testamentary dispositions. Section 1 of this Act is as follows:

> 'A will shall be treated as properly executed if its execution conformed to the internal law in force in the territory where it was executed, or in the territory where, at the time of its execution or of the testator's death, he was domiciled or had his habitual residence, or in a state of which, at either of those times, he was a national,'

and it seems clear that the exercise of a power of appointment in any will or codicil which is admissible by virtue of this section will be accepted as well executed.

1 See p. 777, post. As to the Wills Act 1963, generally, see paras. **3.392** ff., ante.

11.301   Furthermore, under s. 2(1)(d) of the same Act, without prejudice to s. 1, a will, so far as it exercises a power of appointment, is to be treated as properly executed if its execution conformed to the law governing the essential validity of the power.

11.302   There may still be exceptional cases in which only so much of a will as exercises a power of appointment is admissible to proof in this country. If the execution of the will does not comply with any of the alternatives available, in the circumstances of the case, under s. 1 of the Wills Act 1963, s. 2(1)(d) enables only that part of the will which exercises the power to be accepted, if its execution is in accordance with the law governing the essential validity of the power. In such cases the practice set out in paras. **11.315–11.317**, post, should be followed.

Additional formalities required by settlement

11.303 Under s. 2(2) of the Wills Act 1963, a will so far as it exercises a power of appointment is not to be treated as improperly executed by reason only that its execution was not in accordance with any formal requirements contained in the instrument creating the power.

11.304 In relation to persons dying on or after 1 January 1964, this subsection extends the provisions of the latter part of s. 10 of the Wills Act 1837 (quoted in para. **11.298**, ante) so as to apply to all wills which are formally valid: the exercise of a power of appointment in such a will is also formally valid notwithstanding that the settlement creating the power requires compliance with some further formality.

General and special power of appointment

11.305 Under a general power of appointment a person has the right to appoint to whomsoever he pleases, whereas under a special power he is restricted in his choice by the terms of the instrument creating the power (e.g. where he has power to appoint amongst his children).

Exercise of power of appointment

11.306 By s. 27 of the Wills Act 1837, a general bequest or devise of personal or real estate, or a bequest or devise of personal or real property described in a general manner, is to be construed as including any personal or real estate, or any such estate to which the description extends, which the testator may have power to appoint in any manner he may think proper, and operates as an execution of the power of appointment unless a contrary intention appears by the will.

11.307 Section 27 does not apply to special powers. For the exercise by will of a special power of appointment there must be either: (i) a reference to the power; (ii) a reference to the property subject to the power; or (iii) an intention otherwise expressed in the will to exercise the power[1].

1 *Re Weston's Settlement, Neeves v Weston* [1906] 2 Ch 620; *Wrigley v Lowndes* [1908] P 348; *Re Holford's Settlement, Lloyds Bank Ltd v Holford* [1945] Ch 21, [1944] 2 All ER 462; *Re Knight, Re Wynn, Midland Bank Executor and Trustee Co Ltd v Parker* [1957] Ch 441, [1957] 2 All ER 252; *Re Lawrence's Will Trusts, Public Trustee v Lawrence* [1972] Ch 418, [1971] 3 All ER 433.

11.308 A general power of appointment directed to be exercised 'expressly referring to this power as though it were a special power' can be exercised only by a specific reference to the power, and is not exercised merely by a residuary bequest expressed to include 'any property over which I may have any general power of appointment exercisable by will'[1].

1 *Re Priestley's Will Trusts, Hambros Bank Executor and Trustee Co Ltd v Rabagliati* [1971] Ch 858, [1971] 2 All ER 817.

Disposition in will not revoked by subsequent marriage

11.309 Section 18(2) of the Wills Act 1837[1] (as substituted by the Administration of Justice Act 1982) provides that a disposition in a will in exercise of a power of appointment shall take effect notwithstanding the testator's subsequent marriage unless the property so appointed would in default of appointment pass to his personal representatives.

1 See p. 722, post. Section 18(2) is a new provision, introduced by the Administration of Justice Act 1982, and it only applies to *wills made on or after 1 January 1983*, although its effect is similar to the exception formerly contained in s. 18 of the Wills Act 1837, which exception continues to apply to *wills made before 1 January 1983*; see *Re Paul, Public Trustee v Pearce* [1921] 2 Ch 1; *Re Fenwick's Goods* (1867) LR 1 P & D 319.

11.310   The question whether the testamentary exercise of a power of appointment is revoked by the testator's subsequent marriage thus depends upon the destination of the property in default of any appointment. Where, *in respect of a will made on or after 1 January 1983*, a disposition is made in the exercise of a power of appointment and the testator subsequently marries, the exercise of the power is revoked only where the property which is the subject of the power would, in default of appointment, pass to the testator's personal representatives as part of his estate. In respect of *wills made before 1 January 1983*, s. 18 of the Wills Act 1837, as originally enacted, continues to apply: that section contained a similar provision, save that it also made reference to heirship and the since-repealed Statute of Distributions. The following principles have emerged from the earlier legislative provision. If the trust instrument provides that the property vests in the persons entitled on an intestacy—and this includes the widow[1]—or in the executor (of a post-nuptial will) or the administrator of the deceased, then the will is revoked by the marriage; but if, by the terms of the deed, it vests in persons in other categories, or in some (but not all) of the persons entitled on an intestacy, the appointment by the will remains valid, though this may be the only valid portion of the will. In such a case[2], administration (with the unrevoked part of the will) has been granted to the appointee[3].

1 *Re Gilligan* [1950] P 32, [1949] 2 All ER 401.
2 *Re Russell's Goods* (1890) 15 PD 111; *Re Gilligan*, above.
3 But see *Re Poole's Estate, Poole v Poole* [1919] P 10: a general grant was ordered to be made to the widow, and not to the appointee, with so much only of the will annexed as related to the appointed fund.

11.311   For form of oath in such case, see No. 167.

11.312   As to revocation of wills by subsequent marriage see also paras. **3.36** ff., ante and **33.59**, post.

Will must be proved

11.313   The exercise by will of a power of appointment cannot be legally recognised unless the will is proved in England and Wales[1].

1 *Ross v Ewer* (1744) 3 Atk 156.

Will revoked except as to power: practice

11.314   Where a will has been revoked save insofar as it exercises a power (e.g. by subsequent marriage (see above) or by a revocation clause where cogent evidence exists to rebut the presumption that the revocation extends to the exercise of the power[1]), the practice is as follows:

(a)   If there is no valid will, a general grant of administration, with so much only of the revoked will annexed as relates to the appointed fund[2], is usually made to the person entitled on an intestacy.

(b) If there is another (valid) will, which will be proved by the persons entitled to administer the estate of the deceased, the relevant part of the revoked will may be proved by the appointees, or one of them with the consent of the others, but the grant is limited to the property over which the power extends.

1 A later will containing a general revocatory clause will revoke an earlier testamentary exercise of a power of appointment unless there is cogent evidence to rebut the presumption that the revocation extends to the exercise of the power (*Lowthorpe-Lutwidge v Lowthorpe-Lutwidge* [1935] P 151, distinguishing *Smith v Thompson* (1931) 146 LT 14).
2 *Re Poole's Estate*, fn. 3, para. **11.310**, ante; *Re Gibbes' Settlement, White v Randolf* (1887) 37 Ch D 143.

Will invalid save as to exercise of power of appointment

11.315 Although a general grant is usually made to the executor of a valid will which merely exercises a power of appointment and does not dispose of the rest of the testator's estate, it is otherwise in the case of wills which are invalid save as to the exercise of the power. In the rare case where, under the law and practice appropriate to the date of death of the testator (see paras. **11.298** ff., ante) a will is validly executed only as to the exercise of the power, any appointment of executor fails, and administration (with will) will be granted[1]. The normal rules and principles as to the choice of the grantee are applicable.

1 *Murphy v Deichler* [1909] AC 446: the grant in this case, although of administration (with will) and not probate, was ordered to be made to the 'executors and trustees': *Re Vannini's Goods* [1901] P 330: *general* grant of administration (with will) made to the appointees in trust: *Re Roester* (1938) unreported; limited grant made to the appointees in trust.

11.316 If the applicant is the person entitled in priority under the rules to a grant in the estate of the deceased (i.e., under NCPR 22, if the deceased was domiciled in England and Wales, or r. 30 if he was domiciled elsewhere), a general grant may be made to him. If the applicant is not the person entitled to a general grant, it would appear necessary to apply for an order for a grant (whether general or limited to the property appointed) under the court's discretionary powers under s. 116 of the Supreme Court Act 1981: for practice, see paras. **25.91** ff., post[1].

1 The reported cases are all under the pre-1926 practice, and were dealt with by the court on motion, or in an action.

Proof of will

11.317 It should be established by affidavits as to the law and, where necessary, the facts, that the will is invalid under the law of the domicile and, in the case of death on or after 1 January 1964, under any other law which is available by virtue of the Wills Act 1963. The oath must refer to the settlement, and any order of the court. Form of oath, No. 86.

Administration pending suit

Grants 'pending suit'

11.318 The court has power under s. 117 of the Supreme Court Act 1981[1] to grant administration limited during the continuance of a probate action which is pending in the Chancery Division.

1 See p. 845, post.

Order required

11.319   Application for the appointment of an administrator pending suit is made by summons in the Chancery Division (RSC Order 76, r. 14(1)). For practice, see para. **37.01**, post.

11.320   The court has power to appoint a sole administrator pending suit notwithstanding the existence, or possibility, of a life or minority interest[1]. The oath to lead the grant must nevertheless contain the usual clause as to life and minority interests (NCPR 8(4)).

1 *Re Haslip* [1958] 2 All ER 275n, [1958] 1 WLR 583.

Issue of grant

11.321   If an order is made appointing an administrator pending suit, the solicitor should prepare and lodge at the Principal Registry of the Family Division[1] the papers to lead the grant, i.e. the administrator's oath (Form No. 128), an Inland Revenue account (if required, see Chap. 8), and an office copy of the order of the Chancery Division appointing the administrator.

1 The grant cannot be made by a district probate registrar because of the unresolved contention arising from the probate action—NCPR 7(1)(a).

Fees and tax

11.322   The fee for the grant is payable in full, as is also inheritance or capital transfer tax (if any), in respect of all the property of which the deceased was competent to dispose[1].

1 *Re Grimthorpe's Goods, Beal v Grimthorpe* (1905) Times, 8 August (referred to in para. **8.17**, ante) where the pending suit grant was limited as to the property to be dealt with.

Subsequent application for full grant

11.323   As the grant of administration pending suit ceases on the determination of the suit, and not upon the extraction of a grant in substitution, the full grant of probate of the will, or letters of administration, as the case may be, following the limited grant, is not regarded as a cessate grant.

11.324   The value of the whole estate is sworn to in the oath, and all the estate is again disclosed in the Inland Revenue account, if required: see Chap. 8.

Practice

11.325   An office copy of the judgment or order in the probate action must be obtained and lodged with the papers, and the oath must include particulars of the judgment (see also paras. **4.176** and **4.177**, ante), and of the previous grant pending suit.

11.326   The Inland Revenue account for the full grant should be submitted to the Capital Taxes Office before lodgment at the registry, with a request for the transfer of the receipt for the tax (if any) paid on the application for the limited grant. A fee of £2 is payable for the grant[1].

1 Non-Contentious Probate Fees Order 1981, Fee 3(e).

11.327 Application for the full grant may be made at the Principal Registry or at any district probate registry.

Miscellaneous

Grant limited to an action

11.328 Where it is necessary for the personal representative of a deceased person to be made a party to legal proceedings (e.g. an action by or against the estate of the deceased), but the executors or other persons entitled to obtain a grant will not constitute themselves as personal representatives, application may be made for a grant of administration to a nominee, limited to bringing, defending or being a party to the action or proceedings in question. The grant will in no case be a general grant[1]. The action or proceedings must be identified in the oath so far as possible[2] and will be specified in the grant.

1 *Re Chanter's Goods* (1844) 1 Rob Eccl 273; *Davis v Chanter* (1848) 2 Ph 545; *Re Dawson's Goods, Maclean and Maclean v Dawson* (1859) 1 Sw & Tr 425.
2 Circular, 14 March 1956; Registrar's Direction (1964) 23 March.

11.329 For example, where a deceased person against whom a cause of action survives under the Law Reform (Miscellaneous Provisions) Act 1934, s. 1[1], dies insolvent and no grant has been taken in his estate, application may be made for a grant to be made to a nominee of the plaintiff, or such other person as may be considered expedient, limited to defending the specified action[2].

1 See p. 765, post.
2 *Re Simpson's Estate* [1936] P 40; *Re Gunning's Estate* [1936] P 40, *Re Knight's Goods* [1939] 3 All ER 928 (motion), appointment of an administrator ad litem, on the application by the plaintiff to appoint a defendant.

11.330 Difficulties can also arise in those cases where a dependant of a deceased person wishes to bring a claim under the Inheritance (Provision for Family and Dependants) Act 1975 for financial provision from the deceased's estate, but is prevented from bringing proceedings until a grant has issued and a personal representative has been constituted, and there is no person either entitled or (if entitled) willing to apply for a grant. In any such case, the Official Solicitor has intimated that he would be prepared to consider making application for a grant to himself for the purpose of being a party to the proceedings proposed to be brought against the deceased's estate[1]. As to claims under the Inheritance (Provision for Family and Dependants) Act 1975, and the position where the claimant is also the constituted personal representative, see Chap. 41.

1 Secretary's Circular, 11 November 1976.

11.331 Application for a grant limited to an action should be made ex parte to the district judge or registrar under the provisions of s. 116 of the Supreme Court Act

1981: see paras. **25.91** ff., post. The grant should be for a 'nil' estate (see paras. **4.209** and **4.210**, ante).

11.332   Any order for a grant to the Official Solicitor or any other person limited for the purpose of being a party to an action contemplated against the estate of the deceased must specify the action in the limitation. In cases where it is desired to appoint the Official Solicitor his consent will contain the appropriate wording, which should be followed in the oath[1].

1 Registrar's Direction (1964) 23 March.

Proceedings against a deceased's estate

11.333   An alternative method of bringing proceedings against the estate of a deceased person where a cause of action has survived but no personal representative has been constituted is provided by rules of court made under s. 87(2) of the Supreme Court Act 1981: see RSC, Ord. 15, r. 6A.

Court's power to dispense with grant

11.334   RSC Order 15, rule 15 gives power to the court in any proceedings, if it shall appear that any deceased person who was interested in the matter in question has no personal representative, to proceed in the absence of a representative, or to appoint some person to represent his estate for the purposes of the proceedings. The estate of the deceased person is then bound by the proceedings in the same way as if a duly constituted personal representative had been a party. The court may require notice of an application for an order under this rule to be given to such (if any) of the persons having an interest in the estate as it thinks fit. This practice is not appropriate where the estate to which it is desired to appoint a representative is the estate which is the subject of the dispute[1]. The rule is not confined to representation of the estate of a deceased party to the litigation[2].

1 *Silver v Stein* (1852) 1 Drew 295, decided under s. 44 of the repealed Court of Chancery Procedure Act 1852, which RSC Ord. 15, r. 15 replaces.
2 *Lean v Alston* [1947] KB 467, [1947] 1 All ER 261, CA; and see *Wingrove v Thompson* (1879) 11 Ch D 419.

Administration 'ad colligenda bona'

Administration 'ad colligenda bona'

11.335   When the estate of a deceased person may be endangered by delay in administering it, the court is not bound to wait for an application by the person entitled to a grant under the rules, but may grant letters of administration ad colligenda bona for the purpose of preserving the property[1].

1 *Re Clore* [1982] Ch 456, [1982] 3 All ER 419, CA (limited grant made to Official Solicitor following delay of over two years by executors in applying for probate).

11.336   Such grants are always of administration only: where the deceased died testate, the will is not proved or annexed to the grant ad colligenda bona.

11.337 Application for an order for a grant ad colligenda bona should be made ex parte to the district judge or registrar supported by an affidavit[1]. See also paras. **25.173–25.181**, post.

1 NCPR 52(b).

Practice in obtaining grant

11.338 When the order has been made, the papers to lead the grant should be prepared and lodged at the Principal Registry or a district probate registry. The following documents are necessary: administrator's oath (Form No. 139); Inland Revenue account (if required, see Chap. 8); the order appointing the administrator and the supporting affidavits etc.

11.339 In all cases the oath in support of the grant application need not include any statement whether a will exists or whether the deceased died intestate, nor contain any of the usual clearings. It will, however, always be necessary to consider the existence of life or minority interests. It is suggested that the question as to whether any life or minority interest arises in the estate of the deceased be dealt with in the affidavit in support of the application for the order. Every grant ad colligenda bona shall be silent as to the will or the intestacy and the grant is limited 'until further representation be granted'[1].

1 Registrar's Direction (1979) 12 October.

Subsequent application for full grant

11.340 When the object for which the grant was made is completed, application may be made for a general grant by the person entitled to it, no further order of the court being necessary. On the issue of a general grant, the limited grant ceases.

11.341 Details of the former grant must be included in the oath, and, where application for the general grant is made at the Principal Registry, or at a district probate registry other than that from which the limited grant issued, a copy of that grant must be lodged with the papers.

11.342 For form of Inland Revenue account (if required), see paras. **8.36–8.40**, ante.

CHAPTER 12

Grant where deceased died domiciled out of England and Wales

Summary

Domicile

12.01   The determination of the domicile of a deceased person is most important before the application for a grant of representation, not only to ascertain what part of the estate is liable to inheritance tax or capital transfer tax[1], but also for the purpose of determining the validity of the will (if any) and the right to the grant.

1 As to the notional domicile in the United Kingdom which applies under s. 267 of the Inheritance Tax Act 1984 (replacing s. 45 of the Finance Act 1975) (p. 909, post) in certain circumstances in relation to inheritance tax or capital transfer tax, see Chap. 8. This notional domicile has no application to questions of the validity of a will or entitlement to a grant of representation: for these purposes, it is the actual domicile of the deceased that is relevant.

Domicile of origin

12.02   The general rule is that the domicile of origin of a legitimate child is the domicile of its father; of an illegitimate child, that of its mother. It is involuntary, and cannot be changed, being the creation of law. If the father's domicile changes during the child's minority, its domicile of origin remains the father's domicile at the time of its birth[1].

1 *Henderson v Henderson* [1967] P 77, [1965] 1 All ER 179.

12.03   However, s. 4 of the Domicile and Matrimonial Proceedings Act 1973[1] provides an exception to this rule. If the parents of a minor are living apart and the minor has his home with his mother his domicile is that of the mother. Such domicile, once acquired, is retained even though his home is no longer with his mother, or if she dies, so long as he has not since had his home with his father. Section 3 of this Act[2] provides (subject to a transitional modification) that a minor may have an independent domicile from the age of 16 or from the date of marriage if he marries while under age. This Act came into force on 1 January 1974.

1 See p. 807, post.
2 See p. 807, post.

12.04 A person can acquire a domicile of choice, and while this is retained the domicile of origin is in abeyance, but not extinguished. When the domicile of choice is abandoned the domicile of origin revives[1].

1 *Udny v Udny* (1869) LR 1 Sc & Div 441. See also *Re Flynn, Flynn v Flynn* [1968] 1 All ER 49, [1968] 1 WLR 103 (given a physical departure from the country of one's domicile of choice, the ending of the intention to return there, as distinct from the forming of a positive intention not to return, is sufficient to bring that domicile to an end: accordingly the domicile of origin revives until ousted by the acquisition of another domicile of choice).

12.05 The domicile of a fatherless minor does not necessarily change with a change of the domicile of its mother; but only where she exercises the power vested in her of changing the child's domicile for the latter's benefit[1].

1 *Re Beaumont* [1893] 3 Ch 490.

Domicile of choice

12.06 By Rule 10 of Dicey and Morris on the Conflict of Laws 'every independent person can acquire a domicile of choice by the combination of residence and intention of permanent or indefinite residence, but not otherwise'.

12.07 Residence in a country is not, of itself alone, sufficient to create a domicile of choice without evidence of volition to change domicile[1]. A domicile of choice is not acquired merely by accepting and holding a post in a country[2].

1 *IRC v Bullock* [1976] 3 All ER 353, [1976] 1 WLR 1178, CA.
2 *Bowie (or Ramsay) v Liverpool Royal Infirmary* [1930] AC 588; *Cooney v Cooney* (1950) 100 L Jo 705.

12.08 A declaration by a testator in a will that he did not intend to relinquish his English domicile does not operate to prevent a finding that there has been a change of domicile where the physical fact of residence in another country and the intention to reside there permanently are proved[1].

1 *Re Liddell-Grainger's Will Trusts, Dormer v Liddell-Grainger* [1936] 3 All ER 173.

12.09 A domicile of choice, having been abandoned, can be reacquired only by the fulfilment of the same conditions of intention and residence as those by which the domicile of choice was previously acquired[1].

1 *A-G v Yule and Mercantile Bank of India* (1931) 145 LT 9, CA.

Domicile generally

12.10 Under s. 1 of the Domicile and Matrimonial Proceedings Act 1973, the domicile of a married woman as at any time after the coming into force of that section (i.e. 1 January 1974) is, instead of being the same as that of her husband by virtue only of her marriage, to be ascertained by reference to the same factors as in the case of any other individual capable of having an independent domicile.

12.11　But where, immediately before this section came into force, a married woman has her husband's domicile by dependence she is treated as retaining that domicile (as a domicile of choice if it is not also her domicile of origin) unless and until she changes it by the acquisition or revival of some other domicile on or after 1 January 1974[1].

1 Domicile and Matrimonial Proceedings Act 1973, s. 1(2): p. 807, post; and *IRC v Duchess of Portland* [1982] Ch 314, [1982] 1 All ER 784.

12.12　The law of the testator's domicile governs the foreign movable assets of his estate for the purpose of succession and enjoyment. For the purpose of legal representation, though the person entrusted with administration by the court of the domicile is generally recognised by the foreign court as entitled to be appointed, this is not always and necessarily the case; and in administering the estate it is necessary to give foreign creditors priority as regards foreign assets. To this extent, at any rate, foreign movable assets may be governed by the lex loci as regards legal representation and collection, as well as distribution, and not by that of the testator's domicile[1].

1 *Blackwood v R* (1882) 8 App Cas 82, PC.

Domicile to be sworn to

12.13　Unless otherwise directed by a district judge or registrar, every oath to lead a grant of representation must state where the deceased died domiciled[1]. A statement of the domicile sworn to appears in the grant. Where a country has no uniform system of law (e.g. in the case of Australia, Canada, or the United States of America) the particular Province, State or other judicial division must be specified[2].

1 NCPR 8(2).
2 Registrar's Direction (1961) 24 January.

Validity of will: domicile

12.14　The material validity of a will, and its whole operative effect, as regards movable estate, depend on the testator's last domicile[1].

1 *Re Ross, Ross v Waterfield* [1930] 1 Ch 377; *Re Annesley, Davidson v Annesley* [1926] Ch 692.

12.15　As to wills of immovables, see paras. **12.36** ff., post.

12.16　The validity and construction of a will, and the capacity of the testator, as pronounced for by the court of domicile, are followed by the English courts[1]. This rule does not appear to be affected by the Wills Act 1963.

1 *Re Trufort, Trafford v Blanc* (1887) 36 Ch D 600; *Doglioni v Crispin* (1866) LR 1 HL 301; *Re Yahuda's Estate* [1956] P 388, [1956] 2 All ER 262.

Grants where deceased died domiciled out of England and Wales

Normal order of priority usually inapplicable

12.17　In the case of a person who at the time of his death was domiciled out of England and Wales, the normal rules as to priority of right to a grant do not apply[1], except in certain specific cases as provided for by NCPR 30(3)(a) or (b) dealt with later in this chapter—see paras. **12.80–12.87** and **12.118–12.122**. *Where application can be made under these exceptions serious consideration should be given to so doing. It may often be simpler and quicker as it allows practitioners to use law with which they are familiar and often avoids the need to obtain evidence of foreign law.*

1 NCPR 28(2).

12.18 The practice in making grants where the deceased died domiciled out of England and Wales is governed by NCPR 30, and the Registrar's Direction of 20 November 1972 (as modified by the provisions of the NCPR 1987), extracts from which are quoted in the appropriate places on the following pages.

12.19 The former practice, whereby a person who would have been entitled to a grant had the deceased been domiciled in England and Wales was allowed to take a grant in an English title, is no longer applicable, except where the date of death was before 1 January 1926.

Resealing as an alternative

12.20 When deciding whether an English grant of representation is necessary to enable the estate of a deceased person to be administered, if the deceased was domiciled in one of the countries to which the Colonial Probates Acts 1892 and 1927 have been applied (see para. **18.39**, post), and a grant has already been extracted, or will be necessary, in that country, consideration should be given to the alternative of obtaining the resealing of that grant. If this course is possible it is often simpler and less costly than applying for an ancillary English grant. The subject of resealing is dealt with in Chap. 18.

Domicile in Scotland or Northern Ireland

12.21 Where the deceased died domiciled in England and Wales, a grant made by the High Court in England and Wales, which includes a notation of such domicile is, without being resealed, recognised in Northern Ireland and Scotland as if the grant had been made in Northern Ireland or as if confirmation had issued in Scotland to the grantee, as the case may be (Administration of Estates Act 1971, ss. 2 and 3 (see pp. 800–801, post)).

12.22 Similarly a Northern Irish grant stating that the deceased died domiciled in Northern Ireland is recognised in England and Wales and Scotland, and a Scottish confirmation stating that the deceased died domiciled in Scotland is recognised in England and Wales and Northern Ireland, without resealing (ibid., s. 3(1)).

12.23 Where the deceased died domiciled in Scotland or Northern Ireland but representation has not been granted in the country of domicile, application may be made for an English grant if the circumstances make this necessary. Such a grant will be specifically limited to the estate in England and Wales and, to avoid the possibility of dual representation, will also be limited until representation be granted in the country of domicile. Except where the application is for probate of a will in the English or Welsh language containing an effective appointment of an executor, or by the attorney of an executor named in such a will, the application for the grant should be framed in accordance with NCPR 30(1)(b) or 30(1)(c) or

30(3)(b): see paras. **12.105–12.122,** post. It is essential that the oath should show that no grant of representation has been obtained in the country of domicile. The principles normally applicable in cases of domicile out of England and Wales apply in relation to the admissibility of any will left by the deceased: as to this, reference should be made to paras. **12.34** ff., post.

Matters for consideration

12.24   The two principal matters to be considered in cases of foreign domicile are: (i) the admissibility to proof in England and Wales of any will left by the deceased, and (ii) entitlement to an English grant. These subjects are dealt with in detail in the present chapter.

Evidence of the law of the domicile

12.25   Evidence as to the law of the place of domicile may be necessary in respect of one or both of these matters. In non-contentious probate matters, such evidence is given by affidavit, or notarial certificate or act, as appropriate and available. NCPR 19 provides as follows:

> 'Where evidence as to the law of any country or territory outside England and Wales is required on any application for a grant, the district judge or registrar may accept—
>
> (a)   an affidavit from any person whom, having regard to the particulars of his knowledge or experience given in the affidavit, he regards as suitably qualified to give expert evidence of the law in question; or
>
> (b)   a certificate by, or an act before, a notary practising in the country or territory concerned.'

12.26   It should be noted that s. 4(1) of the Civil Evidence Act 1972[1] declares that in civil proceedings a person who is suitably qualified to do so on account of his knowledge or experience is competent to give expert evidence as to the law of any country or territory outside the United Kingdom, or any part of the United Kingdom other than England and Wales, irrespective of whether he has acted or is entitled to act as a legal practitioner there. Accordingly there is no longer an automatic bar on the acceptance of an affidavit of law made by the person claiming to be entitled to the grant or his attorney, or the spouse of either. The acceptability of an affidavit of law made by any such person is a matter for the decision of the district judge or registrar in the light of the circumstances of each particular case. However, an affidavit by an independent expert is obviously to be preferred to one by an interested party.

1   42 Halsbury's Statutes (3rd edn) 351.

12.27   The office of Consul is not of itself regarded as a qualification enabling the holder to speak to the law of his country[1].

1   Registrar's Direction (1972) 20 November.

12.28   Where, as in the Provinces of Canada or the United States of America, there are separate jurisdictions, the law of the particular Province or State must be referred to.

12.29   An affidavit of law made by a person qualified in accordance with r. 19 must set out particulars of the knowledge and experience claimed by the deponent to make him competent to give expert evidence of the law of the country in question.

12.30 Where a certificate by, or an act before, a notary is to be adduced in evidence as to the law of a foreign country or territory, the notary must be one practising in the country or territory concerned.

Reference to law of nationality

12.31 When the law of the country in which a person dies domiciled (he being a national of some other country) provides that the law applicable to the validity of his will and the devolution of his estate is that of his nationality, it is sometimes necessary to ascertain with which part of the 'empire' of which the deceased was a national he was directly associated. For this purpose it may be necessary to ascertain his domicile of origin[1]. As regards persons dying on or after 1 January 1964, reference should be made to the Wills Act 1963 as to nationality and as to the ascertainment of which of several systems of law in force in a territory or state is applicable where the formal validity of a will is to be decided. As to the Wills Act 1963, see paras. **3.392** ff., ante.

1 *Re O'Keefe, Poingdestre v Sherman* [1940] Ch 124, [1940] 1 All ER 216; *Re Ross, Ross v Waterfield* [1930] 1 Ch 377.

Matters to be dealt with in affidavit of law

12.32 When considering whether an affidavit (or notarial certificate) of law is necessary, and, if so, the matters with which it should deal, regard should be had to both Sections I and II below.

12.33 For form of affidavit of law, see No. 9. A certificate of law by a notary should show that the person certifying is a notary practising in the country or territory concerned, contain the same information as should be in an affidavit dealing with the same matters and be dated, signed and sealed by the notary.

Section I. Admissibility to proof of wills of persons dying domiciled abroad

General rule

12.34 Subject to certain exceptions dealt with in the following paragraphs, the general rule is that the will of a person dying domiciled out of England and Wales is admissible to proof in this country if it has been accepted by the country of domicile as a valid testamentary document or if it is executed in accordance with the law of the place of domicile of the deceased at the time of his death[1], or at the time when it was made. So far as regards persons dying on or after 1 January 1964 this rule is modified by the provisions of the Wills Act 1963[2] which provides various alternative tests, any one of which, if satisfied, renders a will admissible to proof in this country. As to the Wills Act 1963, see paras. **3.392** ff., ante.

1 *Re Deshais' Goods* (1865) 4 Sw & Tr 13 at 14, 15, 17.
2 See p. 777, post.

12.35   To be admissible to proof in England and Wales it is normally necessary that a will should dispose of property in this country or contain a valid appointment of an executor (see para. **3.23**, ante), but it is now accepted that the court has power to admit a will notwithstanding that it does not dispose of property in this country[1].

1 *Re Wayland's Estate* [1951] 2 All ER 1041.

Exceptions: (1) Immovable estate in England and Wales

12.36   In the case of death prior to 1 January 1964, in order to be valid to pass immovable estate situate in this country, a will, whether of a British subject or a foreigner, and whatever the domicile of the testator, must have been executed in the form prescribed by the Wills Act 1837[1]. This rule is modified by the Wills Act 1963 so far as regards persons dying on or after 1 January 1964. A will which is properly executed by virtue of s. 1 of that Act is effective to pass both movable and immovable property. The Act also gives statutory force to the common law rule that a will is valid to pass immovables if executed in accordance with the lex situs (see s. 2(1)(b)). As to the Wills Act 1963, see paras. **3.392** ff., ante.

1 See p. 719, post; *Freke v Lord Carbery* (1873) LR 16 Eq 461 at 466; *De Fogassieras v Duport* (1881) 11 LR Ir 123.

12.37   But, as regards British subjects, the rule did not apply to leaseholds, which rank for this purpose as personal estate[1], and were therefore within the provisions of the Wills Act 1861 (Lord Kingsdown's Act). A will (made prior to 1964) of a British subject which is valid in accordance with the provisions of this Act will pass leaseholds in England and Wales even though it be not executed in accordance with the Wills Act 1837 (see also paras. **12.43** ff., post). The Wills Act 1861 is repealed as from 1 January 1964 (though without prejudice to the validity of wills executed prior to the repeal) and replaced by the Wills Act 1963 (see paras. **3.392** ff., ante).

1 *Re Grassi, Stubberfield v Grassi* [1905] 1 Ch 584.

12.38   Where there is a will disposing of, and valid to pass, immovables in England and Wales (either because it was executed in the manner prescribed by the Wills Act 1837, or under s. 2(1)(b) of the Wills Act 1963), it may be proved and a grant (limited to the immovables, where appropriate) made, even though it may be invalid by the law of the testator's domicile.

12.39   Prior to 1964 it was held that revocation of a will so far as it deals with English immovable estate could be effected only by one of the methods prescribed by s. 20 of the Wills Act 1837[1] (but as to persons dying on or after 1 January 1964, see Wills Act 1963, 'Revocation of wills' (paras. **3.404–3.407**, ante)). In cases in which the Act of 1963 is applicable other methods of revocation are also effective.

1 *Re Alberti's Estate* [1955] 3 All ER 730 n, [1955] 1 WLR 1240.

12.40   A testator domiciled in France had made two wills: first, a will in English form appointing executors and disposing of the whole estate, both real and personal, and later a will in French form and not executed in accordance with the Wills Act 1837 disposing of all his movable and immovable estate. There was no formal revocation clause in the latter. It was held that the French will did not revoke the English will so far as immovable estate in England was concerned, but as it was effective to revoke the earlier will in all other respects the executors were not entitled to probate. Administration with the English will annexed was ordered to be granted to one of the residuary legatees, the grant to be limited to realty and lease-hold property in England[1].

1 *Bradby* (1936) unreported motion.

12.41   In cases where there is evidence that only part of a will is valid, the practice is to annex to the grant only that part. This is in accordance with the practice in cases where a will is valid only in so far as it exercises a power of appointment[1].

1 *Re Poole's Estate, Poole v Poole* [1919] P 10.

12.42   For summary of reported cases, see paras. **32.03** and **32.04**, post.

(2) Wills of British subjects made before 1964

12.43   Under ss. 1 and 2 of the Wills Act 1861 (Lord Kingsdown's Act)[1], a will of personal estate made (before 1 January 1964) by a British subject (whatever his domicile) is held to be well executed for the purpose of being admitted to proof in England and Wales:

(a)   if, having been made out of the United Kingdom, it is shown to have been executed according to the forms required, either (i) by the law of the place where it was made; or (ii) by the law of the domicile of the testator at the time when the will was made; or (iii) by the laws then in force in that part of Her Majesty's dominions where the testator had his domicile of origin; or

(b)   if, having been made within the United Kingdom, it was executed according to the forms required by the laws of that part of the United Kingdom in which it was made.

1 See p. 727, post.

12.44   See, further, as to this subject 'Wills Act 1861', paras. **3.374** ff., ante.

12.45   Where a will is admitted under these provisions, unless it is in English form, the grant will be limited to the personal estate of the deceased.

12.46   The Wills Act 1861 is repealed as from 1 January 1964, but without pre-judice to the validity of wills executed before that date, by the Wills Act 1963, s. 7(3), (4): the latter Act reproduces, with extended application, all the provisions of the Act of 1861 except that referred to in subpara. (a)(iii), para. **12.43**, ante. As to the Wills Act 1963, see paras. **3.392** ff., ante.

(3) Wills made in exercise of a power of appointment

12.47   In the case of a person dying before 1 January 1964 domiciled out of England and Wales, so much of his will as exercises a power of appointment under an English settlement may be admitted to proof in this country provided that it is executed in accordance with the provisions of the Wills Act 1837[1], even though the will is not validly executed according to the law of the domicile and is not admis-sible under the Wills Act 1861[2].

1 See p. 719, post.
2 See p. 727, post.

12.48   This subject is dealt with in detail in paras. **11.298–11.317**, ante.

12.49   As to persons dying on or after 1 January 1964, see also Wills Act 1963, 'Exercise of power of appointment', paras. **3.402** and **3.403**, ante.

(4) Change of domicile

12.50   By s. 3 of the Wills Act 1861[1] (repealed 1 January 1964, but without prejudice to wills made prior to that date), no will was to be held to be revoked or to have become invalid, nor was the construction thereof to be altered, by reason of any subsequent change of domicile of the testator. This provision has been held to be of general application, and not merely to apply to the wills of British subjects[2].

1 See p. 727, post.
2 *Re Groos' Estate* [1904] P 269.

12.51   Thus, prior to 1964, a will was admitted to proof in England if it was validly executed in accordance with the law of the domicile of the testator at the time of making it, notwithstanding that he died domiciled in a place by the law of which it was invalid.

12.52   Evidence would be required of the domicile at the date of the will, and, unless this was in England and Wales or in one of the countries referred to in section (B) below, of the validity of the will by the law of the domicile at that date.

12.53   Section 3 of the Wills Act 1861 is partly re-enacted by the Wills Act 1963, s. 4. The effect of the remainder of the repealed section is reproduced by s. 1 of the Act of 1963 (see also para. **3.396**, ante). Under this Act a will is admissible if it was executed in accordance with the law of the place where the deceased was domiciled either at the date of the will or at the date of his death.

(A) Will proved in the country of domicile

12.54   A will which has been accepted by the courts of the place of domicile of the deceased as a valid testamentary instrument is admissible to proof in England and Wales. This rule does not appear to be affected by the Wills Act 1963: see paras. **3.417** ff., ante. It is normally necessary that the will should dispose of estate in England and Wales or contain a valid appointment of an executor: see, however, *Re Wayland's Estate* [1951] 2 All ER 1041, referred to at para. **12.35**, ante.

12.55   The validity and construction of a will, or the capacity of the testator, as pronounced for by the court of domicile, are followed by the courts of England and Wales[1].

1 *Re Trufort, Trafford v Blanc* (1887) 36 Ch D 600; *Doglioni v Crispin* (1866) LR 1 HL 301. See also *Re Yahuda's Estate* [1956] P 388, [1956] 2 All ER 262 (a will disposing of personal estate in the United Kingdom, having been admitted to probate by the court of domicile, admitted to proof in this country although it appeared to have been revoked by a later will).

12.56   If the papers produced contain no clear evidence that the will has been recognised as valid by the court of domicile of the deceased, an affidavit of law (or a certificate of law by a notary practising in the country or territory concerned) must be filed.

12.57 As to the procedure where the original will is not available, see para. **12.73**, post.

(B) Will in English form: domicile in certain specified countries

12.58 A will in English form[1] is normally accepted as validly executed without further enquiry if the deceased was domiciled in Northern Ireland, the Republic of Ireland, Australia, Canada or New Zealand. A domicile in any other British Commonwealth country, colony or protectorate (including the Isle of Man) necessitates the validity of the will being established (unless it has been proved in the court of the domicile) by other evidence[2].

1 I.e., executed in accordance with the provisions of s. 9 of the Wills Act 1837. If there is no attestation clause, or the clause is defective, evidence of due execution is necessary in the same way as if the deceased had been domiciled in England and Wales (see paras. **3.106** ff., ante).
2 Registrar's Direction (1972) 20 November.

12.59 In the case of persons dying on or after 1 January 1964 this practice is extended to cover other circumstances in which the law of the specified countries is in point: see paras. **3.422–3.424**, ante.

12.60 As to Scottish wills, see paras. **12.74–12.76**, post.

(C) Will valid by the law of the domicile

12.61 A will is admissible to proof in England and Wales if it is executed in accordance with the forms required by the law of the testator's domicile at the time of his death[1] (or if executed in accordance with the forms required by the law of his domicile at the time of execution of the will: see 'Change of domicile', paras. **12.50–12.53**, ante).

1 *Re Deshais' Goods* (1865) 4 Sw & Tr 13 at 14, 15, 17. See also para. **32.04**, post.

12.62 It is normally necessary that the will should dispose of estate in England and Wales or contain a valid appointment of an executor: see section (A), paras. **12.54–12.57**, ante.

12.63 As to the procedure where the original will is not available, see para. **12.73**, post.

12.64 Evidence as to the validity of the will and, if necessary, the admissibility of the copy produced, is given by affidavit of law or by a certificate by a notary practising in the country or territory concerned (see 'Evidence of the law of the domicile', paras. **12.25–12.30**, ante).

12.65 As to death on or after 1 January 1964 see also 'Wills Act 1963', paras. **3.392** ff., ante.

Danish wills

12.66 The surviving spouse of a person domiciled in Denmark may take, in Denmark, what is equivalent to a grant of simple administration, notwithstanding any will left by the deceased. Although it is not proved, the will has some legal effect. In such cases a grant of administration with the will annexed will be made in this country, upon a district judge's or registrar's order, to the person entrusted with the administration by the court of the domicile, the validity of the will being established in the usual way[1].

1 Registrar's Direction (1972) 20 November.

English and foreign wills of a testator

12.67 As to cases in which a testator has made two (or more) wills, one dealing only with property in England and Wales and the other (or others) dealing with property elsewhere, see paras. **3.183–3.190**, ante.

Procedure on proving wills

Wills in a foreign language

12.68 If the will is not in the English language, a translation of it and of any endorsement or certificates on or annexed to it must be supplied. The translation must be identifiable with the document translated and usually is annexed to the foreign documents. The translation should, if possible, be verified by the certificate of an English notary public or a British consul. Translations verified in any other way will be referred to a district judge or registrar as to sufficiency. Where an English notarial or consular translation, or a consular verification of a translation, cannot be obtained, and the translator is not a person whose competency is vouched for by his official position, an affidavit by the translator as to his qualifications and verifying the translation is usually required.

12.69 Where the testator's will, written in English, has been lodged with a notary abroad, the notarially certified document lodged may contain a copy of the original will or it may merely contain a translation into a foreign language and a re-translation therefrom into English. In the latter case a photographic copy or a duly verified copy of the original will will be called for. In view of the decision in *Re Rule's Goods* (1878) 4 PD 76, however, if the applicant objects it will not be open to the registry to insist on the production of such photographic or other copy of the original will. If, however, it appears on the face of the document that the re-translation is or may be inaccurate, the registry will require that the re-translation be checked with the original[1].

1 Registrar's Direction (1972) 20 November.

12.70 Where possible, the probate copy of the will is made by the photographic, or similar, process which reproduces a facsimile copy, but where much irrelevant matter is included, or where the document is unsuitable for such reproduction, an engrossment may be necessary (see paras. **4.224–4.226**, ante). In the latter case the Probate Department at the Principal Registry, or the district probate registrar, as the case may be, will, on request, mark the portions required to be copied.

12.71 The original, or official copy of the will, and *not* the translation into English, should be marked with the signatures of the applicant and the person before whom the oath is sworn.

Wills in the Welsh language

12.72 For the practice as to translations, see paras. **4.234–4.236**, ante.

Original will not available

12.73 Where the original will is not available because it is in the custody of a foreign court or official, a copy under seal (where there is a seal) and duly authenticated by the court or official having custody of the original is accepted, and no order for the admission to proof of such a copy is necessary[1]. If the will has been proved in the foreign court the fact that the original is not available is accepted, but if an affidavit of law (or certificate of law by a notary practising in the country or territory concerned) is necessary to establish the validity of the will this should confirm the fact that the original will is not available because it is in the custody of the foreign court or official, and that the copy lodged for proof is admissible in evidence in the courts of the foreign country or territory concerned.

1 NCPR 54(2).

Scottish wills

12.74 The practice in Scotland may be summarised as follows: a will may be 'recorded' in the Commissary Court books, after which it is handed back, even though confirmation of the executor has been issued. Alternatively, a will may be presented for 'registration' in the Books of Council and Session, or the Sheriff Court books: if this is done the will is retained and never given out. Extracts of the will are issued, and are entitled to the same credit and effect as the original will, but registration gives the executor no power, as the registration is for preservation of the will and has no connection with the granting of confirmation.

12.75 If it is sworn that the will has been 'registered'—as opposed to 'recorded'—it follows that the original will cannot be obtained, and an official copy under seal is accepted for proof in this country.

12.76 Neither recording nor registration is in itself an indication that the Scottish court has accepted the will as valid. Validity can be established only by evidence that confirmation has been issued in respect of the will, or, if no confirmation has issued, by an affidavit of law or such other evidence as may satisfy the district judge or registrar[1].

1 Secretary's Circular, 7 November 1955.

Grant made in Ireland: original records burnt at the Four Courts

12.77 To obtain a sealed copy from the court at Dublin in cases where there is no record of the grant or will there, the probate issued by the court in Dublin should be produced to the Principal Probate Registry there, when a record of the grant and will is made. A sealed copy is then issued by that court, and this is accepted for the purpose of proof in England and Wales[1].

1 *Re Selby* (1941) March.

India Office copies

12.78 All records formerly in the custody of the India Office have been transferred to the Foreign and Commonwealth Office. Extracts or copies of any such records will be accepted if under the seal of that Office[1].

1 Registrar's Direction (1950) 18 March, as amended 1954.

Neither original nor official copy will available

12.79   If the original will is lost or unobtainable and no official copy is available, an order of the district judge or registrar is necessary to enable a less formal copy to be admitted. The procedure is the same as in the case of persons dying domiciled in England and Wales (see NCPR 54[1], and paras. **25.46** ff., post).

1 See p. 938, post.

Section II. Entitlement to a grant where deceased died domiciled out of England and Wales

Grant to, or on behalf of, executor where will is in English or Welsh language

12.80   Where the will of a testator, whatever his domicile, is admissible to proof in England and Wales and is in the English or Welsh language, any executor named therein is accepted as having the full rights of executorship[1]. He may obtain probate of the will, or he may appoint an attorney or attorneys to obtain administration (with will) for his use and benefit (as to grants to attorneys, see Chap. 11).

1 NCPR 30(3)(a)(i), and Registrar's Direction (1972) 20 November.

12.81   No expression in a foreign tongue purporting to mean 'executor' will be accepted as constituting an executor: see paras. **12.84** ff., however, as to executors according to the tenor.

12.82   No order for a grant is necessary in these cases. An affidavit (or notarial certificate) of law may be necessary to establish that the will is admissible to proof in this country: see 'Wills Act 1963', paras. **3.392** ff., ante, and Section I, paras. **12.34** ff., ante. If, in the case of a will made before 1 January 1964, it is claimed that it is admissible under ss. 1 or 2 of the Wills Act 1861[1], an affidavit as to British status will be required (see Form No. 12), and an affidavit of facts may be necessary in connection with the proof, by virtue of the Wills Act 1963, of the will of a person dying on or after that date (see para. **3.425**, ante): Form of affidavit, No. 10.

1 See p. 727, post.

12.83   Except where the deceased was domiciled in Scotland, the Inland Revenue account will be required to be submitted to the Capital Taxes Office before the papers are lodged at the probate registry. The grant will cover the estate in England and Wales only. In other respects the procedure is the same as in the case of a grant to an executor, or the attorney of an executor, of a person dying domiciled in England and Wales (see Chaps. 4 and 11).

Will in English, Welsh or foreign language: executor according to the tenor

12.84   If a will, admissible to proof in this country, sets out the duties of a person named therein in terms sufficient to constitute him executor according to the tenor of the will, he may obtain probate, or appoint an attorney, in that capacity[1]. This applies whether the will is written in the English, Welsh or a foreign language.

1 NCPR 30(3)(a)(ii), and Registrar's Direction (1972) 20 November.

12.85   As to the expressions that are sufficient to constitute an executor according to the tenor, see paras. **4.19–4.23**, ante. It is usually necessary to obtain the decision of a district judge or registrar on this point, and it is advisable to consult the Probate Department at the Principal Registry, or the district probate registrar, before preparing the papers for the grant.

12.86   No order for the grant is necessary: the procedure is the same as that set out in paras. **12.82** ff. If the will is in the Welsh or a foreign language a translation into English will be required: see paras. **12.68–12.72**, ante, as to the practice.

Foreign corporation appointed executor

12.87   A foreign corporation appointed executor in a will which would be regarded as giving a right to probate were the executor an individual able to apply may, as executor, appoint an attorney to take a grant for its use and benefit and until further representation be granted. It is immaterial whether the will has been proved in the court of domicile unless there is some other person who has already been entrusted with administration by that court who also applies for an English grant[1]. As to grants to attorneys, see Chap. 11 and see also paras. **12.138** and **12.147**, post.

1   Registrar's Direction (1972) 20 November.

Executor having renounced in the court of domicile

12.88   The renunciation of probate in the court of the country of domicile of the deceased by an executor as qualified in either of the first two paragraphs in this section is not regarded as sufficient to clear off his right to probate in this country. A grant of probate may be made to him notwithstanding his renunciation elsewhere; and, similarly, if a grant is made to, or on behalf of, other executors, then, unless he renounces his right to probate in England and Wales also, his right must be preserved by reserving power to him, or by additional wording in the limitation if the grant is made to an attorney.

Executors and persons entrusted by the court of domicile

12.89   No order of priority is observed as between an executor who qualifies for probate as set out above and a person who has been entrusted by the court of domicile with the administration of the estate.

12.90   'A person who qualifies under r. 30(1)(a) (person entrusted) does not need to clear off an executor.'[1].

1   Registrar's Direction (1972) 20 November.

12.91   On the other hand, an executor who qualifies may obtain probate or apply through an attorney notwithstanding that some other person has been entrusted by the court of domicile[1].

1   This follows from NCPR 30(3)(a), which appears to supersede *Re Meatyard's Goods* [1903] P 125, in non-contentious applications. The position may be otherwise in the event of a dispute. See also observations of Buckley J in *Re Manifold, Slater v Chryssaffinis* [1962] Ch 1 at 18, [1961] 1 All ER 710 at 719.

12.92   If the same person possesses both these capacities he may apply either as the executor or as the person entrusted. In the former case, however, no order of the district judge or registrar will be necessary. If he applies in the capacity of the person entrusted, a district judge's or registrar's order will be necessary: furthermore, if any life or minority interest arises under the will, a grant of administration (with will) must normally be made to not less than two individuals or a trust corporation.

12.93   Whichever capacity is chosen, care should be taken to see that it is followed consistently in preparing all documents.

Person entrusted by the court of domicile

12.94   Application may be made for an order for a grant to the person entrusted with the administration of the estate of the deceased by the court having jurisdiction at the place where the deceased was domiciled at the time of his death, or to his attorney[1].

1   NCPR 30(1)(a). See *Re Earl's Goods* (1867) LR 1 P & D 450 and the other cases quoted at para. **32.04**, post.

12.95   A grant in this capacity is made only where there is a grant, decree or other order of a court clothing some person with authority substantially similar to that conferred upon an English personal representative, i.e. empowering him to collect in and administer the estate. A decree or order merely declaring who are the heirs of the deceased is not normally accepted as sufficient to enable such persons to be treated as entrusted with administration (but may be sufficient evidence as to who are the persons beneficially entitled to the estate by the law of the place where the deceased died domiciled—see paras. **12.105** ff., post). Cases of doubt should be referred to a district judge or registrar for decision.

12.96   The original grant or decree issued by the court of domicile, or an officially certified copy of it, including an official copy of the will, if any, should be lodged: it will be retained in the registry. If the document is in a foreign language, a notarial or other sufficient translation is also required (as to translations, see paras. **12.68–12.71**, ante).

12.97   A district judge's or registrar's order under NCPR 30(1)(a) is necessary; as to the mode of application for this, see paras. **12.127** ff., post. No affidavit of law will be needed to lead the order, nor to establish that the will is valid provided it is clear from the documents that the will has been accepted by the court of the domicile as a valid testamentary instrument (see paras. **12.54–12.57**, ante).

12.98   Where the copies of the grant and will are in separate documents they will be accepted only if it is satisfactorily established that the documents refer to the same deceased person, and to each other.

12.99   The grant is in all cases one of letters of administration, with or without will as the case may be, and consequently the usual rule is that the grant may not issue to a single individual if a life or minority interest arises under the law of the domicile (see 'Minority or life interests', para. **12.140**, post). As to the procedure for joinder of a second administrator when this is necessary, see para. **12.141**, post.

12.100   If the powers of the person entrusted are limited as to time an order for a grant may be made subject to a similar limitation if the district judge or registrar is satisfied that the grant is required for the purpose only of collecting assets in England and Wales, that this can be done within the time limited by the foreign court, and that there are no debts in this country[1].

1 Registrar's Direction (1972) 20 November.

12.101 The district judge or registrar has a general power, under NCPR 30(1), to direct in his order that the grant be limited in such way as he may consider appropriate.

12.102 It should be noted that under the law of Sri Lanka (formerly Ceylon) between 1 January 1974 and 31 December 1977, grants of probate and letters of administration were issued by the Public Trustee, and not by a court of law. It is considered that an executor or administrator constituted by such a grant does not qualify as a person entrusted by the court having jurisdiction in the country of domicile: but such a grant is sufficient evidence of entitlement to administer to support an application for an order for a grant to be made to the grantee or his attorney under r. 30(1)(c). As to applications under r. 30(1)(c), see below. Grants issued by a District Court in Sri Lanka before 1974 and since 1978 will be accepted for the purpose of r. 30(1)(a) without further evidence. Alternatively, application may be made for resealing grants issued by either authority during their respective periods of jurisdiction[1]; as to resealing see Chap. 18.

1 Secretary's Circular, 14 June 1985.

New Zealand and Australia—Public Trustee

12.103 Orders to administer in favour of the Public Trustee of New Zealand and the Public Trustee of Queensland (Australia) (formerly known as the Public Curator of Queensland) and elections to administer by them, have the full force of grants and can be resealed in England and Wales (see paras. **18.84–18.89**, post). Alternatively, such a document may be used to lead an order for a grant to the Public Trustee of New Zealand or the Public Trustee of Queensland as the person entrusted with administration if it is sworn that it is still in force.

12.104 Somewhat similar procedures for the filing of elections by the Public Trustee in respect of relatively small estates exist in the Australian States of Victoria, Western Australia and Tasmania. It should not be assumed without evidence in the particular case under consideration that these qualify as grants which can be resealed. Such an election may, however, be used to lead an order for a grant to the person entrusted on its being sworn that it is still in force[1].

1 Registrar's Direction (1972) 20 November.

Person beneficially entitled to the estate by the law of the domicile

12.105 Where there is no one entrusted with the administration of the estate by the court having jurisdiction at the place where the deceased died domiciled application may be made for an order for a grant to the person beneficially entitled to the estate by the law of the place where the deceased died domiciled or to his attorney[1]. In these circumstances it is not necessary to clear off any executor.[2] If there is more than one person so entitled the district judge or registrar may direct to which of them the grant is to issue. The district judge or register has a general power, under NCPR 30(1), to direct in his order that the grant be limited in such way as he may consider appropriate.

1 NCPR 30(1)(b).
2 Registrar's Direction (1977) 6 December.

12.106 Evidence of the law of the country of domicile is necessary (see paras. **12.25–12.33**, ante). If the evidence is given by affidavit or by a certificate by a notary practising in the country or territory concerned, it should recite the facts of the particular case and state the law applicable. In a case where it is clear to the district judge or registrar from an Act of Notoriety or a Certificate of Inheritance issued abroad in relation to the estate of a deceased person dying domiciled outside England and Wales that the applicant for an English grant under NCPR 30(1)(b) is so entitled, the district judge or registrar may make an order for a grant to the applicant, without calling for an affidavit as to the foreign law.

12.107 If there is a will and there is no evidence that its validity has been accepted by the court of domicile, an affidavit (or certificate by a notary practising in the country or territory of the domicile) of law is required, speaking as to its validity by the law of the domicile and the acceptability of the copy produced.

12.108 The evidence of law must be supported by adequate evidence of the facts themselves (normally an affidavit, or a statement in the oath, by the applicant for the grant)[1].

1 Registrar's Direction (1972) 20 November.

12.109 It is frequently the case that under the law of the domicile more than one person is beneficially entitled to the estate. The district judge or registrar has power, under the rule, to direct to which of them the grant is to issue. If some of the persons beneficially entitled to share in the estate are not joining in the application for the order and the grant (or have not joined in appointing the attorney(s) making the application) it is advisable to make a preliminary enquiry of the Principal of the Probate Department or the district probate registrar, depending upon where the application is to be made, to see if an order will be made in respect of the proposed applicants. A grant can in no case be made to more than four persons[1], though any number may join in executing a power of attorney.

1 Supreme Court Act 1981, s. 114(1) (see p. 844, post).

12.110 A grant may normally be made to a sole individual administrator only if no life or minority interest arises under the law of domicile: see para. **12.140**, post. As to the procedure for joining a second administrator if only one person is qualified, see paras. **12.141** ff., post.

12.111 For procedure for obtaining the district judge's or registrar's order and the grant, see paras. **12.127** ff., post.

Grant under r. 30(1)(c)

12.112 Where there is no person entrusted with administration by the court having jurisdiction at the place where the deceased died domiciled, and no person who is beneficially entitled to the estate by the law of the place where the deceased died domiciled is willing or able to apply for a grant, the district judge or registrar may make an order under the provisions of NCPR 30(1)(c) for a grant to such person as he may think fit. Such an order may also be made if, in the opinion of the district judge or registrar, the circumstances so require notwithstanding that some person has been entrusted with administration or is beneficially entitled to the estate and is willing and able to take a grant.

12.113 An affidavit, normally by the applicant for the grant, setting out the relevant facts is required.

12.114 An affidavit (or certificate by a notary practising in the country concerned) as to the law of the country of domicile is usually necessary. This should show, by reference to the facts of the case, who is beneficially entitled to the estate by the law of the country of domicile, and, in appropriate cases who, according to the law of the domicile, is entitled in priority to administer the estate. It should also deal with the validity of any will, unless this has been proved in the court of the domicile.

12.115 In cases of applications for an order under r. 30(1)(c) the oath should preferably not be sworn until the district judge's or registrar's order has been obtained, as this document should recite the particulars of the order.

12.116 If under the law of the place of domicile a minority or a life interest arises, the grant must normally be made to not less than two individuals or a trust corporation, and the affidavit to lead the district judge's or registrar's order should be framed accordingly.

12.117 As to the procedure for obtaining the district judge's or registrar's order, see paras. **12.127** ff., post.

Whole or substantially whole of estate in England and Wales immovable property

12.118 Where the whole or substantially the whole of the estate in England and Wales of a person who died domiciled out of England and Wales consists of immovable property, a grant in respect of the whole estate in England and Wales may be made to the person who would have been entitled to a grant if the deceased had died domiciled in England and Wales[1].

1 NCPR 30(3)(b).

12.119 This applies whether the deceased died testate or intestate. If there is a will, its admissibility to proof, where the whole of the estate in England and Wales consists of immovable estate and where the date of death was before 1 January 1964, is almost invariably tested by English law (see, however, para. **12.37**, ante, as to leasehold property). In the case of death on or after 1 January 1964 a will executed in accordance with the provisions of the Wills Acts 1963 is to be treated as well executed, and therefore effective to pass immovable estate (see para. **3.401**, ante).

12.120 No evidence of foreign law is necessary in these cases, unless to establish the validity of a will which is not in accordance with s. 9 of the Wills Act 1837.

12.121   The papers required are the same as if the deceased had died domiciled in England and Wales (see Chap. 4, 5 or 6), save that an Inland Revenue account is required in all cases where the deceased died domiciled outside the United Kingdom and the account must be submitted to the Capital Taxes Office before the papers are lodged at the registry.

12.122   The oath must contain a statement that the whole, or substantially the whole, as the case may be, of the estate in England and Wales consists of immovable property. Where it is claimed that the whole of the estate in England and Wales consists of immovable property, a statement accordingly in the oath is normally accepted as sufficient evidence of the fact. Where it is claimed that *substantially* the whole of the estate in England and Wales consists of immovable property, brief details of the immovable estate and the movable estate (in particular their respective total values) should be included in the oath. The oath must contain the usual statement of the domicile of the deceased[1].

1   NCPR 8(2).

Will made in exercise of power of appointment

12.123   As to entitlement to a grant where a will is invalid except as to the exercise of a power of appointment under a settlement, see paras. **11.315** ff., ante.

Wills Acts 1861 and 1963

12.124   Although the Wills Act 1861 (Lord Kingsdown's Act)[1] enables wills of personal estate made before 1 January 1964 by British subjects to be admitted to proof in this country if they are made in accordance with its provisions (see paras. **3.374** ff., ante), it does not affect the entitlement to a grant, which, in the case of persons dying domiciled out of England and Wales, is decided as set out in the foregoing paragraphs of this section.

1   See p. 727, post.

12.125   This is also the case in relation to wills admissible to proof by virtue of the Wills Act 1963[1]: this Act deals with the formal validity of wills and has no effect on the rules as to entitlement to a grant.

1   See p. 777, post.

Death prior to 1926

12.126   Where the death occurred before 1 January 1926, the former practice of allowing an applicant to take a grant under the title which would have applied if the deceased had died domiciled in England and Wales still obtains—see NCPR 23.

Section III. Application for district judge's or registrar's order

Mode of application

12.127   An order for a grant under NCPR 30 may be made by a district judge of the Principal Registry or the registrar of the district probate registry at which the application for the grant has been, or will be, made[1]. Where such an order is necessary, application may be made, except normally in the case of an application under r. 30(1)(c), in either of two ways.

1   NCPR 2 and 30.

(i) *Prior to the application for a grant*

12.128   An application by this method is made by first lodging at the registry the affidavits and other documents required to lead the order, including the will, if any: the application may, if desired, be made by sending the documents to the registry through the post. At the Principal Registry, the documents in support of the application are left in (or posted to) the Probate Department. If the application is approved, the district judge's or registrar's order will be available for collection from the registry or sent to the solicitor through the post. If the papers are defective the solicitor will be informed by post or telephone.

12.129   This mode of application is normally essential in the case of an application for a discretionary order under NCPR 30(1)(c): see paras. **12.112–12.117**, ante.

12.130   When the order has been obtained, the oath and Inland Revenue account should be completed. All the documents, including the district judge's or registrar's order and the affidavits etc., in support, should then be lodged with the Receiver of Papers at the Principal Registry, or at the district registry, in the usual way. Forms of oath, Nos. 164–166.

(ii) *Simultaneously with the application for the grant*

12.131   In straightforward applications for a grant to the person (or the attorney of a person) entrusted with administration, or beneficially entitled to the estate, the oath may, as a concession, be prepared in anticipation of the district judge's or registrar's order, and all necessary documents lodged with (or sent by post to) the Receiver of Papers at the Principal Registry, or the district probate registry. All the relevant matters of fact in support of the application for the order must be deposed to by the applicant, either in the oath or in a separate affidavit. If the papers are approved, the order will first be drawn, and the grant will then be issued and despatched in the normal way. Notice of any defect in the papers will be given by post or telephone.

12.132   No fee is payable in respect of the district judge's or registrar's order.

Requirements in oath

12.133   The oath to lead the grant must state specifically the place of domicile of the deceased[1]. Where, as in the Provinces of Canada or the States of Australia or the United States of America, there are separate jurisdictions, the particular Province or State must be specified. It is not necessary to specify the division of a country where the testamentary law is uniform, as in Switzerland[2].

1   NCPR 8(2).
2   Registrar's Direction (1972) 20 November. Except in the case of wills executed before 1 January 1954, the testamentary law of South Africa is uniform throughout the Republic: it is therefore correct to state that the deceased died domiciled in South Africa (Registrar's Direction (1964) 24 February).

12.134   The estate covered by the grant is that in England and Wales only. Any Scottish or Northern Irish assets, or assets situated outside the United Kingdom, should therefore be excluded in arriving at the figure to be inserted in the oath.

12.135   In cases where, under NCPR 30(1)(a) or (b), *an order has been made* for a grant to the person entrusted with administration by the court of domicile or beneficially entitled to the estate by the law of the domicile, an oath describing the applicant as the person entrusted or beneficially entitled, as the case may be, will normally be accepted whether it recites the order or not. A person who qualifies under r. 30(1)(b) does not need to clear off an executor named in the will of the deceased[1].

1 Registrar's Direction (1977) 6 December.

12.136   Where an order has been made under r. 30(1)(c), the oath should describe the applicant as the person authorised by order under that rule, and specify the date of the order, but where it has been executed before the making of the order, reswearing of the oath may be dispensed with if it is so drawn as to give a sufficient title to the grant, and not to be inconsistent with the order[1].

1 Registrar's Direction (1972) 20 November.

12.137   For forms of oath, see Nos. 164–166.

Attorney grant—form of limitation

12.138   In the case of a grant to attorneys, the limitation 'for his/their use and benefit, and until further representation be granted' is normally used whenever the grant is made in accordance with the law of the domicile (i.e. by order under NCPR 30(1)(a), (b) or (c)), or in the case of a grant to the attorney of an executor entitled to probate, or of any other person under an English title. However, where the district judge or registrar would direct that another limitation be included in the grant if it were issuing to the donor under NCPR 30(1)(a), (b) or (c), such other limitation may be directed to be included in a grant issuing to the attorney in addition to, or instead of, the usual attorney limitation.

Community of property

12.139   As to the additional wording to be included in the oath and as to court fees in cases where, under the law of the domicile of the deceased, community of property existed between him and his spouse, see para. **4.212**, ante.

Minority or life interests

12.140   As stated earlier, where a minority or a life interest arises in any estate, except in the case of a direct grant of probate to an executor, the grant must normally be made to not less than two individuals or to a trust corporation, with or without an individual (Supreme Court Act 1981, s. 114(2)). This is so even if under the law of the domicile a single person may take a grant, although the court has a discretion to allow an individual as a sole administrator if it appears expedient in all the circumstances to do so (s. 114(2)). The statement in the oath as to minority and life interests should be based on the law applicable to the circumstances of the particular case[1]. In straightforward cases the statement by the applicant in the oath that a minority or life interest does or does not exist will be accepted without further evidence. If, however, it appears on the face of the will and in the events which have happened that a minority or life interest does exist and the oath states that it does not, the statement should be verified in the affidavit (or notarial certificate) of law[2].

1 Registrar's Direction (1975) 17 October.
2 Registrar's Direction (1972) 20 November.

Second grantee

12.141 Where, because of the existence of a minority or life interest, the court determines that a grant to a single individual would not be appropriate, the person entitled to the grant may appoint either a trust corporation or not less than two individuals as his attorneys for the purpose of obtaining the grant.

12.142 Otherwise, where by virtue of a life or minority interest, a grant must be made to not less than two administrators, an order may be made under NCPR 30(2) that such person as the district judge or registrar may direct be joined as administrator with a person entrusted with administration by the court of domicile, or beneficially entitled to the estate by the law of the domicile.

12.143 Accordingly, if a minority or life interest arises under the law of the domicile and only one person is qualified to apply as the person entrusted or beneficially entitled, the affidavit of facts, or the oath, as the case may be, should be sworn jointly by that person and the person whom it is proposed to join as second administrator, and should show that application is made for the latter person to be joined as administrator under the provisions of NCPR 30(2).

12.144 In the case of a discretionary order under r. 30(1)(c), where a minority or life interest arises, the affidavit to lead the order should similarly be sworn by both the intended grantees. In this case the district judge or registrar has a discretion to make an order in favour of one or more persons as may be necessary.

12.145 If, notwithstanding the existence of a life or minority interest, it is intended to apply to the court to exercise its discretion and allow the grant to issue to a single individual administrator, it is suggested that the facts be put to the Principal of the Probate Department in London or to the district probate registrar prior to the preparation of the papers.

Grants to attorneys

12.146 Reference has been made in various sections of this chapter to grants to attorneys. For further discussion of this subject, see Chap. 11.

Further grant after grant to attorney

12.147 Where a grant has been made by district judge's or registrar's order to the attorney of a person entrusted by the court of domicile, or of the person beneficially entitled to the estate by the law of the domicile, and the person giving the power of attorney applies later for a direct grant to himself, an affidavit will be called for showing, as the case may be, that the entrusting order is still in force, or that the donor of the power is still beneficially entitled to the estate. A further district judge's or registrar's order will be necessary[1].

1 Registrar's Direction (1972) 20 November.

Settling of papers

12.148   If desired, the Principal of the Probate Department, or the district probate registrar, will, on payment of the requisite fee, settle and approve the oath. In the case of applications under foreign law, however, the papers cannot be settled until after the district judge's or registrar's order has been obtained[1].

1 Registrar's Direction (1972) 20 November.

12.149   It is not the practice to settle affidavits of facts or of foreign law.

Inland Revenue account

12.150   In all cases of domicile outside the United Kingdom, the Inland Revenue account must be submitted to, and assessed by, the Capital Taxes Office prior to the application for the grant[1].

1 Registrar's Direction (1972) 20 November.

Inheritance tax, capital transfer tax or estate duty paid in Scotland or Northern Ireland

12.151   Where a person dies domiciled outside the United Kingdom leaving estate in more than one part of the United Kingdom, separate representation is necessary in each country, for in such circumstances an English grant does not extend to the estate in Scotland or Northern Ireland, nor will a Scottish confirmation or a Northern Irish grant extend to estate in England and Wales[1].

1 See Administration of Estates Act 1971, ss. 1, 3 (pp. 799, 801, post).

12.152   In such circumstances, when the first Inland Revenue account (or inventory, in Scotland) is delivered it should contain particulars of all the assets which may be liable to inheritance tax or capital transfer tax in the United Kingdom and the personal representatives should pay all the tax for which they are liable on delivery of that account or inventory: Finance Act 1975, Sch. 4, paras. 2(2) and 12(2) as consolidated in the Inheritance Tax Act 1984, ss. 216(3) and 226(2). If the applicants for a grant of representation or their legal advisers wish to have the overall tax liability of the deceased's whole estate handled by the Capital Taxes Office in a particular part of the United Kingdom—for example, in Northern Ireland—they should make their first application for a grant of representation in that part. After that first grant has issued (and whether or not tax has been paid) they should send to the Capital Taxes Office in the part of the United Kingdom where the original grant was obtained, the Inland Revenue account or inventory to lead to the further grant. That Office will return the account or inventory with an endorsement showing the tax position and the document should then be sent to the probate registry (or in Scotland to the Commissary Court in Edinburgh) in that part of the United Kingdom in which the further grant of representation is required. It should be noted that where the grant is issued in the Newcastle upon Tyne District Probate Registry the relevant papers are currently being directed to the Capital Taxes Office in Edinburgh.

12.153 The addresses and telephone numbers of the Capital Taxes Offices concerned with the above procedures are as follows:

1. In England and Wales   The Capital Taxes Office,
Ferrers House, PO Box 38,
Castle Meadow Road,
Nottingham NG2 1BB   tel. 0115 9740000
fax 0115 9742432
DX 701201 Nottingham 4

2. In Scotland   16 Picardy Place,
Edinburgh EH1 3NB   tel. 0131 556 8511

3. Northern Ireland   Dorchester House,
52/58 Great Victoria Street,
Belfast BT2 7BB   tel. 01232 236633

Notice to Treasury Solicitor

12.154 In all cases of foreign domicile particular regard must be paid to the provisions of NCPR 38[1]. It must be shown by the applicant that there are kin, or some statutory ultimate heir, who, under the foreign law, will take estate in England and Wales passing under a partial or total intestacy, or that the Treasury Solicitor does not propose to take a grant on behalf of the Crown[2].

1 See p. 934, post.
2 Registrar's Direction (1972) 20 November. See *Re Barnett's Trusts* [1902] 1 Ch 847. Unless there is affirmative evidence that there are successors who, by the law of the place of domicile, inherit the estate of the deceased, the consent of the Treasury Solicitor must be produced by the applicant as the property in England may be bona vacantia. The fact that bona vacantia in the country of domicile vest in the state of that country does not affect the estate in England. But see *Re Maldonado, State of Spain v Treasury Solicitor* [1954] P 223, [1953] 2 All ER 300; affd [1954] P 223, [1953] 2 All ER 1579, CA, where the Spanish State was by statute prescribed to be an alternative heir. See also *Re Mitchell, Hatton v Jones* [1954] Ch 525, [1954] 2 All ER 246, which appears to suggest that the Crown is a statutory heir (as the Republic of Spain was held to be in *Re Maldonado*, above) by virtue of s. 46(1)(vi) of the Administration of Estates Act 1925 (pp. 753, 758, post) and may therefore claim under the provisions of that Act rather than by prerogative right: but see also Ing on *Bona Vacantia*.

CHAPTER 13

Grants 'de bonis non'—Cessate grants—Double probate

Summary

Grants 'de bonis non'

When required

13.01 If the person to whom a grant of representation has been made has died leaving part of the estate of the deceased unadministered then, unless there is a chain of executorship (as to which, see paras. **13.04–13.06**, post), a grant in respect of the unadministered estate may be made to a new personal representative to enable the administration to be completed.

13.02 Where a grant of probate has been made, reserving power to one or more other executors, the latter may at any time obtain double probate.

13.03 As to application for the appointment of an additional personal representative during the subsistence of a life or minority interest where there is only one surviving personal representative, see paras. **7.40–7.47**.

Chain of executorship

13.04 As stated in paras. **4.64** ff., ante, the probate of the will of an executor maintains, by chain, the representation to the estate of the original testator, and this rule applies, so long as the chain continues, to an indefinite succession of testators. As to the circumstances in which a chain of executorship is broken, see para. **4.76**, ante.

13.05 No grant de bonis non can issue while there is already a personal representative of the deceased by chain of executorship.

13.06 As to the position where the chain is in abeyance, see para. **4.83**, ante.

Choice of new grantee: general principles

13.07   The rules of priority in relation to original grants (NCPR 20 and 22: see paras. **5.04** and **6.80** ff., ante) apply equally in the case of second or subsequent grants in the same estate, whether of administration (with will) or of administration.

13.08   The principles may be summarised as follows:

1. A grant de bonis non may be made to any person who had a title to a grant equal to that of the previous grantee.
2. If the deceased grantee was the only person taking a beneficial interest in the residuary estate of the deceased (e.g. the only person entitled to the estate on an intestacy, or the sole residuary legatee and devisee named in a will), a grant de bonis non will be made to his personal representative.
     This may necessitate application for a 'leading grant' in the estate of the deceased grantee prior to the application for the grant de bonis non.
3. On an intestacy (total or partial), where the deceased left a surviving spouse, special considerations apply in view of the nature of the interest of the spouse in the residuary estate.
4. The general rule under which a living person is preferred (except by direction of a district judge or registrar) to the personal representative of a deceased person who had an equal title to a grant[1] applies.

1 NCPR 27(5).

13.09   These principles are dealt with in greater detail in the subsequent pages of this chapter.

Life or minority interests

13.10   It should be noted that if any life or minority interest subsists at the time of the application for a grant de bonis non, the grant must normally be made to not less than two individuals, or to a trust corporation with or without an individual[1].

1 Supreme Court Act 1981, s. 114(2).

Grantee's title. Chancery Court construction

13.11   Where a probate registry has construed a will for the purpose of ascertaining the person who shall be the grantee, and a grant has been made to such person, but subsequently the will is before the Chancery Court for construction, and the finding of that Court differs, the probate registry will adopt the finding of the Chancery Court and act on it. When an original grant of administration (with will) was made to a next-of-kin of a testator on the basis that he had not disposed of his residuary estate, on the death of the grantee administration (with will) de bonis non was granted to the person who the Court of Chancery had in the meantime decided was a residuary legatee[1].

1 *Warren v Kelson* (1859) 1 Sw & Tr 290.

Administration (with will) 'de bonis non'

13.12   Before a grant of administration (with will) de bonis non can be made, it must be established that there is no chain of executorship (see paras. **13.04–13.06**), and all executors named in the will of the deceased must be cleared off (including any to whom power was reserved), i.e. by reciting their death or renunciation[1]. The manner in which the chain of representation is broken must be shown in the oath (e.g. by stating that the sole executor, or the survivor of the proving executors, died intestate, or having made a will but not appointing any executor, or as the case may be).

1 As to citing an executor to whom power was reserved so as to extinguish his rights, see para. **24.15**, post.

13.13   Where the previous grant was one of probate, administration (with will) may be granted to the person next in order of priority under NCPR 20, i.e.:

(i)   any residuary legatee or devisee holding in trust[1] for any other person; or if cleared off,

(ii)   any other residuary legatee or devisee including one for life, or where the residuary estate was not wholly disposed of by the will, any person entitled to or sharing in the undisposed-of estate;

and on clearing off all members of the above classes, to the lower classes under r. 20, in order of priority.

1 An executor who has previously renounced only his right to probate does not thereby lose any right to administration (with will) as residuary legatee and devisee in trust, or in any other capacity, unless he also renounces such right (NCPR 37(1)).

13.14   See also Chap. 7 as to life or minority interests.

13.15   Where the former grant was of administration (with will), the order of priority is the same. If the previous grantee was one of the residuary legatees and devisees, a grant de bonis non may be made to another residuary legatee or devisee; if he was the sole residuary legatee and devisee, the grant should be taken by his personal representative, in accordance with the practice given in paras. **5.119** ff., ante.

13.16   The practice in cases where the estate was not wholly disposed of by the will also corresponds to that in connection with a first grant (see paras. **5.82** ff., ante).

13.17   On clearing off all persons taking an interest in the residuary estate, including the personal representatives of those who have since died, a grant de bonis non may be made to a specific legatee or devisee or a creditor of the deceased. If there be no legatees or devisees or creditors, or if they or their personal representatives have renounced, then a grant de bonis non will be made, without preference, to contingent legatees or devisees. (See NCPR 20.)

13.18   If the original grant was made to a creditor or a legatee on the renunciation of the residuary beneficiaries, any other creditor or legatee may take administration (with will) de bonis non, without any further renunciation on the part of the residuary legatees or devisees; but if they were cited to accept or refuse a grant and did not appear, they would have to be cited again. Their rights are not finally extinguished by the citation as in the case of an executor who does not appear to a citation[1].

1 See Administration of Estates Act 1925, s. 5 (p. 746, post).

13.19   A grant de bonis non may be made to the personal representative of a deceased residuary legatee and devisee who renounced when the original grant was made, or who was cited to accept or refuse a grant and did not appear.

Living interests preferred

13.20   Attention is drawn to NCPR 20(d), under which the personal representative of a residuary legatee or devisee (but not one for life or one holding in trust for any other person, such personal representative having no title to a grant) or of any person entitled to share in any residue not disposed of by the will, now has a lower right of priority to a grant than the deceased he represents.

13.21   Where the will appointed several residuary legatees and devisees, one or some of whom are still alive, but there is some difficulty in making a grant to a living residuary legatee and devisee, or in obtaining the renunciation of those who are alive, those living must be cited to accept or refuse a grant or an application must be made for an order under s. 116 of the Supreme Court Act 1981 by-passing their right to a grant, at the probate registry at which the application for the grant is to be made.

Grant to personal representative of beneficiary

13.22   Where the death occurred on or after 1 January 1926, administration (with the will annexed) de bonis non will not be granted to the personal representative of a child or other beneficiary in whom any property undisposed of by the will of the deceased vested on the statutory trusts, unless such beneficiary attained an absolutely vested interest in the estate by attaining the age of majority or marrying under that age (see Administration of Estates Act 1925, s. 47(2) and (3)[1]).

1   See pp. 755, 759, post,

13.23   Where the first grant of administration in the estate of A has been made to the administrator of the estate of a deceased residuary legatee, and such administrator dies, a further grant of representation in the estate of the residuary legatee would be necessary in order to enable such representative administrator to take a grant to the unadministered estate of the original deceased A.

Codicil proved for the first time

13.24   In ordinary cases the grant of administration (with the will annexed) de bonis non includes only the testamentary papers of which probate was originally granted. But if a codicil is discovered at the time of application for the grant de bonis non, the grant will include the will already proved, and the codicil subsequently found[1]. If the codicil appoints different executors, or if it contains a variation of executors, the former grant must be revoked.

1   *Re Adamson* (1827) July.

13.25   For forms of oath, see Nos. 174 ff.

Orders for provision from estate of deceased

13.26   Section 19 of the Inheritance (Provision for Family and Dependants) Act 1975[1] provides that where an order is made under the Act, then, for all purposes, including the purposes of the enactments relating to inheritance or capital transfer tax, the will or the law relating to intestacy, or both, as the case may be, shall have effect, and shall be deemed to have had effect as from the death of the deceased, subject to the provisions of the order. A memorandum of every order made under the Act (other than an order made under s. 15(1)) must be endorsed on, or permanently annexed to, the grant of probate or administration (see paras. **16.48** ff., post).

1 See p. 819, post. The Act of 1975 applies in relation to deaths on or after 1 April 1976; for deaths prior to that date similar provision is contained in s. 3 of the Inheritance (Family Provision) Act 1938, as amended, which also applies in relation to orders made under ss. 26–28 of the Matrimonial Causes Act 1965.

13.27   Accordingly, upon an application for a second or subsequent grant, in a case where an order under the Act[1] has been made, the memorandum of the order annexed to, and the notation relating thereto on, the original grant must form part of any second or subsequent grant.

1 Or, in respect of a death occurring before 1 April 1976, an order made under the Inheritance (Family Provision) Act 1938, as amended, or under ss. 26–28 of the Matrimonial Causes Act 1965, including an order dismissing an application.

13.28   Where there is a will an office copy is obtained, which must include a memorandum of the order made under the Act, for marking by the applicant and the commissioner for oaths. A copy of both the will and the memorandum will be annexed to the new grant. A notation of the memorandum is made in the margin of the second or subsequent grant in the same form as in the original grant.

13.29   If the alternative procedure of marking the original will, or marking the copy annexed to the original grant, is adopted, the copy memorandum must be included in every case[1].

1 Registrar's Direction (1950) 19 June.

13.30   Where the original grant was made in a district registry an office copy of the will and memorandum must be obtained from the district registry.

13.31   As to applications generally under the Inheritance (Provision for Family and Dependants) Act 1975, see Chap. 41.

Administration 'de bonis non'

Administration 'de bonis non'

13.32   When an administrator dies, leaving part of his deceased's estate unadministered, if the whole estate vested beneficially in the administrator, the grant de bonis non must be made to his personal representative[1]. If no personal representative has been appointed, one must be constituted for this purpose.

1 NCPR 22(4).

13.33   But if there are other persons beneficially entitled who are still alive, they are entitled to the grant in preference to the personal representative of the deceased administrator, unless otherwise directed by a district judge or registrar[1].

1 NCPR 27(5).

13.34 Forms of oath for administration de bonis non, Nos. 169 ff.

Entitlement to grant where spouse survived

13.35 When deciding by whom application for a grant de bonis non should be made, regard must be had to the beneficial entitlement to the estate, for, by NCPR 22, priority of right to a grant is given to persons taking a beneficial interest. In particular, where the intestate was survived by a spouse who has subsequently died, it is necessary to determine whether the grant should be taken by the personal representative of the spouse, or by the issue or other kin of the intestate.

13.36 Under NCPR 22(4), any living kin taking a beneficial interest in the estate are to be preferred to the personal representative of a spouse who has died *without taking a beneficial interest in the whole estate as ascertained at the time of the application for the grant.* Thus, the personal representative of the spouse is entitled to the grant in priority to all other persons either: (a) if the amount of the residuary estate (other than the personal chattels) is such that the whole accrues to the spouse in or towards satisfaction of his or her charge, under s. 46(1) of the Administration of Estates Act 1925 of £125,000 or £200,000[1] (plus interest) according to the circumstances (see para. **6.37**, ante); or (b) if the intestate left no kin within the classes which may share with the spouse in the residuary estate (see tables in para. **6.29**, ante).

1 Where the deceased died on or after 1 December 1993. See para. **6.29**, ante for relevant figures in respect of earlier dates of death.

13.37 If the amount of the residuary estate (other than the personal chattels) is more than sufficient to satisfy the statutory charge, any living person within the classes taking a beneficial interest is preferred to the personal representative of the spouse on an application for a grant (see NCPR 22(4)).

Changes in valuation

13.38 Strictly, the question whether the spouse's statutory charge absorbs the whole known distributable estate (other than personal chattels) is determined by reference to the values prevailing not at the death of the intestate but at the time of payment or appropriation. The earlier values are normally accepted in the probate registries on the footing that any significant change is unlikely, but a substantial change in the value of an asset may change the answer to the question, with appropriate consequences on the application for the grant.

13.39 In cases of doubt, the practitioner may be asked to submit a note showing the basis on which it is claimed that the spouse was (or was not) entitled to the whole of the known estate[1].

1 Secretary's Circular, 9 January 1962.

Death of spouse and all other persons sharing

13.40 Where the surviving spouse and all other kin entitled to share in the estate have died, the personal representative of the spouse is, by virtue of NCPR 22(4), entitled to a grant de bonis non in priority to the personal representatives of the other kin[1]. But if it is sworn that the spouse's beneficial interest in the estate has been entirely satisfied, administration de bonis non may be granted to the personal representative of one of the other kin without clearing off the spouse's personal representative[2].

1 Registrar's Direction (1955) 7 November.
2 Registrar's Direction (1971) 15 November.

To representative of child etc.

13.41   Where the death occurred after 1925, administration de bonis non will not be granted to the personal representative of a child or other beneficiary in whom the estate vested on the statutory trusts arising under the intestacy of the deceased, unless such beneficiary attained an absolutely vested interest in the estate by attaining the age of majority or marrying under that age (Administration of Estates Act 1925, s. 47(2) and (3)[1]); otherwise the grant will be made to the person becoming entitled to the estate[2].

1 See pp. 755, 759, post.
2 *Re Peacock* (1937) 12 March.

When heir-at-law died after 1925, an infant

13.42   Section 51(3) of the Administration of Estates Act 1925[1] (unmarried infant dying after 1925 and being entitled to a vested interest in freehold land deemed to have an entailed interest) applies to notional settlements arising under intestacies, as well as to actual dispositions in a will or deed[2].

1 See p. 761, post.
2 *Re Taylor, Pullan v Taylor* [1931] 2 Ch 242.

13.43   Where, in an intestacy prior to 1926, land had vested in an heir at law who died after 1925, an infant, it was held that by virtue of this subsection the land vested in the next heir to the intestate. Letters of administration had been granted to the widow, who died leaving real estate only unadministered. The grant de bonis non was made to the next heir as 'in the events that have happened the heir at law of the intestate'[1].

1 *Re Hirst* (1938) 27 June.

Particular cases

Resealed grant

13.44   Where a Colonial grant has been resealed in England, on the death of the person to whom the grant was issued, an English grant de bonis non may be obtained. Such a grant is made in accordance with the normal rules and principles applicable according to the place where the deceased died domiciled. For practice in making grants where the deceased died domiciled out of England and Wales, see Chap. 12.

13.45   The resealing of Scottish confirmations and Northern Irish grants in England and Wales, and vice versa, was abolished by the Administration of Estates Act 1971[1] and a grant or confirmation issued in that part of the United Kingdom in which the deceased was domiciled and containing a statement of such domicile, is effective to make title to the estate of the deceased situate in any part of the United Kingdom. This applies to grants and confirmations issued before as well as after the commencement of the Administration of Estates Act 1971.

1 See p. 799, post.

13.46   If, in special circumstances, on the death of the person to whom confirmation was granted in Scotland or a grant was made in Northern Ireland, it is desired to obtain further representation in England and Wales rather than in the country of domicile, the grant will be in respect of the estate in England and Wales only, and will be limited until further representation is granted in the country of domicile: see also para. **12.23**, ante.

Administration, with draft or copy of will annexed, 'de bonis non'

13.47   On the death of an executor who has taken probate of a will as contained in a draft, copy, or reconstruction of the will, without appointing an executor, or of the grantee of letters of administration, with such draft or copy etc. annexed, leaving part of the testator's estate unadministered, letters of administration, with the draft or copy etc. of the will annexed, de bonis non may be granted in accordance with the normal practice, it being again shown by affidavit that the original will has not been found. But if the original will has been found, application should be made for a cessate grant (see paras. **13.85** ff., post).

For the use and benefit of mentally incapable person

13.48   If the person entitled to a grant of administration (with or without will) de bonis non is mentally incapable of managing his affairs, administration de bonis non may be granted for his use and benefit to the persons to whom an original grant would have been made in the same circumstances. The incapacity of the person for whose use the grant is made should be established in the same manner as in the case of an original grant (see paras. **11.225** ff., ante).

Sole grantee becomes incapable

13.49   As to the practice where the sole grantee becomes incapable of managing his affairs, see paras. **17.64** ff., post.

Limited administration (with or without will) 'de bonis non'

13.50   If, on the death of an executor who has taken probate, or of an administrator who has taken administration, limited to a particular part of the estate, that part of the estate is left unadministered, limited letters of administration (with or without will) of the unadministered estate of the deceased will be granted to parties having the same kind of interest as that which the court recognised in the original grant.

Limited administration (with will) 'de bonis non' to legatee

13.51   When an executor has proved his testator's will, and has administered the estate with the exception of a legacy which has been set apart and remains invested in the original testator's name, the court, on the death of the executor and the breaking of the chain of executorship, with the consent or upon the citation of the

residuary legatees, has granted administration (with the will annexed) de bonis non
to the legatee, limited to his legacy[1].

1 *Re Steadman's Goods* (1828) 2 Hag Ecc 59; *Re Biou's Goods, Indigent Blind School and
Westminster Hospital v Flack* (1843) 3 Curt 739 at 741. But see also *Re Watts' Goods* (1860) 1 Sw &
Tr 538 at 540; also *Re Lady Somerset's Goods* (1867) LR 1 P & D 350 (limited grant will not, save
for very strong reasons, be given to a person entitled to a general grant).

13.52   Under the present practice, however, except by order under s. 116 of the
Supreme Court Act 1981[1], the court will not grant limited administration without
the renunciation or citation of persons entitled to a general grant in priority to the
applicant (see NCPR 51(b)).

1 See p. 845, post. For practice on application for such an order, see paras. **25.91** ff., post.

Limited administration 'de bonis non' in respect of legal proceedings

13.53   When the grantee of administration limited to institute or defend legal proceedings dies before the termination of the proceedings, he is considered to have left
the estate unadministered, and a further grant may be made to another person by
order under s. 116 of the Supreme Court Act 1981 (see also paras. **11.328** ff., ante).

Administration 'de bonis non', as distinguished from 'cessate'

13.54   If the donor of a power of attorney, for whose use and benefit administration
has been granted, should die in the lifetime of the attorney administrator, the subsequent grant will be a grant of administration de bonis non and not a cessate grant.

13.55   If, however, the attorney should die in the lifetime of the donor of the
power, a further grant made to another attorney is a cessate grant.

13.56   If a person who is incapable of managing his affairs, for whose use and
benefit a grant has been made, should die in the lifetime of the administrator, a
further grant will be a grant de bonis non; whereas, on the death of the administrator,
a further grant made during the lifetime of the incapable person is a cessate grant.

13.57   As to cessate grants, see paras. **13.81** ff., post.

Settled land

13.58   Where necessary, a grant de bonis non may be made limited to settled land.

Practice in grants 'de bonis non'

Where granted

13.59   Grants de bonis non, and all other second or subsequent grants, may be
extracted from the registry from which the original grant issued or from any other
probate registry.

Oath

13.60   It must be sworn in the oath leading to every grant de bonis non whether
there is (still) any minority or life interest under the will or intestacy and, if the

deceased died on or after 1 January 1926, whether there was land vested in the deceased which was settled previously to his death (and not by his will) and which remained settled land notwithstanding his death[1].

1 NCPR 8(4) and (3).

13.61 If a minority or a life interest still remains, the grant de bonis non must normally be made to a trust corporation[1], with or without an individual, or to not less than two individuals (Supreme Court Act 1981, s. 114(2)[2]).

1 As to grants to trust corporations, see Chap. 9.
2 See p. 844, post.

13.62 Where it is sought to obtain a grant to two individuals not equally entitled, the requirements of NCPR 25 as to the joinder of the second grantee must be considered, as in the case of an application for a first grant. See 'Second administrator', paras. **7.12–7.16**, ante.

13.63 The form of oath differs from that for the first grant in an estate in the following respects:

(a)   Full particulars must be given of the former grant; and the date of the death of the grantee whose death necessitates the grant de bonis non must be sworn to.
(b)   If the original grant was one of probate, the oath must show how the chain of executorship is broken (see also paras. **13.04** and **13.05**, ante).
(c)   The oath should show that part of the estate remains unadministered.

13.64 Where the grant is required for making title only, it may be sworn that the grantee died 'without having completed the administration of the estate'.

13.65 Forms of oath, Nos. 169 ff.

Amount of estate

13.66 The administrator will swear to administer the unadministered estate, and the amount of estate sworn to in the oath will be the value of what remains unadministered at the time.

Letters of administration (with will) 'de bonis non': marking of will or copy

13.67 In all cases of administration (with the will annexed) de bonis non, the applicant, when he swears the oath, must normally swear to and mark the original will, the probate copy annexed to the previous grant, or an office copy of the will issued by the registry in which the original is deposited. An unsealed facsimile copy not issued by the registry is not acceptable unless the district judge or registrar gives leave under NCPR 10(2). Where a copy of the will is marked, the oath should state that the document so marked contains an official copy (or facsimile copy, where the district judge's or registrar's leave has been obtained) of the last will and testament of the testator.

13.68 It should be noted that if the probate copy of the will annexed to the former grant is marked by the applicant, this necessitates its being retained permanently in the registry. It is therefore usually more convenient to bespeak an office copy of the will for marking.

13.69   In particular, where a de bonis non grant is necessary because of the incapacity of the original grantee, the probate copy should not be marked, as the grant may be required in the event of the recovery, or of the death, of the incapable person.

13.70   If the administrator wishes to swear to the original will, he must attend in the registry where the will is deposited, and swear the oath before one of the officers authorised to administer oaths in that registry. In this case the original will must be obtained and a fee of 25p is payable for inspecting it. In addition, a fee of £2 is charged for administering an oath to each deponent, and 50p for marking each exhibit[1].

1 NC Probate Fees Order 1981, Fees 7 and 10.

Foreign will

13.71   Where the former administrator swore to a notarial copy of the will, the applicant for a second grant may swear to and mark the copy already filed, a fresh notarial copy, the copy annexed to the former grant, or an office copy of the document proved in this court[1], or, if the district judge or registrar gives leave under NCPR 10(2), a facsimile copy.

1 Registrar's Direction (1927) 8 December.

Engrossment of will

13.72   In the case of a will proved at a district registry before the introduction of photography, where application for the de bonis non grant is made at that registry, the probate copy for annexing to the de bonis non grant will wherever possible be made by the photographic process (or other process which produces a facsimile copy). If the original will is unsuitable for facsimile reproduction (see paras. **4.224–4.226**, ante) an engrossment will be made in the registry, or may be supplied by the practitioner if he prefers[1].

1 Registrar's Direction (1952) 18 February.

13.73   On an application at the Principal Registry, if the will has been proved and registered at a district registry, no engrossment is required, but a photographic copy is made, in the Registry, of the document sworn to by the applicant.

Inland Revenue account

13.74   For the appropriate form of account, when required, for use on application for a grant de bonis non, see para. **8.36**, ante.

13.75   Copies of Inland Revenue accounts filed at the Capital Taxes Office on obtaining primary grants are not supplied by that Office for the purpose of completing any further account required on a second or subsequent grant. It is necessary only to make reference to the estate remaining unadministered.

13.76   For practice as to submission of the account to the Capital Taxes Office, and certificate as to payment of tax, see paras. **8.37–8.39**, ante.

Papers required

13.77 The practitioner lodges the oath and Inland Revenue account (if required: see Chap. 8) at the Receiver's Department at the Principal Registry or at any district probate registry or sub-registry. If the papers are lodged at the Principal Registry or at a district probate registry other than that from which the previous grant was extracted, the previous grant, or an office copy thereof, must also be lodged. Unless 'marked' by the applicant (see paras. **13.67–13.70**, ante), the former grant or office copy will be returned with the new grant.

13.78 See para. **2.09**, ante, as to lodging papers by post.

Fee for grant

13.79 The fee for a de bonis non grant is £2 in all cases[1].

1 NC Probate Fees Order 1981, Fee 3(e).

13.80 This fee does not include the fee for a copy of the former grant, or of the will for marking, where these are required.

Cessate grants

Nature

13.81 A further grant, commonly called a cessate grant, may be made upon the effluxion of the time or the accomplishment of the event or contingency pending which a limited grant (see Chap. 11) has been made.

13.82 A cessate grant is also made upon the death of the surviving attorney or guardian or other grantee[1] where the grant was made for the use and benefit of a person whom the grantee represented, and was limited in duration, e.g. until that person should obtain a grant. Upon the death of the person for whose use and benefit the grant was made, a subsequent grant is a grant de bonis non (see para. **13.54**, ante).

1 See NCPR 26 and paras. **7.40–7.47**, ante, as to the possible appointment of a substituted administrator upon the death of the first of two grantees, in cases where a minority or a life interest arises under the will or intestacy, by means of which the necessity for a cessate grant might be obviated.

Distinction between cessate and 'de bonis non' grants

13.83 Although a cessate grant is usually required only where the deceased's estate has not been fully administered, it is distinguished from a grant de bonis non, as being a re-grant of the whole of the deceased's estate.

13.84 The estate, however, to be sworn in the oath is that which, at the time of making the application for the second grant, remains unadministered.

Discovery of lost will, or more authentic copy

13.85 When probate has been granted of a reconstruction of a will, or of a will as contained in a copy or draft, limited until the original or a more authentic copy be proved, if the original will or a more authentic copy of this is discovered the grant does not cease until formal steps are taken to prove the document which has been discovered.

13.86   If the document first proved does not correspond in all respects with the original will it may be desirable for the grantee to apply for a cessate grant, but if neither the grantee nor any other person is willing to take the requisite action it is considered by the district judges and registrars that they cannot insist upon it[1].

1 Registrar's Direction (1971) 21 April.

13.87   On an application for a cessate grant, the oath should state that probate of the will of the deceased, as contained in a copy thereof, was granted at, etc., on the   day of   , to A B, limited until the original will or a more authentic copy be proved, and should recite the discovery of the original will or the more authentic copy (as the case may be). If in the meantime the grantee has died, the will may be proved by the person next entitled.

Death of executor for life or other limited period

13.88   Where an executor appointed for his life takes probate, the grant ceases finally on his death, being distinguishable from an ordinary grant of probate which may retain its effectiveness, by chain of executorship, in spite of the death of the grantee. An executor substituted in the will at the decease of the executor for life may take a cessate grant of probate. For form of oath, see No. 78.

13.89   If an executor who was appointed for a limited period other than his life takes probate, the grant ceases upon the expiration of such period, and the substituted executor, if one was appointed by the will, may obtain cessate probate.

13.90   Probate granted to an executrix 'during widowhood' ceases on her remarriage, and a cessate grant of probate may be made to the executor substituted. The oath should state that: 'The probate etc., granted at etc., to A, has ceased and expired by reason of her having intermarried with B on the   day of   '.

13.91   If no executor is substituted in the will, administration (with will) is granted to the person next in order of priority under NCPR 20 (see Chap. 5).

Grant for use of incapable executor

13.92   When administration (with the will annexed) has been granted for the use and benefit of an incapable executor and it is limited 'during his incapacity', it ceases on his recovery; he may then take probate of the will.

13.93   If the administrator should die before the recovery of a mentally incapable executor, further administration (with the will annexed) may be granted to some other person for the use and benefit of the executor, the latter's incapacity being established in the same manner as on the occasion of the first grant. The oath should recite

'That on the   day of   19   letters of administration (with the said will annexed) of the estate of the said deceased were granted at the principal (*or as the case may be*) registry, to A B the residuary legatee named in the said will (*or as the case may be*) for the use and benefit of C D the sole executor therein named and during his incapacity. That the said A B died on the   day of   19   whereby the said letters of administration (with the said will annexed) have ceased and expired. That the said C D is still by reason of mental incapacity incapable of managing his affairs.'

13.94 If the grant had issued, under the previous Non-Contentious Probate Rules, for the use and benefit of an executor who was *physically* incapable of managing his affairs, on the death of the administrator before the recovery of the physically incapable executor, the executor may now appoint an attorney to apply for a further grant for his use and benefit (see paras. **11.31** ff., ante).

13.95 If the grant was for the use and benefit of the incapable person and was limited 'until further representation be granted' it does not cease upon the recovery of the incapable person but continues until such time as a further grant issues to the recovered person (or to somebody else).

13.96 If the incapable executor should die without recovering his capacity, administration (with the will annexed) de bonis non may be granted to the person thereupon entitled to it.

Grant for use of minor executor

13.97 Administration (with the will annexed) which has been granted to guardians or other persons for the use of an executor during his minority ceases when the executor attains his majority, and probate may be granted to the executor. For form of oath, see No. 79.

13.98 Such a grant also ceases by reason of the grantee's death during the executor's minority, and in that case cessate letters of administration (with will) may be granted to new guardians or other persons entitled thereto. See paras. **11.137** and **11.138**, ante.

13.99 In such cases, the oath must give respectively (a) the date upon which the executor came of age, or (b) the date of the grantee's death.

Application by donor of power of attorney for direct grant

13.100 Where administration (with or without will) has been granted to an attorney of the executor, or other person entitled to a grant, the latter may at any time apply for and obtain a cessate grant to himself, whereupon the limited grant ceases. Form of oath, No. 80.

Death of attorney or of donor of power of attorney

13.101 A grant to an attorney for the use and benefit of the executor or other person entitled ceases on the death of the attorney, and a cessate grant may be made to another attorney, or to the person entitled himself[1].

1 In *Re Barton's Goods* [1898] P 11, on the death of an administrator who was the attorney of one of the persons entitled to the estate, cessate administration was granted to the attorney of another person entitled, on notice to the donor of the original power of attorney. (Although described in the report as a grant de bonis non, the grant was in fact a cessate grant.)

13.102 The oath must include particulars of the former grant, and the death of the attorney. Form of oath, No. 136.

13.103   But if the executor, or other person, should die in the lifetime of the attorney administrator and before the administration of the estate has been completed, the grant determines, and a further grant is a grant de bonis non: see para. **13.54**, ante.

Foreign domicile—cessate grants

13.104   Where a grant has been made by order of the district judge or registrar to the attorney of a person entrusted by the court of domicile, or of the person beneficially entitled to the estate by the law of the domicile, limited until further representation be granted, and the donor of the power later applies for a direct grant, an affidavit must be filed showing:

(a)   that the order entrusting is still in force, or
(b)   that the person concerned is still beneficially entitled to the estate,

and a further district judge's or registrar's order will be necessary[1].

1   Registrar's Direction (1972) 20 November.

Grant limited to legal proceedings

13.105   Administration limited to taking or defending legal proceedings ceases on the termination of the suit, or on the prior death of the grantee. Form of oath for a cessate grant, No. 137.

Administration (with or without will) for use of minor beneficiary

13.106   A grant of administration or administration (with will) which has been made to parents or guardians (or a parent or guardian and co-administrator) for the use and benefit of a minor beneficially entitled ceases on the latter attaining full age, and he may then obtain a cessate grant of administration, or administration (with will) as the case may be. Forms of oath, Nos. 135 and 168.

13.107   If the grant was made for the use and benefit of two or more minors sharing in the estate, it ceases when the first of them attains full age: the latter may thereupon take a cessate grant, a co-administrator normally being necessary because of the continued minority interests. As to joinder of a co-administrator, see Chap. 7.

13.108   If one of the administrators should die before majority is attained by any one of the minors, application may be made, under s. 114(4) of the Supreme Court Act 1981[1], for the appointment of an additional administrator (see NCPR 26: for practice see paras. **7.40**–**7.42**, ante).

1   See p. 845, post.

13.109   If the sole minor, or all the minors (where there are several) die before attaining his or their majority, the grant made for their use and benefit is dead, and the form of the subsequent grant is de bonis non. (See, however, paras. **6.157** and **13.41**, ante, as to the divesting of their interests.)

Grant taken by parent or guardian in representative character also ceases

13.110   When parents or guardians or other persons take administration (with will) or administration for the use and benefit of minors limited until one of them shall attain his majority, and afterwards, in their representative character, take administration of the estate of another person, the later grant will be similarly limited and both grants cease as soon as one of the minors attains his majority.

Administration to person on recovering from incapacity

13.111   When administration has been granted to a person authorised by the Court of Protection, or to some other person, for the use of a person who is incapable of managing his affairs limited during the incapacity of that person, the grant ceases on the recovery of that person, or the death of the administrator; and a cessate grant may be made in the one case to the formerly incapable person himself, and in the other to a person authorised by a further order of the Court of Protection (see paras. **11.218** ff., ante), or some other person, for the use of the incapable person (as the case may require).

13.112   In the latter case, where the original grant was made to a person other than the person authorised by the Court of Protection or an attorney acting under a registered enduring power of attorney, evidence must again be adduced as to the incapacity of the person for whose use and benefit administration is to be granted.

13.113   The recovery of the incapable person must be proved (i) where administration has been granted to a person authorised by an order of the Court of Protection, by the production of the order of that Court determining the proceedings, or (ii) where administration has been granted to some other person, by an affidavit of the doctor. Unless the consent of the person who obtained the limited grant is lodged, evidence will be required that notice of the application for a cessate grant has been given to him.

13.114   If the grant for the use and benefit of the incapable person was limited until further representation be granted, it does not cease on the recovery of the formerly incapable person. The recovered person may apply for a grant himself, supported by evidence as to his recovery as in the preceding paragraph, and the limited grant ceases on the issue of the new grant.

13.115   If the incapable person should die, the administration granted for his use is also dead, and administration de bonis non will be granted to the person entitled to the grant, e.g. if he was the only person entitled to the estate, to his personal representative.

Practice on application for cessate grant

13.116   The practice in obtaining cessate grants is, except where otherwise stated, similar to that in obtaining grants de bonis non, as to which, see paras. **13.59** ff., ante.

13.117   The oath must in all cases recite the particulars of the former grant and the circumstances of its cessation. The applicant should swear that he will administer all the estate, but the amount to be inserted in the oath is that remaining unadministered.

Fee on grant

13.118   The fee for a cessate grant is £2 in all cases[1].

1 NC Probate Fees Order 1981, Fee 3(e).

Double probate

13.119   Where a number of executors have been appointed in a will, and probate has been granted to one or some, but not all, of them, power to apply for a like grant is reserved to such other of the executors as at that time have not renounced probate.

13.120   Probate may not be granted to more than four persons in respect of the same part of the estate of a deceased person[1].

1   Supreme Court Act 1981, s. 114(1) (see p. 844, post).

13.121   It follows that, where probate has been granted to four executors, any remaining executors can take up their powers only as vacancies occur among the acting executors.

13.122   Upon application for probate by an executor to whom power has been reserved, the grant is called 'double probate' and it runs concurrently with the first grant if any of the first grantees are still living. It confers the same rights as an original grant.

13.123   Where a grant of probate has been made to two executors, power being reserved to another executor, and the acting executors have both died, and a codicil has since been found, the executor to whom power was reserved may take a grant of double probate of the will together with the codicil.

13.124   Where a will and codicil had been proved by two executors and one had since died, a grant of probate of another codicil, since found, can be made to the surviving executor. Where probate of a will was granted to two executors, a codicil was subsequently found, but both executors had since died, a grant of probate of the codicil was made to the executor of the survivor of the deceased executors[1].

1   *Re Roberts* (1934, unreported).

13.125   As to the practice in cases where the proving executor becomes incapable of managing his affairs, see paras. **17.64** ff., post.

13.126   As to power reserved and double probate in respect of settled land grants, see paras. **10.91** and **10.92**, ante.

Practice

13.127   Double probate may be extracted from the Principal Registry or from any other probate registry: application may be made by post[1].

1   See paras. **2.09** ff., ante.

13.128   A double probate is general in its terms, but the amount of the estate included in the oath to lead the grant is that only which remains unadministered.

Oath

13.129   The oath must give particulars of the former grant, and show that power was reserved to the other executors and, where probate was originally granted to four executors, that a vacancy or vacancies have occurred by death, giving the name and date of death of the executor or executors who have died since the date of the first grant. For forms of oath, see Nos. 74 and 75.

Will or probate to be marked

13.130 The executor may swear to and mark either the original will, or the copy annexed to the first grant of probate (provided, in the latter case for practical reasons, that all the proving executors are dead); or, as is the usual practice, he may swear to an office copy of the will or, with the district judge's or registrar's leave, a facsimile copy of the will. See also paras. **13.67–13.70**, ante.

Renouncing executor permitted to prove will

13.131 An executor who has renounced probate may, in certain circumstances, be permitted, by order of a district judge or registrar, to retract his renunciation (NCPR 37(3): see paras. **15.60** ff., post).

13.132 Where an executor who has renounced probate is permitted to retract his renunciation and prove the will, a notation of the subsequent probate is made upon the original grant of probate or administration (with will): see also paras. **15.69** ff., post.

Photographic copy or engrossment, Inland Revenue account etc.

13.133 For practice as to photographic copy or engrossment of will, Inland Revenue account, office copy of former grant, etc., see 'Practice in grants "de bonis non" ' (paras. **13.59–13.80**, ante), which applies also in relation to double probates.

13.134 If in exceptional cases the applicant for a grant of double probate finds it impossible to complete the Inland Revenue account without information as to the contents of the account filed on the original application the matter should be referred to the Secretary of the Principal Registry of the Family Division[1].

1 Secretary's Circular, 18 August 1952.

Fee for grant

13.135 The fee for a grant of double probate is now £2 in all cases[1].

1 NC Probate Fees Order 1981, Fee 3(e).

CHAPTER 14

Right of the court to select an administrator—'Commorientes'

Summary

Right of the court to select an administrator

14.01   Under certain conditions, the court is called upon to select an administrator.

(a)   Where necessary or expedient, it will exercise the power conferred upon it by s. 116 of the Supreme Court Act 1981, to pass over, by reason of special circumstances, the person entitled to the grant.

(b)   Where there is a dispute between persons with an equal title to a grant, the matter may be decided on summons by a district judge of the Principal Registry or the registrar of the district probate registry in which the application for the grant is being, or is to be, made (NCPR 27(6) and 2(1)).

Persons entitled passed over under section 116 of the Supreme Court Act 1981

14.02   Section 116 of the Supreme Court Act 1981[1] provides as follows:

'(1) If by reason of any special circumstances it appears to the High Court to be necessary or expedient to appoint as administrator[2] some person other than the person who, but for this section, would in accordance with probate rules have been entitled to the grant, the court may in its discretion appoint as administrator such person as it thinks expedient.

(2) Any grant of administration under this section may be limited in any way the court thinks fit.'

1   This section replaces, as from 1 January 1982, the former provisions of s. 162(1) of the Supreme Court of Judicature (Consolidation) Act 1925, and s. 73 of the Court of Probate Act 1857; the new section applies to all cases irrespective of the date of death of the deceased.

2   The court is empowered to apply this section of the Act to cases of testacy as well as intestacy, as 'administration' includes administration with the will annexed (Supreme Court Act 1981, s. 128 (p. 847, post)).

14.03   Applications for grants under this section should, whatever the amount of the estate, be made ex parte to a district judge of the Principal Registry or the registrar of the district probate registry at which the application for the grant is to be made[1]. In the Principal Registry the affidavit (and any other supporting document or documents) should be lodged in the Probate Department.

1   NCPR 52.

14.04   Where it is sought to pass over persons entitled who cannot be traced, in favour of a person having a lower title, a citation served by advertisement may be required unless there are special circumstances (e.g. the small value of the estate) justifying the invocation of the power set out above.

14.05   The district judges and registrars are not in favour of the issue of citations by persons whose only real interest in the estate depends upon the death of an untraced citee (e.g. an application by the kin to pass over a missing spouse who, if alive, is entitled to the whole estate). In such cases it is advisable to apply for an order under s. 116 of the Supreme Court Act 1981. The district judges and registrars may require (i) the insertion of an advertisement for the missing person, and (ii) an indemnity bond[1] by an insurance company, unless circumstances render these precautions unnecessary or impracticable.

1   Indemnity bonds are issued by some insurance companies upon payment of an agreed premium.
   Where an indemnity bond is required the insurers have requested that they be provided with a copy of the affidavit used to lead to the order made under s. 116. It is the solicitor's responsibility, and not the registry's, to provide the company with the copy affidavit (Registrar's Circular, 28 November 1980).

14.06   The issue of citations by persons (e.g. creditors or legatees) who have an immediate interest in the estate is not affected by the above[1].

1   Registrar's Direction (1957) 19 February.

14.07   For the practice in respect of applications under s. 116 of the Supreme Court Act 1981, and instances of the circumstances in which orders are made, see paras. **25.91** ff., post: as to citations, see Chap. 24.

Selection from amongst persons equally entitled

14.08   When there are several claimants for administration, the court is called upon to make a selection from among the applicants. If the interest of one claimant is denied by another, the dispute may have to be resolved by an interest action in the Chancery Division: see Chap. 27.

14.09   By NCPR 27(4) to (8) it is provided:

'(4) A grant of administration may be made to any person entitled thereto without notice to other persons entitled in the same degree.

(5) Unless a district judge or registrar otherwise directs, administration shall be granted to a person of full age entitled thereto in preference to a guardian of a minor, and to a living person entitled thereto in preference to the personal representative of a deceased person.

(6) A dispute between persons entitled to a grant in the same degree shall be brought by summons before a district judge or registrar.

(7) The issue of a summons under this rule in the Principal Registry or a district probate registry shall be notified forthwith to the registry in which the index of pending grant applications is maintained.

(8) If the issue of a summons under this rule is known to the district judge or registrar, he shall not allow any grant to be sealed until such summons is finally disposed of.'

Dispute between executors

14.10   In regard to executors, the court cannot exercise any discretion as to granting or refusing probate, except on the ground of some legal disability recognised and allowed at common law[1].

1   *Smethurst v Tomlin and Bankes* (1861) 2 Sw & Tr 143 at 146; *Re Drawmer* (1913) 108 LT 732.

14.11   One executor cannot dispute the title of another to probate, either on the ground of his insolvency, or even upon a conviction for felony. The testator's choice is considered to overrule all such objections.

14.12   An executor may object or refuse to be joined with his co-executor, if the latter be incapable of managing his affairs; and the court will exclude the latter from the probate, if the objection be proved[1], but power is reserved to him on regaining his capacity; see also 'Other persons having equal right', paras. **11.211** ff., ante.

1   *Evans v Tyler* (1849) 2 Rob Eccl 128 at 131.

14.13   If there are more than four executors who wish to apply for probate at the same time, the dispute between them may be brought by summons before a district judge or registrar under NCPR 27(6).

Dispute between other persons

14.14   In other cases, where the question is that of the relative fitness of parties who are equally entitled to administration, or administration (with will), application may be made to a district judge of the Principal Registry or to the district probate registrar of the district probate registry where the grant application is being, or is proposed to be, made, on summons, supported by affidavits setting out the interest of each party and the grounds upon which the claims to the grant are based and opposed. This type of contest arises only between parties who have equal priority of entitlement to a grant: each must be in a position to take the grant which he seeks to have disallowed to the other. As to practice in relation to such summonses, see paras. **25.193** ff., post.

Considerations acted upon

14.15   The following paragraphs show what considerations have influenced the court in the exercise of its discretion, having regard to the benefit of the estate and to that of the persons interested in the property[1].

1   *Warwick v Greville* (1809) 1 Phillim 123 at 125.

Grounds of objection

14.16   Where objections exist against one of the parties applying for a grant of administration, the court will not compel an unobjectionable person to become a joint administrator with the former[1].

1   *Bell v Timiswood* (1812) 2 Phillim 22.

14.17   Among the grounds of objection are badness of character, bankruptcy or insolvency[1], or extreme ill-health; and if these grounds be satisfactorily established, the court will exclude the objectionable applicant, and grant administration to the other claimant.

1 *Bell v Timiswood* (1812) 2 Phillim 22.

Incompatible interest

14.18   Should one of the applicants have an interest incompatible with the due administration of the estate, the court will exclude him.

14.19   Where a question was likely to arise between the administrators of the estate and a son of one of the applicants respecting the validity of a gift, the court refused to make a grant to the applicant in question on the ground that the claims of the estate might not be sufficiently strongly asserted by the father against his son[1].

1 *Budd v Silver* (1813) 2 Phillim 115.

14.20   Where the persons entitled to the grant, a brother and sister and the children of a predeceasing brother of the intestate, could not agree as to one or more of them acting, the persons entitled being in scattered parts of the country, and the applicants being at the place where the assets were concentrated, a grant was made to two strangers in order to avoid possible litigation and delay[1]. In the case of such disputes this is often the course preferred by the court, a suitable neutral grantee being appointed under the discretionary power given by s. 116 of the Supreme Court Act 1981 (see p. 845, post).

1 *Re Morgans* (1931) 145 LT 392.

14.21   The court would not join a married woman, when, by so doing, it might have defeated a trust created for her by the testator, by giving her control of the property in question, which she and her husband might have dissipated[1].

1 *Dampier and Dampier v Colson* (1812) 2 Phillim 54.

14.22   A next-of-kin, being also a legatee, has been preferred to another next-of-kin who had no such additional interest[1].

1 *Dobson v Cracherode* (1756) 2 Lee 326.

Male formerly preferred to female

14.23   Where all other considerations were equal, the male was formerly preferred to the female[1]. This practice is no longer followed.

1 *Iredale v Ford and Bramworth* (1859) 1 Sw & Tr 305; *Leggatt v Leggatt* (1753) 1 Lee 348; *Chittenden v Knight* (1758) 2 Lee 559.

Majority of interest

14.24   But, above all, the practice has been to prefer the one who has the largest interest, or whom the majority of the other parties interested selects[1].

1 *Mercer v Morland* (1758) 2 Lee 499; *Williams v Wilkins* (1812) 2 Phillim 100 at 101; *Dampier and Dampier v Colson* (1812) 2 Phillim 54; *Jones v Rushall* (1856) 13 March; *Iredale v Ford and Bramworth* (1859) 1 Sw & Tr 305; *Elwes v Elwes* (1728) 2 Lee 573 at 575.

14.25   This is not, however, obligatory upon the court. Sir George Lee said:

> 'Though it is a good general rule to grant administration to the largest interest, yet that is only introduced by practice, and not by any positive law, and the court is not obliged to grant it to the largest interest'[1].

1   *Cardale v Harvey* (1752) 1 Lee 177 at 179, 180; *Re Stainton's Goods* (1871) LR 2 P & D 212.

Half blood—inferior rights

14.26   For many years prior to 1926[1] the next-of-kin of the half blood was considered to have an equal right to a grant with the next-of-kin of the whole blood, and where the first to apply for administration was a next-of-kin of the half blood, and a next-of-kin of the whole blood objected, the court declined to entertain the objection[2].

1   For very early cases in which the whole blood was preferred to the half blood, see *Mercer v Morland* (1758) 2 Lee 499; and *Stratton v Linton* (1861) 31 LJPM & A 48.
2   *Marsden v Simmons* (1896) 16 September.

14.27   But with the enactment of the Administration of Estates Act 1925 the whole blood was given prior right to a grant in the case of brothers and sisters and their issue, and in the case of uncles and aunts and their issue; and where a person dies intestate on or after 1 January 1953, leaving a surviving spouse but no issue, the rights and beneficial interests of brothers and sisters and their issue are confined to those of the whole blood[1].

1   See Administration of Estates Act 1925, s. 46(1)(i), p. 752, post.

Preference of creditors 'inter se'

14.28   Where creditors have contended inter se for administration (with will), or administration, the court has preferred one having a judgment debt[1], or a specialty debt, or a debt of a larger amount[2] than the other creditors can show.

1   *Lord Carpenter v Shelford* (1758) 2 Lee 502. So Dr Bettesworth ruled in *Standwick v Coussemaker* (1730) 4 November (Dr Cottrell's MS).
2   *Kearney v Whitaker* (1756) 2 Lee 324.

14.29   The court has preferred a simple contract creditor, having a large debt against the deceased, to a judgment creditor under the Judgments Act 1838, s. 18[1].

1   18 Halsbury's Statutes (3rd edn) 11; *Re Eustace's Goods, Ernest v Eustace* (1856) Dea & Sw 271 at 273.

14.30   The court has preferred the nominee of the bulk of the deceased's creditors or of the principal creditor to a single creditor[1].

1   *Re Smithson's Goods* (1866) 36 LJP & M 77.

'Prior petens' preferred

14.31   Subject to the above, the first applicant will be preferred, simply as such[1].

1   *Cordeux v Trasler* (1865) 4 Sw & Tr 48.

Commorientes

14.32 Where two or more persons in immediate succession to each other, whether under wills or on intestacy, have died in circumstances rendering it uncertain which of them survived the other or others, if the question of survivorship is relevant to the title to a grant (or grants) of representation, it is necessary for it to be considered by the probate registry before the issue of the grant.

Death before 1926

14.33 Where persons died in circumstances of such uncertainty before 1 January 1926 there was no legal presumption that one survived the other, or that they died at the same moment[1]: it was for the party asserting that one person survived another to establish this affirmatively, failing which representatlon to the estate of each commoriens was granted on the footing that the other had predeceased him or her.

1 *Underwood v Wing* (1855) 4 De GM & G 633; affd sub nom *Wing v Angrave* (1860) 8 HL Cas 183.

Death after 1925: general rule

14.34 Under s. 184 of the Law of Property Act 1925[1], in all cases where, on or after 1 January 1926, two or more persons have died in circumstances rendering it uncertain which of them survived the other or others, such deaths shall (subject to any order of the court[2]), for all purposes affecting the title to property, be presumed to have occurred in order of seniority, and accordingly the younger shall be deemed to have survived the elder.

1 See p. 744, post.
2 The meaning of the words in brackets is somewhat doubtful. They do not give the court a discretion to disregard the statutory presumption on the grounds that it would cause unfairness or injustice; but they enable the court to receive, and act on, evidence rebutting the presumption (*Re Lindop, Lee-Barber v Reynolds* [1942] Ch 377, [1942] 2 All ER 46).

14.35 In order that this section may apply there must be circumstances making it uncertain in what order the deaths occurred, but they need not have taken place in a common disaster[1].

1 *Hickman v Peacey* [1945] AC 304, [1945] 2 All ER 215.

14.36 If the circumstances of the deaths lead to uncertainty, in order to displace the presumption under s. 184 there must be evidence leading to a 'defined and warranted conclusion' that one died before the other[1].

1 *Re Bate, Chillingworth v Bate* [1947] 2 All ER 418, applying dictum of Viscount Simon LC in *Hickman v Peacey*, above.

14.37 *An exception to this general rule applies in the case of a husband and wife dying, in circumstances of such uncertainty, on or after 1 January 1953, where either or both died intestate*: see 'Death of husband and wife after 1952 intestate', paras. **14.41** ff., post.

Presumption avoided by terms of will

14.38 The statutory presumption may be excluded by contrary provisions contained in a will (e.g. by a clause declaring that in the event of the testator and his wife dying simultaneously or in such circumstances that there should be no evidence whether he or she died first, the latter should be deemed to have predeceased[1]). In such a case the terms of the will override the presumption under s. 184.

1 *Re Guggenheim Estate* (1941) Times, 20 June.

'Simultaneous' deaths

14.39   If no such testamentary provision has been made, the statutory presumption applies, even if it appears that the deaths were simultaneous[1]; for s. 184 of the Law of Property Act 1925 proceeds upon the footing that proof of simultaneous death is impossible, i.e. that if survivorship is not established, the only alternative is uncertainty[2].

1 *Hickman v Peacey*, para. **14.35**, ante.
2 Ibid., per Lord Simonds.

14.40   But where a will makes provision for the 'simultaneous deaths' of two persons, this term must be construed so as to give effect to the intentions of the testator, these being gathered from the language of the will read in the light of the circumstances in which it was made, and may generally be taken to mean deaths in such circumstances that the ordinary man would infer that they were simultaneous[1]. Where a husband and wife had each made provision by will for the death of the other 'preceding or coinciding with' that of the respective testator, and they both died in a ship which suddenly sank from an unascertained cause, it was held that their deaths did not 'coincide' within the meaning of the wills, and that the statutory presumption under s. 184 applied[2].

1 *Re Pringle, Baker v Matheson* [1946] Ch 124, [1946] 1All ER 88: death of two persons in an air raid by the same bomb held to have been simultaneous within the meaning of this term in the codicil of one of them.
2 *Re Rowland, Smith v Russell* [1963] Ch 1, [1962] 2 All ER 837.

Death of husband and wife after 1952 intestate

14.41   An exception to the presumption under s. 184 applies in the case of a husband and wife dying on or after 1 January 1953 in circumstances rendering it uncertain which of them survived the other, where one or both spouses died intestate. In such a case, if the elder of the spouses died intestate, then notwithstanding that, under s. 184, the other spouse is deemed to have survived him or her, s. 46 of the Administration of Estates Act 1925 (which governs the distribution of the residuary estate on an intestacy) is nevertheless to have effect as if the other spouse had not survived him or her[1]. *But note also the effect of s. 1 of the Law Reform (Succession) Act 1995 (see p. 900) by which, as respects an intestate dying on or after 1 January 1996, the husband or wife of the intestate has to survive the intestate by a period of 28 days, beginning with the day on which the intestate died, before acquiring a beneficial interest in the estate.*

1 Administration of Estates Act 1925, s. 46(3), added by Intestates' Estates Act 1952 (see p. 754, post).

14.42   If the younger of the spouses died intestate, the statutory presumption, under s. 184 of the Law of Property Act 1925, that the elder spouse predeceased him or her, remains operative. The combined effect of the provisions is thus that the estate of either spouse dying intestate in circumstances of uncertainty as to survivorship is to be distributed on the basis that he or she left no spouse surviving.

14.43 It should be noted that if either spouse leaves a will effectively disposing of the whole estate, the statutory presumption under s. 184 that the deaths occurred in order of seniority operates in relation to his estate; but where there is a partial intestacy, s. 46(3) of the Administration of Estates Act 1925 applies in relation to the estate undisposed of by the will[1]: such estate may thus fall to be distributed on a different basis from that applicable to the estate disposed of by the will. For example, if the husband (the elder of the spouses) leaves part of his estate to his wife, this will pass to her under the will by virtue of s. 184, but any estate undisposed of by the will passes on intestacy as though she did not survive him (but see also final sentence of para. **14.41**, ante).

1 See Administration of Estates Act 1925, s. 49(1) (p. 757, post).

Evidence required

14.44 In every case in which uncertainty as to survivorship arises and is relevant (i.e. to an application for a grant of representation), all the evidence of the circumstances which is readily available should be submitted to a district judge or registrar at the earliest opportunity in order that he may decide whether a grant of representation may issue on that evidence or whether further enquiries should be made. Circumstances vary widely in these cases, but the sort of evidence which is commonly presented consists of an affidavit by the person who found the bodies and an affidavit by the doctor who examined them. This may be sufficient in itself. Although the finding of a coroner's jury cannot be accepted as evidence[1], a copy of the notes of evidence may assist the district judge or registrar in some cases, but solicitors need not delay applications or incur expense in obtaining copy notes of evidence before obtaining the directions of a district judge or registrar[2].

1 *Bird v Keep* [1918] 2 KB 692, CA.
2 Registrar's Direction (1964) 11 June.

14.45 Since the coming into force of the Civil Evidence Acts 1968 and 1972 and the consequential relaxation of the strict rules of evidence, it would seem open to the court, in its discretion, to accept unsworn statements from witnesses, including medical experts, as to the circumstances of the death when considering the question of survivorship in relation to the title to a grant. However, it is normal practice in every case in which this question is relevant to seek the prior directions of the district judge or registrar.

14.46 It will be of assistance if the solicitor produces details of the practical effect of the decision which has to be made and, in particular, whether the ultimate distribution of the estates or the payment of inheritance tax or capital transfer tax will be affected. As to the inheritance tax or capital transfer tax liability, see the Inheritance Tax Act 1984, s. 4(2) (Finance Act 1975, s. 22(9)), p. 903, post and Chap. 8.

14.47 If the district judge or registrar is satisfied that the application may proceed on the basis of uncertainty as to survivorship, it must be sworn in the oath to lead the grant: 'That all possible enquiries as to survivorship have been made, but it appears that the said . . . and . . . died in circumstances rendering it uncertain which of them survived the other(s)'. The oath should also refer to the statutory presumption (e.g. 'That the said . . ., being the younger, is by virtue of section 184 of the Law of Property Act 1925, deemed to have survived the said . . .'). Forms of oath, Nos. 131 to 134.

14.48   In the case of spouses dying on or after 1 January 1953 but before 1 January 1996, on an intestacy it is sufficient to follow the wording given in Form No. 133 without referring to the statutory provisions.

14.49   If there is a contest as to whether the evidence justifies the district judge's or registrar's decision that there is uncertainty as to survivorship, or as to the application of s. 184, the proper course is to appeal to a High Court judge by summons. If the contest arises at an earlier stage, it may be necessary to bring the matter before the court by way of a probate action[1].

1 See *Re Horrocks, Taylor v Kershaw* [1939] P 198 at 208, [1939] 1 All ER 579 at 583.

Deaths in disasters

14.50   Circulars have been issued from time to time by the Principal Registry in connection with the loss of ships or aircraft or other disasters, listing the names of passengers and members of the crew or other persons involved in respect of whom the Senior District Judge is satisfied, from evidence produced to him, that there is uncertainty as to which of them survived the others. Where such a circular has been issued no further evidence relating to commorientes is normally necessary on application for a grant in the estate of a person whose name is listed. Any request for information whether such a circular has been issued in any particular case should be addressed to the Secretary of the Principal Registry of the Family Division, Somerset House, Strand, London WC2R 1LP.

Will must be proved

14.51   If the commoriens to whom representation is sought has left a will, it must be proved, though it may be entirely inoperative in the circumstances[1].

1 *Re Ford, Ford v Ford* [1902] 1 Ch 218; affd [1902] 2 Ch 605.

Specific cases

Death of both spouses after 1952 (one or both intestate)

14.52   On the death of a husband and wife on or after 1 January 1953 but before 1 January 1996 in circumstances of uncertainty as to survivorship, application for a grant in the estate of either spouse dying wholly intestate may be made where appropriate by the person entitled thereto under NCPR 22 on the basis that the intestate left no surviving spouse. Form of oath, No. 133.

14.53   *Entire family intestate*—Where both parents and all their children have died in circumstances rendering the order of their deaths uncertain, and *all the children were of full age, unmarried, and without issue,* and all died intestate, a grant is made to a person entitled to the estate of the youngest, and then grants are made successively, in respect of the estate of each of the other deceased persons, to the personal representative of such youngest child or person; but where the deaths occurred on or after 1 January 1953, neither parent is presumed to have survived the other for the purpose of the devolution of *their* respective estates.

14.54 *Death intestate of widow and children all of full age leaving other issue living*—In the event of a widow and some of her children dying in circumstances of uncertainty as to survivorship leaving one or more other children surviving, if the deceased children all died intestate and were of full age, unmarried, and without issue, and each leaves free estate, the surviving child (or if under age, its guardians) being the person entitled under the intestacy, can take a grant of letters of administration in the estate of each of the deceased persons simultaneously.

14.55 *Children under age*—When a child, being commoriens, dies under the age of 18 years and unmarried, the statutory trusts contained in s. 47(1) of the Administration of Estates Act 1925 fail, and the child's interest becomes divested under s. 47(2) of that Act, as if he or she had not been born; the estate of the other commoriens does not devolve upon him; and consequently no grant thereto can be made to his personal representative[1].

1 In the case of death prior to 1 January 1970, a child's interest becomes absolutely vested on his attaining the age of 21 years or marrying thereunder.

14.56 *Clearing of a minor commoriens in oath*—When the issue of the deceased die unmarried and under the age of 18[1], the clearing in the oath should be: 'died a widow [widower, *or as the case may be*], leaving A. B. and C. D. his [her] children and only issue, who died under the age of eighteen years and unmarried, without having attained an absolutely vested interest in his/her estate. That there is no other person entitled in priority to share in the estate by virtue of any enactment.'

1 In the case of death prior to 1 January 1970, a child's interest becomes absolutely vested on his attaining the age of 21 years or marrying thereunder.

14.57 *Title of deceased minor commoriens, under a will*—Where a minor is a beneficiary under the will of a person whom he is deemed to have survived, the terms of the bequest being such that it vested in him notwithstanding his minority, the person entitled to a grant of the estate of the minor should obtain representation thereto. He is then entitled, on clearing any prior rights, to a grant of the estate of the testator, in his representative capacity.

14.58 As to the circumstances in which a gift is vested notwithstanding the death of the beneficiary during his minority, see paras. **5.89** ff., ante.

Claim under Law Reform (Miscellaneous Provisions) Act 1934

14.59 When a cause of action on behalf of a deceased child survives by virtue of s. 1 of the Law Reform (Miscellaneous Provisions) Act 1934[1], although at the death of the child there may be no other estate vested in it, the resultant damages become part of its estate to be dealt with by its personal representative for the benefit of the persons entitled under s. 46 of the Administration of Estates Act 1925. This does not affect any failure of vesting of other estate by reason of death before attaining the vesting age.

1 See p. 765, post.

Foreign domicile

14.60   Where the deaths of two persons domiciled out of England and Wales occur in circumstances rendering it uncertain which is the survivor, s. 184 of the Law of Property Act 1925 is not applicable. The law of the domicile alone is relevant in determining the distribution of the estates, and is the basis upon which the property is to be administered[1].

1 *Re Cohn* [1945] Ch 5, 171 LT 377.

CHAPTER 15

Renunciation and retraction

Summary

Renunciation

Renunciation

15.01   Renunciation is the act whereby a person having a right to probate or administration waives and abandons it.

Result of renunciation

15.02   Renunciation must be made absolutely and without reserve; it takes effect from the day of its date[1], but can be withdrawn and is not final until filed[2]. It is permanent, and can be acted upon and referred to in all succeeding grants[3]; but there is power to allow a renunciation to be subsequently retracted: see paras. **15.60** ff., post.

1 *Munday and Berry v Slaughter* (1839) 2 Curt 72.
2 *Re Morant's Goods* (1874) LR 3 P & D 151.
3 *Harrison v Harrison* (1846) 1 Rob Eccl 406, 4 Notes of Cases 434.

15.03   Except in the case of executorship, a renunciation does not bind the personal representatives of the renouncing party[1].

1 As to the effect of a renunciation by an executor, see paras. **15.53** ff., post.

15.04   Where the renunciant was the only person entitled to the estate, and died between the date of his renunciation and the application for a grant by a creditor, it was held that the renunciation could not be acted upon against, and did not bind, his personal representative.

Form of renunciation

15.05   A renunciation should be witnessed by a disinterested person; it need not be under seal[1], but if it is it is liable to stamp duty of 50p, except that a renunciation

461

by a corporation (including a trust corporation) whose sealing of the document is equivalent to signature, so that there is no formal delivery, does not require to be stamped. See also paras. **15.09–15.13**, post.

1   By order of the judge, 4 May 1870.

15.06   Forms of renunciation, Nos. 183 ff.

15.07   A renunciation in the English language by a person of a non-English-speaking race will not be accepted unless it was executed before a notary public, or the district judge or registrar is satisfied by some other means that the renunciant understood the meaning and effect of the document.

15.08   As to renunciation by an executor where the domicile is other than in England and Wales, see para. **12.88**, ante.

Renunciation by trust corporation

15.09   The renunciation by a trust corporation is accepted in the form of a renunciation under seal or by an official duly appointed for the purpose of executing renunciations[1] or as executed in accordance with the following paragraph. If the corporation has no seal, or if the renunciation is not under seal or executed as in the following paragraph, a certified copy of a resolution of the governing body showing who is nominated or authorised to execute the form of renunciation must be lodged with the renunciation, which must be attested as in the case of a renunciation by an individual.

1   Secretary's Circular, 19 July 1955.

15.10   A company is no longer required to have a seal. Instead of sealing a deed, a company may now execute a deed (including a deed of renunciation) by either a director and the company secretary or two directors signing it as a deed—Companies Act 1985, s. 36A, as inserted with effect from 31 July 1990.

Renunciation by a corporation other than a trust corporation

15.11   A non-trust corporation wishing to renounce its right to a grant should by special or general resolution appoint a nominee to renounce on its behalf, in the same way that it would appoint a nominee to take a grant for its use and benefit (see paras. **5.201** ff.). When lodged at the registry, the renunciation should be accompanied by a sealed, or otherwise properly authenticated, copy of the resolution.

15.12   In practice, however, a renunciation by resolution of the board of management of the corporation is acceptable.

15.13   See also para. **15.10**, ante.

When made

Before application for grant

15.14   An executor may renounce probate as soon as his testator is dead, and his renunciation can be filed at a probate registry, provided that it is accompanied by the original will. Where the executor is also entitled to a grant under any lower title, his renunciation will not be accepted unless he also renounces administration (with will) in such lower title[1].

1 Registrar's Direction (1954) 5 October. See *Re Fenton's Goods* (1825) 3 Add 35.

15.15 In one case, where the will could not be found, the renunciation of the executor together with a verified copy of the will and an affidavit as to the loss were directed to be filed with the Record Keeper at the Principal Registry in order to break a chain of executorship.

15.16 Where no executor is named in the will, a residuary legatee or devisee, or, if there is none, a person entitled to the undisposed-of estate, may renounce and file the will.

15.17 The testamentary documents, with the renunciation, are filed in, or sent by post to, the Record Keeper's department at the Principal Registry, or a district probate registry. No fee is payable on lodging a will with a renunciation.

15.18 When a will and renunciation are lodged at the Principal Registry or at a district probate registry (other than the registry at which the indexes of all pending grant applications and caveats are maintained) notice is sent to the registry at which the indexes of all pending grant applications and caveats are maintained and an index of all wills filed with renunciations is kept with those other indexes. This index is searched by the registry on every application for a grant.

15.19 Wills lodged at a probate registry on renunciation are not open to public inspection, nor can copies of such wills be obtained as of right. Nevertheless, the fact that such a will exists and, where appropriate, its contents, may be disclosed to any person reasonably establishing an interest[1].

1 Secretary's Circular, 11 November 1975.

15.20 Upon any subsequent application for a grant it may be necessary for the applicant to attend to swear the oath and mark the will before an authorised officer at the registry at which the will is filed; or arrangements may be made for the will to be sent to another registry for this purpose. The district judge or registrar now has a general discretion, under NCPR 10(2), to allow a facsimile copy of the will to be marked in lieu of the original.

Upon application for grant

15.21 The more usual practice is for an applicant for a grant to file, with the other papers, the renunciation of any co-executor, or of any person having an interest prior to his own.

After grant, by executor to whom power was reserved

15.22 An executor to whom power of proving has been reserved (see para. **4.50**, ante) may renounce his right to probate subsequently to the issue of a grant to his co-executor. The renunciation need not refer to the fact of probate having been granted.

15.23   The renunciation is filed at the registry from which the grant issued. In Principal Registry cases it should be lodged at the Record Keeper's department. It is no longer necessary for the original grant or an office copy of the grant to be produced when the renunciation is filed at the registry.

15.24   In district registry cases, the registrar transmits notice of the renunciation to the Record Keeper at the Principal Registry.

15.25   A notation of the renunciation is made on the record. No fee is payable for noting the record.

By whom made

By an executor

15.26   An executor must renounce or be cited (see Chap. 24) before any party having an inferior interest can take. His consent alone is not sufficient for that purpose[1].

1 *Garrard v Garrard* (1871) LR 2 P & D 238.

15.27   An executor's renunciation of probate does not operate as a renunciation of any right which he may have to a grant of administration (with will) in some other capacity unless he expressly renounces that right (NCPR 37(1)).

15.28   Thus, where an executor who is also entitled in another character renounces probate, the form of renunciation must include also a renunciation of his right to letters of administration (with will) in order to enable a grant to be made to some person with a lower title. This does not apply when an application for probate is made by another executor.

15.29   An executor, in renouncing probate of his own testator's will, renounces thereby the executorship of any will of which his testator may have been executor, and of all other wills comprised in the chain. He cannot renounce probate of the first will, and take probate of the second one[1], nor can he take probate of his testator's will and refuse the liability caused by the chain of executorship.

1 *Re Perry's Goods* (1840) 2 Curt 655.

By a personal representative

15.30   An executor, an administrator with the will annexed, or an administrator, may renounce any administration with the will annexed, or administration, which he would be entitled to take in his representative capacity. If the renunciant is the sole personal representative of his own deceased, such renunciation will be a sufficient waiver to enable a grant to be made to a person entitled in a lower degree. If there is another constituted representative, the latter also must be cleared off.

15.31   Where an acting executor was cited, but could not be served personally with the process, the court required the renunciation of the executor to whom power was reserved; but it would seem that the renunciation of the acting executor would have been sufficient if he had not absconded, or if he had been personally served with notice of the application, or with a citation[1].

1 *Re Leach* (1857) 14 May. By Sir John Dodson, and see s. 8, Administration of Estates Act 1925, see p. 746, post.

15.32 If no personal representative has been constituted, all persons who have the prior potential right to obtain a grant to his estate must renounce the rights they would acquire if they became his personal representatives. In such circumstances, in the case of a will, the persons interested in the residuary estate must renounce as well as the executor; and in the case of an intestacy, all persons entitled to share in the estate must renounce. See also para. **5.192**, ante.

By attorney

15.33 An attorney may renounce on behalf of a person living abroad if specifically authorised to do so by a power of attorney appointing him for that purpose[1].

1 *Re Rosser's Goods* (1864) 3 Sw & Tr 490 at 492.

Renunciation on behalf of minors

15.34 Under NCPR 34(2):

'The right of a minor to administration may be renounced only by a person appointed under paragraph (2) of rule 32, and authorised by the district judge or registrar to renounce on behalf of the minor.'

15.35 For forms of affidavit and renunciation, see Nos. 19 and 187.

15.36 See also paras. **11.144** and **11.145**, as to application for the appointment of a person for the purpose of renouncing.

15.37 A mother has been appointed guardian by the court to renounce on behalf of her unborn child[1].

1 *Re Wilmshurst* (1830) August.

15.38 A minor executor's right to *probate* on attaining the age of 18 cannot be renounced by any person on his behalf. (NCPR 34(1).)

15.39 If a minor has been appointed an executor, the appointment does not constitute him a personal representative for any purpose unless and until probate is granted to him[1]. Consequently, on attaining full age he will be able, if so desiring, to renounce probate, notwithstanding that a grant has been taken during his minority by some other person for his use and benefit: the grant for his use and benefit of course ceases on his attaining full age.

1 Supreme Court Act 1981, s. 118 (p. 845, post).

Renunciation by nearest blood relation of claim to be appointed on behalf of minor

15.40 The nearest of kin of a minor may renounce his claim to be appointed under NCPR 32(2), in order to assist an application by a stranger or more distant relative to be appointed under that rule by district judge's or registrar's order.

By person appointed by Court of Protection

15.41   A person appointed by an order made by the Court of Protection under the Mental Health Act 1983 may renounce probate or administration on behalf of a person incapable of managing his affairs, if specifically authorised so to do, except where the incapable person is an executor who is also a minor (see NCPR 34(1)).

15.42   The nearest of kin of a person who is incapable of managing his affairs is not allowed to renounce on behalf of that person.

15.43   When no person has been authorised by the Court of Protection, the only way of clearing off such a person who is entitled to a grant is by citation: but in practice it is usual in such a case to apply for a grant for the use and benefit of the incapable person or, in special circumstances, for a grant under s. 116 of the Supreme Court Act 1981, passing over the incapable person (see paras. **25.91** ff., post). As to grants for the use and benefit of incapable persons, see paras. **11.209** ff., ante.

By attorney acting under a registered enduring power of attorney

15.44   An attorney acting under a registered enduring power of attorney may renounce administration for the use and benefit of the incapable person (see NCPR 35(2)(c)).

Where renunciation invalid. Executor having intermeddled

15.45   An act of a person appointed executor, relating to the belongings of a testator, which shows an intention of assuming the executorship, or an act which will make him liable as an executor de son tort, is regarded as intermeddling[1].

1 See 17 Halsbury's Laws (4th edn) 723–725.

15.46   If an executor has intermeddled in his deceased's estate, the court will not accept his renunciation. It will be declared invalid[1]. It has, however, been doubted by the Court of Appeal whether intermeddling of a trivial and technical character, where the executor never assumed the duties of the office nor acquired any special knowledge as such, has the effect of rendering the renunciation invalid[2].

1 *Long and Feaver v Symes and Hannam* (1832) 3 Hag Ecc 771 at 774; *M'Donnell v Prendergast* (1830) 3 Hag Ecc 212 at 214; *Jackson and Wallington v Whitehead* (1821) 3 Phillim 577; *Rayner v Green* (1839) 2 Curt 248; *Munday and Berry v Slaughter* (1839) 2 Curt 72 at 76; *Pytt v Fendall* (1754) 1 Lee 553 at 557; *Re Badenach's Goods* (1864) 3 Sw & Tr 465; *Mordaunt v Clarke* (1868) LR 1 P & D 592; *Re Lord and Fullerton's Contract* [1896] 1 Ch 228 (though intermeddling was confined to the foreign property).
2 *Holder v Holder* [1968] Ch 353, [1968] 1 All ER 665.

15.47   On no other ground can an executor be precluded from renouncing[1].

1 *Jackson and Wallington v Whitehead* (1821), above.

15.48   The mere act by an executor of being sworn as such, and afterwards changing his mind before probate has issued, is not of itself regarded as intermeddling[1].

1 *M'Donnell v Prendergast* (1830) 3 Hag Ecc 212 at 216.

Compulsion to take a grant

15.49 No person other than an executor can be compelled to take a grant, even though he may have intermeddled[1]. Such persons are therefore entitled to renounce[2]. The method whereby an executor who has intermeddled can be compelled to take a grant is dealt with at paras. **24.28** ff. and **24.93** ff., post. If it is not desired in the circumstances of the case to compel the executor to act, application may be made to pass him over under s. 116 of the Supreme Court Act 1981, notwithstanding that he has intermeddled[3]: see paras. **24.93** ff., post.

1 *Re Davis' Goods* (1860) 4 Sw & Tr 213, 29 LJPM & A 72.
2 *Re Fell's Goods* (1861) 2 Sw & Tr 126.
3 *Re Biggs' Estate* [1966] P 118, [1966] 1 All ER 358: see NCPR 47(5), (7).

Person renouncing administration cannot take in another character

15.50 Under NCPR 37(2):

'Unless a district judge or registrar otherwise directs, no person who has renounced administration in one capacity may obtain a grant thereof in some other capacity[1].'

1 But see *Re Loftus' Goods* (1864) 3 Sw & Tr 307 at 311; *Re Toscani's Estate* [1912] P 1, as to discretion of the court.

15.51 Thus, where a person, other than an executor, has two different characters under the same will, he may not select, but must take administration in the higher capacity.

15.52 Similarly, a residuary legatee or a person sharing in the estate on an intestacy cannot, except by leave of a district judge or registrar, renounce as such and take administration as a creditor. Application for the leave of the district judge or registrar should be made ex parte by lodging an affidavit as to the facts at the registry at which the grant is to be extracted.

Exceptions

15.53 The renunciation of probate by an executor does not operate as a renunciation of any right he may have to a grant in any other capacity, unless he expressly renounces such right[1].

1 NCPR 37(1).

15.54 An executor having renounced probate, for himself as such, and having no other personal right, has been allowed to take administration (will) as the attorney of his co-executors[1].

1 *Re Russell's Goods* (1869) LR 1 P & D 634.

15.55 If an executor has no other capacity in which he can claim, he may in exceptional circumstances be allowed to retract his renunciation of executorship even though a grant may have been made to a person entitled in a lower capacity (see 'Retraction', paras. **15.60** ff., post).

Representative grant: consent of one of two administrators or executors

15.56   If a leading grant has been made to two *administrators*, one of whom is disinclined to take a grant to which they have become entitled in their representative capacity, his renunciation or consent will enable his co-grantee to take it alone, except when a minority or life interest arises in connection with the new grant and the court requires two administrators. In the case of two *executors* no renunciation or consent is required from the other, if one of them applies. See also paras. **6.11–6.15**, ante.

Non-appearance to citation equivalent to renunciation

15.57   The non-appearance to a citation of a party having a superior interest, if he has been served with such process, has the same effect as a renunciation. See Chap. 24.

Non-appearance of executor

15.58   Section 5 of the Administration of Estates Act 1925 contains the provision that where a person appointed executor by a will is cited to take out probate of the will, and does not appear to the citation, his rights in respect of the executorship shall wholly cease; and the representation to the testator and the administration of his real and personal estate shall devolve and be committed in like manner as if that person had not been appointed executor.

15.59   A district judge's or registrar's order is required, directing that a grant be made to the citor. (See paras. **24.73** ff., post, and NCPR 47(5)(a).)

Retraction

Retraction

15.60   The renunciation of a person of his right to a grant may, as a general rule, be taken as final, he not being permitted to retract it except by district judge's or registrar's order.

NCPR 37(3) provides:

> 'A renunciation of probate or administration may be retracted at any time with the leave of a district judge or registrar; provided that only in exceptional circumstances may leave be given to an executor to retract a renunciation of probate after a grant has been made to some other person entitled in a lower degree.'

Retraction by executor

15.61   Under s. 5 of the Administration of Estates Act 1925, where an executor renounces probate of a will his rights in respect of the executorship shall wholly cease, and administration of the estate of the deceased is to be granted as if he had not been appointed executor.

15.62   Notwithstanding this section, the court has the power to permit an executor who has renounced to retract his renunciation and take probate[1]. But, as stated above, permission to retract will be granted only in exceptional circumstances after a grant of representation has been made to another person entitled in a lower degree.

---

1 *Re Stiles' Goods* [1898] P 12, decided under s. 79 of the Court of Probate Act 1857, which was in virtually identical terms. See also NCPR 37(3).

15.63 An executor wishing to retract must be prepared to show that his retraction is for the benefit of the estate, or of those interested under the will of the deceased[1].

1 *Re Gill's Goods* (1873) LR 3 P & D 113.

15.64 An executor who is also the residuary legateee and has renounced in both capacities may, in special circumstances, be permitted to retract his renunciation qua residuary legatee[1].

1 *Re Richardson's Goods* (1859) 1 Sw & Tr 515; *Re Morrison's Goods* (1861) 2 Sw & Tr 129; *Re Wheelwright's Goods* (1878) 3 PD 71.

15.65 In one case an executor who had renounced probate was not allowed to retract his renunciation, but was permitted to take a grant de bonis non as a creditor[1].

1 *Re Toscani's Estate* [1912] P 1.

Effect of retraction of renunciation by executor

15.66 Where an executor who has renounced probate has been permitted, whether before or on or after 1 January 1926, to withdraw the renunciation and prove the will, the probate is to take effect and be deemed always to have taken effect without prejudice to the previous acts and dealings of and notices to any other personal representative who has previously proved the will or taken out letters of administration; and a notation of the subsequent probate is made upon the original probate or letters of administration and the record thereof, or, in the event of the original grant not being available, upon the record; and the grant, when noted, is retained in the registry unless the court shall otherwise direct. See Administration of Estates Act 1925, s. 6[1].

1 See p. 746, post.

Retraction by persons other than executors

15.67 In the case of a person other than an executor, there is no statute or rule requiring the existence of special circumstances to enable him to be permitted to retract, but it should be established that retraction is necessary, e.g. because of difficulty in constituting any other person as administrator to complete the administration of the estate of the deceased[1].

1 For old cases in which retraction was permitted, see *Re Blake's Goods* (1866) 35 LJP & M 91; *Skeffington v White* (1828) 1 Hag Ecc 699. There are no recent reported cases, as the matter is now decided on ex parte application to the district judge or registrar.

Renunciation not binding on personal representative

15.68 A person who has previously renounced by his guardian has been allowed to retract; but the personal representative of a deceased renunciant of administration (with or without will) is not bound by the renunciation, and no retraction is necessary to enable such representative to obtain a grant, if otherwise entitled to it.

Practice

15.69 Application for leave to retract a renunciation should be made ex parte to the district judge or registrar of the registry at which the renunciation is filed[1], supported by an affidavit of the facts, including a statement of the circumstances in which retraction is necessary. The former grant, or an office copy of it, should be lodged with the affidavit.

1 NCPR 37(4).

15.70   If leave is granted, the retraction should be drawn up and executed, and lodged, together with the district judge's or registrar's order and affidavit, at the Principal Registry or district probate registry, as the case may be, with the papers to lead the further grant.

15.71   As to notation of the grant and record in the case of retraction by a renouncing executor, see para. **15.66**, ante.

15.72   Form of retraction, No. 188.

CHAPTER 16

Amendment and notation of grants

Summary

Amendment of grant

16.01   NCPR 41 provides:

'(1) Subject to paragraph (2) below, if a district judge or registrar is satisfied that a grant should be amended or revoked he may make an order accordingly.

(2) Except on the application or with the consent of the person to whom the grant was made, the power conferred in paragraph (1) above shall be exercised only in exceptional circumstances.'

16.02   After a grant has been issued an amendment of it may become necessary for various reasons:

(a)   An error may have been discovered in the grant, or a document may have been found which must be incorporated.
(b)   An error may have been discovered in the probate copy of the will.
(c)   Settled land may have been improperly included or excluded.

Error in grant

16.03   When an error has been discovered in a grant which has been sealed by the registry, it depends upon the nature of the error whether it will be necessary to revoke the grant or to amend it under an order of a district judge or registrar. The revocation of grants is dealt with in Chap. 17: see also 'Death of grantee before issue of grant', paras. **2.49–2.54**, ante.

Error as to deceased

16.04   Amendment of a grant may be allowed where the error was in the Christian name, address, or date of death of the deceased. Where an amendment is desired in the name of the deceased, or in the date of death, the certificate of birth or death must be produced as the case requires.

Surname of deceased

16.05   If the surname of the deceased is wrong the grant should strictly be revoked, but where the mistake has been only in the spelling amendment of the grant is usually allowed.

Christian name of deceased

16.06   If the first Christian name, or the only Christian name, is wrong, the grant is usually revoked, except in cases where the correct name is of the same sound (e.g. 'Ann' and 'Anne', 'Susanna' and 'Susannah'), when an amendment is allowed.

16.07   If a Christian name, other than the first one, is omitted in error, it may be inserted by amendment, on production of a certificate of death, birth, or baptism, as well as the affidavit referred to in para. **16.24**, post.

Alias

16.08   An alias may be added to the true name of the deceased, but where a grant had been made in the alias name and it was subsequently sought to add the true name to the grant, the application was refused and the grant revoked.

Address of deceased

16.09   An additional address may be inserted by amendment[1] where there is a sufficient reason for it to be included.

1 *Re Towgood's Goods* (1872) LR 2 P & D 408.

16.10   Minor errors or omissions in the address given in the grant may be corrected by amendment.

Errors as to grantee

16.11   An executor may have omitted a Christian name of his own, which has been omitted in his appointment in the will, or he may have used the surname stated in the will, without the right to do so. If he can give a sufficient and reasonable explanation, the necessary amendment will be made.

16.12   Although a grant misdescribing the address of the grantee needs amendment, it is not imperfect and remains an effective grant[1].

1 *Cambria Garages v Lodge* (1966) 110 Sol Jo 724.

Error in description of capacity

16.13   Amendment may be allowed in the character in which a person applied for a grant, where the same person was entitled in the new character. It should be noted, however, that as from 1 May 1975 grants of administration (with or without will) no longer include a statement of the way in which prior classes, other than executors, are cleared off, nor the capacity, or title, in which administration is granted. As from 13 October 1993 it has also been the practice not to show how any executor has been cleared off in a grant of administration with will (see paras. **2.24–2.28**, ante).

Addition of limitation

16.14 The district judges and registrars have allowed the insertion of a limitation 'for the use and benefit of minors' etc. and also a note as to reservation of power to make a grant to another executor.

16.15 In limited grants an amendment may be allowed where there has been a misdescription of the property which is to be administered, or where there has been a misrecital of the power in exercise of which a will has been made, or of a deed by which a trust has been created, or under which the settlement arises in settled land cases.

Alteration by unauthorised person

16.16 No grant of probate or letters of administration which has been sealed by the registry may be altered without an order of a district judge or registrar having been previously obtained.

16.17 If an alteration has been made in a grant by an unauthorised person after its issue, the district judges and registrars will in no case adopt such alteration. The grant will be impounded, and a duplicate grant must be obtained, which will then be amended, by district judge's or registrar's order, in the usual course. If the alteration is extensive or of a serious character, the grant will be revoked.

Date of will rectified after probate

16.18 The court will order a memorandum to be endorsed on a probate after it has been issued, showing the true date of a will[1], the affidavit in support being filed with the will.

1 *Re Allchin's Goods* (1869) LR 1 P & D 664.

Probate of codicil subsequent to that of will

16.19 If a codicil is found after probate of a will has been granted, a separate probate of that codicil may, in certain circumstances, be granted, and the first probate undergoes no alteration or amendment whatever. In order to obtain probate of the codicil; an oath must be drawn up, identifying the codicil and reciting the particulars of the grant of probate of the will. The grant must be taken at the registry from which the first grant issued. In applications at the Principal Registry, the probate of the will, or an office copy thereof, should be lodged. A further Inland Revenue account may also be required (see Chap. 8).

16.20 If, however, the appointment of the executors under the will is annulled or varied by the codicil, the probate must be brought in and revoked, and a new grant will be made annexing both the will and the codicil.

16.21 See also paras. **3.152–3.165**, ante.

Settled land

16.22   A general grant may in certain circumstances be amended to exclude settled land but it would no longer appear to be appropriate to amend a general grant to include settled land. See para. **10.128**, ante. Form of affidavit, No. 26.

Official errors

16.23   As to the procedure when a grant contains an official error, see para. **2.47**, ante.

Practice in applications for amendment

16.24   An affidavit of facts is required from the grantee, or grantees, showing the nature of the error, the necessity for its alteration, and the nature of the amendment required. Form of affidavit, No. 25.

16.25   The affidavit and the grant are lodged at, or sent by post to, the registry from which the grant issued. At the Principal Registry the documents should be lodged with, or sent to, the Record Keeper.

16.26   If the district judge or registrar is satisfied, he will make an order, and the amendment will be made in the grant and signed by the district judge or registrar or other authorised officer. Notice of the amendment of any grant made at a district probate registry is sent to the Principal Registry so that the records can be noted.

16.27   No fee is now payable in respect of the amendment of a grant.

Error in probate copy of will

16.28   Where a mistake has been made in an engrossment of a will, an order is required for the amendment. The grant should be lodged at the Record Keeper's Department or district registry, where a district judge's or registrar's order will be drawn up for the correction of the copy in accordance with the original will.

Notation of grants

Undertaking by Public Trustee to administer an estate

16.29   As to notation of grants where an undertaking by the Public Trustee to administer an estate under s. 3 of the Public Trustee Act 1906 is filed, see para. **9.65**, ante.

Executor permitted to retract renunciation

16.30   As to notation on an existing grant of a subsequent grant of probate to an executor who had previously renounced, but has been allowed to retract his renunciation and prove the will, see para. **15.66**, ante.

Notation of domicile

16.31   For the practice as to notation of domicile after the issue of a grant, see para. **18.24**, post.

Addition of a further personal representative

16.32 When an order is made under s. 114(4) of the Supreme Court Act 1981[1], for the addition of a personal representative, the order and the grant are lodged at the Record Keeper's Department of the Principal Registry, or the district registry from which the grant issued, as the case may be; the appointment of the additional personal representative is noted on the grant and on the record. See paras. **7.43–7.47**, ante, as to practice.

1 See p. 845, post.

Substitution or removal of personal representative

16.33 Where an order has been made under s. 50 of the Administration of Justice Act 1985 by the Chancery Court, substituting or removing a personal representative, that court sends the original grant and a sealed copy of the order to the Record Keeper at the Principal Registry, for a memorandum of the order to be endorsed or permanently affixed to the grant, in accordance with RSC Ord. 93, r. 20(5). If the grant was made at a district probate registry, the Record Keeper informs that registry so that its records can be noted.

Bankruptcy Act 1914: administration order

16.34 Administration orders made under s. 130 of the Bankruptcy Act 1914, which in effect transfer the powers of the personal representative of a bankrupt to the person named in the order, are notified by the court making the order to the Record Keeper of the Principal Registry. The record copy of the grant is noted with the particulars and date of the order. Where the grant issued from a district probate registry the information is passed by the Record Keeper to the district registry so that its record can be noted in the same manner[1].

1 Secretary's Circular, 18 May 1953 as amended by Registrar's Direction (1976) 17 December.

Judicial Trustees Act 1896

16.35 Similar arrangements apply in the case of an order made under s. 1(1) of the Judicial Trustees Act 1896, which affects the powers of a person who has obtained a grant of representation. Copies of such orders are filed and open to inspection[1].

1 Secretary's Circular, 6 July 1953.

Election by spouse to have life interest redeemed

Right of surviving spouse to redemption

16.36 By s. 47A of the Administration of Estates Act 1925[1], the surviving husband or wife of an intestate dying on or after 1 January 1953 has the right to require the personal representatives to redeem, at a price to be ascertained in accordance with specific rules[2], any life interest to which he or she is entitled in part of the intestate's estate, being property then in possession.

1 See p. 755, post.
2 See the Intestate Succession (Interest and Capitalisation) Order 1977 (S.I. 1977 No. 1491) and the Intestate Succession (Interest and Capitalisation) Order 1977 (Amendment) Order 1983 (S.I. 1983 No. 1374).

Notice of election

16.37   Where the surviving spouse has become the sole personal representative, then by sub-s. (7) of s. 47A an election under the section is not effective unless written notice is given to the Senior District Judge of the Family Division within twelve months after representation to the estate of the intestate is first taken out, or within such extended period as the court may in special circumstances allow.

16.38   Such notice is given by filing a notice in Form 6 in Schedule 1 to the Non-Contentious Probate Rules 1987[1] either in the Principal Registry or (in duplicate) in the district registry from which the grant issued. Notices so filed are noted on the grant and record and are available for inspection by the public (NCPR 56).

1 See p. 943, post.

16.39   No fee is payable on the filing of a notice of election.

Principal Registry grants

16.40   The personal representative filing the notice should lodge it with the grant at the Record Keeper's Department, which will note the grant and record copy of the grant as to the filing of the election. The grant will be returned and the notice filed by the Record Keeper.

District registry grants

16.41   The personal representative has the option of filing the notice (in duplicate) and lodging the grant at the district registry or the Principal Registry.

16.42   In the district registry, the same notation is made, the grant returned and one copy of the notice filed; the other copy of the notice and a re-photographed act of record are then sent to the Record Keeper, who will file the notice and the substituted act of record.

16.43   If the papers are lodged in London, the Record Keeper will post the grant and the notice, in duplicate, to the district registry, stating the date of filing, for the same procedure to be carried out.

Notice out of time or unaccompanied by grant

16.44   Any notice offered for filing will be accepted, whether apparently in time or not. In the event of a notice being lodged without the grant, it will be accepted, on a satisfactory undertaking to bring in the grant, if the refusal would lead to a risk of its being out of time[1].

1 Circular, 9 December 1952.

Orders for provision out of estate of deceased

Inheritance (Provision for Family and Dependants) Act 1975

16.45   Applications under this Act enabling the court to order provision out of a deceased person's estate are dealt with in detail in Chap. 41. The 1975 Act[1] applies as respects the estates of persons dying after 31 March 1976: for deaths prior to that date reference should be made to the Inheritance (Family Provision) Act 1938 (as amended by the Intestates' Estates Act 1952 and the Family Provision Act 1966)[2] and ss. 26 to 28A of the Matrimonial Causes Act 1965[3].

1 See p. 808, post.
2 13 Halsbury's Statutes (3rd edn) 118.
3 17 Halsbury's Statutes (3rd edn) 197.

16.46   Applications in the High Court under the Act of 1975 are assigned to the Chancery Division or Family Division[1], but where appropriate, the application may be made in the county court[2].

1 See RSC Order 99, r. 2.
2 See para. **41.03**, post.

16.47   A copy of every final order made under the relevant provisions of these Acts[1] is to be sent to the Principal Registry of the Family Division for entry and filing, and a memorandum of the order must be endorsed on, or permanently annexed to, the probate or letters of administration under which the estate is being administered.

1 Other than an order made under s. 15(1) of the Act, but including an order dismissing an application or a final order embodying a consent order or terms of compromise (Registrar's Direction (Divorce), 21 March 1962; *Practice Direction* (Chancery Division: Endorsement of Orders on Grants of Representation): [1978] 3 All ER 1032, [1979] 1 WLR 1).

Practice for recording orders

16.48   The grant of probate, letters of administration (with will) or letters of administration and a copy of the order are sent to the Principal Registry by the Chancery Master, Family Division district judge or county court district judge, as the case may be. A memorandum of the order is prepared by the Record Keeper and photographed. A copy of the memorandum is attached to the grant, and a further copy is sent to the Capital Taxes Office. The order and another copy of the memorandum are filed with the original will, or if there is no will, with the oath to lead the grant of administration.

16.49   A marginal note is made on the grant, as follows: 'Memorandum of order dated   pursuant to section 19(3) of the Inheritance (Provision for Family and Dependants) Act 1975 (*or as the case may be*), annexed hereto' and a note is also made on the record of the grant. The grant, with the copy memorandum attached, is returned to the Chancery Division, Family Division or county court, as the case may be, for handing out to the grantee.

16.50   A similar procedure is followed if a subsequent order varying the original order is made.

16.51   Where the grant issued from a district probate registry the same procedure is followed, save that, after recording at the Principal Registry, the order and copy memorandum are sent to the district registry. Copies of both are annexed to the copy will filed at the Principal Registry, or filed separately where there is no will.

16.52   As to the procedure when obtaining a second or subsequent grant where an order has been made under the Act, see paras. **13.26–13.30**, ante.

Alterations in value of estate

Grant marked by Capital Taxes Office

16.53 It is not the practice of the probate registries to amend the grant or the record where there has been an increase or decrease in the value of the estate. In cases where either the gross or net values of the estate, or the amount of the estate duty[1], has altered, the grant of representation may be lodged with the Capital Taxes Office, if it is desired that the amendment be noted thereon.

1 In the case of a death occurring after 12 March 1975, no statement of the amount of inheritance tax or capital transfer tax paid (if any) appears on the grant of representation following the repeal of s. 30 of the Customs and Inland Revenue Act 1881 by the Finance Act 1975, s. 59 and Schedule 13, Part I: *Practice Note* [1975] CLY 266.

16.54 As to corrective accounts, see para. **8.153**, ante.

16.55 It is still, however, the probate registry practice for the gross and net values of an estate to be stated in grants of representation[1], even in those cases where the estate is sworn at a threshold figure[2].

1 Registrar's Direction (1975) 14 March.
2 *Practice Direction* [1981] 2 All ER 832, [1981] 1 WLR 1185.

16.56 As to grants in which the estate is sworn 'so far as can at present be ascertained', see paras. **4.207–4.208** and **8.18**, ante.

Further security

16.57 If the grant is one of administration (with or without will) *which issued prior to 1 January 1972*, so that an administration bond was filed, and the gross value of the estate is increased, before such a notation can be made by the Capital Taxes Office it is necessary to obtain a certificate from the district judge or registrar of the registry from which the grant issued that the administrator has given sufficient security for due administration of the further assets. This requirement still appears to be operative notwithstanding the abolition of bonds in relation to grants issued on or after 1 January 1972.

Affidavit

16.58 After the amended figures have been agreed by the Capital Taxes Office, the administrator makes an affidavit stating the facts as to the grant, the value of the estate then sworn to, and the true value. Form of affidavit, No. 27. If the grant was made to more than one administrator, all must join in making the affidavit.

Bond or guarantee

16.59 In the case of a grant which issued prior to 1 January 1972, if the bond already given is not sufficient to cover the whole estate, including the increased amount, a further bond should be given with a penalty of double the value of the additional estate. The word 'intended', coming before the word 'administrator' in the bond, should be omitted.

16.60 The district judge or registrar has a discretion to accept as sufficient the bond filed on the issue of the grant if the deficiency is small, i.e. of the order of 5 per cent[1].

1 Registrar's Direction (1952) 29 September.

16.61 In certain circumstances, another person will be permitted to make the affidavit and execute the bond[1]. The sureties to the further bond need not be those who delivered the original bond.

1 *Re Ross's Goods* (1877) 2 PD 274; and also see the case of *Re Sutherland's Goods* (1862) 4 Sw & Tr 189, referred to in that case.

16.62 A person acting under a power of attorney from an absent administrator is allowed to execute the necessary documents.

16.63 Where, in respect of a grant which issued on or after 1 January 1972, a guarantee by sureties has been given, an amended or additional guarantee may be required on noting an increase in the value of the estate.

Practice

16.64 The affidavit, and bond or guarantee (where necessary) must be lodged at, or sent by post to, the Record Keeper's Department of the Principal Registry, or the district registry where the grant was made, as the case may be.

16.65 A certificate that sufficient security has been given is signed by the district judge or registrar (Form No. 47), and a notation to the same effect is made on the record of the grant in cases in which the amount of the estate in the Inland Revenue account was previously stated 'so far as can at present be ascertained'.

16.66 The certificate is then returned to the applicant, in order to be transmitted to the Capital Taxes Office.

Justification by sureties

16.67 In cases where justifying sureties were required on the issue of the grant, a further affidavit of justification by the sureties should be lodged on reswearing the estate at a higher amount.

Further fees

16.68 No additional court fees are taken on reswearing in respect of an increase in the value of the estate, even in cases where the estate was originally sworn 'so far as can at present be ascertained'. Conversely, no repayment of court fees is made in the event of the estate being afterwards sworn at a smaller amount.

CHAPTER 17

Revocation and impounding of grants

Summary

Power of court to revoke

17.01   By s. 25(1)(b) of the Supreme Court Act 1981[1] the court has authority to revoke grants of probate and letters of administration.

1   See p. 837, post.

17.02   A grant may be revoked by a judgment in an action in the Chancery Division or county court for revocation (see paras. **27.13** ff., post); or by order of a district judge or registrar (NCPR 41), or under NCPR 26(2) (see paras. **7.43–7.47**, ante).

17.03   Section 121(1) of the Supreme Court Act 1981[1] gives the court power of its own motion to call in a grant of probate or administration where it appears that the grant ought not to have been made, or that it contains an error, and, if satisfied that it would be revoked at the instance of a party interested, to revoke it.

1   See p. 846, post.

17.04   The grant may be revoked under this subsection without being called in if it cannot be called in (ibid., s. 121(2)).

17.05   A similar power is vested in the court to cancel a grant resealed under the Colonial Probates Acts 1892 and 1927 (Supreme Court Act 1981, s. 121(3) and (4): as to the resealing of grants, see Chap. 18).

Cases in which district judge or registrar may revoke

17.06   Except in exceptional circumstances, a grant may be revoked by a district judge or registrar under NCPR 41 only on the application of, or with the consent of, the person to whom the grant was made[1]. Instances of such exceptional circumstances are given in the following pages. Where the grantee is unwilling for the grant to be revoked, unless the grant is one to which he is clearly not entitled, procedure by way of action for revocation is normally necessary. As to revocation actions, see paras. **27.13** ff., post.

1 NCPR 41.

Grounds for revocation

17.07   The main grounds for revocation of a grant are set out below.

1. False statement

17.08   Where a grant has been made to a person who was not entitled to it, either where he has acted in ignorance of the true facts or where he has acted fraudulently, e.g. by making a false statement or by concealing some material fact from the court.

2. Supervening defect in grant

17.09   Where a grant has been properly made, but has subsequently become ineffective and useless; or which, if allowed to subsist, would prevent the proper administration of the estate.

3. Other cases

17.10   Where a grant should not have been made; e.g. because of the entry of a caveat, or because it was made before the effluxion of the necessary time; or where the grantee had died before its issue.

Cases for revocation under first head

17.11   Examples of cases where a grant will be revoked owing to a false statement by the grantee are:

(a)   A will has been discovered after administration has been granted.

(b)   A later will has been discovered after probate of an earlier will.

(c)   A codicil has been discovered, after a grant of probate, which revokes or alters the appointment of executors: see para. **3.160**, ante.

(d)   Where a will was proved by two executors, power being reserved to two other executors, who died without proving the will, and a codicil which affected the legacies was found several years later, after both proving executors had died, the survivor being intestate, the grant of probate was revoked, and administration (with will) was granted to the person next entitled.

(e)   Administration had been granted to an elected guardian of infants of whom there was a testamentary guardian who had not been cleared off[1].

(f)   Administration (with will) had been granted upon the renunciation of an executor who had previously intermeddled in the estate and was subsequently compelled by the court to take probate[2].

(g)   An executor of a forged or revoked will obtains probate of it.

(h)   An executor obtains probate of a will, whilst an action as to its validity is pending in the court of the deceased's domicile[3].

(i)   An executor, being a minor, obtains probate of the will by which he is appointed, on the tacit suggestion or understanding that he is of full age.

(j)   An executor obtains probate of the will of a living person[4]. Revocation is effected, in the case of supposed deaths on active service, on production of a letter or notification from the appropriate Service department that the person formerly certified dead is now living. When a person is found to be living after a grant has been made following an order for leave to swear to death under NCPR 53, application should be made to the district judge or registrar of the registry from which the grant issued for rescission of the order and for the revocation of the grant[5]. For form of affidavit, see No. 39, mutatis mutandis.

(k)   Administration granted to a woman claiming to be the widow of an intestate, but who had not been legally married[6].

(l)   Administration granted to persons claiming to be an intestate's next of kin, who are in reality illegitimate 'relatives' only, or are impostors, or are not nearest of kin, there being others nearer[7].

(m)   A mother of an intestate spinster had obtained a grant, though there was a natural child of the intestate. The grant was revoked notwithstanding the death of the mother[8].

1   *Re Morris' Goods* (1862) 2 Sw & Tr 360.
2   Comyn's Digest: title 'Administration'.
3   *Lord Trimlestown v Lady Trimlestown* (1830) 3 Hag Ecc 243 at 248.
4   *Re Napier's Goods* (1809) 1 Phillim 83; *Re March* (1940) (testator found to be a prisoner of war).
5   See e.g. *Re Bloch's Estate* [1959] CLY 1251.
6   *Re Moore's Goods* (1845) 3 Notes of Cases 601. In such a case it is unnecessary to allege that the grant was obtained by fraud: it is sufficient for the person claiming revocation to establish his title to the grant (*Re Evon's Estate, Evon v Stevenson* (1963) 107 Sol Jo 893).
7   *Re Bergman's Goods* (1842) 2 Notes of Cases 22.
8   *Re Ayling* (January 1949, unreported).

Cases for revocation under second head

Death of grantee before sealing

17.12   When a grant has been sealed by the registry after the party or any of the parties applying has died. As to the moment when a grant is deemed to have been sealed, and for the practice in cases where the grantee dies before the sealing of the grant, see paras. **2.49–2.54**, ante.

One of two or more grantees becomes incapable

17.13   Where one of two or more grantees becomes incapable of managing his affairs, the grant must be revoked.

17.14   If application for a new grant is made by persons all of whom had a right equal to that of the incapable grantee (whether they are the other grantees or not) a general grant may be made to them.

17.15   If any of them is in a lower category, the new grant will be in accordance with NCPR 35 (see paras. **11.209** ff., ante), for the use and benefit of the incapable person and limited until further representation be granted[1].

1   Registrar's Direction (1956) 16 July (as modified by NCPR 35).

One of several executors becomes incapable of managing his affairs

17.16 When two executors prove a will, but one becomes incapable, probate is revoked and a new grant made to the capable executor, power being reserved to the incapable executor of taking probate again on recovering his capacity[1].

1 *Re Sowerby's Goods* (1891) 65 LT 764; *Re Shaw's Estate* [1905] P 92.

One of several administrators (with or without will) becomes incapable

17.17 Where administration (or administration with will annexed) has been granted to two or more persons, of whom one subsequently becomes incapable[1], the grant is revoked and a fresh grant made to the capable administrator. If any minority or life interest subsists the further grant will normally be made to not less than two individuals, or to a trust corporation with or without an individual.

1 *Re Newton's Goods* (1843) 3 Curt 428; *Re Phillips' Goods* (1824) 2 Add 335. In the latter case, the committees of the person and estate of the incapable administrator consented.

17.18 If the incapable grantee had a superior title to that of the capable grantee, the former's right to a grant on recovering his capacity must be reserved by a limitation in the new grant.

17.19 For the practice when the sole grantee becomes incapable, see paras. **17.64** ff., post.

Both executors incapable

17.20 Where there was the clearest evidence that both the surviving executors were of advanced age and suffering from such a degree of physical and mental infirmity as made continuance of their duties impossible, the court revoked the grant of probate and granted letters of administration (with will) de bonis non to a great-nephew of the testator[1].

1 *Re Galbraith's Goods* [1951] P 422, [1951] 2 All ER 470n.

Grantee wishing to be relieved of duties

17.21 Application is occasionally made for revocation on the ground that the grantee, though not incapable, wishes to be relieved of his responsibility for some reason, such as increasing age. Such an application is allowed only by express direction of a district judge or registrar, which is not readily given.

Disappearance of grantee

17.22 Where a creditor, after taking a grant of administration, had paid himself his debt, and left the country, the court revoked the grant[1].

1 *Re Jenkin's Goods* (1819) 3 Phillim 33.

17.23 Where a creditor, having recovered her debt, wished to retire from the administration of the estate, the court, upon proof of these facts, and:

> 'that there were no actions or suits at law or in equity touching or concerning the estate and effects of the deceased, and the grantee's administration thereof depending between her and any other person,'

revoked the grant and decreed administration de bonis non to one of the intestate's children[1].

1 *Re Hoare's Goods* (1833) 2 Sw & Tr 361, in note, and 5 LTNS 768, in note. A Mrs French lent the intestate certain moneys upon the security of an estate, which the intestate afterwards sold or contracted to sell to another person. Mrs French filed a bill against the purchaser, who eventually paid her the whole of the mortgage debt, with interest. Between filing the bill and the receipt of the money she took administration to the intestate, on the renunciation of his widow and children (through their guardian).

17.24   A grant of administration to one of several residuary legatees, who had absconded, leaving part of the estate unadministered, and of whom there had been no trace for five years, was revoked, and a grant de bonis non was directed to issue to another residuary legatee[1].

1 *Re Covell's Goods* (1889) 15 PD 8. See also *Re Bradshaw's Goods* (1887) 13 PD 18 (creditor absconds).

17.25   A grant of administration to the widow, who had disappeared, leaving part of the estate unadministered, and who could not be traced, was revoked, and a grant de bonis non was made to one of the next-of-kin[1].

1 *Re Loveday's Goods* [1900] P 154.

17.26   A grant of administration to one of the next-of-kin, who had left the country, leaving the estate unadministered, and whose whereabouts was unknown, was revoked, and a grant de bonis non made to the other next-of-kin[1].

1 *Re Colclough's Goods* [1902] 2 IR 499. See *Re Thomas's Estate* [1912] P 177.

17.27   **Note**—*Under the present practice a further grant following a revoked grant is a grant of all the estate, and not a grant de bonis non.*

Other cases for revocation

17.28   There are other cases which do not come under the two general heads before mentioned. Some examples are given below.

Want of due execution discovered since the grant

17.29   If it is discovered after the issue of a grant that a will proved in common form was not duly executed, application should be made for revocation of the grant. The evidence as to lack of execution should first be submitted to the district judge or registrar of the registry from which the grant issued. If he is satisfied that the will was not duly executed, he will make an order revoking the grant and mark the will 'probate refused'.

Codicil found after grant of administration (with will)

17.30   If administration (with a will annexed) has been granted, and later a codicil found, a separate grant cannot be made of the codicil, as in the case of a probate, but the administration (with the will annexed) must be revoked, and a new administration taken, with both the will and the codicil annexed.

Grant issuing before the effluxion of necessary time

17.31   It is stated in Sir S. Toller's *Law of Executors and Administrators* (Book 1, Chap. 3),

> 'that an administration may be repealed *quia improvidè*, that is, where, on a false suggestion in respect to the time of the intestate's death, it is issued before the expiration of a fortnight from that event.'

But he adds that it shall be granted to the same person[1].

1 He quotes Comyn's Digest, Administrator (B. 8), and 1 Sid 293. In *Webb v Field* (1849) (in the Prerogative Court) the question was raised. The defendant had obtained administration one day before the fourteen days had fully expired. The plaintiff called in the grant with a view to revocation, and prayed administration to himself. The defendant admitted the right of the court to revoke under the circumstances, and prayed administration to himself. The suit was finally compromised, and, the administration being revoked, a new grant issued to both parties. In *Faringdon v Blackman* (1729) Hil Term before Dr Bettesworth (Dr Cottrell's MS), 'a next-of-kin took administration within the fourteen days, upon the allegation that the intestate had been dead three months. Grant called in and revoked, having been unduly obtained contrary to an injunction of Archbishop Whitgift, that no administration should pass the seal till fourteen days after deceased's death.' It is not stated to whom the grant was afterwards made.

17.32   The same ruling would seem to apply where the grant has been made through an error in the registry, and without any false suggestion on the part of the applicant, viz. where the day of the deceased's death had been truly stated.

Name wrongly stated

17.33   The court may revoke a grant in which the surname or Christian name of the deceased is incorrectly stated. In many cases, however, the error may be corrected by amendment (see Chap. 16).

By whom revocation is obtained

17.34   An application for revocation of a grant should, if not made by the grantee, be made by a person having an immediate right to the grant which is to take its place, with the consent of the grantee. Such an applicant must ask for, and be prepared to take, the new grant after he has obtained the revocation of the old grant[1].

1 *Phillips v Alcock* (1755) 2 Lee 97.

17.35   A grant, however, may be revoked upon the application of the grantee, even if he has no right to the grant to be substituted.

17.36   It was formerly considered that the court could not revoke on the application of a creditor, whatever might be the merits of the case, because such creditor could not demand a grant to be made to himself of immediate right[1]; but this appears to be no longer so[2]. A creditor now has a right to a grant under NCPR 20 and 22.

1 See *Re Newsom's Goods* (1842) 2 Notes of Cases 15, and the case referred to therein.
2 *Re French's Estate* [1910] P 169. The order for the grant, however, was made under the court's then discretionary powers by virtue of s. 73 of the Court of Probate Act 1857, although not so stated in the report.

Revocation when the grantee is dead

17.37   In proper cases a grant may be revoked notwithstanding that it has ceased owing to the death of the grantee or otherwise[1]. See example quoted in para. **17.11**(m), ante.

1 Registrar's Direction (1924) 15 July.

Revocation by the court of its own motion

17.38   Section 121(1) and (2) of the Supreme Court Act 1981[1] gives the court power of its own volition to call in and revoke any grant which ought not to have been made, or which contains an error. If the grant cannot be called in, the court may revoke it without calling it in.

1 See p. 846, post.

17.39   This procedure is intended for use only in special circumstances where procedure by revocation action is inappropriate, e.g. where a grant is wrongly issued as a result of an official error, or where a grantee is convicted of an offence which destroys his title, but no person competent to take proceedings for revocation is willing to do so[1].

1 Secretary's Circular, 16 July 1956: *Re Davies, Panton v Jones* (1978) Times, 23 May.

Cancellation of resealing

17.40   Section 121(3) and (4) of the Supreme Court Act 1981 introduced a new provision vesting in the court a discretionary power to call in and cancel a resealed grant that ought not to have been resealed: the section provides as follows:

> '(3) Where it appears to the High Court that a grant resealed under the Colonial Probates Acts 1892 and 1927 ought not to have been resealed, the court may call in the relevant document and, if satisfied that the resealing would be cancelled at the instance of a party interested, may cancel the resealing.
>
> In this and the following subsection "the relevant document" means the original grant or, where some other document was sealed by the court under those Acts, that document.
>
> (4) A resealing may be cancelled under subsection (3) without the relevant document being called in, if it cannot be called in.'

17.41   It should be noted that the resealing is cancelled and not revoked.

Practice on application for revocation

17.42   Application for the revocation of a grant issued from the Principal Registry is made at the Record Keeper's Department. If the grant issued from a district registry, the application should be made at that registry[1]. The necessary documents may be lodged on personal attendance, or submitted by post[2].

1 See NCPR 2(1) and 41.
2 Circular, 14 April 1960.

17.43   An affidavit in support of the application should be made by the grantee, or by the applicant for the fresh grant. Where the application for revocation is not made by the grantee himself, his written consent should also be lodged.

17.44   The affidavit should state (i) the details of the first grant, (ii) the grounds for revocation, (iii) the right to the new grant. For form, see No. 39.

Production of grant

17.45   Whenever possible, the grant must be lodged in the registry at the time of application for its revocation.

17.46   If it is impracticable to compel the production of the grant, the court will revoke it, though it cannot so mark it[1], and the record of the grant is marked accordingly.

1 *Baker v Russell* (1752) 1 Lee 167 at 168; *Scotter v Field* (1848) 6 Notes of Cases 182; *Re Langley's Goods* (1851) 2 Rob Eccl 407.

17.47   If the grant has been lost or mislaid, the court will revoke it, notwithstanding that it is not forthcoming. But an undertaking from the grantee to bring it in if it should be found may be required[1].

1 *Re Carr's Goods* (1858) 1 Sw & Tr 111.

17.48   In such cases an office copy of the grant should be lodged with the affidavit in support of the application.

17.49   A revoked grant of administration has been allowed to remain in the hands of the solicitors of the administrator, who had a lien upon it[1].

1 *Barnes v Durham* (1869) LR 1 P & D 728, 38 LJP & M 46.

Other documents required

17.50   If a codicil, or a will of later date, has been found, it must be produced.

17.51   If the grantee died before the grant issued, a certificate of his death is required.

17.52   If one of the grantees has become incapable of managing his affairs, evidence of incapacity is required. The district judge or registrar will normally accept a certificate by the Responsible Medical Officer in the form set out in para. **11.226**, ante, or a certificate by the patient's doctor. If the Responsible Medical Officer or doctor is unable to give such a certificate, the matter should be referred to the district judge or registrar for his directions[1].

1 *Practice Note* [1962] 2 All ER 613, [1962] 1 WLR 738; Registrar's Direction (1969) 31 January.

District judge's or registrar's order

17.53   The order for revocation is drawn up and signed by the district judge or registrar, and the grant is cancelled and filed in the registry.

17.54   No fee is payable for the revocation of a grant.

New grant

17.55   Except as stated in para. **17.57**, post, the executor or administrator who is to take the new grant following upon the revocation cannot swear the papers to lead to the grant until after the revocation of the former grant has been effected.

17.56   In applications lodged at the Principal Registry a 'plain' copy of the revoked grant (see para. **21.17**, post) bearing the note of revocation on it must be lodged with the papers. Forms of oath, Nos. 71 and 119.

Combined application for revocation of probate and new grant

17.57   Where a grant of probate has issued to two or more executors, one of whom has subsequently become incapable of managing his affairs, and it is proposed to revoke it and obtain a new grant of probate to the remaining original grantee or grantees, one sufficient affidavit may be used both to lead the order for revocation and to serve as the oath on which the new grant issues. The will may be referred to as that already proved, and need not be re-marked nor need a copy be annexed. No further Inland Revenue account need be lodged.

17.58   All necessary papers should be lodged with the Receiver of Papers at the Principal Registry (or at the district probate registry, as the case may be). Revocation of the grant will be effected, after which the new grant will be issued.

17.59   This procedure may be applied only to cases strictly within the terms of para. **17.57**, ante[1], or on revocation of a grant of probate because of the death of an executor before its issue: see para. **2.51**, ante. In all other cases the procedure in the preceding paragraphs must be followed.

1 Secretary's Circular, 6 September 1956.

Cases where court will not revoke

17.60   The court has refused to revoke a grant obtained by the administrator on the suggestion that he was the sole person entitled to the estate, though other parties interested were afterwards discovered, and though all parties interested consented that the grant should be revoked and a new grant made to another party interested[1]. Similarly, it is unnecessary for a grant to a trust corporation based on the erroneous statement that certain persons are 'the only persons entitled to share in the estate' to be revoked in order to give to other beneficiaries the shares to which they are entitled as a matter of law[2].

1 *Re Heslop's Goods* (1846) 1 Rob Eccl 457.
2 *Re Ward, National Westminster Bank Ltd v Ward* [1971] 2 All ER 1249, [1971] 1 WLR 1376.

17.61   A grant limited to proceedings in the Chancery Division will not be revoked before the action is ended, merely in order to enable a general grant to issue[1]. Nor will the court revoke such a grant on the application of the executor of a will, unless he can show that inconvenience will result from the continuance of the limited administration.

1 *Re Brown's Goods* (1872) LR 2 P & D 455.

17.62 Where the ultimate object of an application to revoke administration de bonis non was to preserve the right to sue after twenty years, the application was refused as frivolous and vexatious[1].

1 *Willis v Earl Beauchamp* (1886) 11 PD 59.

17.63 The court will not revoke a grant merely on the ground that the administrator has not disclosed all the assets of the deceased, and has failed to furnish satisfactory answers to requests for particulars of the estate[1].

1 *Re Cope's Estate* [1954] 1 All ER 698, [1954] 1 WLR 608.

Incapacity of sole grantee

17.64 Where a sole grantee, or sole surviving grantee, becomes incapable of managing his affairs, a new grant may be made without revocation of the existing grant. The former practice of impounding the old grant in these circumstances has been abandoned[1].

1 Registrar's Direction (1985) 9 July.

17.65 The new grant, whether made to a person equally entitled or, in accordance with NCPR 35 (see paras. **11.209** ff., ante), to some other person, will be a grant de bonis non and for the use and benefit of the incapable grantee, limited during his incapacity—see para. **17.71**, post: except that if the new grantee is an executor to whom power had been reserved, an ordinary grant of double probate (see paras. **13.119** ff., ante) will issue, with a note referring to the incapacity of the other proving, or sole surviving proving, executor[1].

1 Registrar's Direction (1956) 16 July.

17.66 As to the procedure where one of two or more grantees becomes incapable, see paras. **17.13–17.15**, ante.

Impounding grants

When grant impounded

17.67 Where a sole, or sole surviving, grantee becomes incapable, and a new grant is made, the former practice of impounding the old grant has been abandoned[1].

1 Registrar's Direction (1985) 9 July.

17.68 Grants may still be impounded on an application for the addition of a personal representative under NCPR 26(2) (see para. **7.43**, ante); but in practice this is rarely, if ever, directed.

17.69 Where the deceased died domiciled in Eire and the executor (who proved the will in England) became a person of unsound mind, an order for impounding the grant was made before making a grant to the committee appointed by the court of domicile, on the ground that, though appointed by the court of the domicile, the committee was not an officer of the English court, and therefore the grant should not be at large[1].

1 *Re Towell* (1941); *Re Sanders* (1941); *Re Kella* (1942).

Form of new grant

17.70   The new grant is of the *unadministered* estate, except in the case of a grant of double probate which, following the normal practice, is a grant of the whole estate, although the amount shown in the oath and grant is that remaining unadministered (see also paras. **13.119** ff., ante). Form of oath, No. 118.

Grantee's recovery

17.71   In the event of the recovery of the grantee, the temporary grant, together with the original grant when it has remained at large, is lodged at the registry, and, upon evidence of recovery (i.e. if the temporary grant was made to a person authorised by the Court of Protection, the order of that court determining the proceedings, or, in any other case, a doctor's affidavit) and proof that notice has been given to the temporary grantee, the district judge or registrar will order that the temporary grant be noted that it has ceased and expired by reason of the original grantee having recovered his capacity, and that the original grant be re-delivered to the recovered grantee. The temporary grant is also given out after notation.

Death of grantee before recovery

17.72   When the sole or only surviving executor grantee dies without having recovered, having made a will appointing executors who duly prove it, the original grant may be delivered to the executors if it has been impounded under the former practice, by order of a district judge or registrar, for the purpose of establishing the chain of executorship.

CHAPTER 18

Resealing

Summary

History

18.01 Previously to the transfer of probate jurisdiction in this country to the Court of Probate effected by the Court of Probate Act 1857, it often happened that more than one grant of representation was necessary in a given case owing to the assets of the deceased having been situate within the jurisdiction of different probate authorities. With the increasing importance of personal property, which was so marked a feature of the first half of the nineteenth century, the inconvenience of the necessity for multiple grants became more and more acute.

18.02 The institution of one probate authority for the whole of England and Wales went a long way towards meeting the objections that were being voiced against the pre-1857 system; and although the Court of Probate Act 1857 did not itself provide for making English grants effective over property situate in Scotland and Ireland, a considerable step in this direction was taken by two contemporaneous Acts, viz. the Probates and Letters of Administration (Ireland) Act 1857 and the Confirmation of Executors (Scotland) Act 1858 which introduced a simple procedure by which a grant of representation, obtained in any part of the United Kingdom, as then constituted, could be made operative in the other parts of that kingdom simply by having it resealed, or certified, by the competent probate authority.

18.03 The scheme thus originated remained in full force as between England, Scotland and Northern Ireland until 31 December 1971. As from 1 January 1972, however, ss. 168 and 169 of the Supreme Court of Judicature (Consolidation) Act 1925, which had replaced the statutes mentioned above, were repealed, together with the corresponding provisions of the law of Scotland and Northern Ireland, by the Administration of Estates Act 1971 which, as set out in the following paragraphs, provides for extended recognition to be given to grants issued within the United Kingdom, and entirely abolished the resealing of grants as between England and Wales, Scotland and Northern Ireland.

18.04   In the case of grants issued in Ireland where the date of death was prior to 1 April 1923, resealing in England was governed by s. 95 of the Probates and Letters of Administration (Ireland) Act 1857 which remained hitherto unrepealed in respect of such deaths. As from 1 January 1972, however, this section was fully repealed by the Administration of Estates Act 1971, s. 12 and Sch. 2, Part I[1]. The resealing of Irish grants is thus no longer possible whatever the date of death.

1 See p. 803, post.

18.05   By the Colonial Probates Acts 1892[1] and 1927[2], and the Foreign Jurisdiction Act 1913[3], the principle of resealing was extended outside the United Kingdom. The relative provisions of these Acts are dealt with in paras. **18.27** ff., post.

1 See p. 728, post.
2 See p. 764, post.
3 7 Halsbury's Statutes (4th edn) 249.

Extended scope of United Kingdom grants

Recognition of Scottish confirmations in England and Wales

18.06   Section 1(1) of the Administration of Estates Act 1971 is as follows:

'(1) Where a person dies domiciled in Scotland:
(a) a confirmation granted in respect of all or part of his estate and noting his Scottish domicile, and
(b) a certificate of confirmation noting his Scottish domicile and relating to one or more items of his estate
shall, without being resealed, be treated for the purposes of the law of England and Wales as a grant of representation (in accordance with subsection (2) below) to the executors named in the confirmation or certificate in respect of the property of the deceased of which according to the terms of the confirmation they are executors or, as the case may be, in respect of the item or items of property specified in the certificate of confirmation.'

18.07   A Scottish confirmation includes a copy of the inventory of the estate of the deceased as deposed to by the executors and authorises the latter to deal with the items included in such inventory. To facilitate the administration of estates, the Scottish courts also issue on request certificates of confirmation: these show that specific items of the estate of the deceased are included in the confirmation. Such certificates, provided that they include a statement that the deceased died domiciled in Scotland, are under s. 1(1) of the Act treated as the equivalent of an English grant in respect of the specific items of the estate set out in the certificate.

18.08   By s. 6 of the Act[1] the Scottish courts are empowered to include in the inventory of the estate of a person dying domiciled in Scotland any real estate situated in England and Wales and Northern Ireland.

1 See p. 801, post.

18.09   Under s. 1(2) of the Act, where a confirmation or a certificate of confirmation is treated by virtue of s. 1(1) as an English grant, if it appears from it that the executors named in it are executors nominate, the grant is to be treated as a grant of probate: in any other case it is to be treated as a grant of letters of administration. However, notwithstanding that a confirmation may be treated as a grant of probate, it is provided by s. 1(3) of the Act that s. 7 of the Administration of Estates Act 1925[1] is not to apply on the death of an executor named in a confirmation or certificate of confirmation. The expression 'executor named in a confirmation' is somewhat ambiguous: by analogy with s. 1(2) it would appear to signify the executor to whom the confirmation was granted, but the effect of s. 1(3) appears to be that no chain of executorship can be constituted or continued through a Scottish confirmation.

1 See p. 746, post. As to chain of executorship, see also paras. **4.64** ff., ante.

18.10   The foregoing provisions apply in relation to confirmations granted before as well as after the commencement of the Act (1 January 1972). In relation to a confirmation granted before that date the section has effect as if it had come into force immediately before the grant of the confirmation (s. 1(6)).

Recognition of Northern Irish grants in England and Wales

18.11   Section 1 of the Administration of Estates Act 1971 applies also to Northern Irish grants. Section 1(4) is as follows:

'(4) Subject to subsection (5) below, where a person dies domiciled in Northern Ireland, a grant of probate of his will or letters of administration in respect of his estate (or any part of it) made by the High Court in Northern Ireland and noting his domicile there shall, without being resealed, be treated for the purposes of the law of England and Wales as if it had been originally made by the High Court in England and Wales.'

18.12   Section 1(5) provides that a person who is a personal representative according to the law of England and Wales by virtue of the recognition of a Northern Irish grant, shall not be required under s. 25 of the Administration of Estates Act 1925 (as substituted by s. 9 of the Administration of Estates Act 1971[1]) to deliver up his grant to the High Court in England and Wales.

1 See p. 802, post.

18.13   The provision for the recognition of Northern Irish grants applies in relation to grants issued before as well as after the commencement of the Act (1 January 1972). In relation to a grant issued before that date, s. 1 has effect as if it had come into force immediately before the grant was made (s. 1(6)).

18.14   The provisions of s. 7 of the Administration of Estates Act 1925[1] are not disapplied in relation to Northern Irish grants: accordingly a chain of executorship is capable of being created or continued by a Northern Irish grant of probate of the will of a person domiciled in Northern Ireland.

1 See p. 746, post. As to chain of executorship, see also paras. **4.64** ff., ante.

English grant where deceased died domiciled in Scotland or Northern Ireland

18.15   Where a person dies domiciled in Scotland or Northern Ireland leaving estate in England and Wales, the procedure contemplated under the Administration of Estates Act 1971 is for a grant of representation to his estate to be taken in the court of his place of domicile. Where this is done, further representation in England and Wales is unnecessary and should not be applied for. However, if no confirmation or grant has been made in the country of domicile, application may be made, where necessary, for a grant in England and Wales prior to, or in place of, application in Scotland or Northern Ireland, as the case may be. In this event, in order to prevent a possible duality of representation the English grant will be specifically limited to the estate in England and Wales, and further limited until representation is granted in the country of domicile. For the practice on application for such a grant, see para. **12.23**, ante.

Recognition in Northern Ireland of English grants and Scottish confirmations, and in Scotland of English and Northern Irish grants

18.16   Sections 2 and 3 of the Administration of Estates Act 1971[1] contain complementary provisions. Section 2 provides for the recognition in Northern Ireland of grants made in England and Wales in respect of the estates of persons dying domiciled there, and confirmations granted in Scotland in respect of persons dying domiciled there. A grant, confirmation or certificate of confirmation containing a note of such domicile is to be treated, without resealing, as if made in Northern Ireland.

1 See pp. 800, 801, post.

18.17   Section 3 similarly provides that where a person dies domiciled in England and Wales or Northern Ireland, a grant made by the High Court in England and Wales and noting his domicile there, has, without being resealed, the like force and effect and has the same operation in relation to property in Scotland as a confirmation given under the seal of office of the Commissariat of Edinburgh to the grantee.

18.18   Sections 2 and 3 both apply to grants and confirmations issued before as well as after the commencement of the Act.

Estate to be disclosed in Inland Revenue account

18.19   In the case of a person who died domiciled in England and Wales, a grant issued in this country thus makes title to the whole of the estate in the United Kingdom (i.e. in England and Wales, Scotland and Northern Ireland), and all such estate must be disclosed in any Inland Revenue account (see paras. **8.25** ff., ante).

18.20   Probate fees are in such cases payable on the net value of the whole of the estate in the United Kingdom: see paras. **4.258–4.260**, ante.

Evidence of grants or confirmation

18.21   Section 4 contains provisions for the recognition in each country of documents purporting to be grants, confirmations or certificates of confirmations and, in the case of confirmations, duplicates or, in the case of grants, copies thereof, issued in the other countries comprising the United Kingdom.

Trust property

18.22   Section 5 empowers the Scottish courts to include in a confirmation in respect of a person who dies domiciled in Scotland, a note or statement of property in England and Wales or Northern Ireland held by the deceased in trust: the confirmation is to be accepted in England and Wales or Northern Ireland in respect of such trust property as in respect of the remainder of the estate specified in the confirmation.

Notation of domicile in England and Wales

18.23   To entitle a grant in the estate of a person dying domiciled in England and Wales to recognition in Scotland and Northern Ireland, it is necessary for it to contain a statement of such domicile (Administration of Estates Act 1971, ss. 2, 3[1]). Such recognition extends to grants made both before and after the commencement of the Act of 1971. A statement of the place of domicile is required to appear in every oath (NCPR 8(2)), and is reproduced in the grant, but in the case of a grant issued prior to 1 January 1972 a statement of domicile may not have been included. If in such a case there are assets in Scotland or Northern Ireland to be administered, or it is for some other reason necessary for the personal representative to prove his title in one of these countries, the procedure for obtaining a notation of domicile in England and Wales set out in the following paragraph should be followed.

1 See pp. 800, 801, post.

Notation of domicile after grant has issued

18.24   If no statement of domicile in England and Wales has been included in a grant, application for a notation of domicile may be made subsequently. The grant and an affidavit by one of the executors, or by all of the administrators, should be taken or sent by post to the Record Keeper at the Principal Registry, or to the district registry where the grant issued. The affidavit should show that the deceased died domiciled in England and Wales. In the case of grants issued before 1 March 1961 the affidavit should also show that no additional estate has fallen in, and that part of the property is in Scotland or Northern Ireland, as the case may be. (Forms Nos. 28 or 29.) The district judge or registrar will then make an order for the notation.

Where the value of the estate has been increased

18.25   Where a notation of domicile is required in respect of a grant which issued before 1 March 1961 and additional estate has been discovered subsequent to the issue of the grant, the affidavit to lead to the notation should state whether any of such additional estate is situate in Scotland or Northern Ireland. If this be so, the Record Keeper will require to be satisfied that no further estate duty is payable, or that any such duty has been paid.

18.26   No fee is payable for noting the grant as to the domicile of the deceased.

Colonial[1] grants resealed in England and Wales

18.27   By s. 1 of the Colonial Probates Act 1892[2] it is provided that:

> 'Her Majesty the Queen may, on being satisfied that the legislature of any British possession has made adequate provision for the recognition in that possession of probates and letters of administration granted by the courts of the United Kingdom, direct by Order in Council that this Act shall, subject to any exceptions and modifications

specified in the Order, apply to that possession, and thereupon, while the Order is in force, this Act shall apply accordingly.'

1   The term 'colonial' is used for convenience in this chapter, but the Colonial Probates Acts also authorise the resealing of grants issued by a number of former colonies, protectorates, etc. which have attained independence within the Commonwealth, and by South Africa while it was a Republic outside the Commonwealth (see paras. **18.35–18.37**, post).
2   For full text of the Act, see p. 728, post. The term 'British possession' under s. 1 of the Act means, by virtue of Schedule 1 to the Interpretation Act 1978, 'any part of H.M. Dominions outside the United Kingdom', and is thereby not restricted to British dependent territories.

18.28   And by s. 2(1) of the same Act it is provided that:

'Where a court of probate in a British possession to which this Act applies has granted probate or letters of administration in respect of the estate of a deceased person, the probate or letters so granted, may, on being produced to, and a copy thereof deposited with, a court of probate in the United Kingdom, be sealed with the seal of that court, and, thereupon, shall be of like force and effect, and have the same operation in the United Kingdom, as if granted by that court'.

18.29   Under s. 5 of, and the First Schedule to, the Foreign Jurisdiction Act 1890[1] (as amended by the Foreign Jurisdiction Act 1913[2]), Her Majesty may direct by Order in Council that the Colonial Probates Act 1892 shall extend to any foreign country in which, for the time being, Her Majesty has jurisdiction.

1   7 Halsbury's Statutes (4th edn) 241.
2   7 Halsbury's Statutes (4th edn) 249.

18.30   The Colonial Probates (Protected States and Mandated Territories) Act 1927[1] extended the power to apply the Colonial Probates Act 1892 to any territories, being either territories under Her Majesty's protection or those in respect of which a mandate on behalf of the League of Nations had been accepted by Her Majesty, to which it could not be applied by virtue of the Foreign Jurisdiction Acts 1890 and 1913.

1   See p. 764, post.

18.31   On the termination of the League of Nations, the powers under the Act of 1927 were preserved in relation to trust territories administered under the trusteeship system of the United Kingdom.

18.32   Section 3 of the Colonial Probates Act 1892 authorises the resealing in the United Kingdom of grants issued by British courts in foreign countries (see paras. **18.105** ff., post).

18.33   The Act operates to permit resealing only where an Order in Council has been made applying the Act to the country or territory in which the grant issued, but when such an order has been made, the Act authorises the resealing of grants whether issued before or after the date of application of the Act (s. 5).

18.34   Section 6 of the Act[1] defines the documents which are included in the terms 'probate' and 'letters of administration'.

1   See p. 729, post.

Changes in status of former colonies etc.

18.35   In recent years many of the former colonies and protectorates etc. to which the Act had been applied have attained independence. Where such territories have elected to remain within the British Commonwealth, the provisions as to resealing usually remain in force, either by virtue of a specific provision in the particular Independence Act, or by a general provision therein that the existing law of the United Kingdom is not affected by the change in status except in so far as is specifically provided.

18.36   In a few instances the resealing of grants issued by former colonial territories which are not now part of the Commonwealth is no longer possible (e.g. Aden, so far as regards grants issued on or after 1 December 1967).

18.37   In the case of South Africa, s. 2 of, and the Second Schedule to, the South Africa Act 1962 specifically authorised the continued resealing of grants issued in South Africa notwithstanding that it became a Republic outside the Commonwealth.

Territories to which the Act applies

18.38   The Colonial Probates Act Application Order 1965[1] consolidated in one order the provisions of all previous Orders in Council, save that which applied the Act to South Africa, which remains unrevoked (see also previous paragraph).

---

1   S.I. 1965 No. 1530.

18.39   The Colonial Probates Acts now apply to permit the resealing of grants made in the following countries and territories:

[Aden][1]	Ghana
Alberta	Gibraltar
Antigua	Gilbert and Ellice Islands[3]
Australian Capital Territory	Grenada
Bahamas	Guyana (formerly British Guiana)
Barbados	Hong Kong
Belize (formerly British Honduras)	Jamaica
Bermuda	Kenya
Botswana (formerly Bechuanaland)	Kiribati[3]
British Antarctic Territory	Lesotho (formerly Basutoland)
British Columbia	Malawi
British Sovereign Base Areas in	Malaysia[4]
Cyprus	Manitoba
Brunei	Montserrat
Cayman Islands	New Brunswick
Christmas Island (Australian)	New Guinea Territory
Cocos (Keeling) Islands	[New Hebrides[5]]
Cyprus (Republic)[2]	New South Wales
Dominica	New Zealand
Falkland Islands	Newfoundland
Falkland Islands Dependencies	Nigeria
Fiji	Norfolk Island
Gambia	Northern Territory of Australia

North-West Territories of Canada
Nova Scotia
Ontario
Papua (New Guinea)
Prince Edward Island
Queensland
St. Christopher (Kitts), Nevis and Anguilla[6]
St. Helena
St. Lucia
St. Vincent
Saskatchewan
Seychelles (Republic)
Sierra Leone
Singapore[4]
Solomon Islands
South Africa[7]

South Australia
Southern Rhodesia (now Zimbabwe)[8]
Sri Lanka (formerly Ceylon)[9]
Swaziland
Tanzania[10]
Tasmania
Tortola (formerly Virgin Islands)
Trinidad and Tobago (Republic)
Turks and Caicos Islands
Tuvalu (formerly Ellice Islands)[11]
Uganda
Victoria
Western Australia
Zambia
Zimbabwe (formerly Southern Rhodesia)[8]

1 On 30 November 1967 Aden ceased to form part of H.M. Dominions. Grants made in Aden after that date cannot be resealed (Secretary's Circular, 17 January 1968).

2 Only those grants issued by the courts under the jurisdiction of the recognised government of Cyprus may be resealed. Accordingly any document purporting to be a grant issued by a court of the 'Turkish Republic of Northern Cyprus', having only de facto jurisdiction, may not be resealed although such a document may be used to support an application for an order under NCPR 30(1)(c) (see paras. **12.112–12.117**, ante).

3 On 1 January 1976 the Ellice Islands separated from the Gilbert Islands and became a separate colony under the name of Tuvalu. On 1 October 1978 the colony of Tuvalu achieved independence within the Commonwealth. On 19 June 1979, by virtue of the Kiribati Act 1979, the former Gilbert Islands attained full independent status as the Republic of Kiribati. By that Act, the Colonial Probates Acts continue to apply to Kiribati.

4 On 9 August 1965 Singapore seceded from the Federation of Malaysia and became an independent sovereign state. The Colonial Probates Acts continue to apply to Singapore (see Singapore Act 1966).

5 The Act of 1892 applied to the New Hebrides only to the extent of Her Majesty's jurisdiction there. The New Hebrides became an independent country (now known as Vanuatu) on 30 July 1980. Since Her Majesty from that date has no jurisdiction there, the Colonial Probates Acts only apply to grants issued before independence.

6 On 19 December 1980 Anguilla ceased to form part of the territory of the associated states of St. Christopher, Nevis and Anguilla: the Colonial Probates Acts continue to apply to these states.

7 The resealing of grants issued in South Africa, continues under the authority of the South Africa Act 1962, s. 2 and Second Schedule, including the period when South Africa was a Republic outside the Commonwealth. As to South African grants, see also para. **18.62**, post.

8 On 18 April 1980, Southern Rhodesia became an independent country known as Zimbabwe. Provision has been made in the Act granting such independence for the continued application of the Colonial Probates Acts to grants issued by its courts on and after that date. Furthermore, by virtue of an Ordinance enacted on 7 December 1979, provision was made for the recognition of any act done in Southern Rhodesia in reliance upon any law or purported law in operation in that country from 11 November 1965 onwards until its independence. One of the effects of this provision is that grants of representation issued by the courts in Southern Rhodesia, irrespective of the date of issue, may now be resealed in England and Wales under the Colonial Probates Act. (*Practice Direction* [1980] 2 All ER 324, [1980] 1 WLR 553).

9 Grants of probate and letters of administration in Sri Lanka during the period 1 January 1974 to 31 December 1977 were issued by the Public Trustee and not by a court of law. Such grants may be resealed under the Colonial Probates Act 1892 (Secretary's Circular, 14 June 1985).

10 The Colonial Probates Act (Application to Tanzania) Order 1969 provides that the Colonial Probates Act 1892 shall be deemed to have applied to Tanganyika from 9 December 1961 (the date on which Tanganyika attained independence within H.M. Dominions) until immediately before 26 April 1964 (the date on which it entered into a union with Zanzibar).

11 On 1 January 1976 the Ellice Islands separated from the Gilbert Islands and became a separate colony under the name of Tuvalu: on 1 October 1978 the colony of Tuvalu achieved independence within the Commonwealth.

Inland Revenue account

18.40 Before resealing a colonial grant, the court must be satisfied that inheritance tax or capital transfer tax has been paid in respect of so much, if any, of the estate of the deceased as is liable to tax in the United Kingdom[1]. It is accordingly provided by NCPR 39(2) that, on any application for resealing, an Inland Revenue affidavit or account shall be lodged. An Inland Revenue *affidavit* is required when the deceased died before 13 March 1975.

1 Colonial Probates Act 1892, s. 2(2)(a) (see p. 728, post) in relation to estate duty as respects deaths before 13 March 1975, and Supreme Court Act 1981, s. 109 (see p. 843, post) in relation to inheritance tax or capital transfer tax as respects deaths after 12 March 1975.

18.41 The account may be signed by the grantee himself, but it is usually more convenient for it to be signed by the attorney or other agent of the grantee who applies for the resealing.

18.42 As to the practice in relation to Inland Revenue accounts, see Chap. 8. The accounts should be submitted to the Capital Taxes Office for control before the application for resealing is made (see also paras. **18.65–18.71**, post, as to applications lodged by post).

Guarantee

18.43 The Non-Contentious Probate Rules 1987, unlike the previous Rules, contain no provision relating to guarantees. Accordingly a guarantee is not required on an application for resealing proceeding under the current Rules.

Domicile

18.44 Section 2(2) of the Colonial Probates Act 1892[1] provides that the court may require such evidence, if any, as it thinks fit as to the domicile of the deceased. No oath is required on an application for resealing, and the statement as to the domicile of the deceased given in the Inland Revenue account is normally accepted by the registry. Additional evidence as to the domicile may, however, be required by the Capital Taxes Office in relation to the liability for inheritance tax or capital transfer tax.

1 See p. 728, post.

18.45 Where there are separate jurisdictions (e.g. in the case of Australia and Canada) the particular State or Province must be specified. This is not necessary in the case of South Africa, except where the grant being resealed is in respect of a will made before 1 January 1954.

Class of grantee who may normally apply

18.46 NCPR 39(3) provides that, except by leave of a district judge or registrar, no grant shall be resealed unless it was made to such a person as is mentioned in sub-paragraph (a) or (b) of paragraph (1) of NCPR 30, or to a person to whom a grant could be made under sub-paragraph (a) of paragraph (3) of that rule.

Person entrusted by the court of domicile

18.47 NCPR 30(1)(a) provides for a grant to be made to the person entrusted with administration by the court having jurisdiction at the place where the deceased died domiciled. Accordingly, if the court which made the colonial grant is the court having jurisdiction at the place of domicile of the deceased, it may be resealed, even though the grant is not such as would be made in England. Thus a grant made to a corporation having its principal place of business out of England and Wales may be resealed[1].

1   *Re McLaughlin* [1922] P 235; Registrar's Circular, 12 April 1927.

Person beneficially entitled to the estate by the law of the place of domicile

18.48   In relation to resealing, NCPR 30(1)(b) applies where the colonial grant was made by a court other than that having jurisdiction at the place where the deceased died domiciled. For example, if the deceased died domiciled in country 'A', but a colonial grant has been made in country 'B', then, unless the leave of the district judge or registrar is obtained, or the case is within NCPR 30(3)(a) (see next paragraph), the grant may be resealed only upon evidence that the person to whom it has been made is the person, or is one of the persons, beneficially entitled to the estate in accordance with the law of country 'A', the place of domicile. Except where the relevant law is the law of England and Wales, beneficial entitlement is established by affidavit of law, or by a certificate of law by a notary practising in the place of domicile, in accordance with NCPR 19 or by an order or declaration by the court of the place where the deceased died domiciled (see also paras. **12.25–12.33**, ante).

Colonial grantee the executor

18.49   NCPR 30(3)(a) enables probate of any will which is admissible to proof (i.e. in England and Wales) to be granted: (i) where a will is in the English or Welsh language, to the executor named therein; or (ii) whatever the language of the will, to a person who qualifies as executor according to the tenor. Thus, provided that it is established that the will is entitled to proof in this country, a colonial grant of probate to an executor named in the will (if in English or Welsh) or to an executor according to the tenor (whatever the language of the will) may be resealed in England irrespective of the domicile of the deceased.

18.50   This provision becomes relevant only where the colonial grant has been made by a court other than that of the domicile of the deceased.

18.51   Full details of the circumstances in which wills of persons dying domiciled out of England and Wales are admissible to proof in this country are given in paras. **12.34** ff., ante. It may, however, be stated here that a will which is in the English language and in English form is normally accepted as valid where the domicile of the deceased is in Northern Ireland, the Republic of Ireland, Australia, Canada or New Zealand. Moreover, in the case of persons dying on or after 1 January 1964 the Wills Act 1963 enables a will to be accepted as well executed if its execution conformed to any one of a number of alternative tests. If the foregoing provisions do not enable the formal validity of the will to be accepted without further evidence, an affidavit, or a certificate by a notary practising in the relevant country, of law may be necessary.

Grantee not qualified under rule 30

18.52   Where the grant which it is sought to have resealed was made to a person who does not qualify by reference to r. 30(1)(a) or (b), or r. 30(3)(a), the grant may be resealed only by leave of the district judge or registrar (NCPR 39(3)).

18.53   Application for such leave should be made to the Principal of the Probate Department of the Principal Registry or, if the application for resealing is being made at a district probate registry, to the registrar of that district registry.

Documents which may be resealed

18.54   Section 2(1) and (4) of the Act authorise the resealing of the original colonial grant, a duplicate thereof sealed with the seal of the court granting the same, or a copy certified as correct by or under the authority of the court of issue. A copy certified by the proper officer of the court which issued the grant is acceptable, although not under seal[1].

1   Secretary's Circular, 20 July 1955.

18.55   An exemplification of the original grant (when containing all the essential parts of the grant) is held to be a copy within the meaning of the subsection, and may be resealed[1].

1   President's Direction (1902) 13 March.

18.56   The New Zealand statute 'Trustee Companies Act 1967' provides, inter alia, that in certain circumstances a trustee company may, in any case where it would be entitled to obtain a grant of representation in New Zealand, instead file an election to administer in the Supreme Court there. On such election being filed, the trustee company is deemed to be the personal representative in exactly the same way and to the same extent as if a grant of representation had issued.

18.57   Such elections may be resealed under the Colonial Probates Acts, on it being certified on behalf of the trustee company that the election is still in force and an undertaking given that, in the event of further estate in New Zealand being discovered which would place the estate beyond the statutory limit for the election procedure, no further step will be taken in the administration of the estate in England without obtaining further representation in New Zealand: see also 'New Zealand. Public Trustee', paras. **18.84** ff., post.

18.58   A similar procedure may be followed in respect of resealing elections or similar documents from other countries to which the Colonial Probates Acts apply on production of a copy of the local ordinance which establishes that such document has the same effect as a grant[1].

1   *Practice Direction* (1982) 126 Sol Jo 176.

18.59   It is the practice to allow only grants which are in the English language to be resealed.

18.60   Although the English High Court is not granting probate or administration when a colonial grant is resealed, it would appear to be contrary to the principle indicated in the Supreme Court Act 1981, s. 114(1) to reseal a grant issued to more than four persons, if more than four of them are alive at the time resealing is applied for.

Copy will to be lodged

18.61   Every grant lodged for resealing must include a copy of any will to which the grant relates, or be accompanied by a copy thereof certified as correct by or under the authority of the court by which the grant was made: NCPR 39(5). Where the grant and copy will are separate documents, it must be satisfactorily established that they refer to the same deceased, and to each other.

18.62   Grants issued in certain countries, notably South Africa, are described as letters of administration or letters of executorship whether the deceased died testate or intestate, and no copy of the will is annexed to the grant in cases of testacy. When preparing applications to reseal grants made in such countries it should be ascertained whether or not the deceased left a will, so that the copies of the will required by NCPR 39(5) can be lodged. The use of the expression 'executor testamentary' to describe the grantee is an indication that the deceased died testate: on the other hand, the term 'executor dative' and, in the case of South African grants, 'executor', is applicable both to cases of testacy and intestacy.

Practice

18.63   NCPR 39(1) provides:

> 'An application under the Colonial Probates Acts 1892 and 1927 for the resealing of probate or administration granted by the court of a country to which those Acts apply may be made by the person to whom the grant was made or by any person authorised in writing to apply on his behalf.'

18.64   The application may be made by the grantee or any person authorised in writing to apply on his behalf: in the latter case a formal power of attorney is not essential (see 'Power of attorney etc.', paras. **18.77** ff., post).

Mode of application

18.65   The application may be made at the Principal Registry or at any district probate registry. The papers may be lodged there by the grantee, or the person authorised by him, or by a solicitor: the application may be submitted by post (see paras. **2.09** ff. and **2.58**, ante).

18.66   Where a solicitor is not instructed and the application is made at the Principal Registry, it is not essential for the application to be made, as in the case of an application for a grant of representation, through the Personal Application Department. An applicant who is able to obtain and complete the necessary documents may, if he wishes, lodge them with, or send them by post to, the Receiver of Papers at the Principal Registry. But, if desired, the grantee or the person authorised in writing to apply on his behalf may make the application through the Personal Application Department of the Principal Registry, in which case the necessary papers are prepared in that Department. Personal attendance by appointment is, however, in this case essential: the Personal Application Department cannot deal with applications entirely through the post. An additional fee, depending on the value of the estate in this country, is payable in respect of the service of the Department (see NC Probate Fees Order 1981, Fee 2, p. 962, post).

18.67   Similarly, the grantee, or person authorised in writing to apply on his behalf, who is able to obtain and complete the necessary documents may lodge them at (or post them to) a district probate registry or, on payment of the extra fee, have the necessary papers prepared at the district probate registry and attend there on an appointment to complete the application.

Postal applications from abroad

18.68 The requirement that every solicitor through whom an application for a grant is made must give an address within the jurisdiction[1] does not apply to applications for resealing[2]. There is, therefore, no objection in principle to the submission of applications for the resealing of colonial grants through the post by correspondents who are out of this country[3]. In practice, however, there may be difficulties in complying with the requirements set out in this chapter, in particular with regard to the completion of the appropriate English form of Inland Revenue account, and difficulties may also arise in the collection and realisation of the assets unless a solicitor, attorney or other agent in England and Wales is employed.

1 NCPR 4(2).
2 NCPR 2(1).
3 Secretary's Circular, 29 June 1959.

Postal applications generally

18.69 To avoid delay, in any application submitted by post, care should be taken to see that all the requirements detailed in this chapter are observed, and that a remittance for the appropriate fee is enclosed. Remittances for fees should be by crossed cheque, postal or money order, payable to 'H.M. Paymaster General'. Any remittance in respect of inheritance tax or capital transfer tax should be by *separate* crossed cheque or money order payable to 'Inland Revenue'. Postal applications should be addressed to 'The Receiver of Papers, Principal Registry of the Family Division, Somerset House, Strand, London WC2R 1LP' or to one of the district probate registries (see para. **2.58**, ante).

Documents required

18.70 The following documents should be lodged:

(a) The colonial grant, or an officially issued duplicate, copy or exemplification, including, or accompanied by, a copy of the will, if any (see also 'Documents which may be resealed', paras. **18.54–18.60**, ante).

(b) A complete copy of the grant, including a copy of any will, for deposit in accordance with s. 2(1) of the Colonial Probates Act 1892. If desired, a photographic copy will be made in the registry, upon payment of a fee of 25p for each page[1].

(c) Where the application is made by some person on behalf of the grantee, the power of attorney, or other document authorising the agent to apply for resealing (see 'Power of attorney etc.' paras. **18.77** ff., post).

(d) Inland Revenue account (see paras. **18.40–18.42**, ante). This should be submitted to the Capital Taxes Office for control before the papers are lodged at the registry.

1 Secretary's Circular, 17 June 1954: NC Probate Fees Order 1981, Fee 8.

Fees

18.71 The fee for resealing a colonial grant is the same as on application for a normal grant of representation being made[1]: see paras. **4.250** ff., ante.

1 NC Probate Fees Order 1981, Fee 1.

18.72 For a photographic copy of a grant or will made in the registry, the fee is 25p for each sheet, if made on the application for resealing[1].

1 NC Probate Fees Order 1981, Fee 8.

Limited and temporary grants

18.73 No grant which contains a limitation, and no temporary grant, may be resealed, except by leave of a district judge or registrar[1].

1 NCPR 39(4).

18.74 Leave is normally given for the resealing of a temporary grant if it appears probable that the administration of the estate in this country will be completed before the expiry of the grant, and in the absence of special circumstances resealing is permitted in the case of a grant limited for the use and benefit of a minor or an incapable person. Grants limited to part of the estate are usually accepted for resealing unless the form of limitation is such as to exclude the English and Welsh estate: thus, a grant expressly limited to estate within the jurisdiction of the court of issue will not be resealed[1].

1 Registrar's Direction (1951) 16 July.

18.75 The leave of the district judge or registrar is unnecessary for the reseal of a grant expressed to relate to personal estate only[1]: see also paras. **18.91** and **18.92**, post.

1 Registrar's Direction (1936) 26 May.

Grant to attorney

18.76 The former practice, which required the production of the original power of attorney, or a copy of it, where the colonial grant has been made to an attorney, is no longer applicable[1].

1 Registrar's Direction (1974) 11 October.

Power of attorney, or authority to apply for resealing

18.77 Where the application to reseal is made by some person on behalf of the grantee, such person must be authorised in writing by the grantee to make the application[1].

1 NCPR 39(1).

18.78 The authority may take the form of a power of attorney, either limited to the application for resealing, or conferring wider powers (e.g. of collecting and realising the estate) upon the attorney; but any document signed by the actual grantee or grantees, and requesting a named (or otherwise identified or identifiable) person to obtain the resealing of the grant, is sufficient.

18.79 Where the applicant is authorised by a power of attorney, this document is filed with the papers. If it does not specifically authorise the applicant to apply for resealing, its terms should be sufficiently wide to include authority to make such an application.

18.80 For the procedure where the power of attorney contains additional powers and is required to be returned to the applicant, see para. **11.76**, ante. As to powers of attorney, see also Chap. 11.

18.81 A power of attorney which expressly authorises the attorney to obtain a grant in this country is not accepted as authority to apply for resealing of a colonial grant.

18.82 Where a trust corporation, whether acting as attorney or otherwise, applies for the resealing of a colonial grant, no copy of the resolution appointing a nominee to take the necessary steps on behalf of the corporation need be lodged[1].

1 Senior Registrar's decision, January 1956.

Office copy of power of attorney

18.83 Where, prior to the discontinuance of this facility on 1 October 1971[1], a general power of attorney had been filed at the Central Office of the Supreme Court, an office copy issued by the Filing Department of the Central Office will be accepted, but such office copy will not be handed out in exchange for an examined copy. See also paras. **11.51** and **11.52**, ante, as to the acceptability of certified photographic copies of powers of attorney.

1 See Powers of Attorney Act 1971, s. 11(2) and Schedule 2, repealing s. 219(1) of the Supreme Court of Judicature (Consolidation) Act 1925.

New Zealand. Public Trustee

18.84 The effect of certain provisions in the New Zealand statute the Public Trust Office Act 1957 is as follows: (i) the Public Trustee of New Zealand may in various circumstances obtain from the New Zealand court either a grant or an order to administer, which, while in force, has the full effect of a grant; (ii) if the estate in New Zealand is within certain limits (estate out of New Zealand is irrelevant for this purpose), the Public Trustee of New Zealand may file an election to administer. This, while in force, has the full effect of a grant.

18.85 Both orders to administer and elections to administer may be resealed under the Colonial Probates Acts.

18.86 In the case of elections, the document produced should be an official copy showing that the election itself has been filed in the New Zealand court; and the Public Trustee should certify that the election is still in force, and undertake that in the event of further estate in New Zealand beyond the statutory limitation being discovered he will not act further in the administration of the estate in England and Wales without obtaining further representation there[1].

1 Registrar's Direction (1958) 24 March: see also para. **12.103**, ante.

18.87 A general power of attorney has been filed in the Principal Registry by the Public Trustee of New Zealand appointing as his attorney the Public Trustee of England and Wales for the purposes of applying for resealing under the Colonial Probates Acts.

Australia. Public Trustee

18.88 The principles which apply to the resealing of orders to administer in favour of, and elections to administer by, the Public Trustee of New Zealand as set out in the previous section apply equally to orders obtained and elections given by the Public Trustee of Queensland, Australia (formerly known as the Public Curator of Queensland)[1].

1 Registrar's Direction (1979) 18 June.

18.89 Somewhat similar procedures for the filing of elections by the Public Trustee in respect of relatively small estates also exist in the Australian States of Victoria, Western Australia and Tasmania. The present practice is not to assume without evidence in the particular case under consideration that these qualify as grants which can be resealed. They may, however, be used to lead an order for a grant to the person entrusted (see paras. **12.94** ff., ante) on its being sworn that they are still in force[1].

1 Registrar's Direction (1972) 20 November.

Nil estate

18.90 Colonial grants may be resealed notwithstanding that there is no estate in England and Wales. The application must be accompanied by a statement by the applicant as to the reason for which the resealing is required[1].

1 President's Direction (1942) 4 March.

Real estate included

18.91 On resealing any grant not specifically limited to personal (or real) estate, the amount of the estate shown in the certificate on the grant and in the Act of resealing will be the whole value of the estate in England and Wales, including the gross value of the real estate, if any. Where there is real estate but no personalty, the amount will be the gross value of the real estate.

18.92 If the grant is itself specifically limited to personal (or real) estate, the limitation must be shown and the character of the estate stated[1].

1 Registrar's Direction (1951) 31 January.

Settled land

18.93 Where there was settled land in England and Wales which was vested in the deceased as tenant for life and remained settled land notwithstanding his death, difficulties may be caused in dealing with the land if a general colonial grant is resealed. In such a case it may be preferable to obtain separate English grants in accordance with the usual practice in cases where there was settled land (see Chap. 10).

One grantee applying

18.94 Where a colonial grant has been made to more than one person, it cannot be resealed on the application of one of the grantees without the authority of the others.

18.95 Where a colonial grant has been made to two or more executors, one of whom is dead at the time of the application to reseal, the applicant must prove the death of the deceased executor. The district judge's or registrar's fiat to seal the grant, and the record of resealing, will show that the reseal is made 'at the instance of the now-surviving executors'[1].

1 *Pemberton* (1898) September.

Application by personal representative

18.96 Where an application to reseal a grant of probate was made, after the death of the executor to whom it had been granted, by his executors, it was refused. But see also next paragraph.

Chain of executorship

18.97 Where the colonial court in a place to which the Colonial Probates Acts apply has granted probate to an executor, or executors, and such grant has been resealed in England and Wales, and where subsequently the same court has granted probate of the will of the executor (or the last survivor of the proving executors) to his executor, or executors, which grant has also been resealed in England and Wales, a chain of executorship exists, and no further grant to the original estate can be made in this country[1].

1 Registrar's Direction (1949) 24 February.

Amended grants; added grantees etc.

18.98 Where a grant has been resealed in England and Wales and has subsequently been endorsed by the colonial court to show that another grantee has been added, it may be again resealed. A further fiat is endorsed, reading 'Let this grant be resealed at the instance of —— (the added grantee) etc.'.

18.99 Where a grant has been resealed in England and Wales and is subsequently endorsed to show that a non-proving executor appointed by the will 'is deemed to be an executor to whom power was reserved and is deemed to be joint executor', it may be again resealed. A further fiat is endorsed, reading 'Let this grant be resealed at the instance of ——, the joint executor'.

18.100 Where a grant which has not been resealed in England and Wales is produced together with a separate order of the colonial court adding a grantee, it cannot be resealed. But where an exemplification is produced, combining under one seal copies of the grant and an order by which a grantee is added, it may be resealed.

18.101   An exemplification which contains copies of a probate and a double probate may be resealed, provided that the application is at the instance of all parties. The fiat and seal are placed on each copy grant, and a double fee is payable. If a probate and double probate are brought in together, both may be resealed[1].

1   Registrar's Direction (1951) 9 June.

18.102   As to resealing a colonial grant of probate of a will, which will was revoked by a later will, invalid by the law of the domicile, but which could have been proved as being valid in accordance with Lord Kingsdown's Act, see para. **3.388**, ante.

Cancellation of resealing

18.103   As to the cancellation of a resealing of a grant under the Colonial Probates Act, see para. **17.40**, ante.

Duplicate grants

18.104   Upon an application to reseal a duplicate of a colonial grant it is not necessary to produce a letter giving the reason for such application[1]. Fiats on resealing duplicate grants bear the date upon which they are signed, and no reference to the original resealing is made[2].

1   Registrar's Direction (1941) 18 July.
2   Registrar's Direction (1942) 27 January.

Grants of British courts in foreign countries resealed in England and Wales

18.105   By s. 3 of the Colonial Probates Act 1892 it is enacted that:

> 'This Act shall extend to authorise the sealing in the United Kingdom of any probate or letters of administration granted by a British court in a foreign country, in like manner as it authorises the sealing of a probate or letters of administration granted in a British possession to which this Act applies, and the provisions of this Act shall apply accordingly with the necessary modifications.'

18.106   The expression 'British court in a foreign country' means any British court having jurisdiction out of the Queen's dominions in pursuance of an Order in Council, whether made under any Act or otherwise (s. 6).

18.107   No special Order in Council authorising resealing under the Colonial Probates Act 1892 is necessary in these cases.

18.108   The procedure as to resealing grants made in these courts is the same as in resealing colonial grants.

18.109   The fees payable are the same as on resealing a colonial grant (see paras. **18.71** and **18.72**, ante).

Resealing English and Welsh grants in Commonwealth countries and colonies

Reciprocal basis of Colonial Probates Act

18.110 The Colonial Probates Act 1892 is not applied by Order in Council to a particular country or territory unless Her Majesty is satisfied that the legislature of that place has made adequate provision for the recognition there of grants made in the courts of the United Kingdom[1].

1 Colonial Probates Act 1892, s. 1 (p. 728, post).

18.111 Application for the resealing of English and Welsh grants in Commonwealth or colonial courts should be made through an agent in the country concerned: there is no provision for making application through an English or Welsh probate registry.

CHAPTER 19

Inventory and account

Inventory and account

19.01 The duties of a personal representative are set out in s. 25 of the Administration of Estates Act 1925 as follows:

'The personal representative of a deceased person shall be under a duty to:
(a) collect and get in the real and personal estate of the deceased and administer it according to law;
(b) when required to do so by the court, exhibit on oath in the court a full inventory of the estate and when so required render an account of the administration of the estate to the court;
(c) when required to do so by the High Court, deliver up the grant of probate or administration to that court'[1].

1 The powers of the courts in respect of grants issued before the Court of Probate Act 1857 (13 Halsbury's Statutes (3rd edn) 20) were vested in the Chancery Court as regards inventories and accounts. They are now vested in the High Court by s. 25 of the Supreme Court Act 1981. See *Bouverie v Maxwell* (1866) LR 1 P & D 272.

19.02 Any person interested in an estate, e.g. a person sharing in the estate, or a legatee or a creditor, may call upon the personal representative of the deceased, whether he is an executor or an administrator, to exhibit an inventory of the estate and render an account of his administration thereof[1].

1 *Myddleton v Rushout* (1797) 1 Phillim 244.

19.03 A cessate administrator may call upon the original administrator to exhibit an inventory and account[1]. Similarly, an order to exhibit an inventory and account may be made against a former administrator whose grant has been revoked by a decree in a probate action[2].

1 *Taylor v Newton* (1752) 1 Lee 15.
2 *Re Thomas' Estate* [1956] 3 All ER 897, [1956] 1 WLR 1516.

19.04 Subject to the provisions of the Administration of Estates Act 1925, a personal representative is not bound to distribute the estate of the deceased before the expiration of one year from the death (see Administration of Estates Act 1925, s. 44[1]).

1 17 Halsbury's Statutes (4th edn) 289.

19.05 An inventory may be called for at any short period after administration, e.g. before the expiration of six months.

19.06 In regard to the account there does not appear to be any defined limit as to time.

Practice

19.07 Application for an order to exhibit an inventory and account should be made by summons to a district judge of the Principal Registry or the district probate registrar from whose registry the grant issued[1], supported by affidavit.

1 NCPR 61(2) and 2(1).

19.08 For practice as to summonses, see paras. **25.223** ff., post.

19.09 For form of affidavit to lead order, see No. 37.

19.10 For form of inventory, see No. 60.

19.11 An order to file an inventory and account may be enforced by committal[1].

1 *Marshman v Brookes* (1863) 32 LJPM & A 95; *Baker v Baker* (1860) 2 Sw & Tr 380.

CHAPTER 20

Deposit and registration of wills of living persons

Summary

Deposit of wills

20.01   Section 126 of the Supreme Court Act 1981[1] requires the provision of 'safe and convenient depositories for the custody of the wills of living persons' under the control and direction of the High Court, in which any person may deposit his will on payment of such prescribed fee and subject to such conditions as may be prescribed by regulations made by the President of the Family Division with the concurrence of the Lord Chancellor.

1 See p. 847, post.

20.02   The current procedure is contained in the Wills (Deposit for Safe Custody) Regulations 1978 (S.I. 1978 No. 1724) (see pp. 916 ff., post), which Regulations came into operation on 1 February 1979. The Regulations apply to wills (and codicils) whether deposited before or after the coming into operation of the Regulations. In due course, on the coming into operation of the relevant provisions of the Administration of Justice Act 1982 relating to the registration of wills (see paras. **20.21** ff., post), the 1978 Regulations will be replaced by new regulations.

Place and mode of deposit

20.03   The Principal Registry of the Family Division is designated as the sole depository for the safe custody of testamentary documents of living persons under the control and direction of the High Court (*reg. 3(1)*).

20.04   A will may be lodged for safe custody personally by the testator (or by an agent on the written authority of the testator) at the Principal Registry, any district probate registry or at a sub-registry. Alternatively, the testator (or his authorised agent) may send the will by post directly to the Principal Registry for deposit (*reg. 3(2)*). Wills for deposit are not accepted by post at a district probate registry or sub-registry. Where a will is sent in for deposit by a solicitor or other authorised agent of the testator, it is the practice of the Principal Registry to require either a certificate from the solicitor or other agent to the effect that he has been instructed in writing by the testator to deposit the will for safe custody in the Registry or production of the testator's written request for such deposit.

20.05 A will deposited for safe custody must be enclosed in a sealed envelope bearing the prescribed endorsement in Form 1 to the Regulations. The endorsement includes a statement relating to the date or dates of the testamentary documents deposited and the names and addresses of the appointed executors. The testator is also required in the endorsement to undertake to notify the executors of their appointment and of the deposit of the will; he is further required to certify as to his own date of birth (see Form 1 in the Schedule to the Regulations, p. 919, post).

20.06 Where a will is deposited by a testator on personal attendance at a probate registry, he is required to sign the endorsement on the envelope before a countersigning registry official.

Fee

20.07 The prescribed fee on depositing a will for safe custody is £1 (NC Probate Fees Order 1981, Fee 6).

Certificate of deposit

20.08 A written certificate of deposit (Form 2 in the Schedule to the Regulations, see p. 919, post) will be given or sent by the registry to the testator and where the will is deposited by an agent, a copy of the certificate will also be sent to the agent. *It is especially important that the testator should keep the certificate of deposit in a safe place because it will need to be produced should the testator subsequently wish to apply to withdraw his deposited will from the registry.*

Transmission of wills to Principal Registry

20.09 Wills lodged in a district probate registry or a sub-registry on personal attendance are transmitted by that registry by registered post to the Principal Registry for safe keeping (*reg. 6*).

Withdrawal of deposited will during testator's lifetime

20.10 Application for the withdrawal of a deposited will must be made by the testator in writing to the Principal Registry: the application must be supported by the certificate of deposit. No form of request for withdrawal is prescribed by the Regulations. Provided a district judge of the Principal Registry is satisfied as to the identity of the testator and that it would be proper to return the deposited will to him, he may authorise its return (*reg. 8(1) and (2)*).

20.11 No fee is payable on an application to withdraw a deposited will.

20.12 Save where, on the written application of the testator, a district judge of the Principal Registry has authorised the return of a deposited will to him, no will (or codicil) deposited in the Principal Registry for safe custody shall be released from such custody during the lifetime of the testator (*reg. 8(4)*).

Procedure following death of testator

20.13 On the death of the testator being established, a district judge of the Principal Registry may open the envelope containing the will of the testator and, subject to such precautions as he may think necessary (including the lodgment in the registry of a copy of the will), may deliver the will to the executor or to any other person intending to prove it, or (where the will has been effectively revoked or a grant of representation in the estate of the testator is not required) to any person who is entitled to its possession (*reg. 9(1)*). Where application is to be made to prove the will, the district judge may, if he thinks fit, require the person intending to prove the will to attend at a probate registry for that purpose (*reg. 9(1) proviso*). In such a case, the will is not delivered out of the control of the High Court; instead, the person intending to prove it will be required to swear to the will before an authorised officer of a probate registry.

20.14 Whenever, under regulation 9, a deposited will is released from the custody of the Principal Registry, the person to whom the will is delivered will be required to give a receipt for it, together with a written undertaking to lodge the will on any application being made for a grant to the estate of the testator (*reg. 9(2)*).

Records

20.15 Records must be maintained in the Principal Registry of the deposit and the return of wills of living persons (*regs. 7, 8(3) and 9(3)*).

20.16 Printed forms and envelopes for use in connection with the deposit of wills may be obtained from the Record Keeper's Department of the Principal Registry of the Family Division, Somerset House, London WC2R 1LP or from any district probate registry (for the list of district probate registries, see para. **2.58**, ante).

Deposit of wills of soldiers, airmen, etc.

20.17 Under s. 21 of the Regimental Debts Act 1893, where any original will of a person dying while subject to military law, whether he died before or after the commencement of that Act, comes to the hands of a Secretary of State, and representation under the same is not taken out, the Secretary of State may cause the will to be deposited, where the testator's domicile appears to have been other than Scottish or Irish, in the place for the time being appointed in London for the deposit of original wills brought into the High Court in England (i.e. the Principal Registry of the Family Division).

20.18 Where a person dying while subject to military law dies intestate, and under the Act any residue of his property comes into the hands of the Secretary of State and representation to the deceased is not taken out, the Secretary of State may in the like circumstances deposit at the Principal Registry a declaration of his intestacy.

20.19 In either of the above cases the Secretary of State may also deposit an inventory of the personal property of the deceased, showing how it has been applied.

20.20 Wills, declarations and inventories deposited in accordance with the above provisions are to be preserved and dealt with, and may be inspected subject and according to the same rules and orders and on payment of the same fees as any other like documents deposited at the registry, or subject to such special rules and on payment of such special fees as may be fixed.

Registration of wills

Registration Convention

20.21 Sections 23 to 26 of the Administration of Justice Act 1982[1] make statutory provision to enable the United Kingdom to ratify the Council of Europe Convention on the Establishment of a Scheme of Registration of Wills (Cmnd. 5073). The Convention requires each Contracting State to set up a scheme in relation to a limited category of wills under which such wills *must* be registered in that State and *may* be registered in any other Contracting State. The scheme also provides for the registering authorities in each State to receive requests for information from one another after the testator's death, the object being to facilitate the discovery by interested parties of the existence of a will. The Convention was signed by the United Kingdom on 16 May 1972. It came into force on 20 March 1976 and has been ratified by Belgium, Cyprus, France, the Netherlands and Turkey.

1 See pp. 855 ff., post.

20.22 Broadly, the Convention provides that certain classes of will are to be *compulsorily* registrable in the country in which they are made. These are:

(a) formal wills declared to a notary, public authority or any person authorised by law to record them; and
(b) other wills deposited with an authority or person authorised by law to accept deposit.

20.23 In addition, the Convention provides for the creation of a national body in each Contracting State to administer the international aspects of the scheme, which are as follows:

(a) a testator is to be entitled, if he so wishes, to have his will registered in other Contracting States;
(b) national bodies in other States may apply for information as to whether a particular will is registered in the States receiving the request.

20.24 Each of these matters must be dealt with through the national bodies of the States concerned. The remaining provisions of the Convention relate to the amount of information to be supplied, the fees to be charged, etc.

Implementation of Convention

20.25 At present, until the relevant sections of the Administration of Justice Act 1982 are brought into force, there is no system for the *compulsory* registration of wills in the United Kingdom, although in England and Wales facilities do exist for the deposit and safe-keeping of wills of living persons by virtue of s. 126 of the Supreme Court Act 1981 and the Wills (Deposit for Safe Custody) Regulations 1978 (see paras. **20.01–20.12**, above).

20.26   In order to accommodate the Convention in England and Wales, the 1982 Act provides that only those wills which are to be deposited under the Act, or have already been so deposited under s. 126 of the Supreme Court Act 1981 or its predecessor, s. 172 of the Supreme Court of Judicature (Consolidation) Act 1925, are to be registrable compulsorily under the Convention. In other words, wills voluntarily lodged for deposit and safe-keeping in accordance with statutory provision will automatically become registered compulsorily under the Convention, including deposited 'international wills' made in conformity with the Unidroit Convention providing a Uniform Law on the Form of an International Will (Cmnd. 5950) (see paras. **3.446** ff., ante).

20.27   To give effect to the Convention, the Act of 1982 formally provides for the following matters:

(a)   that the Principal Registry of the Family Division shall be the appropriate depository and registering authority for England and Wales;

(b)   that, once deposited in accordance with regulations and on payment of the prescribed fee, wills must be registered in a register maintained by the Registry for that purpose;

(c)   that wills already deposited under s. 126 of the Supreme Court Act 1981 or under s. 172 of the Supreme Court of Judicature (Consolidation) Act 1925 shall on the coming into force of the registration provisions of the Administration of Justice Act 1982, be treated for the purposes of those provisions as having been voluntarily deposited under that Act;

(d)   for the designation of the Principal Registry of the Family Division as the national body for the purposes of performing the functions required by such a body under the Convention; and

(e)   the appropriate regulation-making powers to make detailed provision for deposit and registration of wills, and associated matters.

20.28   Similar provision, as to that above, is made in relation to Scotland and Northern Ireland.

20.29   Note.—*The above provisions of the Administration of Justice Act 1982 relating to registration of wills shall come into operation on such date as the Lord Chancellor and the Secretary of State may by Order jointly appoint. No such commencement Order has yet been made.*

CHAPTER 21

Searches and copies—Exemplifications— Duplicate grants

Summary

Searches and copies

Calendars of grants

21.01 Calendars, or indexes, of all grants of probate or administration issued in the probate registries are available for public search at the Principal and district probate registries[1]. The details which appear in the calendars are: full name, date of death and last address of the deceased; the type of grant, its date and the registry at which it was made; and the gross value of the estate[2].

1 See Supreme Court Act 1981, s. 111 (see p. 844, post), which provides for the keeping of records in such form and containing such particulars as the President of the Family Division may direct. The calendars are now compiled from weekly lists, produced by computer, of grants issued.
2 Registrar's Circular, 22 December 1969.

21.02 Once the entry in the calendar has been found, fuller information may be obtained by ordering a copy of the grant or inspecting the will.

Wills proved since 11 January 1858

Searches and copies

21.03 Any will proved in England and Wales since the institution of the Court of Probate in 1858 can be searched for and a copy read in the Principal Registry. Searches can also be made in the district probate registries.

21.04 No fee is payable on a search for a grant in the calendars if it is made personally at the registry, although on inspection of a copy will or any other document a fee of 25p is charged[1]. Where, however, application is made in the Principal Registry or a district probate registry through the post for a copy of a will or grant (other than on the application for the issue of the original grant), a fee of £2 is payable[2], which fee covers the supplying of a copy of the will and/or grant. If additional copies are requested at the same time the fee for the same is 25p for each page[2].

1 NC Probate Fees Order 1981, Fee 7.
2 Ibid., Fee 9, as amended by NC Probate Fees (Amendment) Order 1986 (S.I. 1986 No. 705) and NC Probate Fees (Amendment No. 2) Order 1986 (S.I. 1986 No. 2185).

21.05 Where the application for copies is made on a personal attendance or on the application for the issue of the original grant, the fee is 25p for each page[1].

1 Ibid., Fee 8(a), as amended by NC Probate Fees (Amendment) Order 1986 (S.I. 1986 No. 705) and NC Probate Fees (Amendment No. 2) Order 1986 (S.I. 1986 No. 2185).

21.06 At the district probate registries, only the originals of the wills proved there can be made available for inspection, whereas at the Principal Registry the originals of the wills proved there and the registered copies of all proved wills can be made available.

21.07 Subject to the control of the High Court and to probate rules, a copy of the whole or any part of a will may be obtained, on payment of the prescribed fee, (i) from the registry in which the will is preserved; or (ii) where the will is preserved in some place other than a registry, from the Principal Registry; or (iii) subject to the approval of the Senior District Judge of the Family Division, from the Principal Registry in any case in which the will was proved in a district probate registry[1].

1 Supreme Court Act 1981, s. 125.

21.08 The following particulars should be supplied by an applicant for the copy of a will: full Christian or other forenames and surname of deceased; exact date of death; date of grant (if known); and the address of deceased.

Standing search for grant of representation

21.09 An application for a standing search for a grant of representation may be made to the Principal Registry or any district probate registry or sub-registry. This facility was introduced originally by a Practice Note[1] especially to assist persons who wish to take action against an estate or to commence proceedings under the Inheritance (Provision for Family and Dependants) Act 1975 (see Chap. 41) or similar legislation once a personal representative is constituted. Before the facility was introduced, a caveat was often entered in such circumstances merely so that the caveator could be aware of the issue of a grant. A standing search offers a procedure better adapted to this situation and obviates the trouble and delay involved in obtaining the removal of the caveat.

1 *Practice Note* (1975) 12 September.

21.10 The facility is now contained in NCPR 43, which provides:

'(1)   Any person who wishes to be notified of the issue of a grant may enter a standing search for the grant by lodging at, or sending by post to any registry or sub-registry, a notice in Form 2.

(2)   A person who has entered a standing search will be sent an office copy of any grant which corresponds with the particulars given on the completed Form 2 and which—

(a) issued not more than twelve months before the entry of the standing search; or

(b) issues within a period of six months after the entry of the standing search.

(3)(a) Where an applicant wishes to extend the said period of six months, he or his solicitor may lodge at, or send by post to, the registry or sub-registry at which the standing search was entered written application for extension.

(b) An application for extension as aforesaid must be lodged, or received by post, within the last month of the said period of six months, and the standing search shall thereupon be effective for an additional period of six months from the date on which it was due to expire.

(c) A standing search which has been extended as above may be further extended by the filing of a further application for extension subject to the same conditions as set out in sub-paragraph (b) above.'

21.11 Application for a standing search is made by lodging with, or sending by post to, the Record Keeper at the Principal Registry or to a district probate registry or sub-registry a request in the form prescribed (see Form No. 189), together with the prescribed fee of £2 (NC Probate Fees Order 1981, Fee 5). Aliases or alternative names for the deceased may be included without additional fee. The form of receipt issued includes provision for extension of the period of search in due course, if required, on payment of a further fee of £2.

21.12 Postal applications should be addressed to the Record Keeper, Principal Registry of the Family Division, Somerset House, Strand, London WC2R 1LP or to any district probate registry or sub-registry. Remittances for fees should be by crossed cheque or postal order payable to 'H.M. Paymaster General'.

21.13 The caveat procedure under NCPR 44 remains available for use by any person who wishes to ensure that no grant is sealed without notice to himself.

Copies of wills, grants and other documents

21.14 NCPR 59 provides that where copies are required of original wills or other documents deposited under s. 124 of the Supreme Court Act 1981[1] such copies may be facsimile copies sealed with the seal of the court and issued either as office copies or certified under the hand of a district judge or registrar to be true copies. Section 124 of the Supreme Court Act 1981 provides that all original wills and other documents which are under the control of the High Court in the Principal Registry or in any district probate registry shall be deposited and preserved in such places as the Lord Chancellor may direct; and any wills or other documents so deposited shall, *subject to the control of the High Court and to probate rules*, be open to inspection. NCPR 58 provides that an original will or other document referred to in s. 124 of the Supreme Court Act 1981 shall not be open to inspection if, in the opinion of the district judge or registrar, such inspection would be undesirable or otherwise inappropriate. Accordingly copies may be obtained of any will or other document unless a district judge or registrar directs that the document is not to be open to inspection.

1 See p. 847, post.

Office copies

21.15 Whenever practicable, and subject to any special direction or any special requirement of the applicant, all copies are made by photography (which for this purpose is treated as including Xerography), and unless required to be sealed and certified, will be issued as 'office copies'[1].

1 Secretary's Circular, 20 August 1954.

21.16   In addition to copies of proved wills and grants, office copies of the following documents may be obtained (unless a district judge or registrar has directed that the will, grant or other document is not open to inspection):

- oaths;
- bonds or guarantees;
- affidavits duly filed (including affidavits of justification by sureties);
- declarations of estates;
- powers of attorney (except where only a plain copy remains on the file);
- renunciations;
- orders (except order for leave to swear death);
- notarial copies of foreign wills, including the accompanying 'proceedings'.

Plain copies

21.17   Plain, unsealed copies of the following documents may be obtained on payment of the appropriate fees (unless a district judge or registrar has directed that the will etc. is not open to inspection):

- an extract, or part only, of a will or other document;
- wills of which probate has been refused;
- wills where probate was granted in the form of a fiat copy;
- unproved wills or codicils (e.g. where the document is inoperative and has merely been filed);
- wills in cases where the grant has been revoked and the will has not been re-proved;
- revoked grants;
- filed copies of colonial grants which have been resealed;
- filed copies of powers of attorney where the original does not remain on the file.

21.18   Wills lodged on renunciation are not open to public inspection, but the fact that such a will is held in the registry and, where appropriate, its contents may be disclosed to any person reasonably establishing an interest[1].

1 Secretary's Circular, 11 November 1975.

Certified and sealed copies

21.19   Where it is not possible to make photographic copies of a will, copies are not ordinarily examined with the original will, but if required such copies may be examined and certified under the hand of a district judge or registrar as true copies. Copies so certified may be sealed with the seal of the court[1].

1 NCPR 59.

21.20   In the latter case it should be stated when ordering the copy that a sealed and certified copy is required.

21.21 A sealed and certified copy of a will can be obtained at the registry where the will was proved or from the Principal Registry. Special arrangements exist for the issue of sealed and certified copies of the official copies of wills deposited at the former Exeter District Probate Registry which were destroyed by enemy action during the 1939–1945 war.

21.22 Sealed copies of proved testamentary documents of a deceased person must include all documents admitted to probate whether proved together or separately[1].

1 Registrar's Direction (1935) 19 July.

21.23 Sealed and certified copies of grants and wills may be ordered, if desired, at the time when the papers to lead the grant are lodged.

Special certificates

21.24 Special forms of certificate have been approved by the President for use in certain foreign courts or for production either abroad or in England and Wales, and copies bearing such certificates should be applied for through the Record Keeper at the Principal Registry or through the district probate registry. See also 'Exemplifications', paras. **21.35** ff., post.

Copies of foreign documents

21.25 A certified and sealed copy of an original document in a foreign language may be supplied by the photographic process, but it is not the practice to issue a sealed and certified copy where the foreign document filed in the registry is a notarial or other certified copy of the original.

Search for caveat

21.26 Any solicitor or member of the public may ask for a search to be made for a caveat in the estate of a specified person: see paras. **23.33** ff., post.

Fees for searches and copies

21.27 Under the Non-Contentious Probate Fees Order 1981, as amended, the fees payable for searches and copies are as follows:

Fee No.

5   Fee for a standing search for a grant (see paras. **21.09–21.12**, ante), for each search period of six months £2

7   On inspection of an original or copy will, or any other document including a copy of a will 25p

8   When applied for on a personal attendance (or on the application for the original grant):

  (a) For a copy of all or part of a document, whether or not issued as an office copy, for each page 25p

  (b) For a sealed and certified copy of any document . . £1

     Plus, for each page after the first 25p

  (c) For an exemplification of a copy signed by a (district judge or) registrar and countersigned by the President, an inclusive fee of . £5

9   For handling a postal application (other than on the application for the original grant), in respect of each estate, and where appropriate supplying—

(a) a copy of any will or grant or other document, whether or not issued as an office copy £2
(b) a sealed and certified copy of any will or grant . . . £3
Only one fee is charged for the purposes of sub-paragraph (a) or (b) on a request for a copy of a will and grant
(c) an additional sealed and certified copy of any will or grant . . £1
and for each page after the first a further fee of . . . 25p
(d) an exemplification of a copy signed by a (district judge or) registrar and countersigned by the President of the Family Division, including the preparation of the necessary documents . . £6
(e) an additional copy of any document, other than a sealed and certified copy, for each page 25p

Production at other courts of documents filed in Probate Registries

21.28   Section 136 of the Supreme Court Act 1981 enables rules to be made for providing that documents filed in, or in the custody of, any office of the Supreme Court, and required to be produced to any court or tribunal sitting elsewhere than at the Royal Courts of Justice may be produced to the court or tribunal by sending them to that court or tribunal with a covering certificate.

21.29   Rules have been made applying this procedure to documents filed in the Central Office of the Supreme Court, but not so far to documents filed in, or in the custody of, the probate registries.

21.30   When it is necessary to produce an original will, oath or other document in the custody of a probate registry at the hearing of a probate action, the Senior District Judge will, on receipt of a request from a Master of the Chancery Division, send to the latter any documents in the custody of the registries which are relevant to the action. The practice as to production of such documents at a county court is set out in para. **40.02**, post.

21.31   From time to time requests are made to the probate registries for a proved original will to be produced for the purposes of court proceedings other than in a probate action (e.g. criminal proceedings in a magistrates' court or a Crown Court). In such a case, unless production of the original will is requested as a matter of urgency, it is usually transmitted by registered post to the probate registry or sub-registry most conveniently situated to the court in which the proceedings are being brought so that an officer of that registry may attend the court with it. As all proved original wills which are under the control of the High Court are required to be deposited and preserved (s. 124 of the Supreme Court Act 1981), the officer attending the court with an original will must arrange to retrieve it at the determination of the proceedings and return it to the registry. Should it be necessary to leave the will with the court for the duration of the proceedings, the officer will obtain a written receipt for the will including an undertaking for its return from the appropriate court official[1].

1 Registrar's Circular, 13 November 1978.

Production of original will for inspection and examination

21.32   Occasionally a request is made to a probate registry for a proved original will to be made available for inspection and forensic examination. Normally, such a request is made by or on behalf of the police authorities. Occasionally, however, the request is made by a solicitor, acting on behalf of his client in contemplation of bringing a probate action, or exceptionally a researcher. Where the request is made by a solicitor or researcher, it will be referred to the district judge or registrar for consideration. Subject to his approval and to such further conditions or restrictions which the district judge or registrar may see fit to impose, it is considered appropriate that any such examination shall normally take place only in a probate registry and that the examination of the will shall be conducted in the presence of a registry official in order that the official may ensure that the will is preserved in its original state and condition. If appropriate, the will may be transmitted by registered post to another probate registry to enable the examination to be made[1]. A fee of 25p is payable for the inspection (NC Probate Fees Order 1981, Fee 7).

1 Registrar's Circular, 13 November 1978.

Wills proved before 1858

Place of deposit

21.33 Wills and testamentary papers in connection with grants made by the ecclesiastical and other courts before the establishment of the probate registries in 1858 have been transferred to County Record Officers or to certain of the principal libraries, etc., under the authority of s. 124 of the Supreme Court Act, 1981[1] (or the earlier provision contained in s. 170 of the Supreme Court of Judicature (Consolidation) Act 1925) and s. 8(5) of the Public Records Act 1958[2]. No pre-1858 records now remain at the probate registries[3].

1 See p. 847, post.
2 See p. 774, post.
3 For a complete list of the places of deposit of pre-1858 wills and records of grants etc., reference should be made to 'Wills and their Whereabouts' by Anthony J. Cramp, BA.

Literary searches

21.34 Special regulations apply in the case of persons wishing to search the records of the probate registries for purposes of research and literary enquiry. Information as to the conditions under which permission is given for such literary enquiry may be obtained from the Record Keeper at the Principal Registry.

Exemplifications

21.35 An exemplification, which is a document sometimes required by foreign courts, contains an exact copy of the will (if any), and a virtual, though not an exact, copy of the grant. A testimonium clause is signed by a district judge or registrar, countersigned by the President of the Family Division and the seal of the Family Division is added. The name and address of the solicitor who extracted the grant are placed in the margin.

21.36 Exemplifications of grants of other countries which have been resealed in England and Wales cannot be issued.

Obtaining exemplification

21.37   At the Principal Registry, application for an exemplification of a probate or letters of administration is made to the Record Keeper's Department.

21.38   Exemplifications of grants issued in a district probate registry must be applied for in such registry.

Fees

21.39   An inclusive fee of £5 is payable for an exemplification applied for on a personal attendance or on the application for the original grant[1]. If applied for by post (other than on the application for the original grant) the fee is £6[2].

1 NC Probate Fees Order 1981 as amended by NC Probate Fees (Amendment) Order 1986 (S.I. 1986 No. 705) and NC Probate Fees (Amendment No. 2) Order 1986 (S.I. 1986 No. 2185), Fee 8(c).
2 NC Probate Fees Order 1981, as amended by NC Probate Fees (Amendment) Order 1986 (S.I. 1986 No. 705) and NC Probate Fees (Amendment No. 2) Order 1986 (S.I. 1986 No. 2185), Fee 9(d).

Duplicate grants

21.40   Any application for a duplicate grant should be in writing, signed by the grantee(s) or the extracting solicitors and stating the reason why the duplicate is required[1].

1 As office copies of grants, which are obtainable in any quantity required on payment of a small fee, are acceptable for the purpose of registration and as evidence of the original (see para. **4.248**), it is usually only where the original grant has been lost or destroyed that it is necessary to obtain a duplicate.

21.41   An application for the issue of two or more duplicates will be referred to a district judge or registrar[1].

1 Registrar's Direction (1975) 20 October.

Procedure

21.42   The application must be made at the registry from which the original grant issued. Application may be made by post.

21.43   The following documents should be lodged with, or posted to, the Record Keeper (or, if applied for at the same time as the original grant, the Receiver of Papers) at the Principal Registry, or at the district probate registry, as the case may be:

(a)   Letter of request (see above).
(b)   If applied for after the issue of the original grant, the grant itself, or an office copy of it. (This is not necessary where the application is made at a district probate registry.)
(c)   Where the application is in respect of a grant issued from the Principal Registry before 1 January 1931, an engrossment of the will (if any) may be required. This is also necessary where the grant issued from a district probate registry prior to the introduction of photography of wills at that registry.
(d)   If the grant issued from the Principal Registry before 1 January 1934, or from a district registry before 1 May 1934, a certificate from the Capital Taxes Office as to the amount of duty paid.

Fees

21.44 The fee for a duplicate grant is £2[1], exclusive of the fee (25p) for an office copy of the original grant, where necessary.

1 NC Probate Fees Order 1981, Fee 3(d).

Form of duplicate grant

21.45 A duplicate grant bears the same date as the original grant, the words 'Duplicate Grant' being placed in the margin at the top, and the date of issue of the duplicate in the right-hand margin[1].

1 Registrar's Direction (1942) 27 January. When issued on the same day as the original grant, the original and each duplicate are noted as to the issue of the duplicates (Registrar's Direction (1932) 4 November).

21.46 Any official amendment or notation made on the original grant after its issue and appearing on the record is reproduced on the duplicate[1].

1 Registrar's Direction (1941) 30 July.

21.47 Where application is made for a duplicate of a grant issued from the Principal Registry before 1 January 1934, or from a district registry before 1 May 1934, the duplicate, being drawn in the same form as the original grant, will not include the addresses and descriptions of the grantees, or the certificate as to, and the amount of, the net personal estate. The duplicate grant will not be photographed, and photographic office copies of the grant will not be obtainable[1].

1 Registrar's Direction (1934) 14 March.

Resealing duplicate grants

21.48 For the practice as to resealing duplicates of colonial grants, see para. **18.104**, ante.

CHAPTER 22

Affidavits, affirmations and statutory declarations

Summary

22.01 There are three methods by which evidence may be given in writing:

(a) By affidavit sworn in accordance with the Oaths Act 1978[1], or by a similar document, called a solemn affirmation, which enables a person who objects to being sworn or to whom it is not reasonably practicable without inconvenience or delay to administer an oath in the manner appropriate to his religious belief to 'solemnly, sincerely and truly declare and affirm'—this having the same force and effect as an oath (Oaths Act 1978, ss. 5 and 6).

(b) By statutory declaration, under the Statutory Declarations Act 1835[2], with a special formula[3]. Such declarations, though not generally admissible in any judicial proceeding in England, may, by s. 16[4], be received in proof of *execution* of a will, codicil, deed or instrument.

(c) In civil proceedings, by a written statement, made admissible by s. 2 of the Civil Evidence Act 1968[5]. Section 3 of the Evidence Act 1938 provides that in civil or criminal proceedings an instrument to the validity of which attestation is necessary may, instead of being proved by an attesting witness, be proved in the same manner as if he was not alive; but this section does not apply to the proof of wills or other testamentary documents. It does, however, apply to evidence other than that in connection with the due execution of a will[6].

---

1 17 Halsbury's Statutes (4th edn) 200.
2 17 Halsbury's Statutes (4th edn) 72.
3 The wording is 'I, AB, do solemnly and sincerely declare, that . . .; and I make this solemn Declaration conscientiously believing the same to be true, and by virtue of the provisions of the Statutory Declarations Act 1835.'
4 17 Halsbury's Statutes (4th edn) 77.
5 17 Halsbury's Statutes (4th edn) 186.
6 So held by Byrne J in *Re Hyman* (1946) 24 July (motion) where the evidence was as to the contents and date. Section 3 of the Evidence Act 1938 is not repealed by the Civil Evidence Act 1968.

22.02   As regards affirmations, NCPR 12 requires that evidence as to due execution be given by affidavit. Rule 8 similarly calls for an oath by the applicants for a grant. However, the Interpretation Act 1978 provides that, unless the contrary intention appears, the words 'oath' and 'affidavit' include affirmations, and they are therefore accepted.

22.03   As regards statutory declarations, it is not considered that the rules above-mentioned exclude the operation of the Statutory Declarations Act 1835; and statutory declarations are accepted in proof of due execution of wills or codicils, but not for any other purpose.

Rules

22.04   NCPR 3 provides:

'Subject to the provisions of these Rules and to any enactment, the Rules of the Supreme Court 1965 shall apply, with the necessary modifications, to non-contentious probate matters, save that nothing in Order 3 shall prevent time from running in the Long Vacation.'

22.05   Affidavits must be drawn in the first person and, unless the court otherwise directs, the place of residence of the deponent and his occupation or, if he has none, his description, must be stated therein. If he is a party, or is employed by a party, to the cause or matter in which the affidavit is sworn, the affidavit must also state that fact.

22.06   In the case of a deponent who is giving evidence in a professional, business or other occupational capacity the affidavit may, instead of stating the deponent's place of residence, state the address at which he works, the position he holds and the name of his firm or employer, if any (RSC Order 41, r. 1(4)).

22.07   As to the description of the deponent, see under *Executor's oath*, paras. **4.107–4.109**, ante. Where a female deponent has an occupation this should be stated, and not her marital status. If she has no occupation her status should be given[1].

1   Secretary's Circular, 12 May 1967.

22.08   Where the deponent appears to the Commissioner to be blind or illiterate it must be stated in the jurat that the affidavit was read in the presence of the Commissioner to such deponent who seemed perfectly to understand the same, and also that he made his mark or signature in the presence of the Commissioner. No such affidavit may be used in the absence of such certificate unless the court or judge is otherwise satisfied that the affidavit was read over to and appeared to be perfectly understood by the deponent (Order 41, r. 3).

22.09   No affidavit is sufficient if sworn before the solicitor acting for the party on whose behalf it is to be used, or before any agent, partner or clerk of that solicitor (Order 41, r. 8).

22.10   Documents for filing in the probate registries should be prepared on A4 ISO size paper of durable quality[1].

1   RSC Ord. 66, r. 1.

Exhibits

22.11 An affidavit to which a testamentary document is exhibited should never refer to it as 'hereunto annexed'; and the document should not be annexed[1]. If it is subsequently admitted to proof, it has to be detached, and loses that form of identification. The proper wording is 'now produced to me marked . . .', and the identification is completed by endorsement, on the back of the document, of the Commissioner's note 'this is the document referred to in the affidavit of', etc., which has to be endorsed on every exhibit, and the exhibit certificate should be entitled in the same manner as the affidavit. The only exception to this is the marking of a will only by the signatures of the applicant for a grant and the person before whom the oath is sworn, as governed by NCPR 10(1)(a).

1 RSC Ord. 41.

Alterations. Erasure

22.12 No affidavit having in the jurat or body thereof any interlineation, alteration or erasure may, without leave of the court or one of the district judges or registrars, be filed or made use of unless the interlineation or alteration (other than by erasure) is authenticated by the initials of the officer taking the affidavit; nor, in the case of an erasure, unless the words or figures appearing at the time of taking the affidavit to be written on the erasure, are re-written and signed or initialled in the margin of the affidavit by the officer taking it. (See RSC Ord. 41, r. 7.)

Must not be made after the affidavit is sworn

22.13 No alteration can properly be made in any affidavit after the same has been sworn, and any Commissioner initialling such an alteration would commit an irregularity, and would render himself liable to the revocation of his commission. (Order of Lord Chancellor, dated 6 February 1882.) In such a case the affidavit must be re-sworn.

Jurats

Several deponents

22.14 In every affidavit made by two or more deponents, the names of the several persons making the affidavits must be inserted in the jurat, except that if the affidavit of all the deponents is taken at one time by the same officer it is sufficient to state that it was sworn by both (or all) the 'above-named' deponents. (See RSC Ord. 41, r. 2.)

Place and date of swearing

22.15 It is the duty of every Commissioner before whom any oath or affidavit is taken or made to state truly in the jurat or attestation at what place and on what date the oath or affidavit is taken or made (Commissioners for Oaths Act 1889, s. 5[1]).

1 17 Halsbury's Statutes (4th edn) 110.

Forms—One deponent

22.16 'Sworn at   in the County of   this   day of   19   .
   Before me,
      [*Signature and designation of Commissioner*].'

Two or more deponents

22.17 'Sworn by the deponents A B and C D [*or* by both, *or* by all of the above-named deponents] at   in the County of   this   day of   19 .

   Before me,
      [*Signature and designation of Commissioner*].'

Illiterate or blind deponent or marksman

22.18 'Sworn by the said A B at   in the County of   this   day of   19   this affidavit having been first truly, distinctly and audibly read over by me (*or* in my presence) to him who seemed perfectly to understand the same and made his mark (*or* signature) thereto in my presence.

   Before me,
      [*Signature and designation of Commissioner*].'

Deponent a member of H.M. Forces

22.19 'Sworn at   by the above-named deponent this   day of   19 .
   Before me,
      [*Signature and full name and rank of officer*].'[1]

1 See paras. **22.36** and **22.37**, post, 'H.M. Forces serving abroad'.

Re-swearing

22.20 In affidavits which require re-swearing it is usual for the Commissioner to leave the original jurat intact and to add a second jurat commencing with the word 're-sworn'.

Forms of oath

Ordinary form

22.21 Commissioner to deponent.—'Take the Book in your right hand, raise your hand (*indicating that the hand holding the Book should be raised above his head*) and repeat after me the following words':

    'I swear by Almighty God that this is my name and handwriting, and that the contents of this, my affidavit, are true'[1].

1 This form of oath is approved for use in the probate registries (Secretary's Circular, 15 January 1959).

Scottish form[1]

22.22 *The deponent holds up his right hand and repeats the words of the oath after the Commissioner.*

    'I swear by Almighty God that this is my name and handwriting, and that the contents of this my affidavit are true.'

No Book is used, the deponent merely raises his right hand above his head while repeating the words of the oath.

1 The Scottish form is a permitted alternative to the ordinary English manner of administering an oath: Oaths Act 1978, s. 3.

Children and young persons

22.23   In relation to any oath administered to and taken by any child or young person (i.e. a person under 17 years of age) s. 1 of the Oaths Act 1978 is to have effect as if the words 'I promise before Almighty God' were set out in it instead of the words 'I swear by Almighty God that'[1].

1   Children and Young Persons Act 1963, s. 28.

22.24   The failure to observe this provision does not, however, invalidate the oath.

Affirmations

Affirmations

22.25   The Oaths Act 1978[1] provides that any person who objects to being sworn or to whom it is not reasonably practicable without inconvenience or delay to administer an oath in the manner appropriate to his religious belief shall be permitted to make his solemn affirmation instead of taking an oath (s. 5(1) and (2)); where such a person may be permitted to make his solemn declaration, he may also be required to do so (s. 5(3)); and a solemn affirmation shall have the same force and effect as an oath (s. 5(4)).

1   17 Halsbury's Statutes (4th edn) 200.

Form of affirmation

22.26   Section 6 of the Oaths Act 1978 provides as follows:

'(1) Subject to subsection (2) below, every affirmation shall be as follows:
"I,   , do solemnly, sincerely and truly declare and affirm,"
and then proceed with the words of the oath prescribed by law, omitting any words of imprecation or calling to witness.
(2) Every affirmation in writing shall commence:
"I,   of   , do solemnly and sincerely affirm"
and the form in lieu of jurat shall be "Affirmed at   this
day of   19   ,   Before me." '

Commissioners etc.

Before whom sworn in England and Wales

22.27   Oaths and other affidavits for use in the probate registries, when sworn in England and Wales, must be sworn before a Commissioner for Oaths or an authorised officer of the Supreme Court[1].

1   Secretary's Circular, 12 April 1967.

22.28   Section 81 of the Solicitors Act 1974 enables affidavits to be sworn in England and Wales before any solicitor who holds a current practising certificate. References in enactments and instruments to Commissioners for Oaths apply also to such solicitors. A solicitor may not exercise the power to administer oaths or take affidavits in proceedings in which he is solicitor to any party or in which he is interested (s. 81(2)). As from 31 July 1995, members of the Institute of Legal Executives have similar powers to solicitors including the right to use the title 'Commissioner for Oaths'[1].

1   Commissioners for Oaths (Prescribed Bodies) Regulations 1995 (S.I. 1995 No. 1676).

22.29 A notary public who is a member of the Incorporated Company of Scriveners and who has been admitted to practise as a notary public within the jurisdiction of that Company has the powers confirmed on a Commissioner for Oaths by the Commissioners for Oaths Act 1889[1] and accordingly may administer an oath in respect of an affidavit to be used in the Supreme Court. The jurat required is similar to that signed by a Commissioner for Oaths but the notary public may either sign or seal it[1]. In addition, any authorised person or general notary, as defined in s. 113(1) of the Courts and Legal Services Act 1990 (and empowered under that Act) has the powers conferred on a Commissioner for Oaths by the Commissioners for Oaths Acts 1889 and 1891.

1 Administration of Justice Act 1985, s. 65.

22.30 Justices of the peace have power (as from 1 July 1991) to administer any oath or take any affidavit which is required for the purposes of an application for a grant of probate or letters of administration (with or without will) made in any non-contentious or common form probate business. The jurat required is similar to that signed by a solicitor. A justice of the peace cannot administer an oath or take an affidavit in any proceedings in which he is interested. (Courts and Legal Services Act 1990, s. 56—see p. 896, post.)

22.31 It should be noted that stipendiary magistrates are not entitled, ex officio, to administer an oath in respect of an affidavit to be used in the Supreme Court.

Before whom sworn out of England and Wales

22.32 When sworn out of England and Wales, oaths may be administered before the persons indicated in the following paragraphs.

Commonwealth countries

22.33 In any part of the British Commonwealth outside England and Wales— before any court, judge, notary public, or other person having authority to administer an oath there. It is accepted without verification that a person before whom an affidavit is sworn in any of these places has the necessary authority[1].

1 RSC Ord. 41, r. 12. In practice this applies also to affidavits sworn in the Republic of Ireland.

In a foreign country

22.34

(i) Before a person holding one of the British diplomatic ranks specified in section 6 of the Commissioners for Oaths Act 1889, as amended (e.g. British ambassador, minister, consul, vice-consul, consular agent, counsellor) in the exercise of his functions in that foreign country; any document duly signed and sealed shall be admitted in evidence without further proof.

(ii) Before a judge of the High Court of such country under the seal of such court.

(iii) Before any person authorised by the law of a foreign country to administer oaths in that country, subject to a certificate being annexed to the affidavit that such person has authority by the laws of the country to administer an oath, the certificate to be signed by a British consul or vice-consul, or verified by the seal of the High Court of the country.

22.35   An affidavit sworn in a foreign country before a notary and duly signed and sealed by him is accepted in the probate registries without verification of his authority to administer oaths[1].

1 Registrar's Direction (1962) 18 May.

H.M. Forces serving abroad

22.36   If the deponent is a person subject to the Naval Discipline Act, or to military law or air force law, or a person not so subject but employed by or in the service of the Secretary of State for the naval purposes of his department, or employed by, in the service of or accompanying, any of H.M. Forces, the affidavit may be sworn before an officer subject to the Naval Discipline Act of or above the rank of lieutenant-commander or equivalent or relative rank or of the rank of lieutenant being a barrister, solicitor or advocate who has been specially appointed for the purpose of taking affidavits and declarations; an officer of the regular Army who is of or above the rank of major or is of the rank of captain and is a member of the legal corps of those forces or an officer of the regular Air Force who is of or above the rank of squadron leader or is of the rank of flight lieutenant and is a member of the legal branch of that force[1].

1 Emergency Laws (Miscellaneous Provisions) Act 1953, s. 10; Army Act 1955, s. 204; Air Force Act 1955, s. 204, as amended by Armed Forces Act 1981, s. 19.

22.37   A document purporting to have subscribed thereto the signature of an authorised officer in testimony of an affidavit or declaration being taken before him in pursuance of the above provisions and containing in the jurat or attestation a statement of the date on which and the place at which the affidavit or declaration was taken and of the full name and rank of that officer is admissible in evidence without proof of the signature being the signature of that officer or of the facts stated.

Statutory declarations

22.38   See also paras. **3.108** and **22.01**(b), ante; and as to the wording of a statutory declaration see footnote 3, para. **22.01**, ante.

Form of attestation

22.39   'Declared at   in the county of
           this   day of   19
           Before me,
           [*Signature and designation of Commissioner*].'

CHAPTER 23

Caveats

Summary

Nature

Definition

23.01 A caveat is a notice in writing lodged in the Principal Registry of the Family Division, or in any district probate registry or sub-registry, by a person wishing to show cause against the sealing of a grant, that no grant is to be sealed in the estate of the deceased named therein without notice to the person who has entered the caveat (NCPR 44). *Note*—If the person does not wish to prevent a grant issuing but requires to know when a grant issues, so that he may pursue a claim against the estate or for any other reason, instead of entering a caveat he should enter a standing search under r. 43—see paras. **21.09–21.12**.

23.02 No grant, other than a grant ad colligenda bona (see paras. **11.335** ff. and **25.173** ff., post) or a grant pending suit (see paras. **11.318** ff., ante), can be sealed if the district judge or registrar has knowledge of an effective caveat, but a caveat is not effective to prevent the sealing of a grant on the day on which it is entered (r. 44(1)).

23.03 The person by whom, or on whose behalf, the caveat is entered, is called *the caveator*.

Purpose

23.04 The following are some of the purposes for which a caveat may be entered:

(a) to give time to the caveator to make enquiries and to obtain such information as may enable him to determine whether or not there are grounds for his opposing the grant;

(b)   to give any person interested in the estate an opportunity of bringing any question arising in respect of the grant before the court on summons;

(c)   as a step preliminary to a probate action[1], or to the issuing of a citation (see para. **24.54**, post).

1   See Chap. 29.

23.05   The proceedings subsequent to the entry of caveat (i.e. the *warning* or notice to appear, issued against the caveator by the party whose application for a grant has been stopped, and the *appearance* to such warning by the caveator) will disclose the names and addresses of the parties and their respective interests in the estate of the deceased, and with this information it is open to either of them, if the interests conflict, to commence an action against the other for the purpose of establishing his own claim.

Effect

23.06   When a caveat has been entered no grant can issue other than a grant ad colligenda bona or a grant pending suit[1], except to the caveator himself, until it has been removed in one of the following ways:

(a)   by the non-appearance of the caveator to the warning (see para. **23.49**, post);

(b)   by the withdrawal of the caveat by the caveator (see paras. **23.45** ff., post);

(c)   by an order of a district judge, registrar or High Court judge; or

(d)   by the expiration of six months from the date of entry or effective extension of the caveat[2].

1   NCPR 44(1) and see *Re Clore* [1982] Fam 113 approved on appeal [1982] Ch 456, [1982] 3 All ER 419, CA.
2   See also 'Date and duration' and 'Extension of caveat', paras. **23.11** ff. and **23.25** ff., post.

23.07   NCPR 44(1) provides that no grant (other than a grant ad colligenda bona or a grant pending suit) shall be sealed if the district judge or registrar has knowledge of an effective caveat, but that no caveat shall operate to prevent the sealing of a grant on the day on which the caveat is entered. For this purpose the seal is deemed to have been impressed immediately before 10 a.m. on the day of the date of the grant. Thus a caveat entered on the day of the date of the grant is ineffective. A grant which has been sealed is operative unless and until the court orders its revocation.

23.08   A caveat is not a notice to a particular person; it is a notice to the court not to allow proceedings to be taken in the matter of the will or estate of the deceased without notice to the caveator[1]. It does not commence litigation, it institutes no proceedings[2], and it is not an 'act' in any proceedings in which the court in the course of its ordinary procedure will order the 'actor' to give security for costs[3].

1   *Moran v Place* [1896] P 214.
2   Ibid.
3   *Re Emery, Emery v Emery* [1923] P 184.

23.09   A caveat also prevents the resealing of a colonial grant (NCPR 2(1)).

Entry of caveat

By whom entered

23.10   A caveat can be entered by any person having or asserting an interest in the estate of the deceased, either by the party himself or his solicitor[1] (NCPR 44(1) and (2)).

1 The actual entry of a caveat is merely a ministerial act, and a person who performs this act on behalf of another is not liable to attachment under s. 18 of the Solicitors Act 1957 (now Solicitors Act 1974, s. 20): *Re Panton* [1901] P 239.

Date and duration

23.11   Except as otherwise provided by NCPR 44, 45 and 46 a caveat remains in force for the period of six months beginning with the date on which it is entered[1] (r. 44(3)(a)). See also 'Extension of caveat', paras. **23.25** ff., post.

1 The date of entry of the caveat is excluded in calculating the six months' period (RSC Ord. 3, r. 2, applied by NCPR 3).

23.12   Unless otherwise directed by order of a district judge of the Principal Registry made on summons, a caveat in force when proceedings by way of citation are commenced remains in force (unless withdrawn by the caveator pursuant to r. 44(11)) until an application for a grant is made by the person shown to be entitled thereto by the decision of the court in such proceedings: on such application any caveat entered by a party who had notice of the proceedings ceases to have effect (r. 46(3)).

23.13   Unless otherwise directed by order of a district judge of the Principal Registry, or where application to discontinue a caveat is made by consent a registrar, made on summons a caveat in respect of which an appearance to a warning has been entered remains in force until the commencement of a probate action (r. 44(13)). As to the position on the commencement of such an action, see paras. **23.15–23.16**, post.

23.14   The life of a caveat is also extended beyond the normal period of six months by the issue of a summons for directions pursuant to r. 44(6) (see paras. **23.64** ff., post) until that summons is disposed of or the district judge or registrar gives a direction, on the summons, for the caveat to cease to have effect (r. 44(8)) unless the caveat is previously withdrawn under r. 44(11), but in the event of a caveat being withdrawn before such a summons has been finally disposed of, no grant will be sealed without reference to a district judge or registrar[1].

1 Registrar's Circular, 12 June 1967.

Commencement of probate action

23.15   When a probate action is commenced, a copy of the writ of summons is sent by the Chancery Division to the Principal Registry of the Family Division. Thereupon, notice of the commencement of the action is given by the Senior District Judge to every person who has already entered a caveat in the estate of the deceased (other than the plaintiff in the action). Similar steps are taken by the Senior District Judge on being notified by the Chancery Division of the commencement of probate proceedings, by way of counterclaim, for a grant of representation (or the revocation of such a grant) in a non-probate action[1]. If any caveat is subsequently entered at any time while the action is pending, notice of the existence of the action is given by the Senior District Judge to the caveator (r. 45(2)). Notice of entry of such a caveat is also given to the Chancery Division.

1 Secretary's Circular, 14 April 1976.

23.16   Whether or not any caveat has been entered, unless otherwise directed by a district judge of the Principal Registry by order on summons, the commencement of a probate action operates to prevent the sealing of any grant (other than a grant of administration pending suit) until application for a grant is made by the person shown to be entitled thereto by the decision of the court in such action. On such application, any caveat entered by the plaintiff in the action, and any caveat in respect of which notice of the action has been given, ceases to have effect (r. 45(4)).

Place and mode of entry

23.17   A caveat may be entered at the Principal Registry or at any district probate registry or sub-registry[1] by attending and completing the prescribed form 'in the appropriate book', or by sending to the registry a notice in the prescribed form (see Form No. 45). Entry by post is at the caveator's risk (r. 44(2)).

1 Supreme Court Act 1981, s. 108 (see p. 843, post); see NCPR 44.

23.18   The person entering a caveat is given or sent a receipt: this must be produced if it is subsequently desired to withdraw the caveat.

23.19   If two or more persons wish to oppose the issue of a grant of representation, separate caveats must be entered: the names of more than one caveator may not appear in any caveat.

Form of caveat

23.20   The following details must be given in the caveat: the full names and last address of the deceased, and the date of death. Full names of the caveator and his address for service, which must be within the jurisdiction (NCPR 49). If the caveat is entered by a solicitor, the name of the caveator must also be stated. Date of entry must be shown and it must be signed by the caveator or his solicitor. For form, see Form No. 45.

23.21   Care should be taken to include in the entry all alternative or alias names for the deceased.

Notice to Principal Registry and to registry where combined index is maintained

23.22   If entry of a caveat is made in a district probate registry, the district probate registrar will immediately send a copy of it to the Principal Registry[1].

1 Supreme Court Act 1981, s. 108(2) (see p. 843, post).

23.23   An index of caveats entered in the Principal Registry or any district probate registry or sub-registry is maintained at the registry where the index of pending grant applications is maintained (r. 44(4)). Under r. 57(1) the Senior District Judge is directed to maintain such an index of pending applications for grants and the indexes are currently maintained at the Leeds District Probate Registry (see para. **2.58**, ante). The Leeds District Probate Registry is notified of all caveats and of all grant applications. On receipt of notice of an application for a grant the indexes are searched and the result of that search is given to the appropriate registry.

Fee

23.24 The fee payable on the entry of a caveat is £4[1]. If sent by post the remittance should be by crossed cheque or postal order made payable to 'H.M. Paymaster General'.

1 NC Probate Fees Order 1981, Fee 4.

Extension of caveat

23.25 By virtue of NCPR 44(3)(a)[1] a caveator may apply for the extension of an existing caveat for a further period of six months from the caveat's expiry date. The application for extension must be made within the last month before the caveat, to which it relates, is due to expire. A caveat may be extended for successive periods of six months' duration by filing a further application for extension and subject to the same conditions (r. 44(3)(c)).

1 See p. 935, post.

23.26 No form of application for the extension of a caveat is prescribed by r. 44(3)(a), other than the requirement that it must be in writing. Application may, therefore, be made by the caveator or his solicitor attending personally at the registry in which the caveat was entered and by endorsing the relevant caveat with a request for its extension or by sending the application to the registry by post. Where postal application is made the related caveat number should be quoted. In every case where a caveat is extended, the registry will issue a receipt[1]. The fee for extending a caveat is £4[2].

1 *Practice Note* (1976) 15 September.
2 NC Probate Fees Order 1981, Fee 4.

23.27 The proviso to NCPR 44(1) (which provides that a caveat is not effective to prevent the sealing of a grant on the day of entry) is not expressly attracted to an application for the extension of a caveat with the result that a successful application for extension made, or received in the registry, on the date upon which the caveat is due to expire will operate to prevent the sealing of a grant. In all other respects, the procedures relating to the entry of a caveat apply to applications for extension[1].

1 Registrar's Circular, 15 September 1976.

23.28 It should be noted that the life of a caveat entered *after* the commencement of proceedings by way of citation is not extended by those proceedings[1].

1 Registrar's Direction (1962) 12 July.

Restriction on entry of further caveat

23.29   Except by leave of a district judge of the Principal Registry, no further caveat may be entered in an estate by or on behalf of a caveator whose caveat is either in force or has ceased to have effect: (i) by filing an affidavit of service of the warning after non-appearance of the caveator to the warning and no summons for directions having been issued; or (ii) following the decision of the court in a probate action or in proceedings by way of citation, the caveator having had notice of such action or proceedings; or (iii) following a direction by a district judge or registrar, given on a summons for directions under r. 44(7), that the caveat cease to have effect (r. 44(14)). An existing caveat may, however, be extended or re-extended under NCPR 44(3) (see paras. **23.25–23.27**).

23.30   If a further caveat is inadvertently accepted without leave, it will be deemed to be of no effect, and the caveator will be so informed[1].

1 Registrar's Direction (1958) 28 January.

23.31   Where leave of a district judge of the Principal Registry for the entry of a further caveat is granted, the further caveat is effective for six months from its entry and not (as in the case of an application for extension of an existing caveat) from the date of expiry of the first caveat[1].

1 Registrar's Direction (1958) 28 January.

Death of caveator

23.32   In a case where papers to lead a grant were lodged, the issue of the grant was stopped by a caveat. The caveator having died since the entry of the caveat, it was decided that an order on summons was required to clear the caveat. Such a summons should normally be served on the personal representative(s) of the deceased caveator, or the person or persons entitled to be constituted such personal representative(s).

Search for caveat

23.33   Any solicitor or member of the public may ask, in the Leeds District Probate Registry (where the index of all current caveats is kept), for a search to be made for an effective caveat against the issue of a grant of representation to the estate of a specified person. The officer in charge of caveats will search the card index and caveat book index and inform the applicant of all effective caveats. If the search reveals an effective caveat the applicant may inspect it and make a note of it, including a note of subsequent proceedings.

23.34   An application may also be made by post to the Leeds District Probate Registry asking for a search to be made and it will be answered by a letter stating whether or not there is an effective caveat, and, if there is a caveat, a copy of it will be posted to the applicant[1].

1 Secretary's Circular, 11 August 1988.

23.35   Fees: For a search made personally at the registry   No fee
            For inspection of a caveat   25p
                (NC Probate Fees Order 1981, Fee 7)

For a copy of a caveat obtained on a personal attendance   25p
     (Ibid., Fee 8(a))
For handling a postal application and, where appropriate,   £2
     supplying a copy of a caveat
(Ibid., Fee 9(a))

Warning of caveats

Caveats warned at the registry where the complete index is maintained—currently Leeds District Probate Registry

23.36 The caveat index is searched before any grant is issued, and if a caveat has been entered the grant is stopped. The person whose application for a grant is stopped by a caveat, or any person wishing to apply for a grant, may thereupon issue a 'warning'. The form of warning is supplied by the officer in charge of caveats and is filled up by the applicant. Form of warning, No. 194.

23.37 Caveats can be warned only at the registry where the index of caveats entered at every registry or sub-registry is maintained (NCPR 44(5)). The index is currently maintained at Leeds District Probate Registry (see para. **2.58**, ante) in accordance with Registrar's Direction of 12 July 1988, [1988] 3 All ER 544.

23.38 When an application for a grant is stopped by the entry of a caveat, the papers to lead the grant are not handed out of the registry without leave of a district judge or registrar until the caveat has been removed.

How warned

23.39 The warning is a notice to the caveator to enter an appearance at the registry in which the caveat index is maintained (currently Leeds District Probate Registry) within eight days, inclusive of the day of service, setting out his interest or, if he has no contrary interest but wishes to show cause against the sealing of a grant, to issue and serve within the same period a summons for directions returnable before a district judge of the Principal Registry or a district probate registrar (see NCPR 44(6)).

23.40 The person warning the caveat must state in the warning the date of the will or codicil under which he claims, and his interest thereunder (e.g. executor or residuary legatee, etc.), or, in the case of intestacy, his interest in the estate of the deceased, and must also give an address within the jurisdiction, which is his address for service (r. 49).

23.41 A warning to a caveat may be issued whether papers to lead a grant have been lodged or not.

23.42 No fee is payable on warning a caveat.

Service of warning

23.43 The warning must be served by leaving it, or a true copy of it, at the place mentioned in the caveat as the address for service of the person who entered it, or sending it, or a copy, there by prepaid ordinary or registered post or by recorded delivery or, if the address for service includes a numbered box at a document exchange, by leaving the warning, or a copy, at that document exchange or one which transmits documents every business day to that document exchange or, in appropriate circumstances by fax—see paras. **25.230–25.233**, post (RSC Ord. 65, r. 5, applied by NCPR 67). After service, an indorsement thereof should be made on the warning.

23.44   Service between 12 noon on a Saturday and midnight on the following day is deemed to be service on the following Monday, and service after 4 p.m. on any other weekday is deemed to be service on the following day[1].

1 RSC Ord. 65, r. 7, applied by NCPR 3.

Withdrawal of caveat

When allowed

23.45   A caveator may withdraw his caveat at any time before he has entered appearance to a warning of it; but if it has been warned, he must give notice of withdrawal forthwith to the person who warned it (r. 44(11)). A caveator *who has not entered an appearance to a warning* may withdraw his caveat notwithstanding the existence of proceedings by way of citation (see NCPR 46(3), which expressly preserves the right to withdraw the caveat given by r. 44(11))[1].

1 Registrar's Direction (1958) 28 January.

23.46   Upon the withdrawal of a caveat which is stopping the issue of a grant, notice of withdrawal will be given to the extracting solicitors, or the personal applicant, by the registry at which the grant is sought, with a request for information as to whether it is desired that the application for the grant should proceed.

23.47   The caveat must be withdrawn *at the registry where it was entered*, and, on the withdrawal of the caveat, the original receipt given when the caveat was entered must be produced and left. At the Principal Registry notice of withdrawal of a caveat must be given to the Probate Department. No fee is payable on the withdrawal of a caveat.

23.48   If a caveat is entered and withdrawn at a registry other than that where the index of all caveats is maintained, a notice of withdrawal is sent by the district judge or registrar to the registrar of the registry maintaining that index.

Non-appearance to warning

Affidavit required

23.49   If no appearance is entered, nor any summons issued, by or on behalf of the caveator within the eight days allowed, the person warning the caveat should file in the Leeds District Probate Registry an affidavit showing that the warning was duly served (r. 44(12)). The search for appearance and for the record of any summons for directions having been issued is made by the registry and if no appearance is found and the time for appearance has expired and if no summons for directions is pending, the caveat will be removed. If the application for a grant has already been lodged, it may then proceed in the normal way.

Fees

23.50 The fees payable in the registry on swearing an affidavit and marking an exhibit are £2 and 50p respectively[1].

1 NC Probate Fees Order 1981, Fee 10.

Appearance to warning

Effect of appearance to warning

23.51 If the caveator enters an appearance to the warning, no grant can issue (except to the caveator himself) without an order of the court. A caveat in respect of which an appearance to a warning has been entered remains in force until proceedings are commenced by probate action, unless otherwise directed by order made on summons by a district judge of the Principal Registry or, if the application to discontinue the caveat is made by consent, a registrar[1].

1 NCPR 44(13).

23.52 The commencement of a probate action operates to prevent the sealing of any grant, except a grant of administration pending suit, until application for a grant is made by the person shown to be entitled to it by the decision of the court in the action[1].

1 NCPR 45(3).

23.53 A caveat may be cleared off by an order on summons, e.g. if agreement is arrived at, or opposition is abandoned, prior to the issue of a writ of summons: in such a case the caveat must be specifically referred to in the order.

23.54 When application for a grant is made after the conclusion of a probate action by the person shown to be entitled to it by the decision of the court in the action, all caveats entered by parties who had notice of the action, or by persons who were notified by the registry of the existence of the action (see paras. **23.15** and **23.16**, ante), cease to have effect[1].

1 NCPR 45(4).

Appearance after time limited

23.55 A caveator who has an interest contrary to that of the person warning the caveat may enter an appearance after the time limited by the warning provided that no affidavit of service has been filed in accordance with NCPR 44(12)[1].

1 NCPR 44(10).

23.56 If such affidavit has been filed the leave of a district judge is necessary before the caveator may enter a further caveat (see paras. **23.29–23.31**, ante).

How entered

23.57   To enter his appearance, a caveator may either attend in person or by his solicitor at the Leeds District Probate Registry and fill up a form of memorandum of appearance, which may be obtained at the registry, or he may send the completed form of appearance by post to that registry. Form of appearance, No. 42.

23.58   No fee is payable on the entry of an appearance.

23.59   In the form of appearance, the party must state his name and address in full, and his interest in the estate, giving the date of the will (if any) under which such interest arises. He must give an address for service within the jurisdiction (r. 49). A sealed copy of the appearance must be served forthwith on the person warning the caveat: see r. 44(10).

Who may appear

23.60   A person seeking to enter an appearance to a warning must have an interest contrary to that of the person who issued the warning (NCPR 44(10)).

23.61   An appearance by an executor, legatee or devisee, the personal representative of a legatee or devisee, or any other person claiming an interest under a will or codicil must state the date of such will or codicil.

23.62   An appearance by a person claiming to be entitled to share in, or interested in, the estate of the deceased on his intestacy or partial intestacy, or as the personal representative of any such person, must set forth the relationship of such person to the deceased[1].

1   The heir-at-law may be interested in cases where the deceased died after 1925, if the deceased was of full age and of unsound mind on and at all times after 1 January 1926; see Administration of Estates Act 1925, s. 51(2) (see p. 761, post).

23.63   The person who warned the caveat may apply by summons to a district judge of the Principal Registry to strike out any appearance which does not comply with the above provisions.

Caveator having no contrary interest

23.64   A caveator who has no interest contrary to that of the person warning the caveat, but wishes to show cause against the issue of a grant to that person, may within eight days of service of the warning upon him (inclusive of the day of service) or at any time thereafter before a step in default has been taken by the person warning (i.e. the filing of an affidavit showing that the warning was duly served), issue and serve a summons for directions returnable before a district judge of the Principal Registry or a district probate registrar (NCPR 44(6)). The district probate registrar of the district probate registry to which the application for the grant has been made or is to be made is the registrar who has jurisdiction to hear the summons.

23.65   It is provided by r. 27(6) that a dispute between persons entitled in the same degree to a grant is to be brought by summons before a district judge or registrar (see paras. **14.10–14.14**, ante and **25.193** ff.). The district probate registrar of the district probate registry to which the application for the grant has been made or is to be made is the registrar who has jurisdiction to hear the summons. If the summons is not issued at the registry where the complete index of pending grant applications is maintained, the registry where the summons is issued notifies that registry forthwith (NCPR 27(7)).

23.66 If the issue of a summons under r. 27(6) is known to the district judge or registrar he must not allow any grant to be sealed until the summons is finally disposed of (NCPR 27(8)). There is similar provision in relation to a summons for directions under r. 44(6). Notice of the issue of such a summons must be notified forthwith to the registry where the combined indexes are maintained (r. 44(9)). The life of the caveat is extended beyond the normal period of six months until either the summons is disposed of or the district judge or registrar directs, on the hearing of the summons, that the caveat ceases to have effect (r. 44(8)), unless the caveat is previously withdrawn under r. 44(11) but, in the event of a caveat being withdrawn before such a summons has been finally disposed of, no grant will be sealed without reference to a district judge or registrar[1].

1 Registrar's Circular, 12 June 1967.

Appearance by persons under disability

23.67 If it is desired to enter an appearance for a minor or other person under disability, the practice is, broadly speaking, similar to that which is adopted in order to appear on behalf of such persons to a writ of summons[1].

1 Registrar's Direction (1922) 21 February and see RSC Ord. 80 as applied by NCPR 3.

Subsequent proceedings

23.68 After entry of appearance, if the parties come to an agreement (which does not involve pronouncing for or against a will or making an order incorporating terms which are properly a matter for the Chancery Division) or if the opposition to the issue of a grant is abandoned, a summons for discontinuance of proceedings should be taken out before a district judge or registrar (see paras. **25.212** ff., post), and an order clearing off the caveat, and for the issue of the grant, may then be made. A district probate registrar has power to make the order where the application to discontinue the caveat is by consent and he has jurisdiction to deal with the summons if the application for the grant has been made or is to be made to his registry.

23.69 Failing this, a probate action is generally commenced by the party who warned the caveat, by the issue of a writ of summons in the Chancery Division.

23.70 If a probate action is determined without any decision of the court indicating entitlement to a grant within the meaning of NCPR 45(3), it may be necessary to apply on summons to a district judge of the Principal Registry for an order that a grant may issue notwithstanding any effective caveats.

CHAPTER 24
Citations

Summary

Object of citations

Definitions

24.01   A citation is an instrument issuing from, and under the seal of, the Principal Registry of the Family Division or a district probate registry, containing a recital of the reason for its issue and the interest of the party extracting it, calling upon the party cited to enter an appearance and take the steps specified in it, with an intimation of the nature of the order the court is asked to and may make unless good cause is shown to the contrary.

Kinds of citations

24.02   Citations are issued in non-contentious probate matters:

(a)   to accept or refuse a grant;
(b)   to take probate;
(c)   to propound a will.

(A) To accept or refuse a grant

24.03   *Citation to accept or refuse. Object.* When a person, having the prior right to take a grant, delays or declines to do so, but will not renounce his right, the court, at the instance of a person having an inferior right, will call upon the former person to take the grant, and, on his failing to do so, may order that a grant issue to the citor.

24.04   The citation, therefore, answers two purposes: (1) it compels those who are primarily entitled to take a grant to decide whether they will do so or not; and (2) where such parties refuse either to take it or to renounce, it provides an alternative grantee.

24.05 *Effect of citation of executor.* Where an executor is cited to accept or refuse probate of a will and does not appear to the citation, his rights in respect of the executorship wholly cease, and representation is granted as though he had not been appointed[1]. He is, however, still entitled to take a grant in a lower capacity (e.g. as residuary legatee) unless he was cited in that capacity also (see para. **15.26**, ante).

1 Administration of Estates Act 1925, s. 5 (see p. 746, post).

24.06 If the executor enters an appearance to the citation, but fails to proceed with reasonable diligence to obtain probate, it would not appear that his rights as executor wholly cease, as s. 5(ii) of the Administration of Estates Act 1925 deals only with non-appearance. However, NCPR 47(7) enables a grant to be made to the citor in such a case.

24.07 In the case of non-appearance by the executor his right is fully cleared off, and it would appear that a grant could, if necessary, be made to a person other than the citor (e.g. if the latter had died or was unable or unwilling to apply).

24.08 For form of citation, see No. 48.

24.09 *Effect of renunciation of executor.* Where an executor renounces probate, his rights cease in the same manner as stated above[1]; but it is open to an executor who has renounced to apply for leave to retract his renunciation (see paras. **15.60–15.72**, ante[2]). Such leave is, however, given only in special circumstances after a grant has been made to another person entitled in a lower capacity[3].

1 Administration of Estates Act 1925, s. 5 (see p. 746, post).
2 *Re Stiles' Goods* [1898] P 12.
3 NCPR 37(3).

24.10 *Alternative to citation.* Where it is sought to pass over persons entitled who cannot be traced, in favour of a lower title, and a citation served by advertisement would normally be required, a district judge or registrar may make an order, if he thinks fit, under s. 116(1) of the Supreme Court Act 1981 after, in appropriate cases, requiring the publication of a suitable advertisement for the person who would normally be cited. This course is usually adopted where the amount of the estate is small.

24.11 See also para. **14.05**, ante, as to applications by persons having no immediate interest in the estate.

24.12 *Where the deceased left a will.* Where the deceased left a will, a residuary legatee or devisee may cite the executor to accept or refuse probate of the testator's will, or to show cause why letters of administration with the will annexed of all the estate which by law devolves to and vests in the personal representative of the testator should not be granted to the citor.

24.13 And if there is no executor, the residuary legatee or devisee in trust may be cited 'to accept or refuse letters of administration with the will annexed of all the estate' etc.

24.14   Legatees, devisees or creditors similarly cite both the executor and the residual legatees and devisees in trust or beneficially entitled, and (*if the whole residue has not been disposed of*) the persons entitled to the undisposed-of estate.

24.15   *Clearing off executors to whom power reserved.* A citation to accept or refuse a grant may also be extracted where it is desired to make use of s. 5 of the Administration of Estates Act 1925[1], and to clear off the right of an executor to whom power has been reserved, so that the chain of executorship, if any, can continue without its being liable to be broken subsequently, or a grant de bonis non can issue to any person entitled thereto. But an executor whose rights as such have been extinguished by his non-appearance to the citation does not lose any alternative rights which he may have as residuary legatee etc., unless he is cited in both capacities.

1   See p. 746, post.

24.16   An executor to whom power was reserved may be cited to accept or refuse a grant by the executors who proved the will, or by the survivor of them, or by the executors of the last survivor of the proving executors[1].

1   NCPR 47(2).

24.17   For form of citation, see No. 52.

24.18   *Will must be filed.* Before any citation can issue every will referred to in it must whenever possible be lodged in the Principal Registry or a district probate registry[1].

1   NCPR 46(5).

24.19   Where the citor has the will in his possession, he should lodge it at the registry where the citation is to be issued before the citation is settled and issued. If the will is at another probate registry, he should communicate with the district judge or registrar of that other registry, and ask him to forward it to the registry where the citation is to be settled and issued.

24.20   Where the will is in the hands of some person who is unwilling to part with it, he should issue a subpoena against that person to bring it into the appropriate registry (see paras. **25.185** ff., post).

24.21   The district judge or registrar has power to dispense with the lodging of the will if it is not in the possession of the citor and the district judge or registrar is satisfied that it is impracticable to require it to be lodged[1].

1   NCPR 46(5).

24.22   *Persons of unsound mind prior to 1926.* When a person of unsound mind, who was living and of full age on the 1 January 1926, but unable by reason of his incapacity to make a will, has a beneficial interest in real estate (not being an interest ceasing on his death) and dies thereafter intestate in respect of such interest without having recovered his capacity, such interest devolves under the general law in force prior to 1926[1] (see also paras. **6.146** and **6.147**, ante).

1   Administration of Estates Act 1925, s. 51(2) (see p. 761, post).

24.23   It is therefore necessary in such a case to cite the heir-at-law in addition to all persons having a prior right to the grant.

24.24   *Where deceased died intestate.* In the case of intestacy, a person who is beneficially interested in the estate may cite all persons with a prior right to the grant. This applies, for example, where the deceased left a surviving spouse whose prior right a child, or other kin, having either an actual or a potential beneficial interest in the estate, wishes to pass over. A creditor must similarly cite all such persons.

24.25   When a person dies without known relations, a creditor must cite 'the kin (if any) and all persons in general', entitled to share in the estate of the deceased, with the intimation that in default of appearance a grant of the estate will be made to him; in such cases it is necessary to serve a copy of the citation on the Treasury Solicitor, or the Solicitor for the Duchy of Lancaster or Cornwall (as the case may be). See, however, 'Alternative to citation', paras. **24.10** and **24.11**, ante.

24.26   For forms of citation, see Nos. 49–51.

24.27   *Citor must have interest in estate.* The district judges of the Principal Registry are not in favour of the issue of citations by persons whose only real interest in the estate depends upon the death of an untraced citee (e.g. an application by the kin to pass over a missing spouse who, if alive, is entitled to the whole estate). In such cases application should be made for an order under s. 116(1) of the Supreme Court Act 1981[1] (for practice, see paras. **14.02–14.07**, ante, **25.91** ff., post).

1   Registrar's Direction (1957) 19 February.

(B) To take probate

24.28   *Citation to take probate.* Where an executor has intermeddled in the estate of his testator and has not taken a grant within six months of his decease, such executor can after that period be cited to take probate (*not* to accept or refuse) by any person interested in the estate, and refusal may render him liable to a fine or committal[1]. It is immaterial that the estate in which he intermeddled is out of the jurisdiction[2]. No such citation may issue while proceedings as to the validity of the will of the deceased are pending[3].

1   NCPR 47(3); see also the Stamp Act 1815, s. 37.
2   *Re Lord and Fullerton's Contract* [1896] 1 Ch 228.
3   NCPR 47(3).

24.29   No action will, however, lie against such an executor for neglect to take out a grant of probate[1].

1   *Re Stevens, Cooke v Stevens* [1897] 1 Ch 422: affd [1898] 1 Ch 162.

24.30   For form of citation, see No. 53.

24.31   *Intermeddling executor may be passed over.* There is a good deal of authority to the effect that an executor who intermeddles cannot subsequently renounce probate[1], and that the court has no power to authorise him to do so. But it was held in 1966 that the executor could, in special circumstances, be passed over by order under s. 162(1) proviso (b) of the Supreme Court of Judicature (Consolidation) Act 1925 (since replaced by s. 116(1) of the Supreme Court Act 1981), notwithstanding that he had intermeddled[2].

1 See paras. **15.45–15.48**, ante, and the cases cited in the footnotes to those paragraphs. But as to the position of an executor who renounces after merely trivial and technical acts of intermeddling, see *Holder v Holder* [1968] Ch 353, [1968] 1 All ER 665.
2 *Re Biggs' Estate* [1966] P 118, [1966] 1 All ER 358, following *Re Potticary's Estate* [1927] P 202 and applying dictum of Merriman P in *Re Leguia's Estate, ex p Ashworth, ex p Meinertzhagen* [1934] P 80 at 83.

24.32   In consequence, NCPR 47(5) and 47(7) provide that a person who cites an intermeddling executor to take probate may, in default of compliance with the citation, apply either for an order directing the executor to take a grant of probate within a specified period, or for a grant to himself or some other person to be specified in the summons (see also paras. **24.91** ff., post).

(C) To propound a will

24.33   *Citation to propound a will.* Any person who becomes aware of the existence of an alleged will which would adversely affect his interest under an intestacy, or under an earlier will, may cite the executors named in it and all the persons interested under it to propound it[1].

1 NCPR 48. See *Re Quick's Goods, Quick v Quick* [1899] P 187; *Re Dennis' Goods* [1899] P 191; *Re Bootle's Goods, Heaton v Whalley* (1901) 84 LT 570; *Re Morton's Goods, Morton v Thorpe* (1863) 3 Sw & Tr 179.

24.34   The will in question must be lodged in the registry where the citation is being settled before the citation issues, or its absence must be accounted for to the satisfaction of the district judge or registrar[1]. It is essential to ascertain and cite all the persons interested under it[2].

1 NCPR 46(5).
2 NCPR 48(1).

24.35   For form of citation, see No. 54.

24.36   *Executor doubtful as to validity of codicil.* An executor of a will who is doubtful of the validity of a codicil should not cite those interested thereunder to propound it[1]. An executor, unless he renounces his office, has a duty to execute the true last wishes of the testator, and the procedure of citing the beneficiary under the codicil to propound the latter and, in default of appearance, seeking probate of the will alone, is inappropriate. If he has reason to believe that the codicil is invalid he should seek probate of the will in solemn form and adduce evidence to satisfy the court as to the invalidity of the codicil. The principle of *Re Morton's Goods*[2] ought not to be extended[3].

1 *Re Benbow's Goods* (1862) 2 Sw & Tr 488.
2 See note 1 to para. **24.33**, above.
3 *Re Muirhead's Estate* [1971] P 263, [1971] 1 All ER 609, following *Re Benbow's Goods*, above.

24.37   *Will already proved in common form.* If a will has been proved in common form, procedure by citation to propound is inappropriate. A person disputing such a will and wishing to compel the grantee to prove it in solemn form should take steps to have the grant called in, and himself commence proceedings for revocation: the Non-Contentious Probate Rules have no application in such circumstances[1].

1 *Re Jolley's Estate, Jolley v Jarvis* [1964] P 262, [1964] 1 All ER 596.

Requirements on extracting citations

Number of citations

24.38   One citation is normally issued against several parties who have different interests so that the interest of each is apparent to the others.

Citations in draft

24.39   In order to extract a citation a draft must first be prepared and lodged for settlement, together with the will (if any), and any necessary papers, e.g. renunciations etc.; these must be left at the registry where the citation is to be settled and issued (in the Probate Department at the Principal Registry, if the citation is to issue out of the Principal Registry). Alternatively the documents may be submitted by post: see paras. **24.57** and **24.58**, post. *Until the citation is settled by the district judge or registrar the affidavit to lead thereto should not be sworn,* see paras **24.45–24.53**, post.

24.40   The principle to keep in mind in drafting all citations is 'that you must set before the parties cited what is their interest and what is yours'[1]. All necessary facts (e.g. dates of wills and codicils) should be stated as concisely as possible and in chronological order.

1 Foster's *Doctors Commons and Probate Court Business.*

24.41   For forms applicable to ordinary cases, see Nos. 48 ff.

Minority or life interest

24.42   Where a citation asks for a grant to the citor and there is a minority or life interest necessitating two grantees, it should be shown who is the proposed co-grantee and that he is equally or next entitled to a grant. Failing this, the citation and the subsequent order should contain the limitation 'if entitled thereto', an application to the district judge or registrar under NCPR 25 for joinder of a co-administrator being necessary before the grant issues unless a co-grantee can be provided under the rules by nomination or otherwise.

24.43   Where it is desired to proceed to a grant to a sole citor notwithstanding that a life or minority interest exists in the estate of the deceased, the facts should be put to the Principal of the Probate Department of the Principal Registry or to the district probate registrar (depending upon where the citation is to be settled and issued) for his consideration on or before the preparation of the draft citation.

Parties 'non sui juris'

24.44   For practice where any citor or citee is a person under disability, see paras. **24.100** ff., post.

Affidavit in support

24.45   The party or parties citing (or, in special circumstances, by leave of the district judge or registrar, the solicitor for the citor or citors) must make an affidavit verifying the statements of fact in the citation (NCPR 46(2)), and, in cases where such citation is to be advertised or served otherwise than by personal service on account of the impossibility of personal service, setting out in detail all the enquiries made and facts demonstrating the impracticability of such service. It is essential that every averment in the citation shall be verified by the affidavit in support. It is for this reason that the affidavit should not be sworn until the draft citation has been settled, and it is known what facts have to be established. Care should also be taken to compare the affidavit with the citation before having it sworn.

24.46   Forms of affidavit, Nos. 30 ff.

24.47   No fee is charged for perusing a draft affidavit in support of a citation.

Additional facts to be sworn to in particular cases

24.48   In the following cases additional facts (which are not set out in the citation) must be sworn to in the affidavit.

Citation to take probate

24.49   In a citation against an executor who has intermeddled, the affidavit must give instances of intermeddling, and should state the fact that the deceased has been dead more than six months. Form of affidavit, No. 34.

Citation by creditor

24.50   If the citation is by a creditor, the affidavit should state the value of the estate, the amount and nature of the debt, and that the applicant holds no security for the same, if such be the fact[1]. If any security is held, the nature of it should be set out. For form of affidavit, see No. 32.

1   As to claims of different creditors to a grant, see *Andrews v Murphy* (1860) 4 Sw & Tr 198.

24.51   Where the creditor is a firm, the affidavit should be made by a partner, who should so describe himself and should confirm that all the remaining partners have been consulted and that each consents to the application being made (see para. **6.329**, ante as to the status of a firm).

24.52   Where the applicant is a nominee of a creditor (e.g. a local authority or other corporate body) this should be stated in the affidavit, and a sealed or certified copy of the nomination must be filed.

Where no known kin, or where address of citee unknown

24.53   In cases where it is alleged that there are no known kin, or where the addresses of the citees are not known, the affidavit should state fully what efforts have been made to trace them.

Caveat to be entered

24.54 Before the citation issues the citor must enter a caveat[1]. As to caveats, see Chap. 23.

1 NCPR 46(3).

Issue of citation

24.55 After the draft has been settled, the practitioner must lodge in the Probate Department (or, if the draft citation was settled at a district probate registry, in that district probate registry) the settled draft, an engrossment of the citation and the affidavit in support duly sworn (together with the perused draft affidavit). These documents are then transmitted to the Principal or the district probate registrar, as the case may be, for the citation to be approved and signed, following which it is sealed and a signed and sealed copy is returned by post to the extracting solicitor.

24.56 The only fee payable on the issue of a citation is a fee of £5 for settling the draft citation[1].

1 NC Probate Fees Order 1981, Fee 12.

Postal application

24.57 Applications for the settling and issue of citations may, if desired, be made through the post.

24.58 The procedure which should be adopted is as follows:

(a) Drafts of the citation and supporting affidavit should be sent for the citation to be settled to the Probate Department at the Principal Registry if that is where the citation is to be issued, or to the district probate registry where the citation is to be issued, together with the originals of any relevant will and codicil. In the event of an original will or codicil being sent, registered post should be used and the registry will retain them unless their return is requested or necessary by reason of the intention to exhibit them to the affidavit.

(b) After the citation has been settled the papers (but not the original wills and codicils except in the circumstances set out in (a) above) will be returned to the solicitor who should then, if he has not already done so, enter a caveat (by post to any probate registry in respect of which a fee of £4[1] is payable: cheques or postal orders should be drawn in favour of 'H.M. Paymaster General'). The solicitor should return to the registry the settled draft citation, an engrossment of the citation, the draft affidavit, the sworn affidavit, any relevant wills and codicils in the solicitor's possession at this stage (e.g. if the draft citation has been provisionally settled in reliance on photographic copies, where the originals were not readily available and it would have been unreasonable to delay the matter until they were produced) and the receipt for the entry of the caveat. A cheque for £5, being the fee for settling the citation, should also be sent.

(c) A signed and sealed citation will be returned to the solicitor. The receipt for the caveat will be returned at the same time.

1 NC Probate Fees Order 1981, Fee 4.

Service

Personal service

24.59   Subject to the power to order substituted service (see paras. **24.62–24.65** below), personal service of a citation is required (NCPR 46(4)) and is effected by serving a copy on the party cited (RSC Ord. 65, r. 2).

24.60   A certificate of service should be indorsed on the citation[1].

1   *Goodburn v Bainbridge* (1860) 2 Sw & Tr 4.

Service out of the jurisdiction

24.61   There is no provision prohibiting service of a citation out of the jurisdiction; but if the party cited has an agent resident in England and Wales, such agent should also be served with a copy of the citation.

Substituted service

24.62   If, either on the issue of the citation or subsequently, it is found that personal service cannot be effected, application may be made to the district judge or registrar for substituted service. This is usually directed to be by advertisement, and an abstract of the citation (see Form No, 55) may be settled and signed by him and inserted as an advertisement in such papers as he may direct (NCPR 46(4)). It must be shown by affidavit to the satisfaction of the district judge or registrar why personal service is not possible, and what (if any) efforts have been made to effect the same. These facts may in many cases be incorporated in the affidavit verifying the citation referred to in paras. **24.45–24.53**, ante; otherwise a separate affidavit should be filed.

24.63   Except as stated in para. **24.65**, the sealed copy of the citation, together with a draft of the abstract of it to be advertised, is left at the Probate Department of the Principal Registry (if the citation was issued there; otherwise at the registry where it was issued) to be settled. If the district judge or registrar directs advertisement, he will give directions as to the papers and the numbers of insertions, and the time for appearance (generally one month after the date of the last insertion, unless in a foreign paper).

24.64   After the advertisements have been inserted, the settled draft and copies of the newspapers containing the advertisements and showing the date of issue and the name of the paper must be lodged in the Probate Department (or the district probate registry, depending upon where the citation was issued) together with the sealed copy citation.

Citations to accept or refuse a grant: short form of advertisement

24.65   A shortened style of advertisement is used when personal service of a citation to accept or refuse a grant is impossible. Examples are shown below. In this case, the advertisement will be drafted in the registry, and a solicitor applying for an abstract to be settled need lodge only a fee sheet imprinted with the fee of £5 (the amount of the estate should be noted on the fee sheet) together with the copy of the sealed citation. A draft abstract brought in by a solicitor will be accepted in lieu of a fee sheet.

SMITH.—The kin of JOHN SMITH, late of 17 Acacia Avenue, London SW13, who died there on 28th February, 1981, are cited to apply within one month to the Principal Registry of the Family Division, Somerset House, London WC2R 1LP (*or*   District Probate Registry at   ) (Estate about £   [1]) ——, District Judge/Registrar. Johnson & Co., 17 Fleet Street, London EC9 2XY, Solicitors.

JONES.—John Henry BUGGINS, last heard of at 23 Oak Avenue, Dorchester, executor named in Will dated 20th December, 1970, of Jack Jones late of 23 Norwood Drive, Worthing, who died at Hammersmith on 17th August, 1981, is cited to apply within one month to the Principal Registry of the Family Division, Somerset House, London WC2R 1LP (*or*   District Probate Registry at   ) ——, District Judge/Registrar. Smith & Howlett, 27 Chancery Lane, London EC6 1AZ, Solicitors.

BINKS.—Emily BINKS, last heard of at 18 Tooting Way, Streatham, SW17, widow of David Binks, late of the same address, who died there on 25th November, 1981, is cited to apply within one month to the Principal Registry of the Family Division, Somerset House, London WC2R 1LP (*or*   District Probate Registry at   ) (Estate £......[1]) —— District Judge/Registrar. Adam Smith, 29 Smith Street, London EC8 9PQ, Solicitor[2].

1 Amount of estate to be inserted.
2 Registrar's Direction (1951) 18 July.

Fees

24.66 The fee for settling a draft advertisement is £5 (NC Probate Fees Order 1981, Fee 12). No fee is payable on filing the settled draft.

Appearance to citation

24.67 Appearances to citations are entered at the registry from which the citation issued[1]. At the Principal Registry they are entered in the Probate Department. An appearance may be entered either on a personal attendance or by post.

1 NCPR 46(6).

24.68 The form of appearance to a citation is shown as No. 42. This form may be obtained in the registry. The caveat number and date of entry; date of citation; full names and last residence of the deceased; full name, address and interest in the estate of the party issuing the citation; full name, address and interest of the person entering the appearance, and an address for service of such person within the jurisdiction must be given in the appearance[1].

1 NCPR 46(6).

24.69 Where the interest claimed is under a will or codicil, the date of such will or codicil must also be given. Where the party cited claims an interest as entitled to share or interested in the estate of the deceased (or as the personal representative of a person having such interest) the relationship to the testator or intestate, on which the claim is founded, must also be set out.

24.70   In addition to filing the appearance, the party cited must forthwith serve a sealed copy of the appearance on the citor: such service may be effected by leaving it at, or sending it by ordinary prepaid or registered post or recorded delivery to, the citor's address for service or, if the address for service includes a numbered box at a document exchange, by leaving it at that document exchange or at a document exchange which transmits documents every business day to that document exchange or, in appropriate cases, by fax—see paras. **25.230** ff., post[1].

1 RSC Ord. 65, r. 5, as applied by NCPR 67.

24.71   Unless the citee is out of the jurisdiction, or the citation is directed to be advertised, the time for appearance is within eight days of the day of service, inclusive of the day of service. If the citee is abroad, or the citation is advertised, the district judge or registrar will fix the time for appearance. A party cited may, however, enter an appearance at any time before a proceeding has been taken in default (r. 46(6)).

24.72   If the citee seeks to enter an appearance in a capacity other than that in which he has been cited, the directions of the district judge or registrar must be obtained.

Subsequent proceedings

(A) Citation to accept or refuse a grant

Citation to accept or refuse. No appearance

24.73   Where a citation has been served personally but no appearance has been entered within the time prescribed, an affidavit of service must be made by the server and filed. This must exhibit the sealed copy citation, which should be indorsed with a certificate of service signed by the server[1]. The affidavit must state the means by which the server knew the identity of the person served[2].

1 *Harenc v Dawson and Clucas* (1863) 3 Sw &Tr 50.
2 Registrar's Direction (1964) 21 April.

24.74   Where the citation has been served abroad the affidavit should show that the citation has also been served on the citee's agent in England and Wales or that 'there is no attorney, agent or correspondent in England and Wales'[1].

1 *Evans v Burrell* (1859) 4 Sw & Tr 185; *Kenworthy v Kenworthy and Watson* (1863) 3 Sw & Tr 64.

24.75   For form of affidavit of service, see No. 40.

24.76   Where the citation has been served by advertisement the newspapers, the sealed copy citation and the settled abstract must be filed.

24.77   No fees are payable for the search for appearance, which is made by an officer of the registry, nor for filing any documents lodged to lead to an order of the district judge or registrar.

Application for order

24.78 The affidavits and other documents detailed above should be lodged in the registry where the citation issued (if at the Principal Registry in the Probate Department) and application made, ex parte, for an order for a grant in favour of the citor[1].

1 NCPR 47(5)(a).

24.79 Form of oath for grant after citation, No. 129.

Renunciation by citee

24.80 If the party cited renounces after being served with the citation, the citor may lodge the necessary papers for a grant to himself without taking any steps to dispose of the citation. The caveat he has entered does not prevent the issue of a grant to him[1].

1 Registrar's Direction (1955) 14 January.

24.81 For forms of renunciation, see Nos. 183 ff.

Acceptance by citee

24.82 If, however, the party cited is willing to take the grant, he should enter an appearance (see paras. **24.67–24.72**, ante) and serve a sealed copy of it on the citor, after which he may obtain an order for a grant ex parte on lodging at the registry where the citation issued and the appearance was entered (in the Principal Registry at the Probate Department) an affidavit that he has been cited, has appeared, is willing to take the grant and that the citor has been served with a sealed copy of the appearance[1].

1 NCPR 47(4).

24.83 Form of affidavit, No. 36.

24.84 After obtaining the order the party cited may apply for a grant in the usual way, the order being lodged with the papers.

Citation to kin. Procedure where issued but not advertised

24.85 Where a citation of the kin of the deceased has been extracted and one of the kin satisfies the citor of his title before service of the citation by advertisement, no formal step to terminate the citation proceedings is necessary. A caveator may at any time withdraw his caveat notwithstanding the existence of proceedings by citation: the only exception being in the case of a caveator who has entered an appearance to a warning[1].

1 NCPR 44(11): Registrar's Direction (1958) 28 January.

Rescission of order or grant to the Crown

24.86 Where an order has been made for a grant to the Treasury Solicitor or to the Solicitor for the Duchy of Lancaster or Cornwall following a citation of the kin (if any) or on application under s. 116(1) of the Supreme Court Act 1981, but kin entitled to the estate are discovered before the issue of a grant, the order may be rescinded on application by the Treasury or Duchy Solicitor or by the person claiming to be kin or otherwise entitled, if the application is not opposed, by district judge's or registrar's order to be obtained on an ex parte application, supported by an affidavit of the facts. If the grant has already been made, it may be revoked by district judge's or registrar's order, on lodging a statement of the facts by the Treasury or Duchy Solicitor[1]. In this latter case the order need not be rescinded[2].

1 In the case of the Duchy of Cornwall an affidavit is necessary.
2 President's Direction (1952) 21 October.

Citee dead

24.87   If after the issue of the citation it appears that the citee is dead, and that his personal representative is entitled to the grant in priority to the citor, and is willing to take it, application should be made by summons to a district judge or registrar for an order for a grant to issue to the personal representative. The summons should be served on the citor. No fee is payable on the issue of the summons.

Appearance but then default

24.88   If the party cited enters an appearance, but does not apply for a grant or prosecute his application with reasonable diligence, the citor should apply to a district judge or registrar by summons for an order for the grant to be made to himself, notwithstanding the appearance to the citation. If some of the parties appear and take no step, and others do not appear, application should be made by the citor to the district judge or registrar on summons for an order that a grant issue to himself notwithstanding the appearances and in default of appearance by the other parties cited (NCPR 47(7)(a)). Affidavit evidence of service of the citation on any person cited who has not appeared will be required.

Citation of executor to whom power was reserved

24.89   Where an executor to whom power was reserved has been cited to accept or refuse a grant of double probate, in default of appearance by the citee application should be made to the district judge or registrar ex parte for an order that the grant be noted, that the executor to whom power was reserved has been duly cited and has not appeared, and that all his rights in respect of the executorship have wholly ceased[1]. The application must be supported by an affidavit of service of the citation[2].

1 NCPR 47(5)(b).
2 NCPR 47(6).

Appearance, then default

24.90   If an executor to whom power was reserved enters an appearance but subsequently fails to apply for a grant, or to prosecute his application for a grant with reasonable diligence, the citor should apply to the district judge or registrar by summons for an order striking out the appearance and that the grant be noted in the manner set out in the preceding paragraph (NCPR 47(7)(b)).

(B) Citation to take probate

Citation to take probate. Appearance by executor

24.91   If a citee, who is an executor and who has intermeddled in the estate, is willing to take a grant he should enter an appearance and serve a sealed copy of it on the citor. He may then, by lodging an affidavit in the registry where the citation was issued and the appearance entered, apply ex parte, as in the case of a person cited to accept or refuse a grant, for an order for a grant to issue to him notwithstanding the caveat and citation (NCPR 47(4)).

24.92 For form of affidavit, see No. 36, duly adapted.

No appearance

24.93 If the citee does not appear, the citor should file an affidavit of service of the citation (see paras. **24.73–24.77**, ante), and may then apply by summons to the district judge or registrar either: (i) for an order directing the executor to take probate within a specified time; or (ii) for an order for a grant to be made to the citor, or to some other person to be specified in the summons, notwithstanding that the executor has intermeddled. The summons must be served on the citee (NCPR 47(5)(c)).

24.94 The court has power to pass over an executor by order under s. 116 of the Supreme Court Act 1981[1] and this applies notwithstanding that he has intermeddled in the estate[2]. Rule 47(5) indicates the alternative method of procedure where it is considered preferable not to compel an unwilling executor to act, but for some other person to be appointed as administrator. A grant to a person other than the executor will take the form of administration (with will), and is made under the authority of s. 116(1) of the Act of 1981.

1 See p. 845, post.
2 *Re Biggs' Estate* [1966] P 118, [1966] 1 All ER 358, following *Re Potticary's Estate* [1927] P 202, being cases relating to s. 162(1) proviso (b) of the Supreme Court of Judicature (Consolidation) Act 1925, since repealed and replaced by s. 116(1) of the Supreme Court Act 1981, but the principle still applies.

24.95 Disobedience of an order to take probate within a specified time renders the executor liable to committal[1]. There must be displayed prominently on the front of the copy of the order served a warning as indicated in RSC Ord. 45, r. 7(4), and the copy of the order must be served personally on the citee. As to enforcement of the order, see paras. **25.248** ff., post.

1 *Mordaunt v Clarke* (1868) LR 1 P & D 592.

24.96 If the citee enters an appearance, but then fails to apply for a grant or to prosecute his application with reasonable diligence, the same procedure should be followed (NCPR 47(7)(c)), but in this case an affidavit of service of the citation is unnecessary.

(C) Citation to propound testamentary papers

Citation to propound. Appearance

24.97 Where a person cited to propound a testamentary paper appears to the citation *and wishes to propound that paper*, his best course is to commence a probate action against the citor.

24.98 If any of the citees has entered an appearance, but not one proceeds with reasonable diligence to propound the testamentary document, the citor may apply by summons to a district judge or registrar for an order for a grant as if the testamentary document were invalid. The summons must be served on every person cited who has entered an appearance: it is not necessary to serve any citee who has not appeared (NCPR 48(2)(b)) but affidavit evidence of service of the citation on any person cited who has not appeared will be required.

No appearance

24.99   When the time for appearance has expired, if none of the persons cited has entered an appearance to the citation the citor, on filing affidavits of service of the citation (see paras. **24.73–24.77**, ante), may apply ex parte to a district judge or registrar for an order for a grant as asked in the citation, as if the testamentary document were invalid (NCPR 48(2)(a)).

Parties under disability

24.100   The Non-Contentious Probate Rules 1987 contain no special provisions as to citations in cases where either the citor or the citee is a person non sui juris but NCPR 3 applies, subject to any enactment, the Rules of the Supreme Court 1965, *with the necessary modifications*, to non-contentious probate matters.

24.101   It would appear that where a proposed citor or citee is a person under disability the provisions of RSC Order 80 as to next friends and guardians ad litem of persons under disability should be applied, with any necessary modifications. Cases of doubt or difficulty should be referred to the Principal of the Probate Department if the citation is to issue, or has issued, at the Principal Registry, or to the registrar at the district probate registry where the citation is to issue or has been issued.

Default of appearance

24.102   In default of acknowledgment of service to a writ by a defendant who is a person under disability, it is necessary for the plaintiff, before proceeding further with the action, to apply to the court for the appointment of a guardian ad litem of such defendant (Order 80, r. 6). This rule is not specifically made applicable to citations by any rule or direction, but it may in many cases be advisable for the party citing to make such an application where there is default as to appearance by a citee who is a person under disability.

24.103   In view of the desirability of protecting the interests of persons under disability, it is possible that in citations under the Non-Contentious Probate Rules the district judge or registrar would decline to allow the citor to proceed further until he has made such an application.

24.104   On an application for the appointment of a guardian ad litem in such circumstances, see RSC Ord. 80, which may be modified to relate to the probate registry in which the citation proceedings are pending.

CHAPTER 25

Applications to district judge, registrar or High Court judge (Non-contentious business)

Summary

25.01   For many years after the establishment of the Court of Probate the standard procedure for obtaining orders or directions preliminary to the issue of grants of representation was by way of motion to the High Court judge in open court.

25.02   With the passage of time the law and practice became more precisely formulated and the powers of the district judges and registrars have been progressively and substantially enlarged.

25.03   The Non-Contentious Probate Rules of 1954 gave the registrars (now district judges) statutory power in most of the cases formerly dealt with by the High Court judges, save in the larger estates. The financial limits imposed by those rules were removed by the Non-Contentious Probate (Amendment) Rules 1967 which, with certain exceptions, extended to district probate registrars many of the powers formerly exercised only by the registrars (now district judges) of the Principal Registry. The Non-Contentious Probate (Amendment) Rules 1985 gave power to district probate registrars to deal with subpoenas to bring in testamentary documents, citations and summonses in relation to applications for grants made, and grants already issued, at the district probate registries, to the same extent as registrars (now district judges) of the Principal Registry. All those powers were retained in the Non-Contentious Probate Rules 1987[1]. The Non-Contentious Probate (Amendment) Rules 1991 further extended the powers of district probate registrars so that a registrar may tax a bill of costs where he made the order for taxation and, where application to discontinue a caveat kept in force because an appearance has been entered to a warning of it, is made by consent, he may make the order. District probate registrars must, however, refer matters about which they are in doubt to a district judge of the Principal Registry for directions[2]. District judges' and registrars' summonses must be issued out of the registry in which they are to be heard[3]. A district judge or registrar to whom any application is made under the Non-Contentious Probate Rules 1987 may order the transfer of the application to another district judge or registrar having jurisdiction[4].

1 See p. 923, post.
2 NCPR 7(1)(b).
3 NCPR 61(3).
4 NCPR 62.

25.04 Although most non-contentious probate applications are dealt with ex parte, the district judges of the Principal Registry and district probate registrars may, if they think fit, require that any application be made by summons to a district judge or registrar[1]. A district judge of the Principal Registry may also direct that an application be made to a High Court judge on summons in chambers or open court and may confirm a district probate registrar's reference to a High Court judge on summons in chambers or open court when a statement of the matter in question is sent to him under r. 7. It is only where the matter is unusually complicated or important, where there is opposition to the order or relief sought, or where it is necessary to give to other persons affected the opportunity to be heard, that one of these modes of procedure is likely to be directed.

1 NCPR 61(1).

25.05 There is a right of appeal by way of summons to a High Court judge from any order or direction of a district judge or registrar[1]: see paras. **25.243** ff., post.

1 NCPR 65(1).

25.06 The present chapter includes all the usual types of application to the district judge or registrar, whether ex parte or by summons, but the list is not necessarily exhaustive. In a number of instances the practice is dealt with in another part of this work, to which a reference is given.

Directions of the district judge or registrar

25.07 It often becomes necessary to obtain a decision or direction of a district judge or registrar in the course of an application for a grant of probate or administration; for example, as to: the applicant's title to a grant (e.g., whether he is executor according to the tenor of a will; whether a will contains any residuary gift[1]; or whether a bequest or devise is absolute or for life only, etc.); whether a will or codicil is conditional[2], or has been revoked; whether a document is entitled to proof as a privileged will; as to incorporation of other documents with a will, or the form in which a will containing alterations is to be proved; whether uncertainty exists as to survivorship between two or more persons; as to the identity of the applicant for a grant; whether the district judge or registrar would be prepared, in all the circumstances, to allow a grant of administration to be made to a single administrator, notwithstanding a minority or life interest arising; etc., etc. The district judge or registrar has power to refuse the issue of a grant until all enquiries which he may see fit to make are answered to his satisfaction[3].

1 See *Re White's Goods* (1882) 7 PD 65 and the cases there cited; *Re Bramley's Goods* [1902] P 106; *Re Lupton's Estate* [1905] P 321; *Re Wilde's Goods* (1887) 13 PD 1; *Re Pool's Goods* (1866) LR 1 P & D 206; *Re M'Auliffe's Goods* [1895] P 290; *Re Last* [1958] P 137, [1958] 1 All ER 316.
2 *Re Vines' Estate, Vines v Vines* [1910] P 147; *Re Hugo's Goods* (1877) 2 PD 73; *Re Mayd's Goods* (1880) 6 PD 17; see also *Re Spratt's Goods* [1897] P 28; *Re O'Connor's Estate* [1942] 1 All ER 546; *Re Hope Brown's Goods* [1942] P 136.
3 NCPR 6(1).

25.08   Such matters as the above are usually referred to the district judge or registrar in an informal way by the Probate Department of the Principal Registry, or Chief Clerk of the district registry, as the case may be. In applications proceeding at a district probate registry the district registrar may, in cases of doubt or difficulty, obtain the directions of a district judge of the Principal Registry[1].

1 NCPR 7; President's Direction (1953) 11 June.

25.09   In relation to matters proceeding at the Principal Registry, certain of the powers and discretions of the district judges have been delegated by the President of the Family Division to the Principal of the Probate Department, subject to reference if necessary to a district judge.

25.10   Where doubt exists, it is advisable for the practitioner to obtain a decision of the registrar or Principal prior to lodgment of the papers to lead the grant. At the Principal Registry, application for any such decision must be made in the first instance to the Probate Department.

Ex parte applications

25.11   The following types of application, which should in all cases be made ex parte at the registry at which the application for the grant is to be, or has been, made, or from which the grant has issued, are dealt with in other parts of this work, in the paragraphs indicated:

Refusal of probate of a will: paras. **3.129–3.134**.
Uncontested applications for omission of words from probate or for rectification or interpretation of a will: paras. **3.249–3.271**.
Application for joinder of a co-administrator having an inferior, or no, title: paras. **7.17–7.19**.
Preference of 'dead' interest to living interest, or of guardians of an infant to a person of full age: paras. **5.101**, **6.07–6.10** and **11.125–11.127**.
Grant where the deceased died domiciled out of England and Wales: paras. **12.127–12.136**.
Appointment of persons to obtain administration (with or without will) for use and benefit of minors: paras. **11.191–11.199**.
Appointment of grantees on behalf of incapable person: paras. **11.245–11.251**.
Direction for grant to person representing incapable person where a person equally entitled is sui juris: paras. **11.211–11.213**.
Amendment or revocation of grant: paras. **16.01–16.28** and **17.01–17.59**.

Application for appointment of additional personal representative after issue of grant: paras. **7.40–7.42**.
Application for leave to retract a renunciation: paras. **15.60–15.72**.

25.12   The following types of application are dealt with later in the present chapter:

Application for leave to swear to death: paras. **25.17–25.42**.
Application for admission of will as contained in a copy etc.: paras. **25.46–25.87**.
Application for a grant under s. 116(1) of the Supreme Court Act 1981: paras. **25.91–25.102**.
Application for grant to part only of an estate: paras. **25.165–25.172**.
Application for grant ad colligenda bona: paras. **25.173–25.181**.
Application for the issue of a subpoena to bring in a testamentary document: paras. **25.185** and **25.186**.

Application for grant after citation

25.13   Where a person has been cited to accept or refuse a grant but has not entered an appearance, or has appeared and wishes to take a grant, an ex parte application must be made to the district judge or registrar of the registry where the citation issued for the requisite order. For the practice on such applications, see paras. **24.78** and **24.82**, ante.

Application to district judge or registrar by summons

25.14   The cases in which application by summons to a district judge or registrar is required by the Non-Contentious Probate Rules are dealt with in paras. **25.193** ff., post.

25.15   A district judge or registrar may require that any application be made by summons to a district judge or registrar in chambers or to a High Court judge in chambers or open court[1].

1   NCPR 61(1).

Exercise of High Court judge's powers during Long Vacation

25.16   During the Long Vacation all powers exercisable under the Non-Contentious Probate Rules 1987 by a High Court judge in chambers may be exercised by a district judge of the Principal Registry (NCPR 64).

Leave to swear death

25.17   Where the applicant for a grant cannot swear in his oath to the death of the deceased, and there is no direct evidence of his being dead[1], but only evidence from which his death may be presumed to have taken place, application must be made for an order giving him leave to swear to the death[2]. Such a presumption may arise: (1) from the disappearance of the presumed deceased at or after a given time, and from the circumstances attending such disappearance, or from his not having been heard of for a prolonged period by those with whom he might reasonably have been expected to communicate[3]; or (2) from his having been on board a ship, which, from its non-arrival in port within a reasonable time, from the absence of tidings of any of those on board, and from other circumstances, is supposed to have been lost at sea; and similarly in the case of a missing or totally destroyed aeroplane.

1 But where death can be sworn to have occurred between two dates, and the fact is not in doubt, the grant can be made in the registry without order (*Re Long-Sutton's Estate* [1912] P 97). In this case the oath should state that the deceased 'was last seen alive [or last known to be alive] on the   day of   19   and that his dead body was found on the   day of   19   '.
2 It must be always remembered in these cases that the court does not presume the death of the deceased; it merely gives the applicant leave to swear the death (*Re Jackson's Goods* (1902) 87 LT 747).
3 The fact that the family or friends of a man whose habit was to communicate with them received no communication from or news of him for seven years leads to the presumption of his death at some time during the seven years, but not at the beginning or at the end of the seven years (*Re How's Goods* (1858) 1 Sw & Tr 53, 31 LT OS 26), provided that there is no assignable cause for the cessation of his communications. The mere fact, however, that he has not been heard of for seven years, where it was not his practice to communicate, does not lead to such an inference, but it may, coupled with other circumstances, induce the court to act on the presumption of his death.
   Where application was made for an order on the ground that a man had not been heard of for nearly seven years, there being also a Chancery suit, it was ordered that the letters of administration were not to be given out (*except for the purposes of the suit*) till the end of the seven years (*Re Winstone's Goods* [1898] P 143).

25.18   As to the certificates issued by the Registrar General of Shipping and Seamen in certain cases of the loss of a ship etc., see paras. **4.154–4.164**, ante.

25.19   Where a person has not been heard of for seven years or more, although there may in the circumstances be a presumption that he is dead, the onus of proof of death at any particular date is on the person to whose title the date is essential[1].

1 *Lal Chand Marwari v Mahant Ramrup Gir* (1925) 42 TLR 159, PC; see also fn. 3 to para. **25.17**, above.

25.20   The force of any presumption arising from the fact that a person has not been heard of for a period of seven years varies with the circumstances; for example, it is of very slight effect as regards persons 'behind the iron curtain'[1]. The question whether a person is or is not to be presumed to be dead is, generally speaking, one of fact[2].

1 *Re Liebeskind* [1952] CLY 1349.
2 *Chard v Chard (otherwise Northcote)* [1956] P 259, [1955] 3 All ER 721.

25.21   Where an order has been made giving leave to swear that death occurred on or since a certain date, the choice of the grantee is regulated by the law in force at the commencing date fixed by the order. But if, owing to a change in the law, important questions as to the right to the grant, or the devolution of the estate, depend on the date of death, it is open to the applicant to apply for an order under s. 116(1) of the Supreme Court Act 1981[1].

1 *Re Parnall's Estate* [1936] P 47.

Uncertainty as to survivorship

25.22   In cases where the death of a person is only presumptive a question of uncertainty as to survivorship may also arise; for example if a beneficiary named in his will, or a person who would inherit on his intestacy, has himself died but it is uncertain whether or not he survived the presumed deceased.

25.23   In such cases, in addition to obtaining an order giving leave to swear to his death it may be necessary to have regard to the law and practice in relation to com-morientes (see paras. **14.32–14.60**, ante). Where the entitlement to a grant is in doubt, it may be appropriate to apply for an order for the grant to be made in the exercise of the court's discretionary powers under s. 116(1) of the Supreme Court Act 1981[1].

1 *Re Harling's Goods* [1900] P 59; *Re Lever's Estate* (1935) 154 LT 270.

Mode of application

25.24   An order for leave to swear to the death may be made by a district judge of the Principal Registry or a district probate registrar[1]. The application should be made ex parte at the registry at which the application for the grant will be made. The application must be made by or on behalf of the person entitled to a grant, and must be supported by an affidavit setting out the grounds of the application and containing particulars of any policies of insurance effected on the life of the presumed deceased together with such further evidence as the district judge or registrar may require[2].

1 NCPR 2(1), 53.
2 NCPR 53.

25.25   Where application is made at the Principal Registry the affidavits and any supporting documents should be lodged in the Probate Department.

25.26   Where application is made to a district probate registrar he may, if he thinks it necessary, take the directions of a district judge of the Principal Registry[1].

1 NCPR 7.

25.27   A district judge or registrar may require any application to be made by summons to a district judge or registrar in chambers or to a High Court judge in chambers or open court[1].

1 NCPR 61(1).

25.28   Orders for leave to swear death are retained in the registry and never given out. The order may be inspected by the solicitor for the applicant and a note of its contents made to enable particulars to be included in the oath to lead the grant[1].

1 Registrar's Direction (1952) 25 January.

Presumed death of several persons in a disaster

25.29   A record is kept at the Principal Registry of disasters resulting in the death of two or more persons in circumstances making it necessary to obtain an order for leave to swear death. The record will give an indication of the type of evidence which should be asked for or expected in the light of any previous application arising out of the same disaster.

25.30   Where it is necessary to obtain an order for leave to swear death following a disaster, an enquiry whether there has been any previous order may be addressed to the Secretary of the Principal Registry[1].

1 Registrar's Circular, 12 June 1967.

Where a person has disappeared

25.31 Where the evidence of the death of the alleged deceased is presumptive in consequence of his sudden disappearance, or of his not having been heard of for several years, the applicant's affidavit should be corroborated on some material points by a member of the family, and, if possible, by a friend of the deceased or of his family, who is not interested in the estate.

25.32 The affidavit of the applicant should state:

(a) When the deceased was last heard of; and his age.

(b) The belief of the applicant that the deceased is now dead[1].

(c) Whether any advertisements for the deceased have been inserted—if so, with what success; if inserted, the newspapers should be filed.

(d) Whether any letters have been received from the deceased (if any exist, they should also be produced)[2].

(e) Whether the life of the deceased was insured—if so, giving particulars of all policies, including the name of, and whether notice of the application has been given to, the insurance company[3], and either producing the reply from the office, or filing an affidavit of service of the notice[4].

(f) Whether the deceased died testate or intestate—in the former case identifying the will (which must be lodged)—and stating who are the persons, if any, entitled to share in his estate in the event of an intestacy.

(g) The value and particulars of the estate of the deceased; and whether his bank accounts, if any, have been operated since his disappearance.

1 This must be averred: see in *Re Hurlston's Goods* [1898] P 27.
2 *Re Clarke's Goods* [1896] P 287.
3 *Re Barber's Goods* (1886) 11 PD 78; see NCPR 53.
4 *Re Saul's Goods* [1896] P 151.

Previous order of another court

25.33 A previous order to the same effect, made by an inferior court of competent jurisdiction, supported by a general affidavit of the facts, is sufficient[1].

1 *Re Rishton's Goods* (1921) 125 LT 863.

Decree under Matrimonial Causes Act

25.34 A decree of presumption of death and dissolution of marriage made by virtue of s. 19 of the Matrimonial Causes Act 1973[1] does not obviate the necessity of applying for an order for leave to swear to the death of the missing former spouse.

1 27 Halsbury's Statutes (4th edn) 720.

Uncertain date in foreign cases

25.35 A grant made in a foreign court of competent jurisdiction in which the date of death is presumed, or leave has been given to swear to death between certain dates, is accepted as being corroborative, but not conclusive, evidence of death[1].

1 *Re Spenceley's Goods* [1892] P 255.

Declaration by court of domicile

25.36   A declaration presuming death made by the court of domicile followed by an order vesting the estate of the presumed deceased is acceptable as sufficient proof of death without requiring death to be proved by independent evidence[1]. An order is nevertheless required to be made giving leave to swear to death on or since the appropriate date, and the district judge or registrar has a discretion to refer such cases to a High Court judge; for circumstances might exist causing doubts as to the trustworthiness of the evidence[2].

1 *Re Schulhof's Goods, Re Wolf's Goods* [1948] P 66, [1947] 2 All ER 841.
2 *Re Dowds' Goods* [1948] P 256.

25.37   Where, however, the court of the domicile of the deceased has made a declaration presuming death but this is not followed by a vesting order, the court will not presume the death without further evidence leading to the presumption[1].

1 *Re Schulhof's Goods, Re Wolf's Goods*, above.

25.38   Where the court of domicile of a person thought to be dead has made a declaration that he died on a particular day (as opposed to a declaration of pre-sumed death on that day), and on this basis a death certificate has been issued by the competent Registrar of Deaths, the death certificate, if shown by an affidavit of law to be conclusive under the law of the domicile, is acceptable as sufficient evid-ence of the fact and date of death. In such a case no order for leave to swear to the death is required[1].

1 *Re Schlesinger's Goods* [1950] CLY 1549; distinguishing *Re Schulhof's Goods, Re Wolf's Goods*, above.

Supposed loss of life at sea, or in a missing aircraft

25.39   Where the death of the deceased is presumptive in consequence of the dis-appearance at sea of the vessel in which he was sailing, the mode of application is as set out at paras. **25.24–25.27**, ante.

25.40   In this case, affidavit evidence of the following facts will be required:

(a)   That the deceased was on board when the vessel sailed from her last port.
(b)   The date and place when and where the vessel was last seen.
(c)   Her non-arrival, within reasonable time, at the port for which she was bound.
(d)   Absence of word from those aboard the vessel from the date when she was last seen.
(e)   Whether the ship and cargo were insured or uninsured, and, if insured, whether the underwriters have paid on the policies as for a total loss. Particulars of all insurance policies on the life of the deceased must also be given[1]. Any certificate granted under the provisions of the Merchant Shipping Acts should be produced[2] (see also paras. **4.154–4.162**, ante).

1 NCPR 53.
2 *Re Dodd's Goods* (1897) 77 LT 137.

25.41   The application should be supported by an affidavit of the owner, managing owner, or agent, of the ship, deposing to all the material facts bearing on the case within his knowledge, as well as by that of the applicant, and by other affidavits, when the circumstances of the case require it.

25.42 Similar evidence is required if the application is in respect of an aircraft which is missing or a total loss.

Oath

25.43 For form of oath to lead to the grant following the order, see No. 117.

Fees

25.44 No fees are payable in respect of an order for leave to swear death.

Person found to be living after order giving leave to swear death

25.45 In such a case, application must be made for the rescission of the order and for revocation of the grant (see para. **17.11**(j), ante).

Original will not available

25.46 When an original will or codicil has been lost, or destroyed without the intention of revoking it, application must be made for an order for leave to prove the will or codicil as contained in a copy, reconstruction or other evidence of its contents (NCPR 54).

25.47 For reported cases, see para. **32.43**, post.

Mode of application

25.48 An application for an order admitting to proof a will as contained in a copy, a completed draft, a reconstruction or other evidence of its contents should be made ex parte at the registry at which the subsequent application for the grant will be made[1].

1 NCPR 2(1), 54(1).

25.49 The application must be supported by an affidavit setting out the grounds of the application, and by such evidence as can be adduced as to:

(a) its existence after the death of the testator or, where there is no such evidence, the facts on which the applicant relies to rebut the presumption that the will has been revoked by destruction;
(b) in respect of a nuncupative will, the contents of that will; and
(c) in respect of a reconstruction of a will, the accuracy of that reconstruction.

25.50 The district judge or registrar may also require additional evidence in the circumstances of a particular case as to due execution of the will or as to the accuracy of the copy will, and may direct that notice be given to persons who would be prejudiced by the application (NCPR 54(4)). If any consents in writing to the application given by any persons not under disability who would be prejudiced by the grant are readily available, they should be lodged with the application.

25.51 A district probate registrar may, if he considers it necessary, obtain the directions of a district judge of the Principal Registry on any such application[1]. A district judge or registrar may require any application to be made by summons to a district judge or registrar in chambers, or to a High Court judge in chambers or open court[2]. For the practice as to summonses, see paras. **25.193** ff., post.

1 NCPR 7.
2 NCPR 61(1).

25.52   In cases when there is any opposition, the practice is to require the will, as contained in the draft, copy or reconstruction, to be propounded in a probate action. Where the consents of the parties affected, if called for, are not given, or where these cannot be given owing to some of the persons interested not being sui juris, but there is no active opposition, it is in the discretion of the district judge or registrar to deal with the matter or to direct a reference on summons to a district judge or registrar in chambers or to a High Court judge in chambers or open court[1].

1 See *Re Apted's Goods* [1899] P 272; as qualifying *Re Pearson's Goods* [1896] P 289; *Re Penson's Estate* (1960) Times, 30 September and NCPR 61(1).

25.53   Application to the district judge or registrar for such an order is made by lodging the affidavits in the Probate Department at the Principal Registry, or at the district probate registry.

25.54   Where a copy or draft of the will is available, the affidavit should show:

(a)   If it is the case, that the original will was in existence at the death of the testator, that it was afterwards lost, and in what circumstances (if known), and what efforts have been made to find it, exhibiting advertisements (if any) and stating whether they have produced any reply. If the original will was not found or available at the death of the testator, the full circumstances in which it was last known to be in existence and the facts on which the applicant relies to rebut the presumption that the will has been revoked by destruction.

(b)   That the copy will was examined with the original and found to be complete and correct.

(c)   If it is a draft, that the original will was prepared from that draft; and if, after execution, the draft was compared with and completed from the original, that fact should be stated.

(d)   Who are the persons prejudiced by the admission of the document sought to be established—their consents being filed, if readily obtainable—and whether they are all sui juris. The persons prejudiced will usually be those who would take a greater interest in the estate under an intestacy than under the will in question. If there is any earlier will this should be stated in the affidavit and, in addition to the consents of the persons who would take a greater interest under an intestacy, the district judge or registrar may require to know the attitude of the persons who would benefit under the earlier will, particularly if there is any doubt as to due execution of the later document or as to whether it contains a revocation clause.

25.55   The district judge or registrar may require additional evidence in the circumstances of a particular case as to due execution of the will or as to the accuracy of the copy will. This is most likely when the document evidencing the contents of the will is not a photocopy, or some other type of facsimile copy, made from the executed original will. If evidence of due execution is called for it should be by affidavit by, whenever possible, one of the attesting witnesses.

25.56 If no copy or draft of the will is available, in addition to items (a) and (d) in para. **25.54**, ante, the affidavit should depose to the contents of the will as set out in a reconstruction, which should be in the form of a separate document exhibited to the affidavit.

Presumption of revocation

25.57 Where a will is known to have been in the possession of the testator and there is no evidence of its having subsequently left his custody but it cannot be found on his death, there is a prima facie presumption that he destroyed it animo revocandi (see para. **33.70**(b), post).

25.58 This presumption may be displaced by evidence (e.g., of declarations of the testator's unchanged intentions, or evidence as to his state of mind etc.) and when it is sought to obtain an order admitting to proof a copy or other evidence of the contents of a will in the above circumstances, affidavit evidence of the facts relied on as rebutting the presumption of destruction animo revocandi should be lodged.

Copy or draft to be lodged

25.59 In all cases where it is sought to prove a will as contained in a copy or draft, the latter should be exhibited to the appropriate affidavits and lodged with the papers to lead the order[1]. It is the actual copy or draft, nearest to the original will, relied on which should be exhibited to the affidavits and not a copy of that copy or draft. A plethora of unnecessary copies is to be avoided.

1 *Re Riley's Goods* [1896] P 9.

25.60 The district judges or registrars do not normally deal with cases where the will was lost or destroyed during the testator's lifetime, nor where there is no examined copy or draft of the missing document, unless the persons prejudiced by the order sought are sui juris and consent: such cases are otherwise usually referred by the district judge or registrar to a High Court judge under NCPR 61.

25.61 Where no copy was made, nor draft preserved, of a will or codicil which has been lost or destroyed, probate may be obtained of its contents, or of its substance and effect, if they can be established by parol evidence[1].

1 As to proving the contents of a lost document generally, see *Brown v Brown* (1858) 8 E & B 876. See also *Sugden v Lord St Leonards* (1876) 1 PD 154 which established that the contents of a lost will may be proved by the evidence of a single witness, though interested. See also paras. **32.40–32.44**, post.

25.62 Where parts of a will were missing, on evidence that at the death of the testator the will was whole and unrevoked, an examined copy of the will was admitted to probate by order of the registrar, the grant being limited until the missing part should be brought into the registry. The parts of the will existing were exhibited to an affidavit as to finding, and were filed. The consents of the parties prejudiced were also filed[1].

1 *Re Pellat* (1938) August. As to the form of the limitation now included in the grant in such cases, see para. **25.87**, post.

25.63   As to proof of wills damaged by enemy action etc., see paras. **11.19–11.30**, ante.

Order of court of domicile

25.64   Where a testator died domiciled out of England and Wales and the court of the domicile had granted probate of his will as contained in a copy, limited until the original will or a more authentic copy should be brought into that court, a grant in this country was made without an order of the court, limited until the original will or a more authentic copy thereof be brought into and proved in the court of the domicile[1]. In view of the wording of NCPR 54 it would appear that an order is now required in such circumstances. It is suggested that verified copies of the affidavits used to support the application to the court of domicile together with confirmation that the original will has not been found should be lodged with the district judge or registrar and his directions sought.

1 *Re Sansbury* (14 June 1949, unreported).

Cases in which copies have been admitted

25.65   After a testator's death a will was in the possession of his solicitors, whose offices were destroyed, no trace of the will being found. A copy of the will, sworn by the solicitor to be a correct copy, was exhibited to his affidavit. An order was made for admission of the will as contained in the copy exhibited[1].

1 *Re Lintott's Estate* (1941) 191 LT Jo 115.

25.66   Where the will was probably destroyed with other papers sent away for salvage, it was admitted as contained in a completed copy[1].

1 *Re Metcalfe* (1943) 196 LT Jo 12.

Destruction by residuary legatee

25.67   A testatrix made her will giving everything to a sister. After the death of the testatrix differences arose between her sisters, and the residuary legatee destroyed the will. The will was pronounced for as contained in a reconstructed copy[1].

1 *Wildmore v Wildmore* (1938) 185 LT Jo 297.

Evidence of substance or contents

25.68   In all these cases, as well as the substance or contents of the will being proved, the district judge or registrar must be satisfied as to due execution of the will[1] and, where appropriate, may require an affidavit as to due execution (see para. **25.55**, ante).

1 *Re Gardner's Goods* (1858) 1 Sw & Tr 109.

25.69   When the contents of a lost will are not completely proved, probate of the contents of the missing will so far as they can be ascertained will be granted[1].

1 *Sugden v Lord St Leonards* (1876) 1 PD 154.

25.70   Evidence of a declaration by the testator as to the contents of a will which is not forthcoming is admissible[1].

1 *Sugden v Lord St Leonards* (1876) 1 PD 154.

Reconstruction required, where no copy or draft available

25.71   Formerly, the court accepted an affidavit of scripts (filed in the action), or a deposition, or an extract from a deposition of a witness, if these documents contained the contents or substance or effect of the lost will or codicil. In *Lord St Leonards'* case[1], the court admitted the will as contained in the declaration which pleaded the contents; but the court now requires the drawing up of a reconstruction representing, as nearly as possible, the will in its original form. This is exhibited to an affidavit verifying it, and is ultimately marked by the applicant and photographed to provide the probate copy to be annexed to the grant.

1 Ibid.

Probate of will limited until a lost codicil be found

25.72   If a codicil has been lost since the testator's death, without a copy having been made, or the draft kept, and its contents or substance cannot be established, the court will grant probate of the will, limited until the original codicil, or an authentic copy thereof, shall be proved.

Probate of a codicil limited until a lost will be found

25.73   Similarly, if the will has been lost since the death of the testator and it is impracticable to prove its contents or substance, the court will grant probate of a codicil to that will containing dispositions independent of and referring to it, limited until the lost will be proved[1].

1 *Re Greig's Goods* (1866) LR 1 P & D 72.

Probate of a copy where the original is in existence

25.74   Where the original will or codicil, or both, are in the possession of a person residing abroad, who has refused or neglected to deliver them up, but a copy has been transmitted to the executor, probate of such copy will be granted to him on his showing, by affidavit, the manner in which it was transmitted, that a better or more authentic copy does not exist in this country, and that it is essential for the interests of the estate that probate be granted forthwith, without awaiting the arrival of the original, or a better or more authentic copy. The grant is limited until the original will, or a more authentic copy thereof, be proved[1].

1 See *Re Lemme's Goods* [1892] P 89; *Re Von Linden's Goods* [1896] P 148; *Re Robinson's Estate* (1941) 191 LT Jo 267.

25.75   If the copy has been transmitted to a person other than the executor, he will be required to give affidavit evidence in addition to that sworn by the executor.

25.76   This affidavit evidence does not speak as to the execution of the will or codicil, as in the case of lost or destroyed instruments of that nature, provided that the document is, on the face of it, duly executed.

25.77   For the form of oath, see No. 73 mutatis mutandis.

25.78   This practice does not apply in cases where the original will is in the official custody of a foreign court or official: for the procedure in this case see para. **12.73**, ante.

Administration (with will) limited

25.79   When the grants before described are made to a residuary legatee, or any person other than the executor, they take the form of letters of administration (with the will annexed), limited in a similar manner.

Contents of will not known

25.80   A person who applies for letters of administration is required to swear that the deceased died intestate. It sometimes happens, though no will is forthcoming on the death of the deceased, that the applicant is unable to depose to an intestacy, for he may know, or have reason to believe, from the deceased's observations, or the statements of others, that there was a will in existence subsequently to the deceased's death.

25.81   If no copy of the will can be produced, and its contents or tenor cannot be substantiated, application may be made for an order for a grant of administration, limited until the original will or a copy be proved[1].

1 *Re Wright's Goods* [1893] P 21.

25.82   Where a foreign court refused to give up the original will or to give a copy of its contents, administration limited to particular property was granted[1].

1 *Re Dost Aly Khan's Goods* (1880) 6 PD 6.

25.83   A testator made his will in the Netherlands where he was domiciled, and left it there with a notary. The will could not be obtained and the contents were not known. The widow was, by the law of domicile, entitled to one-half of the estate, either under a testacy or an intestacy, and to administer on behalf of the son of deceased. Administration was granted to the widow and another person, limited until the original will or an authentic copy be brought into the registry[1].

1 *Re Goudstikker* (1940) July (motion).

25.84   Where a deceased was believed to have left a will but all efforts to obtain it or a copy of it from Romania had failed, administration, with will as contained in a copy of an acte de partage, was granted[1]. In another case where a deceased died in 1944 domiciled in Germany no trace of a will could be found, but the form of the certificate of inheritance issued by the court of domicile indicated that he died testate. The English court granted administration with will (as evidenced by the certificate of inheritance), limited until the original or an authentic copy of the will be brought into the registry[2].

1 *Re Queen Marie of Roumania* [1950] WN 457.
2 *Re Von Wrochem's Estate* (1964) 108 Sol Jo 240.

25.85   A will was alleged to have been destroyed by enemy action, no copy or draft being in existence. A grant of letters of administration, limited until the alleged original will referred to in the applicant's affidavit, or an authentic copy, be brought in, was made to two persons entitled to share in the estate[1].

1 *Boyd* (1942) May (motion).

25.86   Where the court is entirely satisfied that a will has been destroyed, that there is no copy in existence, and that no one has knowledge of its contents, it will allow application to be made for a grant 'as in an intestacy'—imposing no limitations. Application on summons to a High Court judge in open court may be required in such a case. For the practice as to summonses, see paras. **25.223** ff., post.

Order

25.87   If the district judge or registrar grants the application, the order for proof of the will or codicil as contained in the copy, draft or reconstruction thereof will normally direct that the grant be limited until the original will or a more authentic copy thereof be proved, or in some appropriate variation of this wording.

25.88   For practice in obtaining a grant following such an order, see paras. **11.16** and **11.17**, ante.

25.89   Forms of oath, Nos. 72 and 73.

Fees

25.90   No fees are payable in respect of the district judge's or registrar's order.

Grants under s. 116 of the Supreme Court Act 1981[1]

25.91   **Note**. Section 116 of the Act of 1981 replaces, with amendments, s. 162(1) and proviso (b) of the Supreme Court of Judicature (Consolidation) Act 1925 and s. 73 of the Court of Probate Act 1857, with effect from 1 January 1982: the following case law relates to applications made under the earlier statutory provisions, but it is considered that the examples cited also illustrate the 'special circumstances' in respect of which the court may consider it 'necessary or expedient' to exercise its discretionary powers under s. 116 of the Supreme Court Act 1981.

1 See p. 845, post.

25.92   Under s. 116 the court has a discretion, in any special circumstances, to pass over the prior right of the persons first entitled to a grant and to appoint as administrator, or administrator (with will), such other person or persons as it thinks necessary or expedient. The grant may be limited in any way the court thinks fit.

25.93   Section 116 applies as from 1 January 1982[1], irrespective of the date of death of the deceased.

1 Being the date upon which the substantive provisions (including s. 116) of the Supreme Court Act 1981 came into force.

Minority or life interest

25.94 It is considered that the use of the word 'administrator' in the singular does not override the requirement of s. 114(2) of the Supreme Court Act 1981, so that whenever a minority or a life interest arises in an estate the grant must normally be made to not less than two individuals or to a trust corporation with or without an individual[1]. If such an interest arises, application should accordingly be made for the appointment of two or more individuals, or of a trust corporation, with or without an individual, as administrators, unless it is sought to obtain the authority of the court to appoint a sole administrator as being expedient in all the circumstances.

1 *Re White* [1928] P 75, CA; *Re Hall* [1950] P 156, [1950] 1 All ER 718.

Discretion of the court

25.95 Under s. 116 of the Act of 1981 the discretion of the court is practically unlimited[1] and each case is dealt with on its merits; the principles governing the exercise of the court's discretionary powers are to be found in the earlier case of *Teague and Ashdown v Wharton, Re Jeffries' Goods*[2].

1 But see *Re White* [1928] P 75 at 83, per Scrutton LJ, where it is suggested that if no person is entitled to a full grant (e.g. no beneficiary being sui juris) the grant must be limited.
2 (1871) LR 2 P & D 360.

25.96 The court has the power to pass over an executor, even if he has intermeddled in the estate[1].

1 *Re Biggs' Estate* [1966] P 118, [1966] 1 All ER 358.

25.97 But an allegation that the sole beneficiary under a will, a girl aged twenty-one, was immaturely developed and, therefore, unfitted for the time being for the administration and enjoyment of the large fortune to which she had become entitled, has been held not to justify the exercise by the court of its discretionary powers to interfere with the beneficiary's enjoyment of an estate to which she was by law entitled, by making a temporary grant to a trust corporation[1].

1 *Re Edwards-Taylor's Goods* [1951] P 24, [1950] 2 All ER 446.

Mode of application

25.98 An order for a grant under s. 116 of the Supreme Court Act 1981 may be made by a district judge of the Principal Registry or a registrar of a district probate registry, irrespective of the value of the estate. The application must be supported by an affidavit setting out the grounds of the application[1]. The affidavit should, save in exceptional circumstances, be made by the applicant, or at least one of the joint applicants, for the grant.

1 NCPR 52.

25.99 Exceptionally, where a local authority applies as a trust corporation (by virtue of the provisions of the Public Trustee (Custodian Trustee) Rules 1975, as amended: see paras. **9.05–9.08**, ante) on behalf of a person who by reason of age, infirmity or other circumstances is in need of care and attention and occupies residential accommodation provided under s. 21(1)(a) of the National Assistance Act

1948 by that authority, a separate affidavit in support of the application for a district judge's or registrar's order under s. 116 of the Act of 1981 may be dispensed with, provided that the facts are recited fully in the oath and the written consent of the person in care is lodged[1].

1 Registrar's Direction (1976) 30 June. It should be noted that application for an order under s. 116 in these circumstances is an alternative procedure to an application being made under NCPR 31 (see p. 931, post) for a grant to an attorney on behalf of the person in care or made under r. 35 (see p. 932, post) for a grant based on the incapacity of such a person.

25.100 The application should be made ex parte at the registry at which the application for the grant is proposed to be made[1], by lodging the affidavit and other supporting documents. At the Principal Registry the documents should be lodged in the Probate Department.

1 NCPR 2(1).

25.101 A district probate registrar may, if he considers it necessary, obtain the directions of a district judge of the Principal Registry on any such application[1].

1 NCPR 7.

25.102 The district judge or registrar may require any application under s. 116 to be made by summons to a district judge or registrar in chambers or to a High Court judge in chambers or open court[1].

1 NCPR 61(1).

Order

25.103 The order will state that it is made under s. 116. An order for a grant to a creditor of the deceased will describe him as such.

25.104 Details of the order must be included in the oath to lead the grant. The order, affidavit and any other documents in support must be lodged with the papers to lead the grant.

Fees

25.105 No fees are payable in respect of the district judge's or registrar's order.

Oath

25.106 For forms of oath, see Nos. 140 and 163.

Examples of cases in which orders made

25.107 The following paragraphs indicate the class of case in which orders for grants are, or have been, made under the court's discretionary powers:.

(a) Grants to mere nominees and persons having no interest in the estate
25.108 Where the only persons entitled were old and infirm, to their nominee (*Re Roberts' Goods* (1858) 1 Sw & Tr 64; *Re Davis' Estate* [1906] P 330).

25.109   To a local authority applying as a trust corporation (by virtue of the provisions of the Public Trustee (Custodian Trustee) Rules 1975, as amended: see paras. **9.05–9.08**, ante) on behalf of a person who by reason of age, infirmity or other circumstances is in need of care and attention and who occupies residential accommodation provided under s. 21(1)(a) of the National Assistance Act 1948 by that authority[1].

1   Registrar's Direction (1976) 30 June.

25.110   Where all the parties interested agreed, to a stranger with no interest (*Re Hopkins' Goods* (1875) LR 3 P & D 235; *Re Potter's Goods, Potter v Potter* [1899] P 265)[1].

1   Cases of refusal: *Re Richardson's Goods* (1871) LR 2 P & D 244; *Teague and Ashdown v Wharton, Re Jeffries' Goods* (1871) LR 2 P& D 360; *Re Hale's Goods* (1874) LR 3 P & D 207; *Re Prosser's Goods* (1876) IR 11 Eq 37; *Re Brotherton's Goods* [1901] P 139.

25.111   To a party alleging a claim (i.e. having no ascertained interest) as creditor against the estate of the deceased, where the person entitled to represent the estate refused to take the grant after citation (*Re Wensley's Goods* (1882) 7 PD 13).

25.112   Where there were special circumstances making it necessary or expedient to do so, to agreed grantees with a limitation allowing the executors named in the will to apply subsequently for probate (*Re Mathew* [1984] 2 All ER 396, [1984] 1 WLR 1011).

25.113   Where the deceased was a solicitor who was at the time of his death in practice either in his own name or as a sole solicitor under a firm name, the interests of his clients may be jeopardised if the person entitled to a grant to his estate fails to obtain a grant within a reasonable time after his death. In such a case, the court has power in the exercise of its discretion to make an order for a grant in favour of a nominee or nominees of the Law Society: the grant may be general or limited as may be expedient in the circumstances. An affidavit setting out the grounds of the application should first be submitted in draft to the Senior District Judge of the Principal Registry (through the Principal of the Probate Department), who will direct whether the application may be made ex parte to a district judge or registrar without notice to any other person, or on summons to a district judge or registrar or a High Court judge, and on whom such summons should be served. The draft affidavit should therefore show who are the persons first entitled to a general grant so far as their identity has been discovered in the time available, and should deal with the practicability of serving them with the summons[1].

1   President's Direction (1965) 15 March; Secretary's Circular, 12 June 1967. In any case in which it is thought that exercise of this power would be desirable, solicitors should communicate with the Secretary of the Law Society (Professional Purposes) (per *Law Society's Gazette*, June 1965).

(b) Grants without notice to, or citation of, parties having a claim to the grant
25.114   To one of the next of kin, without citation of the heir-at-law, who was abroad and whose address was unknown, notwithstanding s. 2(4) of the Land Transfer Act 1897 (*Re Blenkinsop's Goods* (1901) 49 WR 336).

25.115 To a creditor[1], when the sole executrix and universal legatee was a person of unsound mind (*Re Atherton's Goods* [1892] P 104).

1 It should be noted that where an order is made for a grant to a creditor the latter should be so described in the order (Direction (1935) 7 June).

25.116 To a creditor[1] without citation of the next of kin, where the latter had received notice of the application and the estate was small (*Re Teece's Goods* [1896] P 6; *Re Heerman's Estate* [1910] P 357 (advertisements for next of kin); *Re Bishop's Estate* (1913) 108 LT 928 (notice to widow)).

1 It should be noted that where an order is made for a grant to a creditor the latter should be so described in the order (Direction (1935) 7 June).

25.117 To creditors[1], in the special circumstances of the case, passing over the executor without renunciation or citation, where the estate was insolvent (*Re Leguia's Estate* [1934] P 80. This grant was subsequently revoked on the application of the executor (*Re Leguia's Estate (No 2)* (1936) 155 LT 270).)

1 It should be noted that where an order is made for a grant to a creditor the latter should be so described in the order (Direction (1935) 7 June).

25.118 To one of the only two persons entitled to the estate under the will with the consent of the other, without citing a sole executor who had fled the country (*Re Williams* [1918] P 122).

25.119 The court has power under the section to pass over an executor, even if he has intermeddled in the estate[1]; but only in the most exceptional circumstances will it pass over without citation an executor who is available and is willing to take a grant[2]. It is often desirable that an executor should be cited even if he is missing, but where such an executor has no beneficial interest in the estate it may be possible to avoid the expense and delay of a citation (which would involve service by advertisement) by applying for an order under s. 116 for a grant to be made without citing him.

1 *Re Biggs' Estate* [1966] P 118, [1966] 1 All ER 358; see also paras. **24.31** and **24.32**, ante.
2 See *Re Leguia's Estate* (1936) 155 LT 270; *Re Clore* [1982] Ch 456, [1982] 3 All ER 419, CA; approving [1982] Fam 113 (grant ad colligenda bona to the Official Solicitor passing over the executors to the deceased's English will: see also paras. **25.173** ff., post as to grants ad colligenda bona).

25.120 To a stranger without citing the next of kin, on the consent of some of the beneficiaries (*Re Moffatt's Goods* [1900] P 152).

25.121 Where it is sought to pass over persons entitled who cannot be traced, in favour of a lower title, and a citation served by advertisement would normally be required, a district judge or registrar may, in special circumstances, make an order under s. 116 after requiring the publication of a suitable advertisement, where appropriate, for the person who would normally be cited.

25.122 For practice in cases where the missing person would, if alive, be beneficially entitled to the whole estate, and the applicant has no title which would enable him to extract a citation, see para. **14.05**, ante.

25.123 To the nominee of assignees of residuary legatees (*Re Campion's Goods* [1900] P 13).

25.124 To a person having an inferior right, where the person primarily entitled was shown to have been of bad character and had not been heard of for some time (*Re Stevens' Goods* [1898] P 126; *Re Frost's Estate* [1905] P 140).

25.125 Where the administrator of an intestate had disappeared and the remaining next of kin refused to renounce or apply, the original grant was revoked and a new one issued at the instance of a creditor (*Re French's Estate* [1910] P 169)[1].

1 See also *Re Loveday's Goods* [1900] P 154 (where widow had disappeared), and *Re Colclough's Goods* [1902] 2 IR 499.

25.126 To a specific legatee, where, after payment of debts and legacies, there remained no residue, without citing the residuary legatee, resident overseas, who had taken no notice of letters sent to him suggesting his renunciation in the circumstances (*Re Wilde's Goods* (1887) 13 PD 1).

(c) Direct grants, 'quasi per saltum' (i.e. in spite of the possible existence of a person with a prior right)
25.127 Where a person had not been heard of for seven years, and his sole next of kin died within the seven years, administration of his estate was granted direct to the person who was next of kin at the end of the seven years (*Re Peck's Goods* (1860) 2 Sw & Tr 506; *Re Harling's Goods* [1900] P 59).

25.128 To a grandson of deceased, the son who was sole next of kin having disappeared for over 25 years. The applicant was allowed to say in his oath 'he believed that he was sole next-of-kin' (*Re Callicott's Goods* [1899] P 189; following *Re Reed's Goods* (1874) 29 LT 932. See also *Re Moore's Goods* [1891] P 299; *Re Shoosmith's Goods* [1894] P 23; *Re Pridham's Goods* (1889) 61 LT 302; *Re Harper's Goods* [1899] P 59; *Re Chapman's Goods* [1903] P 192; *Re Byrne's Goods* (1901) 84 LT 570; *Re Jackson's Goods* (1902) 87 LT 747).

(d) Grants in cases of urgency
25.129 To the person authorised by a power of attorney to manage the property of a party who was abroad and was interested in the deceased's estate, and where it was not known when she would return (*Re Escot's Goods* (1858) 4 Sw & Tr 186).

25.130 To the father-in-law of the person entitled, who was in Australia, for the use and benefit of the latter (*Re Jones' Goods* (1858) 1 Sw & Tr 13. See also *Re Cholwill's Goods* (1866) LR 1 P & D 192).

25.131 See also 'Grant ad colligenda bona', paras. **25.173** ff., post, for an alternative procedure.

(e) Grants in pursuance of agreement
25.132 Where there were two claimants to the estate as next of kin, and the kinship of one was doubtful, and the parties agreed to divide the estate, and that the one whose kinship was doubtful should take the grant. Administration decreed to the latter (*Re Minshull's Goods* (1889) 14 PD 151).

(f) Where person entitled is unfit

25.133 Where a sole executor was in prison and refused to renounce, the court passed him over and issued the grant to a residuary legatee (*Re Drawmer's Estate* (1913) 108 LT 732).

25.134 Where the widow had unsuccessfully propounded a will found to be a forgery, she was passed over in favour of her daughter (*Re Paine's Estate* (1916) 115 LT 935).

25.135 Where a woman had been murdered by her husband, letters of administration of her estate were granted under this section (on the ground of public policy) to her next of kin, passing over the husband's personal representative (*Re Crippen's Estate* [1911] P 108). In *Re Hall's Estate, Hall v Knight and Baxter* [1914] P 1, this rule was held to apply in cases of manslaughter. But a murderer found to be insane at the time of the murder retains his rights (*Re Pitts, Cox v Kilsby* [1931] 1 Ch 546, 145 LT 116; *Re Houghton, Houghton v Houghton* [1915] 2 Ch 173); *Re Batten's Will Trusts* (1961) 105 Sol Jo 529: there is no distinction on this point between cases of intestacy and testacy. (The findings of a coroner's jury at an inquest are not admissible as evidence in the High Court (*Re Sigsworth, Bedford v Bedford* [1935] Ch 89, 152 LT 329; *Re Rendell* (1937) (motion); *Bird v Keep* [1918] 2 KB 692). Under s. 11 of the Civil Evidence Act 1968, proof of the conviction of a person for an offence by any court in the United Kingdom or by a court martial is sufficient proof, in any civil proceedings where it is relevant, that he committed such offence, unless the contrary is proved. Properly authenticated copies of certificates of conviction are admissible in evidence.) Where a man killed his wife and then killed himself, and there was no evidence as to his state of mind at the moment when he killed her, no claim on her estate by the husband's representatives was allowed (*Re Pollock, Pollock v Pollock* [1941] Ch 219, [1941] 1 All ER 360). The presumption (rebuttable by admissible evidence of the fact and of the state of mind of the killer) is that the killer was of sound mind (*R v Huntbach, ex p Lockley* [1944] KB 606, [1944] 2 All ER 453). The burden is on his representative to prove there was no felonious intent (*Hollington v F Hewthorn & Co Ltd* [1943] KB 587, [1943] 2 All ER 35).

25.136 The standard of proof that one person feloniously killed another, where both died from gas poisoning, is not that of the criminal law: if the evidence leads to no other conclusion, this is sufficient to disqualify such person, and those taking through him or her, from benefiting under the victim's will (*Re Dellow's Will Trusts, Lloyds Bank Ltd v Institute of Cancer Research* [1964] 1 All ER 771, [1964] 1 WLR 451).

25.137 A wife was convicted of the manslaughter of her husband and sentenced to life imprisonment. She was the sole executrix and beneficiary under his will. It was held in the Probate Division that the destination of the husband's estate was a matter for decision by the Chancery Division, but as the wife was serving a life sentence it was impossible for her to act as executrix. Administration (with will) was granted to the daughters of the deceased (*Re S's Estate* [1968] P 302, [1967] 2 All ER 150).

25.138 A widow convicted of the manslaughter of her husband through diminished responsibility under the Homicide Act 1957 is not entitled to take any benefit from his estate. The principle that the courts will not recognise a benefit accruing to a criminal from his crime does not require that the crime be one deserving of punishment or carrying a degree of moral culpability (*Re Giles, Giles v Giles* [1972] Ch 544, [1971] 3 All ER 1141).

25.139 In the case of *Re Forster* (1963) unreported, a grant issued to the Treasury Solicitor made on the basis that the son of deceased (the residuary legatee under her will) was disqualified from benefiting by reason of his offence under s. 2 of the Suicide Act 1961.

25.140 A murderer's forfeited share in an estate does not pass to the Crown as bona vacantia but to the remaining members of the class beneficially entitled (*Re Callaway, Callaway v Treasury Solicitor* [1956] Ch 559, [1956] 2 All ER 451); see also *Re Peacock, Midland Bank Executor and Trustee Co Ltd v Peacock* [1957] Ch 310, [1957] 2 All ER 98 (if the gift is to a class (or group), the share of a member disqualified by public policy from taking does not lapse but goes to swell the shares of the other members).

25.141 The court will not, however, make a declaration that a beneficiary who murdered the testator be deemed to have predeceased his victim so as to enable a substituted gift in the will to take effect (*Re Robertson's Estate, Marsden v Marsden* (1963) 107 Sol Jo 318).

25.142 Disentitlement by reason of a felonious act is a proper plea in a probate action (*Re G's Estate, M v L* [1946] P 183, [1946] 1 All ER 579). A person whose interest is forfeited by reason of felony is not entitled to contest a probate action in connection with the estate in question, and will be dismissed from the suit if he has become a party to it (*Re Hall's Estate, Hall v Knight and Baxter* [1914] P 1).

25.143 See also now the Forfeiture Act 1982 (p. 852, post) which provides limited relief for persons found guilty of unlawful killing (other than murder) from forfeiture of inheritance and other rights.

25.144 A widow, who had been subject to violent physical attacks by the deceased, had killed him during an altercation and was subsequently convicted of manslaughter. It was held that the forfeiture rule applied to preclude her from benefiting under the deceased's will but the purpose of the Forfeiture Act 1982 was to require the court to form a view of the moral culpability attending the killing to see whether the effect of the rule should be modified. The widow had been a loyal wife and, having regard to the fact that there were no other persons for whom the deceased had been under any moral duty to provide, it would be unjust for her to be deprived of the benefits conferred on her by his will. The forfeiture rule was accordingly modified to allow her to take under the will (*Re K* [1985] Ch 85, [1985] 1 All ER 403).

25.145 It was further held that on the true construction of s. 2(7) of the Forfeiture Act 1982 (see p. 853, post) an interest in property 'acquired' before the coming into force of the Act denoted property which had actually been transferred to the person entitled to it as a result of the forfeiture rule, or who had acquired an indefeasible right to have it transferred to him, and did not include property which, at the time s. 2(7) came into force, was held by a personal representative who had not completed his administration of the estate (*Re K* [1985] Ch 85, [1985] 1 All ER 403).

25.146 A grant was made to the guardian of the heir-at-law passing over the husband of deceased who was of drunken habits (*Re Ardern's Goods* [1898] P 147).

25.147 To a nominee of the widow, passing over the widow (who was old), and the executors who had intermeddled and neglected to prove the will (*Re Potticary's Estate* [1927] P 202).

25.148 Passing over a sole executor without citation on proof of his adverse interest, unfitness, and that he had taken no steps to obtain probate (*Re Ray's Goods* (1926) 136 LT 640).

25.149 Passing over an executor who had intermeddled but refused to take a grant: he was elderly and unwell (*Re Biggs' Estate* [1966] P 118, [1966] 1 All ER 358).

(g) Land ceasing to be settled land. Vesting
25.150 Where a life tenant died leaving no kin and no personalty, a grant limited to the real estate was made to the remainderman (*Re Dalley* (1926) 136 LT 223), but this was before the decision in *Re Bridgett and Hayes' Contract*[1] and cases quoted below, and in the erroneous belief that the land was trust property vested as such in the life tenant.

1 [1928] Ch 163, 97 LJ Ch 33.

25.151 In similar circumstances, but with £250 free estate, a general grant of the estate of the life tenant was made to the remainderman, but it was required, at the instance of the Treasury Solicitor, that the kin (if any) should be cited by advertisement (*Re Bordass' Estate* [1929] P 107).

25.152 Similarly, with personal effects of trifling value, a general grant was made to the remainderman on the consent of the Treasury Solicitor without citation (*Re Birch's Estate* [1929] P 164). See also *Re Mortifee's Estate* cited in para. **25.172** at (e), post.)

(h) To constitute a party to an action
25.153 Where under s. 1 of the Law Reform (Miscellaneous Provisions) Act 1934[1], a cause of action survives, there being no personal representative of a deceased intestate, the court will order that a grant of administration be made to the nominee of a party intending to prosecute the action (*Re Simpson's Estate*; *Re Gunning's Estate* [1936] P 40). See also paras. **11.328** ff., ante.

1 See p. 765, post.

Action by spouse of deceased against estate

25.154 Under the Law Reform (Husband and Wife) Act 1962 each of the parties to a marriage has the like right of action in tort against the other as if they were not married. Where it is desired that a surviving spouse should bring an action against the estate of the deceased it is inappropriate for him or her to become the personal representative under a full grant. Often the ordinary rules of priority will enable a grant to be made to some other person (e.g. on the renunciation of the spouse a grant may be made to the next person entitled, either under the terms of the will of the deceased or under an intestacy). Sometimes, however, it may be necessary to have recourse to the discretionary powers of the court under s. 116 of the Supreme Court Act 1981. The Registrar's Circular reproduced in paras. **25.155–25.161**, post clarifies the practice applicable to the common run of such cases.

25.155   The court prefers the whole of the administration of an estate to be carried out by one person, and therefore if application is made for some person other than the surviving spouse to be appointed as administrator by order under s. 116, it will prefer to appoint that person to administer the whole estate. Such an application must have the approval of the surviving spouse, preferably by the lodging of a written consent to the proposed grant.

25.156   In exceptional cases, e.g. where there is a difficulty in finding someone willing to undertake the whole of the administration or where there is good reason for wishing to leave the main administration of the estate in the spouse's hands, the court will not generally refuse to make a grant to some person limited for the purpose of defending proceedings to be brought against the estate. Such a grant will be made under the authority of s. 116 of which sub-s. (2) enables the court to limit the grant in any way it thinks fit. After such a limited grant has issued, administration of the rest of the estate (i.e. save and except the defence of any action brought against the estate) can be granted to the surviving spouse in his or her ordinary right. It should be noted that application must be made first for the limited grant under s. 116. The power mentioned above to limit the extent of the grant is confined to a grant to a person other than the person ordinarily entitled.

25.157   It follows that where the surviving spouse has already taken out a full grant before realising that this was detrimental to his or her interests, there is no alternative to the revocation of the grant to enable the procedure set out above to be followed.

25.158   Where the surviving spouse has been appointed executor, then upon his or her renunciation, and subject to the right of any co-executor to take probate, a procedure similar to that outlined above should be followed.

25.159   If the spouse-executor has intermeddled, renunciation will not be permitted[1]. If there is a co-executor, probate can be issued to him with power reserved. It would be for the advisers of the surviving spouse to consider whether the proposed action is prejudiced by the intermeddling and consequent reservation of power. If there is no co-executor it will be necessary to apply for an administrator (with will) to be appointed by an order under s. 116, preferably to administer the whole estate.

1   Quaere, if the acts of intermeddling are only trivial or technical: see *Holder v Holder* [1968] Ch 353, [1968] 1 All ER 665.

25.160   As in the case of administration, if the surviving spouse has already proved the will, there is no alternative to revocation.

25.161   It should be noted that s. 113 of the Supreme Court Act 1981 (power of court to grant probate or administration in respect of part of the estate of the deceased) does not cover this class of case[1].

1   Registrar's Circular, 2 February 1967. See *Re Newsham* [1967] P 230, [1966] 3 All ER 681.

25.162   Where a representative of a deceased person was required to be joined as a defendant an order was made under RSC Order 16, r. 46 (now Order 15, r. 15) (*Lean v Alston* [1947] KB 467, [1947] 1 All ER 261, CA).

25.163   Grant to Official Solicitor limited to the purpose of defending the proposed proceedings (*Re Knight's Goods* [1939] 3 All ER 928, 55 TLR 992).

25.164   A person who wishes to bring a claim under the Inheritance (Provision for Family and Dependants) Act 1975 for financial provision from a deceased person's estate is unable to do so until a grant has issued and a personal representative has been constituted (see Chap. 41). Where difficulty arises because there is no person (including the Treasury Solicitor claiming on behalf of the Crown as bona vacantia) either entitled or (if entitled) willing to apply for the grant, the Official Solicitor has intimated that he would be prepared to consider making application under s. 116 of the Supreme Court Act 1981 for an order for a grant to himself for the purpose of being a party to the proceedings proposed to be brought against the deceased's estate[1].

1 Secretary's Circular, 11 November 1976.

Grant to part only of an estate under s. 113 of the Supreme Court Act 1981

25.165   Note.—Section 113 of the Act of 1981 replaced with amendments s. 155 of the Supreme Court of Judicature (Consolidation) Act 1925, with effect from 1 January 1982: the following case law relates to applications made under the earlier statutory provision, but it is considered that the examples cited are illustrative of the court's powers under s. 113 of the 1981 Act.

25.166   Under s. 113, the court may grant probate or administration in respect of any part of the estate of a deceased person, limited in any way the court thinks fit. However, where the estate is insolvent, the grant cannot be severed except as regards a trust estate in which the deceased had no beneficial interest. Otherwise, under this section, the grant can, for example, be in respect of trust property only, or real estate only, or personal estate only.

25.167   Application under this section should be made ex parte at the registry at which the application for the grant is to be made[1]. A district probate registrar may, if he considers it necessary, obtain the directions of a district judge of the Principal Registry on any application made to him[2].

1 NCPR 2(1), 51.
2 NCPR 7.

25.168   A district judge or registrar may require any application to be made by summons to a district judge or registrar in chambers or to a High Court judge in chambers or open court[1].

1 NCPR 61(1).

25.169   The application must be supported by an affidavit setting out the grounds of the application, stating whether the estate is known to be insolvent and showing how any person entitled to a grant in respect of the whole estate in priority to the applicant has been cleared off (r. 51). Where the person in priority has not been cleared off application is also necessary for an order under s. 116 of the Supreme Court Act 1981 under which section the court has the power in proper cases to pass over the persons entitled to a grant in priority (see paras. **25.91** ff., ante) and where this further application is necessary it may be included in the one affidavit.

25.170   The court's powers under s. 113 do not enable it to sever the representation by excepting from a grant of administration to a surviving spouse the defence of an action to be brought against the estate[1]. See also paras. **25.155–25.164**, ante.

1 *Re Newsham's Estate* [1967] P 230, [1966] 3 All ER 681.

25.171   As to the practice in applications under s. 113, see also paras. **11.258 ff.**, ante.

25.172   The following are examples of orders made:

(a)   Grants have been made to the cestui que trust or his nominee after citation of the persons entitled to a general grant, such grant being limited to the grantee's interest unless the other cestuis que trust (if any) consent to the grant covering their interests as well. (See *Pegg v Chamberlain* (1860) 1 Sw & Tr 527; *Re Ratcliffe's Goods* [1899] P 110.)

(b)   Administration de bonis non with will annexed was decreed to a legatee, limited to receive a legacy in the funds and the dividends due thereon, the chain of executorship having been broken, and the person entitled to the general grant de bonis non being in Italy, and not expected to return for some years (*Re Steadman's Goods* (1828) 2 Hag Ecc 59. See also *Re Watson's Goods* (1858) 1 Sw & Tr 110; *Re Baldwin's Goods* [1903] P 61, and contra, *Re Watts' Goods* (1860) 1 Sw & Tr 538.)

(c)   Administration de bonis non of the estate of the person in whose name shares in two foreign railway companies had inadvertently been left, was granted to the trustee in bankruptcy of the beneficial owner of the shares, limited thereto (*Re Agnese's Goods* [1900] P 60).

(d)   Administration was granted to the agent of a foreigner, limited to substantiate proceedings in Chancery for the recovery of a debt, and to the receipt of the debt (*Re Elector of Hesse's Goods* (1827) 1 Hag Ecc 93; *Harris and Wiggins v Milburn* (1828) 2 Hag Ecc 62; *Re Dodgson's Goods* (1859) 1 Sw & Tr 259).

(e)   Where there was land vested in the deceased as tenant for life which ceased to be settled land on his death and the Treasury Solicitor was entitled to a general grant, the court ordered that the grant should exclude the land of which the deceased was tenant for life, and that a grant limited to such land should be made to the remainderman (*Re Mortifee's Estate* [1948] P 274).

Grant 'ad colligenda bona'

25.173   Application may be made for a grant of administration ad colligenda bona defuncti, owing to the impossibility, in the special circumstances of the case, of the court constituting a general personal representative in sufficient time to meet the necessities of the estate. It is now more usual, in appropriate cases, to obtain wider powers by invoking the powers conferred upon the court by s. 116 of the Supreme Court Act 1981 (see paras. **25.91 ff.**, ante).

25.174   A grant ad colligenda bona may be made not only to a person whom the court considers suitable, but also to the persons who are entitled to a full grant but in the interests of the estate cannot wait[1]; or to entire strangers who have been brought into connection with the matter[2].

1 *Re Clarkington's Goods* (1861) 2 Sw & Tr 380.
2 *Re Gudolle's Goods* (1835) cited in 3 Sw & Tr 22; *Re Wyckoff's Goods* (1862) 3 Sw & Tr 20.

25.175 The application must be supported by an affidavit setting out the grounds of the application, and should be made ex parte at the registry at which the application for the grant is to be made[1]. At the Principal Registry the necessary documents should be lodged in the Probate Department. A district probate registrar may, if he considers it necessary, obtain the directions of a district judge of the Principal Registry on any application made to him[2].

1 NCPR 2(1), 52(b).
2 NCPR 7.

25.176 A district judge or registrar may require any application to be made by summons to a district judge or registrar in chambers or to a High Court judge in chambers or open court[1].

1 NCPR 61(1).

25.177 The usual limitation included in the order, which is made under no special section of the Act, is: 'limited for the purpose only of collecting and getting in and receiving the estate and doing such acts as may be necessary for the preservation of the same and until further representation be granted'.

25.178 Ad colligenda bona grants are always grants of letters of administration although there is sometimes in existence a valid will which is ultimately proved. In all cases the oath in support of the grant application (see Form No. 139) need not include any statement whether a will exists or whether the deceased died intestate, nor contain any of the usual clearings. It will always, however, be necessary to consider the existence of life or minority interests. Every grant ad colligenda bona is silent as to the will or the intestacy and is limited 'until further representation be granted'[1]. It is suggested that the question as to whether any life or minority interest arises in the estate of the deceased be dealt with in the affidavit in support of the application for the order.

1 Registrar's Direction (1979) 12 October.

25.179 When a general grant is applied for and obtained in the usual way, the ad colligenda bona grant ceases.

25.180 Where there are no known kin of an intestate entitled to take a grant, and where the Treasury Solicitor or the Solicitor for the Duchy of Lancaster is of opinion that an immediate grant should issue in order to preserve the estate, application for a similar grant of administration may be made, supported by a statement of the facts.

25.181 Grants of administration ad colligenda bona have been made as follows:

(a) To a creditor, limited to collecting the personal estate of the deceased, to giving receipts for his debts on the payment of the same, and to renewing the lease of his business premises which would expire before a general grant could be made (*Re Clarkington's Goods* (1861) 2 Sw & Tr 380; *Re Stewart's Goods* (1869) LR 1 P & D 727).

(b) To a creditor, where the deceased had died without any known relation, and it was impossible to ascertain whether, if ever married, her husband had survived her, upon the affidavit of the solicitor of the creditor that he was informed and believed that she died a widow and intestate (*Re Ashley's Goods* (1890) 15 PD 120).

(c)   Where it is for the benefit of the absent or unknown next of kin, with power to dispose of the property or any portion of it by sale, and give discharges from debts (*Re Schwerdtfeger's Goods* (1876) 1 PD 424; *Re Bolton's Goods* [1899] P 186. See also *Re Roberts' Goods* [1898] P 149, as to real estate.)

(d)   On an application by a creditor (Commissioners of Inland Revenue), grant of administration ad colligenda bona to the Official Solicitor in circumstances where the executors to the deceased's English will had shown a lack of urgency in applying for probate (*Re Clore* [1982] Ch 456, [1982] 3 All ER 419, CA; approving [1982] Fam 113).

Application for order to bring a testamentary paper into the registry

25.182   There are two methods of compelling a person who is, or is believed to be, in possession of a testamentary document to bring it into a probate registry:

(a)   By order of a High Court judge made on an attendance before him following an order of a district judge or registrar obtained on summons, under NCPR 50(1), pursuant to s. 122 of the Supreme Court Act 1981[1]. For practice regarding summonses, see paras. **25.193** ff., post.

(b)   By a subpoena issued by a district judge or registrar under NCPR 50(2), pursuant to s. 123 of the Supreme Court Act 1981[2] (see paras. **25.185–25.192**, post). This simpler procedure is more usual in cases where it is known that the document is in the possession, custody or power of a person who refuses to produce it.

1 See p. 846, post.
2 See p. 847, post.

25.183   In either case, failure to comply with the order of the court or the subpoena constitutes contempt of court.

25.184   Where a probate action is pending, any application under either of these sections to compel the production of a testamentary document must be made in the Chancery Division in accordance with RSC Ord. 76, r. 13. For practice, see paras. **27.16** and **27.17**, post.

Subpoena to bring in a testamentary document

25.185   Application for the issue of a subpoena under s. 123 of the Supreme Court Act 1981[1], in a case where no probate action is pending, is made by lodging at the Probate Department of the Principal Registry or at a district probate registry an affidavit setting out the grounds of the application (NCPR 50(2)) (see Form No. 38), together with two copies of the form of subpoena (Form No. 190), duly completed. If the district judge or registrar directs the issue of the subpoena one of the copies is sealed and returned to the solicitor, the affidavit being indorsed with the district judge's or registrar's direction and filed in the registry.

1 See p. 847, post.

25.186   The subpoena may require the lodgment of the testamentary document in the Principal Registry or at a district probate registry, but lodgment at the registry from which the subpoena issued is usually required.

25.187 The subpoena should be indorsed with the following:

'If you the said .... deny that the testamentary document(s) referred to is/are in your possession, custody or power, you may swear an affidavit to that effect and file it in the .... Registry'. (*Registrar's Direction* (1989) 23 June.)

25.188 No fee is payable on filing the affidavit or sealing the subpoena.

Subsequent procedure

25.189 If the person served with the subpoena is required to bring the testamentary paper into the Principal Registry, he should lodge it with the Record Keeper, who will give a receipt for it, if desired. No fee is payable.

25.190 If the document is not in the possession, custody or power of the person served with the subpoena he should file at the registry from which the subpoena issued an affidavit stating that the document is not in his possession or control (NCPR 50(2)).

25.191 The situation may occur where the will has not been lodged pursuant to the subpoena and no affidavit has been filed by the person served denying that the will is in his possession or control. In such a situation, if there is doubt as to whether the original will is in the possession or under the control of the person subpoenaed (and accordingly no clear evidence that he is in contempt) consideration should be given to applying for an order that the person subpoenaed attend before a High Court judge for examination (see para. **25.182**(a) rather than applying for his committal.

25.192 Disobedience to the subpoena may be enforced by proceedings for committal: see paras. **25.248** ff., post. The court will, however, not necessarily commit a person who disobeys a subpoena. It may make an order for his attendance at court to be examined as to his possession of the document in question[1].

1 *Parkinson v Thornton* (1867) 37 LJP & M 3.

Applications by summons

25.193 District probate registrars have power to hear certain summonses. Where they have such power their jurisdiction relates to matters where the related grant application is made, or is to be made, at their particular registry or the related grant has issued from their particular registry.

25.194 Where the rules require the issue of a district judge's or registrar's summons, or this mode of procedure is directed by a district judge or registrar in a particular case, the summons must be issued out of the registry in which it is to be heard[1].

1 NCPR 61(3).

25.195 The principal matters decided by the district judges of the Principal Registry or a district probate registrar on summons are indicated in the following paragraphs.

Dispute between persons equally entitled to grant

25.196　Where there is a dispute between two or more persons entitled to a grant in the same degree as to which of them shall take the grant, the matter may be determined by a district judge or registrar on summons (NCPR 27(6)): see also paras. **14.13–14.31**, ante.

25.197　A summons for directions returnable before a district judge or registrar may also be issued by a caveator who wishes to oppose the issue of a grant but has no interest contrary to that of the person who warned the caveat (see paras. **23.64–23.66**, ante).

Inventory and account

25.198　A person who desires that an executor or administrator should be ordered to file an inventory of the estate of the deceased and an account of his administration of the estate should apply by summons to the district judge or registrar: see paras. **19.01–19.11**, ante.

Application for leave to sue on guarantee

25.199　In cases where, pursuant to s. 120 of the Supreme Court Act 1981[1] and under the rules in force prior to the commencement of the Non-Contentious Probate Rules 1987, a guarantee by sureties has been given as a condition of granting administration (with or without will), the guarantee enures for the benefit of every person interested in the estate of the deceased as if contained in a contract under seal made by the surety or sureties with every such person, and where there are two or more sureties as if they had bound themselves jointly and severally[2]. No action may, however, be brought on any such guarantee without leave of the court[3].

1　See p. 846, post.
2　Supreme Court Act 1981, s. 120(2).
3　Ibid., s. 120(3).

25.200　Identical provisions apply, under s. 11(4) and (5) of the Administration of Estates Act 1971[1], in the case of a guarantee given under the provisions of the rules in force prior to the commencement of the Non-Contentious Probate Rules 1987 on an application for the resealing of a colonial grant of administration (with or without will).

1　See p. 803, post.

25.201　Application to the court for leave to sue a surety on a guarantee given under either of these provisions is, unless otherwise directed by a district judge or registrar under NCPR 61, made by summons to a district judge of the Principal Registry or a district probate registrar. Under r. 61, the district judge or registrar may require the application to be made to a High Court judge in chambers or open court. In any event, notice of the application must be served on the administrator or administrators, the surety whom it is desired to sue, and any co-surety (NCPR 40).

Order to assign administration bond given prior to 1 January 1972

25.202 Notwithstanding the abolition of administration bonds as from 1 January 1972, a bond filed before that date may still be enforced or assigned[1].

1 Supreme Court Act 1981, s. 152(3) and Sch. 6, para. 10.

25.203 A person interested in the estate of the deceased may call on the sureties to the bond by summons to a district judge of the Principal Registry[1], supported by affidavit, to show cause why, on a prima facie case being shown that the condition of such bond has been broken, an order should not be made that the same be assigned to some person to be named in the order, to entitle such person to sue in his own name on the bond, and further to entitle him to recover as trustee for all persons interested, the full amount recoverable in respect of any breach of the condition of the bond[2]. The administrator and the sureties must all be served with the summons.

1 See *Cope v Bennett* [1911] 2 Ch 488.
2 Section 167 of the Supreme Court of Judicature (Consolidation) Act 1925 (as originally enacted).

25.204 The costs of the summons, in the event of the order being made, are usually ordered to follow the costs of the subsequent action in the county court or the Queen's Bench Division.

25.205 The applicant should by affidavit make out a prima facie case that there has been a breach of the condition of the bond[1].

1 See *Young v Oxley, Re Oxley's Goods* (1858) 1 Sw & Tr 25; where a bond given in the Consistory Court of Chester was ordered to be assigned. See also *Sandrey v Michell* (1862) 3 Sw & Tr 25; *Re Jones' Goods* (1862) 3 Sw & Tr 28; *Baker and Marshman v Brooks, Marshman v Hughes* (1862) 3 Sw & Tr 32; *Re Young's Goods* (1866) LR 1 P & D 186, 35 LJP & M 126.
    As to liability of sureties under a revoked grant, see *Debendra Nath Dutt v Administrator-General of Bengal* (1908) 99 LT 68.

25.206 A formal assignment of the bond is not essential, the person in whose favour the order is made being entitled to sue on the bond by virtue of the order itself. If a formal assignment is desired, however, the practitioner should lodge a blank sheet of foolscap, impressed by a 50p stamp from the Controller of Stamps (Inland Revenue), with the district judge's clerk, who will then draw up the assignment (Form No. 44). The bond is annexed to the assignment and handed to the Record Keeper. The practitioner should make arrangements for the production of the bond and assignment by an officer of the registry at the hearing of the action. If the bond is filed in a district probate registry, the district registrar should be asked to forward it to the Principal Registry.

Grounds for resisting order to assign bond

25.207 The surety, or his personal representative, may resist the order by showing on affidavit that there has in fact been no breach of the condition of the bond, or that there has been undue delay on the part of the applicant; and the district judge has power to reject the application. In *Re Coates* (January 1879, unreported), the Master of the Rolls having made an order in an administration action for an application to be made to the Probate Division for an order to assign the bond for a breach of the condition, by reason of a devastavit by the administratrix, one of the sureties established by affidavit that assets up to the amount of the sum under which the estate had been sworn, and in respect of which amount the bond had been given, had been duly administered, and that the devastavit related to assets in excess of the amount for which the bond was given, whereupon the summons was by consent dismissed with costs, and the order of the Master of the Rolls rescinded.

25.208   So the surety, or his personal representative, may show that there has been a release or waiver of the breach of the condition on the part of the applicant, or on the part of those under whom he claims. Thus it was held[1] that, where a notice had been advertised under s. 29 of the Law of Property Amendment Act 1859[2] by the executor of the administratrix, and the estate had been administered in accordance with the terms thereof, this notice was sufficient, under the statute, to protect the sureties to the bond from liability for the acts of the administratrix.

1 *Newton v Sherry* (1876) 1 CPD 246.
2 Repealed: see now Trustee Act 1925, s. 27.

25.209   There is no invariable rule that it is contrary to law for an attorney-administrator, on the instructions of his principal, to deliver the balance of the estate to a third person. Whether this is a breach of duty must depend on the circumstances. But even if a prima facie case of breach of the condition of the bond is made out, the court has a discretion to refuse an order for assignment of the bond[1].

1 *Re Weiss' Estate* [1962] P 136, [1962] 1 All ER 308.

25.210   These principles would appear to be equally applicable in cases in which the sureties to a guarantee given pursuant to the Supreme Court Act 1981 are sued on the guarantee.

Order for grant etc., after citation

25.211   As to the circumstances in which it is necessary to apply on summons for a grant, or for some other order, following a citation to accept or refuse a grant, to take probate or to propound a will, see paras. **24.73** ff., ante.

Discontinuance of proceedings arising from caveat

25.212   When an appearance has been entered to the warning of a caveat, no grant can issue (except to the caveator himself) until the decision of the court in the proceedings arising from the appearance to warning. But if, prior to the commencement of a probate action, the parties come to terms (which do not involve pronouncing for or against a will or making an order incorporating terms which are properly a matter for the Chancery Division), or the caveator abandons his opposition to the issue of a grant, application may be made by summons to a district judge of the Principal Registry for an order for discontinuance of the caveat and for the issue of a grant notwithstanding the caveat, warning and appearance (NCPR 44(13)). If the application for discontinuance of the caveat is made by consent, the application may be made to the registrar of the district probate registry to which the application for the grant has been, or is to be, made. Form of summons, No. 193.

25.213   A similar application may be made to a district judge of the Principal Registry where a caveator enters an appearance to a warning which shows an insufficient interest.

25.214 As to the right of a caveator who has not appeared to a warning to withdraw his caveat, thus in some cases enabling a grant to issue without an order for discontinuance, see paras. **23.45–23.48**, ante. As to caveats generally, see Chap.23.

Application for order to attend for examination and, if appropriate, to bring in a will

25.215 Where no probate action is pending, application may be made by summons to a district judge of the Principal Registry or the registrar of the district probate registry to which the grant application has been, or is to be, made for an order requiring any person to attend before a High Court judge for the purpose of being examined as to his knowledge of a testamentary document[1]. A district judge or registrar may transfer the application to another district judge or registrar having jurisdiction[2]. When the person is before the High Court judge pursuant to the order he may be required to answer any question relating to the document concerned and, if appropriate, may be ordered to bring in the document in such manner as the court may direct.

1 Supreme Court Act 1981, s. 122 (p. 846, post); NCPR 50(1); *Re Shepherd's Goods* [1891] P 323.
2 NCPR 62.

25.216 The alternative, and more usual, method of procedure is to apply ex parte to the district judge or registrar for the issue of a subpoena requiring the production of the document[1]: for the practice as to the issue of such a subpoena and subsequent action, see paras. **25.185–25.188**, ante.

1 Supreme Court Act 1981, s. 123 (p. 847, post); NCPR 50(2).

25.217 The summons, which should be supported by an affidavit, must be served on the person against whom the order is sought[1].

1 NCPR 50(1).

25.218 If such person shows by affidavit that the document in question is not in his possession or under his control, but it appears that there are reasonable grounds for believing that he has knowledge of it, the district judge or registrar may order him to attend to be examined in open court concerning such document[1].

1 Supreme Court Act 1981, s. 122 (p. 846, post) and see also *Re Laws' Goods* (1872) LR 2 P & D 458; *Banfield v Pickard* (1881) 6 PD 33.

25.219 A copy of the order directing him to attend should be indorsed with the warning notice as required by RSC Ord. 45, r. 7(4), and served personally. Conduct money should be paid or tendered to a person directed to attend for the purpose of being examined[1]. In case of default in attendance, application may be made for enforcement of the order by committal: see paras. **25.248–25.250**, post. The costs of the application are in the discretion of the court.

1 *Re Harvey's Estate* [1907] P 239.

25.220 Where a probate action is pending, any application for an order to bring in a will or to attend for examination must be made in the Chancery Division by summons in the action (RSC Ord. 76, r. 13). For practice, see paras. **27.16** and **27.17**, post.

Discretion of district judge or registrar to direct application by summons

25.221 A district judge of the Principal Registry or a district probate registrar may require any application to be made by summons to a district judge or registrar in chambers, or to a High Court judge in chambers or open court[1], a district probate registrar first referring the matter on statement to a district judge of the Principal Registry, as necessary[2].

1 NCPR 61(1).
2 NCPR 7.

25.222 A district judge or registrar may also transfer an application made to him to another district judge or registrar having jurisdiction[1].

1 NCPR 62.

Practice as to summonses

25.223 The following practice applies in the Family Division in relation both to summonses to a district judge or registrar and summonses to a High Court judge in non-contentious probate matters.

Issue of summons

25.224 Summonses for hearing by a district judge or registrar must be issued out of the registry in which they are to be heard[1]. Those for hearing by a district judge of the Principal Registry are issued in the Probate Department at the Principal Registry of the Family Division. Where a registrar has power to hear a summons his jurisdiction relates to cases where the related application for the grant has been, or is to be, made to his registry or the grant has issued from it. All summonses for hearing by a High Court judge must be issued out of the Principal Registry[2] (Probate Department).

1 NCPR 61(3).
2 NCPR 61(4).

25.225 The summons must be drawn up in duplicate. One copy of the summons is retained in the registry; the other copy, after it has been sealed and the return day and time have been inserted, is returned to the practitioner. Unless otherwise ordered, any evidence relied on in support of the application must be served with the summons (RSC Ord. 32, r. 3(2)(c)). No fee is payable on the issue of the summons or on filing any affidavit in support of the application.

25.226 Except in respect of consent probate summonses (as to which, see para. **25.238**, post), all non-contentious probate summonses for hearing before a High Court or district judge or registrar of the Family Division are specially fixed.

25.227 Orders on summons are sent by post from the Registry.

25.228 See also 'Consent summonses', para. **25.238**, post.

Where reference to be made to Hansard

25.229 Unless the judge otherwise directs, where any party intends to refer at a hearing, as an aid to construing legislation, to the reports of parliamentary proceedings as reported in *Hansard*, that party must not less than five clear working days before the first date of the hearing serve upon all other parties and the court copies of any such extract together with a brief summary of the argument intended to be based upon such extract. Service on the court is to be in accordance with RSC Ord. 65, r. 5 to (a) in the Family Division in cases to be heard in London, the Clerk of the Rules, Room WG4, Royal Courts of Justice, Strand, London WC2A 2LL; in cases to be heard out of London the chief clerk of the relevant district registry, and (b) in the Principal Registry of the Family Division, the Assistant Secretary, Somerset House, London WC2R 1LP. Service upon other parties is also to be effected in accordance with RSC Ord. 65, r. 5 or as otherwise agreed between the parties (*Practice Direction* [1995] 1 All ER 234, [1995] 1 WLR 192).

Service

25.230   Service of a summons must be effected at least two clear days before the return day[1]. Saturdays, Sundays, bank holidays, Christmas Day and Good Friday are excluded in reckoning this period[2]. Unless otherwise ordered the summons must be served within 14 days of its issue (RSC Ord. 32, r. 3(2)(b)).

1 NCPR 66(2).
2 RSC Ord. 3, r. 2(5), applied by NCPR 3.

25.231   A High Court or district judge or registrar may direct that a summons for the service of which no other provision is made under the Non-Contentious Probate Rules shall be served on such person or persons as he may direct (NCPR 66(1)).

25.232   Service is effected by (i) leaving a copy of the summons (or other document) at, or sending it by prepaid ordinary or registered post, or recorded delivery to, the address for service, or (ii) where the address for service includes a numbered box at a document exchange or there is inscribed on the writing paper of the party on whom the document is served (where such party acts in person) or on the writing paper of his solicitor (where such party acts by a solicitor) a document exchange box number, and such a party or his solicitor (as the case may be) has not indicated in writing to the party serving the document that he is unwilling to accept service through a document exchange, by leaving a copy of the summons addressed to that numbered box at that document exchange or at a document exchange which transmits documents every business day to that document exchange, or (iii) by fax where—

(a)   the party serving the document acts by a solicitor,
(b)   the party on whom the document is served acts by a solicitor and service is effected by transmission to the business address of such solicitor,
(c)   the solicitor acting for the party on whom the document is served has indicated in writing to the solicitor serving the document that he is willing to accept service by fax at a specified fax number and the document is transmitted to that number; and for this purpose the inscription of a fax number on the writing paper of a solicitor shall be deemed to indicate that such a solicitor is willing to accept service by fax at that number in accordance with this paragraph unless he states otherwise in writing, and
(d)   as soon as practicable after service by fax the solicitor acting for the party serving the document dispatches a copy of it to the solicitor acting for the other party by leaving it at, or posting it to, his address or by document exchange as indicated above, or

(iv) if there is no address for service by leaving a copy of the summons at or posting it to the usual or last-known address of the person to be served[1].

1   RSC Ord. 65, r. 5, applied by NCPR 3.

25.233   A summons which is served by being left at the address for service and is left after 12 noon on a Saturday or 4 p.m. on any other weekday is deemed, for the purpose of computing time, to have been served on the following Monday, or the day following that other weekday, as the case may be[1].

1   RSC Ord. 65, r. 7, applied by NCPR 3.

When heard

25.234   Summonses are heard by the district judges at the Principal Registry every weekday from Monday to Friday inclusive. A summons to be heard at a district probate registry will be fixed for a weekday, from Monday to Friday inclusive, in consultation with the district probate registrar. If a summons is to be attended by counsel, it should be so marked when issued and served. A considered estimate of the length of hearing must be given when the summons is issued. Failure to request a sufficient length of time for a hearing may result in an adjournment.

25.235   Summonses to a High Court judge are heard in chambers or open court at the Royal Courts of Justice.

25.236   During vacations, High Court judges' summonses are heard on the days notified in the Vacation Notice. It is necessary to obtain the leave of a district judge of the Principal Registry to issue a summons to the High Court judge for hearing during vacations, and if leave is given the practitioner, after issuing the summons in the Registry, must enter the same in the list kept by the Clerk of the Rules at the Royal Courts of Justice. As to the additional powers of the district judges of the Principal Registry during the Long Vacation, see para. **25.16**, ante.

25.237   No costs are allowed for the attendance of counsel before a district judge or registrar in chambers, or of more than one counsel before a High Court judge in chambers, unless the district judge or registrar or High Court judge, as the case may be, has certified the attendance as being proper in the circumstances of the case.

Consent summonses

25.238   It is unnecessary for the parties to attend the hearing of a district judge's or registrar's summons in the Family Division provided that at the time of issue the written consent of the opposite party or parties to the order sought is indorsed on the summons or lodged with it. In such cases, no return date is fixed. If the district judge or registrar who considers the summons finds that there are minor matters which require attention he will note them on the summons and it will be returned to the issuing solicitor by post. Unless the contrary is indicated, such queries can be dealt with without the need for attendance. If the district judge or registrar requires personal attendance, the registry will fix a date and send the sealed copy summons to the issuing solicitor with the date and time of hearing noted on it. The solicitor must then give notice of the appointment to the other parties.

Costs

25.239   In all cases in which an order for costs is sought, an application for costs must be included in the summons[1]. See also para. **25.237**, ante.

1 Registrar's Direction (1975) 25 February.

Reference by district judge or registrar to High Court judge

25.240   The district judge or registrar may require any application brought before him, whether by summons or otherwise, to be brought before a High Court judge by summons in chambers or open court[1]. If a registrar wishes to refer a matter to a High Court judge he must first obtain the confirmation of a district judge of the Principal Registry.

1 NCPR 61(1). It has been suggested that where the application is hotly contested, then directions of the district judge or registrar should be sought at an early stage as to the form of the evidence to be adduced at the hearing before the High Court judge and directions obtained as to the desirability or otherwise of requiring the application to be made in open court (*Van Hoorn v Van Hoorn* (1978) 123 Sol Jo 65).

Adjournment

25.241   When a summons has been adjourned, either to a fixed date or generally, it is necessary for the practitioner to restore it to the list for hearing. A form of restoration of adjourned summons may be obtained in the Probate Department at the Principal Registry or at the district registry, if the matter is proceeding there; it must be filled up and lodged, and notice of the date and time of the adjourned hearing given to the other parties to be heard. No fee is charged for restoring the summons.

Orders

25.242   Orders are drawn up in the registry, and normally bear the date of the day on which they are made; but if some requirement remains to be complied with, e.g. the filing of proof of service, it is the practice to date the order the day on which the requirement is complied with. Orders (or copies of them) are sent by post to the applicant.

Appeal from district judge or registrar

25.243   Any person aggrieved by any decision or requirement of a district judge of the Principal Registry or a district probate registrar may appeal therefrom by way of summons to a High Court judge[1]. If any person besides the appellant appeared, or was represented, before the district judge or registrar, the summons must be issued within seven days of the decision or requirement complained of for hearing on the first available day, and must be served on every such person not less than two clear days before the return day[2].

1 NCPR 65(1).
2 NCPR 65(2) and 66(2).

25.244   Appeals from district judges or registrars are also subject to the Registrar's Direction of 21 February 1985, which provides that:

'Where the appellant is represented, and either party wishes to bespeak a copy of the district judge's or registrar's notes of evidence, the appellant's solicitor shall:

(a) within 21 days from the date upon which the appeal is lodged, certify that either the appellant or the respondent considers that notes of evidence taken before the district judge or registrar are necessary for the purpose of appeal and that notes of evidence will be lodged, and

(b) if he has so certified, unless otherwise directed, not less than 21 days prior to the hearing of the appeal lodge a copy of the notes of evidence (which can be bespoken from the district judge or registrar) and of judgment (being notes prepared by the appellant's solicitor, and where the respondent is represented agreed by his legal advisers, and approved by the district judge or registrar).

Where the appellant is acting in person and the respondent is represented, the respondent's solicitor shall, after service of the notice of appeal, comply with the obligations imposed by paragraph 2(a) and (b) above (save as to the agreement as to notes of judgment) as if he were acting for the appellant, and inform the appellant of the lodging of such notes and (if so required) supply to him a copy thereof on payment of the usual charge.

Where either party is represented but neither party wishes to bespeak a copy of the district judge's or registrar's notes of evidence, a copy of the notes of judgment shall be:

(a) prepared by the appellant's solicitor and, if the respondent is represented, agreed by his solicitor; or

(b) prepared by the respondent's solicitor if the appellant is not represented,

and in any case shall be approved by the district judge or registrar, and not less than 21 days prior to the hearing a copy of the notes shall be lodged by the solicitor who prepared them.

Where both parties to the appeal are acting in person the appellant shall notify the district judge or registrar of the appeal and the district judge or registrar shall, where possible, make a note for the assistance of the High Court judge hearing the appeal and shall furnish each party with a copy of that note or certify that no note can be made.'

Application to the court by motion

25.245 The Non-Contentious Probate Rules 1987, unlike the previous rules, contain no provision for making an application by motion. Where important questions of principle are involved, or persons may be adversely affected by the order sought, and it is thought desirable for the matter to be argued by counsel in open court the district judges or registrars may (subject to a district judge confirming a registrar's direction) direct that the application be made by summons to a High Court judge in open court (see para. **25.221**, ante).

25.246 It has been suggested that where the application is hotly contested and it seems appropriate for the case to be heard in open court on oral evidence, then directions of the district judge or registrar should be sought at an early stage as to the form of the evidence to be adduced at the hearing[1].

1 *Van Hoorn v Van Hoorn* (1978) 123 Sol Jo 65.

25.247 The only application relating to non-contentious probate that must be made by motion is an application for committal[1] (see the following paragraphs).

1 RSC Ord. 52, r. 4(1), applied by NCPR 3.

Application for order of committal

25.248   For the general practice as to committal, including the requirements as to service of orders and judgments it is sought to enforce by this procedure, see Ords. 52 and 45 of the Rules of the Supreme Court 1965, and the notes to them in the Annual Practice.

25.249   Among the orders of the Family Division which may be enforced in this way are:

(a)   Disobedience of an order directing an intermeddling executor to take a grant of probate (see also paras. **24.32** and **24.93**, ante).

(b)   Failure to comply with a subpoena or order to bring in a testamentary document or to attend for examination (see paras. **25.182** ff., ante)[1].

(c)   Failure to comply with an order to file an inventory and account (see also Chap. 19)[2].

1 See *Parkinson v Thornton* (1867) 37 LJP & M 3.
2 *Marshman v Brookes* (1863) 32 LJP M & A 95.

25.250   It should be noted that in non-contentious probate matters an affidavit of service of any document (including an order requiring a person to obey an order or to do an act) must show the means by which the server knew the identity of the person served[1].

1 Registrar's Direction (1964) 21 April.

Practice as to motions in the Family Division

Time for hearing motions

25.251   During Term time, motions in the Family Division are heard at the Royal Courts of Justice by a High Court judge on a date and at a time fixed by the Clerk of the Rules.

25.252   During the Long Vacation the district judges of the Principal Registry may hear summonses in respect of matters normally dealt with by a High Court judge in chambers (NCPR 64), but are not empowered to hear motions or other matters dealt with in open court. If it is necessary to apply by motion during the Long Vacation particulars of the procedure may be obtained on enquiry being made at the Probate Department of the Principal Registry.

Notice of motion

25.253   The notice of motion for an order of committal must be supported by an affidavit[1]. The notice of motion, stating the grounds of the application and accompanied by a copy of the affidavit in support, must be served personally on the person sought to be committed[2], unless the court orders substituted service or dispenses with service[3].

1 RSC Ord. 52, r. 4(1).
2 Ibid., r. 4(2).
3 Ibid., r. 4(3).

25.254   Unless the court gives leave to the contrary the notice of motion must be served not less than two clear days before the date of hearing[1].

1 RSC Ord. 8(2). Saturday, Sunday, bank holidays, Christmas Day and Good Friday are excluded in computing this period.

25.255   There is no fee payable on issuing a motion or filing any document in support.

Order

25.256   After hearing counsel in support of, and (if it be the case) in opposition to, the motion, the court makes its order, which is drawn up and retained in the Registry. Copies of the order can be obtained at the Principal Registry.

25.257   Where it is necessary to serve an order personally, such service is effected by leaving a copy of the order with the person to be served (Ord. 65, r. 2).

Contentious Business

Summary

Introduction

Summary

Contentious business

Definition of non-contentious or 'common form' business

26.01   By the definition in s. 128 of the Supreme Court Act 1981—

' "Non-contentious or common form probate business" means the business of obtaining probate and administration where there is no contention as to the right thereto, including

(a)   the passing of probates and administrations through the High Court in contentious cases where the contest has been terminated,

(b)   all businesses of a non-contentious nature in matters of testacy and intestacy not being proceedings in any action, and

(c)   the business of lodging caveats against the grant of probate or administration.'

Non-contentious probate business extends to the warning of caveats. Although there is no lis pendens until a writ is issued[1], it is the practice to treat the costs of entering and warning a caveat and of appearing to the warning as costs in the cause.

1 *Moran v Place* [1896] P 214; *Salter v Salter* [1896] P 291.

Contentious business

26.02   By Ord. 76, r. 1(2) of the Rules of the Supreme Court 1965 a probate action is defined as 'an action for the grant of probate of the will, or letters of administration of the estate, of a deceased person or for the revocation of such a grant, or for a decree pronouncing for or against the validity of an alleged will, not being an action which is non-contentious or common form probate business'.

Grants in common form and in solemn form distinguished

26.03 Before treating of the various steps to be taken in a probate action, it will be useful here to point out the distinction between grants of representation in common form and those in solemn form. A will is proved in 'common form' where its validity is not contested or questioned. The executor, or the person entitled to administration with the will annexed, brings the will into the Principal Registry or a district probate registry, and obtains the grant notwithstanding the absence of other parties interested, upon his own oath and any further affidavits which may be required.

A will is proved in 'solemn form' by the executor, or a person interested under the will, propounding it in an action to which the persons prejudiced by it have been made parties, and by the court, upon hearing evidence, pronouncing for the validity of the will and ordering the issue of a grant.

As to the effect of probate in common form, see paras. **1.18** and **1.19**, ante.

Any person whose interest is adversely affected by a probate granted in common form may proceed by action for revocation to put the person who obtained it, or his representative, to proof of the will in solemn form. This right is not affected by mere lapse of time, by acquiescence, or by the receipt of legacies under the will[1]. Where a defendant after the lapse of four years from the death of the testator elected to put an executor to proof in solemn form, it was said that he was entitled to do so, but that he was not entitled to any indulgence; he was entitled to have the law strictly administered but nothing beyond it[2].

The difference in effect between a probate which has been granted in common form, and a probate which has been granted in solemn form, is that the former is revocable, and the latter, provided proper notice has been given to all persons interested, is, subject to two exceptions, irrevocable[3].

1 *Hoffman v Norris and White* (1805) 2 Phillim 230n; *Merryweather v Turner* (1844) 3 Curt 802; *Re Topping's Goods* (1853) 2 Rob Eccl 620. But the legatee may be called upon to pay the amount of his legacy into court; see para. **27.05**, post.
2 Per Sir Herbert Jenner Fust in *Blake v Knight* (1843) 3 Curt 547 at 553.
3 *Wytcherley v Andrews* (1871) LR 2 P & D 327; *Young v Holloway* [1895] P 87. The discovery, after the grant in solemn form has issued, of a valid marriage contracted by the testator subsequent to the execution of the will would presumably be a further exception.

Later will

26.04 If the existence of a will of later date is discovered subsequently to the date of the decree, the probate, although granted in solemn form, is liable to be revoked in favour of the later will[1].

1 Wentworth's *Office of Executors* (14th edn) pp. 111, 112.

Fraud

26.05 The judgment may be set aside if it has been obtained by fraud, and though in most cases a judgment obtained by fraud can be set aside only as against the person who committed or procured the fraud, this limitation does not apply to an action to set aside judgment granting probate of a will, inasmuch as a will must be either good or bad as against all the world[1].

1 *Birch v Birch* [1902] P 130.

Parties to a probate action and those privy thereto bound by the result

26.06 With these exceptions probate in solemn form cannot be impeached by any person who has been a party to the action, or who has been privy thereto. A probate action is, in a sense, an action in rem, and anyone who is aware of the probate proceedings and has an interest which would have entitled him to intervene, is bound by the decision of the court and cannot start a fresh action. It matters not that such a party subsequently wishes to claim in a different capacity[1]. And it is to be observed that a person having an interest need not be a party to a probate action to be bound by its results. If he was cognisant of it and had the opportunity of becoming a party, but was content to stand aside while others contested the action, he is precluded from reopening the case[2]. But if he did not at the time know of his interest and thus of his right to intervene he will not be bound by the action although cognisant of the proceedings[3]. Should the probate be subsequently called in by a person adversely affected by it, who was not bound by the decision, and be revoked, such revocation will enure to the benefit of parties and those privy to the first action, who were adversely affected by the revoked probate[4]. Use may also be made of RSC Order 15, r. 13A (see para. **28.04**, post) to obtain a direction as to service of notice of an action, relating to the estate of a deceased, upon any person who is not a party to the action. The persons served in accordance with the direction are bound by the judgment given in the action.

1 *Re Langton's Estate* [1964] P 163, [1964] 1 All ER 749.
2 *Newell v Weeks* (1814) 2 Phillim 224; *Ratcliffe v Barnes* (1862) 2 Sw & Tr 486. It should be noted that under NCPR 45(1) and (2) notice of a probate action is now given by the Senior Registrar to every person (other than the plaintiff) who has entered a caveat or who does so while the action is pending.
3 *Ratcliffe v Barnes*, above; *Young v Holloway* [1895] P 87.
4 *Young v Holloway* [1895] P 87.

Power to set aside judgment by default

26.07 Notwithstanding the fundamental principle that a party to a probate action is bound by the decision if he has had an opportunity to appear and oppose the proceedings, the court's power under Order 35, r. 2 to set aside a judgment given in default of acknowledgment of service is available in appropriate circumstances to a defendant who is, in the real sense of the word, absent, or who does not appear at the trial[1].

1 *Re Barraclough, Barraclough v Young* [1967] P 1, [1965] 2 All ER 311.

Jurisdiction of the court

26.08 The decision of the court, either on the title to probate or on the title to administration, is conclusive in all courts in England and Wales, and where the decision turns upon any particular question, such decision is conclusive upon that question as between the same parties. Thus, if the finding in an action for a grant of letters of administration turns upon the question which of the parties is next of kin or heir-at-law to the intestate, such finding is conclusive upon that question in an action for distribution between or succession to the same parties[1]. When a document has been admitted to probate, all courts in England and Wales must treat it as testamentary[2]. Where there is a question whether legacies or devises are cumulative or substitutive, and it is determinable by the circumstances of the bequests or devises having been given by distinct instruments, and probate has issued of 'a will and codicil', the form of the probate is conclusive of the fact of their being distinct instruments, though written on the same paper[3].

To enable the court to exercise jurisdiction, the question must fairly arise out of the suit for probate or administration—the issue involved in the decision must be fairly raised on the pleadings—all the parties whose interest can be affected by the decision should be before the court, and the court should be of opinion that the question it is asked to determine is ready to be and can be conveniently and properly decided between the parties to the pending action[4]. The court may not only decide on the title to probate but construe the will or make any other declaration normally obtainable in the Chancery Division.

1　*Barrs v Jackson* (1845) 1 Ph 582; *Bouchier v Taylor* (1776) 4 Bro Parl Cas 708.
2　*Re Barrance, Barrance v Ellis* [1910] 2 Ch 419, 103 LT 104.
3　*Baillie v Butterfield* (1787) 1 Cox Eq Cas 392.
4　*Re Tharp's Goods, Tharp v Macdonald* (1878) 3 PD 76, in which it was held, on appeal, to be the duty of the court not only to grant probate of the will of a married woman limited to such property as, under the law then in force, she had power to dispose of, but also to decide, so far as the evidence and pleadings would allow, of what such property consisted, and to add to the decree a declaration in accordance with its findings.

High Court

26.09　Contentious probate business in the High Court is by statute assigned to the Chancery Division[1].

A probate action in the High Court must be begun by writ issued out of Chancery Chambers (that is, the offices of the Chancery Division in the Thomas More Building, Royal Courts of Justice, Strand, London WC2A 2LL) or out of one of the Chancery district registries (that is, one of the district registries of Birmingham, Bristol, Cardiff, Leeds, Liverpool, Manchester, Newcastle upon Tyne and Preston)[2].

A probate action in the High Court may only be transferred to Chancery Chambers or to one of the Chancery district registries[3].

The practice is regulated by Ord. 76 of the Rules of the Supreme Court 1965.

1　Section 61(1) of the Supreme Court Act 1981 and Sch. 1, para. 1(h).
2　Ord. 76, r. 2(1).
3　Ord. 4, r. 5A.

26.10　It is unusual for a county court to try a probate action, even when it has jurisdiction (see Chap. 40). Except where otherwise stated, therefore, this Part deals with contentious probate proceedings in the High Court; and references to the 'court' are references to the Master (or, in a district registry, the district judge) or to the judge or to the court officer (as the case may be) at the Chancery Chambers or at the Chancery district registry, wherever the case is proceeding.

26.11　Practice directions relating to the practice and procedure in the Chancery Division are set out in Part 3 of Vol. 2 of the *Supreme Court Practice 1995*, pp. 158–189; and are hereafter referred to by the initials 'PD' followed by the appropriate direction number.

Procedure and case management in the Chancery Division are now set out in the *Chancery Guide*, copies of which may be obtained from Room E01 and Room

TM2.04 in the Royal Courts of Justice at a cost of £3 per copy. By a Practice Direction of the Vice-Chancellor dated 25 April 1995[1] the provisions of the *Chancery Guide* are to apply to litigation in the Chancery Division and in the case of any inconsistency between the provisions of the *Chancery Guide* and the provisions of any previous directions, the provisions of the *Chancery Guide* are to prevail.

1 [1995] 1 WLR 785.

County court

26.12 See Chap. 40, post.

CHAPTER 27

Actions

Summary

Different forms of probate proceedings

27.01   Actions in probate proceedings fall into three categories: (1) actions for pronouncing for or against a will in solemn form of law; (2) interest actions; (3) actions for the revocation of probates or letters of administration.

(1) Actions for pronouncing for or against a will in solemn form

Question involved

27.02   In these actions the question for the determination of the court is whether a will or other testamentary paper is or is not, in whole or in part, valid as a testamentary instrument.

Who may bring an action

An action can be brought by the executor (or other person interested under a will) for probate in solemn form (i) on his own initiative, or (ii) as the result of a step by some person opposed to the will. Alternatively (iii) a person opposed to the will can bring an action to have the will pronounced against.

(i) An action brought on the plaintiff's own initiative

27.03   The executor of the will to be proved, or failing him a residuary legatee or devisee, or other person interested under the will[1], may issue a writ of summons propounding the will and naming as defendants all persons whose interests are opposed to the will (e.g. all persons who would have a larger interest in the event of an intestacy or the executors and those interested under any other will of the deceased). In practice if there has been no caveat it is unlikely that an executor (or legatee or devisee) will commence a probate action unless he is aware (even without a caveat) of a current or potential argument over the validity of the will. If he is unaware of any such argument and if there has been no caveat the executor would simply seek a grant in common form.

1 If the will has already been proved in common form, the grant must be lodged in the Chancery Registry (*Re Riley's Goods* [1896] P 9).

(ii) An action brought as the result of a step by some person opposed to the will

27.04 The application for a grant in common form may be stopped by a caveat, in which case, after the caveat is warned and the caveator has appeared to the warning (see paras. **23.51** ff., ante), the writ is issued against him and all other persons, as set out above, whose interests are opposed to the will.

An executor or administrator with the will annexed may be compelled to prove a will in solemn form after having proved it in common form. So also may an executor who has intermeddled in the administration of the deceased's estate, i.e. done any act in relation to his estate showing an intention to accept the executorship, or any act which would make him liable as executor de son tort, for he cannot afterwards renounce the executorship[1]. Acts of administration of a minimal character will not be regarded as intermeddling[2]. But a person, other than an executor, who has intermeddled cannot be compelled to take a grant, and is entitled to renounce[3].

Except in the cases referred to in the preceding paragraph, if an executor is unwilling to accept the executorship he should renounce probate. If he has been served with a writ of summons, and is not disposed to be a party to a threatened action, but is not unwilling to take probate if the will is established, his best course will be not to acknowledge service, and if the will is established to apply for probate in common form. Service upon him of such writ has not the same effect as service upon him of a citation to accept or refuse probate under s. 112 of the Supreme Court Act 1981[4], non-appearance to which results in his right to the executorship wholly ceasing[5].

Similarly, a person entitled to a grant of administration with the will annexed may stand aside and not be a party to an action, and yet take a grant if the will is pronounced for.

When an executor fails to acknowledge service to such writ of summons, it is, of course, open to the party entitled to the residue, or a legatee or devisee named in the will, or for the personal representatives of such persons, to acknowledge service and defend the action.

1 *Jackson and Wallington v Whitehead* (1821) 3 Phillim 577.
2 *Holder v Holder* [1968] Ch 353, [1968] 1 All ER 665.
3 *Re Davis' Goods* (1860) 4 Sw & Tr 213; *Re Fell's Goods* (1861) 2 Sw & Tr 126.
4 See p. 844, post.
5 Administration of Estates Act 1925, s. 5 (see p. 746, post).

27.05 *Parties who may compel proof of will in solemn form.* The following persons may put an executor, or other person interested under a will, to proof of that will in solemn form:

1. *Widow or husband and other persons entitled on an intestacy.* The widow or husband of the deceased, or other persons entitled to share in his estate in the event of an intestacy, or the personal representative of any of these. If the deceased died without relation entitled to his estate, (a) domiciled in the Duchy of Lancaster, or, if domiciled abroad, possessed of property there, the Solicitor for the Duchy of Lancaster; (b) domiciled in the Duchy of Cornwall, or, if domiciled abroad, possessed of property there, the Solicitor for the Duchy of Cornwall; (c) wherever else domiciled, the Treasury Solicitor; since, in the event of an intestacy, the property in England may vest in the Crown notwithstanding that the deceased was domiciled abroad. Where an intestate dies domiciled abroad leaving successors in accordance with the law of the foreign domicile such successors take the estate[1]. If there are no such successors the Treasury Solicitor takes as bona vacantia[2].

2. *A legatee in the will.* A legatee or devisee (or his personal representative) named in the will in question, if the person propounding the will intends to submit that the legacy or the clause comprising it is not testamentary, or not valid, and seeks to have it omitted from the probate.

3. *An executor or beneficiary under any other testamentary instrument.* An executor or a legatee, or devisee, who is named in any other testamentary instrument of the deceased and whose interest is adversely affected by the will in question, or the personal representative of any of these. But a legatee who has received his legacy and afterwards disputes the will under which he received it may be called upon to pay the amount of his legacy into court[3].

1 *Re Maldonado's Estate, State of Spain v Treasury Solicitor* [1954] P 223, [1953] 2 All ER 300.
2 *Re Barnett's Trusts* [1902] 1 Ch 847.
3 *Bell v Armstrong* (1822) 1 Add 365 at 374; *Braham v Burchell* (1826) 3 Add 243 at 256. It has been held that where the legatee who has been paid is under age, he cannot be compelled to lodge his legacy in court (*Goddard v Norton* (1846) 5 Notes of Cases 76).

27.06   *When proof in solemn form may be required.* The above persons may put an executor, or other person interested under a will, to proof in solemn form either before or after probate has been taken in common form, but the following two, by reason of their particular status, can only do so before, and not after, probate in common form has issued, namely:

4. *A creditor.* A creditor to whom administration has been granted[1].

5. *An appointee of the court.* Any other person in possession of a grant of administration, as appointee of the court, e.g., by order under s. 116 of the Supreme Court Act 1981, but not having a beneficial interest in the estate.

1 *Menzies v Pulbrook and Ker* (1841) 2 Curt 845 at 851.

(iii) Where a person opposed to the will wishes to bring the action

27.07   Cases occur in practice in which the persons interested under a will purposely refrain from establishing it; and where it is essential in the interests of those who are opposed to the will that it should be pronounced against by a decree of the court, the persons opposed to the will may institute an action claiming a pronouncement against the will on the ground of invalidity.

27.08   *Examination of attesting witnesses.* At the hearing of any cause the court must be satisfied, upon the examination of one or more of the attesting witnesses (if available), of the due execution of the will; although if a satisfactory explanation is given for the failure to trace the witnesses, so that no adverse inference can be drawn from their absence, the will may be pronounced for without their evidence[1]. To prove the due execution of a will, it is necessary to examine one only of the attesting witnesses, provided that his evidence establishes due execution[2]. If the witness called fails to prove its due execution, then the party propounding the will is bound to call the other attesting witness, notwithstanding that he may be an adverse or hostile witness[3]. Even though both witnesses give evidence of incorrect execution, rebutting evidence may be admitted[4].

But when a party is compelled to call the attesting witnesses to a will or codicil he may cross-examine them, as they are not the witnesses of either party, but of the court[5]. As such, they may be cross-examined not only as to due execution but also about collateral matters, such as testamentary capacity[6]. The court is, moreover, entitled (notwithstanding any privileged nature of the document) to see statements made by a witness to the solicitor for the party calling him, to the extent to which they deal with the attestation and execution of the will, and to require their production[7]. See also para. **36.05**, post, 'Statement of solicitor preparing will'.

If the court is dissatisfied with the evidence of the attesting witness examined and the other attesting witness is not called, it is competent to it to decline to grant probate of the instrument propounded.

The Probate Court has always done its best to elicit the facts of the cases it has to try without too rigid an adherence to the rules of evidence practised in other courts[8].

1 *Re Lemon's Estate, Winwood v Lemon* (1961) 105 Sol Jo 1107.
2 *Belbin v Skeats* (1858) 1 Sw & Tr 148.
3 *Owen v Williams* (1863) 4 Sw & Tr 202; *Coles v Coles and Brown* (1866) LR 1 P & D 70.
4 *Re Vere-Wardale, Vere-Wardale v Johnson* [1949] P 395, [1949] 2 All ER 250; and see para. **33.18**, post, and cases there cited.
5 *Jones v Jones* (1908) 24 TLR 839; *Oakes v Uzzell* [1932] P 19.
6 *Re Webster, Webster v Webster* [1974] 3 All ER 822n, [1974] 1 WLR 1641.
7 *Re Fuld's Estate (No 2), Hartley v Fuld* [1965] P 405, [1965] 2 All ER 657.
8 Per Karminski J, *Re Trotman's Estate, Trotman v Trotman* (1964) 108 Sol Jo 159, a revocation action in which he admitted an affidavit of due execution made 19 years earlier by an attesting witness who had since died, and also evidence of a conversation between that witness and the other attesting witness in which the former had said in effect that the testator had not made or acknowledged his signature in his presence.

27.09   *Proof by affidavit.* In an action for probate in solemn form, where neither of the attesting witnesses could be called, an affidavit, sworn by one of them in connection with an application for probate in common form, was admitted as sufficient evidence of due execution[1]. In an undefended action where the estate is of small value, it is entirely appropriate for the witness's evidence to be given on affidavit[2]. Where the action is unopposed and will be heard in the Short Probate List affidavit evidence is encouraged to save the costs of oral evidence[3].

1 *Palin v Ponting* [1930] P 185. See also *Re Trotman*, above.
2 *Re Baldwin, Fletcher v Roulston* (1964) 108 Sol Jo 921.
3 Ord. 76, r. 12.

27.10   *Will pronounced for.* If the instrument or part of it is found to be valid, it is entitled to be admitted in whole or in part to probate, and the court will pronounce for its validity. Upon this pronouncement, a grant of probate or letters of administration with the will annexed may issue in a probate registry to the executor or to a party entitled to administration with the will annexed, upon his lodging the usual documents to lead the grant. (For practice in obtaining the grant, see paras. **4.176** ff., ante, para. **38.14**, post.)

27.11   *Will pronounced against.* If the instrument is found to be invalid, it is not entitled to be admitted to probate, and the court will pronounce against its validity. A grant of probate of a valid testamentary paper, or of letters of administration if as a result of the action there is an intestacy, will, according to the circumstances of the case, issue in a probate registry, on the party entitled thereto applying for the same and lodging the usual documents. (For practice in obtaining the grant, see paras. **4.176** ff., **6.05**, ante, para. **38.14**, post.)

(2) Interest actions

27.12   Where the interest alleged by a person claiming letters of administration, or opposing a will, is disputed, the action becomes what is known as an interest action. The contest is as to the title under which a claim to a grant is made. Such a dispute may arise (1) as an incidental or collateral question in a suit where the interest of a person opposing a will is denied, in which case it may be tried separately from the main issue as to the validity of the will; or (2) as an original suit respecting the right to the administration of the intestate's estate.

By Ord. 76, r. 9(1), in a probate action, where the plaintiff disputes the interest of a defendant, he must allege in his statement of claim that he denies the interest of that defendant.

By Ord. 76, r. 9(2), in a probate action in which the interest by virtue of which a party claims to be entitled to a grant of letters of administration is disputed, the party disputing that interest must show in his pleading that if the allegations made therein are proved, he would be entitled to an interest in the estate[1].

The decision in an interest suit may involve an issue of pedigree or of legitimacy, but a prayer for a declaration of legitimacy may not be included in the writ of summons. Applications for declarations as to legitimacy or legitimation are now made under s. 56 of the Family Law Act 1986 (as substituted by s. 22 of the Family Law Reform Act 1987) and any such declaration may be made only under that section (Family Law Act 1986, s. 58(4)). Any application for a declaration under s. 56 of the Act of 1986 must be made in the form prescribed by rules of court (Family Law Act 1986, s. 60(1)) and r. 3.15 of the Family Proceedings Rules 1991 sets out what should normally be contained in a petition beginning proceedings for such a declaration. The proceedings should be brought in the Family Division or in a county court.

Where an interest action has been heard and determined by the court, the parties, or those claiming through them, cannot afterwards reopen the same question in any other court. The restriction, however, does not extend to other persons whose interest is almost identical with that of one of the parties to the first suit, if they do not actually claim through such parties[2].

---

1 As to subsequent denial of interest, see *Inkson v Jeeves* (1863) 3 Sw & Tr 39.
2 *Spencer v Williams* (1871) LR 2 P & D 230; *Barrs v Jackson* (1845) 1 Ph 582.

(3) Actions for revocation of grants

Actions for revocation when a will has been proved

27.13 An action for the revocation of probate, or administration with will, is instituted when a will has been proved in common form, and it is alleged that the will is invalid, or that the grant was improperly obtained, e.g. by a person not entitled. Cases of the first type, if defended, become actions for proof in solemn form.

A bare executor who has taken probate in common form, or his executor, cannot afterwards take proceedings to contest the validity of the will (except for very special reasons in the interest of justice), as he has no interest in doing so and has no status except under the will[1], but an executor who has a personal interest in the estate (e.g. as next of kin), and who has taken probate, even with knowledge of all the facts, may, if a reasonable explanation be given for his having done so, afterwards institute proceedings for a pronouncement against the will[2].

1 *Re Chamberlain's Goods* (1867) LR 1 P & D 316.
2 *Williams v Evans* [1911] P 175.

Actions for revocation of letters of administration

27.14 An action for the revocation of letters of administration is instituted: (1) On the allegation that they were granted to a person without sufficient title to the grant[1]. The object of such a suit is to compel the party who has obtained the grant of administration to establish such a degree of relationship with the deceased as will entitle him to the grant, and in the result it becomes an interest suit. (2) On the discovery of a will, the validity of which is not admitted by the grantee. This may necessitate an action for the revocation of the grant and for a pronouncement in favour of the will.

1 A grant to the Crown, and the order authorising it, may be revoked by a district judge's or a registrar's order, if kin are discovered. See para. **24.86**, ante. See also Chap. 17, as to the jurisdiction of the district judge or registrar to revoke a grant.

Lodgment of grant

27.15 In an action for the revocation of a grant of probate or of letters of administration, unless the grant has been lodged in the Principal Registry or a district registry, the person to whom the grant was made, if the plaintiff, must lodge the grant at court within seven days of the issue of the writ[1]. If the defendant has the grant in his possession or under his control he must lodge it at court within 14 days after service of the writ on him[2]. The plaintiff should allege in the indorsement of his claim on the writ of summons, and in his statement of claim, the ground for revoking the grant, e.g. the invalidity of the will, or the defendant's want of interest.

No copy of the grant may issue, without leave, after the writ has been issued until the action has been concluded.

1 Ord. 76, r. 4(1)(a). For 'court' see para. **26.10**, ante.
2 Ibid., r. 4(1)(b). For 'court' see para. **26.10**, ante.

Subpoena to bring in script

Production of testamentary papers

27.16   A person who is shown to have any testamentary document in his possession or under his control may be compelled to bring the same into the court.

Section 123 of the Supreme Court Act 1981[1] provides that where it appears that any person has in his possession, custody or power any document which is or purports to be a testamentary document the court may, whether or not any legal proceedings are pending, issue a subpoena requiring him to bring in the document in such manner as the court may in the subpoena direct.

Where a probate action has been commenced, any application under this Act shall be for the issue of a subpoena requiring a person to bring the testamentary paper into the court[2]. The application is made ex parte to the appropriate Master supported by an affidavit setting out the grounds for the application[3]. The Master will authorise the issue of a subpoena accordingly[4] (Form of subpoena, CP51). Any person against whom a subpoena is issued, who denies that the testamentary paper is in his possession, may file an affidavit to that effect[5].

The subpoena must be personally served, indorsed with the penal notice[6].

It is very doubtful whether a subpoena to bring in a script can issue for service out of the jurisdiction. In *Hamborough* (motion, November 1894), the President adjourned, until an action had been brought, an application for leave to issue a subpoena duces tecum for service in Scotland against a person retaining a will. The Irish Court of Appeal in January 1894, in *Ambrose*, decided that where there was no action or suit the court had no power to issue a subpoena for service in England. The decision had reference to a similar section in the Irish Probate Court Act; but in *Matthews* the judge ordered that a subpoena to bring in a script should issue against a person resident in Belfast[7].

If the subpoena be disobeyed, it may be enforced by committal.

But the court will not necessarily commit a person disobeying a subpoena of this nature. It may make an order that he shall attend in court to be examined in reference to his possession of the paper in question[8].

See also Ord. 32, r. 15, RSC.

1   See p. 847, post.
2   Ord. 76, r. 13(3); for 'court' see para. **26.10**, ante.
3   Ibid., r. 13(4).
4   Ibid., r. 13(5).
5   Ibid., r. 13(6).
6   Ord. 45, r. 7.
7   *Re Matthews* (1941) April (motion).
8   *Parkinson v Thornton* (1867) 37 LJPM & A 3.

Examination of party

27.17   By s. 122(1) of the Supreme Court Act 1981, when it appears that there are reasonable grounds for believing that any person has knowledge of any document which is, or purports to be, a testamentary document, the court may, whether or not any legal proceedings are pending, order him to attend for the purposes of being examined in open court.

By s. 122(2) of the same Act the court may:

(a)   require any person who is before it in compliance with an order under sub-s. (1) to answer any question relating to the document concerned; and

(b)   if appropriate, order him to bring in the document in such manner as the court may direct.

By s. 122(3) any person who, having been required by the court to do so, fails to attend for examination, answer any question or bring in any document shall be guilty of contempt of court.

This statutory examination cannot be applied to attesting witnesses who have declined to give information as to the circumstances attending the execution of it[1]. But where attesting witnesses refused to make an affidavit of execution of the will the court has ordered them to attend in person for examination[2].

1   *Evans v Jones* (1867) 36 LJ P & M 70.
2   *Re Sweet's Goods* [1891] P 400; *Re Bays* (1909) 54 Sol Jo 200.

Where no probate action pending

27.18   As to the procedure to obtain a subpoena or an order to bring in a testamentary document where there is no probate action pending, see paras. **25.182–25.192** and paras. **25.215–25.220**, ante.

Limitation of actions

27.19   The statutes of limitation do not apply to the categories of action mentioned at paras. **27.01** ff., ante[1]. In seeking to do justice in actions in any of those categories, the court may apply the doctrine of laches (see paras. **33.78** and **33.79**, post).

1   *Re Coghlan, Briscoe v Broughton* [1948] 2 All ER 68, CA in respect of revocation and propounding. *Re Flynn, Flynn v Flynn* [1982] 1 All ER 882, [1982] 1 WLR 310 in respect of revocation.

Associated actions

27.20   The following three actions are not, strictly, contentious probate actions, but they have sufficient connection to the subject matter of a contentious probate action to warrant mention in this book. They are (1) an action for rectification of a will, (2) an action for the removal of a personal representative and (3) an action under the Inheritance (Provision for Family and Dependants) Act 1975[1].

For applications (in the course of a contentious probate action) for the appointment of an administrator pendente lite, see Chap. 37, post.

1   See Chap. 41, post.

CHAPTER 28

Parties to actions

Summary

Who may be a party

28.01   The foundation of title to be a party to a probate action is *interest*—so that whenever it can be shown that it is competent to the court to make a decree in an action for probate or administration, or for the revocation of probate or of administration, which may affect the interest, or possible interest, of any person, such person has a right to be a party to such a suit[1].

Such was the rule in the Prerogative Court of Canterbury as to the foundation of title to be a party to a cause in that court.

In an action for the revocation of a grant every person who is entitled to administer an estate by virtue of an unrevoked grant of probate or letters of administration shall be made a party to any such action[2].

The rules as to parties in probate actions are now contained in Order 76[3], and are dealt with in detail in the following pages.

1   *Kipping and Barlow v Ash* (1845) 1 Rob Eccl 270, *Crispin v Doglioni* (1860) 2 Sw & Tr 17.
2   Ord. 76, r. 3.
3   See p. 947, post.

Parties generally

28.02   Parties to probate actions are described as plaintiffs and defendants.

Plaintiffs

Joinder of plaintiffs

28.03   Order 15, r. 4(1) provides as follows:

'(1) Subject to rule 5(1), two or more persons may be joined together in one action as plaintiffs or as defendants with the leave of the Court or where—

(a) if separate actions were brought by or against each of them, as the case may be, some common question of law or fact would arise in all the actions, and

(b) all rights to relief claimed in the action (whether they are joint, several or alternative) are in respect of or arise out of the same transaction or series of transactions.'

(Rule 5(1) gives the court power to order separate trials or to make such other order as may be expedient where it appears that the joinder of two or more causes of action, or of two or more plaintiffs or defendants, in the same action may embarrass or delay the trial, or is in some other way inconvenient.)

Defendants

Joinder of defendants

28.04 Order 15, r. 4(1), quoted above ('Joinder of Plaintiffs') applies to the joinder of defendants as well as plaintiffs.

It is important in a probate action to ensure that all persons whose interests may be adversely affected by the relief claimed are either joined as defendants or served with notice of proceedings, in order that such persons may be bound by the decision of the court. When there are a large number of persons who might be affected by an order of the court, e.g. beneficiaries under two disputed wills, it is not always convenient to join them all as parties. In such circumstances the Master may by using RSC Ord. 15, r. 13A direct them to be served thereby allowing them to become parties to the action and in any event causing them to be bound by the result of the action (Form CP6, post). In certain cases it may be appropriate to apply for a representation order.

Representation order

28.05 Order 15, r. 13(1)(a) provides that in any proceedings concerning the estate of a deceased person (which includes probate proceedings) the court may, if it is satisfied that it is expedient so to do, appoint one or more persons to represent an absent person or class of persons if certain conditions are fulfilled. The conditions set out in paragraph (2) are as follows: (a) that the person, class or member of the class cannot be ascertained or readily ascertained; (b) that the person, class or some member of the class, though ascertained, cannot be found; or (c) that the person or class or member of class can be ascertained and found, but that it appears expedient to the court to exercise the power for the purpose of saving expense.

Interveners

Court of Probate

28.06 In the Prerogative Court of Canterbury, and subsequently in the Court of Probate, when a suit was pending, a person whose interest might by possibility be affected by the suit was allowed to intervene to protect his interest. He may now apply to the court to be added as a defendant. If, being cognizant of the proceedings and of an interest enabling him to intervene, such a person fails to apply, he will be bound by the proceedings, although not a party[1]. This does not apply where the parties to a suit compromise it and the decree is founded on a compromise to which he is not a party[2]. An interest, acquired after the death of the deceased, by purchase of part of the estate from the administrator, has been held sufficient to entitle a person to intervene in a suit for revocation of letters of administration[3].

1 *Wytcherley v Andrews* (1871) LR 2 P & D 327; *Young v Holloway* [1895] P 87.
2 *Wytcherley v Andrews* (1871) LR 2 P & D 327.
3 *Lindsay v Lindsay* (1872) LR 2 P & D 459.

Interveners take the action as they find it

28.07 Interveners took the cause as they found it at the time of their intervention. Hence they could *of right* take only such steps, as from the time of their intervention, as they might have done had they been parties in the first instance, or had their intervention occurred at an earlier stage of the cause. An intervener could not, therefore, of right, when a cause was formally concluded by the publication of evidence, give a plea in the cause, but the court might allow him to do so ex gratia on cause shown[1].

1 *Clements v Rhodes* (1825) 3 Add 37 at 40.

Application for leave to intervene

28.08 Application for leave to intervene is made by summons to the Master, supported by an affidavit showing the applicant's interest in the estate of the deceased. The summons must be served on the plaintiff and such other parties to the action as are not in default of acknowledging service[1].

1 Ord. 65, r. 9.

CHAPTER 29

Writ of summons

Summary

Action commenced by writ

Rules applicable

29.01   The practice in probate actions is prescribed by Order 76 of the Rules of the Supreme Court 1965[1], and the remainder of those Rules apply in relation to probate causes and matters, subject to any special provisions in Order 76[2].

1 See p. 947, post.
2 Ord. 76, r. 1(1).

Writ of summons

29.02   A probate action in the High Court must be begun by writ of summons issued out of Chancery Chambers (that is, the offices of the Chancery Division in the Thomas More Building, Royal Courts of Justice, Strand, London WC2A 2LL) or out of one of the Chancery district registries (that is, one of the district registries of Birmingham, Bristol, Cardiff, Leeds, Liverpool, Manchester, Newcastle upon Tyne and Preston)[1].

1 Ibid., r. 2(1).

Notice to caveators: grant may not issue during currency of probate action

29.03   On the commencement of a probate action notice thereof is given by the Senior District Judge of the Principal Registry of the Family Division to every caveator whose caveat is then in force (except the plaintiff, if he has entered a caveat). Similar notice is given to any person who subsequently enters a caveat at any time when the action is pending (NCPR 45).

Unless otherwise directed by order on summons, whether or not any caveat has been entered, the commencement of a probate action operates to prevent the sealing of a grant (other than a grant of administration pending suit) until application for a grant is made by the person shown to be entitled thereto by the decision of the court in the action (NCPR 45).

(As to caveats generally, see Chap. 23.)

Action for revocation of grant: grant to be called in

29.04   When at the commencement of an action for the revocation of a grant of probate or letters of administration the probate or letters of administration has not been lodged at the Principal Registry or district probate registry, if the action is commenced by the person to whom the grant was made, he must lodge the grant at court within seven days of the issue of the writ[1]. If any defendant has the grant he must lodge it at court within fourteen days after the service of the writ on him[2]. Any person who fails to comply with the above provisions may be ordered to lodge the grant within a specified time and will not be entitled to take any step in the action without the leave of the court until he has complied with the order[3].

1 RSC Ord. 76, r. 4(1). For 'the court' see para. **26.10**, ante.
2 Ibid., r. 4(1)(b).
3 Ibid., r. 4(2).

Who may issue a writ

29.05   Where a caveat has been warned and an appearance to the warning has been entered, it is open to either side to issue a writ of summons, although it is usual for the person who warned the caveat to do so.

Heading of writ

29.06   A writ of summons in a probate action must (by PD (23)—see para. **26.11.**, ante) be headed with the name of the deceased as well as the names of the parties, thus:

In the High Court of Justice
Chancery Division   (Probate)
In the estate of AB, deceased.
　　　Between   CD   Plaintiff
　　　　　and   EF   Defendant.

Date

29.07   Every writ of summons must show the date on which it is issued.

Indorsements

Indorsement of interests and claim

29.08   Before issue, a writ beginning a probate action must be indorsed with a statement of the nature of the interest of the plaintiff and of the defendant in the estate of the deceased to which the action relates[1], and with a statement of claim or, if the statement of claim is not indorsed, with a concise statement of the nature of the claim made, or the relief or remedy required, in the action[2].

1 Ord. 76, r. 2(2)(a).
2 Ord. 6, r. 2(1)(a).

Plaintiff's interest

29.09   The indorsement should show in what character the plaintiff claims, and the nature of his interest in the estate of the deceased, e.g. as executor, residuary legatee or devisee, legatee or devisee, creditor, as entitled under an intestacy, etc.

Defendant's interest

29.10   The character in which the defendant is sued, and the nature of his interest, must similarly be indorsed on the writ.

Forms of indorsement

29.11   See Forms CP13 ff.

Party acting in representative capacity

29.12   Where the plaintiff sues, or the defendant is sued, in a representative capacity, the indorsement must include a statement of such capacity[1].

1   Ord. 76, r. 3(1).

Considerations in settling indorsement of claim

29.13   In settling the indorsement of claim, it is of importance to consider:

(1) *Who are entitled to defend the action, and whether all or some of them only shall be made defendants to the writ*

29.14   When the action arises from the entry of a caveat, the indorsement of the defendant's interest follows that disclosed in his appearance to the warning, but all parties whose interests are, or may by any possibility be, affected by the judgment claimed should be made defendants in the action in order that every person interested may be bound by the judgment. If there are a very large number of interested parties it is suggested that only those with major interests should be made parties and that an application be made under RSC Ord. 15, r. 13A (see para. **28.04**, ante, and Form CP6, post).

(2) *The nature of the claim to be put forward*

29.15   In an action for proof of a will in solemn form, it is material to consider whether the plaintiff shall rely on one testamentary instrument, or whether he shall claim in the alternative, e.g. probate of an earlier will in the event of the last will propounded by him being pronounced against, etc.

(3) *The nature of the defendant's interest*

29.16   The indorsement of claim must show the grounds for bringing the defendants into the action, whether as interested in an intestacy, or under another will; and, if interested under another will, the date of the will and the nature of the interest should appear.

(4) *Whether it is intended to serve a separate statement of claim*

29.17   If a statement of claim is indorsed on the writ, it is unnecessary to serve a separate statement of claim after the defendant has acknowledged service. As in any event the nature of the interest of each party, and a concise statement of the nature of the claim, must be given, it is often the more convenient course to frame the indorsement in such a way as to render the service of a subsequent statement of claim unnecessary.

As to the contents of a statement of claim, see Chap. 32, post. Where a statement of claim is long or complex and may need amendment it is better to serve a separate statement of claim as if it is indorsed on the writ the writ will have to be amended and this entails obtaining the Master's fiat to amend and registering the amendments in court.

CHAPTER 30
Scripts

Summary

General 621
Affidavit of scripts 621
Inspection of scripts 623
Practice after decree 624

General

30.01 The requirement for each party to file an affidavit of scripts and lodge the scripts at court (as set out below) is most important. It allows the Master, initially, and later the judge to satisfy himself that the relief sought is correct (and that the plaintiff has not, for example, mistakenly asked the court to pronounce against will 'A' (an alleged last will) and in favour of will 'B' (an earlier will) without realising that there existed a valid intermediate will, which would be the valid will if will 'A' failed). The requirements as to scripts also assists the Master when considering the question which parties should be added (or notified of proceedings).

Definition of script

30.02 The expression 'testamentary script' is defined as a will or draft thereof, written instructions for a will made by, or at the request of, or under the instructions of, the testator, and any document purporting to be evidence of the contents, or to be a copy, of a will which is alleged to have been lost or destroyed[1].

1 Ord. 76, r. 5(5).

Affidavit of scripts

Plaintiff and defendant to swear affidavits of scripts and lodge the scripts

30.03 In a probate action, unless otherwise directed by the court an affidavit of testamentary scripts must be sworn by the plaintiff and by every defendant who has acknowledged service. There is a long established practice that where the Attorney-General is a party he does not have to swear an affidavit but a certificate signed by the Treasury Solicitor is accepted.

The affidavit must describe any testamentary script of the deceased whose estate is the subject of the action of which the deponent has any knowledge or, if it be the case, must state that the deponent knows of no such script[1]. In the case of any script which is not in the possession or under the control of the deponent, the affidavit must give the name and address of the person having possession or control, or, if this is not known, must state that the deponent does not know the name or address of that person[2]. Form of affidavit, CP3. Any script referred to in the affidavit and in the possession or under the control of the deponent must be lodged at court[3].

1 Ord. 76, r. 5(1)(a).
2 Ibid., r. 5(1)(b).
3 Ibid., r. 5(2).

Scripts to be 'described'

30.04   Every script which is in the possession or under the control of the deponent must be described in the affidavit[1]. No script must be marked in any way, even in pencil, and must not be stapled or transfixed with any pin or fastener, nor must it be exhibited to the affidavit of scripts.

1 Ibid., r. 5(1)(a).

By whom sworn

30.05   Under the terms of the present rule, the affidavit of scripts must be sworn by the plaintiff and defendant personally unless the court otherwise directs[1].

1 Ibid., r. 5(1)(a).

Time for filing affidavits and lodging scripts

30.06   Any affidavit of scripts, whether by a plaintiff or a defendant, must be filed and the scripts (including originals) in his possession or under his control lodged within 14 days of acknowledgment of service by a defendant, or if no defendant acknowledges service, before an order for trial is made unless the court otherwise directs[1]. Time runs for each defendant from the date he acknowledges service.

When a party lodges an original script he must at the same time and place lodge a copy thereof. If a script is not lodged by a party, e.g. when it is forwarded by the Family Division to the Chancery Division, the party relying on it must lodge a copy thereof at court before the first hearing at which the script has to be considered.

Photographic copies of scripts are preferred, but typewritten copies are acceptable. Such copies will be used by the Master and sent to the judge if the matter is set down in the short probate list[2].

It is usual to give the other parties notice of the filing of the affidavit.

1 Ibid., r. 5(2). In practice the court will direct the affidavit of scripts to be filed and lodged as soon as possible.
2 PD (19) C; see para. **26.11**, ante.

Supplementary affidavit

30.07   A party may, where necessary, be ordered to file a supplementary affidavit of scripts[1], or may file such affidavit voluntarily.

1 *Peacock and Peake v Lowe* (1867) LR 1 P & D 478n.

Pencil writing on script

30.08 Where a testamentary script or any part thereof is written in pencil, unless otherwise directed by the court a facsimile copy of such script or of the page or pages containing the pencil writing must also be lodged at court, having the words which appear in pencil in the original underlined in red ink on the copy[1].

1 Ord. 76, r. 5(3).

Inspection of scripts

30.09 Except by leave of the court, no party to a probate action is allowed to inspect the affidavit of scripts filed by any other party, or his scripts, unless and until he has filed his own affidavit of scripts[1].

Scripts may be inspected in the Chancery Registry (or Chancery district registry, as the case may be).

1 Ibid., r. 5(4).

Loan of scripts for examination

30.10 If a party wishes his expert to examine a script, his solicitor should attend the Master at ex parte time to give a written undertaking (as to safekeeping and return) against loan of the script for a specified time.

Copies

30.11 Copies of scripts may be ordered by parties to the action from the Chancery Registry (or Chancery district registry, as the case may be). They will be photographic copies except where the document is unsuitable for photography.

Verification of scripts

30.12 When the court orders trial on affidavit evidence it is necessary for an attesting witness to swear an affidavit of due execution, but the scripts are deposited at court. Either an attesting witness can attend at the court and swear an affidavit before an officer of the court, or the solicitor may bespeak from the court a photographic copy of the will or codicil. This will be certified as authentic by the clerk in charge of the office and may be exhibited to an affidavit of due execution in lieu of the original. The affidavit must state that the exhibited document is an authenticated copy of the original[1].

1 PD (19) A; see para. **26.11**, ante.

Transmission of scripts in cases tried outside London

30.13 The more convenient practice is for the action to be set down in London and then all the papers, including the scripts, are sent by the court to the district registrar concerned.

If the action is set down in the district registry the solicitor must forthwith notify the Chancery Registry in writing and ask that the scripts be forwarded to the district registrar[1].

Now that probate actions can (after 1992) be commenced in a Chancery district registry the occasions on which the practice set out in the previous two paragraphs will need to be invoked will be very rare.

1   PD (19) B; see para. **26.11**, ante.

Practice after decree

30.14   Immediately after an order leading to a grant or revocation of a grant of representation has been passed and entered the court sends an office copy of the order together with any script required for the grant to the Principal Registry.

CHAPTER 31

Pleadings generally

Summary

Practice as to pleadings

How indorsed and headed

31.01   All pleadings should be indorsed and headed:

'In the High Court of Justice.
　　Chancery Division (Probate).
　　　In the Estate of AB, deceased
　　　　CB against BD'.

A pleading must bear on its face the year of issue of the writ and the letter and number of the action, the description of the pleading and the date on which it was served[1]. It must be indorsed with the name or firm and business address of the solicitor by whom it was served and, where that solicitor is the agent of another, the name or firm and business address of his principal. A party acting in person must indorse his own name and address[2]. A pleading should also be indorsed with the title and action number of the suit and with the name of the court.

1 Order 18, r. 6(1).
2 Ibid., r. 6(4).

Signature

31.02   Every pleading must be signed by counsel, if settled by him, and if not, by the solicitor for the party, or the party himself if acting in person[1].

1 Ibid., r. 6(5).

Allegation as to condition of mind

31.03   Where a party pleading alleges any condition of the mind of any person, whether any disorder or disability of mind or any malice, fraudulent intention or other condition of mind except knowledge, particulars of the facts on which the party relies must be included in the pleading[1].

1 Ibid., r. 12(1)(b).

Want of knowledge and approval: nature of case to be specified

31.04   Without prejudice to Order 18, r. 7 (i.e. facts, not evidence, to be pleaded), any party who pleads that at the time when a will, the subject of the action, was alleged to have been executed the testator did not know and approve of its contents must specify the nature of the case on which he intends to rely[1].

1 Ord. 76, r. 9(3).

Want of knowledge and approval: other pleas to be specifically pleaded

31.05   No such allegation in support of a plea of want of knowledge and approval of the contents of a will as would with other facts in the pleading establish any of the following other pleas, i.e.,

(a)   that the will was not duly executed;
(b)   that at the time of execution of the will the testator was not of sound mind, or memory or understanding; or
(c)   that the execution of the will was obtained by undue influence or fraud,

shall be made unless that other plea is also expressly pleaded[1].

1 Ibid. Explained in *Re Stott, Klouda v Lloyds Bank Ltd* [1980] 1 All ER 259, [1980] 1 WLR 246.

Denial of interest

31.06   Where the plaintiff disputes the interest of a defendant, he must allege in his statement of claim that he denies the interest of that defendant[1].

Where any party disputes the interest by virtue of which another party claims to be entitled to a grant of administration, his pleading must show that if the allegations made therein are proved he would himself be entitled to an interest in the estate[2].

1 Ibid., r. 9(1).
2 Ibid., r. 9(2).

Undue influence

31.07   When in an action to establish a will the defendant pleads that the testator is of unsound mind, or that the will was obtained by undue influence, the plaintiff is entitled to have stated in the substance of the case particulars of the nature of the unsoundness of mind and of the character of undue influence, and the acts alleged in exercise of such undue influence with necessary dates, but not the names of the persons present. Particulars have been ordered of the deceased's incapacity to manage his own affairs[1].

1 *Re Earl of Shrewsbury's Estate, McLeod v Earl of Shrewsbury* [1922] P 112.

CHAPTER 32

Statement of claim

Summary

Rules and practice

Time for delivery

32.01   The plaintiff in a probate action must, unless

(a)   the court gives leave to the contrary; or
(b)   a statement of claim is indorsed on the writ,

serve a statement of claim on every defendant who acknowledges service.

Where service of a separate statement of claim is necessary, it must be served before the expiration of six weeks after acknowledgment of service by the defendant, or of eight days after the filing by the defendant of his affidavit of testamentary scripts under Order 76, r. 5, whichever is the later[1].

1   Ord. 76, r. 7.

Indorsement of claim on writ

32.02   Every writ beginning a probate action must be indorsed with a statement of the nature of the plaintiff's and the defendant's interest in the estate of the deceased to which the action relates[1], and wherever possible a statement of the plaintiff's claim should be included in the indorsement so as to avoid the necessity for service of a separate statement of claim.

The sequence of the pleadings and the times allowed for their delivery vary according to whether or not a separate statement of claim is delivered, and for this reason the plaintiff should decide at the outset whether a statement of claim is to be indorsed on the writ or served separately.

When a statement of claim is indorsed on the writ it should be specifically described as such, so that the defendant may be aware that the time for service of the defence runs from the last day of the time limited for acknowledgment of service. Where a separate statement of claim is served, the time for defence runs from the date of service of the statement of claim[2].

1 Ibid., r. 2(2)(a).
2 Ord. 18, r. 2.

Denial of interest

32.03 Where the plaintiff disputes the interest of a defendant he must allege this in his statement of claim[1]. If he does not do so he may apply to the court for leave to amend[2]. Further, where the interest by virtue of which the defendant claims to be entitled to a grant of administration is disputed, the plaintiff in his pleading must also show that if the allegations made therein are proved he would himself be entitled to an interest in the estate[3].

1 Ord. 76, r. 9(1).
2 *Medcalf v James* (1876) 25 WR 63.
3 Ord. 76, r. 9(2).

Default of acknowledgment of service

32.04 It is not necessary to serve a statement of claim on a defendant who is in default as to acknowledging service[1].

If no defendant acknowledges service the plaintiff may, after the time limited for acknowledgment of service has expired, apply on summons for an order for discontinuance of the action, or for trial[2].

1 Ibid., r. 7.
2 Ibid., r. 6(3).

Probate in solemn form

Wills under the Wills Acts 1837 and 1852. Due execution

32.05 So far as regards testators dying before 1 January 1964, with certain exceptions a will, to be recognised as validly executed according to English law, must be executed in accordance with the formalities required by the Wills Act 1837[1], as amended by the Wills Act Amendment Act 1852[2].

1 See p. 719, post.
2 See p. 726, post.

In relation to testators dying on or after 1 January 1964, the Wills Act 1963[1] provides a number of alternative tests, any one of which if satisfied entitles a will or other testamentary act to be recognised as well executed (see also paras. **32.21** ff., post).

The form of statement of claim propounding a will in solemn form is given in CP 23 as a guide for the formal parts only, as the indorsement would suffice as the statement of claim in a simple case.

In the following cases special averments are necessary in the statement of claim, to show upon what grounds the will is alleged to be valid.

1 See p. 777, post.

Wills valid under Lord Kingsdown's Act

32.06 The Wills Act 1861 (Lord Kingsdown's Act) is repealed as from 1 January 1964 and replaced by the wider provisions of the Wills Act 1963. This repeal does not, however, invalidate a will executed before that date[1].

The Wills Act 1963 does not operate in relation to persons dying before 1 January 1964.

For text of Wills Act 1861, see p. 727, post.

1 See p. 727, post.

Summary of reported cases

'British subject'

32.07 The term British subject includes naturalised British subjects (*Re Gally's Goods* (1876) 1 PD 438, 45 LJ 107), but does not include natural born British subjects who have become aliens by marriage (*Re Von Buseck's Goods* (1881) 6 PD 211; *Bloxam v Favre* (1883) 8 PD 101; affd (1884) 9 PD 130, CA).

'Personal estate'

32.08 The term personal estate used in the Act includes leaseholds (*Re Grassi, Stubberfield v Grassi* [1905] 1 Ch 584). The term also includes land vesting under a trust for sale (*Re Lyne's Settlement Trusts, Re Gibbs, Lyne v Gibbs* [1919] 1 Ch 80); but the form of the will is relevant in connection with immovables.

Change of domicil (s. 3)

32.09 By s. 3[1] (which is not limited to the wills of British subjects) a will, valid when made and valid up to time of change of domicil, does not become invalid by change of domicil (*Re Groos' Estate* [1904] P 269).

1 See p. 727, post.

Will made where by lex loci no specific form required

32.10 A will made by a British subject residing in a country where by the lex loci no specific form of will is required is valid under s. 2 of Lord Kingsdown's Act if it be proved that the courts of such country would have upheld the will (*Stokes v Stokes* (1898) 78 LT 50).

Prima facie invalidity by foreign law can be rebutted

32.11   Where the will of a British subject residing in a foreign country was by the law of such country prima facie invalid (owing to a mistake in the date), but by such law the validity could be rebutted by proof that the mistake was brought about by accident or inadvertence, it was held, upon proof of these facts, that it could be admitted to proof in England, although the courts of such foreign country had not adjudicated on the matter (*Lyne v De la Ferté and Dunn* (1910) 102 LT 143).

Wills of persons dying domiciled out of England and Wales

Death before 1 January 1964

Will of movables by foreigner domiciled abroad

32.12   To be recognised in this country as valid to dispose of movable estate, the will of a person dying before 1 January 1964, and not being a British subject, should be executed in accordance with the forms required by the law of the place of his domicil, in accordance with the maxim 'mobilia sequuntur personam'.

A form of statement of claim, showing the necessary averment, is CP26.

Summary of reported cases

'Foreigners'

32.13   'Foreigners' includes natural born British subjects who have become aliens by marriage (*Re Von Buseck's Goods* (1881) 6 PD 211; *Bloxam v Favre* (1883) 8 PD 101; affd (1884) 9 PD 130, CA). Cf. now the British Nationality Act 1981.

Law of domicil to be followed

32.14   The courts in this country will follow the law of the deceased's domicil, and will, if the foreign court has entrusted a person with the administration of the estate, as a rule make a grant to such person (*Enohin v Wylie* (1862) 10 HL Cas 1, 31 LJ Ch 402; *Re Earl's Goods* (1867) LR 1 P & D 450), and the grant would generally be given to the persons appointed by the foreign court, if they are not personally disqualified from taking the grant, in preference to the executors named in the will, but not entitled by the law of the domicil (*Re Meatyard's Goods* [1903] P 125). But as to *validity* of the will it has been held that it is not enough to plead that it has been admitted to proof by the court of the domicil; it must be pleaded that it is valid by the law of that place (*Isherwood v Cheetham* (1862) 2 Sw & Tr 607). If the will has been formally recognised and acted upon by the court of competent jurisdiction in the country of domicil and remains unquestioned there, the English court of probate will not allow its validity to be litigated here (*Miller v James* (1872) LR 3 P & D 4: see also *Re Yahuda's Estate* [1956] P 388, [1956] 2 All ER 262). However, recourse need not be had always or necessarily to the courts, but always and necessarily to the law of the domicil (per Lord Selborne in *Ewing v Orr Ewing* (1885) 10 App Cas 453).

As to the system of law to be applied, and the burden of proof, in relation to various issues arising in probate actions in cases of foreign domicil, see *Re Fuld's Estate (No 3)*, *Hartley v*

Fuld [1968] P 675, [1965] 3 All ER 776. Where a British subject, domiciled abroad, left a will valid under Lord Kingsdown's Act[1], and no person had actually been appointed by the court of the domicil, probate was granted to one of the executors (*Re Cocquerel* [1918] P 4). But see *Re Meatyard's Goods*, above. (As to the practice in non-contentious matters, see Chap. 12 and NCPR 30.)

1 See p. 727, post.

Proceedings before foreign court—Stay of proceedings is this country

32.15 If proceedings are actually being taken before a foreign court, the English courts may order the proceedings in this country to be stayed pending a decision by such foreign court (*Trimlestown v Trimlestown* (1830) 3 Hag Ecc 243). But see *Re Cocquerel*, above. But where there is no dispute as to the foreign law and only the construction of English words is in qustion, there will be no stay ordered, and the English courts should decide all questions with regard to the assets of the deceased (*Re Bonnefoi, Surrey v Perrin* [1912] P 233, 107 LT 512).

Change of domicil

32.16 Section 3 of Lord Kingsdown's Act[1] applies to foreigners as well as British subjects, and it would seem that a will valid when made and valid up to the time of change of domicil does not become invalid by such change of domicil (*Re Groos' Estate* [1904] P 269); but a non-British subject cannot invoke the other sections of the Act to establish such validity; see also *Re Reid's Goods* (1866) LR 1 P & D 74, and *Re Martin, Loustalan v Loustalan* [1900] P 211, and 641. (As to persons dying on or after 1 January 1964, see Wills Act 1963.)

The standard of proof of an allegation that the deceased abandoned his domicil of origin and acquired a domicil of choice must be such as to satisfy the conscience of the Court: it is a serious matter not to be lightly inferred from slight indications or casual words (*Re Fuld's Estate (No 3), Hartley v Fuld* [1968] P 675, [1965] 3 All ER 776).

1 Repealed as from 1 January 1964: see now Wills Act 1963.

Change of foreign law

32.17 A will that was valid by the law of the domicil at the date of death of the testator will be admitted to proof in England notwithstanding new legislation under which it would not be valid; and notwithstanding that such new law professes to be retrospective (*Lynch v Paraguay Provisional Government* (1871) LR 2 P & D 268). (As to persons dying on or after 1 January 1964, see Wills Act 1963, s. 6(3).)

Real property in England

32.18 In the case of death before 1 January 1964, for a will (either of a foreigner or a British subject and wherever domiciled) to pass realty in this country, it must be executed in accordance with the Wills Act (*Freke v Lord Carbery* (1873) LR 16 Eq 461 at 466). Where a foreigner domiciled abroad left two wills, one executed according to the law of his domicil, dealing with his foreign assets and English personalty and appointing a foreign executor, and the other executed according to English form dealing with English realty only and appointing English executors, the court made separate grants (a) to the English executors limited to the real estate, and (b) a caeterorum grant to the foreign executors (*Re Von Brentano's Estate* [1911] P 172, 105 LT 78). See also *Re Cartwright, Cartwright v Smith* [1939] Ch 90, [1938]

4 All ER 209, and the motion thereon in the Probate Division, where the deceased was domiciled in England.

As to persons dying on or after 1 January 1964 see Wills Act 1963: a will executed in accordance with s. 1 of this Act is valid to dispose of immovable as well as movable property. See also s. 2(1)(b) of the Act as to wills of immovables.

Leasehold property in England

32.19   In the case of death before 1 January 1964, for the will of a foreigner domiciled abroad to pass leaseholds in England it must be executed in accordance with the Wills Act 1837 (*Freke v Lord Carbery* (1873) LR 16 Eq 461; *De Fogassieras v Duport* (1881) 11 LR Ir 123). As to wills of British subjects dealing with leaseholds, see *Stubberfield v Grassi* [1905] 1 Ch 584. Lord Kingsdown's Act may be invoked. It must be borne in mind that although leaseholds rank as personalty, they are none the less 'immovables', as are chattels real, mortgage debts secured on land in England, any interest in the proceeds of sale of land in England held on trust for sale, and any other immovable property in England. As to persons dying on or after 1 January 1964, see also preceding paragraph.

Wills made in exercise of a power of appointment

32.20   Wills exercising a power of appointment conferred by an English instrument are to be admitted to proof for the purpose, and to the extent to which they are an exercise, of the power, if made in accordance with the provisions of the Wills Act, even though invalid by the law of the deceased's place of domicil (*Murphy v Deichler* [1909] AC 446). See paras. **11.315** ff., ante. (As to persons dying on or after 1 January 1964, see Wills Act 1963, s. 2(1)(d) and s. 2(2).)

Wills Act 1963

Death on or after 1 January 1964 only

32.21   The Wills Act 1963[1] applies only to persons who die on or after the date of its commencement (1 January 1964), but applies to the wills of such persons whether executed before or after the commencement of the Act (s. 7(4)).

The Act is not restricted to British subjects, nor to persons domiciled in any particular place; and a will which is admissible to proof by virtue of s. 1 of the Act is to be treated as properly executed as regards the whole estate. There are additional provisions in s. 2 as to the admissibility of wills of immovable property, wills exercising a power of appointment, and revoking instruments or acts.

1 See p. 777, post.

General rule

32.22   By section 1,

'a will shall be treated as properly executed if its execution conformed to the internal law[1] in force in the territory where it was executed, or in the territory where, at the time of its execution or of the testator's death, he was domiciled or had his habitual residence, or in a state[2] of which, at either of those times, he was a national.'

1 As to internal law, see 'Internal law', para. **32.24**, post.
2 'State' means a territory or group of territories having its own law of nationality (s. 6(1)).

Additional rules

32.23   By section 2,

'(1) Without prejudice to the preceding section, the following shall be treated as properly executed—

(a) a will executed on board a vessel or aircraft of any description, if the execution of the will conformed to the internal law in force in the territory with which, having regard to its registration (if any) and other relevant circumstances, the vessel or aircraft may be taken to have been most closely connected;

(b) a will so far as it disposes of immovable property, if its execution conformed to the internal law in force in the territory where the property was situated;

(c) a will so far as it revokes a will which under this Act would be treated as properly executed or revokes a provision which under this Act would be treated as comprised in a properly executed will, if the execution of the later will conformed to any law by reference to which the revoked will or provision would be so treated;

(d) a will so far as it exercises a power of appointment, if the execution of the will conformed to the law governing the essential validity of the power.

(2) A will so far as it exercises a power of appointment shall not be treated as improperly executed by reason only that its execution was not in accordance with any formal requirements contained in the instrument creating the power.'

Internal law

32.24   Under the Act the law of any territory or state to be applied is its internal law, which is defined as the law which would apply in a case where no question of the law in force in any other territory or state arose (s. 6(1)); thus excluding any question of reference under the law of the territory or state in question to the law of any other place, and any question of renvoi. (See also s. 6(2) of the Act as to the position where there are two or more systems of internal law.)

Decisions of the court of domicil

32.25   It would appear, however, that when recourse is had to the law of the testator's domicil at the time of his death, a will which has been recognised by the competent court of that place as validly executed will be recognised in this country as valid, at any rate to pass movable estate, notwithstanding that the court of domicil may have applied some system of law other than its own internal law. This well-established rule of the common law[1] does not appear to have been superseded by the statute. There has, however, so far been no reported decision on this point.

1 See cases quoted under 'Law of domicil to be followed', para. **32.14**, ante.

Wills Act 1963 generally

32.26   As to the Wills Act 1963, generally, see pp. 777 ff., ante. Form of statement of claim under Wills Act 1963, CP27.

Privileged wills of soldiers and sailors

Under Statute of Frauds, 29 Car. 2, c. 3, s. 22

32.27   The privilege of making wills without the observance of the ordinary formalities was taken from the Roman law, and was expressly reserved to soldiers and sailors by s. 22 of the Statute of Frauds (29 Car. 2, c. 3), which, after providing that 'wills of personal estate shall be in writing or committed to writing within six days after the making of the same', excepted from its operation the wills made by soldiers in actual military service, or by mariners or seamen at sea, in these words:

> 'Provided always that, notwithstanding this Act, any soldier being in actual military service, or any mariner or seaman being at sea may dispose of his movables, wages and personal estate, as he or they might have done before the making of this Act.'

Under the Wills Act 1837, s. 11

32.28   This exception is retained in s. 11 of the Wills Act 1837 in these words:

> 'Provided always, that any soldier being in actual military service, or any mariner or seaman being at sea, may dispose of his personal estate as he might have done before the making of this Act.'

It is further extended by the Wills (Soldiers' and Sailors') Act 1918[1].

The latter Act applied to soldiers, sailors, marines, and members of the Air Force who died after 6 February 1918, notwithstanding that the will in question may have been made before that date (*Re Yates' Estate* [1919] P 93). By s. 1 it was confirmed that any person qualified to make a privileged will might do so under the age of 21 years. By s. 2 it was provided that a member of the naval or marine *forces* might take advantage of the Act not only whilst at sea, and the rules as to 'soldiers in actual military service' were applied to such members and, by s. 5(2), to the Air Force. By s. 3 power was given to dispose of real estate.

By s. 4 power was given to appoint a guardian of infants. Many of the limitations imposed by the reported cases hereunder prior to 6 February 1918 are therefore applicable only to persons who died prior to that date.

It should generally be sufficient for a statement of claim to be indorsed on the writ. For form of indorsement, see CP20.

This subject has been dealt with in Part I at paras. **3.312** ff., ante but the following short summary of decisions may be convenient. Those dealing with who may be considered 'a soldier', and what constitutes being 'in actual military service', must, as regards modern warfare at any rate, be read subject to the decision of the Court of Appeal in *Re Wingham*, and the decision in *Re Jones*, which are fully discussed in paras. **3.338–3.341**, ante.

1 See p. 733, post.

Summary of reported cases

Age of testator

32.29   Will valid if testator of age of 14 and upwards: *Re Farquhar's Goods* (1846) 4 Notes of Cases 651; *Re M'Murdo's Goods* (1868) LR 1 P & D 540; *Re Hiscock's Goods* [1901] P 78. A soldier under 21 years (now 18 years) may exercise by will a power of appointment vested in him (*Re Wernher, Wernher v Beit* [1918] 2 Ch 82).

What may be considered a will?

32.30 An unattested document or nuncupative will (*Drummond v Parish* (1843) 3 Curt 522). For cases of nuncupative wills, see *Morrell v Morrell* (1827) 1 Hag Ecc 51; *Re Scott's Goods* [1903] P 243; *Re J K Spark's Estate* [1941] P 115, [1941] 2 All ER 782. It is not necessary for a testator to have known that he was making a will if it is a deliberate expression of his wishes (*Re Stable, Dalrymple v Campbell* [1919] P 7). To constitute a testamentary act there must be a statement of wishes as to disposition of the estate, not merely imparted as a matter of information but intended to convey a request to see that those wishes are acted upon (*Re Knibb's Estate, Flay v Trueman* [1962] 2 All ER 829). But letters of a testator, stating that he had made his will, and outlining what he thought he had done with his estate, in fact erroneously, but showing no intention to alter his will, are not operative (*Re Beech's Estate, Beech v Public Trustee* [1923] P 46, CA; cf. *Re Macgillivray's Estate* [1946] 2 All ER 301, CA). If it is a clear statement of his final wishes, it is immaterial that it is spoken in reference to a will already made (*Re Spicer, Spicer v Richardson* [1949] P 441, [1949] 2 All ER 659). A will and two letters were admitted as expressing jointly the intention of the testator (*Re Vernon's Estate* (1916) 33 TLR 11); but see *Boughton-Knight v Wilson* (1915) 32 TLR 146. A letter, covering a will, containing alterations to be carried into a fresh will and instructions to destroy the will sent, was admitted to probate (*Re Beavis* (1941) motion). A draft will, not executed, was sent to a solicitor with a covering letter and a memorandum, both signed by the soldier, and indicating his testamentary wishes; the memorandum and the draft will were together admitted to probate (*Re Wood* (1941) October (motion)).

Revocation

32.31 A soldier's will is revoked by marriage (*Re Wardrop's Estate* [1917] P 54). A will, whether formal or informal, may be revoked by a letter or other informal act of a privileged person evincing such intention, without any new will (*Re Gossage's Estate* [1921] P 194, CA). But see *Beech*, above.

Proof of will

32.32 As to affidavit in support of application, see *Re Thorne's Goods* (1865) 4 Sw & Tr 36. As to alterations appearing in will, see *Re Tweedale's Goods* (1874) LR 3 P & D 204.

Who may be considered a soldier?

32.33 A surgeon (*Re Donaldson's Goods* (1840) 2 Curt 386; *Re Taylor's Goods* [1933] IR 709); a volunteer (*Re Hiscock's Goods* [1901] P 78); a member of a force of irregular troops (*Re Cory's Goods* (1901) 84 LT 270); a member of the Women's Auxiliary Air Force (*Re Rowson's Estate* [1944] 2 All ER 36, 171 LT 70); not a member of Home Guard, unless fully mobilised (*Re Anderson's Estate, Anderson v Anderson* [1944] P 1, [1943] 2 All ER 609); not a member of St. John Ambulance Corps (*Re Anderson's Estate, Anderson v Downes* [1916] P 49). But see *Re Wingham*, paras. **3.338–3.347**, ante and the following paragraph.

What is 'actual military service'?

32.34 In *Re Wingham, Andrews v Wingham* [1949] P 187, [1948] 2 All ER 908, the Court of Appeal held that these words meant '*active* military service', and that a testator was privileged if he was actually serving with the armed forces in connection with war operations which were taking place, or were believed to be imminent. Denning LJ stated, obiter, that a wider class of persons was covered by the term 'soldier', but gave no reason for this view. The basis of the decision in this case had no bearing on what *constituted* a 'soldier' for the purposes of the section. The following decisions are therefore retained, though some of them are no longer law at any rate as regards the war of 1939–45. See, further, as to this, the summary in para. **3.346**, ante.

In the following cases the testator was held to be privileged: *Re Hiscock's Goods* [1901] P 78; *Gattward v Knee* [1902] P 99; *May v May* [1902] P 103n; *Stopford v Stopford* (1903) 19 TLR 185; *Re Gordon's Goods* (1905) 21 TLR 653; *Re Kitchen, Kitchen v Allman* (1919) 35 TLR 612; *Re Booth, Booth v Booth* [1926] P 118. For older cases see *Drummond v Parish* (1843) 3 Curt 522; *Herbert v Herbert* (1855) Dea & Sw 10; *Re Thorne's Goods* (1865) 4 Sw & Tr 36. Testator had taken part in military operations and made a will while remaining in the district as escort to delimitation party. He was held to be still in actual military service (*Re Limond, Limond v Cunliffe* [1915] 2 Ch 240). See also *Re Colman's Estate* [1958] 2 All ER 35 (an officer, aged 19, serving in the British Army of the Rhine in Germany in May 1954 was held to be a soldier in actual military service, and a will made by him and executed in accordance with the provisions of s. 9 of the Wills Act 1837 held to be admissible to proof notwithstanding his infancy at the time the will was made). The exact conditions of service must be considered in each individual case (*Re Anderson's Estate, Anderson v Anderson* [1944] P 1 at 4, [1943] 2 All ER 609). A testator received telephone orders to join his battery on 25 August 1939 and made a will in privileged form. He joined next day. Held, that he was 'in actual military service', and it was ordered that the will be admitted as a soldier's privileged will (*Re Rippon's Estate* [1943] P 61, [1943] 1 All ER 676). See also *Re Jones* [1981] Fam 7, [1981] 1 All ER 1, where it was held that a soldier on operations in Northern Ireland in 1978 was on 'actual military service' and that an oral testamentary statement made by him after he had been shot and shortly before his death would be admitted to proof as a soldier's will without the formalities required by the Wills Act 1837.

For applications refused, see *White v Repton* (1844) 3 Curt 818; *Re Hill's Goods* (1845) 1 Rob Eccl 276; *Bowles v Jackson* (1854) 1 Ecc & Ad 294; *Re Phipps' Goods* (1840) 2 Curt 368. A will made in a military hospital one and a half years after returning from service was not admitted (*Re Grey's Estate* [1922] P 140).

Who may be considered a 'mariner or seaman'?

32.35   A merchant seaman (*Morrell v Morrell* (1827) 1 Hag Ecc 51); a surgeon (*Re Saunders' Goods* (1865) LR 1 P & D 16); a purser (*Re Hayes' Goods* (1839) 2 Curt 338). A female nurse employed by the War Office on leave from, but under orders to rejoin, a hospital ship (*Re Stanley's Estate* [1916] P 192). A female typist employed on a ship by a steamship company (*Re Hale's Goods* [1915] 2 IR 362).

What is 'being at sea'?

32.36   *Re Saunders' Goods* (1865) LR 1 P & D 16, 35 LJ 26; *Re Lay's Goods* (1840) 2 Curt 375; *Re Austen's Goods* (1853) 2 Rob Eccl 611; *Re M'Murdo's Goods* (1868) LR 1 P & D 540; *Re Parker's Goods* (1859) 2 Sw & Tr 375; *Re Patterson's Goods* (1898) 79 LT 123 (but see the earlier case of *Re Corby's Goods* (1854) 1 Ecc & Ad 292); *Re Thomas' Estate* (1918) 34 TLR 626; *Re Anderson's Estate, Anderson v Downes* [1916] P 49; but a canal pilot was held not to be privileged (*Re Barnes' Goods, Hodson v Barnes* (1926) 96 LJP 26). A captain of an Irish Channel ship made his will at his house on shore—held, he was not privileged when he signed the document (*Barnard v Birch* [1919] 2 IR 404). But a more liberal view was taken in *Re Newland's Goods* [1952] P 71, [1952] 1 All ER 841, and *Re Wilson, Wilson v Coleclough* [1952] P 92, [1952] 1 All ER 852. *Re Rapley's Estate, Rapley v Rapley* [1983] 3 All ER 248, [1983] 1 WLR 1069.

Extent of probate

32.37 On objection by the military authorities to the whole of a letter, such portion only as was testamentary was admitted (*Re Hey's Estates, Walker v Gaskill* [1914] P 192).

Duration of will

32.38 Return to civil life does not revoke, in the absence of any expression to this effect in the document itself (*Re Coleman's Goods* [1920] 2 IR 332). The rule of Roman law that a soldier's will is only valid for one year after his discharge does not apply to English law (*Re Booth, Booth v Booth* [1926] P 118).

Gift to attesting witness

32.39 The will requiring no attestation, gifts to witnesses are good (*Re Limond* [1915] 2 Ch 240); but see *Re Priest, Belfield v Duncan* [1944] Ch 58, [1944] 1 All ER 51, noted at para. **3.325**, ante.

Lost wills

Probate granted of a lost will

32.40 Where a will which has been destroyed in the testator's lifetime, either by himself unintentionally, or by any other person without his directions, or with his directions but not in his presence[1], or where a will has been destroyed after the testator's death or cannot be found, or where its disappearance is presumably attributable to accident, a copy or a draft of the contents or the substance of the will may be propounded, and the will may be admitted to proof as contained in such copy, draft, or substance until the original will or a more authentic copy thereof be brought into and left in the registry. (For common form practice, see paras. **11.11** ff. and **25.46** ff., ante.)

1 See the Wills Act 1837, s. 20 (see p. 723, post).

Statement of claim propounding a lost will. Contents

32.41 Where there is no draft or copy forthcoming, the contents or substance of the will should be set forth in the statement of claim. Where there is a draft or authenticated copy of the will to be propounded this must be described in the affidavit of scripts.

The essential factor is to ensure that the document which is said to contain the will of the testator, and which may ultimately be published as such, is fully identified throughout the proceedings.

Statement of claim. Form

32.42 For forms of statement of claim propounding a lost will, see CP24, and of indorsement, CP15.

A statement of claim propounding a lost will, in addition to the usual averment as given in the ordinary statement of claim, should allege:

(1)   That the said will was never revoked or destroyed by the testator, nor by any person in his presence and by his direction with the intention of revoking the same, and the same was at the time of his death a valid and subsisting will, but cannot be found.

(2)   That the contents of the said will were in substance or effect as follows: 'This is the last will and testament of me, etc.'—setting out the contents and substance so far as they are capable of proof.

See Wills Act 1837, s. 20[1].

1   See p. 723, post.

Summary of reported cases

Evidence

32.43   Secondary evidence can be given in proof of the contents of a lost will (*Sugden v Lord St Leonards* (1876) 1 PD 154; *Barkwell v Barkwell* [1928] P 91). Contents can be proved by one witness though interested (*Sugden v Lord St Leonards*, above) and the will may be pronounced for even if evidence of execution is incomplete (*Harris v Knight* (1890) 15 PD 170; *Re Webb, Smith v Johnston* [1964] 2 All ER 91, [1964] 1 WLR 509); and although the witnesses are not known (*Re Phibbs' Estate* [1917] P 93); but evidence must be of extreme cogency (*Woodward v Goulstone* (1886) 11 App Cas 469 at 475). The standard of proof required is the ordinary standard of proof in civil cases, i.e. a reasonable balance of probabilities (*Re Wipperman, Wissler v Wipperman* [1955] P 59, [1953] 1 All ER 764). Declarations, written or oral, made by testator before or after execution are admissible as evidence of contents (*Sugden v Lord St Leonards*, above), but declarations made by testator are inadmissible to prove either fact or mode of execution (*Atkinson v Morris* [1897] P 40, CA; see also *Eyre v Eyre* [1903] P 131 at 137); a declaration of the husband of a deceased, against interest, was admitted (*Re Adams' Goods, Benton v Powell* [1922] P 240).

Contents partially proved

32.44   Where contents are not completely proved probate will be granted to the extent to which they are proved (*Sugden v Lord St Leonards*, above). If part of a will has been torn out, the remaining part may be proved[1].

1   *Re Everest* [1975] Fam 44, [1975] 1 All ER 672.

Incorporation

Doctrine of incorporation

32.45   A testamentary paper, although unexecuted, may be entitled to probate by reason of its being incorporated in a duly executed one. Thus where a testamentary paper duly executed refers to a testator's wishes, or a document embodying them, as being in writing and being in existence at the time the will was executed, describing it in such terms that the document may be identified, the unexecuted paper is held to be incorporated in the duly execued one, and will be included in the probate (see also paras. **3.273** ff., ante). If it is claimed that a second page of a will, executed on the first page only, is incorporated by reason of an asterisk[1], the letters 'P.T.O.', or some similar indication, it would seem that such a reference must be *testamentary*—that is to say, above the signature, and not at the foot of the page. See also para. **33.12**, post.

1 *Re Birt's Goods* (1871) LR 2 P & D 214; *Re Greenwood's Goods* [1892] P 7.

Statement of claim

32.46 Where incorporation is relied upon, the statement of claim should refer specifically to the documents said to be incorporated, as well as to the incorporating parts of the duly executed instrument.

The statement of claim may in straightforward cases be indorsed on the writ.

Summary of reported cases

The document to be incorporated

32.47 The document to be incorporated:

(a) *must be in existence at time of execution (Allen v Maddock* (1858) 11 Moo PCC 427; *Wilkinson v Adam* (1813) 1 Ves & B 422 at 445; *Re Goodman* (1944) (motion)).

(b) *And must be described as then existing (Allen v Maddock*, above; *Van Straubenzee v Monck* (1862) 3 Sw & Tr 6; *Re Sunderland's Goods* (1866) LR 1 P& D 198). Therefore a document referred to in a will as a future document cannot be incorporated by codicil confirming the will (*Re Smart's Goods* [1902] P 238); but where a document is referred to in a will as being then existent, although in fact it is later in date, but before the codicil, it can be incorporated by subsequent codicil (*Re Truro's Goods* (1866) LR 1 P & D 201). It must be described as being in writing (*Re Goodman* (1944) (motion)).

(c) *And in such terms that it is capable of being ascertained (Allen v Maddock*, above; *Smart v Prujean* (1801) 6 Ves 560 at 565; *Re Almosnino's Goods* (1859) 1 Sw & Tr 508; *University College of North Wales v Taylor* [1908] P 140, CA; *Van Straubenzee v Monck* (1862) 3 Sw & Tr 6). Therefore where a codicil confirmed will and codicils, such general reference was held insufficient to incorporate unexecuted codicil (*Croker v Marquis of Hertford* (1844) 4 Moo PCC 339); but a coclicil on same piece of paper as an invalid will, described as a codicil to the last will, has been held to incorporate the invalid will—it being proved that there was no other will (*Re Heathcote's Goods* (1881) 6 PD 30; but see *Re Spotten's Goods* (1880) 5 LR Ir 403; *Re Willmott's Goods* (1858) 1 Sw & Tr 36; and *Re Phelps' Goods* (1849) 6 Notes of Cases 695). The document must be described in such a way that the court can be under no mistake (*Smart v Prujean* (1801) 6 Ves 560).

(d) *The will must not state that the document is not to form part of it (Re Louis, Louis v Treloar* (1916) 32 TLR 313).

Evidence, when admissible

32.48 If conditions (a), (b) and (c) are satisfied, parol evidence is admissible to ascertain what document is intended—the only question being sufficiency of such evidence (*Allen v Maddock*, para. **32.47**(a), above).

Evidence, when not admissible

32.49   Parol evidence is excluded if reference is to papers not yet written (*Allen v Maddock*, above); or if reference so vague as to be incapable of application to any particular instrument (*Allen v Maddock*, above; *University College of North Wales v Taylor* [1908] P 140, CA). Direct evidence of intention cannot be received (*Allen v Maddock*, above); *exception*, where reference could apply to one of two or more existent papers (*Paton v Ormerod* [1892] P 247 at 252).

Burden of proof

32.50   The burden of proof is upon party seeking to incorporate (*Singleton v Tomlinson* (1878) 3 App Cas 404; *Smart v Prujean* (1801) 6 Ves at 560).

Part of document incorporated

32.51   Only material parts of document need be incorporated (*Re Dowager Countess of Limerick's Goods* (1850) 2 Rob Eccl 313).

Incorporation excused on account of length of document

32.52   *Sheldon v Sheldon* (1844) 1 Rob Eccl 81 at 86; *Re Marquis of Lansdowne's Goods* (1863) 3 Sw & Tr 194; *Re Balme's Goods* [1897] P 261; document affecting third parties and in their possession (*Sheldon v Sheldon* (1844) 1 Rob Eccl 81 at 87). The practice is to file the document or an examined copy. (See para. **3.300**, ante.)

Alterations in wills

Obliterations, erasures, interlineations or other alterations

32.53   Where obliterations or erasures, interlineations or other alterations, are apparent on the face of the will, the question arises as to whether effect shall or shall not be given to them in the probate.

Section 21 of the Wills Act 1837 provides that:

> 'no obliteration, interlineation, or other alteration made in any will after the execution thereof shall be valid or have any effect, except so far as the words or effect of the will before such alteration shall not be apparent, unless such alteration shall be executed in like manner as hereinbefore is required for the execution of the will; but the will, with such alteration as part thereof, shall be deemed to be duly executed if the signature of the testator and the subscription of the witnesses be made in the margin, or in some other part of the will opposite or near to such alteration, or at the foot or end of or opposite to a memorandum referring to such alteration, and written at the end or some other part of the will.' (See also NCPR 14 and for common form practice, see paras. **3.222** ff., ante.)

In relation to persons dying on or after 1 January 1964, consideration should also be given to the Wills Act 1963. The expression 'will' is therein defined as including any testamentary instrument or act (s. 6(1)), and this term is wide enough to include an alteration to, or partial revocation of, a will. As to the Wills Act 1963, see paras. **3.392** ff. and paras. **32.21** ff., ante.

Form of statement of claim in cases of erasures, etc.

32.54   Where there appears upon the face of the will propounded an erasure, obliteration, interlineation or other alteration, a reference to such erasure, obliteration, interlineation or other alteration should be made in the statement of claim, and the party propounding the will should state whether he claims probate of it in its original or in its altered state.

The statement of claim should normally be indorsed on the writ. (Form of indorsement, CP14.)

Summary of reported cases

What are interlineations and alterations?

32.55   (1) Words written below signature before execution and referred to in body of will may be interlineations (*Re Birt's Goods* (1871) LR 2 P & D 214; *Re Greenwood's Goods* [1892] P 7); (2) the mere circumstance of the amount, or name of a legatee, appearing in different ink or handwriting does not of itself constitute an alteration, etc. The will may have been supplied to the testator with blanks purposely left in it, and then filled in by him in different ink: no presumption arises in such a case against the will having been executed as it appears (*Greville v Tylee* (1851) 7 Moo PCC 320).

Presumptions of law

32.56   In absence of direct evidence as to date, alterations, etc., appearing in will are presumed to have been made after execution (*Cooper v Bockett* (1846) 4 Moo PCC 419). This presumption may, however, be rebutted by proof or internal evidence to the contrary (*Re Adamson* (1875) LR 3 P & D 253 at 255; see also *Re Hindmarch's Goods* (1866) LR 1 P & D 307 at 308). As to declarations of testator, see *Doe d Shallcross v Palmer* (1851) 16 QB 747. This presumption has less weight when applied to alterations, etc., which might involve a question of revocation (*Benson v Benson* (1870) LR 2 P & D 172). Alterations, etc., appearing in a privileged will of a soldier are presumed to have been made during continuance of actual military service if there is no evidence obtainable, and are included in probate (*Re Tweedale's Goods* (1874) LR 3 P & D 204). A declaration, made by a testator *before* execution of a will, as to unattested interlineations is admissible (*Re Jessop* [1924] P 221). Where it is clear on the face of the will that it has been altered, the onus is on the person benefited (*Re Oates' Estate, Callow v Sutton* [1946] 2 All ER 735).

Obliteration, partial or total

32.57   If words obliterated can be read, they will be inserted in the probate unless shown to have been duly revoked (*Townley v Watson* (1844) 3 Curt 761 at 769). And if bequests are obliterated with intention of substituting others, and such other bequests fail, probate will pass of will in original form (*Brooke v Kent* (1841) 3 Moo PCC 334); but see *Re Zimmer's Estate* (1924) 40 TLR 502, as to the intention of the testator.

Means which may be adopted to decipher obliterated words

32.58   As to means which may be adopted, see *Ffinch v Combe* [1894] P 191. Physical interference with document may not be resorted to (ibid.). The use of infra-red rays is not within the Act; but in a case where slips had been pasted over parts of a will it was held that the doctrine of dependent relative revocation applied (*Re Itter, Dedman v Godfrey* [1950] P 130, [1950] 1 All ER 68), and it was permitted, on this footing, to remove the slips, if necessary, the revocation being ineffective (see para. **3.241**, ante).

Attestation of alterations, etc.

32.59   These may be in margin opposite alterations (see *Re Wilkinson's Goods* (1881) 6 PD 100); or at foot, or end of, or opposite to memorandum referring to the alterations (see *Re Treeby's Goods* (1875) LR 3 P & D 242). The initials of the testator and witnesses are sufficient (*Re Blewitt's Goods* (1880) 5 PD 116).

Alterations in will confirmed by subsequent codicil

32.60   Alterations, etc., in a will may be confirmed by the making of a codicil if it be proved that such alterations, etc., were made prior to the execution of the codicil (*Skinner v Ogle* (1845) 4 Notes of Cases 74 at 79; *Re Sykes' Goods* (1873) LR 3 P & D 26 at 28). The wording of the documents may show that the codicil is subsequent in date to the alteration, etc., in the will (*Re Heath's Goods* [1892] P 253).

Interest actions

32.61   For rules of pleading in interest actions, see Ord. 76, r. 9(1) and (2) and para. **27.12**, ante.

A form of statement of claim in an interest action is CP31.

Summary of reported case

Divorce: time at which decree takes effect

32.62   The deceased died between 9 p.m. and 4 a.m. on the night of 5/6 July 1965. A notice of application to make absolute a decree nisi granted to his wife was lodged at the registry at 8.30 a.m. on 6 July. The wife claimed administration as the widow, on the basis that the decree absolute was a nullity. It was held by the Court of Appeal that as the husband had died before the lodgment of the notice of application this was a nullity, and the district registrar had no jurisdiction to make the decree absolute. There was no justification for applying the old common law doctrine under which a judicial act related back to the earliest moment of the day on which it took place. The plaintiff, being the wife of the deceased at the time of his death, was entitled to letters of administration of his estate (*Kruhlak v Kruhlak (No 2)* [1958] 2 All ER 294, [1958] 1 WLR 606, doubted) (*Re Seaford, Seaford v Seifert* [1968] P 53, [1968] 1 All ER 482).

Forfeiture

32.63   A felonious act by a beneficiary, which causes forfeiture, may result in a partial or complete intestacy depending on whether the felon was only one of several beneficaries or the sole executor and beneficiary[1], and on whether the court will grant relief under the Forfeiture Act 1982.

1 *Re G's Estate, M v L* [1946] P 183, [1946] 1 All ER 579 and see paras. **25.133–25.149**, ante.

Actions for the revocation of probate or of letters of administration

32.64 The nature and object of actions for the revocation of probate or of letters of administration have already been briefly described (see ante, paras. **27.13** and **27.14**).

Contents of statement of claim for revocation of probate

32.65 In an action for the revocation of a probate granted in common form, the statement of claim should state—(1) The name, description, and residence of the testator, and the date and place of his death. (2) The fact that probate in common form (with the date of the probate) of an alleged will of the testator (with the date of the will) has been granted to the defendant in the Principal Registry or a district probate registry, and that such probate ought to be revoked. (3) The grounds upon which the revocation of the grant is sought should appear in the statement of claim, indicating why it is claimed. If there is no defence, this method is convenient as entitling the plaintiff to produce evidence at the hearing impeaching its validity, and the court, if satisfied with such evidence, will then be in a position to pronounce against the will. Where the plaintiff, who has called in the probate, relies on a prior will, he should propound it in his statement of claim, and the defendant in his statement of defence should propound his will in a counterclaim at the end of his statement of defence.

(For forms of statement of claim, see CP28 and CP29.)

Where the action is for revocation of a grant of administration with will, the statement of claim is on the same lines, with the necessary adaptations.

Contents of statement of claim for revocation of letters of administration

32.66 In an action for the revocation of a grant of letters of administration, the statement of claim should state—(1) The name, description, address, and date and place of the death of the deceased. (2) The fact of a grant of letters of administration having issued to the defendant, from the Principal Registry or a district probate registry, with the date of the grant. (3) The ground on which the revocation of the grant is claimed, either that the defendant was not entitled to the grant as not being interested in the estate of the deceased either by kinship or otherwise, and that the plaintiff is interested in the estate by kinship or otherwise[1], or that the deceased has died testate, and that the plaintiff has an interest in his estate under his last will; the plaintiff should in the last case propound the will, and claim not only that the court should revoke the grant of administration, but also should pronounce for the force and validity of the will propounded by him[2].

1 In such a case it is not necessary to allege that the grant was obtained by fraud: it is sufficient for the person claiming revocation to establish his title to the grant (*Re Evon's Estate, Evon v Stevenson* (1963) 107 Sol Jo 893).
2 See *Re Jenkins's Goods, Jenkins v Jenkins* (1897) 76 LT 164, where the administator was ordered to deliver an account, on the application of the executor under a will afterwards discovered.

CHAPTER 33

Defence and counterclaim

Summary

Service of defence

33.01   A defendant who acknowledges service and intends to defend an action must, unless the court gives leave to the contrary, serve a defence on the plaintiff before the expiration of 14 days after the time limited for acknowledging service or after the statement of claim is served on him, whichever is the later[1].

If the defendant needs more time to prepare his defence he should in the first instance apply to the plaintiff for further time. If this is not given he must issue a summons for an extension of time.

1   Ord. 18, r. 2(1).

Counterclaim

33.02   In a probate action, a defendant who alleges that he has any claim or is entitled to any relief or remedy in respect of any matter relating to the grant of probate of the will, or letters of administration of the estate, of the deceased must add to his defence a counterclaim in respect of that matter[1]. The alternative of bringing a separate action is not permissible in probate proceedings. If the plaintiff fails to serve a statement of claim any such defendant may apply by summons for leave to serve a counterclaim and the action shall proceed on the basis that the counterclaim is the statement of claim[2].

When a defendant joins another person as a party against whom he is making a counterclaim he must add that person's name to the title of the proceedings and serve on him a copy of the counterclaim. Thereupon that person becomes a party to the action and acknowledges service and pleads in the same way as any other defendant to the action[3].

It is now possible to counterclaim for probate in any other action[4]. A probate counterclaim must contain a statement of the interest of the defendant and the plaintiff in the estate of the deceased to which the counterclaim relates[5]. If the action is not in the Chancery Division the court will, if necessary of its own motion, transfer the action to the Chancery Division and to either the Royal Courts of Justice or a Chancery district registry (if it is not already proceeding in one of those places)[6]. Application may however be made within seven days after the service of a probate counterclaim for the counterclaim to be struck out under Order 15, rule 5(2)[7].

By section 20 of the Administration of Justice Act 1982 (see p. 854, post), if the court is satisfied that a will is expressed in any way that fails to carry out the testator's intentions in consequence of a clerical error or of a failure to understand his instructions it may order that the will shall be rectified so as to carry out those intentions. This can be dealt with by way of a counterclaim in a probate action or by separate proceedings. Except with leave of the court, proceedings must be taken within six months of the date of the grant of representation. See also paras. **3.250** ff., ante and para. **41.01**, post.

1 Ord. 76, r. 8(1).
2 Ibid., r. 8(2).
3 Ord. 15, r. 3(2): for Form of notice to be endorsed on counterclaim, see CP7.
4 Ord. 76, r. 15.
5 Ibid., r. 15(3).
6 Ibid., r. 15(5).
7 Ibid.

Notice of intention merely to cross-examine

33.03   A defendant may, with his defence, serve the plaintiff with notice that he merely insists upon the will of the deceased being proved in solemn form of law and only intends to cross-examine the witnesses produced in support of the will.

When such notice has been served, then, unless the court is of opinion that there was no reasonable ground for opposing the will, no order may be made for the costs of the other side to be paid by the party opposing the will[1]. (Form of notice, CP8.)

The notice must be served with the defence[2]. It may be conditional upon both witnesses being called[3], and includes questions as to the testator's knowledge and approval of the contents of the will. It does not follow, because a defendant fails, that there was no reasonable ground for opposing the will[4].

This rule does not apply to the case of a party applying for revocation of a grant[5]; and a plea of undue influence or fraud is inconsistent with the notice, but questions may be asked as to testamentary capacity[6].

If the opposing party is merely put to proof of due execution, but the notice is *not* given, witnesses to negative due execution may be called[7].

1 Ord. 62, r. 4(3).
2 See *Bone v Whittle* (1886) LR 1 P & D 249.
3 *Leeman v George* (1868) LR 1 P & D 542.
4 *Davies v Jones* [1899] P 161.
5 *Tomalin v Smart* [1904] P 141.
6 *Ireland v Rendall* (1866) LR 1 P & D 194; *Cleare and Forster v Cleare* (1869) LR 1 P & D 655; *Harrington v Bowyer* (1871) LR 2 P & D 264.
7 *Patrick v Hevercroft* (1920) 123 LT 201 .

Precedents of defences

33.04   The following are examples of the more usual defences in probate actions. No particular forms of defence are now specified by rule.

(1) Want of due execution

Form of defence:

33.05   'That the said will and codicil of the deceased were not duly executed according to the provisions of the Wills Act 1837.'

Onus of proof

33.06   The onus of proving that the will propounded was executed as required by law is on the plaintiff or party propounding it. The onus is a shifting one. It is for the person propounding the will to establish a prima facie case by proving due execution. If the will is not irrational, and was not drawn by the person propounding it and benefiting under it, the onus is discharged unless or until, by cross-examination of the witnesses, or by pleading and evidence, the issue of testamentary capacity or want of knowledge and approval is raised. The onus on these points is then again on the person propounding. As to other allegations the onus is, generally speaking, on the party making them.

As to the burden of proof and right to begin, see also para. **38.10**, post.

Form of defence

33.07   The burden of proof being on the party propounding the will, it may be sufficient simply to put him to proof that s. 9 of the Wills Act 1837[1] has been complied with; but where substantive allegations against due execution, supported by evidence, are to be made, the allegations should be pleaded, e.g.

(a)   That on the face of the paper, what purports to be the signature or mark of the testator dying before 1 January 1983 is not placed at the foot or end of the will—nor so placed as to come within the requirements of the Wills Act Amendment Act 1852[2]. (It should be noted that this requirement is relaxed for *deaths on or after 1 January 1983* by the Administration of Justice Act 1982: see p. 854, post.)

(b)   That such signature or mark was not made by the testator himself, nor by any one for him, nor in his presence, nor by his direction.

(c)   That it was neither so made nor acknowledged by the testator as his signature in the presence of two witnesses present at the same time.

(d)   That the two witnesses subsequently to the making or acknowledgment of the testator's signature did not subscribe, or acknowledge, their signatures to the will in the presence of the testator.

For form of defence pleading want of due execution, see CP32.

1   See p. 720, post.
2   See p. 726, post.

Forgery

33.09   The charge that the signature or mark of the testator is a forgery is also raised by this plea, but forgery itself should also be specifically pleaded[1].

1   Ord. 18, rr. 8(1) and 12(1).

Notice under Ord. 62, r. 6(1)(d)

33.10   Where it is proposed merely to put the executors to proof and only to cross-examine their witnesses, the notice as to such cross-examination must be served *with* the defence.

Pleas against validity other than under Wills Act 1837, s. 9

33.11   The will propounded may be alleged to be invalid also either:

(a)   Under the provisions of Lord Kingsdown's Act[1]; see also para. **32.06**, ante.

(b)   Under the foreign laws of the place of domicil; see para. **32.12**.

(c)   In the case of death on or after 1 January 1964 under the Wills Act 1963: see para. **32.21** ff., ante. For precedent of defence, see CP43.

(d)   As the will of a soldier, sailor or airman, under the Wills Act 1837, s. 11[2], and the Wills (Soldiers and Sailors) Act 1918[3]. For precedent of defence, see CP44.

1   See p. 727, post.
2   See p. 721, post.
3   See p. 733, post.

Summary of reported cases as to due execution

33.12   See also Part I, paras. **3.52–3.124**, ante and note the relaxation of the formalities of execution under s. 9 of the Wills Act 1837, as substituted by the Administration of Justice Act 1982, s. 17 (see p. 720, post) in respect of testators dying on or after 1 January 1983. See also paras. **27.08** and **27.09**, ante.

A. *Form of signature*

33.13

(a) *By mark* (*Baker v Dening* (1838) 8 Ad & El 94; *Re Field's Goods* (1843) 2 Curt 752); without name of testator beside it (*Re Bryce's Goods* (1839) 2 Curt 325); with correct name beside it, but testator wrongly described in will (*Re Douce's Goods* (1862) 2 Sw & Tr 593); with wrong name beside it (*Re Clarke's Goods* (1858) 1 Sw & Tr 22); by wrong or assumed name (to be treated as a mark) (*Re Glover's Goods* (1847) 5 Notes of Cases 553; *Re Redding's Goods* (1850) 2 Rob Eccl 339). By uncompleted signature—due to weakness (*Re Chalcraft, Chalcraft v Giles* [1948] P 222, [1948] 1 All ER 700). See also paras. **3.64** ff., ante.

(b) *By a seal* (inscribed with testator's initials) (*Re Emerson's Goods* (1882) 9 LR Ir 443).

(c) *By a thumb mark* (*Re Finn's Estate*) (1935) 154 LT 242.

(d) *Undecipherable scrawls* (treated as mark) *Re Kieran* [1933] IR 222.

(e) *By an impressed stamp* (*Jenkins v Gaisford and Thring, Re Jenkin's Goods* (1863) 3 Sw & Tr 93).

(f) *By initials* (*Re Christian's Goods* (1849) 2 Rob Eccl 110).

(g) *By another person at testator's direction* (signing either his own or testator's name) *Re Clark's Goods* (1839) 2 Curt 329; but a testator cannot adopt or acknowledge a signature pencilled beforehand by another person as an indication (*Reeves v Grainger* (1908) 52 Sol Jo 355).

(h) *By one of the attesting witnesses* (*Re Bailey's Goods* (1838) 1 Curt 914).

(i) *By the person who drew the will* (*Re Elcock's Goods* (1869) 20 LT 757; *Smith v Harris* (1845) 1 Rob Eccl 262).

(j) *By wrong or assumed name* (*Re Glover's Goods* (1847) 5 Notes of Cases 553; *Re Redding's Goods* (1850) 2 Rob Eccl 339).

(k) *By the words 'your loving mother'* (will held to be duly signed (*Re Cook's Estate, Murison v Cook* [1960] 1 All ER 689)).

B. *Position of signature*

33.14   NB *In respect of wills of testators* dying on or after 1 January 1983, *s. 9 of the Wills Act 1837, as substituted by the Administration of Justice Act 1982, s. 17 (see p. 720, post), no longer requires the testator to have signed the will 'at the foot or end thereof'.*

(a) *In testimonium clause* (*Re Mann's Goods* (1858) 28 LJP & M 19).

(b) *In the attestation clause Re Huckvale's Goods* (1867) LR 1 P & D 375; *Re Pearn's Goods* (1875) 1 PD 70; *Re Walker's Goods* (1862) 2 Sw & Tr 354; *Re Casmore's Goods* (1869) LR 1 P & EJ 653; signature on second page, all dispositions being on first page and not visible to witnesses (*Re Moore's Goods* [1901] P 44); testator's signature below those of the witnesses (*Re Puddephatt's Goods* (1870) LR 2 P & D 97).

(c) *Signatures held to be under, beside, or opposite the end of the will*—Entirely above last line with exception of one letter which touched it (*Re Woodley's Goods* (1864) 3 Sw & Tr 429); along lower part of edge of paper (*Re Jones' Goods* (1865) 4 Sw & Tr 1); see also *Re Wright's Goods* (1865) 4 Sw & Tr 35; on second of three pages, crossways (*Re Coombs's Goods* (1866) LR 1 P & D 302; see *Royle v Harris* [1895] P 163); beside last lines of will (*Re Ainsworth's Goods* (1870) LR 2 P & D 151); on third page opposite end of will on second page (*Re Williams' Goods* (1865) LR 1 P & D 4). In margin (*Re Roberts's Estate* [1934] P 102). In an oblong space drawn on right-hand side of the sheet and among the dispositive words (*Re Hornby* [1946] P 171, [1946] 2 All ER 150).

(d) *Signature on page containing no part of the will* (*Re Wright's Goods* (1865) 4 Sw & Tr 35; *Re Williams' Goods* (1865) LR 1 P & D 4; *Re Coombs' Goods* (1866) LR 1 P & D

302; *Re Fuller's Goods* [1892] P 377); signature in attestation clause (*Re Moore's Goods* [1901] P 44).

(e) *Signature on separate sheet of paper attached to will*—Signature pasted on will (*Re Gausden's Goods* (1862) 2 Sw & Tr 362; *Cook v Lambert* (1863) 3 Sw & Tr 46); attached to will by string (*Re Horsford's Goods* (1874) LR 3 P & D 211); sheets held together by testator at time of execution (*Lewis v Lewis* [1908] P 1; *Re Little, Foster v Cooper* [1960] 1 All ER 387, [1960] 1 WLR 495). Where a will is written on several sheets, only the last of which is signed and attested, there is a prima facie presumption (rebuttable by evidence) that all formed part of the will at the time of execution, even though the witnesses only observed the page they signed (*Gregory v Queen's Proctor* (1846) 4 Notes of Cases 620; *Rees v Rees* (1873) LR 3 P & D 84). Where a will was signed by the testator but the witnesses signed a duplicate, probate was refused (*Re Hatton's Goods* (1881) 6 PD 204).

(f) *Signature on envelope in which will enclosed*—A secret will, enclosed in a sealed envelope which was indorsed as to its contents and signed by the testator and wit-nesses, was accepted as valid under the Wills Act 1837 so as to pass real estate in England, on the footing that the two documents were sufficiently 'attached' to each other to constitute one document. It was valid by the law of the (Peruvian) domicil, and there were special circumstances (*Re Nicholls, Hunter v Nicholls* [1921] 2 Ch 11); in *Re Almosnino's Goods* (1859) 1 Sw & Tr 508, followed, though in that case the decision appears to have been based on the principle of incorporation. On envelope, signed by testatrix, the will being then signed by the witnesses and placed in the envelope (*Re Mann's Goods* [1942] P 146, [1942] 2 All ER 193). Held insuffi-cient where spaces in printed indorsement on envelope were filled in by testator, including his name, but he did not indicate that it was intended to be his signature to the will, or that the envelope was part of it; the will was then signed by the witnesses whilst the envelope was lying on the table, visible to them (*Re Bean's Estate* [1944] P 83, [1944] 2 All ER 348).

(g) *Signature in middle of will not necessarily good execution even of the part that pre-cedes it* (*Sweetland v Sweetland* (1865) 4 Sw & Tr 6: all pages signed except the last; *Margary v Robinson* (1886) 12 PD 8); unless the court is satisfied that the second page was incorporated by reference, or could be regarded as being in fact the first page of the will (*Re Anstee's Goods* [1893] P 283); but when a will was written on a printed form and the signature was on first page and will on following pages, it has been held that the signature was really on the last page and that will was duly exe-cuted (*Re Wotton's Goods* (1874) LR 3 P & D 159); see also *Royle v Harris* [1895] P 163; distinguishing *Wotton*; *Re Gilbert's Goods* (1898) 78 LT 762; *Re Coombs's Goods* (1866) LR 1 P & D 302; *Re Powell's Goods* (1865) 4 Sw & Tr 34 (will written on first two sides and part of third side of sheet of notepaper; attestation clause and signatures at bottom of second side, but testator's signature projected slightly on to third side. All three pages admitted to proof on the basis that paper was spread open at time of execution: if not spread open signature might only have referred to second side); and see *Re Smith's Goods* [1931] P 225 (but this case has not been followed). In special circumstances, where a codicil, which had been begun near the bottom of a page of the will, was continued and signed in a space immediately above its com-mencement, the words that were in fact below the signature were admitted (*Re Kimpton's Goods* (1864) 3 Sw & Tr 427); where the whole of the dispositions were on the second page, the front page being confined to the appointment of executors and the execution, whilst all the facts and the appearance of the document justified the presumption that the will began on the second page and was continued on the first— the whole was admitted (*Re Long's Estate* [1936] P 166, [1936] 1 All ER 435); see also *Re Staniforth's Estate, Gilbert v Heining* (1965) 109 Sol Jo 112. Words follow-ing signature may be included in probate if they can be regarded as interlineations or incorporated by reference in the will (*Re Birt's Goods* (1871) LR 2 P & D 214; *Re Greenwood's Goods* [1892] P 7; *Re Watkins's Goods* (1865) LR 1 P & D 19; *Re Dallow's Goods* (1866) LR 1 P & D 189; *Palin v Ponting* [1930] P 185); but in a will signed only at the foot of the first page, the mere fact that an uncompleted sentence, at the end of the first page, is completed on the second page, is not sufficient to justify admission of any part of the second page, in the absence of any reference, asterisk or other mark that can be deemed to constitute incorporation—even though it be established that the whole was written before execution (*Re Gee's Goods* (1898) 78 LT 843; *Royle v Harris* [1895] P 163); an unattested signature, subsequently witnessed under the words 'signed again in the presence', etc., the testator having then signed, was held a good acknowledgment of the earlier signature (*Re Pattison's Goods, Henderson v Priestman* [1918] 2 IR 90); but a will on one sheet with signature at the top was held invalid (*Re Stalman, Stalman v Jones* (1931) 145 LT 339, CA, followed in *Re Harris, Murray v Everard* [1952] 2 All ER 409—signature at top of right-hand margin; *Re Bercovitz's Estate, Canning v Enever* [1962] 1 All ER 552, [1962] 1 WLR 321, witnesses held to have attested a signature at head of will, not that at foot or end: will not duly executed; but cf. *Re Usborne's Goods* (1909) 25 TLR 519; *Re Roberts's Estate* [1934] P 102; signature in margin—*Stalman* distinguished). In *Re Beadle, Mayes v Beadle* [1974] 1 All ER 493, [1974] 1 WLR 417 a will was signed in the presence of one witness and inserted in an envelope. The envelope was signed on one side by the testator and a certificate by the two witnesses indorsed on the back. The court pronounced against the will. In *Wood v Smith* [1993] Ch 90, [1992] 3 All ER 556 it was held by the Court of Appeal that where the testator's signature was written earlier than the rest of the will, the will was nevertheless valid because the signature on the facts of that case was written as part of one transaction with the rest of the will. See also *Weatherhill v Pearce* [1995] 2 All ER 492, [1995] 1 WLR 592: name of testatrix in attestation clause in her own handwriting held a sufficient signature. See also paras. **3.64–3.84**, ante.

C. Acknowledgment of signature by testator

33.15 Witnesses must see or have an opportunity of seeing the signature (*Hudson v Parker* (1844) 1 Rob Eccl 14 at 40; *Re Gunstan's (or Gunston) Goods, Blake v Blake* (1882) 7 PD 102), or part of the signature (*Re Glass' Estate, Hosking v Hutchings* (1961) 105 Sol Jo 612); if signature was there, and witnesses had opportunity of seeing it, it does not matter that they did not actually see it (*Blake v Knight* (1843) 3 Curt 547; *Daintree v Butcher and Fasulo* (1888) 13 PD 67; on appeal 13 PD 102, CA); there is no acknowledgment within s. 9 of the Wills Act 1837 if will is folded up inside testator's coat pocket when he asks witnesses to sign, even though later each separately saw the signature when signing the will (*Re Groffman, Groffman and Block v Groffman* [1969] 2 All ER 108, [1969] 1 WLR 733); in the absence of proof as to existence of signature at time of execution probate may be refused (*Ilott v Genge* (1842) 3 Curt 160; *Fischer v Popham* (1875) LR 3 P & D 246); but as to absence of direct proof, see *Re Huckvale's Goods* (1867) LR 1 P & D 375. See also *Wright v Sanderson* (1884) 9 PD 149, CA. It is not necessary that a witness should know that the document signed is a will (*Re Benjamin's Estate* (1934) 150 LT 417).

33.16 *Acknowledgment may be verbal* (*Gaze v Gaze* (1843) 3 Curt 451; *Blake v Knight* (1843) 3 Curt 547; *Ilott v Genge* (1842) 3 Curt 160 at 172); or by gestures (*Re Davies' Goods* (1850) 2 Rob Eccl 337); or nodding head (*Re Hadler's Estate, Goodall v Hadler* (1960) Times, 20 October, cf. *Re Holtam's Estate, Gillett v Rogers* (1913) 108 LT 732); or by demeanour (*Faulds v Jackson* (1845) 6 Notes of Cases Supp i; *Inglesant v Inglesant* (1874) LR 3 P & D 172; *Re Jones' Goods* (1855) Dea & Sw 3; *Cooke v Henry* [1932] IR 574); or by proffering document as will (*Weatherhill v Pearce* [1995] 2 All ER 492, [1995] 1 WLR 592). See also paras. **3.85** and **3.86**, ante.

D. Presence of witnesses and testator

33.17 Signature must be made or acknowledged in the joint presence of witnesses (*Faulds v Jackson* (1845) 6 Notes of Cases Supp i); and before either of them has signed as witnesses

(*Faulds v Jackson*, above; *Cooper v Bockett* (1846) 4 Moo PCC 419; *Hindmarsh v Charlton* (1861) 8 HL Cas 160; *Re Davies' Estate, Russell v Delaney* [1951] 1 All ER 920; *Re Linley, McDonnell v Linley* (1949) 207 LT Jo 372); the witnesses must both sign in the presence of the testator (*first three cases above*); but need not do so in the presence of each other (*Faulds v Jackson*, above); for what constitutes 'presence' of the testator, see *Re Colman's Goods* (1842) 3 Curt 118; *Brown v Skirrow* [1902] P 3; *Jenner v Ffinch* (1879) 5 PD 106; *Carter v Seaton* (1901) 85 LT 76; it is not sufficient for testator to be corporeally present, he must be mentally aware of what is taking place when witnesses attest his signature (*Right v Price* (1779) 1 Doug KB 241; *Re Killick's Goods* (1864) 3 Sw & Tr 578). It is not essential that the testator should actually see the witnesses sign; it is enough if he might have seen them had he chosen to look. A will attested in an office while testatrix was outside in her carriage was upheld, because she might have seen what occurred through the office window (*Casson v Dade* (1781) 1 Bro CC 99); but where the witnesses left the room in which testator had signed and subscribed their names in an adjoining room, the door being open but testator not being in a position where he could see the witnesses, there was no due execution (*Doe d Wright v Manifold* (1813) 1 M & S 294; *Jenner v Ffinch*, above). See also *Weatherhill v Pearce* [1995] 2 All ER 492, [1995] 1 WLR 592 where, in the absence of contrary evidence and on limited evidence about the configuration of the rooms of the house, the court presumed that the testatrix and the witnesses had been present together at the same time. See also paras. **3.94** and **3.95**, ante.

E. Subscription by witnesses

33.18   **NB.** *In respect of wills of testators* dying on or after 1 January 1983, *s. 9 of the Wills Act 1837, as substituted by the Administration of Justice Act 1982, s. 17 (see p. 720, post), now allows a witness to acknowledge his earlier signature.*

May be by mark (*Re Ashmore's Goods* (1843) 3 Curt 756; *Re Amiss' Goods* (1849) 2 Rob Eccl 116); see also *Hindmarsh v Charlton* (1861) 8 HL Cas 160; or by description of himself (*Re Duggins' Goods* (1870) 39 LJP & M 24; *Re Sperling's Goods* (1863) 3 Sw & Tr 272); but not by signing the name of another person (*Re Leverington's Goods* (1886) 11 PD 80); another person may write name or mark of witness so long as he holds the pen (*Lewis v Lewis* (1861) 2 Sw & Tr 153; *Bell v Hughes* (1880) 5 LR Ir 407); but another person cannot subscribe for witness at his desire (*Re Cope's Goods* (1850) 2 Rob Eccl 335; *Re Duggins' Goods*, above); nor is it sufficient if witness's name is affixed by means of a rubber stamp affixed by the other witness in his presence but without any physical act or participation on his part (*Re Bulloch's Estate* [1968] NI 96, applying dictum in *Bell v Hughes*, above); signature of witness cannot be acknowledged afterwards by any means as can that of a testator, nor is it sufficient to re-write, with a dry pen, a signature written before acknowledgment by the testator in the presence of *both* witnesses (*Re Maddock's Goods* (1874) LR 3 P & D 169; *Hindmarsh v Charlton* above; *Horne v Featherstone* (1895) 73 LT 32); if witness is unable to complete signature the execution is invalid (*Re Maddock's Goods* (1874) LR 3 P & D 169; *McConville v McCreesh* (1879) 13 ILTR 35); the signatures of the witnesses need not appear on any particular part of the instrument (*Re Davis' Goods* (1843) 3 Curt 748; *Re Chamney's Goods* (1849) 1 Rob Eccl 757; *Roberts v Phillips* (1855) 4 E & B 450); but if not on same sheet as signature of testator, the sheets must be physically connected at time of execution (*Re Braddock's Goods* (1876) 1 PD 433); and the court must be satisfied that witnesses intended to attest the signature of the testator (*Re Streatley's Goods* [1891] P 172; *Re Taylor's Goods* (1851) 2 Rob Eccl 411; *Phipps v Hale* (1874) LR 3 P D 166; *Re Denning, Harnett v Elliott* [1958] 2 All ER 1, [1958] 1 WLR 462 (signatures of witnesses upside down on reverse of paper on which will written: see also para. **3.96**, ante)); the signature of third person at end of will may be omitted from probate upon proof that it was not written for purpose of attesting (*Re Sharman's Goods* (1869) LR 1 P & D 661): see also paras. **3.97–3.99**, ante. See also *Re White, Barker v Gribble* [1991] Ch 1, [1990] 3 All ER 1 (witnesses only attested alterations).

F. Presumption of due execution

33.19   If document is ex facie duly executed the court may pronounce for it although the evidence of attesting witnesses is adverse (*Cooper v Bockett* (1846) 4 Moo PCC 419; *Lloyd v Roberts* (1858) 12 Moo PCC 158; see also *Neal v Denston* (1932) 147 LT 460), or though the witness could not speak as to what writing was on the will when executed (*Wright v Sanderson* (1884) 9 PD 149, CA; *Re Coghlan, Briscoe v Broughton* [1948] 2 All ER 68), or although for 20 years no step was taken to prove the will (*Re Musgrove's Estate, Davis v Mayhew* [1927] P 264, CA); for the maxim *omnia praesumuntur rite esse acta* applies (*Woodhouse v Balfour* (1887) 13 PD 2; *Dayman v Dayman* (1894) 71 LT 699; *Wright v Sanderson* (1884) 9 PD 149; *Kavanagh v Fegan* [1932] IR 566); the presumption applies, but with less force, where attestation clause is incomplete (*Vinnicombe v Butler* (1864) 3 Sw & Tr 580); see also *Re Peverett's Goods* [1902] P 205; *Re Denning, Harnett v Elliot* [1958] 2 All ER 1, [1958] 1 WLR 462; and *Re Strong's Estate, Strong v Hadden* [1915] P 211, distinguishing *Peverett*. In *Re Puddephatt's Goods* (1870) LR 2 P & D 97, a will in which the testator's signature appeared below those of the witnesses was pronounced for although no evidence was available from the witnesses or other person present, on the presumption of due execution arising from the wording of the attestation clause. The force of the presumption varies with all the circumstances. It may be very strong if the document is entirely regular in form, but where it is irregular and unusual in form the maxim cannot apply with the same force (*Re Bercovitz's Estate, Canning v Enever* [1961] 2 All ER 481, [1961] 1 WLR 892). As to the presumption, see also *Harris v Knight* (1890) 15 PD 170 at 179. See also paras. **3.106–3.128**, ante, and *Burgoyne v Showler* (1844) 1 Rob Eccl 5.

G. Who else may prove execution

33.20   Evidence of a person present but not a witness (*Mackay v Rawlinson* (1919) 35 TLR 223).

(2) Incapacity

Form of defence

33.21   'That the deceased, at the time the said will and codicil respectively purport to have been executed, was not of sound mind, memory and understanding.'

Particulars required

33.22   'Every pleading must contain the necessary particulars of any claim, defence or other matter pleaded, including . . . (b) where a party pleading alleges any condition of the mind of any person, whether any disorder or disability of mind . . . particulars of the facts on which the party relies'[1].

1 Ord. 18, r. 12(1).

Four classes of persons incapacitated from making a will

33.23   There are four classes of persons who are incapacitated from making a valid will by reason of mental unsoundness:

(a) idiots, i.e. persons whose minds have been continuously unsound since infancy;

(b) persons who are usually insane. They may however have lucid intervals, and during such lucid intervals are competent to make a will;

(c) persons who are mentally unsound from sickness, accident or old age;

(d) persons who are mentally unsound through their own acts, e.g. drunkenness.

In the textbooks and reported cases, insanity is divided into two kinds, general insanity and partial insanity.

General insanity

33.24   General insanity exists where the mind is unsound on multifarious matters, so as to indicate that it is diseased throughout.

A person whose mind is generally unsound is held to be incapable of making a valid will whilst such unsoundness continues.

Partial insanity

33.25   Partial insanity exists in the case of a monomaniac who has insane delusions, limited to a particular subject.

For precedent of defence, see Form CP33.

Summary of reported cases

Presumption of sanity

33.26   A duly executed will, rational on the face of it, is presumed, in the absence of evidence to the contrary, to be that of a person of competent understanding (*Symes v Green* (1859) 1 Sw & Tr 401; *Sutton v Sadler* (1857) 3 CBNS 87). Sanity must be presumed until the contrary is shown (*Burrows v Burrows* (1827) 1 Hag Ecc 109).

Burden of proof

33.27   Where unsoundness of mind is alleged, the burden of proof rests upon those who set up the will, and, a fortiori, when it has already appeared that there was, in some particular, undoubtedly unsoundness of mind, that burden is considerably increased (*Smee v Smee* (1879) 5 PD 84 at 91; but see *Dew v Clark and Clark* (1826) 3 Add 79; *Wheeler and Batsford v Alderson* (1831) 3 Hag Ecc 574 at 598; and *Waring v Waring* (1848) 6 Moo PCC 341). So also where the will is not rational on the face of it (*Arbery v Ashe* (1828) 1 Hag Ecc 214). So where a testator has been found lunatic by inquisition the onus probandi must be upon him who asserts complete or partial recovery (*Prinsep and East India Co v Dyce Sombre, Troup and Solaroli* (1856) 10 Moo PCC 232 at 244; and *Boughton v Knight* (1873) LR 3 P & D 64 (unsoundness of mind extending over many years)).

Foreign domicil

33.28   The general rule is that the testator's capacity is to be determined by the law of his domicil, but as to burden of proof the English court, if conducting the enquiry de novo and not merely giving effect to probate or its equivalent granted abroad, must follow its own lex fori (*Re Fuld's Estate (No 3), Hartley v Fuld* [1968] P 675, [1965] 3 All ER 776).

What is testamentary capacity?

33.29   The testator must understand the nature of the act and effect; the extent of the property of which he is disposing; the claims to which he ought to give effect; and, with a view to the latter object; no disorder of the mind must poison his affections, pervert his sense of right or prevent the exercise of his natural faculties, and no insane delusion must influence his will in disposing of his property, and bring about a disposal of it which, if the mind had been sound, would not have been made (*Banks v Goodfellow* (1870) LR 5 QB 549 at 565; *Harwood v Baker* (1840) 3 Moo PCC 282; *Re Belliss, Polson v Parrott* (1929) 141 LT 245). See also *Boughton v Knight* (1873) LR 3 P & D 64 at 72, note (1).

Partial insanity and delusion

33.30   Monomania, that a brother had administered poison (*Greenwood v Greenwood* (1790) 3 Curt App 1). An insane antipathy to an only daughter (*Dew v Clark and Clark* (1822) 1 Add 279; (1824) 2 Add 102; (1826) 3 Add 79. See also *Smith v Tebbitt* (1867) LR 1 P & D 398). Testator a paranoid psychopath—delusion affected one disposition only (*Re Bohrmann's Estate, Caesar and Watmough v Bohrmann* [1938] 1 All ER 271, 158 LT 180). A repulsion to children or others having natural claims on testator's bounty may amount to a delusion (*Boughton v Knight* (1873) LR 3 P & D 64). If such repulsion be proved, the party setting up the will must prove that it was not operative at the time of execution (ibid.), and the court must regard the contents of the will and the surrounding circumstances (ibid.). Where a delusion has had, or is calculated to have had, an influence on the testamentary disposition it must be held to be fatal to its validity. But where the delusion must be taken neither to have had any influence on the provisions of the will, nor to have been capable of having had any, such delusion does not destroy the capacity to make the will (*Banks v Goodfellow* (1870) LR 5 QB 549; *Boughton v Knight* (1873) LR 3 P & D 64).

Old age or illness

33.31   Testamentary incapacity may arise from old age or illness. As to what constitutes a sound disposing mind, see *Harwood v Baker* (1840) 3 Moo PCC 282 at 290; *Combes' Case* (1604) Moore KB 759; and *Marsh v Tyrrell and Harding* (1828) 2 Hag Ecc 84 at 122. If a testator was of complete capacity when he gave instructions for a will, a very slight degree of capacity at the time of its execution suffices (*Harwood v Baker*, above; *Parker v Felgate* (1883) 8 PD 171). But not if the instructions were given by a third party on the testator's behalf (*Battan Singh v Amirchand* [1948] AC 161, [1948] 1 All ER 152). As to capacity as to part of a will see *Thomas v Jones* [1928] P 162.

Drunkenness

33.32   When a man is drunk, or under the influence of excessive drinking, he is incapable of making a will; but where, although an habitual drunkard, he is not under the excitement of liquor, he is not incapable of making a will (*Billinghurst v Vickers (formerly Leonard)* (1810) 1 Phillim 187 at 193; *Ayrey v Hill* (1824) 2 Add 206 at 210).

Paralysis

33.33   Indication of wishes by nodding, etc. (*Re Holtam's Estate, Gillett v Rogers* (1913) 108 LT 732). See also para. **33.53**, post.

(3) Undue influence

Form of defence

33.34 'That the execution of the said will and codicil was obtained by the undue influence of the plaintiff (and of others acting with him whose names are at present unknown to the defendant).'

The necessary particulars must be included in the defence[1].
For precedent of defence, see Form CP34.

A plea of undue influence ought never to be put forward unless the person who pleads it has reasonable grounds on which to support it[2]. Nor may the plea be used as a screen behind which to make veiled charges of fraud and dishonesty[3].

1 Ord. 18. r. 12(1).
2 *Spiers v English* [1907] P 122 at 124.
3 *Low v Guthrie* [1909] AC 278.

Summary of reported cases

What constitutes undue influence

33.35 To be undue influence there must be coercion (*Wingrove v Wingrove* (1885) 11 PD 81); or fraud (*Boyse v Rossborough* (1857) 6 HL Cas 2 at 45; *Williams v Goude* (1828) 1 Hag Ecc 577 at 581); a testator may be led but not driven; his will must be the offspring of his own volition and not the record of someone else's (*Hall v Hall* (1868) LR 1 P & D 481). See also *Mountain v Bennet* (1787) 1 Cox Eq Cas 353 at 355.

What is not undue influence

33.36 Appeals to affection, ties of kindred, gratitude for past services, or pity for future destitution are legitimate; but not pressure if so exerted as to overpower the volition without convincing the judgment (*Hall v Hall* (1868) LR 1 P & D 481). Even immoral considerations do not amount to undue influence unless the testator is in such a condition that if he could speak his wishes to the last, he would say, 'This is not my wish, but I must do it' (*Baudains v Richardson* [1906] AC 169 at 184).

As to part of a will

33.37 Where only part of a will was obtained by undue influence, the remainder may be admitted, provided that the omissions do not upset the whole tenor of what remains (*Rhodes v Rhodes* (1882) 7 App Cas 192); and similarly where words were included without the instruction or knowledge of the testator (*Re Duane's Goods* (1862) 2 Sw & Tr 590); but the court cannot add or substitute words. See para. **33.51**, post.

The burden of proof

33.38 This is cast upon the person propounding a will and is in general discharged by proof of capacity and the fact of execution (*Barry v Butlin* (1838) 2 Moo PCC 480), together with proof of knowledge and approval if the prima facie case is met, see paras. **33.06**, ante, and **33.50**, post. When this is discharged the burden of proving that a will was executed under undue influence is on the party who alleges it (*Boyse v Rossborough* (1857) 6 HL Cas 2 at 45). Although undue influence will not be presumed, strong proof may be required of intention (*Billinghurst v Vickers* (1810) 1 Phillim 187 at 194), as when the suspicion and vigilance of the court are excited, e.g. by the fact that the will was drawn or prepared by an exceptionally interested party (*Barry v Butlin* (1838) 2 Moo PCC 480; *Greville v Tylee* (1851) 7 Moo PCC 320; *Low v Guthrie* [1909] AC 278; *Spiers v English* [1907] P 122 at 124). See also *Re Liver, Scott v Woods* (1955) 106 L Jo 75; *Wintle v Nye* [1959] 1 All ER 552, [1959] 1 WLR 284, HL; even if the power to overbear the will of the testator is admitted, it must be shown that such power was exercised, and that the circumstances of the execution are inconsistent with any other view but undue influence (*Craig v Lamoureux* [1920] AC 349).

Nature of evidence necessary to establish undue influence

33.39   *Boyse v Rossborough* (1857) 6 HL Cas 2 at 45. See also *Radford v Risdon* (1912) 28 TLR 342, as to evidence of a statement of a deceased person.

Foreign domicil

33.40   The question of undue influence is part of the substantive law of wills and therefore the law of the domicil should be followed, though not blindly: the English court will refuse to apply a law which outrages its sense of justice or decency, but it must consider the foreign law as a whole (*Re Fuld's Estate (No 3), Hartley v Fuld* [1968] P 675, [1965] 3 All ER 776).

(4) Fraud

Form of defence

33.41   'That the execution of the said will and codicil was obtained by the fraud of the plaintiff, such fraud, so far as is within the defendant's present knowledge, being [*state the nature of the fraud*].'

Any allegation of fraud must be specifically pleaded[1]. (See Form CP35.)
Whenever fraud is relied upon, the necessary particulars must be included in the pleading[2].

1 Ord. 18, r. 8(1).
2 Ibid., r. 12(1).

Summary of reported cases

Nature of plea

33.42   Fraud and imposition upon weakness is a sufficient ground to set aside a will (*Lord Donegal's Case* (1751) 2 Ves Sen 408). False representations as to character of person to induce testator to revoke a bequest to him are fraud (*Allen v M'Pherson* (1847) 1 HL Cas 191 at 207). So too are false representations to prevent testator from benefiting his relatives or other persons (*Boyse v Rossborough* (1857) 6 HL Cas 2 at 49). The question of fraud may depend to some extent on that of the capacity of the testator (*Marsh v Tyrrell and Harding* (1828) 2 Hag Ecc 84 at 123).

Fraud must pleaded specifically (Order 18, r. 8(1))

33.43 Evidence of fraud will not be let in by a plea of undue influence (*White v White and Cato* (1862) 2 Sw & Tr 504); leave to amend by alleging fraud may, however, be granted during the hearing (*White v White and Cato* (1862) 2 Sw & Tr 504), even though the case of the party, on whom lay the onus of proof, has been closed (*Riding v Hawkins* (1889) 14 PD 56). In an action in which knowledge and approval are in issue, and no allegation of fraud is made in the pleadings, it is permissible to cross-examine a party to show that if the testator did not know and approve of the contents of the will, it was because that party was fraudulent (*Wintle v Nye* [1959] 1 All ER 552, [1959] 1 WLR 284, HL).

Part of will obtained by fraud

33.44 If part of a will has been obtained by fraud, probate ought to be refused of that part and granted of the rest (*Allen v M'Pherson* (1847) 1 HL Cas 191 at 207, 208).

Probate in solemn form revoked

33.45 A decree pronouncing for a will in solemn form may be set aside if it be proved that the decree was obtained by fraud (*Birch v Birch* [1902] P 130, CA; see also *Priestman v Thomas* (1884) 9 PD 210); but evidence of fraud discovered since the decree must be adduced and be sufficient to raise a reasonable probability of the success of the action (*Birch v Birch*, above).

(5) Want of knowledge and approval

Form of defence

33.46 'The deceased at the time of the execution of the said will and codicil did not know and approve of the contents thereof [*or*] of the contents of the residuary clause in the said will [*as the case may be*].'

Nature of case to be specified: other defences to be specifically pleaded

33.47 'Without prejudice to Order 18, r. 7, any party who pleads that at the time when a will, the subject of the action, was alleged to have been executed the testator did not know and approve of its contents must specify the nature of the case on which he intends to rely, and no allegation in support of that plea which would be relevant in support of any of the following other pleas, that is to say—

(a) that the will was not duly executed,
(b) that at the time of the execution of the will the testator was not of sound mind, memory and understanding, and
(c) that the execution of the will was obtained by undue influence or fraud,

shall be made by that party unless that other plea is also pleaded'[1].

An affirmative plea of undue influence should not be made unless the party pleading had reasonable ground for making it, notwithstanding the provisions of Order 76, r. 9(3)[2].

For precedent of defence, see Form CP36.

1 Ord. 76, r. 9(3).
2 *Re Stott, Klouda v Lloyds Bank Ltd* [1980] 1 All ER 259, [1980] 1 WLR 246.

Summary of reported cases

Knowledge and approval essential

33.48   It is essential to the validity of a will that the testator should know and approve of its contents (*Hastilow v Stobie* (1865) LR 1 P & D 64; *Guardhouse v Blackburn* (1866) LR 1 P & D 109; but see *Parker v Felgate* (1883) 8 PD 171; *Battan Singh v Amirchand* [1948] AC 161, [1948] 1 All ER 152).

Presumption of law

33.49   Unless suspicion attaches to the document, the testator's execution is sufficient evidence of his knowledge and approval (*Guardhouse v Blackburn* (1866) LR 1 P & D 109). Where there is no question of fraud, the fact that a will has been read over to or by a capable testator, or the contents brought to his knowledge in some other way, is (*as a rule*) conclusive evidence that he knew and approved of the contents of it (*Guardhouse v Blackburn* (1866) LR 1 P & D 109; *Atter v Atkinson* (1869) LR 1 P & D 665 at 670). (N.B. The words 'as a rule' above are introduced owing to the case of *Fulton v Andrew* (1875) LR 7 HL 448, where Lord Cairns comments on the two cases cited, and rather questions the unyielding nature of the above proposition of law.) See also *Re Crerar, Rushforth v Rushforth* (1956) 106 L Jo 694; *Wintle v Nye* [1959] 1 All ER 552, [1959] 1 WLR 284; *Re Morris, Lloyds Bank Ltd v Peake* [1971] P 62, [1970] 1 All ER 1057, in which it was held that the rule in *Guardhouse v Blackburn*, above, no longer survives. But if the way in which the will was read over is called in question, the above presumption may be rebutted (*Garnett-Botfield v Garnett-Botfield* [1901] P 335), but only by the clearest evidence (*Gregson v Taylor* [1917] P 256). If knowledge and approval are clearly established at the time of giving instructions for a will, or drafting it, very little evidence of the position at the time of execution is required (*Re Wallace's Estate, Solicitor of the Duchy of Cornwall v Batten* [1952] 2 TLR 925).

Burden of proof

33.50   The burden of proof of the testator's knowledge and approval lies on the party setting up the will (*Barry v Butlin* (1838) 2 Moo PCC 480 at 482; *Cleare and Forster v Cleare* (1869) LR 1 P & D 655), and the burden is discharged prima facie by proof of capacity and due execution (*Barry v Butlin*, above; *Cleare v Cleare*, above; but where this prima facie presumption is met by the cross-examination of the witnesses, the party propounding must prove affirmatively that the testator knew and approved of the contents (*Cleare and Forste v Cleare*, above); *Atter v Atkinson* (1869) LR 1 P & D 665 at 668). Where a will is prepared in suspicious circumstances the onus is cast upon the person propounding it to remove such suspicion, and to prove that the testator knew and approved of its contents (*Tyrrell v Painton* [1894] P 151 at 157, CA, followed in *Re Scott, Huggett v Reichman* (1966) 110 Sol Jo 852. So where a person propounds a will prepared by himself and under which he takes benefit, he must give clear proof that the testator knew and approved of that part under which he takes a benefit (*Hegarty v King* (1880) 5 LR Ir 249; affd 7 LR Ir 18, CA). See also *Re Liver, Scott v Woods* (1955) 106 L Jo 75. This plea refers to the circumstances attending the preparation and execution of the will itself, and not to extraneous matters (*Re R* [1951] P 10, [1950] 2 All ER 117).

It is not the law that in no circumstances can a solicitor or other person who has prepared a will for a testator take a benefit under it; but that fact creates a suspicion that must be removed by the person propounding the will. In all cases the court must be vigilant and jealous. The degree of suspicion will vary with the circumstances of the case. It may be slight and easily dispelled; it may, on the other hand, be so grave that it can hardly be removed (*Wintle v Nye* [1959] 1 All ER 552, [1959] 1 WLR 284, HL). A solicitor beneficiary under a will has a personal obligation to see that the testator was separately advised before he could benefit (*Re a Solicitor* [1975] QB 475, [1974] 3 All ER 853). When a testator is elderly and infirm his will should be witnessed and approved by, a medical practitioner who satisfies himself as to the capacity and understanding of the testator and who records his examination and findings (*Re Simpson, Schaniel v Simpson* (1977) 121 Sol Jo 224).

Mistake

33.51 Where words have been inserted in a will by the mistake of the draftsman, and the will is not read to the testator, such words may be omitted from the probate (*Morrell v Morrell* (1882) 7 PD 68; *Re Walkeley's Goods* (1893) 69 LT 419; *Re Boehm's Goods* [1891] P 247; *Re Reade's Goods* [1902] P 75; *Vaughan v Clerk* (1902) 87 LT 144; *Re White's Estate* (1961) 105 Sol Jo 259 (omission from codicil of words mistakenly confirming an earlier will which had been revoked by a later one)). But where the draftsman has made the mistake owing to misunderstanding the intentions of the testator, or by the language used fails to give effect to them, the mistake must stand (*Harter v Harter* (1873) LR 3 P & D 11; *Collins v Elstone* [1893] P 1.) (But see also *Re Swords' Goods* [1952] P 368, [1952] 2 All ER 281). The court cannot supply words omitted from the will by mistake, or correct an obvious mistake (*Guardhouse v Blackburn* (1866) LR 1 P & D 109 at 114; *Morrell v Morrell* (1882) 7 PD 68 at 70; and see *Re Schott's Goods* [1901] P 190 at 192 where Jeune J deals with decisions of Butt J to the contrary in *Re Bushell's Goods* (1887) 13 PD 7, and *Re Huddleston's Goods* (1890) 63 LT 255). See also *Re Horrocks, Taylor v Kershaw* [1939] P 198, [1939] 1 All ER 579, CA (word 'or' said to have been inserted by mistake for 'and'; no jurisdiction to alter words chosen by testator, *Re Boehm*, above and *Re Schott*, above distinguished). See also paras. **3.249** ff., ante.

Rectification

33.52 In respect of a will of a testator dying on or after 1 January 1983, the court has power by virtue of s. 20 of the Administration of Justice Act 1982 to rectify the will in certain limited instances (see para. **41.01**, post). For earlier deaths, it has been held in a case in which the testator is not bound by a draftsman's error that the Probate Court has power to rectify the matter so far as it can, but has no power to do so by adding words. Where the testator's intention was to revoke clauses 3 and 7(iv) of her will (clause 7 containing a large number of legacies each preceded by a roman numeral) but by mistake the codicil as drafted and executed revoked clauses 3 and 7, it was held that the testator's intentions would be most nearly met by excluding the numeral '7' so that the clause containing the revocation would read 'I revoke clauses 3 and   of my said will'. The court of construction might then deduce from the documents that the intention was to revoke clause 7(iv), or might decide that the gift in the codicil to the particular beneficiary was in substitution for that in clause 7(iv) of the will (*Re Morris, Lloyds Bank Ltd v Peake* [1971] P 62, [1970] 1 All ER 1057).

See also *Re Phelan* [1972] Fam 33, [1971] 3 All ER 1256; and *Re Reynette-James, Wightman v Reynette-James* [1975] 3 All ER 1037, [1976] 1 WLR 161.

Deaf mutes and paralytics

33.53 A will prepared in conformity with instructions made by signs by a testator who was deaf and dumb was proved on an affidavit setting forth the signs by which the testator signified that he understood and approved the provisions of the will (*Re Geale's Goods* (1864) 3 Sw & Tr 431); where testatrix could not speak or write owing to apoplectic stroke (*Re Owston's Goods* (1862) 2 Sw & Tr 461; *Re Holtam's Estate, Gillett v Rogers* (1913) 108 LT 732); where testatrix was paralysed.

Blind or illiterate

33.54   The court must always be satisfied that such testators knew and approved the contents of the will. If the will is proved to be in conformity with instructions of the testator, that will suffice, even though the will may not have been read to the testator (*Fincham v Edwards* (1842) 3 Curt 63).

Foreign domicil

33.55   The court must decide whether the instruments propounded express the intentions of a free and capable testator. The whole point of the rule is evidential: in certain cases it requires of the court vigilant care and circumspection in investigating the facts (see, e.g., *Wintle v Nye*, above). The rule must therefore be applied by the English court as part of its lex fori (*Re Fuld's Estate (No 3), Hartley v Fuld* [1968] P 675, [1965] 3 All ER 776).

(6) Sham will

Form of defence

33.56   'That the said alleged will is not a testamentary document.'

The necessary particulars must be given. For form of defence, see CP37.

Summary of reported cases

Will not made animo testandi

33.57   (1) Upon proof that a document, though testamentary on the face of it, was not executed with intention to effect disposition of property after death, probate of it will be refused (*Lister v Smith* (1863) 3 Sw & Tr 282; *Nichols v Nichols* (1814) 2 Phillim 180); (2) but if a document is clearly testamentary the court cannot look to the effect of it (*King's Proctor v Daines* (1830) 3 Hag Ecc 218). (3) If the wrong document is executed by mistake, probate of the whole must be refused even though some of the testamentary dispositions contained in it were intended by the testator (*Re Meyer's Estate* [1908] P 353). (4) If a document appears on the face of it not to be testamentary, or if its purport be equivocal, the onus of showing that it was made animo testandi is upon the party setting it up (*King's Proctor v Daines* (document appearing to be donatio inter vivos); *Griffin and Amos v Ferard* (1835) 1 Curt 97 (a declaration to his executors that a sum of money standing in deceased's name was held by him in trust); *Coventry v Williams* (1844) 3 Curt 787 (document setting out terms of codicil which deceased intended to execute); *Thorncroft and Clarke v Lashmar* (1862) 2 Sw & Tr 479 (the offer of an appointment at a salary with expression of wish that it should continue after the death)). A document on the face of it not testamentary may be shown to be so by extrinsic evidence (*cases cited above*). See also *Re Berger* [1990] Ch 118, [1989] 1 All ER 591, CA in which a tzava'ah (Hebrew will) in an English translation was admitted to probate. But if a document is executed in accordance with the requirements of the Wills Act

1837 there is a prima facie presumption that it is intended to be testamentary (*Re Meynell* (1949) 93 Sol Jo 466). See also *Corbett v Newey* [1994] Ch 388, [1995] 1 All ER 570, where a will was held valid that had been executed with the intention (not expressed in the will itself) that it should take effect as a testamentary document albeit subject to the fulfilment of a condition (which condition was, on extrinsic evidence accepted by the court, later fulfilled). See also paras. **3.22–3.32**, ante.

(7) Revocation

33.58 As to revocation of wills in cases where the testator died on or after 1 January 1964 see Wills Act 1963, referred to on p. 777, ante. This Act does not alter the internal law of England and Wales as contained in the Wills Act 1837, as to modes of revocation, but provides that in the circumstances specified revocation by other methods is effective.

(i) By marriage or in effect by its annulment or dissolution

33.59 By s. 18 of the Administration of Justice Act 1982, substituting a new s. 18 to the Wills Act 1837 (see p. 722, post), it is provided that a will (including codicils) *made on or after 1 January 1983* shall be revoked by the testator's subsequent marriage, subject to certain exceptions referred to in the section. As regards wills (and codicils) *made before 1 January 1983*, similar provision is contained in the former s. 18 to the 1837 Act and s. 177 of the Law of Property Act 1925 (see pp. 722, 743, post). For an analysis of these exceptions, see Part I, Chap. 3, paras. **3.36** ff., ante.

Revocation of a will by marriage of testator. Form of defence

33.60 'That the deceased, subsequently to the execution of the will, contracted a marriage valid by the law of England.'

Particulars of the date and place of marriage should be included in the defence.

Revocation in effect by annulment or dissolution of marriage

33.61 If a will appoints a spouse as sole executor and sole beneficiary, the subsequent annulment or dissolution of the testator's marriage to that spouse brings about an intestacy (if such will is not then replaced) by virtue of s. 18A of the Wills Act 1837 (see *Re Sinclair, Lloyds Bank plc v Imperial Cancer Research Fund* [1985] Ch 446, [1985] 1 All ER 1066) although the ineffective will still has to be proved as the last will. A new s. 18A has been substituted by s. 3(1) of the Law Reform (Succession) Act 1995 in respect of a will made by a person dying on or after 1 January 1996 (see, ibid., s. 3(2)).

(ii) By subsequent will

Revocation by subsequent testamentary papers. Form of defence

33.62 'That the said will was revoked by a will or other testamentary paper of later date.'

The defence should include the date of the later will, which should be propounded in the counterclaim.

(iii) By destruction

Revocation by destruction. Form of Defence

33.63 'That the said will was revoked by the same having been burnt, torn, or otherwise destroyed, by the testator, or by some person in his presence and by his direction, with the intention to revoke the same.'

The defence should include particulars of when, how, and by whom the will was destroyed or, if such be the case, that the defendant will rely on the presumption of law that, the will not being forthcoming on the death, it was destroyed by the testator animo revocandi.

For precedent of defence, see Form CP40.

(A) Partial revocation (s. 21, Wills Act 1837[1])

33.64 A will may be revoked in part by a duly executed obliteration, interlineation or other alteration, or by such an alteration as renders the former words or effect of the will no longer apparent.

1 See p. 723, post.

(B) Dependent relative, or conditional, revocation

33.65 A will though revoked by the testator may be held good by the doctrine of dependent relative revocation.

> 'A revocation grounded on an assumption of fact which is false takes effect unless, as a matter of construction, the truth of the fact is the condition of the revocation, or, in other words, unless the revocation is contingent upon the facts being true.'

This definition was adopted in *Re Faris, Goddard v Overend (No 2)* [1911] 1 IR 469 at 472 and approved by the Court of Appeal in *Re Southerden's Estate, Adams v Southerden* [1925] P 177.

Summary of reported cases

I. By the marriage of the testator (s. 18, Wills Act 1837[1])

33.66 But see s. 177 of the Law of Property Act 1925[2].

1 See p. 722, post.
2 See p. 743, post.

33.67   NB. The following decisions under this heading 'By the marriage of the Testator' are based on s. 18 of the Wills Act 1837 prior to its replacement by s. 18 of the

Administration of Justice Act 1982 (see p. 854, post). These decisions continue to apply in respect of wills *made before 1 January 1983*. However, in respect of wills *made on or after 1 January 1983*, those decisions must be considered in the light of the revised s. 18 (and in light also of the amendments to s. 18A made by s. 3 of the Law Reform (Succession) Act 1995 in relation to deaths on or after 1 January 1996).

33.68   The will is not revoked by a marriage which is invalid by the law of England (*Mette v Mette* (1859) 1 Sw & Tr 416; *Warter v Warter* (1890) 15 PD 152). A marriage which may be voidable is effective to revoke a will (*Re Roberts, Roberts v Roberts* [1978] 3 All ER 225, [1978] 1 WLR 653, CA). The section does not affect wills of persons domiciled in countries where subsequent marriage does not revoke a will (*Re Reid's Goods* (1866) LR 1 P & D 74); but see *Re Martin, Loustalan v Loustalan* [1900] P 211, CA. The marriage must be valid by English law and contracted by or with a husband who was then domiciled in England. This statement should now be considered in the light of s. 1 of the Domicile and Matrimonial Proceedings Act 1973 under which, as from 1 January 1974, a married woman is capable of having a domicil other than that of her husband. See also Dicey and Morris, *Conflict of Laws*, 11th edition. Subsequent marriage does not revoke such portion of a will as may have exercised a power of appointment, save as provided in s. 18 of the Wills Act 1837 (*Re Fitzroy's Goods* (1858) 1 Sw & Tr 133; *Re Russell's Goods* (1890) 15 PD 111; *Re Paul, Public Trustee v Pearce* [1921] 2 Ch 1). Subsequent marriage does not revoke such portion of a will as may have exercised a power of appointment if the property would not pass to the *widow* and kin in default of appointment (*Re Gilligan* [1950] P 32, [1949] 2 All ER 401). A soldier's will is not excepted from the general rule (*Re Wardrop's Estate* [1917] P 54); nor, it would appear, is a mutual will (*Re Hey's Estate, Walker v Gaskill* [1914] P 192). As to presumption in favour of marriage where no certificate or other confirmation is produced, see *Rumsey v Sterne* (1967) 111 Sol Jo 113. But a will made on or since 1 January 1926, if expressed to be made in contemplation of a marriage, is not revoked by the marriage contemplated: s. 177, Law of Property Act 1925[1]. The marriage contemplated must be identified in the will (*Sallis v Jones* [1936] P 43 (will pronounced against)). A duly executed indorsement on an envelope containing a will revoked by marriage stating that 'The herein named is now my lawful wife' was held to revive the will (*Re Davis' Estate* [1952] P 279, [1952] 2 All ER 509). See also paras. **3.36** and **34.09**. The section does not require that the testator should set out that the will is made because he contemplates marriage: it is sufficient if there is a practical expression of his contemplation of marriage to a particular person. A gift to 'my fiancée' (whom the testator afterwards married) was held to be sufficient (*Re Langston's Estate* [1953] P 100, [1953] 1 All ER 928): see *Pilot v Gainfort* [1931] P 103. It is sufficient if one can collect from the words of the will themselves the fact that the marriage which later took place was mentally in view of the testator at the time when he made the will (*Re Gray's Estate* (1963) 107 Sol Jo 156). The will, not merely some gifts in it, must be in contemplation of marriage (*Re Coleman, Coleman v Coleman* [1976] Ch 1, [1975] 1 All ER 675).

1 See p. 743, post.

II. By another will or codicil (s. 20, Wills Act 1837[1])

33.69

(i)   *Containing express words of revocation.* The expression, 'This is my last will and testament' need not, standing alone, revoke all former testamentary papers (*Cutto v Gilbert* (1854) 9 Moo PCC 131), neither need the words, 'This is the last and only will of me', etc. (*Simpson v Foxon* [1907] P 54). General words of revocation revoke a will exercising a general or special power of appointment (*Sotheran v Dening* (1881) 20 Ch D 99; *Re Kingdon, Wilkins v Pryer* (1886) 32 Ch D 604), unless there is cogent evidence to the contrary (*Lowthorpe-Lutwidge v Lowthorpe-Lutwidge* [1935] P 151 (*Smith v Thompson* (1931) 47 TLR 603, distinguished)). Cf. *Re Wayland's Estate* [1951] 2 All

ER 1041. In *Jones v Treasury Solicitor* (1932) 49 TLR 75, CA, the word 'ungultig' substituted by the word 'cancelled' was held to revoke an earlier will. Revocation of a will does not involve revocation of a codicil to such will (*Black v Jobling* (1869) LR 1 P & D 685; see also *Re Savage's Goods* (1870) LR 2 P & D 78; *Re Turner's Goods* (1872) LR 2 P & D 403; *Gardiner v Courthope* (1886) 12 PD 14; *Farrer v St Catherine's College, Cambridge* (1873) LR 16 Eq 19). Words of revocation inserted per incuriam and without the knowledge of the testator may be omitted from the probate (*Re Moore's Goods* [1892] P 378; *Re Oswald's Goods* (1874) LR 3 P & D 162), but if the testator's mind was directed to the words, even if he did not intend them, they will operate as a revocation (*Collins v Elstone* [1893] P 1; *Re Hope-Brown's Estate* [1942] P 136, [1942] 2 All ER 176). See also *Re Cocke's Goods* [1960] 2 All ER 289, [1960] 1 WLR 491: two wills both appointed the same executor; the later will contained a revocation clause but the residuary clause was inchoate. Both wills admitted to proof, omitting the revocation clause in later will and clauses in the earlier will inconsistent with the later will. In the case of a lost will, prepared hurriedly by a solicitor who was unable to recollect any of its contents, no copy being available, the judge drew the inference that a solicitor-drawn will would contain a revocation clause, and found that all previous wills were revoked (*Re Hampshire's Estate* [1951] WN 174). But a contrary view was taken in *Re Wyatt* [1952] 1 All ER 1030. See further, as to revocation, paras. **3.34** ff., ante.

1 See p. 723, post.

(ii) *Inconsistent wills*. In considering what documents constitute the will, the whole question is one of intention (*Methuen v Methuen* (1817) 2 Phillim 416; see also *Chichester v Quatrefages* [1895] P 186 at 188). Where different testamentary documents are co-extensive and in such terms that probate cannot be granted of both, probate will be granted of the latest in date (*O'Leary v Douglass* (1878) 13 LR Ir 323). Where the priority of two wills (both containing express words of revocation) is uncertain, and their terms are so inconsistent that they cannot stand together, neither will be admitted to probate, but they revoke a previous will (*Re Howard, Howard v Treasury Solicitor* [1944] P 39); if neither contains express words of revocation, the court will, if possible, so construe them that they can both stand as together being the will of the testator (*Townsend v Moore* [1905] P 66, CA). If there is no real inconsistency and no revocation, any number of documents may be admitted as the last will (*Deakin v Garvie* (1919) 36 TLR 122, CA). If the intention of the testator remains in doubt on the face of the two documents, evidence of the surrounding circumstances may be admitted (*Re Bryan's Estate* [1907] P 125), and parol evidence of the testator's intention is admissible (*Thorne v Rooke* (1841) 2 Curt 799; *Jenner v Ffinch* (1879) 5 PD 106). Where the later will is only partly inconsistent the former is only revoked in part, and both are entitled to probate (*Lemage v Goodban* (1865) LR 1 P & D 57): *Re Cocke's Goods*, above. Although the first will disposes of the whole of the property, and a later will contains no words of revocation, and leaves the residue undisposed of, yet the earlier will may be held to be revoked by the later one (*Re Bryan's Estate* [1907] P 125). If a later will partly revoked an earlier will and is in its turn revoked, such revocation will not effect a revival of the revoked portion of the earlier will (*Re Hodgkinson's Goods* [1893] P 339, CA). The general bequest by a later testamentary document, inconsistent with the exercise of a power of appointment by an earlier will, will revoke such will (*Cadell v Wilcocks* [1898] P 21; see also *Wrigley v Lowndes* [1908] P 348; *Re Gibbes' Settlement, White v Randolf* (1887) 37 Ch D 143, but see *Smith v Thompson* (1931) 47 TLR 603 (exercise of power of appointment in first will not revoked by revocatory clause in second)). This case was distinguished in *Lowthorpe-Lutwidge v Lowthorpe-Lutwidge* [1935] P 151. A codicil headed 'codicil' but beginning 'This is the last will and testament', and not referring to the will but effecting a substantial difference in the disposition of the property, was proved with the will (*Kitcat v King* [1930] P 266). See also *Re Mardon's Estate* [1944] P 109, [1944] 2 All ER 397, as to partial revocation, and *Re Swords' Goods* [1952] P 368, [1952] 2 All ER 281, as to exclusion of a revocation clause inserted, in error, in a codicil: *Re White's Estate* (1961) 105 Sol Jo 259 (omission from codicil of words mistakenly confirming a will revoked by one later in date).

(iii) *'By some writing declaring an intention to revoke' (s. 20, Wills Act 1837)*. A document executed and attested as a will, containing a request to destroy a will, has been held to revoke that will (*Re Spracklan's Estate* [1938] 2 All ER 345, CA). The intention need not be express (*Ford v de Pontés* (1861) 30 Beav 572; *Re Hicks' Goods* (1869) LR 1 P & D 683; *Re Durance's Goods* (1872) LR 2 P & D 406); and, in the absence of any other testamentary directions, the written declaration need not be annexed to the grant (*Toomer v Sobinska* [1907] P 106; *Re Eyre's Goods* [1905] 2 IR 540) (see para. **6.06**, ante, as to practice). See also *Re Brennan's Goods* [1932] IR 633 (instructions for new will admitted to probate).

III. By burning, tearing, or otherwise destroying (s. 20, Wills Act 1837[1])

33.70 *(i) Generally:*

(a) *Intention to revoke.* The intention to revoke must accompany the act (*Bibb v Thomas* (1775) 2 Wm Bl 1043; *Clarke v Scripps* (1852) 2 Rob Eccl 563 at 567; *Giles v Warren* (1872) LR 2 P & D 401). Therefore a person of unsound mind cannot revoke his will by destruction (*Brunt v Brunt* (1873) LR 3 P & D 37 at 38; *Re Taylor's Estate, National and Provincial and Union Bank of England v Taylor* (1919) 64 Sol Jo 148). As to standard of capacity required, see *Re Sabatini* (1969) 114 Sol Jo 35. Where the destruction is not with consent of the testator, he cannot subsequently ratify such destruction so as to effect a revocation (*Mills v Millward* (1889) 15 PD 20; *Gill v Gill* [1909] P 157), and subsequent acquiescence does not constitute revocation (*Re Booth, Booth v Booth* [1926] P 118).

(b) *Presumption as to will not forthcoming at testator's death.* Where a will is traced into the testator's custody, and there is no evidence of its having subsequently left his custody, and it is not forthcoming at his death—this will be prima facie evidence of its destruction by him animo revocandi (*Patten v Poulton* (1858) 1 Sw & Tr 55; *Welch v Phillips* (1836) 1 Moo PCC 299 at 302), and it is not necessary for those alleging revocation to show how, in fact, it was lost or destroyed (*Patten v Poulton* (1858) 1 Sw & Tr 55). The presumption may be rebutted by surrounding circumstances, e.g. declaration of unchanged affection or intention (*Patten v Poulton* (1858) 1 Sw & Tr 55; *Welch v Phillips* (1836) 1 Moo PCC 299 at 302; *Re Mackenzie's Estate* [1909] P 305; *Re Sykes, Drake v Sykes* (1906) 22 TLR 741; affd (1907) 23 TLR 747, CA); *Re Wilson's Estate, Walker v Treasury Solicitor* (1961) 105 Sol Jo 531. The strongest proof of the improbability of revocation by destruction arises from the contents of the document itself (*Saunders v Saunders* (1848) 6 Notes of Cases 518 at 522). Where a will which has been in the custody of a testator at a time when he has been of unsound mind as well as of sound mind, is found torn, or is not forthcoming at his death, the burden of showing that it was revoked by him while of sound mind lies on the party who sets up the revocation (*Harris v Berrall* (1858) 1 Sw & Tr 153). See also *Sprigge v Sprigge* (1868) LR 1 P & D 608 (the presumption of destruction animo revocandi does not apply where the testator became of unsound mind after execution of the will and continued so until his death. The burden of showing that the will was revoked before he became of unsound mind lies on the party asserting revocation); *Re Yule's Estate* (1965) 109 Sol Jo 317 (the presumption of destruction animo revocandi and the contrary presumption, in the case where the testator had lost testamentary capacity, that the will was destroyed unintentionally, were not intended to be rigid rules but as indications of the inferences which would always be drawn from a given state of evidence. But the court was not entitled to depart from *Sprigge v Sprigge*, above). In *Re Dickson* [1984] LS Gaz R 3012, CA the presumption that a missing will had been destroyed animo revocandi was rebutted where the only reasonable inference from declarations by the testator and other evidence was that he had intended the missing will to be effective and had intended to benefit the beneficiaries thereunder.

(c)   *Revocation by partial destruction.* Where a testator signed his name, which was attested by both the witnesses, on each of the sheets of his will, and at his death only two of the middle sheets were found among his papers, it was held that the will must be presumed to be revoked (*Re Gullan's Goods* (1858) 1 Sw & Tr 23); so, too, where the testator had replaced the three middle sheets of his will (consisting of five sheets) by three other sheets, and the original sheets could not be found (*Treloar v Lean* (1889) 14 PD 49); see also *Clarke v Scripps* (1852) 2 Rob Eccl 563 (the question is whether the portion destroyed is so important as to raise a presumption that the remainder cannot have been intended to stand without it, or whether it is unimportant and independent of the remainder of the will); *Leonard v Leonard* [1902] P 243. Where part of a will is destroyed, but the part preserved contains the signatures of testator and the witnesses, the onus is normally on the party alleging revocation to prove the necessary animus. But if the part preserved is so mutilated as to be unworkable as a testamentary instrument this raises a presumption that the testator could not have intended it to stand as his will (*Re Green's Estate, Ward v Bond* (1962) 106 Sol Jo 1034). In *Re Adams* [1990] Ch 601, [1990] 2 All ER 97 it was held that the obliteration of his signature by the testator, so that it could not be read with a magnifying glass was by itself sufficient evidence of intention to revoke the whole will.

(d)   *Revocation of duplicate wills.* Where a will is executed in duplicate the revocation of one is the revocation of both (*Boughey v Moreton* (1758) 3 Hag Ecc 191). But there must be evidence that the will was, in fact, executed in duplicate—subsequent declarations by the testator to this effect are inadmissible (*Atkinson v Morris* [1897] P 40, CA; *Eyre v Eyre* [1903] P 131 at 137). See para. **3.201**, ante.

1 See p. 723, post.

33.71   *(ii) Burning.* There must be actual burning, not merely an attempt to burn (*Doe d Reed v Harris* (1837) 6 Ad & El 209); but this may be slight, if done with the intention of revoking (*Bibb v Thomas* (1775) 2 Wm Bl 1043).

33.72   *(iii) Tearing (including cutting).* The tearing need not divide the instrument in two if done with the intention of revoking (*Bibb v Thomas* (1775) 2 Wm Bl 1043; *Elms v Elms* (1858) 1 Sw & Tr 155 at 157); but the process of tearing must be completed. Where the testator was stopped in course of tearing his will and there was evidence of change of intention, it was held that there was no revocation (*Doe d Perkes v Perkes* (1820) 3 B & Ald 489); see also *Elms v Elms* (1858) 1 Sw & Tr 155; in similar circumstances the court may refuse to decree probate on motion (*Re Colberg's Goods* (1841) 2 Curt 832); the tearing must be accompanied by intention to revoke (*Giles v Warren* (1872) LR 2 P & D 401); see *Re Thornton's Goods* (1889) 14 PD 82; *Re Cowling, Jinkin v Cowling* [1924] P 113; cutting away the signature or the signature of either of the attesting witnesses may effect a revocation (*Hobbs v Knight* (1838) 1 Curt 768; *Evans v Dallow, Re Dallow's Goods* (1862) 31 LJPM & A 128; *Bell v Fothergill* (1870) LR 2 P & D 148; though not necessarily, if the piece is preserved (*Re Wheeler's Goods* (1879) 49 LJP 29), for as the intention of the testator is relevant, it must be considered whether he did this for some other purpose, e.g. in an attempt to prevent forfeiture of a legacy to the witness or his spouse; scratching out the signature with a knife (which is lateral cutting) will revoke, but only if carried out by the testator to the extent of making his signature illegible) (*Re Godfrey's Goods* (1893) 69 LT 22); cutting away signature to a will may, on proof of intention, also operate as revocation of a codicil executed on the same paper (*Re Bleckley's Goods* (1883) 8 PD 169); cutting away of portions of a will may operate merely as revocation of such portion (*Clarke v Scripps* (1852) 2 Rob Eccl 563; *Re Nunn's Estate* [1936] 1 All ER 555).

33.73 *(iv) Otherwise destroying,* must be ejusdem generis as burning or tearing (per Sir H. Jenner in *Stephens v Taprell* (1840) 2 Curt 458); see also *Cheese v Lovejoy* (1877) 2 PD 251; cancellation is not such 'otherwise destroying' (*Stephens v Taprell* (1840) 2 Curt 458).

33.74 *(v) In the presence of the testator.* If not effected by the testator, the destruction at his direction must take place in his presence; otherwise there is no revocation (*Re Dadds' Goods* (1857) Dea & Sw 290; *Re De Kremer's Estate, Lundbeck v De Kremer* (1965) 110 Sol Jo 18).

A. Partial revocation

33.75

(a)   *By duly executed obliteration, interlineation, or other alteration.*
(b)   *By such an alteration as will render the former words or effect of the will no longer apparent.* Such obliteration must be complete. If the portion can be read by any means other than physical interference with the document it is not revoked (*Ffinch v Combe* [1894] P 191; *Re Brasier's Goods* [1899] P 36). (See further re obliterations, paras. **3.240–3.247,** ante.)

B. Dependent relative, or conditional, revocation

33.76 *Dependent relative revocation.* Will destroyed in belief that thereby an earlier will would be revived (*Powell v Powell* (1866) LR 1 P & D 209; *Cossey v Cossey* (1900) 82 LT 203); part of will destroyed in belief that its place would be taken by an unexecuted memorandum (*Dancer v Crabb* (1873) LR 3 P & D 98); document destroyed in belief that later will (unexecuted) would take its place (*Re Irvin's Estate* (1908) 25 TLR 41; and *West v West* [1921] 2 IR 34; see also *Dixon v Treasury Solicitor* [1905] P 42); will destroyed in belief that a later will (in fact pronounced against) was properly executed (*Re Bunn, Durber v Bunn* (1926) 134 LT 669); destruction of earlier will after execution of later will in belief later will valid (*Re Davies' Estate, Russell v Delaney* [1951] 1 All ER 920); will mutilated on expressed intention—not fulfilled—of making another (*Re Botting's Estate, Botting v Botting* [1951] 2 All ER 997; *Re Addison's Estate* (1964) 108 Sol Jo 504: testator took will from solicitor's office saying he wanted to make a new will because of his wife's death. No will was found on his death nine months later. The proper inference was that he destroyed the will intending to make a new one. There was no revocation and the will, as contained in a copy, was admitted). See also *Re Bridgewater's Estate* [1965] 1 All ER 717, [1965] 1 WLR 416 (three wills, each with a revocation clause. Testator wrote to solicitor saying he had deposited second will at a bank, having destroyed the third. On his death only the earliest will was found. Held, the letter was admissible as evidence of intention to destroy the third will with a view to reviving the second, and as evidence of the destruction. The third will, as contained in a copy, was admitted); lapse of time immaterial if intention at date of destruction was clear (*Re Bromham's Estate, Wass v Treasury Solicitor* [1952] 1 All ER 110n); will revoked in mistaken belief that certain legatees were dead (*Campbell v French* (1797) 3 Ves

321); a printed form of will, with revocation clause, executed with blanks which were subsequently filled in—probate refused, it being held that the revocation was dependent on another will being made (*Re Irvine's Goods* [1919] 2 IR 485); destruction in mistaken belief as to distribution on intestacy (*Re Southerden's Estate, Adams v Southerden* [1925] P 177, CA). Where a second will which was incomplete revoked the first, both wills were admitted with the revocatory clause excluded (*Re Hope-Brown's Goods* [1942] P 136, [1942] 2 All ER 176: followed in *Re Allen* (1962) 106 Sol Jo 115 (all dispositions in a later will, executed on a printed form which included a revocation clause, were proved to have been added after execution. The revocation clause was held to be conditional upon the later will being effective: the earlier will was therefore not revoked)). See also *Re Cocke's Goods* [1960] 2 All ER 289, [1960] 1 WLR 491 (two inconsistent wills, the later having a revocation clause but no effective residuary gift: both wills admitted, the revocation clause in the second, and clauses in the first will inconsistent with those in the second, being omitted). When a testator destroyed a will under belief that he no longer had anything to leave the revocation was held to be conditional and the will admitted to probate (*Re Carey* (1977) 121 Sol Jo 173).

In the absence of evidence of any direct connection between the destruction of an earlier will and the purported execution of a later will the doctrine was held not applicable (*Re Green's Estate, Ward v Bond* (1962) 106 Sol Jo 1034) and *Re Jones, Evans v Harries* [1976] Ch 200, [1976] 1 All ER 593. Revocation in part of earlier will held not to have been conditional in *Re Feis, Guillaume v Ritz-Remorf* [1964] Ch 106, [1963] 3 All ER 303. See also paras. **3.244–3.247**, ante.

In *Re Finnemore* [1992] 1 All ER 800, [1991] 1 WLR 793, an intention to devise a house gathered from two previous wills was held to give a conditional (and therefore a distributive) effect to a revocation clause contained in the third will. Thus the clause did not destroy the devise in the first or second will, even though the similar devise in the third will was ineffective (that will being witnessed by the husband of the devisee). The clause did, however, operate to revoke the remainder of the earlier wills.

(8) Deceased prevented by threats from altering will

Form of defence

33.77   'That the deceased was prevented by threats on the part of the plaintiffs from making a fresh will or altering the will propounded.'

This was a defence permitted under the Judicature Act 1873, and if established it entitles the court to declare the executors of the will propounded to be trustees for the parties intended to have been benefited by another will[1].

Plea allowed by Hannen P,

> 'that after making the said alleged will of May, 1853, the deceased was prevented by force and threats from executing a further will prepared by and under his instructions whereby the plaintiff would have been deprived of his interest under the said alleged will.'

Where a testator has in a will given a legacy to A. B., and by the threats or undue influence or fraud of the residuary legatee of a subsequent will, has been induced to omit the legacy from the said will, A. B. may plead the fact and ask the court to declare the executors of the last will to be trustees for him of a part of the estate equivalent to the amount of the legacy.

For precedent of defence, see CP42.

---

1 *Betts v Doughty* (1879) 5 PD 26.

(9) Estoppel—Laches

Form of defence

33.78 'The plaintiff is estopped by reason of [as the case maybe].'

The defence should include particulars of the previous action and judgment.

Summary of reported cases

33.79 A plaintiff may be estopped from setting up a will by a previous judgment on the same issue between the same parties (*Priestman v Thomas* (1884) 9 PD 210, CA). Even where the matter was not definitely held to be res judicata, a plaintiff was estopped from prosecuting a claim for a grant of administration as next of kin, where she had practically acquiesced in Chancery proceedings four years before, in which her title as next of kin was involved, and where the property had been distributed by order of the court, it being held that the plaintiff had been guilty of such laches as to disentitle her to maintain her suit (*Mohan v Broughton* [1899] P 211; affd [1900] P 56, CA). As to the binding effect of probate in solemn form, see also para. **26.06**, ante.

As to laches, see also *Mahon v Quinn* [1904] 2 IR 267; *David v Frowd* (1833) 1 My & K 200; and *Sawyer v Birchmore* (1837) 1 Keen 825. The fact that an executor, who is also next of kin, has taken probate, does not estop him from afterwards taking proceedings for a pronouncement against the will (*Williams v Evans* [1911] P 175). A certain amount of delay on the part of such a person, even though he had all along had full knowledge of the facts, in instituting proceedings for revocation of probate does not necessarily amount to laches on his part (ibid.).

(10) Minority

Form of defence

33.80 'That the said alleged will is invalid by reason of the fact that the deceased was under the age of eighteen years at the time the said will purports to have been executed.'

By s. 7 of the Wills Act 1837[1], no will made by any person under the age of 21 years is valid. By the Family Law Reform Act 1969, s. 3(1), the age of 18 years is substituted for 21 years under s. 7 of the Wills Act 1837 and ss. 1 and 3(1) of the Wills (Soldiers and Sailors) Act 1918. For exceptions in the case of soldiers, sailors or airmen being in actual military service, or of mariners or seamen being at sea, see paras. **3.330–3.334**, ante, and paras. **32.27** ff., ante.

For precedent of defence, see CP38.

1 See p. 720, post.

Interest action

33.81 Form of defence, CP46.

Forfeiture

33.82   See para. **32.63**, ante.

CHAPTER 34

Reply and subsequent pleadings

Summary

Rules as to reply

When necessary

34.01   A plaintiff on whom a defendant serves a defence must serve a reply on that defendant if it is needed for compliance with Order 18, r. 8, i.e., if he desires to plead any matter:

(a)   which he alleges makes any claim or defence of the opposite party not maintainable; or

(b)   which, if not specifically pleaded, might take the opposite party by surprise; or

(c)   which raises issues of fact not arising out of the preceding pleading[1].

It is unnecessary to serve a reply if the plaintiff only wishes to deny the allegations contained in the defence since if no reply is served all material facts alleged in the defence are put in issue[2]; but this applies only to a defence and not to a counterclaim.

1   Ord. 18, r. 8(1).
2   Ibid., r. 14(1).

Defence to counterclaim

34.02   A plaintiff who is served with a counterclaim by a defendant must serve a defence to counterclaim on that defendant if he intends to defend the counterclaim[1].
  When the plaintiff serves both a reply and a defence to counterclaim on any defendant, they must both be included in the same document[2].

A defence to counterclaim is subject to the rules governing defences generally.

1 Ord. 18, r. 3(2).
2 Ibid., r. 3(3).

Time for reply and defence to counterclaim

34.03   A reply must be served before the expiration of 14 days after service of the defence, and a defence to counterclaim must be served before the expiration of 14 days after service of the counterclaim[1].

A plaintiff is entitled to reply by traverse, confession and avoidance, or both combined.

> 'There is no limit as to what may be said in reply, except that it must not be scandalous or irrelevant. The plaintiff is left as much at liberty in his reply as in his statement of claim. . . . It is no part of the statement of claim to anticipate the defence, and to state what the plaintiff would have to say in answer to it.'[2].

1 Ord. 18, r. 3(4).
2 Per James LJ, in *Hall v Eve* (1876) 4 Ch D 341 at 345, CA.

No further pleadings without leave

34.04   No pleading subsequent to a reply or a defence to counterclaim may be served except with the leave of the court[1].

Where it is desired to serve a rejoinder or other subsequent pleading, application for leave to do so must be made either by separate summons or by notice on the summons for directions. Leave will not be given unless a pleading is really necessary. If an order is made it will specify the time within which the pleading is to be served.

Further pleadings are called rejoinder, surrejoinder, rebutter and surrebutter; but pleadings beyond rejoinder are rarely allowed.

1 Ord. 18, r. 4.

Joinder of issue

34.05   There can be no joinder of issue, either implied or express, on a statement of claim or a counterclaim[1]; but subject to this, (a) there is, at the close of pleadings, an implied joinder of issue on the pleading last served; and (b) a party may in his pleading expressly join issue on the next preceding pleading[2].

1 Ibid., r. 14(3).
2 Ibid., r. 14(2).

Close of pleadings

34.06   The pleadings in an action are deemed to be closed:

(a)   at the expiration of 14 days after service of the reply or, if there is no reply but only a defence to counterclaim, after service of the defence to counterclaim, or

(b) if neither a reply nor a defence to counterclaim is served, at the expiration of
14 days after service of the defence[1].

The pleadings are deemed to be closed at the time specified notwithstanding that
any request or order for particulars has been made but has not been complied with
at that time[2].

1 Ibid., r. 20(1).
2 Ibid., r. 20(2).

Revival of a revoked will

34.07 Where in the statement of defence it is alleged that the will propounded by
the plaintiff has been revoked by a subsequent will or testamentary paper, the plaintiff might perhaps plead the revival of the will he propounded by a will or other
testamentary paper executed subsequently to the execution of the revoking instrument.

It is probable, however, that such testamentary paper will have been already propounded with the will.

Republication and revival

Republication

34.08 A will or codicil may be republished by a subsequent testamentary instrument. The mere description of a codicil as being a codicil to the will, or a reference
in a testamentary document not described as a codicil to the executor named in the
will has been held sufficient; but a codicil merely referring to a will by date does
not republish an intermediate codicil[1].

Republication may have important consequences to the dispositions in the will,
such as the following:

The will now speaks as from the date of republication.

It may extend the operation of the will to persons and property to whom or to
which a certain description was not applicable at the original date provided that the
will spoke of them as then in existence[2].

It may incorporate documents made since the original will, if they were
described therein (inaccurately) as being then already in existence.

It may give effect to unattested alterations in the will, subject to evidence as to
when they were made.

It may make effective a gift to a witness to the will.

It may make valid a will made during the unsoundness of mind of the testator.

It will not apply so as to defeat the testator's intentions, e.g. by making void a
valid restriction which was barred by a later statute[3].

1 *Burton v Newbery* (1875) 1 Ch D 234; *Re Park, Bott v Chester* [1910] 2 Ch 322.
2 See *Re Hardyman, Teesdale v McClintock* [1925] Ch 287, 133 LT 175.
3 *Re Heath's Will Trusts, Hamilton v Lloyds Bank Ltd* [1949] Ch 170, [1949] 1 All ER 199.

Revival

34.09   A will or codicil that has been revoked, but is still in existence, can be revived by a subsequent testamentary instrument. But there must be evidence of the testator's intention to revive (see also Wills Act 1837, s. 22). See also paras. **3.173–3.178**, ante.

Forms

34.10   For precedent of statement of claim where revival (or republication) is alleged, see CP30.

For precedents of replies see CP47 et seq.

Summary of reported cases

Revival of a revoked will by subsequent testamentary instrument

34.11   In order for a revoked will to be revived by a subsequent testamentary instrument: (i) it must be in existence at the time of execution of such instrument (*Hale v Tokelove* (1850) 2 Rob Eccl 318; *Rogers and Andrews v Goodenough and Rogers* (1862) 2 Sw & Tr 342; *Re Edge's Goods* (1882) 9 LR Ir 516; *Re Reade's Goods* [1902] P 75); (ii) there must be an indication of an intention to revive (Wills Act 1837, s. 22). In the absence of specific words of revival, revival may be effected by words showing with reasonable certainty that such an intention existed. A will cannot be revived by mere implication (*Re Steele's Goods* (1868) LR 1 P & D 575), by oral declaration (*Hale v Tokelove* (1850) 2 Rob Eccl 318 at 325), or by the destruction of the revoking (or inconsistent) document (*Re Brown's Goods* (1858) 1 Sw & Tr 32; *Re Hodgkinson's Goods* [1893] P 339, CA; *Re Debac's Goods, Sanger v Hart* (1897) 77 LT 374). A mere reference in a codicil to a revoked will has been held insufficient to revive it (*Re Steele's Goods* (1868) LR 1 P & D 575); even the formal clause confirming the will may not be sufficient (*Re Sebag-Montefiore, Sebag-Montefiore v Alliance Assurance Co Ltd* [1944] Ch 331, [1944] 1 All ER 672, CA; but see *Re Reynold's Goods* (1873) LR 3 P & D 35), unless there is evidence on the face of the codicil of intention to revive the will or to revoke the intermediate will (*Re Steele's Goods* (1868) LR 1 P & D 575; see also *Re Edge's Goods* (1882) 9 LR Ir 516; and *Goldie v Adam* [1938] P 85, [1938] 1 All ER 586; *Re White's Estate* (1961) 105 Sol Jo 259); the reference in the codicil to a revoked will need not refer to the date of such will, or may even give an inaccurate date so long as the intention to revive the will in question is clear (*Re M'Cabe's Goods* (1862) 2 Sw & Tr 474; *Re Green's Goods* (1899) 79 LT 738; *Marsh v Marsh* (1860) 1 Sw & Tr 528 at 533). A duly attested indorsement on an envelope containing a will revoked by marriage, stating that the beneficiary in the will was now the lawful wife of testator, was held to be a codicil reviving the will (*Re Davis' Estate* [1952] P 279, [1952] 2 All ER 509). Although the mere reference by date to a revoked will in a codicil, if made by mistake, will not revive such revoked will (*Re May's Goods* (1868) LR 1 P & D 575; *Re Wilson's Goods* (1868) LR 1 P & D 575; *Re Lady Isabella Gordon's Goods* [1892] P 228; *Jane v Jane* (1917) 33 TLR 389: see also *Goldie v Adam*, above); yet if the mistake be carried further and details of the revoked will are referred to in the codicil, whether prepared by the testator or by a draftsman on his behalf, the effect may be to revive such will (*Re Stedham's Goods* (1881) 6 PD 205; *Re Dyke's Goods* (1881) 6 PD 205; *Re Chilcott's Goods* [1897] P 223; *Re Baker, Baker v Baker* [1929] 1 Ch 668). In this event the earlier document, being brought up to the date of the codicil by the revival, effects a revocation of the intermediate will and any codicils thereto (*Re Baker*, above): a fortiori if the revived will contains a revocation clause (*Re Pearson, Rowling v Crowther* [1963] 3 All ER 763, [1963] 1 WLR 1358). In the absence of words in the codicil expressly reviving the earlier will and revoking the later, both wills may be included with the codicil in the probate; it is then for the court of construction to interpret the documents (*Re Stedham*, above; *Re Dyke*, above; *Re Chilcott*, above). In a case in which a codicil to a will was, by mistake, indorsed on, and referred to, a revoked earlier will, all three documents were admitted (*Re Carleton's Goods* [1915] 2 IR 9). Where there is ambiguity in the language of a codicil said to revive a revoked will, evidence of the testator's intention is inadmissible (*Re Goodenough's Goods* (1861) 2 Sw & Tr 141; *Re Steele's Goods* (1868) LR 1 P & D 575 at 576); but evidence of surrounding circumstances to explain the language may be received (*Re Steele's Goods* (1868) LR 1 P & D 575 at 576); there may be revival of part only of a will (*Re Mardon's Estate* [1944] P 109, [1944] 2 All ER 397); and if a revoked will or codicil, part of which had been revoked before the revocation of the whole, is revived by a subsequent codicil, such revival will not extend to the part first revoked, unless an intention to revive that part also is shown. See Wills Act 1837, s. 22, and paras. **3.166** ff., ante.

CHAPTER 35

Discovery

Summary

Discovery of documents

General rules as to discovery

35.01   Discovery of documents is governed by RSC Order 24. Although the discovery ordered to be given in a probate action may be somewhat more extensive than in other actions, the basic principles are the same.

As regards documents a distinction must be drawn between discovery and production. All documents relevant to the issues must be included in a party's list or affidavit, though privilege may be claimed, upon various grounds, in respect of certain of them, which should be shown separately in the list or affidavit.

Subject to this, the plaintiff is entitled to discovery of all the documents he has, or has had, in his custody or under his control, relating to the matters in question in the action.

The defendant is similarly entitled to discovery of all documents that are relevant to the issues.

The rule of law whereby a person could not be compelled to produce any document relating solely to his own case and in no way tending to impeach that case or support the case of opposing parties was abrogated by s. 16(2) of the Civil Evidence Act 1968.

It is the duty of solicitors to take positive steps to ensure that their clients appreciate at an early stage of litigation, promptly after issue of the writ, not only the duty of discovery and its width, but also the importance of not destroying documents which might possibly have to be disclosed[1].

---

1   Per Megarry J in *Rockwell Machine Tool Co Ltd v E P Barrus (Concessionaires) Ltd* [1968] 2 All ER 98n, [1968] 1 WLR 693.

Discovery in probate actions

35.02 In consequence of the peculiar nature of the enquiry in probate actions, the court exercises a wider latitude in ordering discovery in these suits than is exercised in other actions. Where the issue raised relates to the testamentary capacity of the deceased the enquiry may legitimately extend to the history of a considerable portion, or of even the whole, of his life; and it is extremely difficult to say before the trial what evidence relating to any particular portion of his life may or may not at the trial turn out to be material to this issue. The same observation, though to a lesser extent, applies in cases where the issue raised is one of undue influence or of fraud, or that the deceased did not know and approve of the contents of a will.

The practice of the court, therefore, is to order discovery of all documents throwing light on the history of the deceased, which might turn out to have any possible bearing on the issues raised.

Right to discovery, of persons believing that they were interested under previous wills

35.03 Where the executors and the solicitor of a deceased testatrix refused to give information as to previous wills alleged to have been executed by the testatrix to persons who believed that they had been benefited by them, they were ordered, under s. 26 of the Court of Probate Act 1857[1], to deposit in the registry all wills and testamentary papers of the deceased in their possession, with liberty to the applicants to take copies of them[2].

1 Since repealed and replaced by s. 122 of the Supreme Court Act 1981: p. 846, post.
2 *Re Shepherd's Goods* [1891] P 323.

Inspection of documents

General rules as to inspection

35.04 Inspection of documents is governed by RSC Order 24.

Inspection of documents belonging to the deceased

35.05 With regard to documents and other papers belonging to the deceased, the court will order inspection by either party, unless the party in whose custody, or under whose control, they happen to be can show that he has any special interest or property in them. Upon the death of the deceased they come, in very many cases, under the control of one of the parties to the suit, by the mere accident of that party having been resident, or in close touch, with him at the time of his death, or being first to take possession of his house, or employing his solicitor, and, unless an administrator pendente lite is appointed, they remain under such person's control pending the enquiry. He ought not, by this accident, to be allowed an advantage in the action over his opponent[1].

By virtue of s. 122 of the Supreme Court Act 1981[2], the High Court has very wide powers to order the production of documents, and such orders are available not only against the parties, but against other persons (see paras. **27.16** and **27.17**, ante).

In a probate action, the function of the court is not only to do justice between the parties, but also to do justice to the deceased, by ascertaining, and ultimately by its decree giving effect to, all duly executed testamentary instruments by which he intended to dispose of his property; and, to ascertain this fact, the court should know as far as possible what he knew; and much of such knowledge may be found in the papers left by him in his depositories. In justice to the testator, therefore, either party may claim to have an opportunity of directing the attention of the court to such papers as he may consider tend to support his own case, and to do this access to very many of them is necessary.

1 See *Hunt v Anderson* (1868) LR 1 P & D 476.
2 See p. 846, post.

In action where deceased's capacity was in dispute, production of briefs prepared on her behalf refused

35.06   In an action where the defendants alleged that the deceased was not of sound mind, memory or understanding, and asked for production of the briefs which had been prepared by one of the plaintiffs as solicitor for the deceased in certain proceedings which had been taken against her, and which the defendants alleged contained certain matter relevant to the issue of the deceased's state of mind, it was held that the defendants were not entitled to production of the briefs[1].

1   *Curtis v Beaney* [1911] P 181, 80 LJP 87.

Inspection of documents which were the property of the testatrix's solicitor refused

35.07   In an action where the plaintiff propounded a will, and the defendants had applied for inspection of documents, and where it appeared that the solicitor for the plaintiff had acted as the solicitor for the testatrix for a long time previous to her death, and had in his possession many books and documents relating to her affairs, an order was refused on the ground that such books and documents were the private property of the solicitor[1].

1   *O'Shea v Wood* [1891] P 286, CA.

Interrogatories

General rules as to interrogatories

35.08   Interrogatories are a means by which facts may be discovered before trial. Interrogatories are governed by RSC Order 26.

Interrogatories in probate action where undue influence is alleged

35.09   In a case in which the defendants (two executors and the universal legatee) were alleged to have exercised undue influence upon the testator, but the executors took no benefit under the will, interrogatories were allowed as to whether the two executors had received loans or gifts from the deceased during his lifetime (as tending to show their influence over him), and as to whether they had received any of the property from the universal legatee since the death of the deceased, and whether this was by arrangement made during his life[1].

1   *Re Holloway, Young v Holloway* (1887) 12 PD 167, CA.

Discovery of facts by other means

Discovery by opening coffin

35.10   Where a question of identity was in dispute a further form of discovery, by opening a coffin buried in consecrated ground, has been allowed on Letters of Request from the President of the Probate Division[1].

1 See *R v Tristram* [1898] 2 QB 371; and *Druce v Young* [1899] P 84.

CHAPTER 36

Summons for directions

Summary

Purpose and time of issue of a summons

36.01   Under Order 25, r. 1:

> 'with a view to providing an occasion for the consideration by the Court of the pre-
> parations for the trial of the action so that: (a) all matters which must or can be dealt
> with on interlocutory applications and have not already been dealt with may so far as
> possible be dealt with, and (b) such directions may be given as to the future course of
> the action as appear best adapted to secure the just, expeditious and economical dis-
> posal thereof',

the plaintiff must, within one month after the pleadings in the action are deemed to
be closed, take out a summons for directions, which must be returnable in not less
than 14 days after the day of issue. (Although Order 25, r. 9 makes provision for
standard directions by consent in Chancery proceedings without the need for a summons, nevertheless in probate proceedings a summons for directions is in practice
always necessary so that the Master can be satisfied that the particular requirements
of probate proceedings are being or will be adhered to.)

Where the time for discovery by exchange of lists of documents under Order 24,
r. 2 is extended (whether by consent or by order or both) beyond the normal period
of 14 days after the pleadings are deemed to be closed, the time within which the
plaintiff must issue the summons for directions is 14 days after the expiration of the
extended time allowed for discovery[1].

In the normal course of events, discovery of documents takes place before the
issue of the summons for directions. A party who wishes the opposite party to
verify his list of documents by affidavit must serve notice requiring this before the
summons for directions is taken out[2].

---

1 Order 24, r. 2(7).
2 Order 25, r. 1(3).

Default of issue of summons

36.02   If the plaintiff does not issue a summons for directions within the required time, the defendant or any defendant may do so[1].

1   Order 25, r. 1(4) and (5).

Issue of summons

36.03   The summons for directions is issued at the Chancery Registry or the Chancery district registry (as the case may be). The plaintiff's solicitors should lodge at the Registry a copy of the pleadings and any request for further and better particulars. Order 25, r. 6(2A) requires a statement of value to be lodged with the Court before the hearing of the summons, if the county court has jurisdiction (i.e. because the gross estate does not exceed £30,000); see also para. **40.01**, post.

Matters to be considered

Duties of the court

36.04   Under Order 25, r. 2, when the summons first comes to be heard, the court must consider whether it is possible to deal then with all the matters which are required to be considered on the hearing of a summons for directions or whether it is expedient to adjourn the consideration of all or any of those matters until a later stage.

The matters which the court must in particular consider (if necessary, of its own motion) are whether any order should be made or direction given in exercise of the powers conferred by any of the following provisions:

(a)   section 40 of the County Courts Act 1984 (as re-enacted by the Courts and Legal Services Act 1990);

(b)   any provision of Part I of the Civil Evidence Act 1968 (hearsay evidence) or of the Civil Evidence Act 1972, or of Part III or of Order 28; and

(c)   Order 38, rr. 2 to 7. These rules permit the court to order:

   (1)   that all or part of the evidence shall be given by affidavit, on such terms as to the filing and giving of copies of the affidavits or proposed affidavits and as to the production of the deponents for cross-examination as the court may think fit. Subject to such terms and to any subsequent order or direction, however, the deponents are not subject to cross-examination and need not attend the trial for this purpose[1];

   (2)   without prejudice to r. 2, that evidence of any particular fact shall be given at the trial in such manner as shall be specified in the order, and in particular,

     (i)   by statement on oath of information or belief;

     (ii)   by the production of documents or entries in books;

     (iii)   by copies of documents or entries in books; or

     (iv)   in the case of a fact which is or was a matter of common knowledge either generally or in a particular district, by the production of a specified newspaper containing a statement of such fact[2];

   (3)   that no more than a specified number of medical or expert witnesses may be called[3];

(4) the exchange of written statements.

The court will also make directions about court bundles[4].

1 Order 38, r. 2(2).
2 Ibid., r. 3.
3 Ibid., r. 4.
4 Order 25, r. 3(2).

Statement of solicitor preparing will

36.05   The Council of the Law Society has stated that a solicitor who acted for a testator in drawing up his will should, if the will becomes the subject matter of a dispute after death, make available a statement of his evidence regarding the execution of the will and the circumstances surrounding it to anyone who asks for such a statement, whether or not the solicitor acted for those propounding the will[1].

1 *Law Society's Gazette* (September 1959), p. 619.

Admissions and agreements

36.06   At the hearing of the summons for directions, the court must endeavour to secure that the parties make all admissions and agreements as to the conduct of the proceedings which they ought reasonably to make. Such admissions or agreements, and (with a view to any special order for costs being made at the trial) any refusal to make admissions or agreements, may be recorded in the order for directions[1].

1 Order 25, r. 4.

Procedure at first hearing of summons

36.07   If the court considers it possible, at the first hearing of a summons for directions, to deal with all the matters set out above, the court will deal with them forthwith, and must endeavour to secure that all other matters which must or can be dealt with on interlocutory applications and have not already been dealt with, are also then dealt with. If, on the other hand, the court thinks it expedient to adjourn the consideration of all or any of the matters set out, such of them as can conveniently be dealt with forthwith will be disposed of and the consideration of the remaining matters adjourned. In this case the court must endeavour similarly to secure that all other interlocutory matters are dealt with either on the original or resumed hearing of the summons[1].

1 Ibid., r. 2(2) and (3).

Summons for directions in probate actions

36.08   Because a probate action is in nature an action in rem with the court taking an investigative role, the Master will be concerned on the first hearing of the summons for directions to satisfy himself that all proper parties are joined (or give directions for their joinder) and that the relief sought is appropriate in light of the affidavits of testamentary scripts filed and the scripts lodged. It is therefore most important (a) that all parties comply with the provisions of Order 76, r. 5 (testamentary scripts) well before the hearing of the summons and (b) that the hearing be estimated (and the appointment fixed) for a sufficient length of time.

Place and mode of trial

36.09 An order made on the summons for directions must determine the place and mode of trial[1].

Except where the parties agree to the making of the order as to the place and mode of trial before all matters required to be considered on the hearing of the summons have been dealt with, no such order may be made until all those matters have been dealt with[2]. At the final hearing of the summons for direction the solicitors must inform the Master of the estimated length of the hearing.

1 Order 33, r. 4(1).
2 Order 25, r. 2(4).

CHAPTER 37

Interlocutory applications

Summary

Particular applications

Administrator pending suit

37.01   When a probate action has begun, application may be made to the court for the appointment of an administrator pending suit. Such an administrator has all the rights and powers of a general administrator other than the right of distributing the estate, and every such administrator is subject to the immediate control of the court and acts under its direction[1]. He is, like a receiver, an officer of the court. A single individual may be appointed as administrator, notwithstanding the fact that a minority or life interest will arise[2].

The application is made by summons in the Chancery Division returnable before a Master[3]. The issue of the writ must precede the application[4]. The application may be made by any party to the action and the court has power to appoint an administrator on the application of a person who is not a party, e.g. a creditor[5]. A person unconnected with the action is the most suitable person to be appointed as administrator[6]. There is no absolute rule that a party to an action cannot be appointed administrator without the consent of all parties. The court will make such an appointment when it is clearly desirable[7].

In some cases the court may refuse the application, e.g. when an executor was appointed under a will and a codicil which was in a dispute did not affect his appointment[8]; or when there was no evidence that the surviving partner of the deceased who was in control of the assets was wasting the estate[9].

It is intended that the practice should be assimilated to the practice relating to receivers[10], and most of the provisions of Order 30 now apply to an administrator. Order 30, r. 5 will not apply to an administrator, and his balances will not be paid into court unless specifically directed in a special case.

The summons for the appointment of an administrator should give the name of the administrator in the summons and ask for all directions required. At least two clear days before the hearing before the Master the applicant should lodge at court an affidavit setting out inter alia the reasons for the application, that there is something to be done and no one empowered to do it[11]; the full name and address and qualification of the proposed administrator; and the value of the property which is likely to come into his hands. The applicant's solicitors should at the same time lodge the consent of the proposed administrator to act and an affidavit of fitness by some disinterested person.

At the hearing if all the evidence is in order, the Master will make an order appointing A. B. as administrator pending suit; fix the security at £X or in an appropriate case dispensing with security; order the administrator to give security for £X by a certain date with liberty to act at once on the applicant giving a undertaking to be answerable in the meantime; order that the administrator do pass his accounts as the court shall from time to time direct; and grant liberty to apply for further directions (Form CP10).

Unless the court otherwise directs, the security is given by guarantee[12]. The guarantee must be filed at court[13]. For form of guarantee, see Form CP5.

1   Supreme Court Act 1981, s. 117.
2   *Re Haslip* [1958] 2 All ER 275n, [1958] 1 WLR 583.
3   Order 76, r. 14(1).
4   *Salter v Salter* [1896] P 291.
5   *Re Cleaver's Estate* [1905] P 319.
6   *De Chatelain v Pontigny* (1858) 1 Sw & Tr 34.
7   *Re Griffin, Griffin v Ackroyd* [1925] P 38.
8   *Mortimer v Paull* (1870) LR 2 P & D 85.
9   *Horrell v Witts and Plumley* (1866) LR 1 P & D 103.
10 Order 76, r. 14(2).
11 *Horrell v Witts and Plumley*, above.
12 Order 30, r. 2(3).
13 Ibid., r. 2(4).

37.02   An administrator pending suit will be allowed such proper remuneration as may be fixed by the court[1], and such remuneration may be paid out of the estate[2].

The parties will often agree to dispense with formal accounts; and the practice now of the court is to direct that the accounts be submitted to the parties interested, and only if a dispute arises on the accounts will the court intervene to determine the matter or matters in dispute. If an account is ordered its form takes the form of a cash account (Form CP1) and an inventory (Form CP2) verified by affidavit. If the administrator fails to submit his accounts as directed, the sanctions provided by Ord. 30, r. 6 in the case of default by a receiver will apply to him also.

On appointment the administrator pending suit applies to the principal registry for a grant: for practice, see para. **11.321**, ante. He has no power to act until the grant is obtained and he should produce the grant in chambers as soon as it has been obtained. The duties of an administrator begin from the date of order appointing him and terminate with the final order in the action. His powers are not formally revoked, but cease with the making of the final order. An appeal operates as an extension of the action, and the administrator continues to act until the action is finally disposed of. The grant continues for this period[3].

An administrator pending suit cannot distribute the residue of the estate, nor can he pay a legacy or annuity given by a disputed will except with the consent of all persons interested in the residue[4]. Where there was a dispute about an alleged debt, an administrator was not permitted to pay the debt until payment had been approved by the court[5]. When a decree has been made by the court the administrator will bring in his final account to be passed in chambers, when his bill of costs will be allowed and the security vacated.

When an unsuccessful party is condemned in the costs of an action, these include all charges of an administrator pending suit including the costs of obtaining the appointment, applying for the grant, passing the accounts (where appropriate) and administrator's remuneration[6]. But if part of the work done was necessary in any event to wind up the estate there should be an apportionment of the costs[7].

1 Order 76, r. 15(2).
2 Supreme Court Act 1981, s. 117(3).
3 *Taylor v Taylor* (1881) 6 PD 29.
4 *Whittle v Keats* (1866) 35 LJ P & M 54.
5 *Charlton v Hindmarsh* (1860) 1 Sw & Tr 519.
6 *Fisher and Joy v Fisher* (1878) 4 PD 231.
7 *Re Howlett, Howlett v Howlett* [1950] P 177, [1950] 1 All ER 485.

Leave to intervene

37.03   A person not a party to a probate action may apply by summons for leave to intervene and be joined as a party. In the Prerogative Court of Canterbury and subsequently in the Court of Probate when a suit was pending, a person whose interest might possibly be affected by the suit was allowed to intervene to protect his interest.

Interveners took the cause as they found it at the time of their intervention. Hence they could of right take only such steps, as from the time of their intervention, as they might have done had they been parties in the first instance, or had their intervention occurred at an earlier stage of the cause. An intervener could not as of right plead after the pleadings were closed but the court might allow him to do so on cause shown[1].

If, being cognisant of the proceedings and of an interest enabling him to intervene, such a person fails to intervene he will be bound by the proceedings although not a party[2], and see RSC Order 15, r. 13A[3]. An applicant who obtains leave to intervene is added as a defendant to the action by the Master and must acknowledge service if he wishes to be heard.

1 *Clement v Rhodes* (1825) 3 Add 37 at 40.
2 *Wytcherley v Andrews* (1871) LR 2 P & D 327; *Young v Holloway* [1895] P 87.
3 See para. **28.04**, ante.

Discontinuance, dismissal and stay of proceedings

37.04   The ordinary rules set out in Order 21 (withdrawal and discontinuance) do not apply to probate actions, and the leave of the court must be obtained in every case. At any stage of the proceedings the plaintiff or any party to the action who has acknowledged service may apply to the court for an order that the action may be discontinued or dismissed. The court may make the order asked for on such terms as to costs or otherwise as it thinks just and may further order the issue of a grant in common form in favour of 'X if entitled'[1]. (Form CP12.)

The application for such an order is made by motion, summons or by notice under Order 25, r. 7 depending on the circumstances[2].

Alternatively an order in 'Tomlin' form staying proceedings on scheduled terms and, if desired, containing an order for the issue of a grant in common form in favour of 'X if entitled thereto' can be made (Form CP11)[3].

Before any proposed order is submitted the parties must file their affidavits of scripts and lodge the scripts (see Chap. 30, ante).

A consent order signed by all parties may be submitted by post. It will be considered by the Master. If he is satisfied he will make the order; otherwise he will raise written queries and may direct one or all parties to attend. If the order seeks approval of a compromise on behalf of a person under a disability the Master will only have jurisdiction if that person's interest in the estate does not exceed £30,000[4].

Once an order is made for discontinuance or dismissal and for the issue of a grant in common form in favour of 'X if entitled thereto', it is then followed by a non-contentious application at the appropriate probate registry[5].

1 Order 76, r. 11(2).
2 Ibid, r. 11(3).
3 If an administrator pendente lite has been appointed an express provision should be made in the operative part of the 'Tomlin' order to discharge him. This is because his functions only cease at the end of the action (see para. **37.02**, ante) whereas a 'Tomlin' order operates only as a stay.
4 PD (13) B(b); see para. **26.11**, ante. See also para. **38.07**, post.
5 An order for this issue of a grant in common form, whether contained in an order for discontinuance or dismissal or in a 'Tomlin' order, is in practice treated as a 'decision' of the court for the purposes of NCPR 45(3).

Dismissal for want of prosecution

37.05 The court will not strike out an action to revoke a grant of probate or letters of administration on the mere grounds of delay but will only strike it out if it is satisfied that it is otherwise frivolous, vexatious or an abuse of the process of the court[1].

1 *Re Flynn, Flynn v Flynn* [1982] 1 All ER 882, [1982] 1 WLR 310, applying *Re Coghlan, Briscoe v Broughton* [1948] 2 All ER 68, CA and dictum of Sir H.I. Fust in *Merryweather v Turner* (1844) 3 Curt 802 at 817. (See also laches, para. **33.78**, ante).

Compromise

37.06 Discontinuance, dismissal and stay of proceedings do not involve the court in making an order in solemn form for or against the validity of a will. At most the order may provide for the issue of a grant in common form.

Section 49 of the Administration of Justice Act 1985 permits a compromise to be effected without a full trial with the court nevertheless making an order in solemn form for or against the validity of a will. Before the court will do this it must be satisfied that every relevant beneficiary as defined in the section (effectively any person who would be affected by a grant for or against) consents to the order. The text of the section is set out at p. 865, post.

The application must be supported by an affidavit showing who all the relevant beneficiaries (as defined) are and their consents must be exhibited or lodged.

A Master may make the order (unless it involves also approval on behalf of a person under a disability whose interest in the estate exceeds £30,000; see PD(13)B(b) and para. **26.11**, ante; see also para. **38.07**, post). Affidavits of scripts must be filed and the scripts lodged (see Chap. 30, ante). Because of the nature of the order and the matters with which the Master has to be satisfied, it would only be in the simplest of cases that a postal application would be appropriate. Attendance before the Master at his ex parte time (2.15 p.m. each day) is also inappropriate because insufficient time is available. The normal procedure is for a summons to be issued and for an appointment (of sufficient length of time) to be obtained on which a party (or the parties) attend.

For a form of order see CP9.

CHAPTER 38
Trial

Summary

Place of trial

38.01   A probate action will normally be tried at the place where the action was commenced (i.e. in London at the Royal Courts of Justice or in one of the Chancery district registries of the High Court in Birmingham, Bristol, Cardiff, Leeds, Liverpool, Manchester, Newcastle upon Tyne and Preston or, rarely, in the county court).

If an action has been commenced in the High Court in London it can be transferred to one of the Chancery district registries (or, rarely and exceptionally, and if the county court has jurisdiction—see Chap. 40, post—to the county court). The transfer will normally be ordered at the hearing of the summons for directions.

There is also power, not to transfer the action, but to direct that the trial shall take place outside London. The procedure is set out in PD (9) (see para. **26.11**, ante).

The lists and Short Probate List procedure

Witness list: Part 1

38.02   If the estimate given by the Master at the summons for directions is over three days it will be allocated to Part 1. Within 28 days of setting down any party may give notice to the clerk of the lists and to all other parties of his intention to apply to fix a date. If this is not done, the clerk of the lists may fix a date at any time after 28 days from the date of setting down. If any party is dissatisfied with any decision of the clerk of the lists that party may apply to the judge in charge of the list (to be ascertained from the Cause List), giving one clear day's notice in writing to the other parties. This application should be made within seven days of the clerk of the lists making his decision[1], and upon a date and time fixed by the judge's clerk.

Within 10 days of setting down the solicitor for each party must lodge with the cause clerk a certificate signed by counsel stating the length of time the trial is expected to take. The certificate may be sent by post, and a single certificate signed by all counsel is preferred[2]. It is good practice to lodge the certificate at the time of setting down. If no agreement can be reached separate certificates must be given[3].

When an action is settled or an estimate of time is altered a letter signed by the solicitors for all parties must be lodged with the clerk of the lists. When the settlement entails a further order from the Master the letter should state this.

Interlocutory applications after setting down, should be made by summons to the Master[4].

1 PD (12)A; see para. **26.11**, ante.
2 Ibid.
3 Ibid.
4 Order 25, r. 7(3) and *Morley v Woolfson* [1954] 3 All ER 378n, [1954] 1 WLR 1363.

Witness list: Part 2

38.03   This consists of actions estimated to last not more than three days where fixed dates are not usually given[1]. Actions may be in the list after 28 days from the date of setting down. In special circumstances a date may be fixed on application to the clerk of the lists. If the application is successful the action will be transferred to Part 1. Counsel's certificate of length of hearing must be lodged as in the case of Part 1. All applications with regard to the hearing of cases in this list are made to the judge notified in the cause list as being in charge of Part 2[2].

1 PD (12)A; see para. **26.11**, ante.
2 Ibid.

Short Probate List procedure

38.04   The procedure for judgment by default under Order 13 and Order 19 does not apply in probate actions. If it is desired that the court should pronounce for or against a will in solemn form this is done in open court unless the procedure under s. 49 of the Administration of Justice Act 1985 can be adopted. Where there is no opposition the proceedings are brought before the Master by summons and he makes an order for trial in the Short Probate List on a date and time to be fixed[1]. This list is used when the defendant is in default of acknowledgment of service, in default of pleadings or sometimes when the parties wish to compromise proceedings.

1 PD (12) B ix; see para. **26.11**, ante.

Default of acknowledgment of service

38.05   When any defendant fails to acknowledge service the plaintiff may by summons apply for an order for trial[1]. The plaintiff's solicitor must file at court an affidavit of service of the writ[2], with the statement of claim if no statement of claim is indorsed on the writ[3] and an affidavit in support of the summons[4]. Evidence should if possible be given by affidavit and not orally. If satisfied with the evidence the Master will order trial in the Short Probate List.

If the plaintiff does not require the will to be proved in solemn form he can issue a summons for the discontinuance of the action and the order can be made by the Master in chambers[5] (Form CP12).

1 Order 76, r. 6(3).
2 Ibid., r. 6(2).
3 Ibid., r. 6(4).
4 Ibid., r. 6(5).
5 Ibid., r. 11.

Default of pleadings

38.06 When any party fails to serve on any other party a pleading which he is required to serve on him, the latter party may, after the expiration of the time allowed for service of such pleading, apply for an order for trial of the action[1]. This usually occurs when there is default in serving a defence, and the same procedure applies as in the preceding paragraph. Evidence is normally given by affidavit[2] and there must be evidence of failure to serve the defence or other pleading.

1 Ibid., r. 10(2).
2 Ibid., r. 10(2).

Compromise

38.07 When, whether before or after service of the defence in a probate action, the parties agree to a compromise a summons can be issued to obtain an order for trial[1]. The summons should be supported by affidavit evidence[2] and accompanied by minutes of the proposed order (Form 228). The application for probate in solemn form can be heard in open court but approval of the compromise on behalf of any minors or any other person under a disability is heard in chambers. See also paras. **37.04** and **37.06**, ante.

Alternatively the section 49 procedure mentioned at para. **37.06** can be adopted, which will usually be the preferred course.

For the trial involving a compromise a summons should be issued with paragraphs, the first asking for the court's approval to the compromise which is heard by the judge in chambers and the second asking for judgment in accordance with the proposed minutes of order which is heard on the same day in the Short Probate List.

The court can approve a compromise on behalf of minors or persons under a disability but cannot force one of them against the opinion of their advisers[3]. The present practice is that the next friend or guardian ad litem of the minor or person under disability swears an affidavit exhibiting case to counsel and his opinion advising that the compromise is for the benefit of the minor or person under disability and stating that he personally approves the compromise. When an action is brought or defended under the sanction of the Court of Protection no compromise can be effected without the sanction of that court.

When it is proposed that there should be a charitable scheme[4] or the court is asked to approve a compromise on behalf of absent charities[5] the Attorney-General should be made a party to the proceedings. Wherever possible the charity should be a party and agree to the compromise itself, but when a compromise has been assented to by the Attorney-General on behalf of charities absent from their own choice they are bound by the compromise[6].

When the court has made an order approving the terms of a compromise the terms are enforceable against all parties to the compromise[7] but (unless the court is acting under Ord. 15, r. 13(4)) are not binding on persons who were not parties to the action or privy to the compromise[8]. The court will only sanction a compromise after a writ has been issued[9]. After the issue of the writ the solicitor of a party has an implied authority to settle the action unless there is a limitation of his authority which had been brought to the notice of the other side[10]. Where a notice has been served under RSC Order 15, r. 13A the court's decree may bind the absent person, but he will not be bound by the terms of compromise.

When a probate action is settled it is usual to order the grant to issue to X 'if entitled thereto'. If these words are omitted they will be inferred, as the right or title to the grant will be determined by the district judge or registrar of the probate registry[11].

1   Ibid., r. 12.
2   Ibid., r. 12.
3   *Re Birchall, Wilson v Birchall* (1880) 16 Ch D 41.
4   *Boughey v Minor* [1893] P 181.
5   *Re King, Jackson v A-G* [1917] 2 Ch 420.
6   Ibid.
7   *Harvey v Allen* (1858) 1 Sw & Tr 151.
8   *Wytcherley v Andrews* (1871) LR 2 P & D 327, and *Re West, Tiger v Handley* [1948] WN 432.
9   *Norman v Strains* (1880) 6 PD 219.
10 *Welsh v Roe* (1918) 118 LT 529.
11 *Practice Note* [1938] WN 222.

Evidence

38.08   At the hearing the court will have to be satisfied by the party propounding the will that it was duly executed, that the testator was of testamentary capacity, and that he knew and approved the contents of the will. For this purpose an affi-davit by one of the attesting witnesses will usually be sufficient[1]. When a will and codicil or codicils are being propounded evidence must of course be called in respect of each document. If a decree pronouncing against a will is sought evidence must be produced to justify such a decree, e.g. that the will was not duly executed or at the time of execution the deceased was not of sound mind.

It is the usual practice to have any later will pronounced against but when proceedings are undefended and evidence has been adduced in favour of an earlier will the court may pronounce for the earlier will without pronouncing against the later will provided it is satisfied that everyone interested under the later will has been served or had proper notice[2].

A grant may be made to the next of kin when the executors and persons interested under the alleged will have not appeared or taken any part in the proceedings. In such circumstances it is not necessary to have the will pronounced against[3].

1 *Re Lemon's Estate, Winwood v Lemon* (1961) 105 Sol Jo 1107.
2 *Re Morton's Goods, Morton v Thorpe* (1863) 3 Sw & Tr 179.
3 *Re Quick's Goods, Quick v Quick* [1899] P 187.

The hearing

38.09　The rules of Order 35 as to proceedings at the trial are in general applicable to probate actions.

If the party opposing a will should not appear at the trial, the party propounding it should proceed to prove it in solemn form.

Burden of proof, and right to begin

38.10　Subject to any direction of the judge, the plaintiff should begin by opening his case unless the burden of proof of all the issues in the action lies on the defendant (or on one of the defendants if there are more than one and they are separately represented), in which case the defendant (or that defendant) has the right to begin (Order 35, r. 7: this rule also prescribes the order of speeches, subject to any direction of the judge).

In a probate action there may well be shifts in the burden of proof, but in broad outline where the issues raised in the suit include those arising out of the alleged condition, act or omission of the testator (e.g. lack of testamentary capacity, want of knowledge and approval or lack of due execution), the burden of proof on those issues is primarily upon the party propounding the will, and it lies with that party to begin[1]. If, however, the validity of the will is not attacked and the sole issue is revocation, it is for the party alleging the revocation of a will to begin[2].

By Order 35, r. 7(6) where the burden of proof of all the issues lies on the defendant he is entitled to begin, but apart from this the court has an unfettered direction to decide who shall begin under Order 35, r. 7(1). Should there be more than one will before the court, it may often be convenient for the defendant to begin when he is setting up the latest will in point of time[3].

The burden of proving affirmative allegations impeaching the will where the fault does not lie with the testator (e.g. undue influence or fraud) is upon the party making them, and if they are pleaded without including the issues referred to above it lies with that party to begin[4]. This applies notwithstanding that the party propounding the will still has the burden of satisfying the court as to due execution, for this remains an essential whatever other issues may be raised in the suit. It is a matter between that party and the court[5].

The same considerations apply in a revocation action[6].

1 *Hutley v Grimstone* (1879) 5 PD 24.
2 *North v North* (1909) 25 TLR 322.
3 *Re Parry's Estate, Parry v Fraser* [1977] 1 All ER 309, [1977] 1 WLR 93n.
4 *Hutley v Grimstone*, above; *Tate v Tate* (1890) 63 LT 112.
5 *Hutley v Grimstone*, above.
6 *Cross v Cross* (1864) 3 Sw & Tr 292.

Witnesses

38.11   The former rule to the effect that witnesses should remain out of court until they had given their evidence no longer applies[1]. But the judge still has a discretion as to whether to exclude them or to require them to remain in court.

1 *Re Nightingale, Green v Nightingale* [1975] 1 WLR 80.

Admission of further evidence while judgment reserved

38.12   While judgment is reserved a judge can accede to a motion to adduce further evidence which was not available at the trial[1].

1 *Acosta v Longsworth, Jones and Turton* [1965] 1 WLR 107, PC, applying *Sugden v Lord St Leonards* (1876) 1 PD 154: the action was for proof of a lost will, and the evidence went not merely to credit, but also to the terms of the will.

Death of party between verdict and judgment

38.13   Where a party to an action dies after the verdict or finding of the issues of fact but before judgment is entered, judgment may be given notwithstanding the death, but the judge, before giving judgment, may, under Order 15, r. 7(2), order that the person upon whom the interest of the deceased has devolved be made a party to the action[1].

1 Order 35, r. 9.

Application for grant following judgment

38.14   The practitioner should order an office copy of the judgment for lodgment with his papers to lead the grant.

On production in the probate registry of a copy of a judgment pronouncing for a will, the original will may be handed out to the solicitor for the purpose of obtaining a grant. A photographic copy of the will (for which the usual fees are payable) is required for retention in the registry, unless a copy is already held.

As to the wording of the oath and the procedure on application for a grant, see paras. **4.176** and **4.177**, ante. As to procedure when a grant pending suit has previously issued, see paras. **11.323** and **11.324**, ante.

Under NC Probate Rule 45(4), upon application for a grant by the person shown to be entitled thereto by the decision of the court in the action, any caveat entered by the plaintiff in the action and any caveat in respect of which notice of the action was given ceases to have effect (see para. **23.16**, ante).

Handing out of a confirmed grant

38.15   Where a grant of representation has previously issued in common form, if the will previously proved is pronounced for in solemn form, or the title to the grant is confirmed by the judgment, the latter should include a direction that the grant be handed out to the grantee or his solicitor.

In the case of a will, the grant is marked as follows: 'The force and validity of the will, a copy whereof is hereunto annexed, was pronounced for in an action entitled AB against CD on the   day of   19   '. This notation is signed by the authorised officer.

The grant is rephotographed, and the records amended accordingly. The grant is returned to the probate registry and may then be handed out to the extracting solicitor.

CHAPTER 39
Costs

Summary

General rules

Costs are in the discretion of the court

39.01   The question of costs of probate actions has always been in the discretion of the court, whether under the practice of the Prerogative Court, under the former Contentious Probate Rules, or under the Judicature Acts and the Rules of the Supreme Court.

By s. 51(1) of the Supreme Court Act 1981:

> 'Subject to the provisions of this or any other Act, and to rules of court, the costs of and incidental to all proceedings in the civil division of the Court of Appeal and in the High Court, including the administration of estates and trusts, shall be in the discretion of the court, and the court shall have full power to determine by whom and to what extent the costs are to be paid.'

Rules as to costs

39.02   The rules as to costs in the High Court are contained in Order 62 of the Rules of the Supreme Court 1965. This Order has effect in relation to all proceedings to which the Rules of the Supreme Court apply, save as excepted by Order 1, r. 2: thus it does not apply in respect of non-contentious or common form probate proceedings[1].

Under Order 62, r. 2(4) the powers and discretion of the court as to costs under s. 51 of the Supreme Court Act 1981 are to be exercised subject to and in accordance with Order 62.

Subject to the specific provisions of Order 62, a party may recover costs from another party only under an order of the court (r. 3(2)).

In general, where the court sees fit to make any order as to costs, the costs will, subject to the provisions of Order 62, be ordered to follow the event except when it appears that in the circumstances some other order should be made (r. 3(3)).

Rule 10 includes provisions as to costs arising from misconduct or neglect, while under r. 11 in certain circumstances a solicitor may be ordered to pay costs personally.

1 As to costs in non-contentious probate proccedings, see paras. **4.266** ff., ante, and Appendix V, p. 975, post.

Restriction of discretion as to costs

39.03 Under Order 62, r. 4(3), where a party opposing a will has given notice (which must be served *with* the defence) that he merely insists on the will being proved in solemn form and only intends to cross-examine the witnesses in support of the will, such party shall not be ordered to pay the costs of the other side unless the court is of opinion that there was no reasonable ground for opposing the will (see also para. **39.17**, post).

Exceptions to the rule that costs follow the event

39.04 Although the general rule is that costs follow the event[1], and should be asked for at the trial[2], there are certain substantial exceptions, and these are dealt with in the following pages.

1 See *Twist v Tye* [1902] P 92.
2 *Re Elmsley's Goods, Dyke v Williams* (1871) LR 2 P & D 239.

Costs of parties propounding a testamentary document

(i) Executors

An executor proving a will in solemn form is entitled to take his costs out of the estate

39.05 An executor who proves a will in solemn form is, as a rule, entitled to have his costs out of the estate[1], and this applies whether he has done so of his own motion, or has been put on proof of the will by parties interested. It is unnecessary for him to make any application to the court for them, as he has a right to take them out of the estate without an order of court[2]. This right would seem to flow as a consequence from the ancient rule that all the expenses incidental to proving a will are a charge upon the estate of the testator, and that the party who takes probate is entitled to recoup himself out of the estate for the costs he may have incurred in obtaining such probate.

Even when an executor propounds a will and codicil, and the court pronounces for the will but against the codicil, he is entitled (unless he is shown to have acted unreasonably) to have his costs out of the estate[3].

1 *Headington v Holloway* (1830) 3 Hag Ecc 280 at 282.
2 It was pointed out by Karminski J that the executor is better off without an order for costs out of the estate, for such an order necessitates taxation of his costs (*Re Cole's Estate, Barclays Bank Ltd v Cole* (1962) 106 Sol Jo 837).
3 *Re Plant's Estate, Wild v Plant* [1926] P 139, CA.

Executor may be ordered to pay costs

39.06   But an executor is not bound to propound a will unless he chooses[1]. If therefore he puts forward a document, and it be proved that he must have known that it could not be supported, he will as a general rule be condemned in costs[2]. If one of two executors is found to have exercised undue influence and the other is exonerated, the action may none the less be dismissed with costs against both[3]. Even if the executor is not guilty of a breach of duty, the court may order him to pay costs[4]. But if an executor had good reason for supposing that a testator was of sound mind and capable of managing his own affairs, he will be allowed his costs out of the estate, even though the will be pronounced against on the ground of the testator's incapacity[5].

If an executor who is also a beneficiary elects to propound a will he does so at risk as to costs[6].

Where executors had obtained a verdict in favour of the validity of a will, and a new trial was granted to parties who had appeared but had not originally pleaded, the court made an order for the executors to have the costs of the first trial out of the estate, up to the time of the ruling for the new trial being made absolute[7].

Where executors, who had proved a will and two codicils, insisted on a third codicil being propounded, they were condemned in the costs[8]; and an executor who insists on asking for probate of clauses found not to be testamentary may be condemned in costs[9].

Where an executrix, who (through carelessness) had lost a will, proved a draft of it in solemn form, she was allowed only such costs as she would have incurred in proving the original will in solemn form, and was condemned in the costs of the defendant[10].

1   *Rennie v Massie* (1866) LR 1 P & D 118 at 119.
2   *Rennie v Massie* (1866), above; see also *Boughton v Knight* (1873) LR 3 P & D 64 at 77; *Rogers v Le Cocq* (1896) 65 LJP 68; *Page v Williamson* (1902) 87 LT 146; *Re Benham's Estate, Saint v Tuckfield* (1961) 105 Sol Jo 511.
3   *Re Barlow's Estate, Haydon v Pring* [1919] P 131, CA.
4   *Re Jeffries, Hill v Jeffries* (1916) 33 TLR 80, CA.
5   *Boughton v Knight* (1873) LR 3 P & D 64 at 79.
6   *Re Scott, Huggett v Reichman* (1966) 110 Sol Jo 852: the court, not being satisfied that the suspicion aroused by the circumstances had been dispelled, or that the testator knew and approved the contents of a will under which the executor was a beneficiary, ordered him to pay the costs. See also *Re Persse's Estate, O'Donnell v Bruce and Dawson* (1962) 106 Sol Jo 432: executors (a solicitor and his clerk) who were also the principal beneficiaries had opportunities of observing the testatrix at a time when, because of their fiduciary relationship with her, it was their duty to exercise the utmost vigilance in her interest. Although they claimed they had been led to believe she was of testamentary capacity by correspondence purporting to come from her which was in fact written by her companion they were condemned in costs.
7   *Boulton v Boulton* (1867) LR 1 P & D 456.
8   *Re Speke's Estate, Speke v Deakin* (1913) 109 LT 719. See also *Wilkinson v Corfield* (1880) 6 PD 27.
9   *Thomas v Jones* [1928] P 162.
10   *Burls v Burls* (1868) LR 1 P & D 472.

(ii) Beneficiaries

When costs allowed out of the estate

39.07   A beneficiary under a will who propounds it in solemn form and obtains a decree in favour of such will, is entitled to have his costs paid out of the estate[1].

But he has not, like an executor, a right to take them ex officio, unless he becomes administrator with the will annexed. When the court pronounces for a will propounded by an executor, the executor takes probate of it himself and is put in possession of the fund out of which he may recoup himself for the expenses he has incurred in the suit. But when the court pronounces for a will propounded by a residuary legatee or a legatee, the residuary legatee or legatee is not always of right entitled to letters of administration with the will annexed. If the will is pronounced for, it is competent to an executor, if he has not renounced (even though he has been cited to propound it and has not done so), to come in and take probate in the usual way, or, if he is cleared off, it is competent to a non-litigant residuary legatee to take letters of administration with the will annexed in preference to the specific legatee who propounded the will[2].

1 *Williams v Goude* (1828) 1 Hag Ecc 577 at 610; *Sutton v Drax* (1815) 2 Phillim 323.
2 *Bewsher v Williams and Ball* (1861) 3 Sw & Tr 62.

Where a legatee propounded a codicil

39.08 A legatee, who has propounded and established a codicil, is entitled to the same costs as an executor in similar circumstances. In a case in which the court awarded a legatee party and party costs against the executor who unsuccessfully opposed the codicil, it further ordered that the legatee should have such sum as the registrar should consider sufficient to cover his extra costs[1]. But where a legatee, who had successfully propounded a codicil, had been guilty of unwise delay in producing it, the court refused to allow him costs out of the estate[2].

1 *Bewsher v Williams*, above.
2 *Headington v Holloway* (1830) 3 Hag Ecc 280.

Application should be made to the court. Order for costs has been made subsequently to decree

39.09 Should a person having a prior title to the grant take it in priority to the party who has established the will, the latter is without control over the estate of the testator, and therefore without power to recoup himself for the expenses incurred by him in obtaining the decree. The most convenient mode of his securing payment of his costs is by applying to the court to include in the decree pronouncing for the will an order that his costs be paid out of the estate. The application should be made on the court pronouncing for the validity of the will. But where no order had been made as to costs when the decree was pronounced, the court has subsequently ordered the costs to be paid out of the estate[1].

1 *Wilkinson v Corfield* (1880) 6 PD 27.

Scale of costs

39.10 The costs will be taxed on the standard basis unless the judge orders otherwise. On a taxation on this basis there are allowed all such costs as were reasonably incurred[1]. Where costs are to be paid to a party either by another party or out of any fund the court may in any case in which it thinks fit to do so order that they be taxed on the indemnity basis[2]. This basis is more generous than the standard basis:

all amounts in respect of costs not unreasonably incurred are to be allowed[3]. Where the costs are to be paid out of a fund, or the party receiving the costs is or was a party in the capacity of trustee or personal representative, no costs are to be disallowed except in so far as those costs or any part thereof should not, in accordance with the duty of the trustee or personal representative as such, have been incurred or paid, and should for that reason be borne by him personally[4].

1 Order 62, r. 12.
2 Ibid, r. 14.
3 Ibid., r. 12(2) (see also *Layzell v British Portland Cement Manufacturers Ltd* [1961] 1 All ER 244n, [1961] 1 WLR 557).
4 Ibid., r. 14(2).

Costs of parties opposing probate

39.11   Probate of a will may be opposed by any person entitled to share in the estate in the event of an intestacy, or by any person interested under another will.

(i) Costs of parties successfully opposing probate

39.12   If a party who successfully opposes probate is entitled to, and obtains, a grant either of letters of administration or of probate of another will, he may recoup himself out of the estate for his costs. He should proceed for recovery of his costs from any party condemned to pay them.

If, however, the successful party is not entitled to, or fails to obtain, a grant, he can only proceed as to his costs under the order of the court. The court may give him his costs either out of the estate or against the unsuccessful party[1]. In the latter case he can only obtain payment of his costs from the party who has been condemned as to them[2] and to the extent of the scale of costs ordered.

1 *Critchell v Critchell* (1863) 3 Sw & Tr 41; *Bewsher v Williams and Ball* (1861) 3 Sw & Tr 62.
2 *Nash v Yelloly* (1862) 3 Sw & Tr 59.

(ii) Costs of parties unsuccessfully opposing probate

39.13   As has been stated above, the general rule is that costs follow the event. Two main principles have, however, been laid down as to the circumstances which justify the court in departing from this rule[1]. These are (1) that where the testator, or those interested in the residue, have been the cause of the litigation, the costs of unsuccessfully opposing probate may be ordered to be paid out of the estate, and (2) that if the circumstances led reasonably to an investigation in regard to a propounded document the costs may be left to be borne by those who respectively incurred them.

These principles are not to be regarded as exact rules, for it is not in the nature of discretion that its exercise should be adjusted by exact rules[2], nor are they exhaustive[3]. However, since the year 1863[4], when they were first enunciated, they have been almost universally acted upon. Decisions as to costs before that date are not as a rule to be relied upon. Whether a probate litigant challenging the validity (as a will) of the whole or part of a testamentary paper should, if unsuccessful, receive his costs out of the estate was a matter for the judge's discretion. The Court of

Appeal so held and that the judge was not bound in deciding whether the challenge was reasonable and proper by *Orton v Smith*[5] which laid down no principle as to what was reasonable and proper[6].

Somewhat different considerations apply when the opposing party has given notice merely to cross-examine under Order 62, r. 4(3), or where undue influence or fraud has been unsuccessfully pleaded. These will be considered separately below.

1 *Spiers v English* [1907] P 122; *Twist v Tye* [1902] P 92 at 94; *Mitchell and Mitchell v Gard and Kingwell* (1863) 3 Sw & Tr 275 at 278; *Re Cutcliffe's Estate, Le Duc v Veness* [1959] P 6, [1958] 3 All ER 642, CA
2 Per Sir J. P. Wilde in *Mitchell and Mitchell v Gard* (1863) 3 Sw & Tr 275 at 277.
3 *Spiers v English* [1907] P 122.
4 I.e. since the decision in *Mitchell v Gard*. As to the principles which prevailed in the Court of Probate, and in the ecclesiastical courts before 1863, see the note to *Summerell v Clements* (1862) 3 Sw & Tr 35, 32 LJPM & A 33, where several decisions are collected.
5 (1873) LR 3 P & D 23.
6 See *Fanshawe's Estate* (1983) Times, 17 November.

(a) Where the litigation has been caused by the testator, or those interested in the residuary estate

Where testator has himself caused the litigation

39.14 If the litigation be caused by the state in which the deceased left his testamentary papers, the costs of both parties will be ordered to be paid out of the estate[1].

So, too, where the testator by his own conduct and habits and mode of life has given reasonable ground for questioning his testamentary capacity, the costs of those opposing probate of his will will be ordered to be paid out of the estate[2], as will also be the case where the testator's statements, to the parties unsuccessfully opposing probate, led them to plead undue influence[3].

But although it is not possible to limit the circumstances in which a testator can be said to have brought about the litigation by leaving his affairs in confusion, they should not extend to cases where the testator has misled other people by his words, written or spoken, and perhaps inspired false hopes that they might benefit on his death[4].

1 *Lemage v Goodban* (1865) LR 1 P & D 57 at 63; *Davies v Gregory* (1873) LR 3 P & D 28; *Mitchell and Mitchell v Gard and Kingwell* (1863) 3 Sw & Tr 275; *Jenner v Ffinch* (1879) 5 PD 106; *Re Hall-Dare, Le Marchant v Lee Warner* [1916] 1 Ch 272, 114 LT 559 (Chancery).
2 *Davies v Gregory* (1873) LR 3 P & D 28.
3 *Cousins v Tubb* (1891) 65 LT 716.
4 *Re Cutcliffe's Estate, Le Duc v Veness* [1959] P 6, [1958] 3 All ER 642, CA.

Where conduct of beneficiary under the will caused the litigation

39.15 Where a party had taken out administration after enquiry, made of the residuary legatee of a will, whether there was a will, to which enquiry he received no answer, and a will was twelve months afterwards produced and proved in solemn form, the court held that the administrator, who was the defendant in the suit, was entitled to have his costs out of the estate, including the costs of taking out administration[1].

An unsuccessful party is usually given his costs where one of the principal beneficiaries under a will has been actively engaged in its preparation, and has not shown by disinterested evidence that its dispositions were read over or explained to and approved of by the testator before its execution[2].

The omission to annex to or mention in the affidavit of scripts the instructions for a will is no ground for allowing out of the estate the costs of an unsuccessful opposition to the will, if such opposition is not founded on the absence of instructions[3].

1 *Smith v Smith* (1865) 4 Sw & Tr 3; see also *Williams v Henery* (1864) 3 Sw & Tr 471.
2 *Dale v Murrell* (March 1879, unreported). See also *Orton v Smith* (1873) LR 3 P & D 23; and *Wilson v Bassil* [1903] P 239.
3 *Foxwell v Poole* (1862) 3 Sw & Tr 5.

(b) Where the circumstances lead reasonably to an investigation

39.16   The losing party will not be condemned in costs if there be a sufficient and reasonable ground, looking to his knowledge and means of knowledge, for him to question either the execution of the will or the capacity of the testator[1]. Thus, where the attesting witnesses gave conflicting accounts as to the due execution of the will[2], or the judge was satisfied with a verdict establishing a will, but would not have been dissatisfied with a contrary verdict[3], or where a next of kin, who had unsuccessfully opposed a will upon information given to him by one of the attesting witnesses, the testator's medical attendant, to the effect that when the will was read over the testator signified his approval of it by gesture only, and that he could not swear that the testator was of sound mind[4], the court refused to condemn the unsuccessful party in costs.

Where the principal beneficiary took instructions for the will himself, and the solicitor who drew the will did not see the testator, it was held that the circumstances so far invited enquiry as to justify the court in refusing to condemn in costs the party opposing the will[5].

1 *Mitchell and Mitchell v Gard and Kingwell* (1863) 3 Sw & Tr 275 at 278; *Spiers v English* [1907] P 122 at 123. In a probate action in which there was a conflict of evidence on the issues of knowledge and approval and incapacity, the widow, who unsuccessfully contested the will, had been supplied with proofs of the evidence of the other side's witnesses before the action was brought. She was ordered to pay one-third of the costs (*Re Coe's Estate* [1957] CLY 3736).
2 *Ferrey v King* (1861) 3 Sw & Tr 51.
3 *Bramley v Bramley* (1864) 3 Sw & Tr 430.
4 *Tippett v Tippett* (1865) LR 1 P & D 54.
5 *Aylwin v Aylwin* [1902] P 203.

(c) Where the opposing party gives notice to cross-examine under Order 62, r. 4(3)

39.17   Under this provision, in probate actions the party opposing a will may, with his defence, serve notice on the party setting up the will that he merely insists upon the will being proved in solemn form of law, and only intends to cross-examine the witnesses produced in support of the will. Thereupon, unless the court is of opinion that there was no reasonable ground for opposing the will, no order may be made for the costs of the other side to be paid by him.

The notice to be efficacious must be served with the defence[1]. Before August 1898 the court had no power to condemn in costs a party who availed himself of the rule[2], but now the point to be considered is—Was there reasonable ground for opposing the will? If so, the party giving notice is not liable to pay the costs of the other side[3]. It does not follow, because a defendant fails, that there was no reasonable ground for opposing the will[4].

The notice may be a conditional one to the effect that if both the attesting witnesses to the will are called, it is merely intended to cross-examine them[5]. The protection afforded by the rule may be relied on if it be pleaded that the deceased did not know or approve of the contents of the will, and the opposing parties may be put to proof of testamentary capacity[6]; but it is lost if undue influence or fraud is pleaded[7].

1 *Bone v Whittle* (1866) LR 1 P &D 249.
2 *Leigh v Green* [1892] P 17; *Tappenden v Lucas* (1891) 65 LT 684.
3 *Davies v Jones* [1899] P 161.
4 *Davies v Jones* [1899] P 161 at 164. For a case under the rule where it was held that there had been no reasonable ground for opposing the will, see *Re Spicer, Spicer v Spicer* [1899] P 38. See also *Re Spicer Perry v Dixon* (1899) 80 LT 297.
5 *Leeman v George* (1868) LR 1 P & D 542.
6 *Cleare and Forster v Cleare* (1869) LR 1 P & D 655. See also *Re Sanders' Estate, Riches and Woodey v Sanders* (1961) 105 Sol Jo 324: the plaintiff not having complied with a request for information of the evidence of the person who arranged for the preparation and execution of a will propounded by him, the judge although pronouncing for the will refused to condemn the defendant in costs.
7 *Ireland v Rendall* (1866) LR 1 P & D 194.

Parties not protected by the rule

39.18 A party who seeks to call in and obtain revocation of a probate is not within the rule, and a notice given thereunder by such a party is bad[1].

1 *Tomalin v Smart* [1904] P 141. See also *Patrick v Hevercroft* (1920) 123 LT 201.

(d) Where undue influence or fraud has been unsuccessfully pleaded

39.19 Where an unsuccessful party has pleaded undue influence or fraud it must be shown that he had reasonable and sufficient ground for so doing, or he will be condemned in the costs of the other side[1].

If there be reasonable ground for putting such a plea forward, costs may be allowed out of the estate, or the unsuccessful party may be ordered to bear his own costs only, according to the circumstances of the case (see paras. **39.14–39.16**, ante).

A party may be condemned in the costs of the other side in respect of his plea of undue influence, and allowed his costs out of the estate in respect of the other pleas put forward by him against the will[2].

Where an order was made allowing costs to a party who had unsuccessfully pleaded undue influence it was held on appeal that, where there are any grounds on which a judge can base such a special order, there is no jurisdiction to interfere with it[3].

1 *Mitchell and Mitchell v Gard and Kingwell* (1863) 3 Sw & Tr 275 at 278; *Spiers v English* [1907] P 122 at 123; *Levy v Leo* (1909) 25 TLR 717; *Re Cutcliffe's Estate, Le Duc v Veness* [1959] P 6, [1958] 3 All ER 642.
2 *Levy v Leo* (1909) 25 TLR 717.
3 *Cummins v Murray* [1906] 2 IR 509.

Costs of particular parties

39.20   The position as to costs of executors or beneficiaries under a will, and of the persons interested on an intestacy, has been discussed above, but a few words should be added as to the position of certain other particular parties.

(i) Defendants intervening

39.21   Where a defendant intervening in a probate action pleads separately, he will not, as a rule, be allowed separate costs, even though he be successful[1], unless his interest is different from those of the other parties to the action[2]. If his interest is the same as that of another party who has already pleaded, he should adopt the pleadings of such party[3]. The next of kin intervening, on a question as to the due execution of a will, in order to take the opinion of the court as to alterations which appeared in the will enhancing their interests, were (although the alterations were pronounced invalid) allowed their costs out of the estate[4]. But where the executor, in his affidavit of scripts, in effect denied the validity of a legacy to a person who intervened, but, subsequently, by his plea, admitted its validity, and such intervener appeared by counsel at the hearing of the cause, the court refused to allow him his costs out of the estate[5].

1 *Twist v Tye* [1902] P 92 at 98.
2 *Bagshaw v Pimm* [1900] P 148.
3 *Twist v Tye* [1902] P 92 at 98; *Colvin v Fraser* (1829) 2 Hag Ecc 266 at 368.
4 *Burgoyne v Showler* (1844) 1 Rob Eccl 5. See also *Cross v Cross* (1864) 3 Sw & Tr 292.
5 *Shawe and Dickens v Marshall* (1858) 1 Sw & Tr 129.

(ii) Parties to an interest suit

39.22   A party who fails to prove his case in an interest suit is, except in special circumstances, condemned in costs[1].

1 *Wiseman v Wiseman* (1866) LR 1 P & D 351.

(iii) Trustees, personal representatives, etc.

39.23   A person who is or has been a party to any proceedings in the capacity of trustee, personal representative or mortgagee is, unless otherwise ordered, entitled to the costs of those proceedings, in so far as they are not recovered from or paid by any other person, out of the fund held by the trustee or personal representative or the mortgaged property, as the case may be. The court may otherwise order only on the ground that he has acted unreasonably or, in the case of a trustee or personal representative, has in substance acted for his own benefit rather than for the benefit of the fund[1].

1 Order 62, r. 6(2). See also *Re Dallaway* [1982] 3 All ER 118, [1982] 1 WLR 756.

(iv) Creditors

39.24   A creditor who obtains a grant may reimburse himself out of the estate for the expense he has been put to in obtaining it.

The costs of a creditor of obtaining the appointment of an administrator pending suit may be allowed out of the estate[1].

1 *Tichborne v Tichborne, ex p Norris* (1869) LR 1 P & D 730.

(v) The Official Solicitor[1]

39.25 To entitle the Official Solicitor to costs as against any other party on other than a standard basis, the order as to costs must specifically direct taxation on an indemnity basis[2].

1 See *White v Duvernay* [1891] P 290; *Gill v Gill* [1909] P 157.
2 *Eady v Elsdon* [1901] 2 KB 460.

(vi) The Treasury Solicitor

39.26 Where the Treasury Solicitor unsuccessfully contested a will on behalf of the Crown, he could not, prior to the Administration of Justice (Miscellaneous Provisions) Act 1933, be condemned in the costs[1], but s. 7 of that Act gives the court discretion in the matter of such costs.

1 *Atkinson v Queen's Proctor* (1871) LR 2 P & D 255.

(vii) Legally aided parties

39.27 The position as to costs of persons admitted under the Legal Aid Act 1988 to take or defend or to be parties to legal proceedings is governed by that Act, and the Regulations thereunder.

More than one set of costs allowed

Two sets of costs

39.28 Separate sets of costs may be allowed in exceptional circumstances where there is a sufficient divergency of interest between the parties appearing on the same side[1].

1 See *Bagshaw v Pimm* [1900] P 148, CA; *Jenner v Ffinch* (1879) 5 PD 106.

Apportionment of costs

39.29 The court is empowered, when ordering costs in a probate action to be paid out of the estate, to direct out of what portion or portions of the estate they are to be paid, by virtue of the general discretion as to costs conferred on the court by the Supreme Court Act 1981, s. 51[1].

Orders have been made, under the predecessor section, that the costs of both plaintiff and defendant be charged on, and paid out of, the corpus of certain real estate devised by the will to successive life tenants[2]; that the costs of all parties be paid out of that portion of the residuary estate passing under the will to four out of six defendants[3], and that the costs of all parties should come out of that portion of the estate which was bequeathed to the persons whose conduct had been the cause of the enquiry, although they had been successful in the litigation[4].

1 See p. 840, post. See also Order 62, r. 2(4).
2 *Dean v Bulmer* [1905] P 1.
3 *Harrington v Butt* [1905] P 3n.
4 *Re Osment's Estate, Child and Jarvis v Osment* [1914] P 129.

CHAPTER 40

County court

Jurisdiction

Where application made in probate registry and net estate under £30,000 county court has jurisdiction

40.01   The county court has all the jurisdiction of the High Court in respect of any contentious matter arising in connection with the grant or revocation of probate or administration in the following circumstances, namely where (a) an application for the grant has been made through the Principal Registry or a district probate registry and (b) the value of the net estate (after payment of expenses and debts) does not exceed the county court limit (currently £30,000)[1].

The need for there to have been a prior application in the probate registry and the limit of £30,000 mean that contentious probate actions are rarely commenced or heard in the county court. There are further reasons for this: the specialist Chancery nature of the proceedings (even now when High Court probate actions can be commenced in a district registry, they may only be commenced in a Chancery district registry); and the administrative requirements associated with the court staff having to receive and preserve in safekeeping the affidavits of scripts and the scripts themselves.

For these reasons it is unusual for probate proceedings to be commenced in the county court even if it has jurisdiction.

For these reasons also it is rare for the High Court to order the transfer of a probate action to the county court under s. 40(2) of the County Courts Act 1984 (regard also being had to the criteria laid down in Art. 7(5) of the High Court and County Courts Jurisdiction Order 1991—see p. 955, post). The court would wish to be satisfied not only that the county court had jurisdiction but also that the particular county court in question had available a judge with the requisite Chancery expertise and that the court officer was acquainted with the procedures regarding scripts. No order can be made in the High Court as to the mode by which a cause sent by it to a county court is to be tried[2].

The parties cannot by agreement confer jurisdiction on a county court[3].

The solicitor should notify the Principal Registry of the commencement of the county court proceedings so that a note can be made in the records[4].

1 Section 32, County Courts Act 1984; County Courts Jurisdiction Order 1981; see also *Re Thomas, Davies v Davies* [1949] P 336, [1949] 1 All ER 1048.
2 *Norris v Allen* (1862) 2 Sw & Tr 601, 32 LJPM & A 3.
3 The only power to do so in other cases is conferred by ss. 18 and 24, County Courts Act 1984, neither of which applies to a probate action.
4 Registrar's Circular, 8 May 1969.

Proceedings in the county court

40.02   Procedure in the county court is regulated by Ord. 41 of the County Court Rules 1981. Where no provision is made by the County Court Rules, the rules and practice of the High Court relating to contentious probate proceedings are to be followed so far as they are appropriate[1].

Proceedings are commenced by summons.

On issuing the summons, the district judge of the county court shall send to the Principal Registry a notice requesting all documents (including scripts) in the Principal Registry or any district probate registry relating to the matter to be sent to him[2]. A copy of those scripts in the registry which are being set up as testamentary by one or other of the parties will be made in the registry, examined free of charge and retained in the registry. In the Principal Registry the photographic copies will be retained in the Probate Department with a list of the documents transmitted to the county court[3].

After the county court has made an order, those testamentary documents which have been pronounced for or against will be endorsed (at the top or the side of the first page whenever convenient) with a memorandum to that effect by the county court district judge. The memorandum will read as follows:

'Pronounced for (against) in an action No. ....entitled
.... v .... in the ....
County Court: order dated the day of   19   .

(Signed) County Court district judge.'

All scripts will then be sent by registered post or delivered by the county court district judge to the probate registry to which, and at the same time as, he sends his certificate of the order under s. 33 of the County Courts Act 1984. The probate registrar will give a receipt for such documents. Testamentary documents which have not been proved may be kept with the papers leading to the grant[4]. A copy of any judgment is to be sent by the court to every party to the proceedings[5].

At the termination of the proceedings the county court district judge transmits to the Principal Registry or a district probate registry, as he thinks convenient, a certificate of the judgment or order (which should show that the evidence of witnesses was taken), under the seal of the county court, and the probate registrar thereupon acts in accordance with the order of the judge on the application of the party in whose favour it was made[6].

For practice in obtaining a grant, see para. **4.180**, ante.

The county court, after a cause has been transferred to it, is to make the final decree and to decide all questions arising in the cause as to costs[7].

1 County Court Rules 1981, Ord. 41, r. 4.
2 Ibid., r. 2(2). For form of notice, see Form No. 59.
3 Direction, 22 May 1950.
4 Direction, 22 May 1950.
5 County Court Rules 1981, Ord. 41, r. 3.
6 County Courts Act 1984, s. 33 (see p. 862, post).
7 *Macleur v Macleur* (1868) LR 1 P & D 604. See also *Re Thomas, Davies v Davies* [1949] P 336, [1949] 1 All ER 1048.

CHAPTER 41

Associated actions

Summary

Rectification of a will

41.01   An action for the rectification of a will under s. 20 of the Administration of Justice Act 1982 is not a probate action within the meaning of Order 76, r. 1. See Order 76, r. 16 'as if'. But rr. 4 and 16 of that Order apply together with other appropriate Rules. Thus it should be commenced by originating summons under Order 5, r. 3. Under Order 28, r. 8 the action can be ordered to continue as if commenced by writ. Actions for the rectification of other kinds of instruments are usually commenced by writ because they involve a determination as to intention, and it is preferable that evidence in chief be given orally. Accordingly an action for the rectification of a will though commenced by originating summons may attract an order under Order 28, r. 8. The standard of proof in the action is the balance of probabilities.

Section 20 of the 1982 Act is set out at p. 854, post. Under the section the court may order rectification to carry out the intentions of the testator if satisfied that the will fails to carry them out in consequence of a clerical error or of a failure to understand the instructions of the testator. The originating summons should include, as part of the relief sought, leave to apply for an order if the summons is issued more than six months after the grant of representation. For the purpose of calculating the six months' period grants limited to property held on trust are ignored, and similarly, any grant limited to either real or personal estate unless a grant limited to the remainder of the estate was made before or at the same time as either such grant.

Subject to RSC Order 15, rr. 1 and 5 such a cause of action can on the originating summons be joined with other cause of action, e.g. construction. (For form of indorsement of originating summons, see CP22.)

When it is necessary to bring an action under s. 20, it is to be commenced in the Chancery Division and Order 7, r. 5(2) applies. The action can be commenced in a Chancery district registry.

If the application for an order of rectification is unopposed and no probate action has been commenced, then the application should be to a district judge of the Principal Registry or to a district probate registrar. See paras. **3.260–3.262**, ante.

Removal of a personal representative

41.02   As an alternative to a beneficiary bringing an administration action or to a personal representative or a beneficiary applying for the appointment of a judicial trustee, section 50 of the Administration of Justice Act 1985 introduces an action for the removal of a personal representative with or without his substitution. The section is at p. 865, post.

In accordance with RSC Order 5, r. 3, the application is made (in the High Court) by originating summons, and the code of procedure includes RSC Order 28.

Under the section, if substitution is not requested, the appointment of a sole personal representative cannot be terminated for it would leave the estate unrepresented. Termination alone can thus not be requested in respect of all personal representatives. To achieve this, *substitution* of all must be sought. The court may treat any application for substitution or termination as an application for the appointment of a judicial trustee under the Judicial Trustees Act 1896.

The date of an order under the section is the effective date of appointment of any new personal representative appointed thereby; and he may be authorised to charge remuneration. As well as an affidavit in support of the summons there will be required an affidavit of fitness and the written consent of any substitute.

There is nothing in the wording of section 50[1] to preclude an application for the removal (or substitution) of an executor before a grant has issued; but equally there is nothing in that wording[1] to allow such an application in respect of an administrator (who before a grant, ex hypothesi, does not exist).

1   Or in the definition of 'administrator' and 'personal representative' in s. 55, Administration of Estates Act 1925.

Family provision

General

41.03   The law governing family provision is contained in the Inheritance (Provision for Family and Dependants) Act 1975[1]. Application is made to the High Court or to a county court[2]. For procedure in the county court, see para. **41.11**, post.

If application is made in the High Court it can be made either to the Chancery Division or to the Family Division in the High Court[3], and the procedure in both Divisions is the same except for modifications dependent on the difference in organisation of the two Divisions. The Masters in the Chancery Division and the district judges in the Family Division have power to hear applications under this Act in chambers[4].

In the High Court the procedure is governed by Order 99 of the Rules of the Supreme Court 1965 (see p. 950, post).

1   As amended by the Law Reform (Succession) Act 1995. See pp. 808 ff., post.
2   By virtue of s. 25 of the County Courts Act 1984 and Art. 2(1)(l) of the High Court and County Courts Jurisdiction Order 1991 (see p. 954, post) the county court has unlimited jurisdiction; but regard must be had to Arts. 7 and 9 of that Order, so that a claim for less than £25,000 should usually be tried in the county court and a claim for more than £50,000 should usually be tried in the High Court.
3   Order 99, r. 2.
4   Ibid., r. 8.

Title and parties

41.04   Application in the High Court is made by originating summons[1], and the summons shall be in Form No. 10 in Appendix A of the Rules of the Supreme Court which is the expedited form of originating summons[2]. The originating summons may be issued out of the Chancery Registry, the Principal Registry of the Family Division or any district registry[3], and is intituled 'In the estate of A.B. deceased' and in the Family Division there are also added the words 'And in the matter of the Inheritance (Provision for Family and Dependants) Act 1975'.

The claimant is the plaintiff and the personal representatives and all beneficiaries who may be affected by an order of the court are made defendants. If a beneficiary only has a small legacy which would not be affected by any order made he is not made a party. The court may at any stage direct that any person be added as a party or that notice of the proceedings be served on any person[4]. If there are a number of beneficiaries with the same interest the court can be asked to make a representation order under Order 15, r. 13[5]. Every person whose rights under the will might be affected ought to be a party or be represented by a party appointed by order to represent him[6]. Where there are two or more claimants whose interests conflict all should be made plaintiffs and the originating summons should be issued by one firm of solicitors. Subsequently the court may order one of the claimants to be a defendant and be represented by separate solicitors[7]. This order is usually drawn up.

Where the claimant is the sole personal representative he should be the plaintiff and the beneficiaries should be the defendants. In such a case, he must in his affidavit give details of the estate as well as particulars of his own circumstances. Where the claimant is one of two or more personal representatives he should be the plaintiff and the other personal representatives and the beneficiaries should be made defendants.

No application under the Act can be made until a personal representative has been constituted[8]. Difficulties can arise if there is no person either entitled or willing to apply for a grant. In such a case the proposed plaintiff should approach the Official Solicitor to see whether he would be prepared to apply for a grant under s. 116 of the Supreme Court Act 1981.

Application can be made by the following persons specified in s. 1 of the Act:

(a)   The wife or husband of the deceased.

(b)   A former wife or husband who has not remarried.

(ba)   (For deaths on or after 1 January 1996) any person (not being a person included in paragraph (a) or (b) above) who during the whole of the period of two years ending immediately before the date when the deceased died, was living in the same household as the deceased, and as the husband or wife of the deceased.

(c)   A child of the deceased.

(d)   Any person who was treated by the deceased as a child of the family.

(e)   Any person who was being maintained wholly or partly by the deceased immediately prior to death. The claimant must show that immediately before his death the deceased was making a substantial contribution in money or money's worth towards the claimant's reasonable needs and this was done other than for full valuable consideration for services rendered.

---

1   Order 99, r. 3(1).
2   Ibid., r. 3(2).
3   Ibid., r. 3(1).

4 Ibid., r. 4(1).
5 Ibid., r. 4(2); and the court may make a direction under Ord. 15, r. 13A.
6 *Re Lidington, Lidington v Thomas (No 2)* [1940] Ch 927, [1940] 3 All ER 600.
7 Order 99, r. 6.
8 *Re McBroom* [1992] 2 FLR 49.

Evidence

41.05 On issuing the summons the plaintiff's solicitors must lodge with the court an affidavit exhibiting an official copy of the grant of representation and will (if any) and a copy of the affidavit must be served on every defendant with the originating summons[1]. The rule does not prescribe the contents of the affidavit but it is important to set out particulars of any known previous proceedings relevant to the application (e.g. any previous pending matrimonial proceedings in the Family Division) and the means of the applicant. A defendant who is a personal representative shall, and any other defendant may, within 21 days after service of the originating summons lodge with the Registry an affidavit in answer[2]. The affidavit lodged by the personal representative shall state to the best of the deponent's ability the following particulars[3]:

(a)   full particulars of the value of the estate;
(b)   the persons or classes of persons beneficially interested in the estate giving names, addresses, and the value of their interest;
(c)   the name of any beneficiary who is a minor or patient;
(d)   any facts known to the deponent which might affect the exercise of the court's powers under the Act.

Every defendant who lodges an affidavit must at the same time serve a copy on the plaintiff and any other defendant[4]. In a Practice Note[5], Vaisey J stated that any suggestion of the testator's weakness of mind ought to be excluded. No suggestion of unsoundness of mind or even want of lucidity could possibly be raised. It could not be one of the reasons for making the bequest. In *Re Blanch*[6], Buckley J said that the Practice Note should be read as indicating only that testamentary capacity or lack of it is not a matter to be investigated and that feebleness of mind or understanding cannot constitute a reason for the deceased's conduct which is relevant for the purposes of the Act. Testamentary capacity is something which must be dealt with in a probate action.

A definition of 'net estate' is set out in s. 8 of the Act and includes nominated property and property subject to a donatio mortis causa. The deceased's share of joint property is also taken into account under section 9 of the Act.

1 Order 99, r. 3(3).
2 Ibid., r. 5(1).
3 Ibid., r. 5(2).
4 Ibid., r. 5(3).
5 *Practice Note* [1945] WN 210.
6 *Re Blanch, Blanch v Honhold* [1967] 2 All ER 468, [1967] 1 WLR 987.

Time limits

41.06 An application under the Act cannot without the leave of the court be made after six months from the date of the grant of representation[1]. If such leave is required it should be sought in a separate paragraph in the originating summons or failing this by a summons in the proceedings.

Applications for leave are usually heard by the Master or district judge prior to the main hearing and the evidence is normally limited to what is required for the application.

When an applicant dies before trial the claim ceases to exist[2].

1 Inheritance (Provision for Family and Dependants) Act 1975, s. 4.
2 See *Whytte (or Whyte) v Ticehurst* [1986] Fam 64, [1986] 2 All ER 158.

The hearing: Chancery Division

41.07   The first hearing of the originating summons is normally the equivalent of a summons for directions. The Master will ensure that all proper parties are before the court and give directions for evidence by the defendants and for time for the plaintiff to reply. A beneficiary is not required to give evidence of his means, but if he does not do so the court will assume that he has no particular compelling financial need. The personal representatives must give full evidence of the value of the estate in accordance with Ord. 99, r. 5. If all the necessary evidence is not ready on the first appointment the Master will give directions and adjourn the summons to another fixed day and time. On the adjourned appointment, the Master will consider the mode of trial. The Master has jurisdiction to hear the main application in chambers[1] or in court under Order 36, r. 11 by consent of the parties. The parties will inform the Master whether they wish to cross-examine witnesses and the Master will adjourn the summons for hearing on a specified date fixed by him. If there is to be cross-examination he will arrange with the Mechanical Recording Department of the court to provide a mechanical recording machine. Sometimes the Master will give judgment immediately the hearing is over, but if the matter is complicated he may reserve his judgment and send a copy of the judgment to all parties by post. The parties are not usually required to attend to hear the judgment pronounced.

If the Master decides that owing to the nature of the case it would be better for it to be heard by a judge he will adjourn the summons into court. Sometimes the Master will adjourn the summons into the witness list with liberty to adduce oral evidence in support of the affidavits already made on both sides. Where cross-examination of deponents is required the Master will ask the solicitor to give undertakings that specified deponents will be available for cross-examination. If they are unable to give such undertakings the Master will make an order for cross-examination.

If the case is heard by consent in open court under Order 36, r. 11 the Master usually hears the case in his private room and a notice saying 'Open Court' is placed on the door. The case is however listed in the Cause List as a hearing in open court and the public are entitled to be admitted. It is not customary for counsel to robe as the Master does not robe.

1 Order 99, r. 8.

The hearing: Family Division

41.08   The initial appointment for hearing of the originating summons is before the district judge and will be for directions only: immediately prior to the issue of the summons, the solicitor should obtain a date and time for the hearing from the district judge's clerk. The date fixed will normally be sufficiently far ahead to allow time for service of the summons by the solicitor together with a period of at least 21 days so as to enable the defendant enough time to file his affidavit in answer.

On the hearing for directions, the district judge will give such directions as are, in his view, appropriate:

(a) for parties to be joined in the proceedings (or given notice of the application);
(b) with regard to the evidence to be filed and the time limits for delivery of that evidence; and
(c) if so requested, for discovery and inspection of documents.

Having given appropriate directions, the summons is normally adjourned to another fixed appointment.

On the restored hearing, the district judge will consider the filed evidence and will give whatever further directions he considers necessary as to the mode of trial (e.g. orders for the attendance of parties to give oral evidence) and will determine the venue and person before whom the substantive hearing should take place. Under Order 99, r. 8 of the Rules of the Supreme Court the district judge has jurisdiction to hear applications and make final orders disposing of proceedings under the Act, subject to a discretionary power to refer any matter to a judge of the Family Division for determination under Order 32, r. 12. Where such a reference is made in respect of a case proceeding in London a date for the hearing before a judge in chambers is fixed through the office of the Clerk of the Rules at the Royal Courts of Justice. Unless any particular case is likely to involve an unduly long or complex issue of fact or a novel point of law or an important question of jurisdiction, the substantive hearing takes place before the district judge. Unless a hearing before the judge has been directed expressly to be heard in chambers, it will be listed for hearing in open court[1].

Where the hearing is not likely to exceed one half day in duration in the estimation of the solicitor for the applicant, application may be made to the district judge's clerk for an appointment once the case is ready for hearing. If the hearing is likely to last for more than one half day, the district judge will require counsel's certificates to be lodged, both giving an estimate of the length of hearing and certifying that the case is ready for trial before a date for hearing is fixed.

Hearings before a district judge normally take place in chambers. At the conclusion of the hearing, the district judge will give judgment, unless reserved for deliberation and subsequent delivery.

The Registry procedure prescribed by the Matrimonial Causes Rules for the drawing up and service of orders in the Family Division applies to orders made under the Inheritance (Provision for Family and Dependants) Act 1975.

1 See *Re F* [1985] CLY 3643, (1985) Times, 11 February.

Interim maintenance

41.09 Where the plaintiff is in immediate need of financial assistance the court may make an interim order for maintenance[1]. In deciding what order to make the court will take into account, so far as is practicable, the same considerations as would be relevant in making a final order. Such an interim order may be, and usually is, made by a Master or district judge.

1 Inheritance (Provision for Family and Dependants) Act 1975, s. 5.

General

41.10   The personal representatives must produce the original grant of representation at the hearing and if an order is made the grant is kept by the court for the purpose of transmitting it to the Principal Registry of the Family Division where a memorandum is indorsed in accordance with s. 19(3) of the Act[1]. The memorandum is indorsed in all cases after trial or on settlement[2].

1 Ord. 99, r. 7.
2 PD (16) B; see para. **26.11**, ante.

Applications to the county court

41.11   In the county court the procedure is regulated by Order 48 of the County Court Rules[1].

1 See p. 952, post.

APPENDIX I
Statutes

Summary

Part I—Probate Business

Part II—Finance Acts etc.

Statutes

Note.—The following text contains extracts from Acts of Parliament having a bearing on the probate practice. In general (with the exception of specific statutes relating to estate duty, as to which see Appendix I to the Twenty-Fifth edition of this work and capital transfer tax, as to which see Appendix I to the Twenty-Sixth edition of this work), those enactments, since repealed, which remain applicable in relation to cases where death occurred prior to the relevant date of repeal have been retained for the purpose of reference.

Part I—Probate Business

WILLS ACT 1837

(7 Will. 4 & 1 Vict. c. 26)

Note to sections 9, 18, 18A and 33 below
New ss. 9, 18 and 33 were substituted, and new s. 18A inserted, by ss. 17–19 of the Administration of Justice Act 1982 (see pp. 854, ff., post). The replaced sections 9 and 33 continue to apply, as previously enacted, to wills (irrespective of date of execution) of *testators dying before 1 January 1983*, whereas s. 18, as previously enacted, continues to apply to *wills made before 1 January 1983,* irrespective of date of death. New s. 18A applies to all deaths on or after 1 January 1983.

1. Meaning of certain words in this Act. The words and expressions hereinafter mentioned, which in their ordinary signification have a more confined or a different meaning, shall in this Act, except where the nature of the provision or the context of the Act shall exclude such construction, be interpreted as follows; (that is to say), the word 'will' shall extend to a testament, and to a codicil, and to an appointment by will or by writing in the nature of a will in exercise of a power, *and also to a disposition by will and testament or devise of the custody and tuition of any child* [and also to an appointment by will of a guardian of a child][1] . . . and to any other testamentary disposition . . .

1 Words in square brackets were substituted for those in italics, as from 14 October 1991, by Children Act 1989, s. 108 (5), Sch. 13, para. 1.

3. All property may be disposed of by will. It shall be lawful for every person to devise, bequeath, or dispose of, by his will executed in manner hereinafter required, all real estate and all personal estate which he shall be entitled to, either at law or in equity, at the time of his death, and which, if not so devised, bequeathed, or disposed of, would devolve [*upon the heir-at-law or customary heir of him, or, if he became entitled by descent of his ancestor, or*] upon his executor or administrator; and that the power hereby given shall extend [*to all real estate of the nature of customary freehold or tenant right, or customary or copyhold, notwithstanding that the testator may not have surrendered the same to the use of his will, or notwithstanding that, being entitled as heir, devisee, or otherwise to be admitted thereto, he shall not have been admitted thereto or notwithstanding that the same, in consequence of the want of a custom to devise or surrender to the use of a will or otherwise, could not at law have been disposed of by will if this Act had not been made, or notwithstanding that the same, in consequence of there being a custom that a will or a surrender to the use of a will should continue in force for a limited time only, or any other special custom, could not have been disposed of by will according to the power contained in this Act, if this Act had not been made; and also to estates pur autre vie, whether there shall or shall not be any special occupant thereof and whether the same shall be freehold, customary freehold, tenant right, customary or copyhold, or of any other tenure, and whether the same shall be a corporeal or an incorporeal hereditament; and also*] to all contingent, executory or other future interests in any real or personal estate, whether the testator may or may not be ascertained as the person or one of the persons in whom the same respectively may become vested, and whether he may be entitled thereto under the instrument by which the same respectively were created, or under any disposition thereof by deed or will; and also to all rights of entry for conditions broken, and other rights of entry; and also to such of the same estates, interests, and rights respectively, and other real and personal estate, as the testator may be entitled to at the time of his death, notwithstanding that he may become entitled to the same subsequently to the execution of his will[2].

7. No will of a person under age valid. No will made by any person under the age of [twenty-one] years shall be valid[3].

Deaths before 1 January 1983
(see note on p. 719, ante)

9. Every will shall be in writing, and signed by the testator in the presence of two witnesses at one time. No will shall be valid unless it shall be in writing and executed in manner hereinafter mentioned; (that is to say,) it shall be signed at the foot or end thereof by the testator, or by some other person in his presence and by his direction[4]; and such signature shall be made or acknowledged by the testator in the presence of two or more witnesses present at the same time, and such witnesses shall attest and shall subscribe the will in the presence of the testator, but no form of attestation shall be necessary[5].

Deaths on or after 1 January 1983
(see note on p. 719, ante)

9. Signing and attestation of wills. No will shall be valid unless:

(a) it is in writing, and signed by the testator, or by some other person in his presence and by his direction; and

---

2   Words in brackets repealed by Statute Law (Repeals) Act 1969, s. 1 and Sch., Pt. III.
3   In relation to wills made on or after 1 January 1970, the age of 18 is substituted (Family Law Reform Act 1969, s. 3 (1) (see p. 789, post)).
4   Amended by Wills Act Amendment Act 1852 (post, p. 726).
5   See ss. 17 and 18 of the Administration of Justice Act 1969 (p. 795, post) and ss. 96 and 97 of the Mental Health Act 1983 (p. 860, post) as to the court's power to direct the execution of a will or codicil on behalf of a person incapable of managing his own affairs.

(b) it appears that the testator intended by his signature to give effect to the will; and

(c) the signature is made or acknowledged by the testator in the presence of two or more witnesses present at the same time; and

(d) each witness either—
   (i) attests and signs the will; or
   (ii) acknowledges his signature,
in the presence of the testator (but not necessarily in the presence of any other witness),

but no form of attestation shall be necessary.

---

10. Appointments by will to be executed like other wills, and to be valid, although other required solemnities are not observed. No appointment made by will, in exercise of any power, shall be valid, unless the same be executed in manner hereinbefore required; and every will executed in manner hereinbefore required shall, so far as respects the execution and attestation thereof, be a valid execution of a power of appointment by will, notwithstanding it shall have been expressly required that a will made in exercise of such power should be executed with some additional or other form of execution or solemnity.

11. Soldiers' and mariners' wills excepted. Provided always, that any soldier being in actual military service, or any mariner or seaman being at sea, may dispose of his personal estate as he might have done before the making of this Act[6].

13. Publication not to be requisite. Every will executed in manner hereinbefore required shall be valid without any other publication thereof.

14. Will not to be void on account of incompetency of attesting witness. If any person who shall attest the execution of a will shall at the time of the execution thereof or at any time afterwards be incompetent to be admitted a witness to prove the execution thereof, such will shall not on that account be invalid.

15. Gifts to an attesting witness to be void. If any person shall attest the execution of any will to whom or to whose wife or husband any beneficial devise, legacy, estate, interest, gift, or appointment, of or affecting any real or personal estate (other than and except charges and directions for the payment of any debt or debts), shall be thereby given or made, such devise, legacy, estate, interest, gift or appointment shall, so far only as concerns such person attesting the execution of such will, or the wife or husband of such person, or any person claiming under such person or wife or husband, be utterly null and void, and such person so attesting shall be admitted as a witness to prove the execution of such will, or to prove the validity or invalidity thereof notwithstanding such devise, legacy, estate, interest, gift, or appointment mentioned in such will[7].

16. Creditor attesting to be admitted a witness. In case by any will any real or personal estate shall be charged with any debt or debts, and any creditor, or the wife or husband of any creditor, whose debt is so charged, shall attest the execution of such will, such creditor, notwithstanding such charge, shall be admitted a witness to prove the execution of such will, or to prove the validity or invalidity thereof.

17. Executor to be admitted a witness. No person shall, on account of his being an executor of a will, be incompetent to be admitted a witness to prove the execution of such will, or a witness to prove the validity or invalidity thereof.

---

6 Explained and extended by Wills (Soldiers and Sailors) Act 1918, post, p. 733.

7 The operation of this section is restricted by the Wills Act 1968 (see p. 787, post). The attestation of a will by a person to whom, or to whose spouse, there is given or made any such disposition as is described in s. 15 is to be disregarded if the will is also attested by at least two 'independent' witnesses.

Wills made before 1 January 1983
(see note on p. 719, ante)

18. Will to be revoked by marriage. Every will made by a man or woman shall be revoked by his or her marriage (except a will made in exercise of a power of appointment, when the real or personal estate thereby appointed would not in default of such appointment pass to his or her heir, customary heir, executor, or administrator, or the person entitled as his or her next-of-kin, under the Statute of Distributions)[8].

Wills made on or after 1 January 1983
(see note on p. 719, ante)

18. Wills to be revoked by marriage except in certain cases. (1) Subject to subsections (2) to (4) below, a will shall be revoked by the testator's marriage.

(2) A disposition in a will in exercise of a power of appointment shall take effect notwithstanding the testator's subsequent marriage unless the property so appointed would in default of appointment pass to his personal representatives.

(3) Where it appears from a will that at the time it was made the testator was expecting to be married to a particular person and that he intended that the will should not be revoked by the marriage, the will shall not be revoked by his marriage to that person.

(4) Where it appears from a will that at the time it was made the testator was expecting to be married to a particular person and that he intended that a disposition in the will should not be revoked by his marriage to that person,—

(a) that disposition shall take effect notwithstanding the marriage; and
(b) any other disposition in the will shall take effect also, unless it appears from the will that the testator intended the disposition to be revoked by the marriage.

Deaths on or after 1 January 1983
(see note on p. 719, ante)

18A. Effect of dissolution or annulment of marriage on wills. (1) Where, after a testator has made a will, a decree of a court [of civil jurisdiction in England and Wales][9] dissolves or annuls his marriage *or declares it void*, [or his marriage is dissolved or annulled and the divorce or annulment is entitled to recognition in England and Wales by virtue of Part II of the Family Law Act 1986][10]

(a) the will shall take effect as if any appointment of the former spouse as an executor or as the executor and trustee of the will were omitted; and
(b) any devise or bequest to the former spouse shall lapse,
[(a) provisions of the will appointing executors or trustees or conferring a power of appointment, if they appoint or confer the power on the former spouse, shall take effect as if the former spouse had died on the date on which the marriage is dissolved or annulled, and

---

8   The Law of Property Act 1925, s. 177, excludes a will made on or after 1 January 1926 and, by virtue of the Administration of Justice Act 1982, before 1 January 1983, *expressed* to be made in contemplation of a particular marriage; see paras. **3. 44** ff., ante. For wills made on or after 1 January 1983, see now the revised s. 18 as substituted by Administration of Justice Act 1982, above. The expression 'heir, etc.' includes the widow: *Re Gilligan's Goods* [1950] P 32, [1949] 2 All ER 401.

9   The words in square brackets were inserted, as from 4 April 1988, by Family Law Act 1986, s. 53 (a)—(see p. 870, post).

10   The words in square brackets were substituted for those in italics, as from 4 April 1988, by Family Law Act 1986, s. 53 (b)—see p. 870, post.

(b) any property which, or an interest in which, is devised or bequeathed to the former spouse shall pass as if the former spouse had died on that date,][11]

except in so far as a contrary intention appears by the will.

(2) Subsection (1) (b) above is without prejudice to any right of the former spouse to apply for financial provision under the Inheritance (Provision for Family and Dependants) Act 1975.

(3) Where:

(a) by the terms of a will an interest in remainder is subject to a life interest; and
(b) the life interest lapses by virtue of subsection (1) (b) above, the interest in remainder shall be treated as if it had not been subject to the life interest and, if it was contingent upon the termination of the life interest, as if it had not been so contingent[12].

19. No will to be revoked by presumption. No will shall be revoked by any presumption of an intention, on the ground of an alteration in circumstances.

20. No will to be revoked but by another will or codicil, or by a writing executed like a will, or by destruction. No will or codicil, or any part thereof, shall be revoked otherwise than as aforesaid, or by another will or codicil executed in manner hereinbefore required, or by some writing declaring an intention to revoke the same and executed in the manner in which a will is hereinbefore required to be executed, or by the burning, tearing, or otherwise destroying the same by the testator, or by some person in his presence and by his direction, with the intention of revoking the same.

21. No alteration in a will shall have any effect unless executed as a will. No obliteration, interlineation, or other alteration made in any will after the execution thereof shall be valid or have any effect, except so far as the words or effect of the will before such alteration shall not be apparent, unless such alteration shall be executed in like manner as hereinbefore is required for the execution of the will; but the will, with such alteration as part thereof, shall be deemed to be duly executed if the signature of the testator and the subscription of the witnesses be made in the margin or on some other part of the will opposite or near to such alteration, or at the foot or end of or opposite to a memorandum referring to such alteration, and written at the end or some other part of the will.

22. No will revoked to be revived otherwise than by re-execution or a codicil to revive it. No will or codicil, or any part thereof, which shall be in any manner revoked, shall be revived otherwise than by the re-execution thereof, or by a codicil executed in manner hereinbefore required, and showing an intention to revive the same; and when any will or codicil which shall be partly revoked, and afterwards wholly revoked, shall be revived, such revivial shall not extend to so much thereof as shall have been revoked before the revocation of the whole thereof, unless an intention to the contrary shall be shown.

23. A devise not to be rendered inoperative by any subsequent conveyance or act. No conveyance or other act made or done subsequently to the execution of a will of or relating to any real or personal estate therein comprised, except an act by which such will shall be revoked as aforesaid, shall prevent the operation of the will with respect to such estate or interest in such real or personal estate as the testator shall have power to dispose of by will at the time of his death.

---

11   Paragraphs (a) and (b) in square brackets substituted for existing paragraphs (a) and (b) as respects a will made by a person dying on or after 1 January 1996 (regardless of the date of the will and the date of the dissolution or annulment)—see s. 3, Law Reform (Succession) Act 1995, p. 901, post.
12   Section 18A (3) is repealed as respects a will made by a person dying on or after 1 January 1996—see s. 5, Law Reform (Succession) Act 1995, p. 902, post.

24. A will shall be construed to speak from the death of the testator. Every will shall be construed, with reference to the real estate and personal estate comprised in it, to speak and take effect as if it had been executed immediately before the death of the testator, unless a contrary intention shall appear by the will.

25. A residuary devise shall include estates comprised in lapsed and void devises. Unless a contrary intention shall appear by the will, such real estate or interest therein as shall be comprised or intended to be comprised in any devise in such will contained, which shall fail or be void by reason of the death of the devisee in the lifetime of the testator, or by reason of such devise being contrary to law or otherwise incapable of taking effect, shall be included in the residuary devise (if any) contained in such will.

26. A general devise of the testator's lands shall include copyhold and leasehold as well as freehold lands. A devise of the land of the testator, or of the land of the testator in any place or in the occupation of any person mentioned in his will, or otherwise described in a general manner, and any other general devise which would describe a [*customary, copyhold, or*] leasehold estate if the testator had no freehold estate which could be described by it, shall be construed to include the [*customary, copyhold, and*] leasehold estates of the testator or his [*customary, copyhold, and*] leasehold estates, or any of them, to which such description shall extend, as the case may be, as well as freehold estates, unless a contrary intention shall appear by the will[13].

27. A general gift shall include estates over which the testator has a general power of appointment. A general devise of the real estate of the testator, or of the real estate of the testator in any place or in the occupation of any person mentioned in his will, or otherwise described in a general manner, shall be construed to include any real estate, or any real estate to which such description shall extend (as the case may be), which he may have power to appoint in any manner he may think proper, and shall operate as an execution of such power, unless a contrary intention shall appear by the will; and in like manner a bequest of the personal estate of the testator, or any bequest of personal property described in a general manner, shall be construed to include any personal estate, or any personal estate to which such description shall extend (as the case may be), which he may have power to appoint in any manner he may think proper, and shall operate as an execution of such power, unless a contrary intention shall appear by the will.

28. A devise without any words of limitation shall be construed to pass the fee. Where any real estate shall be devised to any person without any words of limitation, such devise shall be construed to pass the fee simple, or other the whole estate or interest which the testator had power to dispose of by will in such real estate, unless a contrary intention shall appear by the will.

29. The words 'die without issue', or 'die without leaving issue', shall be construed to mean die without issue living at the death. In any devise or bequest of real or personal estate the words 'die without issue', or 'die without leaving issue', or 'have no issue', or any other words which may import either a want or failure of issue of any person in his lifetime or at the time of his death, or an indefinite failure of his issue, shall be construed to mean a want or failure of issue in the lifetime or at the time of the death of such person, and not an indefinite failure of his issue, unless a contrary intention shall appear by the will, by reason of such person having a prior estate tail, or of a preceding gift, being, without any implication arising from such words, a limitation of an estate tail to such person or issue, or otherwise: Provided, that this Act shall not extend to cases where such words as aforesaid import if no issue described in a preceding gift shall be born, or if there shall be no issue who shall live to attain the age or otherwise answer the description required for obtaining a vested estate by a preceding gift to such issue.

---

13   Words in brackets repealed by Statute Law (Repeals) Act 1969, s. 1 and Sch., Pt. III.

30. No devise to trustees or executors, except for a term or a presentation to a church, shall pass a chattel interest. Where any real estate (other than or not being a presentation to a church) shall be devised to any trustee or executor, such devise shall be construed to pass the fee simple or other the whole estate or interest which the testator had power to dispose of by will in such real estate, unless a definite term of years, absolute or determinable, or an estate of freehold, shall thereby be given to him expressly or by implication.

31. Trustees under unlimited devise, where the trust may endure beyond tbe life of a person beneficially entitled for life, to take the fee. Where any real estate shall be devised to a trustee, without any express limitation of the estate to be taken by such trustee, and the beneficial interest in such real estate, or in the surplus rents and profits thereof, shall not be given to any person for life, or such beneficial interest shall be given to any person for life, but the purposes of the trust may continue beyond the life of such person, such devise shall be construed to vest in such trustee the fee simple or other the whole legal estate which the testator had power to dispose of by will in such real estate, and not an estate determinable when the purposes of the trust shall be satisfied.

32. Devises of estates tail shall not lapse. Where any person to whom any real estate shall be devised for an estate tail or an estate in quasi entail shall die in the lifetime of the testator leaving issue who would be inheritable under such entail, and any such issue shall be living at the time of the death of the testator, such devise shall not lapse, but shall take effect as if the death of such person had happened immediately after the death of the testator, unless a contrary intention shall appear by the will.

Deaths before 1 January 1983
(see note on p. 719, ante)

33. Gifts to children or other issue who leave issue living at the testator's death shall not lapse. Where any person being a child or other issue of the testator to whom any real or personal estate shall be devised or bequeathed for any estate or interest not determinable at or before the death of such person shall die in the lifetime of the testator leaving issue, and any such issue of such person shall be living at the time of the death of the testator, such devise or bequest shall not lapse, but shall take effect as if the death of such person had happened immediately after the death of the testator, unless a contrary intention shall appear by the will[14].

Deaths on or after 1 January 1983
(see note on p. 719, ante)

33. Gifts to children or other issue who leave issue living at the testator's death shall not lapse. (1) Where—

(a) a will contains a devise or bequest to a child or remoter descendant of the testator; and
(b) the intended beneficiary dies before the testator, leaving issue; and
(c) issue of the intended beneficiary are living at the testator's death,

then, unless a contrary intention appears by the will, the devise or bequest shall take effect as a devise or bequest to the issue living at the testator's death.

(2) Where—

(a) a will contains a devise or bequest to a class of persons consisting of children or remoter descendants of the testator; and

14   In the case of deaths on or after 1 January 1970, the definitions of 'child' and 'issue' are extended so as to include illegitimate children and remoter descendants (Family Law Reform Act 1969, s. 16, p. 789, post) (see also Family Law Reform Act 1987, ss. 18 and 19 (p. 876, post) in respect of wills and codicils made on or after 4 April 1988), and, by virtue of the Adoption Act 1976, s. 39 (see p. 828, post), replacing para. 3(1) of Sch. 1 to the Children Act 1975, would seem to include an adopted child in relation to a death occurring on or after 1 January 1976.

(b) a member of the class dies before the testator, leaving issue; and

(c) issue of that member are living at the testator's death,

then, unless a contrary intention appears by the will, the devise or bequest shall take effect as if the class included the issue of its deceased member living at the testator's death.

(3) Issue shall take under this section through all degrees, according to their stock, in equal shares if more than one, any gift or share which their parent would have taken and so that no issue shall take whose parent is living at the testator's death and so capable of taking.

(4) For the purposes of this section—

(a) the illegitimacy of any person is to be disregarded; and

(b) a person conceived before the testator's death and born living thereafter is to be taken to have been living at the testator's death.

---

34. Act not to extend to wills made before 1838, nor to estates pur autre vie of persons who die before 1838. This Act shall not extend to any will made before the first day of January one thousand eight hundred and thirty-eight, and every will re-executed or republished, or revived by any codicil, shall for the purposes of this Act be deemed to have been made at the time at which the same shall be so re-executed, republished, or revived; and this Act shall not extend to any estate pur autre vie of any person who shall die before the first day of January one thousand eight hundred and thirty-eight.

35. Act not to extend to Scotland. This Act shall not extend to Scotland.

WILLS ACT AMENDMENT ACT 1852

(15 & 16 Vict. c. 24)

Lord St. Leonards' Act

Note.—Although the whole of this Act was repealed by the Administration of Justice Act 1982, s. 75 and Sch. 9, Pt. I, its provisions continue to apply to wills of *testators dying before 1 January 1983*.

1. *When signature to a will shall be deemed valid.* *Where by the Wills Act 1837, it is enacted, that no will shall be valid unless it shall be signed at the foot or end thereof by the testator, or by some other person in his presence, and by his direction. Every will shall, so far only as regards the position of the signature of the testator, or of the person signing for him as aforesaid, be deemed to be valid within the said enactment, as explained by this Act, if the signature shall be so placed at or after, or following, or under, or beside, or opposite to the end of the will, that it shall be apparent on the face of the will that the testator intended to give effect by such his signature to the writing signed as his will; and that no such will shall be effected by the circumstance that the signature shall not follow or be immediately after the foot or end of the will, or by the circumstance that a blank space shall intervene between the concluding word of the will and the signature, or by the circumstance that the signature shall be placed among the words of the testimonium clause or of the clause of attestation, or shall follow or be after or under the clause of attestation, either with or without a blank space intervening, or shall follow or be after, or under, or beside the names or one of the names of the subscribing witnesses, or by the circumstance that the signature shall be on a side or page or other portion of the paper or papers containing the will whereon no clause or paragraph or disposing part of the will shall be written above the signature, or by the circumstance that there shall appear to be sufficient space on or at the bottom of the preceding side or page or other portion of the same paper on which the will is written to contain the signature; and the enumeration of the above circumstances shall not*

restrict the generality of the above enactment; but no signature under the said Act or this Act shall be operative to give effect to any disposition or direction which is underneath or which follows it, nor shall it give effect to any disposition or direction inserted after the signature shall be made.

2. Act to extend to certain wills already made. *The provisions of this Act shall extend and be applied to every will already made, where administration or probate has not already been granted or ordered by a court of competent jurisdiction in consequence of the defective execution of such will, or where the property, not being within the jurisdiction of the ecclesiastical courts, has not been possessed or enjoyed by some person or persons claiming to be entitled thereto in consequence of the defective execution of such will, or the right thereto shall not have been decided to be in some other person or persons than the persons claiming under the will, by a court of competent jurisdiction, in consequence of the defective execution of such will.*

3. Interpretation of 'will'. *The word 'will' shall in the construction of this Act be interpreted in like manner as the same is directed to be interpreted under the provisions in this behalf contained in the Wills Act 1837.*

WILLS ACT 1861[15]

(24 & 25 Vict. c. 114)

Lord Kingsdown's Act

An Act to amend the law with respect to Wills of personal estate made by British subjects

1. Wills made out of the UK to be admitted if made according to the law of the place where made. Every will and other testamentary instrument made out of the United Kingdom by a British subject (whatever may be the domicile of such person at the time of making the same or at the time of his or her death) shall as regards personal estate be held to be well executed for the purpose of being admitted in England and Ireland[16] to probate, and in Scotland to confirmation, if the same be made according to the forms required either by the law of the place where the same was made, or by the law of the place where such person was domiciled when the same was made, or by the laws then in force in that part of her Majesty's dominions where he had his domicile of origin.

2. Wills made in the kingdom to be admitted if made according to local usage. Every will and other testamentary instrument made within the United Kingdom by any British subject (whatever may be the domicile of such person at the time of making the same or at the time of his or her death) shall as regards personal estate be held to be well executed, and shall be admitted in England and Ireland[16] to probate, and in Scotland to confirmation, if the same be executed according to the forms required by the laws for the time being in force in that part of the United Kingdom where the same is made.

3. Change of domicile not to invalidate will. No will or other testamentary instrument shall be held to be revoked or to have become invalid, nor shall the construction thereof be altered, by reason of any subsequent change of domicile of the person making the same[17].

---

15 The Wills Act 1861 is repealed with effect from 1 January 1964 (Wills Act 1963, s. 7(3)) but the repeal does not invalidate a will executed before that date (ibid., s. 7 (4)). See now the Wills Act 1963 (p. 777, post), which applies to the wills (whenever made) of persons dying on or after 1 January 1964.

16 The expression 'Ireland' used in this Act now excludes the Republic of Ireland (see Art. 2 of the Irish Free State (Consequential Adaptation of Enactments) Order 1923).

17 Section 3 is not limited to wills of British subjects (*Re Groos' Goods* [1904] P 269).

4. Nothing in this Act to invalidate wills otherwise made. Nothing in this Act contained shall invalidate any will or other testamentary instrument as regards personal estate which would have been valid if this Act had not been passed, except as such will or other testamentary instrument may be revoked or altered by any subsequent will or testamentary instrument made valid by this Act.

5. Extent of Act. This Act shall extend only to wills and other testamentary instruments made by persons who die after the passing of this Act[18].

COLONIAL PROBATES ACT 1892[19]

(55 & 56 Vict. c. 6)

1. Application of Act by Order in Council. Her Majesty the Queen may, on being satisfied that the legislature of any British possession has made adequate provision for the recognition in that possession of probates and letters of administration granted by the courts of the United Kingdom, direct by Order in Council that this Act shall, subject to any exceptions and modifications specified in the Order, apply to that possession, and thereupon, while the Order is in force, this Act shall apply accordingly.

2. Sealing in United Kingdom of colonial probates and letters of administration.—(l) Where a court of probate in a British possession to which this Act applies has granted probate or letters of administration in respect of the estate of a deceased person, [then (subject to section 109 of the Supreme Court Act 1981, section 42 of the Probate and Legacy Duties Act 1808 and section 99A of the Probate and Letters of Administration Act (Ireland) 1857)] the probate or letters so granted may, on being produced to, and a copy thereof deposited with, a court of probate in the United Kingdom, be sealed with the seal of that court, and, thereupon shall be of the like force and effect, and have the same operation in the United Kingdom, as if granted by that court[20].

(2) Provided that the court shall, before sealing a probate or letters of administration under this section, be satisfied—

[(a) *that probate duty has been paid in respect of so much (if any) of the estate as is liable to probate duty in the United Kingdom; and*]
[(b) *in the case of letters of administration, that security has been given in a sum sufficient in amount to cover the property (if any) in the United Kingdom to which letters of administration relate*];

and may require such evidence, if any, as it thinks fit as to the domicile of the deceased person[21].

[(3) *The court may also, if it thinks fit, on the application of any creditor, require, before sealing, that adequate security be given for the payment of debts due from the estate to creditors residing in the United Kingdom.*][21]

18   The Act is repealed with effect from 1 January 1964: see note (15), ante, p. 727.
19   For a list of places to which this Act has been applied, see para **18.39**, ante; see also the Colonial Probates (Protected States and Mandated Territories) Act 1927 (post, p. 764), the powers under which were preserved by the Mandated and Trust Territories Act 1947.
20   Words in brackets, which apply in relation to deaths after 12 March 1975, were inserted by the Finance Act 1975, s. 52 and Sch. 12, and subsequently amended by the Supreme Court Act 1981, s. 152 (1) and Sch. 5. For s. 109 of the Supreme Court Act 1981, see p. 843, post. Section 42 of the Probate and Legacy Duties Act 1808 and s. 99A of the Probate and Letters of Administration Act (Ireland) 1857 make equivalent provision for Scotland and Northern Ireland respectively.
21   Subsection (2) (a) repealed in relation to deaths after 12 March 1975 by the Finance Act 1975, s. 59 and Sch. 13, Pt. I. Subsections (2) (b) and (3) do not apply to the resealing of grants in England and Wales on and after 1 January 1972; see Administration of Estates Act 1971, s. 11 (p. 799, post).

(4) For the purposes of this section, a duplicate of any probate or letters of administration sealed with the seal of the court granting the same, or a copy thereof certified as correct, by or under the authority of the court granting the same, shall have the same effect as the original[22].

(5) Rules of court may be made for regulating the procedure and practice, including fees and costs, in courts of the United Kingdom, on and incidental to an application for sealing a probate or letters of administration granted in a British possession to which this Act applies. [*Such rules shall, so far as they relate to probate duty, be made with the consent of the Treasury, and subject to any exceptions and modifications made by such rules, the enactments for the time being in force in relation to probate duty (including the penal provisions thereof) shall apply as if the person who applies for sealing under this section were a person applying for probate or letters of administration.*][1]

3. Application of Act to British courts in foreign countries. This Act shall extend to authorise the sealing in the United Kingdom of any probate or letters of administration granted by a British court in a foreign country, in like manner as it authorises the sealing of a probate or letters of administration granted in a British possession to which this Act applies, and the provisions of this Act shall apply accordingly with the necessary modifications.

4. Orders in Council.—(1) Every Order in Council made under this Act shall be laid before both Houses of Parliament as soon as may be after it is made, and shall be published under the authority of Her Majesty's Stationery Office.

(2) Her Majesty the Queen in Council may revoke or alter any Order in Council previously made under this Act.

(3) Where it appears to Her Majesty in Council that the legislature of part of a British possession has power to make the provision requisite for bringing this Act into operation in that part, it shall be lawful for Her Majesty to direct by Order in Council that this Act shall apply to that part as if it were a separate British possession, and thereupon, while the Order is in force, this Act shall apply accordingly.

5. Application of Act to probates, etc., already granted. This Act when applied by an Order in Council to a British possession shall, subject to the provisions of the Order, apply to probates and letters of administration granted in that possession either before or after the passing of this Act.

6. Definitions. In this Act—

The expression 'Court of Probate' means any court or authority, by whatever name designated, having jurisdiction in matters of probate, and in Scotland means the sheriff court of the county of Edinburgh;
The expressions 'probate' and 'letters of administration' include confirmation in Scotland, and any instrument having in a British possession the same effect which under English law is given to probate and letters of administration respectively;
[*The expression 'probate duty' includes any duty payable on the value of the estate and effects for which probate or letters of administration is or are granted;*][2]
The expression 'British court in a foreign country' means any British court having jurisdiction out of the Queen's dominions in pursuance of an Order in Council, whether made under any Act or otherwise.

---

22   An exemplification is also accepted; President's Direction (1902) 13 March.
1   Words in brackets repealed in relation to deaths after 12 March 1975 by the Finance Act 1975, s. 52 and Sch. 13, Pt. I.
2   Definition of 'probate duty' repealed in relation to deaths after 12 March 1975 by the Finance Act 1975, s. 52 and Sch. 13, Pt. I.

LAND TRANSFER ACT 1897

(60 & 61 Vict. c. 65)

PART I[3]

ESTABLISHMENT OF A REAL REPRESENTATIVE

1. Devolution of legal interest in real estate on death.—(1) Where real estate is vested in any person without a right in any other person to take by survivorship it shall, on his death, notwithstanding any testamentary disposition, devolve to and become vested in his personal representatives or representative from time to time as if it were a chattel real vesting in them or him.

(2) This section shall apply to any real estate over which a person executes by will a general power of appointment, as if it were real estate vested in him[4].

(3) Probate and letters of administration may be granted in respect of real estate only, although there is no personal estate.

(4) The expression 'real estate', in this Part of this Act, shall not be deemed to include land of copyhold tenure or customary freehold in any case in which an admission or any act by the lord of the manor is necessary to perfect the title of a purchaser from the customary tenant.

(5) This section applies only in cases of death after the commencement of this Act.

2. Provisions as to administration.—(1) Subject to the powers, rights, duties, and liabilities hereinafter mentioned, the personal representatives of a deceased person shall hold the real estate as trustees for the persons by law beneficially entitled thereto, and those persons shall have the same power of requiring a transfer of real estate as persons beneficially entitled to personal estate have of requiring a transfer of such personal estate.

(2) All enactments and rules of law relating to the effect of probate or letters of administration as respects chattels real, and as respects the dealing with chattels real before probate or administration, and as respects the payment of costs of administration and other matters in relation to the administration of personal estate, and the powers, rights, duties, and liabilities of personal representatives in respect of personal estate, shall apply to real estate so far as the same are applicable, as if that real estate were a chattel real vesting in them or him, save that it shall not be lawful for some or one only of several joint personal representatives, without the authority of the court, to sell or transfer real estate[5].

(3) In the administration of the assets of a person dying after the commencement of this Act, his real estate shall be administered in the same manner, subject to the same liabilities for debt, costs, and expenses, and with the same incidents, as if it were personal estate; provided that nothing herein contained shall alter or affect the order in which real and personal assets respectively are now applicable in or towards the payment of funeral and testamentary expenses, debts, or legacies, or the liability of real estate to be charged with the payment of legacies.

3　Part I of this Act was repealed by ss. 147 and 155 of the Law of Property Act 1922 as respects deaths occurring after the year 1925.

4　Sub-ss. (1) and (2) hereof are substantially re-enacted by s. 1 of the Administration of Estates Act 1925.

5　See Conveyancing Act 1911, s. 12:

　　12.—(1) Where probate is granted to one or some of several persons named as executors, power being reserved to the others or other to prove, the sale, transfer or disposition of real estate may, notwithstanding anything contained in sub-s. (2) of the Land Transfer Act 1897, be made by the proving executor or executors without the authority of the court and shall be as effectual as if all the persons named as executors had concurred therein.

　　(2) This section applies to probates granted before as well as after the commencement of this Act, but only as respects dispositions made after the commencement of this Act.

　　Note.—This section was repealed by the Law of Property Act 1925 as respects deaths occurring after the year 1925.

(4) Where a person dies possessed of real estate, the court shall, in granting letters of administration, have regard to the rights and interests of persons interested in his real estate, and his heir-at-law, if not one of the next-of-kin, shall be equally entitled to the grant with the next-of-kin, and provision shall be made by rules of court for adapting the procedure and practice in the grant of letters of administration to the case of real estate.

3. Provision for transfer to heir or devisee.—(1) At any time after the death of the owner of any land, his personal representatives may assent to any devise contained in his will, or may convey the land to any person entitled thereto as heir, devisee, or otherwise, and may make the assent or conveyance, either subject to a charge for the payment of any money which the personal representatives are liable to pay, or without any such charge; and on such assent or conveyance, subject to a charge for all moneys (if any) which the personal representatives are liable to pay, all liabilities of the personal representatives in respect of the land shall cease, except as to any acts done or contracts entered into by them before such assent or conveyance.

(2) At any time after the expiration of one year from the death of the owner of any land, if his personal representatives have failed on the request of the person entitled to the land to convey the land to that person, the court may, if it thinks fit, on the application of that person, and after notice to the personal representatives, order that the conveyance be made, or, in the case of registered land, that the person so entitled be registered as proprietor of the land, either solely or jointly with the personal representatives.

(3) Where the personal representatives of a deceased person are registered as proprietors of land on his death, a fee shall not be chargeable on any transfer of the land by them unless the transfer is for valuable consideration.

(4) The production of an assent in the prescribed form by the personal representatives of a deceased proprietor of registered land shall authorise the registrar to register the person named in the assent as proprietor of the land.

4. Appropriation of land in satisfaction of legacy or share in estate.—(1) The personal representatives of a deceased person may, in the absence of any express provision to the contrary contained in the will of such deceased person, with the consent of the person entitled to any legacy given by the deceased person or to a share in his residuary estate, or, if the person entitled is a lunatic or an infant, with the consent of his committee, trustee, or guardian, appropriate any part of the residuary estate of the deceased in or towards satisfaction of that legacy or share, and may for that purpose value in accordance with the prescribed provisions the whole or any part of the property of the deceased person in such manner as they think fit. Provided that before any such appropriation is effectual, notice of such intended appropriation shall be given to all persons interested in the residuary estate, any of whom may thereupon within the prescribed time apply to the court, and such valuation and appropriation shall be conclusive save as otherwise directed by the court.

(2) Where any property is so appropriated a conveyance thereof by the personal representatives to the person to whom it is appropriated shall not, by reason only that the property so conveyed is accepted by the person to whom it is conveyed in or towards the satisfaction of a legacy or a share in residuary estate, be liable to any higher stamp duty than that payable on a transfer of personal property for a like purpose.

(3) In the case of registered land, the production of the prescribed evidence of an appropriation under this section shall authorise the registrar to register the person to whom the property is appropriated as proprietor of the land.

5. Liability for duty. Nothing in this Part of this Act shall affect any duty payable in respect of real estate or impose on real estate any other duty than is now payable in respect thereof.

PUBLIC TRUSTEE ACT 1906

(6 Edw. 7, c. 55)

1. Office of public trustee.—(l) There shall be established the office of public trustee.

(2) The public trustee shall be a corporation sole under that name, with perpetual succession and an official seal, and may sue and be sued under the above name like any other corporation sole, but any instruments sealed by him shall not, by reason of his using a seal, be rendered liable to a higher stamp duty than if he were an individual.

POWERS AND DUTIES OF PUBLIC TRUSTEE

(1) *In the Administration of Small Estates*

3. Administration of small estates.—(1) Any person who in the opinion of the public trustee would be entitled to apply to the court for an order for the administration by the court of an estate, the gross capital value whereof is proved to the satisfaction of the public trustee to be less than one thousand pounds, may apply to the public trustee to administer the estate, and, where any such application is made and it appears to the public trustee that the persons beneficially entitled are persons of small means, the public trustee shall administer the estate, unless he sees good reason for refusing to do so.

(2) On the public trustee undertaking, by declaration in writing signed and sealed by him, to administer the estate the trust property other than stock shall, by virtue of this Act, vest in him, and the right to transfer or call for the transfer of any stock forming part of the estate shall also vest in him, in like manner as if vesting orders had been made for the purpose by the High Court under the Trustee Act 1893, and that Act shall apply accordingly. As from such vesting any trustee entitled under the trust to administer the estate shall be discharged from all liability attaching to the administration, except in respect of past acts:
  Provided that—

(a) the public trustee shall not exercise the right of himself transferring the stock without the leave of the court; and
(b) this subsection shall not apply to any copyhold land forming part of the estate, but the public trustee shall, as respects such land, have the like powers as if he had been appointed by the court under section thirty-three of the Trustee Act 1893, to convey the land, and section thirty-four of that Act shall apply accordingly.

(3) For the purposes of the administration the public trustee may exercise such of the administrative powers and authorities of the High Court as may be conferred on him by rules under this Act, subject to such conditions as may be imposed by the rules.

(4) Rules shall be made under this Act for enabling the public trustee to take the opinion of the High Court on any question arising in the course of any administration without judicial proceedings, and otherwise for making the procedure under this section simple and inexpensive.

(5) Where proceedings have been instituted in any court for the administration of an estate, and by reason of the small value of the estate it appears to the court that the estate can be more economically administered by the public trustee than by the court, or that for any other reason it is expedient that the estate should be administered by the public trustee instead of the court, the court may order that the estate shall be administered by the public trustee, and thereupon (subject to any directions by the court) this section shall apply as if the administration of the estate had been undertaken by the public trustee in pursuance of this section.

6. Power as to granting probate.—(1) If in pursuance of any rule[6] under this Act, the public trustee is authorised to accept by that name probates of wills or letters of administration,

---

6   By the Public Trustee Rules 1912, rule 6, 'subject to the Act and these Rules the Public Trustee is authorised... to accept by the name of the Public Trustee probate or letters of administration of any kind and either as principal or as agent for any person.'

the court having jurisdiction to grant probate of a will or letters of administration[7] may grant such probate or letters to the public trustee by that name, and for that purpose the court shall consider the public trustee as in law entitled equally with any other person or class of person to obtain the grant of letters of administration[7], save that the consent or citation of the public trustee shall not be required for the grant of letters of administration[7] to any other person, and that, as between the public trustee and the widower widow or next-of-kin of the deceased, the widower widow or next-of-kin shall be preferred, unless for good cause shown to the contrary.

(2) Any executor who has obtained probate or any administrator who has obtained letters of administration[7] and notwithstanding he has acted in the administration of the deceased's estate, may, with the sanction of the court, and after such notice to the persons beneficially interested as the court may direct, transfer such estate to the public trustee for administration either solely or jointly with the continuing executors or administrator, if any. And the order of the court sanctioning such transfer shall, subject to the provisions of this Act, give to the public trustee all the powers of such executor and administrator, and such executor and administrator shall not be in any way liable in respect of any act or default in reference to such estate subsequent to the date of such order, other than the act or default of himself or of persons other than himself for whose conduct he is in law responsible.

SUPPLEMENTAL PROVISIONS AS TO PUBLIC TRUSTEE

11. Mode of action of public trustee.—(3) On behalf of the public trustee such person as may be prescribed may take any oath, make any declaration, verify any account, give personal attendance at any court or place, and do any act or thing whatsoever which the public trustee is required or authorised to take, make, verify, give or do....

(4) Where any bond or security would be required from a private person [*upon the grant to him of administration, or*][8] upon his appointment to act in any capacity, the public trustee, [*if administration is granted to him or*][8] if he is appointed to act in such capacity as aforesaid, shall not be required to give such bond or security, but shall be subject to the same liabilities and duties as if he had given such bond or security.

WILLS (SOLDIERS AND SAILORS) ACT 1918

(7 & 8 Geo. 5, c. 58)   [6 February 1918]

1. Explanation of s. 11 of 7 Will. 4 & 1 Vict. c. 26. In order to remove doubts as to the construction of the Wills Act, 1837, it is hereby declared and enacted that section eleven of that Act authorises and always has authorised any soldier being in actual military service, or any mariner or seaman being at sea, to dispose of his personal estate as he might have done before the passing of that Act, though under the age of [twenty-one years[9]].

2. Extension of s. 11 of Wills Act 1837. Section eleven of the Wills Act 1837, shall extend to any member of His Majesty's naval or marine forces not only when he is at sea but also when he is so circumstanced that if he were a soldier he would be in actual military service within the meaning of that section.

3. Validity of testamentary dispositions of real property made by soldiers and sailors.—(1) A testamentary disposition of any real estate in England or Ireland made by a person to whom section eleven of the Wills Act 1837, applies, and who dies after the passing

---

7   By s. 15 of this Act, 'letters of administration' includes letters of administration with will.
8   Words in brackets repealed, so far as relates to England and Wales, with effect from 1 January 1972 by Administration of Estates Act 1971, s. 12(2) and Sch. 2, Pt. II.
9   In relation to wills made on or after 1 January 1970, the age of 18 years is substituted (Family Law Reform Act 1969, s. 3(1) (see p. 789, post)).

of this Act, shall, notwithstanding that the person making the disposition was at the time of making it under [twenty-one years[9]] of age or that the disposition has not been made in such manner or form as was at the passing of this Act required by law, be valid in any case where the person making the disposition was of such age and the disposition has been made in such manner and form that if the disposition had been a disposition of personal estate made by such a person domiciled in England or Ireland it would have been valid.

(2) [*Repealed by Succession (Scotland) Act 1964, s. 34 (2) and Sch. 3.*]

4. Power to appoint testamentary guardians. Where any person dies after the passing of this Act having made a will which is, or which, if it had been a disposition of property, would have been rendered valid by section eleven of the Wills Act 1837, any appointment contained in that will of any person as guardian of the infant children of the testator shall be of full force and effect.

5. Short title and interpretation.

    *   *   *   *   *

(2) For the purposes of section eleven of the Wills Act 1837, and this Act the expression 'soldier' includes a member of the Air Force, and references in this Act to the said section eleven include a reference to that section as explained and extended by this Act.

SETTLED LAND ACT 1925

(15 & 16 Geo. 5, c. 18)

PART I

GENERAL PRELIMINARY PROVISIONS

Settlements and Settled Land

1. What constitutes a settlement.—(1) Any deed, will, agreement for a settlement or other agreement, Act of Parliament, or other instrument, or any number of instruments, whether made or passed before or after, or partly before and partly after, the commencement of this Act, under or by virtue of which instrument or instruments any land, after the commencement of this Act, stands for the time being—

 (i) limited in trust for any persons by way of succession; or
 (ii) limited in trust for any person in possession—

    (a) for an entailed interest whether or not capable of being barred or defeated;
    (b) for an estate in fee simple or for a term of years absolute subject to an executory limitation, gift, or disposition over on failure of his issue, or in any other event;
    (c) for a base or determinable fee or any corresponding interest in leasehold land;
    (d) being an infant, for an estate in fee simple or for a term of years absolute; or
 (iii) limited in trust for any person for an estate in fee simple or for a term of years absolute contingently on the happening of any event; or
 (iv) [*Repealed by Married Women (Restraint upon Anticipation) Act 1949.*]
 (v) charged, whether voluntarily or in consideration of marriage or by way of family arrangement, and whether immediately or after an interval, with the payment of any rent charge for the life of any person, or any less period, or of any capital, annual, or periodical sums for the portions, advancement, maintenance, or otherwise for the benefit of any persons, with or without any term of years for securing or raising the same;

creates or is for the purposes of this Act a settlement and is in this Act referred to as a settlement, or as the settlement, as the case requires:

Provided that, where land is the subject of a compound settlement, references in this Act to the settlement shall be construed as meaning such compound settlement, unless the context otherwise requires.

(2) Where an infant is beneficially entitled to land for an estate in fee simple or for a term of years absolute and by reason of an intestacy or otherwise there is no instrument under which the interest of the infant arises or is acquired, a settlement shall be deemed to have been made by the intestate, or by the person whose interest the infant has acquired.

(3) An infant shall be deemed to be entitled in possession notwithstanding any subsisting right of dower (not assigned by metes and bounds) affecting the land, and such a right of dower shall be deemed to be an interest comprised in the subject of the settlement and coming to the dowress under or by virtue of the settlement.

Where dower has been assigned by metes and bounds, the letters of administration or probate granted in respect of the estate of the husband of the dowress shall be deemed a settlement made by the husband.

(4) An estate or interest not disposed of by a settlement and remaining in or reverting to the settlor, or any person deriving title under him, is for the purposes of this Act an estate or interest comprised in the subject of the settlement and coming to the settlor or such person under or by virtue of the settlement.

(5) Where—

(a) a settlement creates an entailed interest which is incapable of being barred or defeated, or a base or determinable fee, whether or not the reversion or right of reverter is in the Crown, or any corresponding interest in leasehold land; or

(b) the subject of a settlement is an entailed interest, or a base or determinable fee, whether or not the reversion or right of reverter is in the Crown, or any corresponding interest in leasehold land;

the reversion or right of reverter upon the cesser of the interest so created or settled shall be deemed to be an interest comprised in the subject of the settlement, and limited by the settlement.

(6) Subsections (4) and (5) of this section bind the Crown.

[(7) This section does not apply to land held upon trust for sale[10].]

2. What is settled land. Land which is or is deemed to be the subject of a settlement is for the purposes of this Act settled land, and is in relation to the settlement referred to in this Act as the settled land.

3. Duration of settlements. Land [not held upon trust for sale][11] which has been subject to a settlement shall be deemed for the purposes of this Act to remain and be settled land, and the settlement shall be deemed to be a subsisting settlement for the purposes of this Act so long as—

(a) any limitation, charge, or power of charging under the settlement subsists, or is capable of being exercised; or

(b) the person who, if of full age, would be entitled as beneficial owner to have that land vested in him for a legal estate is an infant.

6. Procedure in the case of settlements by will. Where a settlement is created by the will of an estate owner who dies after the commencement of this Act—

(a) the will is for the purposes of this Act a trust instrument; and

(b) the personal representatives of the testator[12] shall hold the settled land on trust, if and

10   This subsection was added by Law of Property (Amendment) Act 1926.
11   These words were added by Law of Property (Amendment) Act 1926.
12   'Testator' in this section means 'settlor' (*Re Catchpool, Harris v Catchpool* [1928] Ch 429).

when required so to do, to convey it to the person who, under the will, or by virtue of this Act, is the tenant for life or statutory owner, and, if more than one, as joint tenants.

7. Procedure on change of ownership.—(l) If, on the death of a tenant for life or statutory owner, or of the survivor of two or more tenants for life or statutory owners, in whom the settled land was vested, the land remains settled land, his personal representatives shall hold the settled land on trust, if and when required so to do, to convey it to the person who under the trust instrument or by virtue of this Act becomes the tenant for life or statutory owner and, if more than one, as joint tenants.

(2) If a person by reason of attaining full age becomes a tenant for life for the purposes of this Act of settled land, he shall be entitled to require the trustees of the settlement, personal representatives, or other persons in whom the settled land is vested, to convey the land to him.

(3) If a person who, when of full age, will together with another person or other persons constitute the tenant for life for the purposes of this Act of settled land attains that age, he shall be entitled to require the tenant for life, trustees of the settlement, personal representatives or other persons in whom the settled land is vested to convey the land to him and the other person or persons who together with him constitute the tenant for life as joint tenants.

(4) If by reason of forfeiture, surrender, or otherwise the estate owner of any settled land ceases to have the statutory powers of a tenant for life and the land remains settled land, he shall be bound forthwith to convey the settled land to the person who under the trust instrument, or by virtue of this Act, becomes the tenant for life or statutory owner and, if more than one, as joint tenants.

(5) If any person of full age becomes absolutely entitled to the settled land (whether beneficially, or as personal representative, or as trustee for sale, or otherwise) free from all limitations, powers, and charges taking effect under the settlement, he shall be entitled to require the trustees of the settlement, personal representatives, or other persons in whom the settled land is vested, to convey the land to him, and if more persons than one being of full age become so entitled to the settled land they shall be entitled to require such persons as aforesaid to convey the land to them as joint tenants[13].

19. Who is tenant for life.—(l) The person of full age who is for the time being beneficially entitled under a settlement to possession of settled land for his life is for the purposes of this Act the tenant for life of that land and the tenant for life under that settlement.

(2) If in any case there are two or more persons of full age so entitled as joint tenants, they together constitute the tenant for life for the purposes of this Act.

(3) If in any case there are two or more persons so entitled as joint tenants and they are not all of full age, such one or more of them as is or are for the time being of full age is or (if more than one) together constitute the tenant for life for the purposes of this Act, but this subsection does not affect the beneficial interests of such of them as are not for the time being of full age.

(4) A person being tenant for life within the foregoing definitions shall be deemed to be such notwithstanding that, under the settlement or otherwise, the settled land, or his estate or interest therein, is incumbered or charged in any manner or to any extent, and notwithstanding any assignment by operation of law or otherwise of his estate or interest under the settlement, whether before or after it came into possession, other than an assurance which extinguishes that estate or interest.

20. Other limited owners having powers of tenant for life.—(l) Each of the following persons being of full age shall, when his estate or interest is in possession, have the powers of a tenant for life under this Act (namely):

---

13   This section is restricted by the Finance Act 1950.

(i) A tenant in tail, including a tenant in tail after possibility of issue extinct, and a tenant in tail who is by Act of Parliament restrained from barring or defeating his estate tail, and although the reversion is in the Crown, but not including such a tenant in tail where the land in respect whereof he is so restrained was purchased with money provided by Parliament in consideration of public services;

(ii) A person entitled to land for an estate in fee simple or for a term of years absolute with or subject to, in any of such cases, an executory limitation, gift, or disposition over on failure of his issue or in any other event;

(iii) A person entitled to a base or determinable fee, although the reversion or right of reverter is in the Crown, or to any corresponding interest in leasehold land;

(iv) A tenant for years determinable on life, not holding merely under a lease at a rent;

(v) A tenant for the life of another, not holding merely under a lease at a rent;

(vi) A tenant for his own or any other life, or for years determinable on life, whose estate is liable to cease in any event during that life, whether by expiration of the estate, or by conditional limitation, or otherwise, or to be defeated by an executory limitation, gift, or disposition over, or is subject to a trust for accumulation of income for any purpose;

(vii) A tenant by the curtesy;

(viii) A person entitled to the income of land under a trust or direction for payment thereof to him during his own or any other life, whether or not subject to expenses of management or to a trust for accumulation of income for any purpose, or until sale of the land, or until forfeiture, cesser or determination by any means of his interest therein, unless the land is subject to an immediate binding trust for sale;

(ix) A person beneficially entitled to land for an estate in fee simple or for a term of years absolute subject to any estates, interests, charges, or powers of charging, subsisting or capable of being exercised under a settlement;

(x) [*Repealed by Married Women (Restraint upon Anticipation) Act 1949.*]

(2) In every such case as is mentioned in subsection (1) of this section, the provisions of this Act referring to a tenant for life, either as conferring powers on him or otherwise, shall extend to each of the persons aforesaid, and any reference in this Act to death as regards a tenant for life shall, where necessary, be deemed to refer to the determination by death or otherwise of the estate or interest of the person on whom the powers of a tenant for life are conferred by this section.

(3) For the purposes of this Act the estate or interest of a tenant by the curtesy shall be deemed to be an estate or interest arising under a settlement made by his wife.

(4) Where the reversion or right of reverter or other reversionary right is in the Crown, the exercise by a person on whom the powers of a tenant for life are conferred by this section of his powers under this act, binds the Crown.

26. Infants, how to be affected.—(1) Where an infant is beneficially entitled in possession to land for an estate in fee simple or for a term of years absolute or would if of full age be a tenant for life of or have the powers of a tenant for life over settled land, then, during the minority of the infant—

(a) if the settled land is vested in a personal representative, the personal representative, until a principal vesting instrument has been executed pursuant to the provisions of this Act; and

(b) in every other case, the trustees of the settlement;

shall have, in reference to the settled land and capital money, all the powers conferred by this Act and the settlement on a tenant for life, and on the trustees of the settlement.

(2) If the settled land is vested in a personal representative, then, if and when during the minority the infant, if of full age, would have been entitled to have the legal estate in the settled land conveyed to or otherwise vested in him pursuant to the provisions of this Act, a principal vesting instrument shall, if the trustees of the settlement so require, be executed, at the cost of the trust estate, for vesting the legal estate in themselves, and in the meantime the personal representatives shall, during the minority, give effect to the directions of the trustees of the settlement, and shall not be concerned with the propriety of any conveyance

directed to be made by those trustees if the conveyance appears to be a proper conveyance under the powers conferred by this Act or by the settlement, and the capital money, if any, arising under the conveyance is paid to or by the direction of the trustees of the settlement or into court, but a purchaser dealing with the personal representative and paying the capital money, if any, to him shall not be concerned to see that the money is paid to trustees of the settlement or into court, or to inquire whether the personal representative is liable to give effect to any such directions, or whether any such directions have been given.

(3) Subsection (2) of this section applies whether the infant becomes entitled before or after the commencement of this Act, and has effect during successive minorities until a person of full age becomes entitled to require the settled land to be vested in him.

(4) This section does not apply where an infant is beneficially entitled in possession to land for an estate in fee simple or for a term of years absolute jointly with a person of full age (for which case provision is made in the Law of Property Act, 1925), but it applies to two or more infants entitled as aforesaid jointly, until one of them attains full age.

(5) This section does not apply where an infant would, if of full age, constitute the tenant for life or have the powers of a tenant for life together with another person of full age, but it applies to two or more infants who would, if all of them were of full age, together constitute the tenant for life or have the powers of a tenant for life, until one of them attains full age.

(6) Nothing in this section affects prejudicially any beneficial interest of an infant.

Trustees of Settlement

30. Who are trustees for purposes of Act.—(1) Subject to the provisions of this Act, the following persons are trustees of a settlement for the purposes of this Act, and are in this Act referred to as the 'trustees of the settlement' or 'trustees of a settlement', namely—

(i) the persons, if any, who are for the time being under the settlement, trustees with power of sale of the settled land (subject or not to the consent of any person), or with power of consent to or approval of the exercise of such a power of sale, or if there are no such persons; then

(ii) the persons, if any, for the time being, who are by the settlement declared to be trustees thereof for the purposes of the Settled Land Acts 1882 to 1890, or any of them, or this Act, or if there are no such persons; then

(iii) the persons, if any, who are for the time being under the settlement trustees with power of or upon trust for sale of any other land comprised in the settlement and subject to the same limitations as the land to be sold or otherwise dealt with, or with power of consent to or approval of the exercise of such a power of sale, or, if there are no such persons; then

(iv) the persons, if any, who are for the time being under the settlement trustees with future power of sale, or under a future trust for sale of the settled land, or with power of consent to or approval of the exercise of such a future power of sale and whether the power or trust takes effect in all events or not, or, if there are no such persons; then

(v) the persons, if any, appointed by deed to be trustees of the settlement by all the persons who at the date of the deed were together able, by virtue of their beneficial interests or by the exercise of an equitable power, to dispose of the settled land in equity for the whole estate the subject of the settlement.

(2) Paragraphs (i) (iii) and (iv) of the last preceding subsection take effect in like manner as if the powers therein referred to had not by this Act been made exercisable by the tenant for life or statutory owner.

(3) Where a settlement is created by will, or a settlement has arisen by the effect of an intestacy, and apart from this subsection there would be no trustees for the purposes of this Act of such settlement, then the personal representatives of the deceased[14] shall, until other trustees are appointed, be by virtue of this Act the trustees of the settlement, but where there is a sole

14   'Deceased' to be read as 'settlor' (see p. 735, ante).

personal representative, not being a trust corporation, it shall be obligatory on him to appoint an additional trustee to act with him for the purposes of this Act, and the provisions of the Trustee Act 1925, relating to the appointment of new trustees and the vesting of trust property shall apply accordingly.

31. As to trustees of compound settlements.—(1) Persons who are for the time being trustees for the purposes of this Act of an instrument which is a settlement, or is deemed to be a subsisting settlement for the purposes of this Act, shall be the trustees for the purposes of this Act of any settlement constituted by that instrument and any instruments subsequent in date or operation.

[Where there are trustees for the purposes of this Act of the instrument under which there is a tenant for life or statutory owner but there are not trustees for those purposes of a prior instrument, being one of the instruments by which a compound settlement is constituted, those trustees shall, unless and until trustees are appointed of the prior instrument or of the compound settlement, be the trustees for the purposes of this Act of the compound settlement[15].]

(2) This section applies to instruments coming into operation before as well as after the commencement of this Act, but shall have effect without prejudice to any appointment made by the court before such commencement of trustees of a settlement constituted by more than one instrument, and to the power of the court in any case after such commencement to make any such appointment, and where any such appointment has been made before such commencement or is made thereafter this section shall not apply or shall cease to apply to the settlement consisting of the instruments to which the appointment relates.

32. As to trustees of referential settlements.—(1) Where a settlement takes or has taken effect by reference to another settlement, the trustees for the time being of the settlement to which reference is made shall be the trustees of the settlement by reference, but this section does not apply if the settlement by reference contains an appointment of trustees thereof for the purposes of the Settled Land Acts 1882 to 1890, or any of them, or this Act.

(2) This section applies to instruments coming into operation before as well as after the commencement of this Act, but shall have effect without prejudice to any appointment made by the court before such commencement of trustees of a settlement by reference, or of the compound settlement consisting of a settlement and any other settlement or settlements made by reference thereto, and to the power of the court in any case after such commencement to make any such appointment, and where any such appointment has been made before such commencement or is made thereafter this section shall not apply or shall cease to apply.

(3) In this section 'a settlement by reference to another settlement' means a settlement of property upon the limitations and subject to the powers and provisions of an existing settlement, with or without variation.

33. Continuance of trustees in office . . .—(1) Where any persons have been appointed or constituted trustees of a settlement, whether by an order of the court or otherwise, or have by reason of any power of sale, or trust for sale, or by reason of a power of consent to, or approval of, the exercise of a power of sale, or by virtue of this Act, or otherwise at any time become trustees of a settlement for the purposes of the Settled Land Acts 1882 to 1890, or this Act, then those persons or their successors in office shall remain and be trustees of the settlement as long as that settlement is subsisting or deemed to be subsisting for the purposes of this Act.

In this subsection 'successors in office' means the persons who, by appointment or otherwise, have become trustees for the purposes aforesaid.

34. Appointment of trustees by court.—(1) If at any time there are no trustees of a settlement, or where in any other case it is expedient, for the purposes of this Act, that new

---

15   This paragraph was added by Law of Property (Amendment) Act 1926.

trustees of a settlement be appointed, the court may, if it thinks fit, on the application of the tenant for life, statutory owner, or of any other person having, under the settlement, an estate or interest in the settled land, in possession, remainder or otherwise, or, in the case of an infant, of his testamentary or other guardian or next friend, appoint fit persons to be trustees of the settlement.

(2) The persons so appointed, and the survivors and survivor of them, while continuing to be trustees or trustee, and, until the appointment of new trustees, the personal representatives or representative for the time being of the last surviving or continuing trustee, shall become and be the trustees or trustee of the settlement.

120. Short title, commencement and extent.—(1) This Act may be cited as the Settled Land Act 1925.

(2) *This Act shall come into operation on the first day of January, nineteen hundred and twenty-six*[16].

(3) This Act extends to England and Wales only.

TRUSTEE ACT 1925

(15 & 16 Geo. 5, c. 19)

18. Devolution of powers or trusts.—(1) Where a power or trust is given to or imposed on two or more trustees jointly, the same may be exercised or performed by the survivors or survivor of them for the time being.

(2) Until the appointment of new trustees, the personal representatives or representative for the time being of a sole trustee, or, where there were two or more trustees of the last surviving or continuing trustee, shall be capable of exercising or performing any power or trust which was given to, or capable of being exercised by, the sole or last surviving or continuing trustee, or other the trustees or trustee for the time being of the trust.

(3) This section takes effect subject to the restrictions imposed in regard to receipts by a sole trustee, not being a trust corporation.

(4) In this section 'personal representative' does not include an executor who has renounced or has not proved.

36. Power of appointing new or additional trustees.—(1) Where a trustee, either original or substituted, and whether appointed by a court or otherwise, is dead, or remains out of the United Kingdom for more than twelve months, or desires to be discharged from all or any of the trusts or powers reposed in or conferred on him or refuses or is unfit to act therein, or is incapable of acting therein, or is an infant, then, subject to the restrictions imposed by this Act on the number of trustees,

(a) the person or persons nominated for the purpose of appointing new trustees by the instruments, if any, creating the trust; or
(b) if there is no such person, or no such person able and willing to act, then the surviving or continuing trustees or trustee for the time being, or the personal representatives of the last surviving or continuing trustee;

may, by writing, appoint one or more other persons (whether or not being the persons exercising the power) to be a trustee or trustees in the place of the trustee so deceased, remaining out of the United Kingdom, desiring to be discharged, refusing, or being unfit or being incapable, or being an infant, as aforesaid.

16   Repealed by Statute Law Revision Act 1950.

(2) Where a trustee has been removed under a power contained in the instrument creating the trust, a new trustee or new trustees may be appointed in the place of the trustee who is removed, as if he were dead, or, in the case of a corporation, as if the corporation desired to be discharged from the trust, and the provisions of this section shall apply accordingly, but subject to the restrictions imposed by this Act on the number of trustees.

(3) Where a corporation being a trustee is or has been dissolved, either before or after the commencement of this Act, then, for the purposes of this section and of any enactment replaced thereby, the corporation shall be deemed to be and to have been from the date of the dissolution incapable of acting in the trusts or powers reposed in or conferred on the corporation.

(4) The power of appointment given by subsection (1) of this section or any similar previous enactment to the personal representatives of a last surviving or continuing trustee shall be and shall be deemed always to have been exercisable by the executors for the time being (whether original or by representation) of such surviving or continuing trustee who have proved the will of their testator or by the administrators for the time being of such trustee without the concurrence of any executor who has renounced or has not proved.

(5) But a sole or last surviving executor intending to renounce, or all the executors where they all intend to renounce, shall have and shall be deemed always to have had power, at any time before renouncing probate, to exercise the power of appointment given by this section, or by any similar previous enactment, if willing to act for that purpose and without thereby accepting the office of executor.

(6) Where a sole trustee, other than a trust corporation, is or has been originally appointed to act in a trust, or where, in the case of any trust, there are not more than three trustees (none of them being a trust corporation) either original or substituted and whether appointed by the court or otherwise, then and in any such case—

(a) the person or persons nominated for the purpose of appointing new trustees by the instrument, if any, creating the trust; or
(b) if there is no such person, or no such person able and willing to act, then the trustee or trustees for the time being;

may, by writing, appoint another person or other persons to be an additional trustee or additional trustees, but it shall not be obligatory to appoint any additional trustee, unless the instrument, if any, creating the trust, or any statutory enactment provides to the contrary, nor shall the number of trustees be increased beyond four by virtue of any such appointment.

(7) Every new trustee appointed under this section as well before as after all the trust property becomes by law, or by assurance, or otherwise, vested in him, shall have the same powers, authorities, and discretions, and may in all respects act as if he had been originally appointed a trustee by the instrument, if any, creating the trust.

(8) The provisions of this section relating to a trustee who is dead include the case of a person nominated trustee in a will but dying before the testator, and those relative to a continuing trustee include a refusing or retiring trustee, if willing to act in the execution of the provisions of this section.

(9) Where a trustee is incapable, by reason of mental disorder within the meaning of the Mental Health Act 1959, of exercising his functions as trustee and is also entitled in possession to some beneficial interest in the trust property, no appointment of a new trustee in his place shall be made by virtue of paragraph (b) of subsection (1) of this section unless leave to make the appointment has been given by the authority having jurisdiction under Part VIII of the Mental Health Act 1959[17].

40. Vesting of trust property in new or continuing trustees.—(1) Where by a deed a new trustee is appointed to perform any trust, then—

(a) if the deed contains a declaration by the appointor to the effect that any estate or interest

---

17   Subsection substituted by Mental Health Act 1959, s. 149(1) and Sch. 7.

in any land subject to the trust . . . shall vest in the persons who by virtue of the deed become or are the trustees for performing the trust, the deed shall operate, without any conveyance or assignment, to vest in those persons as joint tenants and for the purposes of the trust the estate, interest, or right to which the declaration relates; and

(b) if the deed is made after the commencement of this Act and does not contain such a declaration, the deed shall, subject to any express provision to the contrary therein contained, operate as if it had contained such a declaration by the appointor extending to all the estates, interests, and rights with respect to which a declaration could have been made.

(2) Where by a deed a retiring trustee is discharged under the statutory power without a new trustee being appointed, then—

(a) if the deed contains such a declaration as aforesaid by the retiring and continuing trustees, and by the other person, if any, empowered to appoint trustees, the deed shall, without any conveyance or assignment, operate to vest in the continuing trustees alone, as joint tenants, and for the purposes of the trust, the estate, interest, or right to which the declaration relates; and

(b) if the deed is made after the commencement of this Act and does not contain such a declaration, the deed shall, subject to any express provision to the contrary therein contained, operate as if it had contained such a declaration by such persons as aforesaid extending to all the estates, interests, and rights with respect to which a declaration could have been made.

(3) An express vesting declaration, whether made before or after the commencement of this Act, shall, notwithstanding that the estate, interest, or right to be vested is not expressly referred to, and provided that the other statutory requirements were or are complied with, operate, and be deemed always to have operated (but without prejudice to any express provision to the contrary contained in the deed of appointment or discharge) to vest in the persons respectively referred to in sub-ss. (1) and (2) of this section, as the case may require, such estates, interests, and rights as are capable of being and ought to be vested in those persons.

(4) This section does not extend (a) to land conveyed by way of mortgage for securing money subject to the trust . . .; (b) to land held under a lease which contains any covenant, . . ., against assignment or disposing of the land without licence or consent . . .; (c) to any share,. . ., only transferable in books kept by a company. . . .

PART V

64. Application of Act to Settled Land Act trustees.—(1) All the powers and provisions contained in this Act with reference to the appointment of new trustees, and the discharge and retirement of trustees, apply to and include trustees for the purposes of the Settled Land Act 1925, and trustees for the purpose of the management of land during a minority, whether such trustees are appointed by the court or by the settlement, or under provisions contained in any instrument.

(2) Where, either before or after the commencement of this Act, trustees of a settlement have been appointed by the court for the purposes of the Settled Land Acts 1882 to 1890, or of the Settled Land Act 1925 then, after the commencement of this Act—

(a) the person or persons nominated for the purpose of appointing new trustees by the instrument, if any, creating the settlement, though no trustees for the purposes of the said Acts were thereby appointed; or

(b) if there is no such person, or no such person able and willing to act, the surviving or continuing trustees or trustee for the time being for the purposes of the said Acts or the personal representatives of the last surviving or continuing trustee for those purposes, shall have the powers conferred by this Act to appoint new or additional trustees of the settlement for the purposes of the said Acts.

(3) Appointments of new trustees for the purposes of the said Acts made or expressed to be made before the commencement of this Act by the trustees or trustee or personal representatives referred to in paragraph (b) of the last preceding subsection or by the persons referred to in

paragraph (a) of that subsection are, without prejudice to any order of the court made before such commencement, hereby confirmed.

69. Application of Act.—(1) This Act, except where otherwise expressly provided, applies to trusts including, so far as this Act applies thereto, executorships and administratorships constituted or created either before or after the commencement of this Act.

(2) The powers conferred by this Act on trustees are in addition to the powers conferred by the instrument, if any, creating the trust, but those powers, unless otherwise stated, apply if and so far only as a contrary intention is not expressed in the instrument, if any, creating the trust, and have effect subject to the terms of that instrument.

(3) [*Repealed by Statute Law (Repeals) Act 1978, s. 1 and Sch. 1, Part XVII.*]

71. Short title, commencement, extent.

*　　　　*　　　　*　　　　*　　　　*

(3) This Act, except where otherwise expressly provided, extends to England and Wales only.

LAW OF PROPERTY ACT 1925

(15 & 16 Geo. 5, c. 20)

61. Construction of expressions used in deeds and other instruments. In all deeds, contracts, wills, orders and other instruments executed, made or coming into operation after the commencement of this Act, unless the context otherwise requires—

(a) 'Month' means calendar month;
(b) 'Person' includes a corporation;
(c) The singular includes the plural and vice versa;
(d) The masculine includes the feminine and vice versa.

PART X

175. Contingent and future testamentary gifts to carry the intermediate income.—(1) A contingent or future specific devise or bequest of property, whether real or personal, and a contingent residuary devise of freehold land, and a specific or residuary devise of freehold land to trustees upon trust for persons whose interests are contingent or executory shall, subject to the statutory provisions relating to accumulations, carry the intermediate income of that property from the death of the testator, except so far as such income, or any part thereof, may be otherwise disposed of.

(2) This section applies only to wills coming into operation after the commencement of this Act.

Wills made before 1 January 1983
(see note below)

[**177. Wills in contemplation of marriage.**—*(1) A will expressed to be made in contemplation of a marriage shall notwithstanding anything in section eighteen of the Wills Act 1837, or any other statutory provision or rule of law to the contrary, not be revoked by the solemnization of the marriage contemplated.*

(2) This section only applies to wills made after the commencement of this Act.][18]

18　　Section 177 was repealed and replaced, with effect from 1 January 1983, by s. 18 of the Wills Act 1837, as substituted by s. 18 of the Administration of Justice Act 1982 (see p. 722, ante). Section 177, however, continues to apply to wills made before 1 January 1983.

179. Prescribed forms for reference in wills. The Lord Chancellor may from time to time prescribe and publish forms to which a testator may refer in his will, and give directions as to the manner in which they may be referred to, but, unless so referred to, such forms shall not be deemed to be incorporated in a will[19].

PART XI

184. Presumption of survivorship in regard to claims to property. In all cases where, after the commencement of this Act, two or more persons have died in circumstances rendering it uncertain which of them survived the other or others, such deaths shall (subject to any order of the court), for all purposes affecting the title to property, be presumed to have occurred in order of seniority, and accordingly the younger shall be deemed to have survived the elder[20].

209. Short title, commencement, extent.

*   *   *   *   *

(2) *This Act shall come into operation on the 1st day of January 1926[21].*

(3) This Act extends to England and Wales only.

ADMINISTRATION OF ESTATES ACT 1925

(15 & 16 Geo. 5, c. 23)

PART I

DEVOLUTION OF REAL ESTATE

1. Devolution of real estate on personal representative.—(1) Real estate to which a deceased person was entitled for an interest not ceasing on his death shall on his death, and notwithstanding any testamentary disposition thereof, devolve from time to time on the personal representative of the deceased, in like manner as before the commencement of this Act chattels real devolved on the personal representative from time to time of a deceased person.

(2) The personal representatives for the time being of a deceased person are deemed in law his heirs and assigns within the meaning of all trusts and powers.

(3) The personal representatives shall be the representatives of the deceased in regard to his real estate to which he was entitled for an interest not ceasing on his death as well as in regard to his personal estate.

2. Application to real estate of law affecting chattels real.—(1) Subject to the provisions of this Act, all enactments and rules of law, and all jurisdiction of any court with respect to the appointment of administrators or to probate or letters of administration, or to dealings before probate in the case of chattels real, and with respect to costs and other matters in the administration of personal estate in force before the commencement of this Act, and all powers, duties, rights, equities, obligations, and liabilities of a personal representative in

---

19   The Statutory Will Forms prescribed pursuant to this section are printed in Appendix VII, pp. 1095 ff., post.

20   Where an intestate and his or her spouse die on or after 1 January 1953, in circumstances rendering it uncertain which of them survived the other, and the spouse would, by virtue of this section, be deemed to be the survivor, s. 46 of the Administration of Estates Act 1925 is nevertheless to have effect, as respects the intestate, as if the spouse had not survived him or her (Administration of Estates Act 1925, s. 46(3), added in relation to deaths after 1952 by the Intestates' Estates Act 1952 (see post, p. 767)).

21   Repealed by Statute Law Revision Act 1950.

force at the commencement of this Act with respect to chattels real, shall apply and attach to the personal representative and shall have effect with respect to real estate vested in him, and in particular all such powers of disposition and dealing as were before the commencement of this Act exercisable as respects chattels real by the survivor or survivors of two or more personal representatives, as well as by a single personal representative, or by all the personal representatives together, shall be exercisable by the personal representatives or representative of the deceased with respect to his real estate.

(2) Where as respects real estate there are two or more personal representatives, a conveyance of real estate devolving under this Part of this Act *or a contract for such a conveyance*[1] shall not[, save as otherwise provided as respects trust estates including settled land[1],] be made without the concurrence therein of all such representatives or an order of the court, but where probate is granted to one or some of two or more persons named as executors, whether or not power is reserved to the other or others to prove, any conveyance of the real estate *or contract for such a conveyance*[1] may be made by the proving executor or executors for the time being, without an order of the court, and shall be as effectual as if all the persons named as executors had concurred therein.

(3) Without prejudice to the rights and powers of a personal representative, the appointment of a personal representative in regard to real estate shall not, save as hereinafter provided, affect—

(a) any rule as to marshalling or as to administration of assets;
(b) the beneficial interest in real estate under any testamentary disposition;
(c) any mode of dealing with any beneficial interest in real estate, or the proceeds of sale thereof;
(d) the right of any person claiming to be interested in the real estate to take proceedings for the protection or recovery thereof against any person other than the personal representative.

3. Interpretation of Part I.—(1) In this Part of this Act 'real estate' includes—

(i) Chattels real, and land in possession, remainder, or reversion, and every interest in or over land to which a deceased person was entitled at the time of his death; and
(ii) Real estate held on trust (including settled land) or by way of mortgage or security, but not money to arise under a trust for sale of land, nor money secured or charged on land.

(2) A testator shall be deemed to have been entitled at his death to any interest in real estate passing under any gift contained in his will which operates as an appointment under a general power to appoint by will, or operates under the testamentary power conferred by statute to dispose of an entailed interest.

(3) An entailed interest of a deceased person shall (unless disposed of under the testamentary power conferred by statute) be deemed an interest ceasing on his death, but any further or other interest of the deceased in the same property in remainder or reversion which is capable of being disposed of by his will shall not be deemed to be an interest so ceasing.

(4) The interest of a deceased person under a joint tenancy where another tenant survives the deceased is an interest ceasing on his death.

(5) On the death of a corporator sole his interest in the corporation's real and personal estate shall be deemed to be an interest ceasing on his death and shall devolve to his successor.

This subsection applies on the demise of the Crown as respects all property, real and personal, vested in the Crown as a corporation sole.

---

1   Words in italics added and words in square brackets omitted—see s. 16 of the Law of Property (Miscellaneous Provisions) Act 1994, p. 899, post—as from 1 July 1995.

PART II
EXECUTORS AND ADMINISTRATORS

General provisions

5. Cessor of right of executor to prove. Where a person appointed executor by a will—

(i) survives the testator but dies without having taken out probate of the will; or
(ii) is cited to take out probate of the will and does not appear to the citation; or
(iii) renounces probate of the will;

his rights in respect of the executorship shall wholly cease, and the representation to the testator and the administration of his real and personal estate shall devolve and be committed in like manner as if that person had not been appointed executor.

6. Withdrawal of renunciation.—(1) Where an executor who has renounced probate has been permitted, whether before or after the commencement of this Act, to withdraw the renunciation and prove the will, the probate shall take effect and be deemed always to have taken effect without prejudice to the previous acts and dealings of and notices to any other personal representative who has previously proved the will or taken out letters of administration, and a memorandum of the subsequent probate shall be endorsed on the original probate or letters of administration.

(2) This section applies whether the testator died before or after the commencement of this Act.

7. Executor of executor represents original testator.—(1) An executor of a sole or last surviving executor of a testator is the executor of that testator.

This provision shall not apply to an executor who does not prove the will of his testator, and, in the case of an executor who on his death leaves surviving him some other executor of his testator who afterwards proves the will of that testator it shall cease to apply on such probate being granted.

(2) So long as the chain of such representation is unbroken, the last executor in the chain is the executor of every preceding testator.

(3) The chain of such representation is broken by—

(a) an intestacy; or
(b) the failure of a testator to appoint an executor; or
(c) the failure to obtain probate of a will;

but is not broken by a temporary grant of administration if probate is subsequently granted.

(4) Every person in the chain of representation to a testator—

(a) has the same rights in respect of the real and personal estate of that testator as the original executor would have had if living; and
(b) is, to the extent to which the estate whether real or personal of that testator has come to his hands, answerable as if he were an original executor[2].

8. Right of proving executors to exercise powers.—(1) Where probate is granted to one or some of two or more persons named as executors, whether or not power is reserved to the others or other to prove, all the powers which are by law conferred on the personal representative may be exercised by the proving executor or executors for the time being and shall be as effectual as if all the persons named as executors had concurred therein.

(2) This section applies whether the testator died before or after the commencement of this Act.

---

2   Section 7 does not apply on the death of an executor named in a confirmation or certificate of confirmation which, by virtue of s. 1(1) of the Administration of Estates Act 1971, is treated as a grant made in England and Wales (Administration of Estates Act 1971, s. 1(3): p. 799, post).

9.[4] **Vesting of estate of intestate between death and grant of administration.** Where a person dies intestate, his real and personal estate, until administration is granted in respect thereof, shall vest in the Probate Judge[3] in the same manner and to the same extent as formerly in the case of personal estate it vested in the ordinary.

[9.[4] **Vesting of estate in Public Trustee where intestacy or lack of executors.**—(1) Where a person dies intestate, his real and personal estate shall vest in the Public Trustee until the grant of administration.

(2) Where a testator dies and—

(a) at the time of his death there is no executor with power to obtain probate of the will, or
(b) at any time before probate of the will is granted there ceases to be any executor with power to obtain probate,

the real and personal estate of which he disposes by the will shall vest in the Public Trustee until the grant of representation.

(3) The vesting of real or personal estate in the Public Trustee by virtue of this section does not confer on him any beneficial interest in, or impose on him any duty, obligation or liability in respect of, the property.]

15. Executor not to act while administration is in force. Where administration has been granted in respect of any real or personal estate of a deceased person, no person shall have power to bring any action or otherwise act as executor of the deceased person in respect of the estate comprised in or affected by the grant until the grant has been recalled or revoked.

17. Continuance of legal proceedings after revocation of temporary administration. If, while any legal proceeding is pending in any court by or against an administrator to whom a temporary administration has been granted, that administration is revoked, that court may order that the proceeding be continued by or against the new personal representative in like manner as if the same had been originally commenced by or against him, but subject to such conditions and variations, if any, as that court directs.

21. Rights and liabilities of administrator. Every person to whom administration of the real and personal estate of a deceased person is granted, shall, subject to the limitations contained in the grant, have the same rights and liabilities and be accountable in like manner as if he were the executor of the deceased.

[21A. **Debtor who becomes creditor's executor by representation or administrator to account for debt to estate.**—(1) Subject to subsection (2) of this section, where a debtor becomes his deceased creditor's executor by representation or administrator—

(a) his debt shall thereupon be extinguished; but
(b) he shall be accountable for the amount of the debt as part of the creditor's estate in any case where he would be so accountable if he had been appointed as an executor by the creditor's will.

(2) Subsection (1) of this section does not apply where the debtor's authority to act as executor or administrator is limited to part only of the creditor's estate which does not include the debt; and a debtor whose debt is extinguished by virtue of paragraph (a) shall not be accountable for its amount by virtue of paragraph (b) of that subsection in any case where the debt was barred by the Limitation Act 1939 before he became the creditor's executor or administrator.

---

3   I.e., the President of the Family Division (Administration of Estates Act 1925, s. 55(1)(xv)).
4   New s. 9 in square brackets substituted for existing s. 9 by s. 14 (1) of the Law of Property (Miscellaneous Provisions) Act 1994—p. 898, post—as from 1 July 1995.

(3) In this section 'debt' includes any liability, and 'debtor' and 'creditor' shall be construed accordingly[5].]

Special provisions as to settled land

22. Special executors as respects settled land.—(1) A testator may appoint, and in default of such express appointment shall be deemed to have appointed, as his special executors in regard to settled land, the persons, if any, who are at his death the trustees of the settlement thereof, and probate may be granted to such trustees specially limited to the settled land.

In this subsection 'settled land' means land vested in the testator which was settled previously to his death and not by his will.

(2) A testator may appoint other persons either with or without such trustees as aforesaid or any of them to be his general executors in regard to his other property and assets.

23. Provisions where, as respects settled land, representation is not granted to the trustees of the settlement.—(1) Where settled land becomes vested in a personal representative, not being a trustee of the settlement, upon trust to convey the land to or assent to the vesting thereof in the tenant for life or statutory owner in order to give effect to a settlement created before the death of the deceased and not by his will, or would, on the grant of representation to him, have become so vested, such representative may—

(a) before representation has been granted, renounce his office in regard only to such settled land without renouncing it in regard to other property;
(b) after representation has been granted, apply to the court for revocation of the grant in regard to the settled land without applying in regard to other property.

(2) Whether such renunciation or revocation is made or not, the trustees of the settlement, or any person beneficially interested thereunder, may apply to the High Court for an order appointing a special or additional personal representative in respect of the settled land, and a special or additional personal representative, if and when appointed under the order, shall be in the same position as if representation had originally been granted to him alone in place of the original personal representative, if any, or to him jointly with the original personal representative, as the case may be, limited to the settled land, but without prejudice to the previous acts and dealings, if any, of the personal representative originally constituted or the effect of notices given to such personal representative.

(3) The court may make such order as aforesaid subject to such security, if any, being given by or on behalf of the special or additional personal representative, as the court may direct, and shall, unless the court considers that special considerations apply, appoint such persons as may be necessary to secure that the persons to act as representatives in respect of the settled land shall, if willing to act, be the same persons as are the trustees of the settlement, and an office copy of the order when made shall be furnished to the [principal registry of the Family Division of the High Court[6]] for entry, and a memorandum of the order shall be endorsed on the probate or administration.

(4) The person applying for the appointment of a special or additional personal representative shall give notice of the application to the [principal registry of the Family Division of the High Court[6]] in the manner prescribed.

(5) Rules of court may be made for prescribing for all matters required for giving effect to the provisions of this section, and in particular—

(a) for notice of any application being given to the proper officer;
(b) for production of orders, probates, and administration to the registry;

---

5   Section 21A added by Limitation Amendment Act 1980, s. 10; the reference in sub-section (2) of s. 21A to the Limitation Act 1939 shall be construed as including a reference to the Limitation Act 1980 (Limitation Act 1980, s. 40 and Sch. 3, para. 2).
6   Words in brackets substituted by Administration of Justice Act 1970, s. 1 and Sch. 2.

(c) for the endorsement on a probate or administration of a memorandum of an order, subject or not to any exceptions;
(d) for the manner in which the costs are to be borne;
(e) for protecting purchasers and trustees and other persons in a fiduciary position, dealing in good faith with or giving notices to a personal representative before notice of any order has been endorsed on the probate or administration or a pending action has been registered in respect of the proceedings.

24. Power for special personal representatives to dispose of settled land.—(1) The special personal representatives may dispose of the settled land without the concurrence of the general personal representatives, who may likewise dispose of the other property and assets of the deceased without the concurrence of the special personal representatives.

(2) In this section the expression 'special personal representatives' means the representatives appointed to act for the purposes of settled land and includes any original personal representative who is to act with an additional personal representative for those purposes.

Duties, rights, and obligations

25. Duty of personal representatives. The personal representative of a deceased person shall be under a duty to—

(a) collect and get in the real and personal estate of the deceased and administer it according to law;
(b) when required to do so by the court, exhibit on oath in the court a full inventory of the estate and when so required render an account of the administration of the estate to the court;
(c) when required to do so by the High Court, deliver up the grant of probate or administration to that court[7].

27. Protection of persons acting on probate or administration.—(l) Every person making or permitting to be made any payment or disposition in good faith under a representation shall be indemnified and protected in so doing, notwithstanding any defect or circumstance whatsoever affecting the validity of the representation.

(2) Where a representation is revoked, all payments and dispositions made in good faith to a personal representative under the representation before the revocation thereof are a valid discharge to the person making the same; and the personal representative who acted under the revoked representation may retain and reimburse himself in respect of any payments or dispositions made by him which the person to whom representation is afterwards granted might have properly made.

28. Liability of person fraudulently obtaining or retaining estate of deceased. If any person, to the defrauding of creditors or without full valuable consideration, obtains, receives or holds any real or personal estate of a deceased person or effects the release of any debt or liability due to the estate of the deceased, he shall be charged as executor in his own wrong to the extent of the real and personal estate received or coming to his hands, or the debt or liability released, after deducting—

(a) any debt for valuable consideration and without fraud due to him from the deceased person at the time of his death; and
(b) any payment made by him which might properly be made by a personal representative.

29. Liability of estate of personal representative. Where a person as personal representative of a deceased person (including an executor in his own wrong) wastes or converts to his own use any part of the real or personal estate of the deceased, and dies, his personal repre-

---

7   Revised section substituted, with effect from 1 January 1972, by Administration of Estates Act
    1971, s. 9 (p. 799, post).

sentative shall to the extent of the available assets of the defaulter be liable and chargeable in respect of such waste or conversion in the same manner as the defaulter would have been if living.

30. Provisions applicable where administration granted to nominee of the Crown.—(1) Where the administration of the real and personal estate of any deceased person is granted to a nominee of the Crown (whether the Treasury Solicitor, or a person nominated by the Treasury Solicitor, or any other person), any legal proceeding by or against that nominee for the recovery of the real or personal estate, or any part or share thereof, shall be of the same character, and be instituted and carried on in the same manner, and be subject to the same rules of law and equity (including, except as otherwise provided by this Act, the rules of limitation under the statutes of limitation or otherwise), in all respects as if the administration had been granted to such nominee as one of the persons interested under this Act in the estate of the deceased.

(2) An information or other proceeding on the part of His Majesty shall not be filed or instituted, and a petition of right shall not be presented, in respect of the real or personal estate of any deceased person or any part or share thereof, or any claim thereon, except [*within the same time and*[8]] subject to the same rules of law and equity within and subject to which a proceeding for the like purposes might be instituted by or against a subject.

(3) The Treasury Solicitor shall not be required, when applying for or obtaining administration of the estate of a deceased person for the use or benefit of His Majesty, to deliver, nor shall the [*Probate, Divorce and Admiralty Division of the*[9]] High Court or the Commissioners of Inland Revenue be entitled to receive in connexion with any such application or grant of administration, any affidavit, statutory declaration, account, certificate, or other statement verified on oath; but the Treasury Solicitor shall deliver and the said Division and Commissioners respectively shall accept, in lieu thereof, an account or particulars of the estate of the deceased signed by or on behalf of the Treasury Solicitor.

(4) References in sections two, four, [*six*[10]] and seven of the Treasury Solicitor Act 1876, and in subsection (3) of section three of the Duchy of Lancaster Act 1920, to 'personal estate' shall include real estate.

31. Power to make rules. Provision may be made by rules of court for giving effect to the provisions of this Part of this Act so far as relates to real estate and in particular for adapting the procedure and practice on the grant of letters of administration to the case of real estate.

PART III

ADMINISTRATION OF ASSETS

33. Trust for sale.—(1) On the death of a person intestate as to any real or personal estate, such estate shall be held by his personal representatives—

(a) as to the real estate upon trust to sell the same; and
(b) as to the personal estate upon trust to call in sell and convert into money such part thereof as shall not consist of money,

with power to postpone such sale and conversion for such a period as the personal representatives may think proper. . . .

37. Validity of conveyance not affected by revocation of representation.—(l) All conveyances of any interest in real or personal estate made to a purchaser either before or after the commencement of this Act by a person to whom probate or letters of administration have

---

8   Words in brackets repealed by Limitation Act 1939, s. 34 and Schedule.
9   Words in brackets repealed by Administration of Justice Act 1970, s. 54 and Sch. 11.
10   Word in brackets repealed by Statute Law (Repeals) Act 1981.

been granted are valid, notwithstanding any subsequent revocation or variation, either before or after the commencement of this Act, of the probate or administration.

(2) This section takes effect without prejudice to any order of the court made before the commencement of this Act, and applies whether the testator or intestate died before or after such commencement.

PART IV

DISTRIBUTION OF RESIDUARY ESTATE

45. Abolition of descent to heir, curtesy, dower and escheat.—(l) With regard to the real estate and personal inheritance of every person dying after the commencement of this Act, there shall be abolished—

(a) All existing modes rules and canons of descent, and of devolution by special occupancy or otherwise, of real estate, or of a personal inheritance, whether operating by the general law or by the custom of gavelkind or borough english or by any other custom of any county, locality, or manor, or otherwise howsoever; and

(b) Tenancy by the curtesy and every other estate and interest of a husband in real estate as to which his wife dies intestate, whether arising under the general law or by custom or otherwise: and

(c) Dower and freebench and every other estate and interest of a wife in real estate as to which her husband dies intestate, whether arising under the general law or by custom or otherwise: Provided that where a right (if any) to freebench or other like right has attached before the commencement of this Act which cannot be barred by a testamentary or other disposition made by the husband, such right shall, unless released, remain in force as an equitable interest; and

(d) Escheat to the Crown or the Duchy of Lancaster or the Duke of Cornwall or to a mesne lord for want of heirs.

(2) Nothing in this section affects the descent or devolution of an entailed interest.

Note to sections 46 to 49

Sections 46 to 49 of this Act were extensively amended in relation to deaths occurring on or after 1 January 1953 by the Intestates' Estates Act 1952.

They were further amended in relation to deaths on or after 1 January 1967 by the Family Provision Act 1966, s. 1 (see p. 786, post).

Further minor amendments were made by the Administration of Justice Act 1977, s. 28 and, subject to those amendments, in cases where the death occurred prior to 1 January 1953 the sections apply as originally enacted, see pp. 757 ff., post.

In relation to the estates of persons dying on or after 1 January 1970, Part IV of the Administration of Estates Act 1925 is to have effect as if—

(a) any reference to the issue of the intestate included a reference to any illegitimate child of his and to the issue of any such child;

(b) any reference to the child or children of the intestate included a reference to any illegitimate child or children of his; and

(c) in relation to an intestate who is an illegitimate child, any reference to the parent, parents, father or mother of the intestate were a reference to his natural parent, parents, father or mother (Family Law Reform Act 1969, s. 14(3): see p. 789, post).

In relation to the estates of persons dying on or after 4 April 1988, in Part IV of the Administration of Estates Act 1925 references (however expressed) to any relationship between two persons shall be construed without regard to whether or not the father and mother of either of them, or the father and mother of any person through whom the relationship is deduced, have or had been married to each other at any time (Family Law Reform Act 1987, s. 18(1): see p. 876, post).

See also Law Reform (Succession) Act 1995, p. 900, post.

Deaths on or after 1 January 1953

46. Succession to real and personal estate on intestacy.—(l) The residuary estate of an intestate shall be distributed in the manner or be held on the trusts mentioned in this section, namely:

(i) If the intestate leaves a husband or wife, then in accordance with the following Table:

TABLE

If the intestate—
(1) leaves—

(a) no issue, and (b) no parent, or brother or sister of the whole blood, or issue of a brother or sister of the whole blood	the residuary estate shall be held in trust for the surviving husband or wife absolutely.
(2) leaves issue (whether or not persons mentioned in subparagraph (b) above also survive)	the surviving husband or wife shall take the personal chattels absolutely and, in addition, the residuary estate of the intestate (other than the personal chattels) shall stand charged with the payment of a [fixed net sum][11], free of death duties and costs, to the surviving husband or wife with interest thereon from the date of the death [at such rate as the Lord Chancellor may specify by order][12] until paid or appropriated, and, subject to providing for that sum and the interest thereon, the residuary estate (other than the personal chattels) shall be held— (a) as to one half upon trust for the surviving husband or wife during his or her life, and, subject to such life interest, on the statutory trusts for the issue of the intestate, and (b) as to the other half, on the statutory trusts for the issue of the intestate.
(3) leaves one or more of the following, that is to say, a parent, a brother or sister of the whole blood, or issue of a brother or sister of the whole blood, but leaves no issue	the surviving husband or wife shall take the personal chattels absolutely and, in addition, the residuary estate of the intestate (other than the personal chattels) shall stand charged with the payment of a [fixed net sum][11], free of death duties and costs, to the surviving husband or wife with interest thereon from the date of the death [at such rate as the Lord Chancellor may specify by order][12] until paid or appropriated, and, subject to providing for that sum and the interest thereon, the residuary estate (other than the personal chattels) shall be held—

---

11   Words in square brackets substituted by Family Provision Act 1966, s. 1(2), in relation to persons dying on or after 1 January 1967, for the words 'net sum of five thousand pounds'. The 'fixed net sum' was £8,750 where the date of death was prior to 1 July 1972 (Family Provision Act 1966, s. 1(1)) but is £15,000 where the death occurred on or after that date and before 15 March 1977 (Family Provision (Intestate Succession) Order 1972); is £25,000 where the death occurred on or after 15 March 1977 (Family Provision (Intestate Succession) Order 1977); £40,000 where the death occurred on or after 1 March 1981 (Family Provision (Intestate Succession) Order 1981): £75,000 where the death occurred on or since 1 June 1987 (Family Provision (Intestate Succession) Order 1987 and £125,000 where the death occurred on or since 1 December 1993 (Family Provision (Intestate Succession) Order 1993—see pp. 915, 916, 919, 923, 946, post.

12   Words in square brackets substituted by Administration of Justice Act 1977, s. 28 (1) for the rate of four pounds per cent per annum. The current rate is 6 per cent per annum: Intestate Succession (Interest and Capitalisation) Order 1977 (Amendment) Order 1983 (S.I. 1983 No. 1374). See also footnote 3 to para **6.29**, ante.

Deaths on or after 1 January 1953 (continued)—

    (a) as to one half in trust for the surviving husband or wife absolutely, and

    (b) as to the other half—

        (i) where the intestate leaves one parent or both parents (whether or not brothers or sisters of the intestate of their issue also survive) in trust for the parent absolutely or, as the case may be, for the two parents in equal shares absolutely,

        (ii) where the intestate leaves no parent, on the statutory trusts for the brothers and sisters of the whole blood of the intestate.

        [The fixed net sums referred to in paragraphs (2) and (3) of this Table shall be of the amounts provided by or under section 1 of the Family Provision Act 1966.][13]

(ii) If the intestate leaves issue but no husband or wife the residuary estate of the intestate shall be held on the statutory trusts for the issue of the intestate;

(iii) If the intestate leaves no husband or wife and no issue but both parents, then the residuary estate of the intestate shall be held in trust for the father and mother in equal shares absolutely;

(iv) If the intestate leaves no husband or wife and no issue but one parent, then the residuary estate of the intestate shall be held in trust for the surviving father or mother absolutely;

(v) If the intestate leaves no husband or wife and no issue and no parent, then the residuary estate of the intestate shall be held in trust for the following persons living at the death of the intestate, and in the following order and manner, namely:

    First, on the statutory trusts for the brothers and sisters of the whole blood of the intestate; but if no person takes an absolutely vested interest under such trusts; then

    Secondly, on the statutory trusts for the brothers and sisters of the half blood of the intestate; but if no person takes an absolutely vested interest under such trusts; then

    Thirdly, for the grandparents of the intestate and, if more than one survive the intestate, in equal shares; but if there is no member of this class; then

    Fourthly, on the statutory trusts for the uncles and aunts of the intestate (being brothers or sisters of the whole blood of a parent of the intestate); but if no person takes an absolutely vested interest under such trusts; then

    Fifthly, on the statutory trusts for the uncles and aunts of the intestate (being brothers or sisters of the half blood of a parent of the intestate);

(vi) In default of any person taking an absolute interest under the foregoing provisions, the residuary estate of the intestate shall belong to the Crown or to the Duchy of Lancaster or to the Duke of Cornwall for the time being, as the case may be, as bona vacantia, and in lieu of any right to escheat.

    The Crown or the said Duchy or the said Duke may (without prejudice to the powers reserved by section nine of the Civil List Act 1910, or any other powers), out of the whole or any part of the property devolving on them respectively, provide, in accordance with the existing practice, for dependants, whether kindred or not, of the intestate, and other persons for whom the intestate might reasonably have been expected to make provision.

(1A) The power to make orders under subsection (1) above shall be exercisable by statutory instrument subject to annulment in pursuance of a resolution of either House of Parliament; and any such order may be varied or revoked by a subsequent order made under the power[14].

13   Words in square brackets added by Family Provision Act 1966, in relation to persons dying on or after 1 January 1967. The fixed net sums are at present £125,000 and £200,000 respectively (Family Provision Act 1966, s. 1(1) as modified by Family Provision (Intestate Succession) Order 1993: see p. 786, post).

14   Subsection (1A) inserted by Administration of Justice Act 1977, s. 28(1).

Deaths on or after 1 January 1953 (continued)—

(2) A husband and wife shall for all purposes of distribution or division under the foregoing provisions of this section be treated as two persons.

(2A)   Where the intestate's husband or wife survived the intestate but died before the end of the period of 28 days beginning with the day on which the intestate died, this section shall have effect as respects the intestate as if the husband or wife had not survived the intestate.[15]

(3) Where the intestate and the intestate's husband or wife have died in circumstances rendering it uncertain which of them survived the other and the intestate's husband or wife is by virtue of section one hundred and eighty-four of the Law of Property Act 1925, deemed to have survived the intestate, this section shall, nevertheless, have effect as respects the intestate as if the husband or wife had not survived the intestate.

(4) The interest payable on the [fixed net sum][16] payable to a surviving husband or wife shall be primarily payable out of income.

47. Statutory trusts in favour of issue and other classes of relatives of intestate.—(1) Where under this Part of this Act the residuary estate of an intestate, or any part thereof, is directed to be held on the statutory trusts for the issue of the intestate, the same shall be held upon the following trusts, namely:

(i) In trust, in equal shares if more than one, for all or any of the children or child of the intestate, living at the death of the intestate, who attain the age of twenty-one years[17] or marry under that age, and for all or any of the issue living at the death of the intestate who attain the age of twenty-one years[17] or marry under that age of any child of the intestate who predeceases the intestate, such issue to take through all degrees, according to their stocks, in equal shares if more than one, the share which their parent would have taken if living at the death of the intestate, and so that no issue shall take whose parent is living at the death of the intestate and so capable of taking;

(ii) The statutory power of advancement, and the statutory provisions which relate to maintenance and accumulation of surplus income, shall apply, but when an infant marries such infant shall be entitled to give valid receipts for the income of the infant's share or interest;

(iii) Where the property held on the statutory trusts for issue is divisible into shares, then any money or property which, by way of advancement or on the marriage of a child of the intestate, has been paid to such child by the intestate or settled by the intestate for the benefit of such child (including any life or less interest and including property covenanted to be paid or settled) shall, subject to any contrary intention expressed or appearing from the circumstances of the case, be taken as being so paid or settled in or towards satisfaction of the share of such child or the share which such child would have taken if living at the death of the intestate, and shall be brought into account, at a valuation (the value to be reckoned as at the death of the intestate), in accordance with the requirements of the personal representatives;[18]

(iv) The personal representatives may permit any infant contingently interested to have the use and enjoyment of any personal chattels in such manner and subject to such conditions (if any) as the personal representatives may consider reasonable, and without being liable to account for any consequential loss.

15 Subsection (2A) inserted by s. 1 of the Law Reform (Succession) Act 1995 in respect of an intestate dying on or after 1 January 1996—see p. 900, post.
16 Words in square brackets substituted by Family Provision Act 1966, s. 1(2), in relation to persons dying on or after 1 January 1967, for the words 'net sum of five thousand pounds or, as the case may be, twenty thousand pounds'. As to the fixed net sum, see note 11, p. 752, ante.
17 In relation to intestates dying on or after 1 January 1970, 'eighteen years' is substituted for 'twenty-one years' (Family Law Reform Act 1969, s. 3(2), p. 790, post).
18 Subsection (1)(iii) will cease to have effect as respects an intestate dying on or after 1 January 1996—see ss. 1 and 5, Law Reform (Succession) Act 1995, p. 900, post.

Deaths on or after 1 January 1953 (continued)—

(2) If the trusts in favour of the issue of the intestate fail by reason of no child or other issue attaining an absolutely vested interest—

(a) the residuary estate of the intestate and the income thereof and all statutory accumulations, if any, of the income thereof or so much thereof as may not have been paid or applied under any power affecting the same, shall go, devolve and be held under the provisions of this Part of this Act as if the intestate had died without leaving issue living at the death of the intestate;

(b) references in this Part of this Act to the intestate 'leaving no issue' shall be construed as 'leaving no issue who attain an absolutely vested interest';

(c) references in this Part of this Act to the intestate 'leaving issue' or 'leaving a child or other issue' shall be construed as 'leaving issue who attain an absolutely vested interest'.

(3) Where under this Part of this Act the residuary estate of an intestate or any part thereof is directed to be held on the statutory trusts for any class of relatives of the intestate, other than issue of the intestate, the same shall be held on trusts corresponding to the statutory trusts for the issue of the intestate (other than the provision for bringing any money or property into account) as if such trusts (other than as aforesaid) were repeated with the substitution of references to the members or member of that class for references to the children or child of the intestate.

(4) References in paragraph (i) of subsection (1) of the last foregoing section to the intestate leaving, or not leaving, a member of the class consisting of brothers or sisters of the whole blood of the intestate and issue of brothers or sisters of the whole blood of the intestate shall be construed as references to the intestate leaving, or not leaving, a member of that class who attains an absolutely vested interest.

(5) [*Repealed by Family Provision Act 1966, s. 9 and Schedule 2.*]

47A. Right of surviving spouse to have life interest redeemed.—(1) Where a surviving husband or wife is entitled to a life interest in part of the residuary estate, and so elects, the personal representative shall purchase or redeem the life interest by paying the capital value thereof to the tenant for life, or the persons deriving title under the tenant for life, and the costs of the transaction; and thereupon the residuary estate of the intestate may be dealt with and distributed free from the life interest.

(2) [*Repealed by Administration of Justice Act 1977, s. 32 and Schedule 5, Part VI.*][19]

(3) An election under this section shall only be exercisable if at the time of the election the whole of the said part of the residuary estate consists of property in possession, but, for the purposes of this section, a life interest in property partly in possession and partly not in possession may be treated as consisting of two separate life interests in those respective parts of the property.

(3A) The capital value shall be reckoned in such manner as the Lord Chancellor may by order direct, and an order under this subsection may include transitional provisions.

(3B) The power to make orders under subsection (3A) above shall be exercisable by statutory instrument subject to annulment in pursuance of a resolution of either House of Parliament; and any such order may be carried or revoked by a subsequent order made under the power[20].

(4) [*Repealed by Administration of Justice Act 1977, s. 32 and Schedule 5, Part VI.*]

(5) An election under this section shall be exercisable only within the period of twelve

19 New rules, replacing those formerly enacted by subsection (2) of section 47A, for calculating the capital value of a life interest in favour of a surviving spouse in the residuary estate, are prescribed by the Intestate Succession (Interest and Capitalisation) Order 1977 (S.I. 1977 No. 1491), as amended.

20 Subsections (3A) and (3B) inserted by Administration of Justice Act 1977, s. 28(3).

Deaths on or after 1 January 1953 (continued)—

months from the date on which representation with respect to the estate of the intestate is first taken out;

Provided that if the surviving husband or wife satisfies the court that the limitation to the said period of twelve months will operate unfairly—

(a) in consequence of the representation first taken out being probate of a will subsequently revoked on the ground that the will was invalid, or

(b) in consequence of a question whether a person had an interest in the estate, or as to the nature of an interest in the estate, not having been determined at the time when representation was first taken out, or

(c) in consequence of some other circumstances affecting the administration or distribution of the estate,

the court may extend the said period.

(6) An election under this section shall be exercisable, except where the tenant for life is the sole personal representative, by notifying the personal representative (or, where there are two or more personal representatives of whom one is the tenant for life all of them except the tenant for life) in writing; and a notification in writing under this subsection shall not be revocable except with the consent of the personal representative.

(7) Where the tenant for life is the sole personal representative an election under this section shall not be effective unless written notice thereof is given to the [Senior Registrar of the Family Division of the High Court][21] within the period within which it must be made; and provision may be made by probate rules for keeping a record of such notices and making that record available to the public.

In this subsection the expression 'probate rules' means rules [of court made under section 127 of the Supreme Court Act 1981][22].

(8) An election under this section by a tenant for life who is an infant shall be as valid and binding as it would be if the tenant for life were of age; but the personal representative shall, instead of paying the capital value of the life interest to the tenant for life, deal with it in the same manner as with any other part of the residuary estate to which the tenant for life is absolutely entitled.

(9) In considering for the purposes of the foregoing provisions of this section the question when representation was first taken out, a grant limited to settled land or to trust property shall be left out of account and a grant limited to real estate or to personal estate shall be left out of account unless a grant limited to the remainder of the estate has previously been made or is made at the same time.

48. Powers of personal representative in respect of interests of surviving spouse—

(1) [*Repealed by Intestates' Estates Act 1952, s. 2 (a).*]

(2) The personal representatives may raise

(a) [the fixed net sum][23] or any part thereof and the interest thereon payable to the surviving husband or wife of the intestate on the security of the whole or any part of the residuary estate of the intestate (other than the personal chattels), so far as that estate may be sufficient for the purpose or the said sum and interest may not have been satisfied by an appropriation under the statutory power available in that behalf; and

(b) in like manner the capital sum, if any, required for the purchase or redemption of the life

---

21   Words in brackets substituted by Administration of Justice Act 1970, s. 1 and Sch. 2 and Supreme Court Act 1981, s. 152(1) and Sch. 5.

22   Words in brackets substituted by Supreme Court Act 1981, s. 152(1) and Sch. 5.

23   Words in square brackets substituted by Family Provision Act 1966, s. 1(2), in relation to persons dying on or after 1 January 1967, for the words 'the net sum of five thousand, or as the case may be, twenty thousand pounds'. As to the fixed net sum, see notes 11 and 13), pp. 752, 753, ante.

Deaths on or after 1 January 1953 (continued)—

interest of the surviving husband or wife of the intestate, or any part thereof not satisfied by the application for that purpose of any part of the residuary estate of the intestate; and in either case the amount, if any, properly required for the payment of the costs of the transaction.

49. Application to cases of partial intestacy.—(1) Where any person dies leaving a will effectively disposing of part of his property, this Part of this Act shall have effect as respects the part of his property not so disposed of subject to the provisions contained in the will and subject to the following modifications:

(aa) where the deceased leaves a husband or wife who acquires any beneficial interests under the will of the deceased (other than personal chattels specifically bequeathed) the references in this Part of this Act to [the fixed net sum][24] payable to a surviving husband or wife, and to interest on that sum, shall be taken as references to the said sum diminished by the value at the date of death of the said beneficial interests, and to interest on that sum as so diminished and, accordingly, where the said value exceeds the said sum, this Part of this Act shall have effect as if references to the said sum and interest thereon, were omitted;[25]

(a) the requirements of section forty-seven of this Act as to bringing property into account shall apply to any beneficial interests acquired by any issue of the deceased under the will of the deceased, but not to beneficial interests so acquired by any other persons;[25]

(b) the personal representative shall, subject to his rights and powers for the purpose of administration, be a trustee for the persons entitled under this Part of this Act in respect of the part of the estate not expressly disposed of unless it appears by the will that the personal representative is intended to take such part beneficially.

(2) References in the foregoing provisions of this section to beneficial interests acquired under a will shall be construed as including a reference to a beneficial interest acquired by virtue of the exercise by the will of a general power to appointment (including the statutory power to dispose of entailed interests), but not of a special power of appointment.[25]

(3) For the purposes of paragraph (aa) in the foregoing provisions of this section the personal representative shall employ a duly qualified valuer in any case where such employment may be necessary.[25]

(4) The references in subsection (3) of section forty-seven A of this Act to property are references to property comprised in the residuary estate and, accordingly, where a will of the deceased creates a life interest in property in possession, and the remaining interest in that property forms part of the residuary estate, the said references are references to that remaining interest (which, until the life interest determines, is property not in possession).

Deaths before 1 January 1953[1]

46. Succession to real and personal estate on intestacy.—(1) The residuary estate of an intestate shall be distributed in the manner or be held on the trusts mentioned in this section, namely:

(i) If the intestate leaves a husband or wife (with or without issue) the surviving husband or wife shall take the personal chattels absolutely, and in addition the residuary estate of the intestate (other than the personal chattels) shall stand charged with the payment of a net sum of one thousand pounds, free of death duties and costs, to the surviving husband or

---

24　Words in square brackets substituted by Family Provision Act 1966, s. 1 (2), in relation to persons dying on or after 1 January 1967, for the words 'the net sum of five thousand pounds or twenty thousand pounds'. As to the fixed net sum, see notes 11 and 13, pp. 752, 753, ante.

25　Subsections (1) (aa), (a), (2) and (3) will cease to have effect as respects an intestate dying on or after 1 January 1996—see ss. 1 and 5. Law Reform (Succession) Act 1995, p. 900, post.

1　See headnote to ss. 46 to 49, ante, p. 751, as to the amendments to these sections effected by the Intestates' Estates Act 1952, and the Family Provision Act 1966.

Deaths before 1 January 1953 (continued)[2]—

wife with interest thereon from the date of the death [at such rate as the Lord Chancellor may specify by order][3] until paid or appropriated, and, subject to providing for that sum and the interest thereon, the residuary estate (other than the personal chattels) shall be held—

(a)   If the intestate leaves no issue, upon trust for the surviving husband or wife during his or her life;

(b)   If the intestate leaves issue, upon trust, as to one half, for the surviving husband or wife during his or her life, and, subject to such life interest, on the statutory trusts for the issue of the intestate; and, as to the other half, on the statutory trusts for the issue of the intestate, but if those trusts fail or determine in the lifetime of a surviving husband or wife of the intestate, then upon trust for the surviving husband or wife during the residue of his or her life;

(ii)   If the intestate leaves issue but no husband or wife, the residuary estate of the intestate shall be held on the statutory trusts for the issue of the intestate;

(iii)   If the intestate leaves no issue but both parents, then, subject to the interests of a surviving husband or wife, the residuary estate of the intestate shall be held in trust for the father and mother in equal shares absolutely;

(iv)   If the intestate leaves no issue but one parent, then, subject to the interests of a surviving husband or wife, the residuary estate of the intestate shall be held in trust for the surviving father or mother absolutely;

(v)   If the intestate leaves no issue or parent, then, subject to the interests of a surviving husband or wife, the residuary estate of the intestate shall be held in trust for the following persons living at the death of the intestate, and in the following order and manner, namely:

First, on the statutory trusts for the brothers and sisters of the whole blood of the intestate; but if no person takes an absolutely vested interest under such trusts; then

Secondly, on the statutory trusts for the brothers and sisters of the half blood of the intestate; but if no person takes an absolutely vested interest under such trusts; then

Thirdly, for the grandparents of the intestate and, if more than one survive the intestate, in equal shares; but if there is no member of this class; then

Fourthly, on the statutory trusts for the uncles and aunts of the intestate (being brothers or sisters of the whole blood of a parent of the intestate); but if no person takes an absolutely vested interest under such trusts; then

Fifthly, on the statutory trusts for the uncles and aunts of the intestate (being brothers or sisters of the half blood of a parent of the intestate); but if no person takes an absolutely vested interest under such trusts; then

Sixthly, for the surviving husband or wife of the intestate absolutely;

(vi)   In default of any person taking an absolute interest under the foregoing provisions, the residuary estate of the intestate shall belong to the Crown or to the Duchy of Lancaster or to the Duke of Cornwall for the time being, as the case may be, as bona vacantia, and in lieu of any right to escheat.

The Crown or the said Duchy or the said Duke may (without prejudice to the powers reserved by section nine of the Civil List Act 1910, or any other powers), out of the whole or any part of the property devolving on them respectively, provide, in accordance with the existing practice, for dependants, whether kindred or not, of the intestate, and other persons for whom the intestate might reasonably have been expected to make provision.

2   See headnote to ss. 46 to 49, ante, p. 751, as to the amendments to these sections effected by the Intestates' Estates Act 1952 and the Family Provision Act 1966.

3   Words in square brackets substituted by Administration of Justice Act 1977, s. 28(1) for the rate of five pounds per cent per annum. The current rate is 6 per cent per annum: Intestate Succession (Interest and Capitalisation) Order 1977 (Amendment) Order 1983 (S.I. 1983 No. 1374). See also footnote 3 to para **6.29**, ante.

Deaths before 1 January 1953 (continued)[4]

(2) A husband and wife shall for all purposes of distribution or division under the foregoing provisions of this section be treated as two persons.

47. Statutory trusts in favour of issue and other classes of relatives of intestate.—(1) Where under this Part of this Act the residuary estate of the intestate, or any part thereof, is directed to be held on the statutory trusts for the issue of the intestate, the same shall be held upon the following trusts, namely:

  (i) In trust, in equal shares if more than one, for all or any the children or child of the intestate, living at the death of the intestate, who attain the age of twenty-one years or marry under that age, and for all or any of the issue living at the death of the intestate who attain the age of twenty-one years or marry under that age of any child of the intestate who predeceases the intestate, such issue to take through all degrees, according to their stocks, in equal shares if more than one, the share which their parent would have taken if living at the death of the intestate, and so that no issue shall take whose parent is living at the death of the intestate and so capable of taking;

 (ii) The statutory power of advancement, and the statutory provisions which relate to maintenance and accumulation of surplus income, shall apply, but when an infant marries such infant shall be entitled to give valid receipts for the income of the infant's share or interest;

(iii) Where the property held on the statutory trusts for issue is divisible into shares, then any money or property which, by way of advancement or on the marriage of a child of the intestate, has been paid to such child by the intestate or settled by the intestate for the benefit of such child (including any life or less interest and including, property covenanted to be paid or settled) shall, subject to any contrary intention expressed or appearing from the circumstances of the case, be taken as being so paid or settled in or towards satisfaction of the share of such child or the share which such child would have taken if living at the death of the intestate, and shall be brought into account, at a valuation (the value to be reckoned as at the death of the intestate), in accordance with the requirements of the personal representatives;

(iv) The personal representatives may permit any infant contingently interested to have the use and enjoyment of any personal chattels in such manner and subject to such conditions (if any) as the personal representatives may consider reasonable, and without being liable to account for any consequential loss.

(1A) The power to make orders under subsection (1) above shall be exercisable by statutory instrument subject to annulment in pursuance of a resolution of either House of Parliament; and any such order may be varied or revoked by a subsequent order made under the power[5].

(2) If the trusts in favour of the issue of the intestate fail by reason of no child or other issue attaining an absolutely vested interest—

(a) the residuary estate of the intestate and the income thereof and all statutory accumulations, if any, of the income thereof, or so much thereof as may not have been paid or applied under any power affecting the same, shall go, devolve and be held under the provisions of this Part of this Act as if the intestate had died without leaving issue living at the death of the intestate;

(b) references in this Part of this Act to the intestate 'leaving no issue' shall be construed as 'leaving no issue who attain an absolutely vested interest';

(c) references in this Part of this Act to the intestate 'leaving issue' or 'leaving a child or other issue' shall be construed as 'leaving issue who attain an absolutely vested interest'.

(3) Where under this Part of this Act the residuary estate of an intestate or any part thereof is directed to be held on the statutory trusts for any class of relatives of the intestate, other than

4 See headnote to ss. 46 to 49, ante, p. 751, as to the amendments to these sections effected by the Intestates' Estates Act 1952, and the Family Provision Act 1966.
5 Subsection (1A) inserted by Administration of Justice Act 1977, s. 28(1).

Deaths before 1 January 1953 (continued)[6]—

issue of the intestate, the same shall be held on trusts corresponding to the statutory trusts for the issue of the intestate (other than the provision for bringing any money or property into account) as if such trusts (other than as aforesaid) were repeated with the substitution of references to the members or member of that class for references to the children or child of the intestate.

48. Powers of personal representative in respect of interests of surviving spouse.—(1) Where a surviving husband or wife is entitled to a life interest in the residuary estate or any part thereof the personal representative may, either with the consent of any such tenant for life (not being also the sole personal representative) or, where the tenant for life is the sole personal representative, with the leave of the court, purchase or redeem such life interest (while it is in possession) by paying the capital value thereof (reckoned according to tables selected by the personal representative) to the tenant for life or the persons deriving title under him or her and the costs of the transaction, and thereupon the residuary estate of the intestate may be dealt with or distributed free from such life interest.

(2) The personal representatives may raise—

(a) the net sum of one thousand pounds or any part thereof and the interest thereon payable to the surviving husband or wife of the intestate on the security of the whole or any part of the residuary estate of the intestate (other than the personal chattels), so far as that estate may be sufficient for the purpose or the said sum and interest may not have been satisfied by an appropriation under the statutory power available in that behalf; and

(b) in like manner the capital sum, if any, required for the purchase or redemption of the life interest of the surviving husband or wife of the intestate, or any part thereof not satisfied by the application for that purpose of any part of the residuary estate of the intestate; and in either case the amount, if any, properly required for the payment of the costs of the transaction.

49. Application to cases of partial intestacy. Where any person dies leaving a will effectively disposing of part of his property, this Part of this Act shall have effect as respects the part of his property not so disposed of subject to the provisions contained in the will and subject to the following modifications:

(a) The requirements as to bringing property into account shall apply to any beneficial interests acquired by any issue of the deceased under the will of the deceased, but not to beneficial interests so acquired by any other persons;

(b) The personal representative shall, subject to his rights and powers for the purposes of administration, be a trustee for the persons entitled under this Part of this Act in respect of the part of the estate not expressly disposed of unless it appears by the will that the personal representative is intended to take such part beneficially.

---

50. Construction of documents.—(1) References to any Statutes of Distribution in an instrument inter vivos made or in a will coming into operation after the commencement of this Act, shall be construed as references to this Part of this Act; and references in such an instrument or will to statutory next-of-kin shall be construed, unless the context otherwise requires, as referring to the persons who would take beneficially on an intestacy under the foregoing provisions of this Part of this Act[7,8].

(2) Trusts declared in an instrument inter vivos made, or in a will coming into operation,

---

6   See headnote to ss. 46 to 49, ante, p. 751, as to the amendments to these sections effected by the Intestates' Estates Act 1952, and the Family Provisions Act 1966.

7   Modified by Intestates' Estates Act 1952, s. 6(2), post, p. 767 and, in respect of a will or codicil coming into operation on or after 4 April 1988, by Family Law Reform Act 1987, s. 18(3), post, p. 877.

8   The references in subsection (1) to Part IV of this Act and to the foregoing provisions of that Part shall, in relation to an instrument inter vivos made or a will or codicil coming into operation on or after 1 January 1996 (but not in relation to instruments inter vivos made or wills or codicils coming into operation earlier), be construed as including references to s. 1 of the Law Reform (Succession) Act 1995—see s. 1(4) Law Reform (Succession) Act 1995, p. 901, post.

before the commencement of this Act by reference to the Statutes of Distribution, shall, unless the contrary thereby appears, be construed as referring to the enactments (other than the Intestates' Estates Act 1890) relating to the distribution of effects of intestates which were in force immediately before the commencement of this Act.

(3) In subsection (1) of this section the reference to this Part of this Act, or the foregoing provisions of this Part of this Act, shall in relation to an instrument inter vivos made, or a will or codicil coming into operation, after the coming into force of section 18 of the Family Law Reform Act 1987 (but not in relation to instruments inter vivos made or wills or codicils coming into operation earlier) be construed as including references to that section[9].

51. Savings.—(1) Nothing in this Part of this Act affects the right of any person to take beneficially, by purchase, as heir either general or special.

(2) The foregoing provisions of this Part of this Act do not apply to any beneficial interest in real estate (not including chattels real) to which a lunatic or defective living and of full age at the commencement of this Act, and unable, by reason of his incapacity, to make a will, who thereafter dies intestate in respect of such interest without having recovered his testamentary capacity, was entitled at his death, and any such beneficial interest (not being an interest ceasing on his death) shall, without prejudice to any will of the deceased, devolve in accordance with the general law in force before the commencement of this Act applicable to freehold land, and that law shall, notwithstanding any repeal, apply to the case.

For the purposes of this subsection, a lunatic or defective who dies intestate as respects any beneficial interest in real estate shall not be deemed to have recovered his testamentary capacity unless his receiver has been discharged.

(3) Where an infant dies after the commencement of this Act without having been married, and independently of this subsection he would, at his death, have been equitably entitled under a settlement (including a will) to a vested estate in fee simple or absolute interest in freehold land, or in any property settled to devolve therewith or as freehold land, such infant shall be deemed to have had an entailed interest, and the settlement shall be construed accordingly.

(4) This Part of this Act does not affect the devolution of an entailed interest as an equitable interest.

52. Interpretation of Part IV. In this Part of this Act 'real and personal estate' means every beneficial interest (including rights of entry and reverter) of the intestate in real and personal estate which (otherwise than in right of a power of appointment or of the testamentary power conferred by statute to dispose of entailed interests) he could, if of full age and capacity, have disposed of by his will [and references (however expressed) to any relationship between two persons shall be construed in accordance with section 1 of the Family Law Reform Act 1987][10].

PART V

SUPPLEMENTAL

53. General savings.—(1) Nothing in this Act shall derogate from the powers of the High Court which exist independently of this Act or alter the distribution of business between the several divisions of the High Court, or operate to transfer any jurisdiction from the High Court to any other court.

(2) Nothing in this Act shall affect any unrepealed enactment in a public general Act dispensing with probate or administration as respects personal estate not including chattels real.

---

9   Subsection (3) was added, as from 4 April 1988, by Family Law Reform Act 1987, s. 33(1), Sch. 2, para. 3.

10   The words in square brackets were added, as from 4 April 1988, by the Family Law Reform Act 1987, s. 33(1), Sch. 2, para. 4 (see p. 880, post).

[(3) *Nothing in this Act shall*—

(a) *alter any death duty payable in respect of real estate or impose any new duty thereon;*
(b) *render any real estate liable to legacy duty or exempt it from succession duty;*
(c) *alter the incidence of any death duties*[11].]

54. Application of Act. Save as otherwise expressly provided, this Act does not apply in any case where the death occurred before the commencement of this Act.

55. Definitions. In this Act, unless the context otherwise requires, the following expressions have the meaning hereby assigned to them respectively, that is to say:

(1)   (i) 'Administration' means, with reference to the real and personal estate of a deceased person, letters of administration, whether general or limited, or with the will annexed or otherwise:

     (ii) 'Administrator' means a person to whom administration is granted:

     (iii) 'Conveyance' includes a mortgage, charge by way of legal mortgage, lease, assent, vesting, declaration, vesting instrument, disclaimer, release and every other assurance of property or of an interest therein by any instrument, except a will, and 'convey' has a corresponding meaning and 'disposition' includes a conveyance' also a devise bequest and an appointment of property contained in a will, and 'dispose of' has a corresponding meaning:

     (iv) 'the Court' means the High Court, and also the county court, where that court has jurisdiction[12]:

     (v) 'Income' includes rents and profits:

     (vi) 'Intestate' includes a person who leaves a will but dies intestate as to some beneficial interest in his real or personal estate:

     (vii) 'Legal estates' mean the estates charges and interests in or over land (subsisting or created at law) which are by statute authorised to subsist or to be created at law; and 'equitable interests' mean all other interests and charges in or over land or in the proceeds of sale thereof:

     (viii) 'Lunatic' includes a lunatic whether so found or not, and in relation to a lunatic not so found; and 'defective' includes every person affected by the provisions of section one hundred and sixteen of the Lunacy Act 1890, as extended by section sixty-four of the Mental Deficiency Act 1913, and for whose benefit a receiver has been appointed:

     (ix) 'Pecuniary legacy' includes an annuity, a general legacy, a demonstrative legacy so far as it is not discharged out of the designated property, and any other general direction by a testator for the payment of money, including all death duties free from which any devise, bequest, or payment is made to take effect:

     (x) 'Personal chattels' mean carriages, horses, stable furniture and effects (not used for business purposes), motor cars and accessories (not used for business purposes), garden effects, domestic animals, plate, plated articles, linen, china, glass, books, pictures, prints, furniture, jewellery, articles of household or personal use or ornament, musical and scientific instruments and apparatus, wines, liquors and consumable stores, but do not include any chattels used at the death of the intestate for business purposes nor money or securities for money[13]:

     (xi) 'Personal representative' means the executor, original or by representation, or administrator for the time being of a deceased person, and as regards any liability for the payment of death duties includes any person who takes possession of or intermeddles with the property of a deceased person without the authority of the personal representatives or the court, and 'executor' includes a person deemed to be appointed executor as respects settled land:

11   Subsection (3) repealed, in relation to deaths after 12 March 1975, by Finance Act 1975, s. 59 and Sch. 13, Pt. I.
12   Remainder of para. (iv) repealed by Courts Act 1971, s. 56 and Sch. 11, Pt. II.
13   A collection of clocks and watches is included in the definition of 'personal chattels' (*Re Crispin's Will Trusts* [1975] Ch 245 at 248, [1974] 3 All ER 772).

(xii) 'Possession' includes the receipt of rents and profits or the right to receive the same, if any:

(xiii) Prescribed' means prescribed by rules of court [*or by probate rules made pursuant to this Act*][14]:

(xiv) 'Probate' means the probate of a will:

(xv) 'Probate judge' means the President of the [Family][15] Division of the High Court:

(xvi) [*Repealed by Supreme Court Act 1981, s. 152(4) and Sch. 7.*]

(xvii) 'Property' includes a thing in action and any interest in real or personal property:

(xviii) 'Purchaser' means a lessee, mortgagee or other person who in good faith acquires an interest in property for valuable consideration, also an intending purchaser and 'valuable consideration' includes marriage, but does not include a nominal consideration in money:

(xix) 'Real estate' save as provided in Part IV of this Act means real estate, including chattels real, which by virtue of Part I of this Act devolves on the personal representative of a deceased person:

(xx) Representation' means the probate of a will and administration, and the expression 'taking out representation' refers to the obtaining of the probate of a will or of the grant of administration:

(xxi) 'Rent' includes a rent service or a rentcharge, or other rent, toll, duty, or annual or periodical payment in money or money's worth, issuing out of or charged upon land, but does not include mortgage interest; and 'rentcharge' includes a fee farm rent:

(xxii) [*Repealed by Supreme Court Act 1981, s. 152(4) and Sch. 7.*]

(xxiii) 'Securities' include stocks, funds, or shares:

(xxiv) 'Tenant for life', 'statutory owner', 'land', 'settled land', 'settlement', 'trustees of the settlement', 'term of years absolute', 'death duties', and 'legal mortgage', have the same meanings as in the Settled Land Act 1925, and 'entailed interest' and 'charge by way of legal mortgage' have the same meanings as in the Law of Property Act 1925:

(xxv) 'Treasury solicitor' means the solicitor for the affairs of His Majesty's Treasury, and includes the solicitor for the affairs of the Duchy of Lancaster:

(xxvi) 'Trust corporation' means the public trustee or a corporation either appointed by the court in any particular case to be a trustee or entitled by rules made under subsection (3) of section four of the Public Trustee Act, 1906, to act as custodian trustee[16]:

(xxvii) 'Trust for sale', in relation to land, means an immediate binding trust for sale, whether or not exercisable at the request or with the consent of any person, and with or without a power at discretion to postpone the sale; and 'power to postpone a sale' means power to postpone in the exercise of a discretion:

(xxviii) 'Will' includes codicil:

(2) References to a child or issue living at the death of any person include a child or issue en ventre sa mere at the death.

(3) References to the estate of a deceased person include property over which the deceased exercises a general power of appointment (including the statutory power to dispose of entailed interests) by his will.

57. Application to Crown.—(1) The provisions of this Act bind the Crown and Duchy of Lancaster, and the Duke of Cornwall for the time being, as respects the estates of persons

---

14 Words in brackets repealed by Supreme Court Act 1981, s. 152(4) and Sch. 7.

15 Amended by Administration of Justice Act 1970, s. 1 and Sch. 2. Note—paragraph (xv) repealed by Law of Property (Miscellaneous Provisions) Act 1994, s. 21(2), Sch. 2—see p. 900, post—as from 1 July 1995.

16 Definition extended by Law of Property (Amendment) Act 1926 (see also paras. **9.05–9.07**, ante).

dying after the commencement of this Act but not so as to affect the time within which proceedings for the recovery of real or personal estate vesting in or devolving on His Majesty in right of His Crown, or His Duchy of Lancaster, or on the Duke of Cornwall, may be instituted.

(2) Nothing in this Act in any manner affects or alters the descent or devolution of any property for the time being vested in His Majesty either in right of the Crown or of the Duchy of Lancaster or of any property for the time being belonging to the Duchy of Cornwall.

58. Short title, commencement and extent.—(1) This Act may be cited as the Administration of Estates Act 1925.

(2) This Act shall come into operation on the first day of January, nineteen hundred and twenty-six[17].

(3) This Act extends to England and Wales only.

LAW OF PROPERTY (AMENDMENT) ACT 1926

(16 & 17 Geo. 5, c. 11)

3. Meaning of 'trust corporation'.—(l) For the purposes of the Law of Property Act 1925, the Settled Land Act 1925, the Trustee Act 1925, the Administration of Estates Act 1925, and the [Supreme Court Act 1981][18], the expression 'Trust Corporation' includes the Treasury Solicitor, the Official Solicitor and any person holding any other official position prescribed by the Lord Chancellor, and, in relation to the property of a bankrupt and property subject to a deed of arrangement, includes the trustee in bankruptcy and the trustee under the deed respectively, and, in relation to charitable ecclesiastical and public trusts, also includes any local or public authority so prescribed, and any other corporation constituted under the laws of the United Kingdom or any part thereof which satisfies the Lord Chancellor that it undertakes the administration of any such trusts without remuneration, or that by its constitution it is required to apply the whole of its net income after payment of outgoings for charitable, ecclesiastical or public purposes, and is prohibited from distributing, directly or indirectly, any part thereof by way of profits amongst any of its members, and is authorised by him to act in relation to such trusts as a trust corporation.

(2) For the purposes of this provision, the expression 'Treasury Solicitor' means the solicitor for the affairs of His Majesty's Treasury, and includes the solicitor for the affairs of the Duchy of Lancaster.

COLONIAL PROBATES (PROTECTED STATES AND MANDATED TERRITORIES) ACT 1927[19]

(17 & 18 Geo. 5, c. 43)   [22 December 1927]

1. Extension of Colonial Probates Act 1892 to certain protected states and mandated territories. The power of His Majesty to apply the Colonial Probates Act 1892 to British possessions shall include a power to apply the said Act to any territories, being either territories under His Majesty's protection or territories in respect of which a mandate on behalf

17   Repealed by Statute Law Revision Act 1950.
18   Words in brackets substituted by Supreme Court Act 1981, s. 152(1) and Sch. 5.
19   Upon the termination of the League of Nations the power under this Act was preserved by the Mandated and Trust Territories Act 1947, which provides that as from 13 December 1946: 'Where any enactment passed or made before or after the termination of the League of Nations refers to mandated territories, mandates of the League shall not for the purposes of that enactment be deemed to have come to an end with the termination of the League.'

of the League of Nations has been accepted by His Majesty, to which it cannot be applied by virtue of the provisions of the Foreign Jurisdiction Acts 1890 and 1913, and the said Act shall accordingly have effect as if references therein to British possessions included references to such territories as aforesaid.

2. Short title. This Act may be cited as the Colonial Probates (Protected States and Mandated Territories) Act 1927, and the Colonial Probates Act 1892, and this Act may be cited together as the Colonial Probates Acts 1892 and 1927.

LAW REFORM (MISCELLANEOUS PROVISIONS) ACT 1934

(24 & 25 Geo. 5, c. 41)   [25 July 1934]

1. Effect of death on certain causes of action.—(1) Subject to the provisions of this section, on the death of any person after the commencement of this Act all causes of action subsisting against or vested in him shall survive against, or, as the case may be, for the benefit of, his estate.

(5) The rights conferred by this Act for the benefit of the estates of deceased persons shall be in addition to and not in derogation of any rights conferred on the dependants of deceased persons by the Fatal Accidents Acts 1846 to 1908[20], or the Carriage by Air Act 1932, and so much of this Act as relates to causes of action against the estates of deceased persons shall apply in relation to causes of action under the said Acts as it applies in relation to other causes of action not expressly excepted from the operation of subsection (1) of this section.

EVIDENCE ACT 1938

(1 & 2 Geo. 6, c. 28)

3. Proof of instrument to validity of which attestation is necessary. Subject as hereinafter provided, in any proceedings, whether civil or criminal, an instrument to the validity of which attestation is requisite may, instead of being proved by an attesting witness, be proved in the manner in which it might be proved if no attesting witness were alive:

Provided that nothing in this section shall apply to the proof of wills or other testamentary documents[21].

7.—(2) This Act shall not extend to Scotland or Northern Ireland.

CONSULAR CONVENTIONS ACT 1949

(12, 13 & 14 Geo. 6, c. 29)   [26 April 1949]

1. Powers of consular officers in relation to property in England of deceased persons.—
(1) Where any person who is a national of a State to which this section applies is named as executor in the will of a deceased person disposing of property in England, or is otherwise a

20   Fatal Accidents Acts now consolidated by Fatal Accidents Act 1976: the reference in s. 1(5) of the
     Law Reform (Miscellaneous Provisions) Act 1934, to the Fatal Accidents Acts to include reference
     to the Act of 1976 (Fatal Accidents Act 1976, s. 6 and Sch. 1, para. 2).
21   Held by Byrne J, on motion that the proviso does not apply to evidence as to the contents or date of
     a will (*Re Hyman* (1946) 24 July (motion)).

person to whom a grant of representation to the estate in England of a deceased person may be made, then if the court is satisfied, on the application of a consular officer of the said State, that the said national is not resident in England, and if no application for a grant of such representation is made by a person duly authorised by power of attorney to act for him in that behalf, the court shall make to that officer any such grant of representation to the estate of the deceased as would be made to him if he were so authorised as aforesaid:

Provided that the court may, if it thinks fit, postpone the making of a grant by virtue of this section during such period as the court considers appropriate having regard to the circumstances of the case.

(2) Where any person who is a national of a State to which this section applies—

(a) is entitled to payment or delivery of any money or property in respect of any interest in the estate of a deceased person, or vesting in possession on the death of any person, or is entitled to payment of any money becoming due on the death of any person; or

(b) is a person to whom any money or property comprised in the estate of a deceased person may be paid or delivered in pursuance of any enactment, rule or regulation, whether passed or made before or after the commencement of this Act, authorising the payment or delivery of such money or property without representation to the estate of the deceased being granted,

then if the said national is not resident in England, a consular officer of that State shall have the like right and power to receive and give a valid discharge for any such money or property in England as if he were duly authorised by power of attorney to act for him in that behalf:

Provided that no person shall be authorised or required by this subsection to pay or deliver any money or property to a consular officer if it is within his knowledge that any other person in England has been expressly authorised to receive that money or property on behalf of the said national.

(3) A grant of administration made by virtue of this section may be made to the consular officer by his official title, and to his successors in office; and where a grant is so made, the office of administrator, and all the estate, rights, duties and liabilities of the administrator [(*including liabilities under the administration bond*)][1] shall be vested in and imposed on the person for the time being holding the office, and no fresh grant shall be required by reason only of the death or vacation of office of the person to whom the grant was made or in whom it is vested as aforesaid:

Provided that nothing in this subsection shall affect any limitation contained in the grant, or any power of the court to revoke the grant.

(4) Notwithstanding anything in subsection [(2) of section 114 of the Supreme Court Act 1981][2] (which provides that in the case of a minority or a life interest administration must [in general][3] be granted either to a trust corporation or to not less than two individuals), administration of an estate may in any case be granted by virtue of this section to a consular officer alone; and subsection [(4) of that section][4] (which provides for the appointment of additional personal representatives in the case of a minority or a life interest) shall not apply in any case where the existing personal representative is a consular officer appointed by virtue of this section.

(5) [*Repealed by Administration of Estates Act 1971, s. 12(2) and Sch. 2.*]

6. Application of ss. 1, 2 and 4.—(1) His Majesty may by Order in Council direct that sections one and two or section four of this Act shall apply to any foreign State specified in the Order, being a State with which a consular convention providing for matters for which provision is made by those sections has been concluded by His Majesty.

1   Words in italics repealed by Administration of Estates Act 1971, s. 12(2) and Sch. 2.
2   Words in brackets substituted by Supreme Court Act 1981, s. 152(1) and Sch. 5.
3   Words in brackets inserted by Supreme Court Act 1981, s. 152(1) and Sch. 5.
4   Words in brackets substituted by Supreme Court Act 1981, s. 152(1) and Sch. 5.

8. Repeal of Domicile Act 1861, s. 4. Section four of the Domicile Act 1861 is hereby repealed:

Provided that any Order in Council in force under that section immediately before the commencement of this Act shall continue in force, notwithstanding anything in this section, until revoked by His Majesty by Order in Council.

INTESTATES' ESTATES ACT 1952

(15 & 16 Geo. 6 & 1 E1iz. 2, c. 64)   [30 October 1952]

PART I

AMENDMENTS OF LAW OF INTESTATE SUCCESSION

1. Succession to estate of intestate leaving a surviving spouse.—(1) As respects a person dying intestate after the commencement of this Act sections forty-six, forty-seven and forty-eight of the Administration of Estates Act 1925 (hereafter in this Part of this Act referred to as the 'principal Act'), shall have effect subject to the amendments set out in this section[5].

2. Right of surviving spouse to have life interest redeemed. As respects a person dying intestate after the commencement of this Act—

(a) subsection (1) of section forty-eight of the principal Act (which authorises the personal representative to redeem the surviving spouse's life interest in the residuary estate with his or her consent) shall not have effect, and

(b) Part IV of the principal Act shall have effect as if the following section were added immediately before that section:
'47A.[5]

3. Partial intestacies.—(1) As respects a person dying intestate after the commencement of this Act, section forty-nine of the principal Act (which contains modifications of the general rules of intestacy in cases of partial intestacy) shall have effect subject to the amendments set out in this section.[5]

4. Reproduction of enactments in Administration of Estates Act 1925, as amended. In accordance with the provisions of the foregoing sections, sections forty-six to forty-nine of the principal Act shall have effect as respects a person dying intestate after the commencement of this Act as set out in the First Schedule to this Act.

5. Rights of surviving spouse as respects the matrimonial home. The Second Schedule to this Act shall have effect for enabling the surviving husband or wife of a person dying intestate after the commencement of this Act to acquire the matrimonial home.

6. Interpretation and construction.—(1) In this Part of this Act the expression 'intestate' has the meaning assigned to it by section fifty-five of the principal Act.

(2) The references in subsection (1) of section fifty of the principal Act (which relates to the construction of documents) to Part IV of that Act, or to the foregoing provisions of that Part, shall in relation to an instrument inter vivos made or a will coming into operation after the commencement of this Act, but not in relation to instruments inter vivos made or wills coming into operation earlier, be construed as including references to this Part of this Act and the Schedules to be read therewith.

*   *   *   *   *

---

5   These sections are set out, both in their original form (which still applies to deaths before 1953) and as amended by this Act, in the Administration of Estates Act 1925. For ss. 46 to 49, as amended, see ante, pp. 751 ff. and see the headnote to those sections, ante, p. 751

PART III

GENERAL

9. Short title and commencement.—(l) This Act may be cited as the Intestates' Estates Act 1952.

(2) This Act shall come into operation on the first day of January, nineteen hundred and fifty-three.

SCHEDULES
FIRST SCHEDULE

This Schedule sets out ss. 46 to 49 of the Administration of Estates Act 1925, as amended by this Act. For the sections as thus amended, see ante, pp. 751 ff.

SECOND SCHEDULE   Section 5

RIGHTS OF SURVIVING SPOUSE AS RESPECTS THE MATRIMONIAL HOME

1.—(1) Subject to the provisions of this Schedule, where the residuary estate of the intestate comprises an interest in a dwelling-house in which the surviving husband or wife was resident at the time of the intestate's death, the surviving husband or wife may require the personal representative, in exercise of the power conferred by section forty-one of the principal Act (and with due regard to the requirements of that section as to valuation) to appropriate the said interest in the dwelling-house in or towards satisfaction of any absolute interest of the surviving husband or wife in the real and personal estate of the intestate.

(2) The right conferred by this paragraph shall not be exercisable where the interest is—

(a) a tenancy which at the date of the death of the intestate was a tenancy which would determine within the period of two years from that date; or

(b) a tenancy which the landlord by notice given after that date could determine within the remainder of that period.

(3) Nothing in subsection (5) of section forty-one of the principal Act (which requires the personal representative, in making an appropriation to any person under that section, to have regard to the rights of others) shall prevent the personal representative from giving effect to the right conferred by this paragraph.

(4) The reference in this paragraph to an absolute interest in the real and personal estate of the intestate includes a reference to the capital value of a life interest which the surviving husband or wife has under his Act elected to have redeemed.

(5) Where part of a building was, at the date of the death of the intestate, occupied as a separate dwelling, that dwelling shall for the purposes of this Schedule be treated as a dwelling-house.

2. Where—

(a) the dwelling-house forms part of a building and an interest in the whole of the building is comprised in the residuary estate; or

(b) the dwelling-house is held with agricultural land and an interest in the agricultural land is comprised in the residuary estate; or

(c) the whole or a part of the dwelling-house was at the time of the intestate's death used as a hostel or lodging house; or

(d) a part of the dwelling-house was at the time of the intestate's death used for purposes other than domestic purposes,

the right conferred by paragraph 1 of this Schedule shall not be exercisable unless the court, on being satisfied that the exercise of that right is not likely to diminish the value of assets in the residuary estate (other than the said interest in the dwelling-house) or make them more difficult to dispose of, so orders.

3.—(l) The right conferred by paragraph 1 of this Schedule—

(a) shall not be exercisable after the expiration of twelve months from the first taking out of representation with respect to the intestate's estate;

(b) shall not be exercisable after the death of the surviving husband or wife;

(c) shall be exercisable, except where the surviving husband or wife is the sole personal representative, by notifying the personal representative (or, where there are two or more personal representatives of whom one is the surviving husband or wife, all of them except the surviving husband or wife) in writing.

(2) A notification in writing under paragraph (c) of the foregoing sub-paragraph shall not be revocable except with the consent of the personal representative; but the surviving husband or wife may require the personal representative to have the said interest in the dwelling-house valued in accordance with section forty-one of the principal Act and to inform him or her of the result of that valuation before he or she decides whether to exercise the right.

(3) Subsection (9) of the section forty-seven A added to the principal Act by section two of this Act shall apply for the purposes of the construction of the reference in this paragraph to the first taking out of representation, and the proviso to subsection (5) of that section shall apply for the purpose of enabling the surviving husband or wife to apply for an extension of the period of twelve months mentioned in this paragraph.

4.—(1) During the period of twelve months mentioned in paragraph 3 of this Schedule the personal representative shall not without the written consent of the surviving husband or wife sell or otherwise dispose of the said interest in the dwelling-house except in the course of administration owing to want of other assets.

(2) An application to the court under paragraph 2 of this Schedule may be made by the personal representative as well as by the surviving husband or wife, and if, on an application under that paragraph, the court does not order that the right conferred by paragraph 1 of this Schedule shall be exercisable by the surviving husband or wife, the court may authorise the personal representative to dispose of the said interest in the dwelling-house within the said period of twelve months.

(3) Where the court under sub-paragraph (3) of paragraph 3 of this Schedule extends the said period of twelve months, the court may direct that this paragraph shall apply in relation to the extended period as it applied in relation to the original period of twelve months.

(4) This paragraph shall not apply where the surviving husband or wife is the sole personal representative or one of two or more personal representatives.

(5) Nothing in this paragraph shall confer any right on the surviving husband or wife as against a purchaser from the personal representative.

5.—(1) Where the surviving husband or wife is one of two or more personal representatives, the rule that a trustee may not be a purchaser of trust property shall not prevent the surviving husband or wife from purchasing out of the estate of the intestate an interest in a dwelling-house in which the surviving husband or wife was resident at the time of the intestate's death.

(2) The power of appropriation under section forty-one of the principal Act shall include power to appropriate an interest in a dwelling-house in which the surviving husband or wife was resident at the time of the intestate's death partly in satisfaction of an interest of the surviving husband or wife in the real and personal estate of the intestate and partly in return for a payment of money by the surviving husband or wife to the personal representative.

6.—(1) Where the surviving husband or wife is a person of unsound mind or a defective, a requirement or consent under this Schedule may be made or given on his or her behalf by the committee or receiver, if any, or, where there is no committee or receiver, by the court.

(2) A requirement or consent made or given under this Schedule by a surviving husband or wife who is an infant shall be as valid and binding as it would be if he or she were of age;

and, as respects an appropriation in pursuance of paragraph 1 of this Schedule, the provisions of section forty-one of the principal Act as to obtaining the consent of the infant's parent or guardian, or of the court on behalf of the infant, shall not apply.

7.—(1) Except where the context otherwise requires, references in this Schedule to a dwelling-house include references to any garden or portion of ground attached to and usually occupied with the dwelling-house or otherwise required for the amenity or convenience of the dwelling- house.

(2) This Schedule shall be construed as one with Part IV of the principal Act.

BIRTHS AND DEATHS REGISTRATION ACT 1953

(1 & 2 Eliz. 2, c. 20)   [14 July 1953]

10[6].—**Registration of father where parents not married.**—(1) Notwithstanding anything in the foregoing provisions of this Act, in the case of a child whose father and mother were not married to each other at the time of his birth, no person shall as father of the child be required to give information concerning the birth of the child, and the registrar shall not enter in the register the name of any person as father of the child except—

(a) at the joint request of the mother and the person stating himself to be the father of the child (in which case that person shall sign the register together with the mother); or

(b) at the request of the mother on production of—
  (i) a declaration in the prescribed form made by the mother stating that that person is the father of the child; and
  (ii) a statutory declaration made by that person stating himself to be the father of the child; or

(c) at the request of that person on production of—
  (i) a declaration in the prescribed form by that person stating himself to be the father of the child; and
  (ii) a statutory declaration made by the mother stating that that person is the father of the child; or

(d) at the request of the mother or that person on production of—
  (i) a copy of a parental responsibility agreement made between them in relation to the child; and
  (ii) a declaration in the prescribed form by the person making the request stating that the agreement was made in compliance with section 4 of the Children Act 1989 and has not been brought to an end by an order of a court; or

(e) at the request of the mother or that person on production of—
  (i) a certified copy of an order under section 4 of the Children Act 1989 giving that person parental responsibility for the child; and
  (ii) a declaration in the prescribed form by the person making the request stating that the order has not been brought to an end by an order of a court; or

(f) at the request of the mother or that person on production of—
  (i) a certified copy of an order under paragraph 1 of Schedule 1 to the Children Act 1989 which requires that person to make any financial provision for the child and which is not an order falling within paragraph 4(3) of that Schedule; and
  (ii) a declaration in the prescribed form by the person making the request stating that the order has not been discharged by an order of a court, or

(g) at the request of the mother or that person on production of—
  (i) a certified copy of any of the orders which are mentioned in subsection (1A) of this section which has been made in relation to the child; and
  (ii) a declaration in the prescribed form by the person making the request stating that the order has not been brought to an end or discharged by an order of a court.

6   This s. 10 is as substituted by s. 24 of the Family Law Reform Act 1987 and as further amended by the Children Act 1989 s. 108(7), Sch. 15—see p. 878, post—as from 14 October 1991.

(1A) The orders are—

(a) an order under section 4 of the Family Law Reform Act 1987 that that person shall have all the parental rights and duties with respect to the child;

(b) an order that that person shall have custody or care and control or legal custody of the child made under section 9 of the Guardianship of Minors Act 1971 at a time when such an order could only be made in favour of a parent;

(c) an order under section 9 or 11B of that Act which requires that person to make any financial provision in relation to the child;

(d) an order under section 4 of the Affiliation Proceedings Act 1957 naming that person as putative father of the child.

(2) Where, in the case of a child whose father and mother were not married to each other at the time of his birth, a person stating himself to be the father of the child makes a request to the registrar in accordance with paragraph (c) to (g) of subsection (1) of this section—

(a) he shall be treated as a qualified informant concerning the birth of the child for the purposes of this Act; and

(b) the giving of information concerning the birth of the child by that person and the signing of the register by him in the presence of the registrar shall act as a discharge of any duty of any other qualified informant under section 2 of this Act.

(3) In this section and section 10A of this Act references to a child whose father and mother were not married to each other at the time of his birth shall be construed in accordance with section 1 of the Family Law Reform Act 1987 and 'parental responsibility agreement' has the same meaning as in the Children Act 1989.

10A[7]. Re-registration where parents not married.—(1) Where there has been registered under this Act the birth of a child whose father and mother were not married to each other at the time of the birth, but no person has been registered as the father of the child, the registrar shall re-register the birth so as to show a person as the father—

(a) at the joint request of the mother and that person; or

(b) at the request of the mother on production of—
   (i) a declaration in the prescribed form made by the mother stating that that person is the father of the child; and
   (ii) a statutory declaration made by that person stating himself to be the father of the child; or

(c) at the request of that person on production of—
   (i) a declaration in the prescribed form by that person stating himself to be the father of the child; and
   (ii) a statutory declaration made by the mother stating that that person is the father of the child; or

(d) at the request of the mother or that person on production of—
   (i) a copy of a parental responsibility agreement made between them in relation to the child; and
   (ii) a declaration in the prescribed form by the person making the request stating that the agreement was made in compliance with section 4 of the Children Act 1989 and has not been brought to an end by an order of a court; or

(e) at the request of the mother or that person on production of—
   (i) a certified copy of an order under section 4 of the Children Act 1989 giving that person parental responsibility for the child; and
   (ii) a declaration in the prescribed form by the person making the request stating that the order has not been brought to an end by an order of a court; or

(f) at the request of the mother or that person on production of—
   (i) a certified copy of an order under paragraph 1 of Schedule 1 to the Children Act

---

7   This s. 10A is as substituted by s. 25 of the Family Law Reform Act 1987 and as further amended by the Children Act 1989 s. 108(7), Sch. 15—see p. 878, post—as from 14 October 1991.

1989 which requires that person to make any financial provision for the child and which is not an order falling within paragraph 4(3) of that Schedule; and
  (ii) a declaration in the prescribed form by the person making the request stating that the order has not been discharged by an order of a court; or
(g) at the request of the mother or that person on production of—
  (i) a certified copy of any of the orders which are mentioned in subsection (1A) of this section which has been made in relation to the child; and
  (ii) a declaration in the prescribed form by the person making the request stating that the order has not been brought to an end or discharged by an order of a court.

(1A) The orders are—

(a) an order under section 4 of the Family Law Reform Act 1987 that that person shall have all the parental rights and duties with respect to the child;
(b) an order that that person shall have custody or care and control or legal custody of the child made under section 9 of the Guardianship of Minors Act 1971 at a time when such an order could only be made in favour of a parent;
(c) an order under section 9 or 11B of that Act which requires that person to make any financial provision in relation to the child;
(d) an order under section 4 of the Affiliation Proceedings Act 1957 naming that person as putative father of the child.

(2) On the re-registration of a birth under this section—

(a) the registrar shall sign the register;
(b) in the case of a request under paragraph (a) or (b) of subsection (1) of this section, or a request under any of paragraphs (d) to (g) of that subsection made by the mother of the child, the mother shall also sign the register;
(c) in the case of a request under paragraph (a) or (c) of that subsection, or a request made under any of paragraphs (d) to (g) of that subsection by the person requesting to be registered as the father of the child, that person shall also sign the register; and
(d) if the re-registration takes place more than three months after the birth, the superintendent registrar shall also sign the register.

14. Re-registration of births of legitimated persons.—(1) Where, in the case of any person whose birth has been registered in England or Wales, evidence is produced to the Registrar General which appears to him to be satisfactory that that person has become a legitimated person, the Registrar General may authorise at any time the re-registration of that person's birth, and the re-registration shall be effected in such manner and at such place as may be prescribed:
  Provided that, except where—

(a) the name of a person acknowledging himself to be the father of the legitimated person has been entered in the register in pursuance of section 10 [or 10A][8] of this Act; or
(b) the paternity of the legitimated person has been established by an affiliation order or otherwise by a decree of a court of competent jurisdiction; or
(c) a declaration of the legitimacy of the legitimated person has been made under section 17 of the Matrimonial Causes Act 1950[9] [or section 56 of the Family Law Reform Act 1987][10],

the Registrar General shall not authorise the re-registration unless information with a view to obtaining it is furnished by both parents.

(2) [*Power for Registrar General to call for information from, or attendance by, parents where he believes a person to have become legitimated.*]

8   Words 'or 10A' inserted, with effect from 1 January 1977, by Children Act 1975, s.108 and Sch. 3, para. 13(3).
9   See also Matrimonial Causes Act 1973, s. 45 (p. 806, post).
10   Words in square brackets inserted, as from 4 April 1988, by Family Law Reform Act 1987, s. 33 (1), Sch. 2, para. 16(c) (see p. 880, post).

14A. Re-registration after declaration of parentage.—(1) Where, in the case of a person whose birth has been registered in England and Wales—

(a) the Registrar General receives, by virtue of section 56 (4) of the Family Law Act 1986, a notification of the making of a declaration of parentage in respect of that person; and
(b) it appears to him that the birth of that person should be re-registered.

he shall authorise the re-registration of that person's birth, and the re-registration shall be effected in such manner and at such place as may be prescribed.

(2) This section shall apply with the prescribed modifications in relation to births at sea of which a return is sent to the Registrar General[11].

NAVY AND MARINES (WILLS) ACT 1953

(1 & 2 Eliz. 2, c. 24)   [14 July 1953]

1. Repeal of certain special provisions regulating the wills of seamen and marines.—(1) Section five of the Navy and Marines (Wills) Act 1865 (which regulates the operation of wills made by seamen and marines in respect of wages and other property described in that section) and section six of that Act (which makes special provisions as to wills made by seamen and marines while prisoners of war) shall cease to have effect; and accordingly the whole of that Act, the Navy and Marines (Wills) Act 1930, and the Navy and Marines (Wills) Act 1939, are hereby repealed.

(2) The foregoing provisions of this section shall not apply to the will of any person who has died before the commencement of this Act, nor render invalid any will made before the commencement of this Act which would be valid apart from those provisions; and so much of the said section five as relates to the admission to probate in England (in respect of property described in that section) of wills made by seamen and marines in conformity with that section, and to representation under such wills, shall apply in relation to any will so made before the commencement of this Act as if that section had not been repealed.

2. Short title, commencement and extent.—(1) This Act may be cited as the Navy and Marines (Wills) Act 1953.

(2) This Act shall come into operation one month after the date on which it is passed.

(3) It is hereby declared that this Act extends to Northern Ireland.

PUBLIC RECORDS ACT 1958

(6 & 7 Eliz. 2, c. 51)   [23 July 1958]

5. Access to public records.

       *   *   *   *   *

(5) The Lord Chancellor shall as respects all public records in places of deposit appointed by him under this Act outside the Public Record Office require arrangements to be made for their inspection by the public comparable to those made for public records in the Public Record Office, and subject to restrictions corresponding with those contained in the foregoing provisions of this section.

       *   *   *   *   *

11   Section 14A was added, as from 4 April 1988, by Family Law Reform Act 1987, s. 26 (see p. 878, post).

8. Court records.—(1) The Lord Chancellor shall be responsible for the public records of every court of record or magistrates' court which are not in the Public Record Office or a place of deposit appointed by him under this Act and shall have power to determine in the case of any such records the officer in whose custody they are for the time being to be:

   Provided that in the application of this subsection to public records of the Chancery Court of the County Palatine of Lancaster references to the Chancellor of the Duchy of Lancaster shall be substituted for references to the Lord Chancellor.

(2) [*Repealed by Supreme Court Act 1981, s. 152(4) and Sch. 7.*]

(3) [*Repealed by Administration of Justice Act 1969, s. 27(2).*]

(5) Section three of this Act shall not apply to such of the records of ecclesiastical courts described in paragraph (n) of sub-paragraph (1) of paragraph 4 of the First Schedule to this Act as are not held in any office of the Supreme Court or in the Public Record Office, but, if the Lord Chancellor after consulting the President of the [Family Division][12] so directs as respects any of those records, those records shall be transferred to such place of deposit as may be appointed by the Lord Chancellor and shall thereafter be in the custody of such officer as may be so appointed.

(6) The public records which at the commencement of this Act are in the custody of the University of Oxford and which are included in the index a copy of which was transmitted to the principal probate registrar under section two of the Oxford University Act 1860, shall not be required to be transferred under the last foregoing subsection but the Lord Chancellor shall make arrangements with the University of Oxford as to the conditions under which those records may be inspected by the public.

* * * * *

13. Short title, repeals and commencement.—(1) This Act may be cited as the Public Records Act 1958.

(3) This Act shall come into force on the first day of January, nineteen hundred and fifty-nine.

SCHEDULES
FIRST SCHEDULE   Section 10

DEFINITION OF PUBLIC RECORDS

1. The provisions of this Schedule shall have effect for determining what are public records for the purposes of this Act.

* * * * *

Records of courts and tribunals

4.—(1) Subject to the provisions of this paragraph, records of the following descriptions shall be public records for the purposes of this Act:

(a) records of, or held in any department of, the Supreme Court (including any court held under a commission of assize);

* * * * *

(n) records of ecclesiastical courts when exercising the testamentary and matrimonial jurisdiction removed from them by the Court of Probate Act 1857, and the Matrimonial Causes Act 1857, respectively;

* * * * *

(3) In this paragraph 'records' includes records of any proceedings in the court or tribunal in

---

12 Words in brackets substituted by Administration of Justice Act 1970, s. 1 and Sch. 2.

question and includes rolls, writs, books, decrees, bills, warrants and accounts of, or in the custody of, the court or tribunal in question.

*   *   *   *   *

Interpretation

8. It is hereby declared that any description of government department, court, tribunal or other body or establishment in this Schedule by reference to which a class of public records is framed extends to a government department, court, tribunal or other body or establishment, as the case may be, which has ceased to exist, whether before or after the passing of this Act.

ADOPTION ACT 1958

(7 Eliz. 2, c. 5)   [18 December 1958]

Note

Sections 16 and 17 of the Act of 1958 were repealed as respects things done or events occurring (e.g. deaths) after 31 December 1975, by the Children Act 1975, s. 108 and Sch. 4, Pt. 1. Succession rights of adopted persons were subsequently regulated by Sch. 1 to the Children Act 1975; the relevant provisions of Sch. 1 have since been re-enacted by the Adoption Act 1976, and are contained in Part IV of that Act (see pp. 828, ff., post). The Adoption Act 1976 came into force on 1 January 1988 and repealed the whole of the Adoption Act 1958 then remaining unrepealed. The whole of the Children Act 1975 was repealed, with effect from 14 October 1991, by the Children Act 1989, s. 108(7), Sch. 15 (see p. 893, post).

PART I

ADOPTION ORDERS

16. *English intestacies, wills and settlements.* —(1) *Where, at any time after the making of an adoption order, the adopter or the adopted person or any other person dies intestate in respect of any real or personal property (other than property subject to an entailed interest under a disposition to which subsection (2) of this section does not apply), that property shall devolve in all respects as if the adopted person were the child of the adopter born in lawful wedlock and were not the child of any other person.*

(2) *In any disposition of real or personal property made, whether by instrument inter vivos or by will (including codicil) after the date of an adoption order—*

(a) *any reference (whether express or implied) to the child or children of the adopter shall, unless the contrary intention appears, be construed as, or as including, a reference to the adopted person;*

(b) *any reference (whether express or implied) to the child or children of the adopted person's natural parents or either of them shall, unless the contrary intention appears. be construed as not being, or as not including. a reference to the adopted person; and*

(c) *any reference (whether express or implied) to a person related to the adopted person in any degree shall, unless the contrary intention appears, be construed as a reference to the person who would be related to him in that degree if he were the child of the adopter born in lawful wedlock and were not the child of any other person.*

(3) *Where under any disposition any real or personal property or any interest in such property is limited (whether subject to any preceding limitation or charge or not) in such a way that it would, apart from this section, devolve (as nearly as the law permits) along with a dignity or title of honour, then, whether or not the disposition contains an express reference to the dignity or title of honour, and whether or not the property or some interest in the property may in some event become severed therefrom, nothing in this section shall operate*

to sever the property or any interest therein from the dignity, but the property or interest shall devolve in all respects as if this section had not been enacted.

(4) The references in this section to an adoption order include references to an order authorising an adoption made under the Adoption of Children Act (Northern Ireland) 1950, or any enactment of the Parliament of Northern Ireland for the time being in force[13].

17. Provisions supplementary to s. 16.—*(1) For the purposes of the application of the Administration of Estates Act 1925. to the devolution of any property in accordance with the provisions of the last foregoing section, and for the purposes of the construction of any such disposition as is mentioned in that section, an adopted person shall be deemed to be related to any other person being the child or adopted child of the adopter or (in the case of a joint adoption) of either of the adopters—*

(a) *where he or she was adopted by two spouses jointly, and that other person is the child or adopted child of both of them, as brother or sister of the whole blood;*
(b) *in any other case, as brother or sister of the half blood.*

(2) For the purposes of subsection (2) of the last foregoing section, a disposition made by will or codicil shall be treated as made on the date of the death of the testator.

(3) Notwithstanding anything in the last foregoing section, trustees or personal representatives may convey or distribute any real or personal property to or among the persons entitled thereto without having ascertained that no adoption order has been made by virtue of which any person is or may be entitled to any interest therein, and shall not be liable to any such person of whose claim they have not had notice at the time of the conveyance or distribution; but nothing in this subsection shall prejudice the right of any such person to follow the property, or any property representing it, into the hands of any person, other than a purchaser. who may have received it[14].

(4) Where an adoption order is made in respect of a person who has been previously adopted, the previous adoption shall be disregarded for the purposes of the last foregoing section in relation to the devolution of any property on the death of a person dying intestate after the date of the subsequent adoption order, and in relation to any disposition of property made, or taking effect on the death of a person dying, after that date.

(5) The references in this section to an adoption order shall be construed in accordance with subsection (4) of the last foregoing section[15].

26. Legitimation: revocation of adoption orders . . .—*(1) Where any person adopted by his father or mother alone has subsequently become a legitimated person on the marriage of his father and mother, the court by which the adoption order was made may, on the application of any of the parties concerned, revoke that order.*

PART V

MISCELLANEOUS AND GENERAL

53. Provisional adoption by persons domiciled outside Great Britain.—*(1) If the court is satisfied, upon an application being made by a person who is not domiciled in England or Scotland, that the applicant intends to adopt a child*[16] *under the law of or within the country in which he is domiciled, and for that purpose desires to remove the child*[16] *from Great Britain either immediately or after an interval, the court may, subject to the provisions of this section, make an order (in this section referred to as a provisional adoption order)*

13   The repeal of ss. 16 and 17 by the Children Act 1975, s. 108 and Sch. 4, Pt. I, has effect subject to para. 5(2) of Sch. I to the Act of 1975.
14   Section 17(3) extended to adoption orders made in the Isle of Man or any of the Channel Islands by Adoption Act 1964, s. 1(1).
15   See fn. 13, above.
16   The expression child substituted for 'infant', wherever it appears in the Act, with effect from 1 January 1976, by Children Act 1975, s. 108 and Sch. 3, para. 21.

authorising the applicant to remove the child[16] *for the purpose aforesaid, and giving to the applicant the custody of the child*[16] *pending his adoption as aforesaid.*

*   *   *   *   *

(4) *Subject to the provisions of this section, the provisions of this Act, other than this section and sections sixteen, seventeen and nineteen, shall apply in relation to a provisional adoption order as they apply, in relation to an adoption order, and references in those provisions to adoption, to an adoption order, to an application or applicant for such an order and to an adopter or a person adopted or authorised to be adopted under such an order shall be construed accordingly.*

60. Short title, extent, commencement.—(1) *This Act may be cited as the Adoption Act 1958.*

*   *   *   *   *

(3) *This Act comes into force on the first day of April, nineteen hundred and fifty-nine.*

ADOPTION ACT 1960

(8 & 9 Eliz. 2. c. 59)   [29 July 1960]

Note.—The remaining unrepealed part of this Act was repealed and re-enacted by the Adoption Act 1976 (see p. 826, post) when that latter Act was brought into force on 1 January 1988.

1. Further provision for revocation of adoption orders in cases of legitimation.—(1) *Where any person legitimated by virtue of section one of the Legitimacy Act 1959 had been adopted by his father and mother before the commencement of that Act, the court by which the adoption order was made may, on the application of any of the parties concerned, revoke that order.*

(2) *The revocation of an adoption order under this section, or under section twenty-six of the Adoption Act, 1958, shall not affect the operation of sections sixteen and seventeen of that Act in relation to an intestacy which occurred, or a disposition which was made, before the revocation*[17].

(3) *This section shall be construed as one with section twenty-six of the Adoption Act 1958; and any reference in that Act to that section or to subsection (1) of that section shall be construed as including a reference to subsection (1) of this section.*

3. Short title and extent.—(1) *This Act may be cited as the Adoption Act 1960.*

(2) *This Act does not extend to Northern Ireland.*

WILLS ACT 1963

(1963, c. 44)   [31 July 1963]

1. General rule as to formal validity.—(1) A will shall be treated as properly executed if its execution conformed to the internal law in force in the territory where it was executed, or in the territory where, at the time of its execution or of the testator's death, he was domiciled or had his habitual residence, or in a state of which, at either of those times, he was a national.

---

17   Section 1(2) repealed with effect from 1 January 1976 by Children Act 1975, s. 108 and Sch. 4, Pt. I.

2. Additional rules.—(1) Without prejudice to the preceding section, the following shall be treated as properly executed—

(a) a will executed on board a vessel or aircraft of any description, if the execution of the will conformed to the internal law in force in the territory with which, having regard to its registration (if any) and other relevant circumstances, the vessel or aircraft may be taken to have been most closely connected;

(b) a will so far as it disposes of immovable property, if its execution conformed to the internal law in force in the territory where the property was situated;

(c) a will so far as it revokes a will which under this Act would be treated as properly executed or revokes a provision which under this Act would be treated as comprised in a properly executed will, if the execution of the later will conformed to any law by reference to which the revoked will or provision would be so treated;

(d) a will so far as it exercises a power of appointment, if the execution of the will conformed to the law governing the essential validity of the power.

(2) A will so far as it exercises a power of appointment shall not be treated as improperly executed by reason only that its execution was not in accordance with any formal requirements contained in the instrument creating the power.

3. Certain requirements to be treated as formal. Where (whether in pursuance of this Act or not) a law in force outside the United Kingdom falls to be applied in relation to a will, any requirement of that law whereby special formalities are to be observed by testators answering a particular description, or witnesses to the execution of a will are to possess certain qualifications, shall be treated, notwithstanding any rule of that law to the contrary, as a formal requirement only.

4. Construction of wills. The construction of a will shall not be altered by reason of any change in the testator's domicil after the execution of the will.

5. [*Repealed and replaced by Succession (Scotland) Act 1964, s. 32.*]

6. Interpretation.—(1) In this Act—
'internal law' in relation to any territory or state means the law which would apply in a case where no question of the law in force in any other territory or state arose;
'state' means a territory or group of territories having its own law of nationality;
'will' includes any testamentary instrument or act, and 'testator' shall be construed accordingly.

(2) Where under this Act the internal law in force in any territory or state is to be applied in the case of a will, but there are in force in that territory or state two or more systems of internal law relating to the formal validity of wills, the system to be applied shall be ascertained as follows—

(a) if there is in force throughout the territory or state a rule indicating which of those systems can properly be applied in the case in question, that rule shall be followed; or

(b) if there is no such rule, the system shall be that with which the testator was most closely connected at the relevant time, and for this purpose the relevant time is the time of the testator's death where the matter is to be determined by reference to circumstances prevailing at his death, and the time of execution of the will in any other case.

(3) In determining for the purposes of this Act whether or not the execution of a will conformed to a particular law, regard shall be had to the formal requirements of that law at the time of execution, but this shall not prevent account being taken of an alteration of law affecting wills executed at that time if the alteration enables the will to be treated as properly executed.

7. Short title, commencement, repeal and extent.—(1) This Act may be cited as the Wills Act 1963.

(2) This Act shall come into operation on 1 January 1964.

(3) The Wills Act 1861 is hereby repealed.

(4) This Act shall not apply to a will of a testator who died before the time of the commencement of this Act and shall apply to a will of a testator who dies after that time whether the will was executed before or after that time, but so that the repeal of the Wills Act 1861 shall not invalidate a will executed before that time.

(5) It is hereby declared that this Act extends to Northern Ireland [*Remaining words repealed by Northern Ireland Constitution Act 1973, s. 41(1) and Sch. 6.*]

PERPETUITIES AND ACCUMULATIONS ACT 1964

(1964, c. 55)   [16 July 1964]

4. Reduction of age and exclusion of class members to avoid remoteness.—(1) Where a disposition is limited by reference to the attainment by any person or persons of a specified age exceeding twenty-one years, and it is apparent at the time the disposition is made or becomes apparent at a subsequent time—

(a) that the disposition would, apart from this section, be void for remoteness, but
(b) that it would not be so void if the specified age had been twenty-one years,

the disposition shall be treated for all purposes as if, instead of being limited by reference to the age in fact specified, it had been limited by reference to the age nearest to that age which would, if specified instead, have prevented the disposition from being so void.

(2) Where in the case of any disposition different ages exceeding twenty-one years are specified in relation to different persons—

(a) the reference in paragraph (b) of subsection (1) above to the specified age shall be construed as a reference to all the specified ages, and
(b) that subsection shall operate to reduce each such age so far as is necessary to save the disposition from being void for remoteness.

(3) Where the inclusion of any persons, being potential members of a class or unborn persons who at birth would become members or potential members of the class, prevents the foregoing provisions of this section from operating to save a disposition from being void for remoteness, those persons shall thenceforth be deemed for all the purposes of the disposition to be excluded from the class, and the said provisions shall thereupon have effect accordingly.

(4) Where in the case of a disposition to which subsection (3) above does not apply, it is apparent at the time the disposition is made or becomes apparent at a subsequent time that apart from this subsection, the inclusion of any persons, being potential members of a class or unborn persons who at birth would become members or potential members of the class, would cause the disposition to be treated as void for remoteness, those persons shall, unless their exclusion would exhaust the class, thenceforth be deemed for all the purposes of the disposition to be excluded from the class.

(5) Where this section has effect in relation to a disposition to which section 3 above applies, the operation of this section shall not affect the validity of anything previously done in relation to the interest disposed of by way of advancement, application of intermediate income or otherwise.

(6) Section 163 of the Law of Property Act 1925 (which saves a disposition. from remoteness arising out of a condition requiring the attainment of an age exceeding twenty-one years) is hereby repealed.

(7) For the avoidance of doubt it is hereby declared that a question arising under section 3 of

this Act or subsection (1) (a) above of whether a disposition would be void apart from this section is to be determined as if subsection (6) above had been a separate section of this Act[18].

*　　　　*　　　　*　　　　*　　　　*

15. Short title, interpretation and extent.—(5) The foregoing sections of this Act shall apply (except as provided in section 8 (2) above) only in relation to instruments taking effect after the commencement of this Act, and in the case of an instrument made in the exercise of a special power of appointment shall apply only where the instrument creating the power takes effect after that commencement:

Provided that section 7 above shall apply in all cases for construing the foregoing reference to a special power of appointment.

*　　　　*　　　　*　　　　*　　　　*

ADMINISTRATION OF ESTATES (SMALL PAYMENTS) ACT 1965

(1965, c. 32)   [5 August 1965]

1. Increase in amounts disposable on death without representation.—(1) In the enactments and instruments listed in Schedule 1 to this Act, of which—

(a) those listed in Part I are enactments authorising the disposal of property on death, without the necessity for probate or other proof of title, to persons appearing to be beneficially entitled thereto, to relatives or dependants of the deceased or to other persons described in the enactments, but subject to a limit which is in most cases £100 and which does not in any case exceed £100;

(b) those listed in Part II are enactments giving power to makes rules or regulations containing corresponding provisions subject to a limit of £100; and

(c) those listed in Part III are such rules and regulations as aforesaid and instruments containing corresponding provisions made under other enactments and containing a limit which does not in any case exceed £200;

the said limit shall, subject to the provisions of that Schedule, in each case be [£5,000][19] instead of the limit specified in the enactment or instrument, and for references to the said limits in those enactments and instruments there shall accordingly be substituted references to [£5,000][19].

[(2)   *Repealed: see now National Debt Act 1972, s. 6.*]

2. Increase in amounts disposable on death by nomination—(1) In the enactments and instrument listed in Schedule 2 to this Act (which enable a person by nomination to dispose of property on his death up to a limit of £100 or, in some cases, £200) the said limit shall, subject to the provisions of that Schedule, in each case be [£5,000][19] instead of the limit specified in the enactments or instrument; and for references to the said limits in the said enactments and instrument there shall accordingly be substituted references to [£5,000][19].

(2) This section shall apply in relation to any nomination delivered at or sent to the appropriate office, or made in the appropriate book, after the expiration of a period of one month beginning with the date on which this Act is passed.

18   Section 4(7) added by Children Act 1975, s. 108 and Sch. 3, para. 43.
19   Under the power given by s. 6 of this Act, in relation to deaths occurring on or after 11 May 1984, ss. 1 and 2 have effect as if the figure of £5,000 were substituted in place of £500 (for deaths occurring before 11 May 1984 but on or after 10 August 1975, ss. 1 and 2 have effect as if the figure of £1,500 were substituted for that of £500) so far as they relate to any enactment (Administration of Estates (Small Payments) (Increase of Limit) Orders 1984 and 1975).

3. Extension of certain enactments relating to intestacies to cases where deceased leaves a will.—(1) The enactments mentioned in Schedule 3 to this Act (all of which are listed in Part I of Schedule 1 to this Act) shall have effect subject to the amendments in that Schedule, which are amendments extending the operation of those enactments to cases where the deceased leaves a will.

(2) This section shall not extend to Northern Ireland.

4. Estate duty.—(1) Section 25 (2) of the Local Government Superannuation Act 1953 (under which a certificate as to estate duty may be required before a payment without representation is made under that section), section 24 (4) of the Industrial and Provident Societies Act 1965 (under which a similar certificate is required before a payment is made on a nomination under that Act) and so much of section 61 (11) of the London Midland and Scottish Railway Act 1924, section 99 (12) of the Southern Railway Act 1924 and section 3 (12) of the London and North Eastern Railway Act 1944 (which relate to the railway savings banks) as contains corresponding provisions shall cease to have effect.

(2) *Nothing in this Act shall affect section 8 (1) of the Finance Act 1894 (which applies, in relation to estate duty, certain provisions of the law relating to probate duty).*

(3) *In the last foregoing subsection the reference to the said section 8 (1) includes a reference to that section as it applies in Northern Ireland; but, save as aforesaid, this section shall not extend to Northern Ireland*[20].

5. Power to amend or repeal corresponding or superseded enactments.—(1) If it appears to the Treasury that any provision in an Act (including a local Act) passed before this Act corresponds to any provision amended by section 1 or section 2 of this Act [or to section 66 (1) and (2), 67 or 68 of the Friendly Societies Act 1974][1] [or to section 27 (4) of the Trustee Savings Bank Act 1981][2] [or to section 6 (1) of the National Debt Act 1972][3] and contains a limit of less than [£5,000][4], the Treasury may by order substitute a limit of [£5,000][4] for the limit contained in that provision, but subject to such exceptions, if any, including exceptions as regards the operation of the order in Northern Ireland, the Isle of Man, the Channel Islands or any other place outside Great Britain, as may be specified in the order; and an order under this subsection may make such consequential amendments in the Act to which it relates as appear to the Treasury to be expedient.

(2) If it appears to the Treasury that any provision in a local Act passed before the Local Government Superannuation Act 1953 is wholly or mainly superseded by section 25 (1) of the said Act of 1953 as amended by section 1 of this Act, the Treasury may by order repeal that provision.

(3) An order under subsection (1) of this section amending a local Act may repeal any provision of that Act corresponding to any provision repealed by section 4 of this Act.

(4) No order shall be made under this section in respect of any provision in a local Act the Bill for which was promoted by a local authority except on the application of that authority or their successors.

(5) Any order under this section shall be made by statutory instrument subject to annulment in pursuance of a resolution of either House of Parliament.

---

20   In relation to deaths after 12 March 1975, subsections (2) and (3) are repealed by Finance Act 1975, s. 59, and Sch. 13, Pt. 1.
1   Inserted by Friendly Societies Act 1974, Sch. 10, para. 19.
2   Inserted by Trustee Savings Bank Act 1981, s. 55(1) and Sch. 6.
3   Inserted by National Debt Act 1972, s. 6(3).
4   By virtue of s. 6(3) of this Act, in relation to deaths occurring on or after 11 May 1984 the references to £500 in this subsection are to be read as £5,000. For deaths before 11 May 1984 but on or after 10 August 1975, the references to £500 in this subsection are to be read as £1,500, the Administration of Estates (Small Payments) (Increase of Limit) Orders 1984 and 1975 having increased the limit of £500 appearing in ss. 1 and 2 of the Act in relation to such deaths.

6. Power to provide for further increases.—(1) The Treasury may from time to time by order direct that—

(a) sections 1 and 2 of this Act, so far as they relate to any enactment; and

(b) [*section 8 of the Superannuation Act 1887*[5] section 38 (2) of the Finance Act 1918 [*and*] section 14 (2) of the Ministerial Salaries and Members' Pensions Act 1965 [and section 24 of the Parliamentary and Other Pensions Act 1972][6] (which contain provisions similar to the enactments to which section 1 of this Act relates but subject to a limit of £500); [and

(c) section 66 (2) of the Merchant Shipping Act 1970; and

(d) section 6 (1) of the National Debt Act 1972.][7]

shall have effect as if for references to £500 there were substituted references to such higher amount as may be specified in the order.

(2) Any order under this section shall apply in relation to deaths occurring after the expiration of a period of one month beginning with the date on which the order comes into force, except that, so far as section 2 of this Act has effect by virtue of any such order, subsection (2) of that section shall apply as if for the reference to the date on which this Act is passed there were substituted a reference to the date on which the order comes into force.

(3) Where an order under this section [or section 28 of the Trustee Savings Bank Act 1981][8] specifying any amount is in force, references in section 5 (1) of this Act to £500 shall be construed as references to the amount specified in the order.

(4) Any order under this section may be revoked by a subsequent order and shall be made by statutory instrument; and no such order shall be made unless a draft of the order has been laid before Parliament and approved by a resolution of each House of Parliament.

7. Short title, interpretation, extent, commencement and repeals.—(1) This Act may be cited as the Administration of Estates (Small Payments) Act 1965.

(2) Any reference in this Act to an enactment or instrument shall be construed as including a reference to that enactment or instrument as amended, extended or applied by any other enactment or instrument.

(3) The amendment of any instrument by this Act shall be without prejudice to any power of amending or revoking that instrument.

(4) Save as otherwise expressly provided, so far as this Act amends or gives power to amend, or repeals, any provision which extends to any place outside Great Britain it shall have the same extent.

(5) Subject to sections 2 (2) and 6 (2) of this Act, this Act shall apply in relation to deaths occurring after the expiration of a period of one month beginning with the date on which it is passed.

(6) The enactments mentioned in Schedule 4 to this Act are hereby repealed to the extent specified in the third column of that Schedule, but this subsection shall not affect the operation of those enactments in relation to deaths occurring before the expiration of the said period.

---

5   Words in brackets repealed by Judicial Pensions Act 1981, s. 36 and Sch. 4.
6   Words in brackets inserted by Parliamentary and Other Pensions Act 1972, s. 24(4).
7   Paras. (c) and (d) inserted by Merchant Shipping Act 1970, s. 100 and Sch. 5 and National Debt Act 1972, s. 6(3), respectively.
8   Words in brackets inserted by Trustee Savings Bank Act 1981, s. 55(1) and Sch. 6.

SCHEDULES

SCHEDULE I
Section 1

STATUTORY PROVISIONS AUTHORISING DISPOSAL OF PROPERTY ON DEATH WITHOUT

REPRESENTATION

PART I

ENACTMENTS[9]

Short title and chapter	Provision amended by section 1
The Loan Societies Act 1840 (3 & 4 Vict. c. 110).	Section 11.
The Navy and Marines (Property of Deceased) Act 1865 (28 & 29 Vict. c. 11).	Sections 5, 6 and 8.
The Great Western Railway Act 1885 (48 & 49 Vict. c. cxlvii).	Section 45(8).
The Regimental Debts Act 1893 (56 & 57 Vict. c. 5).	Sections 7 and 9 and, except in relation to liability to estate duty, section 16.
The Taff Vale Railway Act 1895 (58 & 59 Vict. c. cxxii).	Section 18(10).
The Superannuation (Ecclesiastical Commissioners and Queen Anne's Bounty) Act 1914 (4 & 5 Geo. 5, c. 5).	Section 7.
The Constabulary (Ireland) Act 1922 (12 & 13 Geo. 5, c. 55).	Paragraph 15 (3) of Part II of the Schedule.
The London Midland and Scottish Railway Act 1924 (14 & 15 Geo. 5, c. liv).	Section 61 (11) except as it applies in Northern Ireland.
The Southern Railway Act 1924 (14 & 15 Geo. 5, c. lxvi).	Section 99 (12).
The Government Annuities Act 1929 (19 & 20 Geo. 5, c. 29).	Sections 21 and 57.
The Superannuation (Various Services) Act 1938 (1 & 2 Geo. 6, c. 13).	Section 2.
The Greenwich Hospital Act 1942 (5 & 6 Geo. 6, c. 35).	Section 2.
The London and North Eastern Railway Act 1944 (7 & 8 Geo. 6, c. x).	Section 3 (12)(b).
The U.S.A. Veteran's Pensions (Administration) Act 1949 (12, 13 & 14 Geo. 6, c. 45).	Section 1 (3) (c).
The Local Government Superannuation Act 1953 (1 & 2 Eliz. 2, c. 25).	Section 25 (1).
The Building Societies Act 1962 (10 & 11 Eliz. 2, c. 37).	Section 46 (1), but not so as to affect paragraph 7 of Schedule 8.
The Industrial and Provident Societies Act 1965 (1965 c. 12).	Section 25.

PART II

ENABLING ENACTMENTS

Short title and chapter	Provision amended by section 1
The Pensions and Yeomanry Pay Act 1884 (47 & 48 Vict. c. 55).	Section 4.
The Elementary School Teachers (Superannuation) Act 1898 (61 & 62 Vict. c. 57).	Section 6 (1) (d).

9 Various entries in Sch. 1, as originally enacted, are repealed and have been omitted from the text.

Part III

Instruments

Title and number	Provision amended by section 1
Rules of the Supreme Court.	Rule 11 of Order 22.
Amended regulations dated 11 July 1907, and made by the Secretary of State for War under section 4 of the Pensions and Yeomanry Pay Act 1884.	Paragraph 1.
Regulations as to the suitors fund and fee fund accounts (S.R. & 0. 1913/1332).	Regulation 13 (b) and (c) and Form 1 in the Appendix.
The Elementary School Teachers (Superannuation) Rules 1919 (S.R. & O. 1920/2298).	Rule 15.
Regulations dated 27 November 1920, and made by the Secretary of State for Air under section 4 of the Pensions and Yeomanry Pay Act 1884, as applied to the Royal Air Force by the Air Force (Application of Enactments) (No. 2) Order 1918.	Paragraph 1.
The Royal Irish Constabulary Pensions Order 1922 (S.R. & 0. 1922/945).	Article 15 (3).
Supreme Court Fund Rules 1927 (S.R. & O. 1927/1184).	Rule 62 and Forms 63 and 64 in the Appendix.
The Trustee Savings Banks Regulations 1929 (S.R. & O. 1929/1048).	Regulation 28 (1).
The Savings Certificate Regulations 1933 (S.R. & O. 1933/1149).	Regulation 19 (1).
Rules of the Supreme Court (Northern Ireland) 1936 (S.R. & O. 1936/70).	Rule 12 of Order 22.
County Court Rules (S.R. & O. 1936/626).	Rule 22 of Order 48.
Treasury Order dated 8 April 1938, prescribing certain public departments for the purposes of section 8 of the Superannuation Act 1887, and making regulations with respect to the distribution without probate under the said section of sums due from a public department (S.R. & 0. 1938/303).	Article 2 and the Schedule.
The Superannuation (Various Services) Regulations 1938 (S.R. & O. 1938/304).	Article 1 and the Schedule.
The Post Office Savings Bank Regulations 1938 (S.R. & O. 1938/556).	Regulation 39 (1).
The Compensation to Seamen (War Damage to Effects) Scheme 1945 (S.R. &O. 1945/1164).	Article 4.
The Navy and Marines (Property of Deceased) Order 1956 (S.I. 1956/1217).	Article 16.
The Premium Savings Bonds Regulations 1956 (S.I. 1956/1657).	Regulation 9.
The Teachers (Superannuation) (Scotland) Regulations 1957 (S.I. 1957/356).	Regulation 58 (1).
The Military Pensions (Commonwealth Relations Office) Regulations 1959 (S.I. 1959/735).	Regulation 2 and the Schedule.
The Court of Protection Rules 1960 (S.I. 1960/1146).	Rule 83 (2).
The Police Pensions Regulations 1962 (S.I. 1962/2756).	Regulation 57 (3).
The Firemen's Pension Scheme Order 1964 (S.I. 1964/1148).	Article 47 (3).

SCHEDULE 2[10]

Section 2

STATUTORY PROVISIONS AUTHORISING DISPOSAL OF PROPERTY ON DEATH BY NOMINATION

Title and chapter or serial number	Provision amended by section 2
The Trade Union Act Amendment Act 1876 (39 & 40 Vict. c. 22).	Section 10 except as it applies in Northern Ireland.
The Great Western Railway Act 1885 (48 & 49 Vict. c. cxlvii).	Section 45(7).
The Taff Vale Railway Act 1895 (58 & 59 Vict. c. cxxii).	Section 18(9).
The London Midland and Scottish Railway Act 1924 (14 & 15 Geo. 5, c. liv).	Section 61(9).
The Southern Railway Act 1924 (14 & 15 Geo. 5, c. lxvi).	Section 99(10).
The Trustee Savings Bank Regulations 1929 (S.R. & O. 1929/ 1048).	Regulations 11, 21 and 22.
The Industrial and Provident Societies Act 1965 (1965 c. 12).	Section 23(3)(c).

SCHEDULE 3[10]

Section 3

EXTENSION OF ENACTMENTS RELATING TO INTESTACIES
THE LOAN SOCIETIES ACT 1840

(3 & 4 Vict. c. 110)

In section 11—

for the words 'that no will was made and left by such deceased person' there shall be substituted the words 'that no will of the deceased has been or will be proved';

[*the words 'under the Statute of Distribution' and the word 'intestate' in each place where it occurs, shall be omitted*][11]; and

after the words 'although no letters of administration shall have been taken out' there shall be inserted the words 'and no probate of any will has been granted'.

THE GREAT WESTERN RAILWAY ACT 1885

(48 & 49 Vict. c. cxlvii)

In section 45(8) [*the words 'intestate and' shall be omitted, and*][11] after the words 'without letters of administration' there shall be inserted the words 'or probate of any will'.

THE TAFF VALE RAILWAY ACT 1895

(58 & 59 Vict. c. cxxii)

In section 18(10)(c) [*the words 'intestate and' shall be omitted, and*][11] after the words 'without letters of administration' there shall be inserted the words 'or probate of any will'.

THE LONDON MIDLAND AND SCOTTISH RAILWAY ACT 1924

(14 & 15 Geo. 5, c. liv)

In section 61(11) [*the words 'intestate and' shall be omitted, and*][11] after the words 'without letters of administration' there shall be inserted the words 'or probate of any will'.

THE SOUTHERN RAILWAY ACT 1924

(14 &15 Geo. 5, c. lxvi)

In section 99(12) [*the words 'intestate and' shall be omitted, and*][11] after the words 'without letters of administration' there shall be inserted the words 'or probate of any will'.

THE BUILDING SOCIETIES ACT 1962

(10 & 11 Eliz. 2, c. 37)

In section 46—

[*in subsection (1) the word 'intestate' shall be omitted*][11];

in subsection (2), after the words 'without the grant of letters of administration' there shall be inserted the words 'or probate of any will', [*and the words from 'with respect to the distribution' to the end of the subsection shall be omitted*][11];

10 Entries in Schedules 2 and 3, as originally enacted, which have since been repealed are omitted from the text.

11 Words in italics repealed by the Statute Law (Repeals) Act 1974.

in subsection (3), for the words 'died intestate' there shall be substituted the words 'has died'; and in subsection (4) the words 'in the belief that he died intestate' shall be omitted.

THE INDUSTRIAL AND PROVIDENT SOCIETIES ACT 1965

(1965 c. 12)

In section 25(1) [*the word 'intestate' shall be omitted, and*][11] after the words 'without letters of administration' there shall be inserted the words 'or probate of any will'.

MATRIMONIAL CAUSES ACT 1965

(1965, c. 72)   [8 November 1965]

[**11. Legitimacy of children of annulled marriages.** *Where a decree of nullity is granted in respect of a voidable marriage, any child who would have been the legitimate child of the parties to the marriage if at the date of the decree it had been dissolved instead of being annulled shall be deemed to be their legitimate child.*][12]

*   *   *   *   *

20. Judicial separation.

*   *   *   *   *

[(3) *In the case of judicial separation—*

(a) *any property which is acquired by or devolves upon the wife on or after the date of the decree whilst the separation continues; and*

(b) *where the decree is obtained by the wife, any property to which she is entitled for an estate in remainder or reversion on the date of the decree,*

shall, if she dies intestate, devolve as if her husband had then been dead.][13]

*   *   *   *   *

39.—[*Repealed and replaced by Matrimonial Causes Act 1973, s. 45: see p. 806, post.*]

Note.—*Matrimonial Causes Act 1973, s. 45 now repealed by Family Law Act 1986, s. 68(2), Sch. 2, but see also ss. 55 and 56 of that later Act—pp. 870, 871, post.*

FAMILY PROVISION ACT 1966

(1966, c. 35)   [17 November 1966]

1. Increase of net sum payable to surviving husband or wife on intestacy.—(1) In the case of a person dying after the coming into force of this section, section 46 (1) of the Administration of Estates Act 1925, as amended by section 1 of the Intestates' Estates Act 1952, and set out in Schedule 1 to that Act, shall apply as if the net sums charged by paragraph (i) on the residuary estate in favour of a surviving husband or wife were as follows, that is to say—

(a) under paragraph (2) of the Table (which charges a net sum of £5,000 where the intestate leaves issue) a sum of £8,750 or of such larger amount as may from time to time be fixed by order of the Lord Chancellor; and

12   Section 11 repealed by s. 54(1)(b) and Sch. 3 of the Matrimonial Causes Act 1973, but, in relation to decrees of nullity granted before 1 August 1971 in respect of voidable marriages, its effect is preserved by s. 53 of and Sch. 1, Pt. II, para. 12 to the Act of 1973. As to decrees granted on or after 1 August 1971, see. s. 16 of the Act of 1973 (p. 806, post).

13   Repealed, save in relation to deaths occurring before 1 August 1970, by Matrimonial Proceedings and Property Act 1970, s. 40(3): see Matrimonial Causes Act 1973, Sch. 1, Pt. II, para. 13 (p. 806, post).

(b) under paragraph (3) of the Table (which charges a net sum of £20,000 where the intestate leaves certain close relatives but no issue) a sum of £30,000 or of such larger amount as may from time to time be so fixed.

(2) Accordingly in relation to the estate of a person dying after the coming into force of this section sections 46, 48 and 49 (as so amended and set out) of the Administration of Estates Act 1925, shall be further amended as follows—

(a) in the Table in section 46(1)(i) for the words 'net sum of £5,000' in paragraph (2), and for the words 'net sum of £20,000' in paragraph (3), there shall in each case be substituted the words 'fixed net sum', and at the end of the Table there shall be added 'The fixed net sums referred to in paragraphs (2) and (3) of this Table shall be of the amounts provided by or under section 1 of the Family Provision Act, 1966';
(b) in sections 46(4) and 48(2)(a) for the words 'the net sum of £5,000 or, as the case may be, £20,000', and in section 49(1)(aa) for the words 'the net sum of £5,000 or £20,000', there shall in each case be substituted the words 'the fixed net sum';

and any reference in any other enactment to the said net sum of £5,000 or the said net sum of £20,000 shall have effect as a reference to the corresponding net sum of the amount fixed by or under this section.

(3) Any order of the Lord Chancellor under this section fixing the amount of either of the said net sums shall have effect (and, so far as relates to that sum, shall supersede any previous order) in relation to the estate of any person dying after the coming into force of the order.

(4) Any order of the Lord Chancellor under this section shall be made by statutory instrument, and a draft of the statutory instrument shall be laid before Parliament[14].

[NOTE: *This section came into force on 1 January 1967 (Family Provision Act 1966 (Commencement No. 1) Order 1966).*]

* * * * *

10. Short title, repeal, etc.—(1) This Act may be cited as the Family Provision Act 1966.

[(2) *Repealed by Inheritance (Provision for Family and Dependants) Act 1975, s. 26 and Sch.*]

(3) Nothing in this Act extends to Scotland or to Northern Ireland.

WILLS ACT 1968

(1968, c. 28)   [30 May 1968]

1. Restriction of operation of Wills Act 1837, s. 15.—(l) For the purposes of section 15 of the Wills Act 1837 (avoidance of gifts to attesting witnesses and their spouses) the attestation of a will by a person to whom or to whose spouse there is given or made any such disposition as is described in that section shall be disregarded if the will is duly executed without his attestation and without that of any other such person.

14 The Family Provision (Intestate Succession) Order 1972 (see p. 915, post), substituted the sums of £15,000 and £40,000 respectively in relation to persons dying on or after 1 July 1972; the Family Provision (Intestate Succession) Order 1977 (see p. 916, post), increased those sums to £25,000 and £55,000 respectively in relation to deaths occurring on or after 15 March 1977; by the Family Provision (Intestate Succession) Order 1981 (see p. 919, post) those sums were further increased to £40,000 and £85,000 respectively for deaths occurring on or after 1 March 1981, by the Family Provision (Intestate Succession) Order 1987 (see p. 923, post) those sums were further increased to £75,000 and £125,000 for deaths occurring on or after 1 June 1987 and by the Family Provision (Intestate Succession) Order 1993 (see p. 946, post) these sums were further increased to £125,000 and £200,000 for deaths occurring on or after 1 December 1993.

(2) This section applies to the will of any person dying after the passing of this Act, whether executed before or after the passing of this Act.

2. Short title and extent.—(1) This Act may be cited as the Wills Act 1968.

(2) This Act does not extend to Scotland or Northern Ireland.

ADOPTION ACT 1968

(1968, c. 53)   [26 July 1968]

Note.—The remaining unrepealed provisions of this Act were repealed and re-enacted by the Adoption Act 1976 (see p. 826, post) when the latter Act was brought into force on 1 January 1988.

Recognition of adoptions and adoption proceedings taking place overseas

4. Extension of enactments to certain adoptions made overseas.—[(1) *Subject to sections 5 and 6 of this Act, any provision (however expressed) in any enactment passed before the date on which this section comes into force under which a person adopted in pursuance of an adoption order within the meaning of the Act of 1958 is for any purpose treated as the child of the adopter, or any other relationship is deduced by reference to such an order, shall have effect as respects anything done or any event occurring on or after that date as extending to an overseas adoption.*][15]

(2) [*Subject as aforesaid, the following provisions of the Act of 1958, that is to say, sections 14(2), 15(1) to (4), 17(3), 19(1) and 25 (which relate respectively to insurance for funeral expenses, affiliation orders, distribution of property, citizenship and registers of baptism) and section 23 (5) of the Succession (Scotland) Act, 1964 (which defines 'adoption order' for the purposes of Part IV of that Act) shall have effect as if any reference to an adoption order within the meaning of the Act of 1958 included a reference to an overseas adoption.*][15]

(3) In this Act 'overseas adoption' means an adoption of such a description as the Secretary of State may by order specify, being a description of adoptions of infants appearing to him to be effected under the law of any country outside Great Britain; and an order under this subsection may contain provisions as to the manner in which evidence of an overseas adoption may be given.

5. Recognition of determination made overseas in adoption proceedings.—[(1) *Where an authority of a convention country or a specified country having power under the law of that country—*

(a) *to authorise or review the authorisation of a convention adoption or a specified order; or*

(b) *to give or review a decision revoking or annulling a convention adoption, a specified order or an adoption order,*

makes a determination in the exercise of that power, then, subject to section 6 of this Act and any subsequent determination having effect under this subsection, the determination shall have effect in Great Britain for the purpose of effecting, confirming or terminating the adoption in question or confirming its termination, as the case may be.

(2) *In this Act 'convention adoption' means an overseas adoption of a description designated by an order under section 4(3) of this Act as that of an adoption regulated by the Convention.*]

---

15   Section 4(1) and (2) repealed with effect from 1 January 1976, by Children Act 1975, s. 108 and Sch. 4, Pt. I.

6. [*Power to annul revoke. etc., adoptions and determinations made overseas.*]

Miscellaneous and general

11. Interpretation.—[(1) *In this Act the following expressions have the following meanings unless the context otherwise requires. that is to say—*

'*the Act of 1958' means the Adoption Act 1958;*
'*adoption order' means an order made under section 8 of the Children Act 1975 as a Convention adoption order*[16]*;*
'*the Convention' means the Convention mentioned in the preamble to this Act;*
'*convention adoption' has the meaning assigned to it by section 5(2) of this Act;*
'*convention country' means any country (excluding Great Britain and a specified country) for the time being designated by an order of the Secretary of State as a country in which. in his opinion, the Convention is in force;*
'*the court' means the High Court or the Court of Session;*
'*overseas adoption' has the meaning assigned to it by section 4(3) of this Act;*

> *   *   *   *   *

'*reside' means habitually reside and 'resides' shall be construed accordingly;*
'*specified country' means, for the purposes of any provision of this Act, any of the following countries, that is to say, Northern Ireland, any of the Channel Islands, the Isle of Man and a colony, being a country designated for the purposes of that provision by order of the Secretary of State or, if no country is so designated, any of those countries;*
'*Specified order' means an adoption order made under any enactment in force in a specified country and corresponding to sections 8(1) and 24 of the Children Act 1975*[17]*;*

> *   *   *   *   *

(2) Any reference in this Act to any enactment is a reference to it as amended, and includes a reference to it as applied, by or under any other enactment including this Act.]

14. Short title, commencement and extent.—[*(1) This Act may be cited as the Adoption Act 1968.*

(2) This Act shall come into force on such date as the Secretary of State may by order appoint, and different dates may be appointed under this subsection for different purposes of this Act.

(3) This Act [*except the provisions extending section 19 (1) of the Act of 1958 and*][18] [*except sections 9 (5) and*][19] *13 and this section, does not extend to Northern Ireland.*]

[NOTE: *Certain sections of this Act, including ss. 4 (except the figures '19 (1)'), 11 and 14, came into operation on 1 February 1973 (Adoption Act 1968 (Commencement No. 1) Order 1973). Sections 5, 6, 7, 8(1) and 9 were brought into force on 23 October 1978 (Adoption Act 1968 (Commencement No. 2) Order 1978: S.I. 1978 No. 1430). See also Adoption (Designation of Overseas Adoptions) Order 1973, referred to at paras.* **6.257** *ff., ante.*]

FAMILY LAW REFORM ACT 1969

(1969, c. 46)   [25 July 1969]

REDUCTION OF AGE OF MAJORITY AND RELATED PROVISIONS

1. Reduction of age of majority from 21 to 18.—(1) As from the date on which this section comes into force a person shall attain full age on attaining the age of eighteen instead of

---

16   New definition of 'adoption order' substituted by Children Act 1975, s. 108, and Sch. 3, para. 64.
17   New definition of 'specified order' substituted by ibid.
18   Words in brackets repealed by ibid., s. 108 and Sch. 4, Pt. III.
19   Words in brackets repealed by British Nationality Act 1981, s. 52(8) and Sch. 9.

on attaining the age of twenty-one; and a person shall attain full age on that date if he has then already attained the age of eighteen but not the age of twenty-one.

(2) The foregoing subsection applies for the purposes of any rule of law, and, in the absence of a definition or of any indication of a contrary intention, for the construction of 'full age', 'infant', 'infancy', 'minor', 'minority' and similar expressions in—

(a) any statutory provision, whether passed or made before, on or after the date on which this section comes into force; and

(b) any deed, will or other instrument of whatever nature (not being a statutory provision) made on or after that date.

(3) In the statutory provisions specified in Schedule 1 to this Act for any reference to the age of twenty-one years there shall be substituted a reference to the age of eighteen years; but the amendment by this subsection of the provisions specified in Part II of that Schedule shall be without prejudice to any power of amending or revoking those provisions.

(4) This section does not affect the construction of any such expression as is referred to in subsection (2) of this section in any of the statutory provisions described in Schedule 2 to this Act, and the transitional provisions and savings contained in Schedule 3 to this Act shall have effect in relation to this section.

(5) The Lord Chancellor may by order made by statutory instrument amend any provision in any local enactment passed on or before the date on which this section comes into force (not being a provision described in paragraph 2 of Schedule 2 to this Act) by substituting a reference to the age of eighteen years for any reference therein to the age of twenty-one years; and any statutory instrument containing an order under this subsection shall be subject to annulment in pursuance of a resolution of either House of Parliament.

(6) In this section 'statutory provision' means any enactment (including, except where the context otherwise requires, this Act) and any order, rule, regulation, byelaw or other instrument made in the exercise of a power conferred by any enactment.

(7) Notwithstanding any rule of law, a will or codicil executed before the date on which this section comes into force shall not be treated for the purposes of this section as made on or after that date by reason only that the will or codicil is confirmed by a codicil executed on or after that date.

*   *   *   *   *

3. Provisions relating to wills and intestacy.—(1) In the following enactments, that is to say—

(a) section 7 of the Wills Act 1837 (invalidity of wills made by persons under 21);

(b) sections 1 and 3(1) of the Wills (Soldiers and Sailors) Act 1918 (soldier etc. eligible to make will and dispose of real property although under 21),

in their application to wills made after the coming into force of this section, for the words 'twenty-one years' there shall be substituted the words 'eighteen years'.

(2) In section 47(1)(i) of the Administration of Estates Act 1925 (statutory trusts on intestacy), in its application to the estate of an intestate dying after the coming into force of this section, for the words 'twenty-one years' in both places where they occur there shall be substituted the words 'eighteen years'.

(3) Any will which—

(a) has been made, whether before or after the coming into force of this section, by a person under the age of eighteen; and

(b) is valid by virtue of the provisions of section 11 of the said Act of 1837 and the said Act of 1918,

may be revoked by that person notwithstanding that he is still under that age whether or not the circumstances are then such that he would be entitled to make a valid will under those provisions.

(4) In this section 'will' has the same meaning as in the said Act of 1837 and 'intestate' has the same meaning as in the said Act of 1925.

9. Time at which a person attains a particular age.—(1) The time at which a person attains a particular age expressed in years shall be the commencement of the relevant anniversary of the date of his birth.

(2) This section applies only where the relevant anniversary falls on a date after that on which this section comes into force, and, in relation to any enactment, deed, will or other instrument, has effect subject to any provision therein.

*   *   *   *   *

12. Persons under full age may be described as minors instead of infants. A person who is not of full age may be described as a minor instead of as an infant, and accordingly in this Act 'minor' means such a person as aforesaid.

PART II

PROPERTY RIGHTS OF ILLEGITIMATE CHILDREN

14. Right of illegitimate child to succeed on intestacy of parents, and of parents to on intestacy of illegitimate child.—[*(1) Where either parent of an illegitimate child dies intestate as respects all or any of his or her real or personal property, the illegitimate child or, if he is dead, his issue, shall be entitled to take any interest therein to which he or such issue would have been entitled if he had been born legitimate.*

(2) Where an illegitimate child dies intestate in respect of all or any of his real or personal property, each of his parents, if surviving, shall be entitled to take any interest therein to which that parent would have been entitled if the child had been born legitimate.

(3) In accordance with the foregoing provisions of this section, Part IV of the Administration of Estates Act 1925 (which deals with the distribution of the estate of an intestate) shall have effect as if—

(a) any reference to the issue of the intestate included a reference to any illegitimate child of his and to the issue of any such child;
(b) any reference to the child or children of the intestate included a reference to any illegitimate child or children of his; and
(c) in relation to an intestate who is an illegitimate child, any reference to the parent, parents, father or mother of the intestate were a reference to his natural parent, parents, father or mother.

(4) For the purposes of subsection (2) of this section and of the provisions amended by subsection (3)(c) thereof an illegitimate child shall be presumed not to have been survived by his father unless the contrary is shown.

(5) This section does not apply to or affect the right of any person to take any entailed interest in real or personal property.

(6) The reference in section 50(1) of the said Act of 1925 (which relates to the construction of documents) to Part IV of that Act, or to the foregoing provisions of that Part, shall in relation to an instrument inter vivos made, or a will or codicil coming into operation, after the coming into force of this section (but not in relation to instruments inter vivos made or wills or codicils coming into operation earlier) be construed as including references to this section.

(7) Section 9 of the legitimacy Act 1926 (under which an illegitimate child and his issue are entitled to succeed on the intestacy of his mother if she leaves no legitimate issue, and the mother of an illegitimate child is entitled to succeed on his intestacy as if she were the only surviving parent) is hereby repealed.

[(8) *Repealed by Children Act 1975, s. 108 and Sch. 4, Pt. II.*]

(9) This section does not affect any rights under the intestacy of a person dying before the coming into force of this section[20].]

15. Presumption that in dispositions of property references to children and other relatives include references to, and to persons related through, illegitimate children.—[*(1) In any disposition made after the coming into force of this section—*

(a) any reference (whether express or implied) to the child or children of any person shall, unless the contrary intention appears, be construed as, or as including, a reference to any illegitimate child of that person; and

(b) any reference (whether express or implied) to a person or persons related in some other manner to any person shall, unless the contrary intention appears, be construed as, or as including, a reference to anyone who would be so related if he, or some other person through whom the relationship is deduced, had been born legitimate.

(2) The foregoing subsection applies only where the reference in question is to a person who is to benefit or to be capable of benefiting under the disposition or, for the purpose of designating such a person, to someone else to or through whom that person is related; but that subsection does not affect the construction of the word 'heir' or 'heirs' or of any expression which is used to create an entailed interest in real or personal property.

(3) In relation to any disposition made after the coming into force of this section, section 33 of the Trustee Act 1925 (which specifies the trusts implied by a direction that income is to be held on protective trusts for the benefit of any person) shall have effect as if—

(a) the reference to the children or more remote issue of the principal beneficiary included a reference to any illegitimate child of the principal beneficiary and to anyone who would rank as such issue if he, or some other person through whom he is descended from the principal beneficiary, had been born legitimate; and

(b) the reference to the issue of the principal beneficiary included a reference to anyone who would rank as such issue if he, or some other person through whom he is descended from the principal beneficiary, had been born legitimate.

[(4) Repealed by Children Act 1975, s. 108 and Sch. 4, Pt. II.]

(5) Where under any disposition any real or personal property or any interest in such property is limited (whether subject to any preceding limitation or charge or not) in such a way that it would, apart from this section, devolve (as nearly as the law permits) along with a dignity or title of honour, then, whether or not the disposition contains an express reference to the dignity or title of honour, and whether or not the property or some interest in the property may in some event become severed therefrom, nothing in this section shall operate to sever the property or any interest therein from the dignity or title, but the property or interest shall devolve in all respects as if this section had not been enacted.

[(6) Repealed by Children Act 1975, s. 108 and Sch. 4, Pt. II.]

(7) There is hereby abolished, as respects dispositions made after the coming into force of this section, any rule of law that a disposition in favour of illegitimate children not in being when the disposition takes effect is void as contrary to public policy.

(8) In this section 'disposition' means a disposition, including an oral disposition, of real or personal property whether inter vivos or by will or codicil; and, notwithstanding any rule of law, a disposition made by will or codicil executed before the date on which this section comes into force shall not be treated for the purposes of this section as made on or after that

---

20   Section 14 was repealed, as from 4 April 1988, by Family Law Reform Act 1987, s. 33(4), Sch. 4 (see p. 881, *post*) but the repeal does not affect any rights arising under the intestacy of a person dying before the coming into force of the repeal: *ibid.*, s. 33(2), Sch. 3, para. 8 (see p. 881, *post*). See also Family Law Reform Act 1987, s. 18.

date by reason only that the will or codicil is confirmed by a codicil executed on or after that date[1].]

16. Meaning of 'child' and 'issue' in s. 33 of Wills Act 1837.—[*(1) In relation to a testator who dies after the coming into force of this section, section 33 of the Wills Act 1837 (gift to children or other issue of testator not to lapse if they predecease him but themselves leave issue) shall have effect as if—*

(a) *the reference to a child or other issue of the testator (that is, the intended beneficiary) included a reference to any illegitimate child of the testator and to anyone who would rank as such issue if he, or some other person through whom he is descended from the testator, had been born legitimate; and*

(b) *the reference to the issue of the intended beneficiary included a reference to anyone who would rank as such issue if he, or some other person through whom he is descended from the intended beneficiary, had been born legitimate[2].]*

[(2) *Repealed by Legitimacy Act 1976. s. 11, and Sch. 2.*]

17. Protection of trustees and personal representatives. [*Notwithstanding the foregoing provisions of this Part of this Act, trustees or personal representatives may convey or distribute any real or personal property to or among the persons entitled thereto without having ascertained that there is no person who is or may be entitled to any interest therein by virtue of—*

(a) *section 14 of this Act so far as it confers any interest on illegitimate children or their issue or on the father of an illegitimate child; or*

(b) *section 15 or 16 of this Act,*

and shall not be liable to any such person of whose claim they have not had notice at the time of the conveyance or distribution; but nothing in this section shall prejudice the right of any such person to follow the property, or any property representing it, into the hands of any person, other than a purchaser, who may have received it[3].]

*   *   *   *   *

19. Policies of assurance and property in industrial and provident societies.—(l) In section 11 of the Married Women's Property Act 1882, and section 2 of the Married Women's Policies of Assurance (Scotland) Act 1880 (policies of assurance effected for the benefit of children) the expression 'children' shall include illegitimate children.

(2) In section 25(2) of the Industrial and Provident Societies Act 1965 (application of property in registered society where member was illegitimate and is not survived by certain specified relatives) for the words 'and leaves no widow, widower or issue, and his mother does not survive him' there shall be substituted the words 'and leaves no widow, widower or issue (including any illegitimate child of the member) and neither of his parents survives him'.

(3) Subsection (1) of this section does not affect the operation of the said Acts of 1882 and 1880 in relation to a policy effected before the coming into force of that subsection; and

---

1   Section 15 was repealed, as from 4 April 1988, by Family Law Reform Act 1987, s. 33(4), Sch. 4 (see p. 881, post) but the repeal does not affect, or affect the operation of, s. 33 of the Trustee Act 1925 in relation to (a) any disposition inter vivos made before the date on which the repeal came into force; or (b) any disposition by will or codicil executed before that date: ibid., s. 33(2), Sch. 3. para. 9 (see p. 881, post). See also Family Law Reform Act 1987, s. 19.

2   Section 16 repealed by Administration of Justice Act 1982, s. 75 and Sch. 9 with effect from 1 January 1983, although its provisions continue to apply to wills of testators dying before 1 January 1983. For deaths after that date, see now s. 33 of the Wills Act 1837 (as substituted by the Administration of Justice Act 1982) (p. 725, ante).

3   Section 17 ceased to have effect, as from 4 April 1988, Family Law Reform Act 1987, s. 20 (see p. 877, post) but the repeal does not affect the liability of trustees or personal representatives in respect of any conveyance or distribution made before that date: ibid., s. 33(2), Sch. 3, para. 10 (see p. 881, post).

subsection (2) of this section does not affect the operation of the said Act of 1965 in relation to a member of a registered society who dies before the coming into force of the said subsection (2).

PART IV

MISCELLANEOUS AND GENERAL

26. Rebuttal of presumption as to legitimacy and illegitimacy. Any presumption of law as to the legitimacy or illegitimacy of any person may in any civil proceedings be rebutted by evidence which shows that it is more probable than not that that person is illegitimate or legitimate, as the case may be, and it shall not be necessary to prove that fact beyond reasonable doubt in order to rebut the presumption.

*   *   *   *   *

28. Short title, interpretation, commencement and extent.—(1) This Act may be cited as the Family Law Reform Act 1969.

(2) Except where the context otherwise requires, any reference in this Act to any enactment shall be construed as a reference to that enactment as amended, extended or applied by or under any other enactment, including this Act.

(3) This Act shall come into force on such date as the Lord Chancellor may appoint by order made by statutory instrument, and different dates may be appointed for the coming into force of different provisions.

*   *   *   *   *

SCHEDULE 3   Section 1 (4)

TRANSITIONAL PROVISIONS AND SAVINGS

Interpretation

1.—(1) In this Schedule 'the principal section' means section 1 of this Act and 'the commencement date' means the date on which that section comes into force.

(2) Subsection (7) of the principal section shall apply for the purposes of this Schedule as it applies for the purposes of that section.

*   *   *   *   *

Adoption orders

4. The principal section shall not prevent the making of an adoption order or provisional adoption order under the Adoption Act 1958, in respect of a person who has attained the age of eighteen if the application for the order was made before the commencement date, and in relation to any such case that Act shall have effect as if the principal section had not been enacted.

Power of trustees to apply income for maintenance of minor

5.—(1) The principal section shall not affect section 31 of the Trustee Act 1925—

(a) in its application to any interest under an instrument made before the commencement date; or
(b) in its application, by virtue of section 47(1)(ii) of the Administration of Estates Act 1925, to the estate of an intestate (within the meaning of that Act) dying before that date.

(2) In any case in which (whether by virtue of this paragraph or paragraph 9 of this Schedule) trustees have power under subsection (1)(i) of the said section 31 to pay income to the parent or guardian of any person who has attained the age of eighteen, or to apply it for or towards the maintenance, education or benefit of any such person, they shall also have power to pay it to that person himself.

Personal representatives' powers during minority of beneficiary

6. The principal section shall not affect the meaning of 'minority' in sections 33(3) and 39(1) of the Administration of Estates Act 1925, in the case of a beneficiary whose interest arises under a will or codicil made before the commencement date or on the death before that date of an intestate (within the meaning of that Act).

Accumulation periods

7. The change, by virtue of the principal section, in the construction of—

(a) sections 164 to 166 of the Law of Property Act 1925;
(b) section 13(1) of the Perpetuities and Accumulations Act 1964,

(which lay down permissible periods for the accumulation of income under settlements and other dispositions) shall not invalidate any direction for accumulation in a settlement or other disposition made by a deed, will or other instrument which was made before the commencement date.

* * * * *

Statutory provisions incorporated in deeds, wills, etc.

9. The principal section shall not affect the construction of any statutory provision where it is incorporated in and has effect as part of any deed, will or other instrument the construction of which is not affected by that section.

[NOTE: Parts I, II and IV of this Act came into force on 1 January 1970 (Family Law Reform Act 1969 (Commencement No. 1) Order 1969).]

ADMINISTRATION OF JUSTICE ACT 1969

(1969, c. 58)   [22 October 1969]

PART III

POWER TO MAKE WILLS AND CODICILS FOR MENTALLY DISORDERED PERSONS

17. Provision for executing will for patient.—*(1) In the Mental Health Act 1959 (in this Part of this Act referred to as 'the principal Act'), in section 103(1) (powers of the judge as to patient's property and affairs) the following paragraph shall be inserted after paragraph (d)*

    '(dd) the execution for the patient of a will making any provision (whether by way of disposing of property or exercising a power or otherwise) which could be made by a will executed by the patient if he were not mentally disordered, so however that in such cases as a nominated judge may direct the powers conferred by this paragraph shall not be exercisable except by the Lord Chancellor or a nominated judge;'.

(2) At the end of section 103 (3) of the principal Act there shall be inserted the wards 'and the power of the judge to make or give an order, direction or authority for the execution of a will for a patient—

(a) shall not be exercisable at any time when the patient is an infant, and
(b) shall not be exercised unless the judge has reason to believe that the patient is incapable of making a valid will for himself'.

18. Supplementary provisions as to wills executed under s. 103(1)(dd). *The following section shall be inserted in the principal Act after section 103:*

'103A.—*(1) Where under section 103(1) of this Act the judge makes or gives an order, direction or authority requiring or authorising a person (in this section referred to as 'the authorised person') to execute a will for a patient, any will executed in pursuance of that order, direction or authority shall be expressed to be signed by the patient acting by the authorised person, and shall be—*

(a) signed by the authorised person with the name of the patient, and with his own name, in the presence of two or more witnesses present at the same time, and
(b) attested and subscribed by those witnesses in the presence of the authorised person, and
(c) sealed with the official seal of the Court of Protection.

(2) The Wills Act 1837 shall have effect in relation to any such will as if it were signed by the patient by his own hand, except that in relation to any such will—

(a) *section 9 of that Act (which makes provision as to the manner of execution and attestation of wills) shall not apply, and*

(b) *in the subsequent provisions of that Act any reference to execution in the manner therein-before required shall be construed as a reference to execution in the manner required by subsection (1) of this section.*

(3) Subject to the following provisions of this section, any such will executed in accordance with subsection (1) of this section shall have the like effect for all purposes as if the patient were capable of making a valid will and the will had been executed by him in the manner required by the Wills Act 1837.

(4) So much of subsection (3) of this section as provides for such a will to have effect as if the patient were capable of making a valid will—

(a) *shall not have effect in relation to such a will in so far as it disposes of any immovable property, other than immovable property in England or Wales, and*

(b) *where at the time when such a will is executed the patient is domiciled in Scotland or Northern Ireland or in a country or territory outside the United Kingdom, shall not have effect in relation to that will in so far as it relates to any other property or matter, except any property or matter in respect of which, under the law of his domicile, any question of his testamentary capacity would fall to be determined in accordance with the law of England and Wales.*

(5) For the purposes of the application of the Inheritance (Family Provision) Act 1938[4], in relation to a will executed in accordance with subsection (1) of this section, in section 1 (7) of that Act (which relates to the deceased's reasons for disposing of his estate in a particular way)—

(a) *any reference to the deceased's reasons for which anything is done or not done by his will shall be construed as a reference to the reasons for which it is done or (as the case may be) not done by that will, and*

(b) *any reference to a statement in writing signed by the deceased shall be construed as a reference to a statement in writing signed by the authorised person in accordance with a direction given in that behalf by the judge.'*

19. Other amendment of Mental Health Act 1959.—*(1) In section 107 of the principal Act (preservation of interests in patient's property), in subsection (3), after the words 'or other dealing' there shall be inserted the words '(otherwise than by will)'.*

(2) In section 117 of the principal Act (reciprocal arrangements in relation to Scotland and Northern Ireland as to exercise of powers). after subsection (2) there shall be inserted the following subsection:

'(2A) Nothing in this section shall affect any power to execute a will under section 103 (1) (dd) of this Act or the effect of any will executed in the exercise of such a power.'

(3) In section 119 of the principal Act (interpretation of Part VIII). at the end of subsection (1) there shall be inserted the words '"will" includes a codicil'.

*   *   *   *   *

27.—(1) [*Repealed by Supreme Court Act 1981. s. 152 (4) and Sch. 7.*]

(2) [*Repealed by Statute Law (Repeals) Act 1978, s. 1 and Sch. 1, Part 1.*]

*   *   *   *   *

4   In relation to deaths after 31 March 1976, the Inheritance (Family Provision) Act 1938 is repealed and replaced by the Inheritance (Provision for Family and Dependants) Act 1975.

28. [*Repealed by Statute Law (Repeals) Act 1978, s. 1 and Sch. 1, Part 1.*]

Note.—See now Mental Health Act 1983, ss. 94 to 98, pp. 859 ff., post.

ADMINISTRATION OF JUSTICE ACT 1970

(1970, c. 31) [29 May 1970]

PART I

COURTS AND JUDGES

High Court

1. [*Repealed, save as to subsection (6), by the Supreme Court Act 1981, s. 152(4) and Sch. 7.*]

* * * * *

(6) In accordance with the foregoing subsections—

(a) the enactments specified in Schedule 2 to this Act ([*that is to say, the said Act of 1925 and other*][5] enactments relative to the High Court, its jurisdiction, judges, divisions and business) shall be amended as shown in that Schedule; and

(b) references in any other enactment or document to the Probate, Divorce and Admiralty Division, the President of that division, the principal probate registry. the principal (or senior) probate registrar and a probate registrar shall, so far as may be necessary to preserve the effect of the enactment or document, be construed respectively as references to the Family Division and to the President, principal registry, [Senior Registrar][6] and a registrar of that division.

* * * * *

54.—(1) This Act may be cited as the Administration of Justice Act 1970.

[NOTE: Section 1 of the Act came into force on 1 October 1971 (Administration of Justice Act 1970 (Commencement No. 5) Order 1971: S.I. 1971 No. 1244).]

GUARDIANSHIP OF MINORS ACT 1971

(1971, c. 3) [17 February 1971]

Note

The whole of the Act was repealed with effect from 14 October 1991 by the Children Act 1989, s. 108(7), Sch. 15 (see p. 893, post).

* * * * *

Appointment, removal and powers of guardians

3. Rights of surviving parent as to guardianship.—(1) *On the death of the father of a minor, the mother, if surviving, shall, subject to the provisions of this Act, be guardian of the minor either alone or jointly with any guardian appointed by the father; and—*

---

5 Words in square brackets in s. 1(6)(a) repealed by Supreme Court Act 1981, s. 152(4) and Sch. 7, and those in square brackets in s. 1(6)(b) to be deemed by virtue of Supreme Court Act 1981, s. 151(5) and Sch. 4, para. 4.
6 See fn. 5, above.

(a) where no guardian has been appointed by the father; or

(b) in the event of the death or refusal to act of the guardian or guardians appointed by the father,

the court may, if it thinks fit, appoint a guardian to act jointly with the mother.

(2) On the death of the mother of a minor, the father, if surviving, shall, subject to the provisions of this Act, be guardian of the minor either alone or jointly with any guardian appointed by the mother; and—

(a) where no guardian has been appointed by the mother; or

(b) in the event of the death or refusal to act of the guardian or guardians appointed by the mother,

the court may, if it thinks fit, appoint a guardian to act jointly with the father.

[(3) Where the father and mother of a child were not married to each other at the time of his birth, this section does not apply unless the father satisfies the requirements of subsection (4) of this section.

(4) The father of a child satisfies the requirements of this subsection if—

(a) an order is in force under section 4 of the Family Law Reform Act 1987 giving him all the parental rights and duties with respect to the child; or

(b) he has a right to custody, legal or actual custody or care and control of the child by virtue of an order made under any other enactment[7].]

4.   Power of father and mother to appoint testamentary guardians.—*(1) The father of a minor may by deed or will appoint any person to be guardian of the minor after his death.*

(2) The mother of a minor may by deed or will appoint any person to be guardian of the minor after her death.

(3) Any guardian so appointed shall act jointly with the mother or father, as the case may be, of the minor so long as the mother or father remains alive unless the mother or father objects to his so acting.

(4) If the mother or father so objects, or if the guardian so appointed considers that the mother or father is unfit to have the custody of the minor, the guardian may apply to the court, and the court may either—

(a) refuse to make any order (in which case the mother or father shall remain sole guardian); or

(b) make an order that the guardian so appointed—

(i) shall act jointly with the mother or father; or

(ii) shall be the sole guardian of the minor.

(5) Where guardians are appointed by both parents, the guardians so appointed shall, after the death of the surviving parent, act jointly.

(6) If under section 3 of this Act a guardian has been appointed by the court to act jointly with a surviving parent, he shall continue to act as guardian after the death of the surviving parent; but, if the surviving parent has appointed a guardian, the guardian appointed by the court shall act jointly with the guardian appointed by the surviving parent.

[(7) Where the father and mother of a child were not married to each other at the time of his birth—

(a) subsection (1) of this section does not apply, and subsection (3) of this section does not apply in relation to a guardian appointed by the mother, unless the father satisfies the requirements of section 3 (4) of this Act; and

(b) any appointment under subsection (1) of this section shall be of no effect unless the father satisfies those requirements immediately before his death[8].]

---

7   The words in square brackets are added by the Family Law Reform Act 1987, s. 6(1).
8   The words in square brackets are added by the Family Law Reform Act 1987, s. 6(2).

5. Power of court to appoint guardian for minor having no parent, etc.—*(1) Where a minor has no parent, no guardian of the person, and no other person having parental rights with respect to him, the court, on the application of any person, may, if it thinks fit, appoint the applicant to be the guardian of the minor.*

(2) A court may entertain an application under this section to appoint a guardian of a minor notwithstanding[9] that, by virtue of a resolution under [section 3 of the Child Care Act 1980][10], a local authority have parental rights with respect to him; [but where on such an application the court appoints a guardian the resolution shall cease to have effect][11].

[(3) Where the father and mother of a child were not married to each other at the time of his birth, subsection (1) of this section shall have effect as if for the words 'no parent' there were substituted the words 'no mother, no father satisfying the requirements of section 3(4) of this Act'[12].]

*   *   *   *   *

ADMINISTRATION OF ESTATES ACT 1971

(1971, c. 25)   [12 May 1971]

Reciprocal recognition of grants

1. Recognition in England and Wales of Scottish confirmations and Northern Irish grants of representation.—(1) Where a person dies domiciled in Scotland—

(a) a confirmation granted in respect of all or part of his estate and noting his Scottish domicile, and

(b) a certificate of confirmation noting his Scottish domicile and relating to one or more items of his estate,

shall, without being resealed, be treated for the purposes of the law of England and Wales as a grant of representation (in accordance with subsection (2) below) to the executors named in the confirmation or certificate in respect of the property of the deceased of which according to the terms of the confirmation they are executors or, as the case may be, in respect of the item or items of property specified in the certificate of confirmation.

(2) Where by virtue of subsection (1) above a confirmation or certificate of confirmation is treated for the purposes of the law of England and Wales as a grant of representation to the executors named therein then, subject to subsections (3) and (5) below, the grant shall be treated—

(a) as a grant of probate where it appears from the confirmation or certificate that the executors so named are executors nominate; and

(b) in any other case, as a grant of letters of administration.

(3) Section 7 of the Administration of Estates Act 1925 (executor of executor represents original testator), shall not, by virtue of subsection (2) (a) above, apply on the death of an executor named in a confirmation or certificate of confirmation.

(4) Subject to subsection (5) below, where a person dies domiciled in Northern Ireland a grant of probate of his will or letters of administration in respect of his estate (or any part of it) made by the High Court in Northern Ireland and noting his domicile there shall, without

---

9   For the words from 'notwithstanding' to the end there are substituted the words 'notwithstanding that parental rights and duties with respect to the child are vested in a local authority or a voluntary organisation by virtue of a resolution under section 3 or 64 of the Child Care Act 1980': Family Law Reform Act 1987, s.33(1), Sch. 2, para. 29.

10   Words in brackets substituted by Child Care Act 1980, s. 89 and Sch. 5.

11   Words in brackets repealed by Children Act 1975, s. 108 and Sch. 4, Pt. V.

12   Words in square brackets added by Family Law Reform Act 1987, s. 6(3).

being resealed, be treated for the purposes of the law of England and Wales as if it had been originally made by the High Court in England and Wales.

(5) Notwithstanding anything in the preceding provisions of this section, a person who is a personal representative according to the law of England and Wales by virtue only of those provisions may not be required under section 25 of the Administration of Estates Act 1925, to deliver up his grant to the High Court.

(6) This section applies in relation to confirmations, probates and letters of administration granted before as well as after the commencement of this Act, and in relation to a confirmation, probate or letters of administration granted before the commencement of this Act, this section shall have effect as if it had come into force immediately before the grant was made.

(7) In this section 'confirmation' includes an additional confirmation and the term 'executors', where used in relation to a confirmation or certificate of confirmation, shall be construed according to the law of Scotland.

2. Recognition in Northern Ireland of English grants of representation and Scottish confirmations.—(1) Where a person dies domiciled in England and Wales a grant of probate of his will or letters of administration in respect of his estate (or any part of it) made by the High Court in England and Wales and noting his domicile there shall, without being resealed, be treated for the purposes of the law of Northern Ireland as if it had been originally made by the High Court in Northern Ireland.

(2) Where a person dies domiciled in Scotland—

(a) a confirmation granted in respect of all or part of his estate and noting his Scottish domicile, and
(b) a certificate of confirmation noting his Scottish domicile and relating to one or more items of his estate,

shall, without being resealed, be treated for the purposes of the law of Northern Ireland as a grant of representation (in accordance with subsection (3) below) to the executors named in the confirmation or certificate in respect of the property of the deceased of which according to the terms of the confirmation they are executors or, as the case may be, in respect of the item or items of property specified in the certificate of confirmation.

(3) Where by virtue of subsection (2) above a confirmation or certificate of confirmation is treated for the purposes of the law of Northern Ireland as a grant of representation to the executors named therein then, subject to subsection (4) below, the grant shall be treated—

(a) as a grant of probate where it appears from the confirmation or certificate that the executors so named are executors nominate; and
(b) in any other case, as a grant of letters of administration.

(4) Notwithstanding anything in any enactment or rule of law, subsection (3) (a) above shall not operate to entitle an executor of a sole or last surviving executor of a testator, whose will has been proved in Scotland only, to act as the executor of that testator.

(5) This section applies in relation to probates, letters of administration and confirmations granted before as well as after the commencement of this Act, and—

(a) in relation to a probate, letters of administration or confirmation granted, and resealed in Northern Ireland, before the commencement of this Act, this section shall have effect as if it had come into force immediately before the grant was so resealed; and
(b) a probate, letters of administration or confirmation granted but not resealed in Northern Ireland before the commencement of this Act shall, for the purposes of this section, be treated as having been granted at the commencement of this Act.

(6) In this section 'confirmation' includes an additional confirmation, and the term 'executors', where used in relation to a confirmation or certificate of confirmation, shall be construed according to the law of Scotland.

3. Recognition in Scotland of English and Northern Irish grants of representation.—(1) Where a person dies domiciled in England and Wales or in Northern Ireland a grant of probate or letters of administration—

(a) from the High Court in England and Wales and noting his domicile there, or

(b) from the High Court in Northern Ireland and noting his domicile there shall, without being resealed, be of the like force and effect and have the same operation in relation to property in Scotland as a confirmation given under the seal of office of the Commissariat of Edinburgh to the executor or administrator named in the probate or letters of administration.

(2) This section applies in relation to probates and letters of administration granted before as well as after the commencement of this Act, and in relation to a probate or letters of administration granted before the commencement of this Act, this section shall have effect as if it had come into force immediately before the grant was made.

4. Evidence of grants.—(1) In England and Wales and in Northern Ireland—

(a) a document purporting to be a confirmation, additional confirmation or certificate of confirmation given under the seal of office of any commissariat in Scotland shall, except where the contrary is proved, be taken to be such a confirmation, additional confirmation or certificate of confirmation without further proof; and

(b) a document purporting to be a duplicate of such a confirmation or additional confirmation and to be given under such a seal shall be receivable in evidence in like manner and for the like purposes as the confirmation or additional confirmation of which it purports to be a duplicate.

(2) In England and Wales and in Scotland—

(a) a document purporting to be a grant of probate or of letters of administration issued under the seal of the High Court in Northern Ireland or of the principal or district probate registry there shall, except where the contrary is proved, be taken to be such a grant without further proof; and

(b) a document purporting to be a copy of such a grant and to be sealed with such a seal shall be receivable in evidence in like manner and for the like purposes as the grant of which it purports to be a copy.

(3) In Scotland and in Northern Ireland—

(a) a document purporting to be a grant of probate or of letters of administration issued under the seal of the High Court in England and Wales or of the principal or district probate registry there shall, except where the contrary is proved, be taken to be such a grant without further proof; and

(b) a document purporting to be a copy of such a grant and to be sealed with such a seal shall be receivable in evidence in like manner and for the like purposes as the grant of which it purports to be a copy.

5. Property outside Scotland of which deceased was trustee.—(1) A confirmation or additional confirmation granted in respect of property situated in Scotland of a person who died domiciled there, which notes that domicile, may contain or have appended thereto and signed by the sheriff clerk a note or statement of property in England and Wales or in Northern Ireland held by the deceased in trust, being a note or statement which has been set forth in any inventory recorded in the books of the court of which the sheriff clerk is clerk.

(2) Section 1 or, as the case may be, section 2 of this Act shall apply in relation to property specified in such a note or statement as is mentioned in subsection (1) above as it applies in relation to property specified in the confirmation or additional confirmation concerned.

6. Inventory of Scottish estate may include real estate in any part of the United Kingdom.—(1) It shall be competent to include in the inventory of the estate of any person who dies domiciled in Scotland any real estate of the deceased situated in England and

Wales or Northern Ireland, and accordingly in section 9 of the Confirmation of Executors (Scotland) Act 1858, the word 'personal' wherever it occurs is hereby repealed.

(2) Section 14(2) of the Succession (Scotland) Act 1964 (act of sederunt to provide for description of heritable property), shall apply in relation to such real estate as aforesaid as it applies in relation to heritable property in Scotland.

7. Consequential amendments. Schedule 1 to this Act, which contains amendments consequential on the preceding provisions of this Act, shall have effect.

Rights and duties of personal representatives in England and Wales

8. Power to require administrators to produce sureties. [*Repealed by Supreme Court Act 1981, s. 152(4) and Sch. 7.*]

9. Duties of personal representatives. For section 25 of the Administration of Estates Act 1925 (duty of personal representatives as to inventory and account), there shall be substituted the following section:

'**25. Duty of personal representatives.**—The personal representative of a deceased person shall be under a duty to—

(a) collect and get in the real and personal estate of the deceased and administer it according to law;

(b) when required to do so by the court, exhibit on oath in the court a full inventory of the estate and when so required render an account of the administration of the estate to the court;

(c) when required to do so by the High Court, deliver up the grant of probate or administration to that court.'

10. Retainer, preference and the payment of debts by personal representatives.—(1) The right of retainer of a personal representative and his right to prefer creditors are hereby abolished.

(2) Nevertheless a personal representative—

(a) other than one mentioned in paragraph (b) below, who, in good faith and at a time when he has no reason to believe that the deceased's estate is insolvent, pays the debt of any person (including himself) who is a creditor of the estate; or

(b) to whom letters of administration had been granted solely by reason of his being a creditor and who, in good faith and at such a time pays the debt of another person who is a creditor of the estate;

shall not, if it subsequently appears that the estate is insolvent, be liable to account to a creditor of the same degree as the paid creditor for the sum so paid.

Miscellaneous and supplemental

11. Sealing of Commonwealth and Colonial grants.—(1) The following provisions of section 2 of the Colonial Probates Act 1892, that is to say—

(a) subsection (2) (b) (which makes it a condition precedent to sealing in the United Kingdom letters of administration granted in certain overseas countries and territories that a sufficient security has been given to cover property in the United Kingdom); and

(b) subsection (3) (power of the court in the United Kingdom to require that adequate security is given for the payment of debts due to creditors residing in the United Kingdom);

shall not apply to the sealing of letters of administration by the High Court in England and Wales under that section, and the following provisions of this section shall apply instead.

(2) A person to whom letters of administration have been granted in a country or territory to which the said Act of 1892 applies shall on their being sealed by the High Court in England and Wales under the said section 2 have the like duties with respect to the estate of the

deceased which is situated in England and Wales and the debts of the deceased which fall to be paid there as are imposed by section 25(a) and (b) of the Administration of Estates Act 1925 on a person to whom a grant of administration has been made by that court.

(3) As condition of sealing letters of administration granted in any such country or territory, the High Court in England and Wales may, in cases to which section [120 of the Supreme Court Act 1981][13] (power to require administrators to produce sureties) applies and subject to the following provisions of this section and subject to and in accordance with probate rules [*and orders*][14], require one or more sureties, in such amount as the court thinks fit, to guarantee that they will make good, within any limit imposed by the court on the total liability of the surety or sureties, any loss which any person interested in the administration of the estate of the deceased in England and Wales may suffer in consequence of a breach by the administrator of his duties in administering it there.

(4) A guarantee given in pursuance of any such requirement shall enure for the benefit of every person interested in the administration of the estate in England and Wales as if contained in a contract under seal made by the surety or sureties with every such person and, where there are two or more sureties, as if they had bound themselves jointly or severally.

(5) No action shall be brought on any such guarantee without the leave of the High Court.

(6) Stamp duty shall not be chargeable on any such guarantee.

(7) Subsections (2) to (6) above apply to the sealing by the High Court in England and Wales of letters of administration granted by a British court in a foreign country as they apply to the sealing of letters of administration granted in a country or territory to which the Colonial Probates Act 1892 applies.

(8) In this section—
'letters of administration' and 'British court in a foreign country' have the same meaning as in the Colonial Probates Act 1892; and ['probate rules' means rules of court made under section 127 of the Supreme Court Act 1981][15].

12. Repeals and savings.—(1) The enactments specified in Part I of Schedule 2 to this Act (which include an enactment of the Parliament of Northern Ireland) are hereby repealed to the extent specified in the third column of that Schedule and the Government of Ireland (Re-sealing of Probates etc.) Order 1923 is hereby revoked.

(2) So far as they relate to England and Wales only, the enactments specified in Part II of Schedule 2 to this Act are hereby repealed to the extent specified in the third column of that Schedule.

(3) Nothing in this Act shall affect the liability of any person for, or alter the incidence of, estate duty, including estate duty payable under the law for the time being in force in Northern Ireland.

(4) The following provisions of this Act, that is to say—

(a) [*Repealed by Supreme Court Act 1981, s. 152 (4) and Sch. 7.*];
(b) section 11 (other than subsection (2)); and
(c) the repeals specified in Part II of Schedule 2 to this Act, other than the repeal of section 34(2) of the Administration of Estates Act 1925;

shall not apply in relation to grants of administration made by the High Court before the commencement of this Act or to sealing by that court before the commencement of this Act of administration granted in any country or territory outside the United Kingdom.

(5) Any administration bond given before the commencement of this Act [*under section 167*

13   Words in brackets substituted by Supreme Court Act 1981, s. 152(1) and Sch. 5.
14   Words in brackets repealed by Supreme Court Act 1981, s. 152(4) and Sch. 7.
15   Words in brackets substituted by Supreme Court Act 1981, s. 152(1) and Sch. 5.

of the Supreme Court of Judicature (Consolidation) Act 1925, or][16] under the Colonial Probates Act 1892, may be enforced and assigned as if this Act had not been passed.

(6) Section 10 of this Act and the repeal by this section of section 34(2) of the Administration of Estates Act 1925, shall not apply in relation to the estates of persons dying before the commencement of this Act.

[13. Extension of powers of Parliament of Northern Ireland. *Repealed by the Northern Ireland Constitution Act 1973, s. 41 and Sch. 6, Pt. I.*]

14. Short title, commencement and extent.—(1) This Act may be cited as the Administration of Estates Act 1971.

(2) Section 13 of this Act and this section shall come into force on the passing of this Act and the remaining provisions of this Act shall come into force on 1 January 1972; and, notwithstanding anything in section 36 of the Interpretation Act 1889[17], any reference in this Act, or in any Act passed after the passing of this Act, to the commencement of this Act shall be construed as a reference to 1 January 1972.

(3) Sections 1 and [9][18] to 11 of this Act and subsections (2) and (4) to (6) of section 12 of this Act extend to England and Wales only.

(4) Sections 3 and 6 of this Act extend to Scotland only.

(5) Section 2 of this Act extends to Northern Ireland only.

POWERS OF ATTORNEY ACT 1971

(1971, c. 27)   [12 May 1971]

1. Execution of powers of attorney.—(1) An instrument creating a power of attorney shall be signed and sealed[19] by, or by direction and in the presence of, the donor of the power.

(2) Where such an instrument is signed and sealed[19] by a person by direction and in the presence of the donor of the power, two other persons shall be present as witnesses and shall attest the instrument.

(3) This section is without prejudice to any requirement in, or having effect under, any other Act as to the witnessing of instruments creating powers of attorney and does not affect the rules relating to the execution of instruments by bodies corporate.

[2. Abolition of deposit or filing of instruments creating powers of attorney. *Repealed by Supreme Court Act 1981, s. 152(4) and Sch. 7.*]

3. Proof of instruments creating powers of attorney.—(1) The contents of an instrument creating a power of attorney may be proved by means of a copy which—

(a) is a reproduction of the original made with a photographic or other device for reproducing documents in facsimile; and

(b) contains the following certificate or certificates signed by the donor of the power or by a solicitor [duly certified notary public[20]] or stockbroker, that is to say—

16   Words in brackets repealed by Supreme Court Act 1981, s. 152(4) and Sch. 7.
17   The Interpretation Act 1889 is repealed and replaced by the Interpretation Act 1978, with effect from 1 January 1979 (Interpretation Act 1978, s. 25 and Sch. 3).
18   Substituted by Supreme Court Act 1981, s. 152 (1) and Sch. 5.
19   Note that the need for a deed to be sealed by the person executing it was abolished as from 31 July 1990 by s. 1 of the Law of Property (Miscellaneous Provisions) Act 1989.
20   Words in square brackets inserted as from 1 April 1991 by the Courts and Legal Services Act 1990, s. 125(2), Sch. 17, para. 4.

(i) a certificate at the end to the effect that the copy is a true and complete copy of the original; and

(ii) if the original consists of two or more pages, a certificate at the end of each page of the copy to the effect that it is a true and complete copy of the corresponding page of the original.

(2) Where a copy of an instrument creating a power of attorney has been made which complies with subsection (1) of this section, the contents of the instrument may also be proved by means of a copy of that copy if the further copy itself complies with that subsection, taking references in it to the original as references to the copy from which the further copy is made.

(3) In this section ['duly certified notary public' has the same meaning as it has in the Solicitors Act 1974 by virtue of section 87 (1) of that Act and[20]] 'stockbroker' means a member of any stock exchange within the meaning of the Stock Transfer Act 1963, or the Stock Transfer Act (Northern Ireland) 1963.

(4) This section is without prejudice to section 4 of the Evidence and Powers of Attorney Act 1940 (proof of deposited instruments by office copy), and to any other method of proof authorised by law.

(5) For the avoidance of doubt, in relation to an instrument made in Scotland the references to a power of attorney in this section and in section 4 of the Evidence and Powers of Attorney Act 1940 include references to a factory and commission.

*   *   *   *   *

7. Execution of instruments, etc., by donee of power of attorney.—(1) The donee of a power of attorney may, if he thinks fit—

(a) execute any instrument with his own signature and, where sealing is required, with his own seal, and

(b) do any other thing in his own name,

by the authority of the donor of the power; and any document executed or thing done in that manner shall be as effective as if executed or done by the donee with the signature and seal, or, as the case may be, in the name, of the donor of the power.

(2) For the avoidance of doubt it is hereby declared that an instrument to which subsection (3) or (4) of section 74 of the Law of Property Act 1925 applies may be executed either as provided in those subsections or as provided in this section.

(3) This section is without prejudice to any statutory direction requiring an instrument to be executed in the name of an estate owner within the meaning of the said Act of 1925.

(4) This section applies whenever the power of attorney was created.

*   *   *   *   *

10. Effect of general power of attorney in specified form.—(1) Subject to subsection (2) of this section, a general power of attorney in the form set out in Schedule 1 to this Act, or in a form to the like effect but expressed to be made under this Act, shall operate to confer—

(a) on the donee of the power; or

(b) if there is more than one donee, on the donees acting jointly or acting jointly or severally, as the case may be,

authority to do on behalf of the donor anything which he can lawfully do by an attorney.

(2) This section does not apply to functions which the donor has as a trustee or personal representative or as a tenant for life or statutory owner within the meaning of the Settled Land Act 1925.

11. Short title, repeals, consequential amendments, commencement and extent.—(1) This Act may be cited as the Powers of Attorney Act 1971.

(2) The enactments specified in Schedule 2 to this Act are hereby repealed to the extent specified in the third column of that Schedule.

(3) In section 125(2) of the Law of Property Act 1925 for the words 'as aforesaid' there shall be substituted the words 'under the Land Registration Act 1925'; [*remaining words repealed by Supreme Court Act 1981, s. 152(4) and Sch. 7.*]

(4) This Act shall come into force on 1 October 1971.

(5) Section 3 of this Act extends to Scotland and Northern Ireland but, save as aforesaid, this Act extends to England and Wales only.

SCHEDULE 1   Section 10

FORM OF GENERAL POWER OF ATTORNEY FOR PURPOSES OF SECTION 10

THIS GENERAL POWER OF ATTORNEY is made this   day of   19   by AB of

   I appoint CD of   [*or* CD of   and EF of   jointly *or* jointly and severally] to be my attorney[s] in accordance with section 10 of the Powers of Attorney Act 1971.

IN WITNESS etc.,

MATRIMONIAL CAUSES ACT 1973

(1973, c. 18)   [23 May 1973]

PART I

NULLITY

16. Effect of decree of nullity in case of voidable marriage. A decree of nullity granted after 31 July 1971 in respect of a voidable marriage shall operate to annul the marriage only as respects any time after the decree has been made absolute, and the marriage shall, notwithstanding the decree, be treated as if it had existed up to that time.

*   *   *   *   *

18. Effects of judicial separation.—(1) Where the court grants a decree of judicial separation it shall no longer be obligatory for the petitioner to cohabit with the respondent.

(2) If while a decree of judicial separation is in force and the separation is continuing either of the parties to the marriage dies intestate as respects all or any of his or her real or personal property, the property as respects which he or she died intestate shall devolve as if the other party to the marriage had then been dead.

(3) Notwithstanding anything in section 2(1)(a) of the Matrimonial Proceedings (Magistrates' Courts) Act 1960, a provision in force under an order made, or having effect as if made, under that section exempting one party to a marriage from the obligation to cohabit with the other shall not have effect as a decree of judicial separation for the purposes of subsection (2) above.

*   *   *   *   *

PART IV

MISCELLANEOUS AND SUPPLEMENTAL

45. Declarations of legitimacy etc.—[*Repealed by Family Law Act 1986, s. 68(2), Sch. 2.*]

*   *   *   *   *

SCHEDULE 1

TRANSITIONAL PROVISIONS AND SAVINGS

PART II

PRESERVATION FOR LIMITED PURPOSES OF CERTAIN PROVISIONS OF PREVIOUS ENACTMENTS

Nullity

12. Where a decree of nullity was granted on or before 31 July 1971 in respect of a voidable marriage, any child who would have been the legitimate child of the parties to the marriage if at the date of the decree it had been dissolved instead of having being annulled shall be deemed to be their legitimate child.

Succession on intestacy in case of judicial separation

13. Section 18(2) above shall not apply in a case where the death occurred before 1 August 1970, but section 20(3) of the Act of 1965 (which provides that certain property of a wife judicially separated from her husband shall devolve, on her death intestate, as if her husband had then been dead) shall continue to apply in any such case.

*   *   *   *   *

DOMICILE AND MATRIMONIAL PROCEEDINGS ACT 1973

(1973, c. 45)   [25 July 1973]

PART I

DOMICILE

Husband and wife

1. Abolition of wife's dependent domicile.—(l) Subject to subsection (2) below, the domicile of a married woman as at any time after the coming into force of this section shall, instead of being the same as her husband's by virtue only of marriage, be ascertained by reference to the same factors as in the case of any other individual capable of having an independent domicile.

(2) Where immediately before this section came into force a woman was married and then had her husband's domicile by dependence, she is to be treated as retaining that domicile (as a domicile of choice, if it is not also her domicile of origin) unless and until it is changed by acquisition or revival of another domicile either on or after the coming into force of this section.

(3) This section extends to England and Wales, Scotland and Northern Ireland.

*   *   *   *   *

Minors and pupils

3. Age at which independent domicile can be acquired.—(l) The time at which a person first becomes capable of having an independent domicile shall be when he attains the age of sixteen or marries under that age; and in the case of a person who immediately before 1 January 1974 was incapable of having an independent domicile but had then attained the age of sixteen or been married, it shall be that date.

(2) This section extends to England and Wales and Northern Ireland (but not to Scotland).

4. Dependent domicile of child not living with father.—(l) Subsection (2) of this section shall have effect with respect to the dependent domicile of a child as at any time after the coming into force of this section when his father and mother are alive but living apart.

(2) The child's domicile as at that time shall be that of his mother if—

(a) he then has his home with her and has no home with his father; or

(b) he has at any time had her domicile by virtue of paragraph (a) above and has not since had a home with his father.

(3) As at any time after the coming into force of this section the domicile of a child whose mother is dead shall be that which she last had before she had died if at her death he had her domicile by virtue of subsection (2) above and he has not since had a home with his father.

(4) Nothing in this section prejudices any existing rule of law as to the cases in which a child's domicile is regarded as being, by dependence, that of his mother.

(5) In this section, 'child' means a person incapable of having an independent domicile; [*and in its application to a child who has been adopted, references to his father and mother shall be construed as references to his adoptive father and mother.*]

(6) This section extends to England and Wales, Scotland and Northern Ireland.

[NOTE.—The words in square brackets in subs. (5) were repealed with effect from 1 January 1976 by the Children Act 1975, s. 108 and Sch. 4, Pt. I.]

*　*　*　*　*

PART V

MISCELLANEOUS AND GENERAL

15. Extension of Recognition Act to Northern Ireland.—[*Repealed by Family Law Act 1986, s. 68(2), Sch. 2, p. 874, post.*]

16. Non-judicial divorces.—[*Repealed by Family Law Act 1986, s. 68(2), Sch. 2, p. 874, post.*]

17. Citation, etc.—(5) This Act shall come into force on 1 January 1974.

INHERITANCE (PROVISION FOR FAMILY AND DEPENDANTS) ACT 1975

(1975, c. 63)   [12 November 1975]

1. Application for financial provision from deceased's estate.—(1) Where after the commencement of this Act a person dies domiciled in England and Wales and is survived by any of the following persons:

(a) the wife or husband of the deceased;

(b) a former wife or former husband of the deceased who has not remarried;

(ba) any person (not being a person included in paragraph (a) or (b) above) to whom subsection (1A) below applies[1];

(c) a child of the deceased;

(d) any person (not being a child of the deceased) who, in the case of any marriage to which the deceased was at any time a party, was treated by the deceased as a child of the family in relation to that marriage;

(e) any person (not being a person included in the foregoing paragraphs of this subsection) who immediately before the death of the deceased was being maintained, either wholly or partly, by the deceased;

that person may apply to the court for an order under section 2 of this Act on the ground that

---

1   Paragraph (ba) added by s. 2 of the Law Reform (Succession) Act 1995—see p. 901, post.

the disposition of the deceased's estate effected by his will or the law relating to intestacy, or the combination of his will and that law, is not such as to make reasonable financial provision for the applicant.

(1A) This subsection applies to a person if the deceased died on or after 1st January 1996 and, during the whole of the period of two years ending immediately before the date when the deceased died, the person was living—

(a) in the same household as the deceased, and
(b) as the husband or wife of the deceased[2].

(2) In this Act 'reasonable financial provision'—

(a) in the case of an application made by virtue of subsection (1)(a) above by the husband or wife of the deceased (except where the marriage with the deceased was the subject of a decree of judicial separation and at the date of death the decree was in force and the separation was continuing), means such financial provision as it would be reasonable in all the circumstances of the case for a husband or wife to receive, whether or not that provision is required for his or her maintenance;
(b) in the case of any other application made by virtue of subsection (1) above, means such financial provision as it would be reasonable in all the circumstances of the case for the applicant to receive for his maintenance.

(3) For the purposes of subsection (1)(e) above, a person shall be treated as being maintained by the deceased, either wholly or partly, as the case may be, if the deceased, otherwise than for full valuable consideration, was making a substantial contribution in money or money's worth towards the reasonable needs of that person.

2. Powers of court to make orders.—(1) Subject to the provisions of this Act, where an application is made for an order under this section, the court may, if it is satisfied that the disposition of the deceased's estate effected by his will or the law relating to intestacy, or the combination of his will and that law, is not such as to make reasonable financial provision for the applicant, make any one or more of the following orders:

(a) an order for the making to the applicant out of the net estate of the deceased of such periodical payments and for such term as may be specified in the order;
(b) an order for the payment to the applicant out of that estate of a lump sum of such amount as may be so specified;
(c) an order for the transfer to the applicant of such property comprised in that estate as may be so specified;
(d) an order for the settlement for the benefit of the applicant of such property comprised in that estate as may be so specified;
(e) an order for the acquisition out of property comprised in that estate of such property as may be so specified and for the transfer of the property so acquired to the applicant or for the settlement thereof for his benefit;
(f) an order varying any ante-nuptial or post-nuptial settlement (including such a settlement made by will) made on the parties to a marriage to which the deceased was one of the parties, the variation being for the benefit of the surviving party to that marriage, or any child of that marriage, or any person who was treated by the deceased as a child of the family in relation to that marriage.

(2) An order under subsection (1)(a) above providing for the making out of the net estate of the deceased of periodical payments may provide for—

(a) payments of such amount as may be specified in the order,
(b) payments equal to the whole of the income of the net estate or of such portion thereof as may be so specified,
(c) payments equal to the whole of the income of such part of the net estate as the court may direct to be set aside or appropriated for the making out of the income thereof of payments

2   Section (1A) added by s. 2 of the Law Reform (Succession) Act 1995—see p. 901, post.

under this section, or may provide for the amount of the payments or any of them to be determined in any other way the court thinks fit.

(3) Where an order under subsection (1)(a) above provides for the making of payments of an amount specified in the order, the order may direct that such part of the net estate as may be so specified shall be set aside or appropriated for the making out of the income thereof of those payments; but no larger part of the net estate shall be so set aside or appropriated than is sufficient, at the date of the order, to produce by the income thereof the amount required for the making of those payments.

(4) An order under this section may contain such consequential and supplemental provisions as the court thinks necessary or expedient for the purpose of giving effect to the order or for the purpose of securing that the order operates fairly as between one beneficiary of the estate of the deceased and another and may, in particular, but without prejudice to the generality of this subsection—

(a) order any person who holds any property which forms part of the net estate of the deceased to make such payment or transfer such property as may be specified in the order;

(b) vary the disposition of the deceased's estate effected by the will or the law relating to intestacy, or by both the will and the law relating to intestacy, in such manner as the court thinks fair and reasonable having regard to the provisions of the order and all the circumstances of the case;

(c) confer on the trustees of any property which is the subject of an order under this section such powers as appear to the court to be necessary or expedient.

3. Matters to which court is to have regard in exercising powers under s. 2.—(1) Where an application is made for an order under section 2 of this Act, the court shall, in determining whether the disposition of the deceased's estate effected by his will or the law relating to intestacy, or the combination of his will and that law, is such as to make reasonable financial provision for the applicant and, if the court considers that reasonable financial provision has not been made, in determining whether and in what manner it shall exercise its powers under that section, have regard to the following matters, that is to say—

(a) the financial resources and financial needs which the applicant has or is likely to have in the foreseeable future;

(b) the financial resources and financial needs which any other applicant for an order under section 2 of this Act has or is likely to have in the foreseeable future;

(c) the financial resources and financial needs which any beneficiary of the estate of the deceased has or is likely to have in the foreseeable future;

(d) any obligations and responsibilities which the deceased had towards any applicant for an order under the said section 2 or towards any beneficiary of the estate of the deceased;

(e) the size and nature of the net estate of the deceased;

(f) any physical or mental disability of any applicant for an order under the said section 2 or any beneficiary of the estate of the deceased;

(g) any other matter, including the conduct of the applicant or any other person, which in the circumstances of the case the court may consider relevant.

(2) Without prejudice to the generality of paragraph (g) of subsection (1) above, where an application for an order under section 2 of this Act is made by virtue of section 1(1)(a) or 1(1)(b) of this Act, the court shall, in addition to the matters specifically mentioned in paragraphs (a) to (f) of that subsection, have regard to—

(a) the age of the applicant and the duration of the marriage;

(b) the contribution made by the applicant to the welfare of the family of the deceased, including any contribution made by looking after the home or caring for the family;

and, in the case of an application by the wife or husband of the deceased, the court shall also, unless at the date of death a decree of judicial separation was in force and the separation was continuing, have regard to the provision which the applicant might reasonably have expected to receive if on the day on which the deceased died the marriage, instead of being terminated by death, had been terminated by a decree of divorce.

(2A)   Without prejudice to the generality of paragraph (g) of subsection (1) above, where an application for an order under section 2 of this Act is made by virtue of section 1(1)(ba) of this Act, the court shall, in addition to the matters specifically mentioned in paragraphs (a) to (f) of that subsection, have regard to—

(a) the age of the applicant and the length of the period during which the applicant lived as the husband or wife of the deceased and in the same household as the deceased;
(b) the contribution made by the applicant to the welfare of the family of the deceased, including any contribution made by looking after the home or caring for the family.[3]

(3) Without prejudice to the generality of paragraph (g) of subsection (1) above, where an application for an order under section 2 of this Act is made by virtue of section 1(1)(c) or 1(1)(d) of this Act, the court shall, in addition to the matters specifically mentioned in paragraphs (a) to (f) of that subsection, have regard to the manner in which the applicant was being or in which he might expect to be educated or trained, and where the application is made by virtue of section 1(1)(d) the court shall also have regard—

(a) to whether the deceased had assumed any responsibility for the applicant's maintenance and, if so, to the extent to which and the basis upon which the deceased assumed that responsibility and to the length of time for which the deceased discharged that responsibility;
(b) to whether in assuming and discharging that responsibility the deceased did so knowing that the applicant was not his own child;
(c) to the liability of any other person to maintain the applicant.

(4) Without prejudice to the generality of paragraph (g) of subsection (1) above, where an application for an order under section 2 of this Act is made by virtue of section 1(1)(e) of this Act, the court shall, in addition to the matters specifically mentioned in paragraphs (a) to (f) of that subsection, have regard to the extent to which and the basis upon which the deceased assumed responsibility for the maintenance of the applicant and to the length of time for which the deceased discharged that responsibility.

(5) In considering the matters to which the court is required to have regard under this section, the court shall take into account the facts as known to the court at the date of the hearing.

(6) In considering the financial resources of any person for the purposes of this section the court shall take into account his earning capacity and in considering the financial needs of any person for the purposes of this section the court shall take into account his financial obligations and responsibilities.

4.   Time-limit for applications. An application for an order under section 2 of this Act shall not, except with the permission of the court, be made after the end of the period of six months from the date on which representation with respect to the estate of the deceased is first taken out.

5.   Interim orders.—(1) Where on an application for an order under section 2 of this Act it appears to the court—

(a) that the applicant is in immediate need of financial assistance, but it is not yet possible to determine what order (if any) should be made under that section; and
(b) that property forming part of the net estate of the deceased is or can be made available to meet the need of the applicant; the court may order that, subject to such conditions or restrictions, if any, as the court may impose and to any further order of the court, there shall be paid to the applicant out of the net estate of the deceased such sum or sums and (if more than one) at such intervals as the court thinks reasonable; and the court may

3   Section (2A) added by s. 2 of the Law Reform (Succession) Act 1995—see p. 901, post.

order that, subject to the provisions of this Act, such payments are to be made until such date as the court may specify, not being later than the date on which the court either makes an order under the said section 2 or decides not to exercise its powers under that section.

(2) Subsections (2), (3) and (4) of section 2 of this Act shall apply in relation to an order under this section as they apply in relation to an order under that section.

(3) In determining what order, if any, should be made under this section the court shall, so far as the urgency of the case admits, have regard to the same matters as those to which the court is required to have regard under section 3 of this Act.

(4) An order made under section 2 of this Act may provide that any sum paid to the applicant by virtue of this section shall be treated to such an extent and in such manner as may be provided by that order as having been paid on account of any payment provided for by that order.

6. Variation, discharge etc. of orders for periodical payments.—(1) Subject to the provisions of this Act, where the court has made an order under section 2(1)(a) of this Act (in this section referred to as 'the original order') for the making of periodical payments to any person (in this section referred to as 'the original recipient'), the court, on an application under this section, shall have power by order to vary or discharge the original order or to suspend any provision of it temporarily and to revive the operation of any provision so suspended.

(2) Without prejudice to the generality of subsection (1) above, an order made on an application for the variation of the original order may—

(a) provide for the making out of any relevant property of such periodical payments and for such term as may be specified in the order to any person who has applied, or would but for section 4 of this Act be entitled to apply, for an order under section 2 of this Act (whether or not, in the case of any application, an order was made in favour of the applicant);

(b) provide for the payment out of any relevant property of a lump sum of such amount as may be so specified to the original recipient or to any such person as is mentioned in paragraph (a) above;

(c) provide for the transfer of the relevant property, or such part thereof as may be so specified, to the original recipient or to any such person as is so mentioned.

(3) Where the original order provides that any periodical payments payable thereunder to the original recipient are to cease on the occurrence of an event specified in the order (other than the remarriage of a former wife or former husband) or on the expiration of a period so specified, then, if, before the end of the period of six months from the date of the occurrence of that event or of the expiration of that period, an application is made for an order under this section, the court shall have power to make any order which it would have had power to make if the application had been made before that date (whether in favour of the original recipient or any such person as is mentioned in subsection (2)(a) above and whether having effect from that date or from such later date as the court may specify).

(4) Any reference in this section to the original order shall include a reference to an order made under this section and any reference in this section to the original recipient shall include a reference to any person to whom periodical payments are required to be made by virtue of an order under this section.

(5) An application under this section may be made by any of the following persons, that is to say-

(a) any person who by virtue of section 1(1) of this Act has applied, or would but for section 4 of this Act be entitled to apply, for an order under section 2 of this Act,

(b) the personal representatives of the deceased,

(c) the trustees of any relevant property, and

(d) any beneficiary of the estate of the deceased.

(6) An order under this section may only affect—

(a) property the income of which is at the date of the order applicable wholly or in part for the making of periodical payments to any person who has applied for an order under this Act, or

(b) in the case of an application under subsection (3) above in respect of payments which have ceased to be payable on the occurrence of an event or the expiration of a period, property the income of which was so applicable immediately before the occurrence of that event or the expiration of that period, as the case may be,

and any such property as is mentioned in paragraph (a) or (b) above is in subsections (2) and (5) above referred to as 'relevant property'.

(7) In exercising the powers conferred by this section the court shall have regard to all the circumstances of the case, including any change in any of the matters to which the court was required to have regard when making the order to which the application relates.

(8) Where the court makes an order under this section, it may give such consequential directions as it thinks necessary or expedient having regard to the provisions of the order.

(9) No such order as is mentioned in sections 2(1)(d), (e) or (f), 9, 10 or 11 of this Act shall be made on an application under this section.

(10) For the avoidance of doubt it is hereby declared that, in relation to an order which provides for the making of periodical payments which are to cease on the occurrence of an event specified in the order (other than the remarriage of a former wife or former husband) or on the expiration of a period so specified, the power to vary an order includes power to provide for the making of periodical payments after the expiration of that period or the occurrence of that event.

7. Payment of lump sums by instalments.—(1) An order under section 2(1)(b) or 6(2)(b) of this Act for the payment of a lump sum may provide for the payment of that sum by instalments of such amount as may be specified in the order.

(2) Where an order is made by virtue of subsection (1) above, the court shall have power, on an application made by the person to whom the lump sum is payable, by the personal representatives of the deceased or by the trustees of the property out of which the lump sum is payable, to vary that order by varying the number of instalments payable, the amount of any instalment and the date on which any instalment becomes payable.

Property available for financial provision

8. Property treated as part of 'net estate'.—(1) Where a deceased person has in accordance with the provisions of any enactment nominated any person to receive any sum of money or other property on his death and that nomination is in force at the time of his death, that sum of money, after deducting therefrom any capital transfer tax payable in respect thereof, or that other property, to the extent of the value thereof at the date of the death of the deceased after deducting therefrom any capital transfer tax so payable, shall be treated for the purposes of this Act as part of the net estate of the deceased; but this subsection shall not render any person liable for having paid that sum or transferred that other property to the person named in the nomination in accordance with the directions given in the nomination.

(2) Where any sum of money or other property is received by any person as a donatio mortis causa made by a deceased person, that sum of money, after deducting therefrom any capital transfer tax payable thereon, or that other property, to the extent of the value thereof at the date of the death of the deceased after deducting therefrom any capital transfer tax so payable, shall be treated for the purposes of this Act as part of the net estate of the deceased; but this subsection shall not render any person liable for having paid that sum or transferred that other property in order to give effect to that donatio mortis causa.

(3) The amount of capital transfer tax to be deducted for the purposes of this section shall not exceed the amount of that tax which has been borne by the person nominated by the deceased or, as the case may be, the person who has received a sum of money or other property as a donatio mortis causa.

9. Property held on a joint tenancy.—(1) Where a deceased person was immediately before his death beneficially entitled to a joint tenancy of any property, then, if, before the end of the period of six months from the date on which representation with respect to the estate of the deceased was first taken out, an application is made for an order under section 2 of this Act, the court for the purpose of facilitating the making of financial provision for the applicant under this Act may order that the deceased's severable share of that property, at the value thereof immediately before his death, shall, to such extent as appears to the court to be just in all the circumstances of the case, be treated for the purposes of this Act as part of the net estate of the deceased.

(2) In determining the extent to which any severable share is to be treated as part of the net estate of the deceased by virtue of an order under subsection (1) above, the court shall have regard to any capital transfer tax payable in respect of that severable share.

(3) Where an order is made under subsection (1) above, the provisions of this section shall not render any person liable for anything done by him before the order was made.

(4) For the avoidance of doubt it is hereby declared that for the purposes of this section there may be a joint tenancy of a chose in action.

Powers of court in relation to transactions intended to defeat applications for financial provision

10. Dispositions intended to defeat applications for financial provision.—(1) Where an application is made to the court for an order under section 2 of this Act, the applicant may, in the proceedings on that application, apply to the court for an order under subsection (2) below.

(2) Where on an application under subsection (1) above the court is satisfied—

(a) that, less than six years before the date of the death of the deceased, the deceased with the intention of defeating an application for financial provision under this Act made a disposition, and

(b) that full valuable consideration for that disposition was not given by the person to whom or for the benefit of whom the disposition was made (in this section referred to as 'the donee') or by any other person, and

(c) that the exercise of the powers conferred by this section would facilitate the making of financial provision for the applicant under this Act,

then, subject to the provisions of this section and of sections 12 and 13 of this Act, the court may order the donee (whether or not at the date of the order he holds any interest in the property disposed of to him or for his benefit by the deceased) to provide, for the purpose of the making of that financial provision, such sum of money or other property as may be specified in the order.

(3) Where an order is made under subsection (2) above as respects any disposition made by the deceased which consisted of the payment of money to or for the benefit of the donee, the amount of any sum of money or the value of any property ordered to he provided under that subsection shall not exceed the amount of the payment made by the deceased after deducting therefrom any capital transfer tax borne by the donee in respect of that payment.

(4) Where an order is made under subsection (2) above as respects any disposition made by the deceased which consisted of the transfer of property (other than a sum of money) to or for the benefit of the donee, the amount of any sum of money or the value of any property ordered to be provided under that subsection shall not exceed the value at the date of the death of the deceased of the property disposed of by him to or for the benefit of the donee (or if that property has been disposed of by the person to whom it was transferred by the deceased, the value at the date of that disposal thereof) after deducting therefrom any capital transfer tax borne by the donee in respect of the transfer of that property by the deceased.

(5) Where an application (in this subsection referred to as 'the original application') is made for an order under subsection (2) above in relation to any disposition, then, if on an application

under this subsection by the donee or by any applicant for an order under section 2 of this Act the court is satisfied—

(a) that, less than six years before the date of the death of the deceased, the deceased with the intention of defeating an application for financial provision under this Act made a disposition other than the disposition which is the subject of the original application, and

(b) that full valuable consideration for that other disposition was not given by the person to whom or for the benefit of whom that other disposition was made or by any other person,

the court may exercise in relation to the person to whom or for the benefit of whom that other disposition was made the powers which the court would have had under subsection (2) above if the original application had been made in respect of that other disposition and the court had been satisfied as to the matters set out in paragraphs (a), (b) and (c) of that subsection; and where any application is made under this subsection, any reference in this section (except in subsection (2) (b)) to the donee shall include a reference to the person to whom or for the benefit of whom that other disposition was made.

(6) In determining whether and in what manner to exercise its powers under this section, the court shall have regard to the circumstances in which any disposition was made and any valuable consideration which was given therefor, the relationship, if any, of the donee to the deceased, the conduct and financial resources of the donee and all the other circumstances of the case.

(7) In this section 'disposition' does not include—

(a) any provision in a will, any such nomination as is mentioned in section 8 (1) of this Act or any donatio mortis causa, or

(b) any appointment of property made, otherwise than by will, in the exercise of a special power of appointment,

but, subject to these exceptions, includes any payment of money (including the payment of a premium under a policy of assurance) and any conveyance, assurance, appointment or gift of property of any description, whether made by an instrument or otherwise.

(8) The provisions of this section do not apply to any disposition made before the commencement of this Act.

11. Contracts to leave property by will.—(1) Where an application is made to a court for an order under section 2 of this Act, the applicant may, in the proceedings on that application, apply to the court for an order under this section.

(2) Where on an application under subsection (1) above the court is satisfied—

(a) that the deceased made a contract by which he agreed to leave by his will a sum of money or other property to any person or by which he agreed that a sum of money or other property would be paid or transferred to any person out of his estate, and

(b) that the deceased made that contract with the intention of defeating an application for financial provision under this Act, and

(c) that when the contract was made full valuable consideration for that contract was not given or promised by the person with whom or for the benefit of whom the contract was made (in this section referred to as 'the donee') or by any other person, and

(d) that the exercise of the powers conferred by this section would facilitate the making of financial provision for the applicant under this Act,

then, subject to the provisions of this section and of sections 12 and 13 of this Act, the court may make any one or more of the following orders, that is to say—

(i) if any money has been paid or any other property has been transferred to or for the benefit of the donee in accordance with the contract, an order directing the donee to provide, for the purpose of the making of that financial provision, such sum of money or other property as may be specified in the order;

(ii) if the money or all the money has not been paid or the property or all the property has not been transferred in accordance with the contract, an order directing the personal representatives not to make any payment or transfer any property, or not to make any further payment or transfer any further property, as the case may be, in accordance therewith or directing the personal representatives only to make such payment or transfer such property as may be specified in the order.

(3) Notwithstanding anything in subsection (2) above, the court may exercise its powers thereunder in relation to any contract made by the deceased only to the extent that the court considers that the amount of any sum of money paid or to be paid or the value of any property transferred or to be transferred in accordance with the contract exceeds the value of any valuable consideration given or to be given for that contract, and for this purpose the court shall have regard to the value of property at the date of the hearing.

(4) In determining whether and in what manner to exercise its powers under this section, the court shall have regard to the circumstances in which the contract was made, the relationship, if any, of the donee to the deceased, the conduct and financial resources of the donee and all the other circumstances of the case.

(5) Where an order has been made under subsection (2) above in relation to any contract, the rights of any person to enforce that contract or to recover damages or to obtain other relief for the breach thereof shall be subject to any adjustment made by the court under section 12 (3) of this Act and shall survive to such extent only as is consistent with giving effect to the terms of that order.

(6) The provisions of this section do not apply to a contract made before the commencement of this Act.

12. Provisions supplementary to ss. 10 and 11.—(1) Where the exercise of any of the powers conferred by section 10 or 11 of this Act is conditional on the court being satisfied that a disposition or contract was made by a deceased person with the intention of defeating an application for financial provision under this Act, that condition shall be fulfilled if the court is of the opinion that, on a balance of probabilities, the intention of the deceased (though not necessarily his sole intention) in making the disposition or contract was to prevent an order for financial provision being made under this Act or to reduce the amount of the provision which might otherwise be granted by an order thereunder.

(2) Where an application is made under section 11 of this Act with respect to any contract made by the deceased and no valuable consideration was given or promised by any person for that contract then, notwithstanding anything in subsection (1) above, it shall be presumed, unless the contrary is shown, that the deceased made that contract with the intention of defeating an application for financial provision under this Act.

(3) Where the court makes an order under section 10 or 11 of this Act it may give such consequential directions as it thinks fit (including directions requiring the making of any payment or the transfer of any property) for giving effect to the order or for securing a fair adjustment of the rights of the persons affected thereby.

(4) Any power conferred on the court by the said section 10 or 11 to order the donee, in relation to any disposition or contract, to provide any sum of money or other property shall be exercisable in like manner in relation to the personal representative of the donee, and—

(a) any reference in section 10 (4) to the disposal of property by the donee shall include a reference to disposal by the personal representative of the donee, and

(b) any reference in section 10 (5) to an application by the donee under that subsection shall include a reference to an application by the personal representative of the donee;

but the court shall not have power under the said section 10 or 11 to make an order in respect of any property forming part of the estate of the donee which has been distributed by the personal representative; and the personal representative shall not be liable for having distributed any such property before he has notice of the making of an application under the said section

10 or 11 on the ground that he ought to have taken into account the possibility that such an application would be made.

13. Provisions as to trustees in relation to ss. 10 and 11.—(1) Where an application is made for—

(a) an order under section 10 of this Act in respect of a disposition made by the deceased to any person as a trustee, or

(b) an order under section 11 of this Act in respect of any payment made or property transferred, in accordance with a contract made by the deceased, to any person as a trustee,

the powers of the court under the said section 10 or 11 to order that trustee to provide a sum of money or other property shall be subject to the following limitation (in addition, in a case of an application under section 10, to any provision regarding the deduction of capital transfer tax) namely, that the amount of any sum of money or the value of any property ordered to be provided—

 (i) in the case of an application in respect of a disposition which consisted of the payment of money or an application in respect of the payment of money in accordance with a contract, shall not exceed the aggregate of so much of that money as is at the date of the order in the hands of the trustee and the value at that date of any property which represents that money or is derived therefrom and is at that date in the hands of the trustee;

(ii) in the case of an application in respect of a disposition which consisted of the transfer of property (other than a sum of money) or an application in respect of the transfer of property (other than a sum of money) in accordance with a contract, shall not exceed the aggregate of the value at the date of the order of so much of that property as is at that date in the hands of the trustee and the value at that date of any property which represents the first-mentioned property or is derived therefrom and is at that date in the hands of the trustee.

(2) Where any such application is made in respect of a disposition made to any person as a trustee or in respect of any payment made or property transferred in pursuance of a contract to any person as a trustee, the trustee shall not be liable for having distributed any money or other property on the ground that he ought to have taken into account the possibility that such an application would be made.

(3) Where any such application is made in respect of a disposition made to any person as a trustee or in respect of any payment made or property transferred in accordance with a contract to any person as a trustee, any reference in the said section 10 or 11 to the donee shall be construed as including a reference to the trustee or trustees for the time being of the trust in question and any reference in subsection (1) or (2) above to a trustee shall he construed in the same way.

Special provisions relating to cases of divorce, separation etc.

14. Provision as to cases where no financial relief was granted in divorce proceedings etc.—(1) Where, within twelve months from the date on which a decree of divorce or nullity of marriage has been made absolute or a decree of judicial separation has been granted, a party to the marriage dies and—

(a) an application for a financial provision order under section 23 of the Matrimonial Causes Act 1973 or a property adjustment order under section 24 of that Act has not been made by the other party to that marriage, or

(b) such an application has been made but the proceedings thereon have not been determined at the time of the death of the deceased,

then, if an application for an order under section 2 of this Act is made by that other party, the court shall, notwithstanding anything in section 1 or section 3 of this Act, have power, if it thinks it just to do so, to treat that party for the purposes of that application as if the decree of divorce or nullity of marriage had not been made absolute or the decree of judicial separation had not been granted, as the case may be.

(2) This section shall not apply in relation to a decree of judicial separation unless at the date of the death of the deceased the decree was in force and the separation was continuing.

15. Restriction imposed in divorce proceedings etc. on application under this Act.—(1) On the grant of a decree of divorce, a decree of nullity of marriage or a decree of judicial separation or at any time thereafter the court, if it considers it just to do so, may, on the application of either party to the marriage, order that the other party to the marriage shall not on the death of the applicant be entitled to apply for an order under section 2 of this Act.

In this subsection 'the court' means the High Court or, where a county court has jurisdiction by virtue of Part V of the Matrimonial and Family Proceedings Act 1984, a county court.[4]

(2) In the case of a decree of divorce or nullity of marriage an order may be made under subsection (1) above before or after the decree is made absolute, but if it is made before the decree is made absolute it shall not take effect unless the decree is made absolute.

(3) Where an order made under subsection (1) above on the grant of a decree of divorce or nullity of marriage has come into force with respect to a party to a marriage, then, on the death of the other party to that marriage, the court shall not entertain any application for an order under section 2 of this Act made by the first-mentioned party.

(4) Where an order made under subsection (1) above on the grant of a decree of judicial separation has come into force with respect to any party to a marriage, then, if the other party to that marriage dies while the decree is in force and the separation is continuing, the court shall not entertain any application for an order under section 2 of this Act made by the first-mentioned party.

[**Note.** *Section 15A added by Matrimonial and Family Proceedings Act 1984, s. 25. For text see 17 Halsbury's Statutes (4th edn. 1993 Reissue) 406.*]

16. Variation and discharge of secured periodical payments orders made under Matrimonial Causes Act 1973.—(1) Where an application for an order under section 2 of this Act is made to the court by any person who was at the time of the death of the deceased entitled to payments from the deceased under a secured periodical payments order made under the Matrimonial Causes Act 1973, then, in the proceedings on that application, the court shall have power, if an application is made under this section by that person or by the personal representative of the deceased, to vary or discharge that periodical payments order or to revive the operation of any provision thereof which has been suspended under section 31 of that Act.

(2) In exercising the powers conferred by this section the court shall have regard to all the circumstances of the case, including any order which the court proposes to make under section 2 or section 5 of this Act and any change (whether resulting from the death of the deceased or otherwise) in any of the matters to which the court was required to have regard when making the secured periodical payments order.

(3) The powers exercisable by the court under this section in relation to an order shall be exercisable also in relation to any instrument executed in pursuance of the order.

17. Variation and revocation of maintenance agreements.—(1) Where an application for an order under section 2 of this Act is made to the court by any person who was at the time of the death of the deceased entitled to payments from the deceased under a maintenance agreement which provided for the continuation of payments under the agreement after the death of the deceased, then, in the proceedings on that application, the court shall have power, if an application is made under this section by that person or by the personal representative of the deceased, to vary or revoke that agreement.

(2) In exercising the powers conferred by this section the court shall have regard to all the circumstances of the case, including any order which the court proposes to make under

---

4   Section 15(1) as substituted by Matrimonial and Family Proceedings Act 1984, s. 8.

section 2 or section 5 of this Act and any change (whether resulting from the death of the deceased or otherwise) in any of the circumstances in the light of which the agreement was made.

(3) If a maintenance agreement is varied by the court under this section the like consequences shall ensue as if the variation had been made immediately before the death of the deceased by agreement between the parties and for valuable consideration.

(4) In this section 'maintenance agreement', in relation to a deceased person, means any agreement made, whether in writing or not and whether before or after the commencement of this Act, by the deceased with any person with whom he entered into a marriage, being an agreement which contained provisions governing the rights and liabilities towards one another when living separately of the parties to that marriage (whether or not the marriage has been dissolved or annulled) in respect of the making or securing of payments or the disposition or use of any property, including such rights and liabilities with respect to the maintenance or education of any child, whether or not a child of the deceased or a person who was treated by the deceased as a child of the family in relation to that marriage.

18. Availability of court's powers under this Act in applications under ss. 31 and 36 of the Matrimonial Causes Act 1973.—(1) Where—

(a) a person against whom a secured periodical payments order was made under the Matrimonial Causes Act 1973 has died and an application is made under section 31 (6) of that Act for the variation or discharge of that order or for the revival of the operation of any provision thereof which has been suspended, or

(b) a party to a maintenance agreement within the meaning of section 34 of that Act has died, the agreement being one which provides for the continuation of payments thereunder after the death of one of the parties, and an application is made under section 36 (1) of that Act for the alteration of the agreement under section 35 thereof,

the court shall have power to direct that the application made under the said section 31 (6) or 36 (1) shall be deemed to have been accompanied by an application for an order under section 2 of this Act.

(2) Where the court gives a direction under subsection (1) above it shall have power, in the proceedings on the application under the said section 31 (6) or 36 (1), to make any order which the court would have had power to make under the provisions of this Act if the application under the said section 31 (6) or 36 (1), as the case may be, had been made jointly with an application for an order under the said section 2; and the court shall have power to give such consequential directions as may be necessary for enabling the court to exercise any of the powers available to the court under this Act in the case of an application for an order under section 2.

(3) Where an order made under section 15 (1) of this Act is in force with respect to a party to a marriage, the court shall not give a direction under subsection (1) above with respect to any application made under the said section 31 (6) or 36 (1) by that party on the death of the other party.

Miscellaneous and supplementary provisions

19. Effect, duration and form of orders.—(1) Where an order is made under section 2 of this Act then for all purposes, including the purposes of the enactments relating to capital transfer tax, the will or the law relating to intestacy, or both the will and the law relating to intestacy, as the case may be, shall have effect and be deemed to have had effect as from the deceased's death subject to the provisions of the order.

(2) Any order made under section 2 or 5 of this Act in favour of—

(a) an applicant who was the former husband or former wife of the deceased, or

(b) an applicant who was the husband or wife of the deceased in a case where the marriage with the deceased was the subject of a decree of judicial separation and at the date of death the decree was in force and the separation was continuing, shall, in so far as it provides for the making of periodical payments, cease to have effect on the remarriage of the applicant, except in relation to any arrears due under the order on the date of the remarriage.

(3) A copy of every order made under this Act [other than an order made under section 15 (1) of this Act][5] shall be sent to the principal registry of the Family Division for entry and filing, and a memorandum of the order shall be endorsed on, or permanently annexed to, the probate or letters of administration under which the estate is being administered.

20. Provisions as to personal representatives.—(1) The provisions of this Act shall not render the personal representative of a deceased person liable for having distributed any part of the estate of the deceased, after the end of the period of six months from the date on which representation with respect to the estate of the deceased is first taken out, on the ground that he ought to have taken into account the possibility—

(a) that the court might permit the making of an application for an order under section 2 of this Act after the end of that period, or
(b) that, where an order has been made under the said section 2, the court might exercise in relation thereto the powers conferred on it by section 6 of this Act,

but this subsection shall not prejudice any power to recover, by reason of the making of an order under this Act, any part of the estate so distributed.

(2) Where the personal representative of a deceased person pays any sum directed by an order under section 5 of this Act to be paid out of the deceased's net estate, he shall not be under any liability by reason of that estate not being sufficient to make the payment, unless at the time of making the payment he has reasonable cause to believe that the estate is not sufficient.

(3) Where a deceased person entered into a contract by which he agreed to leave by his will any sum of money or other property to any person or by which he agreed that a sum of money or other property would be paid or transferred to any person out of his estate, then, if the personal representative of the deceased has reason to believe that the deceased entered into the contract with the intention of defeating an application for financial provision under this Act, he may, notwithstanding anything in that contract, postpone the payment of that sum of money or the transfer of that property until the expiration of the period of six months from the date on which representation with respect to the estate of the deceased is first taken out or, if during that period an application is made for an order under section 2 of this Act, until the determination of the proceedings on that application.

21. Admissibility as evidence of statements made by deceased. In any proceedings under this Act, a statement made by the deceased, whether orally or in a document or otherwise, shall be admissible under section 2 of the Civil Evidence Act 1968 as evidence of any fact stated therein in like manner as if the statement were a statement falling within section 2 (1) of that Act and any reference in that Act to a statement admissible, or given or proposed to be given, in evidence under section 2 thereof or to the admissibility or the giving in evidence of a statement by virtue of that section or to any statement falling within section 2 (1) of that Act shall be construed accordingly.

[**22. Jurisdiction of county courts.** *Repealed by Administration of Justice Act 1982, s. 75 and Sch. 9; see in substitution County Courts Act 1984, s. 25, p. 862, post.*]

23. Determination of date on which representation was first taken out. In considering for the purposes of this Act when representation with respect to the estate of a deceased person was first taken out, a grant limited to settled land or to trust property shall be left out of account, and a grant limited to real estate or to personal estate shall be left out of account unless a grant limited to the remainder of the estate has previously been made or is made at the same time.

5   Words in square brackets inserted by Administration of Justice Act 1982, s. 52.

24. Effect of this Act on s. 46 (1) (vi) of Administration of Estates Act 1925. Section 46 (1) (vi) of the Administration of Estates Act 1925, in so far as it provides for the devolution of property on the Crown, the Duchy of Lancaster or the Duke of Cornwall as bona vacantia, shall have effect subject to the provisions of this Act.

25. Interpretation.—(1) In this Act—

'beneficiary', in relation to the estate of a deceased person, means—

(a) a person who under the will of the deceased or under the law relating to intestacy is beneficially interested in the estate or would be so interested if an order had not been made under this Act, and

(b) a person who has received any sum of money or other property which by virtue of section 8 (1) or 8 (2) of this Act is treated as part of the net estate of the deceased or would have received that sum or other property if an order had not been made under this Act;

'child' includes an illegitimate child and a child en ventre sa mere at the death of the deceased;

'the court' means [unless the context otherwise requires] the High Court, or where a county court has jurisdiction by virtue of section 22 of this Act, a county court;

'former wife' or 'former husband' means a person whose marriage with the deceased 'was during the lifetime of the deceased either'—

(a) dissolved or annulled by a decree of divorce or a decree of nullity of marriage granted under the law of any part of the British Islands, or

(b) dissolved or annulled in any country or territory outside the British Islands by a divorce or annulment which is entitled to be recognised as valid by the law of England and Wales;

'net estate', in relation to a deceased person, means—

(a) all property of which the deceased had power to dispose by his will (otherwise than by virtue of a special power of appointment) less the amount of his funeral, testamentary and administration expenses, debts, and liabilities, including any capital transfer tax payable out of his estate on his death;

(b) any property in respect of which the deceased held a general power of appointment (not being a power exercisable by will) which has not been exercised;

(c) any sum of money or other property which is treated for the purposes of this Act as part of the net estate of the deceased by virtue of section 8 (1) or (2) of this Act;

(d) any property which is treated for the purposes of this Act as part of the net estate of the deceased by virtue of an order made under section 9 of the Act;

(e) any sum of money or other property which is, by reason of a disposition or contract made by the deceased, ordered under section 10 or 11 of this Act to be provided for the purpose of making of financial provision under this Act;

'property' includes any chose in action;

'reasonable financial provision' has the meaning assigned to it by section 1 of this Act;

'valuable consideration' does not include marriage or a promise of marriage;

'will' includes a codicil.

(2) For the purposes of paragraph (a) of the definition of 'net estate' in subsection (1) above a person who is not of full age and capacity shall be treated as having power to dispose by will of all property of which he would have had power to dispose by will if he had been of full age and capacity.

(3) Any reference in this Act to provision out of the net estate of a deceased person includes a reference to provision extending to the whole of that estate.

(4) For the purposes of this Act any reference to a wife or husband shall be treated as including a reference to a person who in good faith entered into a void marriage with the deceased unless either—

(a) the marriage of the deceased and that person was dissolved or annulled during the lifetime of the deceased and the dissolution or annulment is recognised by the law of England and Wales, or

(b) that person has during the lifetime of the deceased entered into a later marriage.

(5) Any reference in this Act to remarriage or to a person who has remarried includes a reference to a marriage which is by law void or voidable or to a person who has entered into such a marriage, as the case may be, and a marriage shall be treated for the purposes of this Act as a remarriage, in relation to any party thereto, notwithstanding that the previous marriage of that party was void or voidable.

27. Short title, commencement and extent.—(1) This Act may be cited as the Inheritance (Provision for Family and Dependants) Act 1975.

(2) This Act does not extend to Scotland or Northern Ireland.

(3) This Act shall come into force on 1 April 1976.

LEGITIMACY ACT 1976

(1976, c. 31)   [22 July 1976]

1. Legitimacy of children of certain void marriages.—(1) The child of a void marriage, whenever born, shall subject to subsection (2) below and Schedule 1 to this Act, be treated as the legitimate child of his parents if at the time of *the insemination resulting in the birth or, where there was no such insemination, the child's conception* [the act of intercourse resulting in the birth][6] (or at the time of the celebration of the marriage if later) both or either of the parties reasonably believed that the marriage was valid.

(2) This section only applies where the father of the child was domiciled in England and Wales at the time of the birth, or, if he died before the birth, was so domiciled immediately before his death.

(3) It is hereby declared for the avoidance of doubt that subsection (1) above applies notwithstanding that the belief that the marriage was valid was due to a mistake as to law[7].

(4) In relation to a child born after the coming into force of section 28 of the Family Law Reform Act 1987, it shall be presumed for the purposes of subsection (1) above, unless the contrary is shown, that one of the parties to the void marriage reasonably believed at the time of the insemination resulting in the birth or, where there was no such insemination, the child's conception (or at the time of the celebration of the marriage if later) that the marriage was valid[7].

2. Legitimation by subsequent marriage of parents. Subject to the following provisions of this Act, where the parents of an illegitimate person marry one another, the marriage shall, if the father of the illegitimate person is at the date of marriage domiciled in England and Wales, render that person, if living, legitimate from the date of the marriage.

3. Legitimation by extraneous law. Subject to the following provisions of this Act, where the parents of an illegitimate person marry one another and the father of the illegitimate person is not at the time of the marriage domiciled in England and Wales but is domiciled in a country by the law of which the illegitimate person became legitimated by virtue of such subsequent marriage, that person, if living, shall in England and Wales be recognised as having

---

6 The words in italics were substituted for those in square brackets, with effect from 4 April 1988, by Family Law Reform Act 1987, s. 28 (1), p. 879, post).

7 Subsections (3) and (4) were added, with effect from 4 April 1988, by Family Law Reform Act 1987, s. 28 (2), p. 879, post.

been so legitimated from the date of the marriage notwithstanding that, at the time of his birth, his father was domiciled in a country the law of which did not permit legitimation by subsequent marriage.

4. Legitimation of adopted child.—(1) *Section 39 of the Adoption Act 1976* [Paragraph 3 of Schedule 1 to the Children Act 1975][8] does not prevent an adopted child being legitimated under section 2 or 3 above if either natural parent is the sole adoptive parent.

(2) Where an adopted child (with a sole adoptive parent) is legitimated—

(a) *subsection (2) of the said section 39* [sub-paragraph (2) of the said paragraph 3][8] shall not apply after the legitimation to the natural relationship with the other natural parent, and

(b) revocation of the adoption order in consequence of the legitimation shall not affect *section 39, 41 or 42 of the Adoption Act 1976* [Part II of the said Schedule 1][8] as it applies to any instrument made before the date of legitimation.

5. Rights of legitimated persons and others to take interests in property.—(1) Subject to any contrary indication, the rules of construction contained in this section apply to any instrument other than an existing instrument, so far as the instrument contains a disposition of property.

(2) For the purposes of this section, provisions of the law of intestate succession applicable to the estate of a deceased person shall be treated as if contained in an instrument executed by him (while of full capacity) immediately before his death.

(3) A legitimated person, and any other person, shall be entitled to take any interest as if the legitimated person had been born legitimate.

(4) A disposition which depends on the date of birth of a child or children of the parent or parents shall be construed as if—

(a) a legitimated child had been born on the date of legitimation,
(b) two or more legitimated children legitimated on the same date had been born on that date in the order of their actual births,

but this does not affect any reference to the age of a child.

(5) Examples of phrases in wills on which subsection (4) above can operate are—

1. Children of A 'living at my death or born afterwards'.
2. Children of A 'living at my death or born afterwards before any one of such children for the time being in existence attains a vested interest, and who attain the age of 21 years'.
3. As in example 1 or 2, but referring to grandchildren of A, instead of children of A.
4. A for life 'until he has a child' and then to his child or children.

Note.—Subsection (4) above will not affect the reference to the age of 21 years in example 2.

(6) If an illegitimate person or a person adopted by one of his natural parents dies, or has died before the commencement of this Act, and—

(a) after his death his parents marry or have married; and
(b) the deceased would, if living at the time of the marriage, have become a legitimated person,

this section shall apply for the construction of the instrument so far as it relates to the taking of interests by, or in succession to, his spouse, children and remoter issue as if he had been legitimated by virtue of the marriage.

(7) In this section 'instrument' includes a private Act settling property, but not any other enactment.

8   The words in italics were substituted for those in square brackets, with effect from 1 January 1988, by Adoption Act 1976, s. 73(2), Sch. 3, para. 23.

6. Dispositions depending on date of birth.—(1) Where a disposition depends on the date of birth of a child who was born illegitimate and who is legitimated (or, if deceased, is treated as legitimated), section 5 (4) above does not affect entitlement under Part II of the Family Law Reform Act 1969 (illegitimate children).

(2) Where a disposition depends on the date of birth of an adopted child who is legitimated (or, if deceased, is treated as legitimated) section 5 (4) above does not affect entitlement by virtue of *section 42 (2) of the Adoption Act 1976* [paragraph 6 (2) of Schedule 1 to the Children Act 1975].[9]

(3) This section applies for example where—

(a) a testator dies in 1976 bequeathing a legacy to his eldest grandchild living at a specified time,
(b) his daughter has an illegitimate child in 1977 who is the first grandchild,
(c) his married son has a child in 1978,
(d) subsequently the illegitimate child is legitimated,

and in all those cases the daughter's child remains the eldest grandchild of the testator throughout.

7. Protection of trustees and personal representatives.—(1) A trustee or personal representative is not under a duty, by virtue of the law relating to trusts or the administration of estates, to enquire, before conveying or distributing any property, whether any person is illegitimate or has been adopted by one of his natural parents, and could be legitimated (or if deceased be treated as legitimated), if that fact could affect entitlement to the property.

(2) A trustee or personal representative shall not be liable to any person by reason of a conveyance or distribution of the property made without regard to any such fact if he has not received notice of the fact before the conveyance or distribution.

(3) This section does not prejudice the right of a person to follow the property, or any property representing it, into the hands of another person, other than a purchaser, who has received it.

8. Personal rights and obligations. A legitimated person shall have the same rights, and shall be under the same obligations in respect of the maintenance and support of himself or of any other person as if he had been born legitimate, and, subject to the provisions of this Act, the provisions of any Act relating to claims for damages, compensation, allowance, benefit or otherwise by or in respect of a legitimate child shall apply in like manner in the case of a legitimated person.

9. Re-Registration of birth of legitimated person.—(1) It shall be the duty of the parents of a legitimated person or, in cases where re-registration can be effected on information furnished by one parent and one of the parents is dead, of the surviving parent to furnish to the Registrar General information with a view to obtaining the re-registration of the birth of that person within 3 months after the date of the marriage by virtue of which he was legitimated.

(2) The failure of the parents or either of them to furnish information as required by subsection (1) above in respect of any legitimated person shall not affect the legitimation of that person.

(3) This section does not apply in relation to a person who was legitimated otherwise than by virtue of the subsequent marriage of his parents.

(4) Any parent who fails to give information as required by this section shall be liable on summary conviction to a fine not exceeding £2.

10. Interpretation.—(1) In this Act, except where the context otherwise requires—

9   The words in italics were substituted for those in square brackets, with effect from 1 January 1988, by Adoption Act 1976, s. 73(2), Sch. 3, para. 24.

'disposition' includes the conferring of a power of appointment and any other disposition of an interest in or right over property;

'existing', in relation to an instrument, means one made before 1 January 1976;

'legitimated person' means a person legitimated or recognised as legitimated—

(a) under section 2 or 3 above; or

(b) under section 1 or 8 of the Legitimacy Act 1926; or

(c) except in section 8, by legitimation (whether or not by virtue of the subsequent marriage of his parents) recognised by the law of England and Wales and effected under the law of any other country;

and cognate expressions shall be construed accordingly;

'power of appointment' includes any discretionary power to transfer a beneficial interest in property without the furnishing of valuable consideration;

'void marriage' means a marriage, not being voidable only, in respect of which the High Court has or had jurisdiction to grant a decree of nullity, or would have or would have had such jurisdiction if the parties were domiciled in England and Wales.

(2) For the purposes of this Act 'legitimated person' includes, where the context admits, a person legitimated, or recognised as legitimated, before the passing of the Children Act 1975.

(3) For the purpose of this Act, except where the context otherwise requires—

(a) the death of the testator is the date at which a will or codicil is to be regarded as made;

(b) an oral disposition of property shall be deemed to be contained in an instrument made when the disposition was made.

(4) It is hereby declared that references in this Act to dispositions of property include references to a disposition by the creation of an entailed interest.

(5) Except in so far as the context otherwise requires, any reference in this Act to an enactment shall be construed as a reference to that enactment as amended by or under any other enactment, including this Act.

11. Savings, amendments and repeals.—(1) Schedule 1 to this Act, which contains savings and amendments to enactments consequential upon the provisions of this Act, shall have effect.

12. Short title, commencement and extent.—(1) This Act may be cited as the Legitimacy Act 1976.

(2) This Act shall come into force at the end of the period of one month beginning with the date on which it is passed.

(3) This Act does not extend to Scotland or to Northern Ireland.

SCHEDULE I

Section 11

SAVINGS AND CONSEQUENTIAL AMENDMENTS SAVINGS

1.—(1) Notwithstanding the repeal by this Act of sections 1 and 8 of the Legitimacy Act 1926 persons legitimated or recognised as legitimated under that Act shall continue to be legitimated or recognised as legitimated by virtue of section 1 or, as the case may be, section 8 of that Act.

(2) In any enactment whether passed before or after this Act references to persons legitimated or recognised as legitimated under section 1 or section 8 of the Legitimacy Act 1926 or under section 2 or section 3 of this Act shall be construed as including references to persons legitimated or recognised as legitimated under section 2 or section 3 of this Act or under section 1 or section 8 of the said Act of 1926 respectively.

2.—(1) The enactments repealed by Part II of Schedule 4 to the Children Act 1975 (which are superseded by section 5 of this Act) shall notwithstanding those repeals, continue to have effect as respects existing instruments.

In this sub-paragraph 'instrument' has the same meaning as in section 5 of this Act.

(2) Subject to paragraph 3 (b) below, nothing in this Act or in the Legitimacy Act 1926 (in so far as the effect of the Act is preserved by sub-paragraph (1) above) shall affect the operation or construction of any disposition coming into operation before 1 January 1927 or affect any rights under the intestacy of a person dying before that date.

(3) Sub-paragraph (2) above shall apply in relation to a person to whom the said Act of 1926 applied by virtue of section 1 (1) of the Legitimacy Act 1959 with the substitution for '1 January 1927' of '9 October 1959'.

3. Section 1 does not—

(a) affect any rights under the intestacy of a person who dies before 29 October 1959, or
(b) affect the operation or construction of any disposition coming into operation before 29 October 1959 except so far as may be necessary to avoid the severance from a dignity or title of honour of property limited (expressly or not) to devolve (as nearly as the law permits) along with the dignity or title of honour.

4.—(1) Section 1 of this Act, so far as it affects the succession to a dignity or title of honour, or the devolution of property limited as aforesaid, only applies to children born after 28 October 1959.

(2) Apart from section 1, nothing in this Act shall affect the succession to any dignity or title of honour or render any person capable of succeeding to or transmitting a right to succeed to any such dignity or title.

(3) Apart from section 1, nothing in this Act shall affect the devolution of any property limited (expressly or not) to devolve (as nearly as the law permits) along with any dignity or title of honour.

This sub-paragraph applies only if and so far as a contrary intention is not expressed in the instrument, and shall have effect subject to the instrument.

5. It is hereby declared that nothing in this Act affects the Succession to the Throne.

ADOPTION ACT 1976

(1976, c. 36)   [22 July 1976]

Note.—This Act consolidates the enactments having effect in England and Wales in relation to adoption, including the relevant previously unrepealed provisions of the Adoption Acts 1958, 1960, 1964 and 1968 and the Children Act 1975. The Adoption Act 1976 came into force on 1 January 1988.

*   *   *   *   *

PART II

ADOPTION ORDERS

The making of adoption orders

12. Adoption orders.—(1) An adoption order is an order *vesting the parental rights and duties relating to a child in* [giving parental responsibility for a child to][10] the adopters, made on their application by an authorised court.

(2) The order does not affect *the parental rights and duties so far as they relate* [parental responsibility so far as it relates][10] to any period before the making of the order.

(3) The making of an adoption order operates to extinguish—

(a) *any parental right or duty relating to the child which*—

10   The words in square brackets were substituted for those in italics, as from 14 October 1991, by the Children Act 1989, s. 88, Sch. 10, para. 3 (see p. 888, post).

      (i) is vested in a person (not being one of the adopters) who was the parent or guardian of the child immediately before the making of the order, or

      (ii) is vested in any other person by virtue of the order of any court; and

[(a) the parental responsibility which any person has for the child immediately before the making of the order;

(aa) any order under the Children Act 1989;][10]

(b) any duty arising by virtue of an agreement or the order of a court to make payments, so far as the payments are in respect of the child's maintenance *for any period after the making of the order or any other matter comprised in the parental duties and relating to such a period* [or upbringing, for any period after the making of the order][10].

(4) Subsection (3) (b) does not apply to a duty arising by virtue of an agreement—

(a) which constitutes a trust, or

(b) which expressly provides that the duty is not to be extinguished by the making of an adoption order.

(5) An adoption order may not be made in relation to a child who is or has been married.

(6) An adoption order may contain such terms and conditions as the court thinks fit.

(7) An adoption order may be made notwithstanding that the child is already an adopted child.

*   *   *   *   *

17. Convention adoption orders.—(1) An adoption order shall be made as a Convention adoption order if the application is for a Convention adoption order and the following conditions are satisfied both at the time of the application and when the order is made.

(2) The child—

(a) must be a United Kingdom national or a national of a Convention country, and

(b) must habitually reside in British territory or a Convention country.

(3) The applicant or applicants and the child must not all be United Kingdom nationals living in British territory.

(4) If the application is by a married couple, either—

(a) each must be a United Kingdom national or a national of a Convention country, and both must habitually reside in Great Britain, or

(b) both must be United Kingdom nationals, and each must habitually reside in British territory or a Convention country,

and if the applicants are nationals of the same Convention country the adoption must not be prohibited by a specified provision (as defined in subsection (8)) of the internal law of that country.

(5) If the application is by one person, either—

(a) he must be a national of a Convention country, and must habitually reside in Great Britain, or

(b) he must be a United Kingdom national and must habitually reside in British territory or a Convention country,

and if he is a national of a Convention country the adoption must not be prohibited by a specified provision (as defined in subsection (8)) of the internal law of that country.

(6) If the child is not a United Kingdom national the order shall not be made—

(a) except in accordance with the provisions, if any, relating to consents and consultations of the internal law relating to adoption of the Convention country of which the child is a national, and

(b) unless the court is satisfied that each person who consents to the order in accordance with that internal law does so with full understanding of what is involved.

(8) In subsections (4) and (5) 'specified provision' means a provision specified in an order of the Secretary of State as one notified to the Government of the United Kingdom in pursuance of the provisions of the Convention which relate to prohibitions on an adoption contained in the national law of the Convention country in question.

*   *   *   *   *

PART IV

STATUS OF ADOPTED CHILDREN

38. Meaning of 'adoption' in Part IV.—(1) In this Part 'adoption' means adoption—

(a) by an adoption order;
(b) by an order made under the Children Act 1975, the Adoption Act 1958, the Adoption Act 1950 or any enactment repealed by the Adoption Act 1950;
(c) by an order made in Scotland, Northern Ireland, the Isle of Man or in any of the Channel Islands;
(d) which is an overseas adoption; or
(e) which is an adoption recognised by the law of England and Wales and effected under the law of any other country, and cognate expressions shall be construed accordingly.

(2) The definition of adoption includes, where the context admits, an adoption effected before the passing of the Children Act 1975, and the date of an adoption effected by an order is the date of the making of the order.

39. Status conferred by adoption.—(1) An adopted child shall be treated in law—

(a) where the adopters are a married couple, as if he had been born as a child of the marriage (whether or not he was in fact born after the marriage was solemnised);
(b) in any other case, as if he had been born to the adopter in wedlock (but not as a child of any actual marriage of the adopter).

(2) An adopted child shall, subject to subsection (3), be treated in law as if he were not the child of any person other than the adopters or adopter.

(3) In the case of a child adopted by one of its natural parents as sole adoptive parent, subsection (2) has no effect as respects entitlement to property depending on relationship to that parent, or as respects anything else depending on that relationship.

(4) It is hereby declared that this section prevents an adopted child from being illegitimate.

(5) This section has effect—

(a) in the case of an adoption before 1 January 1976, from that date, and
(b) in the case of any other adoption, from the date of the adoption.

(6) Subject to the provisions of this Part, this section—

(a) applies for the construction of enactments or instruments passed or made before the adoption or later, and so applies subject to any contrary indication; and
(b) has effect as respects things done, or events occurring, after the adoption or after 31 December 1975, whichever is the later.

40. [*Repealed by British Nationality Act 1981, s. 52 (8) and Sch. 9.*]

41. Adoptive relatives. A relationship existing by virtue of section 39 may be referred to as an adoptive relationship, and—

(a) a male adopter may be referred to as the adoptive father;
(b) a female adopter may be referred to as the adoptive mother;
(c) any other relative of any degree under an adoptive relationship may be referred to as an adoptive relative of that degree;

but this section does not prevent the term 'parent', or any other term not qualified by the word 'adoptive' being treated as including an adoptive relative.

42. Rules of construction for instruments concerning property.—(1) Subject to any contrary indication, the rules of construction contained in this section apply to any instrument, other than an existing instrument, so far as it contains a disposition of property.

(2) In applying section 39 (1) to a disposition which depends on the date of birth of a child or children of the adoptive parent or parents, the disposition shall be construed as if—

(a) the adopted child had been born on the date of adoption,
(b) two or more children adopted on the same date had been born on that date in the order of their actual births,

but this does not affect any reference to the age of a child[11].

(3) Examples of phrases in wills on which subsection (2) can operate—

1. Children of A 'living at my death or born afterwards'.
2. Children of A 'living at my death or born afterwards before any one of such children for the time being in existence attains a vested interest and who attain the age of 21 years'.
3. As in example 1 or 2, but referring to grandchildren of A instead of children of A.
4 A for life 'until he has a child', and then to his child or children.

(4) Section 39 (2) does not prejudice any interest vested in possession in the adopted child before the adoption, or any interest expectant (whether immediately or not) upon an interest so vested.

(5) Where it is necessary to determine for the purposes of a disposition of property effected by an instrument whether a woman can have a child, it shall be presumed that once a woman has attained the age of 55 years she will not adopt a child after execution of the instrument, and, notwithstanding section 39, if she does so that child shall not be treated as her child or as the child of her spouse (if any) for the purposes of the instrument.

(6) In this section, 'instrument' includes a private Act settling property, but not any other enactment.

43. Dispositions depending on date of birth.—(1) Where a disposition depends on the date of birth of a child who was born illegitimate and who is adopted by one of the natural parents as sole adoptive parent, section 42 (2) does not affect entitlement under Part II of the Family Law Reform Act 1969 (illegitimate children).

(2) Subsection (1) applies for example where—

(a) a testator dies in 1976 bequeathing a legacy to his eldest grandchild living at a specified time,
(b) his daughter has an illegitimate child in 1977 who is the first grandchild,
(c) his married son has a child in 1978,
(d) subsequently the illegitimate child is adopted by the mother as sole adoptive parent,

and in all those cases the daughter's child remains the eldest grandchild of the testator throughout.

44. Property devolving with peerages etc.—(1) An adoption does not affect the descent of any peerage or dignity or title of honour.

(2) An adoption shall not affect the devolution of any property limited (expressly or not) to devolve (as nearly as the law permits) along with any peerage or dignity or title of honour.

(3) Subsection (2) applies only if and so far as a contrary intention is not expressed in the instrument, and shall have effect subject to the terms of the instrument.

---

11   Subsection (2) will not affect the reference to the age of 21 years in example 2.

45. Protection of trustees and personal representatives.—(1) A trustee or personal representative is not under a duty, by virtue of the law relating to trusts or the administration of estates, to enquire, before conveying or distributing any property, whether any adoption has been effected or revoked if that fact could affect entitlement to the property.

(2) A trustee or personal representative shall not be liable to any person by reason of a conveyance or distribution of the property made without regard to any such fact if he has not received notice of the fact before the conveyance or distribution.

(3) This section does not prejudice the right of a person to follow the property, or any property representing it, into the hands of another person, other than a purchaser, who has received it.

46. Meaning of 'disposition'.—(1) In this Part, unless the context otherwise requires,

'disposition' includes the conferring of a power of appointment and any other disposition of an interest in or right over property;
'power of appointment' includes any discretionary power to transfer a beneficial interest in property without the furnishing of valuable consideration.

(2) This Part applies to an oral disposition as if contained in an instrument made when the disposition was made.

(3) For the purposes of this Part, the death of the testator is the date at which a will or codicil is to be regarded as made.

(4) For the purposes of this Part, provisions of the law of intestate succession applicable to the estate of a deceased person shall be treated as if contained in an instrument executed by him (while of full capacity) immediately before his death.

(5) It is hereby declared that references in this Part to dispositions of property include references to a disposition by the creation of an entailed interest.

*   *   *   *   *

47. Miscellaneous enactments.—(2) [*Without prejudice to section 40*][12] section 39 does not apply for the purposes of any provision of—

(a) [the British Nationality Act 1981][13],
(b) the Immigration Act 1971,
(c) any instrument having effect under an enactment within paragraph (a) or (b), or
(d) any other provision of the law for the time being in force which determines [British citizenship, British Dependent Territories citizenship or British Overseas citizenship][14].

(3) [*Repealed by Social Security Act 1986, Sch. 11, as from 6 April 1988.*]

(4) Section 39 does not apply for the purposes of section 70 (3) (b) or section 73 (2) of the Social Security Act 1975 (payment of industrial death benefit to or in respect of an illegitimate child of the deceased and the child's mother).

(5) Subject to regulations made under section 72 of the Social Security Act 1975 (entitlement of certain relatives of deceased to industrial death benefit), section 39 shall not affect the entitlement to an industrial death benefit of a person who would, apart from section 39, be treated as a relative of a deceased person for the purposes of the said section 72.

48. Pensions. Section 39 (2) does not affect entitlement to a pension which is payable to or for the benefit of a child and is in payment at the time of his adoption.

49. Insurance. Where a child is adopted whose natural parent has effected an insurance with a friendly society or a collecting society or an industrial insurance company for the

12   Words in brackets repealed by British Nationality Act 1981, s. 52(8) and Sch. 9.
13   Words in brackets substituted by British Nationality Act 1981, s. 52(6) and Sch. 7.
14   Ibid.

payment on the death of the child of money for funeral expenses, the rights and liabilities under the policy shall by virtue of the adoption be transferred to the adoptive parents who shall for the purposes of the enactments relating to such societies and companies be treated as the person who took out the policy.

PART V

REGISTRATION AND REVOCATION OF ADOPTION ORDERS AND CONVENTION ADOPTIONS

51. Disclosure of birth records of adopted children.—(1) Subject to *subsections (4) and (6)* [what follows][15], the Registrar General shall on an application made in the prescribed manner by an adopted person a record of whose birth is kept by the Registrar General and who has attained the age of 18 years supply to that person on payment of the prescribed fee (if any) such information as is necessary to enable that person to obtain a certified copy

*   *   *   *   *

(3) It shall be the duty of the Registrar General and each local authority and approved adoption society to provide counselling for adopted persons who apply for information under subsection (1).

(4) Before supplying any information to an applicant under subsection (1) the Registrar General shall inform the applicant that counselling services are available to him

(a) at the General Register Officer; or

(b) from the local authority for the area where the applicant is at the time the application is made; or

(c) from the local authority for the area where the court sat which made the adoption order relating to the applicant; or

(d) if the applicant's adoption was arranged by an adoption society which is approved under section 3 of this Act or under section 4 of the Children Act 1975, from that society.

(5) If the applicant chooses to receive counselling from a local authority or an adoption society under subsection (4) the Registrar General shall send to the authority or society of the applicant's choice the information to which the applicant is entitled under subsection (1).

(6) The Registrar General shall not supply a person who was adopted before 12 November 1975 with any information under subsection (1) unless that person has attended an interview with a counsellor either at the General Register Office or in pursuance of arrangements made by the local authority or adoption society from whom the applicant is entitled to receive counselling in accordance with subsection (4).

(7) In this section, 'prescribed' means prescribed by regulations made by the Registrar General.

[(3) Before supplying any information to an applicant under subsection (1), the Registrar General shall inform the applicant that counselling services are available to him—

(a) if he is in England and Wales—
   (i) at the General Register Office;
   (ii) from the local authority in whose area he is living;
   (iii) where the adoption order relating to him was made in England and Wales, from the local authority in whose area the court which made the order sat; or
   (iv) from any other local authority;

(b) if he is in Scotland—
   (i) from the regional or islands council in whose area he is living;
   (ii) where the adoption order relating to him was made in Scotland, from the council in whose area the court which made the order sat; or
   (iii) from any other regional or islands council;

(c) if he is in Northern Ireland—
   (i) from the Board in whose area he is living;

   (ii)   where the adoption order relating to him was made in Northern Ireland, from the
          Board in whose area the court which made the order sat; or
   (iii) from any other Board;
 (d) if he is the United Kingdom and his adoption was arranged by an adoption society—
   (i)   approved under section 3,
   (ii) approved under section 3 of the Adoption (Scotland) Act 1978,
   (iii) registered under Article 4 of the Adoption (Northern Ireland) Order 1987,
from that society.

(4) Where an adopted person who is in England and Wales—

 (a) applies for information under—
   (i)   subscription (1), or
   (ii) Article 54 of the Adoption (Northern Ireland) Order 1987, or
 (b) is supplied with information under section 45 of the Adoption (Scotland) Act 1978,

it shall be the duty of the persons and bodies mentioned in subsection (5) to provide counselling for him if asked by him to do so.

(5) The persons and bodies are—

 (a) the Registrar General;
 (b) any local authority falling within subsection (3)(a)(ii) to (iv);
 (c) any adoption society falling within subsection (3)(d) in so far as it is acting as an adop-
      tion society in England and Wales.

(6) If the applicant chooses to receive counselling from a person or body falling within subsection (3), the Registrar General shall send to the person or body the information to which
the applicant is entitled under subsection (1).

(7) Where a person—

 (a) was adopted before 12 November 1975, and
 (b) applies for information under subsection (1),

the Registrar General shall not supply the information to him unless he has attended an interview with a counsellor arranged by a person or body from whom counselling services are
available as mentioned in subsection (3).

(8) Where the Registrar General is prevented by subsection (7) from supplying information
to a person who is not living in the United Kingdom, he may supply the information to any
body which—

 (a) the Registrar General is satisfied is suitable to provide counselling to that person, and
 (b) has notified the Registrar General that it is prepared to provide such counselling.

(9) In this section—

'a Board' means a Health and Social Services Board established under Article 16 of the
   Health and Personal Social Services (Northern Ireland) Order 1972; and
'prescribed' means prescribed by regulations made by the Registrar General.][15]

52. Revocation of adoptions on legitimation.—(1) Where any person adopted by his father
or mother alone has subsequently become a legitimated person on the marriage of his father
and mother, the court by which the adoption order was made may, on the application of any
of the parties concerned, revoke that order.

(2) Where any person legitimated by virtue of section 1 of the Legitimacy Act 1959 had
been adopted by his father and mother before the commencement of that Act, the court by
which the adoption order was made may, on the application of any of the parties concerned,
revoke that order.

*   *   *   *   *

15   Words in square brackets substituted for those in italics, as from 14 October 1991, by the Children
     Act 1989, s. 88, Sch. 10, para. 20 (see p. 888, post).

PART VI

MISCELLANEOUS AND SUPPLEMENTAL

55. Adoption of children abroad.—(1) Where on an application made in relation to a child by a person who is not domiciled in England and Wales or Scotland or Northern Ireland[16] an authorised court is satisfied that he intends to adopt the child under the law of or within the country in which the applicant is domiciled, the court may, subject to the following provisions of this section, make an order *vesting in him the parental rights and duties relating to the child* [giving him parental responsibility for the child][17].

60. Evidence of adoption in Scotland and Northern Ireland. Any document which is receivable as evidence of any matter—

(a) in Scotland under *section 22 (2) of the Adoption Act 1958* [section 45 (2) of the Adoption (Scotland) Act 1978][18]; or

(b) in Northern Ireland under *section 23 (4) of the Adoption Act (Northern Ireland) 1967 or any corresponding provision contained in a Measure of the Northern Ireland Assembly for the time being in force* [Article 63 (1) of the Adoption (Northern Ireland) Order 1987][18],

shall also be so receivable in England and Wales.

71. Internal law of a country.—(1) In this Act 'internal law' in relation to any country means the law applicable in a case where no question arises as to the law in force in any other country.

(2) In any case where the internal law of a country falls to be ascertained for the purposes of this Act by any court and there are in force in that country two or more systems of internal law, the relevant system shall be ascertained in accordance with any rule in force throughout that country indicating which of the systems is relevant in the case in question or, if there is no such rule, shall be the system appearing to that court to be most closely connected with the case.

72. Interpretation.—(1) In this Act, unless the context otherwise requires—

*   *   *   *   *

'adoption order' means an order under section 12 (1) and, in sections 12 (3) and (4), 18 to 21, 27 and 28 and 30 to 32 includes an order under section 8 of the Children Act 1975 (adoption orders in Scotland); (**Note.** See now section 12, Adoption (Scotland) Act 1978.)

['adoption order'—

(a) means an order under section 12 (1); and

(b) in sections 12 (3) and (4), 18 to 20, 27, 28 and 30 to 32 and in the definition of 'British adoption order' in this subsection includes an order under section 12 of the Adoption (Scotland) Act 1978 and Article 12 of the Adoption (Northern Ireland) Order 1987 (adoption orders in Scotland and Northern Ireland respectively); and

(c) in sections 27, 28 and 30 to 32 includes an order under section 55, section 49 of the Adoption (Scotland) Act 1978 and Article 57 of the Adoption (Northern Ireland) Order 1987 (orders in relation to children being adopted abroad.][19

*   *   *   *   *

'British adoption order' means an adoption order, an order under section 8 of the Children Act 1975 (adoption orders in Scotland), or any provision for the adoption of a child effected under the law of Northern Ireland or any British territory outside the United Kingdom;

16 The words 'or Northern Ireland' were inserted as from 14 October 1991, by the Children Act 1989, s. 108(7), Sch. 10, para. 22 (see p. 889, post).

17 Words in square brackets substituted for those in italics, ibid.

18 Words in square brackets substituted for those in italics, as from 14 October 1991, by the Children Act 1989, s. 108(7), Sch. 10, para. 27 (see p. 889, post).

19 Words in square brackets substituted for those in italics, as from 14 October 1991, by the Children Act 1989, s. 108(7), Sch. 10, para. 30 (see p. 889, post).

['British adoption order' means (a) an adoption order as defined in this subsection, and (b) an order under any provision for the adoption of a child effected under the law of any British territory outside the United Kingdom.][19]

'British territory' means, for the purposes of any provision of this Act, any of the following countries, that is to say, Great Britain, Northern Ireland, the Channel Islands, the Isle of Man and a colony, being a country designated for the purposes of that provision by order of the Secretary of State or, if no country is so designated, any of those countries;

'child', except where used to express a relationship, means a person who has not attained the age of 18 years;

'the Convention' means the Convention relating to the adoption of children concluded at the Hague on 15 November 1965 and signed on behalf of the United Kingdom on that date;

'Convention adoption order' means an adoption order made in accordance with section 17 (1);

'Convention country' means any country outside British territory, being a country for the time being designated by an order of the Secretary of State as a country in which, in his opinion, the Convention is in force;

'existing', in relation to an enactment or other instrument, means one passed or made at any time before 1 January 1976;

'guardian' has the same meaning as in the Children Act 1989[20];

'internal law' has the meaning assigned by section 71;

*   *   *   *   *

'overseas adoption' has the meaning assigned by subsection (2);

'parent' means, in relation to a child, any parent who has parental responsibility for the child under the Children Act 1989[20];

'parental responsibility' and 'parental responsibility agreement' have the same meaning as in the Children Act 1989;[20]

*   *   *   *   *

'relative' in relation to a child means a grandparent, brother, sister, uncle or aunt, whether of the full blood or half-blood or by affinity and includes, where the child is illegitimate, the father of the child and any person who would be a relative within the meaning of this definition if the child were the legitimate child of his mother and father;

*   *   *   *   *

'specified order' means any provision for the adoption of a child effected under enactments similar to section 12 (1) and 17 in force in Northern Ireland or any British territory outside the United Kingdom;

'United Kingdom national' means, for the purposes of any provision of this Act, a citizen of the United Kingdom and colonies[1] satisfying such conditions, if any, as the Secretary of State may by order specify for the purposes of that provision;

'upbringing' has the same meaning as in the Children Act 1989.[20]

(1A) In this Act, in determining with what person, or where, a child has his home, any absence of the child at a hospital or boarding school and any other temporary absence shall be disregarded.[20]

---

20   Words substituted or inserted as from 14 October 1991, by the Children Act 1989, s. 88, Sch. 10, para. 30 (see p. 889, post)
1   Section 51(3)(a) of the British Nationality Act 1981 provides that 'a citizen of the United Kingdom and colonies' means a person who, under the British Nationality Act 1981, is a British citizen, a British Dependent Territories citizen or a British Overseas citizen.

(1B) In this Act, references to a child who is in the care of or looked after by a local authority have the same meaning as in the Children Act 1989.[20]

*   *   *   *   *

(2) In this Act 'overseas adoption' means an adoption of such a description as the Secretary of State may by order specify, being a description of adoptions of children appearing to him to be effected under the law of any country outside Great Britain; and an order under this subsection may contain provision as to the manner in which evidence of an overseas adoption may be given.

*   *   *   *   *

74. Short title, commencement and extent.—(1) This Act may be cited as the Adoption Act 1976.

(2) This Act shall come into force on such date as the Secretary of State may by order appoint and different dates may be appointed for different provisions.

*   *   *   *   *

SCHEDULE 2   Section 73

TRANSITIONAL PROVISIONS AND SAVINGS

Rights relating to property

6.—(1) Section 39—

(a) does not apply to an existing instrument or enactment in so far as it contains a disposition of property, and
(b) does not apply to any public general Act in its application to any disposition of property in an existing instrument or enactment.

(2) Sections 16 and 17 of the Adoption Act 1958 and provisions containing references to those sections shall continue to apply in relation to dispositions of property effected by existing instruments notwithstanding the repeal of those sections, and such provisions, by the Children Act 1975.

(3) Section 46 shall apply in relation to this paragraph as if it were contained in Part IV.

Note.—The Act came into force on 1 January 1988.

SUPREME COURT ACT 1981

(1981, c. 54)   [28 July 1981]

PART I

CONSTITUTION OF SUPREME COURT

The Supreme Court

1. The Supreme Court.—(1) The Supreme Court of England and Wales shall consist of the Court of Appeal, the High Court of Justice and the Crown Court, each having such jurisdiction as is conferred on it by or under this or any other Act.

(2) The Lord Chancellor shall be president of the Supreme Court.

*   *   *   *   *

The High Court

4. The High Court.—(1) The High Court shall consist of—

(a) the Lord Chancellor;

(b) the Lord Chief Justice;

(c) the President of the Family Division;

(d) the Vice-Chancellor; and

(e) not more than eighty puisne judges of that court.

(2) The puisne judges of the High Court shall be styled 'Justices of the High Court'.

(3) All the judges of the High Court shall, except where this Act expressly provides otherwise, have in all respects equal power, authority and jurisdiction.

*   *   *   *   *

5. Divisions of High Court.—(1) There shall be three divisions of the High Court, namely—

(a) the Chancery Division, consisting of the Lord Chancellor, who shall be president thereof, the Vice-Chancellor, who shall be vice-president thereof, and such of the puisne judges as are for the time being attached thereto in accordance with this section;

(b) the Queen's Bench Division, consisting of the Lord Chief Justice, who shall be president thereof, and such of the puisne judges as are for the time being so attached thereto; and

(c) the Family Division, consisting of the President of the Family Division and such of the puisne judges as are for the time being so attached thereto.

*   *   *   *   *

(5) Without prejudice to the provisions of this Act relating to the distribution of business in the High Court, all jurisdiction vested in the High Court under this Act shall belong to all the Divisions alike.

*   *   *   *   *

PART II

JURISDICTION

THE COURT OF APPEAL

*   *   *   *   *

16. Appeals from High Court.—(1) Subject as otherwise provided by this or any other Act (and in particular to the provision in section 13 (2) (a) of the Administration of Justice Act 1969 excluding appeals to the Court of Appeal in cases where leave to appeal from the High Court directly to the House of Lords is granted under Part II of that Act), the Court of Appeal shall have jurisdiction to hear and determine appeals from any judgment or order of the High Court.

*   *   *   *   *

17. Applications for new trial.—(1) Where any cause or matter, or any issue in any cause or matter, has been tried in the High Court, any application for a new trial thereof, or to set aside a verdict, finding or judgment therein, shall be heard and determined by the Court of Appeal except where rules of court made in pursuance of subsection (2) provide otherwise.

(2) As regards cases where the trial was by a judge alone and no error of the court at the trial is alleged, or any prescribed class of such cases, rules of court may provide that any such application as is mentioned in subsection (1) shall be heard and determined by the High Court.

*   *   *   *   *

18. Restrictions on appeals to Court of Appeal.—(1) No appeal shall lie to the Court of Appeal—

*   *   *   *   *

(b) from any order of the High Court or any other court or tribunal allowing an extension of time for appealing from a judgment or order;

(c) from any order, judgment or decision of the High Court or any other court or tribunal which, by virtue of any provision (however expressed) of this or any other Act, is final;

*   *   *   *   *

[(f)—repealed by the Courts and Legal Services Act 1990 s. 125 (7), Sch. 20 as from 1 October 1993—see p. 898, post.
(h) Ibid.
(2) Ibid.]

THE HIGH COURT

General jurisdiction

19. General jurisdiction of High Court.—(1) The High Court shall be a superior court of record.

(2) Subject to the provisions of this Act, there shall be exercisable by the High Court—

(a) all such jurisdiction (whether civil or criminal) as is conferred on it by this or any other Act; and

(b) all such other jurisdiction (whether civil or criminal) as was exercisable by it immediately before the commencement of this Act (including jurisdiction conferred on a judge of the High Court by any statutory provision).

(3) Any jurisdiction of the High Court shall be exercised only by a single judge of that court, except in so far as it is—

(a) by or by virtue of rules of court or any other statutory provision required to be exercised by a divisional court; or

(b) by rules of court made exercisable by a master, registrar or other officer of the court, or by any other person.

(4) The specific mention elsewhere in this Act of any jurisdiction covered by subsection (2) shall not derogate from the generality of that subsection.

*   *   *   *   *

Other particular fields of jurisdiction

25. Probate jurisdiction of High Court.—(1) Subject to the provisions of Part V, the High Court shall, in accordance with section 19 (2), have the following probate jurisdiction, that is to say all such jurisdiction in relation to probates and letters of administration as it had immediately before the commencement of this Act, and in particular all such contentious and non-contentious jurisdiction as it then had in relation to—

(a) testamentary causes or matters;

(b) the grant, amendment or revocation of probates and letters of administration; and

(c) the real and personal estate of deceased persons.

(2) Subject to the provisions of Part V, the High Court shall, in the exercise of its probate jurisdiction, perform all such duties with respect to the estates of deceased persons as fell to be performed by it immediately before the commencement of this Act.

31. Application for judicial review.—(1) An application to the High Court for one or more of the following forms of relief, namely—

(a) an order of mandamus, prohibition or certiorari;

(b) a declaration or injunction under subsection (2); or

(c) an injunction under section 30 restraining a person not entitled to do so from acting in an office to which that section applies, shall be made in accordance with rules of court by a procedure to be known as an application for judicial review.

(2) A declaration may be made or an injunction granted under this subsection in any case where an application for judicial review, seeking that relief has been made and the High Court considers that, having regard to—

(a) the nature of the matters in respect of which relief may be granted by orders of mandamus, prohibition or certiorari;
(b) the nature of the persons and bodies against whom relief may be granted by such orders; and
(c) all the circumstances of the case,

it would be just and convenient for the declaration to be made or the injunction to be granted, as the case may be.

(3) No application for judicial review shall be made unless the leave of the High Court has been obtained in accordance with rules of court; and the court shall not grant leave to make such an application unless it considers that the applicant has a sufficient interest in the matter to which the application relates.

(4) On an application for judicial review the High Court may award damages to the applicant if—

(a) he has joined with his application a claim for damages arising from any matter to which the application relates; and
(b) the court is satisfied that, if the claim had been made in an action begun by the applicant at the time of making his application, he would have been awarded damages.

(5) If, on an application for judicial review seeking an order of certiorari, the High Court quashes the decision to which the application relates, the High Court may remit the matter to the court, tribunal or authority concerned, with a direction to reconsider it and reach a decision in accordance with the findings of the High Court.

(6) Where the High Court considers that there has been undue delay in making an application for judicial review, the court may refuse to grant—

(a) leave for the making of the application; or
(b) any relief sought on the application, if it considers that the granting of the relief sought would be likely to cause substantial hardship to, or substantially prejudice the rights of, any person or would be detrimental to good administration.

(7) Subsection (6) is without prejudice to any enactment or rule of court which has the effect of limiting the time within which an application for judicial review may be made.

*   *   *   *   *

36. Subpoena issued by High Court to run throughout United Kingdom.—(1) If in any cause or matter in the High Court it appears to the court that it is proper to compel the personal attendance at any trial of a witness who may not be within the jurisdiction of the court, it shall be lawful for the court, if in the discretion of the court it seems fit so to do, to order that a writ of subpoena ad testificandum or writ of subpoena duces tecum shall issue in special form commanding the witness to attend the trial wherever he shall be within the United Kingdom; and the service of any such writ in any part of the United Kingdom shall be as valid and effectual for all purposes as if it had been served within the jurisdiction of the High Court.

(2) Every such writ shall have at its foot a statement to the effect that it is issued by the special order of the High Court, and no such writ shall issue without such a special order.

(3) If any person served with a writ issued under this section does not appear as required by the writ, the High Court, on proof to the satisfaction of the court of the service of the writ and of the default, may transmit a certificate of the default under the seal of the court or under the hand of a judge of the court—

(a) if the service was in Scotland, to the Court of Session at Edinburgh; or

(b) if the service was in Northern Ireland, to the High Court of Justice in Northern Ireland at Belfast;

and the court to which the certificate is sent shall thereupon proceed against and punish the person in default in like manner as if that person had neglected or refused to appear in obedience to process issued out of that court.

(4) No court shall in any case proceed against or punish any person for having made such default as aforesaid unless it is shown to the court that a reasonable and sufficient sum of money to defray—

(a) *the expenses of coming and attending to give evidence and of returning from giving evidence; and*

(b) *any other reasonable expenses which he has asked to be defrayed in connection with his evidence,*

was tendered to him at the time when the writ was served upon him[2].

(5) Nothing in this section shall affect—

(a) the power of the High Court to issue a commission for the examination of witnesses out of the jurisdiction of the court in any case in which, notwithstanding this section, the court thinks fit to issue such a commission; or

(b) the admissibility at any trial of any evidence which, if this section had not been enacted, would have been admissible on the ground of a witness being outside the jurisdiction of the court.

(6) In this section references to attendance at a trial include references to attendance before an examiner or commissioner appointed by the High Court in any cause or matter in that court, including an examiner or commissioner appointed to take evidence outside the jurisdiction of the court.

37. Powers of High Court with respect to injunctions and receivers.—(1) The High Court may by order (whether interlocutory or final) grant an injunction or appoint a receiver in all cases in which it appears to the court to be just and convenient to do so.

(2) Any such order may be made either unconditionally or on such terms and conditions as the court thinks just.

(3) The power of the High Court under subsection (1) to grant an interlocutory injunction restraining a party to any proceedings from removing from the jurisdiction of the High Court, or otherwise dealing with, assets located within that jurisdiction shall be exercisable in cases where that party is, as well as in cases where he is not, domiciled, resident or present within that jurisdiction.

39. Execution of instrument by person nominated by High Court.—(1) Where the High Court has given or made a judgment or order directing a person to execute any conveyance, contract or other document, or to indorse any negotiable instrument, then, if that person—

(a) neglects or refuses to comply with the judgment or order; or
(b) cannot after reasonable inquiry be found,

the High Court may, on such terms and conditions, if any, as may be just, order that the conveyance, contract or other document shall be executed, or that the negotiable instrument shall be indorsed, by such person as the court may nominate for that purpose.

(2) A conveyance, contract, document or instrument executed or indorsed in pursuance of an order under this section shall operate, and be for all purposes available, as if it had been executed or indorsed by the person originally directed to execute or indorse it.

*   *   *   *   *

2   The words in italics in sub-s. (4) were substituted for former words by the Courts and Legal Services Act 1990, s. 125(7), Sch. 17, para. 13—see p. 897, post).

GENERAL PROVISIONS

Law and equity

49. Concurrent administration of law and equity.—(1) Subject to the provisions of this or any other Act, every court exercising jurisdiction in England or Wales in any civil cause or matter shall continue to administer law and equity on the basis that, wherever there is any conflict or variance between the rules of equity and the rules of the common law with reference to the same matter, the rules of equity shall prevail.

(2) Every such court shall give the same effect as hitherto—

(a) to all equitable estates, titles, rights, reliefs, defences and counterclaims, and to all equitable duties and liabilities; and

(b) subject thereto, to all legal claims and demands and all estates, titles, rights, duties, obligations and liabilities existing by the common law or by any custom or created by any statute,

and, subject to the provisions of this or any other Act, shall so exercise its jurisdiction in every cause or matter before it as to secure that, as far as possible, all matters in dispute between the parties are completely and finally determined, and all multiplicity of legal proceedings with respect to any of those matters is avoided.

(3) Nothing in this Act shall affect the power of the Court of Appeal or the High Court to stay any proceedings before it, where it thinks fit to do so, either on its own motion or on the application of any person, whether or not a party to the proceedings.

50. Power to award damages as well as, or in substitution for, injunction or specific performance. Where the Court of Appeal or the High Court has jurisdiction to entertain an application for an injunction or specific performance, it may award damages in addition to, or in substitution for, an injunction or specific performance.

Costs

51. Costs in civil division of Court of Appeal and High Court.—(1) Subject to the provisions of this or any other Act and to rules of court, the costs of and incidental to all proceedings in the civil division of the Court of Appeal and in the High Court, including the administration of estates and trusts, shall be in the discretion of the court, and the court shall have full power to determine by whom and to what extent the costs are to be paid.

*   *   *   *   *

(3) Provision may be made by rules of court for regulating any matters relating to the costs of proceedings in the civil division of the Court of Appeal or in the High Court, including the administration of estates and trusts.

*   *   *   *   *

Other provisions

*   *   *   *   *

60. Rules of court, and decision of Court of Appeal, as to whether judgment or order is final or interlocutory.—(1) Rules of court may provide for orders or judgments of any prescribed description to be treated for any prescribed purpose connected with appeals to the Court of Appeal as final or as interlocutory.

(2) No appeal shall lie from a decision of the Court of Appeal as to whether a judgment or order is, for any purpose connected with an appeal to the court, final or interlocutory.

THE HIGH COURT

Distribution of business

61. Distribution of business among Divisions.—(1) Subject to any provision made by or under this or any other Act (and in particular to any rules of court made in pursuance of subsection (2) and any order under subsection (3)), business in the High Court of any description mentioned in Schedule 1, as for the time being in force, shall be distributed among the Divisions in accordance with that Schedule.

(2) Rules of court may provide for the distribution of business in the High Court among the Divisions, but any rules made in pursuance of this subsection shall have effect subject to any orders for the time being in force under subsection (3).

(3) Subject to subsection (5), the Lord Chancellor may by order—

(a) direct that any business in the High Court which is not for the time being assigned by or under this or any other Act to any Division be assigned to such Division as may be specified in the order;

(b) if at any time it appears to him desirable to do so with a view to the more convenient administration of justice, direct that any business for the time being assigned by or under this or any other Act to any Division be assigned to such other Division. as may be specified in the order; and

(c) amend Schedule 1 so far as may be necessary in consequence of provision made by order under paragraph (a) or (b).

(4) The powers conferred by subsection (2) and subsection (3) include power to assign business of any description to two or more Divisions concurrently.

(5) No order under subsection (3) (b) relating to any business shall be made without the concurrence of the senior judge of—

(a) the Division or each of the Divisions to which the business is for the time being assigned; and

(b) the Division or each of the Divisions to which the business is to be assigned by the order.

(6) Subject to rules of court, the fact that a cause or matter commenced in the High Court falls within a class of business assigned by or under this Act to a particular Division does not make it obligatory for it to be allocated or transferred to that Division.

(7) Without prejudice to subsections (1) to (5) and section 63, rules of court may provide for the distribution of the business (other than business required to be heard by a divisional court) in any Division of the High Court among the judges of that Division.

(8) Any order under subsection (3) shall be made by statutory instrument, which shall be laid before Parliament after being made.

*   *   *   *   *

64. Choice of Division by plaintiff.—(1) Without prejudice to the power of transfer under section 65, the person by whom any cause or matter is commenced in the High Court shall in the prescribed manner allocate it to whichever Division he thinks fit.

(2) Where a cause or matter is commenced in the High Court, all subsequent interlocutory or other steps or proceedings in the High Court in that cause or matter shall be taken in the Division to which the cause or matter is for the time being allocated (whether under subsection (1) or in consequence of its transfer under section 64).

65. Power of transfer.—(1) Any cause or matter may at any time and at any stage thereof, and either with or without application from any of the parties, be transferred, by such authority and in such manner as rules of court may direct, from one Division or judge of the High Court to another Division or judge thereof.

(2) The transfer of a cause or matter under subsection (1) to a different Division or judge of the High Court shall not affect the validity of any steps or proceedings taken or order made in that cause or matter before the transfer.

*   *   *   *   *

Mode of conducting business

67. Proceedings in court and in chambers. Business in the High Court shall be heard and disposed of in court except in so far as it may, under this or any other Act, under rules of court or in accordance with the practice of the court, be dealt with in chambers.

*   *   *   *   *

RULES OF COURT

84. Power to make rules of court.—(1) Rules of court may be made for the purpose of regulating and prescribing the practice and procedure to be followed in the Supreme Court.

(2) Without prejudice to the generality of subsection (1), the matters about which rules of court may be made under this section include all matters of practice and procedure in the Supreme Court which were regulated or prescribed by rules of court immediately before the commencement of this Act.

(3) No provision of this or any other Act, or contained in any instrument made under any Act, which—

(a) authorises or requires the making of rules of court about any particular matter or for any particular purpose; or

(b) provides (in whatever words) that the power to make rules of court under this section is to include power to make rules about any particular matter or for any particular purpose,

shall be taken as derogating from the generality of subsection (1).

(4) Rules made under this section shall have effect subject to any special rules for the time being in force in relation to proceedings in the Supreme Court of any particular kind.

(5) Special rules may, to any extent and with or without modifications, apply any rules made under this section to proceedings to which the special rules apply; and rules under this section may, to any extent and with or without modifications, apply any special rules to proceedings in the Supreme Court to which those special rules would not otherwise apply.

(6) Special rules which apply any rules made under this section may apply them as amended from time to time; and rules under this section which apply any special rules may apply them as amended from time to time.

*   *   *   *   *

(9) In this section 'special rules' means rules applying to proceedings of any particular kind in the Supreme Court, being rules made by an authority other than the Supreme Court Rule Committee or the Crown Court Rule Committee under any provision of this or any other Act which (in whatever words) confers on that authority power to make rules in relation to proceedings of that kind in the Supreme Court.

87. Particular matters for which rules of court may provide.—(1) Rules of court may make provision for regulating the means by which particular facts may be proved, and the mode in which evidence thereof may be given, in any proceedings in the High Court or in the civil division of the Court of Appeal or on any application in connection with or at any stage of any such proceedings.

(2) Rules of court may make provision—

(a) for enabling proceedings to be commenced in the High Court against the estate of a deceased person (whether by the appointment of a person to represent the estate or otherwise) where no grant of probate or administration has been made;

(b) for enabling proceedings purporting to have been commenced in that court against a person to be treated, if he was dead at their commencement, as having been commenced against his estate, whether or not a grant of probate or administration was made before their commencement; and

(c) for enabling any proceedings commenced or treated as commenced in that court against the estate of a deceased person to be maintained (whether by substitution of parties, amendment or otherwise) against a person appointed to represent the estate or, if a grant of probate or administration is or has been made, against the personal representatives.

(3) Rules of court may amend or repeal any statutory provision relating to the practice and procedure of the Supreme Court so far as may be necessary in consequence of provision made by the rules.

*   *   *   *   *

PART IV

OFFICERS AND OFFICES

District probate registries

104. District probate registries.—(1) The Lord Chancellor may by order direct that there shall be district probate registries of the High Court at such places and for such districts as are specified in the order.

(2) Any order under this section shall be made by statutory instrument, which shall be laid before Parliament after being made.

PART V

PROBATE CAUSES AND MATTERS

Procedure in probate registries in relation to grants of representation

105. Applications. Applications for grants of probate or administration and for the revocation of grants may be made to—

(a) the Principal Registry of the Family Division (in this Part referred to as 'the Principal Registry'); or
(b) a district probate registry.

106. Grants by district probate registrars.—(1) Any grant made by a district probate registrar shall be made in the name of the High Court under the seal used in the registry.

(2)[3]

(3)[3]

(4)[3]

107. No grant where conflicting applications. Subject to probate rules, no grant in respect of the estate, or part of the estate, of a deceased person shall be made out of the Principal Registry or any district probate registry on any application if, at any time before the making of a grant, it appears to the registrar concerned that some other application has been made in respect of that estate or, as the case may be, that part of it and has not been either refused or withdrawn.

108. Caveats.—(1) A caveat against a grant of probate or administration may be entered in the Principal Registry or in any district probate registry.

(2) On a caveat being entered in a district probate registry, the district probate registrar shall immediately send a copy of it to the Principal Registry to be entered among the caveats in that Registry.

109. Refusal of grant where capital transfer tax unpaid.—(1) Subject to subsections (2) and (3), no grant shall be made, and no grant made outside the United Kingdom shall be

---

3   Omitted, as from 1 October 1986, by Administration of Justice Act 1985, s. 51(2), p. 866, post. See also NCPR 7, p. 926, post.

resealed, except on the production of an account prepared in pursuance of Part III of the Finance Act 1975[4] showing by means of such receipt or certification as may be prescribed by the Commissioners of Inland Revenue (in this and the following section referred to as 'the Commissioners') either—

(a) that the capital transfer tax payable on the delivery of the account has been paid; or

(b) that no such tax is so payable.

(2) Arrangements may be made between the President of the Family Division and the Commissioners providing for the purposes of this section in such cases as may be specified in the arrangements that the receipt or certification of an account may be dispensed with or that some other document may be substituted for the account required by Part III of the Finance Act 1975[5].

(3) Nothing in subsection (1) applies in relation to a case where the delivery of the account required by that Part of that Act has for the time being been dispensed with by any regulations under section 94 (1) (a) of the Finance Act 1980 [6].

110. Documents to be delivered to Commissioners of Inland Revenue. Subject to any arrangements which may from time to time be made between the President of the Family Division and the Commissioners, the Principal Registry and every district probate registry shall, within such period after a grant as the President may direct, deliver to the Commissioners or their proper officer the following documents—

(a) in the case of a grant of probate or of administration with the will annexed, a copy of the will;

(b) in every case, such certificate or note of the grant as the Commissioners may require.

111. Records of grants.—(1) There shall continue to be kept records of all grants which are made in the Principal Registry or in any district probate registry.

(2) Those records, shall be in such form, and shall contain such particulars, as the President of the Family Division may direct.

Powers of court in relation to personal representatives

112. Summons of executor to prove or renounce. The High Court may summon any person named as executor in a will to prove, or renounce probate of, the will, and to do such other things concerning the will as the court had power to order such a person to do immediately before the commencement of this Act.

113. Power of court to sever grant.—(1) Subject to subsection (2), the High Court may grant probate or administration in respect of any part of the estate of a deceased person, limited in any way the court thinks fit.

(2) Where the estate of a deceased person is known to be insolvent, the grant of representation to it shall not be severed under subsection (1) except as regards a trust estate in which he had no beneficial interest.

114. Number of personal representatives.—(1) Probate or administration shall not be granted by the High Court to more than four persons in respect of the same part of the estate of a deceased person.

(2) Where under a will or intestacy any beneficiary is a minor or a life interest arises, any grant of administration by the High Court shall be made either to a trust corporation (with or without an individual) or to not less than two individuals, unless it appears to the court to be expedient in all the circumstances to appoint an individual as sole administrator.

4   See now Inheritance Tax Act 1984, s. 276, Sch. 8, para. 20(a).
5   See now ibid., s. 276, Sch. 8, para. 20(b).
6   See now ibid., s. 256(1)(a).

(3) For the purpose of determining whether a minority or life interest arises in any particular case, the court may act on such evidence as may be prescribed.

(4) If at any time during the minority of a beneficiary or the subsistence of a life interest under a will or intestacy there is only one personal representative (not being a trust corporation), the High Court may, on the application of any person interested or the guardian or receiver of any such person, and in accordance with probate rules, appoint one or more additional personal representatives to act while the minority or life interest subsists and until the estate is fully administered.

(5) An appointment of an additional personal representative under subsection (4) to act with an executor shall not have the effect of including him in any chain of representation.

115. Grants to trust corporations.—(1) The High Court may—

(a) where a trust corporation is named in a will as executor, grant probate to the corporation either solely or jointly with any other person named in the will as executor, as the case may require; or

(b) grant administration to a trust corporation, either solely or jointly with another person;

and the corporation may act accordingly as executor or administrator, as the case may be.

(2) Probate or administration shall not be granted to any person as nominee of a trust corporation.

(3) Any officer authorised for the purpose by a trust corporation or its directors or governing body may, on behalf of the corporation, swear affidavits, give security and do any other act which the court may require with a view to the grant to the corporation of probate or administration; and the acts of an officer so authorised shall be binding on the corporation.

116. Power of court to pass over prior claims to grant.—(1) If by reason of any special circumstances it appears to the High Court to be necessary or expedient to appoint as administrator some person other than the person who, but for this section, would in accordance with probate rules have been entitled to the grant, the court may in its discretion appoint as administrator such person as it thinks expedient.

(2) Any grant of administration under this section may be limited in any way the court thinks fit.

117. Administration pending suit.—(1) Where any legal proceedings concerning the validity of the will of a deceased person, or for obtaining, recalling or revoking any grant, are pending, the High Court may grant administration of the estate of the deceased person in question to an administrator pending suit, who shall, subject to subsection (2), have all the rights, duties and powers of a general administrator.

(2) An administrator pending suit shall be subject to the immediate control of the court and act under its direction; and, except in such circumstances as may be prescribed, no distribution of the estate, or any part of the estate, of the deceased person in question shall be made by such an administrator without the leave of the court.

(3) The court may, out of the estate of the deceased, assign an administrator pending suit such reasonable remuneration as it thinks fit.

118. Effect of appointment of minor as executor. Where a testator by his will appoints a minor to be an executor, the appointment shall not operate to vest in the minor the estate, or any part of the estate, of the testator, or to constitute him a personal representative for any purpose, unless and until probate is granted to him in accordance with probate rules.

119. Administration with will annexed.—(1) Administration with the will annexed shall be granted, subject to and in accordance with probate rules, in every class of case in which the High Court had power to make such a grant immediately before the commencement of this Act.

(2) Where administration with the will annexed is granted, the will of the deceased shall be performed and observed in the same manner as if probate of it had been granted to an executor.

120. Power to require administrator to produce sureties.—(1) As a condition of granting administration to any person the High Court may, subject to the following provisions of this section and subject to and in accordance with probate rules, require one or more sureties to guarantee that they will make good, within any limit imposed by the court on the total liability of the surety or sureties, any loss which any person interested in the administration of the estate of the deceased may suffer in consequence of a breach by the administrator of his duties as such.

(2) A guarantee given in pursuance of any such requirement shall enure for the benefit of every person interested in the administration of the estate of the deceased as if contained in a contract under seal made by the surety or sureties with every such person and, where there are two or more sureties, as if they had bound themselves jointly and severally.

(3) No action shall be brought on any such guarantee without the leave of the High Court.

(4) Stamp duty shall not be chargeable on any such guarantee.

(5) This section does not apply where administration is granted to the Treasury Solicitor, the Official Solicitor, the Public Trustee, the Solicitor for the affairs of the Duchy of Lancaster or the Duchy of Cornwall or the Crown Solicitor for Northern Ireland, or to the consular officer of a foreign state to which section 1 of the Consular Conventions Act 1949 applies, or in such other cases as may be prescribed.

Revocation of grants and cancellation of resealing at instance of court

121. Revocation of grants and cancellation of resealing at instance of court.—(1) Where it appears to the High Court that a grant either ought not to have been made or contains an error, the court may call in the grant and, if satisfied that it would be revoked at the instance of a party interested, may revoke it.

(2) A grant may be revoked under subsection (1) without being called in, if it cannot be called in.

(3) Where it appears to the High Court that a grant resealed under the Colonial Probates Acts 1892 and 1927 ought not to have been resealed, the court may call in the relevant document and, if satisfied that the resealing would be cancelled at the instance of a party interested, may cancel the resealing. In this and the following subsection 'the relevant document' means the original grant or, where some other document was sealed by the court under those Acts, that document.

(4) A resealing may be cancelled under subsection (3) without the relevant document being called in, if it cannot be called in.

Ancillary powers of court

122. Examination of person with knowledge of testamentary document.—(1) Where it appears that there are reasonable grounds for believing that any person has knowledge of any document which is or purports to be a testamentary document, the High Court may, whether or not any legal proceedings are pending, order him to attend for the purpose of being examined in open court.

(2) The court may—

(a) require any person who is before it in compliance with an order under subsection (1) to answer any question relating to the document concerned; and
(b) if appropriate, order him to bring in the document in such manner as the court may direct.

(3) Any person who, having been required by the court to do so under this section, fails to attend for examination, answer any question or bring in any document shall be guilty of contempt of court.

123. Subpoena to bring in testamentary document. Where it appears that any person has in his possession, custody or power any document which is or purports to be a testamentary document, the High Court may, whether or not any legal proceedings are pending, issue a subpoena requiring him to bring in the document in such manner as the court may in the subpoena direct.

Provisions as to documents

124. Place for deposit of original wills and other documents. All original wills and other documents which are under the control of the High Court in the Principal Registry or in any district probate registry shall be deposited and preserved in such places as the Lord Chancellor may direct; and any wills or other documents so deposited shall, subject to the control of the High Court and to probate rules, be open to inspection.

125. Copies of wills and grants. An office copy, or a sealed and certified copy, of any will or part of a will open to inspection under section 124 or of any grant may, on payment of the prescribed fee, be obtained—

(a) from the registry in which in accordance with section 124 the will or documents relating to the grant are preserved; or

(b) where in accordance with that section the will or such documents are preserved in some place other than a registry, from the Principal Registry; or

(c) subject to the approval of the Senior Registrar of the Family Division, from the Principal Registry in any case where the will was proved in or the grant was issued from a district probate registry.

[**126. Depositories for wills of living persons**—*(1) There shall be provided, under the control and direction of the High Court, safe and convenient depositories for the custody of the wills of living persons; and any person may deposit his will in such a depository on payment of the prescribed fee and subject to such conditions as may be prescribed by regulations made by the President of the Family Division with the concurrence of the Lord Chancellor.*

(2) Any regulations made under this section shall be made by statutory instrument which shall be laid before Parliament after being made; and the Statutory Instruments Act 1946 shall apply to a statutory instrument containing regulations under this section in like manner as if they had been made by a Minister of the Crown.[7]]

Probate rules

127. Probate rules.—(1) The President of the Family Division may, with the concurrence of the Lord Chancellor, make rules of court (in this Part referred to as 'probate rules') for regulating and prescribing the practice and procedure of the High Court with respect to non-contentious or common form probate business.

(2) Without prejudice to the generality of subsection (1), probate rules may make provision for regulating the classes of person entitled to grants of probate or administration in particular circumstances and the relative priorities of their claims thereto.

(3) Probate rules shall be made by statutory instrument subject to annulment in pursuance of a resolution of either House of Parliament; and the Statutory Instruments Act 1946 shall apply to a statutory instrument containing probate rules in like manner as if they had been made by a Minister of the Crown.

Interpretation of Part V and other probate provisions

128. Interpretation of Part V and other probate provisions. In this Part, and in the other provisions of this Act relating to probate causes and matters, unless the context otherwise requires—

'administration' includes all letters of administration of the effects of deceased persons,

---

7   Section 126 is repealed by the Administration of Justice Act 1982, s. 75 and Sch. 9, Pt. I, and, once the relevant provisions are brought into force will be replaced by ss. 23 to 26 of the 1982 Act.

whether with or without a will annexed, and whether granted for general, special or limited purposes;

'estate' means real and personal estate, and 'real estate' includes—

(a) chattels real and land in possession, remainder or reversion and every interest in or over land to which the deceased person was entitled at the time of his death, and

(b) real estate held on trust or by way of mortgage or security, but not money to arise under a trust for sale of land, nor money secured or charged on land;

'grant' means a grant of probate or administration;

'non-contentious or common form probate business' means the business of obtaining probate and administration where there is no contention as to the right thereto, including—

(a) the passing of probates and administrations through the High Court in contentious cases where the contest has been terminated,

(b) all business of a non-contentious nature in matters of testacy and intestacy not being proceedings in any action, and

(c) the business of lodging caveats against the grant of probate or administration;

'Principal Registry' means the Principal Registry of the Family Division;

'probate rules' means rules of court made under section 127;

'trust corporation' means the Public Trustee or a corporation either appointed by the court in any particular case to be a trustee or authorised by rules made under section 4 (3) of the Public Trustee Act 1906 to act as a custodian trustee;

'will' includes a nuncupative will and any testamentary document of which probate may be granted.

PART VI

Miscellaneous and Supplementary

Miscellaneous provisions

130. Fees to be taken in Supreme Court.—(1) The Lord Chancellor may by order under this section prescribe the fees to be taken in the Supreme Court, other than fees which he or some other authority has power to prescribe apart from this section.

(2) The concurrence of the Treasury shall be required for the making of any order under this section; and in addition—

(a) the concurrence of the Lord Chief Justice, the Master of the Rolls, the President of the Family Division and the Vice-Chancellor or any three of them, shall be required for the making of any such order not relating exclusively to fees to be taken in connection with proceedings in the Crown Court;

*   *   *   *   *

(3) Nothing in subsection (1) shall be taken to prevent any authority having power apart from this section to prescribe fees to be taken in the Supreme Court from applying to any extent any provisions contained in any order made under this section; and where any instrument made in the exercise of any such power applies any provisions so contained, then, unless the contrary intention appears, it shall be taken to apply those provisions as amended from time to time.

(4) Any order under this section shall be made by statutory instrument, which shall be laid before Parliament after being made.

*   *   *   *   *

132. Proof of documents bearing seal or stamp of Supreme Court or any office thereof.
Every document purporting to be sealed or stamped with the seal or stamp of the Supreme

Court or of any office of the Supreme Court shall be received in evidence in all parts of the United Kingdom without further proof.

*　　　　　*　　　　　*　　　　　*　　　　　*

134. Powers of attorney deposited before October 1971.—(1) This section applies to any instrument creating, or verifying the execution of, a power of attorney which was deposited in the Central Office of the Supreme Court before 1 October 1971.

(2) A separate file of such instruments shall continue to be kept and, subject to payment of any prescribed fee—

(a) any person may search that file, and may inspect any such instrument; and

(b) an office copy of any such instrument shall be issued to any person on request.

(3) A document purporting to be an office copy of any such instrument shall, in any part of the United Kingdom, without further proof be sufficient evidence of the contents of the instrument and of its having been deposited as mentioned in subsection (1).

*　　　　　*　　　　　*　　　　　*　　　　　*

136. Production of documents filed in, or in custody of Supreme Court.—(1) The Lord Chancellor may, with the concurrence of the Lord Chief Justice, the Master of the Rolls, the President of the Family Division and the Vice-Chancellor, or any three of them, make rules for providing that, in any case where a document filed in, or in the custody of, any office of the Supreme Court is required to be produced to any court or tribunal (including an umpire or arbitrator) sitting elsewhere than at the Royal Courts of Justice—

(a) it shall not be necessary for any officer, whether served with a subpoena in that behalf or not, to attend for the purpose of producing the document; but

(b) the document may be produced to the court or tribunal by sending it to the court or tribunal, in the manner prescribed in the rules, together with a certificate, in the form so prescribed, to the effect that the document has been filed in, or is in the custody of, the office; and such certificate shall be prima facie evidence of the facts stated in it.

(2) Rules under this section may contain—

(a) provisions for securing the safe custody and return to the proper office of the Supreme Court of any document sent to a court or tribunal in pursuance of the rules; and

(b) such incidental and supplementary provisions as appear to the Lord Chancellor to be necessary or expedient.

(3) Rules under this section shall be made by statutory instrument, which shall be laid before Parliament after being made.

*　　　　　*　　　　　*　　　　　*　　　　　*

151. Interpretation of this Act, and rules of construction for other Acts and documents.—(1) In this Act, unless the context otherwise requires—

'action' means any civil proceedings commenced by writ or in any other manner prescribed by rules of court;

'appeal', in the context of appeals to the civil division of the Court of Appeal, includes—

(a) an application for a new trial,

*　　　　　*　　　　　*　　　　　*　　　　　*

'cause' means any action;

*　　　　　*　　　　　*　　　　　*　　　　　*

'judgment' includes a decree;

'jurisdiction' includes powers;

'matter' means any proceedings in court not in a cause;

'party', in relation to any proceedings, includes any person who pursuant to or by virtue of rules of court or any other statutory provision has been served with notice of, or has intervened in, those proceedings;

'prescribed' means—

(a) except in relation to fees, prescribed by rules of court; and
(b) in relation to fees, prescribed by an order under section 130;

'senior judge', where the reference is to the senior judge of a Division, means—

(a) in the case of the Chancery Division, the Vice-Chancellor;
(b) in any other case, the president of the Division in question;

'solicitor' means a solicitor of the Supreme Court;

'statutory provision' means any enactment, whenever passed, or any provision contained in subordinate legislation (as defined in section 21 (1) of the Interpretation Act 1978), whenever made;

'this or any other Act' includes an Act passed after this Act.

(2) Section 128 contains definitions of expressions used in Part V and in the other provisions of this Act relating to probate causes and matters.

(3) Any reference in this Act to rules of court under section 84 includes a reference to rules of court under any provision of this or any other Act which confers on the Supreme Court Rules Committee or the Crown Court Rule Committee power to make rules of court.

(4) Except where the context otherwise requires, in this or any other Act—

*   *   *   *   *

'judge of the Supreme Court' means—

(a) a judge of the Court of Appeal other than an ex-officio judge within paragraph (b) or (c) of section 2 (2), or
(b) a judge of the High Court,

and accordingly does not include, as such, a judge of the Crown Court;

*   *   *   *   *

'Rules of the Supreme Court' means rules of court made by the Supreme Court Rule Committee.

(5) The provisions of Schedule 4 (construction of references to superseded courts and officers) shall have effect.

152. Amendments to other Acts, transitional provisions, savings and repeals.

*   *   *   *   *

(3) This Act shall have effect subject to the transitional provisions and savings contained in Schedule 6.

*   *   *   *   *

(5) The following instruments are hereby revoked—

(a) the District Probate Registries Order 1968;

*   *   *   *   *

153. Citation, commencement and extent.—(1) This Act may be cited as the Supreme Court Act 1981.

(2) This Act, except the provisions mentioned in subsection (3), shall come into force on 1 January 1982; and references to the commencement of this Act shall be construed as references to the beginning of that day.

(3) Sections 72, 143 and 152 (2) and this section shall come into force on the passing of this Act.

*   *   *   *   *

SCHEDULE 1

DISTRIBUTION OF BUSINESS IN HIGH COURT

Chancery Division

1. To the Chancery Division are assigned all causes and matters relating to—

*   *   *   *   *

(d)   the administration of the estates of deceased persons;

*   *   *   *   *

(h)   probate business, other than non-contentious or common form business;

*   *   *   *   *

Family Division

3. To the Family Division are assigned—

*   *   *   *   *

(b)   all causes and matters (whether at first instance or on appeal) relating to—

*   *   *   *   *

(iv)   non-contentious or common form probate business;

SCHEDULE 4

CONSTRUCTION OF REFERENCES TO SUPERSEDED COURTS AND OFFICERS

*   *   *   *   *

Principal registrar of Family Division

4. In any enactment or document passed or made before the commencement of this Act any reference to the principal registrar of the Family Division shall be read as a reference to the Senior Registrar of that Division.

*   *   *   *   *

Scheme for establishment of district probate registries

6. The scheme for the establishment of district probate registries as set out in Schedule 2 to the 1925 Act and in force immediately before the commencement of this Act shall continue to have effect, but as if it were contained in an order under section 104 of this Act; and accordingly it may be amended or revoked by an order under that section.[8]

Inland Revenue affidavits

7. In relation to deaths occurring before 13 March 1975 (the date on which the Finance Act 1975 was passed)—

(a)   section 109 shall not apply; and
(b)   section 110 shall have effect as if at the end of paragraph (b) there were added the words 'and the Inland Revenue affidavit within the meaning of Part I of the Finance Act 1894'.

Grants of representation made under provisions of 1925 Act not reproduced in this Act

8. Nothing in the repeals made by this Act shall affect—

---

8   Since revoked: see now the District Probate Registries Order 1982: p. 921, post.

(a) any grant made before the commencement of this Act under any of the following provisions of the 1925 Act, namely section 162 (1) and proviso (a) thereto and sections 164 and 165; or

(b) the continued operation of subsections (2) and (3) of section 164 of that Act in relation to any grant so made under that section.

Minor executors

9. Any appointment of a minor as executor which, immediately before the commencement of this Act, was by virtue of section 165 (2) of the 1925 Act rendered ineffective for the purposes mentioned in that subsection shall continue to be ineffective for those purposes unless and until probate is granted to the person in question in accordance with probate rules.

Administration bonds given before 1 January 1972

10. Nothing in this Act shall affect the continued operation of section 167 of the 1925 Act, as in force before 1 January 1972 (the date on which the Administration of Estates Act 1971 came into force), in relation to the enforcement or assignment of any administration bond given under that section before that date.

Grants and resealings liable to revocation or cancellation at instance of court

11. Section 121 applies whether the grant in question was made or (as the case may be) resealed before or after the commencement of this Act.

*   *   *   *   *

Interpretation

13.—(1) In this Schedule 'the 1925 Act' means the Supreme Court of Judicature (Consolidation) Act 1925.

(2) Nothing in this Schedule shall be taken as prejudicing the operation of the provisions of the Interpretation Act 1978 as respects the effect of repeals.

FORFEITURE ACT 1982

(1982, c. 34)   [13 July 1982]

1. The 'forfeiture rule'.—(1) In this Act, the 'forfeiture rule' means the rule of public policy which in certain circumstances precludes a person who has unlawfully killed another from acquiring a benefit in consequence of the killing.

(2) References in this Act to a person who has unlawfully killed another include a reference to a person who has unlawfully aided, abetted, counselled or procured the death of that other and references in this Act to unlawful killing shall be interpreted accordingly.

2. Power to modify the rule.—(1) Where a court determines that the forfeiture rule has precluded a person (in this section referred to as 'the offender') who has unlawfully killed another from acquiring any interest in property mentioned in subsection (4) below, the court may make an order under this section modifying the effect of that rule.

(2) The court shall not make an order under this section modifying the effect of the forfeiture rule in any case unless it is satisfied that, having regard to the conduct of the offender and of the deceased and to such other circumstances as appear to the court to be material, the justice of the case requires the effect of the rule to be so modified in that case.

(3) In any case where a person stands convicted of an offense of which unlawful killing is an element, the court shall not make an order under this section modifying the effect of the forfeiture rule in that case unless proceedings for the purpose are brought before the expiry of the period of three months beginning with his conviction.

(4) The interests in property referred to in subsection (1) above are—

(a) any beneficial interest in property which (apart from the forfeiture rule) the offender would have acquired—

    (i) under the deceased's will (including, as respects Scotland, any writing having testamentary effect) or the law relating to intestacy or by way of ius relicti, ius relictae or legitim;

   (ii) on the nomination of the deceased in accordance with the provisions of any enactment;

  (iii) as a donatio mortis causa made by the deceased; or

  (iv) under a special destination (whether relating to heritable or moveable property); or

(b) any beneficial interest in property which (apart from the forfeiture rule) the offender would have acquired in consequence of the death of the deceased, being property which, before the death, was held on trust for any person.

(5) An order under this section may modify the effect of the forfeiture rule in respect of any interest in property to which the determination referred to in subsection (1) above relates and may do so in either or both of the following ways, that is—

(a) where there is more than one such interest, by excluding the application of the rule in respect of any (but not all) of those interests; and

(b) in the case of any such interest in property, by excluding the application of the rule in respect of part of the property.

(6) On the making of an order under this section the forfeiture rule shall have effect for all purposes (including purposes relating to anything done before the order is made) subject to the modifications made by the order.

(7) The court shall not make an order under this section modifying the effect of the forfeiture rule in respect of any interest in property which, in consequence of the rule, has been acquired before the coming into force of this section by a person other than the offender or a person claiming through him.

(8) In this section—

'property' includes any chose in action or incorporeal moveable property; and

'will' includes codicil.

3. Application for financial provision not affected by the rule.—(1) The forfeiture rule shall not be taken to preclude any person from making any application under a provision mentioned in subsection (2) below or the making of any order on the application.

(2) The provisions referred to in subsection (1) above are—

(a) any provision of the Inheritance (Provision for Family and Dependants) Act 1975; and

*   *   *   *   *

5. Exclusion of murderers.—Nothing in this Act or in any order made under section 2 or referred to in section 3 (1) of this Act shall affect the application of the forfeiture rule in the case of a person who stands convicted of murder.

7. Short title etc.—(1) This Act may be cited as the Forfeiture Act 1982.

(2) sections 1 to 3 and 5 of this Act shall come into force on the expiry of the period of three months beginning with the day on which it is passed.

*   *   *   *   *

(4) Subject to section 2 (7) of this Act, an order under section 2 of this Act or an order referred to in section 3 (1) of this Act and made in respect of a person who has unlawfully killed another may be made whether the unlawful killing occurred before or after the coming into force of those sections.

Note.—Section 7 above came into force on 13 July 1982, the day on which the Act was passed.

ADMINISTRATION OF JUSTICE ACT 1982

(1982, c. 53)   [28 October 1982]

PART IV

WILLS

Amendments of Wills Act 1837

17. Relaxation of formal requirements for making wills.

(For text, see s. 9 of the Wills Act 1837, p. 720, ante.)

18. Effect of marriage or its termination on wills.

(For text, see s.18 of the Wills Act 1837, p. 722, ante.)

19. Gifts to children etc. who predecease testator.

(For text, see s. 33 of the Wills Act 1837, p. 725, ante.)

Rectification and interpretation of wills

20. Rectification.—(1) If a court is satisfied that a will is so expressed that it fails to carry out the testator's intentions, in consequence—

(a) of a clerical error; or
(b) of a failure to understand his instructions,

it may order that the will shall be rectified so as to carry out his intentions.

(2) An application for an order under this section shall not, except with the permission of the court, be made after the end of the period of six months from the date on which representation with respect to the estate of the deceased is first taken out.

(3) The provisions of this section shall not render the personal representatives of a deceased person liable for having distributed any part of the estate of the deceased, after the end of the period of six months from the date on which representation with respect to the estate of the deceased is first taken out, on the ground that they ought to have taken into account the possibility that the court might permit the making of an application for an order under this section after the end of that period; but this subsection shall not prejudice any power to recover, by reason of the making of an order under this section, any part of the estate so distributed.

(4) In considering for the purposes of this section when representation with respect to the estate of a deceased person was first taken out, a grant limited to settled land or to trust property shall be left out of account, and a grant limited to real estate or to personal estate shall be left out of account unless a grant limited to the remainder of the estate has previously been made or is made at the same time.

21. Interpretation of wills—general rules as to evidence.—(1) This section applies to a will—

(a) in so far as any part of it is meaningless;
(b) in so far as the language used in any part of it is ambiguous on the face of it;
(c) in so far as evidence, other than evidence of the testator's intention, shows that the language used in any part of it is ambiguous in the light of surrounding circumstances.

(2) In so far as this section applies to a will extrinsic evidence, including evidence of the testator's intention, may be admitted to assist in its interpretation.

22. Presumption as to effect of gifts to spouses. Except where a contrary intention is shown it shall be presumed that if a testator devises or bequeaths property to his spouse in terms which in themselves would give an absolute interest to the spouse, but by the same instrument purports to give his issue an interest in the same property, the gift to the spouse is absolute notwithstanding the purported gift to the issue.

Registration of wills

23. Deposit and registration of wills of living persons.—(1) The following, namely—

(a) the Principal Registry of the Family Division of the High Court of Justice;
(b) the Keeper of the Registers of Scotland; and
(c) the Probate and Matrimonial Office of the Supreme Court of Northern Ireland,

shall be registering authorities for the purposes of this section.

(2) Each registering authority shall provide and maintain safe and convenient depositories for the custody of the wills of living persons.

(3) Any person may deposit his will in such a depository in accordance with regulations under section 25 below and on payment of the prescribed fee.

(4) It shall be the duty of a registering authority to register in accordance with regulations under section 25 below—

(a) any will deposited in a depository maintained by the authority; and
(b) any other will whose registration is requested under Article 6 of the Registration Convention.

(5) A will deposited in a depository provided—

(a) under section 172 of the Supreme Court of Judicature (Consolidation) Act 1925 or section 126 of the Supreme Court Act 1981; or
(b) under Article 27 of the Administration of Estates (Northern Ireland) Order 1979,

shall be treated for the purposes of this section as if it had been deposited under this section.

(6) In this section 'prescribed' means—

(a) in the application of this section to England and Wales, prescribed by an order under section 130 of the Supreme Court Act 1981;

24. Designation of Principal Registry as national body under Registration Convention.—(1) The Principal Registry of the Family Division of the High Court of Justice shall be the national body for the purposes of the Registration Convention, and shall accordingly have the functions assigned to the national body by the Registration Convention including, without prejudice to the general application of the Convention to the Principal Registry by virtue of this section, the functions—

(a) of arranging for the registration of wills in other Contracting States as provided for in Article 6 of the Convention;
(b) of receiving and answering requests for information arising from the national bodies of other Contracting States.

(2) In this Part of this Act 'the Registration Convention' means the Convention on the Establishment of a Scheme of Registration of Wills concluded at Basle on 16 May 1972.

25. Regulations to deposit and registration of wills etc.—(1) Regulations may make provision—

(a) as to the conditions for the deposit of a will;
(b) as to the manner of and procedure for—
     (i)   the deposit and registration of a will; and
     (ii) the withdrawal of a will which has been deposited; and
     (iii) the cancellation of the registration of a will; and
(c) as to the manner in which the Principal Registry of the Family Division is to perform its functions as the national body under the Registration Convention.

(2) Regulations under this section may contain such incidental or supplementary provisions as the authority making the regulations considers appropriate.

(3) Any such regulations are to be made—

(a) for England and Wales, by the President of the Family Division of the High Court of Justice, with the concurrence of the Lord Chancellor;

*   *   *   *   *

(4) Regulations made by virtue of subsection (1) (c) above shall be made by the Lord Chancellor.

(5) Subject to subsection (6) below, regulations under this section shall be made by statutory instrument and shall be laid before Parliament after being made.

(7) The Statutory Instruments Act 1946 shall apply to a statutory instrument containing regulations made in accordance with subsection (3) (a) . . . above as if the regulations had been made by a Minister of the Crown.

(8) Any regulations made under section 172 of the Supreme Court of Judicature (Consolidation) Act 1925 or section 126 of the Supreme Court Act 1981 shall have effect for the purposes of this Part of this Act as they have effect for the purposes of the enactment under which they were made.

*   *   *   *   *

27. The form of an international will.—(1) The Annex to the Convention on International Wills shall have the force of law in the United Kingdom.

(2) The Annex is set out in Schedule 2 to this Act.

(3) In this Part of this Act
'international will' means a will made in accordance with the requirements of the Annex, as set out in Schedule 2 to this Act; and
'the Convention on International Wills' means the Convention providing a Uniform Law on the Form of an International Will concluded at Washington on 26 October 1973.

28. International wills—procedure.—(1) The persons authorised to act in the United Kingdom in connection with international wills are—

(a) solicitors; and
(b) notaries public.

(2) A person who is authorised under section 6 (1) of the Commissioners for Oaths Act 1889 to do notarial acts in any foreign country or place is authorised to act there in connection with international wills.

(3) An international will certified by virtue of subsection (1) or (2) above may be deposited in a depository provided under section 23 above.

(4) Section 23 above shall accordingly have effect in relation to such international wills.

(5) Subject to subsection (6) below, regulations under section 25 above shall have effect in relation to such international wills as they have effect in relation to wills deposited under section 23 above.

(6) Without prejudice to the generality of section 25 above, regulations under that section may make special provision with regard to such international wills.

(7) In section 10 of the Consular Relations Act 1968 (by virtue of which diplomatic agents and consular officials may administer oaths and do notarial acts in certain cases)—

(a) at the end of subsection (1) (b) there shall be added the words 'or
(c) in connection with an international will.'; and
(b) at the end of subsection (4) there shall be added the words 'and "international will" has the meaning assigned to it by section 27 of the Administration of Justice Act 1982'.

PART IX

GENERAL AND SUPPLEMENTARY

73. Transitional provisions and savings.

(6) Nothing in the following provisions of this Act—

(a) section 17;
(b) section 18 (2);
(c) sections 19 to 22;
(d) section 75, so far as it relates—
    (i) to the Wills Act Amendment Act 1852; and
    (ii) to the Family Law Reform Act 1969,

affects the will of a testator who dies before the commencement of the provision in question.

(7) Neither section 18 (1) above nor the repeal of this Act or section 177 of the Law of Property Act 1925 affects a will made before the commencement of section 18 (1) above.

     *   *   *   *   *

76. Commencement.

(5) The provisions of this Act specified in subsection (6) below shall come into operation on such day as the Lord Chancellor and the Secretary of State may by order jointly appoint.

(6) The provisions of this Act mentioned in subsection (5) above are—

(a) sections 23 to 25;
(b) sections 27 and 28;
(c) section 75, so far as it relates—
    (i) to section 126 of the Supreme Court Act 1981;

     *   *   *   *   *

(7) Any order under this section shall be made by statutory instrument.

(8) Any such order may appoint different days for different provisions and for different purposes.

     *   *   *   *   *

(11) Subject to the foregoing provisions of this section, this Act shall come into operation on 1 January 1983.

77. Extent.—(1) Subject to subsection (6) below, the following provisions of this Act—

     *   *   *   *   *

(c) sections 17 to 22;

     *   *   *   *   *

extend to England and Wales only.

     *   *   *   *   *

(5) The repeal of the Wills Act Amendment Act 1852 by section 75 above does not extend to Northern Ireland.

(6) Subject to subsection (5) above, where any enactment repealed or amended or instrument revoked by this Act extends to any part of the United Kingdom, the repeal, amendment or revocation extends to that part.

78. Citation.—This Act may be cited as the Administration of Justice Act 1982.

SCHEDULE 2

THE ANNEX TO THE CONVENTION ON INTERNATIONAL WILLS

UNIFORM LAW ON THE FORM OF AN INTERNATIONAL WILL

ARTICLE 1

1. A will shall be valid as regards form, irrespective particularly of the place where it is made, of the location of the assets and of the nationality, domicile or residence of the testator, if it is made in the form of an international will complying with the provisions set out in Articles 2 to 5 hereinafter.

2. The invalidity of the will as an international will shall not affect its formal validity as a will of another kind.

ARTICLE 2

This law shall not apply to the form of testamentary dispositions made by two or more persons in one instrument.

ARTICLE 3

1. The will shall be made in writing.
2. It need not be written by the testator himself.
3. It may be written in any language, by hand or by any other means.

ARTICLE 4

1. The testator shall declare in the presence of two witnesses and of a person authorised to act in connection with international wills that the document is his will and that he knows the contents thereof.
2. The testator need not inform the witnesses, or the authorised person, of the contents of the will.

ARTICLE 5

1. In the presence of the witnesses and of the authorised person, the testator shall sign the will or, if he has previously signed it, shall acknowledge his signature.
2. When the testator is unable to sign, he shall indicate the reason therefor to the authorised person who shall make note of this on the will. Moreover, the testator may be authorised by the law under which the authorised person was designated to direct another person to sign on his behalf.
3. The witnesses and the authorised person shall there and then attest the will by signing in the presence of the testator.

ARTICLE 6

1. The signatures shall be placed at the end of the will.
2. If the will consists of several sheets, each sheet shall be signed by the testator or, if he is unable to sign, by the person signing on his behalf or, if there is no such person, by the authorised person. In addition, each sheet shall be numbered.

ARTICLE 7

1. The date of the will shall be the date of its signature by the authorised person.
2. This date shall be noted at the end of the will by the authorised person.

ARTICLE 8

In the absence of any mandatory rule pertaining to the safekeeping of the will, the authorised person shall ask the testator whether he wishes to make a declaration concerning the safekeeping of his will. If so and at the express request of the testator the place where he intends to have his will kept shall be mentioned in the certificate provided for in Article 9.

ARTICLE 9

The authorised person shall attach to the will a certificate in the form prescribed in Article 10 establishing that the obligations of this Law have been complied with.

ARTICLE 10

The certificate drawn up by the authorised person shall be in the following form or in a substantially similar form:

CERTIFICATE

(CONVENTION OF OCTOBER 26, 1973)

1. I .... (name, address and capacity),
   a person authorised to act in connection with international wills

2. Certify that on . . . . (date) at . . . .
. . . . (place)
3. (testator) . . . . (name, address, date
and place of birth) in my presence and that of the witnesses
4. (a) . . . . (name, address, date and place of birth)
(b) . . . . (name, address, date and place of birth)
has declared that the attached document is his will and that he knows the contents thereof.
5. I furthermore certify that:
6. (a) in my presence and in that of the witnesses
   (1) the testator has signed the will or has acknowledged his signature previously affixed.
   *(2) following a declaration of the testator stating that he was unable to sign his will for the following reason

   . . . .
   —I have mentioned this declaration on the will
   *—the signature has been affixed by . . . . (name, address)
7. (b) the witnesses and I have signed the will;
8. *(c) each page of the will has been signed by . . . .
   and numbered:
9. (d) I have satisfied myself as to the identity of the testator and of the witnesses as designated above;
10. (e) the witnesses met the conditions requisite to act as such according to the . . . .
    law under which I am acting;
11. *(f) the testator has requested me to include the following statement concerning the safekeeping of his will:

    . . . .
    . . . .

12. PLACE
13. DATE
14. SIGNATURE and, if necessary, SEAL
              *To be completed if appropriate.

ARTICLE 11

The authorised person shall keep a copy of the certificate and deliver another to the testator.

ARTICLE 12

In the absence of evidence to the contrary, the certificate of the authorised person shall be conclusive of the formal validity of the instrument as a will under this Law.

ARTICLE 13

The absence or irregularity of a certificate shall not affect the formal validity of a will under this Law.

ARTICLE 14

The international will shall be subject to the ordinary rules of revocation of wills.

ARTICLE 15

In interpreting and applying the provisions of this Law, regard shall be had to its international origin and to the need for uniformity in its interpretation.

MENTAL HEALTH ACT 1983

(1983, c. 20)   [9 May 1983]

PART VII

94.—(1) [Subject to subsection (1A) below,] the functions expressed to be conferred by this Part of this Act on the judge shall be exercisable by the Lord Chancellor or by any nominated judge, and shall also be exercisable by the Master of the Court of Protection[, by the Public Trustee] or by any nominated officer, but—

(a)   in the case of the Master[, the Public Trustee] or any nominated officer, subject to any express provision to the contrary in this Part of this Act or any rules made under this Part of this Act,

[(aa) in the case of the Public Trustee, subject to any directions of the Master and so far only as may be provided by any rules made under this Part of this Act or (subject to any such rules) by directions of the Master,]

(b)   in the case of any nominated officer, subject to any directions of the Master and so far only as may be provided by the instrument by which he is nominated;

and references in this Part of this Act to the judge shall be construed accordingly.

[(1A) In such cases or circumstances as may be prescribed by any rules under this Part of this Act or (subject to any such rules) by directions of the Master, the functions of the judge under this Part of this Act shall be exercised by the Public Trustee (but subject to any directions of the Master as to their exercise).]

(2) The functions of the judge under this Part of this Act shall be exercisable where, after considering medical evidence, he is satisfied that a person is incapable, by reason of mental disorder, of managing and administering his property and affairs; and a person as to whom the judge is so satisfied is referred to in this Part of this Act as a patient.[9]

95.—(1) The judge may, with respect to the property and affairs of a patient, do or secure the doing of all such things as appear necessary or expedient—

(a) for the maintenance or other benefit of the patient,
(b) for the maintenance or other benefit of members of the patient's family,
(c) for making provision for other persons or purposes for whom or which the patient might be expected to provide if he were not mentally disordered, or
(d) otherwise for administering the patient's affairs.

(2) In the exercise of the powers conferred by this section regard shall be had first of all to the requirements of the patient, and the rules of law which restricted the enforcement by a creditor of rights against property under the control of the judge in lunacy shall apply to property under the control of the judge; but, subject to the foregoing provisions of this subsection, the judge shall, in administering a patient's affairs, have regard to the interests of creditors and also to the desirability of making provision for obligations of the patient notwithstanding that they may not be legally enforceable.

96.—(1) Without prejudice to the generality of section 95 above, the judge shall have power to make such orders and give such directions and authorities as he thinks fit for the purposes of that section and in particular may for those purposes make orders or give directions or authorities for—

(a) the control (with or without the transfer or vesting of property or the payment into or lodgment in the Supreme Court of money or securities) and management of any property of the patient;
(b) the sale, exchange, charging or other disposition of or dealing with any property of the patient;
(c) the acquisition of any property in the name or on behalf of the patient;
(d) the settlement of any property of the patient, or the gift of any property of the patient to any such persons or for any such purposes as are mentioned in paragraphs (b) and (c) of section 95 (1) above;
(e) the execution for the patient of a will making any provision (whether by way of disposing of property or exercising a power or otherwise) which could be made by a will executed by the patient if he were not mentally disordered;
(f) the carrying on by a suitable person of any profession, trade or business of the patient;
(g) the dissolution of a partnership of which the patient is a member;

---

9   The words in square brackets in s. 94 were added, as from 2 January 1987, by the Public Trustee and Administration of Funds Act 1986.

(h) the carrying out of any contract entered into by the patient;

(i) the conduct of legal proceedings in the name of the patient or on his behalf;

(j) the reimbursement out of the property of the patient, with or without interest, of money applied by any person either in payment of the patient's debts (whether legally enforceable or not) or for the maintenance or other benefit of the patient or members of his family or in making provision for other persons or purposes for whom or which he might be expected to provide if he were not mentally disordered;

(k) the exercise of any power (including a power to consent) vested in the patient, whether beneficially, or as guardian or trustee, or otherwise.

(2) If under subsection (1) above provision is made for the settlement of any property of a patient, or the exercise of a power vested in a patient of appointing trustees or retiring from a trust, the judge may also make as respects the property settled or trust property such consequential vesting or other orders as the case may require, including (in the case of the exercise of such a power) any order which could have been made in such a case under Part IV of the Trustee Act 1925.

(3) Where under this section a settlement has been made of any property of a patient, and the Lord Chancellor or a nominated judge is satisfied, at any time before the death of the patient, that any material fact was not disclosed when the settlement was made, or that there has been any substantial change in circumstances, he may by order vary the settlement in such manner as he thinks fit, and give any consequential directions.

(4) The power of the judge to make or give an order, direction or authority for the execution of a will for a patient—

(a) shall not be exercisable at any time when the patient is a minor, and

(b) shall not be exercised unless the judge has reason to believe that the patient is incapable of making a valid will for himself.

(5) The powers of a patient as a patron of a benefice shall be exercisable by the Lord Chancellor only.

97.—(1) Where under section 96 (1) above the judge makes or gives an order, direction or authority requiring or authorising a person (in this section referred to as 'the authorised person') to execute a will for a patient, any will executed in pursuance of that order, direction or authority shall be expressed to be signed by the patient acting by the authorised person, and shall be—

(a) signed by the authorised person with the name of the patient, and with his own name, in the presence of two or more witnesses present at the same time, and

(b) attested and subscribed by those witnesses in the presence of the authorised person, and

(c) sealed with the official seal of the Court of Protection.

(2) The Wills Act 1837 shall have effect in relation to any such will as if it were signed by the patient by his own hand, except that in relation to any such will—

(a) section 9 of that Act (which makes provision as to the signing and attestation of wills) shall not apply, and

(b) in the subsequent provisions of that Act any reference to execution in the manner required by the previous provisions of that Act shall be construed as a reference to execution in the manner required by subsection (1) above.

(3) Subject to the following provisions of this section, any such will executed in accordance with subsection (1) above shall have the same effect for all purposes as if the patient were capable of making a valid will and the will had been executed by him in the manner required by the Wills Act 1837.

(4) So much of subsection (3) above as provides for such a will to have effect as if the patient were capable of making a valid will—

(a) shall not have effect in relation to such a will in so far as it disposes of any immovable property, other than immovable property in England or Wales, and

(b) where at the time when such a will is executed the patient is domiciled in Scotland or Northern Ireland or in a country or territory outside the United Kingdom, shall not have effect in relation to that will in so far as it relates to any other property or matter, except any property or matter in respect of which, under the law of his domicile, any question of his testamentary capacity would fall to be determined in accordance with the law of England and Wales.

98.—Where it is represented to the judge, and he has reason to believe, that a person may be incapable, by reason of mental disorder, of managing and administering his property and affairs, and the judge is of the opinion that it is necessary to make immediate provision for any of the matters referred to in section 95 above, then pending the determination of the question whether that person is so incapable the judge may exercise in relation to the property and affairs of that person any of the powers conferred on him in relation to the property and affairs of a patient by this Part of this Act so far as is requisite for enabling that provision to be made.

COUNTY COURTS ACT 1984

(1984, c. 28)   [26 June 1984]

PART II

FAMILY PROVISION PROCEEDINGS

25. Jurisdiction under Inheritance (Provision for Family and Dependants) Act 1975. A county court shall have jurisdiction to hear and determine any application for an order under section 2 of the Inheritance (Provision for Family and Dependants) Act 1975 (including any application for permission to apply for such an order and any application made, in the proceedings on an application for such an order under any other provision of that Act).

      *   *   *   *   *

PROBATE PROCEEDINGS

32. Contentious probate jurisdiction.—(1) Where—

(a) an application for the grant or revocation of probate or administration has been made through the principal registry of the Family Division or a district probate registry under section 105 of the Supreme Court Act 1981; and

(b) it is shown to the satisfaction of a county court that the value at the date of the death of the deceased of his net estate does not exceed the county court limit,

the county court shall have the jurisdiction of the High Court in respect of any contentious matter arising in connection with the grant or revocation.

(2) In subsection (1) 'net estate', in relation to a deceased person, means the estate of that person exclusive of any property he was possessed of or entitled to as a trustee and not beneficially, and after making allowances for funeral expenses and for debts and liabilities.

33. Effect of order of judge in probate proceedings. Where an order is made by a judge of a county court for the grant or revocation of probate or administration, in pursuance of any jurisdiction conferred upon him by section 32—

(a) the registrar of the county court shall transmit to the principal registry of the Family Division or a district probate registry, as he thinks convenient, a certificate under the seal of the court certifying that the order has been made; and

(b) on the application of a party in favour of whom the order has been made, probate or administration in compliance with the order shall be issued from the registry to which the certificate was sent or, as the case may require, the probate or letters of administration previously granted shall be recalled or varied by, as the case may be, a registrar of the principal registry of the Family Division or the district probate registrar according to the effect of the order.

TRANSFER OF PROCEEDINGS

40. Transfer of proceedings to county court.—(1) Where the High Court is satisfied that any proceedings before it are required by any provision of a kind mentioned in subsection (8) to be in a county court it shall—

(a) order the transfer of the proceedings to a county court; or
(b) if the court is satisfied that the person bringing the proceedings knew, or ought to have known, of that requirement order that they be struck out.

(2) Subject to any such provision, the High Court may order the transfer of any proceedings before it to a county court.

(3) An order under this section may be made either on the motion of the High Court itself or on the application of any party to the proceedings.

(4) Proceedings transferred under this section shall be transferred to such county court as the High Court considers appropriate, having taken into account the convenience of the parties and that of any other persons likely to be affected and the state of business in the courts concerned.

(5) The transfer of any proceedings under this section shall not affect any right of appeal from the order directing the transfer.

(6) Where proceedings for the enforcement of any judgment or order of the High Court are transferred under this section—

(a) the judgment or order may be enforced as if it were a judgment or order of a county court; and
(b) subject to subsection (7), it shall be treated as a judgment or order of that court for all purposes.

(7) Where proceedings for the enforcement of any judgment or order of the High Court are transferred under this section—

(a) the powers of any court to set aside, correct, vary or quash a judgment or order of the High Court, and the enactments relating to appeals from such a judgment or order, shall continue to apply; and
(b) the powers of any court to set aside, correct, vary or quash a judgment or order of a county court, and the enactments relating to appeals from such a judgment or order, shall not apply.

(8) The provisions referred to in subsection (1) are any made—

(a) under section 1 of the Courts and Legal Services Act 1990; or
(b) by or under any other enactment.

(9) This section does not apply to family proceedings within the meaning of Part V of the Matrimonial and Family Proceedings Act 1984.

41. Transfer to High Court by order of High Court.—(1) If at any stage in proceedings commenced in a county court or transferred to a county court under section 40, the High Court thinks it desirable that the proceedings, or any part of them, should be heard and determined in the High Court, it may order the transfer to the High Court of the proceedings or, as the case may be, of that part of them.

(2) The power conferred by subsection (1) is without prejudice to section 29 of the Supreme Court Act 1981 (power of High Court to issue prerogative orders) but shall be exercised in relation to family proceedings (within the meaning of Part V of the Matrimonial and Family Proceedings Act 1984) in accordance with any directions given under section 37 of that Act (directions as to distribution and transfer of family business and proceedings).

(3) The power conferred by subsection (1) shall be exercised subject to any provision made—

(a) under section 1 of the Courts and Legal Services Act 1990; or
(b) by or under any other enactment

42. Transfer to High Court by order of a county court.—(1) Where a county court is satisfied that any proceedings before it are required by any provision of a kind mentioned in subsection (7) to be in the High Court, it shall—

(a) order the transfer of the proceedings to the High Court; or
(b) if the court is satisfied that the person bringing the proceedings knew, or ought to have known, of that requirement order that they be struck out.

(2) Subject to any such provision, a county court may order the transfer of any proceedings before it to the High Court.

(3) An order under this section may be made either on the motion of the court itself or on the application of any party to the proceedings.

(4) The transfer of any proceedings under this section shall not affect any right of appeal from the order directing the transfer.

(5) Where proceedings for the enforcement of any judgment or order of a county court are transferred under this section—

(a) the judgment or order may be enforced as if it were a judgment or order of the High Court; and
(b) subject to subsection (6), it shall be treated as a judgment or order of that court for all purposes.

(6) Where proceedings for the enforcement of any judgment or order of a county court are transferred under this section—

(a) the powers of any court to set aside, correct, vary or quash a judgment or order of a county court, and the enactments relating to appeals from such a judgment or order, shall continue to apply; and
(b) the powers of any court to set aside, correct, vary or quash a judgment or order of the High Court, and the enactments relating to appeals from such a judgment or order, shall not apply.

(7) The provisions referred to in subsection (1) are any made—

(a) under section 1 of the Courts and Legal Services Act 1990, or
(b) by or under any other enactment.

(8) This section does not apply to family proceedings within the meaning of Part V of the Matrimonial and Family Proceedings Act 1984.

45. Costs in transferred cases.—(1) Where an action, counterclaim or matter is ordered to be transferred—

(a) from the High Court to a county court; or
(b) from a county court to the High Court; or
(c) from one county court to another county court,

the costs of the whole proceedings both before and after the transfer shall, subject to any order of the court which ordered the transfer, be in the discretion of the court to which the proceedings are transferred; and that court shall have power to make orders with respect to the costs and the costs of the whole proceedings shall be taxed in that court.

ADMINISTRATION OF JUSTICE ACT 1985

(1985, c. 61) [30 October 1985]

PART IV

THE SUPREME COURT AND COUNTY COURTS

49. Powers of High Court on compromise of probate action.—(1) Where on a compromise of a probate action in the High Court—

(a) the court is invited to pronounce for the validity of one or more wills, or against the validity of one or more wills, or for the validity of one or more wills and against the validity of one or more other wills; and

(b) the court is satisfied that consent to the making of the pronouncement or, as the case may be, each of the pronouncements in question has been given by or on behalf of every relevant beneficiary, the court may without more pronounce accordingly.

(2) In this section—

'probate action' means an action for the grant of probate of the will, or letters of administration of the estate, of a deceased person or for the revocation of such a grant or for a decree pronouncing for or against the validity of an alleged will, not being an action which is non-contentious or common form probate business; and

'relevant beneficiary', in relation to a pronouncement relating to any will or wills of a deceased person, means—

(a) a person who under any such will is beneficially interested in the deceased's estate; and

(b) where the effect of the pronouncement would be to cause the estate to devolve as on an intestacy (or partial intestacy), or to prevent it from so devolving, a person who under the law relating to intestacy is beneficially interested in the estate.[10]

50. Power of High Court to appoint substitute for, or to remove, personal representative.—(1) Where an application relating to the estate of a deceased person is made to the High Court under this subsection by or on behalf of a personal representative of the deceased or a beneficiary of the estate, the court may in its discretion—

(a) appoint a person (in this section called a substituted personal representative) to act as personal representative of the deceased in place of the existing personal representative or representatives of the deceased or any of them; or

(b) if there are two or more existing personal representatives of the deceased, terminate the appointment of one or more, but not all, of those persons.

(2) Where the court appoints a person to act as substituted personal representative of a deceased person then—

(a) if that person is appointed to act with an executor or executors the appointment shall (except for the purpose of including him in any chain of representation) constitute him executor of the deceased as from the date of the appointment; and

(b) in any other case the appointment shall constitute that person administrator of the deceased's estate as from the date of the appointment.

(3) The court may authorise a person appointed as a substituted personal representative to charge remuneration for his services as such, on such terms (whether or not involving the submission of bills of charges for taxation by the court) as the court may think fit.

(4) Where an application relating to the estate of a deceased person is made to the court under subsection (1), the court may if it thinks fit, proceed as if the application were, or included, an application for the appointment under the Judicial Trustees Act 1896 of a judicial trustee in relation to that estate.

10   Section 49 came into force on 1 January 1986: s. 69(4)(a) of the Act.

(5) In this section 'beneficiary', in relation to the estate of a deceased person, means a person who under the will of the deceased or under the law relating to intestacy is beneficially interested in the estate.

(6) In section 1 of the Judicial Trustees Act 1896, after subsection (6) there shall be added—

'(7) Where an application relating to the estate of a deceased person is made to the court under this section, the court may, if it thinks fit, proceed as if the application were, or included, an application under section 50 of the Administration of Justice Act 1985 (power of High Court to appoint substitute for, or to remove, personal representative)'[11].

51. Contentious probate jurisdiction.—(1) [This subsection provides for the substitution of s. 32 of the County Courts Act 1984 (for text see p. 862, ante).

(2) In section 106 of the Supreme Court Act 1981 (grants by district probate registrars), subsections (2) to (4) shall be omitted.[12]

56. Interpretation of Part IV.—In this Part—

'action' means any civil proceedings commenced by writ or in any other manner prescribed by rules of court;
'judgment' includes an order;
'will' includes a nuncupative will and any testamentary document of which probate may be granted.

FAMILY LAW ACT 1986

(1986, c. 55)   [7 November 1986]

PART II

RECOGNITION OF DIVORCES, ANNULMENTS AND LEGAL SEPARATIONS

Divorces, annulments and judicial separations granted in the British Islands

44. Recognition in United Kingdom of divorces, annulments and judicial separations granted in the British Islands.—(1) Subject to section 52 (4) and (5) (a) of this Act, no divorce or annulment obtained in any part of the British Islands shall be regarded as effective in any part of the United Kingdom unless granted by a court of civil jurisdiction.

(2) Subject to section 51 of this Act, the validity of any divorce, annulment or judicial separation granted by a court of civil jurisdiction in any part of the British Islands shall be recognised throughout the United Kingdom.

Overseas divorces, annulments and legal separations

45. Recognition in the United Kingdom of overseas divorces, annulments and legal separations. Subject to sections 51 and 52 of this Act, the validity of a divorce, annulment or legal separation obtained in a country outside the British Islands (in this Part referred to as an overseas divorce, annulment or legal separation) shall be recognised in the United Kingdom if, and only if it is entitled to recognition—

(a) by virtue of sections 46 to 49 of this Act, or
(b) by virtue of any enactment other than this Part.

46. Grounds for recognition.—(1) The validity of an overseas divorce, annulment or legal separation obtained by means of proceedings shall be recognised if—

---

11   Section 50 came into force on 28 April 1986, S.I. 1986 No. 1503.
12   This subsection came into operation on 1 October 1986, S.I. 1986 No. 1503.

(a) the divorce, annulment or legal separation is effective under the law of the country in which it was obtained; and

(b) at the relevant date either party to the marriage—
   (i) was habitually resident in the country in which the divorce, annulment or legal separation was obtained; or
   (ii) was domiciled in that country; or
   (iii) was a national of that country.

(2) The validity of an overseas divorce, annulment or legal separation obtained otherwise than by means of proceedings shall be recognised if—

(a) the divorce, annulment or legal separation is effective under the law of the country in which it was obtained;

(b) at the relevant date—
   (i) each party to the marriage was domiciled in that country; or
   (ii) either party to the marriage was domiciled in that country and the other party was domiciled in a country under whose law the divorce, annulment or legal separation is recognised as valid; and

(c) neither party to the marriage was habitually resident in the United Kingdom throughout the period of one year immediately preceding that date.

(3) In this section 'the relevant date' means—

(a) in the case of an overseas divorce, annulment or legal separation obtained by means of proceedings, the date of the commencement of the proceedings;

(b) in the case of an overseas divorce, annulment or legal separation obtained otherwise than by means of proceedings, the date on which it was obtained.

(4) Where in the case of an overseas annulment, the relevant date fell after the death of either party to the marriage, any reference in subsection (1) or (2) above to that date shall be construed in relation to that party as a reference to the date of death.

(5) For the purpose of this section, a party to a marriage shall be treated as domiciled in a country if he was domiciled in that country either according to the law of that country in family matters or according to the law of the part of the United Kingdom in which the question of recognition arises.

47. Cross-proceedings and divorces following legal separations.—(1) Where there have been cross-proceedings, the validity of an overseas divorce, annulment or legal separation obtained either in the original proceedings or in the cross-proceedings shall be recognised if—

(a) the requirements of section 46 (1) (b) (i), (ii) or (iii) of this Act are satisfied in relation to the date of the commencement either of the original proceedings or of the cross-proceedings, and

(b) the validity of the divorce, annulment or legal separation is otherwise entitled to recognition by virtue of the provisions of this Part.

(2) Where a legal separation, the validity of which is entitled to recognition by virtue of the provisions of section 46 of this Act or of subsection (1) above is converted, in the country in which it was obtained, into a divorce which is effective under the law of that country, the validity of the divorce shall be recognised whether or not it would itself be entitled to recognition by virtue of those provisions.

48. Proof of facts relevant to recognition.—(1) For the purpose of deciding whether an overseas divorce, annulment or legal separation obtained by means of proceedings is entitled to recognition by virtue of sections 46 and 47 of this Act, any finding of fact made (whether expressly or by implication) in the proceedings and on the basis of which jurisdiction was assumed in the proceedings shall—

(a) if both parties to the marriage took part in the proceedings, be conclusive evidence of the fact found; and

(b) in any other case, be sufficient proof of that fact unless the contrary is shown.

(2) In this section `finding of fact' includes a finding that either party to the marriage—

(a) was habitually resident in the country in which the divorce, annulment or legal separation was obtained; or

(b) was under the law of that country domiciled there; or

(c) was a national of that country.

(3) For the purposes of subsection (1) (a) above, a party to the marriage who has appeared in judicial proceedings shall be treated as having taken part in them.

Supplemental

49. Modifications of Part II in relation to countries comprising territories having different systems of law.—(1) In relation to a country comprising territories in which different systems of law are in force in matters of divorce, annulment or legal separation, the provisions of this Part mentioned in subsections (2) to (5) below shall have effect subject to the modifications there specified.

(2) In the case of a divorce, annulment or legal separation the recognition of the validity of which depends on whether the requirements of subsection (1) (b) (i) or (ii) of section 46 of this Act are satisfied, that section and, in the case of a legal separation, section 47 (2) of this Act shall have effect as if each territory were a separate country.

(3) In the case of a divorce, annulment or legal separation the recognition of the validity of which depends on whether the requirements of subsection (1) (b) (iii) of section 46 of this Act are satisfied—

(a) that section shall have effect as if for paragraph (a) of subsection (1) there were substituted the following paragraph—

'(a) the divorce, annulment or legal separation is effective throughout the country in which it was obtained;'; and

(b) in the case of a legal separation, section 47 (2) of this Act shall have effect as if for the words 'is effective under the law of that country' there were substituted the words 'is effective throughout that country'.

(4) In the case of a divorce, annulment or legal separation the recognition of the validity of which depends on whether the requirements of subsection (2) (b) of section 46 of this Act are satisfied, that section and section 52 (3) and (4) of this Act and, in the case of a legal separation, section 47 (2) of this Act shall have effect as if each territory were a separate country.

(5) Paragraphs (a) and (b) of section 48 (2) of this Act shall each have effect as if each territory were a separate country.

50. Non-recognition of divorce or annulment in another jurisdiction no bar to remarriage.—Where, in any part of the United Kingdom—

(a) a divorce or annulment has been granted by a court of civil jurisdiction, or

(b) the validity of a divorce or annulment is recognised by virtue of this Part, the fact that the divorce or annulment would not be recognised elsewhere shall not preclude either party to the marriage from re-marrying in that part of the United Kingdom or cause the remarriage of either party (wherever the remarriage takes place) to be treated as invalid in that part.

51. Refusal of recognition.—(1) Subject to section 52 of this Act, recognition of the validity of—

(a) a divorce, annulment or judicial separation granted by a court of civil jurisdiction in any part of the British Islands, or

(b) an overseas divorce, annulment or legal separation,

may be refused in any part of the United Kingdom if the divorce, annulment or separation was granted or obtained at a time when it was irreconcilable with a decision determining the question of the subsistence or validity of the marriage of the parties previously given (whether before or after the commencement of this Part) by a court of civil jurisdiction in that part of the United Kingdom or by a court elsewhere and recognised or entitled to be recognised in that part of the United Kingdom.

(2) Subject to section 52 of this Act, recognition of the validity of—

(a) a divorce or judicial separation granted by a court of civil jurisdiction in any part of the British Islands, or
(b) an overseas divorce or legal separation,

may be refused in any part of the United Kingdom if the divorce or separation was granted or obtained at a time when, according to the law of that part of the United Kingdom (including its rules of private international law and the provisions of this Part), there was no subsisting marriage between the parties.

(3) Subject to section 52 of this Act, recognition by virtue of section 45 of this Act of the validity of an overseas divorce, annulment or legal separation may be refused if—

(a) in the case of a divorce, annulment or legal separation obtained by means of proceedings, it was obtained—
  (i) without such steps having been taken for giving notice of the proceedings to a party to the marriage as, having regard to the nature of the proceedings and all the circumstances, should reasonably have been taken; or
  (ii) without a party to the marriage having been given (for any reason other than lack of notice) such opportunity to take part in the proceedings as, having regard to those matters, he should reasonably have been given; or
(b) in the case of a divorce, annulment or legal separation obtained otherwise than by means of proceedings—
  (i) there is no official document certifying that the divorce, annulment or legal separation is effective under the law of the country in which it was obtained; or
  (ii) where either party to the marriage was domiciled in another country at the relevant date, there is no official document certifying that the divorce, annulment or legal separation is recognised as valid under the law of that other country; or
(c) in either case, recognition of the divorce, annulment or legal separation would be manifestly contrary to public policy.

(4) In this section—

'official', in relation to a document certifying that a divorce, annulment or legal separation is effective, or is recognised as valid, under the law of any country, means issued by a person or body appointed or recognised for the purpose under that law;
'the relevant date' has the same meaning as in section 46 of this Act; and subsection (5) of that section shall apply for the purposes of this section as it applies for the purposes of that section.

(5) Nothing in this Part shall be construed as requiring the recognition of any finding of fault made in any proceedings for divorce, annulment or separation or of any maintenance, custody or other ancillary order made in any such proceedings.

52. Provisions as to divorces, annulments etc, obtained before commencement of Part II.—(1) The provisions of this Part shall apply—

(a) to a divorce, annulment or judicial separation granted by a court of civil jurisdiction in the British Islands before the date of the commencement of this Part, and
(b) to an overseas divorce, annulment or legal separation obtained before that date, as well as to one granted or obtained on or after that date.

(2) In the case of such a divorce, annulment or separation as is mentioned in subsection (1) (a) or (b) above, the provisions of this Part shall require or, as the case may be, preclude the recognition of its validity in relation to any time before that date as well as in relation to any subsequent time, but those provisions shall not—

(a) affect any property to which any person became entitled before that date, or

(b) affect the recognition of the validity of the divorce, annulment or separation if that matter has been decided by any competent court in the British Islands before that date.

(3) Subsections (1) and (2) above shall apply in relation to any divorce or judicial separation granted by a court of civil jurisdiction in the British Islands before the date of the commencement of this Part whether granted before or after the commencement of section 1 of the Recognition of Divorces and Legal Separations Act 1971.

(4) The validity of any divorce, annulment or legal separation mentioned in subsection (5) below shall be recognised in the United Kingdom whether or not it is entitled to recognition by virtue of any of the foregoing provisions of this Part.

(5) The divorces, annulments and legal separations referred to in subsection (4) above are—

(a) a divorce which was obtained in the British Islands before 1 January 1974 and was recognised as valid under rules of law applicable before that date;
(b) an overseas divorce which was recognised as valid under the Recognition of Divorces and Legal Separations Act 1971 and was not affected by section 16 (2) of the Domicile and Matrimonial Proceedings Act 1973 (proceedings otherwise than in a court of law where both parties resident in United Kingdom);
(c) a divorce of which the decree was registered under section 1 of the Indian and Colonial Divorce Jurisdiction Act 1926;
(d) a divorce or annulment which was recognised as valid under section 4 of the Matrimonial Causes (War Marriages) Act 1944; and
(e) an overseas legal separation which was recognised as valid under the Recognition of Divorces and Legal Separations Act 1971.

53. Effect of divorces and annulments on wills.—In subsection (1) of section 18A of the Wills Act 1837 (effect of a decree of divorce or nullity of marriage on wills)—

(a) after the word 'court' there shall be inserted the words 'of civil jurisdiction in England and Wales'; and
(b) for the words 'or declares it void' there shall be substituted the words 'or his marriage is dissolved or annulled and the divorce or annulment is entitled to recognition in England and Wales by virtue of Part II of the Family Law Act 1986'.

54. Interpretation of Part II.—(1) In this Part—

'annulment' includes any decree or declaration of nullity of marriage, however expressed;
'part of the United Kingdom' means England and Wales, Scotland or Northern Ireland;
'proceedings' means judicial or other proceedings.

(2) In this Part 'country' includes a colony or other dependent territory of the United Kingdom but for the purposes of this Part a person shall be treated as a national of such a territory only if it has a law of citizenship or nationality separate from that of the United Kingdom and he is a citizen or national of that territory under that law.

PART III

DECLARATIONS OF STATUS

55. Declarations as to marital status.—(1) Subject to the following provisions of this section, any person may apply to the court for one or more of the following declarations in relation to a marriage specified in the application, that is to say—

(a) a declaration that the marriage was at its inception a valid marriage;.
(b) a declaration that the marriage subsisted on a date specified in the application;
(c) a declaration that the marriage did not subsist on a date so specified;
(d) a declaration that the validity of a divorce, annulment or legal separation obtained in any country outside England and Wales in respect of the marriage is entitled to recognition in England and Wales;

(e) a declaration that the validity of a divorce, annulment or legal separation so obtained in respect of the marriage is not entitled to recognition in England and Wales.

(2) A court shall have jurisdiction to entertain an application under subsection (1) above if, and only if, either of the parties to the marriage to which the application relates—

(a) is domiciled in England and Wales on the date of the application, or
(b) has been habitually resident in England and Wales throughout the period of one year ending with that date, or
(c) died before that date and either—
   (i) was at death domiciled in England and Wales, or
   (ii) had been habitually resident in England and Wales throughout the period of one year ending with the date of death.

(3) Where an application under subsection (1) above is made by any person other than a party to the marriage to which the application relates, the court shall refuse to hear the application if it considers that the applicant does not have a sufficient interest in the determination of that application.

56. Declarations of parentage, legitimacy or legitimation[13].—(1) Any person may apply to the court for a declaration—

(a) that a person named in the application is or was his parent; or
(b) that he is the legitimate child of his parents.

(2) Any person may apply to the court for one (or for one or, in the alternative, the other) of the following declarations, that is to say—

(a) a declaration that he has become a legitimated person;
(b) a declaration that he has not become a legitimated person.

(3) A court shall have jurisdiction to entertain an application under this section if, and only if the applicant—

(a) is domiciled in England and Wales on the date of the application; or
(b) has been habitually resident in England and Wales throughout the period of one year ending with that date.

(4) Where a declaration is made on an application under subsection (1) above, the prescribed officer of the court shall notify the Registrar General, in such a manner and within such period as may be prescribed, of the making of that declaration.

(5) In this section 'legitimated person' means a person legitimated or recognised as legitimated—

(a) under section 2 or 3 of the Legitimacy Act 1976;
(b) under section 1 or 8 of the Legitimacy Act 1926; or
(c) by a legitimation (whether or not by virtue of the subsequent marriage of his parents) recognised by the law of England and Wales and effected under the law of another country.

57. Declarations as to adoptions effected overseas.—(1) Any person whose status as an adopted child of any person depends on whether he has been adopted by that person by either—

(a) an overseas adoption as defined by section 72 (2) of the Adoption Act 1976, or
(b) an adoption recognised by the law of England and Wales and effected under the law of any country outside the British Islands,

may apply to the court for one (or for one or, in the alternative, the other) of the declarations mentioned in subsection (2) below.

(2) The said declarations are—

13   Section 56 is as substituted by s. 22 of the Family Law Reform Act 1987.

(a) a declaration that the applicant is for the purposes of section 39 of the Adoption Act 1976 the adopted child of that person;

(b) a declaration that the applicant is not for the purposes of that section the adopted child of that person.

(3) A court shall have jurisdiction to entertain an application under subsection (1) above if, and only if, the applicant—

(a) is domiciled in England and Wales on the date of the application, or

(b) has been habitually resident in England and Wales throughout the period of one year ending with that date.[14]

58. General provisions as to the making and effect of declarations.—(1) Where on an application for a declaration under this Part the truth of the proposition to be declared is proved to the satisfaction of the court, the court shall make that declaration unless to do so would manifestly be contrary to public policy.

(2) Any declaration made under this Part shall be binding on Her Majesty and all other persons.

(3) The court, on the dismissal of an application for a declaration under this Part, shall not have power to make any declaration for which an application has not been made.

(4) No declaration which may be applied for under this Part may be made otherwise than under this Part by any court.

(5) No declaration may be made by any court, whether under this Part or otherwise—

(a) that a marriage was at its inception void;

(b) that any person is or was illegitimate.

(6) Nothing in this section shall affect the powers of any court to grant a decree of nullity of marriage.

*　　　　*　　　　*　　　　*　　　　*

63. Interpretation of Part III. In this Part 'the court' means the High Court or a county court.

PART IV

*　　　　*　　　　*　　　　*　　　　*

68. Minor and consequential amendments, repeals and savings.—(1) The enactments and orders mentioned in Schedule 1 to this Act shall have effect subject to the amendments specified in that Schedule, being minor amendments and amendments consequential on the provisions of this Act.

(2) The enactments mentioned in Schedule 2 to this Act (which include some that are spent or no longer of practical utility) are hereby repealed to the extent specified in the third column of that Schedule.

(3) Nothing in this Act shall affect—

(a) any proceedings under section 45 of the Matrimonial Causes Act 1973 begun before the date of the commencement of Part III of this Act;

*　　　　*　　　　*　　　　*　　　　*

(c) any proceedings for a declaration begun in the High Court before that date by virtue of rules of court relating to declaratory judgments.

14　This subsection contained provisional matters which were not effective as they were dependent upon the Adoption Act 1976 not coming into force before the commencement of this Act.

(4) The repeal of section 2 of the Legitimacy Declaration Act (Ireland) 1868 shall not affect any proceedings under that section begun before the commencement of that repeal.

69. Short title, commencement and extent.—(1) This Act may be cited as the Family Law Act 1986.

(2) Sections 64 to 67 of this Act shall come into force at the end of the period of two months beginning with the day on which this Act is passed.

(3) Subject to subsection (2) above, this Act shall come into force on such day as the relevant Minister or Ministers may by order made by statutory instrument appoint; and different days may be so appointed for different provisions or for different purposes.

(4) In subsection (3) above 'the relevant Minister or Ministers' means—

(a) in the case of an order which appoints a day only for Part III of this Act and its associated amendments and repeals, the Lord Chancellor;

(b) in any other case, the Lord Chancellor and the Lord Advocate.

(5) The following provisions of this Act, namely—

*   *   *   *   *

section 53
Part III

*   *   *   *   *

section 68 (3)

*   *   *   *   *

extend to England and Wales only,

*   *   *   *   *

(7) The following provisions of this Act, namely—

*   *   *   *   *

section 68 (4)

*   *   *   *   *

extend to Northern Ireland only;

SCHEDULE 1

Minor and consequential amendments

*   *   *   *   *

10.—(1) Section 15 of the Guardianship of Minors Act 1971 shall be amended as follows[15]—

*   *   *   *   *

12. In section 17 of that Act subsection (2) shall cease to have effect.

---

15   Note, para. 10 of Sch. 1 was repealed, with effect from 14 October 1991, by the Children Act 1989, s. 108(7), Sch. 15 (see p. 894, post).

SCHEDULE 2

Repeals

Chapter	Short title	Extent of repeal
*	* * *	* *
1971 c. 3	The Guardianship of Minors Act 1971	Section 17(2)
1971 c. 53	Recognition of Divorces and Legal Separations Act 1971	The whole Act
1973 c. 18	The Matrimonial Causes Act 1973	Section 45
*	* * *	* *
1973 c. 45	Domicile and Matrimonial Proceedings Act 1973	Section 2 Sections 15 and 16
*	* * *	* *

[**Note.**—The whole of the Family Law Act 1986 came into force on 4 April 1988.]

FAMILY LAW REFORM ACT 1987

(1987 c. 42)   [15 May 1987]

PART I

GENERAL PRINCIPLE

1. General principle.[16]—(1) In this Act and enactments passed and instruments made after the coming into force of this section, references (however expressed) to any relationship between two persons shall, unless the contrary intention appears, be construed without regard to whether or not the father and mother of either of them, or the father and mother of any person through whom the relationship is deduced, have or had been married to each other at any time.

(2) In this Act and enactments passed after the coming into force of this section, unless the contrary intention appears—

(a) references to a person whose father and mother were married to each other at the time of his birth include; and

(b) references to a person whose father and mother were not married to each other at the time of his birth do not include,

references to any person to whom subsection (3) below applies, and cognate references shall be construed accordingly.

(3) This subsection applies to any person who—

(a) is treated as legitimate by virtue of section 1 of the Legitimacy Act 1976;

(b) is a legitimated person within the meaning of section 10 of that Act;

(c) is an adopted child within the meaning of Part IV of the Adoption Act 1976; or

(d) is otherwise treated in law as legitimate.

(4) For the purpose of construing references falling within subsection (2) above, the time of a person's birth shall be taken to include any time during the period beginning with—

(a) the insemination resulting in his birth; or

(b) where there was no such insemination, his conception,

and (in either case) ending with his birth.

16   Section 1 came into force on 4 April 1988.

PART II

RIGHTS AND DUTIES OF PARENTS ETC.

Parental rights and duties: general

2. Construction of enactments relating to parental rights and duties.—(1) In the following enactments, namely—

(a) section 42 (1) of the National Assistance Act 1948;
(b) section 6 of the Family Law Reform Act 1969;
(c) the Guardianship of Minors Act 1971 (in this Act referred to as 'the 1971 Act');
(d) Part I of the Guardianship Act 1973 (in this Act referred to as 'the 1973 Act');
(e) Part II of the Children Act 1975;
(f) the Child Care Act 1980 except Part I and sections 13, 24, 64 and 65;
(g) section 26 (3) of the Social Security Act 1986,

references (however expressed) to any relationship between two persons shall be construed in accordance with section 1 above.

(2) In subsection (7) of section 1 of the 1973 Act (equality of parental rights) for the words from 'or be taken' to the end there shall be substituted the words 'and nothing in subsection (1) above shall be taken as applying in relation to a child whose father and mother were not married to each other at the time of his birth'.

3. Agreements as to exercise of parental rights and duties. *For subsection (2) of section 1 of the 1973 Act (agreements between parents to give up parental rights) there shall be substituted the following subsection—*

  '(2) Notwithstanding anything in section 85(2) of the Children Act 1975, an agreement may be made between the father and mother of a child as to the exercise by either of them, during any period when they are not living with each other in the same household, of any of the parental rights and duties with respect to the child; but no such agreement shall be enforced by any court if the court is of opinion that it will not be for the benefit of the child to give effect to it.'

Parental rights and duties where parents not married

4. Parental rights and duties of father.—*(1) Where the father and mother of a child were not married to each other at the time of his birth, the court may, on the application of the father, order that he shall have all the parental rights and duties with respect to the child.*

(2) Where the father of a child is given all the parental rights and duties by an order under this section, he shall, subject to any order made by the court otherwise than under this section, have those rights and duties jointly with the mother of the child or, if the mother is dead, jointly with any guardian of the child appointed under the 1971 Act.

(3) An order under this section may be discharged by a subsequent order made on the application of the father or mother of the child or, if the mother is dead, any guardian of the child appointed under the 1971 Act.

(4) This section and the 1971 Act shall be construed as if this section were contained in that Act.

5. Exercise of parental rights and duties. *At the beginning of subsection (3) of section 1 of the 1973 Act (which enables application to be made for the direction of the court where parents disagree on a question affecting the child's welfare) there shall be inserted the words 'Subject to subsection (3A) below' and after that subsection there shall be inserted the following subsection—*

  '(3A) Where a child's father and mother were not married to each other at the time of his birth, subsection (3) above does not apply unless—

  (a) an order is in force under section 4 of the Family Law Reform Act 1987 giving the father all the parental rights and duties with respect to the child; or

(b) the father has a right to custody, legal or actual custody or care and control of the child by virtue of an order made under any other enactment.'

6. Appointment of guardians.—*(1) At the end of section 3 of the 1971 Act (rights of surviving parent as to guardianship) there shall be added the following subsections—*

'*(3) Where the father and mother of a child were not married to each other at the time of his birth, this section does not apply unless the father satisfies the requirements of subsection (4) of this section.*

(4) The father of a child satisfies the requirements of this subsection if—

(a) an order is in force under section 4 of the Family Law Reform Act 1987 giving him all the parental rights and duties with respect to the child; or
(b) he has a right to custody, legal or actual custody or care and control of the child by virtue of an order made under any other enactment.'

(2) At the end of section 4 of that Act (power of father and mother to appoint testamentary guardians) there shall be added the following subsection—

'*(7) Where the father and mother of a child were not married to each other at the time of his birth—*

(a) subsection (1) of this section does not apply, and subsection (3) of this section does not apply in relation to a guardian appointed by the mother, unless the father satisfies the requirements of section 3 (4) of this Act; and
(b) any appointment under subsection (1) of this section shall be of no effect unless the father satisfies those requirements immediately before his death.'

(3) At the end of section 5 of that Act (power of court to appoint guardian for child having no parent etc.) there shall be added the following subsection—

'*(3) Where the father and mother of a child were not married to each other at the time of his birth, subsection (1) of this section shall have effect as if for the words "no parent" there were substituted the words "no mother, no father satisfying the requirement of section 3(4) of this Act".'*

7. Rights with respect to adoption.—*(1)* *   *   *   *   *

(2) In section 72 (1) of that Act* (interpretation) in the definition of 'guardian' for paragraph (b) there shall be substituted the following paragraph—

'*(b) in the case of a child whose father and mother were not married to each other at the time of his birth, includes the father where—*
   (i) an order is in force under section 4 of the Family Law Reform Act 1987 giving him all the parental rights and duties with respect to the child; or
   (ii) he has a right to custody, legal or actual custody or care and control of the child by virtue of an order made under any enactment.'

*   *   *   *   *

[*The Adoption Act 1976.]

[**Note.** Sections 3 to 7 above were repealed, as from 14 October 1991, by the Children Act 1989, s. 108(7), Sch. 15 (see p. 894, post).]

*   *   *   *   *

PART III

PROPERTY RIGHTS

18. Succession on intestacy.—(1) In Part IV of the Administration of Estates Act 1925 (which deals with the distribution of the estate of an intestate), references (however expressed) to any relationship between two persons shall be construed in accordance with section 1 above.

(2) For the purposes of subsection (1) above and that Part of that Act, a person whose father and mother were not married to each other at the time of his birth shall be presumed not to have been survived by his father, or by any person related to him only through his father, unless the contrary is shown.

(3) In section 50 (1) of that Act (which relates to the construction of documents), the reference to Part IV of that Act, or to the foregoing provisions of that Part, shall in relation to an instrument inter vivos made, or a will or codicil coming into operation, after the coming into force of this section (but not in relation to instruments inter vivos made or wills or codicils coming into operation earlier) be construed as including references to this section.

(4) This section does not affect any rights under the intestacy of a person dying before the coming into force of this section.

19. Dispositions of property.—(1) In the following dispositions, namely—

(a) dispositions inter vivos made on or after the date on which this section comes into force; and

(b) dispositions by will or codicil where the will or codicil is made on or after that date,

references (whether express or implied) to any relationship between two persons shall be construed in accordance with section 1 above.

(2) It is hereby declared that the use, without more, of the word 'heir' or 'heirs' or any expression which is used to create an entailed interest in real or personal property does not show a contrary intention for the purposes of section 1 as applied by subsection (1) above.

(3) In relation to the dispositions mentioned in subsection (1) above, section 33 of the Trustee Act 1925 (which specifies the trust implied by a direction that income is to be held on protective trusts for the benefit of any person) shall have effect as if any reference (however expressed) to any relationship between two persons were construed in accordance with section 1 above.

(4) Where under any disposition of real or personal property, any interest in such property is limited (whether subject to any preceding limitation or charge or not) in such a way that it would, apart from this section, devolve (as nearly as the law permits) along with a dignity or title of honour, then—

(a) whether or not the disposition contains an express reference to the dignity or title of honour; and

(b) whether or not the property or some interest in the property may in some event become severed from it,

nothing in this section shall operate to sever the property or any interest in it from the dignity or title, but the property or interest shall devolve in all respects as if this section had not been enacted.

(5) This section is without prejudice to section 42 of the Adoption Act 1976 (construction of dispositions in cases of adoption).

(6) In this section 'disposition' means a disposition, including an oral disposition, of real or personal property whether inter vivos or by will or codicil.

(7) Notwithstanding any rule of law, a disposition made by will or codicil executed before the date on which this section comes into force shall not be treated for the purposes of this section as made on or after that date by reason only that the will or codicil is confirmed by a codicil executed on or after that date.

20. No special protection for trustees and personal representatives. Section 17 of the Family Law Reform Act 1969 (which enables trustees and personal representatives to distribute property without having ascertained that no person whose parents were not married to each other at the time of his birth, or who claims through such a person, is or may be entitled to an interest in the property) shall cease to have effect.

21. Entitlement to grant of probate etc.—(1) For the purpose of determining the person or persons who would in accordance with probate rules be entitled to a grant of probate or administration in respect of the estate of a deceased person, the deceased shall be presumed, unless the contrary is shown, not to have been survived—

(a) by any person related to him whose father and mother were not married to each other at the time of his birth; or

(b) by any person whose relationship with him is deduced through such a person as is mentioned in paragraph (a) above.

(2) In this section 'probate rules' means rules of court made under section 127 of the Supreme Court Act 1981.

(3) This section does not apply in relation to the estate of a person dying before the coming into force of this section.

PART IV

DETERMINATION OF RELATIONSHIPS

22. Declarations of parentage.—For section 56 of the Family Law Act 1986 (declarations of legitimacy or legitimation) there shall be substituted the following section[17]—

[Note. Sections 18 to 22 above came into force on 4 April 1988.]

PART V

REGISTRATION OF BIRTHS

24. Registration of father where parents not married. For section 10 of the Births and Deaths Registration Act 1953 (in this Act referred to as 'the 1953 Act') there shall be substituted the following section[18]—

25. Re-registration where parents not married. For section 10A of the 1953 Act there shall be substituted the following section[19]—

26. Re-registration after declaration of parentage[20]. After section 14 of the 1953 Act there shall be inserted the following section[1]—

PART VI

MISCELLANEOUS AND SUPPLEMENTAL

Miscellaneous

27. Artificial insemination.—(1) Where after the coming into force of this section a child is born in England and Wales as the result of the artificial insemination of a woman who—

(a) was at the time of the insemination a party to a marriage (being a marriage which had not at that time been dissolved or annulled); and

17   For text see p. 871, ante.
18   For text, as subsequently amended, see p. 770, ante.
19   For text, as subsequently amended, see p. 772, ante.
20   Section 26 came into force on 4 April 1988.
 1   For text see p. 773, ante.

(b) was artificially inseminated with the semen of some person other than the other party to that marriage,

then, unless it is proved to the satisfaction of any court by which the matter has to be determined that the other party to that marriage did not consent to the insemination, the child shall be treated in law as the child of the parties to that marriage and shall not be treated as the child of any person other than the parties to that marriage.

(2) Any reference in this section to a marriage includes a reference to a void marriage if at the time of the insemination resulting in the birth of the child both or either of the parties reasonably believed that the marriage was valid; and for the purposes of this section it shall be presumed, unless the contrary is shown, that one of the parties so believed at that time that the marriage was valid.

(3) Nothing in this section shall affect the succession to any dignity or title of honour or render any person capable of succeeding to or transmitting a right to succeed to any such dignity or title.

28. Children of void marriages.—(1) In subsection (1) of section 1 of the Legitimacy Act 1976 (legitimacy of children of certain void marriages), for the words 'the act of intercourse resulting in the birth' there shall be substituted the words 'the insemination resulting in the birth or, where there was no such insemination, the child's conception'.

(2) At the end of that section there shall be added the following subsections[2]—

*   *   *   *   *

Supplemental

30. Orders applying section 1 to other enactments.[3]—(1) The Lord Chancellor may by order make provision for the construction in accordance with section 1 above of such enactments passed before the coming into force of that section as may be specified in the order.

(2) An order under this section shall so amend the enactments to which it relates as to secure that (so far as practicable) they continue to have the same effect notwithstanding the making of the order.

(3) An order under this section shall be made by statutory instrument which shall be subject to annulment in pursuance of a resolution of either House of Parliament.

31. Interpretation[4]**. In this Act—**

'the 1953 Act' means the Births and Deaths Registration Act 1953;
'the 1971 Act' means the Guardianship of Minors Act 1971;
'the 1973 Act' means the Guardianship Act 1973.

*   *   *   *   *

33. Amendments, transitional provisions, savings and repeals.—(1) The enactments mentioned in Schedule 2 to this Act shall have effect subject to the amendments there specified, being minor amendments and amendments consequential on the provisions of this Act.

(2) The transitional provisions and savings in Schedule 3 to this Act shall have effect.

(3) The inclusion in this Act of any express saving or amendment shall not be taken as prejudicing the operation of sections 16 and 17 of the Interpretation Act 1978 (which relate to the effect of repeals).

---

2   For text see pp. 822, 823, ante.
3   Section 30 above is to come into force on a day to be appointed.
4   Section 31 above came into force on 4 April 1988.

(4) The enactments mentioned in Schedule 4 to this Act are hereby repealed to the extent specified in the third column of that Schedule[5].

34. Short title, commencement and extent.—(1) This Act may be cited as the Family Law Reform Act 1987.

(2) This Act shall come into force on such day as the Lord Chancellor may by order made by statutory instrument appoint; and different days may be so appointed for different provisions or different purposes.

(3) Without prejudice to the transitional provisions contained in Schedule 3 to this Act, an order under subsection (2) above may make such further transitional provisions as appear to the Lord Chancellor to be necessary or expedient in connection with the provisions brought into force by the order, including—

(a) such adaptations of the provisions so brought into force; and
(b) such adaptations of any provisions of this Act then in force, as appear to him necessary or expedient in consequence of the partial operation of this Act.

(4) The following provisions of this Act extend to Scotland and Northern Ireland, namely—

(a) section 33(1) and paragraphs 12, 13 and 74 of Schedule 2;
(b) section 33(2) and paragraph 7 of Schedule 3 so far as relating to the operation of the Maintenance Orders Act 1950;
(c) section 33 (4) and Schedule 4 so far as relating to that Act and the Interpretation Act 1978; and
(d) this section.

(5) Subject to subsection (4) above, this Act extends to England and Wales only[5].

SCHEDULE 2

*   *   *   *   *

3. At the end of section 50 of the Administration of Estates Act 1925 there shall be added the following subsection[6]—

4. At the end of section 52 of that Act there shall be added the words 'and references (however expressed) to any relationship between two persons shall be construed in accordance with section 1 of the Family Law Reform Act 1987'.

*   *   *   *   *

16. In the proviso to section 14 (1) of that Act[7]—

(a) ...
(b) ...
(c) at the end of paragraph (c) there shall be added the words 'or section 56 of the Family Law Reform Act 1987'.

*   *   *   *   *

SCHEDULE 3

TRANSITIONAL PROVISIONS AND SAVINGS

Applications pending under amended or repealed enactments

1. This Act (including the repeals and amendments made by it) shall not have effect in relation to any application made under any enactment repealed or amended by this Act if that application is pending at the time when the provision of this Act which repeals or amends that enactment comes into force.

*   *   *   *   *

5   Section 33 above, as regards parts of Schedules 2, 3 and 4 of the Act (the parts relevant to this work are set out below) and s. 34 above came into force on 4 April 1988.
6   For text, see p. 760, ante.
7   The Births and Deaths Registration Act 1953.

Property rights

8. The repeal by this Act of section 14 of the Family Law Reform Act 1969 shall not affect any rights arising under the intestacy of a person dying before the coming into force of the repeal.

9. The repeal by this Act of section 15 of the Family Law Reform Act 1969 shall not affect, or affect the operation of section 33 of the Trustee Act 1925 in relation to—

(a) any disposition inter vivos made before the date on which the repeal comes into force or
(b) any disposition by will or codicil executed before that date.

10. The repeal by this Act of section 17 of the Family Law Reform Act 1969 shall not affect the liability of trustees or personal representatives in respect of any conveyance or distribution made before the coming into force of the repeal.

SCHEDULE 4

Repeals

Chapter	Short title	Extent of repeal
*	*	*	*	*
1969 c. 46	The Family Law Reform Act 1969	Sections 14 and 15 Section 17
*	*	*	*	*

[**Note.**—The matters set out above in Schedules 2, 3 and 4 took effect on 4 April 1988.]

CHILDREN ACT 1989

(1989, c. 41)   [16 November 1989]

[**Note.** *The relevant parts shown here save for section 5(11) and (12) came into force on 14 October 1991—S.I. 1991 No. 828. Sections 5(11) and (12) came into force on 1 February 1992.*]

PART I

*   *   *   *   *

2.—(1) Where a child's father and mother were married to each other at the time of his birth, they shall each have parental responsibility for the child.

(2) Where a child's father and mother were not married to each other at the time of his birth—

(a) the mother shall have parental responsibility for the child;
(b) the father shall not have parental responsibility for the child, unless he acquires it in accordance with the provisions of this Act.

(3) References in this Act to a child whose father and mother were, or (as the case may be) were not, married to each other at the time of his birth must be read with section 1 of the Family Law Reform Act 1987 (which extends their meaning).

(4) The rule of law that a father is the natural guardian of his legitimate child is abolished.

(5) More than one person may have parental responsibility for the same child at the same time.

(6) A person who has parental responsibility for a child at any time shall not cease to have that responsibility solely because some other person subsequently acquires parental responsibility for the child.

(7) Where more than one person has parental responsibility for a child, each of them may act alone and without the other (or others) in meeting that responsibility; but nothing in this Part shall be taken to affect the operation of any enactment which requires the consent of more than one person in a matter affecting the child.

(8) The fact that a person has parental responsibility for a child shall not entitle him to act in any way which would be incompatible with any order made with respect to the child under this Act.

(9) A person who has parental responsibility for a child may not surrender or transfer any part of that responsibility to another but may arrange for some or all of it to be met by one or more persons acting on his behalf.

(10) The person with whom any such arrangement is made may himself be a person who already has parental responsibility for the child concerned.

(11) The making of any such arrangement shall not affect any liability of the person making it which may arise from any failure to meet any part of his parental responsibility for the child concerned.

3.—(1) In this Act 'parental responsibility' means all the rights, duties, powers, responsibilities and authority which by law a parent of a child has in relation to the child and his property.

(2) It also includes the rights, powers and duties which a guardian of the child's estate (appointed, before the commencement of section 5, to act generally) would have had in relation to the child and his property.

(3) The rights referred to in subsection (2) include, in particular, the right of the guardian to receive or recover in his own name, for the benefit of the child, property of whatever description and wherever situated which the child is entitled to receive or recover.

(4) The fact that a person has, or does not have, parental responsibility for a child shall not affect—

(a) any obligation which he may have in relation to the child (such as a statutory duty to maintain the child); or
(b) any rights which, in the event of the child's death, he (or any other person) may have in relation to the child's property.

$$* \qquad * \qquad * \qquad * \qquad *$$

4.—(1) Where a child's father and mother were not married to each other at the time of his birth—

(a) the court may, on the application of the father, order that he shall have parental responsibility for the child; or
(b) the father and mother may by agreement ('a parental responsibility agreement') provide for the father to have parental responsibility for the child.

(2) No parental responsibility agreement shall have affect for the purposes of this Act unless—

(a) it is made in the form prescribed by regulations made by the Lord Chancellor; and
(b) where regulations are made by the Lord Chancellor prescribing the manner in which such agreements must be recorded, it is recorded in the prescribed manner.

(3) Subject to section 12(4), an order under subsection (1)(a), or a parental responsibility agreement, may only be brought to an end by an order of the court made on the application—

(a) of any person who has parental responsibility for the child; or
(b) with leave of the court, of the child himself.

$$* \qquad * \qquad * \qquad * \qquad *$$

5.—(1) Where an application with respect to a child is made to the court by any individual, the court may by order appoint that individual to be the child's guardian if—

(a) the child has no parent with parental responsibility for him; or

(b) a residence order has been made with respect to the child in favour of a parent or guardian of his who has died while the order was in force.

(2) The power conferred by subsection (1) may also be exercised in any family proceedings if the court considers that the order should be made even though no application has been made for it.

(3) A parent who has parental responsibility for his child may appoint another individual to be the child's guardian in the event of his death.

(4) A guardian of a child may appoint another individual to take his place as the child's guardian in the event of his death.

(5) An appointment under subsection (3) or (4) shall not have effect unless it is made in writing, is dated and is signed by the person making the appointment or—

(a) in the case of an appointment made by a will which is not signed by the testator, is signed at the direction of the testator in accordance with the requirements of section 9 of the Wills Act 1837; or

(b) in any other case, is signed at the direction of the person making the appointment, in his presence and in the presence of two witnesses who each attest the signature.

(6) A person appointed as a child's guardian under this section shall have parental responsibility for the child concerned.

(7) Where—

(a) on the death of any person making an appointment under subsection (3) or (4), the child concerned has no parent with parental responsibility for him; or

(b) immediately before the death of any person making such an appointment, a residence order in his favour was in force with respect to the child,

the appointment shall take effect on the death of that person.

(8) Where, on the death of any person making an appointment under subsection (3) or (4)—

(a) the child concerned has a parent with parental responsibility for him; and

(b) subsection (7)(b) does not apply,

the appointment shall take effect when the child no longer has a parent who has parental responsibility for him.

(9) Subsections (1) and (7) do not apply if the residence order referred to in paragraph (b) of those subsections was also made in favour of a surviving parent of the child.

(10) Nothing in this section shall be taken to prevent an appointment under subsection (3) or (4) being made by two or more persons acting jointly.

(11) Subject to any provision made by rules of court, no court shall exercise the High Court's inherent jurisdiction to appoint a guardian of the estate of any child[8].

(12) Where rules of court are made under subsection (11) they may prescribe the circumstances in which, and conditions subject to which, an appointment of such a guardian may be made.[8]

(13) A guardian of a child may only be appointed in accordance with the provisions of this section.

6.—(1) An appointment under section 5(3) or (4) revokes an earlier such appointment (including one made in an unrevoked will or codicil) made by the same person in respect of

---

8 Subsections (11) and (12) came into force 1 February 1992.

the same child, unless it is clear (whether as the result of an express provision in the later appointment or by any necessary implication) that the purpose of the later appointment is to appoint an additional guardian.

(2) An appointment under section 5(3) or (4) (including one made in an unrevoked will or codicil) is revoked if the person who made the appointment revokes it by a written and dated instrument which is signed—

(a) by him; or
(b) at his direction, in his presence and in the presence of two witnesses who each attest the signature.

(3) An appointment under section 5(3) or (4) (other than one made in a will or codicil) is revoked if, with the intention of revoking the appointment, the person who made it—

(a) destroys the instrument by which it was made; or
(b) has some other person destroy that instrument in his presence.

(3A) An appointment under section 5(3) or (4) (including one made in an unrevoked will or codicil) is revoked if the person appointed is the spouse of the person who made the appointment and either—

(a) a decree of a court of civil jurisdiction in England and Wales dissolves or annuls the marriage, or
(b) the marriage is dissolved or annulled and the divorce or annulment is entitled to recognition in England or Wales by virtue of Part II of the Family Law Act 1986,

unless a contrary intention appears by the appointment[9].

(4) For the avoidance of doubt, an appointment under section 5(3) or (4) made in a will or codicil is revoked if the will or codicil is revoked.

(5) A person who is appointed as a guardian under section 5(3) or (4) may disclaim his appointment by an instrument in writing signed by him and made within a reasonable time of his first knowing that the appointment has taken effect.

(6) Where regulations are made by the Lord Chancellor prescribing the manner in which such disclaimers must be recorded, no such disclaimer shall have effect unless it is recorded in the prescribed manner.

(7) Any appointment of a guardian under section 5 may be brought to an end at any time by order of the court—

(a) on the application of any person who has parental responsibility for the child;
(b) on the application of the child concerned, with leave of the court; or
(c) in any family proceedings, if the court considers that it should be brought to an end even though no application has been made.

*   *   *   *   *

PART II

8.—(1) In this Act—

*   *   *   *   *

'a residence order' means an order settling the arrangements to be made as to the person with whom a child is to live; and

*   *   *   *   *

---

9   Subsection (3A) inserted by s. 4, Law Reform (Succession) Act 1995—see p. 902, post—and has effect as respects an appointment made by a person dying on or after 1 January 1996 (regardless of the date of the dissolution or annulment).

(2) In this Act 'a section 8 order' means any of the orders mentioned in subsection (1) and any order varying or discharging such an order.

* * * * *

12.—(1) Where the court makes a residence order in favour of the father of a child it shall, if the father would not otherwise have parental responsibility for the child, also make an order under section 4 giving him that responsibility.

* * * * *

(4) Where subsection (1) requires the court to make an order under section 4 in respect of the father of a child, the court shall not bring that order to an end at any time while the residence order concerned remains in force.

* * * * *

PART IV

31.—(1) On the application of any local authority or authorised person, the court may make an order—

(a) placing the child with respect to whom the application is made in the care of a designated local authority; or

* * * * *

(11) In this Act—

'a care order' means (subject to section 105(1)) an order under subsection (1)(a) and (except where express provision to the contrary is made) includes an interim care order made under section 38; and

* * * * *

33.—(1) Where a care order is made with respect to a child it shall be the duty of the local authority designated by the order to receive the child into their care and to keep him in their care while the order remains in force.

* * * * *

39.—(1) A care order may be discharged by the court on the application of—

(a) any person who has parental responsibility for the child;
(b) the child himself; or
(c) the local authority designated by the order.

* * * * *

PART XII

* * * * *

88.—(1) The Adoption Act 1976 shall have effect subject to the amendments made by Part I of Schedule 10.

* * * * *

91.—(1) The making of a residence order with respect to a child who is the subject of a care order discharges the care order.

(2) The making of a care order with respect to a child who is the subject of any section 8 order discharges that order.

(3) The making of a care order with respect to a child who is the subject of a supervision order discharges that other order.

(4) The making of a care order with respect to a child who is a ward of court brings that wardship to an end.

*   *   *   *   *

(7) Any order made under section 4(1) or 5(1) shall continue in force until the child reaches the age of eighteen, unless it is brought to an end earlier.

*   *   *   *   *

(8) Any—

(a) agreement under section 4; or
(b) appointment under section 5(3) or (4),

shall continue in force until the child reaches the age of eighteen, unless it is brought to an end earlier.

(10) A section 8 order shall, if it would otherwise still be in force, cease to have effect when the child reaches the age of sixteen, unless it is to have effect beyond that age by virtue of section 9(6).

(11) Where a section 8 order has effect with respect to a child who has reached the age of sixteen, it shall, if it would otherwise still be in force, cease to have effect when he reaches the age of eighteen.

(12) Any care order, other than an interim care order, shall continue in force until the child reaches the age of eighteen, unless it is brought to an end earlier.

(13) Any order made under any other provision of this Act in relation to a child shall, if it would otherwise still be in force, cease to have effect when he reaches the age of eighteen.

*   *   *   *   *

92.—

*   *   *   *   *

(7) For the purposes of this Act 'the court' means the High Court, a county court or a magistrates' court.

*   *   *   *   *

96.—(1) Subsection (2) applies where a child who is called as a witness in any civil proceedings does not, in the opinion of the court, understand the nature of an oath.

(2) The child's evidence may be heard by the court if, in its opinion—

(a) he understands that it is his duty to speak the truth; and
(b) he has sufficient understanding to justify his evidence being heard.

*   *   *   *   *

(7) In this section—

'civil proceedings' and 'court' have the same meaning as they have in the Civil Evidence Act 1968 by virtue of section 18 of that Act; and

105.—(1) In this Act—

*   *   *   *   *

'care order' has the meaning given by section 31(11) and also includes any order which by or under any enactment has the effect of, or is deemed to be, a care order for the purposes of this Act; and any reference to a child who is in the care of an authority is a reference to a child who is in their care by virtue of a care order;
'child' means, subject to paragraph 16 of Schedule 1, a person under the age of eighteen;

*   *   *   *   *

'guardian of a child' means a guardian (other than a guardian of the estate of a child) appointed in accordance with the provisions of section 5;

* * * * *

'local authority' means, in relation to England and Wales, the council of a county, a metropolitan district, a London Borough or the Common Council of the City of London and, in relation to Scotland, a local authority within the meaning of section 1(2) of the Social Work (Scotland) Act 1968;

* * * * *

'parental responsibility' has the meaning given in section 3;

'parental responsibility agreement' has the meaning given in section 4(1);

'prescribed' means prescribed by regulations made under this Act;

* * * * *

'residence order' has the meaning given by section 8(1);

* * * * *

'signed', in relation to any person, includes the making by that person of his mark;

* * * * *

'supervision order' has the meaning given by section 31(11);

* * * * *

(2) References in this Act to a child whose father and mother were, or (as the case may be) were not, married to each other at the time of his birth must be read with section 1 of the Family Law Reform Act 1987 (which extends the meaning of such references).

* * * * *

108.—(1) This Act may be cited as the Children Act 1989.

(2) Sections 89 and 96(3) to (7), and paragraph 35 of Schedule 12, shall come into force on the passing of this Act and paragraph 36 of Schedule 12 shall come into force at the end of the period of two months beginning with the day on which this Act is passed but otherwise this Act shall come into force on such date as may be appointed by order made by the Lord Chancellor or the Secretary of State, or by both acting jointly.

(3) Different dates may be appointed for different provisions of this Act and in relation to different cases.

(4) The minor amendments set out in Schedule 12 shall have effect.

(5) The consequential amendments set out in Schedule 13 shall have effect.

(6) The transitional provisions and savings set out in Schedule 14 shall have effect.

(7) The repeals set out in Schedule 15 shall have effect.

* * * * *

SCHEDULE 3 SUPERVISION ORDERS

* * * * *

PART II

* * * * *

10. The making of a supervision order with respect to any child brings to an end earlier care or supervision order which—

* * * * *

(a) was made with respect to that child; and
(b) would otherwise continue in force.

*   *   *   *   *

SCHEDULE 10   Amendments of Adoption Legislation

Part I

Amendments of Adoption Act 1976

3.—(1) In section 12 (adoption orders), in subsection (1) for the words 'vesting the parental rights and duties relating to a child in' there shall be substituted 'giving parental responsibility for a child to'.

(2) In subsection (2) of that section for the words 'the parental rights and duties so far as they relate' there shall be substituted 'parental responsibility so far as it relates'.

(3) In subsection (3) of that section for paragraph (a) there shall be substituted—

'(a)   the parental responsibility which any person has for the child immediately before the making of the order;
(aa)   any order under the Children Act 1989';

and in paragraph (b) for the words from 'for any period' to the end there shall be substituted 'or upbringing for any period after the making of the order'.

*   *   *   *   *

20.—(1) In section 51 (disclosure of birth records of adopted children), in subsection (1) for the words 'subsections (4) and (6)' there shall be substituted 'what follows'.

(2) For subsections (3) to (7) of that section there shall be substituted—

'(3) Before supplying any information to an applicant under subsection (1), the Registrar General shall inform the applicant that counselling services are available to him—

(a)   if he is in England and Wales—
    (i)   at the General Register Office;
    (ii)   from the local authority in whose area he is living;
    (iii)   where the adoption order relating to him was made in England and Wales, from the local authority in whose area the court which made the order sat; or
    (iv)   from any other local authority;
(b)   if he is in Scotland—
    (i)   from the regional or islands council in whose area he is living;
    (ii)   where the adoption order relating to him was made in Scotland, from the council in whose area the court which made the order sat; or
    (iii)   from any other regional or islands council;
(c)   if he is in Northern Ireland—
    (i)   from the Board in whose area he is living;
    (ii)   where the adoption relating to him was made in Northern Ireland, from the Board in whose area the court which made the order sat; or
    (iii)   from any other Board;
(d)   if he is in the United Kingdom and his adoption was arranged by an adoption society—
    (i)   approved under section 3,
    (ii)   approved under section 3 of the Adoption (Scotland) Act 1978,
    (iii)   registered under Article 4 of the Adoption (Northern Ireland) Order 1987,

from that society.

(4) Where an adopted person who is in England and Wales—

(a)   applies for information under—
    (i)   subsection (1), or
    (ii)   Article 54 of the Adoption (Northern Ireland) Order 1987, or
(b)   is supplied with information under section 45 of the Adoption (Scotland) Act 1978,

it shall be the duty of the persons and bodies mentioned in subsection (5) to provide counselling for him if asked by him to do so.

(5) The persons and bodies are—

(a)   the Registrar General;
(b)   any local authority falling within subsection (3)(a)(ii) to (iv);
(c)   any adoption society falling within subsection (3)(d) in so far as it is acting as an adoption society in England and Wales.

(6) If the applicant chooses to receive counselling from a person or body falling within subsection (3), the Registrar General shall send to the person or body the information to which the applicant is entitled under subsection (1).

(7) Where a person—

(a) was adopted before 12 November 1975, and
(b) applies for information under subsection (1),

the Registrar General shall not supply the information to him unless he has attended an interview with a counsellor arranged by a person or body from whom counselling services are available as mentioned in subsection (3).

(8) Where the Registrar General is prevented by subsection (7) from supplying information to a person who is not living in the United Kingdom, he may supply the information to any body which—

(a) the Registrar General is satisfied is suitable to provide counselling to that person, and
(b) has notified the Registrar General that it is prepared to provide such counselling.

(9) In this section—

"a Board" means a Health and Social Services Board established under Article 16 of the Health and Personal Social Servides (Northern Ireland) Order 1972; and

"prescribed" means prescribed by regulations made by the Registrar General.'

*   *   *   *   *

22.—(1) In section 55 (adoption of children abroad), in subsection (1) after the word 'Scotland' there shall be inserted 'or Northern Ireland' and for the words 'vesting in him the parental rights and duties relating to the child' there shall be substituted 'giving him parental responsibility for the child'.

*   *   *   *   *

27. In section 60 (evidence of adoption in Scotland and Northern Ireland), in paragraph (a) for the words 'section 22(2) of the Adoption Act 1958' there shall be substituted 'section 45(2) of the Adoption (Scotland) Act 1978' and in paragraph (b) for the words from 'section 23(4)' to 'in force' there shall be substituted 'Article 63(1) of the Adoption (Northern Ireland) Order 1987'.

*   *   *   *   *

30.—

*   *   *   *   *

(3) For the definition of 'adoption order' there shall be substituted—

'"adoption order"—

(a) means an order under section 12(1); and
(b) in sections 12(3) and (4), 18 to 20, 27, 28 and 30 to 32 and in the definition of "British adoption order" in this subsection includes an order under section 12 of the Adoption (Scotland) Act 1978 and Article 12 of the Adoption (Northern Ireland) Order 1987 (adoption orders in Scotland and Northern Ireland respectively); and
(c) in sections 27, 28 and 30 to 32 includes an order under section 55, section 49 of the Adoption (Scotland) Act 1978 and Article 57 of the Adoption (Northern Ireland) Order 1987 (orders in relation to children being adopted abroad).'

(4) For the definition of 'British adoption order' there shall be substituted—

'"British adoption order" means—

(a) an adoption order as defined in this subsection, and
(b) an order under any provision for the adoption of a child effected under the law of any British territory outside the United Kingdom.'

(5) For the definition of 'guardian' there shall be substituted—

'"guardian" has the same meaning as in the Children Act 1989.'

*   *   *   *   *

(7) After the definition of 'overseas adoption' there shall be inserted—

'"parent" means, in relation to a child, any parent who has parental responsibility for the child under the Children Act 1989;

"parental responsibility" and "parental responsibility agreement" have the same meaning as in the Children Act 1989.'

(8) After the definition of 'United Kingdom national' there shall be inserted—

'"upbringing" has the same meaning as in the Children Act 1989.'

(9) For section 72(1A) there shall be substituted the following subsections—

'(1A) In this Act, in determining with what person, or where, a child has his home, any absence of the child at a hospital or boarding school and any other temporary absence shall be disregarded.

(1B) In this Act, references to a child who is in the care of or looked after by a local authority have the same meaning as in the Children Act 1989.'

*   *   *   *   *

SCHEDULE 12   MINOR AMENDMENTS

*   *   *   *   *

The Births and Deaths Registration Act 1953 (c.20)

6.—(1) Sections 10 and 10A of the Births and Deaths Registration Act 1953 (registration of father, and re-registration, where parents not married) shall be amended as follows.

(2) In sections 10(1) and 10A(1) for paragraph (d) there shall be substituted—

'(d) at the request of the mother or that person on production of—
    (i) a copy of a parental responsibility agreement made between them in relation to the child; and
    (ii) a declaration in the prescribed form by the person making the request stating that the agreement was made in compliance with section 4 of the Children Act 1989 and has not been brought to an end by an order of a court; or
(e) at the request of the mother or that person on production of—
    (i) a certified copy of an order under section 4 of the Children Act 1989 giving that person parental responsibility for the child; and
    (ii) a declaration in the prescribed form by the person making the request stating that the order has not been brought to an end by an order of a court; or
(f) at the request of the mother or that person on production of—
    (i) a certified copy of an order under paragraph 1 of Schedule 1 to the Children Act 1989 which requires that person to make any financial provision for the child and which is not an order falling within paragraph 4(3) of that Schedule; and
    (ii) a declaration in the prescribed form by the person making the request stating that the order has not been discharged by an order of a court; or
(g) at the request of the mother or that person on production of—
    (i) a certified copy of any of the orders which are mentioned in subsection (1A) of this section which has been made in relation to the child; and
    (ii) a declaration in the prescribed form by the person making the request stating that the order has not been brought to an end or discharged by an order of a court.'

(3) After sections 10(1) and 10A(1) there shall be inserted—

'(1A) The orders are—

(a) an order under section 4 of the Family Law Reform Act 1987 that that person shall have all the parental rights and duties with respect to the child;
(b) an order that the person shall have custody or care and control or legal custody of the child made under section 9 of the Guardianship of Minors Act 1971 at a time when such an order could only be made in favour of a parent;
(c) an order under section 9 or 11B of that Act which requires that person to make any financial provision in relation to the child;
(d) an order under section 4 of the Affiliation Proceedings Act 1957 naming that person as putative father of the child.'

(4) In section 10(2) for the words 'or (d)' there shall be substituted 'to (g)'.

(5) In section 10(3) for the words from 'relevant order' to the end there shall be substituted ' "parental responsibility agreement" has the same meaning as in the Children Act 1989'.

*   *   *   *   *

(6) In section 10A(2) in paragraphs (b) and (c) for the words 'paragraph (d)' in both places where they occur there shall be substituted 'any of paragraphs (d) to (g)'.

*   *   *   *   *

SCHEDULE 13 CONSEQUENTIAL AMENDMENTS

The Wills Act 1837 (c.26)

1. In section 1 of the Wills Act 1837 (interpretation), in the definition of 'will', for the words 'and also to a disposition by will and testament or devise of the custody and tuition of any child' there shall be substituted 'and also to an appointment by will of a guardian of a child'.

* * * * *

SCHEDULE 14 TRANSITIONALS AND SAVINGS

1.—(1) Subject to sub-paragraph (1A) and (4), nothing in any provision of this Act (other than the repeals mentioned in sub-paragraph (2)) shall affect any proceedings which are pending immediately before the commencement of that provision.

(1A) Proceedings pursuant to section 7(2) of the Family Law Reform Act 1969 (committal of wards of court to care of local authority) or in the exercise of the High Court's inherent jurisdiction with respect to children which are pending in relation to a child who has been placed or allowed to remain in the care of a local authority shall not be treated as pending proceedings after 13th October 1992 for the purposes of this Schedule if no final order has been made by that date pursuant to section 7(2) of the 1969 Act or in the exercise of the High Court's inherent jurisdiction in respect of the child's care[10].

(2) The repeals are those of—

(a) section 42(3) of the Matrimonial Causes Act 1973 (declaration by court that party to marriage unfit to have custody of children of family); and

(b) section 38 of the Sexual Offences Act 1956 (power of court to divest person of authority over girl or boy in cases of incest).

(3) For the purposes of the following provisions of this Schedule, any reference to an order in force immediately before the commencement of a provision of this Act shall be construed as including a reference to an order made after that commencement in proceedings pending before that commencement.

(4) Sub-paragraph (3) is not to be read as making the order in question have effect from a date earlier than that on which it was made.

* * * * *

The Family Law Reform Act 1987 (c.42)

Conversion of orders under section 4

4. Where, immediately before the day on which Parts I and II come into force, there was in force an order under section 4(1) of the Family Law Reform Act 1987 (order giving father parental rights and duties in relation to a child), then, on and after that day, the order shall be deemed to be an order under section 4 of this Act giving the father parental responsibility for the child.

Orders to which paragraphs 6 to 11 apply

5.—(1) In paragraphs 6 to 11 'an existing order' means any order which—

(a) is in force immediately before the commencement of Parts I and II;
(b) was made under any enactment mentioned in sub-paragraph (2);
(c) determines all or any of the following—
    (i) who is to have custody of a child;
    (ii) who is to have care and control of a child;
    (iii) who is to have access to a child;
    (iv) any matter with respect to a child's education or upbringing; and
(d) is not an order of a kind mentioned in paragraph 15(1).

(2) The enactments are—

(a) the Domestic Proceedings and Magistrates' Courts Act 1978;
(b) the Children Act 1975;
(c) the Matrimonial Causes Act 1973;
(d) the Guardianship of Minors Acts 1971 and 1973;
(e) the Matrimonial Causes Act 1965;
(f) the Matrimonial Proceedings (Magistrates' Courts) Act 1960.

10 Para. (1A) inserted by the Children Act 1989 (Commencement No. 2—Amendment and Transitional Provisions) Order 1991: S.I. 1991 No. 1990.

(3) For the purposes of this paragraph and paragraphs 6 to 11 'custody' includes legal custody and joint as well as sole custody but does not include access.

Parental responsibility of parents

6.—(1) Where—

(a) a child's father and mother were not married to each other at the time of his birth; and
(b) there is an existing order with respect to the child,

each parent shall have parental responsibility for the child in accordance with section 2 as modified by sub-paragraph (3).

(2) Where—

(a) a child's father and mother were not married to each other at the time of his birth; and
(b) there is an existing order with respect to the child,

section 2 shall apply as modified by sub-paragraphs (3) and (4).

(3) The modification is that for section 2(8) there shall be substituted—

'(8) The fact that a person has parental responsibility for a child does not entitle him to act in a way which would be incompatible with any existing order or any order made under this Act with respect to the child.'

(4) The modifications are that—

(a) for the purposes of section 2(2), where the father has custody or care and control of the child by virtue of any existing order, the court shall be deemed to have made (at the commencement of that section) an order under section 4(1) giving him parental responsibility for the child; and
(b) where by virtue of paragraph (a) a court is deemed to have made an order under section 4(1) in favour of a father who has care and control of a child by virtue of an existing order, the court shall not bring the order under section 4(1) to an end at any time while he has care and control of the child by virtue of the order.

*   *   *   *   *

GUARDIANS

Existing guardians to be guardians under this Act

12.—(1) Any appointment of a person as guardian of a child which—

(a) was made—
      (i)   under sections 3 to 5 of the Guardianship of Minors Act 1971;
      (ii) under section 38(3) of the Sexual Offences Act 1956; or
      (iii) under the High Court's inherent jurisdiction with respect to children; and
(b) has taken effect before the commencement of section 5,

shall (subject to sub-paragraph (2)) be deemed, on and after the commencement of section 5, to be an appointment made and having effect under that section.

(2) Where an appointment of a person as guardian of a child has effect under section 5 by virtue of sub-paragraph (1)(a)(ii), the appointment shall not have effect for a period which is longer than any period specified in the order[11].

Appointment of guardian not yet in effect

13. Any appointment of a person to be a guardian of a child—

(a) which was made as mentioned in paragraph 12(1)(a)(i); but
(b) which, immediately before the commencement of section 5, had not taken effect,

shall take effect in accordance with section 5 (as modified, where it applies, by paragraph[11] 8(2)).

Persons deemed to be appointed as guardians under existing wills

14. For the purposes of the Wills Act 1837 and of this Act any disposition by will and testament or

11   References in paragraphs 12, 13 and 14 to the commencement of s. 5 shall be construed as references to the commencement of sub-ss. (1) to (10) and (13) of that section except in relation to the appointment of a guardian of the estate of any child in which case they shall be construed as a reference to the commencement of sub-ss. (11) and (12) of that section. (Inserted by the Children Act 1989 (Commencement No. 2—Amendment and Transitional Provisions) Order 1991: S.I. 1991 No. 1990.)

devise of the custody and tuition of any child, made before the commencement of section 4 and paragraph 1 of Schedule 13, shall be deemed to be an appointment by will of a guardian of the child.[11]

Children in compulsory care

15.—(1) Sub-paragraph (2) applies where, immediately before the day on which Part IV comes into force, a person was—

(a) in care by virtue of—
    (i) a care order under section 1 of the Children and Young Persons Act 1969;
    (ii) a care order under section 15 of that Act, on discharging a supervision order made under section 1 of that Act; or
    (iii) an order or authorisation under section 25 or 26 of that Act;
(b) deemed, by virtue of—
    (i) paragraph 7(3) of Schedule 5A to the Army Act 1955;
    (ii) paragraph 7(3) of Schedule 5A to the Air Force Act 1955; or
    (iii) paragraph 7(3) of Schedule 4A to the Naval Discipline Act 1957,

to be the subject of a care order under the Children and Young Persons Act 1969;

(c) in care—
    (i) under section 2 of the Child Care Act 1980; or
    (ii) by virtue of paragraph 1 of Schedule 4 to that Act (which extends the meaning of a child in care under section 2 to include children in care under section 1 of the Children Act 1948),

and a child in respect of whom a resolution under section 3 of the Act of 1980 or section 2 of the Act of 1948 was in force;

(d) a child in respect of whom a resolution had been passed under section 65 of the Child Care Act 1980;
(e) in care by virtue of an order under—
    (i) section 2(1)(e) of the Matrimonial Proceedings (Magistrates' Courts) Act 1960;
    (ii) section 7(2) of the Family Law Reform Act 1969;
    (iii) section 43(1) of the Matrimonial Causes Act 1973;
    (iv) section 2(2)(b) of the Guardianship Act 1973; or
    (v) section 10 of the Domestic Proceedings and Magistrates' Courts Act 1978,

(orders having effect for certain purposes as if the child had been received into care under section 2 of the Child Care Act 1980);

(f) in care by virtue of an order made, on the revocation of a custodianship order, under section 36 of the Children Act 1975;
(g) in care by virtue of an order made, on the refusal of an adoption order, under section 25 of the Adoption Act 1976 or any order having effect (by virtue of paragraph 1 of Schedule 2 to that Act) as if made under that section; or
(h) in care by virtue of an order of the court made in the exercise of the High Court's inherent jurisdiction with respect to children[12].

(2) Where this sub-paragraph applies, then, on and after the day on which Part IV commences—

(a) the order or resolution in question shall be deemed to be a care order;
(b) the authority in whose care the person was immediately before that commencement shall be deemed to be the authority designated in that deemed care order; and
(c) any reference to a child in the care of a local authority shall include a reference to a person who is the subject of such a deemed care order,

and the provisions of this Act shall apply accordingly, subject to paragraph 16.

*   *   *   *   *

SCHEDULE 15 REPEALS

Short title	Extent of repeal
<p align="center">* * * * *</p>	
The Guardianship of Minors Act 1971	The whole Act.
<p align="center">* * * * *</p>	

12   Para (h) added by the Courts and Legal Services Act 1990, Sch. 16.

The Guardianship Act 1973.   The whole Act.

   *   *   *   *   *

The Children Act 1975.   The whole Act.

   *   *   *   *   *

The Child Care Act 1980.   The whole Act.

   *   *   *   *   *

The Family Law Act 1986.   In Schedule 1, paragraphs 10, . . .

   *   *   *   *   *

The Family Law Reform Act 1987.   Section 3, Sections 4 to 7.

   *   *   *   *   *

COURTS AND LEGAL SERVICES ACT 1990

(1990, c. 41)   **[1 November 1990]**

   *   *   *   *   *

PART II

LEGAL SERVICES

Probate services

54.[13]—(1) In section 23 of the Solicitors Act 1974 (preparation of papers for probate etc. by unqualified persons), the following subsections shall be substituted for subsections (2) and (3)—

'(2) Subsection (1) does not apply to—

(a) a barrister;

(b) a duly certificated notary public;

(c) the Public Trustee;

(d) the Official Solicitor;

(e) any institution which—

 (i) is authorised by the Bank of England, under Part I of the Banking Act 1987, to carry on a deposit-taking business; and

 (ii) satisfies the conditions mentioned in subsection (2A);

(f) any building society which—

 (i) is authorised to raise money from its members by the Building Societies Commission under section 9 of the Building Societies Act 1986; and

 (ii) satisfies those conditions;

(g) any insurance company which—

 (i) is authorised under section 3 or 4 of the Insurance Companies Act 1982; and

 (ii) satisfies those conditions;

(h) any subsidiary (as defined by section 736(1) of the Companies Act 1985) of a body falling within paragraph (e), (f) or (g)—

 (i) whose business, or any part of whose business, consists of acting as trustee or executor; and

 (ii) which satisfies those conditions.

(2A) The conditions are that the body is a member of, or otherwise subject to, a scheme which—

(a) has been established (whether or not exclusively) for the purpose of dealing with complaints about the provision of probate services; and

13 Sections 54 and 55 are to come into force on a date to be appointed.

(b) complies with such requirements as may be prescribed by regulations made by the Lord Chancellor with respect to matters relating to such complaints.

(3) Subsection (1) also does not apply to—

(a) any act done by an officer or employee of a body corporate at a time when it is exempt from subsection (1) by virtue of any of paragraphs (e) to (h) of subsection (2) or by virtue of section 55 of the Courts and Legal Services Act 1990 (preparation of probate papers etc.); or

(b) any act done by any person at the direction and under the supervision of another person if—

   (i) that other person was at the time his employer, a partner of his employer or a fellow employee; and

   (ii) the act could have been done by that other person for or in expectation of any fee, gain or reward without committing an offence under this section.

(4) For the avoidance of doubt, where a person does any act which would constitute an offence under subsection (1) but for an exemption given to him by this section or by or under any other enactment, he shall not be guilty of an offence under section 22 by virtue of having done that act.'

(2) In section 115 of the Supreme Court Act 1981 (grants to trust corporations) the following subsection shall be added at the end—

'(4) Subsections (1) to (3) shall also apply in relation to any body which is exempt from the provisions of section 23(1) of the Solicitors Act 1974 (unqualified persons not to prepare papers for probate etc.) by virtue of any of paragraphs (e) to (h) of subsection (2) of that section.'

(3) If a person who applies for any grant of probate or letters of administration—

(a) makes a statement in his application, or supports his application with a document, which he knows to be false or misleading in a material particular; or

(b) recklessly makes a statement in his application, or supports his application with a document, which is false or misleading in a material particular,

he shall be guilty of an offence.

(4) Any person guilty of an offence under subsection (3) shall be liable—

(a) on conviction on indictment, to imprisonment for a term not exceeding two years or to a fine or to both;

(b) on summary conviction, to imprisonment for a term not exceeding six months or to a fine not exceeding the statutory maximum or to both.

(5) In subsection (3) 'letters of administration' includes all letters of administration of the effects of deceased persons, whether with or without a will annexed, and whether granted for general, special or limited purposes.

55.[13]—(1) The provisions of section 23(1) of the Solicitors Act 1974 (preparation of papers for probate etc. by unqualified persons) shall not apply to any person to whom exemption from those provisions is granted by an approved body.

(2) An approved body may only grant such an exemption to a person who is one of its members and who satisfies it—

(a) that his business is, and is likely to continue to be, carried on by fit and proper persons or, in the case of an individual, that he is a fit and proper person;

(b) that he, and any person employed by him in the provision of probate services, is suitably trained;

(c) that satisfactory arrangements will at all times be in force for covering adequately the risk of any claim made against him in connection with the provision of probate services by him, however arising;

(d) that he is a member of, or otherwise subject to, a scheme which—
    (i) has been established (whether or not exclusively) for the purposes of dealing with complaints about the provision of probate services; and
    (ii) complies with such requirements as may be prescribed by regulations made by the Lord Chancellor with respect to matters relating to such complaints; and
(e) that he has in force satisfactory arrangements to protect his clients in the event of his ceasing to provide probate services.

(3) In this section 'approved body' means a professional or other body which is approved by the Lord Chancellor under Schedule 9.

(4) The approval of any body under Schedule 9 may be revoked under that Schedule.

56.—(1) Every justice shall have power to administer any oath or take any affidavit which is required for the purposes of an application for a grant of probate or letters of administration made in any non-contentious or common form probate business.

(2) A justice before whom any oath or affidavit is taken or made under this section shall state in the jurat or attestation at what place and on what date the oath or affidavit is taken or made.

(3) No justice shall exercise the powers conferred by this section in any proceedings in which he is interested.

(4) A document purporting to be signed by a justice administering an oath or taking an affidavit shall be admitted in evidence without proof of the signature and without proof that he is a justice.

(5) In this section—

'affidavit' has the same meaning as in the Commissioners for Oaths Act 1889;

'justice' means a justice of the peace;

'letters of administration' includes all letters of administration of the effects of deceased persons, whether with or without a will annexed, and whether granted for general, special or limited purposes; and

'non-contentious or common form probate business' has the same meaning as in section 128 of the Supreme Court Act 1981[14].

          *   *   *   *   *

124.—(1) The following provisions come into force on the passing of this Act—

(a) sections 1, 5, 119 to 123, this section and section 125(1); and
(b) paragraphs 2 and 3 of Schedule 17.

(2) The following provisions come into force at the end of the period of two months beginning on the day on which this Act is passed—

(a) sections 6, 8, 11, 16, 64, 65, 72, 73, 85, 87 and 88, 90 to 92, 94 to 97, 98 and 108 to 110;
(b) paragraphs 1, 11, 12, 16 and 20 of Schedule 17;
(c) paragraphs 7, 8, 14 to 16, 55 and 57 of Schedule 18; and
(d) paragraph 1 of Schedule 19.

(3) The other provisions of this Act shall come into force on such date as may be appointed by order made by the Lord Chancellor or by the Secretary of State or by both, acting jointly.

(4) Different dates may be appointed for different provisions of this Act and for different purposes.

125.—(1) This Act may be cited as the Courts and Legal Services Act 1990.

---

14 Section 56 came into force on 1 July 1991—Courts and Legal Services Act 1990 (Commencement No. 5) Order 1991, S.I. 1991 No. 1364.

(2) The minor amendments set out in Schedule 17 shall have effect.

(3) The consequential amendments set out in Schedule 18 shall have effect.

(4) The Lord Chancellor may by order make such amendments or repeals in relevant enactments as appear to him to be necessary or expedient in consequence of any provision made by Part II with respect to advocacy, litigation, conveyancing or probate services.

(5) In subsection (4) 'relevant enactments' means such enactments or instruments passed or made before or in the same Session as this Act as may be specified in the order.

(6) The transitional provisions and savings set out in Schedule 19 shall have effect.

(7) The repeals set out in Schedule 20 (which include repeals of certain enactments that are spent or of no further practical utility) shall have effect.

* * * * *

SCHEDULE 16

CHILDREN ACT 1989

PART I

AMENDMENT OF ACT AND OTHER ENACTMENTS AFFECTED

* * * * *

The Children Act 1989 (c.41)

33.—(1) Schedule 14 to the Act of 1989 (transitionals and savings) shall be amended as follows:

(2) In paragraph 15 (children in compulsory care) at the end of sub-paragraph (1) there shall be added ';
or
(h) in care by virtue of an order of the court made in the exercise of the High Court's inherent jurisdiction with respect to children.'

* * * * *

SCHEDULE 17 MINOR AMENDMENTS

* * * * *

The Powers of Attorney Act 1971 (c. 27)

4. In section 3 of the Powers of Attorney Act 1971 (proof of instruments creating powers of attorney)—

(a) in subsection (1)(b), after the word 'solicitor' there shall be inserted 'duly certificated notary public' and
(b) in subsection (3), after the word 'section' there shall be inserted ' "duly certificated notary public" has the same meaning as it has in the Solicitors Act 1974 by virtue of section 87(1) of that Act and'.

* * * * *

The Supreme Court Act 1981 (c.54)

* * * * *

13. In section 36(4) of that Act (witness not to be punished for failing to appear if he is not offered payment of his reasonable expenses of attending), for the words from 'the expenses', to the end, there shall be substituted '—

(a) the expenses of coming and attending to give evidence and of returning from giving evidence; and
(b) any other reasonable expenses which he has asked to be defrayed in connection with his evidence,

was tendered to him at the time when the writ was served upon him.'

SCHEDULE 20   REPEALS

Chapter	Short title	Extent of repeal
	* * * *	*
1981 c. 54	The Supreme Court Act 1981	In section 18, in subsection (1) paragraphs (f) and (h) and subsection (2)
	* * * *	*
1989 c. 41	The Children Act 1989	*
		In Schedule 14, in paragraph 15(1), the word 'or' immediately preceding paragraph (g)
	* * * *	*

LAW OF PROPERTY (MISCELLANEOUS PROVISIONS) ACT 1994

(1994, c. 36)   [3 November 1994]

[Note

The following provisions of this Act came into force on 1 July 1995]

PART II

MATTERS ARISING IN CONNECTION WITH DEATH

14.—(1) For section 9 of the Administration of Estates Act 1925 (vesting of estate of intestate between death and grant of administration) substitute—

9. 'Vesting of estate in Public Trustee where intestacy or lack of executors.—(1) Where a person dies intestate, his real and personal estate shall vest in the Public Trustee until the grant of administration.

(2) Where a testator dies and—

(a) at the time of his death there is no executor with power to obtain probate of the will, or
(b) at any time before probate of the will is granted there ceases to be any executor with power to obtain probate,

the real and personal estate of which he disposes by the will shall vest in the Public Trustee until the grant of representation.

(3) The vesting of real or personal estate in the Public Trustee by virtue of this section does not confer on him any beneficial interest in, or impose on him any duty, obligation or liability in respect of, the property.'

(2) Any real or personal estate of a person dying before the commencement of this section shall, if it is property to which this subsection applies, vest in the Public Trustee on the commencement of this section.

(3) Subsection (2) above applies to any property—

(a) if it was vested in the Probate Judge under section 9 of the Administration of Estates Act 1925 immediately before the commencement of this section, or
(b) if it was not so vested but as at commencement there has been no grant of representation in respect of it and there is no executor with power to obtain such a grant.

(4) Any property vesting in the Public Trustee by virtue of subsection (2) above shall—

(a) if the deceased died intestate, be treated as vesting in the Public Trustee under section 9(1) of the Administration of Estates Act 1925 (as substituted by subsection (1) above) and

(b) otherwise be treated as vesting in the Public Trustee under section 9(2) of that Act (as so substituted).

(5) Anything done by or in relation to the Probate Judge with respect to property vested in him as mentioned in subsection (3)(a) above shall be treated as having been done by or in relation to the Public Trustee.

(6) So far as may be necessary in consequence of the transfer to the Public Trustee of the functions of the Probate Judge under section 9 of the Administration of Estates Act 1925, any reference in an enactment or instrument to the Probate Judge shall be construed as a reference to the Public Trustee.

*　　　*　　　*　　　*　　　*

16.—(1) In section 2(2) of the Administration of Estates Act 1925 (concurrence of all personal representatives required for conveyance of real estate)—

(a) after 'a conveyance of real estate devolving under this Part of this Act' insert 'or a contract for such a conveyance';
(b) omit the words ', save as otherwise provided as respects trust estates including settled land,' (which are unnecessary); and
(c) after 'any conveyance of the real estate' insert 'or contract for such a conveyance'.

(2) Section 2(2) of the Administration of Estates Act 1925 as amended by subsection (1) above (concurrence of all personal representatives required for conveyance of real estate or contract for such conveyance) applies in relation to an interest under a trust for sale of land as in relation to real estate.

(3) The amendments made by subsection (1) apply to contracts made after the commencement of this section; and subsection (2) applies to contracts made after the commencement of this section and to conveyances so made otherwise than in pursuance of a contract made before commencement.

*　　　*　　　*　　　*　　　*

19.—(1) The Public Trustee may give directions as to the office or offices at which documents may be served on him—

(a) by virtue of section 9 of the Administration of Estates Act 1925 (as substituted by section 14(1) above), or
(b) in pursuance of section 18(1)(b) above (service on Public Trustee of copy of certain notices affecting land);

and he shall publish such directions in such manner as he considers appropriate.

(2) The Lord Chancellor may by regulations make provision with respect to the functions of the Public Trustee in relation to such documents; and the regulations may make different provision in relation to different descriptions of document or different circumstances.

(3) The regulations may, in particular, make provision requiring the Public Trustee—

(a) to keep such documents for a specified period and thereafter to keep a copy or record of their contents in such form as may be specified;
(b) to keep such documents, copies and records available for inspection at such reasonable hours as may be specified; and
(c) to supply copies to any person on request.

In this subsection 'specified' means specified by or under the regulations.

(4) Regulations under this section shall be made by statutory instrument which shall be subject to annulment in pursuance of a resolution of either House of Parliament.

(5) The following provisions of the Public Trustee Act 1906, namely—

(a) section 8(5) (payment of expenses out of money provided by Parliament), and
(b) section 9(1), (3) and (4) (provisions as to fees),

apply in relation to the functions of the Public Trustee in relation to documents to which this section applies as in relation to his functions under that Act.

PART III   GENERAL PROVISIONS

*   *   *   *   *

21.—(1) . . .

(2) The enactment specified in Schedule 2 are repealed to the extent specified.

(3) . . .

(4) . . .

22.—(1) The provisions of this Act extend to England and Wales.

(2) In addition—

(a) the provisions of Schedules 1 and 2 (consequential amendments and repeals) extend to Scotland so far as they relate to enactments which so extend; and

(b) . . . .

23.—(1) The provisions of this Act come into force on such day as the Lord Chancellor may appoint by order made by statutory instrument.

(2) Different days may be appointed for different provisions and for different purposes.

24. This Act may be cited as the Law of Property (Miscellaneous Provisions) Act 1994.

*   *   *   *   *

SCHEDULE 2   REPEALS

Chapter	Short title	Extent of repeal
* * * *		*
15 & 16 Geo. 5 c. 23.	Administration of Estates Act 1925.	In section 2(2), the words ', save as otherwise provided as respects trust estates including settled land,'.
		*
		In section 55(1), paragraph (xv)
* * * *		*

LAW REFORM (SUCCESSION) ACT 1995

(1995, c. 41)   [8 November 1995]

Distribution of estates

1.—(1) In the Administration of Estates Act 1925 ('the 1925 Act'), in section 46 (succession on intestacy) the following subsection shall be inserted after subsection (2)—

'(2A) Where the intestate's husband or wife survived the intestate but died before the end of the period of 28 days beginning with the day on which the intestate died, this section shall have effect as respects the intestate as if the husband or wife had not survived the intestate.'

(2) The following provisions of the 1925 Act (which require certain payments made by an

intestate, and certain interests acquired under a will of an intestate, to be brought into account) shall cease to have effect—

(a) in section 47 (statutory trusts in favour of issue and other relatives of intestate), subsection (1)(iii);

(b) in section 49 (partial intestacy), in subsection (1) paragraphs (aa) and (a), and subsections (2) and (3).

(3) Subsections (1) and (2) above have effect as respects an intestate dying on or after 1st January 1996.

(4) In section 50 of the 1925 Act (construction of documents), the references in subsection (1) to Part IV of that Act and to the foregoing provisions of that Part shall, in relation to an instrument inter vivos made or a will or codicil coming into operation on or after 1st January 1996 (but not in relation to instruments inter vivos made or wills or codicils coming into operation earlier), be construed as including references to this section.

(5) In this section 'intestate' shall be construed in accordance with section 55(1)(vi) of the 1925 Act.

2.—(1) The Inheritance (Provision for Family and Dependants) Act 1975 shall be amended as follows.

(2) In section 1 (application for financial provision from deceased's estate), in subsection (1) (persons who may apply) the following paragraph shall be inserted after paragraph (b)—

'(ba) any person (not being a person included in paragraph (a) or (b) above) to whom subsection (1A) below applies;'.

(3) In that section, the following subsection shall be inserted after subsection (1)—

'(1A) This subsection applies to a person if the deceased died on or after 1st January 1996 and, during the whole of the period of two years ending immediately before the date when the deceased died, the person was living—

(a) in the same household as the deceased, and
(b) as the husband or wife of the deceased.'

(4) In section 3 (matters to which court is to have regard in exercising its powers to make orders), the following subsection shall be inserted after subsection (2)—

'(2A) Without prejudice to the generality of paragraph (g) of subsection (1) above, where an application for an order under section 2 of this Act is made by virtue of section 1(1)(ba) of this Act, the court shall, in addition to the matters specifically mentioned in paragraphs (a) to (f) of that subsection, have regard to—

(a) the age of the applicant and the length of the period during which the applicant lived as the husband or wife of the deceased and in the same household as the deceased;
(b) the contribution made by the applicant to the welfare of the family of the deceased, including any contribution made by looking after the home or caring for the family.'

Effect of dissolution or annulment of marriage

3.—(1) In section 18A of the Wills Act 1837 (effect of dissolution or annulment of marriage on will), in subsection (1), for paragraphs (a) and (b) (abrogation of appointment of spouse as executor and lapse of devise or bequest to spouse) there shall be substituted—

'(a) provisions of the will appointing executors or trustees or conferring a power of appointment, if they appoint or confer the power on the former spouse, shall take effect as if the former spouse had died on the date on which the marriage is dissolved or annulled, and
'(b) any property which, or an interest in which, is devised or bequeathed to the former spouse shall pass as if the former spouse had died on that date,'.

(2) Subsection (1) above has effect as respects a will made by a person dying on or after 1st January 1996 (regardless of the date of the will and the date of the dissolution or annulment).

4.—(1) In section 6 of the Children Act 1989 (revocation of appointment of guardian), the following subsection shall be inserted after subsection (3)—

'(3A) An appointment under section 5(3) or (4) (including one made in an unrevoked will or codicil) is revoked if the person appointed is the spouse of the person who made the appointment and either—

(a) a decree of a court of civil jurisdiction in England and Wales dissolves or annuls the marriage, or
(b) the marriage is dissolved or annulled and the divorce or annulment is entitled to recognition in England and Wales by virtue of Part II of the Family Law Act 1986,

unless a contrary intention appears by the appointment.'

(2) Subsection (1) above has effect as respects an appointment made by a person dying on or after 1st January 1996 (regardless of the date of the appointment and the date of the dissolution or annulment).

Supplemental

5. The enactments mentioned in the Schedule to this Act are repealed in accordance with that Schedule.

6.—(1) This Act may be cited as the Law Reform (Succession) Act 1995.

(2) This Act extends to England and Wales only.

SCHEDULE   Repeals

Chapter	Short title	Extent of repeal
7 Will. 4 & 1 Vict. c. 26.	The Wills Act 1837.	Section 18A(3).
15 & 16 Geo. 5 c. 23.	The Administration of Estates Act 1925.	Section 47(1)(iii). In section 49, in subsection (1) paragraphs (aa) and (a), and subsections (2) and (3).
15 & 16 Geo. 6 & 1 Eliz. 2 c. 64.	The Intestates' Estates Act 1952.	Section 3(2).

The repeal in the Wills Act 1837 has effect as respects a will made by a person dying on or after 1st January 1996 and the other repeals have effect as respects an intestate (within the meaning of section 1) dying on or after that date.

Part II—Finance Acts etc.

Notes. For the earlier statutes, since repealed, relating to estate duty, see Appendix I to the Twenty-fifth edition of this work; the provisions of the Finance Acts 1975 et seq, consolidated in the Inheritance Tax/Capital Transfer Tax Act 1984, are to be found in Appendix 1 to the Twenty-sixth edition of this work.

For Tables of Rates of Inheritance Tax and Capital Transfer Tax, see Appendix IV, post.

For Inheritance Tax and Capital Transfer Tax (Delivery of Accounts) Regulations, see Appendix III, post.

INHERITANCE TAX ACT 1984[1]

(1984, c. 51)   [31 July 1984]

PART I

GENERAL

Main charges and definitions

1. Charge on transfers. Inheritance tax[1] shall be charged on the value transferred by a chargeable transfer.

*   *   *   *   *

4. Transfers on death.—(1) On the death of any person tax shall be charged as if, immediately before his death, he had made a transfer of value and the value transferred by it had been equal to the value of his estate immediately before his death.

(2) For the purposes of this section, where it cannot be known which of two or more persons who have died survived the other or others they shall be assumed to have died at the same instant.

5. Meaning of estate.—(1) For the purposes of this Act a person's estate is the aggregate of all the property to which he is beneficially entitled, except that the estate of a person immediately before his death does not include excluded property.

(2) A person who has a general power which enables him, or would if he were sui juris enable him, to dispose of any property other than settled property, or to charge money on any property other than settled property, shall be treated as beneficially entitled to the property or money; and for this purpose 'general power' means a power or authority enabling the person by whom it is exercisable to appoint or dispose of property as he thinks fit.

6. Excluded property.—(1) Property situated outside the United Kingdom is excluded property if the person beneficially entitled to it is an individual domiciled outside the United Kingdom.

*   *   *   *   *

Rates

7. Rates.—(1) [Subject to subsections (2), (4) and (5) below[2]] the tax charged on the value transferred by a chargeable transfer made by any transferor shall be charged at the following rate or rates, that is to say—

---

1   See FA 1986, s. 100, post as to the change in nomenclature—previously capital transfer tax.
2   Ibid., s. 101 and Sch. 19, para. 2(1)(a) in relation to events on and after 18 March 1986.

(a) if the transfer is the first chargeable transfer made by that transferor in the period of [seven[3]] years ending with the date of the transfer, at the rate or rates applicable to that value under the *appropriate*[4] Table in Schedule 1 to this Act;

(b) in any other case, at the rate or rates applicable under that Table to such part of the aggregate of—
  (i) that value, and
  (ii) the values transferred by previous chargeable transfers made by him in that period, as is the highest part of that aggregate and is equal to that value.

(2) [Except as provided by subsection (4) below, the tax charged on the value transferred by a chargeable transfer made before the death of the transferor shall be charged at one-half of the rate or rates referred to in subsection (1) above[5].]

(3) In [the Table[6]] in Schedule 1 to this Act any rate shown in the third column is that applicable to such portion of the value concerned as exceeds the lower limit shown in the first column but does not exceed the upper limit (if any) shown in the second column.

[(4) Subject to subsection (5) below, subsection (2) above does not apply in the case of a chargeable transfer made at any time within the period of seven years ending with the death of the transferor but, in the case of a chargeable transfer made within that period but more than three years before the death, the tax charged on the value transferred shall be charged at the following percentage of the rate or rates referred to in subsection (1) above—

(a) where the transfer is made more than three but not more than four years before the death, 80 per cent;

(b) where the transfer is made more than four but not more than five years before the death, 60 per cent;

(c) where the transfer is made more than five but not more than six years before the death, 40 per cent; and

(d) where the transfer is made more than six but not more than seven years before the death, 20 per cent.

(5) If, in the case of a changeable transfer made before the death of the transferor, the tax which would fall to be charged in accordance with subsection (4) above is less than the tax which would have been chargeable (in accordance with subsection (2) above) if the transferor had not died within the period of seven years beginning with the date of the transfer, subsection (4) above shall not apply in the case of that transfer[7].]

*   *   *   *   *

PART III

SETTLED PROPERTY

CHAPTER I

Preliminary

*   *   *   *   *

48. Excluded property.—(1) A reversionary interest is excluded property unless—

---

3   Ibid., s. 101 and Sch. 19, para. 2(1)(b) in relation to events on and after 18 March 1986. Formerly 'ten'.

4   Repealed by FA 1986, s. 101 and Sch. 19, para. 2(1)(c) with effect from 18 March 1986.

5   FA 1986, s. 101 and Sch. 19, para. 2(2) in relation to events on and after 18 March 1986. Formerly:
   '(2) Except as otherwise provided, the first Table in Schedule 1 to this Act is the appropriate Table for a transfer made on or at any time within three years of the death of the transferor, and the second Table in that Schedule is the appropriate Table for any other transfer.'

6   Ibid., s. 101 and Sch. 19, para. 2(3) with effect from 18 March 1986. Formerly 'each of the Tables'.

7   Ibid., s. 101 and Sch. 19, para. 4 in relation to events on and after 18 March 1986.

(a) it has at any time been acquired (whether by the person entitled to it or by a person pre-viously entitled to it) for a consideration in money or money's worth, or
(b) it is one to which either the settlor or his spouse is or has been beneficially entitled, or
(c) it is the interest expectant on the determination of a lease treated as a settlement by virtue of section 43 (3) above.

(2) In relation to a reversionary interest under a settlement made before 16 April 1976, sub-section (1) above shall have effect with the omission of paragraph (b); and, if the person entitled to a reversionary interest under a settlement made on or after 16 April 1976 acquired the interest before 10 March 1981, that subsection shall have effect with the omission of the words 'or has been' in paragraph (b).

*   *   *   *   *

CHAPTER II

Interests in possession and reversionary interests

*   *   *   *   *

55. Reversionary interest acquired by beneficiary.—(1) Notwithstanding section 5(1) above, where a person entitled to an interest (whether in possession or not) in any settled property acquires a reversionary interest expectant (whether immediately or not) on that interest, the reversionary interest is not part of his estate for the purposes of this Act.

*   *   *   *   *

PART VII

LIABILITY

General rules

199. Dispositions by transferor.—(4) For the purposes of this section—

(a) any person who takes possession of or intermeddles with, or otherwise acts in relation to, property so as to become liable as executor or trustee (or, in Scotland, any person who intromits with property or has become liable as a vitious intromitter), and
(b) any person to whom the management of property is entrusted on behalf of a person not of full legal capacity, shall be treated as a person in whom the property is vested.

200. Transfer on death.—(1) The persons liable for the tax on the value transferred by a chargeable transfer made (under section 4 above) on the death of any person are—

(a) so far as the tax is attributable to the value of property which either—
   (i) was not immediately before the death comprised in a settlement, or
   (ii) was so comprised and consists of land in the United Kingdom which devolves upon or vests in the deceased's personal representatives,
the deceased's personal representatives;
(b) so far as the tax is attributable to the value of property which, immediately before the death, was comprised in a settlement, the trustees of the settlement;
(c) so far as the tax is attributable to the value of any property, any person in whom the property is vested (whether beneficially or otherwise) at any time after the death, or who at any such time is beneficially entitled to an interest in possession in the property;
(d) so far as the tax is attributable to the value of any property which, immediately before the death, was comprised in a settlement, any person for whose benefit any of the prop-erty or income from it is applied after the death.

(2) A purchaser of property, and a person deriving title from or under such a purchaser, shall not by virtue of subsection (1) (c) above be liable for tax attributable to the value of the prop-erty unless the property is subject to an Inland Revenue charge.

(3) For the purposes of subsection (1) above a person entitled to part only of the income of

any property shall, notwithstanding anything in section 50 above, be deemed to be entitled to an interest in the whole of the property.

(4) Subsections (4) and (5) of section 199 above shall have effect for the purposes of this section as they have effect for the purposes of that section.

*   *   *   *   *

204. Limitation of liability.—(1) A person shall not be liable under section 200 (1) (a) above for any tax as a personal representative of a deceased person, except to the extent of the following assets, namely—

(a) so far as the tax is attributable to the value of any property other than such as is mentioned in paragraph (b) below, the assets (other than property so mentioned) which he has received as personal representative or might have so received but for his own neglect or default; and

(b) so far as the tax is attributable to property which, immediately before the death, was comprised in a settlement and consists of land in the United Kingdom, so much of that property as is at any time available in his hands for the payment of the tax, or might have been so available but for his own neglect or default.

205. More than one person liable. Except as otherwise provided, where under this Act two or more persons are liable for the same tax, each of them shall be liable for the whole of it.

*   *   *   *   *

Burden of tax, etc.

211. Burden of tax on death.—(1) Where personal representatives are liable for tax on the value transferred by a chargeable transfer made on death, the tax shall be treated as part of the general testamentary and administration expenses of the estate, but only so far as it is attributable to the value of property in the United Kingdom which—

(a) vests in the deceased's personal representatives, and
(b) was not immediately before the death comprised in a settlement.

(2) Subsection (1) above shall have effect subject to any contrary intention shown by the deceased in his will.

(3) Where any amount of tax paid by personal representatives on the value transferred by a chargeable transfer made on death does not fall to be borne as part of the general testamentary and administration expenses of the estate, that amount shall, where occasion requires, be repaid to them by the person in whom the property to the value of which the tax is attributable is vested.

(4) References in this section to tax include references to interest on tax.

*   *   *   *   *

PART VIII

ADMINISTRATION AND COLLECTION

Management

215. General. The tax shall be under the care and management of the Board.

Accounts and information

216. Delivery of accounts.—(1) Except as otherwise provided by this section or by regulations under section 256 below, the personal representatives of a deceased person and every person who—

(a)   is liable as transferor for tax on the value transferred by a chargeable transfer, or would be so liable if tax were chargeable on that value, or

(b)   is liable as trustee of a settlement for tax on the value transferred by a transfer of value, or would be so liable if tax were chargeable on that value, or

[(bb) is liable under section 199 (1) (b) above for tax on the value transferred by a potentially exempt transfer which proves to be a chargeable transfer, or would be so liable if tax were chargeable on that value, or

(bc) is liable under section 200 (1) (c) above for tax on the value transferred by a chargeable transfer made on death, so far as the tax is attributable to the value of property which, apart from section 102 (3) of the Finance Act 1986, would not form part of the deceased's estate, or would be so liable if tax were chargeable on the value transferred on the death, or[8]]

(c)   is liable as trustee of a settlement for tax on an occasion on which tax is chargeable under Chapter III of Part III of this Act (apart from section 79), or would be so liable if tax were chargeable on the occasion,

shall deliver to the Board an account specifying to the best of his knowledge and belief all appropriate property and the value of that property.

(2) Where in the case of the estate of a deceased person no grant of representation or confirmation has been obtained in the United Kingdom before the expiration of the period of twelve months from the end of the month in which the death occurred—

(a) every person in whom any of the property forming part of the estate vests (whether beneficially or otherwise) on or at any time after the deceased's death or who at any such time is beneficially entitled to an interest in possession in any such property, and

(b) where any of the property is at any such time comprised in a settlement and there is no person beneficially entitled to an interest in possession in that property, every person for whose benefit any of that property (or income from it) is applied at any such time,

shall deliver to the Board an account specifying to the best of his knowledge and belief the appropriate property vested in him, in which he has an interest or which (or income from which) is applicable for his benefit and the value of that property.

(3) Where an account is to be delivered by personal representatives (but not where it is to be delivered by a person who is an executor of the deceased only in respect of settled land in England and Wales), the appropriate property is all property which formed part of the deceased's estate immediately before his death [other than property which would not, apart from section 102(3) of the Finance Act 1986, form part of his estate[9]]; but—

(a) if the personal representatives, after making the fullest enquiries that are reasonably practicable in the circumstances, are unable to ascertain the exact value of any particular property, their account shall in the first instance be sufficient as regards that property if it contains a statement to that effect, a provisional estimate of the value of the property and they undertake to deliver a further account of it as soon as its value is ascertained; and

(b) the Board may from time to time give such general or special directions as they think fit for restricting the property to be specified in pursuance of this subsection by any class of personal representatives.

(4) Where subsection (3) above does not apply the appropriate property is any property to the value of which the tax is or would be attributable.

(5) Except in the case of an account to be delivered by personal representatives, a person shall not be required to deliver an account under this section with respect to any property if a full and proper account of the property, specifying its value, has already been delivered to the Board by some other person who—

(a) is or would be liable for the tax attributable to the value of the property, and

(b) is not or would not be liable with him jointly as trustee;

8   FA 1986, s. 101 and Sch. 19, para. 29(1) in relation to events on and after 18 March 1986.
9   FA 1986, s. 101 and Sch. 19, para. 29(2) in relation to events on and after 18 March 1986.

and a person within subsection (2) above shall not be required to deliver an account under that subsection if he or another person within that subsection has satisfied the Board that an account will in due course be delivered by the personal representatives.

(6) An account under the preceding provisions of this section shall be delivered—

(a)   in the case of an account to be delivered by personal representatives, before the expiration of the period of twelve months from the end of the month in which the death occurs, or, if it expires later, the period of three months beginning with the date on which the personal representatives first act as such;

[(aa) in the case of an account to be delivered by a person within subsection (1) (bb) above, before the expiration of the period of twelve months from the end of the month in which the death of the transferor occurs;

(ab) in the case of an account to be delivered by a person within subsection (1) (bc) above, before the expiration of the period of twelve months from the end of the month in which the death occurs;[10]]

(b)   in the case of an account to be delivered by a person within subsection (2) above, before the expiration of the period of three months from the time when he first has reason to believe that he is required to deliver an account under that subsection:

*   *   *   *   *

Payment

226. Payment: general rules.—(1) Except as otherwise provided by the following provisions of this Part of this Act, the tax on the value transferred by a chargeable transfer shall be due six months after the end of the month in which the chargeable transfer is made or, in the case of a transfer made after 5 April and before 1 October in any year otherwise than on death, at the end of April in the next year.

(2) Personal representatives shall, on delivery of their account, pay all the tax for which they are liable and may, on delivery of that account, also pay any part of the tax chargeable on the death for which they are not liable, if the persons liable for it request them to make the payment.

*   *   *   *   *

Penalties

245. Failure to provide information.—(1) A person who—

(a) fails to deliver an account under section 216 or 217 above

*   *   *   *   *

shall be liable to a penalty not exceeding £50 and, if the failure continues after it has been declared by a court or the Special Commissioners, to a further penalty not exceeding £10 for each day on which it continues.

*   *   *   *   *

Miscellaneous

*   *   *   *   *

256. Regulations about accounts, etc.—(1) The Board may make regulations[11]—

(a) dispensing with the delivery of accounts under section 216 above in such cases as may be specified in the regulations;

(b) discharging, subject to such restrictions as may be so specified, property from an Inland Revenue charge and persons from further claims for tax in cases other than those mentioned in section 239 above;

(c) requiring information to be furnished to the Board, in such circumstances as may be so

---

10   Ibid., s. 101 and Sch. 19, para. 29(3) in relation to deaths on and after 18 March 1986.
11   See the Capital Transfer Tax (Delivery of Accounts) Regulations 1981 as amended at Appendix II, post.

specified, by persons who have not delivered accounts under section 216 above or who have produced documents other than an account or inventory in pursuance of arrangements made under the enactments mentioned in subsection (2) below;

(d) modifying section 264 (8) below in cases where the delivery of an account has been dispensed with under the regulations.

(2) The enactments referred to in subsection (1) (c) above are section 109 (2) of the Supreme Court Act 1981, the proviso to section 42 of the Probate and Legacy Duties Supreme Court Act 1981, the proviso to section 42 of the Probate and Legacy Duties Act 1808 and Article 20 of the Administration of Estates (Northern Ireland) Order 1979.

(3) Regulations under this section may contain such supplementary or incidental provisions as the Board think fit.

(4) The power to make regulations under this section shall be exercisable by statutory instrument, which shall be subject to annulment in pursuance of a resolution of the House of Commons.

257. Form etc. of accounts.—(1) All accounts and other documents required for the purposes of this Act shall be in such form and shall contain such particulars as may be prescribed by the Board.

(2) All accounts to be delivered to the Board under this Act shall be supported by such books, papers and other documents, and verified (whether on oath or otherwise) in such manner, as the Board may require.

(3) For the purposes of this Act, an account delivered to a probate registry pursuant to arrangements made between the President of the Family Division and the Board or delivered to the Probate and Matrimonial Office in Northern Ireland pursuant to arrangements made between the Lord Chancellor and the Board shall be treated as an account delivered to the Board.

* * * * *

PART IX

MISCELLANEOUS AND SUPPLEMENTARY

Miscellaneous

* * * * *

267. Persons treated as domiciled in the United Kingdom.—(1) A person not domiciled in the United Kingdom at any time (in this section referred to as 'the relevant time') shall be treated for the purposes of this Act as domiciled in the United Kingdom (and not elsewhere) at the relevant time if—

(a) he was domiciled in the United Kingdom within the three years immediately preceding the relevant time, or

(b) he was resident in the United Kingdom in not less than seventeen of the twenty years of assessment ending with the year of assessment in which the relevant time falls.

(2) Subsection (1) above shall not apply for the purposes of section 6 (2) or (3) or 48 (4) above and shall not affect the interpretation of any such provision as is mentioned in section 158 (6) above.

(3) Paragraph (a) of subsection (1) above shall not apply in relation to a person who (apart from this section) has not been domiciled in the United Kingdom at any time since 9 December 1974, and paragraph (b) of that subsection shall not apply in relation to a person who has not been resident there at any time since that date; and that subsection shall be disregarded—

(a) in determining whether settled property which became comprised in the settlement on or before that date is excluded property,

(b) in determining the settlor's domicile for the purposes of section 65 (8) above in relation to settled property which became comprised in the settlement on or before that date, and

(c) in determining for the purposes of section 65 (8) above whether the condition in section 82 (3) above is satisfied in relation to such settled property.

(4) For the purposes of this section the question whether a person was resident in the United Kingdom in any year of assessment shall be determined as for the purposes of income tax[12].

* * * * *

Interpretation

* * * * *

272. General interpretation.—In this Act, except where the context otherwise requires,—

* * * * *

'personal representatives' includes any person by whom or on whose behalf an application for a grant of administration or for the resealing of a grant made outside the United Kingdom is made, and any such person as mentioned in section 199 (4) (a) above;

* * * * *

FINANCE ACT 1986

(1986, c. 41)   [25 July 1986]

PART V

INHERITANCE TAX

100. Capital transfer tax to be known as inheritance tax.—(1) On and after the passing of this Act, the tax charged under the Capital Transfer Tax Act 1984 (in this Part of this Act referred to as 'the 1984 Act') shall be known as inheritance tax and, accordingly, on and after that passing,—

(a) the 1984 Act may be cited as the Inheritance Tax Act 1984; and

(b) subject to subsection (2) below, any reference to capital transfer tax in the 1984 Act, in any other enactment passed before or in the same Session as this Act or in any document executed, made, served or issued on or before the passing of this Act or at any time thereafter shall have effect as a reference to inheritance tax.

(2) Subsection (1) (b) above does not apply where the reference to capital transfer tax relates to a liability to tax arising before the passing of this Act.

(3) In the following provisions of this Part of this Act, any reference to tax except where it is a reference to a named tax is a reference to inheritance tax and, in so far as it occurs in a provision which relates to a time before the passing of this Act, includes a reference to capital transfer tax.

* * * * *

102. Gifts with reservation.—(1) Subject to subsections (5) and (6) below, this section applies where, on or after 18 March 1986, an individual disposes of any property by way of gift and either—

(a) possession and enjoyment of the property is not bona fide assumed by the donee at or before the beginning of the relevant period; or

(b) at any time in the relevant period the property is not enjoyed to the entire exclusion, or

12   Prior to 27 July 1993 the phrase 'but without regard to any dwelling house available in the United Kingdom for his use' was included. Removed by s. 208(3), Finance Act 1993.

virtually to the entire exclusion, of the donor and of any benefit to him by contract or otherwise;

and in this section 'the relevant period' means a period ending on the date of the donor's death and beginning seven years before that date or, if it is later, on the date of the gift.

(2) If and so long as—

(a) possession and enjoyment of any property is not bona fide assumed as mentioned in sub-section (1) (a) above, or

(b) any property is not enjoyed as mentioned in subsection (1) (b) above,

the property is referred to (in relation to the gift and the donor) as property subject to a reservation.

(3) If, immediately before the death of the donor, there is any property which, in relation to him, is property subject to a reservation then, to the extent that the property would not, apart from this section, form part of the donor's estate immediately before his death, that property shall be treated for the purposes of the 1984 Act as property to which he was beneficially entitled immediately before his death.

(4) If, at a time before the end of the relevant period, any property ceases to be property subject to a reservation, the donor shall be treated for the purposes of the 1984 Act as having at that time made a disposition of the property by a disposition which is a potentially exempt transfer.

(5) This section does not apply if or, as the case may be, to the extent that the disposal of property by way of gift is an exempt transfer by virtue of any of the following provisions of Part II of the 1984 Act,—

(a) section 18 (transfers between spouses);
(b) section 20 (small gifts);
(c) section 22 (gifts in consideration of marriage);
(d) section 23 (gifts to charities);
(e) section 24 (gifts to political parties);
(f) section 25 (gifts for national purposes, etc.);
(g) section 26 (gifts for public benefit);
(h) section 27 (maintenance funds for historic buildings); and
(i) section 28 (employee trusts).

(6) This section does not apply if the disposal of property by way of gift is made under the terms of a policy issued in respect of an insurance made before 18 March 1986 unless the policy is varied on or after that date so as to increase the benefits secured or to extend the terms of the insurance; and, for this purpose, any change in the terms of the policy which is made in pursuance of an option or other power conferred by the policy shall be deemed to be a variation of the policy.

(7) If a policy issued as mentioned in subsection (6) above confers an option or other power under which benefits and premiums may be increased to take account of increases in the retail prices index (as defined in section 8 (3) of the 1984 Act) or any similar index specified in the policy, then, to the extent that the right to exercise that option or power would have been lost if it had not been exercised on or before 1 August 1986, the exercise of that option or power before that date shall be disregarded for the purposes of subsection (6) above.

(8) Schedule 20 to this Act has effect for supplementing this section.

*   *   *   *   *

Rules, Orders and Regulations

Summary

Rules, Orders and Regulations

Part I—Non-Contentious Business

THE FAMILY PROVISION (INTESTATE SUCCESSION) ORDER 1972

S.I. 1972 No. 916

Dated 21 June 1972

The Lord Chancellor, in exercise of the powers conferred on him by section 1 (1) (a) and (b) of the Family Provision Act 1966, hereby makes the following order:

1.—(l) This Order may be cited as the Family Provision (Intestate Succession) Order 1972 and shall come into operation on 1 July 1972.

(2) The Interpretation Act 1889 shall apply to the interpretation of this Order as it applies to the interpretation of an Act of Parliament.

2. In the case of a person dying after the coming into operation of this Order, section 46 (1) of the Administration of Estates Act 1925 as amended by section 1 of the Intestates' Estates Act 1952 and section 1 of the Family Provision Act 1966 shall apply as if the net sums charged by paragraph (i) on the residuary estate were:

(a) under paragraph (2) of the Table, the sum of £15,000; and
(b) under paragraph (3) of the Table, the sum of £40,000.

THE ADMINISTRATION OF ESTATES (SMALL PAYMENTS) (INCREASE OF LIMIT) ORDER 1975

S.I. 1975 No. 1137

Dated 9 July 1975

1. This Order may be cited as the Administration of Estates (Small Payments) (Increase of Limit) Order 1975, and shall come into operation on 10 July 1975.

2. The Interpretation Act 1889 shall apply for the interpretation of this Order as it applies for the interpretation of an Act of Parliament.

3. The following provisions (which relate to property which may be disposed of on death without representation or in pursuance of a nomination subject to a limit of £500), namely—

(a) sections 1 and 2 of the Administration of Estates (Small Payments) Act 1965, so far as they relate to any enactment;
(b) section 14 (2) of the Ministerial Salaries and Members' Pensions Act 1965;
(c) paragraph 12 of Schedule 1 to the Forestry Act 1967;

(d) section 28 (5) of the Trustee Savings Banks Act 1969[1];
(e) section 66 (2) of the Merchant Shipping Act 1970;
(f) section 9 (1) of the National Savings Bank Act 1971;
(g) section 4 (1) of the Superannuation Act 1972;
(h) section 24 of the Parliamentary and other Pensions Act 1972;
(i) section 6 (1) of the National Debt Act 1972;
(j) section 119 (1) of the Local Government Act 1972; and
(k) sections 66, 67 and 68 of the Friendly Societies Act 1974;

shall have effect as if for the references to £500 there were substituted references to £1,500.

[**Note.** In respect of deaths on or after 11 May 1984, see the Administration of Estates (Small Payments) (Increase of Limit) Order 1984, p. 922, post.]

THE FAMILY PROVISION (INTESTATE SUCCESSION) ORDER 1977

S.I. 1977 No. 415

Dated 4 March 1977

The Lord Chancellor, in exercise of the powers conferred on him by section 1 (1) (a) and (b) of the Family Provision Act 1966 hereby makes the following Order:

1.—(1) This Order may be cited as the Family Provision (Intestate Succession) Order 1977 and shall come into operation on 15 March 1977.

(2) The Interpretation Act 1889 shall apply to the interpretation of this Order as it applies to the interpretation of an Act of Parliament.

2. In the case of a person dying after the coming into operation of this Order, section 46 (1) of the Administration of Estates Act 1925, as amended by section 1 of the Intestates' Estates Act 1952 and section 1 of the Family Provision Act 1966 shall apply as if the net sums charged by paragraph (i) on the residuary estate were:

(a) under paragraph (2) of the Table, the sum of £25,000; and
(b) under paragraph (3) of the Table, the sum of £55,000.

THE WILLS (DEPOSIT FOR SAFE CUSTODY) REGULATIONS 1978[2]

S.I. 1978 No. 1724

Dated 13 November 1978

Citation, commencement and application

1.—(1) These Regulations may be cited as the Wills (Deposit for Safe Custody) Regulations 1978 and shall come into operation on 1 February 1979.

(2) These Regulations shall apply to wills whether deposited before or after the coming into operation of these Regulations.

1   See now s. 27(4) of the Trustee Savings Banks Act 1981.
2   These Regulations were made by the President of the Family Division under and by virtue of the power contained in s. 172 of the Supreme Court of Judicature (Consolidation) Act 1925. Notwithstanding the repeal and replacement of the Act of 1925 by the Supreme Court Act 1981 as from 1 January 1982, by virtue of the Interpretation Act 1978, the Regulations continue to apply until revoked or replaced.

Interpretation

2.—(1) The Interpretation Act 1978 shall apply to these Regulations as it applies to subordinate legislation made after the commencement of that Act.

(2) In these Regulations, unless the context otherwise requires—

'the Act' means the Supreme Court of Judicature (Consolidation) Act 1925[3];
'prescribed' means prescribed by the Supreme Court (Non-Contentious Probate) Fees Order 1975[4];
'the principal registry' means the Principal Registry of the Family Division;
'registrar' means a registrar of the principal registry and includes the registrar of a district probate registry;
'registry' means the principal registry or a district probate registry, including a sub- registry;
'the Senior Registrar' means the Senior Registrar of the principal registry;
'will' includes a codicil to a will.

(3) In these Regulations a form referred to by number means the form so numbered in the Schedule to these Regulations, or a form substantially to the like effect, with such variations as the circumstances of the particular case may require.

Place and mode of deposit

3.—(1) The place of deposit for the wills of living persons pursuant to section 172 of the Act[5] shall be the principal registry and a testator may deposit his will there subject to, and in accordance with, these Regulations and on payment of the prescribed fee.

(2) A will may be deposited for safe custody on personal attendance by the testator, or by an agent authorised in writing by the testator to do so, at any registry or may be sent by post for deposit by the testator, or any agent so authorised, to the principal registry.

(3) A will deposited for safe custody shall be enclosed in a sealed envelope bearing an endorsement in Form 1.

Deposit on personal attendance by testator

4. Where the testator attends at a registry to deposit his will he shall sign the endorsement on the envelope containing the will in the presence of an officer of the registry who shall append his signature to the endorsement and shall give the testator a certificate of deposit in Form 2 and shall file a copy of the certificate with the will.

Deposit by post or by agent

5.—(1) A will presented for deposit at a registry by an agent, or sent by post to the principal registry for deposit, shall be accepted if the endorsement on the envelope containing the will purports to be signed by the testator and, in the case of deposit by an agent, the registrar is satisfied that the agent is authorised by the testator to deposit the will.

(2) On accepting a will for deposit, the registrar shall send to the testator by post a certificate of such deposit in Form 2 and, in the case of deposit by an agent shall also give or send to the agent a copy of the certificate, and shall in every case file a copy of the certificate with the will.

The Administration of Justice Act 1982, ss. 23–26 makes new statutory provision for the deposit *and registration* of wills so as to enable the United Kingdom to ratify the Council of Europe Convention on the Establishment of a Scheme of Registration of Wills (see Chap. 20). These provisions shall come into operation on such date as shall be appointed. No commencement order has yet been made. Under the new provisions, regulation making power for England and Wales is vested in the President of the Family Division with the concurrence of the Lord Chancellor. This power, once exercised, will replace the power at present contained in s. 126 of the Supreme Court Act 1981. The Act of 1982 further provides that wills deposited under either s. 172 of the Act of 1925 or s. 126 of the Act of 1981 shall be treated as deposited for the purposes of the 1982 Act.

3   Ibid., this Act was repealed and replaced by the Supreme Court Act 1981.
4   The current Fees Order is the NC Probate Fees Order 1981 (pp. 961 ff., post).
5   See now s. 126 of the Supreme Court Act 1981 (p. 847, ante), and note 2, ante.

Transmission of will to principal registry

6. On the lodgment at a registry (other than at the principal registry) of a will for deposit, the district registrar shall forward the sealed envelope containing the will and a copy of the certificate of deposit by registered post to the principal registry and shall retain in his registry a further copy of the certificate.

Entry in records

7. On the deposit of a will at the principal registry, the Senior Registrar shall make such entries in the records as are requisite to enable the fact of the deposit to be known on any application for a grant of representation in the estate of the testator.

Withdrawal of deposited will

8.—(1) A testator whose will is deposited under section 172 of the Act[6] may make a written request to the principal registry for the return of the will to him, and the request shall be accompanied by the certificate of deposit given or sent to him.

(2) Where, on receipt of a request under paragraph (1) above, a registrar of the principal registry is satisfied—

(a) as to the identity of the testator, and
(b) that it would be proper to return the said will to him,

the registrar may authorise the return of the deposited will to the testator, and the Senior Registrar shall cause the record of deposit of the will to be noted accordingly.

(3) The Senior Registrar shall retain the record of the deposit and return of a will for so long as he considers it necessary to do so.

(4) Subject to paragraph (2) above, a will deposited under section 172 of the Act[6] shall not be released from the custody of the principal registry until the death of the testator is established to the satisfaction of a registrar of the principal registry.

Procedure on death of testator

9.—(1) On production of—

(a) a certificate of the death of a testator who has deposited his will in the principal registry or such other evidence of death as may satisfy a registrar of the principal registry, and
(b) unless otherwise directed by the registrar, the certificate of deposit of the will,

a registrar of the principal registry may open the envelope containing the will and, subject to such precautions as he may think necessary (including the lodgment in the registry of a copy of the will), may—

(i) deliver the will to the executor or to any other person who satisfies the registrar that he intends to prove the will, or
(ii) where the will has been effectively revoked or a grant of representation in the estate of the testator is not required, deliver the will to any person who is entitled to possession of the will.

Provided that the registrar may, if he thinks fit, require the person intending to prove the will to attend at a registry for that purpose.

(2) Where a registrar releases a deposited will from the custody of the principal registry under this regulation, the person to whom the will is delivered shall give a receipt for it together with a written undertaking to lodge the will on any application for a grant of representation to the estate of the testator.

(3) The Senior Registrar shall retain the record of the deposit and return of the will and of any copy of a will as is required to be lodged pursuant to this regulation.

6   See note 2, ante.

SCHEDULE

FORM 1

Endorsement of envelope containing Will

This sealed packet contains the last Will and Testament (with a codicil thereto) (*or* codicil to the last Will and Testament: *or as the case may be*) bearing date (respectively) (*state date of all testamentary documents enclosed*) of me (*full name*) of (*full postal address*)
in which   of   and   of   are appointed Executors, which I hereby lodge for deposit in the Principal Registry of the Family Division for safe custody.

I undertake to notify the above named Executors of their appointment and of the deposit of the will (and) (codicil).
I certify that the date of my birth was the   19
Dated this   day of   19

Testator

Signed in the presence of

FORM 2

Certificate of deposit of will

In the High Court of Justice
Family Division (Probate)

It is hereby certified that the will (codicil)
of
of
bearing date (respectively)
in which
of
(and
of
are appointed executors has been (deposited in the Principal Registry) (lodged at the Registry for deposit in the Principal Registry) of the Family Division, Somerset House, Strand, London WC2R 1LP for safe custody pursuant to section 172 of the Supreme Court of Judicature (Consolidation) Act 1925[6a]
Except by leave of a registrar of the Principal Registry the will may not be given out during the lifetime of the testator.

Dated this   day of   19

Senior Registrar

THE FAMILY PROVISION (INTESTATE SUCCESSION) ORDER 1981

S.I. 1981 No. 255

Dated 23 February 1981

The Lord Chancellor, in exercise of the powers conferred on him by section 1 (1) (a) and (b) of the Family Provision Act 1966, hereby makes the following Order:

1. This Order may be cited as the Family Provision (Intestate Succession) Order 1981 and shall come into operation on 1 March 1981.

2. In the case of a person dying after the coming into operation of this Order, section 46(1) of the Administration of Estates Act 1925 shall apply as if the net sums charged by paragraph (i) on the residuary estate were:

(a) under paragraph (2) of the Table, the sum of £40,000; and
(b) under paragraph (3) of the Table, the sum of £85,000.

6a See note 2, ante.

THE CAPITAL TRANSFER TAX (DELIVERY OF ACCOUNTS) REGULATIONS 1981[7]

S.I. 1981 No. 880

Dated 22 June 1981

The Commissioners of Inland Revenue, in exercise of the powers conferred on them by section 94 (1) of the Finance Act 1980, hereby make the following regulations:

Citation, commencement and extent

1. These Regulations may be cited as the Capital Transfer Tax (Delivery of Accounts) Regulations 1981 and shall come into operation on 1 August 1981.

2. These Regulations do not extend to Scotland or Northern Ireland.

Interpretation

3. In these Regulations, unless the context otherwise requires:

'an excepted estate' means the estate of a person immediately before his death where:

(a) the value of the estate is attributable wholly to property passing under that person's will or intestacy or under a nomination of an asset taking effect on death or by survivorship in beneficial joint tenancy;

(b) the total gross value of that property did not exceed £145,000[8];

(c) of that property not more than £15,000[9] represented value attributable to property then situated outside the United Kingdom; and

(d) that person died on or after 1 April 1995[10], domiciled in the United Kingdom and without having made any chargeable transfer during his lifetime;

'the prescribed period' in relation to any person is the period beginning with that person's death and ending 35 days after the making of the first grant of representation in respect of that person in England and Wales (not being a grant limited in duration, in respect of property or to any special purpose);

'value' means value for the purposes of tax.

Accounts

4. Notwithstanding anything in paragraph 2 of Schedule 4 to the Finance Act 1975 or section 94 of the Finance Act 1980, no person shall be required to deliver to the Board an account of the property comprised in an excepted estate, unless the Board so require by a notice in writing issued to that person within the prescribed period.

5. If any person who has not delivered an account in reliance on Regulation 4 discovers at any time that the estate is not an excepted estate, the delivery to the Board within six months of that time of an account of the property comprised in that estate shall satisfy any requirement to deliver an account imposed on that person.

7   These Regulations, as amended, have equal application to inheritance tax on and after 25 July 1986 by virtue of the Finance Act 1986, s. 100.

8   S.I. 1995, No. 1461 with effect from 1 April 1995. Previously, by S.I. 1991, No. 1248 with effect from 1 April 1991, by S.I. 1990 No. 1110 with effect from 1 April 1990, S.I. 1989 No. 1078 with effect from 1 April 1989 and S.I. 1987 No. 1127 with effect from 1 April 1987. Previously, by S.I. 1983 No. 1039 with effect from 1 September 1983, £40,000. Originally '£25,000'.

9   S.I. 1989 No. 1078 with effect from 1 April 1989. Previously, by S.I. 1987 No. 1127 with effect from 1 April 1987, £10,000. Previously, by S.I. 1983 No. 1039 with effect from 1 April 1983, '10 per cent. of the total gross value or £2,000, whichever figure is the higher'. Originally as first amended but with a figure of '£1,000'.

10   S.I. 1995, No. 1461 with effect from 1 April 1995. Previously, by S.I. 1991 No. 1248 with effect from 1 April 1991, by S.I. 1990 No. 1110 with effect from 1 April 1990, S.I. 1989 No. 1078 with effect from 1 April 1989, and S.I. 1987 No. 1127 with effect from 1 April 1987. Previously, by S.I. 1983 No. 1039 with effect from 1 April 1983. Originally by 1981.

Discharge of persons and property from tax

6. Subject to Regulation 7 and unless within the prescribed period the Board issue a notice requiring an account of the property comprised in an excepted estate, all persons shall at the expiration of that period be discharged from any claim for tax on the value transferred by the chargeable transfer made on the deceased's death and attributable to the value of that property and any Inland Revenue charge for that tax shall then be extinguished.

7. Regulation 6 shall not discharge any person from tax in the case of fraud or failure to disclose material facts and shall not affect any tax that may be payable if further property is later shown to form part of the estate and, in consequence of that property, the estate is not an excepted estate.

Transfers reported late

8. Where no account of a person's excepted estate is required by the Board, an account of that estate shall, for the purposes of section 114 (6) of the Finance Act 1976 (delivery of account to be treated as payment where tax rate nil), be treated as having been delivered on the last day of the prescribed period in relation to that person.

THE DISTRICT PROBATE REGISTRIES ORDER 1982

S.I. 1982 No. 379

Dated 25 February 1982

[**Note.** Shown as amended by the District Probate Registries (Amendment) Order 1994, S.I. 1994 No. 1103 as from 23 May 1994, and the District Probate Registries (Amendment No. 2) Order 1994, S.I. 1994 No. 3079, as from 16 January 1995.]

The Lord Chancellor, in exercise of the power conferred on him by section 104 of the Supreme Court Act 1981, hereby makes the following Order:

1. This Order may be cited as the District Probate Registries Order 1982 and shall come into operation on 20 April 1982.

2.—(1) District probate registries shall be established at the places specified in column 1 of the Schedule to this Order.

(2) The name of every place so specified shall be the name of the district probate registry at that place except that the name of the district probate registry at Cardiff shall be the Probate Registry of Wales.

3. District probate sub-registries shall be established at the places specified in column 2 of the Schedule to this Order, and each sub-registry shall be attached to and under the control of the registrar of the district probate registry appearing opposite it in column 1 of the Schedule to this Order.

4. Every district probate registrar shall arrange for an officer of a district probate registry or of a district probate sub-registry to attend, for the purpose of personal applications for a grant of probate or administration, at such places and such times as may be specified by the Lord Chancellor, and any such place may be styled a probate office.

5. The District Probate Registries Order 1968 and the District Probate Registries (Amendment) Order 1981 are hereby revoked.

SCHEDULE

Column 1	Column 2
District Probate Registries	Sub-registries
Birmingham	Stoke-on-Trent
Brighton	Maidstone
Bristol	Bodmin, Exeter
Cardiff	Bangor, Carmarthen
Ipswich	Norwich, Peterborough
Leeds	Lincoln, Sheffield
Liverpool	Chester, Lancaster
Manchester	Nottingham
Newcastle-upon-Tyne	Carlisle, Middlesbrough, York
Oxford	Gloucester, Leicester
Winchester	

THE ADMINISTRATION OF ESTATES (SMALL PAYMENTS) (INCREASE OF LIMIT) ORDER 1984

S.I. 1984 No. 539

Dated 10 April 1984

1. This Order may be cited as the Administration of Estates (Small Payments) (Increase of Limit) Order 1984 and shall come into operation on 11 April 1984.

2. The following provisions (which relate to property which may be disposed of on death without representation or in pursuance of a nomination subject to a limit of £1,500), namely—

(a) sections 1 and 2 of the Administration of Estates (Small Payments) Act 1965, so far as they relate to any enactment;
(b) section 14 (2) of the Ministerial Salaries and Members' Pensions Act 1965;
(c) paragraph 12 of Schedule 1 to the Forestry Act 1967;
(d) section 66 (2) of the Merchant Shipping Act 1970;
(e) section 9 (1) of the National Savings Bank Act 1971;
(f) section 4 (1) of the Superannuation Act 1972;
(g) section 24 (1) of the Parliamentary and other Pensions Act 1972;
(h) section 6 (1) of the National Debt Act 1972;
(i) section 119 (1) of the Local Government Act 1972;
(j) sections 66, 67 and 68 of the Friendly Societies Act 1974;
(k) paragraph 31 (1) (b) of Part IV of Schedule 1 to the Trade Union and Labour Relations Act 1974;
(1) section 27 (4) of the Trustee Savings Banks Act 1981;

shall have effect as if for the references to £1,500 there were substituted references to £5,000.

3. Paragraph 20 (1) of Part IV of Schedule 1 to the Judicial Pensions Act 1981 (which relates to property which may be disposed of on death without representation subject to a limit of £500), shall have effect as if for the reference to £500 there was substituted a reference to £5,000.

4. The Administration of Estates (Small Payments) (Increase of Limit) Order 1975 is hereby revoked.

THE FAMILY PROVISION (INTESTATE SUCCESSION) ORDER 1987

S.I. 1987 No. 799

Dated 1 May 1987

The Lord Chancellor, in exercise of the powers conferred on him by section 1 (1) (a) and (b) of the Family Provision Act 1966, hereby makes the following Order:

1. This Order may be cited as the Family Provision (Intestate Succession) Order 1987 and shall come into force on 1 June 1987.

2. In the case of a person dying after the coming into force of this Order, section 46 (1) of the Administration of Estates Act 1925 shall apply as if the net sums charged by paragraph (i) on the residuary estate were:

(a) under paragraph (2) of the Table, the sum of £75,000; and
(b) under paragraph (3) of the Table, the sum of £125,000.

THE NON-CONTENTIOUS PROBATE RULES 1987

S.I. 1987 No. 2024 (L.10)

Dated 24 November 1987

[**Note.** Shown as amended by the Non-Contentious Probate (Amendment) Rules 1991, S.I. 1991 No. 1876, as from 14 October 1991.]

ARRANGEMENT OF RULES

The President of the Family Division, in exercise of the powers conferred upon him by section 127 of the Supreme Court Act 1981, and section 2 (5) of the Colonial Probates Act 1892, and with the concurrence of the Lord Chancellor, hereby makes the following Rules:

1. Citation and commencement.—These Rules may be cited as the Non-Contentious Probate Rules 1987, and shall come into force on 1 January 1988.

2.   Interpretation.—(1) In these Rules, unless the context otherwise requires—

'the Act' means the Supreme Court Act 1981;
'authorised officer' means any officer of a registry who is for the time being authorised by the President to administer any oath or to take any affidavit required for any purpose connected with this duties;
'the Crown' includes the Crown in right of the Duchy of Lancaster and the Duke of Cornwall for the time being;
'district judge' means a district judge of the Principal Registry;

'grant' means a grant of probate or administration and includes, where the context so admits, the resealing of such a grant under the Colonial Probates Acts 1892 and 1927;

'gross value' in relation to any estate means the value of the estate without deduction for debts, incumbrances, funeral expenses or inheritance tax (or other capital tax payable out of the estate);

'judge' means a judge of the High court;

'oath' means the oath required by rule 8 to be sworn by every applicant for a grant;

'personal applicant' means a person other than a trust corporation who seeks to obtain a grant without employing a solicitor, and 'personal application' has a corresponding meaning;

'registrar' means the district probate registrar of the district probate registry—

   (i) to which an application for a grant is made or is proposed to be made,

  (ii) in rules 26, 40, 41 and 61 (2), from which the grant issued, and

 (iii) in rules 46, 47 and 48, from which the citation has issued or is proposed to be issued;

'registry' means the Principal Registry or a district probate registry;

'the senior district judge' means the Senior District Judge of the Family Division or, in his absence, the senior of the district judges in attendance at the Principal Registry;

'the Treasury Solicitor' means the solicitor for the affairs of Her Majesty's Treasury and includes the solicitor for the affairs of the Duchy of Lancaster and the solicitor of the Duchy of Cornwall;

'trust corporation' means a corporation within the meaning of section 128 of the Act as extended by section 3 of the Law of Property (Amendment) Act 1926.

(2) A form referred to by number means the form so numbered in the First Schedule; and such forms shall be used wherever applicable, with such variations as a district judge or registrar may in any particular case direct or approve.

3. Application of other rules.—Subject to the provisions of these Rules and to any enactment, the Rules of the Supreme Court 1965 shall apply, with the necessary modifications, to non-contentious probate matters, save that nothing in Order 3 shall prevent time from running in the Long Vacation.

4. Applications for grants through solicitors.—(1) A person applying for a grant through a solicitor may apply at any registry or sub-registry.

(2) Every solicitor through whom an application for a grant is made shall give the address of his place of business within England and Wales.

5. Personal applications.—(1) A personal applicant may apply for a grant at any registry or sub-registry.

(2) Save as provided for by rule 39 a personal applicant may not apply through an agent, whether paid or unpaid, and may not be attended by any person acting or appearing to act as his adviser.

(3) No personal application shall be proceeded with if—

(a) it becomes necessary to bring the matter before the court by action or summons;

(b) an application has already been made by a solicitor on behalf of the applicant and has not been withdrawn; or

(c) the district judge or registrar so directs.

(4) After a will has been deposited in a registry by a personal applicant, it may not be delivered to the applicant or to any other person unless in special circumstances the district judge or registrar so directs.

(5) A personal applicant shall produce a certificate of the death of the deceased or such other evidence of the death as the district judge or registrar may approve.

(6) A personal applicant shall supply all information necessary to enable the papers leading to the grant to be prepared in the registry.

(7) Unless the district judge or registrar otherwise directs, every oath or affidavit required on a personal application shall be sworn or executed by all the deponents before an authorised officer.

(8) No legal advice shall be given to a personal applicant by any officer of a registry and every such officer shall be responsible only for embodying in proper form the applicant's instructions for the grant.

6. Duty of district judge or registrar on receiving application for grant.—(1) A district judge or registrar shall not allow any grant to issue until all inquiries which he may see fit to make have been answered to his satisfaction.

(2) Except with the leave of a district judge or registrar, no grant of probate or of administration with the will annexed shall issue within seven days of the death of the deceased and no grant of administration shall issue within fourteen days thereof.

7. Grants by registrars.—(1) No grant shall be made by a registrar—

(a) in any case in which there is contention, until the contention is disposed of; or
(b) in any case in which it appears to him that a grant ought not to be made without the directions of a judge or a district judge.

(2) In any case in which paragraph (1) (b) applies, the registrar shall send a statement of the matter in question to the Principal Registry for directions.

(3) A district judge may either confirm that the matter be referred to a judge and give directions accordingly or may direct the registrar to proceed with the matter in accordance with such instructions as are deemed necessary, which may include a direction to take no further action in relation to the matter.

8. Oath in support of grant.—(1) Every application for a grant other than one to which rule 39 applies shall be supported by an oath by the applicant in the form applicable to the circumstances of the case, and by such other papers as the district judge or registrar may require.

(2) Unless otherwise directed by a district judge or registrar, the oath shall state where the deceased died domiciled.

(3) Where the deceased died on or after 1 January 1926, the oath shall state whether or not, to the best of the applicant's knowledge, information and belief, there was land vested in the deceased which was settled previously to his death and not by his will and which remained settled land notwithstanding his death.

(4) On an application for a grant of administration the oath shall state in what manner all persons having a prior right to a grant have been cleared off and whether any minority or life interest arises under the will or intestacy.

9. Grant in additional name.—Where it is sought to describe the deceased in a grant by some name in addition to his true name, the applicant shall depose to the true name of the deceased and shall specify some part of the estate which was held in the other name, or give any other reason for the inclusion of the other name in the grant.

10. Marking of wills.—Subject to paragraph (2) below, every will in respect of which an application for a grant is made—

(a) shall be marked by the signatures of the applicant and the person before whom the oath is sworn; and
(b) shall be exhibited to any affidavit which may be required under these Rules as to the validity, terms, condition or date of execution of the will.

(2) The district judge or registrar may allow a facsimile copy of a will to be marked or exhibited in lieu of the original document.

11. Engrossment for purposes of record.—(1) Where the district judge or registrar considers that in any particular case a facsimile copy of the original will would not be satisfactory for purposes of record, he may require an engrossment suitable for facsimile reproduction to be lodged.

(2) Where a will—

(a) contains alterations which are not to be admitted to proof; or

(b) has been ordered to be rectified by virtue of section 20 (1) of the Administration of Justice Act 1982,

there shall be lodged an engrossment of the will in the form in which it is to be proved.

(3) Any engrossment lodged under this rule shall reproduce the punctuation, spacing and division into paragraphs of the will and shall follow continuously from page to page on both sides of the paper.

12. Evidence as to due execution of will.—(1) Subject to paragraphs (2) and (3) below, where a will contains no attestation clause or the attestation clause is insufficient, or where it appears to the district judge or registrar that there is doubt about the due execution of the will, he shall before admitting it to proof require an affidavit as to due execution from one or more of the attesting witnesses or, if no attesting witness is conveniently available, from any other person who was present when the will was executed; and if the district judge or registrar, after considering the evidence, is satisfied that the will was not duly executed, he shall refuse probate and mark the will accordingly.

(2) If no affidavit can be obtained in accordance with paragraph (1) above, the district judge or registrar may accept evidence on affidavit from any person he may think fit to show that the signature on the will is in the handwriting of the deceased, or of any other matter which may raise a presumption in favour of due execution of the will, and may if he thinks fit require that notice of the application be given to any person who may be prejudiced by the will.

(3) A district judge or registrar may accept a will for proof without evidence as aforesaid if he is satisfied that the distribution of the estate is not thereby affected.

13. Execution of will of blind or illiterate testator.—Before admitting to proof a will which appears to have been signed by a blind or illiterate testator or by another person by direction of the testator, or which for any other reason raises doubt as to the testator having had knowledge of the contents of the will at the time of its execution, the district judge or registrar shall satisfy himself that the testator had such knowledge.

14. Evidence as to terms, condition and date of execution of will.—(1) Subject to paragraph (2) below, where there appears in a will any obliteration, interlineation, or other alteration which is not authenticated in the manner prescribed by section 21 of the Wills Act 1837, or by the re-execution of the will or by the execution of a codicil, the district judge or registrar shall require evidence to show whether the alteration was present at the time the will was executed and shall give directions as to the form in which the will is to be proved.

(2) The provisions of paragraph (1) above shall not apply to any alteration which appears to the district judge or registrar to be of no practical importance.

(3) If a will contains any reference to another document in such terms as to suggest that it ought to be incorporated in the will, the district judge or registrar shall require the document to be produced and may call for such evidence in regard to the incorporation of the document as he may think fit.

(4) Where there is a doubt as to the date on which a will was executed, the district judge or registrar may require such evidence as he thinks necessary to establish the date.

15. Attempted revocation of will.—Any appearance of attempted revocation of a will by burning, tearing, or otherwise destroying and every other circumstance leading to a presumption of revocation by the testator, shall be accounted for to the district judge's or registrar's satisfaction.

16. Affidavit as to due execution, terms, etc., of will.—A district judge or registrar may require an affidavit from any person he may think fit for the purpose of satisfying himself as to any of the matters referred to in rules 13, 14 and 15, and in any such affidavit sworn by an attesting witness or other person present at the time of the execution of a will the deponent shall depose to the manner in which the will was executed.

17. Wills proved otherwise than under section 9 of the Wills Act 1837.—(1) Rules 12 to 15 shall apply only to a will that is to be established by reference to section 9 of the Wills Act 1837 (signing and attestation of wills).

(2) A will that is to be established otherwise than as described in paragraph (1) of this rule may be so established upon the district judge or registrar being satisfied as to its terms and validity, and includes (without prejudice to the generality of the foregoing)—

(a) any will to which rule 18 applies; and

(b) any will which, by virtue of the Wills Act 1963, is to be treated as properly executed if executed according to the internal law of the territory or state referred to in section 1 of that Act.

18. Wills of persons on military service and seamen.—Where the deceased died domiciled in England and Wales and it appears to the district judge or registrar that there is prima facie evidence that a will is one to which section 11 of the Wills Act 1837 applies, the will may be admitted to proof if the district judge or registrar is satisfied that it was signed by the testator or, if unsigned, that it is in the testator's handwriting.

19. Evidence of foreign law.—Where evidence as to the law of any country or territory outside England and Wales is required on any application for a grant, the district judge or registrar may accept—

(a) an affidavit from any person whom, having regard to the particulars of his knowledge or experience given in the affidavit, he regards as suitably qualified to give expert evidence of the law in question; or

(b) a certificate by, or an act before, a notary practising in the country or territory concerned.

20. Order of priority for grant where deceased left a will.—Where the deceased died on or after 1 January 1926 the person or persons entitled to a grant in respect of a will shall be determined in accordance with the following order of priority, namely—

(a) the executor (but subject to rule 36 (4) (d) below);

(b) any residuary legatee or devisee holding in trust for any other person;

(c) any other residuary legatee or devisee (including one for life) or where the residue is not wholly disposed of by the will, any person entitled to share in the undisposed of residue (including the Treasury Solicitor when claiming bona vacantia on behalf of the Crown), provided that—

　(i) unless a district judge or registrar otherwise directs, a residuary legatee or devisee whose legacy or devise is vested in interest shall be preferred to one entitled on the happening of a contingency, and

　(ii) where the residue is not in terms wholly disposed of the district judge or registrar may, if he is satisfied that the testator has nevertheless disposed of the whole or substantially the whole of the known estate, allow a grant to be made to any legatee or devisee entitled to, or to share in, the estate so disposed of, without regard to the persons entitled to share in any residue not disposed of by the will;

(d) the personal representative of any residuary legatee or devisee (but not one for life, or one holding in trust for any other person), or of any person entitled to share in any residue not disposed of by the will;

(e) any other legatee or devisee (including one for life or one holding in trust for any other person) or any creditor of the deceased, provided that, unless a district judge or registrar otherwise directs, a legatee or devisee whose legacy or devise is vested in interest shall be preferred to one entitled on the happening of a contingency;

(f) the personal representative of any other legatee or devisee (but not one for life or one holding in trust for any other person) or of any creditor of the deceased.

21. Grants to attesting witnesses, etc.—Where a gift to any person fails by reason of section 15 of the Wills Act 1837, such person shall not have any right to a grant as a beneficiary named in the will, without prejudice to his right to a grant in any other capacity.

22. Order of priority for grant in case of intestacy.—(1) Where the deceased died on or after 1 January 1926, wholly intestate, the person or persons having a beneficial interest in the estate shall be entitled to a grant of administration in the following classes in order of priority, namely—

(a) the surviving husband or wife;

(b) the children of the deceased and the issue of any deceased child who died before the deceased;

(c) the father and mother of the deceased;

(d) brothers and sisters of the whole blood and the issue of any deceased brother or sister of the whole blood who died before the deceased;

(e) brothers and sisters of the half blood and the issue of any deceased brother or sister of the half blood who died before the deceased;

(f) grandparents;

(g) uncles and aunts of the whole blood and the issue of any deceased uncle or aunt of the whole blood who died before the deceased;

(h) uncles and aunts of the half blood and the issue of any deceased uncle or aunt of the half blood who died before the deceased.

(2) In default of any person having a beneficial interest in the estate, the Treasury Solicitor shall be entitled to a grant if he claims bona vacantia on behalf of the Crown.

(3) If all persons entitled to a grant under the foregoing provisions of this rule have been cleared off, a grant may be made to a creditor of the deceased or to any person who, notwithstanding that he has no immediate beneficial interest in the estate, may have a beneficial interest in the event of an accretion thereto.

(4) Subject to paragraph (5) of rule 27, the personal representative of a person in any of the classes mentioned in paragraph (1) of this rule or the personal representative of a creditor of the deceased shall have the same right to a grant as the person whom he represents provided that the persons mentioned in sub-paragraphs (b) to (h) of paragraph (1) above shall be preferred to the personal representative of a spouse who has died without taking a beneficial interest in the whole estate of the deceased as ascertained at the time of the application for the grant.

23. Order of priority for grant in pre-1926 cases.—Where the deceased died before 1 January 1926, the person or persons entitled to a grant shall, subject to the provisions of any enactment, be determined in accordance with the principles and rules under which the court would have acted at the date of death.

24. Right of assignee to a grant.—(1) Where all the persons entitled to the estate of the deceased (whether under a will or on intestacy) have assigned their whole interest in the estate to one or more persons, the assignee or assignees shall replace, in the order of priority for a grant of administration, the assignor or, if there are two or more assignors, the assignor with the highest priority.

(2) Where there are two or more assignees, administration may be granted with the consent of the others to any one or more (not exceeding four) of them.

(3) In any case where administration is applied for by an assignee the original instrument of assignment shall be produced and a copy of the same lodged in the registry.

25. Joinder of administrator.—(1) A person entitled in priority to a grant of administration may, without leave, apply for a grant with a person entitled in a lower degree, provided that there is no other person entitled in a higher degree to the person to be joined, unless every other such person has renounced.

(2) Subject to paragraph (3) below, an application for leave to join with a person entitled in priority to a grant of administration a person having no right or no immediate right thereto shall be made to a district judge or registrar, and shall be supported by an affidavit by the person entitled in priority, the consent of the person proposed to be joined as administrator and such other evidence as the district judge or registrar may direct.

(3) Unless a district judge or registrar otherwise directs, there may without any such application be joined with a person entitled in priority to administration—

(a) any person who is nominated under paragraph (3) of rule 32 or paragraph (3) of rule 35;
(b) a trust corporation.

26. Additional personal representatives.—(1) An application under section 114 (4) of the Act to add a personal representative shall be made to a district judge or registrar and shall be supported by an affidavit by the applicant, the consent of the person proposed to be added as personal representative and such other evidence as the district judge or registrar may require.

(2) On any such application the district judge or registrar may direct that a note shall be made on the original grant of the addition of a further personal representative, or he may impound or revoke the grant or make such other order as the circumstances of the case may require.

27. Grants where two or more persons entitled in same degree.—(1) Subject to paragraphs (1A), (2) and (3) below, where, on an application for probate, power to apply for a like grant is to be reserved to such other of the executors as have not renounced probate, notice of the application shall be given to the executor or executors to whom power is to be reserved; and unless the district judge or registrar otherwise directs, the oath shall state that such notice has been given.

(1A) Where power is to be reserved to executors who are appointed by reference to their being partners in a firm, and not by their names, notice need not be given to them under paragraph (1) above if probate is applied for by another partner in that firm.

(2) Where power is to be reserved to partners of a firm, notice for the purposes of paragraph (1) above may be given to the partners by sending it to the firm at its principal or last known place of business.

(3) A district judge or registrar may dispense with the giving of notice under paragraph (1) above if he is satisfied that the giving of such a notice is impracticable or would result in unreasonable delay or expense.

(4) A grant of administration may be made to any person entitled thereto without notice to other persons entitled in the same degree.

(5) Unless a district judge or registrar otherwise directs, administration shall be granted to a person of full age entitled thereto in preference to a guardian of a minor, and to a living person entitled thereto in preference to the personal representative of a deceased person.

(6) A dispute between persons entitled to a grant in the same degree shall be brought by summons before a district judge or registrar.

(7) The issue of a summons under this rule in the Principal Registry or a district probate registry shall be notified forthwith to the registry in which the index of pending grant applications is maintained.

(8) If the issue of a summons under this rule is known to the district judge or registrar, he shall not allow any grant to be sealed until such summons is finally disposed of.

28. Exceptions to rules as to priority.—(1) Any person to whom a grant may or is required to be made under any enactment shall not be prevented from obtaining such a grant notwithstanding the operation of rules 20, 22, 25 or 27.

(2) Where the deceased died domiciled outside England and Wales rules 20, 22, 25 or 27 shall not apply except in a case to which paragraph (3) of rule 30 applies.

29. Grants in respect of settled land.—(1) In this rule 'settled land' means land vested in the deceased which was settled prior to his death and not by his will and which remained settled land notwithstanding his death.

(2) The person or persons entitled to a grant of administration limited to settled land shall be determined in accordance with the following order of priority:

(i) the special executors in regard to settled land constituted by section 22 of the Administration of Estates Act 1925;
(ii) the trustees of the settlement at the time of the application for the grant; and
(iii) the personal representatives of the deceased.

(3) Where there is settled land and a grant is made in respect of the free estate only, the grant shall expressly exclude the settled land.

30. Grants where deceased died domiciled outside England and Wales.—(1) Subject to paragraph (3) below, where the deceased died domiciled outside England and Wales, a district judge or registrar may order that a grant, limited in such way as the district judge or registrar may direct, do issue to any of the following persons—

(a) to the person entrusted with the administration of the estate by the court having jurisdiction at the place where the deceased died domiciled; or
(b) where there is no person so entrusted, to the person beneficially entitled to the estate by the law of the place where the deceased died domiciled or, if there is more than one person so entitled, to such of them as the district judge or registrar may direct; or
(c) if in the opinion of the district judge or registrar the circumstances so require, to such person as the district judge or registrar may direct.

(2) A grant made under paragraph (1) (a) or (b) above may be issued jointly with such person as the district judge or registrar may direct if the grant is required to be made to not less than two administrators.

(3) Without any order made under paragraph (1) above—

(a) probate of any will which is admissible to proof may be granted—
(i) if the will is in the English or Welsh language, to the executor named therein; or
(ii) if the will describes the duties of a named person in terms sufficient to constitute him executor according to the tenor of the will, to that person; and
(b) where the whole or substantially the whole of the estate in England and Wales consists of immovable property, a grant in respect of the whole estate may be made in accordance with the law which would have been applicable if the deceased had died domiciled in England and Wales.

31. Grants to attorneys.—(1) Subject to paragraphs (2) and (3) below, the lawfully constituted attorney of a person entitled to a grant may apply for administration for the use and benefit of the donor, and such grant shall be limited until further representation be granted, or in such other way as the district judge or registrar may direct.

(2) Where the donor referred to in paragraph (1) above is an executor, notice of the application shall be given to any other executor unless such notice is dispensed with by the district judge or registrar.

(3) Where the donor referred to in paragraph (1) above is mentally incapable and the attorney is acting under an enduring power of attorney, the application shall be made in accordance with rule 35.

32. Grants on behalf of minors.—(1) Where a person to whom a grant would otherwise be made is a minor, administration for his use and benefit, limited until he attains the age of eighteen years, shall, unless otherwise directed, and subject to paragraph (2) of this rule, be granted to—

(a) a parent of the minor who has, or is deemed to have, parental responsibility for him in accordance with—
　　(i) section 2 (1), 2 (2) or 4 of the Children Act 1989,
　(ii) paragraph 4 or 6 of Schedule 14 to that Act, or
　(iii) an adoption order within the meaning of section 12 (1) of the Adoption Act 1976, or
(b) a guardian of the minor who is appointed, or deemed to have been appointed, in accordance with section 5 of the Children Act 1989 or in accordance with paragraph 12, 13 or 14 of Schedule 14 to that Act;

provided that where the minor is sole executor and has no interest in the residuary estate of the deceased, administration for the use and benefit of the minor limited as aforesaid, shall, unless a district judge or registrar otherwise directs, be granted to the person entitled to the residuary estate.

(2) A district judge or registrar may by order appoint a person to obtain administration for the use and benefit of the minor, limited as aforesaid, in default of, or jointly with, or to the exclusion of, any person mentioned in paragraph (1) of this rule; and the person intended shall file an affidavit in support of his application to be appointed.

(3) Where there is only one person competent and willing to take a grant under the foregoing provisions of this rule, such person may, unless a district judge or registrar otherwise directs, nominate any fit and proper person to act jointly with him in taking the grant.

33. Grants where a minor is a co-executor.—(1) Where a minor is appointed executor jointly with one or more other executors, probate may be granted to the executor or executors not under disability with power reserved to the minor executor, and the minor executor shall be entitled to apply for probate on attaining the age of eighteen years.

(2) Administration for the use and benefit of a minor executor until he attains the age of eighteen years may be granted under rule 32 if, and only if, the executors who are not under disability renounce or, on being cited to accept or refuse a grant, fail to make an effective application therefor.

34. Renunciation of the right of a minor to a grant.—(1) The right of a minor executor to probate on attaining the age of eighteen years may not be renounced by any person on his behalf.

(2) The right of a minor to administration may be renounced only by a person appointed under paragraph (2) of rule 32, and authorised by the district judge or registrar to renounce on behalf of the minor.

35. Grants in case of mental incapacity.—(1) Unless a district judge or registrar otherwise directs, no grant shall be made under this rule unless all persons entitled in the same degree as the incapable person referred to in paragraph (2) below have been cleared off.

(2) Where a district judge or registrar is satisfied that a person entitled to a grant is by reason of mental incapacity incapable of managing his affairs, administration for his use and benefit, limited until further representation be granted or in such other way as the district judge or registrar may direct, may be granted in the following order of priority—

(a) to the person authorised by the Court of Protection to apply for a grant;
(b) where there is no person so authorised, to the lawful attorney of the incapable person acting under a registered enduring power of attorney;
(c) where there is no such attorney entitled to act, or if the attorney shall renounce administration for the use and benefit of the incapable person, to the person entitled to the residuary estate of the deceased.

(3) Where a grant is required to be made to not less than two administrators, and there is only one person competent and willing to take a grant under the foregoing provisions of this rule, administration may, unless a district judge or registrar otherwise directs, be granted to such person jointly with any other person nominated by him.

(4) Notwithstanding the foregoing provisions of this rule, administration for the use and benefit of the incapable person may be granted to such two or more other persons as the district judge or registrar may by order direct.

(5) Notice of an intended application under this rule shall be given to the Court of Protection.

36. Grants to trust corporations and other corporate bodies.—(1) An application for a grant to a trust corporation shall be made through one of its officers, and such officer shall depose in the oath that the corporation is a trust corporation as defined by these Rules and that it has power to accept a grant.

(2)(a) Where the trust corporation is the holder of an official position, any officer whose name is included on a list filed with the Senior District Judge of persons authorised to make affidavits and sign documents on behalf of the office holder may act as the officer through whom the holder of that official position applies for the grant.

(b) In all other cases a certified copy of the resolution of the trust corporation authorising the officer to make the application shall be lodged, or it shall be deposed in the oath that such certified copy has been filed with the Senior District Judge, that the officer is therein identified by the position he holds, and that such resolution is still in force.

(3) A trust corporation may apply for administration otherwise than as a beneficiary or the attorney of some person, and on any such application there shall be lodged the consents of all persons entitled to a grant and of all persons interested in the residuary estate of the deceased save that the district judge or registrar may dispense with any such consents as aforesaid on such terms, if any, as he may think fit.

(4)(a) Subject to sub-paragraph (d) below, where a corporate body would, if an individual, be entitled to a grant but is not a trust corporation as defined by these Rules, administration for its use and benefit, limited until further representation be granted, may be made to its nominee or to its lawfully constituted attorney.

(b) A copy of the resolution appointing the nominee or the power of attorney (whichever is appropriate) shall be lodged, and such resolution or power of attorney shall be sealed by the corporate body, or be otherwise authenticated to the district judge's or registrar's satisfaction.

(c) The nominee or attorney shall depose in the oath that the corporate body is not a trust corporation as defined by these Rules.

(d) The provisions of paragraph (4) (a) above shall not apply where a corporate body is appointed executor jointly with an individual unless the right of the individual has been cleared off.

37. Renunciation of probate and administration.—(1) Renunciation of probate by an executor shall not operate as renunciation of any right which he may have to a grant of administration in some other capacity unless he expressly renounces such right.

(2) Unless a district judge or registrar otherwise directs, no person who has renounced administration in one capacity may obtain a grant thereof in some other capacity.

(3) A renunciation of probate or administration may be retracted at any time with the leave of a district judge or registrar; provided that only in exceptional circumstances may leave be given to an executor to retract a renunciation of probate after a grant has been made to some other person entitled in a lower degree.

(4) A direction or order giving leave under this rule may be made either by the registrar of a district probate registry where the renunciation is filed or by a district judge.

38. Notice to Crown of intended application for grant.—In any case in which it appears that the Crown is or may be beneficially interested in the estate of a deceased person, notice of intended application for a grant shall be given by the applicant to the Treasury Solicitor, and the district judge or registrar may direct that no grant shall issue within 28 days after the notice has been given.

39. Resealing under Colonial Probates Acts 1892 and 1927.—(1) An application under the Colonial Probates Acts 1892 and 1927 for the resealing of probate or administration granted by the court of a country to which those Acts apply may be made by the person to whom the grant was made or by any person authorised in writing to apply on his behalf.

(2) On any such application an Inland Revenue affidavit or account shall be lodged.

(3) Except by leave of a district judge or registrar, no grant shall be resealed unless it was made to such a person as is mentioned in sub-paragraph (a) or (b) of paragraph (1) of rule 30 or to a person to whom a grant could be made under sub-paragraph (a) of paragraph (3) of that rule.

(4) No limited or temporary grant shall be resealed except by leave of a district judge or registrar.

(5) Every grant lodged for resealing shall include a copy of any will to which the grant relates or shall be accompanied by a copy thereof certified as correct by or under the authority of the court by which the grant was made, and where the copy of the grant required to be deposited under subsection (1) of section 2 of the Colonial Probates Act 1892 does not include a copy of the will, a copy thereof shall be deposited in the registry before the grant is resealed,

(6) The district judge or registrar shall send notice of the resealing to the court which made the grant.

(7) Where notice is received in the Principal Registry of the resealing of a grant issued in England and Wales, notice of any amendment or revocation of the grant shall be sent to the court by which it was resealed.

40. Application for leave to sue on guarantee.—An application for leave under section 120 (3) of the Act or under section 11 (5) of the Administration of Estates Act 1971 to sue a surety on a guarantee given for the purposes of either of those sections shall, unless the district judge or registrar otherwise directs under rule 61, be made by summons to a district judge or registrar and notice of the application shall be served on the administrator, the surety and any co-surety.

41. Amendment and revocation of grant.—(1) Subject to paragraph (2) below, if a district judge or registrar is satisfied that a grant should be amended or revoked he may make an order accordingly.

(2) Except on the application or with the consent of the person to whom the grant was made, the power conferred in paragraph (1) above shall be exercised only in exceptional circumstances.

42. Certificate of delivery of Inland Revenue affidavit.—Where the deceased died before 13 March 1975 the certificate of delivery of an Inland Revenue affidavit required by section 30 of the Customs and Inland Revenue Act 1881 to be borne by every grant shall be in Form 1.

43. Standing searches.—(1) Any person who wishes to be notified of the issue of a grant may enter a standing search for the grant by lodging at, or sending by post to any registry or sub-registry, a notice in Form 2.

(2) A person who has entered a standing search will be sent an office copy of any grant which corresponds with the particulars given on the completed Form 2 and which—

(a) issued not more than twelve months before the entry of the standing search; or

(b) issues within a period of six months after the entry of the standing search.

(3)(a) Where an applicant wishes to extend the said period of six months, he or his solicitor may lodge at, or send by post to, the registry or sub-registry at which the standing search was entered written application for extension.

(b) An application for extension as aforesaid must be lodged, or received by post, within the last month of the said period of six months, and the standing search shall thereupon be effective for an additional period of six months from the date on which it was due to expire.

(c) A standing search which has been extended as above may be further extended by the filing of a further application for extension subject to the same conditions as set out in sub-paragraph (b) above.

44. Caveats.—(1) Any person who wishes to show cause against the sealing of a grant may enter a caveat in any registry or sub-registry, and the district judge or registrar shall not allow any grant to be sealed (other than a grant ad colligenda bona or a grant under section 117 of the Act) if he has knowledge of an effective caveat; provided that no caveat shall prevent the sealing of a grant on the day on which the caveat is entered.

(2) Any person wishing to enter a caveat (in these Rules called 'the caveator'), or a solicitor on his behalf, may effect entry of a caveat—

(a) by completing Form 3 in the appropriate book at any registry or sub-registry; or

(b) by sending by post at his own risk a notice in Form 3 to any registry or sub-registry and the proper officer shall provide an acknowledgment of the entry of the caveat.

(3)(a) Except as otherwise provided by this rule or by rules 45 or 46, a caveat shall be effective for a period of six months from the date of entry thereof, and where a caveator wishes to extend the said period of six months, he or his solicitor may lodge at, or send by post to, the registry or sub-registry at which the caveat was entered a written application for extension.

(b) An application for extension as aforesaid must be lodged, or received by post, within the last month of the said period of six months, and the caveat shall thereupon (save as otherwise provided by this rule) be effective for an additional period of six months from the date on which it was due to expire.

(c) A caveat which has been extended as above may be further extended by the filing of a further application for extension subject to the same conditions as set out in sub-paragraph (b) above.

(4) An index of caveats entered in any registry or sub-registry shall be maintained at the same registry in which the index of pending grant applications is maintained, and a search of the caveat index shall be made—

(a) on receipt of an application for a grant at that registry; and

(b) on receipt of a notice of an application for a grant made in any other registry,

and the appropriate district judge or registrar shall be notified of the entry of a caveat against the sealing of a grant for which application has been made in that other registry.

(5) Any person claiming to have an interest in the estate may cause to be issued from the registry in which the caveat index is maintained a warning in Form 4 against the caveat, and the person warning shall state his interest in the estate of the deceased and shall require the caveator to give particulars of any contrary interest in the estate; and the warning or a copy thereof shall be served on the caveator forthwith.

(6) A caveator who has no interest contrary to that of the person warning, but who wishes to show cause against the sealing of a grant to that person, may within eight days of service of the warning upon him (inclusive of the day of such service), or at any time thereafter if no affidavit has been filed under paragraph (12) below, issue and serve a summons for directions.

(7) On the hearing of any summons for directions under paragraph (6) above the district judge or registrar may give a direction for the caveat to cease to have effect.

(8) Any caveat in force when a summons for directions is issued shall remain in force until the summons has been disposed of unless a direction has been given under paragraph (7) above or until it is withdrawn under paragraph (11) below.

(9) The issue of a summons under this rule shall be notified forthwith to the registry in which the caveat index is maintained.

(10) A caveator having an interest contrary to that of the person warning may within eight days of service of the warning upon him (inclusive of the day of such service) or at any time thereafter if no affidavit has been filed under paragraph (12) below, enter an appearance in the registry in which the caveat index is maintained by filing Form 5; and he shall serve forthwith on the person warning a copy of Form 5 sealed with the seal of the court.

(11) A caveator who has not entered an appearance to a warning may at any time withdraw his caveat by giving notice at the registry or sub-registry at which it was entered, and the caveat shall thereupon cease to have effect; and, where the caveat has been so withdrawn, the caveator shall forthwith give notice of withdrawal to the person warning.

(12) If no appearance has been entered by the caveator or no summons has been issued by him under paragraph (6) of this rule, the person warning may at any time after eight days after service of the warning upon the caveator (inclusive of the day of such service) file an affidavit in the registry in which the caveat index is maintained as to such service and the caveat shall thereupon cease to have effect provided that there is no pending summons under paragraph (6) of this rule.

(13) Unless a district judge or, where application to discontinue a caveat is made by consent, a registrar by order made on summons otherwise directs, any caveat in respect of which an appearance to a warning has been entered shall remain in force until the commencement of a probate action.

(14) Except with the leave of a district judge no further caveat may be entered by or on behalf of any caveator whose caveat is either in force or has ceased to have effect under paragraphs (7) or (12) of this rule or under rule 45 (4) or rule 46 (3).

45. Probate actions.—(1) Upon being advised by the court concerned of the commencement of a probate action the Senior District Judge shall give notice of the action to every caveator other than the plaintiff in the action in respect of each caveat that is in force.

(2) In respect of any caveat entered subsequent to the commencement of a probate action the Senior District Judge shall give notice to that caveator of the existence of the action.

(3) Unless a district judge by order made on summons otherwise directs, the commencement of a probate action shall operate to prevent the sealing of a grant (other than a grant under section 117 of the Act) until application for a grant is made by the person shown to be entitled thereto by the decision of the court in such action.

(4) Upon such application for a grant, any caveat entered by the plaintiff in the action, and any caveat in respect of which notice of the action has been given, shall cease to have effect.

46. Citations.—(1) Any citation may issue from the Principal Registry or a district probate registry and shall be settled by a district judge or registrar before being issued.

(2) Every averment in a citation, and such other information as the district judge or registrar may require, shall be verified by an affidavit sworn by the person issuing the citation (in these Rules called the 'citor'), provided that the district judge or registrar may in special circumstances accept an affidavit sworn by the citor's solicitor.

(3) The citor shall enter a caveat before issuing a citation and, unless a district judge by order made on summons otherwise directs, any caveat in force at the commencement of the citation proceedings shall, unless withdrawn pursuant to paragraph (11) of rule 44, remain in

force until application for a grant is made by the person shown to be entitled thereto by the decision of the court in such proceedings, and upon such application any caveat entered by a party who had notice of the proceedings shall cease to have effect.

(4) Every citation shall be served personally on the person cited unless the district judge or registrar, on cause shown by affidavit, directs some other mode of service, which may include notice by advertisement.

(5) Every will referred to in a citation shall be lodged in a registry before the citation is issued, except where the will is not in the citor's possession and the district judge or registrar is satisfied that it is impracticable to require it to be lodged.

(6) A person who has been cited to appear may, within eight days of service of the citation upon him (inclusive of the day of such service), or at any time thereafter if no application has been made by the citor under paragraph (5) of rule 47 or paragraph (2) of rule 48, enter an appearance in the registry from which the citation issued by filing Form 5 and shall forthwith thereafter serve on the citor a copy of Form 5 sealed with the seal of the registry.

47. Citation to accept or refuse or to take a grant.—(1) A citation to accept or refuse a grant may be issued at the instance of any person who would himself be entitled to a grant in the event of the person cited renouncing his right thereto.

(2) Where power to make a grant to an executor has been reserved, a citation calling on him to accept or refuse a grant may be issued at the instance of the executors who have proved the will or the survivor of them or of the executors of the last survivor of deceased executors who have proved.

(3) A citation calling on an executor who has intermeddled in the estate of the deceased to show cause why he should not be ordered to take a grant may be issued at the instance of any person interested in the estate at any time after the expiration of six months from the death of the deceased, provided that no citation to take a grant shall issue while proceedings as to the validity of the will are pending.

(4) A person cited who is willing to accept or take a grant may, after entering an appearance, apply ex parte by affidavit to a district judge or registrar for an order for a grant to himself.

(5) If the time limited for appearance has expired and the person cited has not entered an appearance, the citor may—

(a) in the case of a citation under paragraph (1) of this rule, apply to a district judge or registrar for an order for a grant to himself;

(b) in the case of a citation under paragraph (2) of this rule, apply to a district judge or registrar for an order that a note be made on the grant that the executor in respect of whom power was reserved has been duly cited and has not appeared and that all his rights in respect of the executorship have wholly ceased; or

(c) in the case of a citation under paragraph (3) of this rule, apply to a district judge or registrar by summons (which shall be served on the person cited) for an order requiring such person to take a grant within a specified time or for a grant to himself or to some other person specified in the summons.

(6) An application under the last foregoing paragraph shall be supported by an affidavit showing that the citation was duly served.

(7) If the person cited has entered an appearance but has not applied for a grant under paragraph (4) of this rule, or has failed to prosecute his application with reasonable diligence, the citor may—

(a) in the case of a citation under paragraph (1) of this rule, apply by summons to a district judge or registrar for an order for a grant to himself;

(b) in the case of a citation under paragraph (2) of this rule, apply by summons to a district judge or registrar for an order striking out the appearance and for the endorsement on the grant of such a note as is mentioned in sub-paragraph (b) of paragraph (5) of this rule; or

(c) in the case of a citation under paragraph (3) of this rule, apply by summons to a district judge or registrar for an order requiring the person cited to take a grant within a specified time or for a grant to himself or to some other person specified in the summons;

and the summons shall be served on the person cited.

48. Citation to propound a will.—(1) A citation to propound a will shall be directed to the executors named in the will and to all persons interested thereunder, and may be issued at the instance of any citor having an interest contrary to that of the executors or such other persons.

(2) If the time limited for appearance has expired, the citor may—

(a) in the case where no person has entered an appearance, apply to a district judge or registrar for an order for a grant as if the will were invalid and such application shall be supported by an affidavit showing that the citation was duly served; or

(b) in the case where no person who has entered an appearance proceeds with reasonable diligence to propound the will, apply to a district judge or registrar by summons, which shall be served on every person cited who has entered an appearance, for such an order as is mentioned in paragraph (a) above.

49. Address for service.—All caveats, citations, warnings and appearances shall contain an address for service in England and Wales.

50. Application for order to attend for examination or for subpoena to bring in a will.—(1) An application under section 122 of the Act for an order requiring a person to attend for examination may, unless a probate action has been commenced, be made to a district judge or registrar by summons which shall be served on every such person as aforesaid.

(2) An application under section 123 of the Act for the issue by a district judge or registrar of a subpoena to bring in a will shall be supported by an affidavit setting out the grounds of the application, and if any person served with the subpoena denies that the will is in his possession or control he may file an affidavit to that effect in the registry from which the subpoena issued.

51. Grants to part of an estate under section 113 of the Act.—An application for an order for a grant under section 113 of the Act to part of an estate may be made to a district judge or registrar, and shall be supported by an affidavit setting out the grounds of the application, and—

(a) stating whether the estate of the deceased is known to be insolvent; and

(b) showing how any person entitled to a grant in respect of the whole estate in priority to the applicant has been cleared off.

52. Grants of administration under discretionary powers of court, and grants ad colligenda bona.—An application for an order for—

(a) a grant of administration under section 116 of the Act, or

(b) a grant of administration ad colligenda bona,

may be made to a district judge or registrar and shall be supported by an affidavit setting out the grounds of the application.

53. Applications for leave to swear to death.—An application for leave to swear to the death of a person in whose estate a grant is sought may be made to a district judge or registrar, and shall be supported by an affidavit setting out the grounds of the application and containing particulars of any policies of insurance effected on the life of the presumed deceased together with such further evidence as the district judge or registrar may require.

54. Grants in respect of nuncupative wills and copies of wills.—(1) Subject to paragraph (2) below, an application for an order admitting to proof a nuncupative will, or a will contained in a copy or reconstruction thereof where the original is not available, shall be made to a district judge or registrar.

(2) In any case where a will is not available owing to its being retained in the custody of a foreign court or official, a duly authenticated copy of the will may be admitted to proof without the order referred to in paragraph (1) above.

(3) An application under paragraph (1) above shall be supported by an affidavit setting out the grounds of the application, and by such evidence on affidavit as the applicant can adduce as to—

(a) the will's existence after the death of the testator or, where there is no such evidence, the facts on which the applicant relies to rebut the presumption that the will has been revoked by destruction;
(b) in respect of a nuncupative will, the contents of that will; and
(c) in respect of a reconstruction of a will, the accuracy of that reconstruction.

(4) The district judge or registrar may require additional evidence in the circumstances of a particular case as to due execution of the will or as to the accuracy of the copy will, and may direct that notice be given to persons who would be prejudiced by the application.

55. Application for rectification of a will.—(1) An application for an order that a will be rectified by virtue of section 20 (1) of the Administration of Justice Act 1982 may be made to a district judge or registrar, unless a probate action has been commenced.

(2) The application shall be supported by an affidavit, setting out the grounds of the application, together with such evidence as can be adduced as to the testator's intentions and as to whichever of the following matters as are in issue:—

(a) in what respects the testator's intentions were not understood; or
(b) the nature of any alleged clerical error.

(3) Unless otherwise directed, notice of the application shall be given to every person having an interest under the will whose interest might be prejudiced by the rectification applied for and any comments in writing by any such person shall be exhibited to the affidavit in support of the application.

(4) If the district judge or registrar is satisfied that, subject to any direction to the contrary, notice has been given to every person mentioned in paragraph (3) above, and that the application is unopposed, he may order that the will be rectified accordingly.

56. Notice of election by surviving spouse to redeem life interest.—(1) Where a surviving spouse who is the sole or sole surviving personal representative of the deceased is entitled to a life interest in part of the residuary estate and elects under section 47A of the Administration of Estates Act 1925 to have the life interest redeemed, he may give written notice of the election to the Senior District Judge in pursuance of subsection (7) of that section by filing a notice in Form 6 in the Principal Registry or in the district probate registry from which the grant issued.

(2) Where the grant issued from a district probate registry, the notice shall be filed in duplicate.

(3) A notice filed under this rule shall be noted on the grant and the record and shall be open to inspection.

57. Index of grant applications.—(1) The Senior District Judge shall maintain an index of every pending application for a grant made in any registry.

(2) Notice of every application for a grant shall be sent by the registry in which the application is made to the registry in which the index is maintained and shall be in the form of a document stating the full name of the deceased and the date of his death.

(3) On receipt of the notice referred to in paragraph (2) above, the registry shall search its current index and shall give a certificate as to the result of that search to the registry which sent the notice.

(4) The requirements of paragraph (2) above shall not apply in any case in which the application for a grant is made in the registry in which the index is maintained.

(5) In this rule 'registry' includes a sub-registry.

58. Inspection of copies of original wills and other documents.—An original will or other document referred to in section 124 of the Act shall not be open to inspection if, in the opinion of a district judge or registrar, such inspection would be undesirable or otherwise inappropriate.

59. Issue of copies of original wills and other documents.—Where copies are required of original wills or other documents deposited under section 124 of the Act, such copies may be facsimile copies sealed with the seal of the court and issued either as office copies or certified under the hand of a district judge or registrar to be true copies.

60. Taxation of costs.—Every bill of costs, other than a bill delivered by a solicitor to his client which falls to be taxed under the Solicitors Act 1974, shall be referred for taxation—

(a) where the order for taxation was made by a district judge, to a district judge, or to a taxing officer of the Principal Registry authorised to tax costs in accordance with Order 62, rule 19 of the Rules of the Supreme Court 1965;

(b) where the order for taxation was made by a registrar, to that registrar.

61. Power to require application to be made by summons.—(1) Subject to rule 7 (2), a district judge or a registrar may require any application to be made by summons to a district judge or registrar in chambers or a judge in chambers or open court.

(2) An application for an inventory and account shall be made by summons to a district judge or registrar.

(3) A summons for hearing by a district judge or registrar shall be issued out of the registry in which it is to be heard.

(4) A summons to be heard by a judge shall be issued out of the Principal Registry.

62. Transfer of applications.—A district judge or registrar to whom any application is made under these Rules may order the transfer of the application to another district judge or registrar having jurisdiction.

63. Power to make orders for costs.—On any application dealt with by him on summons, the registrar shall have full power to determine by whom and to what extent the costs are to be paid.

64. Exercise of powers of judge during Long Vacation.—All powers exercisable under these Rules by a judge in chambers may be exercised during the Long Vacation by a district judge.

65. Appeals from district judges or registrars.—(1) An appeal against a decision or requirement of a district judge or registrar shall be made by summons to a judge.

(2) If, in the case of an appeal under the last foregoing paragraph, any person besides the appellant appeared or was represented before the district judge or registrar from whose decision or requirement the appeal is brought, the summons shall be issued within seven days thereof for hearing on the first available day and shall be served on every such person as aforesaid.

66. Service of summons.—(1) A judge or district judge or, where the application is to be made to a district probate registrar, that registrar, may direct that a summons for the service of which no other provision is made by these Rules shall be served on such person or persons as the judge or district judge may direct.

(2) Where by these Rules or by any direction given under the last foregoing paragraph a summons is required to be served on any person, it shall be served not less than two clear

days before the day appointed for the hearing, unless a judge or district judge or registrar at or before the hearing dispenses with service on such terms, if any, as he may think fit.

67. Notices, etc.—Unless a district judge or registrar otherwise directs or these Rules otherwise provide, any notice or other document required to be given to or served on any person may be given or served in the manner prescribed by Order 65, rule 5 of the Rules of the Supreme Court 1965.

68. Application to pending proceedings.—Subject in any particular case to any direction given by a judge or district judge or registrar, these Rules shall apply to any proceedings which are pending on the date on which they come into force as well as to any proceedings commenced on or after that date.

69. Revocation of previous rules.—(1) Subject to paragraph (2) below, the rules set out in the Second Schedule are hereby revoked.

(2) The rules set out in the Second Schedule shall continue to apply to such extent as may be necessary for giving effect to a direction under rule 68.

FIRST SCHEDULE   Rule 2 (2)

FORMS

FORM 1   Rule 42

Certificate of Delivery of Inland Revenue Affidavit

And it is hereby certified that an Inland Revenue affidavit has been delivered wherein it is shown that the gross value of the said estate in the United Kingdom (exclusive of what the said deceased may have been possessed of or entitled to as a trustee and not beneficially) amounts to £ and that the net value of the estate amounts to £

And it is further certified that it appears by a receipt signed by an Inland Revenue officer on the said affidavit that £   on account of estate duty and interest on such duty has been paid.

FORM 2   Rule 43 (1)

Standing Search

In the High Court of Justice

Family Division

The Principal [or ....District Probate] Registry.

I/We apply for the entry of a standing search so that there shall be sent to me/us an office copy of every grant of representation in England and Wales in the estate of—

Full name of deceased:

Full address:

Alternative or alias names:

Exact date of death:

which either has issued not more than 12 months before the entry of this application or issues within 6 months thereafter.

Signed

Name in block letters

Full address

Reference No. (if any)

FORM 3   Rule 44 (2)

Caveat

In the High Court of Justice

Family Division

The Principal [*or*   District Probate] Registry.

Let no grant be sealed in the estate of (*full name and address*) deceased, who died on the   day
of   19   without notice to (*name of party by whom or on whose behalf the caveat is entered*).

Dated this   day of   19

(*Signed*)   (*to be signed by the caveator's solicitor or by the caveator if acting in person*)
whose address for service is:

Solicitor for the said   (*If the caveator is acting in person, substitute 'In person'.*)

FORM 4   Rule 44 (5)

Warning to Caveator

In the High Court of Justice

Family Division

[*The Registry in which the caveat index is maintained*]

To   of   a party who has entered a caveat in the estate of   deceased.

You have eight days (starting with the day on which this warning was served on you):

  (i) to enter an appearance either in person or by your solicitor, at the [*name and address of the reg-
      istry in which the caveat index is maintained*] setting out what interest you have in the estate of the
      above-named   of   deceased contrary to that of the party at whose instance
      this warning is issued; or
 (ii) if you have no contrary interest but wish to show cause against the sealing of a grant to such party,
      to issue and serve a summons for directions by a district judge of the Principal Registry or a regis-
      trar of a district probate registry.

If you fail to do either of these, the court may proceed to issue a grant of probate or administration in the
said estate notwithstanding your caveat.

Dated the   day of   19

Issued at the instance of

[*Here set out the name and interest (including the
date of the will, if any, under which the interest
arises) of the party warning, the name of his solicitor and the address for service. If the party warning
is acting in person, this must be stated.*]   Registrar

FORM 5   Rules 44 (10), 46 (6)

Appearance to Warning or Citation

In the High Court of Justice

Family Division

The Principal [*or*   District Probate] Registry

Caveat   No.   dated the   day of   19

[Citation dated the   day of   19   ]

Full name and address of deceased:

Full name and address of person warning [*or* citor]:

(*Here set out the interest of the person warning, or citor, as shown in warning or citation.*)

Full name and address of caveator [or person cited].
(*Here set out the interest of the caveator or person cited, stating the date of the will (if any) under which such interest arises.*)
Enter an appearance for the above-named caveator [or person cited] in this matter.

Dated the   day of   19

(*Signed*)

whose address for service is:

                                                                    Solicitor (*or* 'In person').

FORM 6   Rule 56

Notice of Election to Redeem Life Interest

In the High Court of Justice

Family Division

The Principal [*or*   District Probate] Registry

In the estate of   deceased.

Whereas   of   died on the   day of   19
wholly/partially intestate leaving his/her lawful wife/husband and   lawful issue of the said deceased;

    And whereas Probate/Letters of Administration of the estate of the said   were granted
to me, the said   [and to   of   ] at the Probate Registry on the   day of   19 ;

    And whereas [the said   has ceased to be a personal
representative because   ] and I am [now] the sole
personal representative;

Now I, the said   hereby give notice in accordance with
section 47A of the Administration of Estates Act 1925 that I elect to redeem the life interest to which I
am entitled in the estate of the late   by retaining £   its capital value, and £   the
costs of the transaction.

Dated the   day of   19

(Signed)

To the Senior District Judge of the Family Division.

SECOND SCHEDULE   Rule 69
REVOCATIONS

Rules revoked	References
The Non-Contentious Probate Rules 1954	S.I. 1954/796
The Non-Contentious Probate (Amendment) Rules 1961	S.I. 1961/72
The Non-Contentious Probate (Amendment) Rules 1962	S.I. 1962/2653
The Non-Contentious Probate (Amendment) Rules 1967	S.I. 1967/748
The Non-Contentious Probate (Amendment) Rules 1968	S.I. 1968/1675
The Non-Contentious Probate (Amendment) Rules 1969	S.I. 1969/1689
The Non-Contentious Probate (Amendment) Rules 1971	S.I. 1971/1977
The Non-Contentious Probate (Amendment) Rules 1974	S.I. 1974/597
The Non-Contentious Probate (Amendment) Rules 1976	S.I. 1976/1362
The Non-Contentious Probate (Amendment) Rules 1982	S.I. 1982/446
The Non-Contentious Probate (Amendment) Rules 1983	S.I. 1983/623
The Non-Contentious Probate (Amendment) Rules 1985	S.I. 1985/1232

THE PARENTAL RESPONSIBILITY AGREEMENT REGULATIONS 1991

S.I. 1991 No. 1478

Dated 14 October 1991

[**Note.**—the Schedule to these regulations is shown as substituted by the Parental Responsibility Agreement (Amendment) Regulations 1994. S.I. 1994 No. 3157—which came into force on 3 January 1995.]

Citation, commencement and interpretation

1.—(1) These Regulations may be cited as the Parental Responsibility Agreement Regulations 1991 and shall come into force on 14 October 1991.

(2) In these Regulations, 'the Principal Registry' means the principal registry of the Family Division of the High Court.

Form of parental responsibility agreement

2. A parental responsibility agreement shall be made in the form set out in the Schedule to these Regulations.

Recording of parental responsibility agreement

3.—(1) A parental responsibility agreement shall be recorded by the filing of the agreement, together with two copies, in the Principal Registry.

(2) Upon the filing of documents under paragraph (1), an officer of the Principal Registry shall seal the copies and send one to the child's mother and one to the child's father.

(3) The record of an agreement under paragraph (1) shall be made available, during office hours, for inspection by any person upon—

(a) written request to an officer of the Principal Registry, and
(b) payment of such fee as may be prescribed in an Order under section 41 of the Matrimonial and Family Proceedings Act 1984 (Fees in family proceedings).

SCHEDULE   Regulation 2

Parental Responsibility Agreement
Section 4(1)b) Children Act 1989

Read the notes on the other side before you make this agreement.

Keep this form in a safe place

Date recorded at the Principal Registry of the Family Division

This is a Parental Responsibility Agreement regarding

the Child   *Name*

_____   _____   _____
              Boy or Girl   *Date of birth*   *Date of 18th birthday*

Between   _____

the Mother   *Name*

               Address

and   the Father   *Name*

_____

Address

_____

We declare that   we are the mother and father of the above child and we agree that the child's father shall have parental responsibility for the child (in addition to the mother having parental responsibility).

_____   _____
Signed (**Mother**)   Signed (**Father**)

_____   _____
Date   Date

Certificate of Witness

| The following evidence of identity was produced by the person signing above: | The following evidence of identity was produced by the person signing above: |

_____   _____
Signed in the presence of: Signed in the presence of:
Name of Witness   *Name of Witness*

_____   _____
Address   *Address*

_____   _____
Signature of Witness   Signature of Witness

_____   _____
[A Justice of the Peace]   [A Justice of the Peace]
[Justices' Clerk]   [Justices' Clerk]
[An Officer of the Court   [An Officer of the Court
authorised by the judge   authorised by the judge
to administer oaths]   to administer oaths]

Notes about the Parental Responsibility Agreement

Read these notes before you make the agreement.

About the Parental Responsibility Agreement

The making of this Agreement will affect the legal position of the mother and the father. You should both seek legal advice before you make the Agreement. You can obtain the name and address of a solicitor from the Children Panel (0171–242–1222) or from

—your local family proceedings court, or country court

—a Citizens Advice Bureau

—a Law Centre

—a local library.

You may be eligible for legal aid.

When you fill in the Agreement

Please use black ink (the Agreement will be copied). Put the name of one child only. If the father is to have parental responsibility for more than one child, fill in a separate form for each child. **Do not sign the Agreement.**

When you have filled in the Agreement

Take it to a local family proceedings court, or county court, or the Principal Registry of the Family Division (the address is below).

A justice of the peace, a justices' clerk, or a court official who is authorised by the judge to administer oaths, will witness your signature and he or she will sign the certificate of the witness.

To the mother: When you make the declaration you will have to prove that you are the child's mother so take to the court the child's full birth certificate.

You will also need evidence of your identity showing a photograph and signature (for example, a photocard, official pass or passport).

To the father: You will need evidence of your identity showing a photograph and signature (for example, a photocard, official pass or passport).

When the certificate has been signed and witnessed

Make 2 copies of the other side of this form. You do not need to copy these notes.

Take, or send, this form and the copies to the Principal Registry of the Family Division, Somerset House, Strand, London WC2R 1LP.

The Registry will record the Agreement and keep this form. The copies will be stamped and sent back to each parent at the address on the Agreement. The Agreement will not take effect until it has been received and recorded at the Principal Registry of the Family Division.

Ending the Agreement

Once a parental responsibility agreement has been made it can only end

—by an order of the court made on the application of any person who has parental responsibility for the child

—by an order of the court made on the application of the child with leave of the court

—when the child reaches the age of 18.

THE FAMILY PROVISION (INTESTATE SUCCESSION) ORDER 1993

S.I. 1993 No. 2906

Dated 29 November 1993

1. This Order may be cited as the Family Provision (Intestate Succession) Order 1993 and shall come into force on 1st December 1993.

2.   In the case of a person dying after the coming into force of this Order, section 46(1) of the Administration of Estates Act 1925 shall apply as if the net sums charged by paragraph (i) on the residuary estate were:—

(a)   under paragraph (2) of the Table, the sum of £125,000; and
(b)   under paragraph (3) of the Table, the sum of £200,000.

Part II—Contentious Business

THE RULES OF THE SUPREME COURT 1965

ORDER 76

CONTENTIOUS PROBATE PROCEEDINGS

1. Application and interpretation.—(1) This Order applies to probate causes and matters, and the other provisions of these rules apply to those causes and matters including applications for the rectification of a will subject to the provisions of this Order.

(2) In these Rules 'probate action' means an action for the grant of probate of the will, or letters of administration of the estate, of a deceased person or for the revocation of such a grant or for a decree pronouncing for or against the validity of an alleged will, not being an action which is non-contentious or common form probate business.

(3) In this Order, 'will' includes a codicil.

(4) In this Order, 'relevant office' means

(a) if the action is proceeding in a Chancery District Registry, that registry, and
(b) in any other case, Chancery Chambers.

2. Requirements in connection with issue of writ.—(1) A probate action must be begun by writ, and the writ must be issued out of Chancery Chambers or one of the Chancery district registries.

(2) Before a writ beginning a probate action is issued it must be indorsed with a statement of the nature of the interest of the plaintiff and of the defendant in the estate of the deceased to which the action relates.

3. Parties to action for revocation of grant. Every person who is entitled or claims to be entitled to administer the estate of a deceased person under or by virtue of an unrevoked grant of probate of his will or letters of administration of his estate shall be made a party to any action for revocation of the grant.

4. Lodgment of grant in action for revocation.—(1) Where, at the commencement of an action for the revocation of a grant of probate of the will or letters of administration of the estate of a deceased person, the probate or letters of administration, as the case may be, have not been lodged in court, then—

(a) if the action is commenced by a person to whom the grant was made, he shall lodge the probate or letters of administration in the relevant office within 7 days after the issue of the writ;
(b) if any defendant to the action has the probate or letters of administration in his possession or under this control, he shall lodge it or them in the relevant office within 14 days after the service of the writ upon him.

In this paragraph 'court' includes the principal registry of the Family Division or a district probate registry.

(2) Any person who fails to comply with paragraph (1) may, on the application of any party to the action, be ordered by the Court to lodge the probate or letters of administration in the relevant office within a specified time; and any person against whom such an order is made shall not be entitled to take any step in the action without the leave of the Court until he has complied with the order.

5. Affidavit of testamentary scripts.—(1) Unless the Court otherwise directs, the plaintiff and every defendant who has acknowledged service of the writ in a probate action must swear an affidavit:

(a) describing any testamentary script of the deceased person, whose estate is the subject of the action, of which he has any knowledge or, if such be the case, stating that he knows of no such script, and

(b) if any such script of which he has knowledge is not in his possession or under his control, giving the name and address of the person in whose possession or under whose control it is or, if such be the case, stating that he does not know the name or address of that person.

(2) Any affidavit required by this rule must be filed, and any testamentary script referred to therein which is in the possession or under the control of the deponent, must be lodged in the relevant office within 14 days after the acknowledgment of service by a defendant to the action or, if no defendant acknowledges service and the Court does not otherwise direct, before an order is made for the trial of the action.

(3) Where any testamentary script required by this rule to be lodged in the relevant office or any part thereof is written in pencil, then, unless the Court otherwise directs, a facsimile copy of that script, or of the page or pages thereof containing the part written in pencil, must also be lodged in Chancery Chambers and the words which appear in pencil in the original must be underlined in red ink in the copy.

(4) Except with the leave of the Court, a party to a probate action shall not be allowed to inspect an affidavit filed, or any testamentary script lodged by any other party to the action under this rule, unless and until an affidavit sworn by him containing the information referred to in paragraph (1) has been filed.

(5) In this rule 'testamentary script' means a will or draft thereof, written instructions for a will made by or at the request or under the instructions of the testator and any document purporting to be evidence of the contents, or to be a copy, of a will which is alleged to have been lost or destroyed.

6. Failure to acknowledge service.—(1) Order 13 shall not apply in relation to a probate action.

(2) Where any of several defendants to a probate action fails to acknowledge service of the writ, the plaintiff may, after the time for acknowledging service has expired and upon filing an affidavit proving due service of the writ, or notice of the writ, on that defendant proceed with the action as if that defendant had acknowledged service.

(3) Where the defendant, or all the defendants, to a probate action, fails or fail to acknowledge service of the writ, then, unless on the application of the plaintiff the Court orders the action to be discontinued, the plaintiff may after the time limited for acknowledging service by the defendant apply to the Court for an order for trial of the action.

(4) Before applying for an order under paragraph (3) the plaintiff must file an affidavit proving due service of the writ, or notice of the writ, on the defendant, and, if no statement of claim is indorsed on the writ, he must lodge a statement of claim in the judge's chambers.

(5) Where the Court grants an order under paragraph (3), it may direct the action to be tried on affidavit evidence.

7. Service of statement of claim. The plaintiff in a probate action must, unless the Court gives leave to the contrary or unless a statement of claim is indorsed on the writ, serve a statement of claim on every defendant who acknowledges service of the writ in the action and must do so before the expiration of 6 weeks after acknowledgment of service by that defendant or of 8 days after the filing by that defendant of an affidavit under rule 5, whichever is the later.

8. Counterclaim.—(1) Notwithstanding anything in Order 15, rule 2 (1), a defendant to a probate action who alleges that he has any claim or is entitled to any relief or remedy in respect of any matter relating to the grant of probate of the will, or letters of administration of the estate, of the deceased person which is the subject of the action must add to his defence a counterclaim in respect of that matter.

(2) If the plaintiff fails to serve a statement of claim, any such defendant may, with the leave of the Court, serve a counterclaim and the action shall then proceed as if the counterclaim were the statement of claim.

9. Contents of pleadings.—(1) Where the plaintiff in a probate action disputes the interest of a defendant he must allege in his statement of claim that he denies the interest of that defendant.

(2) In a probate action in which the interest by virtue of which a party claims to be entitled to a grant of letters of administration is disputed, the party disputing that interest must show in his pleading that if the allegations made therein are proved he would be entitled to an interest in the estate.

(3) Without prejudice to Order 18, rule 7, any party who pleads that at the time when a will, the subject of the action, was alleged to have been executed the testator did not know and approve of its contents must specify the nature of the case on which he intends to rely, and no allegation in support of that plea which would be relevant in support of any of the following other pleas, that is to say—

(a) that the will was not duly executed,
(b) that at the time of the execution of the will the testator was not of sound mind, memory and understanding, and
(c) that the execution of the will was obtained by undue influence or fraud,

shall be made by that party unless that other plea is also pleaded.

10. Default of pleadings.—(1) Order 19 shall not apply in relation to a probate action.

(2) Where any party to a probate action fails to serve on any other party a pleading which he is required by these rules to serve on that other party, then, unless the Court orders the action to be discontinued or dismissed, that other party may, after the expiration of the period fixed by or under these rules for service of the pleading in question, apply to the Court for an order for trial of the action; and if an order is made the Court may direct the action to be tried on affidavit evidence.

11. Discontinuance and dismissal.—(1) Order 21 shall not apply in relation to a probate action.

(2) At any stage of the proceedings in a probate action the Court may, on the application of the plaintiff or of any party to the action who has acknowledged service of the writ therein, order the action to be discontinued or dismissed on such terms as to costs or otherwise as it thinks just, and may further order that a grant of probate of the will, or letters of administration of the estate, of the deceased person, as the case may be, which is the subject of the action, be made to the person entitled thereto.

(3) An application for an order under this rule may be made by motion or summons or by notice under Order 25, rule 7.

12. Compromise of action: trial on affidavit evidence. Where, whether before or after the service of the defence in a probate action, the parties to the action agree to a compromise, the Court may order the trial of the action on affidavit evidence.

13. Application for order to bring in will, etc.—(1) Any application in a probate action for an order under section 122 of the Act shall be for an order requiring a person to bring a will or other testamentary paper into the relevant office or to attend in court for examination.

(2) An application under paragraph (1) shall be made by summons in the action, which must be served on the person against whom the order is sought.

(3) Any application in a probate action for the issue of a subpoena under section 123 of the Act shall be for the issue of a subpoena requiring a person to bring into the relevant office a will or other testamentary paper.

(4) An application under paragraph (3) may be made ex parte and must be supported by an affidavit setting out the grounds of the application.

(5) An application under paragraph (3) shall be made to a master who may, if the application is granted, authorise the issue of a subpoena accordingly.

(6) Any person against whom a subpoena is issued under section 123 or the Act and who denies that the will or other testamentary paper referred to in the subpoena is in his possession or under his control may file an affidavit to that effect.

14. Administration pending suit.—(1) An application under section 117 of the Act for an order for the grant of administration may be made by summons issued in the Chancery Division.

(2) Where an order for a grant of administration is made under the said section 117, Order 30, rules 2, 4 and 6 and (subject to subsection (3) of the said section) rule 3, shall apply as if the administrator were a receiver appointed by the court; and every application relating to the conduct of the administration shall be made in the Chancery Division.

15. Probate counterclaim in other proceedings.—(1) In this rule 'probate counterclaim' means a counterclaim in any action other than a probate action by which the defendant claims any such relief as is mentioned in rule 1 (2).

(2) Subject to the following paragraphs, this Order shall apply with the necessary modifications to a probate counterclaim as it applies to a probate action.

(3) A probate counterclaim must contain a statement of the nature of the interest of the defendant and of the plaintiff in the estate of the deceased to which the counterclaim relates.

(4) [*Revoked.*]

(5) Unless an application under Order 15, rule 5 (2), is made within seven days after the service of a probate counterclaim for the counterclaim to be struck out and the application is granted, the Court shall, if necessary of its own motion, order the transfer of the action to the Chancery Division (if it is not already assigned to that Division) and to either the Royal Courts of Justice or a Chancery district registry (if it is not already proceeding in one of those places).

16. Rectification of wills.—(1) Where an application is made for the rectification of a will, and the grant has not been lodged in court, rule 4 shall apply, with the necessary modifications, as if the proceedings were a probate action.

(2) A copy of every order made for the rectification of a will shall be sent to the principal registry of the Family Division for filing, and an memorandum of the order shall be endorsed on, or permanently annexed to, the grant under which the estate is administered.

ORDER 99

INHERITANCE (PROVISION FOR FAMILY AND DEPENDANTS) ACT 1975

1. Interpretation. In this Order 'the Act' means the Inheritance (Provision for Family and Dependants) Act 1975 and a section referred to by number means the section so numbered in that Act.

2. Assignment to Chancery or Family Division. Proceedings in the High Court under the Act may be assigned to the Chancery Division or to the Family Division.

3. Application for financial provision.—(1) Any originating summons by which an application under section 1 is made may be issued out of Chancery Chambers, the principal registry of the Family Division or any district registry.

(2) The summons shall be in Form No. 10 in Appendix A.

(3) There shall be lodged with the Court an affidavit by the applicant in support of the summons, exhibiting an official copy of the grant of representation to the deceased's estate and of every testamentary document admitted to proof, and a copy of the affidavit shall be served on every defendant with the summons.

4. Powers of Court as to parties.—(1) Without prejudice to its powers under Order 15, the Court may at any stage of proceedings under the Act direct that any person be added as a party to the proceedings or that notice of the proceedings be served on any person.

(2) Order 15, rule 13, shall apply to proceedings under the Act as it applies to the proceedings mentioned in paragraph (1) of that rule.

5. Affidavit in answer.—(1) A defendant to an application under section 1 who is a personal representative of the deceased shall and any other defendant may, within 21 days after service of the summons on him, inclusive of the day of service, lodge with the Court an affidavit in answer to the application.

(2) The affidavit lodged by a personal representative pursuant to paragraph (1) shall state to the best of the deponent's ability—

(a) full particulars of the value of the deceased's net estate, as defined by section 25 (1);
(b) the person or classes of persons beneficially interested in the estate, giving the names and (in the case of those who are not already parties) the addresses of all living beneficiaries, and the value of their interests so far as ascertained;
(c) if such be the case, that any living beneficiary (naming him) is a minor or a patient within the meaning of Order 80, rule 1; and
(d) any facts known to the deponent which might affect the exercise of the Court's powers under the Act.

(3) Every defendant who lodges an affidavit shall at the same time serve a copy on the plaintiff and on every other defendant who is not represented by the same solicitor.

6. Separate representation. Where an application under section 1 is made jointly by two or more applicants and the originating summons is accordingly issued by one solicitor on behalf of all of them, they may, if they have conflicting interests, appear on any hearing of the summons by separate solicitors or counsel or in person; and where at any stage of the proceedings it appears to the Court that one of the applicants is not but ought to be separately represented, the Court may adjourn the proceedings until he is.

7. Endorsement of memorandum on grant. On the hearing of an application under section 1 the personal representative shall produce to the Court the grant of representation to the deceased's estate and, if an order is made under the Act, the grant shall remain in the custody of the Court until a memorandum of the order has been endorsed on or permanently annexed to the grant in accordance with section 19 (3).

8. Disposal of proceedings in chambers. Any proceedings under the Act may, if the Court so directs, be disposed of in chambers and Order 32, rule 14 (1), shall apply in relation to proceedings in the Family Division as if for the words 'The masters of the Chancery Division shall' there were substituted the words 'A registrar of the Family Division shall'.

9. Subsequent applications in proceedings under section 1. Where an order has been made on an application under section 1, any subsequent application under the Act, whether made by a party to the proceedings or by any other person, shall be made by summons in those proceedings.

10. Drawing up and service of orders. The provisions of the Family Proceedings Rules relating to the drawing up and service of orders shall apply to proceedings in the Family Division under this Order as if they were proceedings under those Rules.

In this rule 'Family Proceedings Rules' means rules made under section 40 of the Matrimonial and Family Proceedings Act 1984.

11. Transfer to county court. [*Revoked by R.S.C. (Amendment) 1992 (S.I. 1992 No. 638).*]

COUNTY COURT RULES 1981

ORDER 41

PROBATE ACTIONS

1. Interpretation. In this Order 'probate action' means an action in respect of any contentious matter arising in connection with an application through the principal registry of the Family Division or a district probate registry for the grant or revocation of probate or administration.

2. Commencement of probate action.—On issuing a summons in a probate action the proper officer of the county court shall send to the principal registry a notice requesting all documents in the principal registry or any district probate registry relating to the matter to be sent to him.

3. Judgment to be sent to every party. A copy of any judgment given in a probate action brought in or transferred to a county court under section 32 or 40 of the Act shall be sent by the proper officer to every party to the proceedings.

4. Application of RSC. Except as otherwise provided by these rules, the provisions of the RSC relating to contentious probate proceedings shall, so far as appropriate, apply to probate actions in the county court as they apply to probate actions in the High Court.

ORDER 48

FAMILY PROVISION

1. Interpretation. In this Order—

'the Act of 1975' means the Inheritance (Provision for Family and Dependants) Act 1975;
'the deceased' means, in the case of an application under section 1 of the Act of 1975, the
  person to whose estate the application relates.

2. Mode of application.—(1) An application to a county court under section 1 of the Act of 1975 for provision to be made out of the estate of a deceased person shall be made by originating application stating—

(a) the name of the deceased, the date of his death and his country of domicile at that date;
(b) the relationship of the applicant to the deceased or other qualification of the applicant for making the application;
(c) the date on which representation with respect to the deceased's estate was first taken out and the names and addresses of the personal representatives;
(d) [*Omitted.*][1992];
(e) whether the disposition of the deceased's estate effected by his will or the law relating to intestacy was such as to make any provision for the applicant and, if it was, the nature of the provision;
(f) to the best of the applicant's knowledge and belief, the persons or classes of persons interested in the deceased's estate and the nature of their interests;

(g) particulars of the applicant's present and foreseeable financial resources and financial needs and any other information which he desires to place before the court on the matters to which the court is required to have regard under section 3 of the Act of 1975;

(h) where appropriate, a request for the court's permission to make the application notwithstanding that the period of six months has expired from the date on which representation in regard to the estate of the deceased was first taken out, and the grounds of the request; and

(i) the nature of the provision applied for.

3. Filing of application.—(1) An application to which rule 2 (1) or (2) relates shall be filed—

(a) in the court for the district in which the deceased resided at the date of his death, or

(b) if the deceased did not then reside in England or Wales, in the court for the district in which the respondent or one of the respondents resides or carries on business or the estate or part of the estate is situate, or

(c) if neither of the foregoing sub-paragraphs is applicable, in the court for the district in which the applicant resides or carries on business.

(2) The applicant shall file with this originating application an official copy of the grant of representation to the deceased's estate and of every testamentary document admitted to proof.

(3) Unless the court otherwise directs, the return day of the originating application shall be a day fixed for the pre-trial review of the proceedings.

4. Parties.—(1) Without prejudice to its powers under Orders 5 and 15, the court may, at any stage of the proceedings, direct that any person be added as a party to the proceedings or that notice of the proceedings be served on any person.

(2) Order 5, rule 6, shall apply to an application under section 1 of the Act of 1975 as it applies to the proceedings mentioned in that rule.

5. Answer. Every respondent shall, within 21 days after service of the originating application on him, file an answer, which, if the respondent is a personal representative, shall state to the best of his ability—

(a) full particulars of the value of the deceased's net estate, as defined by section 25 (1) of the Act of 1975;

(b) the persons or classes of persons beneficially interested in the estate, giving the names and (in the case of those who are not already parties) the addresses of all living beneficiaries, and the value of their interests so far as ascertained;

(c) if such be the case, that any living beneficiary (naming him) is a minor or a mental patient; and

(d) in the case of an application under section 1 of the Act of 1975, any facts known to the personal representative which might affect the exercise of the court's powers under that Act.

6. Subsequent application. Where an order has been made on an application under section 1 of the Act of 1975, any subsequent application, whether made by a party to the proceedings or by any other person, shall be made in those proceedings in accordance with Order 13, rule 1.

7. Hearing. Any application under section 1 of the Act of 1975 may be heard and determined by the registrar and may, if the court thinks fit, be dealt with in chambers.

8. Endorsement of memorandum on grant. On the hearing of an application under section 1 of the Act of 1975, the personal representative shall produce to the court the grant of representation to the deceased's estate and, if an order is made under the Act, the proper officer shall send a sealed copy thereof, together with the grant of representation, to the principal registry of the Family Division for a memorandum of the order to be endorsed on, or permanently annexed to, the grant in accordance with section 19 (3) of the Act of 1975.

9. Transfer to High Court.—An order transferring an application under section 1 of the Act of 1975 to the High Court shall state whether it is desired that the proceedings be assigned to the Chancery Division or to the Family Division of the High Court.

THE HIGH COURT AND COUNTY COURTS JURISDICTION ORDER 1991 (as amended 1993)

S.I. 1991 No. 724

1. Title and commencement. This Order may be cited as the High Court and County Courts Jurisdiction Order 1991 and shall come into force on 1 July 1991.

2. Jurisdiction.—(1) A county court shall have jurisdiction under—

(a) sections 30, 146 and 147 of the Law of Property Act 1925,
(b) section 58C of the Trade Marks Act 1938,
(c) section 26 of the Arbitration Act 1950,
(d) section 63 (2) of the Landlord and Tenant Act 1954,
(e) section 28 (3) of the Mines and Quarries (Tips) Act 1969,
(f) section 66 of the Taxes Management Act 1970,
(g) section 41 of the Administration of Justice Act 1970,
(h) section 139 (5) (b) of the Consumer Credit Act 1974,
(i) section 13 of the Torts (Interference with Goods) Act 1977,
(j) section 87 of the Magistrates' Courts Act 1980,
(k) sections 19 and 20 of the Local Government Finance Act 1982
(l) sections 15, 16, 21, 25 and 139 of the County Courts Act 1984,
(m) section 39 (4) of, and paragraph 3 (1) of Schedule 3 to, the Legal Aid Act 1988,
(n) sections 99, 102 (5), 114, 195, 204, 230, 231 and 235 (5) of the Copyright, Designs and Patents Act 1988, and
(o) section 40 of the Housing Act 1988,

whatever the amount involved in the proceedings and whatever the value of any fund or asset connected with the proceedings.

7. Allocation trial.—(1) Subject to the following provisions of this article, proceedings in which both the High Court and the county courts have jurisdiction may be tried in the High Court or in a county court.

(2) The following provisions of this article apply to proceedings in which both the High Court and the county courts have jurisdiction, other than proceedings mentioned in section 23, 24 or 32 of the Country Courts Act 1984, save that paragraphs (3) and (4) do not apply to proceedings which have no quantifiable value.

(3) An action of which the value is less than £25,000 shall be tried in a country court unless—

(a) a county court, having regard to the criteria set out in sub-paragraphs (a) to (d) of paragraph (5), considers that it ought to transfer the action to the High Court for trial and the High Court considers that it ought to try the action; or
(b) it is commenced in the High Court and the High Court, having regard to the said criteria, considers that it ought to try the action.

(4) An action of which the value is £50,000 or more shall be tried in the High Court unless—

(a) it is commenced in a county court and the county court does not, having regard to the criteria set out in sub-paragraphs (a) to (d) of paragraph (5), consider that the action ought to be transferred to the High Court for trial: or

(b) the High Court, having regard to the said criteria, considers that it ought to transfer the case to a county court for trial.

(5) The High court and the county courts, when considering whether to exercise their powers under sections 40 (2), 41 (1) or 41 (2) of the Country Courts Act 1984 (Transfer) shall have regard to the following criteria—

(a) the financial substance of the action, including the value of any counterclaim,

(b) whether the action is otherwise important and, in particular, whether it raises questions of importance to persons who are not parties or questions of general public interest,

(c) the complexity of the facts, legal issues, remedies or procedures involved, and

(d) whether transfer is likely to result in a more speedy trial of the action,

but no transfer shall be made on the grounds of sub-paragraph (d) alone.

9. Definition of value of action.—(1) For the purposes of articles 5 and 7—

(a) the value of an action for a sum of money, whether specified or not, is the amount which the plaintiff or applicant reasonably expects to recover;

(b) an action for specified relief other than a sum of money—

(i) has a value equal to the amount of money which the plaintiff or applicant could reasonably state to be the financial worth of the claim to him, or

(ii) where there is no such amount, has no quantifiable value;

(c) an action which includes more than one claim—

(i) if one or more of the claims is of a kind specified in paragraph (b) (ii), has no quantifiable value;

(ii) in any other case, has a value which is the aggregate of the values of the claims as determined in accordance with paragraphs (a) and (b) (i).

(2) In determining the value of an action under paragraph (1), claims for—

(a) unspecified further or other relief,

(b) interest, other than interest pursuant to a contract, and

(c) costs,

shall be disregarded.

(4) In determining the value of an action under paragraph (1) (a)—

(a) the sum which the plaintiff or applicant reasonably expects to recover shall be reduced by the amount of any debt which he admits that he owes to a defendant in that action and which arises from the circumstances which give rise to the action;

(b) no account shall be taken of a possible finding of contributory negligence, except to the extent, if any, that such negligence is admitted;

(c) where the plaintiff seeks an award of provisional damages as described in section 32A (2) (a) of the Supreme Court Act 1981, no account shall be taken of the possibility of a future application for further damages;

(d) the value shall be taken to include sums which, by virtue of section 22 of the Social Security Act 1989 [now Part IV of the Social Security Administration Act 1992], are required to be paid to the Secretary of State.

10. The value of an action shall be determined—

(a) for the purposes of article 5, as at the time when the action is commenced, and

(b) for the purposes of article 7, as at the time when the value is declared in accordance with rules of court.

APPENDICES III, IV AND V

III Fees (Non-Contentious Business)

IV Rates of Inheritance Tax and Capital Transfer Tax

V Costs (Non-Contentious Business)

APPENDIX III

Fees

to be taken in the Principal Registry and District Probate Registries in respect of
Non-Contentious Business

Fees (Non-Contentious Business)

NON-CONTENTIOUS PROBATE FEES ORDER 1981[1]

S.I. 1981 No. 861

Dated 12 June 1981

1. Citation and commencement. This Order may be cited as the Non-Contentious Probate Fees Order 1981 and shall come into operation on 3 August 1981.

2. Interpretation.—(1) In this Order, unless the context otherwise requires—
'assessed value' means the value of the net real and personal estate (excluding settled land if any) passing under the grant as shown—

(i) in the Inland Revenue affidavit (for a death occurring before 13 March 1975), or

(ii) in the Inland Revenue account (for a death occurring on or after 13 March 1975), or

(iii) in a case in which, in accordance with arrangements made between the President of the Family Division and the Commissioners of Inland Revenue or regulations made under section 94 (1)[2] of the Finance Act 1980 and from time to time in force, no such affidavit or account is required to be delivered, in the oath which is sworn to lead to the grant;

and in the case of an application to reseal a grant means the said value, as so shown, passing under the grant upon its being resealed;
'authorised place of deposit' means any place in which, by virtue of a direction given under section 170 of the Supreme Court of Judicature (Consolidation) Act 1925[3] original wills and other documents under the control of the High Court (either in the principal registry or in any district registry) are deposited and preserved;
'grant' means a grant of probate or letters of administration;
'district registry' includes the probate registry of Wales, any district probate registry and any sub-registry attached thereto;
'the principal registry' means the Principal Registry of the Family Division and any sub-registry attached thereto.

(2) A fee referred to by number means the fee so numbered in the Schedule to this Order.

3. Taking of fees.—(1) The fees set out in column 2 of the Schedule to this Order shall be taken in the principal registry and in each district registry in respect of the items set out opposite thereto in column 1.

(2) The fees prescribed by this Order shall be taken in cash.

4. Exclusion of certain death gratuities. In determining the value of any personal estate for the purpose of this Order there shall be excluded the value of a death gratuity payable

---

1   This Fees Order is printed as amended by the NC Probate Fees (Amendment) Orders 1981, 1983, 1986 (2), 1987 and 1989.
2   For regulations, see Appendix II, p. 920, ante.
3   Section 170 of the Act of 1925 was repealed and replaced by s. 124 of the Supreme Court Act 1981 with effect from 1 January 1982 (see p. 847, ante).

under section 17 (2) of the Judicial Pensions Act 1981 or payable to the personal representatives of a deceased civil servant by virtue of a scheme made under section 1 of the Superannuation Act 1972.

5. Reduction, remission and exemption.—(1) Where it appears to the Lord Chancellor that the payment of any fee specified in the Schedule would, owing to the exceptional circumstances of the particular case, involve undue hardship, the Lord Chancellor may reduce or remit the fee in that case.

(2) Where by any convention entered into by Her Majesty with any foreign power it is provided that no fee shall be required to be paid in respect of any proceedings, the fees specified in this Order shall not be taken in respect of those proceedings.

(3) Where any application for a grant is withdrawn before the issue of the grant, a registrar may reduce or remit a fee.

(4) Where, on application for a grant by a personal applicant, the papers leading to the grant are prepared by the applicant himself, a registrar may remit up to one-half of the fee prescribed by fee No. 2.

(5) Fee No. 7 shall not be taken where a search is made for research or similar purposes by permission of the President of the Family Division for a document over 100 years old filed in the principal registry or a district registry or another authorised place of deposit.

6. Revocation of orders. The Supreme Court (Non-Contentious Probate) Fees Order 1975, The Supreme Court (Non-Contentious Probate) Fees (Amendment) Order 1976, The Supreme Court (Non-Contentious Probate) Fees (Amendment) Order 1978, and The Supreme Court (Non-Contentious Probate) Fees (Amendment) Order 1980 are hereby revoked.

SCHEDULE

rule 3(1)

Column 1	*Column 2*
Item	Fee £
Application for grant: general	
1. On an application for a grant (or for resealing a grant) other than an application to which fee No. 3 applies:	
(*a*) if the assessed value	
does not exceed £10,000	No fee
exceeds £10,000 but does not exceed £25,000	40.00
exceeds £25,000 but does not exceed £40,000	80.00
exceeds £40,000 but does not exceed £70,000	150.00
exceeds £70,000 but does not exceed £100,000	215.00
(*b*) if the assessed value exceeds £100,000 but does not exceed £200,000	300.00
and, for every additional £100,000 or part thereof, a further fee of	50.00
Personal application fee	
2. On application for a grant by a personal applicant (or for resealing such a grant if the application is prepared in the registry) save where fee No. 3 (*a*) is payable, in addition to any other fee:	
(a) if the assessed value	
does not exceed £500	1.00
exceeds £500 but does not exceed £1,000	2.00
exceeds £1,000 but does not exceed £5,000	5.00
(*b*) if the assessed value exceeds £5,000, for each £1,000 or part thereof	1.00

Column 1	Column 2
Item	Fee £

Special applications

3. On an application for:

(*a*) a grant in respect of an estate exempt from estate duty by virtue of section 71 of the Finance Act 1952[4] or from capital transfer tax by virtue of paragraph 1 of Schedule 7 to the Finance Act 1975[5] (exemption for members of the armed forces, etc.);
(*b*) a grant limited to settled land;
(*c*) a grant limited to trust property;
(*d*) a duplicate grant;
(*e*) any second or subsequent grant (including one following a revoked grant) in respect of the same deceased person, other than a grant preceded only by a grant limited to settled land, to trust property or to a part of the estate 2.00

Caveats

4. For the entry or the extension of a caveat . . . 4.00

Search

5. On an application for a standing search to be carried out in an estate, for each search period of six months 2.00

Deposits of wills

6. On depositing a will for safe custody in the principal registry or a district registry 1.00

Inspection

7. On inspection of an original will or any other document including a copy of a will 0.25

Copies of documents—Personal attendance or on application for grant

8.—(*a*) For a copy of all or part of any document, whether or not issued as an office copy, for each page. 0.25
(*b*) For a sealed and certified copy of any document. . . 1.00
and for each page after the first, a further fee of . . 0.25
(*c*) For an exemplification of a copy signed by a registrar and countersigned by the President of the Family Division, including the fees for preparing the necessary documents 5.00

Copies of documents—Postal applications other than on application for grant

9. For handling a postal application in respect of each estate, and where appropriate supplying—

(*a*) a copy of any will or grant or other document, whether or not issued as an office copy 2.00
(*b*) a sealed and certified copy of any will or grant . . . 3.00
Only one fee shall be charged for the purposes of sub-paragraph (*a*) or (*b*) on a request for a copy of a will and a grant.
(*c*) an additional sealed and certified copy of any will or grant . . 1.00
and for each page after the first a further fee of . . 0.25
(*d*) an exemplification of a copy signed by a registrar and countersigned by the President of the Family Division, including the preparation of the necessary document 6.00
(*e*) an additional copy of any document, other than a sealed and certified copy, for each page 0.25

---

4 1952 c. 33; section 71 was repealed (with savings) by the Finance Act 1975 (c. 7), sections 50, 52 (2), (3), 59 and Schedule 13, Part 1.
5 1975 c. 7.

Column 1	Column 2
Item	Fee £
Oaths and guarantees	
10. Save on a personal application for a grant—	
(*a*) for administering an oath, for each deponent to each affidavit . .	2.00
(*b*) for marking each exhibit	0.50
(*c*) for superintending and attesting execution of a guarantee, for each surety	1.00
Taxation of costs	
11. For taxing a bill of costs in the principal registry inclusive of the registrar's certificate	The same fees as are payable in an action.
Settling documents	
12. For perusing and settling citations, advertisements, oaths, affidavits or other documents, for each document settled	5.00

Rates of Inheritance Tax and Capital Transfer Tax

Rates of Inheritance Tax and Capital Transfer Tax

Deaths on or after 13 March 1975 and prior to 27 October 1977. First Table of rates of Capital Transfer Tax (Finance Act 1975, s. 37; s. 49 and Schedule 11, para. 1).

Range of value		Cumulative tax to bottom of range	Rate of tax on value within range
Exceeding	Not exceeding		
£	£	£	%
15,000	20,000	Nil	10
20,000	25,000	500	15
25,000	30,000	1,250	20
30,000	40,000	2,250	25
40,000	50,000	4,750	30
50,000	60,000	7,750	35
60,000	80,000	11,250	40
80,000	100,000	19,250	45
100,000	120,000	28,250	50
120,000	150,000	38,250	55
150,000	500,000	54,750	60
500,000	1,000,000	264,750	65
1,000,000	2,000,000	589,750	70
2,000,000		1,289,750	75

Deaths on or after 27 October 1977 and prior to 26 March 1980. First Table of rates of Capital Transfer Tax (Finance Act 1978, s. 62 and Schedule 10).

Range of value		Cumulative tax to bottom of range	Rate of tax on value within range
Exceeding	Not exceeding		
£	£	£	%
25,000	30,000	Nil	10
30,000	35,000	500	15
35,000	40,000	1,250	20
40,000	50,000	2,250	25
50,000	60,000	4,750	30
60,000	70,000	7,750	35
70,000	90,000	11,250	40
90,000	110,000	19,250	45
110,000	130,000	28,250	50
130,000	160,000	38,250	55
160,000	510,000	54,750	60
510,000	1,010,000	264,750	65
1,010,000	2,010,000	589,750	70
2,010,000		1,289,750	75

Deaths on or after 26 March 1980 and prior to 9 March 1982. First Table of rates of Capital Transfer Tax (Finance Act 1980, s. 85 and Schedule 14).

Range of value		Cumulative tax to bottom of range	Rate of tax on value within range
Exceeding	Not exceeding		
£	£	£	%
50,000	60,000	Nil	30
60,000	70,000	3,000	35
70,000	90,000	6,500	40
90,000	110,000	14,500	45
110,000	130,000	23,500	50
130,000	160,000	33,500	55
160,000	510,000	50,000	60
510,000	1,010,000	260,000	65
1,010,000	2,010,000	585,000	70
2,010,000		1,285,000	75

Deaths on or after 9 March 1982 and prior to 15 March 1983. First Table of rates of Capital Transfer Tax (Finance Act 1982, s. 90 and Schedule 14).

Range of value		Cumulative tax to bottom of range	Rate of tax on value within range
Exceeding	Not exceeding		
£	£	£	%
55,000	75,000	Nil	30
75,000	100,000	6,000	35
100,000	130,000	14,750	40
130,000	165,000	26,750	45
165,000	200,000	42,500	50
200,000	250,000	60,000	55
250,000	650,000	87,500	60
650,000	1,250,000	327,500	65
1,250,000	2,500,000	717,500	70
2,500,000		1,592,500	75

Deaths on or after 15 March 1983 and prior to 13 March 1984. First Table of rates of Capital Transfer Tax (Finance (No. 2) Act 1983, s. 8).

Range of value		Cumulative tax to bottom of range	Rate of tax on value within range
Exceeding	Not exceeding		
£	£	£	%
60,000	80,000	Nil	30
80,000	110,000	6,000	35
110,000	140,000	16,500	40
140,000	175,000	28,500	45
175,000	220,000	44,250	50
220,000	270,000	66,750	55
270,000	700,000	94,250	60
700,000	1,325,000	352,250	65
1,325,000	2,650,000	758,500	70
2,650,000		1,686,000	75

Deaths on or after 13 March 1984 and before 6 April 1985. First Table of rates of Capital Transfer Tax (Finance Act 1984, s. 101).

Range of value		Cumulative tax to bottom of range	Rate of tax on value within range
Exceeding	Not exceeding		
£	£	£	%
64,000	85,000	Nil	30
85,000	116,000	6,300	35
116,000	148,000	17,150	40
148,000	185,000	29,950	45
185,000	232,000	46,600	50
232,000	285,000	70,100	55
285,000		99,250	60

Deaths on or after 6 April 1985 and prior to 18 March 1986. First Table of rates of Capital Transfer Tax (S.I. 1985 No. 429).

Range of value		Cumulative tax to bottom of range	Rate of tax on value within range
Exceeding	Not exceeding		
£	£	£	%
67,000	89,000	Nil	30
89,000	122,000	6,600	35
122,000	155,000	18,150	40
155,000	194,000	31,350	45
194,000	243,000	48,900	50
243,000	299,000	73,400	55
299,000		104,200	60

Deaths on or after 18 March 1986 and before 17 March 1987. Table of rates of tax (Finance Act 1986, s. 101 and Sch. 19, para. 36).

Range of value		Cumulative tax to bottom of range	Rate of tax on value within range
Exceeding	Not exceeding		
£	£	£	%
71,000	95,000	Nil	30
95,000	129,000	7,200	35
129,000	164,000	19,100	40
164,000	206,000	33,100	45
206,000	257,000	52,000	50
257,000	317,000	77,500	55
317,000		110,500	60

Deaths on or after 17 March 1987 and before 15 March 1988. Table of rates of tax (Finance Act 1987, s. 57).

Range of value		Cumulative tax to bottom of range	Rate of tax on value within range
Exceeding	Not exceeding		
£	£	£	%
90,000	140,000	Nil	30
140,000	220,000	15,000	40
220,000	330,000	47,000	50
330,000		102,000	60

Deaths on or after 15 March 1988 and before 6 April 1989. Table of rates of tax (Finance Act 1988, s. 136).

Range of value		Cumulative tax to bottom of range	Rate of tax on value within range
Exceeding	Not exceeding		
£	£	£	%
110,000		Nil	40

Deaths on or after 6 April 1989 and before 6 April 1990 (S.I. 1989 No. 468).

Range of value		Cumulative tax to bottom of range	Rate of tax on value within range
Exceeding	Not exceeding		
£	£	£	%
118,000		Nil	40

Deaths on or after 6 April 1990 and before 6 April 1991 (S.I. 1990 No. 680).

Range of value		Cumulative tax to bottom of range	Rate of tax on value within range
Exceeding	Not exceeding		
£	£	£	%
128,000		Nil	40

Deaths on or after 6 April 1991 and before 10 March 1992 (S.I. 1991 No. 735).

Range of value		Cumulative tax to bottom of range	Rate of tax on value within range
Exceeding	Not exceeding		
£	£	£	%
140,000		Nil	40

Deaths on or after 10 March 1992 and before 6 April 1995 (section 72, F.A. (No. 2) 1992).

Range of value		Cumulative tax to bottom of range	Rate of tax on value within range
Exceeding	Not exceeding		
£ 150,000	£	£ Nil	% 40

Deaths on or after 6 April 1995 (S.I. 1994 No. 3011).

Range of value		Cumulative tax to bottom of range	Rate of tax on value within range
Exceeding	Not exceeding		
£ 154,000	£	£ Nil	% 40

APPENDIX V

Costs (Non-Contentious Business)

Costs (Non-Contentious Business)

The Solicitors' (Non-Contentious Business) Remuneration Order 1994

S.I. 1994 No. 2616 (L. 16)

Dated 5 October 1994

1. Citation, commencement and revocation.—(1) This Order may be cited as the Solicitors' (Non-Contentious Business) Remuneration Order 1994.

(2) This Order shall come into force on 1 November 1994 and shall apply to all non-contentious business for which bills are delivered on or after that date.

(3) The Solicitors' Reumeration Order 1972 is hereby revoked except in its application to business for which bills are delivered before this Order comes into force.

2. Interpretation.—(1) In this Order:—

'client' means the client of a solicitor;

'costs' means the amount charged in a solicitor's bill, exclusive of disbursements and value added tax, in respect of non-contentious business or common form probate business;

'entitled person' means a client or an entitled third party;

'entitled third party' means a residuary beneficiary absolutely and immediately (and not contingently) entitled to an inheritance, where a solicitor has charged the estate for his professional costs for acting in the administration of the estate, and either

(a) the only personal representatives are solicitors (whether or not acting in a professional capacity); or

(b) the only personal representatives are solicitors acting jointly with partners or employees in a professional capacity;

'paid disbursements' means disbursements already paid by the solicitor;

'recognised body' means a body corporate recognised by the Council under section 9 of the Administration of Justice Act 1985;

'remuneration certificate' means a certificate issued by the Council pursuant to this Order;

'residuary beneficiary' includes a person entitled to all or part of the residue of an intestate estate;

'solicitor' includes a recognised body;

'the Council' means the Council of the Law Society.

3. Solicitors' costs. A solicitor's costs shall be such sum as may be fair and reasonable to both solicitor and entitled person, having regard to all the circumstances of the case and in particular to:—

(a) the complexity of the matter or the difficulty or novelty of the questions raised;

(b) the skill, labour, specialised knowledge and responsibility involved;

(c) the time spent on the business;

(d) the number and importance of the documents prepared or perused, without regard to length;

(e) the place where and the circumstances in which the business or any part thereof is transacted.

(f) the amount or value of any money or property involved;

(g) whether any land involved is registered land;

(h) the importance of the matter to the client; and

(i) the approval (express or implied) of the entitled person or the express approval of the
testator to:—
  (i) the solicitor undertaking all or any part of the work giving rise to the costs or
  (ii) the amount of the costs.

4. Right to certification.—(1) Without prejudice to the provisions of sections 70, 71 and
72 of the Solicitors Act 1974 (which relate to taxation of costs), an entitled person may, subject to the provisions of this Order, require a solicitor to obtain a remuneration certificate
from the Council in respect of a bill which has been delivered where the costs are not more
than £50,000.

(2) The remuneration certificate must state what sum, in the opinion of the Council, would
be a fair and reasonable charge for the business covered by the bill (whether it be the sum
charged or a lesser sum). In the absence of taxation the sum payable in respect of such costs
is the sum stated in the remuneration certificate.

5. Disciplinary and other measures.—(1) If on a taxation the taxing officer allows less
than one half of the costs, he must bring the facts of the case to the attention of the Council.

(2) The provisions of this Order are without prejudice to the general powers of the Council
under the Solicitors Act 1974.

6. Commencement of proceedings against a client. Before a solicitor brings proceedings
to recover costs against a client on a bill for non-contentious business he must inform the
client in writing of the matters specified in article 8, except where the bill has been taxed.

7. Costs paid by deduction.—(1) If a solicitor deducts his costs from monies held for or on
behalf of a client or of an estate in satisfaction of a bill and an entitled person objects in writing to the amount of the bill within the prescribed time, the solicitor must immediately
inform the entitled person in writing of the matters specified in article 8, unless he has
already done so.

(2) In this article and in article 10, 'the prescribed time' means:—

(a) in respect of a client, three months after delivery of the relevant bill, or a lesser time
(which may not be less than one month) specified in writing to the client at the time of
delivery of the bill, or
(b) in respect of an entitled third party, three months after delivery of notification to the
entitled third party of the amount of the costs, or a lesser time (which may not be less than
one month) specified in writing to the entitled third party at the time of such notification.

8. Information to be given in writing to entitled person. When required by articles 6 or 7,
a solicitor must inform an entitled person in writing of the following matters:—

(a) where article 4(1) applies—
  (i) that the entitled person may, within one month of receiving from the solicitor the
  information specified in this article or (if later) of delivery of the bill or notification
  of the amount of the costs, require the solicitor to obtain a remuneration certificate;
  and
  (ii) that (unless the solicitor has agreed to do so) the Council may waive the requirements of article 11(1), if satisfied from the client's written application that
  exceptional circumstances exist to justify granting a waiver;
(b) that sections 70, 71 and 72 of the Solicitors Act 1974 set out the entitled person's rights
in relation to taxation;
(c) that (where the whole of the bill has not been paid, by deduction or otherwise) the solicitor
may charge interest on the outstanding amount of the bill in accordance with article 14.

9. Loss by client of right to certification. A client may not require a solicitor to obtain a
remuneration certificate:—

(a) after a bill has been delivered and paid by the client, other than by deduction;
(b) where a bill has been delivered, after the expiry of one month from the date on which the client was informed in writing of the matters specified in article 8 or from delivery of the bill if later;
(c) after the solicitor and client have entered into a non-contentious business agreement in accordance with the provisions of section 57 of the Solicitors Act 1974;
(d) after a court has ordered the bill to be taxed;—
(e) if article 11(2) applies.

10. Loss by entitled third party of right to certification. An entitled third party may not require a solicitor to obtain a remuneration certificate:

(a) after the prescribed time (within the meaning of article 7(2)(b)) has elapsed without any objection being received to the amount of the costs;
(b) after the expiry of one mnth from the date on which the entitled third party was (in compliance with article 7) informed in writing of the matters specified in article 8 or from notification of the costs if later;
(c) after a court has ordered the bill to be taxed.

11. Requirement to pay a sum towards the costs.—(1) On requiring a solicitor to obtain a remuneration certificate a client must pay to the solicitor the paid disbursements and value added tax comprised in the bill together with 50% of the costs unless:—

(a) the client has already paid the amount required under this article, by deduction from monies held or otherwise; or
(b) the solicitor or (if the solicitor refuses) the Council has agreed in writing to waive all or part of this requirement.

(2) The Council shall be under no obligation to provide a remuneration certificate, and the solicitor may take steps to obtain payment of his bill, if the client, having been informed of his right to seek a waiver of the requirements of paragraph (1), has not:—

(a) within one month of receipt of the information specified in article 8, either paid in accordance with paragraph (1) or applied to the Council in writing for a waiver of the requirements of paragraph (1); or
(b) made payment in accordance with the requirements of paragraph (1) within one month of written notification that he has been refused a waiver of those requirements by the Council.

12. Miscellaneous provisions.—(1) After an application has been made by a solicitor for a remuneration certificate the client may pay the bill in full without invalidating the application.

(2) A solicitor and entitled person may agree in writing to waive the provisions of sub-paragraphs (a) or (b) of articles 9 and 10.

(3) A solicitor may take from his client security for payment of any costs, including the amount of any interest to which the solicitor may become entitled under article 14.

13. Refunds by solicitor.—(1) If a solicitor has received payment of all or part of his costs and a remuneration certificate is issued for less than the sum already paid, the solicitor must immediately pay to the entitled person any refund which may be due (after taking into account any other sums which may properly be payable to the solicitor whether for costs, paid disbursements, value added tax or otherwise) unless the solicitor has applied for an order for taxation within one month of receipt by him of the remuneration certificate.

(2) Where a solicitor applies for taxation, his liability to pay any refund under paragraph (1) shall be suspended for so long as the taxation is still pending.

(3) The obligation of the solicitor to repay costs under paragraph (1) is without prejudice to any liability of the solicitor to pay interest on the repayment by virtue of any enactment, rule of law or professional rule.

14. Interest.—(1) After the information specified in article 8 has been given to an entitled person in compliance with articles 6 or 7, a solicitor may charge interest on the unpaid amount of his costs plus any paid disbursements and value added tax, subject to paragraphs (2) and (3) below.

(2) Where an entitlement to interest arises under paragraph (1), and subject to any agreement made between a solicitor and client, the period for which interest may be charged may run from one month after the date of delivery of a bill, unless the solicitor fails to lodge an application within one month of receipt of a request for a remuneration certificate under article 4, in which case no interest is payable in respect of the period between one month after receiving the request and the actual date on which the application is lodged.

(3) Subject to any agreement made between a solicitor and client, the rate of interest must not exceed the rate for the time being payable on judgment debts.

(4) Interest charged under this article must be calculated, where applicable, by reference to the following:—

(a) if a solicitor is required to obtain a remuneration certificate, the total amount of the costs certified by the Council to be fair and reasonable plus paid disbursements and value added tax;
(b) if an application is made for the bill to be taxed, the amount ascertained on taxation;
(c) if an application is made for the bill to be taxed or a solicitor is required to obtain a remuneration certificate and for any reason the taxation or application for a remuneration certificate does not proceed, the unpaid amount of the costs shown in the bill or such lesser sum as may be agreed between the solicitor and the client, plus paid disbursements and value added tax.

15. Application by solicitor. A solicitor, when making an application for a remuneration certificate in accordance with the provisions of this Order, must deliver to the Council the complete relevant file and working papers, and any other information or documentation which the Council may require for the purpose of providing a remuneration certificate.

VI Forms
VII Instructions, Statutory Will Forms, Probate Offices

APPENDIX VI

Forms

SUMMARY OF CONTENTS

Part I—Forms for use in Non-contentious Probate Matters

Part II—Forms for use in Probate Actions

Alphabetical Index of Forms

[All references are to form numbers]

Forms

Part I—Forms for use in Non-Contentious Probate Matters

AFFIDAVITS

1. General heading of affidavit (and other forms)

In the High Court of Justice
Family Division
The Principal [*or*   District Probate] Registry [*or* The Probate Registry of Wales].
In the estate of AB deceased.

[**Note.**—*Every affidavit must be expressed in the first person and unless the court otherwise directs must state the place of residence of the deponent and his occupation or, if he has none, his description (Order 41, r. 1(4)). The occupation (if any) of a female deponent should therefore be stated, but if she has none, her marital status should be given.*]

2. Affidavit of execution of a will or codicil

(Heading as in Form No. 1)

I, C D, of   make oath and say that:

1. I am one of the subscribing witnesses to the [*codicil to the*] last will and testament of A B of   deceased, the said will [*codicil*] bearing date the   day of   19   being now produced to me and marked 'A'.
2. The said testator executed the said will [*codicil*] on the day of the date thereof [*or* on the day of   19] by signing his [*name at the foot or end thereof**] as the same now appears thereon, in the presence of me and of E F the other subscribed witness thereto, both of us being present at the same time, and we thereupon (after the testator had so signed) attested and subscribed the said will [*codicil*] in the presence of the said testator.

Sworn by the above-named deponent at   in the County
of   this   day of
   19   *(Signed)* CD

Before me
A Commissioner for Oaths.
[**Where the testator died on or after I January 1983, it is not necessary for the will or codicil, irrespective of its date of execution, to have been signed at the foot or end thereof. Furthermore, for deaths on or after 1 January 1983, it is permissible for an attesting witness to acknowledge his own signature (see s. 9 of the Wills Act 1837, as substituted, p. 720, ante).*]

Modifications of Form No. 2

2. (a) *Will signed in attestation clause or testimonium clause*

For paragraph 2 above, substitute:

2. The said testator executed the said will [*codicil*] on the day of the date thereof [*or* on the   day of   19] by signing his name in the attestation clause [*or* in the testimonium clause] thereof, as the same now appears thereon, meaning and intending the same for his final signature to the said will in the presence of me and of E F [etc.—*continue as in Form No. 2*].

2. (b) *Execution by acknowledgment of signature*

For paragraph 2 above, substitute:

2. The said testator executed the said will [*codicil*] on the day of the date thereof [*or on the day of   19] by acknowledging his signature 'A B', as the same now appears [*at the foot or end thereof**], to be his signature to the said will [*codicil*] in the presence of me and of E F, the other subscribed witness thereto, both of us being present at the same time, in the following manner, namely [by producing the said will [*codicil*] to us, pointing to his signature visible thereon and saying to us 'Will you witness my signature' or words to that effect] [*or as the case may be*], and we thereupon [etc. *—continue as in Form No. 2*].

[**See note to Form No. 2 above.*]

2. (c) *Imperfect signature, or will signed by mark: knowledge of contents*

For paragraph 2 above, substitute:

2. The testator executed the said will [*codicil*] on the day of the date thereof [*or on the   day of   19] by signing his name [*or* making his mark] [*or as the case may be*] [*at the foot or end thereof**], as the same now appears thereon, in the presence of me and of E F, the other subscribed witness thereto, both of us being present at the same time, and we thereupon attested and subscribed the said will [*codicil*] in the presence of the said testator.
3. Prevously to the execution of the said will [*codicil*] by the said testator, the same was read over to him by me [*or* by E F in my presence] [*or* the testator himself read the same in my presence] and the said testator at such time seemed perfectly to understand the same and to have full knowledge of the contents thereof.
   Sworn etc.

[**See note to Form No. 2 above.*]

2. (d) *Will signed by another person by direction of testator*

For paragraph 2 above, substitute:

2. The said testator executed the said will [*codicil*] on the day of the date thereof [*or on the   day of   19] by G H signing the testator's name [*or his own name, as the case may be*] [*at the foot or end thereof**], as the same now appears thereon, in the presence of and by the direction of the said testator and in the presence of me and of E F the other subscribed witness thereto, both of us being present at the same time, and the said testator thereupon acknowledged the said signature to be his signature to the said will [*codicil*] in our presence, and we thereupon attested and subscribed the said will [*codicil*] in the presence of the said testator.
3. [*Continue with paragraph 3 from Form No. 2 (c), above, as to the reading over of the will and the testator's knowledge of its contents.*]

[**See note to Form No. 2 above.*]

2. (e) *Signature of testator appears below those of the witnesses*

For paragraph 2 above, substitute:

2. The said testator executed the said will on the day of the date thereof by signing his name [*at the foot or end thereof**], as the same now appears thereon, meaning and intending the same as his final signature to the said will, in the presence of me and of E F, the other subscribed witness thereto, both of us being present at the same time, and we thereupon, after the testator had so signed, attested and subscribed the said will in the presence of the said testator.
3. The said E F and I signed our names above that of the testator because no space was left for our signatures to be placed below that of the said testator [*or as the case may be*].
   Sworn etc.

[**See note to Form No. 2 above.*]

3. Affidavit in support of due execution (evidence of execution not available)

(Heading as in Form No. 1)

I, C D, of   make oath and say that:

1. I am the sole executor [*or as the case may be*] named in the last will and testament of A B of   deceased, who died on the   day of   19   domiciled in England and Wales the said will, bearing date the   day of   19   being now produced to me and marked 'A'.
2. Referring to the fact that the said will is subscribed by E F and G H as attesting witnesses, I say that the said E F and G H are both dead, having died on or about the   day of   19   and the   day of   19   respectively [*or that I have caused enquiries to be made as to the whereabouts of the said E F and G H but they have not been traced despite such enquiries*] [*adapt as necessary*].
3. I have been unable to ascertain that any person other than the said E F and G H was present with the said A B at the execution of the said will.
4. The said testator died a [bachelor without issue or parent [*or as the case may be*] or any other person entitled in priority to share in his estate by virtue of any enactment] leaving I K and L M his lawful* nephews of the whole blood (being the lawful* sons of N O the lawful* sister of the whole blood of the said testator who died in his lifetime) and myself the deponent his lawful* brother of the whole blood, together the only persons who would be entitled to share in his estate if he had died intestate, who are all sui juris (and have consented to the admission of the said will to proof without further proof of due execution, as appears from the consents now produced to me and marked 'B' and 'C' respectively**).
   Sworn etc.

[*Where the deceased died on or after 4 April 1988 it is not necessary for the relationship, other than that of a spouse, to be lawful. Accordingly, with that exception, the word 'lawful' may be omitted.*
***If the consents are readily available they should be exhibited. The district judge or registrar may direct that notice be given to any person prejudiced by the will.*]

[**Note.**—*Form of consent to proof of will, No. 56. An affidavit establishing that the signature of the will is in the true and proper handwriting of the testator is also necessary (see Form No. 4). If affidavits of the handwriting of the witnesses can also be obtained, the consents of persons prejudiced may often be dispensed with.*]

4. Affidavit of handwriting

(Heading as in Form No. 1)

I, C D, of   make oath and say that:

1. I knew and was well acquainted with A B of   deceased, for many years before and down to the time of his death.
2. During such period I have frequently seen him write and also subscribe his name to documents, whereby I have become well acquainted with his handwriting.
3. Having now carefully perused and inspected the paper writing now produced to me and marked 'A', purporting to be and contain the last will and testament of the said deceased, bearing date   and being subscribed thus 'A B', I verily believe [the whole of the said will, together with] the signature 'A B', subscribed thereto as aforesaid, to be of the true and proper handwriting of the said deceased.
   Sworn etc.

[**Note.**—*This form may be adapted for use as an affidavit of handwriting of an attesting witness.*]

5. Affidavit of plight and condition and finding

(Heading as in Form No. 1)

I, C D, of   make oath and say that:

I. I am the sole executor named in the last will and testament of A B of   deceased, the said will bearing date the   day of   19   being now produced to me and marked 'A'.

2. Having viewed and perused the said will and particularly observed [*here recite the various obliterations, interlineations, erasures, and alterations (if any), or describe the plight and condition of the will, or any other matters requiring to be accounted for, and set forth the finding of the will in its present state, and, if possible, trace the will from the possession of the deceased in his lifetime up to the time of making the affidavit*] the same is now in all respects in the same state, plight and condition as when found [*or as the case may be*] by me as aforesaid.

Sworn etc.

6. Affidavit of search for will

(Heading as in Form No. 1)

I, C D, of   make oath and say that:

1. I am the sole executor named in the last will and testament of A B of   deceased, the said will bearing date the   day of   19   being now produced to me and marked 'A'.

2. Referring to the fact that the blank spaces originally left in the said will for the insertion of the day and month of the date thereof have never been supplied [*or that the said will is without date, or as the case may be*], I have made all possible searches and enquiries for any other will including a thorough search of the deceased's home and of all places where he usually kept important papers or valuables, but have been unable to discover any other will, codicil or testamentary paper whatever except the said will.

3. I know of no other person, such as a solicitor or bank manager, who might have kept papers for the deceased [except (*give details of any such persons and show that enquiries have been made of them*)].

4. I verily believe the said deceased died without having left any will, codicil, or testamentary paper whatever, other than the said will hereinbefore referred to.

Sworn. etc.

[**Note.**—*Where it is necessary to have an affidavit in both Forms 5 and 6, they may be conveniently combined in one document.*]

7. Affidavit as to alterations in a will (deponent an attesting witness)

(Heading as in Form No. 1)

I, C D, of   make oath and say that:

1. I am one of the subscribing witnesses to the last will and testament of A B of   deceased, the said will bearing date the   day of   19   being now produced to me and marked 'A'.

2. The said testator executed the said will on the day of the date thereof by signing his name [*at the foot or end thereof**], as the same now appears thereon, in the presence of me and of E F the other subscribed witness thereto, both of us being present at the same time, and we thereupon attested and subscribed the said will in the presence of the said testator.

3. Having particularly observed the words   interlined between the   and   lines of the   sheet of the said will [*or as the case may be*], I confirm that the said interlineation [*or alteration etc.*] was written and made in the said will previously [*or subsequently*] to the execution thereof [*or, that I am unable to say whether the said interlineation (or alteration) was made previously or subsequently to the execution of the said will*].

Sworn etc.

[**See note to Form No. 2 above.*]

8. Affidavit verifying alterations in a will (deposed to by the writer thereof)

(Heading as in Form No. 1)

I, C D, of   make oath and say that:

1. I was the writer of the last will and testament of A B of   deceased, bearing date

the   day of   19   the said will being now produced to me and marked 'A'.

2. Referring to an erasure appearing at the beginning of the   line of the   page thereof, immediately before the name   and to an interlineation of the word   between the   and   lines of the said page, I confirm that the said erasure and interlineation were made by me in the said will, in manner and form as the same now appear, previously to the execution of the said will.

Sworn etc.

[Note.—*If the deponent was present at the time of execution of the will he must also depose to the manner in which the will was executed (NCPR 16).*]

9. Affidavit as to foreign law

(Heading as in Form No. 1)

I, C D, of   [*an advocate or other person conversant with the laws of the country*], make oath and say that:

1. I am conversant with the laws and constitution of X and practise [*or* have practised for   years] as an advocate in the courts of that country [*or, if the deponent is other than an advocate, his full qualifications should be stated*].

2. I have referred to the [official (*or* notarial) copy of the] last will and testament of A B of   deceased, bearing date the   day of   19   and now produced to me and marked 'A'; and I say that the said will was made in conformity with the internal law of X and is valid by the aforesaid laws and constitution [*or* is accepted as valid under the said laws and constitution of X if it is valid under the internal law of Y, to which the question of validity is referred by the law of X because . . .]. [*Add where necessary:* Under the aforesaid laws and constitution the original of the said will is deposited permanently at the (Wills Registry at   ) (office of MN, notary at   ) and cannot be removed from such custody. The aforesaid copy of the said will is acceptable in the courts of X as evidence of the contents of the original will.]

3. [I am informed and verily believe (*set out facts leading to deponent's conclusions—see Note 2 to this form*).

4. In the aforesaid circumstances I say that E F and G H are according to the aforesaid laws and constitution the persons beneficially entitled to the estate of the said deceased.]

Sworn etc.

[Notes.—*(1) When it is sought to establish the validity of execution of a will under the Wills Act 1963, the affidavit of law should deal with the internal law of the territory or state concerned excluding any question of reference to the law of any other country. In order to comply with s. 6(2) of the Act, the affidavit should show whether a single system of law relating to the formal validity of wills obtains throughout the territory or state, or whether there is more than one such system. If the latter is the case, the affidavit should also show whether there is in force throughout the territory or state a rule indicating which system is to be applied to the case in question: if so, the deponent's opinion as to the validity of the execution of the will etc. should be based on the application of that rule. If there is no such rule, the deponent should state upon which system his conclusions are based. In this latter case, it will also be necessary to show in the affidavit of facts upon what grounds it is claimed that the deceased was most closely connected, at the time of execution of the will or at the time of his death (whichever is the relevant time: see s. 6(2)(b) of the Act), with the system of law referred to in the affidavit of law.*

(2) On an application for a grant under NCPR 30, the affidavit of law should refer to the facts and state the law applicable, but this must be supported by adequate evidence (normally on affidavit, or statement in the oath) as to the facts themselves (Registrar's Direction (1992) 20 November).

Form of affidavit of facts, No. 10.]

10. Affidavit of facts: Wills Act 1963

(Heading as in Form No. 1)

I, C D, of   make oath and say that:

1. I am the sole executor [*or as the case may be*] named in the last will and testament [*or codicil to the last will and testament*] dated the   day of   19   of A B of   who died on the   day of   19   the said will [codicil] being now produced to me and marked 'A'.
2. The said will [codicil] was executed at   in
[*or*]
At the time of execution of the said will [codicil] [*or at the date of his death*] the said A B [was domiciled in   ] [*or had his habitual residence at (address) in   ] [*or was a national of (name of state)*].
[*Add, if necessary (see s. 6(2), Wills Act 1963)*]
3. Of the systems of internal law in force in   relating to the formal validity of wills at the time of execution of the said will [codicil] [*or at the date of his death*] the said A B was most closely connected with the   system of internal law [*state grounds on which this connection is claimed* (e.g. place of birth, habitual residence, religion, caste, etc.)].
   Sworn etc.

11. Affidavit verifying the translation of a will

(Heading as in Form No. 1)

I, C D, of   make oath and say that:

1. I am well acquainted with the [*Welsh*] and English languages, and have had experience in the translation of documents from [*Welsh*] into English for   years. [*Set out brief details of any academic or other qualifications.*]
2. The paper writing now produced to me and marked 'A' is a true, faithful and complete translation of the last will and testament of A B deceased, which will bears date the   day of   and is written in the [*Welsh*] language and is now produced to me and marked 'B'.
   Sworn etc.

12. Affidavit as to British status of testator

(Heading as in Form No. 1)

I, C D, of   make oath and say that:

1. I am the sole executor named in the last will and testament of A B of   deceased, bearing date the   day of   19   and now produced to me and marked 'A'.
2. The said will was made at
3. The said A B was at the date of the said will a British subject [having been born of (*English*) parents at   ] [*or having been naturalised by certificate dated the   day of   19   ] [*or as the case may be, stating grounds on which British nationality is claimed— see Note (2) to this form*] and that his domicile of origin was [*English*].
   Sworn etc.

[**Notes.**—*(1) This form is used in connection with the proof of a will which it is sought to establish under the Wills Act 1861 (Lord Kingsdown's Act). This Act is repealed as from 1 January 1964, but without prejudice to wills executed before that date (Wills Act 1963, s. 7). See also paras. 3.374 ff., ante.*
(2) As to British nationality, see paras. 3.390 and 3.391, ante.]

13. Affidavit as to military service

(Heading as in Form No. 1)

I, C D, of   make oath and say that:

1. I believe the paper writing now produced to me and marked 'A' to contain the true and original last will and testament of A B of   who died on the   day of   19   at the said will bearing date the   day of   19
2. At the date of execution of the said will the said deceased was serving as a soldier [*or an airman*] in actual military service [*or as a seaman in actual naval service*] and was domiciled in England and Wales.

[*or* At the date of execution of the said will the said deceased was a seaman at sea, being on board   [*name of vessel*] [*or as the case may be*], and was domiciled in England and Wales.]

Sworn etc.

[**Notes.**—*In the case of a will made by a member of the forces at a time when a state of war does not exist, the affidavit should include the details establishing that the testator was at the date of the will on actual military service as understood at the relevant time (see paras. 3.346 and 3.347, ante).*

If the testator was under age at the date of execution of the will, his age should be stated in the affidavit.]

14. Affidavit of identity of executor

(Heading as in Form No. 1)

I, George William Smithson, of   make oath and say that:

1. A B of   deceased, died on the   day of   19   having made and duly executed his last will and testament bearing date the   day of   19   and therein appointed 'William Smithson, of 12, High Street, Highgate, butcher' [*or* 'Mr Smithson, of 12, High Street, Highgate'] sole executor.
2. At the date of the said will no one of the name of William Smithson [*or* no person other than myself bearing the name of Smithson] was living at 12, High Street, aforesaid.
3. I was living at that address at the date of the will, and was the only butcher named Smithson trading there; and I am usually known as [*or* the testator always referred to me as] William Smithson and that the testator informed me he had appointed me as [*or* had asked me to be] his executor [*adapt in accordance with the circumstances*].

Sworn etc.

15. Affidavit as to alias (will)

(Heading as in Form No. 1)

In the estate of John Winston, otherwise John Wanstone, deceased.
I, A B, of   make oath and say that:

1. John Winston, otherwise John Wanstone, of   deceased, died on the   day of   19   having made and duly executed his last will and testament, bearing date the day of   19   and thereof appointed me one of the executors.
2. The true name of the deceased was John Winston.
3. The said deceased purchased certain freehold property at   , and such property was conveyed to him in the name of John Wanstone.
[*or*]
At the time of the death of the said deceased, there was standing to his credit in X Bank Ltd a sum of money in the name of John Wanstone.
4. In the circumstances it is desired that the grant of probate of the will of the said deceased should issue in the names of John Winston, otherwise John Wanstone.

Sworn etc.

16. Affidavit as to alias (administration)

(Heading as in Form No. 1)

In the estate of John Henry Jones, otherwise John Jones, deceased.
I, A J, of   make oath and say that:

1. I am the lawful son of John Henry Jones, otherwise John Jones, of   deceased, who died on the   day of   19   intestate.
2. The true name of the deceased was John Henry Jones.
3. The said deceased effected a policy of insurance on his own life in the name of John Jones in the X Insurance Society Limited.

[*or*]
At the time of the death of the said deceased a sum of money was standing to his credit in the National Savings Bank in the name of John Jones.
4. In order to deal with the said property, it is desired that the grant should issue in the names of John Henry Jones, otherwise John Jones.
    Sworn etc.

17. Affidavit to lead order for grant under s. 116 of the Supreme Court Act 1981

(Heading as in Form No. 1)

I, E F, of   make oath and say that:

1. A B of   died on the   day of   19   intestate a widow, domiciled in England and Wales, leaving C D her lawful* son, the only person entitled to her estate.
2. I am informed by my solicitors, Messrs X and Y, and verily believe that the bundle now produced to me and marked 'A' contains true copies of the letters sent to the said C D by them and the replies thereto received from him, from which it appears that the said C D is willing neither to apply for letters of administration of the estate of the said deceased nor to renounce his right thereto.
3. I am a creditor of the said deceased in the sum of £   in respect of goods sold and delivered [*or as the case may be*].
4. The gross value of the estate of the said deceased amounts to £   and after deduction of debts and incumbrances the net value of the estate is £
5. No minority or life interest arises under the intestacy.
6. In the aforesaid circumstances I apply for an order that letters of administration of the estate of the said deceased be granted to me, a creditor of the said deceased, under and by virtue of section 116 of the Supreme Court Act 1981.
    Sworn etc.

[*Where the deceased died on or after 4 April 1988 it is not necessary for the relationship of anyone except a spouse to be lawful. Accordingly, with that exception, the word 'lawful' may be omitted.*]

[**Note.**—*Paragraphs 1, 4, 5 and 6 indicate the formal parts of an affidavit of this nature, and these, with the necessary adaptations, should be included in all cases. The facts which necessitate the application will, of course, vary in each case. In the case of a missing beneficiary or other person having a prior right to a grant full details of the enquiries made and attempts to trace him or her should be set out. See also Form No. 22 as to the insertion of advertisements, the contents of which may be embodied in this affidavit, where appropriate.*]

18. Affidavit to lead district judge's or registrar's order appointing persons to obtain administration for the use and benefit of a minor

[**Note.**—*This form can be adapted to the case of the minority of a sole executor or residuary legatee, or other person entitled to a grant where the deceased died testate.*]

(Heading as in Form No. 1)

We, C D of   and E F of   jointly and severally make oath and say that:

1. A B of   died on the   day of   19   intestate a widower, domiciled in England and Wales, leaving G B his lawful* son the only person entitled to his estate, who is now a minor of the age of   years.
2. There is no parent, guardian or other person with parental responsibility for the said minor.
3. No application has been made to make the said minor a ward of court and no such application is currently contemplated.
4. We are the lawful grandparents [*or the lawful uncle and aunt of the whole blood or as the case may be*] (and nearest of kin) of the said minor.
[*or*]
J K the lawful grandfather and only nearest-of-kin of the said minor has renounced his right to take a grant for the use and benefit of the said minor.
5. [*Here state who has had the care and charge of the minor since the death of the*

deceased, and any other facts relied on in support of the application.]

6. The gross value of the estate of the said deceased is £   and that after deduction of debts and incumbrances the net value of the estate is £

7. We hereby apply for an order appointing us to obtain letters of administration of the estate of the said deceased for the use and benefit of the said minor limited until he shall attain the age of eighteen years.

    Sworn etc.

[**Where the deceased died on or after 4 April 1988 it is not necessary for the relationship to be specified as either lawful or natural.*]

[**Notes.**—*This form should be adapted in accordance with the circumstances.*

If there is a parent or guardian with parental responsibility, unless such parent or guardian has renounced his or her right to a grant for the use and benefit of the minor it should be shown for what reason it is desired to pass him or her over.]

19. Affidavit to lead district judge's or registrar's order for appointment of a person for the purpose of renouncing on behalf of a minor

(Heading as in Form No. 1)

I, C D, of   make oath and say that:

1. A B of   deceased, died on the   day of   19   intestate a widower, domiciled in England and Wales, leaving E B his lawful* son, and the only person entitled to his estate, who is now a minor of the age of   years.

2. There is no parent, guardian or other person with parental responsibility for the said minor.

3. No application has been made to make the said minor a ward of court and no such application is currently contemplated.

4. I am the lawful grandmother and only [*or* one of the] nearest of kin of the said minor, and I hereby apply for an order appointing me for the purpose of renouncing on his behalf all right and title to letters of administration of the estate of the said A B deceased.

5. The gross value of the said estate is £   and after deduction of debts and incumbrances the net value of the estate is £

    Sworn etc.

[**See note* to Form No. 18, above.*]

20. Affidavit of heir-at-law in support of claim to grant (where the death occurred before 1926)

(Heading as in Form No. 1)

I, E B, of   make oath and say that:

1. The above-named A B of   died on the   day of   19   seised of two freehold dwelling-houses, being Nos. 4 and 5, Barking Road, Chester, in the county of Chester, which were devised to him by the will of   who died on the   day of   19 .

2. The said A B was also seised of a plot of freehold building land situate at   in the county of   which was purchased by him.

3. That the said A B was married once only, namely, to C B, formerly C S, and had issue three lawful children and no more.

4. I, the said E B, am the eldest born son and heir-at-law of the said A B, being one of the said three children of the said A B and C B.

    Sworn etc.

(See also No. 21)

21. Affidavit of heirship: another form

(Heading as in Form No. 1)

I, C D, of   make oath and say that:

1. The above-named A B (wife of E B), of   was married once only, namely, to the said E B now residing at   .

2. The said A B died on   19   without leaving any parent or other ancestor, and without ever having had any issue.

3. I am the heir-at-law of the said A B being the lawful child and the eldest born son of J S and E S his wife, who were respectively the lawful father and lawful mother of the said A B.

4. The said A B died possessed of certain real estate to which she became entitled under the will of E H proved in the Principal Probate Registry on the   day of   19   being part of the real estate of the said E H and devised by him to trustees upon trust to pay the rents thereof to the said A B's mother, the said E S, during her life, and after her death to the use of the children of the said E S in fee simple.

5. The said E S died on the   day of   19 .

Sworn etc.

22. Affidavit as to the insertion of advertisements for kin

(Heading as in Form No. 1)

I, E F, of   make oath and say that:

1. I am the solicitor for C D who is applying for letters of administration of the estate of A B of   deceased.

2. Acting on behalf of the said C D, I caused an advertisement requesting the relations (if any) of the said deceased to apply to me to be inserted once in the London morning newspaper called the   on the   day of   and once in the London morning newspaper called the   on the   day of   and once in the London evening newspaper called the   on the   day of   as appears from the said newspapers now produced to me in a bundle marked 'A'.

3. No application whatever has been made to me in consequence of or in answer to the said advertisement, nor have I been able to obtain any information respecting the relations (if any) of the said deceased.

Sworn etc.

23. Affidavit as to the insertion of advertisements for the recovery of a lost will

(Heading as in Form No. 1)

I, C D, of   make oath and say that:

1. I am the solicitor for E F the sole executrix named in the last will and testament of A B of   deceased, and the person applying for probate of the said will as contained in a copy thereof.

2. On the   day of   19   I caused to be inserted in the London newspaper called the ' ' an advertisement in the following terms: 'A B deceased.

Any person having knowledge of any will made by the above-named, late of   who died on   at   is requested to communicate with C D, solicitor, of   . It is believed that the said deceased made a will in or about the year 19   but the same cannot be found.'

3. The said newspaper is now produced to me and marked 'A' [*and so on with any other newspaper*].

4. No application has been made to me in consequence of or in answer to the said advertisement, nor have I been able to obtain any information respecting the original will therein referred to.

Sworn etc.

24. Affidavit in proof of incapacity

(Heading as in Form No. 1)

I, C D, of   make oath and say that:

1. I am [*state qualifications*] and I have for the last   years attended E F of   in my professional capacity.

2.　The said E F is now, and has been for　　　　　years, in my opinion incapable by reason of mental disorder of managing his property and affairs, and is unlikely to recover the use of his mental faculties.

　　Sworn etc.

[**Note.**—*A certificate in the form given in para. **11.226**, ante, by the Responsible Medical Officer (where the incapable person is a patient who is resident in an institution) or by the incapable person's doctor (in other cases) is normally sufficient in lieu of an affidavit.*]

25. Affidavit to lead amendment of grant

(Heading as in Form No. I)

I, C D, of　　　　make oath and say that:

1.　On the　　　　day of　　　　19　　letters of administration of the estate of A B of
　　　　deceased, were granted at the Principal [*or*　　　　District Probate] Registry to me the lawful father and only person entitled to the estate of the said deceased.
2.　In the said letters of administration the date of the deceased's death is stated to be the 14th day of November 19　　whereas the true date was the 24th day of the same month and year, as appears by the certificate of death now produced to me and marked 'A'.
3.　The error arose by my not observing when I read the oath to lead the grant that the wrong day, namely, the '14th', had been inadvertently inserted in that document.
4.　I apply for an order that the said letters of administration be amended by substituting '24th' for the '14th' in the date of death of the deceased.

　　Sworn etc.

26. Affidavit to lead amendment to 'save and except settled land'

(Heading as in Form No. 1)

We, A B of　　　　and C D of　　　　make oath and say that:

1.　E F of　　　　died on the　　　　day of　　　　19　　at　　　　having by his last will appointed us executors.
2.　On the　　　　day of　　　　19　　probate of the said will was granted to us at the Principal [*or* District Probate] Registry.
3.　There was land vested in the deceased immediately before his death which was settled previously thereto (and not by his will) and remained settled land notwithstanding his death, namely under the will of　　　which was proved at the　　　Registry on the　　　day of　　of which the present trustees [*or* under a Deed of Settlement dated　　　of which the present trustees], for the purposes of the Settled Land Act 1925, are L M and N O.
4.　The value of the said settled land was [*or* was not] included in the said grant [and is in addition to the value of the estate in the said grant].
5.　We apply for an order that the said grant be amended by the addition thereto of the limitation 'save and except settled land'.

　　Sworn etc.

27. Affidavit—increase of estate—further security

(Heading as in Form No. 1)

I, C D, of　　　　make oath and say that:

1.　On the　　　　day of　　　　19　　letters of administration of the estate of A B of
　　　　deceased, were granted to me at the Principal [*or*　　　　District Probate] Registry.
2.　The gross value of the said estate was then sworn to amount to £
3.　I have since discovered that the value of the said estate exceeds that amount; and that the true gross value thereof is £

　　Sworn etc.

28. Affidavit to lead order for notation of domicile (estate in Scotland)

(Heading as in Form No. 1)

I, C D, of   make oath and say that:

1. A B of   deceased, died on the   day of   19   domiciled in England and Wales.
2. On the   day of   19   probate of the will [*or as the case may be*] of the said deceased was granted to me at the Principal [*or   District Probate*] Registry.
[3. The gross value of the estate in respect of which the grant was made was then sworn to be £
4. No additional estate has since come to my knowledge [*or* Additional estate has since come to my knowledge, of which the value is £   and none of such additional estate is situate in Scotland].
5. Part of the said estate amounting to £   , further particulars of which are set forth in the schedule, now produced to me marked 'A', is in Scotland.]
6. I apply for an order that it be noted on the said grant that the deceased died domiciled in England and Wales.
    Sworn etc.

[**Note.**—*Where the grant issued on or after 1 March 1961, the inclusion of the contents of paragraphs 3, 4 and 5 is unnecessary.*]

29. Affidavit to lead order for notation of domicile (estate in Northern Ireland)

(Heading as in Form No. 1)

I, C D, of   make oath and say that:

1. A B, of   deceased, died on the   day of   19   domiciled in England and Wales.
2. On the   day of   19   probate of the will [*or as the case may be*] of the said deceased was granted to me at the Principal [*or   District Probate*] Registry.
[3. The gross value of the estate in respect of which the grant was made was then sworn to be £
4. No additional estate has since come to my knowledge [*or* Additional estate has since come to my knowledge, of which the value is £   and none of such additional estate is situate in Scotland [*or as the case may be*].]
5. In addition to the said estate the deceased possessed estate amounting to £   , further particulars of which are set forth in the schedule now produced to me marked 'A', in Northern Ireland].
6. I apply for an order that it be noted on the said grant that the deceased died domiciled in England and Wales.
    Sworn etc.

[**Note.**—*Where the grant issued on or after 1 March 1961, the inclusion of the contents of paragraphs 3, 4 and 5 is unnecessary.*]

30. Affidavit to lead citation to accept or refuse probate

(NCPR 47(1))

(Heading as in Form No. 1)

I, C D, of   make oath and say that:

1. A B of   deceased, died on the   day of   19   domiciled in England and Wales, having made and duly executed his last will and testament bearing date the   day of   19   [now remaining in the Principal Registry of the Family Division *or* in the   District Probate Registry] and thereof appointed E F of   sole executor.
2. The said E F has not as yet taken upon himself probate of the said will.
3. I am the residuary legatee and devisee named in the said will [*or* The said deceased did not in his said will name any residuary legatee or devisee, and he died a widower without

issue or parent [*or as the case may be*] or any other person entitled in priority to share in the undisposed-of estate by virtue of any enactment, and I am the lawful* [*brother of the whole blood*] of the said deceased and one of the persons entitled to share in the estate undisposed of by the said will], and I wish to obtain letters of administration (with will) of the estate of the said deceased.

4. No minority or life interest arises in the estate of the said deceased.

5. To the best of my knowledge information and belief, there was no land vested in the deceased which was settled previously to his death and not by his will and which remained settled land notwithstanding his death.

Sworn etc.

[**Notes.**—(*1*) *Where the deceased died on or after 4 April 1988 it is not necessary for the relationship of anyone, except a spouse, to be lawful. Accordingly, with that exception, the word 'lawful' may be omitted.*

(*2*) *For practice where a life or minority interest arises, see para.* **24.42**, *ante.*

(*3*) *The affidavit should not be sworn until after the draft citation has been settled—see paras.* **24.45** *ff., ante.*

(*4*) *Form of citation, No. 48.*]

31. Affidavit to lead citation to accept or refuse administration

(NCPR 47(1))

(Heading as in Form No. 1)

We, C B of   tailor and D B of   carpenter, make oath and say that:

1. A B of   deceased, died on the   day of   19   intestate, domiciled in England and Wales, without issue or parent or any other person entitled in priority to share in his estate by virtue of any enactment, leaving E B of   his lawful widow and relict him surviving.

2. The said E B has not as yet taken upon herself letters of administration of the estate of the said deceased.

3. We are the lawful* brothers of the whole blood and two of the persons entitled to share in the estate of the said deceased, and wish to obtain letters of administration of the estate of the said deceased.

4. No life or minority interest [*or as the case may be*] arises under the intestacy.

5. To the best of our knowledge, information and belief there was no land vested in the deceased which was settled previously to his death and which remained settled land notwithstanding his death.

Sworn etc.

[**See notes 1–3 to Form No. 30, above.*]

(Form of citation, No. 49.)

32. Affidavit of creditor to lead citation (no known kin)

(NCPR 47(1))

(Heading as in Form No. 1)

I, C D, of   make oath and say that:

1. A B of   deceased, died on the   day of   19   intestate, domiciled in England and Wales, a widower without known issue, parent, brother or sister of the whole or half blood or their issue, grandparent, uncle or aunt of the whole or half blood or their issue or any other person entitled in priority to share in his estate by virtue of any enactment.

2. [*Set out in detail the nature of the inquiries which have been made to trace the kin of the deceased.*]

3. The said deceased was at the time of his death justly and truly indebted to me in the sum of £   for goods sold and delivered [*or as the case may be*], and no part of such sum has been since received by me or by any person on my behalf but the whole thereof still remains

justly due and owing to me, and I hold no security whatever for the same or any part thereof.

4. No life or minority interest arises under the intestacy.

5. To the best of my knowledge, information and belief, there was no land vested in the deceased which was settled previously to his death and which remained settled land notwithstanding his death.

6. The gross value of the estate of the said deceased is £

Sworn etc.

(Form of citation, No. 50.)

[**Notes.**—*(1) Where a creditor desires to cite the persons entitled to share in the estate, Form 31, adapted as necessary, should be used.*
(2) See note (3) to Form 30, above.]

33. Affidavit to lead citation against executor to whom power is reserved to accept or refuse double probate

(NCPR 47(2))

(Heading as in Form No. 1)

I, John Jones, of   grocer, make oath and say that:

1. A B of   died on the   day of   19   domiciled in England and Wales having made and duly executed his last will and testament bearing date the   day of   19   wherein he named C D of   and E F of   as executors.

2. On the   day of   19   probate of the said will was granted at the Principal [*or* District Probate] Registry to the said C D power being reserved of making the like grant to the said E F.

3. The said C D died on the   day of   19   leaving part of the estate of the said deceased unadministered.

4. The said E F has not as yet taken upon himself probate and execution of the said will.

5. I am the sole executor of the will of the said C D probate thereof having been granted to me at the   Registry on the   day of   19   and I wish to act as executor (by chain of representation) of the will of the said deceased.

6. The gross value of the estate of the said deceased left unadministered is £

Sworn etc.

[*See note (3) to Form 30, above.*]

(Form of citation, No. 52.)

34. Affidavit to lead citation requiring an intermeddling executor to take probate

(NCPR 47(3))

(Heading as in Form No. 1)

I, C D, of   bookmaker, make oath and say that:

1. A B of   made and duly executed his last will and testament, bearing date the   day of   19   [now remaining in the Principal Registry of the Family Division *or* in the District Probate Registry] and thereof appointed E F sole executor and me this deponent residuary legatee and devisee.

2. The said A B died on the   day of   19   domiciled in England and Wales.

3. More than six calendar months have elapsed since the date of the death of the said deceased, and no proceedings concerning the validity of the said will are pending.

4. The said E F has neglected to prove the said will.

5. The said E F has intermeddled in the estate of the said deceased by collecting the rents owing to the said deceased [*or as the case may be. Instances must be set out*].

6. I wish to compel the said E F to take probate of the said will.

Sworn etc.

[*See note (3) to Form 30, above.*]

(*Form of citation, No. 53.*)

35. Affidavit to lead citation to propound a will

(NCPR 48)

(*Heading as in Form No. 1*)

We, C D of   grocer, and E F of   baker, make oath and say that:

1. A B of   died on the   day of   19   domiciled in England and Wales, a widower leaving us, his lawful* sons, the only persons entitled to share in his estate in case he died intestate [*or* having made and duly executed his last will and testament dated the day of   [now remaining in the Principal Registry of the Family Division *or* in the   District Probate Registry] wherein he named us executors].

2. The said deceased left a certain paper writing dated the   day of   19   purporting to be a will [now remaining in the Principal Registry of the Family Division *or* in the   District Probate Registry], wherein he appointed G H of   sole executrix and residuary legatee and devisee.

3. We seek to issue a citation against the said G H to propound the said will or paper writing dated the   day of   should she think it for her interest so to do, and that in default letters of administration of the estate of the said A B as having died intestate be granted to us [*or* that in default probate of the said last will and testament of the said deceased dated the   day of   be granted to us].

   Sworn etc.

[**See notes to Form No. 30, above.*]

(*Form of citation, No. 54.*)

36. Affidavit of party cited—accepting grant

(*Heading as in Form No. 1*)

I, C D, of   research chemist, make oath and say that:

1. By a citation issued on the   day of   19   and served upon me on the   day of   19   I was duly cited to accept or refuse letters of administration of the estate of A B the deceased in this matter [*or* to take probate of the will *etc*].

2. On the   day of   19   I entered an appearance to such citation by my solicitors herein, and a sealed copy of the appearance was, on the   day of   19   duly served by my said solicitors on Messrs   of   the solicitors for the citors.

3. I am ready and willing to take letters of administration as aforesaid.
   Sworn etc.

37. Affidavit to lead summons to exhibit an inventory and account

(*Heading as in Form No. 1*)

I, C D, of   [*occupation*] make oath and say that:

1. A B of   deceased, died on the   day of   19   intestate, domiciled in England and Wales, leaving M B his lawful widow, and I am his lawful* daughter, and one of the persons entitled to share in his estate [*or* I am a creditor of the said deceased].

2. On the   day of   19   letters of administration of the estate of the said deceased were granted at the   Probate Registry to the said M B and E F.

3. The said M B and E F have sworn the value of the estate of the said deceased to amount to £   , but I verily believe this to be considerably less than the true value thereof.

[4. Part of the said estate consists of stock and growing crops, which should be forthwith valued and appraised before the same are removed or sold, in order that the true value thereof as assets belonging to the said estate may be satisfactorily ascertained.] [*or* The said deceased was at the date of his death justly and truly indebted to me in the sum of £   for goods sold and delivered, and I have not received from the said M B and E F payment of the said sum or any part thereof.]

5. In the circumstances, I apply for an order calling upon the said M B and E F to exhibit, upon oath, a true and perfect inventory of the estate of the said deceased and to render a just and true account of their administration of the estate of the said deceased and to file the same in the   Registry within   days from the date of service of the order upon them.
    Sworn etc.

[*See note (1) to Form No. 30, above.]

38. Affidavit to lead subpoena to bring in testamentary document

(NCPR 50(2))

(Heading as in Form No. 1)

I, C D, of   tailor, make oath and say that:

1. A B of   deceased, died on the   day of   19   domiciled in England and Wales having made and duly executed his last will and testament, bearing date the   day of   19   and thereof appointed E F and G H executors, and me residuary legatee.

2. The said will is now in the possession, custody or power of the said E F and G H or one of them, and that they, the said E F and G H, have neglected or declined to prove the said will or renounce probate thereof, and I request that the said will should be brought into the Principal Registry [*or the   District Probate Registry*] of this Division in order that I may prove the same or otherwise act as I may be advised.

3. The said E F resides at   and the said G H resides at
    Sworn etc.

(For form of subpoena see Form No. 190.)

39. Affidavit to lead revocation of grant by consent

(Heading as in Form No. 1)

I, C D, of   grocer, make oath and say that:

1. A B of   died on the   day of   19   intestate, domiciled in England and Wales a widower, without issue or parent or brother or sister of the whole blood, brother or sister of the half blood or their issue or grandparent or any other person entitled in priority to share in his estate by virtue of any enactment.

2. I verily believed (until I had, as hereinafter deposed, ascertained to the contrary) that the said deceased left surviving him no issue of brother or sister of the whole blood, and being a lawful* uncle of the whole blood of the said deceased I applied at the Principal [*or   District Probate*] Registry for, and on the   day of   19   I obtained therefrom, letters of administration of the estate of the said deceased, which were granted to me on the basis that I was one of the persons entitled to share in the estate of the said deceased.

3. Since the date last mentioned I have caused further inquiries to be made respecting the relatives of the said deceased, and I have thereby ascertained that E F of   is the lawful* nephew of the whole blood and the only person entitled to the estate of the said deceased.

4. I therefore seek an order that the letters of administration shall be revoked and declared null and void.
    Sworn etc.

[*See note (1) to Form No. 30, above.]

40. Affidavit of service of citation

(Heading as in Form No. 1)

I, E F, of   clerk to   of   solicitor, make oath and say that:

1. I did on the   day of   duly serve C D of   with a true copy of a citation issued out of the Principal Registry of the Family Division [*or out of the   District Probate Registry*]

in the above-named matter, by delivering to and leaving the copy with him at   and a sealed copy of the citation is now produced to me and marked 'A'.

2. [*State the means by which the deponent knew the identity of the person served.*]
    Sworn etc.

[**Note.**—*In non-contentious probate business an affidavit of personal service of any document should include a statement of the means by which the server knew the identity of the person served (Registrar's Direction (1964) 21 April).*]

41. Affidavit of service of warning

(NCPR 44, 67)

(Heading as in Form No. 1)

I, C D, of   clerk to   of   solicitor, make oath and say that:

1. On the   day of   19   I duly served   with a true copy of the warning now produced to me and marked 'A', by delivering to and leaving the said copy with a clerk of Messrs   of   at their office aforesaid [*or* leaving the same at the office of Messrs   of   ], that being the address for service on the said   given in his caveat, before the hour of 4 in the afternoon (12 noon on Saturdays) [*or* by sending the same by prepaid ordinary post or registered post or recorded delivery to   , the address for service of the said   given in his caveat *or* by leaving the same at the   document exchange for box number   included in the address for service on the said   given in his caveat *or* by leaving the same at the   document exchange for transmission to the   document exchange for box number   included in the address for service on the said   given in his caveat].
    Sworn etc.

APPEARANCE

42. Appearance to warning or citation

(NCPR 44(10), 46(6))

In the High Court of Justice
Family Division
The Principal [*or*   District Probate] Registry
    Caveat No.   dated the   day of   19   .
    [Citation dated the   day of   19   .]
    Full name and address of deceased:
    Full name and address of person warning [*or* citor]:
[*Here set out the interest of the person warning, or citor, as shown in warning or citation.*]
    Full name and address of caveator [*or* person cited].
[*Here set out the interest of the caveator or person cited, stating date of the will (if any) under which such interest arises.*]
    Enter an appearance for the above-named caveator [*or* person cited] in this matter.
    Dated the   day of   19
    (Signed)
whose address for service is: Solicitor [*or* 'In person'].

[*NCPR 1987, Form 5.*]

APPOINTMENT

43. Appointment of nominee of a county council to take grant

(Heading as in Form No. 1)

At a meeting of the Committee of the County Council of the County of   held at   on   the   day of   19

It was resolved

That C D the Officer for   be, and is hereby, appointed nominee of the County Council of the County of   for the purpose of taking out letters of administration of the estate of A B of   in the county of   who died on the   day of   19   and of whom the said County Council is a creditor.

I certify the above to be a true copy of the minute of the Resolution duly passed at the above-mentioned meeting.

> (*Signed*)
> Clerk of the Council.

ASSIGNMENT

44. Assignment of bond

(Heading as in Form No. 1)

KNOW ALL MEN by these presents, that I, B C, Senior District Judge of the Principal Registry of the Family Division of the High Court of Justice, pursuant to section 167 of the Supreme Court of Judicature (Consolidation) Act 1925, and by virtue of an order [*quote the order for assignment made on summons*] made on the   day of   19   have assigned and by these presents do assign to C D of   in the county of   farmer, the annexed bond bearing date the   day of   19   for the due administration of the estate of A B deceased, of and all benefit and advantage arising therefrom.

> (L.S.)
> Senior District Judge.

Signed, sealed and delivered by the within-named BC in the presence of

[**Note.**—*This form is obsolete save in respect of grants of representation issued before 1 January 1972.*]

CAVEAT

45. Caveat

(NCPR 44(2))

In the High Court of Justice
Family Division
The Principal [*or*   District Probate] Registry

Let no grant be sealed in the estate of [*full name and address*] deceased, who died on the   day of   19   without notice to [*name of party by whom or on whose behalf the caveat is entered*].

Dated this   day of   19   .

(*Signed*)   [*to be signed by the caveator's solicitor or by the caveator if acting in person*] whose address for service is:

Solicitor for the said   [*If the caveator is acting in person, substitute 'In person'.*]

[*NCPR 1987, Form 3.*]

CERTIFICATES

[**Note.**—*See para. 11.226, ante for certificate as to mental incapacity.*]

46. Certificate as to grant, estate and security

(Heading as in Form No. 1)

I,   , one of the District Judges of the Principal Registry of the Family Division of the High Court of Justice in England and Wales, hereby certify that letters of administration [with will annexed] of all the estate which by law devolves to and vests in the personal

representative of A B late of   deceased, were granted by the court on the   day
of   19   to E F of   , that the said estate was sworn in the oath to lead the grant of such
letters of administration [with will annexed] to amount in value to the sum of £   and that
the said E F has given security in this court in the sum of £   such security being in the guarantee of G H of   and JK of   as sureties.
Dated the   day of   19   District Judge.

47. Certificate of further security

(Heading as in Form No. 1)

In the estate of A B deceased.

I, the undersigned District Judge of the Principal [*or* Registrar of the   District
Probate] Registry of the Family Division of the High Court of Justice do hereby certify that
the gross value of the estate of A B of   deceased, originally sworn to amount to the sum
of £   has now been sworn to amount to the sum of £   and security has been given for the
increased amount.

Dated the   day of   19   .
Letters of administration(   )
were granted at the
Probate Registry on the
day of   .   District Judge/Registrar.

CITATIONS

48. Citation to accept or refuse probate

(NCPR 47(1))

(Heading as in Form No. 1)

Elizabeth the Second, by the grace of God, of the United Kingdom of Great Britain and
    Northern Ireland and of our other realms and territories Queen, Head of the
    Commonwealth, Defender of the Faith:

To E F of
    Take notice that C D has stated in an affidavit sworn the   day of   19   that A B
of   died on the   day of   19   domiciled in England and Wales having made and
duly executed his last will and testament dated the   day of   19   [now remaining in
the Principal Registry of the Family Division *or* in the   District Probate Registry],
that you the said E F are named in that will as sole executor, that there is no residuary legatee
or devisee named in that will, that the said deceased died a widower without issue or parent,
and that the said C D is the lawful* brother of the whole blood and one of the persons
entitled to share in the undisposed-of estate of the said deceased:
    Now this is to command you the said E F that within eight days after service hereof on
you, inclusive of the day of such service, you do cause an appearance to be entered in the
Principal Registry of the Family Division of the High Court of Justice, at Somerset House,
Strand, London WC2R 1LP [*or* in the   District Probate Registry at   ] and accept or
refuse probate of the said will, or show cause why letters of administration, with the said will
annexed, of all the estate which by law devolves to and vests in the personal representative
of the said deceased, should not be granted to the said C D. And take further notice that, in
default of your so appearing and accepting and extracting probate of the said will, our said
court will proceed to grant letters of administration, with the said will annexed, of the said
estate to the said C D, your absence notwithstanding.
    Dated at   this   day of   19   .

Extracted by   .
of   *(Signed)*
Solicitor.   District Judge/ Registrar.

[*See notes to Form No. 30, above.*]

(*Form of affidavit to lead citation, No. 30*)

49. Citation to accept or refuse administration

(NCPR 47(1))

(*Heading as in Form No. 1*)

Elizabeth the Second etc. (*as in Form No. 48*).

To E B of   .

Take notice that C B and D B have stated in a joint affidavit, sworn the   day
of   19   that A B of   died on the   day of   19   domiciled in England
and Wales intestate, leaving you the said E B his lawful widow and one of the persons entitled to share in his estate and the said C B and D B his lawful* [*or* natural*] sons and two
of the persons entitled to share in the estate of the said deceased:

Now this is to command the said E B that within eight days after service hereof on
you, inclusive of the day of such service, you do cause an appearance to be entered in the
Principal Registry of the Family Division of the High Court of Justice at Somerset House,
Strand, London WC2R lLP [*or* in the   District Probate Registry at   ] and accept or
refuse letters of administration of all the estate which by law devolves to and vests in the personal representative of the said deceased, or show cause why the same should not be granted to
the said C B and D B. And take further notice that, in default of your so appearing and accepting and extracting the said letters of administration, our said court will proceed to grant letters
of administration of the said estate to the said C B and D B, your absence notwithstanding.

Dated at   this   day of   19   .

Extracted by   .
of   (*Signed*)
Solicitor.   District Judge/Registrar.

[*If the deceased died on or after 4 April 1988 the word 'lawful' or 'natural' can be
omitted.*]

[**Note.**—*This form may be adapted for use in cases where specific persons are cited by a
creditor.*]

(*Form of affidavit to lead citation, No. 31.*)

50. Citation by creditor against kin (if any) to accept or refuse administration

(NCPR 47(1))

(*Heading as in Form No. 1*)

Elizabeth the Second etc. (*as in Form No. 48*):

To the kin (if any) who are entitled to share and all other persons having or claiming any
interest in the estate of A B deceased.

Take notice that C D has stated in an affidavit sworn the   day of   19   that
A B of   died on the   day of   19   domiciled in England and Wales intestate, a
widower without known issue or parent, brother or sister of the whole or half blood or their
issue, grandparent, uncle or aunt of the whole or half blood or their issue, or any other person
entitled in priority to share in his estate by virtue of any enactment, and that the said C D is a
creditor of the said deceased:

Now this is to command you that within one month after service by publication hereof on
you, inclusive of the day of such service, you do cause an appearance to be entered in the
Principal Registry of the Family Division of the High Court of Justice at Somerset House,
Strand, London WC2R 1LP [*or* in the   District Probate Registry at   ] and accept or
refuse letters of administration of all the estate which by law devolves to and vests in the
personal representative of the said deceased, or show cause why letters of administration of
his estate should not be granted to the said C D. And take further notice that, in default of
your so appearing and accepting and extracting letters of administration as aforesaid, our

said court will proceed to grant letters of administration of the estate of the said deceased to the said C D, your absence notwithstanding.

Dated at   this   day of   19   .

Extracted by   .
of   *(Signed)*
Solicitor.   District Judge/Registrar.

[**Note.**—*If the applicant is the nominee of a county council, he should be so described, and the sealed or certified appointment lodged (see Form No. 43).*]

(Form of affidavit to lead citation, No. 32.)

51. Citation by creditor against a minor to accept or refuse administration

(NCPR 47(1); RSC Order 80, r. 16(2))

(Heading as in Form No. 1)

Elizabeth the Second etc. *(as in Form No. 48)*:
    To G H of   .
    Take notice that E F has stated in an affidavit sworn the   day of   19   that A B of   died on the   day of   19   domiciled in England and Wales intestate, a bachelor without issue or parent or any other person entitled in priority to share in his estate by virtue of any enactment, leaving you the said G H, his lawful* brother of the whole blood and the only person entitled to his estate, that the said E F is a creditor of the said deceased, that you the said G H are a minor, and that C D is your lawful father [*or* your guardian *or* the person with whom you reside or under whose care you are [*as the case may be*]]:
    Now this is to command you the said G H that within eight days after service hereof on you, inclusive of the day of such service, you do cause an appearance to be entered in the Principal Registry of the Family Division of the High Court of Justice at Somerset House, Strand, London WC2R 1LP [*or* in the   District Probate Registry at   ] and accept or refuse letters of administration of all the estate which by law devolves to and vests in the personal representative of the said deceased, or show cause why the same should not be granted to the said E F and another. And take further notice that, in default of your so appearing and accepting and extracting the said letters of administration, our said court will proceed to grant letters of administration of the said estate to the said E F and another, your absence notwithstanding.

Dated at   this   day of   19   .

Extracted by   .
of   *(Signed)*
Solicitor.   District Judge/Registrar.

[*If the deceased died on or after 4 April 1988 the relationship, except in the case of a spouse, need not be lawful and, with that exception, the word 'lawful' may be omitted.*]

52. Citation, by executor of executor, against executor to whom power was reserved, to accept or refuse probate

(NCPR 47(2))

(Heading as in Form No. 1)

Elizabeth the Second etc. *(as in Form No. 48)*:
    To E F of   .
    Take notice that G H has stated in an affidavit sworn the   day of   19   that probate of the will of A B of   deceased, was on the   day of   granted by our High Court of Justice at the Principal Registry of the Family Division [*or* at the   District Probate Registry] thereof to C D one of the executors named therein, power being reserved of making a like grant to you E F the other executor named therein, that the said C D died on the   day of   leaving part of the estate of the said deceased unadministered and that on the   day of   19   probate of the will of the said C D deceased, was granted by this

court at the said registry [*or* at the   District Probate Registry] to the said G H the sole executor thereof:

Now this is to command you the said E F that within eight days after service hereof on you, inclusive of the day of such service, you do cause an appearance to be entered in the Principal Registry of the Family Division of this court at Somerset House, Strand, London WC2R lLP [*or* in the   District Probate Registry at   ] and accept or refuse probate of the will of the said A B deceased. And take further notice that, in default of your so appearing and accepting and extracting probate of the said will, your rights as such executor will wholly cease, and the representation to the said A B deceased will devolve as if you had not been appointed executor.

Dated at   this   day of   19   .

Extracted by   .
of   (*Signed*)
Solicitor.   District Judge/Registrar.

(*Form of affidavit to lead citation, No. 33.*)

53. Citation to take probate against an executor who has intermeddled

(NCPR 47(3))

(*Heading as in Form No. 1*)

Elizabeth the Second etc. (*as in Form No. 48*):
    To E F of   .

Take notice that C D has stated in an affidavit sworn the   day of   19   that A B of   died on the   day of   19   domiciled in England and Wales, having made and duly executed his last will and testament bearing date the   day of   19   [now remaining in the Principal Registry of the Family Division of the High Court of Justice *or* in the   District Probate Registry], that you the said E F are appointed sole executor in that will, that the said C D is interested in the estate of the said deceased under the said will and that you the said E F have intermeddled in the estate of the said deceased:

Now this is to command you the said E F that within eight days after service hereof on you, inclusive of the day of such service, you do cause an appearance to be entered in the Principal Registry of the Family Division at Somerset House, Strand, London WC2R 1LP [*or* in the   District Probate Registry at   ] and show cause why you should not be ordered to take probate of the said will.

Dated at   this   day of   19   .

Extracted by   .
of   (*Signed*)
Solicitor.   District Judge/Registrar.

(*Form of affidavit to lead citation, No. 34.*)

54. Citation to propound paper writing

(NCPR 48)

(*Heading as in Form No. 1*)

Elizabeth the Second etc. (*as in Form No. 48*):
    To E F of   .

Take notice that C D has stated in an affidavit sworn the   day of   19   that A B of   died on the   day of   19   domiciled in England and Wales a widower leaving the said C D, his lawful* [*or* natural*] son and the only person entitled to his estate and that the said deceased left a certain paper writing dated the   day of   19   purporting to be a will [now remaining in the Principal Registry of the Family Division *or* in the   District Probate Registry] whereby he appointed you the said E F sole executrix and residuary legatee and devisee:

Now this is to command you the said E F that within eight days after service hereof on you, inclusive of the day of such service, you do cause an appearance to be entered in the Principal Registry of the Family Division of the High Court of Justice at Somerset House, Strand, London WC2R 1LP [*or* in the   District Probate Registry at   ] and propound the said paper writing should you think it for your interest so to do, or show cause why letters of administration of all the estate which by law devolves to and vests in the personal representative of the said deceased should not be granted to the said C D. And take further notice that in default of your so appearing and doing as aforesaid our said court will proceed to issue a grant of representation of the said estate as if the said purported will were invalid, your absence notwithstanding.

Dated at   this   day of   19 .

Extracted by   .
  of   *(Signed)*
  Solicitor.   District Judge/Registrar.

[**If the deceased died on or after 4 April 1988 the word 'lawful' or 'natural' can be omitted.*]

(*Form of affidavit to lead citation, No. 35.*)

55. Abstract of citation for advertisement

SMITH. Jane Smith, last heard of at   widow of   [*or* A B, last heard of at   executor named in will dated   of] John Smith, late of   who died at   on   19   is cited to apply within one month to the Principal Registry of the Family Division, Somerset House, Strand, London WC2R 1LP [*or* the   District Probate Registry at   ] (Estate about £   )
                                                                          (Signed)
                                                          District Judge/Registrar.

Solicitors.
[*or*]
SMITH. The kin of John Smith, late of   who died there on   19   are cited to apply within one month to the Principal Registry of the Family Division, Somerset House, Strand, London WC2R 1LP [*or* the   District Probate Registry at   ] (Estate about £   )

                                                                          (Signed)
                                                          District Judge/Registrar.

Solicitors.
   To be advertised in the following newspapers:

CONSENTS

56. Consent to proof of will

(*Heading as in Form No. 1*)

1. A B of   died on the   day of   19   domiciled in England and Wales leaving his last will and testament bearing date the   day of   19   wherein he named C D as sole executor and residuary legatee and devisee;

2. The said will contains no [*or* a defective] attestation clause [*or state circumstances calling for evidence of due execution*];

3. E F and G H, the subscribed witnesses to the said will, are both dead [*or* have not been traced] [*or as the case may be*];

4. The said deceased died a widow without issue or parent or any person entitled in priority to share in her estate by virtue of any enactment leaving I J her lawful* sister of the whole blood, who would be the only person entitled to her estate if she had died intestate;

5. Now I, the said I J of   do hereby consent to probate of the said will being granted to the said C D without proof of due execution.

   Dated this   day of   19

Signed by the within-named ⎫
I J in the presence of   (*Signed*) I J
[*signature and address of* ⎬
witness] ⎭

[**See note* to Form No. 51, above.*]

57. Consent by assignee to grant to other assignees

(Heading as in Form No. 1)

1. A B of   died on the   day of   19   domiciled in England and Wales intestate,
leaving C D his lawful widow and relict and E F his lawful* [*or* natural*] son, together the
only persons entitled to share in his estate;
[*or* having made and duly executed his last will and testament bearing date the   day of
19   wherein he appointed no executor but named C D as residuary legatee and devisee for
life and E F as residuary legatee and devisee substituted];
2. The said C D and E F by an instrument in writing dated the   day of
19   have assigned to G H, I J and K L all their right and title to and interest in the estate of
the said deceased;
3. Now I, the said G H of   do hereby consent to letters of administration [with will] of
the estate of the said deceased being granted to the said I J and K L.
4. Dated this   day of   19 .
Signed by the within-named ⎫
G H in the presence of   (*Signed*) G H
[*signature and address of* ⎬
witness] ⎭

[**If the deceased died on or after 4 April 1988 the relationship, except in the case of a
spouse, need not be lawful and, with that exception, the word 'lawful' or 'natural' may be
omitted.*]

58. Consent to trust corporation applying

(Heading as in Form No. 1)

1. A B of   died on the   19   domiciled in England and Wales [intestate a widower
leaving E F his lawful* [*or* natural*] son the only person entitled to his estate [*or as the case
may be*]] [*or* having made and duly executed his last will and testament bearing date the
     day of   19   wherein he named C D sole executor and E F residuary legatee and
devisee; the said C D has renounced probate of the said will];
2. Now I, the said E F of   hereby consent to letters of administration [with the said
will annexed] of the estate of the said deceased being granted to X and Company Limited.
3. Dated this   day of   19 .
Signed by the within-named ⎫
E F in the presence of   (*Signed*) E F
[*signature and address of* ⎬
witness] ⎭

[**See note* to Form No. 57.*]

[**Note.**—*Executors must renounce probate, and, if entitled to share in the residuary estate,
or to a grant in some other capacity, e.g. as residuary legatees and devisees in trust, must
also consent to the grant.*]

[*See also Form No. 186 (Renunciation and consent to grant to trust corporation).*]

COUNTY COURT FORM

59. Notice to Principal Registry to produce documents

In the   County Court.
   No.

Between   A B   Plaintiff,
                         and
                         C D   Defendant

1. An application has been made to this court to revoke the grant of probate of the will [*or* letters of administration of the estate] of [*here insert the name and address of the testator or intestate*] granted out of the   Probate Registry on the   day of   19 .

2. Such application will be heard by this court at   on the   day of   at a.m. [*or* p.m.]:

3. I therefore request that you will cause to be produced before the court on that day [the will and*] all documents which are in the principal registry or any district probate registry relating to the matter.

     Dated this   day of   19 .

                                           (Property Officer)

[*See County Court Rules 1981, Order 41, rule 2.*]

[**To be left out when administration without will annexed has been granted.*]

INVENTORY AND ACCOUNT

60. Inventory and account

(Heading as in Form No. 1)

I, C D, of   make oath and say that:

1. The following constitutes a true inventory of the estate of A B of   showing all items of which he was possessed, or was entitled to at the time of his death, and which have, at any time since his death, come to the hands or knowledge of me, the sole executor of the will of the deceased [*or* administrator of the estate of the deceased], namely:

                                                       £   p

Household goods, furniture, plate and jewellery at his residence at   which have been valued by   of   at the sum of   .   .   .   .
Leasehold house and premises at   whereof   years remain unexpired under his lease at the annual rent of £   valued   by   of   at the sum of .   .
Cash in the house or which has come to my hands   .   .   .   .
Cash at   Bank .   .   .   .
Stocks and shares .   .   .   .
Real estate at   .   .   .   .
Other securities, investments or reversions   .   .   .   .   .
                                     Total   .   .   £

[2. The document now produced to me and marked 'A' is a just and true account of my administration of the estate of the said deceased.]

3. No other estate of, or belonging to, the said deceased has at any time since his death come to the hands or knowledge of me.

     Sworn etc.

MOTION

61. Notice of motion

(RSC Order 8, r. 3)

(Heading as in Form No. 1)

Take notice that the court will be moved on   day the   day of   19   at o'clock, or so soon thereafter as counsel can be heard by counsel for the above named plaintiff   . that
and that the costs of the application be   .

     Dated the   day of   19   .

                     (*Signed*)   of

                                   Solicitor for the [*plaintiff*].

To
Solicitor for the   .

NOMINATION

62. Nomination of a second administrator; minority interest

(NCPR 32(3))

(Heading as in Form No. 1)

1. A B of   deceased, died on the   day of   19   domiciled in England and Wales intestate, leaving C D his lawful widow, and E F and G H his lawful* sons, together the only persons entitled to share in his estate;
2. The said E F and G H are now both minors of the ages of   and   respectively;
3. I, the said C D, am the mother [*or as the case may be*] of the said minors;
4. There is no other parent or guardian with parental responsibility for the said minors competent and willing to take a grant;
5. I, the said C D, hereby nominate J K of   to be my co-administrator in the estate of the said intestate, he being a fit and proper person to act in that capacity.
    Dated this   day of   19 .
Signed by the said C D
in the presence of
[*Name and address of witness.*]

[**See note* to Form 51, above.*]

[**Note.**—*A person entitled to a grant in his own right may nominate a second administrator only if he is the only parent or guardian of the minor with parental responsibility for him who is competent and willing to take a grant—see NCPR 32(3). In any other case application should be made for an order appointing the proposed second grantee for the purpose of joining in the grant (see Registrar's Direction (1955) 7 November).*]

[*For form of appointment of nominee of a county council, see No. 43.*]

63. Nomination of a second administrator; mental incapacity and minority or life interest

(NCPR 35(3))

(Heading as in Form No. I)

1. A B of   deceased, died on the   day of   19   domiciled in England and Wales having made and duly executed his last will and testament bearing date the   day of 19   ;
2. C D the sole executor and residuary legatee and devisee named in the said will is by reason of mental incapacity incapable of managing her affairs;
3. I, E F, am the person authorised by the Court of Protection to apply for a grant of representation of the estate of the said deceased for the use and benefit of the said C D [*or* No one has been authorised by the Court of Protection to apply for a grant of representation of the estate of the said deceased for the use and benefit of the said C D and I, E F, am her lawful attorney acting under a registered enduring power of attorney];
4. A life [*or* a minority] interest arises under the said will;
5. I, the said E F, hereby nominate G H of   to be my co-administrator in the estate of the said deceased, he being a fit and proper person to act in that capacity.
    Dated this   day of   19 .
Signed by the said E F
in the presence of
[*Name and address of witness.*]

[**Note.**—*This form can be adapted where the person nominating is the person entitled to the residuary estate or where the deceased died intestate.*]

NOTICES

64. Notice under s. 47A of Administration of Estates Act 1925 of election to redeem life interest

(NCPR 56)

(Heading as in Form No. 1)

Whereas   of   died on the   day of   19   wholly/partially intestate leaving his/her lawful wife/husband and   lawful issue of the said deceased;
   And whereas probate/letters of administration of the estate of the said   were granted to me, the said   [and to   of   ] at the Probate Registry on the   day of   19   ;
   And whereas [the said   has ceased to be a personal representative because   ] and I am [now] the sole personal representative;
   Now I, the said   hereby give notice in accordance with section 47A of the Administration of Estates Act 1925 that I elect to redeem the life interest to which I am entitled in the estate of the late   by retaining £   its capital value, and £   the costs of the transaction.
   Dated the   day of   19   .
   (Signed)
To the Senior District Judge of the Family Division.

[Form 6 in the First Schedule to the Non-Contentious Probate Rules 1987.]

65. Notice of application for probate to executor to whom power is to be reserved

(Heading as in Form No. 1)

To E F of
Take notice that:
1. A B of   died on the   day of   19   having made and duly executed his last will and testament dated the   day of   19   ;
2. C D of   and you the said E F are named as the executors in that will;
3. The said C D is applying for probate of that will with power to be reserved to you the said E F to apply for double probate.
   Dated the   day of   19   .
(Signed)
Y Z & Co. of   , Solicitors for the said C D.

OATHS

General notes.—*Except where otherwise stated, the following forms are applicable in cases where the deceased died on or after 1 January 1926.*
   In every oath to lead a grant of administration (with or without will annexed), the deponent must state whether there is a life interest or a minority interest (NCPR 8(4).)
   Where there is a life interest or a minority interest, the grant must be made to a trust corporation, with or without an individual, or to not less than two individuals, unless it appears to the court to be expedient in all the circumstances to appoint an individual as sole administrator.
   Where the death occurred on or after 1 January 1926, in every oath to lead a grant of probate or administration (with or without will annexed), the deponent must swear to the best of his knowledge, information and belief whether there was land vested in the deceased which was settled previously to his death (and not by his will) and which remained settled land notwithstanding his death (NCPR 8(3)).
   The name, address and occupation of the deponent or status (if a female with no occupation) and, in certain cases, his relationship to the deceased, if any, must be shown (see para. 4.91).
   As from 3 August 1981, every oath must state the age of the deceased. In those cases in which the exact age is not known, the applicant should give the best estimate he can (Practice Direction [1981] 2 All ER 832, [1981] 1 WLR 1185).

66. Oath for probate (general form)

(Heading as in Form No. 1)

I, C D [*or* we C D and E F] of   make oath and say that:

1. I [we] believe the paper writing now produced to and marked by me [us] to contain the true and original last will and testament [with two codicils, *or as the case may be*] of A B of   formerly of   deceased, who died on the   day of   19   aged   years, domiciled in England and Wales;

2. To the best of my [our] knowledge, information and belief, there was [no] land vested in the said deceased which was settled previously to his death, and not by his will, and which remained settled land notwithstanding his death*;

3. I am [We are] the son[s] of the said deceased and the sole executor [*or* two of the executors] [*or* the surviving executors] named in the said will;

[4. Notice of this application has been given to the executor(s) to whom power is to be reserved, save   **;]

5. I [We] will:

  (i)   collect, get in and administer according to law the real and personal estate of the said deceased;

  (ii) when required to do so by the Court exhibit in the Court a full inventory of the said estate and render an account thereof to the Court; and

  (iii) when required to do so by the High Court, deliver up to that Court the grant of probate;

6. To the best of my [our] knowledge, information and belief the gross estate passing under the grant [does not exceed/amounts to†] £   and that the net estate [does not exceed/amounts to†] £   [and that this is not a case in which an Inland Revenue account is required to be delivered]†.

    Sworn by (both) the
    above-named deponent(s)
    at
    this   day of   19
    Before me,
    A Commissioner for Oaths.

[*If there is settled land, a general executor may take a grant 'save and except settled land' on swearing simply that there was such settled land, but the value of the settled land must not be included in the oath. In such a case the word 'estate' should be followed by the words 'save and except settled land' in each place where it occurs. For form of oath for probate save and except settled land where there has been a previous grant limited to settled land, see No. 85.*
**Where there are several executors and they do not all prove, power is reserved to the non-proving executors. See paras. 4.50 ff., ante as to the requirements for giving notice to the other executor(s) or dispensing with giving such notice and the relevant statement in the oath.*
†*The alternatives so marked should be deleted as appropriate. In those cases in which an Inland Revenue account is not required to be delivered (see Chap. 8, and the Capital Transfer Tax (Delivery of Accounts) Regulations, pp. 920 ff., ante), it will be sufficient to state in the oath the threshold figures into which the estate falls (see paras 4.199 and 4.200, ante).*]

67. Oath for probate to a trust corporation

(Heading as in Form No. 1)

I, C D, of   [bank official] in the employ of X Bank Limited ('the Bank'), whose registered office is situated at   in the   of   make oath and say that:

1. I believe the paper writing now produced to and marked by me to contain the true and original last will and testament of A B of   deceased who died on the   day of   19   aged   years, domiciled in England and Wales, having in his said will appointed the Bank sole executor;

2. The Bank has by a resolution dated the   day of   19   , a certified copy of which is lodged herewith, appointed me [*or* a certified copy of which has been filed with the Senior District Judge, in which I am identified by the position I hold and which is still in force, appointed me] for the purpose of applying for probate of the said will [*or* for grants of probate] on its behalf;

3. The Bank is a trust corporation as defined by rule 2(1) of the Non-Contentious Probate Rules 1987 and has power to accept the grant now applied for;

4. The Bank is the sole executor named in the said will;

5. To the best of my knowledge, information and belief there was [no] land vested in the said deceased which was settled previously to his death, and not by his will, and which remained settled land notwithstanding his death;

6. The Bank will:

(i) collect, get in and administer according to law the real and personal estate of the said deceased;

(ii) when required to do so by the Court exhibit in the Court a full inventory of the said estate and render an account thereof to the Court; and

(iii) when required to do so by the High Court, deliver up to that Court the grant of probate;

[etc.—*continue as in Form No. 66*].

[**Note.**—*Where the corporation has been appointed as executor on terms and conditions specifically referred to as being in existence at the date of the will or its republication, as the case may be, the oath should contain a statement to the effect that nothing in those terms or conditions limits the corporation's powers to take a full grant:* Practice Direction *[1981]* 2 *All ER 1104.*]

68. Oath for probate to the Public Trustee

(Heading as in Form No. 1)

I, A B, of the Public Trust Office, Kingsway, London, WC2,   on behalf of C D the Public Trustee, make oath and say that:

1. I believe the paper writing now produced to and marked by me to contain the true and original last will and testament [with a codicil *or as the case may be*] of A B of   formerly of   deceased, who died on the   day of   19   aged   years, domiciled in England and Wales;

[2. *add statement as to settled land.*]

3. The said C D is the Public Trustee constituted by the Public Trustee Act 1906, and the Public Trustee is the sole executor named in the said will;

4. He will:

(i) collect, get in and administer [etc.—*continue as in Form No. 66*].

69. Oath for probate where partners in a firm appointed as executors by reference to them being such partners

(Heading as in Form No. 1)

I, C D, of   solicitor, make oath and say that:

1. I believe the paper writing now produced to and marked by me to contain the true and original last will and testament of A B of   deceased, who died on the   day of   19   aged   years, domiciled in England and Wales;

2. To the best of my knowledge, information and belief there was [no] land vested in the said deceased which was settled previously to his death, and not by his will, and which remained settled land notwithstanding his death;

3. The deceased named as executors, in the said will, the partners at the date of his death in the firm of Y Z of   ;

4. At the date of death of the deceased I was one of the partners in the said firm and as such I am one of the executors named in the will;

5. E F the only other partner at the date of death of the deceased in the said firm is to have

power reserved to him [*or* has renounced probate *or* has since died];
6. I will:
(i) collect, get in and administer [etc.—*continue as in Form No. 66*].

70. Oath for probate where partners in a successor firm appointed as executors

(Heading as in Form No. 1)

I, C D, of   solicitor, make oath and say that:

1. I believe the paper writing now produced to and marked by me to contain the true and original last will and testament of A B of   deceased, who died on the   day of   19   aged   years, domiciled in England and Wales;
2. To the best of my knowledge, information and belief there was [no] land vested in the said deceased which was settled previously to his death, and not by his will, and which remained settled land notwithstanding his death;
3. The deceased named as executors, in the said will, the partners at the date of his death in the firm of Y Z of   or the firm which at that date had succeeded to and carried on its practice;
4. At the date of death of the deceased the firm W X of   had succeeded to and was carrying on the practice of Y Z of   ;
5. At the date of death of the deceased I was one of the partners in the said firm of W X and as such I am one of the executors named in the will;
6. E F the only other partner at the date of death of the deceased in the said firm of W X is to have power reserved to him [*or* has renounced probate *or* has since died];
7. I will:
(i) collect, get in and administer [etc.—*continue as in Form No. 66*].

71. Oath of executor, former probate having been revoked

(Heading as in Form No. 1)

I, C D, of   make oath and say that:

1. A B of   deceased, died on the   day of   19   aged   years domiciled in England and Wales, having made and duly executed his last will and testament, bearing date the   day of   19   .
2. [*add statement as to settled land*].
3. Probate of an earlier will of the said testator, dated the   day of   19   was on the   day of   19   granted at the Principal [*or*   District Probate] Registry of the Family Division to E F, the sole executor therein named.
4. The said probate has since been voluntarily brought in by the said E F, and revoked.
5. I believe the paper writing now produced to and marked by me to contain the true and original last will and testament of the said deceased.
6. I am the sole executor named in the said will.
7. I will:
(i) collect, get in and administer [etc.—*continue as in Form No. 66*].

72. Oath after judgment pronouncing for a will as contained in a draft

(Heading as in Form No. 1)

I, C D, of   make oath and say that:

1. A B of   deceased, died on the   day of   19   aged   years, domiciled in England and Wales;
2. [*add statement as to settled land*];
3. The said deceased made and duly executed her last will and testament, bearing date the   day of   and thereof appointed me the deponent, sole executor;
4. On the   day of   the Honourable Sir   , one of the Justices of the Chancery Division, in an action entitled 'S and others against T and another', pronounced for the force and validity of the said will as contained in a draft thereof, and ordered that the said will be

admitted to proof as contained in the said draft limited until the original will or a more authentic copy thereof be proved;

5. I believe the paper writing now produced to and marked by me to contain the true last will and testament (the same being the said draft thereof) of the said deceased;

6. I am the sole executor named in the said will, and that I will:

(i) collect, get in and administer according to law the real and personal estate of the said deceased limited until the original will or a more authentic copy thereof be proved;

(ii) when required to do so by the Court exhibit in the Court a full inventory of the said estate and render an account thereof to the Court; and

(iii) when required to do so by the High Court, deliver up to that Court the grant of probate;

[etc.—*continue as in Form No. 66*].

73. Oath on proving a lost will as contained in a copy or draft etc.

(Heading as in Form No. 1)

I, C D, of   make oath and say that:

1. I believe the paper writing now produced to and marked by me to contain the last will and testament, as contained in [*the draft, completed draft, copy, or reconstruction*] exhibited to the affidavit of E F sworn on the day of   19   and marked 'A', of A B of   who died on the   day of   19   , aged   years, domiciled in England and Wales;

2. [*add statement as to settled land*];

3. On   day of   19   it was ordered by Mr District Judge [*or* Mr   Registrar] of this Division that the last will and testament of the said deceased be admitted to proof as contained in the said [*draft, copy, reconstruction*];

4. I am the sole executor named in the said will;

5. I will:

(i) collect, get in and administer according to law the real and personal estate of the said deceased, limited until the original will or a more authentic copy thereof be proved [*or as the case may be, according to the limitation imposed by the order*];

(ii) when required to do so [etc.—*continue as in Form No. 66*].

74. Oath for double probate, where not more than four executors were appointed

(Heading as in Form No. 1)

I, C D, of   make oath and say that:

1. I believe the paper writing now produced to and marked by me to contain the true and original [*or an official copy of the true and original, as the case may be*] last will and testament of A B of   deceased, who died on the   aged   years, domiciled in England and Wales;

2. [*add statement as to settled land*];

3. On the   day of   19   probate of the said will was granted at the   Probate Registry to E F, one of the executors named in the said will, power being reserved to the other executor;

4. I am the other executor named in the said will;

5. I will:

(i) collect, get in and administer according to law the real and personal estate of the said deceased;

(ii) when required to do so by the Court, exhibit in the Court a full inventory of the said estate and render an account thereof to the Court; and

(iii) when required to do so by the High Court, deliver up to that Court the grant of double probate;

[etc.—*continue as in Form 66, but with reference to the value of the unadministered estate*].

75. Oath for double probate, where more than four executors were appointed

(Heading as in Form No. 1)

I, C D, of   make oath and say that:

1. I believe the paper writing now produced to and marked by me to contain the true and

original [*or an official copy of the true and original, as the case may be*] last will and testament of A B of   deceased, who died on the   day of   19   aged
          years, domiciled in England and Wales;

2. [*add statement as to settled land*];

3. On the   day of   19   probate of the said will was granted at the   Probate
Registry to E F, G H, I J and K L, four of the executors named therein, power being reserved
to the other executor;

4. The said E F died on the   day of   19   ;

5. I am the other executor named in the said will;

6. I will:

(i) collect, get in and administer [etc.—*continue as in Form No. 74, but with reference to the
value of the unadministered estate*].

76. Oath for probate 'save and except'

(Heading as in Form No. 1)

I, C D, of   make oath and say that:

1. A B of   deceased, died on the   day of   19   aged   years, domiciled in
England and Wales;

2. [*add statement as to settled land*];

3. The said deceased made and duly executed his last will and testament, bearing date the
          day of   19   and therein named me, his son, executor, save and except as regards
the business of bookseller carried on by him at   ;

4. I believe the paper writing now produced to and marked by me to contain the true and
original last will and testament of the said deceased;

5. I am the executor therein named, save and except as aforesaid;

6. I will:

  (i) collect, get in and administer according to law the real and personal estate of the said
     deceased, save and except so far as relates to the said business of bookseller;

 (ii) when required to do so by the Court, exhibit in the Court a full inventory of the said
     estate, save and except as aforesaid, and render an account thereof to the Court; and

(iii) when required to do so by the High Court, deliver up to that Court the grant of probate;

[etc. *as in Form No. 66, save and except as aforesaid*].

77. Oath for probate caeterorum

(Heading as in Form No. 1)

I, C D, of   make oath and say that:

1. A B of   deceased, died on the   day of   19   aged   years, domiciled in
England and Wales;

2. The said deceased made and duly executed his last will and testament bearing date the
          day of   19   and therein named E F executor in respect of his literary papers and
documents, and me executor as to the rest of his estate;

3. On the   day of   19   probate of the said will, limited to the literary papers and
documents of the said testator, was granted at the   Probate Registry to the said E F;

4. [*add statement as to settled land*];

5. I believe the paper writing now produced to and marked by me to contain [an official
copy of] the true and original last will and testament of the said deceased;

6. I am the executor therein named in the said will as to the rest of his estate;

7. I will:

  (i) collect, get in and administer according to law the rest of the real and personal estate of
     the said deceased;

 (ii) when required to do so by the Court, exhibit in the Court a full inventory of the rest of
     the said estate and render an account thereof to the Court; and

(iii) when required to do so by the High Court, deliver up to that Court the grant of probate;

[etc. *as in Form No. 66, with reference to the value of the rest of the estate*].

78. Oath for cessate probate to a substituted executor

(Heading as in Form No. I)

I, C D, of   make oath and say that:

1. A B of   deceased, died on the   day of   19   aged   years, domiciled in England and Wales, having made and duly executed his last will and testament;
2. On the   day of   19   probate of the said will was granted at the Principal [*or* District] Probate Registry to E F, the executrix for life named in the said will;
3. The said E F died on the   day of   19   whereby the said probate has ceased and expired;
4. [*add statement as to settled land*];
5. I believe the paper writing now produced to and marked by me to contain [an official copy of] the true and original last will and testament of the said deceased;
6. I am the executor substituted in the said will;
7. I will: [*continue as in Form No. 66*].

79. Oath for cessate probate, the executor having attained his majority

(Heading as in Form No. 1)

I, C D, of   make oath and say that:

1. A B of   deceased, died on the   day of   19   aged   years, domiciled in England and Wales, having made and duly executed his last will and testament;
2. I am the sole executor named in the said will;
3. On the   day of   19   letters of administration (with the said will annexed) of the estate of the said deceased were granted at the Principal [*or*   District Probate] Registry to my mother E F, and to G H, the person nominated by her as co-administrator, for my use and benefit and until I should attain the age of eighteen years;
4. On the   day of   19   I attained the age of eighteen years, whereby the said letters of administration (with will annexed) have ceased and expired;
5. [*add statement as to settled land*];
6. I believe the paper writing now produced to and marked by me to contain [an official copy of] the true and original last will and testament of the said deceased;
7. I will: [*continue as in Form No. 66*].

80. Oath for cessate probate to executor where attorney has proved

(Heading as in Form No. 1)

I, C D, of   make oath and say that:

1. A B of   deceased, died on the   day of   19   aged   years, domiciled in England and Wales, having made and duly executed his last will and testament;
2. I am the sole executor named in the said will;
3. On the   day of   19   letters of administration (with the said will annexed) of the estate of the said deceased were granted at the Principal [*or*   District Probate] Registry to E F, my lawful attorney, for my use and benefit, and until I should obtain probate of the said will [*or* until further representation be granted];
4. [*add statement as to settled land*];
5. I believe the paper writing now produced to and marked by me to contain [an official copy of] the true and original last will and testament of the said deceased;
6. I will: [*continue as in Form No. 66*].

81. Oath of special executors for letters of administration limited to settled land after probate 'save and except', or letters of administration (with will) 'save and except'

(Heading as in Form No. 1)

We, C D of   and E F of   make oath and say that:

1. A B of   deceased, died on the   day of   19 aged   years, domiciled in England and Wales having made and duly executed his last will and testament [with a codicil, *or as the case may be*];

2. Probate of the said will [and codicil] [*or* letters of administration (with will [and codicil]) of the estate of the said deceased] save and except settled land was [were] granted at the Principal [*or*   District Probate] Registry on the   day of   19 to G H and K L, the executors [*or* the residuary legatees and devisees] named in the said will;

3. There was land vested in the said deceased which was settled previously to his death (and not by his will) and which remained settled land notwithstanding his death, namely, under an indenture of settlement dated the   day of   19 [*or* under the will of   deceased, which was proved at the Principal [*or*   District Probate] Registry on the   day of 19];

4. We were the trustees at the date of death of the said A B, deceased, of the settled land, and that as such we are the executors as to the said settled land;

5. We will:

  (i) collect, get in and administer according to law the estate of the said deceased, limited to the said settled land;
 (ii) when required to do so by the Court, exhibit in the Court a full inventory of the said estate, limited as aforesaid, and render an account thereof to the Court; and
(iii) when required to do so by the High Court, deliver up to that Court the grant of administration;

[etc. *as in Form No. 66, limited to the said settled land*].

82. Oath for administration limited to settled land to the trustees where deceased died intestate

(Heading as in Form No. 1)

We, C D of   and E F of   make oath and say that:

1. A B of   deceased, died on the   day of   19 aged   years, intestate, a widower, domiciled in England and Wales;

2. On the   day of   19 letters of administration of the estate of the said deceased save and except settled land were granted at the Principal [*or*   District Probate] Registry to G B, the son and only person entitled to the estate of the said deceased;

3. There was land vested in the said deceased which was settled previously to his death and which remained settled land notwithstanding his death, namely, under an indenture of settlement dated the   day of   19 [*or* under the will of   deceased, which was proved at the Principal [*or*   District Probate] Registry on the   day of   19];

4. We are the trustees of the said settled land;

5. We will:

  (i) collect, get in and administer according to law the estate of the said deceased limited to the said settled land;
 (ii) when required to do so by the Court, exhibit in the Court a full inventory of the said · estate, limited as aforesaid, and render an account thereof to the Court; and
(iii) when required to do so by the High Court, deliver up to that Court the grant of letters of administration;

[etc. *as in Form No. 66, limited to the said settled land*].

83. Oath for administration limited to settled land to trustees (no former grant) where deceased left a will

(Heading as in Form No. 1)

We, C D of   and E F of   make oath and say that:

1. A B of   deceased, died on the   day of   19 aged   years, domiciled in England and Wales having made and duly executed his last will and testament which has not yet been proved;

2. There was land vested in the said deceased which was settled previously to his death (and not by his will) and which remained settled land notwithstanding his death, namely, under the will of M N deceased, which was proved at the Principal [*or*   District Probate] Registry on the   day of   19   ; [*or* under an indenture of settlement dated the   day of   19   ];

3. [*Clear off trustees at the date of death of the deceased, e.g.* At the date of death of the said deceased there were no trustees of the said settled land; *or* G H, the surviving trustee at the date of death of the said deceased of the said settled land and as such the executor as to the said settled land has since died without having taken upon himself a grant of representation limited to the said settled land, *or* has renounced administration limited to the said settled land.]

4. We are the present trustees of the said settled land.

5. We will:

(i) collect, get in and administer [etc.—*complete as in Form No. 82*].

   Sworn etc.

84. Oath for letters of administration limited to settled land to personal representatives of the settlor as special executors (after grant 'save and except')

(Heading as in Form No. 1)

We, C D of   and E F of   make oath and say that:

1. A B of   deceased, died on the   day of   19   aged   years, domiciled in England and Wales, having made and duly executed his last will and testament [with a codicil *or as the case may be*];

2. Letters of administration (with will [and codicil]) of the estate of the said deceased save and except settled land were granted on the   day of   19   at the Principal [*or*   District Probate] Registry, to G H and K L, the residuary legatees and devisees named in the said will;

3. There was land vested in the said deceased which was settled previously to his death (and not by his will) and which remained settled land notwithstanding his death, namely, under the will of M N, deceased, which was proved at the Principal [*or*   District Probate] Registry on the   day of   19   ;

4. There were no trustees of the said settled land at the date of death of the said deceased save and except ourselves, and none have since been appointed [*or as the case may be*];

5. We are the executors of the will of the said M N, deceased, and, having been such at the date of death of the said A B, deceased, we are, by virtue of section 30(3) of the Settled Land Act 1925, the executors as to the said settled land;

6. We will:

(i) collect, get in and administer [etc.—*complete as in Form No. 82*].

   Sworn etc.

85. Oath for probate save and except settled land (after grant limited to settled land)

(Heading as in Form No. 1)

We, C D of   and E F of   make oath and say that:

1. We believe the paper writing now produced to and marked by us to contain [an official copy of] the true and original last will and testament of A B of   deceased, who died on the   day of   19   aged   years, domiciled in England and Wales;

2. There was land vested in the said deceased which was settled previously to his death (and not by his will) and which remained settled land notwithstanding his death;

3. On the   day of   19   probate of the said will [*or* letters of administration (with will) of the estate of the said deceased] limited to settled land was [were] granted at the Principal [*or*   District Probate] Registry to G H, the executor as to the said settled land [*or as the case may be*];

4. We are the executors named in the said will;

5. We will:

(i) collect, get in and administer according to law the real and personal estate of the said deceased save and except settled land;

(ii) when required to do so by the Court, exhibit in the Court a full inventory of the said estate save and except settled land and render an account thereof to the Court; and

(iii) when required to do so by the High Court, deliver up to that Court the grant of probate;

[etc. *as in Form No. 66, save and except the said settled land*].

86. Oath for administration (with will) (will admissible only as to part of estate)

(Heading as in Form No. 1)

I, C D of   make oath and say that:

1. I believe the paper writing now produced to and marked by me to contain [an official copy of] the true and original last will and testament of A B, of   deceased, who died on the   day of   19   aged   years, domiciled in   ;

2. The said will is not valid by the law of the place where the said deceased died domiciled [and is not admissible to proof in England and Wales [in its entirety] by virtue of the Wills Act 1963] [*or* is admissible to proof in England and Wales [by virtue of the Wills Act 1963] so far only as it disposes of immovable property [*or* so far only as it exercises the power of appointment possessed by the said deceased under [*give particulars of the instrument*]]];

3. [*Statement as to minority and life interests and settled land.*]

4. I am [*applicant's title to grant*];

5. I will:

(i) collect, get in and administer according to law the estate of the said deceased, limited to [the immovable estate disposed of by the said will] [*or* the immovable estate of the said deceased in England and Wales] [*or* limited to such estate as the said deceased had a right or power to appoint or dispose of, and did in the said will appoint or dispose of], but no further or otherwise;

(ii) when required to do so by the Court exhibit in the Court a full inventory of the said estate and render an account thereof to the Court; and

(iii) when required to do so by the High Court deliver up to that Court the grant of letters of administration;

[etc. *as in Form No. 66 limited as aforesaid*].

[**Note.**—*The Wills Act 1963 applies in the case of testators dying on or after 1 January 1964.*

Whatever the date of death, if the whole, or substantially the whole, estate of the deceased in England and Wales consists of immovable property, a grant in respect of the whole estate may be made in accordance with the law which would have been applicable if the deceased had died domiciled in England and Wales (NCPR 30(3)(b)).

As to title to grant where the deceased died domiciled out of England and Wales, see Chap. 12.]

87. Oath for administration to husband or widow—net estate not exceeding £125,000 (where deceased left issue surviving) or £200,000 (where deceased left no issue) for death on or after 1 December 1993 [*or the appropriate lesser sums depending on date of death—see para. 6.85, ante*]

(Heading as in Form No. 1)

I, C B, of   make oath and say that:

1. A B of   deceased, died on the   day of   19 , aged   years, domiciled in England and Wales intestate;

2. No minority or life interest arises under the intestacy;

3. To the best of my knowledge, information, and belief there was no land vested in the deceased which was settled previously to his death and which remained settled land notwithstanding his death;

4. I am the lawful husband [*or* the lawful widow *as the case may be*] and the only person now entitled to the estate of the said deceased;

5. I will:

  (i) collect, get in and administer according to law the real and personal estate of the said deceased;

  (ii) when required to do so by the Court, exhibit in the Court a full inventory of the said estate and render an account thereof to the Court; and

  (iii) when required to do so by the High Court, deliver up to that Court the grant of letters of administration;

[etc. *as in Form No. 66*].

[**Note.**—*For the wording to be added when the gross estate exceeds £125,000 or £200,000, or as the case may be, but the net estate, after making the permissible deductions, is below whichever amount is appropriate, see paras. 6.92 ff., ante.*

Where the deceased left a spouse but no issue and the net estate exceeds £125,000 but does not exceed £200,000 or as the case may be the words 'without issue or any other person entitled in priority to share in the estate by virtue of any enactment' should be included in para. 1 after 'intestate', so as to establish that the applicant is the 'only person now entitled to the estate' (see fn. 2 to para. 6.85, ante).]

88. Oath for administrators where net value of the estate exceeds £125,000 for death on or after 1 December 1993 and there are issue (husband or widow applying with next person entitled under NCPR 22) [*for the appropriate lesser sums depending on date of death see para. 6.85, ante*]

(Heading as in Form No. 1)

We, C B, of   and E B, of   make oath and say that:

1. A B of   deceased, died on the   day of   19   aged   years, domiciled in England and Wales intestate;

2. No minority but a life interest arises under the intestacy;

3. To the best of our knowledge, information and belief, there was no land vested in the deceased which was settled previously to [his] death and which remained settled land notwithstanding [his] death;

4. I the said C B am the lawful husband [*or* the lawful widow *as the case may be*] of the said deceased, and I the said E B am the lawful* [*or* natural*] son and one of the persons entitled to share in the estate of the said deceased;

5. We will:

  (i) collect, get in and administer according to law the real and personal estate of the said deceased;

  (ii) when required to do so by the Court, exhibit in the Court a full inventory of the said estate and render an account thereof to the Court; and

  (iii) when required to do so by the High Court, deliver up to that Court the grant of letters of administration;

[etc. *as in Form No. 66*].

[**If the deceased died on or after 4 April 1988 it is not necessary for the relationship of anyone, except a spouse, to be lawful. Accordingly, with that exception, the word 'lawful' or 'natural' may be omitted.*]

[**Note.**—*Where the person next entitled to the first applicant has renounced and the second person applying is next in order under NCPR 22, an order under rule 25 for joinder of the second grantee is necessary.*]

89. Oath for administrators—net estate exceeding £125,000 for death on or after 1 December 1993: widow (or husband) and minor child survive: application by spouse and nominated co-administrator [*for the appropriate lesser sums depending on date of death see para. 6.85, ante*]

(Heading as in Form No. 1)

We, C D, of　　　and E F, of　　make oath and say that:

1. A B of　　　deceased, died on the　　day of　　19　aged　　years domiciled in England and Wales intestate, leaving the said C D, his lawful widow [*or* her lawful husband] and G H, his [her] lawful* son, together the only persons entitled to share in his [her] estate;
2. The said G H is now a minor of the age of　　years;
3. There is no guardian with parental responsibility for the said minor;
4. The said C D is the mother of the said minor [*or* is the father of the said minor with parental responsibility for him under s. 2(1) of the Children Act 1989 *or* is the father of the said minor and has acquired parental responsibility for him under s. 4 of the Children Act 1989 under an order [*or* under a duly recorded parental responsibility agreement)];
5. A minority and a life interest arise under the intestacy;
6. To the best of our knowledge, information and belief there was no land vested in the said deceased which was settled previously to his [her] death and which remained settled land notwithstanding his [her] death;
7. The said E F is the person nominated by the said C D as co-administrator of the estate of the said deceased;
8. We will:

(i) collect, get in and administer [etc.—*complete as in Form 88*].

[**See note* to Form No. 88.]*
[*When the father is relying on s. 4 of the Children Act 1989 a sealed copy of the order or of the recorded parental responsibility agreement, as the case may be, must be produced on the application.*]

90. Oath for administrator—spouse applies alone on assignment by children (net estate exceeding £125,000 for death on or after 1 December 1993) [*for the appropriate lesser sums depending on date of death see para. 6.85, ante*]

(Heading as in Form No. 1)

I, C D, of　　make oath and say that:

1. A B of　　　deceased, died on the　　day of　　19　aged　　years, domiciled in England and Wales intestate, leaving me the said C D, his lawful widow [*or* her lawful husband] and E F and G H his [her] lawful* [*or* natural*] son and daughter [*or as the case may be*], together the only persons entitled to share in his [her] estate.
2. The said E F and G H have by deed of assignment dated the　　day of 19　assigned to me, the said C D, all their right and title to and interest in the estate of the said intestate;
3. No minority interest and now no life interest arises under the intestacy;
4. [*add statement as to settled land*];
5. I will:

(i) collect, get in and administer [etc.—*complete as in Form No. 88*].

[**See note* to Form No. 88.*]

91. Oath for administrator (husband's, or widow's, representative applies, whole estate having passed to surviving spouse)

(Heading as in Form No. 1)

I, C D, of　　make oath and say that:

1. A B of　　　deceased, died on the　　day of　　19　aged　　years, domiciled in England and Wales intestate, leaving E B, her lawful husband [*or* his lawful widow] and the only

person entitled to her [his] estate, who has since died without having taken letters of administration of the estate of the said intestate;

2. I am the sole executor of the will [*or* administrator of the estate] of the said E B, deceased, probate thereof [*or* letters of administration [with will] thereof] having been granted to me at the   Registry on the   day of   19 ;

3. No minority and no life interest arises under the intestacy;

4. [*add statement as to settled land*];

5. I will:

(i) collect, get in and administer [etc.—*complete as in Form 88*].

92. Oath for administrator where net estate exceeds in value £125,000 for death on or after 1 December 1993—issue apply on renunciation of surviving spouse [*for the appropriate lesser sums depending on date of death see para. 6.85, ante*]

(Heading as in Form No. 1)

We, C B of   and D B of   make oath and say that:

1. A B of   deceased, died on the   day of   19   aged   years domiciled in England and Wales intestate, leaving E B, her lawful husband [*or* his lawful widow [*as the case may be*]], who has renounced letters of administration of the estate of the said deceased;

2. A minority and a life interest arise [*or* No minority but a life interest arises] under the intestacy;

3. To the best of our knowledge, information, and belief, there was no land vested in the deceased which was settled previously to her [his] death and which remained settled land notwithstanding her [his] death;

4. We are the lawful* son and grandson respectively [*or as the case may be*] and two of the persons entitled to share in the estate of the said deceased (the said D B being the lawful* son of F B the lawful* son of the said deceased who died in the lifetime of the said deceased);

5. We will:

(i) collect, get in and administer [etc.—*complete as in Form 88*].

[*See note* to Form No. 88.]

93. Oath for administrator where the net estate is under £125,000 for death on or after 1 December 1993—son or daughter applies on renunciation of surviving spouse [*for the appropriate lesser sums depending on date of death see para. 6.85, ante*]

(Heading as in.Form No. 1)

I, C D, of   make oath and say that:

1. A B of   deceased, died on the   day of   19   aged   years, domiciled in England and Wales intestate leaving C B, his lawful widow [*or* her lawful husband] and the only person now entitled to his [her] estate who has renounced letters of administration thereof;

2. [*statements as to minority or life interests and settled land*];

3. I am a lawful* [*or* natural*] son [daughter] of the said deceased and a person who may have a beneficial interest in his [her] estate in the event of an accretion thereto;

4. I will:

(i) collect, get in and administer [etc.—*complete as in Form No. 88*].

[*See note* to Form No. 88.]

[**Note.**—*A creditor is equally entitled to this grant, and the form can be adapted for his use.*]

94. Oath for administration to child, or other issue having a beneficial interest—spouse survived but has since died

(Heading as in Form No. 1)

I, C D, of   make oath and say that:

1. A B of   deceased, died on the   day of   19 aged   years, domiciled in England and Wales intestate leaving E F, his lawful widow [*or* her lawful husband] who has since died without having taken upon herself [himself] letters of administration of his [her] estate;
2. No minority and now no life interest arises under the intestacy;
3. To the best of my knowledge, information, and belief there was no land vested in the said deceased which was settled previously to his [her] death and which remained settled land notwithstanding his [her] death;
4. I am the lawful* [*or* natural*] son and one of the persons entitled to share in the estate of the said deceased;
5. I will:

(i) collect, get in and administer [etc.—*complete as in Form No. 88*].

[**See note* to Form No. 88.*]

95. Oath for administration to child (on assignment by surviving spouse)

(Heading as in Form No. 1)

I, E F, of   make oath and say that:

1. A B of   deceased, died on the   day of   19 aged   years, domiciled in England and Wales, intestate, leaving C D, his lawful widow [*or* her lawful husband] and me, the said E F and G H his [her] lawful* [*or* natural*] son and daughter [*or as the case may be*] together the only persons entitled to share in his [her] estate;
2. The said C D has by deed of assignment dated the   day of   19 assigned to the said E F and G H all her [his] right and title to and interest in the estate of the said intestate, and has renounced letters of administration of the estate of the said intestate;
3. No life interest now arises, and no minority interest arises under the intestacy;
4. [*add statement as to settled land*];
5. I will:

(i) collect, get in and administer [etc.—*complete as in Form 88*].

[**See note* to Form No. 88.*]

96. Oath for administration to child or other issue having a beneficial interest—no surviving spouse

(Heading as in Form No. 1)

I, C D, of   make oath and say that:

1. A B of   deceased, died on the   day of   19 aged   years, domiciled in England and Wales, intestate, a widow [*or* a widower] [*or* a single man] [*or* a single woman] [*or* a bachelor] [*or* a spinster];
2. No life or minority interest arises under the intestacy;
3. [*add statement as to settled land*];
4. I am the lawful* [*or* natural*] son [*or* daughter] and the only person entitled to the estate [*or* one of the persons entitled to share in the estate] of the said intestate;
   [*Or* I am the lawful* grandson [*or* granddaughter] (being the lawful* son [*or* daughter] of E F, the lawful* son [*or* daughter] of the said intestate who died in the lifetime of the said intestate) [*or* the lawful* son [*or* daughter] of E F, the natural* son [*or* daughter] of the said intestate who died in the lifetime of the said intestate] and the only person entitled to the estate [*or* one of the persons entitled to share in the estate] of the said intestate;]
5. I will:

(i) collect, get in and administer [etc.—*complete as Form No. 88*].

[**See note* to Form No. 88.*]

[*For additional wording which must be included in the oath when the deceased was a divorced man or woman, see Form 102 and para. 6.120, ante.*]

97. Oath for administration to a person entitled, jointly with attorney of person equally entitled

(Heading as in Form No. 1)

We, C D of   and E F of   make oath and say that:

1. A B of   deceased, died on the   day of   19   aged   years, domiciled in England and Wales, intestate a widow [*or as the case may be*], leaving the said C D and G H, her lawful* [*or* natural*] son and daughter, and two of the persons entitled to share in her estate;
2. A minority but no life interest arises under the intestacy;
3. [*add statement as to settled land*];
4. The said C D is the lawful* [*or* natural*] son and one of the persons entitled to share in the estate of the said intestate, and that the said E F is the lawful attorney of the said G H;
5. We will:

   (i) collect, get in and administer according to law the real and personal estate of the said intestate, limited until further representation be granted;
   (ii) when required to do so by the Court, exhibit in the Court a full inventory of the said estate and render an account thereof to the Court; and
   (iii) when required to do so by the High Court, deliver up to that Court the grant of letters of administration;

[etc. *as in Form No. 88*].
   And I, the said C D, further say that I hereby consent to the grant of administration being limited in the manner hereinbefore set out.
   Sworn etc.

[**See note* to Form No. 66.*]

98. Oath for administration to child or children the only issue, save and except others alienated by adoption order made during the lifetime of intestate

(Death on or after 1 January 1950)

(Heading as in Form No. 1)

I, C B, of   make oath and say that:

1. A B of   deceased, died on the   day of   19   aged   years, domiciled in England and Wales, intestate a widow[er] leaving me the said C B her [his] lawful* [*or* natural*] son [daughter] the only person entitled to her [his] estate;
2. By virtue of an adoption order made under the authority of the Adoption Act 1958 [*or as the case may be*], which order is still subsisting, D B the lawful* [*or* natural*] son [daughter] of the said deceased was duly adopted and the estate of the said deceased devolves in all respects as if the said D B were the lawful child of the adopter [*or* adopters] and not the child of the said deceased;
3. No life or minority interest arises under the intestacy;
4. [*add statement as to settled land*];
5. I am the lawful* [*or* natural*] son [daughter] and the only person entitled to the estate of the said deceased;
6. I will:

(i) collect, get in and administer [etc.—*complete as in Form No. 88*].

[**See note* to Form No. 88.*]

[**Note.**—*The adoption order should not be exhibited to the oath, and the child should be referred to by the name by which he was known prior to the adoption (Registrar's Circular, 2 March 1966).*]

99. Oath for administration to person entitled, issue being alienated by adoption order made during the lifetime of intestate

(Death on or after 1 January 1950)

(Heading as in Form No. 1)

I, E F, of   make oath and say that:

1. A B of   deceased, died on the   day of   19   aged   years, domiciled in England and Wales intestate a widow[er] without issue entitled to her [his] estate or any other person entitled in priority to share in the estate by virtue of any enactment;
2. By virtue of an adoption order made under the authority of the Adoption Act 1958 [*or as the case may be*], which order is still subsisting, C D, the lawful* son [*or* daughter] [*or* the natural* son [*or* daughter]] and only issue of the said deceased was duly adopted and the estate of the said deceased devolves in all respects as if the said C D were the lawful child of the adopter [*or* adopters] and not the child of the said deceased;
    [*Clear off any intervening classes.*]
3. No life or minority interest arises under the intestacy.
4. [*add statement as to settled land*];
5. I am the lawful*   and only person entitled to [*or* one of the persons entitled to share in] the estate of the said deceased;
6. I will:

(i) collect, get in and administer [etc.—*complete as in Form No. 88*].

[**See note* to Form No. 88.*]

[**Note.**—*The adoption order should not be exhibited to the oath, and the child should be referred to by the name by which he was known prior to the adoption (Registrar's Circular, 2 March 1966).*]

100. Oath for administration to adopted child

(Death on or after 1 January 1950)

(Heading as in Form No. 1)

I, C D, of   make oath and say that:

1. A B of   died on the   day of   aged   years, domiciled in England and Wales intestate a widow [*or* a widower, *or* a spinster, *or* a bachelor];
2. By an order dated the   day of   19   made by the   Court at   under authority of the Adoption Act 1958 [*or as the case may be*] I was duly adopted by the said intestate [and E F, his deceased wife, *or* her deceased husband] and that the said order is still subsisting;
3. [*Statement as to minority and life interest.*]
4. [*Statement as to settled land.*]
5. I am the lawful adopted son [*or* daughter], and the only person entitled to the estate [*or* one of the persons entitled to share in the estate] of the said intestate.
6. I will:

(i) collect, get in and administer [etc.—*complete as in Form No. 88*].

101. Oath for administration to adopter or adopters

(Death on or after 1 January 1950)

(Heading as in Form No. 1)

I, C D [*or* we C D and E F] of   make oath and say that:

1. A B of   died on the   day of   19   aged   years, domiciled in England and Wales, intestate, a bachelor [spinster] [widower] [widow] without issue or any other person entitled in priority to share in the estate by virtue of any enactment;

2. By an order dated the   day of   19   made by the   Court at   under authority of the Adoption Act 1958 [*or as the case may be*] the said intestate was duly adopted by me [us], and that the said order is still subsisting;

3. [*Statement as to minority and life interest.*]

4. [*Statement as to settled land.*]

5. I am [we are] [one of] the lawful adopter[s] and one of the persons [*or* the only person[s]] entitled to [share in] the estate of the said intestate;

6. I [We] will:

(i) collect, get in and administer [etc.—*complete as in Form No. 88*].

102. Oath for administrator: deceased a divorced man or woman

(Heading as in Form No. 1)

I, D B, of   make oath and say that:

1. A B of   deceased, died on the   day of   19   aged   years, domiciled in England and Wales intestate, a single man [*or* a single woman] [*insert any further clearings, e.g.* 'without issue or parent' *etc. as the case may require*];

2. The marriage of the said A B with E B was, on the   day of   19   dissolved by final decree of the High Court of Justice [*or* of the   County Court] in [England and Wales]** and that the said A B did not remarry;

3. [*Add statement as to minority or life interest.*]

4. [*Statement as to settled land.*]

5. I am the lawful* [*or* natural*] daughter and only person entitled to the estate of the said deceased;

6. I will:

(i) collect, get in and administer [etc.—*complete as in Form No. 88*].

[**See note** *to Form No. 88.*]
[***As to the practice and wording of oath in cases where the marriage was dissolved by a court other than in England or Wales see paras. 6.136 ff., ante.*]

103. Oath for administrator (father or mother takes)

(Heading as in Form No. 1)

I, C D, of   make oath and say that:

1. A B of   deceased, died on the   day of   19   aged   years, domiciled in England and Wales intestate, a bachelor [spinster] [widower] [widow] without issue or any other person entitled in priority to share in the estate by virtue of any enactment;

2. [*add statement as to life or minority interest*];

3. [*add statement as to settled land*];

4. I am the lawful* [*or* natural*] father [*or* mother] and only person entitled to [*or* one of the persons entitled to share in] the estate of the said deceased;

5. I will:

(i) collect, get in and administer [etc.—*complete as in Form No. 88*].

[**See note** *to Form No. 88.*]

[**Note.**—(*1*) *As to the evidence required on an application by the natural father where the deceased died before 4 April 1988, see para. 6.275, ante.*
(*2*) *For additional wording which must be included in the oath when the deceased was a divorced man or woman, see Form 102 and para. 6.120, ante.*]

104. Oath for administration to personal representative of father or mother

(Heading as in Form No. 1)

I, C D, of   make oath and say that:

1. A B of   deceased, died on the   day of   19   aged   years, domciled in England and Wales intestate, a bachelor [spinster] [widower] [widow] without issue or any other person entitled in priority to share in the estate by virtue of any enactment, leaving E F, his [*or* her] lawful* [*or* natural*] father [*or* mother] and the only person entitled to his [*or* her] estate, who has since died without having taken upon himself [*or* herself] letters of administration of his [*or* her] estate;
2. [*add statement as to minority or life interest*];
3. [*add statement as to settled land*];
4. I am the sole executor [*or* one of the executors] of the will [*or* the administrator of the estate] of the said E F, deceased, probate of the said will [*or* letters of administration of the said estate] having been granted to me at the Principal [*or*   District Probate] Registry on the   day of   19   ;
5. I will:

(i) collect, get in and administer [etc.—*complete as in Form No. 88*].

[**See note* to Form No. 88.*]

[**Note.**—*If both parents survived the deceased but have since died, application may be made by the personal representative of either parent.*]

105. Oath for administration to brother and sister of the whole blood

(Heading as in Form No. 1)

I, C D, of   make oath and say that:

1. A B of   deceased, died on the   day of   19   aged   years, domiciled in England and Wales intestate, a bachelor [spinster] [widower] [widow] without issue or parent or any other person entitled in priority to share in the estate by virtue of any enactment;
2. [*add statement as to minority or life interest*];
3. [*add statement as to settled land*];
4. I am the lawful* brother [*or* sister] of the whole blood, and the only person entitled to the estate [*or* one of the persons entitled to share in the estate] of the said intestate;
5. I will:

(i) collect, get in and administer [etc.—*complete as in Form No. 88*].

[**See note* to Form No. 88.*]

106. Oath for administration to nephew or niece of the whole blood

(Heading as in Form No. 1)

I, C D, of   make oath and say that:

1. A B of   deceased, died on the   day of   19   aged   years, domiciled in England and Wales intestate, a bachelor [spinster] [widower] [widow] without issue or parent or any other person entitled in priority to share in the estate by virtue of any enactment;
2. I am the lawful* nephew [*or* niece] of the whole blood and the only person entitled to the estate [*or* one of the persons entitled to share in the estate] of the said intestate, being the lawful* son [*or* daughter] of E F, the lawful* brother [*or* sister] of the whole blood of the said intestate, who died before the said intestate;
3. [*add statement as to minority or life interest*];
4. [*add statement as to settled land*];
5. I will:

(i) collect, get in and administer [etc.—*complete as in Form No. 88*].

[*See note* to Form No. 88.]

107. Oath for administration to brother or sister of the half blood

(Heading as in Form No. 1)

I, C D, of   make oath and say that:

1. A B of   deceased, died on the   day of   19   aged   years, domiciled in England and Wales intestate a bachelor [spinster] [widower] [widow] without issue, parent, brother or sister of the whole blood or their issue or any other person entitled in priority to share in the estate by virtue of any enactment;
2. [*add statement as to minority or life interest*];
3. [*add statement as to settled land*];
4. I am the lawful* brother [*or* sister] of the half blood and the only person entitled to the estate [*or* one of the persons entitled to share in the estate] of the said intestate;
5. I will:

(i) collect, get in and administer [etc.—*complete as in Form No. 88*].

[*See note* to Form No. 88.]

108. Oath for administration to nephew or niece of the half blood

(Heading as in Form No. 1)

I, C D, of   make oath and say that:

1. A B of   deceased, died on the   day of   19   aged   years, domiciled in England and Wales intestate, a bachelor [spinster] [widower] [widow] without issue, parent, brother or sister of the whole blood or their issue or any other person entitled in priority to share in the estate by virtue of any enactment;
2. [*add statement as to minority or life interest*];
3. [*add statement as to settled land*];
4. I am the lawful* nephew [*or* niece] of the half blood and the only person entitled to the estate [*or* one of the persons entitled to share in the estate] of the said intestate, being the lawful* son [*or* daughter] of I K, the lawful* brother of the half blood of the said intestate who died before the said intestate;
5. I will:

(i) collect, get in and administer [etc.—*complete as in Form No. 88*].

[*See note* to Form No. 88.]

109. Oath for administration to uncle or aunt

(Heading as in Form No. 1)

I, C D, of   make oath and say that:

1. A B of   deceased, died on the   day of   19   aged   years, domiciled in England and Wales intestate, a bachelor [spinster] [widower] [widow] without issue, parent, brother or sister of the whole or half blood or their issue, grandparent or any other person entitled in priority to share in the estate by virtue of any enactment;
2. [*add statement as to minority or life interest*];
3. [*add statement as to settled land*];
4. I am the lawful* uncle [*or* aunt] of the whole blood, and the only person entitled to the estate [*or* one of the persons entitled to share in the estate] of the said intestate;
5. I will:

(i) collect, get in and administer [etc.—*complete as in Form No. 88*].

[*See note* to Form No. 88.]

[**Note.**—*On an application by an uncle or aunt of the half blood, it must also be shown that the intestate died without uncle or aunt of the whole blood or their issue.*]

110. Oath for administration to cousin german

(Heading as in Form No. 1)

I, C D, of   make oath and say that:

1. A B of   deceased, died on the   day of   19   aged   years, domiciled in England and Wales intestate, a bachelor [spinster] [widower] [widow] without issue, parent, brother or sister of the whole or half blood or their issue, grandparent or any other person entitled in priority to share in the estate by virtue of any enactment;
2. [*add statement as to minority or life interest*];
3. [*add statement as to settled land*];
4. I am the lawful* cousin german of the whole blood and the only person entitled to the estate [*or* one of the persons entitled to share in the estate] of the said intestate, being the lawful* son [*or* daughter] of E F, the lawful* uncle [*or* aunt] of the whole blood of the said intestate who died in the lifetime of the said intestate;
5. I will:

(i) collect, get in and administer [etc.—*complete as in Form No. 88*].

[*See note* to Form No. 88.]

[**Note.**—*On an application by a cousin german of the half blood, it must also be shown that the intestate died without uncle or aunt of the whole blood or their issue.*]

111. Oath for administration to a trust corporation

(Heading as in Form No. 1)

I, I K, of   [trustee manager] of Z Bank Limited, whose registered office is situated at   ('the Bank') make oath and say that:

1. A B of   deceased, died on the   day of   19   aged   years, domiciled in England and Wales intestate [leaving C D his lawful widow, the only person now entitled to his estate] [*or* a widower without issue or parent or any other person entitled in priority to share in the estate by virtue of any enactment *or* [*as the case may be*] leaving C D, E F, and G H, his lawful* brother and sisters of the whole blood the only persons entitled to share in his estate], who has [have] consented to letters of administration of the estate of the said intestate being granted to the Bank;
2. The Bank is a trust corporation as defined by rule 2(1) of the Non-Contentious Probate Rules 1987, and has power to accept the grant now applied for;
3. The Bank has by a resolution dated the   day of   19   , a certified copy whereof is lodged herewith, appointed me [*or* a certified copy of which has been filed with the Senior District Judge, in which I am identified by the position I hold and which resolution is still in force, appointed me] for the purpose of applying for letters of administration of the estate of the said intestate [*or* for the purpose of applying for grants of letters of administration on its behalf];
4. No minority or life interest arises under the intestacy;
5. [*add statement as to settled land*];
6. The Bank will:

(i) collect, get in and administer according to law the real and personal estate of the said deceased;
(ii) when required to do so by the Court, exhibit in the Court a full inventory of the said estate and render an account thereof to the Court; and
(iii) when required to do so by the High Court, deliver up to that Court the grant of letters of administration;

[etc. *as in Form No. 66*].

112. Oath for administration to a creditor (on the renunciation of the persons entitled)

(Heading as in Form No. 1)

I, C D, of   make oath and say that:

1. A B of   deceased, died on the   day of   19   aged   years, domiciled in England and Wales intestate, a bachelor [spinster] [widower] [widow] without issue or parent or any other person entitled in priority to share in the estate by virtue of any enactment leaving E F and G H, his lawful* brother and sister of the whole blood respectively and the only persons entitled to share in his estate, who have renounced letters of administration of his said estate;

2. [*add statement as to minority or life interest*];

3. [*add statement as to settled land*];

4. I am a creditor of the said deceased;

5. I will:

(i) collect, get in and administer [etc.—*complete as in Form No. 88*].

[**See note* to Form No. 88.*]

113. Oath for administration to assignee of persons entitled on intestacy

(NCPR 24)

(Heading as in Form No. 1)

I, G H, of   make oath and say that:

1. A B of   deceased, died on the   day of   19   aged   years, domiciled in England and Wales intestate a bachelor [spinster] [widower] [widow] without issue or parent [*clear other prior classes as appropriate*] or any other person entitled in priority to share in the estate by virtue of any enactment, leaving C D [and E F] her lawful* sister[s] of the whole blood [*or as the case may be*] and the only person[s] entitled to [share in] her estate;

2. By deed of assignment dated the   day of   19   the said C D [and E F] has [have] assigned to me [and to I J and K L] all her [their] right and title to and interest in the estate of the said intestate;

3. No minority or life interest arises under the intestacy;

4. [*add statement as to settled land*];

5. I will:

(i) collect, get in and administer [etc.—*complete as in Form No. 88*].

114. Oath for administration to attorneys of intestate's husband or widow

(Heading as in Form No. 1)

We, C D of   and F G of   make oath and say that:

1. A B of   deceased, died on the   day of   19   aged   years, domiciled in England and Wales, intestate, leaving E B her lawful husband [*or* his lawful widow];

2. No minority but a life interest arises under the intestacy;

3. [*add statement as to settled land*];

4. We are the lawful attorneys of the said E B;

5. We will:

(i) collect, get in and administer according to law the real and personal estate of the said deceased for the use and benefit of the said E B until further representation be granted;

(ii) when required to do so by the Court, exhibit in the Court a full inventory of the said estate and render an account thereof to the Court; and

(iii) when required to do so by the High Court, deliver up to the Court the grant of letters of administration;

[etc. *as in Form No. 66*].

115. Oath for administration to attorney of intestate's father or mother

(Heading as in Form No. 1)

I, C D, of   make oath and say that:

1. A B of   deceased, died on the   day of   19   aged   years, domiciled in England and Wales intestate, a bachelor [spinster] [widower] [widow] without issue or any other person entitled in priority to share in the estate by virtue of any enactment, leaving E F, his [*or* her] lawful* [*or* natural*] father [*or* mother] and the only person entitled to his [*or* her] estate;

2. No minority or life interest arises under the intestacy;

3. [*add statement as to settled land*];

4. I am the lawful attorney of the said E F;

5. I will:

  (i) collect, get in and administer according to law the real and personal estate of the said deceased, for the use and benefit of the said E F until further representation be granted;

  (ii) when required to do so by the Court exhibit in the Court a full inventory of the said estate and render an account thereof to the Court; and

  (iii) when required to do so by the High Court, deliver up to that Court the grant of letters of administration;

[etc. *as in Form No. 66*].

[**See note* to Form No. 88.*]

116. Oath for administration to attorneys of intestate's child—another child being a minor

(Heading as in Form No. 1)

We, C D of   and G H of   make oath and say that:

1. A B of   deceased, died on the   day of   19   aged   years, domiciled in England and Wales intestate, a widow [*or* a widower] leaving E F her [*or* his] lawful* [*or* natural*] son and one of the persons entitled to share in her [*or* his] estate;

2. A minority but no life interest arises under the intestacy;

3. [*add statement as to settled land*];

4. We are the lawful attorneys of the said E F;

5. We will:

  (i) collect, get in and administer according to law the real and personal estate of the said deceased, for the use and benefit of the said E F until further representation be granted;

  (ii) when required to do so [etc.—*complete as in Form No. 88*].

[**See note* to Form No. 88.*]

117. Oath for administration (leave having been given to swear to the death)

(Heading as in Form No. 1)

I, C D, of   make oath and say that:

1. A B of   deceased, died on or since the   day of   19   aged   years, domiciled in England and Wales intestate, a bachelor [*or as the case may be, clearing off all prior classes*];

2. By an order of Mr District Judge [*or* Registrar]   of this Division dated the   day of   19   it was ordered that, on an application being made for letters of administration of the estate of the said deceased, the death of the said deceased may be sworn to have occurred on or since the   day of   19   ;

3. No minority or life interest arises under the intestacy;

4. [*add statement as to settled land*];

5. I am the lawful* [*or* natural*] mother and only person entitled to the estate of the said deceased [*or as the case may be*];

6. I will:

  (i) collect, get in and administer [etc.—*complete as in Form No. 88*].

[**See note* to Form No. 88.*]

118. Oath for administrator (former grantee having become mentally incapable)

(Heading as in Form No. 1)

I, C D, of   make oath and say that:

1. A B of   deceased, died on the   day of   19   aged   years, domiciled in England and Wales, intestate, a widower [*or as the case may be*];

2. On the   day of   19   letters of administration of the estate of the said deceased were granted at the Principal [*or*   District Probate] Registry to E B, the lawful* son and only person entitled to the estate of the said deceased;

3. The said E B is now by reason of mental incapacity incapable of managing his affairs, no person has been authorised by the Court of Protection to apply for a grant in the estate of the said deceased, and part of the estate of the said deceased remains unadministered;

4. [*Add statement as to minority and life interests.*]

5. [*Add statement as to settled land.*]

6. I am the lawful attorney of the said E B acting under a registered enduring power of attorney;

7. I will:

  (i) collect, get in and administer according to law the unadministered estate of the said deceased, for the use and benefit of the said E B and during his incapacity;

  (ii) when required to do so by the Court, exhibit in the Court a full inventory of the said estate and render an account thereof to the Court; and

  (iii) when required to do so by the High Court, deliver up to that Court the grant of letters of administration;

[*etc. as in Form No. 88, but with reference to the unadministered estate*].

[**See note* to Form No. 88.*]

[**Note.**—*This form may be adapted for use where the former grantee was one of the persons entitled to share in the estate, in which case the applicant should be one of the other persons entitled to share.*]

119. Oath for administrator (a former grant having been revoked)

(Heading as in Form No. 1)

I, C D, of   make oath and say that:

1. A B of   deceased, died on the   day of   19   aged   years, domiciled in England and Wales intestate, a widower, without issue, parent, or brother or sister of the whole blood or any other person entitled in priority to share in his estate by virtue of any enactment [*or as the case may be*];

2. Letters of administration of the estate of the said deceased were, on the   day of   19   granted at the Principal [*or*   District Probate] Registry to E F, the lawful* cousin german of the whole blood of the said deceased, on the basis that the said deceased died intestate, a widower, without issue, parent, brother or sister of the whole or half blood or their issue, grandparent or uncle or aunt of the whole blood or any other person entitled in priority to share in the estate by virtue of any enactment, and that the said E F was one of the persons entitled to share in the estate of the said deceased;

3. The said letters of administration have been since voluntarily brought in by or on behalf of the said E F, and have been duly revoked and declared null and void;

4. [*Add statement as to minority and life interests.*]

5. [*Add statement as to settled land.*]

6. I am the lawful* nephew of the whole blood and one of the persons entitled to share in the estate of the said deceased;

7. I will:

  (i) collect, get in and administer [*etc.—complete as in Form No. 88*].

[**See note* to Form No. 88.*]

120. Oath for administration to mother of minor and nominated co-administrator

(Heading as in Form No. 1)

We, E F of   and G H of   make oath and say that:

1. A B of   deceased, died on the   day of   19   aged   years, domiciled in England and Wales intestate, a single man leaving C D his lawful* son and the only person entitled to his estate, who is now a minor aged   years;
2. The marriage of the said intestate with the deponent E F was dissolved by final decree of the High Court of Justice [*or* of the   County Court] in England and Wales dated the   day of   19   and that the said intestate did not thereafter remarry;
3. The said E F is the mother of the said minor and that there is no guardian of the said minor with parental responsibility for him;
4. That the said E F has by a nomination dated the   day of   19   nominated the deponent G H to be her co-administrator;
5. A minority but no life interest arises under the intestacy.
6. [*Add statement as to settled land.*]
7. We will:

(i) collect, get in and administer according to law the real and personal estate of the said intestate, for the use and benefit of the said minor until he attains the age of eighteen years;
(ii) when required to do so by the Court, exhibit in the Court a full inventory of the said estate and render an account thereof to the Court; and
(iii) when required to do so by the High Court, deliver up to that Court the grant of letters of administration;

[etc. *as in Form No. 88*].

[*See note *to Form No. 88.*]

[*This form may be adapted where the mother has parental responsibility by virtue of an adoption order made within the meaning of s. 12 of the Adoption Act 1976. The oath must state that she is the adopter or one of the adopters of the minor by such order and a copy of the order must be produced.*]

121. Oath for administration to father of minor and nominated co-administrator

(Heading as in Form No. 1)

We E F of   and G H of   make oath and say that:

1. A B of   deceased, died on the   day of   19   aged   years, domiciled in England and Wales intestate, a single woman leaving C D her lawful* son and the only person entitled to her estate who is now a minor aged   years;
2. The marriage of the said intestate with the deponent E F was dissolved by final decree of the High Court of Justice [*or* of the   County Court] in England and Wales dated the day of   19   and the said intestate did not thereafter remarry;
3. The said E F is the father of the said minor with parental responsibility for him under s. 2(1) of the Children Act 1989 [*or* has acquired parental responsibility for him under s. 4 of the Children Act 1989 under an order] [*or as the case may be*];
4. There is no guardian of the said minor with parental responsibility for him;
5. The said E F has by a nomination dated the   day of   19   nominated the said G H to be his co-administrator;
6. A minority but no life interest arises under the intestacy;
7. [*Add statement as to settled land.*]
8. We will:
[*as in Form No. 120*].

[*See note* to Form No. 88.*]

[*This form may be adapted where the father has parental responsibility by virtue of an adoption order made within the meaning of s. 12 of the Adoption Act 1976. The oath must state that he is the adopter or one of the adopters by such order and a copy of the order must be produced.*]

122. Oath for administration to guardian of minor and nominated co-administrator

(Heading as in Form No. 1)

We, C D of   and M N of   make oath and say that:

1. A B of   deceased, died on the   day of   19   aged   years, domiciled in England and Wales intestate, a widow, leaving E B and G B, her lawful* children and the only persons entitled to share in her estate, who are both now minors, aged   years and   years respectively;

2. I B, deceased, the father of the said minors and having parental responsibility for them, by his will dated the   day of   19   and proved on the   day of   19   at the Principal [*or*   District Probate] Registry, appointed the said C D to be guardian of his said children;

3. There is no other guardian of the said minors with parental responsibility for them, or either of them;

4. The said C D has by an instrument in writing dated the   day of   19   nominated the said M N to be his co-administrator;

5. The said C D is the guardian of the said minors having parental responsibility for them by virtue of the said appointment and the said M N is the person nominated as co-administrator;

6. A minority but no life interest arises under the intestacy;

7. [*add statement as to settled land*]

8. We will:

   (i) collect, get in and administer according to law the real and personal estate of the said intestate, for the use and benefit of the said minors, and until one of them attains the age of eighteen years;

   (ii) when required to do so [etc.—*complete as in Form No. 88*].

[**See note* to Form No. 88.*]

[**Note.**—*This form may be adapted where the guardian has parental responsibility under one of the other parts of s. 5 of the Children Act 1989 or in accordance with para. 12, 13 or 14 of Sch. 14 to that Act.*]

123. Oath for persons appointed to obtain administration for the use of minors

(Heading as in Form No. 1)

We, C D of   and K L of   make oath and say that:

1. AB of   deceased, died on the   day of   19   aged   years, domiciled in England and Wales intestate, a widower, leaving E F and G H, his lawful* children and the only persons entitled to share in his estate, who are now minors aged   years and   years respectively;

2. We have been appointed by order of Mr District Judge [*or* Registrar]   dated the   day of   19   to obtain letters of administration of the estate of the said deceased, for the use and benefit of the said minors until one of them attains the age of eighteen years;

3. [*add statement as to minority and life interests*];

4. [*add statement as to settled land*];

5. We will:

(i) collect, get in and administer [etc.—*complete as in Form No. 88*].

[**See note* to Form No. 88.*]

124. Oath for administration to guardians of a minor as personal representatives of the person entitled

(Heading as in Form No. 1)

We, C D of   and R F of   make oath and say that:

1. A B of   deceased, died on the   day of   19   aged   years, domiciled in England and Wales intestate, a widower [*or as the case may be*], leaving E B, his lawful* [*or natural**] son and the only person entitled to his estate, who has since died without

having taken upon himself letters of administration of the estate of the said intestate;

2. No minority or life interest arises under the intestacy;

3. [*add statement as to settled land*];

4. We are the administrators (as guardians and for the use and benefit of F B, who is now a minor) of the estate of the said E B, letters of administration of his estate having been granted to us at the Principal [*or   District Probate*] Registry on the   day of   19   ;

5. We will:

  (i) collect, get in and administer according to law the real and personal estate of the said deceased, for the use and benefit of the said F B until he attains the age of eighteen years;

  (ii) when required to do so by the Court, exhibit [etc.—*complete as in Form No. 88*].

[**See note* to Form No. 88*.]

125. Oath for person appointed by the Court of Protection for use of incapable person

(Heading as in Form No. 1)

I, C D, of   make oath and say that:

1. A B of   deceased, died on the   day of   19   aged   years, domiciled in England and Wales intestate, a bachelor [spinster] [widower] [widow] without issue or any other person entitled in priority to share in the estate by virtue of any enactment leaving E B, his lawful* [*or* natural*] father and the only person entitled to his estate;

2. The said E B is now by reason of mental incapacity incapable of managing his affairs;

3. I am the person authorised by an order of the Court of Protection dated the   day of   19   in the matter of the said E B, to apply for letters of administration of the estate of the said A B;

4. No minority or life interest arises under the intestacy;

5. [*add statement as to settled land*];

6. I will:

  (i) collect, get in and administer according to law the real and personal estate of the said deceased, for the use and benefit of the said E B until further representation be granted;

  (ii) when required to do so [etc.—*complete as in Form No. 88*].

[**See note* to Form No. 88*.]

[**Note.**—*See also Form No. 118 for oath for further grant where original grantee becomes incapable.*]

126. Oath for administrator by attorney acting under a registered enduring power of attorney for the use of incapable person

(Heading as in Form No. 1)

I, C D, of   make oath and say that:

1. A B of   deceased, died on the   day of   19   aged   years, domiciled in England and Wales intestate, a widower [*or as the case may be*], leaving E F, his lawful* [*or* natural*] son and the only person entitled to his estate;

2. The said E F is now by reason of mental incapacity incapable of managing his affairs;

3. No person has been authorised by the Court of Protection to apply for a grant in the estate of the said deceased;

4. No minority or life interest arises under the intestacy;

5. [*add statement as to settled land*];

6. I am the lawful attorney of the said E F, acting under a registered enduring power of attorney;

7. I will:

  (i) collect, get in and administer according to law the real and personal estate of the said deceased, for the use and benefit of the said E F until further representation be granted;

  (ii) when required to do so [etc.—*complete as in Form No. 88*].

127. Oath for administrators appointed by district judge or registrar for the use of incapable person

(Heading as in Form No. 1)

We, C D of   and G H of   make oath and say that:

1. A B of   deceased, died on the   day of   19 aged   years, domiciled in England and Wales intestate, a bachelor [spinster] [widower] [widow] without issue or parent or any other person entitled in priority to share in the estate by virtue of any enactment leaving E F, his lawful* brother of the whole blood and the only person entitled to his estate, who is now by reason of mental incapacity incapable of managing his affairs;
2. No minority or life interest arises under the intestacy;
3. [*add statement as to settled land*];
4. By order of Mr District Judge [*or* Registrar]   dated the   day of   19 it was ordered that letters of administration of the estate of the said deceased be granted to us under and by virtue of rule 35(4) of the Non-Contentious Probate Rules 1987, the grant to be for the use and benefit of the said E F limited until further representation be granted;
5. We will:

   (i) collect, get in and administer according to law the real and personal estate of the said deceased, for the use and benefit of the said E F until further representation be granted;
   (ii) when required to do so [etc.—*complete as in Form No. 88*].

[*See note* to Form No. 88.]

128. Oath for administrator pending suit

(Heading as in Form No. 1)

I, C D, of   make oath and say that:

1. A B of   widow, deceased, died on the   day of   19 aged   years, domiciled in England and Wales;
2. There is now pending in the Chancery Division of the High Court an action entitled E against F, concerning the validity of the will of the said deceased [*or* the estate of the said deceased];
3. By order of the said Chancery Division dated the   day of   19 it was ordered that letters of administration of the estate of the said deceased be granted to me, pending the said action;
4. [*add statement as to life or minority interest*];
5. [*add statement as to settled land*];
6. I will:

   (i) collect, get in and administer according to law the real and personal estate of the said deceased, pending the said action, under the directions and control of this court, save distributing the residue thereof;
   (ii) when required to so by the Court [etc.—*complete as in Form No. 88*].

[**Note.**—*If the order of the court contains any limitation, this form must be varied accordingly. The grant may be made to one individual administrator notwithstanding any life or minority interest, but the oath must state whether or not such interests arise. Application for the grant may only be made to the Principal Registry because the contention in the case has not been disposed of—see NCPR 7(1)(a).*]

129. Oath for administrator, after citation to accept or refuse a grant

(Heading as in Form No. 1)

We, D B of   and E B of   make oath and say that:

1. A B of   deceased, died on the   day of   19 aged   years, domiciled in England and Wales, intestate;
2. C B, the lawful widow of the said intestate, has been duly cited to accept or refuse letters of administration of the estate of the said intestate;

3. In default of appearance of the said C B to the said citation, it was ordered by Mr District Judge [*or* Registrar]   of this Division on the   day of   19   that letters of administration of the estate of the said intestate be granted to us;

4. No minority but a life interest arises under the intestacy;

5. [*add statement as to settled land*];

6. We are the lawful* [*or* natural*] sons and two of the persons entitled to share in the estate of the said intestate;

7. We will:

(i) collect, get in and administer [etc.—*complete as in Form No. 88*].

[**See note* to Form No. 88.*]

130. Oath for administrator, after citation to propound will

(NCPR 48)

(Heading as in Form No. 1)

I, C D, of   make oath and say that:

1. A B of   deceased, died on the   day of   19   aged   years, domiciled in England and Wales, intestate;

2. In default of appearance of the persons cited to propound the purported will dated 19   it was ordered by Mr District Judge [*or* Registrar]   of this Division on the   day of   19   that a grant of representation of the estate of the deceased be issued as if the said purported will were invalid;

3. [*add statement as to minority or life interest*];

4. [*add statement as to settled land*];

5. The said deceased died [etc.—*clearances*], and I am the lawful*   and only [one of the] person[s] entitled to [share in] the estate of the deceased;

6. I will:

(i) collect, get in and administer [etc.—*complete as in Form No. 88*].

[**See note* to Form No. 88.*]

131. Oath for administrator (commoriens spouses)

(Death after 1925 but before 1953)

(Estate exceeding £1,000 net)

(Heading as in Form No. 1)

I, C D, of   make oath and say that:

1. A B of   deceased, died on the   day of   19   aged   years, domiciled in England and Wales, intestate;

2. All possible enquiries as to survivorship have been made, but it appears that the said A B and E F, his lawful wife [*or* her lawful husband] [and G H, his [her] lawful daughter and only issue] died in circumstances rendering it uncertain which of them survived the other [others];

3. [That the said G H died an infant and unmarried without having attained an absolutely vested interest in the estate of the said intestate];

4. The said A B, being the younger of the spouses is, by virtue of section 184 of the Law of Property Act 1925, deemed to have survived the said E F;

5. That no life or minority interest arises under the intestacy;

6. [*add statement as to settled land*];

7. I am the lawful [father] and only person [*or* one of the persons] entitled to [share in] the estate of the said intestate;

8. I will:

(i) collect, get in and administer [etc.—*complete as in Form No. 88*].

[**Note.**—*Evidence of the circumstances must be submitted previously to the district judge or registrar for his decision whether more enquiries must be made, or whether it may be sworn that the circumstances render survivorship uncertain.*

If the relationship of the applicant is more remote than parent, it must be sworn that the intestate died without relations nearer than the applicant in the order as set out in NCPR 22.]

132. Oath for administrator (commorientes) to representative of person deemed to have survived

(Heading as in Form No. 1)

I, C D, of   make oath and say that:

1. A B of   died on the   day of   19   aged   years, domiciled in England and Wales, intestate, a bachelor [spinster] [widower] [widow] without issue or parent or any other person entitled in priority to share in the estate by virtue of any enactment [*or as the case may be*];
2. All possible enquiries as to survivorship have been made, but it appears that the said A B and E F, his lawful* sister of the whole blood, died in circumstances rendering it uncertain which of them survived the other;
3. The said E F, being the younger is, by virtue of section 184 of the Law of Property Act 1925, deemed to have survived the said intestate, and was the only person entitled to the estate of the said intestate;
4. [*Statement as to minority and life interests.*]
5. [*Statement as to settled land.*]
6. I am the sole executor of the will [*or* administrator of the estate] of the said E F, probate [*or* letters of administration] thereof having been granted to me at the Principal [*or* District Probate] Registry on the day of   19 ;
7. I will:

(i) collect, get in and administer [etc.—*complete as in Form No. 88*].

[**See note* to Form No. 88.*]

[**Note.**—*Evidence of the circumstances must be submitted previously to the district judge or registrar for his decision whether more enquiries must be made, or whether it may be sworn that the circumstances render survivorship uncertain.*]

133. Oath for administrator (commoriens spouses)

(Death after 1952 but before 1996)

(Heading as in Form No. 1)

I, C D, of   make oath and say that:

1. A B of   died on the   day of   19   aged   years, domiciled in England and Wales, intestate;
2. All possible enquiries as to survivorship have been made, but it appears that the said A B and E F, his lawful wife [*or* her lawful husband] died in circumstances rendering it uncertain which of them survived the other.
3. [*Statement as to minority and life interests.*]
4. [*Statement as to settled land.*]
5. I am the lawful* son and one of the persons entitled to share in the estate of the said intestate;
6. I will:

(i) collect, get in and administer [etc.—*complete as in Form No. 88*].

[**See note* to Form No. 88.*]

[**Note.**—*Evidence of the circumstances must be submitted previously to the district judge or registrar for his decision whether more enquiries must be made, or whether it may be sworn that the circumstances render survivorship uncertain.*]

134. Oath for administration (with will) (commorientes)

(Heading as in Form No. 1)

I, C D, of   make oath and say that:

1. I believe the paper writing now produced to and marked by me to contain the true and original last will and testament of A B of   deceased, who died on the   day of   19   aged   years, domiciled in England and Wales;
2. All possible enquiries as to survivorship have been made, but it appears that the said deceased and E F, the sole executrix and residuary legatee and devisee named in the said will, died in circumstances rendering it uncertain which of them survived the other;
3. No life or minority interest arises in the estate of the said deceased;
4. [*add statement as to settled land*];
5. The said E F, being the younger, is by virtue of section 184 of the Law of Property Act 1925, deemed to have survived the said deceased;
6. I am the sole executor of the will of the said E F [*or* the administrator [with will] of the estate of the said E F], probate [*or* letters of administration [with will]] thereof having been granted to me at the Principal [*or*   District Probate] Registry on the   day of   19   [*or*, The said E F, being the elder, is by virtue of section 184 of the Law of Property Act 1925, deemed to have died in the lifetime of the said deceased who died a spinster without issue or parent or any other person entitled in priority to share in her estate by virtue of any enactment [*or as the case may be*];
7. I am the lawful* brother of the whole blood and one of the persons entitled to share in the undisposed-of estate of the said deceased;]
8. I will:

(i) collect, get in and administer [etc.—*complete as in Form 88*].

[**See note* to Form No. 88.*]

[**Note.**—*Evidence of the circumstances must be submitted previously to the district judge or registrar for his decision whether more enquiries must be made, or whether it may be sworn that the circumstances render survivorship uncertain.*]

135. Oath for cessate administration to person entitled on attaining his majority

(Heading as in Form No. 1)

I, C D, of   make oath and say that:

1. A B of   deceased, died on the   day of   19   aged   years, domiciled in England and Wales, intestate, a widower leaving me his lawful* son and only person entitled to his estate;
2. On the   day of   19   letters of administration of the estate of the said deceased were granted at the Principal [*or*   District Probate] Registry to E F and G H, for my use and benefit, and until I should attain the age of twenty-one [*or* eighteen] years;
3. On the   day of   19   I attained the age of twenty-one [*or* eighteen] years, by reason of which the said letters of administration have ceased and expired;
4. No life interest and now no minority interest arises under the intestacy;
5. [*add statement as to settled land*];
6. I am the lawful* son and only person entitled to the estate of the said deceased;
7. I will:

(i) collect, get in and administer according to law the real and personal estate of the said deceased;
(ii) when required to do so by the Court, exhibit in the Court a full inventory of the said estate and render an account thereof to the Court; and
(iii) when required to do so by the High Court, deliver up to that Court the grant of letters of administration;

[etc. *as in Form No. 88, but with reference to the unadministered estate*].

[**See note* to Form No. 88.*]

136. Oath for cessate administration, the attorney administrator having died

(Heading as in Form No. 1)

I, C D, of   make oath and say that:

1. A B of   deceased, died on the   day of   19   aged   years, domiciled in England and Wales, intestate, leaving me her lawful husband and only person entitled to her estate;

2. On the   day of   19   letters of administration of the estate of the said deceased were granted at the Principal [*or*   District Probate] Registry to E F, my lawful attorney, for my use and benefit, and until I should obtain letters of administration of the said estate [*or* until further representation be granted];

3. The said E F died on the   day of   19   by reason of which the said letters of administration have ceased and expired;

4. [*add statement as to minority and life interests*];

5. [*add statement as to settled land*];

6. I am the lawful husband and only person now entitled to the estate of the said deceased;

7. I will:

(i) collect, get in and administer [etc.—*complete as in Form No. 135*].

137. Oath for cessate administration, following a grant limited to an action

(Heading as in Form No. 1)

I, C D, of   make oath and say that:

1. A B of   deceased, died on the   day of   19   aged   years, domiciled in England and Wales, intestate, a bachelor [*or as the case may be*];

2. On the   day of   19   letters of administration of the estate of the said deceased were granted at the Principal [*or*   District Probate] Registry under and by virtue of section 116 of the Supreme Court Act 1981 [*or as the case may be*], to J K, limited to prosecuting [*or defending*] an action in the   Division of the High Court to be brought against the personal representative of the deceased [*or as the case may be*];

3. The proceedings in the said action have since terminated, whereby the said letters of administration have ceased and expired;

4. [*add statement as to minority and life interests*];

5. [*add statement as to settled land*];

6. I am the lawful* father and only person entitled to the estate of the said deceased [*or as the case may be*];

7. I will:

(i) collect, get in and administer [etc.—*complete as in Form No. 135*].

[**See note* to Form No. 88.]

138. Oath for administration limited to prosecuting or defending an action

(Heading as in Form No. 1)

I, C D, of   make oath and say that:

1. A B of   deceased, died on the   day of   19   aged   years, domiciled in England and Wales, intestate;

2. I am the person authorised by order of Mr District Judge [*or* Registrar]   under section 116 of the Supreme Court Act 1981, dated   to apply for and obtain letters of administration of the estate of the said deceased, limited as hereinafter mentioned;

3. [*add statement as to minority or life interest*];

4. [*add statement as to settled land*];

5. I will:

(i) collect, get in and administer according to law the real and personal estate of the said deceased, limited for the purpose only of prosecuting [defending] [becoming a party to] an action in the   Division of the High Court [*or as the case may be*] to be brought against E F [*or to be brought by E F*], but no further or otherwise;

(ii) when required to do so by the Court, exhibit in the Court a full inventory of the said estate, limited as aforesaid, and render an account thereof to the Court; and

(iii) when required to do so by the High Court, deliver up to that Court the grant of letters of administration;

[etc. *as in Form No. 66, but with reference to the limited estate, as aforesaid, amounting to the sum of nil.*]

[**Note.**—*The action should be identified in the oath (Registrar's Direction, 23 March 1964).*]

139. Oath for administration ad colligenda bona

(Heading as in Form No. 1)

I, C D, of   make oath and say that:

1. A B of   deceased, died on the   day of   19   aged   years, domiciled in England and Wales;
2. [*Statement as to minority or life interest.*]
3. [*Statement as to settled land.*]
4. By order of Mr District Judge [*or* Registrar]   dated the   day of   19   it was ordered that letters of administration of the estate of the said deceased be granted to me limited as hereinafter mentioned;
5. I will:

(i) collect, get in and administer according to law the real and personal estate of the said deceased limited to collecting, getting in and receiving the estate, and doing such acts as may be necessary for the preservation of the same† and until further representation be granted, but no further or otherwise;

(ii) when required to do so by the Court, exhibit in the Court a full inventory of the said estate and render an account thereof to the Court; and

(iii) when required to do so by the High Court, deliver up to that Court the grant of letters of administration;

[etc. *as in Form No. 66*].

[†*If express powers beyond these have been included in the order they must be recited here.*]

140. Oath for administration under s. 116 of the Supreme Court Act 1981

(Heading as in Form No. 1)

I, C D, of   make oath and say that:

1. A B of   widow, deceased, died on the   day of   19   aged   years, domiciled in England and Wales, intestate;
2. No minority or life interest arises under the intestacy;
3. [*Statement as to settled land.*]
4. On the   day of   19   it was ordered by Mr District Judge [*or* Registrar]   that letters of administration of the estate of the said deceased be granted to me under and by virtue of section 116 of the Supreme Court Act 1981 [*recite any limitations given in order*];
5. I will:

(i) collect, get in and administer according to law the real and personal estate of the deceased [*add, if applicable,* limited as aforesaid];

(ii) when required to do so by the court [etc.—*complete as in Form No. 88*].

(Form of oath for grant limited to an action, No. 138; Oath for administration (with will) under s. 116, No. 163.)

141. Oath for limited administration—married woman separated from her husband by separation order or decree (death prior to 1 August 1970)

(Heading as in Form No. 1)

I, C D, of   make oath and say that:

1. A B of   deceased, died on the   day of   19   aged   years, domiciled in England and Wales, intestate, leaving surviving her E F, her lawful husband;
2. On the   day of   19   the Right Honourable   the President [*or* the Honourable Sir   one of the Judges] of the Probate, Divorce, and Admiralty Division of the said High Court, by his final decree, decreed that the said A B be judicially separated from the said E F [*or* By an order dated the   day of   19   made by the Court under the Summary Jurisdiction (Separation and Maintenance) Acts 1895–1949 [*or* under the Matrimonial Proceedings (Magistrates' Courts) Act 1960] it was ordered that the said intestate be no longer bound to cohabit with the said E F [*follow terms of order*];
3. The separation under the said decree [order] continued from the making thereof to the time of the death of the said deceased;
4. The said deceased died without issue or parent;
5. [*Add statement as to minority or life interest.*]
6. [*Add statement as to settled land.*]
7. I am the lawful brother of the whole blood, and one of the persons entitled to share in the estate of the said deceased;
8. I will:

   (i) collect, get in and administer according to law the real and personal estate of the said deceased, limited to all such estate as she acquired since the date of the said decree [*or* order], but no further or otherwise;
   (ii) when required to do so by the Court, exhibit in the Court a full inventory of the said estate, limited as aforesaid, and render an account thereof to the Court; and
   (iii) when required to do so by the High Court, deliver up to that Court the grant of letters of administration;

[etc. *as in Form No. 66, but limited as aforesaid*].

142. Oath for administration—judicially separated spouse (death on or after 1 August 1970)

(Heading as in Form No. 1)

I, C D, of   make oath and say that:

1. A B of   deceased, died on the   day of   19   aged   years, domiciled in England and Wales, intestate, leaving him [*or* her] surviving E F, his lawful widow [*or* her lawful husband];
2. By decree of the High Court of Justice [*or* of the   County Court] in England and Wales, dated the   day of   19   it was decreed that the said A B be judicially separated from the said E F;
3. At the date of death of the said deceased the said decree remained in force and the separation thereunder continued;
4. [*Insert clearings, e.g.* The said deceased died without issue or parent or any other person entitled in priority to share in the estate by virtue of any enactment;]
5. [*Add statement as to minority and life interests.*]
6. [*Add statement as to settled land.*]
7. I am the lawful* brother of the whole blood and only person entitled to [*or* one of the persons entitled to share in] the estate of the said deceased;
8. I will:

(i) collect, get in and administer [etc.—*complete as in Form No. 88*].

[**See note* to Form No. 88.*]

143. Oath for administration (will) to residuary legatee and devisee

(Heading as in Form No. 1)

I, C D, of   make oath and say that:

1. I believe the paper writing now produced to and marked by me to contain the true and original last will and testament of A B, of   deceased, who died on the   day of 19 aged   years, domiciled in England and Wales;

2. No executor or residuary legatee or devisee in trust is named in the will; [*or* E F, the sole executor [and residuary legatee and devisee in trust] named in the said will died in the lifetime of the said deceased [*or* survived the said deceased but has since died without having taken upon himself probate of the said will [*or* letters of administration with the said will annexed]]; [*or* E F, the sole [*or* surviving] executor [and residuary legatee and devisee in trust] named in the said will has renounced probate thereof [and letters of administration with the said will annexed]];

3. No life or minority interest arises in the estate of the said deceased;

4. [*add statement as to settled land*];

5. I am the residuary legatee [*or* the residuary devisee, *or* the residuary legatee and devisee] named in the said will;

6. I will:

   (i) collect, get in and administer according to law the real and personal estate of the said deceased;

   (ii) when required to do so by the Court, exhibit in the Court a full inventory of the said estate and render an account thereof to the Court; and

   (iii) when required to do so by the High Court, deliver up to that Court the grant of letters of administration;

[etc. *as in Form No. 66.*]

[**Note.**—*Under NCPR 20(c) the class of residuary legatee or devisee includes one for life and under NCPR 20(c)(i) a* **contingent** *residuary legatee or devisee is in the same class of priority as a residuary legatee or devisee having a vested interest, but, unless a district judge or registrar otherwise directs, a residuary beneficiary whose interest is vested is preferred to one entitled on the happening of a contingency.*]

144. Oath for administration (will) to residuary legatee and devisee for life and residuary legatee and devisee substituted

(Heading as in Form No. 1)

We, E F of   and G H of   make oath and say that:

1. We believe the paper writing now produced to and marked by us to contain the true and original last will and testament [with a codicil thereto], of A B of   deceased, who died on the   day of   19 aged   years, domiciled in England and Wales;

2. C D, the sole executor and residuary legatee and devisee in trust named in the said will, has renounced probate of the said will [and codicil] and administration (with will [and codicil]) of the estate of the said deceased;

3. No minority but a life interest arises in the estate of the said deceased;

4. [*add statement as to settled land*];

5. The deponent E F is the residuary legatee and devisee for life named in the said will, and the deponent G H is the residuary legatee and devisee substituted in the said will;

6. We will:

   (i) collect, get in and administer according to law the real and personal estate of the said deceased;

   (ii) when required to do so by the Court, exhibit in the Court a full inventory of the said estate and render an account thereof to the Court; and

   (iii) when required to do so by the High Court, deliver up to that Court the grant of letters of administration:

[etc. *as in Form No. 66.*]

145. Oath for administration (will) to residuary legatee and devisee and a specific legatee or devisee, or a creditor

(Heading as in Form No. 1)

We, E F of   and G H of   make oath and say that:

1. We believe the paper writing now produced to and marked by us to contain the true and original last will and testament of A B of   deceased, who died on the   day of 19   aged   years, domiciled in England and Wales;
2. C D, the sole executor named in the said will, died in the lifetime of the deceased [*or* survived the said deceased, and has since died without having taken upon himself probate of the said will] [*or* has renounced probate of the said will];
3. A minority but no life interest arises in the estate of the said deceased;
4. [*add statement as to settled land*];
5. The deponent E F is the residuary legatee and devisee named in the said will, and the deponent G H is a legatee [*or* a devisee] named in the said will [*or* a creditor of the said deceased];
6. We will:

(i) collect, get in and administer [etc.—*complete as in Form No. 143*].

146. Oath for administration (will) to representative of residuary legatee and devisee

(Heading as in Form No. 1)

I, C D, of   make oath and say that:

1. I believe the paper writing now produced to and marked by me to contain the true and original last will and testament of A B of   deceased, who died on the   day of 19   aged   years, domiciled in England and Wales;
2. E B, the sole executor and residuary legatee and devisee named in the said will survived the said deceased and has since died without having proved the said will;
3. [*add statement as to life and minority interests*];
4. [*add statement as to settled land*];
5. I am the executor of the will [*or* administrator of the estate] of the said E B, probate [*or* letters of administration] thereof having been granted to me out of the   Probate Registry on the   day of   19   ;
6. I will:

(i) collect, get in and administer [etc.—*complete as in Form No. 143*].

147. Oath for administration (will) to substituted residuary legatees

(Heading as in Form No. 1)

We, C D of   and G H of   make oath and say that:

1. We believe the paper writing now produced to and marked by us to contain the true and original last will and testament of A B of   deceased, who died on the   day of 19   aged   years, domiciled in England and Wales;
2. E F the sole executrix and residuary legatee and devisee for life named in the said will, has renounced probate thereof and administration (with will) of the estate of the said deceased;
3. No minority but a life interest arises in the estate of the said deceased;
4. [*add statement as to settled land*];
5. We are two of the residuary legatees and devisees substituted in the said will;
6. We will:

(i) collect, get in and administer according to law [etc.—*complete as in Form No. 143*].

148. Oath for administration (will) to person entitled to undisposed-of estate

(Heading as in Form No. 1)

I, C D, of   make oath and say that:

1. I believe the paper writing now produced to and marked by me to contain the true and original last will and testament of A B of   deceased, who died on the   day of 19   aged   years, domiciled in England and Wales;
2. No executor or residuary legatee or devisee is named in the will;
3. The said deceased died a bachelor [spinster] [widower] [widow] without issue or parent or any other person entitled in priority to share in the estate by virtue of any enactment [*or as the case may be*];
4. I am the lawful* brother of the whole blood and only person entitled to [*or* one of the persons entitled to share in] the undisposed-of estate of the said deceased;
5. No life or minority interest arises in the estate of the said deceased;
6. [*add statement as to settled land*];
7. I will:

(i) collect, get in and administer [etc.—*complete as in Form No. 143*].

[**See note** to Form No. 88.]

[*If a residuary gift in a will fails by reason of s. 15 of the Wills Act 1837, the following wording, adapted as necessary, should be used:* 'The residuary bequest and devise to E F in the said will is void by reason that he was an attesting witness to the said will [*or* that at the date of the said will he was the lawful husband of G F, an attesting witness to the said will].']

149. Oath for administration (will) to legatee, devisee or creditor

(Heading as in Form No. 1)

I, C D, of   make oath and say that:

1. I believe the paper writing now produced to and marked by me to contain the true and original last will and testament of A B of   deceased, who died on the   day of   19   aged   years, domiciled in England and Wales;
2. E F, the sole executor and residuary legatee and devisee named in the said will has renounced probate thereof and letters of administration (with will) of the estate of the said deceased;
3. [*add statement as to minority or life interest*];
4. [*add statement as to settled land*];
5. I am a legatee [*or* devisee] named in the said will [*or* a creditor of the said deceased];
6. I will:

(i) collect, get in and administer [etc.—*complete as in Form No. 143*].

[*If the residuary gift in a will fails by reason of s. 15 of the Wills Act 1837, the following wording, adapted as necessary, should be used:* 'The residuary bequest and devise to E F in the said will is void by reason that he was an attesting witness to the said will [*or* that at the date of the said will he was the lawful husband of G F, an attesting witness to the said will].']

[**Note.**—*Under NCPR 20(e) a* **contingent** *legatee or devisee is in the same class of priority as a legatee or devisee having a vested interest but, unless a district judge or registrar otherwise directs, a legatee or devisee whose interest is vested is preferred to one entitled on the happening of a contingency.*]

150. Oath for administration (will) to legatee in accordance with NCPR 20(c)(ii); whole, or substantially whole, of known estate disposed of by enumeration

(Heading as in Form No. 1)

I, C D, of   make oath and say that:

1. I believe the paper writing now produced to and marked by me to contain the true and original last will and testament of A B of   deceased, who died on the   day of 19   aged   years, domiciled in England and Wales;

2. E F, the sole executor named in the said will has renounced probate thereof [*or,* No executor is named in the said will];

3. [*add statement as to minority and life interests*];

4. [*add statement as to settled land*];

5. I am a legatee [*or* devisee] named in the said will which disposes of the whole [*or* substantially the whole] of the known estate;

6. I will:

   (i) collect, get in and administer according to law the real and personal estate of the said deceased;

   (ii) when required to do so by the Court, exhibit in the Court a full inventory of the said estate and render an account thereof to the Court; and

   (iii) when required to do so by the High Court, deliver up to that Court the grant of letters of administration;

[etc.—*complete as in Form No. 66.*]

[**Note.**—*Where application is made by a legatee (or devisee) on the ground that substantially the whole estate is disposed of the case must be submitted to the district judge or registrar for his decision whether the facts bring the case within the terms of the rule, having regard to the size of the estate and the amount disposed of. The following statement should then be added at the end of the oath:* '£   of the total value of the known estate of £   is disposed of by the said will'.

Unless it is clear from the papers that there are kin entitled to share in any undisposed-of estate, a statement to this effect should (if such be the case) be included in the oath. If there are no such kin, notice of the application should be given to the Treasury Solicitor under NCPR 38 (Registrar's Direction, 5 August 1954).]

151. Oath for administration (will) to the Public Trustee

(Heading as in Form No. 1)

I,   of the Public Trust Office, Kingsway, London, WC2, on behalf of C D, the Public Trustee, make oath and say that:

1. A B of   deceased, died on the   day of   19   aged   years, domiciled in England and Wales, having made and duly executed his last will and testament;

2. [*Clear off executors.*]

3. The said deceased by his said will appointed E F and G H residuary legatees and devisees [*or* did not in his said will name any residuary legatee or devisee and died a bachelor [spinster, *etc.*], leaving E F, G H, and I J his lawful*   the only persons entitled to share in his undisposed-of estate];

4. The said C D is the Public Trustee constituted by the Public Trustee Act 1906;

5. Notice in writing has been duly given to all persons above mentioned as residuary legatees or devisees [*or* persons entitled to share in the undisposed-of estate] [except the said   whose address the Public Trustee has been unable to discover] that the Public Trustee is about to apply for a grant of letters of administration (with will annexed) of the estate of the said deceased, and all the said persons have in writing consented to the said grant being made to him [except the said   who has not within due time after the posting of the said notice applied for a like grant or entered any caveat];

6. I believe the paper writing now produced to and marked by me to contain the true and original last will and testament of the said deceased;

7. [*Add statement as to life and minority interests.*]

8. [*Add statement as to settled land.*]

9. The Public Trustee will:

   (i) collect, get in and administer [etc.—*complete as in Form No. 143, duly adapted*].

[*See note* to Form No. 88.]

152. Oath for administration (will) to testator's widow and a person entitled to share in estate (there being no executor or residuary legatee or devisee)

(Heading as in Form No. 1)

We, E B of   and C B of   make oath and say that:

1. We believe the paper writing now produced to and marked by us to contain the true and original last will and testament of A B of   deceased, who died on the   day of 19   aged   years, domiciled in England and Wales;
2. No executor or residuary legatee or devisee is named in the will;
3. No minority but a life interest arises in the estate of the said deceased;
4. [*add statement as to any settled land*];
5. We are respectively the lawful widow, and a lawful* [*or* natural*] son and one of the persons entitled to share in the undisposed-of estate of the said deceased;
6. We will:

(i) collect, get in and administer [etc.—*complete as in Form No. 143*].

[*See note* to Form No. 88.]

153. Oath for administration (will) to a person interested in the event of an accretion (estate below £125,000 (where deceased left issue), or £200,000 (where deceased left no issue)) for death on or after 1 December 1993 [*for the appropriate lesser sums depending on date of death see para. 6.85, ante*]

(Heading as in Form No. 1)

I, C D, of   make oath and say that:

1. I believe the paper writing now produced to and marked by me to contain the true and original last will and testament of A B of   deceased, who died on the   day of   19   aged   years, domiciled in England and Wales;
2. No executor or residuary legatee or devisee is named in the will;
3. E B, the lawful widow and the only person now entitled to the undisposed-of estate of the said deceased has renounced letters of administration (with will) of the estate of the said deceased;
4. [*add statement as to life and minority interests*];
5. [*add statement as to settled land*];
6. I am the lawful* [*or* natural*] son of the said deceased and a person who may have a beneficial interest in this estate in the event of an accretion thereto;
7. I will:

(i) collect, get in and administer [etc.—*complete as in Form No. 143*].

[*See note* to Form No. 88.]

154. Oath for administration (will)—gift to child or other issue saved by s. 33 of the Wills Act 1837

(Death before 1 January 1983)

(Heading as in Form No. 1)

I, C D, of   make oath and say that:

1. I believe the paper writing now produced to and marked by me to contain the true and original last will and testament of A B of   deceased, who died on the   day of 19   aged   years, domiciled in England and Wales;
2. No executor or residuary legatee or devisee in trust is named in the will;
3. [*add statement as to life and minority interests*];
4. [*add statement as to settled land*];
5. E B, the lawful daughter of the said deceased and the residuary legatee and devisee named in the said will, died in the lifetime of the said deceased leaving lawful issue who survived the said deceased;

6. I am the executor of the will [*or* administrator of the estate] of the said E B, probate [*or* letters of administration] thereof having been granted out of the Principal [*or* District Probate] Registry on the   day of   19   ;
7. I will:

(i) collect, get in and administer [etc.—*complete as in Form No. 143*].

[**Note.**—*Where the death occurred on or after 1 January 1970, the provisions of s. 33 of the Wills Act 1837 are extended by s. 16 of the Family Law Reform Act 1969 so that references to children or other issue of the testator, and to issue of the intended beneficiary, include illegitimate children and persons who would rank as such issue but for their own illegitimacy or that of some other person through whom they have descended from the testator, or the intended beneficiary, as the case may be; furthermore, by virtue of s. 39 of the Adoption Act 1976 (which replaced para. 3(1) of Sch. 1 to the Children Act 1975) it would appear that as respects deaths after 31 December 1975, the references in s. 33 of the Wills Act 1837 to children or other issue of the testator are to include children adopted by the testator (see paras. 5.136 ff., ante).*
  Where a gift is saved by these extended provisions, the reference in this form to 'lawful issue' should be adapted accordingly.]

155. Oath for administration (will)—gift to child or other issue saved by s. 33 of the Wills Act 1837

(Death on or after 1 January 1983)

(Heading as in Form No. 1)

I, C D, of   make oath and say that:

1. I believe the paper writing now produced to and marked by me to contain the true and original last will and testament of A B of   deceased, who died on the   day of   19   aged   years, domiciled in England and Wales;
2. No executor or residuary legatee or devisee in trust is named in the will;
3. [*add statement as to life and minority interests*];
4. [*add statement as to settled land*];
5. E B, the lawful daughter of the said deceased and the residuary legatee and devisee named in the said will, died in the lifetime of the said deceased leaving lawful issue who survived the said deceased;
6. I am [one of] the said lawful issue of the said E B being her lawful son [*or as the case may be*] and [one of the persons] the person now entitled to [share in] the residue under the said will;
7. I will:

(i) collect, get in and administer [etc.—*complete as in Form No. 143*].

[*See note to Form No. 154.*]

156. Oath for administration (will) to assignee

(NCPR 24)

(Heading as in Form No. 1)

I, E F, of   make oath and say that:

1. I believe the paper writing now produced to and marked by me to contain the true and original last will and testament of A B of   deceased, who died on the   day of   19   aged   years, domiciled in England and Wales;
2. No executor or residuary legatee or devisee in trust is named in the will [*or* G H, the sole executor (and residuary legatee and devisee in trust) named in the said will, died in the lifetime of the said deceased [*or* has renounced probate thereof (and letters of administration with will annexed of the deceased's estate)]];
3. That no life or minority interest arises in the estate of the said deceased;
4. [*add statement as to settled land*];

5. By deed of assignment dated the   day of   19   C D [and I J], son [and daughter] of the said deceased, the universal legatee[s] and devisee[s] named in the said will, has [have] assigned to me the deponent [and to K L] all his [their] right and title to an interest in the estate of the said deceased;
6. I will:

(i) collect, get in and administer [etc.—*complete as in Form No. 143*].

157. Oath for administration (will) to the attorney of an executor

(Heading as in Form No. 1)

I, C D, of   make oath and say that:

1. A B of   deceased, died on the   day of   19   aged   years, domiciled in England and Wales, having made and duly executed his last will and testament, and thereof appointed E F sole executor;
2. [*add statement as to minority or life interest*];
3. [*add statement as to settled land*];
4. I am the lawful attorney of the said E F;
5. I believe the paper writing now produced to and marked by me to contain the true and original last will and testament of the said deceased;
6. I will:

(i)   collect, get in and administer according to law the real and personal estate of the said deceased for the use and benefit of the said E F, until further representation be granted;
(ii) when required to do so by the Court, exhibit in the Court a full inventory of the said estate and render an account thereof to the Court; and
(iii) when required to do so by the High Court, deliver up to that Court the grant of letters of administration;

[etc. *as in Form No. 66*].

158. Oath for administration (will) to nominee of an executor or residuary legatee or devisee (a non-trust corporation)

(Heading as in Form No. 1)

I, C D, of   make oath and say that:

1. I believe the paper writing now produced to and marked by me to contain the true and original last will and testament of A B of   deceased, who died on the   day of   19   aged   years, domiciled in England and Wales;
2. E F [*the corporation or association*] the sole executor [*or the residuary legatee and devisee in trust, or residuary legatee and devisee*] named in the said will is not a trust corporation as defined by rule 2(1) of the Non-Contentious Probate Rules 1987;
3. [*statement as to minority and life interests*];
4. [*statement as to settled land*];
5. By resolution dated the   day of   I was duly appointed by the said E F as its nominee for the purpose of applying for letters of administration (with will) of the estate of the said deceased;
6. I will:

(i) collect, get in and administer according to law the real and personal estate of the said deceased for the use and benefit of the said E F, until further representation be granted;
(ii) when required to do so by the Court [etc.—*complete as in Form No. 143*].

[**Note.**—*If the corporation is an executor, it must be established (e.g. by producing a copy of its constitution) that it has power to take a grant through a nominee. In the case of a corporation, association, or public or charitable or private body of persons, entitled as beneficiary or creditor, it is sufficient to lodge an authenticated copy of a resolution of the committee or other body most completely representing the corporation or association etc. appointing the nominee (Registrar's Direction, 2 January 1956).*]

159. Oath for administration (will) to both parents of a minor jointly

(Heading as in in Form No. 1)

We, E D   and F D, both of   make oath and say that:

1. A B of   deceased, died on the   day of   19   aged   years, domiciled in England and Wales, having made and duly executed his last will and testament;
2. No executor or residuary legatee or devisee in trust is named in the will [*or* G H, the sole executor [and residuary legatee and devisee in trust] named in the said will died in the life-time of the said deceased *or* has renounced probate of the said will [and letters of administration with will annexed of the deceased's estate] *or as the case may be*];
3. C D the residuary legatee and devisee named in the said will is now a minor of the age of   years;
4. We believe the paper writing now produced to and marked by us to contain the true and original last will and testament of the said deceased;
5. A minority but no life interest arises in the estate of the said deceased;
6. [*Add statement as to settled land.*]
7. We are the parents of the said C D and have parental responsibility for him under s. 2(1) of the Children Act 1989, and we will:

(i) collect, get in and administer [etc.—*complete as in Form No. 120*].

160. Oath for administration (will) to person authorised by Court of Protection where executor is incapable

(Heading as in Form No. 1)

I, C D, of   make oath and say that:

1. A B of   deceased, died on the   day of   19   aged   years, domiciled in England and Wales, having made and duly executed his last will and testament and thereof appointed E F sole executor;
2. The said E F is now by reason of mental incapacity incapable of managing his affairs;
3. By an order of the Court of Protection dated the   day of   19   I was duly authorised to apply for letters of administration (with will) of the estate of the said deceased for the use and benefit of the said E F;
4. [*add statement as to minority or life interest*];
5. [*add statement as to settled land*];
6. I believe the paper writing now produced to and marked by me to contain the true and original last will and testament of the said deceased;
7. I will:

(i) collect, get in and administer according to law the real and personal estate of the said deceased for the use and benefit of the said E F until further representation be granted;
(ii) when required to do so by the Court [etc.—*complete as in Form No. 143*].

161. Oath for administration (will) to attorney acting under a registered enduring power of attorney; for the use of incapable executor

(Heading as in Form No. 1)

I, C D, of   make oath and say that:

1. A B of   deceased, died on the   day of   19   aged   years, domiciled in England and Wales, having made and duly executed his last will and testament;
2. E F, the sole executor named in the said will, is now by reason of mental incapacity incapable of managing his affairs;
3. No one has been authorised by the Court of Protection to apply for a grant of representa-tion of the estate of the said deceased for the use and benefit of the said E F;
4. I am the lawful attorney of the said E F acting under a registered enduring power of attorney;
5. [*add statement as to minority or life interest*];
6. [*add statement as to settled land*];

7. I believe the paper writing now produced to and marked by me to contain the true and original last will and testament of the said deceased;

8. I will:

(i)   collect, get in and administer according to law the real and personal estate of the said deceased for the use and benefit of the said E F until further representation be granted;

(ii) when required to do so [etc.—*complete as in Form No. 143*].

162. Oath for administration (will) to person entitled to the residuary estate; for the use of incapable executor

(Heading as in Form No. 1)

I, C D, of   make oath and say that:

I. A B of   deceased, died on the   day of   19   aged   years, domiciled in England and Wales, having made and duly executed his last will and testament;

2. E F, the sole executor named in the said will, is now by reason of mental incapacity incapable of managing his affairs;

3. No one has been authorised by the Court of Protection to apply for a grant of representation of the estate of the said deceased for the use and benefit of the said E F;

4. There is no lawful attorney of the said E F acting under a registered enduring power of attorney [*or* G H, the lawful attorney of the said E F acting under a registered enduring power of attorney, has renounced administration for the use and benefit of the said E F];

5. I am the residuary legatee and devisee named in the said will;

6. [*add statement as to minority or life interest*];

7. [*add statement as to settled land*];

8. I believe the paper writing now produced to and marked by me to contain the true and original last will and testament of the said deceased;

9. I will:

(i)   collect, get in and administer according to law the real and personal estate of the said deceased for the use and benefit of the said E F until further representation be granted;

(ii) when required to do so [etc.—*complete as in Form No. 143*].

163. Oath for administration (will) under s. 116 of the Supreme Court Act 1981

(Heading as in Form No. 1)

I, C D, of   make oath and say that:

1. A B of   deceased, died on the   day of   19   aged   years, domiciled in England and Wales, having made and duly executed his last will and testament;

2. On the   day of   19   it was ordered by   of this Division that letters of administration (with will annexed) of the estate of the said deceased be granted to me under and by virtue of s. 116 of the Supreme Court Act 1981 [*recite any limitations given in order*];

3. [*Add statement as to life and minority interests.*]

4. [*Add statement as to settled land.*]

5. I believe the paper writing now produced to and marked by me to contain the true and original last will and testament of the said deceased;

6. I will:

(i)   collect, get in and administer according to law the real and personal estate of the said deceased [*add, if applicable*, limited as aforesaid];

(ii) when required to do so by the Court [etc.—*complete as in Form No. 143*].

164. Oath for administration (will) where deceased died domiciled out of England and Wales; attorney of person entrusted with administration by court of domicile

(Heading as in Form No. 1)

I, E F, of   make oath and say that:

1. A B of   , deceased, died on the   day of   19   aged   years domiciled in the State of Texas in the United States of America having made and duly executed his last will and testament [with a codicil thereto];

2. I believe the paper writing now produced to and marked by me to contain an official copy of the true and original last will and testament of the said deceased;

3. C D is the person entrusted with the administration of the estate of the said deceased by the Court having jurisdiction at the place where the deceased died domiciled [*if order made under r. 30(1)(a) of the Non-Contentious Probate Rules 1987 on prior application add here the relevant details of the order*];

4. [*add statement as to minority and life interests*];

5. [*add statement as to settled land*];

6. I am the lawful attorney of the said C D, and [*if order not made on prior application*, I hereby apply for an order under r. 30(1)(a) of the Non-Contentious Probate Rules 1987 directing that letters of administration, with the said will annexed, of the estate of the said deceased be granted to me for the use and benefit of the said C D until further representation be granted and] I will:

   (i) collect, get in and administer according to law the real and personal estate of the said deceased for the use and benefit of the said C D, until further representation be granted;

   (ii) when required to do so by the Court, exhibit in the Court a full inventory of the said estate and render an account thereof to the Court; and

   (iii) when required to do so by the High Court, deliver up to that Court the grant of letters of administration;

7. To the best of my knowledge, information and belief the gross value of the estate in England and Wales of the said deceased passing under the grant amounts to the sum of £   and the net value amounts to £

[**Note.**—*The grant is made by order of a district judge or registrar founded on the oath, or an affidavit of facts, supported by the grant issued by the court of domicile. If the deceased died intestate the above form should be adapted accordingly.*]

165. Oath for administration (will) where deceased died domiciled out of England and Wales; person beneficially entitled to the estate by the law of the place where the deceased died domiciled

(Heading as in Form No. 1)

I, E F, of   make oath and say that:

1. A B of   deceased, died on the   day of   19   aged   years, domiciled in Spain having made and duly executed his last will and testament;

2. I believe the paper writing now produced to and marked by me to contain [an official copy of] the true and original last will and testament of the said deceased;

3. No one has been entrusted with the administration of the estate of the said deceased by the court having jurisdiction at the place where the deceased died domiciled;

4. [*If order made under r. 30(1)(b) of the Non-Contentious Probate Rules 1987 on a prior application, recite here the relevant details of the order. If, instead, the order is to be applied for in the oath, confirm here all the relevant facts upon which the expert relies, e.g. nationality of deceased, no one in class(es) of kin entitled to a reserved share etc. or, if relying on a certificate of inheritance issued by the court of domicile, exhibit an official copy of it*];

5. [*add statement as to minority and life interests*];

6. [*add statement as to settled land*];

7. I am the person beneficially entitled to the estate of the said deceased by the law of the place where he died domiciled and [*if order not made on prior application*, I hereby apply for an order under r. 30(1)(b) of the Non-Contentious Probate Rules 1987 directing that letters of administration, with the said will annexed, of the estate of the said deceased be granted to me and] I will:

   (i) collect, get in and administer according to law the real and personal estate of the said deceased;

   (ii) when required to do so [etc.—*complete as in Form No. 164*].

[**Notes.**—*The grant is made by order of a district judge or registrar founded on the oath, or an affidavit of facts, supported by an affidavit of law or other sufficient evidence of the law in question.*

If the deceased died intestate the above form should be adapted accordingly.]

166. Oath for administration or administration (with will) where deceased died domiciled out of England and Wales—discretionary order made under NCPR 30(1)(c)

(Heading as in Form No. 1)

I, E F, of   make oath and say that:

1. A B of   deceased, died on the   day of   19   aged   years domiciled in Spain, intestate [*or* having made and duly executed his last will and testament and I believe the paper writing now produced to and marked by me to contain [an official copy of] the true and original said last will and testament];
2. [*add statement as to minority and life interests*];
3. [*add statement as to settled land*];
4. On the   day of   19   it was ordered by Mr District Judge [*or* Registrar]   that letters of administration [with will annexed] of the estate of the said deceased be granted to me under and by virtue of r. 30(1)(c) of the Non-Contentious Probate Rules 1987;
5. I will:

   (i) collect, get in and administer according to law the real and personal estate of the said deceased;
   (ii) when required to do so [etc.—*complete as in Form No. 164*].

[**Note.**—*The grant is made by order of a district judge or registrar founded on an affidavit of facts supported by an affidavit of law or other sufficient evidence of the law in question.*]

167. Oath—limited administration (with will)—will made under power and not revoked by subsequent marriage (Wills Act 1837, s. 18)

(Heading as in Form No. 1)

I, J H R, of   widow (formerly J H S spinster), make oath and say that:

1. G B R of   deceased, died on   aged   years, domiciled in England and Wales, having made and duly executed a will dated the   day of   19   whereby, in exercise of a power of appointment vested in him under the will of his mother, E R, deceased, dated the   day of   and proved at the Principal [*or*   District Probate] Registry on the   day of   19   he gave and bequeathed all such estate over which at the time of his decease he should have power of appointment to me, the said J H R, in his will described as J H S, and by his said will he appointed me sole executrix;
2. The said G B R on the   day of   19   intermarried with me, the said J H R, whereby the said will was revoked except so far as it was made in exercise of the said power;
3. [*Add statement as to minority or life interest.*]
4. [*Add statement as to settled land.*]
5. I believe the paper writing now produced to and marked by me to contain the true and original last will and testament of the said deceased;
6. I am the appointee named in the said will;
7. I will:

   (i) collect, get in and administer according to law the real and personal estate of the said deceased, limited to such estate as the said deceased, by virtue of the will of the said E R, had power to appoint or dispose of, and has, in and by his said will, appointed or disposed of accordingly, but not further or otherwise;
   (ii) when required to do so by the Court [etc.—*complete as in Form No. 143*].

168. Oath for cessate administration (will) to residuary legatee [*or* devisee] on his attaining his majority

(Heading as in Form No. 1)

I, C D, of   make oath and say that:

1. A B of   deceased, died on the   day of   19   aged   years, domiciled in England and Wales, having made and duly executed his last will and testament and thereof appointed E F sole executor [and residuary legatee and devisee in trust], and me, this deponent, residuary legatee [and devisee];

2. The said E F heretofore renounced probate of the said will [and letters of administration with will annexed of the deceased's estate], and on the   day of   19   letters of administration (with the said will annexed) of the estate of the said deceased were granted at the Principal [or   District Probate] Registry to G H and J H for my use and benefit, and until I should attain the age of eighteen [or twenty-one] years;

3. On the   day of   19   I attained the age of eighteen [or twenty-one] years, by reason of which the said letters of administration with will annexed ceased and expired;

4. No life interest and now no minority interest arises in the estate of the said deceased;

5. [add statement as to settled land];

6. I believe the paper writing now produced to and marked by me to contain [an official copy of] the true last will and testament of the said deceased;

7. I am the residuary legatee [and devisee] named in the said will, and I will:

(i) collect, get in and administer [etc.—*complete as in Form No. 135*].

169. Oath for administration de bonis non to intestate's child

(Heading as in Form No. 1)

I, C B, of   make oath and say that:

1. A B of   deceased, died on the   day of   19   aged   years, domiciled in England and Wales, intestate;

2. On the   day of   19   letters of administration of the estate of the said deceased were granted at the Principal [or   District Probate] Registry to E B, his lawful widow, and G B one of his lawful* [or natural*] sons and one of the persons entitled to share in the said estate;

3. The said G B survived his co-administrator and died on the   day of   19   leaving part of the said estate unadministered**;

4. There is no minority, and now no life interest in the estate;

5. [add statement as to settled land];

6. I am a lawful* [or natural*] son and one other of the persons entitled to share in the estate of the said deceased;

7. I will:

(i) collect, get in and administer according to law the unadministered real and personal estate of the said deceased;

(ii) when required to do so by the Court, exhibit in the Court a full inventory of the said estate and render an account thereof to the Court; and

(iii) when required to do so by the High Court, deliver up to that Court the grant of letters of administration;

[etc. *as in Form No. 66, but with reference to the unadministered estate*].

[*See note* to Form No. 88.]
[**If no estate remains unadministered, but it is necessary to constitute a personal representative for some other purpose, substitute 'without having completed the administration of the estate': the oath must include a statement of the reason for the application.]*

170. Oath for administration de bonis non to personal representative of spouse

(Heading as in Form No. 1)

I, E F, of   make oath and say that:

1. A B, of   deceased, died on the   day of   19   aged   years, domiciled in England and Wales, intestate, leaving C D, his lawful widow [or her lawful husband] and the only person entitled to his [her] estate;

2. On the   day of   19   letters of administration of the estate of the said deceased were granted at the Principal [*or*   District Probate] Registry to the said C D, who died on the   day of   19   leaving part of the said estate unadministered**;
3. No life or minority interest arises under the intestacy;
4. [*add statement as to settled land*];
5. I am the sole executor of the will [*or* the administrator [with will] of the estate] of the said C D, probate [*or* letters of administration [with will]] thereof having been granted to me at the Principal [*or*   District Probate] Registry on the   day of   19   ;
6. I will:

(i) collect, get in and administer [etc.—*complete as in Form No. 169*].

[**Notes.**—*As to the circumstances in which the personal representative of the spouse is entitled in priority to a grant de bonis non, see paras. 13.35–13.37, ante.*

**See note to Form No. 169.*]

171. Oath for administration de bonis non to personal representative of only person entitled

(Heading as in Form No. 1)

I, C D, of   make oath and say that:

1. A B of   deceased, died on the   day of   19   aged   years, domiciled in England and Wales, intestate, a bachelor [spinster] [widower] [widow] without issue or parent or any other person entitled in priority to share in the estate by virtue of any enactment [*or as the case may be*] leaving E B, his [*or* her] lawful* father and the only person entitled to his [*or* her] estate;
2. On the   day of   19   letters of administration of the estate of the said deceased were granted at the Principal [*or*   District Probate] Registry to the said E B, who died on the   day of   19   leaving part of the said estate unadministered**;
3. [*add statement as to minority or life interest*];
4. [*add statement as to settled land*];
5. I am the sole executor of the will [*or* administrator of the estate] of the said E B, probate thereof [*or* letters of administration thereof] having been granted to me at the Principal [*or*   District Probate] Registry on the   day of   19   ;
6. I will:

(i) collect, get in and administer [etc.—*complete as in Form No. 169*].

[**See note** to Form No. 88.*]
[****See note**** to Form No. 169.*]

172. Oath for administration de bonis non to intestate's brother or sister entitled in distribution

(Death before 1926 only)

(Heading as in Form No. 1)

I, C B, of   make oath and say that:

1. A B of   deceased, died on the   day of   19   aged   years, domiciled in England and Wales, intestate, a bachelor [*or* a spinster], without father, and not possessed of real estate*, leaving E B, widow, his [*or* her] lawful mother and only next-of-kin him [*or* her] surviving;
2. On the   day of   19   letters of administration of the estate of the said deceased were granted at the Principal [*or*   District Probate] Registry to the said E B, who died on the   day of   19   leaving part of the said estate unadministered**;
3. [*add statement as to minority or life interest*];
4. I am the lawful brother [*or* sister] and one of the persons entitled in distribution to the personal estate of the said deceased;

5. I will:

(i) collect, get in and administer [etc.—*complete as in Form No. 169*].

[*If the deceased left real estate the heir-at-law must be cleared off.*]
[**See note** to Form No. 169.*]

173. Oath for administration de bonis non to another person sharing on intestacy

(Heading as in Form No. 1)

I, C D, of   make oath and say that:

1. A B of   deceased, died on the   day of   19   aged   years, domiciled in England and Wales, intestate, a bachelor [spinster] [widower] [widow] without issue or parent or any other person entitled in priority to share in the estate by virtue of any enactment [*or as the case may be*];
2. On the   day of   19   letters of administration of the estate of the said deceased were granted at the Principal [*or   District Probate*] Registry to E B, a lawful* brother of the whole blood, and one of the persons entitled to share in the estate of the said deceased, who died on the   day of   19   leaving part of the said estate unadministered**;
3. [*add statement as to minority or life interest*];
4. [*add statement as to settled land*];
5. I am the lawful* nephew of the whole blood and one other of the persons entitled to share in the estate of the said deceased, being the lawful* son of G B, a lawful* brother of the whole blood of the said deceased, who died in his lifetime;
6. I will:

(i) collect, get in and administer [etc.—*complete as in Form No. 169*].

[*See note* to Form No. 88.*]
[**See note** to Form No. 169.*]

174. Oath for administration (will) de bonis non to residuary legatee or devisee

(Heading as in Form No. 1)

I, C D, of   make oath and say that:

1. A B of   deceased, died on the   day of   19   aged   years, domiciled in England and Wales, having made and duly executed his last will and testament;
2. On the   day of   19   probate of the said will was granted at the Principal [*or   District Probate*] Registry, to E F, the sole executor named in the said will, who died on the   day of   19   intestate [*or as the case may be, showing how the chain of executorship is broken*], leaving part of the estate of the said deceased unadministered**;
3. [*add statement as to minority or life interest*];
4. [*add statement as to settled land*];
5. I believe the paper writing now produced to and marked by me to contain [an official copy of] the true and original last will and testament of the said deceased;
6. No residuary legatee or devisee in trust is named in the will [*or otherwise clear off any such trustee*];
7. I am the residuary legatee [and/*or* devisee] named in the said will, and I will:

(i) collect, get in and administer [etc.—*complete as in Form No. 169*].

[**See note** to Form No. 169.*]

175. Oath for administration (will) de bonis non to representative of residuary legatee and devisee

(Heading as in Form No. 1)

I, C D, of   make oath and say, that:

1. A B of   deceased, died on the   day of   19   aged   years, domiciled in

England and Wales, having made and duly executed his last will and testament, and thereof appointed E B and G B executors (*and residuary legatees and devisees in trust*), and the said G B residuary legatee and devisee;

2. On the   day of   19   probate of the said will was granted at the Principal [*or* District Probate] Registry to the said E B and G B;

3. The said E B survived his co-executor and died on the   day of   19   intestate [*or as the case may be, showing how the chain of executorship is broken*] leaving part of the estate of the deceased unadministered**;

4. [*add statement as to minority or life interest*];

5. [*add statement as to settled land*];

6. I believe the paper writing now produced to and marked by me to contain [an official copy of] the true and original last will and testament of the said A B;

7. I am the administrator (with will annexed) [*or as the case may be*] of the estate of the said G B, deceased, under a grant of administration (with will) made to me at the   Registry on the   day of   19   ;

8. I will:

(i) collect, get in and administer [etc.—*complete as in Form No. 169*].

[**See note** *to Form No. 169.*]

176. Oath for administration (will) de bonis non to specific legatee or devisee or creditor

(Heading as in Form No. 1)

I, C D, of   make oath and say that:

1. A B of   deceased, died on the   day of   19   aged   years, domiciled in England and Wales, having made and duly executed his last will and testament, and thereof appointed E F sole executor [and residuary legatee and devisee in trust];

2. On the   day of   19   probate of the said will was granted at the Principal [*or* District Probate] Registry to the said E F, who died on the   day of   19   intestate [*or as the case may be, showing how the chain of executorship is broken*], leaving part of the estate of the said deceased unadministered**;

3. G H, the residuary legatee and devisee named in the said will has renounced letters of administration (with will annexed) of the unadministered estate of the said deceased [*or* No residuary legatee or devisee is named in the will and the deceased died a widower leaving G H, his lawful* son, the only person entitled to his undisposed-of estate, who has renounced letters of administration (with will annexed) of the unadministered estate of the said deceased];

4. [*add statement as to minority or life interest*];

5. [*add statement as to settled land*];

6. I believe the paper writing now produced to and marked by me to contain an official copy of the last will and testament of the said deceased;

7. I am a creditor of the said deceased [*or* a legatee [*or* a devisee] named in the said will], and I will:

(i) collect, get in and administer [etc.—*complete as in Form No. 169*].

[*See note* *to Form No. 88.*]
[**See note** *to Form No. 169.*]

177. Oath for administration caeterorum to only person entitled to the estate, after limited administration

(Heading as in Form No. 1)

I, C D, of   make oath and say that:

1. A B of   deceased, died on the   day of   19   aged   years, domiciled in England and Wales, intestate, a bachelor [spinster] [widower] [widow] without issue or any other person entitled in priority to share in the estate by virtue of any enactment;

2. On the   day of   19   letters of administration of the estate of the said deceased, limited to prosecuting [*or* defending] an action in the Queen's Bench Division [*or as the*

case may be] were granted at the Principal [*or   District Probate*] Registry to G H, under and by virtue of s. 116 of the Supreme Court Act 1981 [*or as the case may be*];

3. I am the lawful* [*or* natural*] mother and only person entitled to the estate of the said intestate;

4. No minority or life interest arises under the intestacy;

5. [*add statement as to settled land*];

6. I will:

  (i) collect, get in and administer according to law the rest of the real and personal estate of the said deceased;

 (ii) when required to do so by the Court, exhibit in the Court a full inventory of the said estate and render an account thereof to the Court; and

(iii) when required to do so by the High Court, deliver up to that Court the grant of letters of administration;

[etc. *as in Form No. 66, but with reference to the value of the remainder of the estate*].

[**See note* to Form No. 88.*]

ORDER

178. Order for grant after caveat

(Heading as in Form No. 1)

Upon hearing   and by consent, it is ordered that probate of the will dated   [*or* letters of administration [with will] of the estate] of A B, of   , the deceased herein, be granted to   , the sole executor named in the said will [*or as the case may be*], if entitled thereto.

And that on application for a grant by the said   Caveat No.   entered on the   day of   19   do cease to have effect.

Dated the   day of   19   .

(*Signed*)

District Judge/Registrar.

POWERS OF ATTORNEY

179. Power of attorney to take administration

(Heading as in Form No. 1)

A B of   deceased, died on the   day of   19   domiciled in England and Wales intestate, leaving C D, his lawful widow and relict [and the only person now entitled to his estate]:

I, the said C D, of   do hereby nominate, constitute, and appoint E F of   and G H of   jointly [*or* jointly and severally] to be my lawful attorneys for the purpose of obtaining letters of administration of the estate of the said deceased, to be granted to them [*or* to them or either of them] by the High Court of Justice for my use and benefit, limited until further representation be granted; and I hereby promise to ratify and confirm whatever my said attorneys shall lawfully do or cause to be done in the premises.

In witness whereof I have hereunto set my hand this   day of   19   .

Signed as a deed and delivered ⎞
by the said C D   ⎬
in the presence of   ⎠

(Witness's name, address and occupation)

[**Notes.**—*If a minority or life interest arises, the power must be given to a trust corporation, to a trust corporation and an individual, or to not less than two individuals, unless the court considers it expedient in all the circumstances to appoint an individual as a sole administrator.*

As to execution of powers of attorney in non-English speaking countries, see paras. 11.45–11.47, ante.

If it is known that it will be necessary for the attorney subsequently to take, in his representative capacity, a grant in the estate of another deceased, the power of attorney may, if desired, contain additional words authorising this (see Form No. 182, which may be adapted to suit the facts).]

180. Power of attorney to take administration (will) given by executors

(Heading as in Form No. 1)

A B of   deceased, died on the   day of   19   having made and duly executed his last will and testament, bearing date the   day of   19   and thereof appointed C D and E F executors:

We, the said C D of   and E F of   do hereby nominate, constitute, and appoint G H of   to be our lawful attorney for the purpose of obtaining letters of administration (with the said will annexed) of the estate of the said deceased, to be granted to him by the High Court of Justice for our use and benefit, limited until further representation be granted; and we hereby promise to ratify and confirm whatever our said attorney shall lawfully do or cause to be done in the premises.

In witness whereof we have hereunto set our hands this   day of   19   .

Signed as a deed and delivered ⎤
by the said C D and E F in the   ⎬
presence of   .   ⎦

(Witness's name, address and occupation)

[*See notes to Form No. 179.*]

181. Power of attorney to take administration (will) given by residuary legatee

(Heading as in Form No. 1)

A B of   deceased, died on the   day of   19   having made and duly executed his last will and testament, with a codicil thereto, the said will bearing date the   day of   19   and the said codicil bearing date the   day of   19   and therein named C D and E F executors and G H residuary legatee and devisee; and the said C D and E F both died in the lifetime of the said deceased:

I, the said G H of   do hereby nominate, constitute, and appoint I K of   to be my lawful attorney for the purpose of obtaining letters of administration (with the said will and codicil annexed) of the estate of the said deceased, to be granted to him by the High Court of Justice for my use and benefit, limited until further representation be granted; and I hereby promise to ratify and confirm whatever my said attorney shall lawfully do or cause to be done in the premises.

In witness whereof I have hereunto set my hand this   day of   19   .

Signed as a deed and delivered ⎤
by the said G H in the   ⎬
presence of   .   ⎦

(Witness's name, address and occupation)

[*See notes to Form No. 179.*]

182. Power of attorney where further grant to attorney in his representative capacity is required

(Heading as in Form No. 1)

A B of   died on the   day of   19   , intestate a widow, leaving D B, her [lawful son] and the only person entitled to her estate;

C B of   died on the   day of   19   , having made and duly executed his last will and testament wherein he named no executor or residuary legatee or devisee in trust, but named the said A B as residuary legatee and devisee:

I, the said D B of   do hereby nominate, constitute and appoint E F of   to be my lawful attorney for the purpose of obtaining letters of administration of the estate of the said A B and for the purpose of obtaining (as administrator of the estate of the said A B) letters of administration (with will) of the estate of the said C B deceased, both grants to be for my use and benefit and limited until further representation be granted in the estate of the said A B:

And I hereby promise to ratify and confirm whatever my said attorney shall lawfully do or cause to be done in the premises.

In witness whereof I have hereunto set my hand this   day of   19   .

Signed as a deed and delivered ⎤
by the said D B in the   ⎬
presence of   .   ⎦

(Witness's name, address and occupation)

RENUNCIATIONS

183. Renunciation of probate

(Heading as in Form No. 1)

A B of   deceased, died on the   day of   19   having made and duly executed his last will and testament, bearing date the   day of   19   and thereof appointed the under-signed C D sole executor [and residuary legatee and devisee [in trust]]:

I, the said C D of   do hereby declare that I have not intermeddled in the estate of the said deceased, and will not hereafter intermeddle therein with intent to defraud creditors, and I do hereby renounce all my right and title to probate and execution of the said will [and to letters of administration (with the said will annexed) of the estate of the said deceased]*.

Signed by the said C D as a deed this ⎤
day of   19   in the   ⎬
presence of   .   ⎦

(Witness's name, address and occupation)

[*These words must be included in the form where the executor is also entitled in a lower character under NCPR 20 and has to be cleared off in that character by the applicant for the grant (Registrar's Direction (1952) 27 November).]*

184. Renunciation of administration

(Heading as in Form No. 1)

A B of   deceased, died on the   day of   19   intestate, a widow, leaving C D, her son and the only person entitled to her estate:

Now I, the said C D of   do hereby renounce all my right and title to letters of admini-stration of the estate of the said deceased.

Signed by the said C D as a deed this ⎤
day of   19   in the   ⎬
presence of   .   ⎦

(Witness's name, address and occupation)

185. Renunciation of administration (with will annexed)

(Heading as in Form No. 1)

A B of   deceased, died on the   day of   19   having made and duly executed his last will and testament, bearing date the   day of   19   wherein he did not name any execu-tor, but appointed me, the undersigned C D, residuary legatee and devisee:

I, the said C D of   do hereby renounce all my right and title to letters of administration, with the said will annexed, of the estate of the said deceased.

Signed by the said C D as a deed this ⎤
day of   19   in the   ⎬
presence of   .   ⎦

(Witness's name, address and occupation)

186. Renunciation and consent to grant to a trust corporation

(Heading as in Form No. 1)

A B of   deceased, died on the   day of   19   having made and duly executed his last will and testament [with a codicil thereto] bearing date [respectively] the   day of
     19   [and the   day of   19   ] and therein named C D as sole executor and residuary legatee and devisee in trust, and E F as residuary legatee and devisee;
I, the said C D of   do hereby renounce all my right and title to probate of the said will [and codicil];
     And we, the said C D and E F of   do hereby consent to letters of administration (with will [and codicil]) of the estate of the said deceased being granted to X Y Limited;
     And I, the said C D, hereby declare that I have not intermeddled in the estate of the said deceased, and will not hereafter intermeddle therein with intent to defraud creditors.

> Signed by the said C D
> and E F as a deed this   day
> of   19   in the presence
> of   .

(Witness's name, address and occupation)

187. Renunciation, by person appointed for the purpose, of minor's right to a grant

(NCPR 34(2))

(Heading as in Form No. 1)

A B of   deceased, died on the   day of   19   intestate, a widower, leaving C B, his son and the only person entitled to his estate;
     The said C B is now a minor of the age of   years only and on the   day of   19   by order of Mr District Judge [*or* Registrar]   G H was appointed and authorised for the purpose of renouncing on the minor's behalf letters of administration of the estate of the said deceased:
I, the said G H of   do hereby renounce all the minor's right and title to letters of administration of the said estate.

> Signed by the said G H as a deed this
>   day of   19   in the
> presence of   .

(Witness's name, address and occupation)

188. Retraction of renunciation

(Heading as in Form No. 1)

A B of   deceased, died on the   day of   19   having made and duly executed his last will and testament, bearing date the   day of   19   and thereof appointed C D sole executor, and me, the undersigned E F, residuary legatee and devisee;
     The said C D renounced probate and execution of the said will, and I renounced letters of administration (with will annexed) of the estate of the said deceased;
     Letters of administration (with will annexed) of the said estate were on the   day of   granted at the   Probate Registry to G H, a creditor of the said deceased, who died on the   day of   19   leaving part of the said estate unadministered:
I, the said E F of   do hereby retract my said renunciation of letters of administration (with will annexed) of the estate of the said A B deceased.

> Signed by the said E F as a deed this
>   day of   19   in the
> presence of   .

(Witness's name, address and occupation)

[**Note.**—*An order of the district judge or registrar must first be obtained giving leave to retract (NCPR 37(3)).*]

STANDING SEARCH

189. Standing search

(NCPR 43(1))

In the High Court of Justice
Family Division
The Principal [*or*   District Probate] Registry

I/We apply for the entry of a standing search so that there shall be sent to me/us an office copy of every grant of representation in England and Wales in the estate of—

Full name of deceased:
Full address:
Alternative or alias names:
Exact date of death:

which either has issued not more than 12 months before the entry of this application or issues within 6 months thereafter.

Signed:
Name in block letters:
Full address:
Reference No. (if any):

(NCPR 1988, Form 2.)

SUBPOENAS

190. Subpoena to bring in a testamentary document

(Heading as in Form No. 1)

Elizabeth the Second, by the grace of God, of the United Kingdom of Great Britain and Northern Ireland and of our other realms and territories Queen, Head of the Commonwealth, Defender of the Faith.
    To   of

It appears by an affidavit of   sworn on the   day of   and filed in the Principal Registry of the Family Division of our High Court of Justice [*or* in the   District Probate Registry], that a certain document, being or purporting to be testamentary, namely [*here describe the document*], bearing date the   day of 19   of A B, deceased, late of   who died on the   day of   19 is now in your possession, custody or power:

We command you that, within eight days after service hereof on you, inclusive of the day of such service, you do bring into and leave with the proper officer of the Principal Registry of the Family Division [*or* in the   District Probate Registry] aforesaid the said document now in the possession, custody or power of you the said   :
Witness, the Right Honourable [   ] Lord High Chancellor of Great Britain, the   day of   19 .

> *(Signed)*
> District Judge/Registrar.

    Subpoena issued by   of   solicitor for
[*To be indorsed prominently on the front of the copy to be served:*] You the within-named   are warned that disobedience to this subpoena by the time therein limited would be a contempt of court punishable by imprisonment.
[*Also to be indorsed on the copy to be served:*] 1. N.B.—The Principal Registry of the Family Division of the High Court of Justice is at Somerset House, Strand, London WC2R 1LP and the proper officer referred to is the Record Keeper [*or* The   District Probate Registry is at   and   the proper officer referred to is the   ].

2. If you the said   deny that the testamentary document(s) referred to is/are in your possession, custody or power, you may swear an affidavit to that effect and file it in the (issuing) registry. (*Registrar's Direction (1989) 23 June.*)

[*For form of affidavit to lead subpoena see Form No. 38.*]

[*For subpoena to bring in a testamentary document in a probate action, see No. CP51.*]

191. Order for examination of person with knowledge of testamentary document

(Heading as in Form No. 1)

Elizabeth the Second, [etc. *as in Form No. 190*]:

   To   of
We command you to appear before the [Right] Honourable Sir   Knight, the President [*or* Judge] of the Family Division of our High Court of Justice at the Royal Courts of Justice, Strand, London WC2 on the   day of   19   at   o'clock, to testify the truth according to your knowledge [*or* to answer any question to be put to you], relating to a certain document, being or purporting to be testamentary, namely [*here describe the document, and give its date as accurately as possible*], of which said document there are reasonable grounds for believing that you have knowledge.
Witness the Right Honourable [Lord Chancellor], the   day of   19   .

(*Signed*)
District Judge/Registrar.

[*Name and address of solicitor.*]
[**Note.**—*To be indorsed prominently on the front of the copy to be served:*] You the within-named   are warned that disobedience to this order would be a contempt of court punishable by imprisonment.

SUMMONSES

192. Summons (general form) (Family Division)

(Heading as in Form No. 1)

Let all parties concerned attend one of the judges of this Division in Chambers at the Royal Courts of Justice [*or* one of the district judges at the Principal Registry of the Family Division, Somerset House], Strand, London WC2 [*or* the District Registrar at the   District Probate Registry at   ], on   day the   day of   19   at   o'clock, on the hearing of an application on the part of [*or* to show cause why   ].
This summons was taken out by   of   solicitor for the   .
   To   [solicitor for] the   .

193. Summons for discontinuance of caveat after appearance to warning (Family Division)

(Heading as in Form No. 1)

Let E F attend one of the district judges at the Principal Registry of the Family Division of the High Court of Justice, Somerset House, Strand, London WC2, on   day the   day of   19   at   o'clock, to show cause why the caveat no.   entered on the   day of   19   in this matter should not be discontinued, and why probate of the will dated the   day of   19   [*or as the case may be*] of A B of   the deceased herein, should not be granted to C D, the sole executor named in the said will [*or as the case may be*], if entitled thereto, and that on application for a grant by the said C D the said caveat do cease to have effect.

This summons was taken out by   of   solicitor for the   .
   To   [solicitor for] the   .

[**Note.**—*If the application to discontinue the caveat is made by consent, the summons may be issued in the district probate registry where the application for the grant has been, or is to be, made for hearing by the registrar at that registry.*]

WARNING

194. Warning to caveat

(NCPR 44(5))

In the High Court of Justice
Family Division
The   Registry [*that in which the caveat index is maintained*]
To   of   a party who has entered a caveat in the estate of   deceased.

You have eight days (starting with the day on which this warning was served on you):

(i) to enter an appearance either in person or by your solicitor, at the [*name and address of the registry in which the caveat index is maintained*], setting out what interest you have in the estate of the above-named   of   deceased contrary to that of the party at whose instance this warning is issued; or

(ii) if you have no contrary interest but wish to show cause against the sealing of a grant to such party, to issue and serve a summons for directions by a district judge of the Principal Registry or a registrar of a district probate registry.

If you fail to do either of these, the court may proceed to issue a grant of probate or administration in the said estate notwithstanding your caveat.

Dated the   day of   19   .
Issued at the instance of

[*Here set out the name and interest (including
the date of the will, if any, under which the
interest arises) of the party warning, the name
of his solicitor and the address for service. If
the party warning is acting in person, this
must be stated.*]   Registrar

[**Note.**—*The caveat index is currently maintained at the Leeds District Probate Registry.*]

Part II—Forms for use in Probate Actions

CP0. Heading for all actions (hereinafter called 'Heading')

In the High Court of Justice   19   No.
   Chancery Division (Probate)
In the Estate of A B, deceased
       BETWEEN   CD   ..   ..   .. Plaintiff
                      and
                      EF   ..   ..   .. Defendant

ADMINISTRATOR'S ACCOUNT

CP1. Administrator's cash account

(Heading)

The [first] account of XY, the Administrator appointed by order dated the   day of
19   from the   day of   19   to the   day of   19   both dates inclusive.

No. of item	Date when received	Names of persons from whom received	On what account received	Amount received	No. of Item	Date when paid or allowed	Names of persons to whom paid or allowed	For what purpose paid or allowed	Amount paid or allowed

CP2. Administrator's inventory

(Heading)

Inventory as at the   day of   19   .

Particulars of property in estate	Date of disposal

AFFIDAVITS

CP3. Affidavit of testamentary scripts

(Order 24, r. 5)

(Heading)

I, C D, of   the plaintiff [*or* defendant] in this action, make oath and say as follows:

1. I have no knowledge of any document being or purporting to be, or having the form or effect of, a will or codicil, or other testamentary instrument, of A B, late of   deceased,

the deceased in this action, or being or purporting to be a draft of any will, codicil or other testamentary instrument of the said deceased, or written instructions for such an instrument made by or at the request of or under the instructions of the said deceased, or being or purporting to be evidence of the contents, or to be a copy, of any will, codicil or other testamentary instrument of the said deceased which is alleged to have been lost or destroyed, save and except the true last will of the said deceased, now produced and shown to me, the said will bearing date the   day of   19   [also save and except*].

[*Here add the dates and particulars of all other testamentary scripts of which the deponent has any knowledge: any such script which is in the possession or under the control of the deponent being referred to in the affidavit. If any such script is not in his possession or under his control the deponent must give the name and address of the person in whose possession or under whose control it is, or if he does not know this, must state that he does not know the name or address of that person (Order 76, r. 5(1)(b)).]

CP4. Affidavit verifying administrator's account

(Order 76, r. 1))

(Heading)

I, G H, of   the administrator pending suit appointed in this action, make oath and say as follows:

1. The account marked with the letter A, now produced and shown to me, and purporting to be my account of the estate of   the deceased in this action, from the   day of   19   to the   day of   19   both inclusive, contains a true account of all and every sum of money received by me or by any other person or persons by my order, pursuant to order dated the   day of   19 .
2. The several sums of money mentioned in the said account, hereby verified, to have been paid and allowed, have been actually and truly so paid and allowed for the several purposes in the said account mentioned.
3. The said account is just and true in all and every one of the items and particulars therein contained, according to the best of my knowledge and belief.

Sworn, etc.

GUARANTEE

CP5. Guarantee for the acts and defaults of an administrator pending suit

(Heading)

I,   of   in the county of   the administrator pending suit appointed by order dated   [or proposed to be appointed] in this action hereby undertake with the Court duly to account for all moneys and property received by me as such administrator pending suit at such times and in such manner in all respects as the Court shall direct.

And we   hereby jointly and severally [in the case of a guarantee or other company strike out 'jointly and severally'] undertake with the Court and guarantee to be answerable for any default by the said   as such administrator pending suit and upon such default to pay to any person or persons or otherwise as the Court shall direct any sum or sums not exceeding in the whole £   that may from time to time be certified by a Master of the Supreme Court [or by the District Judge] to be due from the said administrator pending suit and we submit to the jurisdiction of the Court in this action to determine any claim made under this undertaking.

Date this   day of   19

Signed as a deed by the above named   in the presence of   [and/or the Common Seal of   was hereunto affixed in the presence of]:

NOTICES

CP6. Notice of proceedings

(Order 15 r. 13A)

(Heading)

TAKE NOTICE THAT:

(1) An action has been begun in the High Court of Justice in accordance with the writ of summons attached hereto.

(2) You are or may be one of the persons who are interested in the estate to which the action relates.

(3) You may within 14 days after service of this notice acknowledge service of the writ by properly completing the attached acknowledgment and handing it in at, or sending it by post to Chancery Chambers, Royal Courts of Justice, Strand, London WC2A 2LL [*or*   District Registry] and thereby become a party to the action.

(4) If you do not acknowledge service of the writ you will be bound by any judgment given in the action as if you were a party to it.

Dated
To
Signed

CP7. Notice to be indorsed on copy of counterclaim

(Order 15, r. 3(6))

To X Y

Take notice that, within [14 days] after service of this defence and counterclaim on you, counting the day of service, you must acknowledge service and state in your acknowledgment whether you intend to contest the proceedings. If you fail to do so or if your acknowledgment does not state your intention to contest the proceedings, judgment may be given against you without further notice.

IMPORTANT
Directions for acknowledgment of service are given with the accompanying form.

CP8. Notice under Order 62, r. 4(3)

(Heading)

Take notice that upon the hearing of this action the defendant will merely insist upon the plaintiff proving the will propounded in solemn form of law, and that he only intends to cross examine the witnesses produced by the plaintiff in support of the said will.

Solicitors for the defendant.

   To
      Solicitors for the plaintiff.

ORDERS

CP9. Order in probate action involving compromise

(Heading)

UPON the application of [   ]
by summons dated [   ]
AND upon hearing [   ] for the [   ] and for the [   ]
AND upon reading the documents recorded on the court file as having been read and [probate of the alleged last will and testament of the above named deceased bearing date
    granted on   to   ] [*or* letters of administration of the estate of the above named deceased granted on   to   ]
   And the Court being satisfied

(1) that consents by or on behalf of every relevant beneficiary (as defined by s. 49, Administration of Justice Act 1985) have been given to the making of this order hereinafter made and

(2) that the said order is for the benefit of those relevant beneficiaries who are minors

The Court hereby pronounces for [against] the force and validity of the last will and testament of the above named deceased a completed copy of which is the script bearing the date [   ] being the exhibit marked [   ] referred to in the affidavit of scripts [   ] sworn [   ] and against the force and validity of the last will and testament of the above named deceased a completed copy of which is the script bearing the date [   ] being the exhibit marked [   ] referred to in the affidavit of scripts of [   ] sworn [   ]

AND it is ordered

(1) that this action [and counterclaim] be discontinued.

( ) that the said probate [letters of administration] be revoked.

( ) that the terms set out in the Schedule be carried into effect

( ) that [probate of the will] [and   codicil] [letters of administration of the estate] of the above named deceased late of [   ] be granted to the plaintiff/the defendant [   ] the executor named therein

( ) that on application for such a grant the caveat numbered [   ] and entered on [   ] do if still subsisting cease to have effect

( ) that there be taxed if not agreed

    (a) the costs of this action [and counterclaim] of the plaintiff/defendant [   ] the executor named in the said will

    (b) the costs of this action [and counterclaim] of the plaintiff/defendant [   ] and [   ]

    (c) the costs of the plaintiff/defendant pursuant to the Legal Aid Act 1988

( ) that the costs specified in (a) and (b) above be paid out of the estate of the said deceased in the due course of administration

Schedule
[Set out the agreed terms]

CP10. Order appointing administrator pending suit

(Order 76, r. 14)

(Heading)

Upon the application of the plaintiff by summons dated the   day of   19 .

And upon hearing [etc. *as Form CP9*]

And upon reading [etc. *as Form CP9*]

The Court hereby appoints   of   administrator of the estate of the above-named deceased pending the disposal of this action.

And the said   having given security to the satisfaction of the Court in the sum of

It is ordered that a grant of administration pending suit pursuant to section 117 of the Supreme Court Act 1981 be made to the said

And it is ordered that the said   do pass his accounts as the Court shall from time to time direct.

Liberty to apply for further directions.

CP11. Order staying proceedings in 'Tomlin' form

(Heading)

Upon hearing the solicitors for the plaintiff and the defendant, and both parties by their solicitors consenting to this order

And upon reading [etc. *as Form CP9*]

It is ordered that probate of the will dated   the day of   19   [*or* letters of administration [with will] of the estate] of A B of   , the deceased herein, be granted to C D, the sole executor named in the said will, if entitled thereto

And it is ordered [*set out costs order*]

It is ordered that all further proceedings be stayed on the terms set out in the Schedule hereto,

Liberty to apply to enforce such terms.

THE SCHEDULE
[*Agreed terms of settlement*]

CP12. Order for discontinuance of action and grant

(Heading)

Upon hearing the solicitors for the plaintiff and defendant and by consent,

It is ordered that the contentious proceedings in this action arising from the writ of summons issued on the   day of   19   be discontinued and that probate of the will dated the   day of   19   [*or* letters of administration [with will] of the estate] of A B of   , the deceased herein, be granted to C D, the sole executor named in the said will [*or as the case may be*], the plaintiff [*or* defendant] in this action, if entitled thereto.

And it is ordered [*set out costs order*]

PLEADINGS

I. INDORSEMENTS OF CLAIM

[**Notes.**—(i) *The indorsements are not pleadings. but precedents for indorsements of claim are for convenience included under this heading.*

(ii) *In a probate action, unless the court gives leave to the contrary, or a statement of claim is indorsed on the writ of summons, the plaintiff must serve a statement of claim on every defendant who acknowledges sertice of the writ (Order 76, r. 7). As the defendant's time for acknowledgment of service varies according to whether or not a separate statement of claim is served, it is important that the plaintiff should decide when preparing his writ of summons whether a statement of claim is to be indorsed thereon. If the statement of claim is indorsed on the writ it must be clearly stated to be the statement of claim.*

(iii) *For formal indorsements which must appear on a writ of summons, see paras.* **29.08** *ff., ante.*]

CP13. Executor or residuary legatee propounds will—defendant interested on an intestacy

The plaintiff claims as the sole executor [*or* the residuary legatee and devisee *or as the case may be*] named in the last will and testament dated the   day of   19   of A B, late of   , deceased, who died on the   day of   19   that the Court shall pronounce for the said will in solemn form of law.

This writ is issued against you because you have entered a caveat and appeared to the warning thereto as the lawful brother of the whole blood and one of the persons entitled to share in the estate of the said deceased in the event of an intestacy [*or as the case may be*].

[*Signature of counsel or solicitors*]

CP14. Residuary legatee propounds will omitting interlineation—defendants interested (1) in the interlineation, and (2) on intestacy

The plaintiff claims as the residuary legatee and devisee named in the last will and testament dated the   day of   19   of A B, late of   deceased, who died on the   day of   19   that the Court shall pronounce for the said will in solemn form, excluding the interlineation   appearing on the   page thereof.

This writ is issued against you, the said C D, as a legatee named in the said interlineation and being adversely affected in the event of the same not being admitted to probate, and against you, the said E F, as the lawful nephew of the whole blood of the said deceased and the only person who would be entitled to his estate in the event of an intestacy.

[**Note.**—*The statement of claim should give concise particulars of the grounds on which the plaintiff claims that the interlineation is not admissible to proof.*]

CP15. Executor propounds lost will—defendants executors under earlier will

The plaintiff claims, as executor named in the will undated but executed on or about
19   , of A B, late of   in the county of   spinster, deceased, who died on
19   to have the contents of the said will as contained in a completed draft thereof pronounced for in solemn form.

This writ is issued against you because you have entered a caveat and appeared to the warning thereto as the sole executor named in an earlier will of the deceased dated 6 September 1977 [*follow title as shown in the appearance to warning*].

CP16. Executors propound will and codicil—defendant a beneficiary under an alleged second codicil

The plaintiffs claim as the executors named in the last will and testament dated the   day of
19   with a codicil thereto dated the   day of   19   of A B, late of   deceased,
who died on the   day of   19   that the Court shall pronounce for the said will and codicil and against a pretended second codicil purporting to have been executed on the
day of   19 .

This writ is issued against you because you have entered a caveat and appeared to the warning thereto as a legatee named in the said pretended second codicil.

[**Note.**—*The statement of claim should include particulars of the grounds on which the plaintiff claims that the second codicil is not admissible to proof.*]

CP17. Executor or residuary legatee under an earlier will claims revocation—defendant the executor under a later will

The plaintiff claims as the sole executor [*or residuary legatee and devisee*] named in the true last will and testament, dated the   day of   19   of A B, late of   deceased, who died
on the   day of   19   to have the probate of the pretended will of the said deceased
dated the   day of   19   granted to you on the   day of   19   revoked and the said
will pronounced against, and further to have the said will dated the   day of   19   pronounced for in solemn form of law.

This writ is issued against you as the executor named in the pretended will dated the
day of   19 .

CP18. Party entitled on an intestacy claims revocation—defendants executors and beneficiaries under a will

The plaintiff claims as the lawful father and one of the persons entitled, in the event of an intestacy, to share in the estate of A B, late of   deceased, who died on the   day of
19   to have the probate of a pretended will of the said deceased dated the   day of
19   granted on the   day of   19   revoked, and the said will pronounced against,
and to have a grant of letters of administration of the estate of the said deceased.

This writ is issued against you the said C D and E F as the executors named in the pretended will dated the   day of   19   and against you, the said G H and I J as respectively the residuary legatee and devisee, and a legatee named therein.

CP19. Executor or residuary legatee propounds will and claims revocation of grant of administration—defendant the party who has obtained the grant

The plaintiff claims as the sole executor [*or residuary legatee and devisee*] named in the last will and testament dated the   day of   19   of A B, late of   deceased, who died on
the   day of   19   that the Court shall pronounce for the said will in solemn form of law, and shall revoke the grant of letters of administration of the estate of the said deceased dated the   day of   19 .

This writ is issued against you as having obtained the said grant of letters of administration.

CP20. Residuary legatee propounds privileged will—defendants entitled on an intestacy

The plaintiff claims as the residuary legatee and devisee named in the last will and testament, undated but in fact executed on the   day of   19   of A B, deceased, late of   who died on the   day of   19   the said will being in the form of a letter, and made by the said deceased while a soldier in actual military service [*or* as a seaman while at sea], to have the said will pronounced for in solemn form.

This writ is issued against you because you have entered a caveat and appeared to the warning thereto, the said C D as the lawful uncle of the whole blood, and the said E F and G H as the lawful cousins german of the whole blood, and together the only persons entitled to share in the estate of the said deceased in the event of an intestacy [*follow title as shown in appearance to warning*].

CP21. Interest action

The plaintiff claims to be the lawful brother of the whole blood, and only person entitled to the estate of A B of   deceased, late of   who died on the   day   of   19   intestate, and to have as such a grant of letters of administration of the estate of the said deceased.

This writ is issued against you because you have entered a caveat and appeared to the warning thereto as the lawful widow and relict and one of the persons entitled to share in the estate of the said deceased [*or as the case may be—follow title as shown in the appearance to warning*] [and the plaintiff denies your interest].

CP22. Claim by originating summons for, inter alia, rectification

By this summons which is issued on the application of the plaintiff A B, of   the plaintiff claims against the defendants:

1. An order that the will [codicil] of the said deceased made   19   , [and proved by the grant of representation issued with respect to the estate of the said deceased on   19   ,] be rectified in the following manner—

(a) [In clause   by deletion/substitution/addition of   *etc.*];
(b) [In clause   *etc.*].

[2. An order giving leave to ask for an order as in paragraph 1 above notwithstanding that since the date of issue of the said grant more than six months have elapsed before the issue of this summons.]
[3. An order that upon their true construction, the words '. . . ' in clause   of the said will [codicil] mean [include]   .]

II. STATEMENTS OF CLAIM

[**Note.**—*In many cases it is possible for the statement of claim to be indorsed on the writ of summons.*]

CP23. Executor propounds will

(Heading)

STATEMENT OF CLAIM

1. The plaintiff is the sole executor named in the last will and testament of A B, deceased, late of   who died on the   day of   19   the said will bearing date the   day of
     19   with a codicil thereto dated the   day of   19   .
     The plaintiff claims:
     That the Court shall pronounce for the force and validity of the said will and codicil in solemn form of law.

(Signature of counsel)

     Served this   day of   19   by G H, of   solicitor, agents for I and K of   the solicitors for the plaintiff.

CP24. Executor propounds a lost will

(Heading)

STATEMENT OF CLAIM

1. The plaintiff is the sole executor named in the true last will and testament of A B, deceased, late of   who died on the   day of   19   the said will bearing date the   day of   19   .
2. The said will was never revoked or destroyed by the said deceased or by any other person in his presence or by his direction with the intention of revoking the same, but was at the time of his death a valid and subsisting will, but the same cannot now be found.
3. The contents of the said will were in substance and to the effect as follows: [*here set out contents of will*]

[*or* The contents of the said will are contained in a completed draft thereof [*or as the case may be*] marked   and annexed to the plaintiff's affidavit of testamentary scripts filed in this action.]

The plaintiff claims:

That the court shall pronounce for the force and validity of the said will as set out in paragraph 3 hereof [*or* as contained in the said draft], and decree probate thereof in solemn form of law.

(Signature)

Served, etc.

CP25. Executrix propounds will destroyed by deceased whilst incapable

(Heading)

STATEMENT OF CLAIM

1. The plaintiff is the sole executrix named in the true last will and testament of A B, deceased, late of   spinster, who died on the   day of   19   .
2. The said will was never revoked by the said deceased, but was destroyed by her whilst not of testamentary capacity.

PARTICULARS

[*Particulars of the facts relied upon in support of any allegation of a condition of mind must be given in the pleading (Order 18, r. 12(1)).*]
3. The contents of the said will are contained in a copy [*or* completed draft] thereof [*or as the case may be*] marked   and annexed to the plaintiff's affidavit of testamentary scripts filed in this action.

The plaintiff claims:

That the Court shall pronounce for the force and validity of the said will, as contained in the said copy [draft] and decree probate thereof in solemn form of law.

(Signature)

Served, etc.

CP26. Executor propounds will of person domiciled abroad

(Heading)

STATEMENT OF CLAIM

1. The plaintiff is the sole executor named in the last will and testament dated the   day of   19   of A B, late of   deceased, who died on the   day of   19   domiciled in [France].
2. The said will was executed in accordance with the laws and constitutions of [France].

The plaintiff claims:

That the Court shall pronounce for the form and validity of the said will in solemn form of law.

(Signature)

Served, etc.

CP27. Executor propounds will under Wills Act 1963 (death on or after 1 January 1964)

(Heading)

STATEMENT OF CLAIM

1. The plaintiff is the sole executor* [*or as the case may be*] named in the last will and testament dated the　　day of　　19　of A B, late of　　deceased, who died on the　　day of 19 .

2. The said deceased, at the time of execution of the said will [*or at the date of his death*] was domiciled in　　[*or* had his habitual residence at　　in　　] [*or* was a national of　　] [*Add if necessary:* 3. At the time of execution of the said will [*or* at the date of his death] the said deceased was most closely connected with the　　system of internal law relating to the formal validity of wills [*state grounds on which this connection is claimed*]].

4. The said will was executed in accordance with the internal law of　　.

The plaintiff claims:

That the Court shall pronounce for the force and validity of the said will in solemn form of law.

(Signature)

Served, etc.

[**The capacity of executor is available only if the will is in the English language or if the will describes the duties of the plaintiff in terms sufficient to constitute him executor according to the terms of the will, in which case he should be so described in paragraph 1.*]

CP28. Plaintiff (entitled on an intestacy) claims revocation of probate, and grant of administration

(Heading)

STATEMENT OF CLAIM

1. The plaintiff is the lawful nephew of the whole blood and the only person entitled to the estate of A B, late of　　deceased, who died on the　　day of　　19　intestate a widower without issue or parent, or brother or sister of the whole blood or any other person entitled in priority to share in the estate by virtue of any enactment.

2. On the　　day of　　19　probate of an alleged will of the said deceased, bearing date the　　day of　　19　was granted to the defendant, as sole executor therein named, at the Principal [*or* District Probate] Registry of the Family Division.

3. The said alleged will was not duly executed in accordance with the provisions of the Wills Act 1837.

PARTICULARS

[*Every pleading must contain the necessary particulars of any claim, defence or other matter pleaded (Order 18. r. 12).*]

4. The said deceased at the time the said alleged will purports to have been executed was not of sound mind, memory or understanding.

PARTICULARS

[*Particulars of the facts relied on in support of any allegation of a condition of mind must be included in the pleading (Order 18, r. 12(1)).*]

5. The execution of the said alleged will was obtained by the undue influence of the defendant.

PARTICULARS

[*Particulars of any allegation of misrepresentation, fraud, breach of trust, wilful default or undue influence must be included in the pleading (Order 18, r. 12(1)).*]

6. The execution of the said alleged will was obtained by the fraud of the defendant.

PARTICULARS

[Particulars must be given: see note to paragraph 5.]
7. The said deceased at the time the said alleged will purports to have been executed did not know or approve of the contents thereof.

NATURE OF CASE

[Any party who pleads that a testator did not know and approve of the contents of the will propounded must specify the nature of the case on which he intends to rely (Order 76, r. 9(3)).]
    The plaintiff claims:
    That the Court shall revoke the said grant of probate and pronounce against the force and validity of the said alleged will.

(Signature)

    Served, etc.

CP29. Plaintiff (executor) claims revocation of probate and grant of probate of earlier will

(Heading)

STATEMENT OF CLAIM

1. The plaintiff is the sole executor named in the true last will and testament bearing date the   day of   19   of A B, late of   deceased, who died on the   day of   19   .
[Continue as in such of paragraphs 2 to 7 of Form No. CP28 as are applicable, or as the case may be.]
    The plaintiff claims:
1. That the Court shall revoke the said grant of probate and pronounce against the force and validity of the said alleged will dated the   day of   19   .
2. That the Court shall pronounce for the force and validity of the said true last will and testament dated the   day of   19   in solemn form of law.

(Signature)

    Served, etc.

CP30. Executor propounds will which has been revoked, and codicil reviving the same (or as re-executed)

(Heading)

STATEMENT OF CLAIM

1. A B, late of   who died there on the   day of   19   made and duly executed a will on the   day of   19   , whereof he appointed the plaintiff sole executor.
2. On the   day of   19   , the said deceased made and duly executed a further will whereby he revoked the said will dated   19   .
3. On the   day of   19   , the said deceased made and duly executed a codicil whereby he expressly revived the said will dated   19   *[or* duly re-executed the said will dated the   day of   19   , whereby he revived its force and validity].
    The plaintiff claims:
    That the Court shall pronounce for the force and validity of the said will dated   19   , and the codicil dated   19   , in solemn form of law *[or* for the force and validity of the said will dated   19   , as re-executed on   19   , in solemn form of law].

(Signature)

    Served, etc.

CP31. Interest action

(Heading)

STATEMENT OF CLAIM

1. The plaintiff is the lawful cousin german of the whole blood and one of the persons entitled to share in the estate of A B, late of   deceased, who died on the   day of
19   intestate a widower without issue, parent, brother or sister of the whole or half blood or their issue, grandparent or uncle or aunt of the whole blood or any other person entitled in priority to share in the estate by virtue of any enactment.
2. The plaintiff denies the defendant's claim to be the lawful brother of the whole blood of the said deceased and will allege that he is the illegitimate son of G H, the lawful mother of the deceased, and he denies that the defendant has any interest in the said estate.
    The plaintiff claims:
    That the Court shall grant him letters of administration of the estate of the said deceased.

(Signature)

Served, etc.

[**Note.**—*Where the plaintiff disputes the interest of a defendant. he must allege in his statement of claim that he denies such interest (Order 76, r. 9(1)).*
    The plaintiff's pleading must show that if the allegations made therein are proved he would be entitled to an interest in the estate of the deceased (ibid., r. 9(2)).]

III. DEFENCES

CP32. Plea—will not duly executed

(Heading)

DEFENCE

The defendant says that:
1. The alleged will and codicil of the deceased were not duly executed in accordance with the provisions of the Wills Act 1837.

PARTICULARS

The testator did not sign or acknowledge his signature to the said alleged will in the joint presence of the attesting witnesses.
    The alleged witnesses to the said alleged will did not attest and subscribe the same in the presence of the testator [*or as the case may be*].

[*or* 1. The defendant does not admit that the alleged will and codicil of the deceased were duly executed in accordance with the provisions of the Wills Act 1837.

PARTICULARS

The defendant puts the plaintiff to proof that the provisions of the said statute were complied with.]

(Signature)

Served, etc.

CP33. Plea—testator not of sound mind, memory and understanding

(Heading)

DEFENCE

The defendant says that:
1. The deceased at the time the alleged will dated the   day of   19   purports to have been executed was not of sound mind, memory and understanding.

PARTICULARS

At the time the deceased executed the said alleged will she was 87 years of age and suffering from senile dementia. Her memory was so defective and untrustworthy that there was an almost total loss of memory for recent events. She was at the time of execution of the said alleged will in such a condition of mind and memory as to be unable to understand the nature of the act and its effects, the extent of the property of which she was disposing, or to comprehend and appreciate the claims to which she ought to give effect [*or as the case may be*].

(Signature)

Served, etc.

CP34. Plea—undue influence

(Heading)

DEFENCE

The defendant says that:

1. The execution of the alleged will dated the   day of   19   was procured by the undue influence of the plaintiff [and of   ].

PARTICULARS

For a year prior to his death the plaintiff had been living in the house of the deceased, being employed to look after him during such time as the defendant (his only son) was necessarily resident abroad. The plaintiff so took advantage of the extreme old age of the deceased and of his weak and emotional state as to assume complete domination over him and his household; she frequently contrived to keep from the deceased the letters the defendant wrote to him, she encouraged the deceased falsely to believe the defendant had abandoned him, and she persuaded him that she was the only person to whom he owed any duty; she herself gave the instructions for the alleged will and was present when the deceased purported to execute it. The defendant will allege that the influence of the plaintiff over the deceased was such that he was not a free agent, and that the said alleged will was not the product of his own volition but was procured by the importunity of the plaintiff [*or as the case may be*].

(Signature)

 Served, etc.

CP35. Plea—fraud

(Heading)

DEFENCE

The defendant says that:

1. The execution of the alleged will dated the   day of   19   was obtained by the fraud of the plaintiff.

PARTICULARS

The said deceased had given instructions to the plaintiff to prepare a will for him bequeathing the whole of his estate to the defendant. The plaintiff thereupon induced the said deceased to sign the said alleged will in the presence of the witnesses whose names appear thereon by falsely and fraudulently representing that it carried out the said instructions [*or as the case may be*].

(Signature)

 Served, etc.

CP36. Plea—want of knowledge and approval

(Heading)

DEFENCE

The defendant says that:

1. The deceased at the time of execution of the alleged will dated the   day of 19   did not know and approve of the contents thereof.

NATURE OF CASE*

The said deceased never gave any instructions for the alleged will, and the said alleged will was not read over or properly explained to him, nor did he read it himself before it was executed, and he was not aware of its nature and effect [*or as the case may be*] [*and if pleaded in conjunction with Form No. CP35*, nor was he capable of comprehending or appreciating its provisions and effect for the causes pleaded in paragraph [2] of this defence].

[**Any party who pleads that at the time when a will was alleged to have been executed the testator did not know and approve of its contents must specify the nature of the case on which he intends to rely (Order 76, r. 9(3)).*

 No allegation in support of such a plea which would be relevant in support of any of the following other pleas:

(a) that the will was not duly executed;
(b) that at the time of execution of the will the testator was not of sound mind, memory and understanding; and
(c) that the execution of the will was obtained by undue influence or fraud,
may be made unless such other plea is also pleaded (ibid).]

(Signature)

 Served, etc.

CP37. Plea—pretended will

(Heading)

DEFENCE

The defendant says that:
1. The alleged will dated the   day of   19   is not a testamentary document.

PARTICULARS

The said alleged will is not testamentary, as clearly appears from the language thereof. The said deceased did not intend it to take effect as a will in any event, but as a donation inter vivos only [*or as the case may be*].

And by way of counterclaim the defendant says that:
2. The said deceased duly executed his true last will on the   day of   19   whereby he appointed the defendant his residuary legatee and devisee.
    The defendant claims:
1. That the Court shall pronounce against the alleged will propounded by the plaintiff.
2. That the Court shall pronounce for the will dated the   day of   19   in solemn form of law.

(Signature)

Served, etc.

CP38. Plea—testator not of age

(Heading)

DEFENCE

The defendant says that:
1. The alleged will is invalid by reason that the deceased was under the age of 18 years at the time at which the said alleged will purports to have been executed, having been born on the   day of   19   .

(Signature)

Served, etc.

CP39. Plea—testator prevented by force and threats from making a fresh will

(Heading)

DEFENCE

The defendant says that:
1. After making the said alleged will dated the   day of   19   the deceased was prevented by force and threats from executing a further will prepared by and under his instructions, whereby the plaintiff would have been deprived of his interest under the said will*.

PARTICULARS

In the month of May 1978, the deceased gave oral instructions to her solicitor to prepare a will bequeathing all her property to the defendant. The draft of the said will was approved by the deceased, who was at the time residing with the plaintiff and remained with her until her death. The clerk of the solicitor attended at the house with the said proposed will for the purpose of getting it executed, but the deceased was prevented by force exercised by the plaintiff from seeing him or executing the proposed will. The plaintiff further threatened the deceased, who was then 80 years of age and in infirm health, that if she executed the said will she would be turned out of the house [*or as the case may be*].
    The defendant claims:
    That the Court shall pronounce that the plaintiff holds upon trust for the defendant absolutely that share of the deceased's estate which devolves on the plaintiff under the said will dated the   day of   19   .

[**Plea allowed by Hannen P in* Betts v Doughty *(1879) 5 P D 26.*]

(Signature)

Served, etc.

CP40. Defendant pleads that will propounded by plaintiff was revoked by destruction

(Heading)

DEFENCE

1. The defendant denies that the said alleged will was never revoked or destroyed by the deceased or by any other person in his presence or by his direction with the intention of revoking it. The defendant denies that at the time of the death of the deceased the same was a valid and subsisting will.

PARTICULARS

The defendant will allege that the said alleged will was destroyed by the deceased on or about the   day of   19   by burning the same at   with the intention of revoking it; and further that [the said alleged will was last known to be in the possession of the deceased but was not forthcoming at his death; and the defendant will rely on the presumption of law that the said will was destroyed animo revocandi].

[**Note.**—*If such is the case, the words in brackets may stand alone as particulars.*]

The defendant counterclaims:
That the Court shall pronounce against the force and validity of the said will.

(Signature)

Served, etc.

CP41. Defendant pleads against will propounded by plaintiff and claims probate of earlier will

(Heading)

DEFENCE

The defendant says that:
[*Insert grounds of defence, including the necessary particulars: see Forms CP32–CP40.*]
And by way of counterclaim the defendant says:
1. That the deceased made his true will dated the   day of   19   and thereof appointed the defendant sole executor.
  The defendant claims:
1. That the Court shall pronounce against the said alleged will and codicil propounded by the plaintiff.
2. That the Court shall pronounce for the force and validity of the last will and testament of the said deceased dated the   day of   19   in solemn form of law.

(Signature)

Served, etc.

[*For form of notice to be indorsed on a counterclaim, see Form CP7.*]

CP42. Defendant pleads against will propounded by plaintiff and claims an intestacy

(Heading)

DEFENCE

The defendant says that:
1. He is the lawful [*or* natural] son and only person entitled to the estate of the said A B, late of   in the county of   who died on the   intestate, a widower [*continue as in Forms CP32 to CP40, or as the case may be*].
  The defendant claims:
That the Court shall pronounce against the said alleged will and codicil propounded by the plaintiff.

(Signature)

Served, etc.

CP43. Plaintiff propounds will under Wills Act 1963: defendant pleads that it was not duly executed

(Death on or after I January 1964 only)

(Heading)

DEFENCE

The defendant says that:

1. The alleged will dated the   day of   19   was not duly executed in accordance with the provisions of the Wills Act 1963.

PARTICULARS

(1) The defendant does not admit that the said alleged will was executed in England, or that at the date thereof or at the date of his death the said deceased had his habitual residence in England.
(2) The defendant denies that at the date of the said alleged will or at the date of his death the deceased was a citizen of the United Kingdom and Colonies, and that at either of those times his closest connection was with the English system of internal law relating to the formal validity of wills.
    The defendant says that at all material times the deceased was a French citizen.
(3) The defendant denies that at the time of execution of the said alleged will or of his death the deceased was domiciled in Scotland [*or as the case may be*].

2. The deceased died intestate, and the defendant is the lawful widow and relict and the only person entitled to the estate of the said deceased.
    The defendant claims:
    That the Court shall pronounce against the force and validity of the said alleged will.
                                                                        (Signature)
    Served, etc.

CP44. Plaintiff propounds privileged will

(Heading)

DEFENCE AND COUNTERCLAIM

The defendant says that:
1. The alleged will dated the   day of   19   was not executed in accordance with the provisions of the Wills Act 1837.

PARTICULARS

[*As in Form CP32, or as the case may be.*]

2. The said letter is not a will.

PARTICULARS

The said letter is not in the form of a will and was not intended to take effect as such, as clearly appears from the language thereof.

3. The deceased was not in actual military service at the time the said letter purports to have been written.

PARTICULARS

The said letter was written before the outbreak of war and before any order for mobilisation had been issued.

4. That the deceased was not at the time the said letter purports to have been written domiciled in England and Wales.

PARTICULARS

The deceased was born in Scotland of Scottish parents. His domicile of origin was in Scotland, and he at all times retained such domicile.

    And by way of counterclaim:
5. The defendant is the surviving executor named in the true last will and testament dated the day of   19   of the said deceased.
    The defendant counterclaims:
1. That the Court shall pronounce against the force and validity of the said alleged will dated the   day of   19   .
2. That the Court shall pronounce for the force and validity of the said true last will and testament dated the   day of   19   in solemn form of law.
                                                                        (Signature)
    Served, etc.

[*For form of notice to be indorsed on a counterclaim, see Form CP7.*]

CP45. Defendant sets up further testamentary document in addition to those propounded by plaintiff

(Heading)

DEFENCE AND COUNTERCLAIM

The defendant says that:
1. He admits that the will and two codicils bearing date respectively the   day of
19 , the   day of   19 and the   day of   19 were duly executed by the testator.
2. The said testator duly executed a further codicil to the said will bearing date the   day
of   19 [*or* undated but in fact executed on the   day of   19].
3. The defendant is a legatee named in the said further codicil.
    The defendant counterclaims:
    That the Court shall pronounce for the force and validity of the said third codicil together
with the will and two codicils propounded by the plaintiff as together constituting the true
last will and codicils of the testator.

(Signature)

Served, etc.

[*For form of notice to be indorsed on a counterclaim, see Form CP7.*]

CP46. Interest action

(Heading)

DEFENCE

The defendant says that:
1. He denies that the plaintiff is the lawful brother of the whole blood of the said deceased
and that as such he is one of the persons entitled to share in the estate of the said deceased.
    The defendant says that the plaintiff is in fact the illegitimate son of C D, the lawful
mother of the said deceased, and that he has no interest in the estate of the said deceased.
2. The defendant is the lawful nephew of the whole blood and only person entitled to the
estate of the deceased, being the lawful son of G B, the lawful brother of the whole blood of
the deceased, who died in his lifetime.
    The defendant claims:
    That the Court shall pronounce that the defendant is the lawful nephew of the whole blood
and only person entitled to the estate of the deceased, and entitled to a grant of letters of
administration of the estate of the deceased.

(Signature)

Served, etc.

IV. REPLIES AND DEFENCES TO COUNTERCLAIMS

CP47. Defendant having pleaded against will and claimed an intestacy—plaintiff sets up earlier will in the alternative

(Heading)

REPLY

The plaintiff says that:
1. He admits that the said will was not read over to the deceased before execution but denies
that the deceased did not himself read the will. He says that the deceased did read the will
and was fully aware of its contents [*or as the case may be*].
2. [Save as expressly admitted in paragraph 1 hereof] he denies each and every allegation
contained in paragraphs   to   of the Defence, and joins issue thereon.
    And by way of defence to counterclaim the plaintiff says that:
3. He is also one of the executors named in a prior will of the deceased dated the   day of
    19 . If for any reason the will dated the   day of   19 is not entitled to probate,
then the said will dated the   day of   19 is entitled to probate.
    The plaintiff claims:
1. As before or in the alternative:
2. That the Court shall pronounce for the said will dated the   day of   19 in solemn
form of law.

(Signature)

Served, etc.

CP48. Defendant having propounded earlier will, plaintiff pleads that it was revoked by a later will which was in turn revoked by last will

(Heading)

REPLY AND DEFENCE TO COUNTERCLAIM

1. The plaintiff denies that [*set out matters denied*]
    And by way of defence to the counterclaim: the plaintiff will say that the said will dated the   day of   19   was revoked by the will dated the   day of   19   which was in turn revoked by the true last will of the deceased dated the   day of   19 .

CP49. Plaintiffs propound will—defendants propound later will revoking it—plaintiffs reply that later will was executed while deceased was not of sound mind; alternatively that it was in its turn revoked

(Heading)

REPLY

The plaintiffs say that:
1. They deny each and every allegation contained in paragraphs 1 and 2 of the defence and join issue thereon.
    And by way of defence to counterclaim the plaintiffs say:
2. That the purported will dated the   day of   19   was not duly executed in accordance with the provisions of the Wills Act 1837.

PARTICULARS

[*As in Form CP32 or as the case may be.*]

3. That at the time of execution of the said purported will the deceased was not of sound mind, memory and understanding.

PARTICULARS

[*As in Form CP33 or as the case may be.*]

4. That if the deceased duly executed the purported will dated the   day of   19   while in a sound state of mind she duly revoked the same by a subsequent will dated the   day of   19   duly executed by her in accordance with the provisions of the Wills Act 1837, while in a similar state of mind.

CP50. Plaintiff propounds will—defendants claim intestacy: plaintiff in reply claims in the alternative probate of earlier will destroyed by testator (dependent relative revocation)

(Heading)

REPLY AND DEFENCE TO COUNTERCLAIM

1. The plaintiff denies [*set out matters denied*].
    And by way of defence to counterclaim, the plaintiff says that:
2. The deceased duly executed a will dated the   day of   19   wherein he named L M and N O as executors, and the plaintiff as residuary legatee and devisee.
    The said L M and N O both died in the lifetime of the deceased.
3. The said will dated the   day of   19   was revoked by the will dated the   day of   19   propounded by the plaintiff.
4. Upon the execution of the will propounded by the plaintiff, the deceased destroyed the said will dated the   day of   19   . The contents of the said will are set out in an examined copy thereof annexed to the plaintiff's affidavit of testamentary scripts in this action and marked '   '.
5. If for any reason the will propounded by the plaintiff is not entitled to probate then the will dated the   day of   19   is entitled to probate.

PARTICULARS

The deceased destroyed the said will dated the   day of   19   by burning the same upon the execution of the will propounded by the plaintiff, in the mistaken belief that the said will was invalid owing to the death of the executors named therein.

The plaintiff will contend that such destruction operates as a revocation only in the event of the will propounded by the plaintiff being held to be valid.

The plaintiff claims:
1. As before.
   Or in the alternative:
2. That the Court shall pronounce for the will dated the   day of   19   as contained in the said copy, in solemn form of law.

(Signature)

Served, etc

SUBPOENA

CP51. Subpoena to bring in a testamentary document in a probate action

Issued pursuant to the authority of Master/District Judge   dated   19   .

In the High Court of Justice (District Registry)   19   ,   No.
Chancery Division (Probate)
In the Estate of   , deceased
    Between   Plaintiff
            and
                                             Defendant
Elizabeth the Second, by the Grace of God, of the United Kingdom of Great Britain and Northern Ireland and of Our other Realms and Territories Queen, Head of the Commonwealth, Defender of the Faith
    To [*name*]   of [*address*]
    Whereas it appears by an affidavit of   filed on   19   in the Chancery Division of our High Court of Justice, that a certain original paper or script, being or purporting to be testamentary, namely [the last will and testament dated   19   of   deceased late of [*address*] who died on   19   *or as the case may be*] is now in your possession, within your power or under your control
    We command you that, within eight days after service hereof on you, exclusive of the day of such service, you do bring into and leave with the proper officer in Chancery Chambers Room TM7.09, Thomas More Buildings, Royal Courts of Justice, Strand, London WC2A 2LL [*or* in the   District Registry at [*address*]] the said original paper or script now in the possession, within the power and under control of you the said
    Witness, the Right Honorable   , Lord High Chancellor of Great Britain the   day of
    19

(Signature)
Master of the Supreme Court [*or*
District Judge].

    Subpoena to bring in a script issued by [*name of solicitor*]
            of
Solicitors.
[*To be indorsed on the copy to be served:*]
Disobedience to this writ would be a contempt of Court punishable by imprisonment.
    If you the within-named   neglect to obey this subpoena by the time therein limited you will be liable to process of execution for the purpose of compelling you to obey the same.

Instructions, Statutory Will Forms, Probate Offices

SUMMARY

Instructions, Statutory Will Forms, Probate Offices

I. INTESTATES' REAL ESTATE

The rules of descent of an estate in fee simple, where the deceased died before 1 January 1926

Notwithstanding the Land Transfer Act 1897, the title of an heir is still ascertained by the same rules as were in force before the passing of that Act[1]: although since that Act his interest, in the case of estates in fee simple, is at first equitable only and he does not obtain the legal estate in the lands descended to him until the same has been expressly conveyed to him by the deceased tenant's personal representatives.

By the Land Transfer Act 1897, s. 2(4), 'Where a person dies possessed of real estate, the Court shall in granting letters of administration have regard to the rights and interests of persons interested in his real estate, and his heir-at-law, if not one of the next-of-kin, shall be equally entitled to the grant with the next-of-kin . . .'

When the heir-at-law applies for letters of administration (with or without will) an affidavit is required in proof of his heirship; the following rules of descent, taken from *Williams and Eastwood on Real Property*, may be of use in framing the affidavit:

Rules of descent

(See also Inheritance Act 1833)

1. Inheritances shall lineally descend, in the first place, to the issue of the last purchaser[2] in infinitum.
2. The male issue shall be admitted before the female.
3. Where two or more of the male issue are in equal degree of consanguinity to the purchaser, the eldest only shall inherit; but the females shall inherit all together.
4. All the lineal descendants in infinitum of any person deceased shall represent their ancestor; that is, shall stand in the same place as the person himself would have done had he been living.
5. On failure of lineal descendants, or issue of the purchaser, the inheritance shall descend to his nearest lineal ancestor.
6. The father and all the male paternal ancestors of the purchaser, and their descendants, shall be admitted before any of the female paternal ancestors or their heirs; all the female paternal ancestors and their heirs before the mother or any of the maternal ancestors, or her or their descendants; and the mother and all the male maternal ancestors, and her and their descendants, before any of the female maternal ancestors, or their heirs.
7. A kinsman of the half blood shall be capable of being heir; and such kinsman shall inherit next after a kinsman in the same degree of the whole blood, and after the issue of such kinsman when the common ancestor is a male, and next after the common ancestor, when such ancestor is a female.
8. In the admission of female paternal ancestors, the mother of the more remote male paternal ancestor, and her heirs, shall be preferred to the mother of a less remote male paternal

---

1 But see *Re Higham* (p. 1098, post).
2 'Purchaser' is 'the person who last acquired the land otherwise than by descent, or than by any escheat, partition or inclosure by the effect of which the land shall have become part of, or descendible in the same manner as, other land acquired by descent' (Inheritance Act 1833, s. 1). 'Descent' means the title to inherit land by reason of consanguinity, as well where the heir shall be an ancestor or collateral relation as where he shall be a child or other issue, and 'descendant' of any ancestor extends to all persons who must trace their descent through such ancestor (ibid.).

ancestor, and her heirs; and, in the admission of female maternal ancestors, the mother of the more remote male maternal ancestor, and her heirs, shall be preferred to the rnother of a less remote male maternal ancestor, and her heirs.

9. Where there shall be a total failure of heirs of the purchaser; or where any land shall be descendible as if an ancestor had been the purchaser thereof, and there shall be a total failure of the heirs of such ancestor, then and in every such case the land shall descend, and the descent shall thenceforth be traced, from the person last entitled to the land, as if he had been the purchaser thereof[3].

Descent according to the custom of Gavelkind which applied chiefly to land in the county of Kent

To all sons equally—failing sons or their issue—to all daughters equally (Statute de Prerogativa Regis (*temp. incert.*), c. 18).

If no issue, to father, if living, and through him, if dead, the brothers and sisters will claim, males, however, before females. The husband of the intestate had a courtesy title in a moiety of the land whether there had been issue or not. The widow had a dower interest in a moiety.

In Borough English or other special cases the rule of descent prevailing in such cases must be proved by affidavit.

As from 1 January 1926, all customs of heirship have been abolished. The heir-at-law according to the general law before that date is now the only recognised heir-at-law[4].

II. INSTRUCTIONS UNDER THE LAND TRANSFER ACT 1897

These instructions are still effective where the deceased died before 1926

1. If the deceased did not die possessed of any real estate the Act does not apply. If it be necessary to clear off a prior right that would exist if there were real estate, it should be done by a statement in the oath (which should also be inserted in the grant) that 'the deceased did not die possessed of real estate'.

2. A residuary legatee and a residuary devisee are equally entitled to a grant.

3. Where there is a residuary devisee in trust he should be cleared off before a grant can be made to a residuary legatee, and where there is a residuary legatee in trust he should be cleared off before a grant can be made to a residuary devisee.

4. The next-of-kin and heir-at-law are equally entitled to a grant. [But see No. 8.]

5. If there be no executor or residuary legatee, a grant should not be made to a next-of-kin without clearing off the residuary devisee, and if there be no executor or residuary devisee, a grant should not be made to the heir-at-law without clearing off the residuary legatee.

6. A grant should not be made to the representative of a deceased residuary legatee without clearing off the residuary devisee.

7. The prior right of the husband or widow of an intestate to a grant is not affected by the Act.

8. Although the next-of-kin and heir-at-law are equally entitled to a grant, yet, in the case of the renunciation of the husband of an intestate, the heir-at-law should be cleared off before a grant is made to the next-of-kin (who has no interest in the estate).

9. But on the renunciation of the widow of an intestate, it is not necessary to clear off the heir-at-law before making a grant to the next-of-kin.

10. On the renunciation of the husband of an intestate a grant should not be made to the husband's receiver in bankruptcy without clearing off the heir-at-law.

11. A grant should not be made to a person who (though not one of the next-of-kin) is entitled in distribution to the personal estate, without clearing off the heir-at-law as well as the next-of-kin of the intestate.

12. A grant should not be made to the representative of a next-of-kin of an intestate without clearing off the heir-at-law.

3   Law of Property Amendment Act 1859, s. 19.
4   *Re Higham* [1937] 2 All ER 17.

13. Guardians of minors and infants are not entitled to a grant without clearing off all persons of age equally entitled with such minors and infants whether as interested in real or personal estate.

14. A grant will not be made to a person for the use of a lunatic without clearing off all other persons equally entitled with the lunatic whether as having an interest in real or personal estate.

15. A person acting under a power of attorney has the same equality and priority as the donor of the power would have if applying personally.

16. When a grant is made to an heir-at-law, his relationship to the deceased should not appear in the grant.

17. The value of any real estate in Scotland or Ireland accounted for in the Inland Revenue affidavit should not be included in the oath or certificate on the grant.

[*Paragraphs 18 and 19 are obsolete.*]

20. The foregoing instructions are to be considered provisional. Should any case arise in which a departure from them might seem to be expedient, such case should be referred to the registrars of the principal registry.

D.H.OWEN
Senior Registrar

December 1898

III. STATUTORY WILL FORMS

(Prescribed by the Lord Chancellor in exercise of the powers conferred by s. 179 of the Law of Property Act 1925 (15 & 16 Geo. 5, c. 20))

1. Short title.—The Forms hereinafter contained may be cited as the Statutory Will Forms, 1925, and are divided into two groups called Part I and Part II respectively.

2. Manner of application.—The Forms in Part I may be incorporated in a will by a general reference to that Part, and the Forms in Part I and Part II or any of them may be incorporated in a will in manner indicated in the Schedule hereto or in any other manner indicating an intention to incorporate them, and in the case of Forms in Part II also indicating what property or disposition is to be affected thereby.

3. Interpretation.—In any form when incorporated in a will—

(i) The provisions thereof shall have effect subject to the express provisions of the will;
(ii) 'Disposition' means a devise, bequest, and testamentary appointment, whether in exercise of a general or special power and includes a disposition under the statutory power to dispose of entailed interests by will; 'dispose of' has a corresponding meaning; and references to a testator's property include property which he disposes of in exercise of a power;
(iii) 'The trustees' mean the trustees appointed by the testator either generally or for a specific purpose, as the case may require, and the persons who by appointment by the court or otherwise become the trustees, and include his personal representatives, when acting as his trustees;
(iv) 'Authorised investments' mean investments authorised by the will creating the trust, for the investment of any money subject to the trusts of the will, or by law;
(v) Other words and expressions have the same meanings as in the Law of Property Act 1925.

FORMS

PART I.—FORMS WHICH MAY BE APPLIED EITHER GENERALLY OR BY SPECIFIC REFERENCE

Form 1. Confirmation of settlements

I confirm every settlement of property made by me which is subsisting at my death, and subject to any express provision to the contrary in my will, the provisions made by my will for the benefit of persons beneficially interested under any such settlement, shall be in addition to, and not in satisfaction of, those made, or covenanted to be made by me in such settlement.

Form 2. Meaning of 'personal chattels'

(1) 'Personal chattels' shall mean 'carriages, horses, stable furniture and effects (not used for business purposes), motor cars and accessories (not used for business purposes), garden effects, domestic animals, plate, plated articles, linen, china, glass, books, pictures, prints, furniture, jewellery, articles of household or personal use or ornament (including wearing apparel), also musical and scientific instruments and apparatus, wines, liquors, and consumable stores, but shall not include any chattels used at my death for business purposes, nor money or securities for money'.

(2) But a general disposition of personal chattels shall take effect subject to any specific disposition.

Form 3. Inventories and provisions respecting chattels

(1) An inventory of chattels given by my will, otherwise than by way of absolute gift, shall be made in duplicate, one part shall be retained by the trustees and the other part shall be delivered to the person of full age for the time being entitled to the use or possession of chattels, in this clause called the 'usufructuary'.

(2) A receipt shall be signed by the usufructuary, at the foot of the inventory retained by the trustees.

(3) The inventory delivered to the usufructuary shall, if he so requires, be signed at the foot thereof by the trustees.

(4) On any change of the right to the use or possession of the chattels, a new receipt shall be signed by the usufructuary at the foot of the inventory retained by the trustees.

(5) Where, by reason of the exercise of any power to sell, exchange, purchase, alter the fashion of, or otherwise deal with the chattels, or of any destruction or loss of any chattel, the inventories become inaccurate, the inventories shall be altered and re-signed, or new inventories shall, if convenient, be made and signed.

(6) The trustees may, at their discretion, exclude from an inventory, any chattels which, by reason of their trifling value or wearing out nature, they may consider ought to be so excluded.

(7) Where the chattels have been delivered to the usufructuary and a receipt is given therefor, the trustees, so long as the usufructuary remains entitled to the use of the chattels, shall not be liable in any way—

   (a) for any unauthorised disposition thereof or dealing therewith,
   (b) to see to the insurance (so far as the same are capable of being insured), repair, or safe custody of the chattels,

   unless and until required, in writing, to insure the chattels or to take any proceedings in reference thereto, by some person beneficially interested in the chattels or by his guardian, committee or receiver, and unless also due provision be made, to the satisfaction of the trustees, for the payment of the costs of insurance or of any proceedings required to be taken.

(8) Where there is no person of full age and capacity entitled to the use of the chattels, the trustees may, during the period of disability, make such arrangements for the safe custody, repair, insurance and use of the chattels as, having regard to the circumstances of the case, they may in their absolute discretion, think expedient.

Form 4. Legacies to charity

The receipt of the treasurer or other proper officer of a charitable benevolent or philanthropic institution, society or body of persons (corporate or incorporate), to which a legacy is given by my will shall be a complete discharge of my personal representatives.

Form 5. Directions respecting annuities

The following provisions shall have effect in regard to any annuities or annuity given by my will—

(1) The trustees may, and (if so requested by or on behalf of any person beneficially interested in the property affected), shall, as soon as may be after annuity commences to accrue, set apart in their names or under their control authorised investments to provide a fund the income whereof will be sufficient, in the opinion of the trustees, to produce an annual sum equal to the amount of the annuities for the time being payable under my will.

(2) The income or, if necessary, the capital of the fund so appropriated, shall be applied in payment of every subsisting annuity.

(3) Until a fund shall be so appropriated, my residuary estate shall stand charged with the payment of every subsisting annuity, but, after appropriation, the said estate shall be thereby discharged therefrom.

(4) The appropriated fund, or, where more than one annuity is bequeathed, such parts thereof as, in the opinion of the trustees, may not be required to answer any subsisting annuity, shall, on the cesser of an annuity, fall into my residuary personal estate.

(5) Accordingly, as each annuity ceases, the trustees may treat as part of my residuary personal estate, the whole or a corresponding part of the appropriated fund, as the case may require, retaining only such part thereof (if any) as may, from time to time, in their opinion, be sufficient to produce, by the income thereof an annual sum equal to the amount of any subsisting annuities.

(6) Any surplus income of the appropriated fund shall be applied in the same manner as the income of my residuary personal estate.

(7) The trustees may, at their discretion, vary any of the investments for the time being representing the appropriated fund for other authorised investments.

(8) In this clause 'annuity' includes any periodical payment (not being a rentcharge) for life or other terminable interest.

Form 6. Power of appropriation

(1) The power of appropriation conferred by the Administration of Estates Act 1925 shall be exercisable by the trustees, without any of the consents made requisite by that Act.

(2) So far as practicable, the trustees shall give one month's notice, at least, of an intended appropriation, to the persons whose consent would, but for this clause, be required under that Act; but a purchaser shall not be concerned to see or inquire whether any such notices have been given.

(3) In this clause 'trustees' includes my personal representatives.

PART II.—FORMS WHICH CAN ONLY BE APPLIED BY SPECIFIC REFERENCE

Form 7. Trusts of a settled legacy

Any legacy of money or investments to which this clause is applied shall be subject to the following provisions:

(1) The trustees shall stand possessed of the legacy upon trust to invest the same in their names or under their control in any authorised investments, with power, at the like discretion, to vary the investments thereof for others of a like nature.

(2) The trustees shall stand possessed of the legacy, and of the investments representing the same and all statutory accumulations, if any, of income thereof hereinafter included in the description of such legacy upon trust to pay the income thereof to the legatee during the life of the legatee.

(3) After the death of the legatee, the capital and income of the legacy shall be held—

In trust for all or any one or more exclusively of the other or others, of the issue of the legatee, whether children or remoter descendants, at such time, and if more than one in such shares, with such provisions for maintenance, education, advancement, and otherwise, at the discretion of any person or persons, and with such gifts over, and generally in such manner, for the benefit of such issue, or some or one of them, as the legatee shall, by deed, revocable or irrevocable, or by will appoint; but so that, under any appointment a child shall not, otherwise than by way of advancement, take a vested interest, except upon attaining the age of twenty-one years or upon marriage.

And in default of and until and subject to any such appointment—

In trust for all or any of the children or child of the legatee, who attain the age of twenty-one years, or marry under that age, and if more than one in equal shares.

(4) Any child of the legatee, who, or whose issue, takes any part of the legacy under any appointment by the legatee, shall not, in the absence of any direction by the legatee to the contrary, take any share in the unappointed part without bringing the share or shares appointed to him or his issue into hotchpot and accounting for the same accordingly.

(5) If the legatee shall not have any child who, under the trusts in default of appointment hereinbefore contained, attains a vested interest in the legacy, then, subject to the trusts and powers hereinbefore expressed in favour of the legatee and his issue, the legacy and the income thereof and all statutory accumulations, if any, of income shall fall into and form part of my residuary personal estate.

(6) The legatee may, notwithstanding any of the trusts hereinbefore expressed concerning his legacy, from time to time or at any time by deed, revocable or irrevocable, or by will, appoint to or for the benefit of any spouse who may survive the legatee, during the residue of the life of such spouse or for any less period (and subject or not to any conditions, and with such gifts over, and discretionary or other trusts for the benefit of the spouse and issue of the legatee, as the legatee may think fit), all or any part of the annual income of the legacy of the legatee, or of so much thereof as shall not, before the death of the legatee, have been paid or applied under any power affecting the same.

And, upon any such appointment, the trusts and powers limited to take effect after the death of the legatee, shall take effect subject to the interest limited by any such appointment:

Provided that the power last aforesaid, to appoint by deed, shall not be exercisable by a woman while under coverture.

Form 8. Administration trusts

Any property disposed of by my will (otherwise than in exercise of a special power) to which this clause is applied shall be subject to the following provisions:

(1) The property shall be held—

(a) as to the real property, if any, including chattels real, upon trust to sell the same, and
(b) as to the personal property, if any, upon trust to call in, sell, and convert into money such part thereof as may not consist of money.

(2) The trustees shall have power to postpone such sale and conversion for such a period as they, without being liable to account, may think proper.

(3) A reversionary interest shall not be sold until it falls into possession, unless the trustees see special reason for sale.

(4) The trustees shall out of the net money to arise from the sale and conversion of the property (after payment of costs), and out of any ready money of mine, included in the disposition, pay or provide for—

(a) my funeral and testamentary expenses;
(b) my debts, except charges on other property of mine so far as those charges are discharged out of the property primarily charged therewith under the Administration of Estates Act, 1925;
(c) the duties, payable out of capital on my death, and not charged on or primarily payable out of other property;
(d) any other liabilities properly payable out of the property, or the proceeds of sale thereof;
(e) the legacies (including money directed to be paid by my will), and annuities bequeathed by me, but so that all legacies and annuities, and the duty on all legacies and annuities bequeathed free of duty, shall be paid primarily out of personal property, if any, included in the disposition.

(5) The trustees may invest, in their names or under their control, the residue of the said money, or so much thereof as may not have been distributed, in any authorised invest-

ments, with power, at their discretion, to vary such investments for others of a like nature.

(6) The income (including net rents and profits of real property and chattels real, after payment of rates, taxes, rent, costs of insurance and of repairs and other outgoings properly attributable to income) of so much of the property as is not required for the administration purposes aforesaid, shall, however the property is invested, as from my death, be treated and applied as income; and for that purpose any necessary apportionment may be made between capital and income.

(7) Provided that—

(a) statutory accumulations of income made during a minority, or pending a contingency, or accumulations made under an express trust for accumulation, may be added to capital;

(b) income may be applied in effecting and maintaining a leasehold sinking fund policy, or may be set aside and invested for providing a fund to answer any liabilities which in the opinion of the trustees ought to be borne by income;

(c) the trustees may in their discretion adjust, in such manner as they shall think fit, having regard to the circumstances of the case, the incidence, as between capital and income, of the payments made in due course of administration.

Form 9. Trusts for spouse for life with power to appoint to issue and gift over to them

Any property disposed of by my will (otherwise than in exercise of a special power) to which this clause is applied shall be subject to the following provisions:

(1) The property (including the investments for the time being representing the same) shall be held upon trust to pay the income thereof to my spouse for life.

(2) After the death of my spouse, the capital and income of the property shall be held—

(i) In trust for all or any one or more, exclusively of the other or others, of my issue, whether children or remoter descendants, at such time, and if more than one in such shares, with such provisions for maintenance, education, advancement and otherwise, at the discretion of any person or persons, and with such gifts over, and generally in such manner, for the benefit of such issue, or some or one of them, as my spouse shall, by deed, revocable or irrevocable, or by will, appoint; but so that, under any appointment, a child shall not, otherwise than by way of advancement, take a vested interest, except upon attaining the age of twenty-one years or upon marriage.

(ii) And in default of and until and subject to any such appointment in trust, in equal shares if more than one, for all or any of my children or child who survive me and attain the age of twenty-one years or marry under that age, and for all or any of the issue living at my death who attain the age of twenty-one years or marry under that age of any child of mine who predeceases me, such issue to take through all degrees, according to their stocks, in equal shares if more than one, the share or shares which his or their parent would have taken if living at my death, and so that no issue shall take whose parent is living at my death and so capable of taking.

(3) Any person who, or whose issue, takes any part of the property, under any appointment by my spouse, shall not, in the absence of any direction by my spouse to the contrary, take any share in the unappointed part, without bringing the shares appointed to such person or his issue into hotchpot, and accounting for the same accordingly.

Form 10. Trusts for spouse and issue, without power of appointment

Any property disposed of by my will (otherwise than in exercise of a special power) to which this clause is applied shall be subject to the following provisions:

(1) The property (including the investments for the time being representing the same) shall be held upon trust to pay the income thereof to my spouse for life.

(2) After the death of my spouse the capital and income of the property shall be held in trust, in equal shares if more than one, for all or any of my children or child, who

survive me and attain the age of twenty-one years or marry under that age, and for all or any of the issue living at my death, who attain the age of twenty-one years or marry under that age, of any child of mine who predeceases me, such issue to take through all degrees, according to their stocks, in equal shares, if more than one, the share or shares which his or their parent would have taken if living at my death; and so that no issue shall take whose parent is living at my death and so capable of taking.

SCHEDULE

INCORPORATION OF ALL THE FORMS IN PART I

All the Forms contained in Part I of the Statutory Will Forms 1925 are incorporated in my will [subject to the following modifications, namely*   ].

* Here insert the modifications (if any).

INCORPORATION OF SPECIFIED FORMS FROM PART I

The following Forms contained in Part I of the Statutory Will Forms 1925 shall be incorporated in my will:

[*Specify those of the following Forms which it is desired to incorporate.*]
Form 1 (Confirmation of settlements).
Form 2 (Meaning of 'personal chattels').
Form 3 (Inventories and provisions respecting chattels).
Form 4 (Legacies to charity).
Form 5 (Directions respecting annuities).
Form 6 (Power of appropriation)

[Subject to the following modifications, namely*   .]

* Here insert the modifications (if any).

INCORPORATION OF SPECIFIED FORMS FROM PART II

Form 7. Trusts of a settled legacy

Form 7 of the Statutory Will Forms 1925 is incorporated in my will, and shall apply to the following legacies*   [subject to the following modifications†   ].

* Here insert the legacies of money or investments to be settled.
† Here insert the modifications (if any).

Form 8. Administration trusts

Form 8 of the Statutory Will Forms 1925 is incorporated in my will, and shall apply to *
[subject to the following modifications†   ].

* Here insert description of property to be held upon administration trusts.
† Here insert the modifications (if any).

Form 9. Trusts for spouse for life with power to appoint to issue and gift over to them

Form 9 of the Statutory Will Forms 1925 is incorporated in my will, and shall apply to*   [subject to the following modifications†   ].

* Here insert description of the property to be held on trusts for spouse for life with power to appoint to issue and gift over to them.
† Here insert the modifications (if any).

Form 10. Trusts for spouse and issue, without power of appointment

Form 10 of the Statutory Will Forms 1925 is incorporated in my will, and shall apply to *   [subject to the following modifications†   ].

* Here insert description of the property to be held on trusts for spouse and issue without power of appointment.
† Here insert the modifications (if any).

IV. PROBATE OFFICES AT WHICH PERSONAL APPLICATIONS FOR GRANTS MAY BE MADE

The following is a list of local probate offices at which, in addition to the registries and sub-registries (see paras. **2.10** and **2.11** and para. **2.58**, ante), personal applications for grants of probate and letters of administration may be made. These offices are open in most cases on either one or two days in the week normally by appointment only. In tending applicants should first apply to the appropriate main registry or sub-registry for the necessary forms.

It should be noted that applications in which solicitors are instructed cannot be accepted at probate offices.

This list is subject to alteration.

County and Town	Main Registry or Sub-Registry	County and Town	Main Registry or Sub-Registry
AVON		DURHAM	
Bath	Bristol	Darlington	Middlesbrough
Weston-super-Mare	Bristol	Durham	Middlesbrough
		DYFED	
BEDFORDSHIRE		Aberystwyth	Carmarthen
Bedford	Leicester	Haverfordwest	Carmarthen
Luton	Principal	EAST SUSSEX	
BERKSHIRE		Hastings	Brighton
Reading	Oxford	ESSEX	
Slough	Oxford	Chelmsford	Ipswich
		Colchester	Ipswich
BUCKINGHAMSHIRE		Harlow	Principal
Aylesbury	Oxford	Southend-on-Sea	Principal
High Wycombe	Oxford	GLOUCESTERSHIRE	
CAMBRIDGESHIRE		Cheltenham	Gloucester
Cambridge	Peterborough	GREATER LONDON	
CHESHIRE		Croydon	Principal
Crewe	Stoke-on-Trent	Edmonton	Principal
Warrington	Manchester	Kingston-upon-Thames	Principal
CLWYD		Woolwich	Principal
Rhyl	Bangor	GREATER MANCHESTER	
Wrexham	Bangor	Bolton	Manchester
CORNWALL		Oldham	Manchester
Truro	Bodmin	Stockport	Manchester
CUMBRIA		Wigan	Manchester
Barrow	Lancaster	GWENT	
Workington	Carlisle	Newport	Cardiff
DERBYSHIRE		HAMPSHIRE	
Chesterfield	Sheffield	Basingstoke	Winchester
Derby	Nottingham	Portsmouth	Winchester
DEVON		Southampton	Winchester
Barnstaple	Exeter	HEREFORD AND WORCESTER	
Newton Abbot	Exeter	Hereford	Gloucester
Penzance	Bodmin	Kidderminster	Birmingham
Plymouth	Bodmin	Worcester	Gloucester
DORSET			
Bournemouth	Winchester		
Dorchester	Winchester		

County and Town	Main Registry or Sub-Registry	County and Town	Main Registry or Sub-Registry
HUMBERSIDE		SALOP	
Grimsby	Lincoln	Shrewsbury	Stoke-on-Trent
Hull	York		
ISLE OF WIGHT		SOMERSET	
Newport	Winchester	Taunton	Exeter
		Yeovil	Exeter
KENT			
Canterbury	Maidstone	SOUTH YORKSHIRE	
Chatham	Maidstone	Doncaster	Sheffield
Folkestone	Maidstone		
Tunbridge Wells	Maidstone	STAFFORDSHIRE	
		Lichfield	Birmingham
LANCASHIRE		Stafford	Stoke-on-Trent
Blackpool	Lancaster		
Nelson	Manchester	SUFFOLK	
Preston	Lancaster	Lowestoft	Norwich
MERSEYSIDE		SURREY	
St Helens	Liverpool	Guildford	Winchester
Southport	Liverpool		
Wallasey	Liverpool	TYNE AND WEAR	
		Sunderland	Middlesbrough
MID GLAMORGAN			
Bridgend	Cardiff	WEST GLAMORGAN	
Pontypridd	Cardiff	Swansea	Carmarthen
NORFOLK		WEST MIDLANDS	
King's Lynn	Peterborough	Coventry	Birmingham
		Wolverhampton	Birmingham
NORTHAMPTONSHIRE			
Kettering	Leicester	WEST SUSSEX	
Northampton	Birmingham	Crawley	Brighton
		Chichester	Brighton
NORTHUMBERLAND			
Morpeth	Newcastle-upon-Tyne	WEST YORKSHIRE	
		Bradford	Leeds
NORTH YORKSHIRE		Huddersfield	Leeds
Harrogate	Leeds	Wakefield	Leeds
Scarborough	York		
		WILTSHIRE	
NOTTINGHAMSHIRE		Salisbury	Winchester
Mansfield	Nottingham	Swindon	Oxford

Index

Money
meaning, 160–161
Moneys
meaning, 160–161
Motion
form, 1019
practice as to, 597–598
Murder or manslaughter
letters of administration with will annexed,
184–185
Mutual wills, 72–73
community of property, 73
exclusion of direction as to proof, 73
revocation, 73

National insurance, 17
National Savings Bank, 13–14
New Zealand
Public Trustee, 505–506
Next of kin
meaning, 162
Nominated assets, 11–12
Nominations, 42–43
forms, 1020
Non-contentious business
fees, 961–964
meaning, 601
Non-Contentious Probate Rules, 923–943
definitions, 924–925
Northern Ireland grants of representation
recognition in England and Wales, 799–800
recognition of grants and confirmations in, 800
Notation of grants, 474–475
Notice
form, 1021
Notice of intention merely to cross-examine,
645–646
Nullity of marriage
effect of decree, 806
Nuncupative wills
grants in respect of, 938–939
privileged, 91

Oath in support of grant, 926
Oaths, 24–26. *See also* EXECUTOR'S OATH
administration abroad, 531–532
form, 529–530, 1021–1069
Order
form, 1069
Order of priority for grant, 928–929, 931
Orders for provision out of estate of deceased,
476–477. *See also* FAMILY PROVISION
Original will not available, 567–573
administration limited, 572
cases in which copies admitted, 570
contents not known, 572–573
copy or draft to be lodged, 569–570
destruction by residuary legatee, 570
evidence of substance or contents, 570–571
fees, 573
mode of application, 567–569
order, 573
order of court of domicile, 570

Original will not available—*contd*
presumption of revocation, 569
probate of codicil limited until lost will found,
571
probate of copy where original in existence,
571
reconstruction required where no copy or draft
available, 571

Parental responsibility agreement, 944–946
Parental rights and duties, 875–876, 881–886,
892
Parents
grants for use of minors, 377–379. *See also*
MINORS
Parties to actions, 614–616
defendants, 615
interveners, 615–616
plaintiffs, 615
who may be, 614
Perpetuities and accumulations, 779–780
Personal applications, 34–36, 925–926
administration guarantee, 36
capital transfer tax, 36
fees, 36
grant, for, 34–35
inheritance tax, 36
probate offices, 1105–1107
procedure, 35–36
resealing, 35
where made, 35
Personal effects
meaning, 161
Personal representatives
additional, 930
devolution of real estate on, 744
duties, 802
powers of court, 844–846
removal of, 711
Persons incapable of managing affairs, 16–17
Plaintiffs, 615
Pleadings, 625–626
allegation as to condition of mind, 625–626
close of, 672
contents, 949
default, 949
denial of interest, 626
forms, 1080–1093
heading, 625
indorsement, 625
practice as to, 625–626
signature, 625
undue influence, 626
want of knowledge and approval, 626
Power of appointment, 400–403
exercise, 401
general, 401
proof of will, 403
special, 401
subsequent marriage, and, 401–402
will invalid save as to exercise of, 403
will revoked except as to, 402–403
wills in exercise of, 400–403